STRATEGIC MANAGEMENT

CONCEPTS & CASES

STRATEGIC MANAGEMENT

CONCEPTS & CASES

SEVENTH EDITION

ARTHUR A. THOMPSON, JR.
&
A.J. STRICKLAND III

BOTH OF THE UNIVERSITY OF ALABAMA

IRWIN

HOMEWOOD, IL 60430
BOSTON, MA 02116

Cover image: "October in Massachusetts"
© Diana Kan/VAGA, New York 1993
Photograph by Sing-Si Schwartz

© RICHARD D. IRWIN, INC., 1978, 1981, 1984, 1987, 1990, 1992, and 1993

Senior sponsoring editor: *Kurt L. Strand*
Developmental editor: *Libby Rubenstein*
Marketing manager: *Kurt Messersmith*
Project editor: *Paula M. Buschman*
Production manager: *Bette K. Ittersagen*
Interior designer: *Heidi J. Baughman*
Cover designer: *Julie Smith*
Art coordinator: *Mark Malloy*
Compositor: *Weimer Incorporated*
Typeface: *10.5/12 Palatino*
Printer: *Von Hoffmann Press*

Library of Congress Cataloging-in-Publication Data

Thompson, Arthur A.,
   Strategic management: concepts and cases / Arthur A. Thompson
Jr., A. J. Strickland III.—7th ed.
      p.   cm.
   Includes bibliographical references and indexes.
   ISBN 0-256-12707-7
   1. Strategic planning. 2. Strategic planning—Case studies.
I. Strickland, A. J. (Alonzo J.) II. Title
HD30.28.T53 1993
658.4'012—dc20   92–37023

Printed in the United States of America
1 2 3 4 5 6 7 8 9 0 VH 0 9 8 7 6 5 4 3

To Hasseline and Kitty

This seventh edition, coming right on the heels of last year's sixth edition, represents an innovative response to the market's unrelenting appetite for the freshest possible cases. While new developments in the concepts of strategic management are not sufficiently fast-paced to warrant our revising the text chapters annually, there's plenty of merit and justification for the practice of regularly refurbishing the set of assigned cases. Since many business schools offer the strategic management course every term, there's a tendency for the case collection in any one edition to "wear out" after a few terms—or sooner. Sometimes current events can make certain cases prematurely obsolete. The legitimate need for fresh cases, together with welcome and much-needed growth in the supply of first-rate cases being researched and written each year, has prompted us to shorten our case revision cycle and provide a second collection of 34 cases from which to choose. The only carryover case from the sixth edition is the timeless two-page Robin Hood case. Other than the cases, the content of this seventh edition matches that of the sixth; the 10 chapters of text material have been untouched except for redesigned artwork and minor editing.

If you are a sixth edition user, shifting to the seventh edition becomes attractive whenever you feel it is time to incorporate a new case collection into your course offering. If you haven't adopted the sixth edition, then it makes sense to base your choice between the sixth and seventh editions on which group of cases appeals to you most. Because only the cases differentiate the sixth and seventh editions, both editions will remain simultaneously available from the publisher, thus allowing adopters the freedom to select whichever case set they prefer.

The Case Collection in the Seventh Edition

Thirty-three of the 34 cases are new to this edition and nearly all are the product of current research. To facilitate tight linkage between the cases and strategic management concepts, we have grouped the cases into five sections. In the first section, 4 cases spotlight the role and tasks of the manager as chief strategy-maker and chief strategy-implementer. The second section, consisting of 13 cases, deals with analyzing and crafting business-level strategy. There are 4 cases involving strategy formation in diversified companies and a 9-case grouping that covers the managerial challenges of implementing strategy. The last section contains 4 cases highlighting the links between strategy, ethics, and social responsibility. Scattered throughout the lineup are 9 cases concerning international companies, globally competitive industries, and cross-cultural situations. These cases, in conjunction with the globalized content of the text chapters, permit solid international coverage—in keeping with new AACSB standards and the ongoing globalization of the world economy. Five cases have videotape segments for use during the class discussion. Then there are 6 cases about young start-up companies, 10 cases dealing with the strategic problems of family-owned or relatively small entrepreneurial businesses, 1 nonprofit organization case, and 14 cases involving public companies about which students can do further research in the library.

This seventh edition again reflects our strong preference for cases that feature interesting products and companies and that trigger lively classroom discussions. At least 19 of the cases involve companies, products, or people that students will have heard of or will know about from personal experience. The case researchers whose work appears in this edition have done an absolutely first-class job of preparing cases that contain valuable teaching points, that illustrate the important strategic challenges managers face, and that allow students to apply the strategic analysis tools. We believe you will find the seventh edition's case collection chock full of interest, effective in the classroom, and tightly linked to the text treatments in Chapters 1 through 10. This is as attractive a case lineup as any we have previously been able to assemble.

How the Text Chapters Differ from the Fifth Edition

The speed at which new concepts and analytical tools are appearing in the strategic management literature mandates frequent text changes to keep the presentation close to the cutting edge. This sixth-seventh edition version of the text chapters (1) covers the full gamut of global issues in strategic management, (2) provides treatments of best-cost producer strategies, strategic alliances, the concept of strategic intent, core competencies, profit sanctuaries, and economies of scope, and (3) includes a series of margin inserts for each chapter to draw prominent attention to strategic management principles, basic concepts, and major conclusions. Extensive rewriting to achieve better economy of presentation has allowed us to include the new material and still cover everything in less than 280 pages.

While the organization of the text chapters parallels that of the fifth edition (1990), you'll see some noteworthy refinements in both content and emphasis:

- Chapters 1 and 2 contain new discussions of a company's need for both strategic objectives and financial objectives, the role of each in the strategic management process, and the trade-offs between actions to strengthen long-term competitive position and actions to improve short-term financial performance.
- The strategic role and relevance of a company's *core competencies* have been woven into the discussions of company strengths, crafting strategy around what a company does best, and building a capable organization (Chapters 2, 4, and 9).
- To help students differentiate between good and bad strategies, we've added a section on the tests of a winning strategy (Chapter 2).
- A section describing how to build sustainable competitive advantage via a strategy of being a *best-cost producer* (as opposed to a low-cost producer) has been added to Chapter 5.
- There are expanded and improved treatments of multicountry (or multidomestic) competition versus global competition, the pros and cons

of strategic alliances, the ways to achieve competitive advantage with a global strategy, and how global competitors can build profit sanctuaries and use cross-subsidization to outcompete domestic competitors (Chapter 6).

- To draw together the main lessons from the three-chapter module on business strategy, we've added a summary section that presents 13 "commandments" for successful strategy-making in single-business enterprises (Chapter 6).
- How diversified multinational enterprises can rely upon *economies of scope* and cross-subsidization to gain competitive advantage over single-business domestic firms is prominently featured in Chapter 7. Chapter 7 also contains new treatments of how to test whether diversification builds shareholder value and of the relationships between strategic fit, economies of scope, and competitive advantage.
- In Chapter 8, we've added more methodological detail in the explanations of how to compare industry attractiveness and business-unit strength in diversified companies.
- There's updated and expanded coverage of how shared values, ethical considerations, and corporate social responsibility enter into the process of crafting and implementing strategy (Chapters 2 and 10).
- There are eight new Illustration Capsules.

The most visible addition to the chapters is the use of "margin notes" highlighting basic concepts, major conclusions, and "core truths" about strategic behavior in competitive markets. Most of these notes represent an effort to distill the subject matter into a series of concise "principles" expressing what every student should know about strategic management. The teaching-learning objectives underlying these margin notes are to bring the text discussion into sharper focus for readers, point them more directly to what is important, and make it easier for them to learn to think strategically.

Substantial effort has gone into improving content, clarity, and style. As a result, we believe you will find the material crisply written, forcefully presented, comfortably mainstream, and as close to the frontiers of theory and practice as a basic textbook can be.

The Business Strategy Game Option

Version one of *The Business Strategy Game*, published in 1990, was very well received and rekindled interest in PC-based simulations. The second version, now available, has features that make the use of a simulation exercise in the strategy course even more appealing. Based on our experience of having used a simulation game every semester for over 15 years, we are convinced that simulation games are the *single best exercise* available for helping students pull the pieces of the business puzzle together and giving them an integrated, capstone experience.

The Value a Simulation Adds   First and foremost, the exercise of running a simulated company over a number of decision periods helps develop students' business judgment. They learn about risk taking. They have to react to changing market conditions, study the actions of competitors, and weigh alternative courses of action. They get valuable practice in spotting market opportunities, evaluating threats to their company's well-being, and assessing the long-term consequences of short-term decisions. And by having to live with the decisions they make, they experience what it means to be accountable and responsible for achieving satisfactory results. All of these activities have a positive and meaningful impact on students' business acumen and managerial judgment.

Second, students learn an enormous amount from working with the numbers, exploring options, and trying to unite production, marketing, finance, and human resource decisions into a coherent strategy. The effect is to help students integrate a lot of material, look at decisions from the standpoint of the company as a whole, and see the importance of thinking strategically about a company's competitive position and future prospects. Since a simulation game is, by its very nature, a hands-on exercise, the lessons learned are forcefully planted in students' minds: the impact is far more lasting than what is remembered from lectures. Third, students' entrepreneurial instincts blossom as they get caught up in the competitive spirit of the game. The resulting entertainment value helps maintain an unusually high level of student motivation and emotional involvement in the course throughout the term.

We think you will find *The Business Strategy Game* a welcome course option. It will add a dimension to your course that can't be matched by any other teaching-learning tool. Moreover, with the aid of today's high-speed personal computers and the technical advances in software capability, there's minimal gearup time on the instructor's part. You'll find that the time and effort required to administer *The Business Strategy Game* is well within tolerable limits.

About the Simulation   The product for *The Business Strategy Game* is athletic footwear—chosen because it is a product students personally know about, buy themselves, and wear regularly. The industry setting is global; companies can manufacture and sell their brands in the United States, Europe, or Asia. Competition is head-to-head; each team of students must match its strategic wits against the other company teams. Companies can focus their efforts on one geographic market or two or all three; they can establish a one-country production base or they can manufacture in all three of the geographic markets. Demand conditions, tariffs, and wage rates vary from area to area.

The company that students manage has plants to operate, a work force to compensate, distribution expenses and inventories to control, capital expenditure decisions to make, marketing and sales campaigns to wage, sales forecasts to consider, and changes in exchange rates, interest rates, and the stock market to take into account. Students must evaluate whether to pursue a low-cost producer strategy, a differentiation strategy, or a focus strategy. They have to decide whether to produce "off-shore" in Asia where wage rates are very low or whether to avoid import tariffs and transocean shipping costs by having a producing base in every primary geographic market. And they must endeavor to maximize shareholder wealth via increased dividend payments and stock price appreciation. Each team of students is challenged to use its entrepreneurial and strategic skills to become the next Nike or Reebok and ride the wave of growth to the top of the worldwide athletic footwear industry.

There's a built-in planning and analysis feature that allows students to (1) craft a five-year strategic plan, (2) make five-year financial projections, (3) do all kinds of "what-iffing," (4) assess the revenue-cost-profit consequences of alternative strategic actions, and (5) develop a tentative five-year set of decisions (in effect, a five-year strategic plan) which can easily be revised and updated as the game unfolds. A special "Calc" feature allows all the number-crunching to be done in a matter of seconds.

The Business Strategy Game can be used with any IBM or compatible PC with 640K memory and it is suitable for both senior-level and MBA courses. The game is programmed to accommodate a wide variety of computer setups as concerns disk drives, monitors, and printers.

Features of the Latest Edition   The latest version of *The Business Strategy Game* makes things easier and better for both the players and the game administrator:

- No longer is access to Lotus 1-2-3 (or any other spreadsheet software) required as a supporting tool for either players or game administrators. By completely eliminating the need for any kind of outside software supplement, we've cast aside a requirement that complicated the procedures and that proved inconvenient for some and burdensome for others.
- We've enhanced the visual appeal of the screens by using color throughout (something that will be appreciated by those with color monitors).
- The scoring algorithm has been reworked to include a "power rating" for each company's strategy. In addition, the stock price performance measure has been replaced with a stock value measure (stock price × number of shares outstanding) to create a more inclusive measure of how successful the players have been in boosting shareholder value.
- The *Player's Manual* now has an index, and those parts of the manual that students found unclear have been rewritten to improve the explanations of how things work.
- We've recast the treatment of exchange rate fluctuations to impact costs rather than profits. The effect is to make the decision-making implications of exchange rate fluctuations more straightforward and understandable to students.
- A new manufacturing decision variable has been added to give companies another option for increasing the efficiency of existing plants over time. By making expenditures for *production methods improvement,* company managers can reduce production run set-up costs, cut supervision costs, and boost worker productivity.
- The company operations reports provide more extensive cost analysis figures, and the "Footwear Industry Report" provides more complete financial information for each company.
- Based on the experiences and suggestions of users, we've added print options for both dot-matrix and laser printers and reprogrammed several things to reduce the potential for glitches (disk problems and disk errors). We've improved the procedures for processing decisions and done all kinds of behind-the-scenes programming to make things run faster and more trouble-free on almost any kind of IBM or 100 percent-IBM compatible computer setup. Both players and game administrators will find Version 2.0 more user-friendly in virtually every respect.

At the same time, though, we've retained the features that made Version 1.0 so popular:

- Everything is done on disks. Students enter their decisions on disks and, during processing, a complete set of industry and company results is written back on the disks. It takes only a few minutes to collect the disks and return them. A printout of the industry scoreboard and a printout of the instructor's report are automatically generated during processing.

- Decisions can be processed in 40 minutes (less than 25 minutes on a fast PC); simple procedures allow most or all of the processing to be delegated to a student assistant.

- Students will find it convenient and uncomplicated to use the PC to play *The Business Strategy Game* even if they have had no prior exposure to PCs; *no programming of any kind is involved* and full instructions are presented in the *Player's Manual* and on the screens themselves.

- A scoreboard of company performance is automatically calculated each decision period. Instructors determine the weights to be given to each of six performance measures—revenues, after-tax profits, return on stockholders' investment, stock value, bond rating, and strategy rating.

- An *Instructor's Manual* describes how to integrate the game into your course, provides pointers on how to administer the game, and contains step-by-step processing instructions.

The STRAT-ANALYST Software Option

The STRAT-ANALYST software supplement was introduced six years ago as a way of incorporating the calculating power of PCs into the case analysis part of the strategic management course. Whereas earlier versions of the software package required using Lotus 1-2-3 to drive the STRAT-ANALYST disks, now everything that students need to use STRAT-ANALYST is contained on the disks themselves. The self-contained programming feature that we've incorporated into the STRAT-ANALYST supplement is a big plus, especially for students who have their own personal computers but don't have the Lotus 1-2-3 package. It also opens the door for STRAT-ANALYST's use at universities whose PC labs don't have the Lotus 1-2-3 package available for general student access. This STRAT-ANALYST edition also has color screens to enhance visual appeal. STRAT-ANALYST works on all IBM or 100 percent-compatible personal computers with 640K memories.

The version of STRAT-ANALYST accompanying this seventh edition has three main sections. The first section contains preprogrammed, customized templates for each of 12 cases where substantial number-crunching is called for. With these templates, students can

- Obtain calculations showing financial ratios, profit margins and rates of return, common-size income statements and balance sheets, and annual compound rates of change.

- Calculate Altman's bankruptcy index (a method for predicting when a company may be headed into deep financial trouble).

- Do "What-If" scenarios and compare the projected outcomes for one strategic option versus another.

- Make five-year best-case, expected-case, and worst-case projections of financial performance using the what-if approach.
- Get report-ready printouts of all these calculations.

Not only is this section of STRAT-ANALYST a big time-saver for students but it also gets them into the habit of always looking at the story the numbers tell about a company's performance and situation. Since students can do a more systematic number-crunching analysis with STRAT-ANALYST than without it, instructors can insist on and expect thorough financial assessments. The "What-If" features make it easier to quantify the effects of particular strategic actions and to examine the outcomes of alternative scenarios. Five-year financial performance projections can be generated in less than 10 minutes.

The second section of STRAT-ANALYST features an easy-to-use, step-by-step generic procedure for using various analytical tools and doing situation analysis. The three part menu includes:

- Industry and competitive situation analysis (keyed to Table 3-5 in the text).
- Company situation analysis (keyed to Table 4-4 in the text).
- Business portfolio analysis (keyed to Chapter 8's discussion of how to compare industry attractiveness and business strength in diversified firms).

Students can choose to use whatever situation analysis tools are appropriate and, when finished, get a neatly organized, final-copy printout of their analysis in a report format. (This report can then be conveniently graded by the instructor.) Hints for using each situational analysis tool are provided directly on STRAT-ANALYST to guide the student in the right direction. The benefit of these three menu options is that students are prompted to consider the full array of concepts and tools and to do a *systematic* situation analysis rather than trying to get by with spotty analysis and weakly justified opinions.

The third section offers two menu selections for developing action recommendations:

1. Action recommendations pertaining to strategy formulation— development of a basic strategic direction (mission and objectives), proposing an overall business strategy, specifying functional strategies, and recommending specific action steps to develop the strategy and gain competitive advantage.
2. Action recommendations for implementing/executing the chosen strategy and correcting whatever assortment of internal administrative and operating problems may exist.

Both selections walk students step-by-step through areas where actions may need to be taken. A "Hints" screen appears at each step.

The whole intent of the STRAT-ANALYST software package is to give students a major assist in doing higher-caliber strategic analysis and to cut the time that it takes to do a thorough job of case preparation. It also helps build student comfort levels and skills in the use of PCs for managerial analysis purposes. The instructor profits too—from improved student performance and from increased flexibility in varying the nature of case analysis assignments.

Start-up instructions for STRAT-ANALYST are included here in the book (see pages 926-932); once the disks are booted up, all other directions needed by the user appear right on the screens.

The Readings Book Option

For instructors who want to incorporate samples of the strategic management literature into the course, a companion *Readings in Strategic Management* containing 43 selections is available. Twenty-six of the 43 readings are new to the current edition. Over two-thirds have appeared since 1985. All are quite readable, and all are suitable for seniors and MBA students. Most of the selections are articles reprinted from leading journals; they add in-depth treatment to important topic areas covered in the text and put readers at the cutting edge of academic thinking and research on the subject. Some of the articles are drawn from practitioner sources and stress how particular tools and concepts relate directly to actual companies and managerial practices. Nine articles examine the role of the general manager and strategy; 10 articles concern strategic analysis and strategy formation at the business-unit level; 8 articles deal with strategy in diversified companies; 10 articles relate to various aspects of strategy implementation; and 6 articles are about strategy and ethics management. Eight of these articles deal with the international dimensions of strategic management. In tandem, the readings package provides an effective, efficient vehicle for reinforcing and expanding the text-case approach.

The Instructor's Package

A full complement of instructional aids is available to assist adopters in using the seventh edition successfully. The *Instructor's Manual* contains suggestions for using the text materials, various approaches to course design and course organization, a sample syllabus, alternative course outlines, a set of over 850 multiple-choice and essay questions, a comprehensive teaching note for each case, plus eight "classic" cases from previous editions. There is a computerized test bank for generating examinations, a set of color transparencies depicting the figures and tables in the 10 text chapters, and a package of lecture and transparency masters that thoroughly covers the text (concepts) part of the book and can be used to support the instructor's classroom presentations. To help instructors enrich and vary the pace of class discussions of cases, there are video supplements for use with the Manna Grocery, Sonic Corp., World Tire Industry, Bama Pie, and SIFCO cases.

   In concert, the textbook, the three companion supplements, and the comprehensive instructor's package provide a complete, integrated lineup of teaching materials. The package offers wide latitude in course design, full access to the range of computer-assisted instructional techniques, an assortment of visual aids, and plenty of opportunity to keep the nature of student assignments varied and interesting. Our goal has been to give you everything you need to offer a course that is very much in keeping with the strategic management challenges and issues of the 1990s and that is capable of winning enthusiastic student approval.

Acknowledgments

We have benefited from the help of many people during the evolution of this book. Students, adopters, and reviewers have generously supplied an untold number of insightful comments and helpful suggestions. Our intellectual debt to those academics, writers, and practicing managers who have blazed new trails in the strategy field will be obvious to any reader familiar with the literature of strategic management.

We are particularly indebted to the case researchers whose casewriting efforts appear herein and to the companies whose cooperation made the cases possible. To each one goes a very special thank-you. The importance of timely, carefully researched cases cannot be overestimated in contributing to a substantive study of strategic management issues and practices. From a research standpoint, cases in strategic management are invaluable in exposing the generic kinds of strategic issues which companies face, in forming hypotheses about strategic behavior, and in drawing experience-based generalizations about the practice of strategic management. Pedagogically, cases about strategic management give students essential practice in diagnosing and evaluating strategic situations, in learning to use the tools and concepts of strategy analysis, in sorting through various strategic options, in crafting strategic action plans, and in figuring out successful ways to implement and execute the chosen strategy. Without a continuing stream of fresh, well-researched, and well-conceived cases, the discipline of strategic management would quickly fall into disrepair, losing much of its energy and excitement. There's no question, therefore, that first-class case research constitutes a valuable scholarly contribution.

The following reviewers made valuable contributions to improving the content of the text chapters in this edition: Tuck Bounds, Lee Burke, Ralph Catalanello, William Crittenden, Vince Luchsinger, Stan Mendenhall, John Moore, Will Mulvaney, Sandra Richard, Ralph Roberts, Thomas Turk, Gordon VonStroh, and Fred Zimmerman.

We are also indebted to S. A. Billion, Charles Byles, Gerald L. Geisler, Rose Knotts, Joseph Rosenstein, James B. Thurman, Ivan Able, W. Harvey Hegarty, Roger Evered, Charles B. Saunders, Rhae M Swisher, Claude I. Shell, R. Thomas Lenz, Michael C. White, Dennis Callahan, R. Duane Ireland, William E. Burr, II, C. W. Millard, Richard Mann, Kurt Christensen, Neil W. Jacobs, Louis W. Fry, D. Robley Wood, George J. Gore, and William R. Soukup, all of whom guided our efforts at various stages in the evolution of the manuscript through the first five editions.

Naturally, as custom properly dictates, we are responsible for whatever errors of fact, deficiencies in coverage or in exposition, and oversights that remain. As always, we value your recommendations and thoughts about the book. Your comments regarding coverage and content will be most welcome, as will your calling our attention to specific errors. Please write us at P.O. Box 870225, Department of Management and Marketing, The University of Alabama, Tuscaloosa, Alabama 35487-0225

Arthur A. Thompson, Jr.
A. J. Strickland III

The ground that strategic management covers is challenging, wide-ranging, and exciting. The center of attention is *the total enterprise*—the environment in which it operates, the direction management intends to head, management's strategic plan for getting the enterprise moving in this direction, and the managerial tasks of implementing and executing the chosen strategy successfully. We'll be examining the foremost issue in running a business enterprise: What must managers do, and do well, to make the company a winner rather than a loser in the game of business?

The answer that emerges again and again, and which becomes the theme of the course is that good strategy making and good strategy implementing are always the most reliable signs of good management. The task of this course is to expose you to the reasons why good strategic management nearly always produces good company performance and to instruct you in the methods of crafting a well-conceived strategy and then successfully executing it.

During the course, you can expect to learn what the role and tasks of the strategy-maker are. You will grapple with what strategy means and with all the ramifications of figuring out which strategy is best in light of a company's overall situation. You will get a workout in sizing up a variety of industry and competitive situations, in using the tools of strategic analysis, in considering the pros and cons of strategic alternatives, and in crafting an attractive strategic plan. You will learn about the principal managerial tasks associated with implementing the chosen strategy successfully. You will become more skilled as a strategic thinker and you will develop your powers of business judgment. The excitement comes, believe it or not, from the extra savvy you will pick up about playing the game of business and from the blossoming of your entrepreneurial and competitive instincts.

In the midst of all this, another purpose is accomplished: to help you integrate and apply what you've learned in prior courses. Strategic management is a big picture course. It deals with the grand sweep of how to manage. Unlike your other business courses where the subject matter was narrowly aimed at a particular function or piece of the business—accounting, finance, marketing, production, human resources, or information systems—this course deals with the company's entire makeup and situation from both inside and outside. Nothing is ignored or assumed away. The task is to arrive at solid judgments about how all the relevant factors add up. This makes strategic management an integrative, capstone course in which you reach back to use concepts and techniques covered in previous courses. For perhaps the first time you'll see how the various pieces of the business puzzle fit together and why the different parts of a business need to be managed in strategic harmony for the organization to operate in winning fashion.

   No matter what your major is, the content of this course has all the ingredients to be the best course you've taken—best in the sense of learning a lot about business and holding your interest from beginning to end. Dig in, get involved, and make the most of what the course has to offer. As you tackle the subject matter, ponder Ralph Waldo Emerson's observation, "Commerce is a game of skill which many people play, but which few play well." What we've put between these covers is aimed squarely at helping you become a wiser, shrewder player. Good luck!

A. A. T.
A. J. S.

CONTENTS

Strategic Management

Concepts & cases

THE CONCEPTS AND TECHNIQUES OF STRATEGIC MANAGEMENT

The Strategic Management Process

*"Cheshire Puss," she [Alice] began . . . "would you please tell me which way I ought
to go from here?"*
"That depends on where you want to get to," said the cat.
~Lewis Carroll

• • • • • • •

My job is to make sure the company has a strategy and that everybody follows it.
~Kenneth H. Olsen
CEO, Digital Equipment Corp.

• • • • • • •

A strategy is a commitment to undertake one set of actions rather than another.
~Sharon M. Oster
Professor, Yale University

This book is about the managerial tasks of crafting and implementing company strategies. *An organization's strategy consists of the moves and approaches devised by management to produce successful organization performance.* Strategy, in effect, is management's game plan for the business. Managers develop strategies to guide *how* an organization conducts its business and *how* it will achieve its target objectives. Without a strategy, there is no established course to follow, no roadmap to manage by, no cohesive action plan to produce the intended results.

Crafting and implementing a strategy for the business are *core* management functions. Among all the things that managers do, few affect organizational performance more lastingly than how well the management team handles the tasks of charting the organization's long-term direction, developing effective strategic moves and approaches, and then executing the strategy in ways that produce the intended results. Indeed, *good strategy and good implementation are the most trustworthy signs of good management.*

There is strong reason to associate "good management" with how well managers develop and execute strategy. Managers cannot be awarded a top grade

To qualify as excellently-managed, an organization must exhibit excellent execution of an excellent strategy.

for designing shrewd strategies but failing to carry them out well—weak implementation opens the door for organizational performance to fall short of full potential. Competent execution of a mediocre strategy scarcely qualifies managers for a gold-star award either. But powerful execution of a powerful strategy is a proven recipe for business success—the instances where a company with a well-conceived, well-executed strategy is unable to build a leading market position are few and far between. The standards for judging whether an organization is well managed, therefore, are grounded in good strategy-making *combined* with good strategy execution. The better conceived an organization's strategy and the more flawless its execution, the greater the chance that the organization will be a peak performer in its industry.

However, superior strategy-making and strategy-implementing don't *guarantee superior organizational performance continuously*. Even well-managed organizations can hit the skids for short periods because of adverse conditions beyond management's ability to foresee or react to. But the bad luck of adverse events never excuses weak performance year after year. It is management's responsibility to adjust to negative conditions by undertaking strategic defenses and managerial approaches that can overcome adversity. Indeed, the essence of good strategy-making is to build a position strong and flexible enough to produce successful performance despite unforeseeable and unexpected external factors.

THE FIVE TASKS OF STRATEGIC MANAGEMENT

The strategy-making, strategy-implementing function of managers consists of five interrelated components:

1. *Developing a concept of the business and forming a vision of where the organization needs to be headed*—in effect, infusing the organization with a sense of purpose, providing long-term direction, and establishing a *mission*.
2. *Converting the mission into specific performance objectives*.
3. *Crafting a strategy* to achieve the targeted performance.
4. *Implementing and executing the chosen strategy* efficiently and effectively.
5. *Evaluating performance, reviewing the situation, and initiating corrective adjustments* in mission, objectives, strategy, or implementation in light of actual experience, changing conditions, new ideas, and new opportunities.

Figure 1–1 shows a model of the process. Together, these five components define what we mean by the term *strategic management*. Let's explore this basic conceptual model in more detail to set the stage for the chapters that follow.

Developing a Vision and a Mission

The foremost direction-setting question senior managers of any enterprise need to ask is "What is our business and what will it be?" Developing a carefully reasoned answer to this question pushes managers to consider what the organization's business makeup should be and to develop a clearer vision of where the organization needs to be headed over the next 5 to 10 years.

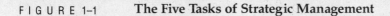

FIGURE 1–1   **The Five Tasks of Strategic Management**

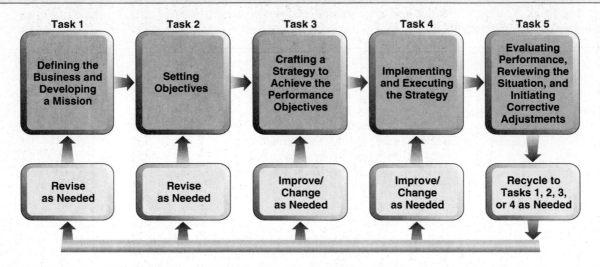

Management's answer to "What is our business and what will it be?" begins the process of carving out a meaningful direction for the organization to take and of establishing a strong organizational identity. Management's vision of what the organization seeks to do and to become is commonly termed the organization's *mission*. A mission statement establishes the organization's future course and outlines "who we are, what we do, and where we're headed." In effect, it sets forth the organization's intent to stake out a particular business position. Some examples of *company mission statements* are presented in Illustration Capsule 1.

Setting Objectives

The purpose of setting objectives is to convert the statement of organizational mission and direction into specific performance targets, something the organization's progress can be measured by. Objective-setting implies challenge, establishing a set of desired outcomes that require stretch and disciplined effort. The challenge of trying to close the gap between actual and desired performance pushes an organization to be more inventive, to exhibit some urgency in improving both its financial performance and its business position, and to be more intentional and focused in its actions. Setting *challenging but achievable* objectives thus helps guard against complacency, drift, internal confusion over what to accomplish, and status quo organizational performance. The set of objectives management establishes should ideally embrace a time horizon that is both near-term and far-term. *Short-range objectives* spell out the immediate improvements and outcomes management desires. *Long-range objectives* prompt managers to consider what they can do *now* to enhance the organization's strength and performance capabilities over the long term.

Objective-setting is required of *all managers*. Every unit in an organization needs concrete, measurable performance targets indicating its contribution to the organization's overall objectives. When organizationwide objectives are

---

 ILLUSTRATION CAPSULE **1** EXAMPLES OF COMPANY MISSION STATEMENTS

Presented below are seven actual company mission statements:

Otis Elevator

Our mission is to provide any customer a means of moving people and things up, down, and sideways over short distances with higher reliability than any similar enterprise in the world.

Deluxe Checks

The mission of Deluxe Checks is to provide all banks, S&L's, and investment firms with error-free financial instruments delivered in a timely fashion.

McCormick & Company

The primary mission of McCormick & Company is to expand our worldwide leadership position in the spice, seasoning, and flavoring markets.

Hewlett-Packard Company

Hewlett-Packard is a major designer and manufacturer of electronic products and systems for measurement and computation. HP's basic business purpose is to provide the capabilities and services needed to help customers worldwide improve their personal and business effectiveness.

The Saturn Division of General Motors

To market vehicles developed and manufactured in the United States that are world leaders in quality, cost, and customer satisfaction through the integration of people, technology, and business systems and to transfer knowledge, technology, and experience throughout General Motors.

Public Service Company of New Mexico

Our mission is to work for the success of the people we serve by providing our CUSTOMERS reliable electric service, energy information, and energy options that best satisfy their needs.

American Red Cross

The mission of the American Red Cross is to improve the quality of human life; to enhance self-reliance and concern for others; and to help people avoid, prepare for, and cope with emergencies.

Source: Company annual reports.

---

broken down into specific targets for each unit and lower-level managers are held accountable for achieving them, a results-oriented climate emerges, with each part of the organization striving to achieve results that will move the whole organization in the intended direction.

Two types of performance yardsticks are called for: *financial objectives* and *strategic objectives*. Financial objectives are needed because acceptable financial performance is critical to preserving an organization's vitality and well-being. Strategic objectives are needed to provide consistent direction in strengthening a company's overall business position. Financial objectives typically focus on such measures as earnings growth, return on investment, and cash flow. Strategic objectives, however, relate more directly to a company's overall competitive situation and involve such performance yardsticks as growing faster than the industry average and making gains in market share, overtaking key competitors on product quality or customer service, achieving lower overall costs than rivals, boosting the company's reputation with customers, winning a stronger foothold in international markets, exercising technological leadership, and developing attractive growth opportunities. Strategic objectives make it explicit that management not only must deliver good financial performance but also must deliver on strengthening the organization's long-term business and competitive position.

Examples of the kinds of strategic and financial objectives companies set are shown in Illustration Capsule 2.

••••••••••••

Strategic Management Principle
Strategic objectives are, at the very least, coequal in importance to financial objectives.

ILLUSTRATION CAPSULE | **2** | **EXAMPLES OF CORPORATE OBJECTIVES**
Nike, La-Z-Boy, Owens-Corning, and McCormick & Company

Nike's Objectives (as stated in 1987)

- Protect and improve NIKE's position as the number one athletic brand in America, with particular attention to the company's existing core businesses in running, basketball, tennis, football, baseball, and kid's shoes and newer businesses with good potential like golf and soccer.
- Build a strong momentum in the growing fitness market, beginning with walking, workout, and cycling.
- Intensify the company's effort to develop products that women need and want.
- Explore the market for products specifically designed for the requirements of maturing Americans.
- Direct and manage the company's international business as it continues to develop.
- Continue the drive for increased margins through proper inventory management and fewer, better products.

La-Z-Boy's Objectives (as stated in 1990)

- To position La-Z-Boy as a full-line furniture manufacturer.
- To strengthen La-Z-Boy's brand name image with American families and businesspeople.
- To improve the quality of the company's distribution network.
- To expand production capacity and make it more efficient.
- To continue to gain financial strength.

Owens-Corning's Objectives (as stated in 1990)

- To anticipate our customers' requirements and provide them with the products which meet their market, quality, and service needs.
- To maintain our number one market positions through continued leadership in technology, manufacturing, and marketing.
- To maximize cash flow for continued debt reduction.
- To focus on operating profit improvements through productivity programs and focused market development.
- To make the most of the talents of our people and provide them with the opportunity and training to reach their full potential.

McCormick & Company's Objectives (as stated in 1990)

- Improve the returns from each of our existing operating groups—consumer, industrial, food service, international, and packaging.
- Dispose of those parts of our business which do not or cannot generate adequate returns or do not fit with our business strategy.
- Make selective acquisitions which complement our current businesses and can enhance our overall returns.
- Achieve a 20% return on equity.
- Achieve a net sales growth rate of 10% per year.
- Maintain an average earnings per share growth rate of 15% per year.
- Maintain total debt to total capital at 40% or less.
- Pay out 25% to 35% of net income in dividends.

Source: Company annual reports.

Crafting a Strategy

An organization's strategy for achieving its performance objectives consists of actions and approaches already in place and scheduled for continuation, supplemented with new actions just underway and additional future moves being mapped out.

Strategy-making brings into play the critical managerial issue of *how* to achieve the targeted results in light of the organization's situation and prospects. Objectives are the "ends," and *strategy* is the "means" of achieving them. In effect, strategy is a management tool for achieving strategic targets. The task of forming a strategy starts with hard analysis of the organization's internal and external situation. Armed with an understanding of the "big picture," managers can better devise a strategy to achieve targeted strategic and financial results.

Definitionally, *strategy is the pattern of organizational moves and managerial approaches used to achieve organizational objectives and to pursue the organization's mission.* The pattern of moves and approaches already taken indicates what the prevailing strategy is; the planned moves and approaches signal how the prevailing strategy is to be embellished or changed. Thus, while strategy represents the managerial game plan for running an organization, this plan does not consist of just good intentions and actions yet to be taken. An organization's strategy is nearly always a blend of prior moves, approaches already in place, and new actions being mapped out. Indeed, the biggest part of an organization's strategy usually consists of prior approaches and practices that are working well enough to continue. An organization's strategy that is mostly new most of the time signals erratic decision-making and weak "strategizing" on the part of managers. Quantum changes in strategy can be expected occasionally, especially in crisis situations, but they cannot be made too often without creating undue organizational confusion and disrupting performance.

Strategy and Entrepreneurship Crafting strategy is an exercise in *entrepreneurship*. Some degree of venturesomeness and risk-taking is inherent in choosing among alternative business directions and devising the next round of moves and approaches. Managers face an ever-present entrepreneurial challenge keeping the organization's strategy fresh, responding to changing conditions, and steering the organization into the right business activities at the right time. Consideration of strategy changes thus cannot and should not be avoided. Often, there is more risk in coasting along with the status quo than there is in assuming the risk of making strategic changes. When managers become reluctant entrepreneurs, they get complacent about current strategy and become overly analytical or hesitant to make strategic decisions that blaze new trails. How boldly or cautiously managers push in new directions and how vigorously they initiate actions for boosting organizational performance are good indicators of their entrepreneurial spirit.

> *Strategy-making is fundamentally an entrepreneurial activity—risk-taking, venturesomeness, business creativity, and an eye for spotting emerging market opportunities are all involved in crafting a strategic action plan.*

All managers, not just senior executives, need to exercise entrepreneurship in strategy-making. Entrepreneurship is involved when a district customer service manager crafts a strategy to cut the response time on service calls by 25 percent and commits $15,000 to equip all service trucks with mobile telephones. Entrepreneurship is involved when a warehousing manager develops a strategy to reduce the error frequency on filling orders from 1 error per every hundred orders to 1 error per every thousand orders. A sales manager exercises strategic entrepreneurship in deciding to run a special advertising promotion and cut sales prices by 5 percent. A manufacturing manager exercises strategic entrepreneurship in deciding to source an important component from a lower-priced South Korean supplier instead of making it in-house. Strategy-making is not something just top managers do; it is something all managers do—every manager needs an entrepreneurial game plan for the area he/she is in charge of.

Why Strategy Is Constantly Evolving From the perspective of the whole organization, the task of "strategizing" is always an ongoing exercise.[1] "The whats" of an organization's mission and long-term objectives, once chosen,

> *A company's strategic action plan is dynamic, undergoing continuous review, refinement, enhancement, and occasional major revision.*

---

[1]Henry Mintzberg, "Crafting Strategy," *Harvard Business Review* 65, no. 4 (July–August 1987), pp. 66–75; and James B. Quinn, *Strategies for Change: Logical Incrementalism* (Homewood, Ill.: Richard D. Irwin, 1980), chap. 2, especially pp. 58–59.

may remain unaltered for several years. But "the hows" of strategy evolve constantly, partly in response to an ever-changing external environment, partly from managers' efforts to create new opportunities, and partly from fresh ideas about how to make the strategy work better. On occasion, quantum changes in strategy emerge when a big strategic move is put to test in the real world or when crisis strikes and managers see that the organization's strategy needs radical reorientation. Refinements and additions, interspersed with periodic quantum leaps, are a normal part of managerial "strategizing."

Because strategic moves and new action approaches are made in an ongoing stream, an organization's strategy forms over a period of time and then reforms, always consisting of a mix of holdover approaches, fresh actions in process, and unrevealed moves being planned. Aside from crisis situations (where many strategic moves are often made quickly to produce a substantially new strategy almost overnight) and new company start-ups (where strategy exists mostly in the form of plans and intended actions), a company's strategy is crafted in bits and pieces as events unfold and as managerial experience accumulates. Everything cannot be planned out in advance, and even the best-laid plans must be responsive to changing conditions and unforeseen events. Strategy-making thus proceeds on two fronts—one proactively thought through in advance, the other conceived in response to new developments, special opportunities, and experiences with the successes and failures of prior strategic moves, approaches, and actions. Figure 1–2 depicts the kinds of actions that form a company's strategy.

Strategy and Strategic Plans   The three tasks of defining the business, setting objectives, and crafting a strategy all involve direction-setting. Together, they specify where the organization is headed and how management intends to achieve the targeted results. Together, they constitute a *strategic plan*. In some companies, especially large corporations committed to regular strategy reviews and formal strategic planning, the strategic plan is explicit and written (although parts of the plan may be omitted if they are too sensitive to reveal before they are actually undertaken). In other companies, the strategic plan is not put on paper but rather exists in the form of understandings among managers about what is to be carried over from the past and what new actions are to be taken. Organizational objectives are the part of the strategic plan that are most often written and circulated among managers and employees.

Illustration Capsule 3 presents an outline of Sara Lee Corporation's mission, objectives, and strategies as an example of how the three direction-setting steps join together.

Strategy Implementation and Execution

Strategy implementation is fundamentally an administrative activity—organizing, budgeting, motivating, culture-building, supervising, and leading are all part of "making it happen" and achieving the intended strategic and financial outcomes.

The strategy-implementing function consists of seeing what it will take to make the strategy work and to reach the targeted performance on schedule—*the skill comes in knowing how to achieve results.* The job of implementing strategy is primarily an action-driven *administrative task* that cuts across many internal matters. The principal administrative aspects associated with putting the strategy into place include:

- Building an organization capable of carrying out the strategy successfully.

FIGURE 1–2   The Components of Company Strategy

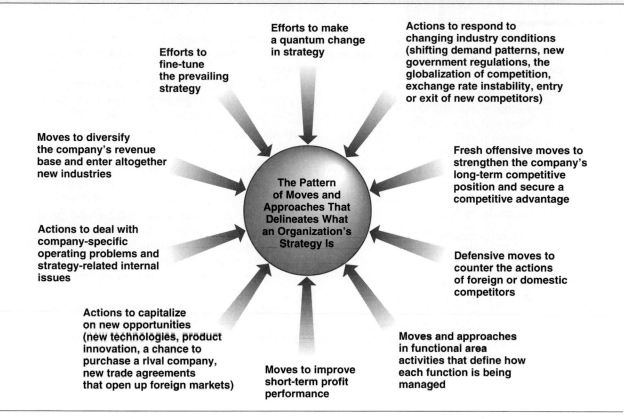

Efforts to make
a quantum change
in strategy

Actions to respond to
changing industry conditions
(shifting demand patterns, new
government regulations, the
globalization of competition,
exchange rate instability, entry
or exit of new competitors)

Efforts to
fine-tune
the prevailing
strategy

Moves to diversify
the company's revenue
base and enter altogether
new industries

Fresh offensive moves to
strengthen the company's
long-term competitive
position and secure a
competitive advantage

The Pattern
of Moves and
Approaches That
Delineates What
an Organization's
Strategy Is

Actions to deal with
company-specific
operating problems and
strategy-related internal
issues

Defensive moves to
counter the actions
of foreign or domestic
competitors

Actions to capitalize
on new opportunities
(new technologies, product
innovation, a chance to
purchase a rival company,
new trade agreements
that open up foreign markets)

Moves and approaches
in functional area
activities that define how
each function is being
managed

Moves to improve
short-term profit
performance

- Developing budgets that steer resources into those internal activities critical to strategic success.
- Motivating people in ways that induce them to pursue the target objectives energetically and, if need be, modifying their duties and job behavior to better fit the requirements of successful strategy execution.
- Tying the reward structure tightly to the achievement of the targeted results.
- Creating a work environment conducive to successful strategy implementation.
- Installing strategy-supportive policies and procedures.
- Developing an information and reporting system to track progress and monitor performance.
- Exerting the internal leadership needed to drive implementation forward and to keep improving on how the strategy is being executed.

The administrative aim is to create "fits" between the way things are done and what it takes for effective strategy execution. The stronger the fits, the better the execution of strategy. The most important fits are between strategy and organizational capabilities, between strategy and the reward structure, between

---

ILLUSTRATION CAPSULE | **3** | SARA LEE CORPORATION: MISSION, OBJECTIVES, AND STRATEGY

In a recent annual report, the management of Sara Lee Corporation set forth the company's mission, objectives, and strategy:

Mission

Sara Lee Corporation's mission is to be the leading brand-name food and consumer packaged goods company with major market share positions in key consumer markets worldwide.

We manufacture and market high-quality, marketing-sensitive products with growth potential. These products, which are sold through common distribution channels, include

- Packaged food products,
- Food products and services for the foodservice industry,
- Consumer personal products, and
- Household and personal care products.

Objectives

Size alone—that is, being the largest by some quantitative measure—does not define leadership. We aspire to be a larger company only to the extent that size and scale contribute to achieving more important measures of pre-eminence.

First, and above all, the leading company must be an outstanding financial performer for its stockholders. We must produce dependable and consistent financial returns which rank high in absolute terms as well as relative to our peer competitors.

Second, our product positions must be very high quality, compete in significant market segments, and command exceptionally strong market shares.

Third, our management people and processes must be of the highest caliber and appropriate to the times.

And fourth, we must be recognized as a corporation with an especially high sense of responsibility to our employees and public constituencies.

Corporate Strategies

1. Invest to accelerate internal growth. Direct and focus investment spending on strategic opportunities to build share and to accelerate unit volume growth in key product positions.

2. Develop the lowest cost position in all product categories. Emphasize and measure operating efficiencies and cost structures in all areas of the corporation to reduce costs consistently and to increase return on sales without sacrificing quality.

3. Make acquisitions. Acquire businesses which fit Sara Lee Corporation's strategic focus and which provide increased opportunity for growth consistent with our mission.

4. Leverage brand names and strategically link businesses for synergy. Generate growth by building and extending brand positions, and improve returns by strategically combining divisions and developing synergies among businesses.

5. Pursue cross-channel distribution for established products, brands and positions. Increase unit volume and return on sales with cross-channel distribution.

Source: 1987 Annual Report.

---

strategy and internal policies and procedures, and between strategy and the organization's culture (the latter emerges from the values and beliefs shared by organizational members and from management's human relations practices). Fitting the ways the organization does things internally to what it takes for effective strategy execution is what unites the organization firmly behind the accomplishment of strategy.

The strategy-implementing task is easily the most complicated and time-consuming part of strategic management. It cuts across virtually all facets of managing and must be initiated from many points inside the organization. The strategy-implementer's agenda for action emerges from careful assessment of what the organization must do differently and better to carry out the strategic plan proficiently. Each manager has to think through the answer to "What has to be done in my area of responsibility to carry out my piece of the overall strategic plan and how can I best get it done?" How much internal change is needed to put the strategy into effect depends on the degree of strategic change, whether internal practices deviate very far from what the strategy requires, and how well strategy and organizational culture already match. As needed changes and actions are identified, management must supervise all the details of implementation and apply enough pressure on the organization to convert objectives into actual results. Depending on the amount of internal change involved, full implementation can take several months to several years.

Evaluating Performance, Reviewing the Situation, and Initiating Corrective Adjustments

None of the previous four tasks are one-time exercises. New circumstances always crop up that make corrective adjustments desirable. Long-term direction may need to be altered, the business redefined, and management's vision of the organization's future course narrowed or broadened. Performance targets may need raising or lowering in light of past experience and future prospects. Strategy may need to be modified because of shifts in long-term direction, because new objectives have been set, or because of changing conditions in the environment.

　　The search for even better strategy execution is also continuous. Sometimes an aspect of implementation does not go as well as intended and changes have to be made. Progress typically proceeds unevenly—faster in some areas and slower in others. Some tasks get done easily; others prove nettlesome. Implementation occurs through the pooling effect of many administrative decisions about how to do things and how to create stronger fits between strategy and internal operating practices. Budget revisions, policy changes, reorganization, personnel changes, culture-changing actions, and revised compensation practices are typical ways of trying to make the chosen strategy work better.

A company's mission, objectives, strategy, or approach to strategy implementation is never final; evaluating performance, reviewing changes in the surrounding environment, and making adjustments are normal and necessary parts of the strategic management process.

WHY STRATEGIC MANAGEMENT IS AN ONGOING PROCESS

Because each one of the five tasks of strategic management requires constant evaluation and a decision whether to continue with things as they are or to make changes, *the process of managing strategy is ongoing*. Nothing is final— all prior actions are subject to modification as conditions in the surrounding environment change and ways to improve emerge. Strategic management is a process filled with constant motion. Changes in the organization's situation, either from the inside or outside or both, constantly drive strategic adjustments. This is why, in Figure 1–1, we refer to recycling.

　　The task of evaluating performance and initiating corrective adjustments is both the end and the beginning of the strategic management cycle. The march of external and internal events guarantees revision in the four previous components will be needed sooner or later. It is always incumbent on management to push for better performance—to find ways to improve the existing strategy and how it is being executed. Changing external conditions add further impetus to the need for periodic revisions in a company's mission, performance objectives, strategy, and approaches to strategy execution. Adjustments usually involve fine-tuning, but occasions for a major strategic reorientation do arise— sometimes prompted by significant external developments and sometimes by sharply sliding financial performance. Strategy managers must stay close enough to the situation to detect when changing conditions require a strategic response and when they don't. It is their job to read the winds of change, recognize significant changes early, and capitalize on events as they unfold.[2]

Characteristics of the Process

Although the tasks of developing a mission, setting objectives, forming a strategy, implementing and executing the strategic plan, and evaluating performance constitute the elements of the strategic management function, actually performing these five tasks is not so cleanly divided and neatly sequenced. There is much interplay among the five tasks. For example, considering what strategic actions to take raises issues about whether and how the strategy can be satisfactorily implemented. Deciding on a company mission shades into setting objectives for the organization to achieve (both involve directional priorities). To establish challenging but achievable objectives, managers must consider both current performance and the strategy options available to improve performance. Deciding on a strategy is entangled with decisions about long-term direction and whether objectives have been set too high or too low.

Second, the five strategic management tasks are not done in isolation. They are carried out in the midst of all other managerial responsibilities—supervising day-to-day operations, dealing with crises, going to meetings, preparing reports, handling people problems, and taking on special assignments and civic duties. Thus, while the job of managing strategy is the most important function management performs insofar as organizational success or failure is concerned, it isn't all managers must do or be concerned about.

Third, strategic management makes erratic demands on a manager's time. An organization's situation does not change in an orderly or predictable way. The events that prompt reconsideration of strategy can build quickly or gradually; they can emerge singly or in rapid-fire succession; and the implications they have for strategic change can be easy or hard to diagnose. Hence strategic issues and decisions take up big chunks of management time some months and little or none in other months. As a practical matter, there is as much skill in knowing *when* to institute strategic changes as there is in knowing *what* to do.[3]

Last, the big day-in, day-out time-consuming aspect of strategic management is trying to get the best strategy-supportive performance out of every individual and trying to perfect the current strategy by refining its content and execution. Managing strategy is mostly improving bits and pieces of the strategy in place, not developing and instituting radical strategic changes.

---

[2]Mintzberg, "Crafting Strategy," p. 74.
[3]Ibid., p. 73.

Excessive changes in strategy can be disruptive to employees and confusing to customers, and they are usually unnecessary. Most of the time, there's more to be gained from improving execution of the present strategy. Persistence in trying to make a sound strategy work better is often the key to managing the strategy to success.

WHO ARE THE STRATEGY MANAGERS?

An organization's chief executive officer is the most visible and important *strategy manager.* The CEO, as captain of the ship, bears full responsibility for leading the tasks of formulating and implementing the strategic plans of the whole organization, even though many other managers have a hand in the process. The CEO functions as chief direction-setter, chief objective-setter, chief strategy-maker, and chief strategy-implementer for the total enterprise. What the CEO views as important usually moves to the top of every manager's priority list, and the CEO has the final word on big decisions.

Vice presidents for production, marketing, finance, human resources, and other functional departments have important strategy-making and strategy-implementing responsibilities as well. Normally, the production VP oversees production strategy; the marketing VP heads up the marketing strategy effort; the financial VP is in charge of financial strategy; and so on. Usually, functional vice presidents are also involved in proposing and developing key elements of the overall strategy, working closely with the CEO to hammer out a consensus and make certain parts of the strategy more effective. Only rarely does a CEO personally craft all the key pieces of organization strategy.

But managerial positions with strategy-making and strategy-implementing responsibility are by no means restricted to these few senior executives. *Every manager is a strategy-maker and strategy-implementer for the area he/she has authority over and supervises.* Every part of a company—business unit, division, operating department, plant, or district office—has a strategic role to carry out. And the manager in charge of that unit, with guidance from superiors, usually ends up doing some or most of the strategy-making for the unit and implementing whatever strategic choices are made. However, managers farther down in the managerial hierarchy have a narrower, more specific strategy-making/strategy-implementing role than managers closer to the top.

All managers are involved in the strategy-making and strategy-implementing process.

Another reason lower-echelon managers are strategy-makers and strategy-implementers is that the more geographically scattered and diversified an organization's operations are, the more impossible it becomes for a few senior executives to handle all the strategic planning that needs to be done. Managers in the corporate office don't know all the situational details in all geographical areas and operating units to be able to prescribe appropriate strategies. Usually, they delegate some of the strategy-making responsibility to the lower-level managers who head the organizational subunits where specific strategic results must be achieved. Delegating a lead strategy-making role to those managers who will be deeply involved in carrying it out in their areas fixes accountability for strategic success or failure. When the managers who implement the strategy are also its architects, it is hard for them to shift the blame or make excuses if they don't achieve the target results.

In diversified companies where the strategies of several different businesses have to be managed, there are usually four distinct levels of strategy managers:

- *The chief executive officer and other senior corporation-level executives* who have primary responsibility and personal authority for big strategic decisions affecting the total enterprise and the collection of individual businesses the enterprise has diversified into.
- *Managers who have profit-and-loss responsibility for one specific business unit* and who are delegated a major leadership role in formulating and implementing strategy for that unit.
- *Functional area managers within a given business unit* who have direct authority over a major piece of the business (manufacturing, marketing and sales, finance, R&D, personnel) and whose role it is to support the business unit's overall strategy with strategic actions in their own areas.
- *Managers of major operating departments and geographic field units* who have front-line responsibility for developing the details of strategic efforts in their areas and for implementing and executing the overall strategic plan at the grassroots level.

Single-business enterprises need no more than three of these levels (business-level strategy managers, functional area strategy managers, and operating-level strategy managers). In a large single-business company, the team of strategy managers consists of the chief executive, who functions as chief strategist with final authority over both strategy and its implementation; the vice presidents in charge of key functions (R&D, production, marketing, finance, human resources, and so on); plus as many operating-unit managers of the various plants, sales offices, distribution centers, and staff support departments as it takes to handle the company's scope of operations. Proprietorships, partnerships, and owner-managed enterprises, however, typically have only one or two strategy managers since in small-scale enterprises the whole strategy-making/strategy-implementing function can be handled by just a few key people.

Managerial jobs involving strategy formulation and implementation abound in not-for-profit organizations as well. For example, a multicampus state university has four strategy-managing levels: (1) the president of the university system is a strategy manager with broad direction-setting responsibility and strategic decision-making authority over all the campuses; (2) the chancellor for each campus customarily has strategy-making/strategy-implementing authority over all academic, student, athletic, and alumni matters, plus budgetary, programmatic, and coordinative responsibilities for that campus; (3) the academic deans have lead responsibility for charting future direction at the college level, steering resources into high-demand programs and out of low-demand programs, and otherwise devising a collegewide plan to fulfill the college's teaching-research-service mission; and (4) the heads of various academic departments are strategy managers with first-line strategy-making/strategy-implementing responsibility for the department's undergraduate and graduate program offerings, faculty research efforts, and all other activities relating to the department's mission, objectives, and future direction. In federal and state government, heads of local, district, and regional offices function as strategy managers in their efforts to respond to the needs and situations of the areas they serve (a district manager in Portland may need a slightly different strategy than a district manager in Orlando). In municipal government, the heads of various departments (fire, police, water and sewer, parks and recreation, health, and so on) are strategy managers because they have line authority for the operations of their departments and thus can influence departmental objectives, the formation of a strategy to achieve these objectives, and how the strategy is implemented.

Managerial jobs with strategy-making/strategy-implementing roles are thus the norm rather than the exception. The job of crafting and implementing strategy touches virtually every managerial job in one way or another, at one time or another. Strategic management is basic to the task of managing; it is not something just top-level managers deal with.[4]

The Role and Tasks of Strategic Planners

If senior and middle managers have the lead roles in strategy-making and strategy-implementing in their areas of responsibility, what should strategic planners do? Is there a legitimate place in big companies for a strategic planning department staffed with specialists in planning and strategic analysis? The answer is yes. But the planning department's role and tasks should consist chiefly of helping to gather and organize information that strategy managers need, establishing and administering an annual strategy review cycle whereby all strategy managers reconsider and refine their strategic plans, and coordinating the process of reviewing and approving the strategic plans developed for all the various parts of the company. Strategic planners are valuable because they help managers at all levels crystallize the strategic issues that ought to be addressed; in addition, they can provide data, help analyze industry and competitive conditions, and distribute information on the company's strategic performance. But strategic planners should *not* make strategic decisions, prepare strategic plans (for someone else to implement), or make strategic action recommendations that usurp the strategy-making responsibilities of managers in charge of major operating units.

When strategic planners are asked to go beyond providing staff assistance and actually prepare a strategic plan for management's consideration, either of two adverse consequences may occur. First, some managers will gladly toss tough strategic problems in their areas onto the desks of strategic planners to let the planners do their strategic thinking for them. The planners, not knowing as much about the situation as managers do, are in a weaker position to design a workable action plan. And they can't be held responsible for implementing what they recommend. Giving planners responsibility for strategy-making and line managers responsibility for implementation makes it hard to fix accountability for poor results. It also deludes line managers into thinking they don't

- - - - - - - - - - - - - -

Strategic Management Principle
Strategy-making is not a proper task for strategic planners.

---

[4]Since the scope of a manager's strategy-making/strategy-implementing role varies according to the manager's position in the organizational hierarchy, our use of the word "organization" includes whatever kind of unit the strategy manager is in charge of—an entire company or not-for-profit organization, a business unit within a diversified company, a major geographic division, an important functional area within a business, or an operating department or field unit reporting to the functional area head. It should be clear from the context of the discussion whether the subject applies to the total enterprise or to most or all management levels.

have to be personally involved in crafting a strategy for their own organizational unit or in finding strategic solutions to strategic problems in their area of responsibility. The hard truth is that strategy-making is not a staff function, nor is it something that can be handed off to an advisory committee of lower-ranking managers. Second, when line managers have no ownership stake in or personal commitment to the strategic agenda proposed by the planners, they give it lip service, make a few token implementation efforts, and quickly get back to "business as usual," knowing that the formal written plan concocted by the planners does not match their own "real" managerial agenda. The written strategic plan, because it lacks credibility and true top-management commitment, soon collects dust on managers' shelves. The result is that few managers take the work product of the strategic planning staff seriously enough to pursue implementation—strategic planning comes to be seen as just another bureaucratic exercise.

Either consequence renders formal strategic planning efforts ineffective and opens the door for a strategy-making vacuum conducive to organizational drift or to fragmented, uncoordinated strategic decisions. The odds are then heightened that the organization will have no strong strategic rudder and insufficient top-down direction. The flaws in having staffers or advisory committees formulate strategies for areas they do not manage are: (1) they can't be held accountable if their recommendations don't produce the desired results since they don't have authority for directing implementation, and (2) what they recommend won't be well accepted or enthusiastically implemented by those who "have to sing the song the planners have written." But when line managers are expected to be the chief strategy-makers and strategy-implementers for the areas they head, it is their own strategy and their own implementation approach that are being put to the test of workability. They are likely to be more committed to making the plan work (their future careers with the organization are at more risk!), and they can be held strictly accountable for achieving the target results in their area.

The Strategic Role of the Board of Directors

Strategic Management Principle
A board of directors' role in the strategic management process is to critically appraise and ultimately approve strategic action plans but rarely, if ever, to participate directly in the details of strategy-making.

Since lead responsibility for crafting and implementing strategy falls to key managers, the chief strategic role of an organization's board of directors is to see that the overall task of managing strategy is adequately done.[5] Boards of directors normally review important strategic moves and officially approve the strategic plans submitted by senior management—a procedure that makes the board ultimately responsible for the strategic actions taken. But directors rarely can or should play a direct role in formulating strategy. The immediate task of directors in ratifying strategy and new direction-setting moves is to ensure that all proposals have been adequately analyzed and considered and that the proposed strategic actions are superior to available alternatives; flawed proposals are customarily withdrawn for revision by management.[6] The longer-range task of directors is to evaluate the caliber of senior executives'

[5]Kenneth R. Andrews, *The Concept of Corporate Strategy*, 3rd ed. (Homewood, Ill.: Richard D. Irwin, 1987), p. 123.
[6]Ibid.

strategy-making and strategy-implementing skills. The board must determine whether the current CEO is doing a good job of strategic management (as a basis for awarding salary increases and bonuses and deciding on retention or removal) and evaluate the strategic skills of other senior executives in line to succeed the current CEO.

THE BENEFITS OF A "STRATEGIC APPROACH" TO MANAGING

The message of this book is that doing a good job of managing inherently requires doing a good job of strategic management. Today's managers have to think strategically about their company's position and about the impact of changing conditions. They have to monitor the external situation closely enough to know *when* to institute strategy change. They have to know the business well enough to know *what kind* of strategic changes to initiate. Simply said, the fundamentals of strategic management need to drive the whole approach to managing organizations.[7] The chief executive officer of one successful company put it well when he said:

> In the main, our competitors are acquainted with the same fundamental concepts and techniques and approaches that we follow, and they are as free to pursue them as we are. More often than not, the difference between their level of success and ours lies in the relative thoroughness and self-discipline with which we and they develop and execute our strategies for the future.

The advantages of first-rate strategic thinking and conscious strategy management (as opposed to freewheeling improvisation, gut feel, and drifting along) include (1) providing better guidance to the entire organization on the crucial point of "what it is we are trying to do and to achieve," (2) making managers more alert to the winds of change, new opportunities, and threatening developments, (3) providing managers with a rationale to evaluate competing budget requests for investment capital and new staff—a rationale that argues strongly for steering resources into strategy-supportive, results-producing areas, (4) helping to unify the numerous strategy-related decisions by managers across the organization, and (5) creating a more *proactive* management posture and counteracting tendencies for decisions to be reactive and defensive.[8]

The fifth advantage of being proactive rather than merely reactive is that trail-blazing strategies can be the key to better long-term performance. Business history shows that high-performing enterprises often *initiate* and *lead*, not just *react* and *defend*. They launch strategic *offensives* to secure sustainable competitive advantage and then use their market edge to achieve superior financial performance. Aggressive pursuit of a creative, opportunistic strategy can propel a firm into a leadership position, paving the way for its products/services to become the industry standard.

---

[7]For a lucid discussion of the importance of the strategic management function, see V. Ramanujam and N. Venkatraman, "Planning and Performance: A New Look at an Old Question," *Business Horizons* 30, no. 3 (May–June, 1987), pp. 19–25; and Henry Mintzberg, "The Strategy Concept: Another Look at Why Organizations Need Strategies," *California Management Review* 30, no. 1 (Fall 1987), pp. 25–32.

[8]Kenneth R. Andrews, *The Concept of Corporate Strategy*, rev. ed. (Homewood, Ill.: Richard D. Irwin, 1980), pp. 15–16, 46, 123–29; and Seymour Tilles, "How to Evaluate Corporate Strategy," *Harvard Business Review* 41, no. 4 (July–August 1963), p. 116

A RECAP OF
IMPORTANT
TERMS

We conclude this introductory overview by defining key terms that will be used again and again in the chapters to come:

Organization mission—management's customized answer to the question "What is our business and what will it be?" A mission statement broadly outlines the organization's future direction and serves as a guiding concept for what the organization is to do and to become.

Performance objectives—the organization's targets for achievement.

Financial objectives—the targets management has established for the organization's financial performance.

Strategic objectives—the targets management has established for strengthening the organization's overall position and competitive vitality.

Long-range objectives—the results to be achieved either within the next three to five years or else on an ongoing basis year after year.

Short-range objectives—the organization's near-term performance targets; the amount of short-term improvement signals how fast management is trying to achieve the long-range objectives.

Strategy—the managerial action plan for achieving organizational objectives; strategy is mirrored in the *pattern* of moves and approaches devised by management to produce the targeted outcomes. Strategy is the *how* of pursuing the organization's mission and achieving the desired objectives.

Strategic plan—a statement outlining an organization's mission and future direction, near-term and long-term performance targets, and strategy in light of the organization's external and internal situation.

Strategy formulation—the entire direction-setting management function of conceptualizing an organization's mission, setting performance objectives, and crafting a strategy. The end product of strategy formulation is a strategic plan.

Strategy implementation—the full range of managerial activities associated with putting the chosen strategy into place, supervising its pursuit, and achieving the targeted results.

In the chapters to come, we will probe the strategy-related tasks of managers and the methods of strategic analysis more intensively. When you get to the end of the book, we think you will see that two factors separate the best-managed organizations from the rest: (1) superior strategy-making and entrepreneurship, and (2) competent implementation and execution of the chosen strategy. There's no escaping the fact that the quality of managerial strategy-making and strategy-implementing has a significant impact on organization performance. A company that lacks clear-cut direction, has vague or undemanding objectives, or has a muddled or flawed strategy is a company whose performance is probably suffering, whose business is at long-term risk, and whose management is less than capable.

Andrews, Kenneth R. *The Concept of Corporate Strategy*. 3rd ed. Homewood, Ill.: Richard D. Irwin, 1987, chap. 1.

Gluck, Frederick W. "A Fresh Look at Strategic Management." *Journal of Business Strategy* 6, no. 2 (Fall 1985), pp. 4–21.

Hax, Arnoldo C., and Nicolas S. Majluf. *The Strategy Concept and Process: A Pragmatic Approach* (Englewood Cliffs, N.J.: Prentice Hall, 1991), chaps. 1 and 2.

Kelley, C. Aaron. "The Three Planning Questions: A Fable." *Business Horizons* 26, no. 2 (March–April 1983), pp. 46–48.

Kotter, John P. *The General Managers*. New York: Free Press, 1982.

Levinson, Harry, and Stuart Rosenthal. *CEO: Corporate Leadership in Action*. New York: Basic Books, 1987.

Mintzberg, Henry. "The Strategy Concept: Five Ps for Strategy." *California Management Review* 30, no. 1 (Fall 1987), pp. 11–24.

———. "The Strategy Concept: Another Look at Why Organizations Need Strategies." *California Management Review* 30, no. 1 (Fall 1987), pp. 25–32.

———. "Crafting Strategy." *Harvard Business Review* 65, no. 4 (July–August 1987), pp. 66–75.

Quinn, James B. *Strategies for Change: Logical Incrementalism*. Homewood, Ill.: Richard D. Irwin, 1980, chaps. 2 and 3.

Ramanujam, V., and N. Venkatraman. "Planning and Performance: A New Look at an Old Question." *Business Horizons* 30, no. 3 (May–June 1987), pp. 19–25.

Yip, George S. "Who Needs Strategic Planning?" *Journal of Business Strategy* 6, no. 2 (Fall 1985), pp. 22–29.

SUGGESTED READINGS

CHAPTER 2

The Three
Strategy-Making Tasks

Developing a Mission, Setting Objectives, and Forming a Strategy

Management's job is not to see the company as it is . . . but as it can become.
~John W. Teets
CEO, Greyhound Corp.

• • • • • • •

Without a strategy the organization is like a ship without a rudder, going around in circles. It's like a tramp; it has no place to go.
~Joel Ross and Michael Kami

• • • • • • •

You've got to come up with a plan. You can't wish things will get better.
~John F. Welch
CEO, General Electric

In this chapter, we provide a more in-depth look at each of the three strategy-making tasks: defining the business and developing a mission, setting performance objectives, and crafting a strategy to produce the desired results. We also examine the nature of strategy-making at each managerial level in the organizational hierarchy and discuss the four basic ways managers perform the strategy-making task.

DEVELOPING A MISSION: THE FIRST DIRECTION-SETTING TASK

Management's vision of what the organization is trying to do and to become over the long term is commonly referred to as the organization's *mission*. A *mission statement* specifies what activities the organization intends to pursue and what course management has charted for the future. It outlines "who *we* are, what *we* do, and where *we* are headed." Mission statements are thus personalized in the sense that they set an organization apart from others in its industry and give it its own special identity, character, and path for development. For example, the mission of a globally active New York bank like Citicorp has little in common with that of a locally owned small town bank even though both are in the banking industry. Without a concept of what the organization should and should not do and a vision of where the organization needs to be going, a manager cannot function effectively as either leader or strategy-maker. There are three distinct aspects to the task of developing a company mission:

- Understanding what business a company is really in.
- Deciding when to change the mission and alter the company's strategic course.
- Communicating the mission in ways that are clear, exciting, and inspiring.

Effective strategic leadership starts with a concept of what the organization should and should not do and a vision of where the organization needs to be headed.

Understanding and Defining the Business

Deciding what business an organization is in is neither obvious nor easy. Is IBM in the computer business (a product-oriented definition) or the information and data processing business (a customer service or customer needs type of definition) or the advanced electronics business (a technology-based definition)? Is Coca-Cola in the soft-drink business (in which case its strategic vision can be trained narrowly on the actions of Pepsi, 7Up, Dr Pepper, Canada Dry, and Schweppes)? Or is it in the beverage industry (in which case management must think strategically about positioning Coca-Cola products in a market that includes fruit juices, alcoholic drinks, milk, bottled water, coffee, and tea)? This is not a trivial question for Coca-Cola. Many young adults get their morning caffeine fix by drinking cola instead of coffee; with a beverage industry perspective as opposed to a soft-drink industry perspective, Coca-Cola management is more likely to perceive a long-term growth opportunity in winning youthful coffee drinkers over to its colas.

Defining what business an organization is in requires taking three factors into account:[1]

1. Customer needs, or *what* is being satisfied.
2. Customer groups, or *who* is being satisfied.
3. The technologies used and functions performed—*how* customers' needs are satisfied.

A company's business is defined by what needs it is trying to satisfy, by which customer groups it is targeting, and by the technologies it will use and the functions it will perform in serving the target market.

Defining a business in terms of what to satisfy, who to satisfy, and how the organization will go about producing the satisfaction adds completeness to the definition. It also directs management to look outward toward customers and markets as well as inward in forming its concept of "who we are and what we

---

[1]Derek F. Abell, *Defining the Business: The Starting Point of Strategic Planning* (Englewood Cliffs, N.J.: Prentice Hall, 1980), p. 169.

ILLUSTRATION CAPSULE 4   CIRCLE K'S MISSION STATEMENT

We believe our primary business is not so much retail as it is service oriented.

Certainly, our customers buy merchandise in our stores. But they can buy similar items elsewhere, and perhaps pay lower prices.

But they're willing to buy from Circle K because we give them added value for their money.

That added value is service and convenience.

Our Mission

As a service company, our mission is to:

Satisfy our customers' immediate needs and wants by providing them with a wide variety of goods and services at multiple locations.

Our Customers

We will not place a limit on the conveniences we offer customers.

They buy at Circle K much differently than at a supermarket. They come to our stores for specific purchases, which they make as quickly as possible. They want immediate service and are willing to pay a premium for it.

Our Stores

We will build our stores at locations most accessible to our customers.

We will organize our merchandise to (1) facilitate quick purchases and (2) encourage other purchases.

We will maintain our stores so they will always be brightly lit, colorful, clean, and comfortable places for our customers and our employees.

Our Goods and Services

We will not be one store—but a dozen stores in one.

We are a gas station, a fast-food restaurant, a grocery store, drugstore, liquor store, newsstand, video rental shop, small bank—and more.

Source: 1987 Annual Report.

do."[2] A good example of a business definition that incorporates all three aspects is a paraphrase of Polaroid's business definition during the early 1970s: "perfecting and marketing instant photography to satisfy the needs of more affluent U.S. and West European families for affection, friendship, fond memories, and humor." For years, McDonald's business definition has centered on "serving hot, tasty food quickly in a clean restaurant for a good value" to a broad base of customers worldwide (McDonald's now serves over 25 million customers daily at some 14,000 restaurants in over 40 countries). Illustration Capsule 4 describes how Circle K, the second largest convenience store retailer in the United States, views its mission and business.

The Polaroid, McDonald's, and Circle K examples all adhere closely to the three necessary components of a mission statement: the specific needs served by the company's basic product(s) or service(s), the targeted customer groups, and the technology and functions the company employs in providing its product/service. It takes all three to define what business a company is really in. Just knowing what products or services a firm provides is never enough. Products or services per se are not important to customers; what turns a product or service into a business is the need or want being satisfied. Without the need or want there is no business. Customer groups are relevant because they indicate

---

[2]There is a tendency sometimes for companies to view their mission in terms of making a profit. However, profit is more correctly an *objective* and a *result* of what the company does. Missions based on making a profit are incapable of distinguishing one type of profit-seeking enterprise from another—the mission and business of Sears are plainly different from the mission and business of Delta Airlines, even though both endeavor to earn a profit.

the market to be served: the geographic area to be covered and the types of buyers the firm is going after. Technology and functions performed are important because they indicate how the company will satisfy customers' needs and how much of the industry's production chain its own activities will span. For instance, a firm can be *specialized*, participating in one aspect of the whole industry's production chain, or *fully integrated*, operating in all parts of the industry chain. Circle K is a specialized firm operating only in the retail end of the chain; it doesn't manufacture the items it sells. Major international oil companies like Exxon, Mobil, and Chevron, however, are fully integrated; they lease drilling sites, drill wells, pump oil, transport the oil in their own ships and pipelines to their own refineries, and sell gasoline and other refined products through their own distributors and service stations. Because of the disparity in functions performed and technology employed, the business of a retailer like Circle K is much narrower and quite different from a fully integrated enterprise like Exxon. Between these two extremes, firms can stake out *partially integrated* positions, participating only in selected stages of the industry. So one way of distinguishing a firm's business, especially among firms in the same industry, is by looking at which functions it performs in the chain and how far its scope of operation extends across the industry.

A Broad or Narrow Business Definition?   A small Hong Kong printing company that defines its business broadly as "Asian-language communications" gains no practical guidance in making direction-setting decisions; with such a definition the company could pursue limitless courses, most well beyond its scope and capability. To have managerial value, mission statements and business definitions must be narrow enough to pin down the real arena of business interest. Otherwise they cannot serve as boundaries for what to do and not do and as beacons of where managers intend to take the company. Consider the following definitions based on broad-narrow scope:

Broad Definition	Narrow Definition
Beverages	Soft drinks
Footwear	Athletic footwear
Furniture	Wrought iron lawn furniture
Global mail delivery	Overnight package delivery
Travel and tourism	Ship cruises in the Caribbean

Broad-narrow definitions are relative, of course. Being in "the furniture business" is probably too broad a concept for a company intent on being the largest manufacturer of wrought iron lawn furniture in North America. On the other hand, soft drinks has proved too narrow a scope for a growth-oriented company like Coca-Cola, which, with its beverage industry perspective, acquired Minute-Maid and Hi-C (to capitalize on growing consumer interest in fruit juice products) and Taylor Wine Company (using the California Cellars brand to establish a foothold in wines).[3] The U.S. Postal Service operates with a broad definition—providing global mail delivery services to all types of senders.

---

[3]Coca-Cola's foray into wines evidently was not successful enough; the division was divested about five years after initial acquisition.

Federal Express, however, operates with a narrow business definition based on handling overnight package delivery for customers who have unplanned emergencies and tight deadlines.

· · · · · · · · · · · ·

Diversified companies have broader missions and business definitions than single-business enterprises.

Diversified firms have more expansive business definitions than single-business enterprises. Their mission statements typically use narrow terms to define current customer-market-technology arenas but are open-ended and adaptable enough to incorporate expansion into desirable new businesses. Alcan, Canada's leading aluminum company, used this type of language in its mission statement:

> Alcan is determined to be the most innovative diversified aluminum company in the world. To achieve this position, Alcan will be one, global, customer-oriented enterprise committed to excellence and lowest cost in its chosen aluminum businesses, with significant resources devoted to building an array of new businesses with superior growth and profit potential.

Morton-Thiokol, a substantially more diversified enterprise, used simultaneous broad-narrow terms to define its business:

> We are an international, high-technology company serving the diverse needs of government and industry with products and services ranging from massive solid rocket motors to small ordnance devices, from polymers to disc brake pads, from heavy denier yarns to woven carpet backing, from snow-grooming vehicles to trigger sprayers.

John Hancock's mission statement communicates a shift from its long-standing base in insurance to a broader mission in insurance, banking, and diversified financial services:

> At John Hancock, we are determined not just to compete but to advance, building our market share by offering individuals and institutions the broadest possible range of products and services. Apart from insurance, John Hancock encompasses banking products, full brokerage services and institutional investment, to cite only a few of our diversified activities. We believe these new directions constitute the right moves . . . the steps that will drive our growth throughout the remainder of this century.

Where Entrepreneurship Comes In

A member of Maytag's board of directors summed it up well when commenting on why the company acquired a European appliance-maker and shifted its long-term focus to include international markets as well as domestic ones: "Times change, conditions change." The swirl of new events and altered circumstances make it incumbent on managers to continually reassess their company's position and prospects, always checking for *when* it's time to steer a new course and adjust the mission. The key question here is "What new directions should we be moving in *now* to get ready for the changes we see coming in our business?" Repositioning an enterprise in light of emerging developments lessens the chances of getting caught in a poor market position or being dependent on the wrong business at the wrong time. For example, Philip Morris, the leading U.S. manufacturer of cigarettes, in anticipation of long-term deterioration in the demand for tobacco products, positioned itself as a major contender in the food products industry by acquiring two of the largest manufacturers, General Foods and Kraft. Many U.S. companies are broadening their missions geographically and forming joint ventures with European companies to try to capitalize on the dismantling of trade barriers in the European Community in 1992 and the opening of markets in Eastern Europe.

Good entrepreneurs are alert to changing customer wants and needs, customer dissatisfaction with current products and services, emerging technologies, changing international trade conditions, and other important signs of growing or shrinking business opportunity. Appraising new customer-market-technology developments ultimately leads to entrepreneurial judgments about which of several roads to take. A strategy leader must peer down each of the roads, evaluate the risks and prospects of each, and make direction-setting decisions to position the enterprise for success in the years ahead. *A well-chosen mission prepares a company for the future.* Many companies in consumer electronics and telecommunications, believing that their future products will incorporate microprocessors and other elements of computer technology, are expanding their missions and establishing positions in the computer business to have access to the needed technology. Numerous companies in manufacturing, seeing the swing to internationalization and global competition, are broadening their missions from serving domestic markets to serving global markets. Coca-Cola, Kentucky Fried Chicken, and McDonald's are pursuing market opportunities in China, Europe, Japan, and the Soviet Union. Japanese automobile companies are working to establish a bigger presence in the European car market. CNN, Turner Broadcasting's successful all-news cable channel, is pushing hard to become the first global all-news channel. Thus, a company's mission always has a time dimension; it is subject to change whenever top management concludes that the present mission is no longer adequate.

The entrepreneurial challenge in developing a mission is to recognize when emerging opportunities and threats in the surrounding environment make it desirable to revise the organization's long-term direction.

Communicating the Mission

How to phrase the mission statement and communicate it to lower-level managers and employees is almost as important as the soundness of the mission itself. A mission statement phrased in words that inspire and challenge can help build committed effort from employees, thus serving as a powerful motivational tool.[4] Bland language, platitudes, and motherhood-and-apple-pie-style verbiage should be scrupulously avoided. Companies should communicate their mission in words that induce employee buy-in and convey a sense of organizational purpose. In organizations with freshly changed missions, executives need to provide a convincing rationale for the new direction; otherwise a new mission statement does little to change employees' attitudes and behavior or to win their commitment—outcomes that make it harder to move the organization down the chosen path.

The best mission statements use simple, concise terminology; they speak loudly and clearly, generate enthusiasm for the firm's future course, and encourage personal effort and dedication from everyone in the organization. They need to be repeated over and over in a challenging, convincing fashion. A short, clear, often-repeated, inspiring mission statement has the power to turn heads in the intended direction and begin a new organizational march. As this occurs, the first step in organizational direction-setting has been com-

A well-worded mission statement creates enthusiasm for the future course management has charted; the motivational goal in communicating the mission is to challenge and inspire everyone in the organization.

---

[4]Tom Peters, *Thriving on Chaos* (New York: Harper & Row, 1988), pp. 486–87.

ILLUSTRATION CAPSULE | **5** | NOVACARE'S BUSINESS MISSION AND VISION

NovaCare is a fast-growing health care company specializing in providing patient rehabilitation services on a contract basis to nursing homes. Rehabilitation therapy is a $10 billion industry, of which 35% is provided contractually; the contract segment is highly fragmented with over 1,000 competitors. In 1990 NovaCare was a $100 million company, with a goal of being a $275 million business by 1993. The company stated its business mission and vision as follows:

NovaCare is people committed to making a difference . . . enhancing the future of all patients . . . breaking new ground in our professions . . . achieving excellence . . . advancing human capability . . . changing the world in which we live.

We lead the way with our enthusiasm, optimism, patience, drive and commitment.

We work together to enhance the quality of our patients' lives by reshaping lost abilities and teaching new skills. We heighten expectations for the patient and family. We rebuild hope, confidence, self-respect and a desire to continue.

We apply our clinical expertise to benefit our patients through creative and progressive techniques. Our ethical and performance standards require us to expend every effort to achieve the best possible results.

Our customers are national and local health care providers who share our goal of enhancing the patients' quality of life. In each community, our customers consider us a partner in providing the best possible care. Our reputation is based on our responsiveness, high standards and effective systems of quality assurance. Our relationship is open and proactive.

We are advocates of our professions and patients through active participation in the professional, regulatory, educational and research communities at national, state and local levels.

Our approach to health care fulfills our responsibility to provide investors with a high rate of return through consistent growth and profitability.

Our people are our most valuable asset. We are committed to the personal, professional and career development of each individual employee. We are proud of what we do and dedicated to our Company. We foster teamwork and create an environment conducive to productive communication among all disciplines.

NovaCare is a company of people in pursuit of this Vision.

Source: Company annual report.

---

pleted successfully. Illustration Capsule 5 illustrates an inspiration-oriented mission statement.

A well-conceived, well-said mission statement has real managerial value: (1) it crystallizes top management's own view about the firm's long-term direction and makeup, (2) it helps keep the direction-related actions of lower-level managers on the right path, (3) it conveys an organizational purpose and identity that motivates employees to do their best, (4) it helps managers avoid either visionless or rudderless management, and (5) it helps an organization prepare for the future.

ESTABLISHING OBJECTIVES: THE SECOND DIRECTION-SETTING TASK

Establishing objectives converts the mission and directional course into designated performance outcomes. Objectives represent a managerial commitment to produce specified results in a specified time. They spell out *how much* of *what kind* of performance *by when*. They direct attention and energy to what needs to be accomplished.

The Managerial Value of Establishing Objectives

Unless an organization's mission and direction are translated into *measurable* performance targets, and managers are pressured to show progress in reaching these targets, an organization's mission statement is just window-dressing. Experience tells a powerful story about why objective-setting is a critical task in the strategic management process: *Companies whose managers set objectives for each key result area and then aggressively pursue actions calculated to achieve their performance targets are strong candidates to outperform the companies whose managers operate with hopes, prayers, and good intentions.*

> *Objectives are a managerial commitment to achieve specific performance targets by a certain time.*

For performance objectives to have value as a management tool, they must be stated in *quantifiable* or measurable terms, and they must contain a *deadline for achievement*. This means avoiding statements like "maximize profits," "reduce costs," "become more efficient," or "increase sales" which specify neither how much or when. Spelling out organization objectives in measurable terms and then holding managers accountable for reaching their assigned targets within a specified time frame (1) substitutes purposeful strategic decision-making for aimless actions and confusion over what to accomplish and (2) provides a set of benchmarks for judging the organization's performance.

What Kinds of Objectives to Set

Objectives are needed for each *key result* that managers deem important to success.[5] Two types of key result areas stand out: those relating to *financial performance* and those relating to *strategic performance*. Achieving acceptable financial performance is a must; otherwise the organization's survival ends up at risk. Achieving acceptable strategic performance is essential to sustaining and improving the company's long-term market position. Specific kinds of financial and strategic performance objectives are shown below:

> **Strategic Management Principle**
> *Every company needs to establish both strategic objectives and financial objectives.*

---

[5]The literature of management is filled with references to *goals* and *objectives*. These terms are used in a variety of ways, many of them conflicting. Some writers use the term *goals* to refer to the long-run results an organization seeks to achieve and the term *objectives* to refer to immediate, short-run performance targets. Some writers reverse the usage. Others use the terms interchangeably. And still others use the term *goals* to refer to broad organizationwide performance targets and the term *objectives* to designate specific targets set by subordinate managers in response to the broader, more inclusive goals of the whole organization. In our view, little is gained from semantic distinctions between *goals* and *objectives*; the important thing is to recognize that the results an enterprise seeks to attain vary both in scope and in time perspective. Nearly always, organizations need to have broad and narrow performance targets for both the near term and long term. It is inconsequential which targets are called "goals" and which are called "objectives." To avoid a semantic jungle, we will use the single term *objectives* to refer to the performance targets and results an organization seeks to attain. We will use the adjectives *long-range* (or long-run) and *short-range* (or short-run) to identify the relevant time frame, and we will try to describe objectives in words that indicate their intended scope and level in the organization.

Strategic objectives tend
to be competitor-focused,
often aiming at unseating
a competitor considered
to be the best in a
particular category.

Financial Objectives	Strategic Objectives
• Faster revenue growth	• A bigger market share
• Faster earnings growth	• A higher, more secure industry rank
• Higher dividends	• Higher product quality
• Wider profit margins	• Lower costs relative to key competitors
• Higher returns on invested capital	• Broader or more attractive product line
• Stronger bond and credit ratings	• A stronger reputation with customers
• Bigger cash flows	• Superior customer service
• A rising stock price	• Recognition as a leader in technology and/or product innovation
• Recognition as a "blue chip" company	• Increased ability to compete in international markets
• A more diversified revenue base	• Expanded growth opportunities
• Stable earnings during recessionary periods	

Illustration Capsule 6 provides a sampling of strategic and financial objectives of some well-known corporations.

Strategic Objectives versus Financial Objectives: Which Take Precedence?

Strategic Management Principle

A market leader can become an ex-market leader by putting more emphasis on the financial objective of boosting next quarter's profits than on the strategic objective of strengthening long-term market position.

Although both financial and strategic objectives carry top priority because of their key results character, a dilemma arises when trade-offs must be made between actions to boost short-term financial performance and efforts to build a stronger business position for the long term. Managers with strong financial instincts often focus on short-term financial performance at the expense of actions with a longer-term and more uncertain market and competitive payoff. This is especially true when an organization's financial performance is poor. Yet, once an organization's financial results are healthy enough to avert crisis, the objective of building a stronger competitive position for the long term outweighs better financial payoffs in the short term. A company that consistently passes up opportunities to strengthen its long-term competitive position (opting instead for immediate improvements in its financial performance) risks diluting its competitiveness, losing momentum in its markets, and impairing its ability to stave off market challenges from ambitious rivals. The risks are especially great when a company has growth-minded competitors who place more value on achieving long-term industry leadership than on current profits. Competitors who will accept lower prices and lower profit margins for long periods in return for annual gains in market share can in time build a leading market position at the expense of companies that are preoccupied with their short-term profitability. One need look no further than the long-range strategic efforts of Japanese companies to gain market ground on their more profit-centered American and European rivals to appreciate the pitfall of letting short-term financial objectives dominate the strategic objective of building a sustainable competitive position.

The Concept of Strategic Intent

A company's strategic objectives are important for another reason—they delineate its *strategic intent* to stake out a particular business position.[6] The strategic intent of a large company may be to exercise

---

[6]The concept of strategic intent is described in more detail in Gary Hamel and C. K. Prahalad, "Strategic Intent," *Harvard Business Review* 89, no. 3 (May–June 1989), pp. 63–76. This section draws on their pioneering discussion.

ILLUSTRATION CAPSULE 6 STRATEGIC AND FINANCIAL OBJECTIVES OF WELL-KNOWN CORPORATIONS

Ford Motor Company:	To be a low-cost producer of the highest quality products and services that provide the best customer value.
Federal Express:	To continue the expansion of Federal Express's global network linking key markets around the world by merging dissimilar networks, providing service to additional countries, increasing the number of flight destinations, expanding our fleet of aircraft, opening new hubs, and adding U.S. gateways for the distribution of packages and freight.
Eastman Kodak:	To be the world's best in chemical and electronic imaging.
Alcan Aluminum:	To be the lowest cost producer of aluminum and to outperform the average return on equity of the Standard & Poor's Industrial Stock Index.
General Electric:	To become the most competitive enterprise in the world by being number one or number two in market share in every business the company is in.
Apple Computer:	To offer the best possible personal computing technology, and to put that technology in the hands of as many people as possible.
Atlas Corporation:	To become a low-cost, medium-size gold producer, producing in excess of 125,000 ounces of gold a year and building gold reserves of 1,500,000 ounces.
Quaker Oats Company:	To achieve return on equity at 20 percent or above, "real" earnings growth averaging 5 percent or better over time, be a leading marketer of strong consumer brands, and improve the profitability of low-return businesses or divest them.

Source: Company annual reports.

industry leadership on a national or global scale. The strategic intent of a small company may be to dominate a market niche and gain recognition as an up-and-coming enterprise. The time horizon underlying the concept of strategic intent is long term. Companies that rise to prominence in their markets almost invariably begin with strategic intents that are out of proportion to their immediate capabilities and market positions. But they set ambitious long-term strategic objectives and then pursue them relentlessly, sometimes even obsessively, over a 10- to 20-year period. In the 1960s, Komatsu, Japan's leading earth-moving equipment company, was less than one-third the size of Caterpillar, had little market presence outside Japan, and depended on its small bulldozers for most of its revenue. Komatsu's strategic intent was to "encircle Caterpillar" with a broader product line and compete globally against Caterpillar. By the late 1980s, Komatsu was the industry's second-ranking company, with a strong sales presence in North America, Europe, and Asia plus a product line that included industrial robots and semiconductors as well as a broad array of earth-moving equipment.

Often, a company's strategic intent takes on a heroic character, serving as a rallying cry for managers and employees alike to go all out and do their very best. Canon's strategic intent in copying equipment was to "beat Xerox." The strategic intent of the U.S. government's Apollo space program was to land a person on the moon ahead of the Soviet Union. Wal-Mart's strategic intent has been to "overtake Sears" as the largest U.S. retailer. In such instances, strategic intent signals a deep-seated commitment to winning—unseating the industry leader, remaining the industry leader (and becoming more dominant in the process), or otherwise beating long odds to gain a significantly stronger

• • • • • • • • • • • •
Basic Concept
A company exhibits
strategic intent *when it*
relentlessly pursues a
long-term strategic
objective and concentrates
its actions on achieving
that objective.

business position. A capably managed enterprise whose strategic objectives go well beyond its present reach and resources is potentially a more formidable competitor than a company with modest strategic intent.

Long-Range versus Short-Range Objectives   An organization needs both long-range and short-range objectives. Long-range objectives serve two purposes. First, setting performance targets five or more years ahead raises the issue of what actions to take *now* in order to achieve the targeted long-range performance *later* (a company can't wait until the end of year 4 of its 5-year strategic plan to begin building the competitive market position it wants to have in year 5!). Second, having explicit long-range objectives pushes managers to weigh the impact of today's decisions on longer-range performance. Without the pressure to make progress in meeting long-range performance targets, it is human nature to base decisions on what is most expedient and worry about the future later. The problem with short-sighted decisions, of course, is that they put a company's long-term business position at greater risk.

Short-range objectives spell out the immediate and near-term results to be achieved. They indicate the *speed* at which management wants the organization to progress as well as the *level of performance* being aimed for over the next two or three periods. Short-range objectives can be identical with long-range objectives any time an organization is already performing at the targeted long-term level. For instance, if a company has an ongoing objective of 15 percent profit growth every year and is currently achieving this objective, the company's long-range and short-range profit objectives coincide. The most important situation where short-range objectives differ from long-range objectives occurs when managers are trying to elevate organizational performance and cannot reach the long-range/ongoing target in just one year. Short-range objectives then serve as stairsteps for reaching the ultimate target.

The "Challenging but Achievable" Test

*Company performance
targets should
be challenging
but achievable.*

Objectives should not represent whatever levels of achievement management decides would be "nice." Wishful thinking has no place in objective-setting. For objectives to serve as a tool for *stretching* an organization to reach its full potential, they must meet the criterion of being *challenging but achievable*. Satisfying this criterion means setting objectives in the light of several important "inside-outside" considerations:

- What performance levels will industry and competitive conditions realistically allow?
- What results will it take for the organization to be a successful performer?
- What performance is the organization capable of *when pushed*?

To set challenging but achievable objectives, managers must judge what performance is possible in light of external conditions and what performance the organization is capable of achieving. The tasks of objective-setting and strategy-making often become intertwined at this point. Strategic choices, for example, cannot be made in a financial vacuum; the money has to be available to execute whatever strategy is chosen. Consequently, decisions about strategy are contingent on setting the organization's financial performance objectives high enough to (1) execute the chosen strategy, (2) fund other needed actions, and (3) please investors and the financial community. Objectives and strategy also intertwine when it comes to matching the means (strategy) with the ends (objectives). If a company can't achieve established objectives by following its current strategy (either because the objectives are unrealistic or because the strategy is), the objectives or the strategy need adjustment to produce a better fit.

The Need for Objectives at All Management Levels

For strategic thinking and strategy-driven decision-making to penetrate the organizational hierarchy, performance targets must be established not only for the organization as a whole but also for each of the organization's separate businesses and product lines down to each functional area and department within the business-unit/product-line structure.[7] Only when every manager, from the chief executive officer to the lowest level manager, is held accountable for achieving specific results in their units is the objective-setting process complete enough to ensure that the whole organization is headed down the chosen path and that each part of the organization knows what it needs to accomplish.

The objective-setting process is more top-down than it is bottom-up. To see why strategic objectives at one managerial level tend to drive objectives and strategies at the next level down, consider the following example. Suppose the senior executives of a diversified corporation establish a corporate profit objective of $5 million for next year. Suppose further, after discussion between corporate management and the general managers of the firm's five different businesses, that each business is given the challenging but achievable profit objective of $1 million by year-end (i.e., if the five business divisions contribute $1 million each in profit, the corporation can reach its $5 million profit objective). A concrete result has thus been agreed on and translated into measurable action commitments at two levels in the managerial hierarchy. Next, suppose the general manager of business unit X, after some analysis and discussion with functional area managers, concludes that reaching the $1 million profit objective will require selling 100,000 units at an average price of $50 and producing them at an average cost of $40 (a $10 profit margin × 100,000 units = $1 million profit). Consequently, the general manager and the manufacturing manager may settle on a production objective of 100,000 units at a unit cost of $40. The general manager and the marketing manager may agree on a sales objective of 100,000 units and a target selling price of $50. In turn, the marketing manager may break the 100,000-unit sales objective into unit sales targets for each sales territory, each item in the product line, and each salesperson.

A top-down approach of establishing performance targets is a logical way to divide organizationwide targets into pieces that lower-level units and managers are responsible for achieving. Such an approach also provides a valuable degree of *unity* and *cohesion* to the objective-setting and strategy-making occurring in different parts of the organization. Generally speaking, organizationwide objectives and strategy need to be established first so they

• • • • • • • • • • • •
Strategic Management Principle
Objective-setting should be more of a top-down than a bottom-up process in order to guide lower-level units toward objectives that support overall business and company objectives.

---

[7]Peter F. Drucker, *Management: Tasks, Responsibilities, Practices* (New York: Harper & Row, 1974), p. 100. See also Charles H. Granger, "The Hierarchy of Objectives," *Harvard Business Review* 42, no. 3 (May–June 1963), pp. 63–74.

can *guide* objective-setting and strategy-making at lower levels. Top-down objective-setting and strategizing steer lower-level units toward objectives and strategies that take their cues from those of the total enterprise. When objective-setting and strategy-making begin at the bottom levels of an organization and organizationwide objectives and strategies reflect the aggregate of what has bubbled up from below, the resulting strategic action plan won't be consistent, cohesive, or coordinated. Bottom-up objective-setting, with no guidance from above, nearly always signals an absence of strategic leadership on the part of senior executives.

CRAFTING A STRATEGY: THE THIRD DIRECTION-SETTING TASK

. . . .

Basic Concept

An organization's strategy consists of the combined actions that management has taken and intends to take in achieving strategic and financial objectives and pursuing the organization's mission.

Organizations need strategies to guide *how* to achieve objectives and *how* to pursue the organization's mission. Strategy-making is all about *how*—how to reach performance targets, how to outcompete rivals, how to seek and maintain competitive advantage, how to strengthen the enterprise's long-term business position. An organization's overall strategy and managerial game plan emerge from the *pattern* of actions already initiated and the plans managers have for making fresh moves. In forming a strategy out of many possible options, the strategist forges responses to market change, seeks new opportunities, and synthesizes different approaches taken at various times in various parts of the organization.[8]

An organization's strategy evolves over time. One would be hard pressed to find a company whose strategy was conceived in advance and followed exactly for a sustained time period. As a rule, companies revise their strategies in response to changes inside the company or in the surrounding environment. The unknowable or unpredictable character of competition and market change make it impossible to anticipate and plan for everything in advance. There is always something new to react to and some new strategic window opening up. This is why the task of strategizing is always ongoing, involving continuous review and reconsideration and fresh strategic initiatives to embellish or modify the current strategy.

As we emphasized in the opening chapter, strategy-making is not just a task for senior executives. In large, diversified enterprises, decisions about what approaches to take and what new moves to initiate involve corporate senior executives, heads of business units and product divisions, heads of major functional areas within a business or division (manufacturing, marketing and sales, finance, human resources, and the like), plant managers, product managers, district and regional sales managers, and lower-level supervisors. In diversified enterprises, strategies are initiated at four distinct organization levels. There's a strategy for the company and all of its businesses as a whole (*corporate strategy*). There's a strategy for each separate business the company has diversified into (*business strategy*). Then there is a strategy for each specific functional unit within a business (*functional strategy*)—each business usually has a production

---

[8]Henry Mintzberg, "The Strategy Concept II: Another Look at Why Organizations Need Strategies," *California Management Review* 30, no. 1 (Fall 1987), pp. 25–32.

TABLE 2–1 **The Strategy-Making Hierarchy** *(Who has primary responsibility for what kinds of strategy actions)*

Strategy Level	Primary Strategy-Development Responsibility	Strategy-Making Functions and Areas of Focus
Corporate strategy	CEO, other key executives (decisions are typically reviewed/approved by boards of directors)	• Building and managing a high-performing portfolio of business units (making acquisitions, strengthening existing business positions, divesting businesses that no longer fit into management's plans) • Capturing the synergy among related business units and turning it into competitive advantage • Establishing investment priorities and steering corporate resources into businesses with the most attractive opportunities • Reviewing/revising/unifying the major strategic approaches and moves proposed by business-unit managers
Business strategies	General manager/head of business unit (decisions are typically reviewed/approved by a senior executive or a board of directors)	• Devising moves and approaches to compete successfully and to secure a competitive advantage • Forming responses to changing external conditions • Uniting the strategic initiatives of key functional departments • Taking action to address company-specific issues and operating problems
Functional strategies	Functional managers (decisions are typically reviewed/approved by business-unit head)	• Crafting moves and approaches to support business strategy and to achieve functional/departmental performance objectives • Reviewing/revising/unifying strategy-related moves and approaches proposed by lower-level managers
Operating strategies	Field-unit heads/lower-level managers within functional areas (decisions are reviewed/approved by functional area head/department head)	• Crafting still narrower and more specific approaches/moves aimed at supporting functional and business strategies and at achieving operating-unit objectives

strategy, a marketing strategy, a finance strategy, and so on. And, finally, there are still narrower strategies for basic operating units—plants, sales districts and regions, and departments within functional areas (*operating strategy*). Single-business enterprises have only three levels of strategy-making (business strategy, functional strategy, and operating strategy) unless diversification into other businesses becomes an active consideration. Table 2–1 highlights which level of management usually has lead responsibility for which level of strategy and indicates the kinds of strategic actions that distinguish each of the four strategy-making levels.

Corporate Strategy

Corporate strategy is the overall managerial game plan for a diversified company. Corporate strategy extends companywide—an umbrella over all businesses that a diversified company is in. It consists of the moves made to establish

. . . .
Basic Concept
Corporate strategy *concerns a diversified company's moves to establish business positions in different industries and the actions and approaches it uses in managing its diversified businesses.*

F I G U R E 2–1   **Identifying the Corporate Strategy of a Diversified Company**

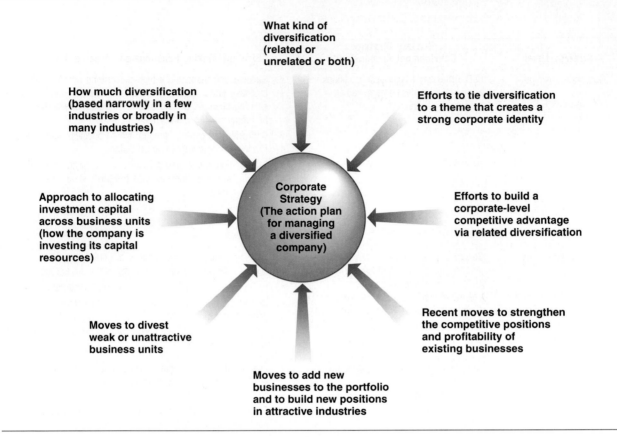

business positions in different industries and the approaches used to manage the company's group of businesses. Figure 2–1 depicts what to look for in profiling a diversified company's corporate strategy. Crafting corporate strategy for a diversified company involves four kinds of initiatives:

1. *Making the moves to accomplish diversification.* The first concern in diversification is what the portfolio of businesses should consist of—specifically, what industries to diversify into and whether to enter those industries by starting a new business or acquiring a company already in the industry (an established leader, an up-and-coming company, or a troubled company with turnaround potential). This piece of corporate strategy establishes whether diversification is based narrowly in a few industries or broadly in many industries, and it shapes how the company will be positioned in each of the target industries.

2. *Initiating actions to boost the combined performance of the businesses the firm has diversified into.* As positions are created in the chosen industries, corporate strategy-making concentrates on ways to get better performance out of the business-unit portfolio. Decisions must be

reached about how to strengthen the long-term competitive positions and profitabilities of the businesses the corporation has invested in. Corporate parents can help their business subsidiaries be more successful by financing additional capacity and efficiency improvements, by supplying missing skills and managerial know-how, by acquiring another company in the same industry and merging the two operations into a stronger business, and/or by acquiring new businesses that strongly complement existing businesses. The overall plan for managing a group of diversified businesses usually involves pursuing rapid-growth strategies in the most promising businesses, keeping the other core businesses healthy, initiating turnaround efforts in weak-performing businesses with potential, and divesting businesses that are no longer attractive or that don't fit into management's long-range plans.

3. *Finding ways to capture the synergy among related business units and turn it into competitive advantage.* When a company diversifies into businesses with related technologies, similar operating characteristics, the same distribution channels, common customers, or some other synergistic relationship, it gains competitive advantage potential not open to a company that has diversified into totally unrelated businesses. With related diversification companies can usually transfer skills, share expertise, or share facilities across businesses, thereby reducing overall costs, strengthening the competitiveness of some of the corporation's products, or enhancing the capabilities of particular business units— any of which can represent a significant source of competitive advantage. The greater the relatedness among the businesses of a diversified company, the greater the opportunities for skills transfer and/or sharing across businesses and the bigger the window for creating competitive advantage. Indeed, what makes related diversification so attractive is the synergistic *strategic fit* across related businesses that allows company resources to be leveraged into a combined performance *greater* than the units could achieve operating independently. The 2 + 2 = 5 aspect of strategic fit makes related diversification a very appealing strategy for boosting corporate performance and shareholder value.

4. *Establishing investment priorities and steering corporate resources into the most attractive business units.* A diversified company's different businesses are usually not equally attractive from the standpoint of investing additional funds. Corporate executives need to rank the attractiveness of investing more capital in each business so they can channel resources into areas where earnings potentials are higher. Corporate strategy may include divesting businesses that are chronically poor performers or those in an unattractive industry. Divestiture frees up unproductive funds for redeployment to promising businesses or for financing attractive new acquisitions.

Corporate strategy is crafted at the highest levels of management. Senior corporate executives normally have lead responsibility for devising corporate strategy and for synthesizing whatever recommendations bubble up from lower-level managers. Key business-unit heads may also be influential, especially in strategic decisions affecting the businesses they head. Major strategic decisions are usually reviewed and approved by the company's board of directors.

Business Strategy

The term *business strategy* (or business-level strategy) refers to the managerial game plan for a single business. It is mirrored in the pattern of approaches and moves management devises to produce successful performance in *one specific line of business*. The various elements of business strategy are shown in Figure 2–2. For a stand-alone single-business company, corporate strategy and business strategy are one and the same since there is only one business to form a strategy for; the distinction between corporate strategy and business strategy is relevant only when diversification enters the firm's picture.

The central thrust of business strategy is how to build and strengthen the company's long-term competitive position in the marketplace. Toward this end, business strategy is concerned principally with (1) forming responses to changes underway in the industry, the economy at large, the regulatory and political arena, and other relevant areas, (2) crafting competitive moves and market approaches that can lead to sustainable competitive advantage, (3) uniting the strategic initiatives of functional departments, and (4) addressing specific strategic issues the business faces.

Clearly, business strategy encompasses whatever moves and new approaches managers deem prudent in light of competitive forces, economic trends and market developments, buyer demographics, new legislation and regulatory requirements, and other broad external factors. *A good strategy is well matched to the external situation*; as the external environment changes in significant ways, adjustments in strategy eventually become desirable. Whether a company's response to external change is quick or slow tends to be a function of how long events must unfold before managers can assess any implications for the business and how much longer it takes them to form a strategic response. Some external changes, of course, require little or no response, while others call for significant strategy alterations. On occasions, external factors change in ways that pose a formidable strategic hurdle—for example, cigarette manufacturers face a tough challenge holding their own against the mounting antismoking campaign.

What separates a powerful business strategy from a weak one is the strategist's ability *to forge a series of moves and approaches capable of producing sustainable competitive advantage*. With a competitive advantage, a company has good prospects for above-average profitability and success in the industry. Without competitive advantage, a company risks being outcompeted by stronger rivals and locked into mediocre performance. Crafting a business strategy that yields sustainable competitive advantage has several facets: deciding where a firm has the best chance to win a competitive edge, developing product/service attributes that have strong buyer appeal and set the company apart from rivals, and neutralizing the competitive moves of rival companies. A company's strategy for competing is typically both offensive and defensive—some aggressive actions amount to direct attacks on competitors' market positions; others neutralize fresh moves made by rivals. The three basic competitive approaches are: (1) striving to be the industry's low-cost pro-

---

FIGURE 2–2   **Identifying Strategy for a Single-Business Company**

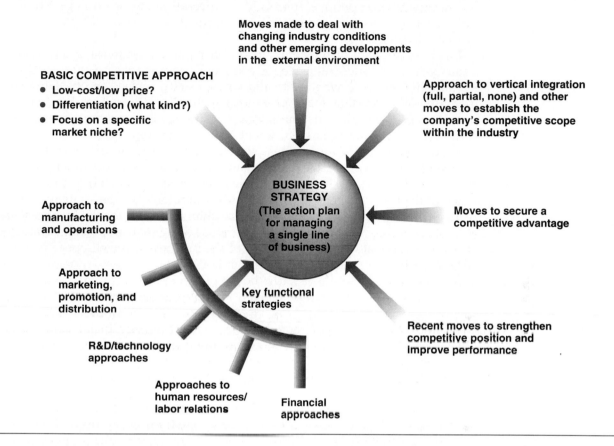

ducer (thereby aiming for a cost-based competitive advantage over rivals); (2) pursuing differentiation based on such advantages as quality, performance, service, styling, technological superiority, or unusually good value; and (3) focusing on a narrow market niche and winning a competitive edge by doing a better job than rivals of serving the special needs and tastes of buyers in the niche.

Internally, business strategy involves taking actions to develop the skills and capabilities needed to achieve competitive advantage. Successful business strategies usually aim at building the company's competence in one or more core activities crucial to strategic success and then using the core competence as a basis for winning a competitive edge over rivals. A *core competence* is something a firm does especially well in comparison to rival companies. It thus represents a source of competitive strength. Core competences can relate to R&D, mastery of a technological process, manufacturing capability, sales and distribution, customer service, or anything else that is a competitively important aspect of creating, producing, or marketing the company's product or service. *A core competence is a basis for competitive advantage because it represents specialized expertise that rivals don't have and can't readily match.*

On a broader internal front, business strategy must also aim at uniting strategic initiatives in the various functional areas of business (purchasing, production, R&D, finance, human resources, sales and marketing, and distribution). Strategic actions are needed in each functional area to *support* the company's competitive approach and overall business strategy. Strategic unity and coordination across the various functional areas add power to the business strategy.

Business strategy also extends to action plans for addressing any special strategy-related issues unique to the company's competitive position and internal situation (such as whether to add new capacity, replace an obsolete plant, increase R&D funding for a promising technology, or reduce burdensome interest expenses). Such custom-tailoring of strategy is one of the reasons every company in an industry has a different business strategy.

Lead responsibility for business strategy falls in the lap of the manager in charge of the business. Even if the business head does not personally wield a heavy hand in the business strategy-making process, preferring to delegate much of the task to others, he or she is still accountable for the strategy and the results it produces. The business head, as chief strategist for the business, has at least two other responsibilities. The first is seeing that supporting strategies in each of the major functional areas of the business are well-conceived and consistent with each other. The second is getting major strategic moves approved by higher authority (the board of directors and/or corporate-level officers) if needed, and keeping them informed of important new developments, deviations from plan, and potential strategy revisions. In diversified companies, business-unit heads may also have to ensure that business-level objectives and strategy conform to corporate-level objectives and strategy.

Functional Strategy

. . . .

Basic Concept

Functional strategy concerns the managerial game plan for running a major functional activity within a business—R&D, production, marketing, customer service, distribution, finance, human resources, and so on; a business needs as many functional strategies as it has major functional activities.

Functional strategy refers to the set of strategic initiatives taken in one part of a business. A company needs a functional strategy for every major functional activity—an R&D strategy, a production strategy, a marketing strategy, a customer service strategy, a distribution strategy, a finance strategy, a human resources strategy, and so on. Functional strategies add detail to business strategy and govern *how* functional activities will be managed. A company's marketing strategy, for example, represents the managerial game plan for running the marketing part of the business. The primary role of a functional strategy is to *support* the company's overall business strategy and competitive approach. Another role is to create a managerial roadmap for achieving functional area performance objectives. Thus, functional strategy in the production/manufacturing area represents the game plan for *how* manufacturing activities will be managed to support business strategy and achieve manufacturing objectives. Functional strategy in the finance area consists of *how* financial activities will be managed in supporting business strategy and achieving specific financial objectives.

Lead responsibility for strategy-making in functional areas is normally delegated to the functional area heads, unless the business-unit head decides to exert a strong influence. In crafting strategy, a functional department head ideally works closely with key subordinates and often touches base with the heads of other functional areas and the business head. Coordinated and mutually supportive functional strategies are essential for the overall business strategy to have maximum impact. Plainly, a business's marketing strategy, production strategy, finance strategy, and human resource strategy should be working in concert rather than at cross-purposes. Coordination across functional area strategies is best accomplished during the deliberation stage. If inconsistent functional strategies are sent up the line for approval, it is up to the business head to spot the conflicts and get them resolved.

Operating Strategy

Operating strategies concern the even narrower strategic initiatives and approaches for managing key operating units (plants, sales districts, distribution centers) and for handling daily operating tasks with strategic significance (advertising campaigns, materials purchasing, inventory control, maintenance, shipping). Operating strategies, while of lesser scope than the higher levels of strategy-making, add relevant detail and completeness to the overall business plan. Lead responsibility for operating strategies is usually delegated to operating-level managers, subject to review and approval by higher ranking managers.

Even though operating strategy is at the bottom of the strategy-making hierarchy, its importance should not be downplayed. For example, a plant that fails to achieve production volume, unit cost, and quality targets can undercut sales and profit objectives and wreak havoc with the whole company's strategic efforts to build a quality image with customers. One can't always judge the importance of a strategic initiative by the managerial level where it originated.

Operating managers are part of an organization's strategy-making team because numerous operating-level units have strategy-critical performance targets and need to have strategic action plans in place to achieve them. A regional manager needs a strategy customized to the region's particular situation and objectives. A plant manager needs a strategy for accomplishing the plant's objectives, carrying out the plant's part of the company's overall manufacturing game plan, and dealing with any strategy-related problems at the plant. A company's advertising manager needs a strategy for getting maximum audience exposure and sales impact from the ad budget. The following two examples illustrate how operating strategy supports higher-level strategies.

- A company with a low-price, high-volume business strategy and a need to achieve low manufacturing costs launches a companywide effort to boost worker productivity by 10 percent. To contribute to this objective: (1) the manager of employee recruiting develops a strategy for interviewing and testing job applicants that weeds out all but the most highly motivated, best-qualified candidates; (2) the manager of information systems devises a way to use technology to boost the productivity of office workers; (3) the employee benefits manager devises an improved incentive-compensation plan to reward manufacturing employees for increased output; (4) the purchasing manager launches a program to obtain new efficiency-increasing equipment faster and easier.

- A distributor of plumbing equipment emphasizes quick delivery and accurate order-filling as keystones of its customer service approach. To support this strategy, the warehouse manager (1) develops an inventory-stocking strategy that allows 99 percent of all orders to be completely filled without back ordering any item and (2) institutes a warehouse staffing strategy that allows any order to be shipped within 24 hours.

• • • • • • • • • • • •
Basic Concept
Operating strategy concerns the game plan for managing key organizational units within a business (plants, sales districts, distribution centers) and for handling strategically significant operating tasks (materials purchasing, inventory control, maintenance, shipping, advertising campaigns).

Uniting the Strategy-Making Effort

The previous discussion underscores that *an organization's strategic plan is a collection of strategies* devised by different managers at different levels in the organizational hierarchy. The larger the enterprise, the more points of strategic initiative it has. Management's direction-setting effort is not complete until managers unify the separate layers of strategy into a coherent, supportive pattern. Ideally the pieces and layers of strategy should fit together like the pieces of a picture puzzle. Unified objectives and strategies don't emerge from an undirected process where managers at each level set objectives and craft strategies *independently*. Indeed, functional and operating-level managers have a duty to set performance targets and invent strategic actions that will help achieve business objectives and make business strategy more effective.

Harmonizing objectives and strategies piece-by-piece and level-by-level can be tedious and frustrating, requiring numerous consultations and meetings, annual strategy review and approval processes, trial and error, and months (sometimes years) of consensus-building. The politics of gaining strategic consensus and the battle of trying to keep all managers and departments focused on what's best for the total enterprise (as opposed to what's best for their departments or their careers) are often big obstacles in unifying the layers of objectives and strategies.[9] Gaining broad consensus is particularly difficult when there is ample room for opposing views and disagreement. It is not unusual for discussions about the organization's mission and basic direction, what objectives to set, and what strategies to employ to provoke heated debates and strong differences of opinion.

Figure 2–3 portrays the networking of objectives and strategies down through the managerial hierarchy. The two-way arrows indicate that there are simultaneous bottom-up and top-down influences on the objectives and strategies at each level. These vertical linkages, if managed in a way that promotes coordination, can help unify the objective-setting and strategy-making activities of many managers into a mutually reinforcing pattern. The tighter coordination is enforced, the tighter the linkages in the objectives and strategies of the various organizational units. Tight linkages safeguard against organizational units straying from the direction top management has charted.

As a practical matter, however, corporate and business missions, objectives, and strategies need to be clearly outlined and communicated down the line before much progress can be made in objective-setting and strategy-making at the functional and operating levels. Direction and guidance needs to flow from the corporate level to the business level and from the business level to the functional and operating levels. The strategic disarray that occurs in an organization when senior managers don't exercise strong top-down direction-setting and strategic leadership is akin to what would happen to a football team's offensive performance if the quarterback decided not to call a play for the team, but instead, gave each player the latitude to pick whatever play he thought would work best at his respective position.

---

[9]Functional managers can sometimes be more interested in doing what is best for their own areas, in building their own empire, and in consolidating their personal power and influence than they are in cooperating with other functional managers to unify behind the overall business strategy. As a consequence, it's easy for functional area support strategies to conflict, thereby forcing the general manager to spend time and energy refereeing differences and building support for a more unified approach.

The Networking of Missions, Objectives, and Strategies through the Managerial Hierarchy

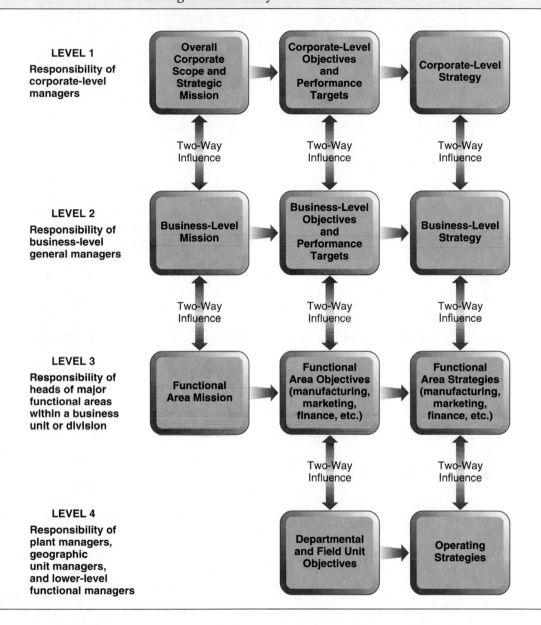

THE FACTORS THAT SHAPE STRATEGY

Many factors enter into the forming of a company's strategy. Figure 2–4 is a simple model of the primary factors that shape the choice of a strategy. The interplay of these factors is frequently complex and always industry- and company-specific. No two strategic choices are made in exactly the same context; the situational factors always differ, if only slightly. This is why managers need to assess all the various situational factors, both external and internal, before they begin crafting strategy.

Societal, Political, Regulatory, and Citizenship Considerations

Societal, political, regulatory, and citizenship factors limit the strategic actions a company can take.

What an enterprise can and cannot do strategywise is always constrained by what is legal, by what is in compliance with government policies and regulations, by what is considered socially acceptable, and by what constitutes community citizenship. Outside pressures also come from other sources—special interest groups, the glare of investigative reporting, a fear of unwanted political action, and the stigma of negative opinion. Societal concerns over health and nutrition, alcohol and drug abuse, hazardous waste disposal, sexual harassment, and the impact of plant closings on local communities have impacted many companies' strategies. American concerns over the growing volume of foreign imports and political debate over whether to impose tariffs and import quotas to help reduce the chronic U.S. trade deficit have been key factors in the strategic decisions of Japanese and European companies to locate plants in the United States. Heightened awareness of the dangers of cholesterol has driven food products companies to substitute low-fat ingredients despite extra costs.

More and more companies now consider societal values and priorities, community concerns, and the potential for onerous legislation and regulatory requirements when analyzing their external situation. Intense public pressure and adverse media coverage have made such a practice prudent. The task of making an organization's strategy "socially responsible" means (1) conducting organizational activities within the bounds of what is considered ethical and in the general public interest; (2) responding positively to emerging societal priorities and expectations; (3) demonstrating a willingness to take action ahead of regulatory confrontation; (4) balancing stockholder interests against the larger interests of society; and (5) being a "good citizen" in the community.

The concept of corporate social responsibility is showing up in company mission statements. John Hancock, for example, concludes its mission statement with the following sentence:

> In pursuit of this mission, we will strive to exemplify the highest standards of business ethics and personal integrity; and shall recognize our corporate obligation to the social and economic well-being of our community.

Union Electric, a St. Louis–based utility company, includes the following statement in its official corporate policy:

> As a private enterprise entrusted with an essential public service, we recognize our civic responsibility in the communities we serve. We shall strive to advance the growth and welfare of these communities and shall participate in civic activities which fulfill that goal . . . for we believe this is both good citizenship and good business.

Illustration Capsule 7 describes Anheuser-Busch's efforts to be socially responsible.

Industry Attractiveness and Competitive Conditions

Strategic Management Principle
A company's strategy ought to be closely matched to industry and competitive conditions.

Industry attractiveness and competitive conditions are big strategy-determining factors. A company's assessment of the industry and competitive environment directly affects how it should try to position itself in the industry and what its basic competitive strategy approach should be. When a firm concludes its industry environment has grown unattractive, and it is better off investing

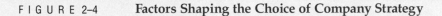

F I G U R E 2–4   Factors Shaping the Choice of Company Strategy

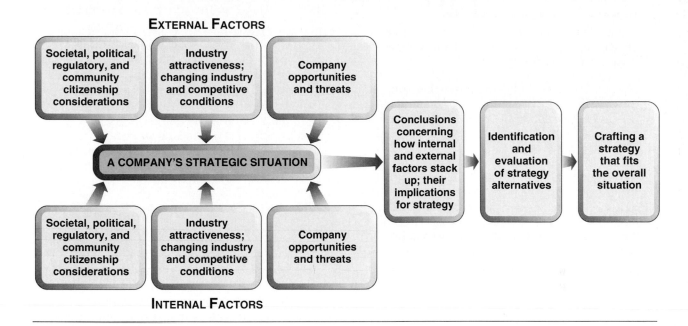

company resources elsewhere, it may craft a strategy of disinvestment and abandonment. When competitive conditions intensify significantly, a company must respond with strategic actions to protect its position. Fresh moves on the part of rival companies, changes in the industry's price-cost-profit economics, and new technological developments can alter the requirements for competitive success and mandate that a firm reconsider its strategy. A strategist, therefore, has to be a student of industry and competitive conditions.

Specific Company Opportunities and Threats

The particular business opportunities a company has and the threats to its position that it faces are key influences on strategy. Strategy needs to be deliberately crafted to capture some or all of a company's best growth opportunities, especially the ones that can enhance its long-term competitive position and profitability. Likewise, strategy should be geared to providing a defense against external threats to the company's well-being and future performance. For strategy to be successful, it has to be well matched to company opportunities and threats.

Organizational Strengths, Weaknesses, and Competitive Capabilities

Experience shows that in matching strategy to a firm's internal situation, management should build strategy around what the company does well and avoid strategies whose success depends heavily on something the company does poorly or has never done at all. In short, *strategy must be well matched to company strengths, weaknesses, and competitive capabilities.* Pursuing an opportunity

- - - - - - - - - - -
Strategic Management Principle

A well-conceived strategy aims at capturing a company's best growth opportunities and defending against external threats to its well-being and future performance.

ILLUSTRATION CAPSULE 7   SOCIAL RESPONSIBILITY EFFORTS AT ANHEUSER-BUSCH

In a recent annual report, Anheuser-Busch described three main areas in which it was exercising social responsibility:

Alcohol Issues—Anheuser-Busch has long believed it is in the company's best interest, and in the interest of society as a whole, to play an important role in the fight against the abuse of alcoholic beverages. Although the company's efforts were already the most extensive in the brewing industry, in 1989 Anheuser-Busch created a Department of Consumer Awareness and Education to (1) educate consumers and servers of alcohol about the appropriate use of its products and (2) aggressively defend the right of brewers and beer consumers to make and enjoy beer without the fear of being stigmatized. One of the current activities of this department was an expanded "Know When to Say When" advertising campaign featuring well-known sports celebrities. In addition, Anheuser-Busch supported scientific research into the causes and possible cures of alcoholism and alcohol abuse. More than $15 million was contributed in 1989 to such organizations as the Alcoholic Beverage-Medical Research Foundation in Baltimore, Md., and the Alcohol Research Center at UCLA.

Minority Development—Anheuser-Busch supports minority organizations engaged in economic development, cultural heritage, education and leadership development. As the founder and national sponsor of the Lou Rawls Parade of Stars telethon, Anheuser-Busch commissioned a traveling exhibit to commemorate this television special's 10th anniversary and its success in raising more than $75 million since 1980. The company also contributed $15 million in 1989 to the National Hispanic Scholarship Fund to support its development and scholarship efforts. Anheuser-Busch is the NHSF's largest corporate supporter.

Community Support—Anheuser-Busch tries to enrich the communities in which it operates breweries and other major facilities by supporting local nonprofit organizations such as the United Way, social service agencies, arts and cultural groups, health care institutions, youth groups and colleges and universities. In addition, through the Anheuser-Busch Employee Volunteer Grant Program, the company recognizes its employees who actively volunteer their services to nonprofit organizations by making grants to these organizations. The company also has an employee Matching Gift program for educational institutions.

Source: 1989 Annual Report.

• • • • • • • • • • • •
Strategic Management Principle

A company's strategy ought to be grounded in what it is good at doing (i.e., its organizational strengths and competitive capabilities) and avoid what it is not so good at doing (i.e., its organizational and competitive weaknesses).

without the organizational competences and resources to capture it is foolish. An organization's strengths make some opportunities and strategies attractive; likewise its internal weaknesses and its present competitive market position make certain strategies risky or even out of the question.

One of the most pivotal strategy-shaping internal considerations is whether a company has or can build the core strengths or competences needed to execute the strategy proficiently. An organization's core strengths—the things it does especially well—are an important strategy-making consideration because of (1) the skills and capabilities they provide in capitalizing on a particular opportunity, (2) the competitive edge they may give in the marketplace, and (3) the potential they have for becoming a cornerstone of strategy. The best path to competitive advantage is found where a firm has core strengths in one or more of the key requirements for market success, where rivals do not have matching or offsetting competences, and where rivals can't develop comparable strengths except at high cost and/or over an extended period of time.[10]

---

[10]David T. Kollat, Roger D. Blackwell, and James F. Robeson, *Strategic Marketing* (New York: Holt, Rinehart & Winston, 1972), p. 24.

Even if an organization has no outstanding core competences (and many do not), it still must shape its strategy to suit its particular skills and available resources. It never makes sense to develop a strategic plan that cannot be executed with the skills and resources a firm is able to muster.

The Personal Ambitions, Business Philosophies, and Ethical Beliefs of Managers

Managers do not dispassionately assess what strategic course to steer. Their decisions are often influenced by their own vision of how to compete and how to position the enterprise and by what image and standing they want the company to have. Both casual observation and formal studies indicate that managers' ambitions, values, business philosophies, attitudes toward risk, and ethical beliefs have important influences on strategy.[11] Sometimes the influence of the manager's personal values and experiences is conscious and deliberate; at other times it is unconscious. As Professor Andrews has noted in explaining the relevance of personal factors to strategy, "People have to have their hearts in it."[12]

Several examples of how business philosophies and personal values enter into strategy-making are particularly noteworthy. Japanese managers are strong proponents of strategies that take a long-term view and that aim at building market share and competitive position. In contrast, some corporate executives and Wall Street financiers have drawn criticism for overemphasizing short-term profits at the expense of long-term competitive positioning and for being more attracted to strategies involving a financial play on assets (leveraged buyouts and stock buybacks) rather than using corporate resources to make long-term strategic investments. Japanese companies also display a different philosophy regarding the role of suppliers. They prefer to establish long-term partnership arrangements with key suppliers to improve the quality and reliability of component parts and to reduce inventory requirements. In the United States and Europe the prevailing managerial philosophy has been to play suppliers off against one another, doing business on a short-term basis with whoever offers the best price and delivery.

Attitudes toward risk also have a big influence on strategy. Risk-avoiders favor "conservative" strategies that minimize downside risk, have a quick payback, and produce sure short-term profits. Risk-takers lean more toward opportunistic strategies where bold moves can produce a big payoff over the long term. Risk-takers prefer innovation to imitation and strategic offensives to defensive conservatism.

Managerial values also shape the ethical quality of a firm's strategy. Managers with strong ethical convictions take pains to see that their companies observe a strict code of ethics in all aspects of the business. They expressly forbid such practices as accepting or giving kickbacks, badmouthing rivals' products, and

Managers' personal ambitions, business philosophies, and ethical beliefs are usually woven into the strategies they craft.

---

[11]See, for instance, William D. Guth and Renato Tagiuri, "Personal Values and Corporate Strategy," *Harvard Business Review* 43, no. 5 (September–October 1965), pp. 123–32; Kenneth R. Andrews, *The Concept of Corporate Strategy*, 3rd ed. (Homewood Ill.: Richard D. Irwin, 1987), chap. 4; and Richard F. Vancil, "Strategy Formulation in Complex Organizations," *Sloan Management Review* 17, no. 2 (Winter 1986), pp. 4–5.

[12]Andrews, *The Concept of Corporate Strategy*, p. 63.

buying political influence with political contributions. Instances where a company's strategic actions run counter to high ethical standards include charging excessive interest rates on credit card balances, employing bait-and-switch sales tactics, continuing to market products suspected of having safety problems, and using ingredients that are known health hazards.

The Influence of Shared Values and Company Culture on Strategy

An organization's policies, practices, traditions, philosophical beliefs, and ways of doing things combine to give it a distinctive culture. A company's strategic actions typically reflect its cultural traits and managerial values. In some cases a company's core beliefs and culture even dominate the choice of strategic moves. This is because culture-related values and beliefs become so embedded in management's thinking and actions that they condition how the enterprise responds to external events. Such firms have a culture-driven bias about how to handle strategic issues and what kinds of strategic moves it will consider or reject. Strong cultural influences partly account for why companies gain reputations for such strategic traits as technological leadership, product innovation, dedication to superior craftsmanship, a proclivity for financial wheeling and dealing, growth through acquisitions, a strong people-orientation, or unusual emphasis on customer service and total customer satisfaction.

In recent years, more companies have begun to articulate the core beliefs and values underlying their business approaches. One company expressed its core beliefs and values this way:

> We are market-driven. We believe that functional excellence, combined with teamwork across functions and profit centers, is essential to achieving superb execution. We believe that people are central to everything we will accomplish. We believe that honesty, integrity, and fairness should be the cornerstone of our relationships with consumers, customers, suppliers, stockholders, and employees.

IBM's founder, Thomas Watson, once stated, "We must be prepared to change all the things we are in order to remain competitive in the environment, but we must never change our three basic beliefs: (1) respect for the dignity of the individual, (2) offering the best customer service in the world, and (3) excellence." For nearly a century, AT&T's value system has emphasized (1) universal service, (2) fairness in handling personnel matters, (3) a belief that work should be balanced with commitments to family and community, and (4) relationships (from one part of the organization to another). AT&T's management views these values as essential in a technologically dynamic, highly structured company. Both the IBM and AT&T value systems are deeply ingrained and widely shared by managers and employees. Whenever this happens, values and beliefs become more than an expression of nice platitudes; they become a way of life within the company.[13]

---

[13]For more details, see Richard T. Pascale, "Perspectives on Strategy: The Real Story behind Honda's Success," in Glenn Carroll and David Vogel, *Strategy and Organization: A West Coast Perspective* (Marshfield, Mass.: Pitman Publishing, 1984), p. 60.

LINKING STRATEGY WITH ETHICS

Strategy ought to be ethical. It should involve rightful actions, not wrongful ones, or it won't pass the test of moral scrutiny. This means more than conforming to what is legal. Ethical and moral standards go beyond the prohibitions of law and the language of "thou shalt not" to the issues of *duty* and the language of "should do and should not do." Ethics concerns human duty and the principles on which these duties rest.[14]

Every strategic action a company takes should be ethically acceptable.

Every business has an ethical duty to each of five constituencies: owners/ shareholders, employees, customers, suppliers, and the community at large. Each of these constituencies affects the organization and is affected by it. Each is a stakeholder in the enterprise, with certain expectations as to what the enterprise should do and how it should do it.[15] Owners/shareholders, for instance, expect a return on their investment. Even though individual investors differ in their preferences for profits now versus profits later, their desire to take risks, and their willingness to exercise social responsibility, business executives have a moral duty to profitably manage the owners' investment.

A company has ethical duties to owners, employees, customers, suppliers, and the public.

A company's duty to employees arises out of respect for the worth and dignity of individuals who devote their energies to the business and depend on the business for their economic well-being. Principled strategy-making requires that employee-related decisions be made equitably and compassionately, with concern for due process and for the impact that strategic change has on employees' lives. At best, the chosen strategy should promote employee interests in areas such as wage and salary levels, career opportunities, job security, and overall working conditions. At least, the chosen strategy should not disadvantage employees. Even in crisis situations where adverse employee impact cannot be avoided, businesses have an ethical duty to minimize whatever hardships have to be imposed in the form of workforce reductions, plant closings, job transfers, relocations, retraining, and loss of income.

A company's duty to the customer arises out of expectations that attend the purchase of a good or service. Inadequate appreciation of this duty has led to product liability laws and a host of regulatory agencies to protect consumers. All kinds of strategy-related ethical issues still arise here, however. Should a seller inform consumers *fully* about the contents of its product, especially if it contains ingredients that, though officially approved for use, are suspected of having potentially harmful effects? Is it ethical for the makers of alcoholic beverages to sponsor college events, given that many college students are under 21? Is it ethical for cigarette manufacturers to advertise at all (even though it is legal)? Is it ethical for airlines to withhold information about terrorist bomb threats from the public? Is it ethical for manufacturers to produce and sell products they know have faulty parts or defective designs that may not become apparent until after the warranty expires? In submitting bids on a contract, is it unethical to seek access to inside information not available to other bidders? Is it ethical to give some customers special treatment?

---

[14]Harry Downs, "Business Ethics: The Stewardship of Power," forthcoming in *Strategic Management Planning*.
[15]Ibid.

A company's ethical duty to its suppliers arises out of the market relationship that exists between them—they are both partners and adversaries. They are partners in the sense that the quality of suppliers' parts affects the quality of a firm's own product. They are adversaries in the sense that the supplier wants the highest price and profit it can while the buyer wants a cheaper price, better quality, and speedier service. A business confronts several ethical issues in its supplier relationships. Is it ethical to threaten to cease doing business with a supplier unless the supplier agrees not to do business with key competitors? Is it ethical to reveal one supplier's price quote to a rival supplier? Is it ethical to accept gifts from suppliers? Is it ethical to pay a supplier in cash?

The ethical duty to the community-at-large stems from the business's status as a citizen of the community and as an institution of society. Communities and society are reasonable in expecting businesses to be good citizens—to pay their fair share of taxes for fire and police protection, waste removal, streets and highways, and so on and to exercise care in the impact their activities have on the environment and on the communities in which they operate. The community should be accorded the same recognition and attention as the other four constituencies. Whether a company is a good community citizen is ultimately demonstrated by the way it supports community activities, encourages employees to participate in community activities, handles the health and safety aspects of its operations, accepts responsibility for overcoming environmental pollution, relates to regulatory bodies and employee unions, and exhibits high ethical standards.

NCR Corporation, a $6 billion computer and office equipment company, recently cast its entire mission statement in terms of its duty to stockholders, customers, employees, suppliers, and the community at large. See Illustration Capsule 8.

Carrying Out Ethical Responsibilities   It is management, not constituent groups, who is responsible for managing the enterprise. Thus, it is management's perceptions of its ethical duties and of constituents' claims that determine whether and how strategy is linked to ethical behavior. Ideally, managers weigh strategic decisions from each constituent's viewpoint and, where conflicts arise, strike a rational, objective, and equitable balance among the interests of all five. If any of the five constituencies conclude that management is not doing its duty, they have their own avenues for recourse. Concerned investors can complain at the annual shareholders' meeting, appeal to the board of directors, or sell their stock. Concerned employees can unionize and bargain collectively, or they can seek employment elsewhere. Customers can buy from competitors. Suppliers can find other buyers or pursue other market alternatives. The community and society can do anything from staging protest marches to stimulating political and governmental action.[16]

A company that truly cares about business ethics and corporate social responsibility is proactive rather than reactive in linking strategy and ethics. It steers away from ethically or morally questionable business opportunities. It won't do business with suppliers that engage in activities the company does not condone. Its products are safe for its customers to use. Its workplace

---

[16]Ibid.

ILLUSTRATION CAPSULE 8 ETHICS AND VALUES AT NCR CORPORATION

NCR's corporate mission statement formally recognizes the company's duty to serve the interests of all stakeholders, not just those of stockholders, and represents a blend of ethical principles and values. As management stated in a recent annual report:

NCR is a successful, growing company dedicated to achieving superior results by assuring that its actions are aligned with stakeholder expectations. Stakeholders are all constituencies with a stake in the fortunes of the company. NCR's primary mission is to create value for our stakeholders.

We believe in conducting our business activities with integrity and respect while building mutually beneficial and enduring relationships with all of our stakeholders.

We take customer satisfaction personally: we are committed to providing superior value in our products and services on a continuing basis.

We respect the individuality of each employee and foster an environment in which employees' creativity and productivity are encouraged, recognized, valued and rewarded.

We think of our suppliers as partners who share our goal of achieving the highest quality standards and the most consistent level of service.

We are committed to being caring and supportive corporate citizens within the worldwide communities in which we operate.

We are dedicated to creating value for our shareholders and financial communities by performing in a manner that will enhance returns on investments.

Source: 1987 Annual Report.

---

environment is safe for employees. It recruits and hires employees whose values and behavior are consistent with the company's principles and ethical standards. It acts to reduce any environmental pollution it causes. It cares about *how* it does business and whether its actions reflect integrity and high ethical standards. Illustration Capsule 9 describes Harris Corporation's ethical commitments to its stakeholders.

Tests of a Winning Strategy

How can a manager judge which strategic option is best for the company? What are the standards for determining whether a strategy is successful or not? Three tests can be used to evaluate the merits of one strategy over another and to gauge how good a strategy is:

The Goodness of Fit Test—A good strategy is well matched to the company's situation—both internal and external factors and its own capabilities and aspirations.

The Competitive Advantage Test—A good strategy leads to sustainable competitive advantage. The bigger the competitive edge that a strategy helps build, the more powerful and effective it is.

The Performance Test—A good strategy boosts company performance. Two kinds of performance improvements are the most telling: gains in profitability and gains in the company's long-term business strength and competitive position.

Strategic options with low potential on one or more of these criteria do not merit strong consideration. The strategic option with the highest potential on all three counts can be regarded as the best or most attractive strategic

• • • • • • • • • • • •
Strategic Management Principle
A strategy is not a true winner unless it exhibits good fit with the enterprise's situation, builds sustainable competitive advantage, and boosts company performance.

Harris Corp. is a major supplier of information, communication, and semiconductor products, systems, and services to commercial and governmental customers throughout the world. The company utilizes advanced technologies to provide innovative and cost-effective solutions for processing and communicating data, voice, text, and video information. The company's sales exceed $2 billion, and it employs nearly 23,000 people. In a recent annual report, the company set forth its commitment to satisfying the expectations of its stakeholders:

Customers—For customers, our objective is to achieve ever-increasing levels of satisfaction by providing quality products and services with distinctive benefits on a timely and continuing basis worldwide. Our relationships with customers will be forthright and ethical, and will be conducted in a manner to build trust and confidence.

Shareholders—For shareholders, the owners of our company, our objective is to achieve sustained growth in earnings-per-share. The resulting stock-price appreciation combined with dividends should provide our shareholders with a total return on investment that is competitive with similar investment opportunities.

Employees—The people of Harris are our company's most valuable asset, and our objective is for every employee to be personally involved in and share the success of the business. The company is committed to providing an environment which encourages all employees to make full use of their creativity and unique talents; to providing equitable compensation, good working conditions, and the opportunity for personal development and growth which is limited only by individual ability and desire.

Suppliers—Suppliers are a vital part of our resources. Our objective is to develop and maintain mutually beneficial partnerships with suppliers who share our commitment to achieving increasing levels of customer satisfaction through continuing improvements in quality, service, timeliness, and cost. Our relationships with suppliers will be sincere, ethical, and will embrace the highest principles of purchasing practice.

Communities—Our objective is to be a responsible corporate citizen. This includes support of appropriate civic, educational, and business activities, respect for the environment, and the encouragement of Harris employees to practice good citizenship and support community programs. Our greatest contribution to our communities is to be successful so that we can maintain stable employment and create new jobs.

Source: 1988 Annual Report.

alternative. Once a strategic commitment has been made and enough time has elapsed to see results, these same tests can be used to determine how well a company's current strategy is performing. The bigger the margins by which a strategy satisfies all three criteria when put to the test in the marketplace, the more it qualifies as a winning strategy.

There are, of course, some additional criteria for judging the merits of a particular strategy: clarity, internal consistency among all the pieces of strategy, timeliness, match to the personal values and ambitions of key executives, the degree of risk involved, and flexibility. These can be used to supplement the three tests posed above whenever it seems appropriate.

APPROACHES TO PERFORMING THE STRATEGY-MAKING TASK

Companies and managers perform the strategy-making task differently. In small, owner-managed companies, strategy-making is developed informally. Often the strategy is never written but exists mainly in the entrepreneur's own mind and in oral understandings with key subordinates. The largest firms, however, tend to develop their plans via an annual strategic planning cycle (complete with prescribed procedures, forms, and timetables) that includes broad management participation, lots of studies, and multiple meetings to probe and question. The larger and more diverse an enterprise, the more managers feel it is better to have a structured annual process with written plans, management scrutiny, and official approval at each level.

Along with variations in the organizational process of formulating strategy are variations in how managers personally participate in analyzing the company's situation and deliberating what strategy to pursue. The four basic strategy-making styles managers use include:[17]

The Master Strategist Approach—Here the manager personally functions as chief strategist and chief entrepreneur, exercising *strong* influence over assessments of the situation, over the strategy alternatives that are explored, and over the details of strategy. This does not mean that the manager personally does all the work; it means the manager personally becomes the chief architect of strategy and wields a proactive hand in shaping some or all of the major pieces of strategy. The manager acts as strategy commander and has a big ownership stake in the chosen strategy.

The Delegate-It-to-Others Approach—Here the manager in charge delegates the exercise of strategy-making to others, perhaps a strategic planning staff or a task force of trusted subordinates. The manager then stays off to the side, keeps in touch via reports and conversations, offers guidance if needed, reacts to informal "trial balloon" recommendations, then puts a stamp of approval on the "strategic plan" after it has been formally presented and discussed and a consensus emerges. But the manager rarely has much ownership in the recommendations and, privately, may not see much urgency in pushing *truly hard* to implement some or much of what has been written down in the company's "official strategic plan." Also, it is generally understood that "of course, we may have to proceed a bit differently if conditions change"—which gives the manager flexibility to go slow or ignore those approaches/moves that "on further reflection may not be the thing to do at this time." This strategy-making style has the advantage of letting the manager pick and choose from the smorgasbord of strategic ideas that bubble up from below, and it allows room for broad participation and input from many managers and areas. The weakness is that a manager can end up so detached from the process of formal strategy-making that he or she exercises no real strategic leadership—indeed, subordinates are likely to conclude that strategic planning isn't important enough to warrant a claim on the boss's personal time and attention. The stage is then set for rudderless direction-setting. Often the strategy-making that does occur is short-run-oriented and reactive; it deals more with today's problems than with positioning the enterprise to capture tomorrow's opportunities.

---

[17]This discussion is based on David R. Brodwin and L. J. Bourgeois, "Five Steps to Strategic Action," in Glenn Carroll and David Vogel, *Strategy and Organization: A West Coast Perspective* (Marshfield, Mass.: Pitman Publishing, 1984), pp. 168–78.

The Collaborative Approach—This is a middle approach whereby the manager enlists the help of key subordinates in hammering out a consensus strategy that all the key players will back and do their best to implement successfully. The biggest strength of this strategy-making style is that those who are charged with crafting the strategy also have to implement it. Giving subordinate managers such a clear-cut ownership stake in the strategy they subsequently must implement enhances commitment to successful execution. When subordinates have a hand in proposing their part of the overall strategy, they can be held accountable for making it work—the "I told you it was a bad idea" alibi won't fly.

The Champion Approach—In this style, the manager is interested neither in personally crafting the details of strategy nor in the time-consuming task of leading a group to brainstorm a consensus strategy. Rather, the manager encourages subordinate managers to develop, champion, and implement sound strategies. Here strategy moves upward from the "doers" and the "fast-trackers." Executives serve as judges, evaluating the strategy proposals that reach their desks. This approach works best in large diversified corporations where the CEO cannot personally orchestrate strategy-making in each business division. Headquarters executives depend on ambitious and talented entrepreneurs at the business-unit level who can see strategic opportunities that the executives cannot. Corporate executives may articulate general strategic themes as organizationwide guidelines. But the key to strategy-making is stimulating and rewarding new strategic initiatives conceived by champions who believe in the opportunity and badly want the blessing to go after it. With this approach, total "strategy" is shaped by the sum of the championed initiatives that get approved.

These four basic managerial approaches illuminate several aspects about how strategy emerges. In situations where the manager in charge personally functions as the chief architect of strategy, the strategy is a product of his/her own vision, ambitions, values, business philosophies, and sense of what moves to make next. Highly centralized strategy-making works fine when the manager in charge has a powerful, insightful vision of what needs to be done and how to do it. The primary weakness of the master strategist approach is that the caliber of the strategy depends so heavily on one person's strategy-making skills. It also breaks down in large enterprises, where many strategic initiatives are needed and the strategy-making task is too complex for one person to handle.

Of the four basic approaches managers can use in crafting strategy, none stands out as inherently superior— each has strengths and weaknesses.

The group approach to strategy-making has its risks too. Sometimes, the strategy that emerges is a middle-of-the-road compromise that lacks bold, creative initiative. Other times, it represents political consensus, with the outcome shaped by influential subordinates, powerful functional departments, or majority coalitions that have a common interest in promoting their own version of what the strategy ought to be. "Politics" and power plays are most likely in situations where there is no strong consensus on what strategy to adopt. The collaborative approach is especially conducive to political strategy formation, since powerful departments and individuals have ample opportunity to try to build a consensus for their favored strategic approach. However, the big danger of a delegate-it-to-others approach is a serious lack of top-down direction and strategic leadership.

The strength of the champion approach is also its weakness. The value of championing is that it encourages people at lower organizational levels to propose new strategic initiatives and stay on the lookout for good opportunities to pursue. Individuals with attractive strategic proposals are given the latitude and resources to try them out, thus helping keep strategy fresh and renewing an organization's capacity for innovation. On the other hand, the championed actions, because they come from many parts of the organization, are not likely to form a coherent pattern or promote clear strategic direction. With championing, the chief executive has to work at ensuring that what is championed adds power to the overall organization strategy; otherwise, strategic initiatives may be launched in directions that have no integrating links or overarching rationale.

KEY POINTS

Management's direction-setting task involves developing a mission, setting objectives, and forming a strategy. Early on in the direction-setting process, managers need to form a vision of where to lead the organization and to answer the question, "What is our business and what will it be?" A well-conceived mission statement helps channel organizational efforts along the course management has charted and builds a strong sense of organizational identity. Effective visions are clear, challenging, and inspiring; they prepare a firm for the future, and they make sense in the marketplace. A well-conceived, well-said mission statement serves as a beacon of long-term direction and creates employee "buy-in."

The second direction-setting step is to establish strategic and financial objectives for the organization to achieve. Objectives convert the mission statement into specific performance targets. The agreed-on objectives need to be challenging but achievable, and they need to spell out precisely how much by when. In other words, objectives should be measurable and should involve deadlines for achievement. Objectives are needed at all organizational levels.

The third direction-setting step entails forming strategies to achieve the objectives set in each area of the organization. A corporate strategy is needed to achieve corporate-level objectives; business strategies are needed to achieve business-unit performance objectives; functional strategies are needed to achieve the performance targets set for each functional department; and operating-level strategies are needed to achieve the objectives set in each operating and geographic unit. In effect, an organization's strategic plan is a collection of unified and interlocking strategies. As shown in Table 2–1, different strategic issues are addressed at each level of managerial strategy-making. Typically, the strategy-making task is more top-down than bottom-up. Lower-level strategy supports and complements higher-level strategy and contributes to the achievement of higher-level, companywide objectives.

Strategy is shaped by both outside and inside considerations. The major external considerations are societal, political, regulatory, and community factors; industry attractiveness; and the company's market opportunities and threats. The primary internal considerations are company strengths, weaknesses, and competitive capabilities; managers' personal ambitions, philosophies, and ethics; and the company's culture and shared values. A good strategy must be well matched to all these situational considerations.

There are essentially four basic ways to manage the strategy formation process in an organization: the master strategist approach where the manager in charge personally functions as the chief architect of strategy, the delegate-it-to-others approach, the collaborative approach, and the champion approach. All four have strengths and weaknesses. All four can succeed or fail depending on how well the approach is managed and depending on the strategy-making skills and judgments of the individuals involved.

SUGGESTED READINGS

Andrews, Kenneth R. *The Concept of Corporate Strategy*, 3rd ed. Homewood, Ill.: Dow Jones-Irwin, 1987, chaps. 2, 3, 4, and 5.

Foster, Lawrence W. "From Darwin to Now: The Evolution of Organizational Strategies," *Journal of Business Strategy* 5, no. 4 (Spring 1985), pp. 94–98.

Hamel, Gary, and C. K. Prahalad. "Strategic Intent." *Harvard Business Review* 89, no. 3 (May–June, 1989), pp. 63–76.

McLellan, R., and G. Kelly. "Business Policy Formulation: Understanding the Process." *Journal of General Management* 6, no. 1 (Autumn 1980), pp. 38–47.

Morris, Elinor. "Vision and Strategy: A Focus for the Future." *Journal of Business Strategy* 8, no. 2 (Fall 1987), pp. 51–58.

Mintzberg, Henry. "Crafting Strategy." *Harvard Business Review* 65, no. 4 (July–August 1987), pp. 66–77.

Quinn, James Brian. *Strategies for Change: Logical Incrementalism*. Homewood, Ill.: Richard D. Irwin, 1980, chaps. 2 and 4.

Industry and Competitive Analysis

Analysis is the critical starting point of strategic thinking.
~Kenichi Ohmae

• • • • • • •

Awareness of the environment is not a special project to be undertaken only when warning of change becomes deafening . . .
~Kenneth R. Andrews

Crafting strategy is an analysis-driven exercise, not an activity where managers can succeed by sheer effort and creativity. Judgments about what strategy to pursue should ideally be grounded in a probing assessment of a company's external environment and internal situation. Unless a company's strategy is well-matched to the full range of external and internal situational considerations, its suitability is suspect.

THE ROLE OF SITUATION ANALYSIS IN STRATEGY-MAKING

While the phrase *situation analysis* tends to conjure up images of collecting reams of data and developing all sorts of facts and figures, such impressions don't apply here. From a strategy-making standpoint, *the purpose of situation analysis is to determine the features in a company's internal/external environment that will most directly affect its strategic options and opportunities*. The effort concentrates on generating solid answers to a well-defined set of strategic questions, then using these answers first to form an understandable picture of the company's strategic situation and second to identify what its realistic strategic options are.

In studying the methods of strategic situation analysis, it is customary to begin with single-business companies instead of diversified enterprises. This is because strategic analysis of diversified companies draws on many of the concepts and techniques used in evaluating the strategic situations of single-business companies. In single-business strategic analysis, the two biggest situational considerations are (1) industry and competitive conditions (the heart of a single-business company's "external environment") and (2) the company's own internal situation and competitive position. This chapter examines the techniques of *industry and competitive analysis*, the terms used to refer to external situation analysis of a single-business company. Chapter 4 covers the tools of *company situation analysis*. Industry and competitive analysis looks broadly at a company's *macroenvironment*; company situation analysis examines the narrower field of its *microenvironment*.

• • • • • • • • • • • • •
Analysis of industry and competitive conditions is the starting point in evaluating a company's strategic situation and market position.

Figure 3–1 presents the external-internal framework of strategic situation analysis for a single-business company. It indicates both the analytical steps involved and the connection to developing business strategy. Note the logical flow from analysis of the company's external and internal situation to evaluation of alternatives to choice of strategy. Also note that situation analysis is the starting point in the process. Indeed, as we shall see in the rest of this chapter and in Chapter 4, managers must understand a company's macro- and microenvironments to do a good job of establishing a mission, setting objectives, and crafting business strategy. The three criteria for deciding whether a strategy is "good" are whether it fits the situation, whether it helps build competitive advantage, and whether it is likely to boost company performance.

THE METHODS OF INDUSTRY AND COMPETITIVE ANALYSIS

Industries differ widely in their economic characteristics, competitive situations, and future outlooks. The pace of technological change can range from fast to slow. Capital requirements can be big or small. The market can be worldwide or local. Sellers' products can be standardized or highly differentiated. Competitive forces can be strong or weak and can center on price, quality, service, or other variables. Buyer demand can be rising briskly or declining. Industry conditions differ so much that leading companies in unattractive industries can find it hard to earn respectable profits, while even weak companies in attractive industries can turn in good performances.

Industry and competitive analysis utilizes a tool kit of concepts and techniques to get a clear fix on changing industry conditions and on the nature and strength of competitive forces. It is a way of thinking strategically about an industry's overall situation and drawing conclusions about whether the industry is an attractive investment for company funds. The framework for industry and competitive analysis hangs on developing probing answers to seven questions:

• • • • • • • • • • • •
There are seven questions to ask in thinking strategically about market conditions in a given industry.

1. What are the chief economic characteristics of the industry?
2. What factors are driving change in the industry, and what impact will they have?
3. What competitive forces are at work in the industry, and how strong are they?
4. Which companies are in the strongest/weakest competitive positions?

FIGURE 3–1   From Situation Analysis to Strategic Choices

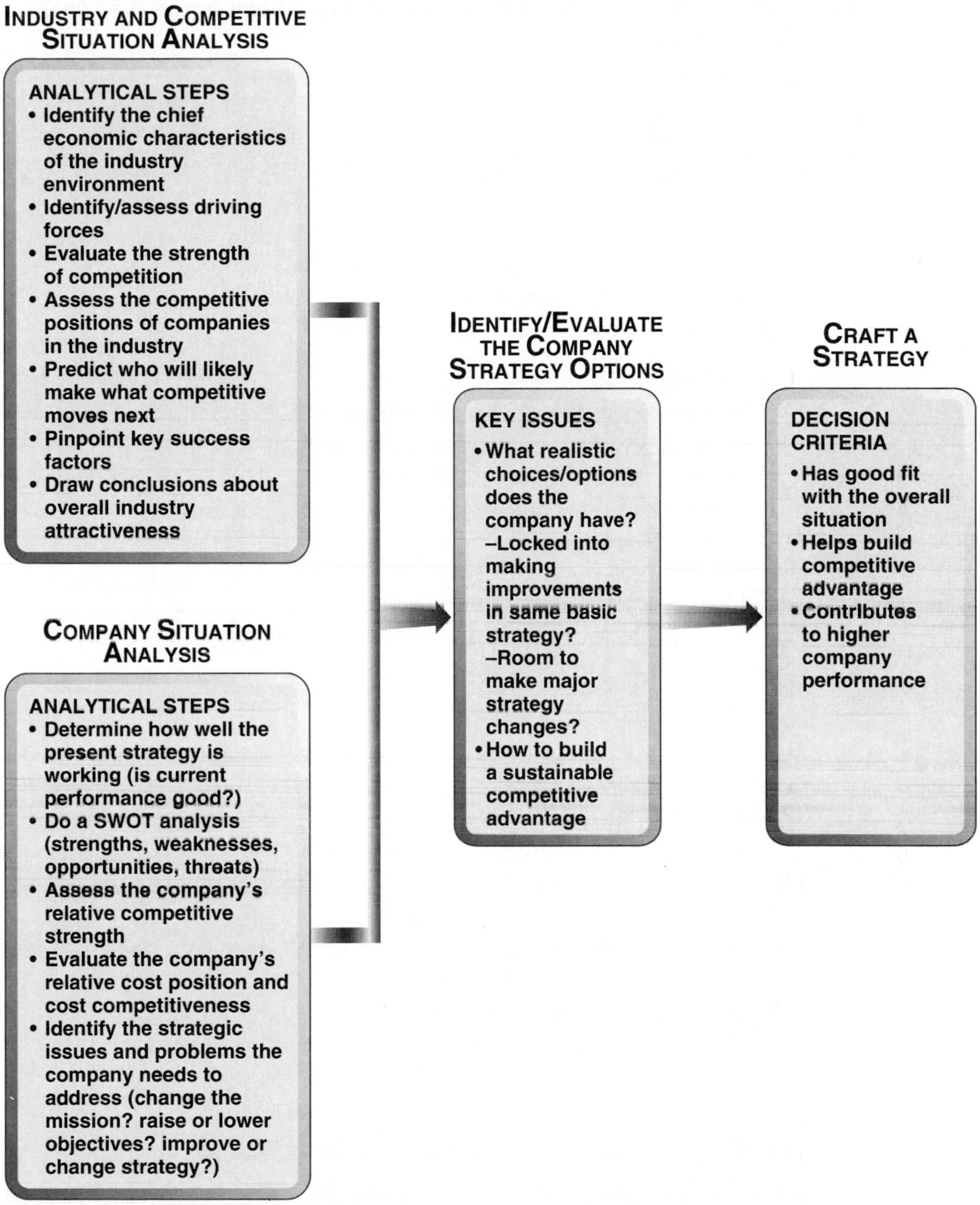

INDUSTRY AND COMPETITIVE SITUATION ANALYSIS

ANALYTICAL STEPS
- Identify the chief economic characteristics of the industry environment
- Identify/assess driving forces
- Evaluate the strength of competition
- Assess the competitive positions of companies in the industry
- Predict who will likely make what competitive moves next
- Pinpoint key success factors
- Draw conclusions about overall industry attractiveness

COMPANY SITUATION ANALYSIS

ANALYTICAL STEPS
- Determine how well the present strategy is working (is current performance good?)
- Do a SWOT analysis (strengths, weaknesses, opportunities, threats)
- Assess the company's relative competitive strength
- Evaluate the company's relative cost position and cost competitiveness
- Identify the strategic issues and problems the company needs to address (change the mission? raise or lower objectives? improve or change strategy?)

IDENTIFY/EVALUATE THE COMPANY STRATEGY OPTIONS

KEY ISSUES
- What realistic choices/options does the company have?
  - Locked into making improvements in same basic strategy?
  - Room to make major strategy changes?
- How to build a sustainable competitive advantage

CRAFT A STRATEGY

DECISION CRITERIA
- Has good fit with the overall situation
- Helps build competitive advantage
- Contributes to higher company performance

---

5. Who will likely make what competitive moves next?
6. What key factors will determine competitive success or failure?
7. How attractive is the industry in terms of its prospects for above-average profitability?

The collective answers to these questions build understanding of a firm's surrounding environment and form the basis for matching strategy to changing industry conditions and to competitive forces. Let's see what each question involves and consider some concepts and techniques that help managers answer them.

Identifying the Industry's Dominant Economic Characteristics

Because industries differ significantly in their basic character and structure, industry and competitive analysis begins with an overview of the industry's dominant economic traits. As a working definition, we use the word *industry* to mean a group of firms whose products have so many of the same attributes that they compete for the same buyers. The factors to consider in profiling an industry's economic features are fairly standard:

- Market size.
- Scope of competitive rivalry (local, regional, national, or global).
- Market growth rate and where the industry is in the growth cycle (early development, rapid growth and takeoff, early maturity, late maturity and saturation, stagnant and aging, decline and decay).
- Number of rivals and their relative sizes—is the industry fragmented with many small companies or concentrated and dominated by a few large companies?
- The number of buyers and their relative sizes.
- The prevalence of backward and forward integration.
- Ease of entry and exit.
- The pace of technological change in both production processes and new product introductions.
- Whether the product(s)/service(s) of rival firms are highly differentiated, weakly differentiated, or essentially identical.
- Whether there are economies of scale in manufacturing, transportation, or mass marketing.
- Whether high rates of capacity utilization are crucial to achieving low-cost production efficiency.
- Whether the industry has a strong learning and experience curve such that average unit cost declines as *cumulative* output (and thus the experience of "learning by doing") builds up.
- Capital requirements.
- Whether industry profitability is above/below par.

Table 3–1 illustrates a profile of an industry's chief economic characteristics.

. . . .
An industry's economic characteristics have important implications for crafting an effective strategy.

An industry's economic characteristics are important because of the implications they have for strategy. For example, in capital-intensive industries, where investment in a single plant can run several hundred million dollars, a firm can ease the resulting burden of high fixed costs by pursuing a strategy that promotes high utilization of fixed assets and generates more revenue per dollar of fixed-asset investment. Thus commercial airlines employ strategies to boost the revenue productivity of their expensive jet aircraft fleets by cutting

TABLE 3–1   **A Sample Profile of an Industry's Dominant Economic Characteristics**

Market Size: $400–$500 million annual revenues; 4 million tons, total volume.

Scope of Competitive Rivalry: Primarily regional; producers rarely sell outside a 250-mile radius of plant due to high cost of shipping long distances.

Market Growth Rate: 2–3 percent annually.

Stage in Life Cycle: Mature.

Number of Companies in Industry: About 30 companies with 110 plant locations and capacity of 4.5 million tons. Market shares range from a low of 3 percent to a high of 21 percent.

Customers: About 2,000 buyers; most are industrial chemical firms.

Degree of Vertical Integration: Mixed; 5 of the 10 largest companies are integrated backward into mining operations and also forward in that sister industrial chemical divisions buy over 50 percent of the output of their plants; all other companies are engaged solely in manufacturing.

Ease of Entry/Exit: Moderate entry barriers exist in the form of capital requirements to construct a new plant of minimum efficient size (cost equals $10 million) and ability to build a customer base inside a 250-mile radius of plant.

Technology/Innovation: Production technology is standard and changes have been slow; biggest changes are occurring in products—about 1–2 newly formulated specialty chemicals products are being introduced annually, accounting for nearly all of industry growth.

Product Characteristics: Highly standardized; the brands of different producers are essentially identical (buyers perceive little real difference from seller to seller).

Scale Economies: Moderate; all companies have virtually equal manufacturing costs but scale economies exist in shipping in multiple carloads to same customer and in purchasing large quantities of raw materials.

Experience Curve Effects: Not a factor in this industry.

Capacity Utilization: Manufacturing efficiency is highest between 90–100 percent of rated capacity; below 90 percent utilization, unit costs run significantly higher.

Industry Profitability: Subpar to average; the commodity nature of the industry's product results in intense price-cutting when demand slackens, but prices firm up during periods of strong demand. Profits track the strength of demand for the industry's products.

ground time at airport gates (to get in more flights per day with the same plane) and by discounting fares to fill up otherwise empty seats on each flight. In industries characterized by one product advance after another, companies are driven to invest enough time and money in R&D to keep their technical skills and innovative capability abreast of competitors—a strategy of continuous product innovation becomes a condition of survival.

In industries like semiconductors, the presence of a *learning/experience* curve effect in manufacturing causes unit costs to decline about 20 percent each time *cumulative* production volume doubles. With a 20 percent experience curve effect, if the first 1 million chips cost $1 each, by a production volume of 2 million the unit cost would be $.80 (80 percent of $1); by a production volume of 4 million the unit cost would be $.64 (80 percent of $0.80); and so on. When an industry is characterized by a strong experience curve effect in its manufacturing operations, a company that moves first to initiate production of a new-style product and develops a strategy to capture the largest market share can win the competitive advantage of being the low-cost producer. The bigger the experience curve effect, the bigger the cost advantage of the company with the largest *cumulative* production volume, as shown in Figure 3–2.

• • • • • • • • • • • •
Basic Concept
When a strong learning/ experience curve effect causes unit costs to decline as production volume builds, a high-volume manufacturer can have the competitive advantage of being the industry's lowest-cost producer.

FIGURE 3–2   **Comparison of Experience Curve Effects for 10 Percent, 20 Percent, and 30 Percent Cost Reductions for Each Doubling of Cumulative Production Volume**

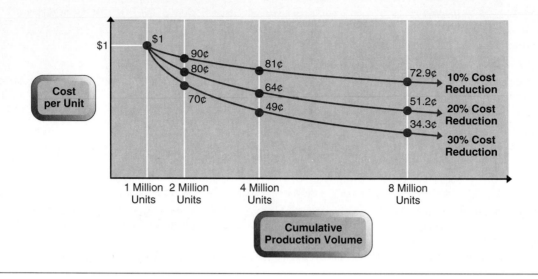

Table 3–2 presents some additional examples of how an industry's economic characteristics can be relevant to managerial strategy-making.

The Concept of Driving Forces: Why Industries Change

An industry's economic features say a lot about the basic nature of the industry environment but very little about the ways in which the environment may be changing. All industries are characterized by trends and new developments that, either gradually or speedily, produce changes important enough to require a strategic response from participating firms. The popular hypothesis about industries going through evolutionary growth phases or life-cycle stages helps explain why industry conditions change but is still incomplete.[1] The life-cycle stages are strongly keyed to the overall industry growth rate (which is why stages are described with such terms as rapid growth, early maturity, saturation, and decline). Yet there are more causes of industry and competitive change than moving to a new position on the growth curve.

While it is important to judge what growth stage an industry is in, there's more analytical value in identifying the specific factors causing industry change. Industry conditions change *because forces are in motion that create incen-*

[1]For a more extended discussion of the problems with the life-cycle hypothesis, see Michael E. Porter, *Competitive Strategy: Techniques for Analyzing Industries and Competitors* (New York: Free Press, 1980), pp. 157–62.

> **Basic Concept**
> *Industry conditions change because important forces are driving industry participants (competitors, customers, suppliers) to alter their actions; the driving forces in an industry are the major underlying causes of changing industry and competitive conditions.*

TABLE 3–2   **Examples of the Strategic Importance of an Industry's Key Economic Characteristics**

Factor/Characteristic	Strategic Importance
• Market size	• Small markets don't tend to attract big/new competitors; large markets often draw the interest of corporations looking to acquire companies with established competitive positions in attractive industries.
• Market growth rate	• Fast growth breeds new entry; growth slowdowns spawn increased rivalry and a shake-out of weak competitors.
• Capacity surpluses or shortages	• Surpluses push prices and profit margins down; shortages pull them up.
• Industry profitability	• High-profit industries attract new entrants; depressed conditions encourage exit.
• Entry/exit barriers	• High barriers protect positions and profits of existing firms; low barriers make existing firms vulnerable to entry.
• Product is a big-ticket item for buyers	• More buyers will shop for lowest price.
• Standardized products	• Buyers have more power because it is easier to switch from seller to seller.
• Rapid technological change	• Raises risk factor; investments in technology facilities/equipment may become obsolete before they wear out.
• Capital requirements	• Big requirements make investment decisions critical; timing becomes important; creates a barrier to entry and exit.
• Vertical integration	• Raises capital requirements; often creates competitive differences and cost differences among fully versus partially versus nonintegrated firms.
• Economies of scale	• Increases volume and market share needed to be cost competitive.
• Rapid product innovation	• Shortens product life cycle; increases risk because of opportunities for leapfrogging.

tives or pressures for change.[2] The most dominant forces are called *driving forces* because they have the biggest influences on what kinds of changes will take place in the industry's structure and environment. Driving forces analysis has two steps: (1) identifying what the driving forces are and (2) assessing the impact they will have on the industry.

The Most Common Driving Forces   Many events affect an industry powerfully enough to qualify as driving forces. Some are one-of-a-kind, but most fall into one of several basic categories. The most common driving forces are shown here.[3]

- **Changes in the Long-Term Industry Growth Rate.** Shifts in industry growth up or down are a force for industry change because they affect the balance between industry supply and buyer demand, entry and exit, and how hard it will be for a firm to capture additional sales. A strong upsurge in long-term demand frequently attracts new firms and encourages

• • • • • • • • • • • • •
Several different factors can affect an industry powerfully enough to act as driving forces.

[2]Ibid., p. 162.
[3]What follows draws on the discussion in Porter, *Competitive Strategy,* pp. 164–83.

established ones to invest in additional capacity. In a shrinking market, some firms will exit the industry, and the remaining ones may postpone further capacity investments.

- **Changes in Who Buys the Product and How They Use It.** Shifts in buyer demographics and the emergences of new ways to use the product can force adjustments in customer service offerings (credit, technical assistance, maintenance and repair), open the way to market the industry's product through a different mix of dealers and retail outlets, prompt producers to broaden/narrow their product lines, increase/decrease capital requirements, and change sales and promotion approaches. The computer industry has been transformed by the surge of interest in personal and mid-size computers. Consumer interest in cordless telephones and mobile telephones has opened a major new buyer segment for telephone equipment manufacturers.

- **Product Innovation.** Product innovation can broaden an industry's customer base, rejuvenate industry growth, and widen the degree of product differentiation among rival sellers. Successful new product introductions strengthen a company's position, usually at the expense of companies who stick with their old products or are slow to follow with their own versions of the new product. Industries where product innovation has been a key driving force include copying equipment, cameras and photographic equipment, computers, electronic video games, toys, prescription drugs, frozen foods, and personal computer software.

- **Technological Change.** Advances in technology can dramatically alter an industry's landscape, making it possible to produce new and/or better products at a lower cost and opening up whole new industry frontiers. Technological change can also affect capital requirements, minimum efficient plant sizes, desirability of vertical integration, and learning or experience curve effects.

- **Marketing Innovation.** When firms are successful in introducing new ways to market their products, they can spark a burst of buyer interest, widen industry demand, increase product differentiation, and/or lower unit costs—any or all of which can alter the competitive positions of rival firms and force strategy revisions.

- **Entry or Exit of Major Firms.** The entry of one or more foreign companies into a market once dominated by domestic firms nearly always produces a big shakeup in industry conditions. Likewise, when an established domestic firm in another industry attempts entry either by acquisition or by launching its own startup venture, it usually intends to apply its skills and resources in some innovative fashion. Entry by a major firm often produces a "new ballgame" not only with new key players but also with new rules for competing. Similarly, exit of a major firm changes industry structure by reducing the number of market leaders (perhaps increasing the dominance of the leaders who remain) and causing a rush to capture the exiting firm's customers.

- **Diffusion of Technical Know-How.** As knowledge about how to perform a particular activity or to execute a particular manufacturing technology spreads, any technically-based competitive advantage held by firms possessing this know-how erodes. Diffusion of technical know-how occurs through scientific journals, trade publications, on-site plant tours, word-of-mouth among suppliers and customers, and the hiring away of knowledgeable employees. It can also occur when the possessors of technological know-how license others to use it for a fee or team up with a company interested in turning the technology into a new business venture. Often companies acquire technical know-how by buying a company with the desired skills, patents, or manufacturing capabilities. In recent years technology transfer across national boundaries has emerged as one of the most important driving forces in globalizing markets and competition. As companies in more countries gain access to technical know-how, they upgrade their manufacturing capabilities to compete with established companies. Technology transfer has turned many domestic industries into global ones (e.g., automobiles, tires, consumer electronics, telecommunications, and computers).

- **Increasing Globalization of the Industry.** Global competition usually changes patterns of competitive advantage among key players. Industries move toward globalization for several reasons. Certain firms may launch aggressive long-term strategies to win a globally dominant market position. Demand for the industry's product may emerge in more countries. Trade barriers may drop. Technology-transfer may open the door for more companies in more countries to enter the industry on a major scale. Significant labor cost differences among countries may create a strong reason to locate plants for labor-intensive products in low-wage countries (wages in South Korea, Taiwan, and Singapore, for example, are about one-fourth those in the United States). Significant cost economies may accrue to firms with world-scale volumes as opposed to national-scale volumes. The growing ability of multinational companies to transfer their production, marketing, and management know-how from country to country at significantly lower cost than companies with a one-country production base may give multinational competitors a significant competitive advantage over domestic-only competitors. Globalization is most likely to be a driving force in industries (*a*) based on natural resources (supplies of crude oil, copper, and cotton, for example, are geographically scattered all over the globe), (*b*) where low-cost production is a critical consideration (making it imperative to locate plant facilities in countries where the lowest costs can be achieved), and (*c*) where one or more growth-oriented, market-seeking companies are pushing hard to gain a significant competitive position in as many attractive country markets as they can.

- **Changes in Cost and Efficiency.** In industries where significant economies of scale are emerging or strong learning curve effects are allowing firms with the most production experience to undercut rivals' prices, large market share becomes such a distinct advantage that all firms are pressured to adopt volume-building strategies—a "race for growth" dominates the industry. Likewise, sharply rising costs for a key input (either raw materials or labor) can cause a scramble to either (*a*) line up reliable supplies at affordable prices or (*b*) search out lower-cost substitutes. Any time important changes in cost or efficiency take place, firms' positions can change radically concerning who has how big a cost advantage.

- **Emerging Buyer Preferences for a Differentiated Instead of a Commodity Product (or for a more standardized product instead of strongly differentiated products).** Sometimes growing numbers of buyers decide that a standard product at a bargain price meets their needs as effectively as premium priced brands offering more features and options. These swings in buyer demand can drive industry change by shifting patronage to sellers of cheaper commodity products and creating a price-competitive market environment. Such a development may so dominate the market that industry producers can't do much more than compete hard on price. On the other hand, a shift away from standardized products occurs when sellers are able to win a bigger and more loyal buyer following by introducing new features, making style changes, offering options and accessories, and creating image differences via advertising and packaging. Then the driver of change is the struggle among rivals to out-differentiate one another. Industries evolve differently depending on whether the forces in motion are acting to increase or decrease the emphasis on product differentiation.

- **Regulatory Influences and Government Policy Changes.** Regulatory and governmental actions can often force significant changes in industry practices and strategic approaches. Deregulation has been a major driving force in the airline, banking, natural gas, and telecommunications industries. Drunk driving laws and drinking age legislation recently became driving forces in the alcoholic beverage industry. In international markets, newly enacted regulations of host governments to open up their domestic markets to foreign participation or to close off foreign participation to protect domestic companies are a major factor in shaping whether the competitive struggle between foreign and domestic companies occurs on a level playing field or whether it is one-sided (owing to government favoritism).

- **Changing Societal Concerns, Attitudes, and Life-styles.** Emerging social issues and changing attitudes and life-styles can be powerful instigators of industry change. Consumer concerns about salt, sugar, chemical additives, cholesterol, and nutrition are forcing the food industry to reexamine food processing techniques, redirect R&D efforts, and introduce healthier products. Safety concerns are driving change in the automobile, toy, and outdoor power equipment industries. Increased interest in physical fitness is producing whole new industries to supply exercise equipment, jogging clothes and shoes, and medically super-vised diet programs. Social concerns about air and water pollution are affecting industries that discharge waste products. Growing anti-smoking sentiment is posing a major long-term threat to the cigarette industry.

- **Reductions in Uncertainty and Business Risk.** A young, emerging industry is typically characterized by an unproven cost structure and much uncertainty over potential market size, R&D costs, and distribution channels. Emerging industries tend to attract only the most entrepreneurial companies. Over time, however, if pioneering firms succeed and uncertainty about the industry's viability fades, more conservative firms are usually enticed to enter the industry. Often, the entrants are larger, financially strong firms hunting for attractive growth industries. In international markets, conservatism is prevalent in the early stages of globalization. Firms tend to minimize their risk by relying initially on exporting, licensing, and joint ventures. Then, as their experience accumulates and as perceived risk levels decline, companies move more quickly and aggressively to form wholly owned subsidiaries and to pursue full-scale, multicountry competitive strategies.

The foregoing list of *potential* driving forces in an industry indicates why it is too simplistic to view industry change only in terms of moving from one growth stage to another and why it is essential to probe for the *causes* underlying the emergence of new industry conditions.

However, while *many* forces of change may be at work in an industry, no more than three or four are likely to be *driving* forces in the sense that they act as *the major determinants* of how the industry evolves and operates. Strategic analysts must resist the temptation to label everything they see changing as driving forces; the analytical task is to evaluate the forces of industry change carefully enough to separate major factors from minor ones.

Analyzing driving forces has practical strategy-making value. First, the driving forces in an industry indicate to managers what external factors will have the greatest effect on the company's business over the next one to three years. Second, to position the company to deal with these forces, managers must assess the implications and consequences of each driving force—that is, they must project what impact the driving forces will have on the industry. Third, strategy-makers need to craft a strategy that is responsive to the driving forces and their effects on the industry.

> • • • • • • • • • • • • •
> *The task of driving forces analysis is to separate the major causes of changing industry conditions from minor ones; usually no more than three or four factors qualify as driving forces.*

Environmental Scanning Techniques   One way to predict future driving forces is to utilize environmental scanning techniques. *Environmental scanning* involves studying and interpreting social, political, economic, ecological, and technological events in an effort to spot budding trends and conditions that could eventually affect the industry. It attempts to look broadly at "first of its kind" happenings, what kinds of new ideas and approaches are catching on, and extrapolate their possible implications 5 to 20 years into the future. For example, environmental scanning could involve judgments about the demand for energy in the year 2000, uses for computers 20 years from now, or the condition of forests in the 21st century given the growing demand for paper. Environmental scanning raises managers' awareness of potential developments that could have an important impact on industry conditions and pose new opportunities and threats.

Environmental scanning can be accomplished by systematically monitoring and studying current events, constructing scenarios, and employing the Delphi method (a technique for finding consensus among a group of "knowledgeable experts"). Although highly qualitative and subjective, environmental scanning helps managers lengthen their planning horizon, translate vague inklings into clearer strategic issues (for which they can begin to develop a strategic answer), and think strategically about future developments in the

> • • • • • • • • • • • •
> **Basic Concept**
> *Strategists use environmental scanning to spot budding trends and developments that could emerge as new driving forces.*

surrounding environment.[4] Companies that undertake formal environmental scanning include General Electric, AT&T, Coca-Cola, Ford, General Motors, Du Pont, and Shell Oil.

Analyzing the Strength of Competitive Forces

One of the big cornerstones of industry and competitive analysis involves carefully studying the industry's competitive process to discover the main sources of competitive pressure and how strong they are. This analytical step is essential because managers cannot devise a successful strategy without understanding the industry's special competitive character.

Even though competitive pressures differ in different industries, competition itself works similarly enough to use a common framework in gauging its nature and intensity. As a rule, *competition in an industry is a composite of five competitive forces*:

1. The rivalry among competing sellers in the industry.
2. The market attempts of companies in other industries to win customers to their own *substitute* products.
3. The potential entry of new competitors.
4. The bargaining power and leverage exercisable by suppliers of key raw materials and components.
5. The bargaining power and leverage exercisable by buyers of the product.

The *five-forces model*, as diagrammed in Figure 3–3, is extremely helpful in systematically diagnosing the principal competitive pressures in a market and assessing how strong and important each one is.[5] Not only is it the most widely used technique of competition analysis, but it is also straightforward to use.

The Rivalry among Competing Sellers   The most powerful of the five competitive forces is *usually* the competitive battle among rival firms.[6] How vigorously sellers use the competitive weapons at their disposal to jockey for a stronger market position and win a competitive edge over rivals shows the strength of this competitive force. *Competitive strategy is the narrower portion of business strategy dealing with a company's competitive approaches for achieving market success, its offensive moves to secure a competitive edge over rival firms, and its defensive moves to protect its competitive position.*[7]

---

[4]For further discussion of the nature and use of environmental scanning, see Roy Amara and Andrew J. Lipinski, *Business Planning for an Uncertain Future: Scenarios and Strategies* (New York: Pergamon Press, 1983); Harold E. Klein and Robert U. Linneman, "Environmental Assessment: An International Study of Corporate Practice," *Journal of Business Strategy* 5, no. 1 (Summer 1984), pp. 55–75; and Arnoldo C. Hax and Nicolas S. Majluf, *The Strategy Concept and Process* (Englewood Cliffs, N.J.: Prentice Hall, 1991), chaps. 5 and 8.

[5]For a thorough treatment of the five-forces model by its originator, see Porter, *Competitive Strategy*, chap. 1.

[6]Parts of this section are based on the discussion in Arthur A. Thompson, "Competition as a Strategic Process," *Antitrust Bulletin* 25, no. 4 (Winter 1980), pp. 777–803.

[7]The distinction between *competitive strategy* and *business strategy* is useful here. As we defined it in Chapter 2, business strategy not only addresses the issue of how to compete, it also embraces all of the functional area support strategies, how management plans to respond to changing industry conditions of all kinds (not just those that are competition-related), and how management intends to address the

---

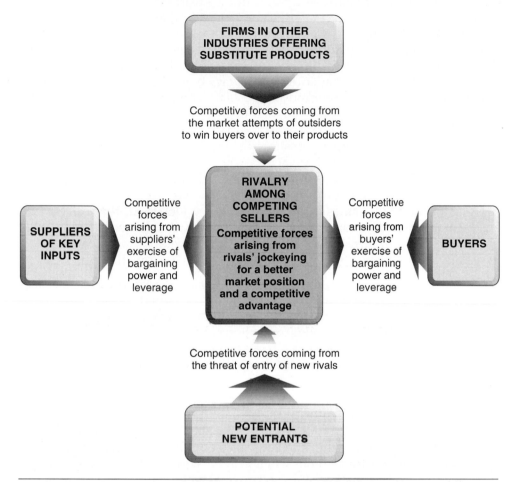

Source: Adapted from Michael E. Porter, "How Competitive Forces Shape Strategy," *Harvard Business Review* 57, no. 2 (March–April 1979), pp.137–45.

The challenge in crafting a winning competitive strategy, of course, is *how to gain an edge over rivals.* The big complication is that the success of any one firm's strategy hinges on what strategies its rivals employ and the resources rivals are willing and able to put behind their strategies. The "best" strategy for one firm in maneuvering for competitive advantage depends on the competitive strength and strategies of its rivals. Whenever one firm makes a strategic move, rivals often retaliate with offensive or defensive countermoves. Thus, competitive rivalry turns into a game of strategy, of move and countermove, played under "warlike" conditions according to the rules of business competition—in effect, *competitive markets are economic battlefields.*

---

full range of strategic issues. Competitive strategy, however, is narrower in scope. It focuses on the firm's competitive approach, the competitive edge strived for, and specific moves to outmaneuver rival companies.

· · · · · · · · · · · ·
Principle of Competitive Markets
Competitive jockeying among rivals is ever-changing as firms initiate new offensive and defensive moves and as emphasis swings from one mix of competitive weapons to another.

Competitive battles among rival sellers can assume many forms and degrees of intensity. The weapons used for competing include price, quality, features, services, warranties and guarantees, advertising, better networks of wholesale distributors and retail dealers, innovation, and so on. The relative dependence that competitors place on each of these weapons can change over time, as first one then another is used more extensively to catch buyers' attention and as competitors initiate fresh offensive and defensive moves. Rivalry is thus dynamic; current conditions are always being modified as companies initiate new moves and countermoves and as the competitive emphasis swings from one weapons mix to another. Two principles of competitive rivalry are particularly important: (1) a powerful competitive strategy used by one company intensifies competitive pressures on the other companies, and (2) the manner in which rivals employ various competitive weapons to try to out-maneuver one another shapes "the rules of competition" in the industry and determines the requirements for competitive success.

Once an industry's rules of competition are understood, then judgments can be made regarding whether competitive rivalry is cutthroat, intense, normal to moderate, or attractively weak. There are several factors that, industry after industry, influence the *strength* of rivalry among competing sellers:[8]

· · · · · · · · · · · ·
There are many reasons why the rivalry among competing sellers can grow stronger or weaker.

1. *Rivalry tends to intensify as the number of competitors increases and as they become more equal in size and capability.* Up to a point, the greater the number of competitors the greater the probability of fresh, creative strategic initiatives. In addition, when rivals are more equal in size and capability, they compete on a fairly even footing, making it harder for one or two firms to "win" the competitive battle and dominate the market.

2. *Rivalry is usually stronger when demand for the product is growing slowly.* In a rapidly expanding market, there tends to be enough business for everybody to grow. Indeed, it may take all of a firm's financial and managerial resources just to keep pace with buyer demand, much less steal rivals' customers. But when growth slows or when market demand drops unexpectedly, expansion-minded firms and/or firms with excess capacity often cut prices and use other sales-increasing tactics. The ensuing battle for market share can result in a shake out of the weak and less-efficient firms. The industry then "consolidates" into a smaller, but individually stronger, group of sellers.

3. *Rivalry is more intense when industry conditions tempt competitors to use price cuts or other competitive weapons to boost unit volume.* Whenever fixed costs account for a large fraction of total cost, unit costs tend to be lowest at or near full capacity since fixed costs can be spread over more units of production. Unused capacity thus imposes a significant cost-increasing penalty because there are fewer units to carry the fixed cost burden. In such cases, if market demand weakens and capacity utilization begins to fall off, the pressure of rising unit costs pushes firms into secret price concessions, special discounts, rebates, and other

---

[8]These indicators of what to look for in evaluating the intensity of interfirm rivalry are based on Porter, *Competitive Strategy*, pp. 17–21.

sales-increasing tactics, thus heightening competition. Likewise, when a product is perishable, seasonal, or costly to inventory, competitive pressures build quickly anytime one or more competitors decides to dump its excess supplies on the market.

4. *Rivalry is stronger when the costs incurred by customers to switch their purchases from one brand to another are low.* The lower the costs of switching, the easier it is for rival sellers to raid one another's customers. On the other hand, high switching costs give a seller some protection against the efforts of rivals to raid its customers.

5. *Rivalry is stronger when one or more competitors is dissatisfied with its market position and launches moves to bolster its standing at the expense of rivals.* Firms that are losing ground or find themselves in financial trouble often take such aggressive actions as acquiring smaller rivals, introducing new products, increasing advertising, promoting special prices, and so on. Such actions can trigger a new round of competitive maneuvering and a heightened battle for market share.

6. *Rivalry increases in proportion to the size of the payoff from a successful strategic move.* The greater the potential reward, the more likely some firm will aggressively pursue a strategy to capture it. The size of the strategic payoff depends partly on how fast rivals retaliate. When competitors respond slowly (or not at all), the initiator of a fresh competitive strategy can reap benefits in the intervening period and perhaps gain a first-mover advantage that is not easily surmounted. The greater the benefits of moving first, the more likely some firm will accept the risk and try it.

7. *Rivalry tends to be more vigorous when it costs more to get out of a business than to stay in and compete.* The higher the exit barriers (thus the more costly it is to abandon a market), the stronger the incentive for firms to remain and compete as best they can, even though they may be earning low profits or even incurring a loss.

8. *Rivalry becomes more volatile and unpredictable the more diverse competitors are in terms of their strategies, personalities, corporate priorities, resources, and countries of origin.* A diverse group of sellers is more likely to spawn one or more mavericks willing to rock the boat with unconventional moves and approaches, thus generating a more lively and uncertain competitive environment. The added presence of new, lower-cost foreign-based competitors intent on gaining market share is a surefire factor in boosting the intensity of rivalry.

9. *Rivalry increases when strong companies outside the industry acquire weak firms in the industry and launch aggressive, well-funded moves to transform their newly-acquired firms into major market contenders.* For example, Philip Morris, a leading cigarette firm with excellent marketing know-how, shook up the whole beer industry's marketing approach when it acquired stodgy Miller Brewing Company in the late 1960s. In short order, Philip Morris revamped the marketing plan for Miller High Life and pushed it to the number two best-selling brand. PM also pioneered low-calorie beers with the introduction of Miller Lite—a move that made light beer the fastest-growing segment in the beer industry.

Such jockeying for position among competitors unfolds in round after round of moves and countermoves. The strategist has to identify the current competitive weapons, stay on top of how the game is being played, and judge how much pressure competitive rivalry is going to put on profitability. Competitive rivalry is "intense" when competitors' actions are driving down industry profits; rivalry is "moderate" when most companies can earn acceptable profits; and rivalry is "weak" when most companies in the industry can earn above-average returns on investment. Chronic outbreaks of cutthroat competition make an industry brutally competitive.

The Competitive Force of Potential Entry   New entrants to a market bring new production capacity, the desire to establish a secure place in the market, and sometimes substantial resources with which to compete.[9] How serious the threat of entry is in a particular market depends on two factors: *barriers to entry* and the *expected reaction of incumbent firms to new entry.* A barrier to entry exists whenever it is hard for a newcomer to break into a market and/or economic factors put a potential entrant at a disadvantage relative to its competitors. There are several types of entry barriers:[10]

- **Economies of scale.** Scale economies deter entry because they force potential entrants either to enter on a large-scale basis (a costly and perhaps risky move) or to accept a cost disadvantage (and consequently lower profitability). Firms that do attempt large-scale entry can cause overcapacity problems in the industry and so threaten the market shares of existing firms that they retaliate aggressively (with price cuts, increased advertising and sales promotion, and similar steps) to maintain their position. Either way, a new entrant can expect to earn lower profits. Entrants may encounter scale-related barriers not just in production, but in advertising, marketing and distribution, financing, after-sale customer service, raw materials purchasing, and R&D as well.
- **Inability to gain access to technology and specialized know-how.** Many industries require technological capability and skills not readily available to a new entrant. Key patents can bar entry as can lack of technically skilled personnel and an inability to execute complicated manufacturing techniques. Existing firms often carefully guard know-how that gives them an edge in technology and manufacturing capability. Unless new entrants can gain access to such knowledge, they will lack the technical capability to compete on an equal footing.
- **Learning and experience curve effects.** When lower unit costs are partly or mostly a result of experience and other learning curve benefits, a new entrant is faced with a cost disadvantage in competing against existing firms with more accumulated know-how.

[9]Michael E. Porter, "How Competitive Forces Shape Strategy," *Harvard Business Review* 57, no. 2 (March–April 1979), p. 138.
[10]Porter, *Competitive Strategy,* pp. 7–17.

- **Brand preferences and customer loyalty.** Buyers are often attached to existing brands. European consumers, for example, are fiercely loyal to European brands of major household appliances. High brand loyalty means that a potential entrant must be prepared to spend enough money on advertising and sales promotion to overcome customer loyalties and build its own clientele. Substantial time and money can be involved. In addition, if it is difficult or costly for a customer to switch to a new brand, a new entrant must persuade buyers that its brand is worth the switching costs. To overcome the switching cost barrier, new entrants may have to offer buyers a bigger price cut or extra quality or service. All this can mean lower profit margins for new entrants—something that increases the risk to startup companies dependent on sizable, early profits to support their new investment.

- **Capital requirements.** The larger the total dollar investment needed to enter the market successfully, the more limited the pool of potential entrants. The most obvious capital requirements are associated with manufacturing plant and equipment, working capital to finance inventories and customer credit, introductory advertising and sales promotion to establish a clientele, and covering startup losses.

- **Cost disadvantages independent of size.** Existing firms may have cost advantages not available to potential entrants regardless of the entrant's size. These advantages can include access to the best and cheapest raw materials, possession of patents and proprietary technological know-how, the benefits of learning and experience curve effects, having built and equipped plants years earlier at lower costs, favorable locations, and lower borrowing costs.

- **Access to distribution channels.** In the case of consumer goods, a potential entrant may face the barrier of gaining adequate access to distribution channels. Wholesale distributors may be reluctant to take on a product that lacks buyer recognition. A network of retail dealers may have to be set up from scratch. Retailers may have to be convinced to give a new brand ample display space and an adequate trial period. The more existing producers have tied up present distribution channels, the tougher entry will be. To overcome this barrier, entrants may have to "buy" distribution access by offering better margins to dealers and distributors or by giving advertising allowances and other promotional incentives. As a consequence, a potential entrant's profits may be squeezed until its product gains such acceptance that distributors and retailers want to carry it.

- **Regulatory policies.** Government agencies can limit or even bar entry by requiring licenses and permits. Regulated industries like banking, insurance, radio and television stations, liquor retailing, and railroads feature government-controlled entry. In international markets, host governments commonly limit foreign entry and must approve all foreign investment applications. Stringent government-mandated safety regulations and environmental pollution standards are entry barriers because they raise entry costs.

- **Tariffs and international trade restrictions.** National governments commonly use tariffs and trade restrictions (antidumping rules, local content requirements, and quotas) to raise entry barriers for foreign firms. In 1988, due to tariffs imposed by the South Korean government, a Ford Taurus cost South Korean car buyers over $40,000. European governments require that certain Asian products, from electronic typewriters to copying machines, contain European-made parts and labor equal to 40 percent of the selling price. And to protect European chipmakers from low-cost Asian competition, European governments instituted a rigid formula to calculate floor prices for computer memory chips.

Even if a potential entrant is willing to tackle the problems of entry barriers, it still faces the issue of how existing firms will react.[11] Will incumbent firms react passively, or will they aggressively defend their market positions with price cuts, increased advertising, product improvements, and whatever else will give a new entrant (as well as other rivals) a hard time? A potential entrant often has second thoughts when incumbents send strong signals that they will stoutly defend their market positions against entry and when they have the financial resources to do so. A potential entrant may also turn away when incumbent firms can use leverage with distributors and customers to keep their business.

The best test of whether potential entry is a strong or weak competitive force is to ask if the industry's growth and profit prospects are attractive enough to induce additional entry. When the answer is no, potential entry is not a source of competitive pressure. When the answer is yes (as in industries where lower-cost foreign competitors are seeking new markets), then potential entry is a strong force. The stronger the threat of entry, the greater the motivation of incumbent firms to fortify their positions against newcomers to make entry more costly or difficult.

One additional point: the threat of entry changes as industry prospects grow brighter or dimmer and as entry barriers rise or fall. For example, the expiration of a key patent can greatly increase the threat of entry. A technological discovery can create an economy of scale and advantage where none existed before. New actions by incumbent firms to increase advertising, strengthen distributor-dealer relations, step up R&D, or improve product quality can erect higher roadblocks to entry. In international markets, entry barriers for foreign-based firms ease when tariffs are lowered; domestic wholesalers and dealers seek out lower-cost foreign-made goods, and domestic buyers become more willing to purchase foreign brands.

• • • • • • • • • • • • •

Principle of Competitive Markets
The competitive threat posed by substitute products is strong when prices of substitutes are attractive, buyers' switching costs are low, and buyers believe substitutes have equal or better features.

The Competitive Force of Substitute Products   Firms in one industry are, quite often, in close competition with firms in another industry because their respective products are good substitutes. The producers of eyeglasses compete with the makers of contact lenses. The sugar industry competes with companies that produce artificial sweeteners. The producers of plastic containers confront strong competition from makers of glass bottles and jars, paperboard cartons, and tin and aluminum cans.

The competitive force of substitute products comes into play in several ways. First, the presence of readily available and competitively priced substi-

---

[11]Porter, "How Competitive Forces Shape Strategy," p. 140; and Porter, *Competitive Strategy*, pp. 14–15.

tutes places a ceiling on the prices companies in an industry can afford to charge without giving customers an incentive to switch to substitutes and thus eroding their own market position.[12] This price ceiling, at the same time, puts a lid on the profits that industry members can earn unless they find ways to cut costs. When substitutes are cheaper than an industry's product, industry members come under heavy competitive pressure to reduce prices and find ways to absorb the price cuts with cost reductions. Second, the availability of substitutes invites customers to compare quality and performance as well as price. For example, firms that buy glass bottles and jars from glassware manufacturers monitor whether they can just as effectively package their products in plastic containers, paper cartons, or tin cans. Because of competitive pressure from substitute products, industry rivals have to convince customers their product is more advantageous than substitutes. Usually this requires devising a competitive strategy to differentiate the industry's product from substitute products via some combination of lower cost, better quality, better service, and more desirable performance features.

Another determinant of whether substitutes are a strong or weak competitive force is whether it is difficult or costly for customers to switch to substitutes.[13] Typical switching costs include employee retraining costs, the costs of purchasing additional equipment, costs for technical help needed to make the changeover, the time and cost to test the quality and reliability of the substitute, and the psychic costs of severing old supplier relationships and establishing new ones. If switching costs are high, sellers of substitutes must offer a major cost or performance benefit to steal the industry's customers. When switching costs are low, it's much easier for the sellers of substitutes to convince buyers to change over to their product.

As a rule, then, the lower the price of substitutes, the higher their quality and performance, and the lower the user's switching costs, the more intense are the competitive pressures posed by substitute products. The best indicators of the competitive strength of substitute products are the rate at which their sales are growing, the market inroads they are making, the plans the sellers of substitutes have for expanding production capacity, and the size of their profits.

The Power of Suppliers   Whether the suppliers to an industry are a weak or strong competitive force depends on market conditions in the supplier industry and the significance of the item they supply.[14] The competitive force of suppliers is greatly diminished whenever the item they provide is a standard commodity available on the open market from a large number of suppliers with ample ability to fill orders. Then it is relatively simple to multiple-source whatever is needed, choosing to buy from whichever suppliers offer the best deal. In such cases, suppliers can win concessions only when supplies become tight and users are so anxious to secure what they need that they agree to terms more favorable to suppliers. Suppliers are also in a weak bargaining position whenever there are good substitute

---

[12]Ibid., p. 142; and pp. 23–24.
[13]Porter, *Competitive Strategy*, p. 10.
[14]Ibid., pp. 27–28.

Principle of Competitive Markets

The suppliers to an industry are a strong competitive force whenever they have sufficient bargaining power to command a price premium for their materials or components and whenever they can affect the competitive well-being of industry rivals by the reliability of their deliveries or by the quality and performance of the items they supply.

inputs and switching is neither costly nor difficult. For example, soft drink bottlers check the power of aluminum can suppliers by using plastic containers and glass bottles. Suppliers also have less leverage when the industry they are supplying is a *major* customer. In this case, the well-being of suppliers becomes closely tied to the well-being of their major customers. Suppliers then have a big incentive to protect the customer industry via reasonable prices, improved quality, and new products and services that might enhance their customers' positions, sales, and profits. When industry members form a close working relationship with major suppliers, they may gain substantial benefit in the form of better-quality components, just-in-time deliveries, and reduced inventory costs.

On the other hand, powerful suppliers can put an industry in a profit squeeze with price increases that can't be fully passed on to the industry's own customers. Suppliers become a strong competitive force when their product makes up a sizable fraction of the costs of an industry's product, is crucial to the industry's production process, and/or significantly affects the quality of the industry's product. Likewise, a supplier (or group of suppliers) gains bargaining leverage the more difficult or costly it is for users to switch suppliers. Big suppliers with good reputations and growing demand for their output are harder to wring concessions from than struggling suppliers striving to broaden their customer base.

Suppliers are also more powerful when they can supply a component cheaper than industry members can make it themselves. For instance, the producers of outdoor power equipment (lawnmowers, rotary tillers, snowblowers, and so on) find it cheaper to buy small engines from outside manufacturers rather than make their own because the quantity they need is too small to justify the investment and master the process. Small-engine manufacturers, by supplying many kinds of engines to the whole power equipment industry, sell enough to capture scale economies, become proficient in the manufacturing techniques, and keep costs well below what power equipment firms would incur on their own. Small engine suppliers can price the item below what it would cost the user to self-manufacture but far enough above their own costs to generate an attractive profit margin. In such situations, suppliers' bargaining position is strong *until* a customer needs enough parts to justify backward integration. Then the balance of power shifts away from the supplier. The more credible the threat of backward integration, the more leverage companies have in negotiating favorable terms with suppliers.

A final instance in which an industry's suppliers play an important competitive role is when suppliers, for one reason or another, do not have the manufacturing capability or a strong enough incentive to provide items of adequate quality. Suppliers who lack the ability or incentive to provide quality parts can seriously damage their customers' business. For example, if auto parts suppliers provide lower-quality components to U.S. automobile manufacturers, they can so increase the warranty and defective goods costs that they seriously impair U.S. auto firms' profits, reputation, and competitive position in world markets.

The Power of Buyers   Just as with suppliers, the competitive strength of buyers can range from strong to weak. Buyers have substantial bargaining leverage in a number of situations.[15] The most obvious is when buyers are large and purchase a sizable percentage of the industry's output. The bigger buyers are and the larger the quantities they purchase, the more clout they have in negotiating with sellers. Often, large buyers successfully leverage their size and volume purchases to obtain price concessions and other favorable terms. Buyers also gain power when the cost of switching to competing brands or substitutes is relatively low. Any time buyers can meet their needs by sourcing from several sellers, they have added room to negotiate. When sellers' products are virtually identical, buyers can switch with little or no cost. However, if sellers' products are strongly differentiated, buyers are less able to switch without incurring sizable switching costs.

One last point: all buyers don't have equal bargaining power with sellers; some may be less sensitive than others to price, quality, or service. For example, in the apparel industry, major manufacturers confront significant customer power when they sell to retail chains like Sears or Kmart. But they can get much better prices selling to small owner-managed boutiques.

Strategic Implications of the Five Competitive Forces   The contribution of Figure 3–3 is the assist it provides in exposing the makeup of competitive forces. *To analyze the competitive environment, the strength of each one of the five competitive forces must be assessed.* The collective impact of these forces determines what competition is like in a given market. As a rule, the stronger competitive forces are, the lower the collective profitability of participating firms. The most brutally competitive situation occurs when the five forces are tough enough to cause prolonged subpar profitability or even losses for most or all firms. The competitive structure of an industry is clearly "unattractive" from a profit-making standpoint if rivalry among sellers is very strong, entry barriers are low, competition from substitutes is strong, and both suppliers and customers have considerable bargaining leverage. On the other hand, when an industry offers superior long-term profit prospects, competitive forces are not unduly strong and the competitive structure of the industry is "favorable" and "attractive." The "ideal" competitive environment from a profit-making perspective is one in which both suppliers and customers are in a weak bargaining position, there are no good substitutes, entry barriers are relatively high, and rivalry among present sellers is only moderate. However, even where some of the five competitive forces are strong, an industry can be competitively attractive to those firms whose market position and strategy provide a good enough defense against competitive pressures to preserve their competitive advantage and retain an ability to earn above-average profits.

In coping with competitive forces, successful strategists craft competitive approaches that will (1) insulate the firm as much as possible from the five competitive forces, (2) influence the industry's competitive rules in the company's favor, and (3) provide a strong, secure position of advantage from which to "play the game" of competition as it unfolds in the industry. Strategists cannot do this task well without first perceptively analyzing the whole competitive picture of the industry via the five forces model.

> **• • • • • • • • • • • • • •**
> *Principle of Competitive Markets*
> Buyers become a stronger competitive force the more they are able to exercise bargaining leverage over price, quality, service, or other terms or conditions of sale.

> **• • • • • • • • • • • • • •**
> *Competitive Strategy Principle*
> A company's competitive strategy is increasingly effective the more it provides good defenses against the five competitive forces, influences the industry's competitive rules in the company's favor, and helps create sustainable competitive advantage.

---

[15]Ibid., pp. 24–27.

Assessing the Competitive Positions of Rival Companies

Strategic group mapping is a technique for displaying the different competitive positions that rival firms occupy in an industry.

The next step in examining the industry's competitive structure is studying the market positions of rival companies. One technique for comparing the competitive positions of industry participants is *strategic group mapping*.[16] This analytical tool bridges the gap between looking at the industry as a whole and considering the standing of each firm separately. It is most useful when an industry has too many competitors to examine each one in depth.

A strategic group consists of those rival firms with similar competitive approaches and positions in the market.[17] Companies in the same strategic group can resemble one another in several ways: they may have comparable product lines, be vertically integrated to the same degree, offer buyers similar services and technical assistance, appeal to similar types of buyers with the same product attributes, emphasize the same distribution channels, depend on identical technology, and/or sell in the same price/quality range. An industry has only one strategic group if all sellers use essentially identical strategies. At the other extreme, there are as many strategic groups as there are competitors if each one pursues a distinctively different competitive approach and occupies a substantially different position in the marketplace.

To construct a strategic group map, analysts need to:

1. Identify the competitive characteristics that differentiate firms in the industry—typical variables are price/quality range (high, medium, low), geographic coverage (local, regional, national, global), degree of vertical integration (none, partial, full), product-line breadth (wide, narrow), use of distribution channels (one, some, all), and degree of service offered (no frills, limited, full service).
2. Plot the firms on a two-variable map using pairs of these differentiating characteristics.
3. Assign firms that fall in about the same strategy space to the same strategic group.
4. Draw circles around each strategic group, making the circles proportional to the size of the group's respective share of total industry sales revenues.

This produces a two-dimensional *strategic group map* such as the one for the beer industry shown in Illustration Capsule 10.

To map the positions of strategic groups accurately in the industry's overall "strategy space," several guidelines must be observed.[18] First, the two variables selected as axes for the map should *not* be highly correlated; if they are, the circles on the map will fall along a diagonal and analysts will learn nothing more than they would by considering only one variable. For instance, if companies with broad product lines use multiple distribution channels while companies with narrow lines use a single distribution channel, one of the variables is redundant. Second, the variables chosen as axes for the map should expose big differences in how rivals have positioned themselves to compete in the

---

[16]Ibid., chap. 7.
[17]Ibid., pp. 129–30.
[18]Ibid., pp. 152–54.

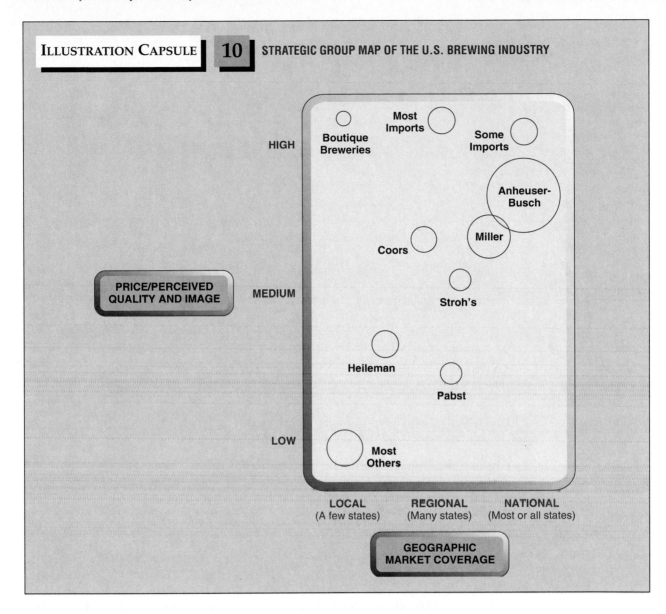

ILLUSTRATION CAPSULE | **10** | STRATEGIC GROUP MAP OF THE U.S. BREWING INDUSTRY

marketplace. This means that analysts must identify the characteristics that differentiate rival firms and use these differences as variables for the axes and as the basis for deciding which firm belongs in which group. Third, the variables used for the axes don't have to be either quantitative or continuous; they can be discrete variables or defined in terms of distinct classes and combinations. Fourth, the circles on the map should be drawn proportional to the combined sales of the firms in each group so that the map will reflect the relative size of each strategic group. Fifth, if more than two good competitive variables can be used for axes, several maps can be drawn to give different exposures to the competitive relationships. Because there is not necessarily one best map, it is advisable to experiment with different pairs of competitive variables.

• • • • • • • • • • • •
Principle of Competitive Markets
Some strategic groups are usually more favorably positioned than others because driving forces and competitive pressures do not affect each group evenly and profit prospects vary among groups based on the relative attractiveness of their market positions.

Strategic group analysis helps deepen understanding of competitive rivalry.[19] To begin with, *driving forces and competitive pressures often favor some strategic groups and hurt others.* Firms in adversely affected strategic groups may try to shift to a more favorably situated group; how hard such a move proves to be depends on whether the entry barriers in the target group are high or low. Attempts by rival firms to enter a new strategic group nearly always increase competitive pressures. If certain firms are known to be changing their competitive positions, arrows can be added to the map to show the targeted direction and help clarify the picture of competitive jockeying among rivals.

Second, *the profit potential of different strategic groups may vary due to the strengths and weaknesses in each group's market position.* Differences in profitability can occur because of different bargaining leverage with suppliers or customers and different exposure to competition from substitute products.

Generally speaking, *the closer strategic groups are on the map, the stronger competitive rivalry among member firms tends to be.* Although firms in the same strategic group are the closest rivals, the next closest rivals are in the immediately adjacent groups. Often, firms in strategic groups that are *far apart* on the map hardly compete at all. For instance, Heineken Brewing Co. in Amsterdam and Dixie Brewing Co. in New Orleans both sell beer, but the prices and perceived qualities of their products are much too different to generate any real competition between them. For the same reason, Timex is not a meaningful competitor of Rolex, and Subaru is not a close competitor of Lincoln or Mercedes-Benz.

Competitor Analysis: Predicting What Moves Which Rivals Are Likely to Make Next

• • • • • • • • • • • •
Competitive Strategy Principle
Successful strategists take great pains in scouting competitors—understanding their strategies, watching their actions, sizing up their strengths and weaknesses, and trying to anticipate what moves they will make next.

Studying the actions and behavior of close competitors is essential. Unless a company pays attention to what competitors are doing, it ends up "flying blind" into battle. A firm can't outmaneuver its rivals without monitoring their actions and anticipating what moves they are likely to make next. The strategies rivals are using and the actions they are likely to take next have direct bearing on what a company's own best strategic moves are—whether it will need to defend against rivals' actions or whether rivals' moves provide an opening for a new offensive thrust.

Identifying Competitors' Strategies   Strategists can get a quick profile of key competitors by studying where they are in the industry, their strategic objectives (as revealed by their recent actions), and their basic competitive approaches. Table 3–3 provides an easy-to-use scheme for categorizing rivals' objectives and strategies. Such a summary, along with a strategic group map, usually suffices to diagnose the competitive intent of rivals.

Evaluating Who the Industry's Major Players Are Going to Be   It's usually obvious who the *current* major contenders are, but these same firms are not necessarily positioned strongly for the future. Some may be losing ground or be ill-equipped to compete on the industry's future battleground. Smaller

---

[19]Ibid., pp. 130, 132–38, and 154–55.

T A B L E 3–3   **Categorizing the Objectives and Strategies of Competitors**

Competitive Scope	Strategic Intent	Market Share Objective	Competitive Position/Situation	Strategic Posture	Competitive Strategy

• Local
• Regional
• National
• Multicountry
• Global
	• Be the dominant leader
	• Overtake the present industry leader
	• Be among the industry leaders (top 5)
	• Move into the top 10
	• Move up a notch or two in the industry rankings
	• Overtake a particular rival (not necessarily the leader)
	• Maintain position
	• Just survive
		• Aggressive expansion via both acquisition and internal growth
		• Expansion via internal growth (boost market share at the expense of rival firms)
		• Expansion via acquisition
		• Hold on to present share (by growing at a rate equal to the industry average)
		• Give up share if necessary to achieve short-term profit objectives (stress profitability, not volume)
			• Getting stronger; on the move
			• Well-entrenched; able to maintain its present position
			• Stuck in the middle of the pack
			• Going after a different market position (trying to move from a weaker to a stronger position)
			• Struggling; losing ground
			• Retrenching to a position that can be defended
				• Mostly offensive
				• Mostly defensive
				• A combination of offense and defense
				• Aggressive risk-taker
				• Conservative follower
					• Striving for low cost leadership
					• Mostly focusing on a market niche
					  – High end
					  – Low end
					  – Geographic
					  – Buyers with special needs
					  – Other
					• Pursuing differentiation based on
					  – Quality
					  – Service
					  – Technological superiority
					  – Breadth of product line
					  – Image and reputation
					  – Other attributes

Note: Since a focus strategy can be aimed at any of several market niches and a differentiation strategy can be keyed to any of several attributes, it is best to be explicit about what kind of focus strategy or differentiation strategy a given firm is pursuing. All focusers do not pursue the same market niche, and all differentiators do not pursue the same differentiating attributes.

companies may be poised for an offensive against larger but vulnerable rivals. In fast-moving, high-technology industries and in globally competitive industries, companies can and do fall from leadership; others end up being acquired. Today's industry leaders don't automatically become tomorrow's.

In deciding whether a competitor is favorably positioned to gain market ground, attention needs to center on *why* there is potential for it to do better or worse than other rivals. Usually, how securely a company holds its present market share is a function of its vulnerability to driving forces and competitive pressures, whether it has a competitive advantage or disadvantage, and whether it is the likely target of offensive attacks from other industry participants. Trying to identify which rivals are poised to gain or lose market position helps a strategist figure out what kinds of moves key rivals are likely to make next.

Predicting Competitors' Next Moves   Predicting rivals' moves is the hardest yet most useful part of competitor analysis. Good clues about what moves a specific competitor may make next come from finding out how much pressure the rival is under to improve its financial performance. Aggressive rivals usually undertake some type of new strategic initiative. Content rivals are likely to continue their present strategy with only minor fine-tuning. Ailing rivals can be performing so poorly that fresh strategic moves, either offensive or defensive, are virtually certain. Since managers generally operate from assumptions about the industry's future and beliefs about their own firm's situation, strategists can gain insights into the strategic thinking of rival managers by examining their public pronouncements about where the industry is headed and what it will take to be successful, listening to what they are saying about their firm's situation, gathering information about what they are doing, and studying their past actions and leadership styles. Strategists also need to consider whether a rival is flexible enough to make major strategic changes.

To predict a competitor's next moves, an analyst must get a good "feel" for the rival's situation, how its managers think, and what its options are. The detective work can be tedious and time-consuming since the information comes in bits and pieces from many sources. But it is a task worth doing well because the information gives managers more time to prepare countermoves and a chance to beat rivals to the punch by moving first.

Pinpointing the Key Factors for Competitive Success

Key success factors (KSFs) are the major determinants of financial and competitive success in a particular industry. Key success factors highlight the specific outcomes crucial to success in the marketplace and the competences and capabilities with the most bearing on profitability. In the beer industry, the KSFs are full utilization of brewing capacity (to keep manufacturing costs low), a strong network of wholesale distributors (to gain access to as many retail outlets as possible), and clever advertising (to induce beer drinkers to buy a particular brand and thereby pull beer sales through the established wholesale/retail channels). In apparel manufacturing, the KSFs are appealing designs and color combinations (to create buyer interest) and low-cost manufacturing efficiency (to permit attractive retail pricing and ample profit margins). In tin and aluminum cans, where the cost of shipping empty cans is substantial, the KSFs are having plants located close to end-use customers and the ability to market plant output within economical shipping distances (regional market share is far more crucial than national share).

Identifying key success factors is a top-priority strategic consideration. At the very least, management needs to know the industry well enough to conclude what is more important to competitive success and what is less important. At most, KSFs can serve as *the cornerstones* for building a company's strategy. Companies frequently win competitive advantage by concentrating on being distinctively better than rivals in one or more of the industry's key success factors.

Key success factors vary from industry to industry, and even over time in the same industry, as driving forces and competitive conditions change. Table 3–4 lists the most common types of key success factors. Only rarely does an industry have more than three or four key success factors at any one time. And even among these three or four, one or two usually outrank the others in importance. Strategic analysts, therefore, have to resist the temptation to include factors that have only minor importance—the purpose of identifying KSFs is to make judgments about what things are more important to competitive success and what things are less important. To compile a list of every factor that matters even a little bit defeats the purpose of training management's eyes on the factors truly crucial to long-term competitive success.

Basic Concept
Key success factors spell the difference between profit and loss and, ultimately, between competitive success and failure. A key success factor can be a skill or talent, a competitive capability, or a condition a company must achieve; it can relate to technology, manufacturing, distribution, marketing, or organizational resources.

Drawing Conclusions about Overall Industry Attractiveness

The final step of industry and competitive analysis is to review the overall industry situation and develop reasoned conclusions about the relative attractiveness or unattractiveness of the industry, both near-term and long-term. An assessment that the industry is attractive typically calls for some kind of aggressive, expansion-oriented strategic approach. If the industry and competitive situation is judged relatively unattractive, companies are drawn to consider strategies aimed at protecting their profitability. Weaker companies may consider leaving the industry or merging with a rival.

Important factors to consider in drawing conclusions about industry attractiveness are:

- The industry's growth potential.
- Whether the industry will be favorably or unfavorably impacted by the prevailing driving forces.
- The potential for the entry/exit of major firms (probable entry reduces attractiveness to existing firms; the exit of a major firm or several weak firms opens up market share growth opportunities for the remaining firms).
- The stability/dependability of demand (as affected by seasonality, the business cycle, the volatility of consumer preferences, inroads by substitutes, and the like).
- Whether competitive forces will become stronger or weaker.
- The severity of problems/issues confronting the industry as a whole.
- The degrees of risk and uncertainty in the industry's future.
- Whether the industry's overall profit prospects are above or below average.

Whether an industry is relatively attractive or unattractive depends on several situational considerations.

Technology-Related KSFs
- Scientific research expertise (important in such fields as pharmaceuticals, medicine, space exploration, other "high-tech" industries)
- Production process innovation capability
- Product innovation capability
- Expertise in a given technology

Manufacturing-Related KSFs
- Low-cost production efficiency (achieve scale economies, capture experience curve effects)
- Quality of manufacture (fewer defects, less need for repairs)
- High utilization of fixed assets (important in capital intensive/high fixed-cost industries)
- Low-cost plant locations
- Access to adequate supplies of skilled labor
- High labor productivity (important for items with high labor content)
- Low-cost product design and engineering (reduces manufacturing costs)
- Flexibility to manufacture a range of models and sizes/take care of custom orders

Distribution-Related KSFs
- A strong network of wholesale distributors/dealers
- Gaining ample space on retailer shelves
- Having company-owned retail outlets
- Low distribution costs
- Fast delivery

Marketing-Related KSFs
- A well-trained, effective sales force
- Available, dependable service and technical assistance
- Accurate filling of buyer orders (few back orders or mistakes)
- Breadth of product line and product selection
- Merchandising skills
- Attractive styling/packaging
- Customer guarantees and warranties (important in mail-order retailing, big ticket purchases, new product introductions)

Skills-Related KSFs
- Superior talent (important in professional services)
- Quality control know-how
- Design expertise (important in fashion and apparel industries)
- Expertise in a particular technology
- Ability to come up with clever, catchy ads
- Ability to get newly developed products out of the R&D phase and into the market very quickly

Organizational Capability
- Superior information systems (important in airline travel, car rental, credit card, and lodging industries)
- Ability to respond quickly to shifting market conditions (streamlined decision-making, short lead times to bring new products to market)
- More experience and managerial know-how

Other Types of KSFs
- Favorable image/reputation with buyers
- Overall low cost (not just in manufacturing)
- Convenient locations (important in many retailing businesses)
- Pleasant, courteous employees
- Access to financial capital (important in newly emerging industries with high degrees of business risk and in capital-intensive industries)
- Patent protection
- Overall low cost (not just in manufacturing)

However, even if an industry is relatively unattractive overall, it can still be attractive to a company already favorably situated in the industry or to an outsider with the resources and skills to acquire an existing company and turn it into a major contender. Appraising industry attractiveness from the standpoint of a particular company in the industry means looking at the following *additional aspects*:

Strategic Management Principle
A company well situated in an unattractive industry can still earn good profits.

- The company's competitive position in the industry and whether its position is likely to grow stronger or weaker (a well-entrenched leader in a lackluster industry can still generate good profits).
- The company's potential to capitalize on the vulnerabilities of weaker rivals (thereby converting an unattractive *industry* situation into a potentially rewarding *company* opportunity).
- Whether the company is insulated from, or able to defend against, the factors that make the industry unattractive.
- Whether continued participation in the industry adds significantly to the firm's ability to be successful in other industries in which it has business interests.

Conclusions drawn about an industry's attractiveness and competitive situation have a major bearing on a company's strategic options and ultimate choice of strategy.

KEY POINTS

Thinking strategically about a company's external situation involves probing for answers to the following seven questions:

1. What are the chief economic characteristics of the industry?
2. What are the drivers of change in the industry, and what impact will they have?
3. What competitive forces are at work in the industry, and how strong are they?
4. Which companies are in the strongest/weakest competitive positions?
5. Who will likely make what competitive moves next?
6. What key factors will determine competitive success or failure?
7. How attractive is the industry in terms of its prospects for above-average profitability?

To answer these questions, several concepts and techniques are useful—driving forces, the five forces model of competition, strategic groups and strategic group mapping, competitor analysis, key success factors, and industry attractiveness.

Table 3–5 provides a *format* for conducting industry and competitive analysis. It pulls together the relevant concepts and considerations and makes it easier to do a concise, understandable analysis of the industry and competitive environment.

Two final points are worth keeping in mind. First, the task of analyzing a company's external situation is not a mechanical exercise in which

TABLE 3-5   Industry and Competitive Analysis Summary Profile

1. **DOMINANT ECONOMIC CHARACTERISTICS OF THE INDUSTRY ENVIRONMENT** (market growth, geographic scope, industry structure, scale economies, experience curve effects, capital requirements, and so on)

2. **DRIVING FORCES**

3. **COMPETITION ANALYSIS**
   - Rivalry among competing sellers (a strong, moderate, or weak force / weapons of competition)

   - Threat of potential entry (a strong, moderate, or weak force/assessment of entry barriers)

   - Competition from subsitutes (a strong, moderate, or weak force/why)

   - Power of suppliers (a strong, moderate, or weak force/why)

   - Power of customers (a strong, moderate, or weak force/why)

4. **COMPETITIVE POSITION OF MAJOR COMPANIES/ STRATEGIC GROUPS**
   - Favorably positioned/why

   - Unfavorably positioned/why

5. **COMPETITOR ANALYSIS**
   - Strategic approaches/predicted moves of key competitors

   - Who to watch and why

6. **KEY SUCCESS FACTORS**

7. **INDUSTRY PROSPECTS AND OVERALL ATTRACTIVENESS**
   - Factors making the industry attractive

   - Factors making the industry unattractive

   - Special industry issues/problems

   - Profit outlook (favorable/unfavorable)

analysts plug in data and definitive conclusions come out. There can be several appealing scenarios about how an industry will evolve and what future competitive conditions will be like. For this reason, strategic analysis always leaves room for differences of opinion about how all the factors add up and how industry and competitive conditions will change. However, while no strategic analysis methodology can guarantee a single conclusive diagnosis, it doesn't make sense to shortcut strategic analysis and rely on opinion and casual observation. Managers become better strategists when they know what analytical questions to pose, can use situation analysis techniques to find answers, and have the skills to read clues about industry and competitive change.

Second, in practice, industry and competitive analysis is an incremental and ongoing process, the result of gradually accumulated knowledge and continuous rethinking and retesting. Sweeping industry and competitive analyses need to be done periodically; in the interim, managers must update and reexamine the picture as events unfold. Important strategic actions usually result from a *gradual* build-up of clues and documentation that important changes in the external environment are occurring, a *gradual* understanding of the implications of these changes, and *gradually* reached conclusions about upcoming conditions in the industry.

Ghemawat, Pankaj. "Building Strategy on the Experience Curve." *Harvard Business Review* 64, no. 2 (March–April 1985), pp. 143–49.

Linneman, Robert E., and Harold E. Klein. "Using Scenarios in Strategic Decision Making." *Business Horizons* 28, no. 1 (January–February 1985), pp. 64–74.

Ohmae, Kenichi. *The Mind of the Strategist*. New York: Penguin Books, 1983, chaps. 3, 6, 7, and 13.

Porter, Michael E. "How Competitive Forces Shape Strategy." *Harvard Business Review* 57, no. 2 (March–April 1979), pp. 137–45.

————. *Competitive Strategy: Techniques for Analyzing Industries and Competitors*. New York: Free Press, 1980, chap. 1.

————. *Competitive Advantage*. New York: Free Press, 1985, chap. 2.

Company Situation Analysis

Understand what really makes a company "tick."
~Charles R. Scott
CEO, Intermark Corp.

• • • • • • •

If you think what exists today is permanent and forever true,
you inevitably get your head handed to you.
~John Reed
Chairman, Citicorp

• • • • • • •

The secret of success is to be ready for opportunity when it comes.
~Disraeli

In the last chapter, we saw how to use industry and competitive analysis to assess the attractiveness of a company's external environment. In this chapter, we discuss how to evaluate a particular company's strategic situation in that environment. Company situation analysis centers on five questions:

There are five questions to answer in analyzing a company's strategic situation.

1. How well is the present strategy working?
2. What are the company's strengths, weaknesses, opportunities, and threats?
3. Is the company competitive on cost?
4. How strong is the company's competitive position?
5. What strategic issues does the company face?

To explore these questions, strategists use three analytical techniques: SWOT analysis, strategic cost analysis, and competitive strength assessment. These tools are widely used in strategic analysis because they indicate how strongly a company holds its industry position and whether the present strategy is capable of boosting long-term performance.

HOW WELL IS THE PRESENT STRATEGY WORKING?

To evaluate how well a company's present strategy is working, one needs to start with what the strategy is (see Figure 2–2 in Chapter 2 to refresh your recollection of the key components of business strategy). The first thing to understand is the company's competitive approach—whether it is striving for low-cost leadership, trying to differentiate itself from rivals, or focusing narrowly on specific customer groups and market niches. Another important consideration is the firm's competitive scope within the industry—its degree of vertical integration and geographic market coverage. The company's functional area support strategies in production, marketing, finance, human resources, and so on need to be identified and understood as well. In addition, the company may have initiated some recent strategic moves (for instance, a price cut, stepped-up advertising, entry into a new geographic area, or merger with a competitor) that are integral to its strategy and that aim at securing a particular competitive advantage and/or improved competitive position. Examining the rationale for each piece of the strategy—for each competitive move and each functional approach—should clarify what the present strategy is.

While there's merit in evaluating a strategy from a qualitative standpoint (i.e., its completeness, internal consistency, rationale, and suitability), the best evidence of how well a strategy is working comes from the company's recent strategic and financial performance. The most obvious indicators of a firm's strategic and financial performance include: (1) whether the firm's market share is rising or falling, (2) whether the firm's profit margins are increasing or decreasing and how large they are relative to rival firms, (3) trends in the firm's net profits and return on investment, (4) whether the firm's sales are growing faster or slower than the market as a whole, (5) whether the firm enjoys a competitive advantage or is at a disadvantage, and (6) whether its long-term competitive position is becoming stronger or weaker. The better a company's current overall performance, the less likely the need for radical changes in strategy. The weaker a company's strategic and financial performance, the more its current strategy should be questioned.

The stronger a company's strategic and financial performance, the more likely it has a well-conceived, well-executed strategy.

SWOT ANALYSIS

SWOT is an acronym for a company's strengths, weaknesses, opportunities, and threats. A SWOT analysis consists of evaluating a firm's internal strengths and weaknesses and its external opportunities and threats. It is an easy-to-use tool for getting a quick *overview* of a firm's strategic situation. SWOT analysis underscores the basic point that strategy must produce a good fit between a company's internal capability (its strengths and weaknesses) and its external situation (reflected in part by its opportunities and threats).

Identifying Strengths and Weaknesses

Table 4–1 lists the considerations used to identify a company's internal strengths and weaknesses. A *strength* is something a company is good at doing or a characteristic that gives it an important capability. A strength can be

T A B L E 4–1   SWOT Analysis—What to Look for in Sizing up a Company's Strengths, Weaknesses, Opportunities, and Threats

Potential Internal Strengths

- Core competences in key areas
- Adequate financial resources
- Well thought of by buyers
- An acknowledged market leader
- Well-conceived functional area strategies
- Access to economies of scale
- Insulated (at least somewhat) from strong competitive pressures
- Proprietary technology
- Cost advantages
- Better advertising campaigns
- Product innovation skills
- Proven management
- Ahead on experience curve
- Better manufacturing capability
- Superior technological skills
- Other?

Potential Internal Weaknesses

- No clear strategic direction
- Obsolete facilities
- Subpar profitability because . . .
- Lack of managerial depth and talent
- Missing some key skills or competences
- Poor track record in implementing strategy
- Plagued with internal operating problems
- Falling behind in R & D
- Too narrow a product line
- Weak market image
- Weak distribution network
- Below-average marketing skills
- Unable to finance needed changes in strategy
- Higher overall unit costs relative to key competitors
- Other?

Potential External Opportunities

- Serve additional customer groups
- Enter new markets or segments
- Expand product line to meet broader range of customer needs
- Diversify into related products
- Vertical integration (forward or backward)
- Falling trade barriers in attractive foreign markets
- Complacency among rival firms
- Faster market growth
- Other?

Potential External Threats

- Entry of lower-cost foreign competitors
- Rising sales of substitute products
- Slower market growth
- Adverse shifts in foreign exchange rates and trade policies of foreign governments
- Costly regulatory requirements
- Vulnerability to recession and business cycle
- Growing bargaining power of customers or suppliers
- Changing buyer needs and tastes
- Adverse demographic changes
- Other?

· · · · · · · · · · · ·
Basic Concept
A company's internal strengths usually represent competitive assets; its internal weaknesses usually represent competitive liabilities. A company's strengths/assets should outweigh its weaknesses/liabilities by a hefty margin.

a skill, a competence, a valuable organizational resource or competitive capability, or an achievement that gives the company a market advantage (like having a better product, stronger name recognition, superior technology, or better customer service). A *weakness* is something a company lacks or does poorly (in comparison to others) or a condition that puts it at a disadvantage. A weakness may or may not make a company competitively vulnerable, depending on how much it matters in the competitive battle.

Once a company's internal strengths and weaknesses are identified, the two lists have to be carefully evaluated. Some strengths are more important than others because they count for more in determining performance, in competing successfully, and in forming a powerful strategy. Likewise, some internal weaknesses can prove fatal, while others don't matter much or can be easily remedied. A SWOT analysis is like constructing a *strategic balance sheet*—strengths are *competitive assets* and weaknesses are *competitive liabilities*. The

issue is whether the strengths/assets adequately overcome the weaknesses/
liabilities (a 50–50 balance is definitely not desirable!), how to meld strengths
into an effective strategy, and whether strategic actions are needed to tilt the
strategic balance more toward the asset side and away from the liability side.

From a strategy-making perspective, a company's strengths are significant
because they can be used as the cornerstones of strategy and the basis on
which to build competitive advantage. If a company doesn't have strong competences and competitive assets around which to craft an attractive strategy,
management must move quickly to build capabilities on which a strategy
can be grounded. At the same time, a good strategy needs to aim at correcting competitive weaknesses that make the company vulnerable, hurt its
performance, or disqualify it from pursuing an attractive opportunity. The
point here is simple: *an organization's strategy should be well-suited to company
strengths, weaknesses, and competitive capabilities.* As a rule, management should
build its strategy around what the company does best and should avoid
strategies whose success depends heavily on areas where the company is
weak or has unproven ability.

Core Competences   One of the "trade secrets" of first-rate strategic management is consolidating a company's technological, production, and marketing
know-how into competences that enhance its competitiveness. *A core competence is something a company does especially well in comparison to its competitors.*[1] In practice, there are many possible types of core competences: manufacturing excellence, exceptional quality control, the ability to provide better
service, more know-how in low-cost manufacturing, superior design capability, unique ability to pick out good retail locations, innovativeness in developing new products, better skill in merchandising and product display, mastery
of an important technology, a strong understanding of customer needs and
tastes, an unusually effective sales force, outstanding skill in working with customers on new applications and uses of the product, and expertise in integrating multiple technologies to create families of new products. *The importance
of a core competence to strategy-making rests with (1) the added capability it gives an
organization in going after a particular market opportunity, (2) the competitive edge
it can yield in the marketplace, and (3) its potential for being a cornerstone of strategy.*
It is easier to build competitive advantage when a firm has a core competence
in an area important to market success, when rivals do not have offsetting
competences, and when it is costly and time-consuming for rivals to match the
competence. Core competences are thus valuable competitive assets.

Identifying Opportunities and Threats

Table 4–1 also lists factors that help identify a company's external opportunities and threats. Market opportunity is a big factor in shaping a company's
strategy. However, there is an important distinction between *industry opportunities* and *company opportunities*. Not every company in an industry is
well positioned to pursue each opportunity that exists in the industry—
some companies are always better situated than others and several may

• • • • • • • • • • • •
***Strategic Management
Principle***
*Successful strategists
seek to exploit what a
company does best—its
expertise, strengths, core
competences, and
strongest competitive
capabilities.*

• • • • • • • • • • • •
***Strategic Management
Principle***
*Core competences
empower a company
to build
competitive advantage.*

---

[1]For a fuller discussion of the core competence concept, see C. K. Prahalad and Gary Hamel, "The Core
Competence of the Corporation," *Harvard Business Review* 90, no. 3 (May–June 1990), pp. 79–93.

be hopelessly out of contention. A company's strengths and weaknesses make it better suited to pursuing some opportunities than others. *The industry opportunities most relevant to a particular company are those that offer important avenues for growth and those where a company has the most potential for competitive advantage.*

Often certain factors in a company's external environment pose *threats* to its well-being. Threats can stem from the emergence of cheaper technologies, rivals' introduction of new or better products, the entry of low-cost foreign competitors into a company's market stronghold, new regulations that are more burdensome to a company than to its competitors, vulnerability to a rise in interest rates, the potential for a hostile takeover, unfavorable demographic shifts, adverse changes in foreign exchange rates, political upheaval at a company's foreign facilities, and the like.

Opportunities and threats not only affect the attractiveness of a company's situation but point to the need for strategic action. To be adequately matched to a company's situation, strategy must (1) be aimed at pursuing opportunities well suited to the company's capabilities and (2) provide a defense against external threats. SWOT analysis is therefore more than an exercise in making four lists. The important part of SWOT analysis involves *evaluating* the strengths, weaknesses, opportunities, and threats and *drawing conclusions* about the attractiveness of the company's situation and the need for strategic action. Some of the pertinent strategy-making questions to consider, once the SWOT listings have been compiled, are:

- Does the company have any internal strengths or core competences an attractive strategy can be built around?
- Do the company's weaknesses make it competitively vulnerable and/or do they disqualify the company from pursuing certain opportunities? Which weaknesses does strategy need to correct?
- Which opportunities does the company have the skills and resources to pursue with a real chance of success? (*Remember*: Opportunity without the means to capture it is an illusion.)
- What threats should managers be worried about most, and what strategic moves should they consider in crafting a good defense?

. . . .
Strategic Management Principle
Successful strategists aim at capturing a company's best growth opportunities and creating defenses against threats to its competitive position and future performance.

STRATEGIC COST ANALYSIS AND ACTIVITY-COST CHAINS

. . . .
Assessing whether a company's costs are competitive with those of its close rivals is a necessary and crucial part of company situation analysis.

One of the most telling signs of the strength of a company's strategic position is its cost position relative to competitors. Cost comparisons are especially critical in a commodity-product industry where price competition typically dominates and lower-cost companies have the upper hand. But even in industries where products are differentiated and competition is based on factors other than price, companies have to keep costs *in line with* rivals or risk jeopardizing their competitive position.

Competitors do not necessarily, or even usually, incur the same costs in supplying their products to end-users. Disparities in costs among rival producers can stem from:

- Differences in the prices paid for raw materials, component parts, energy, and other items purchased from suppliers.

- Differences in basic technology and the age of plants and equipment. (Because rivals usually invest in plants and key pieces of equipment at different times, their facilities usually have different technological efficiencies and different fixed costs. Older facilities are typically less efficient, but if they were less expensive to construct or cheaply acquired, they *may* still be reasonably cost competitive with modern facilities.)

- Differences in internal operating costs due to the economies of scale associated with different size plants, learning and experience curve effects, different wage rates, different productivity levels, different administrative overhead expenses, different tax rates, and the like.

- Differences in rivals' exposure to inflation and changes in foreign exchange rates (as can occur in global industries where competitors have plants located in different nations).

- Differences in marketing costs, sales and promotion expenditures, and advertising expenses.

- Differences in inbound transportation costs and outbound shipping costs.

- Differences in forward channel distribution costs (the costs and markups of distributors, wholesalers, and retailers who get the product from the manufacturer to the end-user).

Cost differences among close rivals can stem from many factors.

For a company to be competitively successful, its costs must be in line with those of rival producers. However, some cost disparity is justified when the products of competing companies are *differentiated*. The need to be cost competitive is not so stringent as to *require* the costs of every firm in the industry to be *equal*, but, as a rule, the higher a firm's costs above low-cost producers, the more vulnerable its market position becomes. Given the numerous opportunities for cost disparities, a company must be aware of how its costs compare with rivals'. This is where *strategic cost analysis* comes in.

Strategic cost analysis focuses on a firm's cost position relative to its rivals'. The primary analytical tool of strategic cost analysis is an *activity-cost chain* showing the buildup of value from raw materials supply to the price paid by ultimate customers.[2] The activity-cost chain goes beyond a company's own internal cost structure to cover all the stages in the industry chain: raw materials supply, manufacturing, wholesale distribution, and retailing, as shown in Figure 4–1. An activity-cost chain is especially revealing for a manufacturing firm because its ability to supply its product to end-users at a competitive price can easily depend on costs that originate either *backward* in suppliers' portion of the activity-cost chain, or *forward* in the wholesale and retail stages of the chain.

The data requirements for activity-cost chain analysis are formidable. It requires breaking a firm's own historical cost accounting data out into several principal cost categories and also developing cost estimates for the backward and forward channel portions. To see how the firm's cost position compares with rivals, the same cost elements for each rival must likewise be estimated—an advanced art in competitive intelligence in itself. But despite the tediousness of the task and the imprecision of some of the estimates the payoff

Strategic Management Principle
The higher a company's costs are above those of rivals, the more competitively vulnerable it becomes.

Basic Concept
Strategic cost analysis involves comparing a company's cost position relative to key competitors, activity by activity, from raw materials purchase to the price paid by ultimate customers.

---

[2]Strategic cost analysis is described at greater length in Michael E. Porter, *Competitive Advantage* (New York: Free Press, 1985), chap. 2. What follows is a distilled adaptation of the analytical method pioneered by Porter.

Generic Activity-Cost Chain for a Representative Industry Situation

TOTAL INDUSTRY ACTIVITY-COST CHAIN

SUPPLIER-RELATED ACTIVITIES

MANUFACTURING-RELATED ACTIVITIES

FORWARD CHANNEL ACTIVITIES

Purchased Materials, Components, Inputs, and Inbound Logistics	Production Activities and Operations	Marketing and Sales Activities	Customer Service and Outbound Logistics Activities	In-House Staff Support Activities	General and Administrative Activities	Profit Margin	Wholesale Distributor and Dealer Network Activities	Retailer Activities
Specific activities/costs	Specific activities/costs	Specific activities/costs	Specific activities/costs	Specific activities/costs	Specific activities/costs			

Purchased Materials, Components, Inputs, and Inbound Logistics — Specific activities/costs
- Ingredient raw materials and component parts supplied by outsiders
- Energy
- Inbound shipping
- Inbound materials handling
- Warehousing

Production Activities and Operations — Specific activities/costs
- Facilities and equipment
- Processing
- Assembly and packaging
- Labor and supervision
- Maintenance
- Product design and testing
- Quality and inspection
- Inventory management

Marketing and Sales Activities — Specific activities/costs
- Salesforce operations
- Advertising and promotion
- Market research
- Technical literature
- Travel and entertainment
- Dealer/distributor relations

Customer Service and Outbound Logistics Activities — Specific activities/costs
- Service reps
- Order processing
- Spare parts
- Other outbound logistics costs

In-House Staff Support Activities — Specific activities/costs
- Payroll and benefits
- Recruiting and training
- Internal communications
- Computer services
- Procurement functions
- R&D
- Safety and security
- Union relations

General and Administrative Activities — Specific activities/costs
- Finance and accounting services
- Legal services
- Public relations
- Executive salaries
- Interest on borrowed funds
- Tax-related costs
- Regulatory compliance

Wholesale Distributor and Dealer Network Activities / Retailer Activities

Includes all of the activities, associated costs, and markups of distributors, wholesale dealers, retailers, and any other forward channel allies whose efforts are utilized to get the product into the hands of end-users/customers in exposing the cost competitiveness of one's position makes it a valuable analytical tool. Illustration Capsule 11 on page 94 shows a simplified activity-cost chain comparison for various brands of beer produced by Anheuser-Busch (the industry leader) and Adolph Coors (the third-ranking brewer).

The most important application of the activity-cost technique is to expose how a particular firm's cost position compares with those of its rivals. What is needed is competitor versus competitor cost estimates for a given product. The size of a company's cost advantage/disadvantage can vary from item to item in the product line, from customer group to customer group (if different distribution channels are used), and from geographic market to geographic market (if cost factors vary across geographic regions).

Looking again at Figure 4–1, observe that there are three main areas in the cost chain where important differences in competitors' *relative* costs can occur: in suppliers' part of the cost chain, in each company's activity segments, or in the forward channel portion. If a firm's lack of cost competitiveness lies either in the backward or forward sections of the chain, the task of reestablishing cost competitiveness may have to extend beyond its own operations. When a firm's cost disadvantage is principally associated with items purchased from suppliers (the backward end of the activity-cost chain), it can pursue any of several strategic actions to correct the problem:

Strategic actions to eliminate a cost disadvantage need to be linked to the location in the activity-cost chain where the cost differences originate.

- Negotiate more favorable prices with suppliers.
- Work with suppliers to help them achieve lower costs.
- Integrate backward to gain control over the costs of purchased items.
- Try to use lower-priced substitute inputs.
- Try to save on inbound shipping costs.
- Try to make up the difference by cutting costs elsewhere in the chain.

A company's strategic options for eliminating cost disadvantages in the forward end of the chain include:

- Pushing distributors and other forward channel allies to reduce their costs and markups.
- Changing to a more economical distribution strategy, including forward integration.
- Trying to make up the difference by cutting costs earlier in the chain.

When the source of a firm's cost disadvantage is internal, it can use any of nine strategic approaches to restore cost parity:

- Initiate internal budget-tightening measures.
- Improve production methods and work procedures (to boost the productivity of workers and increase utilization of high-cost equipment).
- Try to eliminate some cost-producing activities altogether.
- Relocate high-cost activities to geographical areas where they can be performed cheaper.
- See if certain activities can be farmed out to contractors cheaper than they can be done internally.
- Invest in cost-saving technological improvements (automation, robotics, flexible manufacturing techniques, computerized controls).

ILLUSTRATION CAPSULE   **11**   **ACTIVITY-COST CHAINS FOR ANHEUSER-BUSCH AND ADOLPH COORS BEERS**

In the table below are average cost estimates for the combined brands of beer produced by Anheuser-Busch and Coors. The example shows raw material costs, other manufacturing costs, and forward channel distribution costs. The data are for 1982.

Activity-Cost Elements	Estimated Average Cost Breakdown for Combined Anheuser-Busch Brands		Estimated Average Cost Breakdown for Combined Adolph Coors Brands	
	Per 6-Pack of 12-oz. Cans	Per Barrel Equivalent	Per 6-Pack of 12-oz. Cans	Per Barrel Equivalent
1. Manufacturing costs:				
Direct production costs:				
Raw material ingredients.	$0.1384	$ 7.63	$0.1082	$ 5.96
Direct labor.	0.1557	8.58	0.1257	6.93
Salaries for nonunionized personnel	0.0800	4.41	0.0568	3.13
Packaging	0.5055	27.86	0.4663	25.70
Depreciation on plant and equipment	0.0410	2.26	0.0826	4.55
Subtotal	0.9206	50.74	0.8396	46.27
Other expenses:				
Advertising.	0.0477	2.63	0.0338	1.86
Other marketing costs and general				
administrative expenses	0.1096	6.04	0.1989	10.96
Interest	0.0147	0.81	0.0033	0.18
Research and development	0.0277	1.53	0.0195	1.07
Total manufacturing costs	$1.1203	$ 61.75	$1.0951	$ 60.34
2. Manufacturer's operating profit	0.1424	7.85	0.0709	3.91
3. Net selling price.	1.2627	69.60	1.1660	64.25
4. Plus federal and state excise taxes				
paid by brewer.	0.1873	10.32	0.1782	9.82
5. Gross manufacturer's selling price to				
distributor/wholesaler	1.4500	79.92	1.3442	74.07
6. Average margin over manufacturer's cost	0.5500	30.31	0.5158	28.43
7. Average wholesale price charged to retailer (inclusive of taxes in item 4 above but exclusive of other taxes)	$2.00	$110.23	$1.86	$102.50
8. Plus other assorted state and local taxes levied on wholesale and retail sales (this varies from locality to locality)	0.60		0.60	
9. Average 20% retail markup over wholesale cost	0.40		0.38	
10. Average price to consumer at retail	$3.00		$2.84	

Note: The difference in the average cost structures for Anheuser-Busch and Adolph Coors is, to a substantial extent, due to A-B's higher proportion of super-premium beer sales. A-B's super-premium brand, Michelob, was the bestseller in its category and somewhat more costly to brew than premium and popular-priced beers.

Source: Compiled by Tom McLean, Elsa Wischkaemper, and Arthur A. Thompson, Jr., from a wide variety of documents and field interviews.

- Innovate around the troublesome cost components as new investments are made in plant and equipment.
- Simplify the product design and make it easier to manufacture.
- Try to make up the internal cost disadvantage by cutting costs in the backward and forward portions of the chain.

Activity-cost chains reveal a great deal about a firm's cost competitiveness. Examining the makeup of a company's own activity-cost chain and comparing it to rivals' indicate who has how much of a cost advantage/disadvantage and which cost components are responsible. Such information is vital in crafting strategies to eliminate a cost disadvantage or create a cost advantage.

COMPETITIVE STRENGTH ASSESSMENT

In addition to the cost competitiveness diagnosis that activity-cost chain analysis provides, a more broad-based assessment needs to be made of a company's competitive position and competitive strength. Particular elements to single out for evaluation are: (1) how strongly the firm holds its present competitive position, (2) whether the firm's position can be expected to improve or deteriorate if the present strategy is continued (allowing for fine-tuning), (3) how the firm ranks *relative to key rivals* on each important measure of competitive strength and industry key success factor, (4) whether the firm has a net competitive advantage or disadvantage, and (5) the firm's ability to defend its position in light of industry driving forces, competitive pressures, and the anticipated moves of rivals.

Systematic assessment of whether a company's competitive position is strong or weak relative to close rivals is an essential step in company situation analysis.

Table 4–2 lists some indicators of whether a firm's competitive position is improving or slipping. But more is needed than just a listing of the signs of improvement or slippage. The important thing is to develop some judgments about whether the company's position will improve or deteriorate under the current strategy and to consider what strategic actions are needed to improve the company's market position.

The really telling part of competitive position assessment, however, is the formal appraisal of whether the company is stronger or weaker than close rivals on each key success factor and indicator of competitive strength. Much of the information for competitive position assessment comes from previous analyses. Industry and competitive analysis reveals the key success factors and competitive strength measures that will separate industry winners and losers. Competitor analysis provides a basis for judging the strengths and capabilities of key rivals. Step one is to make a list of the industry's key success factors and measures of competitive strength or weaknesses (6 to 10 measures usually suffice). Step two is to rate the firm and its key rivals on each factor. Rating scales from 1 to 5 or 1 to 10 are straightforward and simple to use although ratings of stronger (+), weaker (–), and about equal (=) may be appropriate when numerical scores are too subjective. Step three is to sum the individual strength ratings to get an overall measure of competitive strength for each competitor. Step four is to draw conclusions about the size and extent of the company's net competitive advantage or disadvantage, noting areas where the company's competitive position is strongest and weakest.

T A B L E 4–2   **The Signs of Strength and Weakness in a Company's Competitive Position**

Signs of Competitive Strength	Signs of Competitive Weakness
• Important core competences	• Confronted with competitive disadvantages
• Strong market share (or a leading market share)	• Losing ground to rival firms
• A pacesetting or distinctive strategy	• Below-average growth in revenues
• Growing customer base and customer loyalty	• Short on financial resources
• Above-average market visibility	• A slipping reputation with customers
• In a favorably situated strategic group	• Trailing in product development
• Concentrating on fastest-growing market segments	• In a strategic group destined to lose ground
• Strongly differentiated products	• Weak in areas where there is the most market potential
• Cost advantages	• A higher-cost producer
• Above-average profit margins	• Too small to be a major factor in the marketplace
• Above-average technological and innovational capability	• Not in good position to deal with emerging threats
• A creative, entrepreneurially alert management	• Weak product quality
• In position to capitalize on opportunities	• Lacking skills and capabilities in key areas

• • • • • • • • • • • •

High competitive strength ratings signal a strong competitive position and possession of competitive advantage; low ratings signal a weak position and competitive disadvantage.

Table 4–3 gives two examples of competitive strength assessments. The first one employs an *unweighted rating scale*; with unweighted ratings each key success factor/competitive strength measure is assumed to be equally important. Whichever company has the highest strength rating on a given measure has implied competitive edge on that factor. The size of its edge is reflected in the margin of difference between its rating and the ratings assigned to rivals. Summing a company's strength ratings on all the measures produces an overall strength rating. The higher a company's overall strength rating, the stronger its competitive position. The bigger the difference between a company's overall rating and a rival's rating, the greater its implied net competitive advantage. Thus, ABC's score of 61 (see the top half of Table 4–3) signals a greater net competitive advantage over Rival 4 (with a score of 32) than Rival 1 (with a score of 58).

• • • • • • • • • • •

A weighted competitive strength analysis is conceptually stronger than an unweighted analysis because of the inherent weakness in assuming that all the strength measures are equally important.

However, it is conceptually stronger to use a weighted rating system because the different measures of competitive strength are unlikely to be *equally* important. In a commodity-product industry, for instance, low unit costs relative to rivals are the biggest determinant of competitive strength. In an industry with strong product differentiation, the most significant measures of competitive strength may be brand awareness, amount of advertising, reputation for quality, and distribution capability. In a *weighted rating system*, each measure of competitive strength is assigned a weight based on its perceived importance in shaping competitive success. The largest weight could be as high as .75 (or higher) if a variable is overwhelmingly decisive, or as low as .20 when two or three measures are more important than the rest. Lesser indicators can carry weights of .05 or .10. However, *the sum of the weights must add up to 1.0.*

Weighted strength ratings are calculated by deciding how a company stacks up on each strength measure (using the 1 to 5 or 1 to 10 rating scale) and multiplying the rating by the assigned weight (a rating score of 4 times a weight of .20 gives a weighted rating of .80). Again, the company with the highest rating on a given measure has an implied competitive edge on that measure,

TABLE 4-3   Illustrations of Unweighted and Weighted Competitive
                 Strength Assessments

A. Sample of an Unweighted Competitive Strength Assessment
Rating scale: 1 = Very weak; 10 = Very strong

Key Success Factor/Strength Measure	ABC Co.	Rival 1	Rival 2	Rival 3	Rival 4
Quality/product performance	8	5	10	1	6
Reputation/image	8	7	10	1	6
Raw material access/cost	2	10	4	5	1
Technological skills	10	1	7	3	8
Advertising effectiveness	9	4	10	5	1
Marketing/distribution	9	4	10	5	1
Financial resource	5	10	7	3	1
Relative cost position	5	10	3	1	4
Ability to compete on price	5	7	10	1	4
Unweighted overall strength rating	61	58	71	25	32

B. Sample of a Weighted Competitive Strength Assessment
Rating scale: 1 = Very weak; 10 = Very strong

Key Success Factor/Strength Measure	Weight	ABC Co.	Rival 1	Rival 2	Rival 3	Rival 4
Quality/product performance	0.10	8/0.80	5/0.50	10/1.00	1/0.10	6/0.60
Reputation/image	0.10	8/0.80	7/0.70	10/1.00	1/0.10	6/0.60
Raw material access/cost	0.10	2/0.20	10/1.00	4/0.40	5/0.50	1/0.10
Technological skills	0.05	10/0.50	1/0.05	7/0.35	3/0.15	8/0.40
Manufacturing capability	0.05	9/0.45	4/0.20	10/0.50	5/0.25	1/0.05
Marketing/distribution	0.05	9/0.45	4/0.20	10/0.50	5/0.25	1/0.05
Financial strength	0.10	5/0.50	10/1.00	7/0.70	3/0.30	1/0.10
Relative cost position	0.35	5/1.75	10/3.50	3/1.05	1/0.35	4/1.40
Ability to compete on price	0.15	5/0.75	7/1.05	10/1.50	1/0.15	4/1.60
Sum of weights	1.00					
Weighted overall strength rating		6.20	8.20	7.00	2.10	2.90

with the size of its edge reflected in the difference between its rating and rivals' ratings. Summing a company's weighted strength ratings for all measures yields an overall strength rating. Comparisons of the weighted overall strength scores indicate which competitors are in the strongest and weakest competitive positions and who has how big a net competitive advantage over whom.

The bottom half of Table 4–3 shows a sample competitive strength assessment for ABC Company using a weighted rating system. Note that the unweighted and weighted rating schemes produce a different ordering of the companies. In the weighted system, ABC Company dropped from second to third in strength, and Rival 1 jumped from third into first because of its high ratings on the two most important factors. Weighting the importance of the strength measures can thus make a significant difference in the outcome of the assessment.

The foregoing competitive strength assessment procedure yields useful conclusions about a company's competitive situation. The ratings show how a company compares against rivals, factor by factor or measure by measure, thus revealing where it is strongest and weakest. Moreover, the overall competitive strength scores indicate whether the company is at a net competitive advantage or disadvantage against each rival. The firm with the largest overall competitive strength rating has a net competitive advantage over each rival.

Knowing where a company is competitively strong and where it is weak is essential in crafting a strategy to strengthen its long-term competitive position. Generally, a company should try to convert its competitive strengths into sustainable competitive advantage and take strategic actions to protect against its competitive weaknesses. At the same time, competitive strength ratings clearly indicate which rivals may be vulnerable to competitive attack and the areas where they are weakest. When a company has important strengths in areas where one or more rivals are weak, it should consider offensive moves to exploit rivals' weaknesses.

· · · · · · · · · · · · ·

Strategic Management Principle

Competitive strengths and competitive advantages empower a company to improve its long-term market position.

DETERMINING WHAT STRATEGIC ISSUES NEED TO BE ADDRESSED

· · · · · · · · · · · · ·

Strategic Management Principle

Effective strategy-making requires a thorough understanding of the strategic issues a company faces.

The final analytical task is to hone in on the strategic issues management needs to address in forming an effective strategic action plan. This step should be taken very seriously because it entails putting the company's overall situation into perspective and getting a lock on exactly where management needs to focus its strategic attention. Without a clear fix on the issues, strategists are ill-prepared for strategy-making.

To pinpoint issues for the company's strategic action agenda, strategists should consider the following:

- Whether the present strategy is adequate in light of driving forces at work in the industry.
- How closely the present strategy matches the industry's *future* key success factors.
- How good a defense the present strategy offers against the five competitive forces—future ones, not necessarily past or present ones.
- In what ways the present strategy may not adequately protect the company against external threats and internal weaknesses.
- Where and how the company may be vulnerable to competitive attack from one or more rivals.
- Whether the company has competitive advantage or must work to offset competitive disadvantage.
- Where the strong spots and weak spots are in the present strategy.
- Whether additional actions are needed to improve the company's cost position, capitalize on emerging opportunities, and strengthen the company's competitive position.

These considerations should indicate whether the company can continue the same basic strategy with minor adjustments or whether it should undertake a major overhaul.

The better matched a company's strategy is to its external environment and internal situation, the less need there is for big shifts in strategy. On the other hand, when the present strategy is not well suited for the future, crafting a new strategy has to take top priority.

KEY POINTS

There are five steps to conducting a company situation analysis:

1. *Evaluating how well the current strategy is working.* This involves looking at the company's recent strategic performance and determining whether the various pieces of strategy are logically consistent.

2. *Doing a SWOT analysis.* A company's strengths are important because they can serve as major building blocks for strategy; company weaknesses are important because they may represent vulnerabilities that need correction. External opportunities and threats come into play because a good strategy aims at capturing attractive opportunities and defending against threats to the company's well-being.

3. *Evaluating the company's cost position relative to competitors* (using the concepts of strategic cost analysis and activity-cost chains if appropriate). Strategy must always aim at keeping costs sufficiently in line with rivals to preserve the company's ability to compete.

4. *Assessing the company's competitive position and competitive strength.* This step looks at how a company matches rivals on the chief determinants of competitive success. The competitive strength rankings indicate where a company is strong and weak; as a rule, a company's competitive strategy should be built on its competitive strengths and attempt to shore up areas where it is competitively vulnerable. A company has the best potential for offensive attack in areas where it is strong and rivals are weak.

5. *Determining the strategic issues and problems the company needs to address.* The purpose of this analytical step is to develop a complete strategy-making agenda using the results of both company situation analysis and industry and competitive analysis. This step helps management draw conclusions about the strengths and weaknesses of its strategy and pinpoint the issues strategy-makers need to consider.

Table 4–4, on page 100, provides a format for company situation analysis. It incorporates the concepts and analytical techniques discussed in this chapter and makes it easier to perform the analysis in a systematic, concise manner.

SUGGESTED READINGS

Andrews, Kenneth R. *The Concept of Corporate Strategy*, 3rd ed. Homewood, Ill.: Richard D. Irwin, 1987, chap. 3.

Fahey, Liam, and H. Kurt Christensen. "Building Distinctive Competences into Competitive Advantages." Reprinted in Liam Fahey, *The Strategic Planning Management Reader.* Englewood Cliffs, N.J.: Prentice Hall, 1989, pp. 113–18.

Hax, Arnoldo C., and Nicolas S. Majluf. *Strategic Management: An Integrative Perspective.* Englewood Cliffs, N.J.: Prentice Hall, 1984, chap. 15.

T A B L E 4–4   **Company Situation Analysis**

1. STRATEGIC PERFORMANCE INDICATORS

Performance Indicator	19__	19__	19__	19__	19__
Market share	——	——	——	——	——
Sales growth	——	——	——	——	——
Net profit margin	——	——	——	——	——
Return on equity investment	——	——	——	——	——
Other?	——	——	——	——	——

2. INTERNAL STRENGTHS

INTERNAL WEAKNESSES

EXTERNAL OPPORTUNITIES

EXTERNAL THREATS

3. COMPETITIVE STRENGTH ASSESSMENT
Rating scale: 1 = Very weak; 10 = Very strong.

Key Success Factor/ Competitive Variable	Weight	Firm A	Firm B	Firm C	Firm D	Firm E
Quality/product performance	——	——	——	——	——	——
Reputation/image	——	——	——	——	——	——
Raw material access/cost	——	——	——	——	——	——
Technological skills	——	——	——	——	——	——
Manufacturing capability	——	——	——	——	——	——
Marketing/distribution	——	——	——	——	——	——
Financial strength	——	——	——	——	——	——
Relative cost position	——	——	——	——	——	——
Other?	——	——	——	——	——	——
Overall strength rating	——	——	——	——	——	——

4. CONCLUSIONS CONCERNING COMPETITIVE POSITION
(Improving/slipping? Competitive advantages/disadvantages?)

5. MAJOR STRATEGIC ISSUES/PROBLEMS THE COMPANY MUST ADDRESS

Henry, Harold W. "Appraising a Company's Strengths and Weaknesses." *Managerial Planning,* July–August 1980, pp. 31–36.

Paine, Frank T., and Leonard J. Tischler. "Evaluating Your Costs Strategically." Reprinted in Laim Fahey, *The Strategic Planning Management Reader.* Englewood Cliffs, N.J.: Prentice Hall, 1989, pp. 118–23.

Prahalad, C. K., and Gary Hamel. "The Core Competence of the Corporation." *Harvard Business Review* 90, no. 3 (May–June 1990), pp. 79–93.

Stevenson, Howard H. "Defining Corporate Strengths and Weaknesses." *Sloan Management Review* 17, no. 2 (Winter 1976), pp. 1–18.

CHAPTER 5

Strategy and Competitive Advantage

Competing in the marketplace is like war. You have injuries and casualties, and the best strategy wins.
~John Collins

· · · · · · ·

Competitive advantage is at the heart of a firm's performance in competitive markets.
~Michael E. Porter

Competitive Strategy Principle
Successful companies invest aggressively in creating sustainable competitive advantage for it is the single most dependable contributor to above-average profitability.

Winning business strategies are grounded in sustainable competitive advantage. A company has *competitive advantage* whenever it has an edge over rivals in securing customers and defending against competitive forces. There are many sources of competitive advantage: making the highest-quality product, providing superior customer service, achieving lower costs than rivals, having a more convenient geographic location, designing a product that performs better than competing brands, making a more reliable and longer-lasting product, and providing buyers more value for the money (a combination of good quality, good service, and acceptable price). To succeed in building a competitive advantage, a firm must try to provide what buyers will perceive as "superior value"—either a good product at a low price or a "better" product that is worth paying more for.

This chapter focuses on how a company can achieve or defend a competitive advantage.[1] We begin by describing the basic types of competitive strategies and then examine how these approaches rely on offensive moves to build competitive advantage and defensive moves to protect competitive advantage. In the concluding two sections, we survey the pros and cons of a vertical

---

[1]The definitive work on this subject is Michael E. Porter, *Competitive Advantage* (New York: Free Press, 1985). The treatment in this chapter draws heavily on Porter's pioneering effort.

integration strategy and look at the competitive importance of timing strategic moves—when it is advantageous to be a first-mover or a late-mover.

THE THREE GENERIC TYPES OF COMPETITIVE STRATEGY

Competitive strategy consists of all the moves and approaches a firm has taken and is taking to attract buyers, withstand competitive pressures, and improve its market position. In plainer terms, competitive strategy concerns what a firm is doing to try to knock the socks off rival companies and gain competitive advantage. A firm's strategy can be mostly offensive or mostly defensive, shifting from one to the other as market conditions warrant.

Companies the world over have tried every conceivable approach to outcompeting rivals and winning an edge in the marketplace. And because managers tailor strategy to fit the specifics of their own company's situation and market environment, there are countless variations. In this sense, there are as many competitive strategies as there are companies trying to compete. However, beneath all the nuances, the approaches to competitive strategy fall into three categories:

1. Striving to be the overall low-cost producer in the industry (a *low-cost leadership strategy*).
2. Seeking to differentiate one's product offering from rivals' products (a *differentiation strategy*).
3. Focusing on a narrow portion of the market rather than the whole market (a *focus* or *niche strategy*).[2]

Table 5–1 highlights the distinctive features of these three generic competitive strategy approaches.

Striving to Be the Low-Cost Producer

Striving to be the low-cost producer is a powerful competitive approach in markets where many buyers are price-sensitive. The aim is to open up a sustainable cost advantage over competitors and then use lower cost as a basis for either underpricing competitors and gaining market share at their expense or earning a higher profit margin selling at the going price. A cost advantage will generate superior profitability unless it is used up in aggressive price-cutting efforts to win sales from rivals. Firms that achieve low-cost leadership typically make low cost *relative to competitors* the theme of their entire business strategy—though they must be careful not to pursue low cost so zealously that their products end up being too stripped down and cheaply made to generate buyer appeal.

A low-cost leader's basis for competitive advantage is lower overall costs than competitors.

Opening up a Cost Advantage   To achieve a cost advantage, a firm's cumulative costs across its activity-cost chain must be lower than competitors' cumulative costs. There are two ways to accomplish this:

---

[2]The classification scheme follows that presented in Michael E. Porter, *Competitive Strategy: Techniques for Analyzing Industries and Competitors* (New York: Free Press, 1980), chap. 2, especially pp. 35–39 and 44–46.

T A B L E 5–1   Distinctive Features of the Generic Competitive Strategies

Type of Feature	Low-Cost Leadership	Differentiation	Focus
Strategic target	• A broad cross-section of the market.	• A broad cross-section of the market.	• A narrow market niche where buyer needs and preferences are distinctively different from the rest of the market.
Basis of competitive advantage	• Lower costs than competitors.	• An ability to offer buyers something different from competitors.	• Lower cost in serving the niche or an ability to offer niche buyers something customized to their requirements and tastes.
Product line	• A good basic product with few frills (acceptable quality and limited selection).	• Many product variations, wide selection, strong emphasis on the chosen differentiating features.	• Customized to fit the specialized needs of the target segment.
Production emphasis	• A continuous search for cost reduction without sacrificing acceptable quality and essential features.	• Invent ways to create value for buyers.	• Tailor-made for the niche.
Marketing emphasis	• Try to make a virtue out of product features that lead to low cost.	• Build in whatever features buyers are willing to pay for. • Charge a premium price to cover the extra costs of differentiating features.	• Communicate the focuser's unique ability to satisfy the buyer's specialized requirements.
Sustaining the strategy	• Economical prices/good value. • All elements of strategy aim at contributing to a sustainable cost advantage—the key is to manage costs down, year after year, in every area of the business.	• Communicate the points of difference in credible ways. • Stress constant improvement and use innovation to stay ahead of imitative competitors. • Concentrate on a few key differentiating features; use them to create a reputation and brand image.	• Remain totally dedicated to serving the niche better than other competitors; don't blunt the firm's image and efforts by entering other segments and adding other product categories to widen market appeal.

ILLUSTRATION CAPSULE | **12** | **WINNING A COST ADVANTAGE:**
IOWA BEEF PACKERS AND FEDERAL EXPRESS

Iowa Beef Packers and Federal Express have been able to win strong competitive positions by restructuring the traditional activity-cost chains in their industries. In beef packing, the traditional cost chain involved raising cattle on scattered farms and ranches, shipping them live to labor-intensive, unionized slaughtering plants, and then transporting whole sides of beef to grocery retailers whose butcher departments cut them into smaller pieces and package them for sale to grocery shoppers.

Iowa Beef Packers revamped the traditional chain with a radically different strategy—large automated plants employing nonunion labor were built near economically transportable supplies of cattle, and the meat was partially butchered at the processing plant into smaller high-yield cuts (sometimes sealed in plastic casing ready for purchase), boxed, and shipped to retailers. IBP's inbound cattle transportation expenses, traditionally a major cost item, were cut significantly by avoiding the weight losses that occurred when live animals were shipped long distances; major outbound shipping cost savings were achieved by not having to ship whole sides of beef with their high waste factor. Iowa Beef's strategy was so successful that it was, in 1985, the largest U.S. meatpacker, surpassing the former industry leaders, Swift, Wilson, and Armour.

Federal Express innovatively redefined the activity-cost chain for rapid delivery of small parcels. Traditional firms like Emery and Airborne Express operated by collecting freight packages of varying sizes, shipping them to their destination points via air freight and commercial airlines, and then delivering them to the addressee. Federal Express opted to focus only on the market for overnight delivery of small packages and documents. These were collected at local drop points during the late afternoon hours, flown on company-owned planes during early evening hours to a central hub in Memphis where from 11 P.M. to 3 A.M. each night, all parcels were sorted, then reloaded on company planes, and flown during the early morning hours to their destination points, where they were delivered the next morning by company personnel using company trucks. The cost structure so achieved by Federal Express was low enough to permit it to guarantee overnight delivery of a small parcel anywhere in the United States for a price as low as $11. In 1986, Federal Express had a 58 percent market share of the air-express package delivery market versus a 15 percent share for UPS, 11 percent for Airborne Express, and 10 percent for Emery/Purolator.

Source: Based on information in Michael E. Porter, *Competitive Advantage* (New York: Free Press, 1985), p. 109.

- Do a better job of improving efficiency and controlling costs along the existing activity-cost chain.
- Revamp the firm's activity-cost chain to bypass some cost-producing activities altogether.

Achieving a cost advantage entails (a) outmanaging rivals on efficiency and cost control and/or (b) finding creative ways to cut cost-producing activities out of the activity-cost chain.

Both approaches can be used simultaneously. Successful low-cost producers usually achieve their cost advantages by exhaustively pursuing cost savings throughout the activity-cost chain. No area is overlooked. Normally, low-cost producers have a very cost-conscious organizational culture symbolically reinforced by spartan facilities, limited perks for executives, intolerance of waste, intensive screening of budget requests, and broad employee participation in cost control efforts. But while low-cost producers are champions of frugality, they tend to commit funds aggressively to cost-saving improvements.

A firm intent on being a low-cost producer has to scrutinize each cost-creating activity and identify what drives the cost of the activity. Then it has to use its knowledge about the cost drivers to manage the costs of each activity down further year after year. Where possible, whole activities are eliminated from the activity-cost chain entirely. Companies can achieve dramatic cost advantages from restructuring the cost-chain and eliminating unnecessary cost-producing activities. Illustration Capsule 12 describes how two companies won strong competitive positions by revamping the makeup of their industry's traditional activity-cost chain.

Firms well known for their low-cost leadership strategies include: Lincoln Electric in arc welding equipment, Briggs and Stratton in small horsepower gasoline engines, BIC in ballpoint pens, Black and Decker in tools, Design and Manufacturing in dishwashers (marketed under Sears' Kenmore brand), Beaird-Poulan in chain saws, Ford in heavy-duty trucks, General Electric in major home appliances, Wal-Mart in discount retailing, and Southwest Airlines in commercial airline travel.

The Appeal of Being a Low-Cost Producer   Being the low-cost producer in an industry provides some attractive defenses against the five competitive forces:

Competitive Strategy Principle
A low-cost leader is in the strongest position to set the floor on market price.

- As concerns *rival competitors*, the low-cost company is in the best position to compete offensively on the basis of price, to defend against price war conditions, to use the appeal of a lower price to win sales (and market share) from rivals, and to earn above-average profits (based on bigger profit margins or greater sales volume) in markets where price competition thrives.

- As concerns *buyers*, the low-cost company has partial profit margin protection from powerful customers, since such customers are rarely able to bargain price down past the survival level of the next most cost-efficient seller.

- As concerns *suppliers*, the low-cost producer is more insulated than competitors from powerful suppliers *if* greater internal efficiency is the primary source of its cost advantage.

- As concerns *potential entrants*, the low-cost producer can use price-cutting to make it harder for a new rival to win customers; the pricing power of the low-cost producer acts as a barrier for a new entrant.

Competitive Strategy Principle
The competitive power of low-cost leadership is greatest when rivals' products are essentially identical, price competition dominates, most buyers use the product similarly and want similar features, buyer switching costs are low, and large customers shop aggressively for the best price.

- As concerns *substitutes*, a low-cost producer is better positioned than higher-cost rivals to use low price as a defense against substitutes trying to gain market inroads.

A low-cost producer's ability to set the industry's price floor and still earn a profit erects barriers around its market position. Anytime price competition becomes a major market force, less efficient rivals get squeezed the most. Firms in a low-cost position relative to rivals have a significant edge in appealing to buyers who base their purchase decision on low price.

A competitive strategy based on low-cost leadership is particularly powerful when:

1. Price competition among rival sellers is a dominant competitive force.
2. The industry's product is an essentially standardized, commodity-type item readily available from a variety of sellers (a condition that allows buyers to shop for price).
3. There are few ways to achieve product differentiation that have value to buyers (put another way, the differences from brand to brand don't matter much to buyers).

4. Most buyers use the product in the same ways—with common user requirements, a standardized product can fully satisfy the needs of all buyers, in which case price, not features or quality, becomes the dominant competitive force.

5. Buyers incur low switching costs in changing from one seller to another, thus giving them flexibility to shop for the best price.

6. Buyers are large and have significant power to bargain down prices.

The Risks of a Low-Cost Producer Strategy A low-cost competitive approach has its drawbacks. Technological breakthroughs can open up cost reductions for rivals that nullify a low-cost producer's past investments and hard-won gains in efficiency. Rival firms may find it easy and/or inexpensive to imitate the leader's low-cost methods, thus making any advantage short-lived. A company driving hard to push its costs down can become so fixated on cost reduction that it fails to pick up on such significant market changes as growing buyer preference for added quality or service, subtle shifts in how buyers use the product, or declining buyer sensitivity to price and thus gets left behind as buyer interest swings to quality, performance, service, and other differentiating features. In sum, heavy investments in cost reduction can lock a firm into both its present technology and its present strategy, leaving it vulnerable to new technologies and to growing customer interest in something other than a cheaper price.

Differentiation Strategies

Differentiation strategies come into play whenever buyers' needs and preferences are too diverse to be satisfied by a standardized product. A successful differentiator studies buyers' needs and behavior carefully to learn what they consider important and valuable. Then the differentiator incorporates one or several of those features into its product offering to encourage buyer preferences for its brand over the brands of rivals. Competitive advantage results when enough buyers become strongly attached to the attributes of a differentiator's product offering. Successful differentiation allows a firm to

With a differentiation strategy, the basis for competitive advantage is a product whose attributes differ significantly from the products of rivals.

- command a premium price for its product, and/or
- sell more units (because additional buyers are won over by the differentiating features), and/or
- gain greater buyer loyalty to its brand (because some buyers are strongly attracted to the differentiating features).

Differentiation enhances profitability whenever the extra price the product commands outweighs the added costs of achieving differentiation. Differentiation is unsuccessful when buyers don't value the additional features highly enough to buy the product in profitable quantities. And differentiation is unprofitable when the price premium buyers are willing to pay won't cover the extra costs of achieving brand distinctiveness.

The approaches to differentiating a product take many forms: a different taste (Dr Pepper and Listerine), special features (Jenn-Air's indoor cooking tops with a vented built-in grill for barbecuing), superior service (Federal Express in overnight package delivery), spare parts availability (Caterpillar guarantees 48-hour spare parts delivery to any customer anywhere in the world or else the part is furnished free), overall value to the customer

(McDonald's), engineering design and performance (Mercedes), prestige and distinctiveness (Rolex), product reliability (Johnson & Johnson baby products), quality manufacture (Honda), technological leadership (3M in bonding and coating products), a full range of services (Merrill Lynch), a complete line of products (Campbell soups), and top-of-the-line image and reputation (Brooks Brothers and Ralph Lauren in menswear, Kitchen Aid in dishwashers, and Cross in writing instruments).

Achieving Differentiation

Anything a firm can do to create buyer value represents a potential basis for differentiation. Once a firm finds good sources of buyer value, it must build the value-creating attributes into its product at an acceptable cost. A differentiator can incorporate attributes that raise the product's performance or make it more economical to use. Or a firm can incorporate features that enhance buyer satisfaction in tangible or intangible ways during use. Differentiation possibilities can grow out of activities performed anywhere in the activity-cost chain. McDonald's gets high ratings on its french fries partly because it has very strict specifications on the potatoes it purchases from its supplier. The quality of Japanese cars stems primarily from Japanese automakers' skills in manufacturing and quality control. IBM boosts buyer value by providing its customers with an extensive array of services and technical support. L. L. Bean makes its mail-order customers feel secure by providing an unconditional guarantee with no time limit: "All of our products are guaranteed to give 100 percent satisfaction in every way. Return anything purchased from us at anytime if it proves otherwise. We will replace it, refund your purchase price, or credit your credit card, as you wish." Commercial airlines use their empty seats during off-peak travel periods (i.e., their excess capacity) as the basis for awarding free travel to frequent flyers.

What Makes Differentiation Attractive

Differentiation provides some buffer against rivals' strategies because buyers become loyal to the brand or model they like best and often are willing to pay a little (perhaps a lot!) more for it. In addition, successful differentiation (1) erects entry barriers in the form of customer loyalty and uniqueness that newcomers find hard to overcome, (2) mitigates the bargaining power of large buyers since rivals' products are less attractive to them, and (3) helps a firm fend off threats from substitutes. If differentiation allows a firm to charge a higher price and boost profit margins, it will be in a stronger position to withstand powerful suppliers' efforts to raise their prices. Thus, as with cost leadership, successful differentiation creates lines of defense for dealing with the five competitive forces.

As a rule, differentiation strategies work best in situations where (1) there are many ways to differentiate the product or service and many buyers perceive these differences as valuable, (2) buyer needs and uses of the item are diverse, and (3) few rival firms are following a similar differentiation approach.

The most appealing types of differentiation strategies are those least subject to quick or inexpensive imitation. Here is where having core competences becomes a major competitive asset. When a firm has skills and expertise that competitors cannot match easily, it can use them as a basis for successful differentiation. Differentiation is most likely to produce an attractive, longer-lasting competitive edge if it is based on:

· · · · · · · · · · · ·
Competitive Strategy Principle
The competitive power of a differentiation strategy is greatest when buyer needs are diverse, there are many ways to differentiate that have value to buyers, few rivals choose the same approach, and the firm's product can't be quickly or cheaply imitated.

- Technical superiority.
- Quality.
- More customer support services.
- More value for the money.

Such differentiating attributes tend to be harder for rivals to copy quickly and profitably.

Real Value, Perceived Value, and Signals of Value   Buyers seldom pay for value they don't perceive, no matter how real the unique features may be.[3] Thus the price premium a differentiation strategy commands reflects *the value actually delivered* to the buyer and *the value the buyer perceives* (even if it is not actually delivered). Actual and perceived value can differ whenever buyers have trouble assessing in advance what their experience with the product will be. Buyers with incomplete knowledge of the product often judge value based on such *signals* as seller's word-of-mouth reputation, attractive packaging, extensive ad campaigns (i.e., how "well known" the product is), ad content and image, brochures and sales presentations, the seller's facilities, the seller's list of customers, the firm's market share, length of time the firm has been in business, price (where price connotes "quality"), and the professionalism, appearance, and personality of the seller's employees. Such signals of value may be as important as actual value (1) when the nature of differentiation is subjective or hard to quantify, (2) when buyers are making a first-time purchase, (3) when repurchase is infrequent, and (4) when buyers are unsophisticated.

Keeping the Cost of Differentiation in Line   Attempts to achieve differentiation usually raise costs. The trick to profitable differentiation is either to keep the costs of achieving differentiation below the price premium the differentiating attributes can command in the marketplace (thus increasing the profit margin per unit sold) or to offset thinner profit margins with enough added volume to increase total profits (larger volume can make up for smaller margins provided differentiation adds enough extra sales). In pursuing differentiation, a firm must be careful not to get its overall unit costs so far out of line with competitors that it has to charge a higher price than buyers are willing to pay. There may also be good reason to add extra differentiating features that are not costly but add to buyer satisfaction—fine restaurants typically provide such extras as a slice of lemon in the water glass, valet parking, and complimentary after-dinner mints.

The Risks of a Differentiation Strategy   There are, of course, no guarantees that differentiation will produce a meaningful competitive advantage. If buyers see little value in uniqueness (i.e., a standard item meets their needs), a low-cost strategy can easily defeat a differentiation strategy. In addition, differentiation can be defeated from the outset if competitors can quickly copy the attempt at differentiating. Rapid imitation means that firms never

- - - - - - - - - - - -
Competitive Strategy Principle
A firm whose differentiation strategy delivers only modest extra value but signals that value effectively may command a higher price than a firm that actually delivers higher value but signals it poorly.

- - - - - - - - - - - -
Competitive Strategy Principle
A low-cost producer strategy can defeat a differentiation strategy when buyers are satisfied with a standard product and don't think "extra" attributes are worth a higher price.

---

[3]This discussion draws from Porter, *Competitive Advantage* pp. 138–42. Porter's insights here are particularly important to formulating differentiating strategies because they highlight the relevance of "intangibles" and "signals."

achieve real differentiation because competing brands keep changing in like ways despite continued efforts to create uniqueness. Thus, to be successful at differentiation, a firm must search out durable sources of uniqueness that cannot be quickly or cheaply imitated. Aside from these considerations, other common pitfalls include:[4]

- Trying to differentiate on the basis of something that does not lower a buyer's cost or enhance a buyer's well-being (as perceived by the buyer).
- Overdifferentiating so that price is too high relative to competitors or product quality or service levels exceed buyers' needs.
- Trying to charge too high a price premium (the bigger the premium, the more buyers can be lured away by lower-priced competitors).
- Ignoring the need to signal value and depending only on tangible product attributes to achieve differentiation.
- Not understanding or identifying what buyers consider as value.

The Strategy of Being a Best-Cost Producer   A differentiation strategy aimed at giving customers *more value for the money* usually means combining an emphasis on low-cost with an emphasis on *more than minimally acceptable* quality, service, features, and performance. The idea is to create superior value by meeting or exceeding buyer expectations on quality-service-features-performance attributes and beating their expectations on price. Strategy-wise, the aim is to be the low-cost producer of a product with *good-to-excellent* product attributes, then use the cost advantage to underprice brands with comparable attributes. Such a competitive approach is termed a *best-cost producer strategy* because the producer has the best (lowest) cost relative to producers whose brands are comparably positioned on the quality-service-features-performance scale. The competitive advantage of a best-cost producer comes from matching close rivals on key attributes and beating them on cost. To become a best-cost producer, a company must match quality at a lower cost than rivals, match features at a lower cost than rivals, match product performance at a lower cost than rivals, and so on. What distinguishes a successful best-cost producer is expertise in incorporating upscale product attributes at a low cost; or, to put it a bit differently, an ability to contain the costs of providing customers with a better product. The most successful best-cost producers have the skills to simultaneously manage unit costs down and product caliber up.

A best-cost producer strategy has great appeal from the standpoint of competitive positioning. It produces superior customer value by balancing strategic emphasis on low cost against strategic emphasis on differentiation. In effect, such a *hybrid* strategy allows a company to combine the competitive advantage appeals of both low-cost and differentiation. In markets where buyer diversity makes product differentiation the norm and buyers are price and value sensitive, a best-cost producer strategy can be more advantageous than either a pure low-cost producer strategy or a pure differentiation strategy keyed to product superiority. This is because a best-cost producer can position itself near the middle of the market with either a medium-quality product

Competitive Strategy Principle

The most powerful competitive approach a company can pursue is relentlessly striving to become a lower and lower cost producer of a higher and higher caliber product, with the intent of eventually becoming the industry's absolute lowest cost producer and, simultaneously, the producer of the industry's overall best product.

---

[4]Ibid., pp. 160–62.

at a below-average price or a very good product at a medium price. Many buyers prefer a mid-range product rather than the cheap, basic product of a low-cost producer or the expensive product of a top-of-the-line differentiator.

Focus and Specialization Strategies

Focusing starts by choosing a market niche where buyers have distinctive preferences or requirements. The niche can be defined by geographic uniqueness, by specialized requirements in using the product, or by special product attributes that appeal only to niche members. *A focuser's basis for competitive advantage is either lower costs than competitors in serving the market niche or an ability to offer niche members something different from other competitors.* A focus strategy based on low cost depends on there being a buyer segment whose needs are less costly to satisfy compared to the rest of the market. A focus strategy based on differentiation depends on there being a buyer segment that demands unique product attributes.

What sets a focus strategy apart is concentrated attention on a narrow piece of the total market.

Examples of firms employing a focus strategy include Tandem Computers (a specialist in "nonstop" computers for customers who need a "fail-safe" system), Rolls Royce (in super luxury automobiles), Apple Computer in desktop publishing (Apple computers produce typeset-quality reports and graphics), Fort Howard Paper (specializing in paper products for industrial and commercial enterprises only), commuter airlines like Skywest and Atlantic Southeast (specializing in low-traffic, short-haul flights linking major airports with smaller cities 50 to 250 miles away), and Bandag (a specialist in truck tire recapping that promotes its recaps aggressively at over 1,000 truck stops).

Using a focus strategy to achieve a cost breakthrough is a fairly common technique. Budget-priced motel chains like Days Inn, Motel 6, and LaQuinta have lowered their investment and operating cost per room by using a no-frills approach and catering to price-conscious travelers. Discount stock brokerage houses have lowered costs by focusing on customers mainly interested in buy-sell transactions who are willing to forgo the investment research, investment advice, and financial services offered by full-service firms like Merrill Lynch. Pursuing a cost advantage via focusing works well when a firm can find ways to lower costs by limiting its customer base to a well-defined buyer segment.

Competitive Strategy Principle
The competitive power of a focus strategy is greatest when: (a) fast-growing segments are big enough to be profitable but small enough not to interest large competitors, (b) no other rivals are concentrating on the segment, and (c) segment buyers require special expertise or custom products.

When Focusing Is Attractive   A focus strategy becomes increasingly attractive as more of the following conditions are met:

- The segment is big enough to be profitable.
- The segment has good growth potential.
- The segment is not crucial to the success of major competitors.
- The focusing firm has the skills and resources to serve the segment effectively.
- The focuser can defend itself against challengers based on the customer goodwill it has built up and its superior ability to serve buyers in the segment.

A focuser's specialized skills in serving the target market niche provide a basis for defending against the five competitive forces. Multisegment rivals do not have the same competitive capability to serve the target clientele. The focused firm's competence in serving the market niche raises entry barriers, thus making it harder for companies outside the niche to enter. A focuser's unique capabilities in serving the niche also present a hurdle that makers of substitute products must overcome. The bargaining leverage of powerful customers is blunted somewhat by their own unwillingness to shift their business to rival firms less capable of serving their needs.

Focusing works best (1) when it is costly or difficult for multisegment competitors to meet the specialized needs of the niche, (2) when no other rival is attempting to *specialize* in the same target segment; (3) when a firm doesn't have enough resources to pursue a wider part of the total market; and (4) when the industry has many different segments, thereby allowing a focuser to pick an attractive segment suited to its strengths and capabilities.

The Risks of a Focus Strategy   Focusing carries several risks. One is the chance that competitors will find ways to match the focused firm in serving the narrow target market. Second is the potential for the niche buyer's preferences and needs to shift toward the product attributes desired by the market as a whole; such erosion opens the way for rivals with broad market appeal. Third is the chance that the segment will become so attractive that it becomes inundated with competitors, causing profits to be splintered.

USING OFFENSIVE STRATEGIES TO SECURE COMPETITIVE ADVANTAGE

. . . .

Competitive Strategy Principle

Competitive advantage is usually acquired by employing a creative offensive strategy that isn't easily thwarted by rivals.

An offensive strategy, if successful, can open up a competitive advantage over rivals.[5] How long this process takes depends on the industry's competitive characteristics. The *buildup period*, shown in Figure 5–1, can be short as in service businesses which need little in the way of equipment and distribution support to implement a new offensive move. Or the buildup can take much longer, as in capital intensive and technologically sophisticated industries where firms may need several years to debug a new technology, bring new capacity on line, and win consumer acceptance of a new product. Ideally, an offensive move builds competitive advantage quickly; the longer it takes the more likely rivals will spot the move, see its potential, and begin responding. The size of the advantage (indicated on the vertical scale in Figure 5–1) can be large (as in pharmaceuticals where patents on new drugs produce a substantial advantage) or small (as in apparel where popular new designs can be imitated quickly).

Following a successful competitive offensive, there is a *benefit period* during which the fruits of competitive advantage can be enjoyed. The length of the benefit period depends on how much time it takes rivals to launch counteroffensives and begin closing the competitive gap. A lengthy benefit period gives a firm valuable time to earn above-average profits and recoup the investment made in creating the advantage. The best strategic offensives produce big competitive advantages and long benefit periods.

---

[5]Ian C. MacMillan, "How Long Can You Sustain a Competitive Advantage," reprinted in Liam Fahey, *The Strategic Planning Management Reader* (Englewood Cliffs, N.J.: Prentice Hall, 1989), pp. 23–24.

FIGURE 5–1   The Building and Eroding of Competitive Advantage

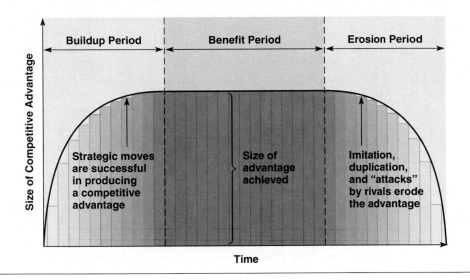

As competitors respond with counteroffensives, the *erosion period* begins. Any competitive advantage a firm currently holds will eventually be eroded by the actions of competent, resourceful competitors.[6] Thus, to sustain its initial advantage, a firm must devise a second strategic offensive. The groundwork for the second offensive needs to be laid during the benefit period so that the firm is ready for launch when competitors respond to the earlier offensive. To successfully sustain a competitive advantage, a firm must stay a step ahead of rivals by mounting one creative strategic offensive after another.

There are six basic ways to mount strategic offensives:[7]

- Attacks on competitor strengths.
- Attacks on competitor weaknesses.
- Simultaneous attack on many fronts.
- End-run offensives.
- Guerrilla offensives.
- Preemptive strikes.

Attacking Competitor Strengths

There are two good reasons to go head-to-head against rivals, pitting one's own strengths against theirs, price for price, model for model, promotion tactic for promotion tactic, and geographic area by geographic area. The first is to try to

---

[6]Ian C. MacMillan, "Controlling Competitive Dynamics by Taking Strategic Initiative," *The Academy of Management Executive* 2, no. 2 (May 1988), p. 111.

[7]Philip Kotler and Ravi Singh, "Marketing Warfare in the 1980's," *The Journal of Business Strategy* 1, no. 3 (Winter 1981), pp. 30–41; Philip Kotler, *Marketing Management*, 5th ed. (Englewood Cliffs, N.J.: Prentice Hall, 1984), pp. 401–6; and Ian MacMillan, "Preemptive Strategies," *Journal of Business Strategy* 14, no. 2 (Fall 1983), pp. 16–26.

gain market share by overpowering weaker rivals; challenging weaker rivals where they are strongest is attractive whenever a firm can win a decisive market victory and a commanding edge over struggling competitors. The other reason is to whittle away at a strong rival's competitive advantage; here success is measured by how much the competitive gap is narrowed. The merits of a strength-against-strength offensive challenge, of course, depend on how much the offensive costs compared to its benefits. To succeed, the initiator needs enough competitive strength and resources to take at least some market share from the targeted rivals.

One of the most powerful offensive strategies is to challenge rivals with an equally good or better product and a lower price.

All-out attacks on competitor strengths can involve initiatives on any of several fronts—price-cutting, comparison ads, new features that appeal to a rival's customers, new plant capacity in a rival's backyard, or new models that match rivals'. One of the best ploys is for the aggressor to attack with an equally good product offering and a lower price.[8] This can produce market share gains if the targeted rival has strong reasons for not cutting its prices and if the challenger convinces buyers that its product is just as good. However, such a strategy will increase profits only if volume gains offset the impact of thinner margins per unit sold.

In another type of price-aggressive attack, firms first achieve a cost advantage and then attack competitors with a lower price.[9] Price-cutting supported by a cost advantage is the strongest basis for launching and sustaining a price-aggressive offensive. Without a cost advantage, price-cutting works only if the aggressor has more financial resources and can outlast its rivals in a war of attrition.

Competitive Strategy Principle
Challenging larger, entrenched competitors with aggressive price-cutting is foolhardy unless the aggressor has either a cost advantage or greater financial strength.

Attacking Competitor Weaknesses

In this offensive approach, firms concentrate their competitive attention directly on the weaknesses of rivals. There are a number of weaknesses which can prove fruitful to challenge:

Competitive Strategy Principle
Challenging rivals where they are most vulnerable is more likely to succeed than challenging them where they are strongest, especially if the challenger has advantages in the areas where rivals are weak.

- Attack geographic regions where a rival has a weak market share or is exerting less competitive effort.
- Attack buyer segments that a rival is neglecting or is weakly equipped to serve.
- Attack rivals that lag on quality, features, or product performance; in such cases, a challenger with a better product can often convince the most performance-conscious customers of lagging rivals to switch to its brand.
- Attack rivals that have done a poor job of servicing customers; in such cases, a service-oriented challenger can win a rival's disenchanted customers.
- Attack rivals with weak advertising and brand recognition; a challenger with strong marketing skills and a good image can often move in on lesser-known rivals.
- Attack market leaders that have gaps in their product line; challengers can exploit opportunities to develop these gaps into strong, new market segments.

---

[8]Kotler, *Marketing Management*, p. 402.
[9]Ibid., p. 403.

- Attack market leaders who are ignoring certain buyer needs by introducing product versions that satisfy these needs.

As a rule, attacks on competitor weaknesses have a better chance of succeeding than attacks on competitor strengths, provided the weaknesses represent important vulnerabilities and the rival is caught by surprise with no ready defense.[10]

Simultaneous Attack on Many Fronts

Sometimes aggressors launch a grand competitive offensive involving several major initiatives in an effort to throw a rival off-balance, scatter its attention, and force it into channeling resources to protect all its sides simultaneously. Hunt's tried such an offensive several years ago in an attempt to wrest market share from Heinz ketchup. The attack began when Hunt's introduced two new ketchup flavors to disrupt consumers' taste preferences, try to create new product segments, and capture more shelf space in retail stores. Simultaneously, Hunt's lowered its price to 70 percent of Heinz's; it offered sizable trade allowances to retailers; and it raised its advertising budget to over twice that of Heinz's.[11] The offensive failed because not enough Heinz users tried the Hunt's brands, and many of those who did soon switched back to Heinz. Grand offensives have their best chance of success when a challenger, because of superior resources, can overpower its rivals by outspending them across-the-board long enough to buy its way into a position of market leadership and competitive advantage.

End-Run Offensives

End-run offensives seek to avoid head-on challenges tied to aggressive price-cutting, escalated advertising, or costly efforts to outdifferentiate rivals. Instead the idea is to maneuver *around* competitors and lead the way into unoccupied market territory. Examples of end-run offensives include moving aggressively into geographic areas where close rivals have no market presence, trying to create new segments by introducing products with different attributes and performance features to better meet the needs of selected buyers, and leapfrogging into next-generation technologies to supplant existing products and/or production processes. With an end-run offensive, a firm can gain a significant first-mover advantage in a new arena and force competitors to play catch-up. The most successful end-runs change the rules of the competitive game in the aggressor's favor.

> • • • • • • • • • • • •
> *End-run offensives dodge head-to-head confrontations, concentrating instead on innovative product attributes, technological advances, and early entry into less contested geographic markets.*

Guerrilla Offensives

Guerrilla offensives are particularly well-suited to small challengers who have neither the resources nor the market visibility to mount a full-fledged attack on industry leaders. A guerrilla offensive uses the hit-and-run principle, selectively attacking where and when an underdog can temporarily exploit the

---

[10]For a discussion of the use of surprise, see William E. Rothschild, "Surprise and the Competitive Advantage," *Journal of Business Strategy* 4, no. 3 (Winter 1984), pp. 10–18.

[11]As cited in Kotler, *Marketing Management*, p. 404.

situation to its own advantage. There are several ways to wage a guerrilla offensive:[12]

1. Attack a narrow, well-defined segment that is weakly defended by competitors.

2. Attack areas where rivals are overextended and have spread their resources most thinly (possibilities include going after their customers in less-populated geographic areas, enhancing delivery schedules at times when competitors' deliveries are running behind, adding to quality when rivals have quality control problems, and boosting technical services when buyers are confused by the number of competitors' models and features).

3. Make small, scattered, random raids on leaders with such tactics as occasional lowballing on price (to win a big order or steal a key account), intense bursts of promotional activity, and legal actions charging antitrust violations, patent infringement, and unfair advertising.

Preemptive Strategies

Preemptive strategies create competitive advantage by catapulting the aggressor into a prime competitive position which rivals are prevented or discouraged from matching.

Preemptive strategies involve moving first to secure an advantageous position that rivals are foreclosed or discouraged from duplicating. There are several ways to win a prime strategic position with preemptive moves:[13]

- Expand production capacity ahead of market demand in hopes of discouraging rivals from following suit. When rivals are "bluffed" out of adding capacity by a fear of creating long-term excess supply and underutilized plants, the preemptor can win a bigger market share if market demand grows and its own plant capacity fills.

- Tie up the best (or the most) raw material sources and/or the most reliable, high-quality suppliers via long-term contracts or backward vertical integration. This move can relegate rivals to struggling for second-best supply positions.

- Secure the best geographic locations. An attractive first-mover advantage can often be locked up by moving to obtain the most favorable site along a heavily traveled thoroughfare, at a new interchange or intersection, in a new shopping mall, in a natural beauty spot, close to cheap transportation or raw material supplies or market outlets, and so on.

- Obtain the business of prestigious customers.

- Build a "psychological" image in the minds of consumers that is unique and hard to copy and that establishes a compelling appeal and rallying cry. Examples include Avis's well-known "We try harder" theme, Frito-Lay's guarantee to retailers of "99.5% service," Holiday Inn's assurance of

---

[12]For more details, see MacMillan, "How Business Strategists Can Use Guerrilla Warfare Tactics," *Journal of Business Statistics* 1, no. 2 (Fall 1980), pp. 63–65; Kathryn R. Harrigan, *Strategic Flexibility* (Lexington, Mass.: Lexington Books, 1985), pp. 30–45; and Liam Fahey, "Guerrilla Strategy: The Hit- and-Run Attack," in Fahey, *The Strategic Planning Management Reader*, pp. 194–97.

[13]The use of preemptive moves is treated comprehensively in Ian C. MacMillan, "Preemptive Strategies," *Journal of Business Strategy*, pp. 16–26. What follows in this section is based on MacMillan's article .

"no surprises," and Prudential's "piece of the rock" image of safety and permanence.

- Secure exclusive or dominant access to the best distributors in an area.

Preemption has been used successfully by a number of companies. General Mills' Red Lobster restaurant chain has gained a prime position in the restaurant business by establishing strong relationships with very dependable seafood suppliers. DeBeers became the dominant world distributor of diamonds by buying the production of most of the important diamond mines. Du Pont's aggressive capacity expansions in titanium dioxide, while not blocking all competitors from expanding, did discourage enough to give it a leadership position in the titanium dioxide industry.

To be successful, a preemptive move doesn't have to totally block rivals from following or copying; it merely needs to give a firm a "prime" position. A prime position is one that puts rivals at a competitive disadvantage and is not easily circumvented.

Choosing Who to Attack

Aggressor firms need to analyze which of their rivals to attack as well as how to attack them. There are basically three types of firms that can be attacked offensively:[14]

1. *Market leader(s).* Waging an offensive against strong leader(s) risks squandering valuable resources in a futile effort and even precipitating a fierce and profitless industrywide battle for market share. Offensive attacks on a major competitor make the best sense when the leader in terms of size and market share is not the "true leader" in terms of serving the market well. Signs of leader vulnerability include unhappy buyers, sliding profits, strong emotional commitment to a technology the leader has pioneered, outdated plants and equipment, a preoccupation with diversification into other industries, a product line that is clearly not superior to rivals', and a competitive strategy that lacks real strength based on low-cost leadership or differentiation. Attacks on leaders can also succeed when the challenger is able to revamp its activity-cost chain or innovate to gain a fresh cost-based or differentiation-based competitive advantage.[15] Attacks on leaders need not have the objective of making the aggressor the new leader; a challenger may "win" by simply wresting enough sales from the leader to make the aggressor a stronger runner-up.

2. *Runner-up firms.* Offensives against weaker, vulnerable runner-up firms entail relatively low risk. Attacking a runner-up is an especially attractive option when a challenger's competitive strengths match the runner-up's weaknesses.

3. *Struggling enterprises that are on the verge of going under.* Challenging a hard-pressed rival in ways that further sap its financial strength and

---

[14]Kotler, *Marketing Management*, p. 400.
[15]Porter, *Competitive Advantage*, p. 518.

competitive position can weaken its resolve enough to prompt its exit from the market.

4. *Small local and regional firms.* Because these firms typically have limited expertise, a challenger with broader capabilities is well-positioned to raid their biggest and best customers—particularly those who are growing rapidly, have increasingly sophisticated needs, and may already be thinking about switching to a supplier with more full-service capability.

As we have said, successful strategies are grounded in competitive advantage. This goes for offensive strategies too. The competitive advantage potentials that offer the strongest basis for a strategic offensive include:[16]

- Developing a lower-cost product design.
- Making changes in production operations that lower costs or enhance differentiation.
- Developing product features that deliver superior performance or lower user costs.
- Giving buyers more responsive after-sale support.
- Escalating the marketing effort in an undermarketed industry.
- Pioneering a new distribution channel.
- Bypassing wholesale distributors and selling direct to the end-user.

A strategic offensive *must* be tied to what a firm does best—its competitive strengths and capabilities. As a rule, these strengths take the form of a *key skill* (cost reduction capabilities, customer service skills, technical expertise) or a uniquely *strong functional competence* (engineering and product design, manufacturing expertise, advertising and promotion, marketing know-how).[17]

USING DEFENSIVE STRATEGIES TO PROTECT COMPETITIVE ADVANTAGE

The foremost purpose of defensive strategy is to protect competitive advantage and fortify the firm's competitive position.

In a competitive market, all firms are subject to attacks from rivals. Offensive attacks can come both from new entrants and from established firms seeking to improve their market positions. The purpose of defensive strategy is to lower the risk of being attacked, weaken the impact of any attack that occurs, and influence challengers to aim their efforts at other rivals. While defensive strategy usually doesn't enhance a firm's competitive advantage, it should help fortify a firm's competitive position and sustain whatever competitive advantage it has.

There are several basic ways for a firm to protect its competitive position. One approach involves trying to block challengers' avenues for mounting an offensive; the options include:[18]

- Broadening the firm's product line to close off vacant niches and gaps to would-be challengers.

---

[16]Ibid., pp. 520–22.

[17]For more details, see Macmillan, "Controlling Competitive Dynamics," pp. 112–16.

[18]Porter, *Competitive Advantage*, pp. 489–94.

- Introducing models or brands that match the characteristics challengers' models already have or might have.
- Keeping prices low on models that most closely match competitors' offerings.
- Signing exclusive agreements with dealers and distributors to keep competitors from using the same ones.
- Granting dealers and distributors sizable volume discounts to discourage them from experimenting with other suppliers.
- Offering free or low-cost training to buyers' personnel in the use of the firm's product.
- Making it harder for competitors to get buyers to try their brands by (1) giving special price discounts to buyers who are considering trial use of rival brands, (2) resorting to high levels of couponing and sample giveaways to buyers most prone to experiment, and (3) making early announcements about impending new products or price changes so buyers postpone switching.
- Raising the amount of financing provided to dealers and/or buyers.
- Reducing delivery times for spare parts.
- Increasing warranty coverages.
- Patenting alternative technologies.
- Protecting proprietary know-how in products, production technologies, and other parts of the activity-cost chain.
- Signing exclusive contracts with the best suppliers to block access of aggressive rivals.
- Purchasing natural resource reserves ahead of present needs to keep them from competitors.
- Avoiding suppliers that also serve competitors.
- Challenging rivals' products or practices in regulatory proceedings.

There are many ways to blunt offensive challenges from rival firms.

Moves such as these not only buttress a firm's present position, they also present competitors with a moving target. It is not enough just to try to protect the status quo. A good defense entails adjusting quickly to changing industry conditions and, on occasion, being a first-mover to block or preempt moves by would-be aggressors. A mobile defense is always preferable to a stationary defense.

A second approach to defensive strategy entails signaling strong retaliation if a challenger attacks. The goal is to dissuade challengers from attacking at all (by raising their expectations that the resulting battle will be more costly than it is worth) or divert challengers to options less threatening to the defender. Would-be challengers can be signaled by:[19]

One of the best defensive strategies is to signal challengers that aggressive actions will be met with strong retaliatory countermeasures.

- Publicly announcing management's commitment to maintain the firm's present market share.
- Publicly announcing plans to construct adequate production capacity to meet forecast demand growth, and sometimes building ahead of demand.

---

[19]Porter, *Competitive Advantage*, pp. 495–97. The listing here is selective; Porter offers a greater number of options.

- Giving out advance information about a new product, technological breakthrough, or the planned introduction of important new brands or models, in hopes that challengers will be induced to delay moves of their own until they see if the signaled actions are true.
- Publicly committing the firm to a policy of matching the prices or terms offered by competitors.
- Maintaining a war chest of cash and marketable securities.
- Making an occasional strong counterresponse to the moves of weak competitors to enhance the firm's image as a tough defender.

Another way to dissuade rivals involves trying to lower the profit inducement for challengers to launch an offensive. When a firm's or industry's profitability is enticingly high, challengers are more willing to tackle high defensive barriers and combat strong retaliation. A defender can deflect attacks, especially from new entrants, by deliberately forgoing some short-run profits and by using accounting methods that obscure profitability.

VERTICAL INTEGRATION STRATEGIES

Vertical integration strategies aim at extending a firm's competitive scope within the same industry. Firms can expand their range of activities backward into sources of supply and/or forward toward end-users. A manufacturer that builds a new plant to make component parts rather than purchase them from suppliers remains in essentially the same industry as before. The only change is that it has business units in two stages of production in the industry's total activity-chain. Similarly, if a personal computer manufacturer elects to integrate forward by opening retail stores to market its brands, it remains in the personal computer business even though its competitive scope extends further forward in the industry chain.

Moves to vertically integrate can aim at *full integration* (participating in all stages of the process of getting products in the hands of final-users) or *partial integration* (building positions in just some stages of the industry's total production-distribution chain). A firm can accomplish vertical integration by starting its own company in other stages of the industry's activity chain or by acquiring a company already positioned in the stage it wishes to integrate.

Competitive Strategy Principle

A vertical integration strategy has appeal only if it significantly strengthens a firm's competitive position.

The Appeal of Vertical Integration

The only good reason for investing company resources in vertical integration is to strengthen the firm's competitive position.[20] Unless vertical integration produces sufficient cost-savings to justify the extra investment or yields a competitive advantage, it has no real profit or strategic payoff.

Integrating backward generates cost-savings only when the volume needed is big enough to capture the same scale economies suppliers have and when it can match or exceed suppliers' production efficiency. Backward integration

---

[20]See Kathryn R. Harrigan, "Matching Vertical Integration Strategies to Competitive Conditions," *Strategic Management Journal* 7, no. 6 (November–December 1986), pp. 535–56; for a fuller discussion of the advantages and disadvantages of vertical integration, see Kathryn R. Harrigan, *Strategic Flexibility* (Lexington, Mass.: Lexington Books, 1985), p. 162.

usually generates the largest cost advantage when suppliers have sizable profit margins, when the item being supplied is a major cost component, and when the needed technological skills are easily mastered. Backward vertical integration can produce a differentiation-based competitive advantage when a company, by supplying its own parts, ends up with a better-quality part and thereby significantly enhances the performance of its final product.

Backward integration can also spare a firm the uncertainty of being dependent on suppliers of crucial raw materials or support services, and it can lessen the firm's vulnerability to powerful suppliers intent on raising prices at every opportunity. Stockpiling, fixed-price contracts, or the use of substitute inputs may not be attractive ways for dealing with uncertain supply conditions or economically powerful suppliers. When this is the case, backward integration can be an organization's most profitable and competitively secure option for accessing reliable supplies of essential materials and support services at favorable prices.

The strategic impetus for forward integration has much the same roots. Undependable sales and distribution channels can give rise to costly inventory pileups and frequent underutilization of capacity, thereby undermining the economies of a steady, near-capacity production operation. In such cases, it is often advantageous for a firm to set up its own wholesale-retail distribution network in order to gain dependable channels through which to push its products to end-users. Sometimes even a small percentage increase in the average rate of capacity utilization can boost manufacturing margins enough to make forward integration economical. On other occasions, forward integration into distribution and retailing is cheaper than dealing with independent distributors and retailers, thus providing a source of cost advantage.

Integrating forward into manufacturing may help a raw materials producer achieve greater product differentiation and escape the price-oriented competition of a commodity business. Often, in the early phases of vertical product flow, intermediate goods are "commodities" in the sense that they have essentially identical technical specifications irrespective of producer (as is the case with crude oil, poultry, sheet steel, cement, and textile fibers). Competition in commodity or commodity-like markets is usually fiercely price-competitive, with shifting supply and demand conditions causing volatile profits. However, the closer the production stage to the ultimate consumer, the greater the opportunities for a firm to break out of a commodity-like competitive environment and differentiate its end-product via design, service, quality features, packaging, promotion, and so on. Product differentiation often reduces the importance of price in comparison with other product attributes and allows for improved profit margins.

For a manufacturer, integrating forward may mean building a chain of closely supervised dealer franchises or establishing company-owned and operated retail outlets. Or it may entail simply establishing a sales force instead of selling through manufacturer's agents or independent distributors.

The Strategic Disadvantages of Vertical Integration

Vertical integration has some potential weaknesses, however. First, it boosts a firm's capital investment in the industry, perhaps denying financial resources

. . . .
The big disadvantage of vertical integration is that it locks a firm deeper into an industry; unless vertical integration builds competitive advantage, it is a questionable strategic move.

to more worthwhile pursuits. Second, integration introduces additional risks, since it extends the enterprise's scope of activity across the industry chain. Third, vertical integration increases a firm's interest in protecting its present technology and production facilities even though they are becoming obsolete. Because of the high cost of abandoning such investments before they are worn out, fully integrated firms are more vulnerable to new technologies and new products than partially integrated or nonintegrated firms.

Fourth, vertical integration can pose problems of balancing capacity at each stage in the activity chain. The most efficient scale of operation at each step in the chain can vary substantially. Exact self-sufficiency at each interface is the exception not the rule. Where internal capacity is deficient to supply the next stage, the difference has to be bought externally. Where internal capacity is excessive, customers need to be found for the surplus. And if by-products are generated, they must be disposed of.

All in all, a strategy of vertical integration can have both strengths and weaknesses. Which direction the scales tip depends on (1) how compatible vertical integration is with the organization's long-term strategic interests and performance objectives, (2) how much it strengthens an organization's position in the overall industry, and (3) the extent to which it creates competitive advantage. Unless these considerations yield solid benefits, vertical integration is unlikely to be an attractive business strategy option.[21]

First-Mover Advantages and Disadvantages

When to make a strategic move is often as crucial as *what* move to make. Timing is especially important when *first-mover advantages* or *disadvantages* exist.[22] Being first to initiate a strategic move can have a high payoff when (1) pioneering helps build a firm's image and reputation with buyers, (2) early commitments to supplies of raw materials, new technologies, distribution channels, and so on can produce an absolute cost advantage over rivals, (3) first-time customers remain strongly loyal to pioneering firms in making repeat purchases, and (4) moving first constitutes a preemptive strike, making imitation extra hard or unlikely. The bigger the first-mover advantages, the more attractive that making the first move becomes.

However, a "wait and see" approach doesn't always carry a competitive penalty. Making the first move may carry greater risks than a late move. First-mover disadvantages (or late-mover advantages) arise when: (1) pioneering leadership is much more costly and only negligible experience curve effects accrue to the leader, (2) technological change is so rapid that early investments are soon obsolete (thus allowing following firms to gain the advantages of next-generation newest products and more efficient processes), (3) it is easy for late-comers to crack the market because customer loyalty to pioneering firms is weak, and (4) skills and know-how developed by the market leaders can be

---

[21]For an extensive, well-researched look at the whole family of approaches to vertical integration, see Kathryn R. Harrigan, "Formulating Vertical Integration Strategies," *Academy of Management Review* 9, no. 4 (October 1984), pp. 638–52.

[22]Porter, *Competitive Strategy*, pp. 232–33.

easily copied or even surpassed by late movers. Good timing, therefore, is an important ingredient in deciding whether to be aggressive or cautious.

The challenge of competitive strategy—low-cost, differentiation, or focus—is to create a competitive advantage for the firm. Competitive advantage comes from positioning a firm in the marketplace so it has an edge in coping with competitive forces and in attracting buyers.

A strategy of trying to be the low-cost producer works well in situations where

- The industry's product is pretty much the same from seller to seller.
- The marketplace is dominated by price competition (buyers are prone to shop for the lowest price).
- There are only a few ways to achieve product differentiation that have much value to buyers.
- Most buyers use the product in the same ways and thus have common user requirements.
- Buyers' costs in switching from one seller or brand to another are low (or even zero).
- Buyers are large and have significant bargaining power.

To achieve a low-cost advantage, a company must become more skilled than rivals in controlling cost drivers and/or it must find innovative cost-saving ways to revamp the activity-cost chain.

Differentiation strategies can produce a competitive edge based on technical superiority, quality, service, or more value for the money. Differentiation strategies work *best* when:

- There are many ways to differentiate the product/service that buyers think have value.
- Buyer needs or uses of the product/service are diverse.
- Not many rivals are following a similar differentiation strategy.

Anything a firm can do to create buyer value represents a potential basis for differentiation. Successful differentiation is usually keyed to lowering the buyer's cost of using the item, raising the performance the buyer gets, giving the buyer more value for the money, or boosting a buyer's psychological satisfaction. A best-cost producer strategy works especially well in market situations where product differentiation is the rule and buyers are price sensitive.

The competitive advantage of focusing comes from achieving lower costs in serving the target market niche or from offering niche buyers something different from rivals—in other words, the advantage a firm gains with a focus strategy is either *cost-based* or *differentiation-based*. Focusing works best when:

- Buyer needs or uses of the item are diverse.
- No other rival is attempting to *specialize* in the same target segment.
- A firm lacks the ability to go after a wider part of the total market.

- Buyer segments differ widely in size, growth rate, profitability, and intensity in the five competitive forces, making some segments more attractive than others.

A variety of offensive strategic moves can be used to secure a competitive advantage. Strategic offensives can be aimed at competitors' strengths or weaknesses; they can involve end-runs or grand offensives; they can be designed as guerrilla actions or as preemptive strikes; and the target of the offensive can be a market leader, a runner-up firm, or the smallest and/or weakest firms in the industry.

To defend its current position, a company can: (1) make moves that fortify its current position, (2) present competitors with a moving target to avoid "out-of-date" vulnerability, and (3) dissuade rivals from even trying to attack.

Vertical integration forward or backward makes strategic sense if it strengthens a company's position via either cost reduction or enhanced product differentiation.

The timing of strategic moves is important. First-movers sometimes gain strategic advantage; at other times, it is cheaper and easier to be a follower than a leader.

SUGGESTED
READINGS

Aaker, David A. "Managing Assets and Skills: The Key to a Sustainable Competitive Advantage." *California Management Review* 31, no. 2 (Winter 1989), pp. 91–106.

Cohen, William A. "War in the Marketplace." *Business Horizons* 29, no. 2 (March–April 1986), pp. 10–20.

Coyne, Kevin P. "Sustainable Competitive Advantage—What It Is, What It Isn't." *Business Horizons* 29, no. 1 (January–February 1986), pp. 54–61.

Harrigan, Kathryn R. "Guerrilla Strategies of Underdog Competitors." *Planning Review* 14, no. 16 (November 1986), pp. 4–11.

———. "Formulating Vertical Integration Strategies." *Academy of Management Review* 9, no. 4 (October 1984), pp. 638–52.

Hout, Thomas, Michael E. Porter, and Eileen Rudden. "How Global Companies Win Out." *Harvard Business Review* 60, no. 5 (September–October 1982), pp. 98–108.

MacMillan, Ian C. "Preemptive Strategies." *Journal of Business Strategy* 14, no. 2 (Fall 1983), pp. 16–26.

———. "Controlling Competitive Dynamics by Taking Strategic Initiative." *The Academy of Management Executive* 2, no. 2 (May 1988), pp. 111–18.

Porter, Michael E. *Competitive Advantage* (New York: Free Press, 1985), chaps. 3, 4, 5, 7, 14, and 15.

Rothschild, William E. "Surprise and the Competitive Advantage." *Journal of Business Strategy* 4, no. 3 (Winter 1984), pp. 10–18.

Thompson, Arthur A. "Strategies for Staying Cost Competitive." *Harvard Business Review* 62, no. 1 (January–February 1984), pp. 110–17.

Matching Strategy to the Situation

*Strategy isn't something you can nail together in slap-dash fashion
by sitting around a conference table . . .*
~Terry Haller

· · · · · · ·

*The essence of formulating competitive strategy is relating a company to its
environment . . . the best strategy for a given firm is ultimately a unique
construction reflecting its particular circumstances.*
~Michael E. Porter

· · · · · · ·

You do not choose to become global. The market chooses for you; it forces your hand.
~Alain Gomez
CEO, Thomson, S.A.

What kind of strategy best suits a company's business is conditioned partly by
the industry environment in which it competes and partly by the company's situation. To demonstrate the kinds of considerations involved in matching strategy to the situation, this chapter examines strategy-making in eight classic
types of industry environments and company situations:

1. Competing in a young, emerging industry.
2. Competing during the transition to industry maturity.
3. Competing in mature or declining industries.
4. Competing in fragmented industries.
5. Competing in international markets.
6. Strategies for industry leaders.
7. Strategies for runner-up firms.
8. Strategies for weak and crisis-ridden firms.

STRATEGIES FOR COMPETING IN EMERGING INDUSTRIES

An emerging industry is one in the early formative stage. Most companies are in a start-up mode, adding people, acquiring or constructing facilities, gearing up production, trying to broaden distribution and gain buyer acceptance. Often, such firms have to work out important product design and technological problems as well. Emerging industries present strategy-makers with some unique challenges:[1]

- Because the market is new and unproven, there are many uncertainties about how it will function, how fast it will grow, and how big it will get; the little historical data available is virtually useless in projecting future trends.

- Much of the technological know-how tends to be proprietary and closely guarded, having been developed in-house by pioneering firms; patent protection is sought for competitive advantage.

- Often, there is no consensus on which production technologies will be most efficient and which product attributes buyers will prefer. The result is industrywide absence of product and technological standardization, wide differences in product quality and performance, and a situation where each firm has to pioneer its own approach to technology, product design, marketing, and distribution.

- Entry barriers tend to be relatively low; additional start-up companies and large outsiders will enter if it becomes more evident that the industry's future is promising.

- Experience curve effects often permit significant cost reductions as volume builds.

- Firms have little hard information about competitors, how fast products are gaining buyer acceptance, and users' experiences with the product; there are no trade associations gathering and distributing information.

- Since all buyers are first-time users, the marketing task is to induce initial purchase and overcome customer concerns about product features, performance reliability, and conflicting claims of rival firms.

- Many buyers expect first-generation products to be rapidly improved, so they wait to buy until technology and product design mature.

- Firms may have trouble securing ample supplies of raw materials and components (until suppliers gear up to meet the industry's needs).

- Many companies find themselves short of funds to support needed R&D and to get through several lean years until the product catches on.

The two critical strategic issues confronting firms in an emerging industry are (1) how to finance the start-up phase and (2) what market segments and competitive advantage to go after to secure a leading industry position.[2] Competitive strategies keyed either to low-cost or differentiation are usually viable. Focusing should be considered when finances are limited and the industry has

---

[1]Michael E. Porter, *Competitive Strategy* (New York: Free Press, 1980), pp. 216–23.
[2]Charles W. Hofer and Dan Schendel, *Strategy Formulation: Analytical Concepts* (St. Paul, Minn.: West Publishing, 1978), pp. 164–65.

too many technological frontiers to pursue at once; one option for financially constrained enterprises is to form a strategic alliance or joint venture with another company to gain access to needed skills and resources. Dealing with all the risks and opportunities of an emerging industry is one of the most challenging business strategy problems. To be successful in an emerging industry, companies need to observe the following guidelines:[3]

1. Try to win the early race for industry leadership by employing a bold, creative entrepreneurial strategy. Because an emerging industry has no established rules of the game and industry participants often try a variety of strategic approaches, a pioneering firm with a powerful strategy can shape the rules and become the industry leader.

2. Push hard to perfect the technology, improve product quality, and develop attractive performance features.

3. Try to capture any first-mover advantages associated with more models, better styling, early commitments to technologies and raw materials suppliers, experience curve effects, and new distribution channels.

4. Search out new customer groups, new geographical areas to enter, and new user applications. Make it easier and cheaper for first-time buyers to try the industry's new product.

5. Gradually shift the advertising emphasis from building product awareness to increasing frequency of use and creating brand loyalty.

6. Move quickly when technological uncertainty clears and a "dominant" technology emerges; try to pioneer the "dominant design" (but be cautious when technology is evolving so rapidly that early investments are likely to become obsolete).

7. Use price cuts to attract price-sensitive buyers into the market.

8. Expect large, established firms looking for growth opportunities to enter the industry as their perceived risk of investing in the industry lessens. Try to prepare for the entry of powerful competitors by forecasting (*a*) who will enter (based on present and future entry barriers) and (*b*) the types of strategies they will employ.

Strategic success in an emerging industry calls for bold entrepreneurship, a willingness to pioneer and take risks, an intuitive feel for what buyers will like and how they will use the product, quick response to new developments, and opportunistic strategy-making.

The short-term value of winning the early race for growth and market share has to be balanced against the longer-range need to build a durable competitive edge and a defendable market position.[4] New entrants, attracted by the growth and profit potential, may crowd the market. Aggressive newcomers, aspiring for industry leadership, can quickly become major players by acquiring and merging the operations of weaker competitors. A young, single-business enterprise in a fast-developing industry can help its cause by selecting knowledgeable members for its board of directors, hiring entrepreneurial managers with experience in guiding young businesses through the development and takeoff, or merging with another firm to gain added expertise and a stronger resource base.

---

[3]Phillip Kotler, *Marketing Management*, 5th ed. (Englewood Cliffs, N.J.: Prentice Hall, 1984), p. 366; and Porter, *Competitive Strategy*, chap. 10.

[4]Hofer and Schendel, *Strategy Formulation*, pp. 164–65.

STRATEGIES FOR COMPETING DURING THE TRANSITION TO INDUSTRY MATURITY

Principle of Competitive Markets

Slower rates of market growth cause competitive pressures to intensify, often producing a shakeout of weaker competitors and slimmer profit margins industrywide.

Rapid industry growth doesn't last forever. However, the transition to a slower-growth, maturing environment does not begin on any easily predicted schedule and it can be forestalled by a steady stream of technological advances, product innovations, or other driving forces that keep rejuvenating market demand. Nonetheless, as growth rates slack off, the transition usually produces fundamental changes in the industry's competitive environment:[5]

1. *Slowing growth in buyer demand generates more head-to-head competition for market share.* Firms that want to continue on a rapid-growth track start looking for ways to take customers from competitors. Outbreaks of price-cutting, increased advertising, and other aggressive tactics are common.

2. *Buyers become more sophisticated, often driving a harder bargain on repeat purchases.* Since buyers have experience with the product and are familiar with competing brands, they are better able to evaluate different brands, and will negotiate with sellers to get a better deal.

3. *Competition often produces a greater emphasis on cost and service.* As all sellers begin to offer the product attributes buyers prefer, buyer choices increasingly depend on which seller offers the best combination of price and service.

4. *Firms have a "topping out" problem in adding production capacity.* Slower rates of industry growth mean slowdowns in capacity expansion. Each firm has to monitor rivals' expansion plans and time its own carefully to minimize oversupply conditions in the industry. Adding too much capacity too soon can adversely affect company profits well into the future.

5. *Product innovation and new end-use applications are harder to come by.* Producers find it increasingly difficult to develop new product features, find further uses for the product, and sustain buyer excitement.

6. *International competition increases.* Growth-minded domestic firms start to seek out sales opportunities in foreign markets. Some companies, looking for ways to cut costs, relocate plants to countries with lower wage rates. Greater product standardization and diffusion of technological know-how reduce entry barriers and make it possible for enterprising foreign companies to become serious market contenders in more countries. Industry leadership passes to companies with the biggest global market shares and strong competitive positions in most of the world's major geographic markets.

7. *Industry profitability falls temporarily or permanently.* Slower growth, increased competition, more sophisticated buyers, and occasional periods of overcapacity put pressure on industry profit margins. Weaker, less-efficient firms are usually the hardest hit.

8. *The resulting competitive shakeout induces a number of mergers and acquisitions among former competitors, drives some firms out of the industry, and,*

---

[5]Porter, *Competitive Strategy*, pp. 238–40.

in general, produces industry consolidation. Inefficient firms and firms with weak competitive strategies can survive in a rapid-growth industry. But the much stiffer competition in the industry maturity stage exposes competitive weakness and results in a survival-of-the-fittest market contest.

As market growth slows and competitive pressures build, firms can make several strategic moves to strengthen their competitive positions.[6]

As industry growth slows, strategic emphasis shifts to efficiency-increasing, profit-preserving measures: pruning the product line, improving production methods, reducing costs, expanding internationally, and acquiring distressed rivals.

Pruning the Product Line A wide selection of models, features, and options has competitive value during the growth stage when buyers' needs are still evolving. But such variety can become too costly as price competition stiffens and profit margins are squeezed. Too many product versions prevent firms from achieving the economies of long production runs. In addition, the prices of slow-selling versions may not cover their true costs. Pruning product lines and concentrating sales efforts on items whose margins are highest and/or where the firm has a competitive advantage reduces costs and helps keep strategy matched to company strengths.

More Emphasis on Process Innovation Efforts to "re-invent" the manufacturing process can have a twofold payoff: lower costs and better quality control. Process innovation can involve mechanizing high-cost activities, revamping production lines to improve labor efficiency, and increased use of advanced technology (robotics, computerized controls, and automatic guided vehicles). Japanese firms have successfully used manufacturing process innovation to become lower-cost producers of higher-quality products.

A Stronger Focus on Cost Reduction Stiffening price competition gives firms extra incentive to reduce unit costs. Such efforts can cover a broad front: firms can negotiate with suppliers for better prices, switch to lower-priced components, develop more economical product designs, cut unnecessary tasks out of the activity-cost chain, increase manufacturing and distribution efficiency, and trim administrative overhead.

Increasing Sales to Present Customers In a mature market, growing by taking customers from rivals may not be as appealing as expanding sales to existing customers. Strategies to increase purchases to existing customers can involve broadening the lines offered to include complementary products and ancillary services, finding more ways for customers to use the product, and performing more functions for the buyers (assembling components prior to shipment). Convenience food stores, for example, have boosted average sales per customer by adding video rentals, automatic bank tellers, and deli counters.

Purchasing Rival Firms at Bargain Prices Sometimes distressed rivals can be acquired cheaply. Bargain-priced acquisitions can help create a low-cost position if they present opportunities for greater operating efficiency. In addition, an acquired firm's customer base can provide expanded market coverage. The most desirable acquisitions are those that will significantly enhance the acquiring firm's competitive strength.

---

[6]The following discussion draws on Porter, *Competitive Strategy,* pp. 241–46.

Expanding Internationally   As its domestic market matures, a firm may seek to enter foreign markets where attractive growth potential still exists and competitive pressures are not so strong. Foreign expansion is particularly attractive if equipment no longer suitable for domestic operations is usable for export production or for plants in less developed foreign markets (a condition that lowers entry costs). Such possibilities arise when (1) foreign buyers have less sophisticated needs, (2) end-use applications are much simpler, and (3) foreign competitors are smaller, less formidable, and do not employ the latest production technology. Strategies to expand internationally make particular sense when a domestic firm's skills and reputation are readily transferable to foreign markets.

Strategic Pitfalls

Perhaps the biggest mistake a firm can make during the transition to industry maturity is steering a middle course between low cost, differentiation, and focusing. Such a compromise guarantees that the firm will end up with a fuzzy strategy, no clearly staked out market position, an "average" image with buyers, and no competitive advantage. Other pitfalls include sacrificing long-term competitive position for short-term profit, waiting too long to respond to price-cutting, getting caught with too much capacity as growth slows, overspending on marketing efforts to boost sales growth, and failing to pursue cost reduction soon enough and aggressively enough.

STRATEGIES FOR FIRMS IN MATURE OR DECLINING INDUSTRIES

Many firms operate in industries where demand is growing slower than the economy average—or even declining. Although cash-flow maximization, selling out, and closing down are obvious strategies for uncommitted competitors with dim long-term prospects, strong competitors can still achieve good performance in a stagnant market environment.[7] Stagnant demand by itself is not enough to make an industry unattractive. Selling out may or may not be practical, and closing down operations is always a last resort.

Businesses competing in slow-growth/declining industries have to accept the difficult realities of continuing stagnancy and they must set performance goals consistent with available market opportunities. Although cash flow and return on investment are more appropriate criteria than growth-oriented performance measures, firms don't have to rule out sales and market share growth. Strong competitors may be able to take sales from weaker rivals, and the acquisition or exit of weaker firms may help remaining companies capture greater market share.

In general, companies that have succeeded in stagnant industries have relied heavily on one of the following strategic themes:[8]

1. *Pursue a focus strategy by identifying, creating, and exploiting the growth segments within the industry.* Slow-growth or declining markets, like

---

[7]R. G. Hamermesh and S. B. Silk, "How to Compete in Stagnant Industries," *Harvard Business Review* 57, no. 5 (September–October 1979), p. 161.

[8]Ibid., p. 162.

other markets, are composed of numerous segments and subsegments. Frequently, one or more of these segments is growing rapidly, despite a lack of growth in the industry as a whole. An astute competitor who is first to concentrate on the most attractive segments can escape stagnating sales and profits and achieve competitive advantage in the target segments.

2. *Stress differentiation based on quality improvement and product innovation.* Either enhanced quality or innovation can rejuvenate demand by creating important new growth segments or inducing buyers to trade up. Successful product innovation opens up an avenue for competing besides meeting or beating rivals' prices. Differentiation based on innovation has the additional advantage of being difficult and expensive for rivals to imitate.

3. *Work diligently and persistently to drive costs down.* When increases in sales cannot be counted on to generate increased earnings, firms can improve profit margins and return on investment by continuously reducing operating costs and increasing efficiency. They can achieve a lower-cost position by: (1) improving the manufacturing process via automation and increased specialization, (2) consolidating underutilized production facilities, (3) adding more distribution channels to ensure the unit volume needed for low-cost production, (4) closing low-volume, high-cost distribution outlets, and (5) revamping the activity-cost chain to eliminate some cost-producing tasks.

These three themes are not mutually exclusive.[9] Attempts to introduce innovative versions of a product can *create* a fast-growing market segment. Similarly, increased operating efficiencies permit price reductions that create price-conscious growth segments. Note that all three themes are spin-offs of the three generic competitive strategies, adjusted to fit the circumstances of a tough industry environment.

The most attractive declining industries are those in which decline is reasonably slow, there is big built-in demand, and some profitable niches remain. Dangers in a stagnating market include: (1) getting trapped in a profitless war of attrition, (2) diverting too much cash out of a business too quickly (thus accelerating a company's demise), and (3) being overly optimistic about the industry's future and waiting complacently for things to get better.

Illustration Capsule 13 describes the creative approach taken by Yamaha to reverse declining market demand for pianos.

STRATEGIES FOR COMPETING IN FRAGMENTED INDUSTRIES

A number of industries are populated with hundreds, even thousands, of small and medium-sized companies, many privately held and none with a substantial share of total industry sales.[10] The outstanding feature of a fragmented industry is the absence of market leaders with king-sized market shares who have the clout and visibility to set the tone of competition. Examples of

---

[9] Ibid., p. 165.

[10] This section is summarized from Porter, *Competitive Strategy*, chap. 9.

ILLUSTRATION CAPSULE | **13** | YAMAHA'S STRATEGY IN THE PIANO INDUSTRY

For some years now, worldwide demand for pianos has been declining—in the mid-1980s the decline was 10 percent annually. Modern-day parents have not put the same stress on music lessons for their children as prior generations of parents did. In an effort to see if it could revitalize its piano business, Yamaha conducted a market research survey to learn what use was being made of pianos in households that owned one. The survey revealed that the overwhelming majority of the 40 million pianos in American, European, and Japanese households were seldom used. In most cases, the reasons the piano had been purchased no longer applied. Children had either stopped taking piano lessons or were grown and had left the household; adult household members played their pianos sparingly, if at all—only a small percentage were accomplished piano players. Most pianos were serving as a piece of fine furniture and were in good condition despite not being tuned regularly. The survey also confirmed that the income levels of piano owners were well above average.

Yamaha's piano strategists saw the idle pianos in these upscale households as a potential market opportunity. The strategy that emerged entailed marketing an attachment that would convert the piano into an old-fashioned automatic player piano capable of playing a wide number of selections recorded on $3\frac{1}{2}$-inch floppy disks (the same kind used to store computer data). The player piano conversion attachment carried a $2,500 price tag. Concurrently, Yamaha introduced Disklavier, an upright acoustic player piano model that could play *and record* performances up to 90 minutes long; the Disklavier retailed for $8,000. At year-end 1988 Yamaha offered 30 prerecorded disks for $29.95 each. Another 30 selections were scheduled for release in 1989. Yamaha believed that these new high-tech products held potential to reverse the downtrend in piano sales.

---

fragmented industries include book publishing, landscaping and plant nurseries, kitchen cabinets, oil tanker shipping, auto repair, restaurants and fast-food, public accounting, women's dresses, metal foundries, meat packing, paperboard boxes, log homes, hotels and motels, and furniture.

Any of several factors can account for why the supply side of an industry is fragmented.

* * * * * * * * * * * *

Many reasons account for why an industry has hundreds or even thousands of small competitors rather than a few large competitors.

- Low entry barriers allow small firms to enter quickly and cheaply.
- An absence of large-scale production economies permits small companies to compete on an equal cost footing with larger firms.
- Buyers require relatively small quantities of customized products (as in business forms, interior design, and advertising); because demand for any particular product version is small, sales volumes can't support producing, distributing, or marketing on a scale that favors a large firm.
- The market for the industry's product/service is local (dry cleaning, residential construction, medical services, automotive repair), giving competitive advantage to local businesses familiar with local buyers and market conditions.
- Market demand is so large and diverse that it takes large numbers of firms to accommodate buyer requirements (health care, energy, apparel).
- High transportation costs limit the radius a plant can economically service—as in concrete blocks, mobile homes, milk, and gravel.

- Local regulatory requirements make each geographic area unique.
- The industry is so new that no firms have yet developed the skills and resources to command a significant market share.

Some fragmented industries consolidate naturally as they mature. The stiffer competition that accompanies slower growth produces a shake-out of weak, inefficient firms and a greater concentration of larger, more visible sellers. Other industries remain fragmented because it is inherent to the nature of their business. And still others remain "stuck" in a fragmented state because existing firms lack the resources or ingenuity to employ a strategy that might promote industry consolidation.

Firms in fragmented industries usually are in a weak bargaining position with buyers and suppliers. New entrants are an ongoing threat. Competition from substitutes may or may not be a major factor. Rivalry among competitors can vary from moderately strong to fierce. In such an environment, the best a firm can expect is to cultivate a loyal customer base and grow a bit faster than the industry average. Competitive strategies based on low cost, some kind of differentiation theme, or focusing are all viable except when the industry's product is highly standardized; then competitors must rely on low cost or focused specialization. Suitable competitive strategy options in a fragmented industry include:

- **Constructing and operating "formula" facilities**—This is an attractive approach to achieving low cost when firms must operate facilities at multiple locations. Such firms design a standard facility, construct outlets in favorable locations at minimum cost, and then operate them in a superefficient manner. McDonald's and 7-Eleven have pursued this strategy to perfection, earning excellent profits in their respective industries.

  Competitive advantage in a fragmented industry usually comes from low cost, successful differentiation on well-chosen product attributes, or focusing on a particular market segment.

- **Becoming a low-cost operator**—When price competition is intense and profit margins are under constant pressure, firms can pursue no-frills operations featuring low overhead, use of high-productivity/low-cost labor, tight budget control, and total operating efficiency. Successful low-cost producers can play the price-cutting game and still earn profits above the industry average.

- **Increasing customer value through integration**—Backward or forward integration may contain opportunities to lower costs or enhance the value given to customers (like cutting to size, assembling components before shipment to customers, or providing technical advice).

- **Specializing by product type**—When products come in many models and styles, a focus strategy based on specialization in one area of the line can be very effective. Some firms in the furniture industry specialize in only one furniture type such as brass beds, rattan and wicker, lawn and garden, and early American. In auto repair, firms specialize in transmission repair; body work; and mufflers, brakes, and shocks.

- **Specializing by customer type**—A firm can cope with the intense competition of a fragmented industry by catering to those customers (1) who have the least bargaining leverage (because they are small in size or purchase small amounts), (2) who are the least price sensitive, (3) who are interested in additional services, unique product attributes, or other "extras," (4) who place custom orders, or (5) who have special needs or tastes.

- **Focusing on a limited geographic area**—Even though a firm in a fragmented industry is blocked from winning a big industrywide market share, it can still gain significant internal operating economies by blanketing a local/regional geographic area. Concentrating facilities and marketing activities on a limited territory can produce greater sales force efficiency, speed delivery and customer services, and permit saturation advertising—while avoiding the diseconomies of trying to employ the strategy on a national scale. Convenience food stores, banks, and department store retailers have been successful in operating multiple locations within a limited geographic area.

In fragmented industries, firms have a wide degree of strategic freedom—many different strategic approaches can exist side by side.

STRATEGIES FOR COMPETING IN INTERNATIONAL MARKETS

Firms "go international" for any of three basic reasons: a desire to seek out new markets, a competitive need to achieve lower costs, or a desire to access natural resource deposits in other countries. Whatever the reason, an international strategy has to be situation-driven and requires careful analysis of the industry's international aspects. Special attention has to be paid to how national markets differ in buyer needs and habits, distribution channels, long-run growth potential, driving forces, and competitive pressures. In addition to basic market differences from country to country, four other situational considerations are unique to international operations: cost variations among countries, fluctuating exchange rates, host government trade policies, and the pattern of international competition.

Competing in international markets poses a bigger strategy-making challenge than competing in only the company's home market.

Manufacturing Cost Variations   Differences in wage rates, worker productivity, inflation rates, energy costs, tax rates, and the like create sizable variations in manufacturing costs from country to country. Plants in some countries often have major manufacturing cost advantages because of their lower input costs (especially labor) or their unique natural resources. In such cases, the low-cost countries become principal production sites, and most of the output is exported to markets in other parts of the world. Companies with facilities in these locations (or which source their products from contract manufacturers in these countries) typically have a competitive advantage over those that do not. The importance of this consideration is most evident in low-wage countries like Taiwan, South Korea, Mexico, and Brazil, which have become production havens for goods with high labor content.

Another important manufacturing cost consideration in international competition is the concept of *manufacturing share* as distinct from brand share or market share. For example, although less than 40 percent of all the video recorders sold in the United States carry a Japanese brand, Japanese companies do 100 percent of the manufacturing—all sellers source their video recorders from Japanese manufacturers.[11] In microwave ovens, Japanese

---

[11]C. K. Prahalad and Yves L. Doz, *The Multinational Mission* (New York: Free Press, 1987), p. 60.

brands have less than a 50 percent share of the U.S. market, but Japanese companies have a manufacturing share of over 85 percent. *Manufacturing share is significant because it is a better indicator than market share of which competitor is the industry's low-cost producer.* In a globally competitive industry where some competitors are intent on global dominance, being the worldwide low-cost producer is a powerful competitive advantage. Achieving low-cost producer status often requires a company to have the largest worldwide manufacturing share, with production centralized in one or a few superefficient plants. However, important marketing and distribution economies associated with multinational operations can also yield low-cost leadership.

Fluctuating Exchange Rates   The volatility of exchange rates greatly complicates the issue of locational cost advantages. Exchange rates can fluctuate as much as 20 to 40 percent annually. Changes of this magnitude can totally wipe out a country's low-cost advantage or transform a former high-cost location into a competitive-cost location. A strong U.S. dollar makes it more attractive for U.S. companies to manufacture in foreign countries. A declining dollar can eliminate much of the cost advantage foreign manufacturers have over U.S. manufacturers and can even prompt foreign companies to establish production plants in the United States.

Host Government Trade Policies   National governments have enacted all kinds of measures affecting international trade and the operation of foreign companies in their markets. Host governments may impose import tariffs and quotas, set local content requirements on goods made inside their borders by foreign-based companies, and regulate the prices of imported goods. In addition, firms may face a web of regulations regarding technical standards, product certification, prior approval of capital spending projects, withdrawal of funds from the country, and minority (sometimes majority) ownership by local citizens. Some governments also provide subsidies and low-interest loans to domestic companies to help them compete against foreign-based companies. Other governments, anxious to obtain new plants and jobs, offer foreign companies subsidies, privileged market access, and technical assistance.

Multicountry Competition versus Global Competition

There are important differences in the patterns of international competition from industry to industry.[12] At one extreme, competition can be termed *multicountry* or *multidomestic* because it takes place country-by-country; competition in each national market is essentially independent of competition in other national markets. For example, there is a banking industry in France, one in Brazil, and one in Japan, but competitive conditions in banking differ markedly in all three countries. Moreover, a bank's reputation, customer base, and competitive position in one nation have little or no bearing on its ability to compete successfully in another. While a company may compete internationally, the power of its strategy in any one nation and any competitive advantage it yields are largely confined to that nation and do not spill over to other countries where it operates. With multicountry competition there is no "international

* * * * * * * * * * * * *
Basic Concept
Multicountry (or multidomestic) competition exists when competition in one national market is independent of competition in another national market—there is no "international market," just a collection of self-contained country markets.

---

[12]Michael E. Porter, *The Competitive Advantage of Nations* (New York: Free Press, 1990), pp. 53–54.

market," just a collection of self-contained country markets. Industries characterized by multicountry competition include many types of food products (coffee, cereals, canned goods, frozen foods), many types of retailing, beer, life insurance, apparel, and metals fabrication.

At the other extreme is *global competition* where prices and competitive conditions across country markets are strongly linked and the term *international* or *global market* has true meaning. In a globally competitive industry, a company's competitive position in one country both affects and is affected by its position in other countries. Rival companies compete against each other in many different countries, but especially so in countries where sales volumes are large and where having a competitive presence is strategically important to building a strong global position in the industry. In global competition, a firm's overall competitive advantage grows out of its entire worldwide operations. The competitive advantage it has created at its home base is supplemented by advantages growing out of its foreign operations (plants in low-wage countries, an ability to serve customers with multinational operations of their own, and brand reputation that is transferable from country to country). *A global competitor's strength is directly proportional to its portfolio of country-based competitive advantages.* Global competition exists in automobiles, television sets, tires, telecommunications equipment, copiers, watches, and commercial aircraft.

An industry can have segments that are globally competitive and segments where competition takes place country-by-country.[13] In the hotel-motel industry, for example, the low- and medium-priced segments are characterized by multicountry competition because competitors mainly serve travelers within the same country. In the business and luxury segments, however, competition is more global; companies like Marriott, Sheraton, and Hilton have hotels in many countries and use worldwide reservation systems and common quality and service standards to service international travelers. In lubricants, the marine engine segment is globally competitive because ships move from port to port and require the same oil everywhere they stop. Brand reputations have a global scope, and successful marine engine lubricant producers (Exxon, British Petroleum, and Shell) operate globally. In automotive motor oil, however, multicountry competition dominates. Countries have different weather conditions and driving patterns, production is subject to limited scale economies and shipping costs are high, and retail distribution channels differ markedly from country to country. Thus domestic firms, like Quaker State and Pennzoil in the United States and Castrol in Great Britain, can be market leaders.

All these situational considerations, along with the obvious cultural and political differences among countries, shape a company's strategic approach in international markets.

Types of International Strategies

There are six distinct strategic options for a firm participating in international markets. It can:

1. *License foreign firms to use the company's technology or produce and distribute the company's products* (in which case international revenues will equal the royalty income from the licensing agreement).

---

[13]Ibid., p. 61.

2. *Maintain a national (one-country) production base and export goods to foreign markets,* using either company-owned or foreign-controlled forward distribution channels.

3. *Follow a multicountry strategy* whereby a company's international strategy is crafted country-by-country to be responsive to buyer needs and competitive conditions in each country where it operates. Strategic moves in one country are made independent of actions taken in another country; strategy coordination across countries is secondary to the need to match company strategy to national conditions.

4. *Follow a global low-cost strategy* where strategy is based on the company being a low-cost supplier to buyers in most or all strategically important markets of the world. The company's strategic efforts are coordinated worldwide to achieve a low-cost position relative to competitors.

5. *Follow a global differentiation strategy* where a firm differentiates its product on the same attributes in all countries to create a consistent image and a consistent competitive theme. The firm's strategic moves are coordinated across countries to achieve consistent worldwide differentiation.

6. *Follow a global focus strategy* where company strategy is aimed at serving the same identifiable niche in each of many strategically important country markets. Strategic actions are coordinated globally to achieve a consistently focused approach in each country market.

Licensing makes sense when a firm with valuable technical know-how or a unique patented product has neither the internal organizational capability nor the resources to compete in foreign markets. By licensing the technology or the production rights to foreign-based firms, it at least realizes income from royalties.

Using domestic plants as a production base for exporting goods to foreign markets is an excellent initial strategy for achieving international sales growth. It minimizes both risk and capital requirements, and it is a conservative way to test the international waters. With an export strategy, a manufacturer can limit its involvement in foreign markets by letting foreign wholesalers experienced in importing assume the entire distribution and marketing function in their countries or regions of the world. If it is more advantageous to maintain control over these functions, a firm can establish its own distribution and sales organizations in some or all of its foreign markets. Either way, a firm minimizes its direct investment in foreign countries because of its home-base production and export strategy. Such strategies are commonly favored by Korean and Italian companies—products are designed and manufactured at home and only marketing activities are performed abroad. Whether such a strategy can be successful over the long run hinges on the relative cost competitiveness of a home-country production base. In some industries, firms gain additional scale economies and experience curve benefits from centralizing production in one or several giant-scale plants whose output capability exceeds demand in any one national market; to capture such economies a company must export to markets in other countries. However, this strategy is competitively vulnerable when manufacturing costs in the home country are substantially higher than in countries where rivals have plants.

The pros and cons of a multicountry versus global strategy are a bit more complex.

A Multicountry Strategy or a Global Strategy?

The logic and appeal of a multicountry strategy derives from the sometimes vast differences in cultural, economic, political, and competitive conditions in different countries. The more diverse national market conditions are, the stronger the case for a *multicountry strategy* where the company tailors its strategic approach to fit each host country's market situation. In such cases, the company's overall international strategy is a collection of its country strategies.

While multicountry strategies are best suited for industries where multicountry competition dominates, global strategies are best suited for globally competitive industries. A *global strategy* is one that is mostly the same in all countries. Although *minor* county-to-country differences do exist to accommodate specific competitive conditions in host countries, the company's fundamental competitive approach (low-cost, differentiation, or focus) remains the same worldwide. Moreover, a global strategy involves (1) integrating and coordinating the company's strategic moves worldwide and (2) selling in many or all nations where there is significant buyer demand. Table 6–1 provides a point-by-point comparison of multicountry versus global strategies. The question of which to pursue is the foremost strategic issue firms face when they compete in international markets.

The strength of a multicountry strategy is that it matches strategy to host-country circumstances. Such a strategy is essential when there are significant national differences in customers' needs and buying habits, when buyers in a country insist on special-order or highly customized products, when buyer demand for the product exists in comparatively few national markets, when host governments enact regulations requiring that products sold locally meet strict manufacturing specifications or performance standards, and when the trade restrictions of host governments are so diverse and complicated they preclude a uniform, coordinated worldwide market approach. However, a multicountry strategy has pitfalls; it entails very little strategic coordination across countries and it is not tightly tied to competitive advantage. Because the primary orientation of a multicountry strategy is responsiveness to local country conditions, it does not help a firm build a multinational-based competitive advantage over other international competitors and the domestic companies of host countries. A global strategy, because it is more uniform from country to country, helps a firm concentrate on securing a sustainable competitive advantage over both international and domestic rivals. Whenever country-to-country differences are small enough to be accommodated within the framework of a global strategy, a global strategy is preferable because of its broader-based competitive advantage potential.

Global Strategy and Competitive Advantage

There are two ways a firm can gain competitive advantage (or offset domestic disadvantages) with a global strategy approach.[14] One involves a global com-

---

[14]Ibid., p. 54.

TABLE 6–1   Differences between Multicountry and Global Strategies

	Multicountry Strategy	Global Strategy
Strategic arena	Selected target countries and trading areas	Most countries which constitute critical markets for the product (at least North America, the European Community, and the Pacific Rim [Australia, Japan, South Korea, and Southeast Asia])
Business strategy	Custom strategies to fit the circumstances of each host country situation; little or no strategy coordination across countries	Same basic strategy worldwide; minor country-by-country variations where essential
Product-line strategy	Adapted to local needs	Mostly standardized products sold worldwide
Production strategy	Plants scattered across many host countries	Plants located on the basis of maximum competitive advantage (in low-cost countries, close to major markets, geographically scattered to minimize shipping costs, or use of a few world-scale plants to maximize economies of scale—as most appropriate)
Source of supply for raw materials and components	Suppliers in host country preferred (local facilities meeting local buyer needs; some local sourcing may be required by host government)	Attractive suppliers from anywhere in the world
Marketing and distribution	Adapted to practices and culture of each host country	Much more worldwide coordination; minor adaption to host country situations if required
Company organization	Form subsidiary companies to handle operations in each host country; each subsidiary operates more or less autonomously to fit host country conditions	All major strategic decisions are closely coordinated at global headquarters; a global organizational structure is used to unify the operations in each country

petitor's ability to locate its activities (R&D, parts manufacture, assembly, distribution centers, sales and marketing, customer service centers) among nations in a manner that lowers costs or achieves greater product differentiation. The other concerns a global competitor's ability to coordinate its activities in ways that a domestic-only competitor cannot.

Locating Activities   To use location to build competitive advantage, a global firm must consider two issues: (1) whether to concentrate each activity it performs in one or two countries or disperse performance of the activity to many nations and (2) in which countries to locate particular activities. Activities tend to be concentrated in one or two locations when there are significant economies of scale in performing an activity, when there are advantages in locating related activities in the same area to achieve better coordination, and when there is a steep learning or experience curve associated with concentrating performance of an activity in a single location. In some industries, scale economies in parts manufacture or assembly are so great that a company establishes one large plant from which it serves the world market. Where just-in-time inventory practices yield big cost-savings, parts manufacturing plants may be clustered around final assembly plants.

With global strategy a firm can pursue sustainable competitive advantage by locating activities in the most advantageous nations and coordinating strategic actions worldwide; a domestic-only competitor forfeits such opportunities.

Dispersing activities is more advantageous than concentrating activities in several instances. Buyer-related activities—such as distribution to dealers, sales and advertising, and after-sale service—usually must take place close to buyers. This means physically locating the capability to perform such activities in every country where a global firm has major customers (unless buyers in several adjoining countries can be served quickly from a nearby central location). For example, firms that make mining and oil drilling equipment maintain operations in many international locations to support customers' needs for speedy equipment repair and technical assistance. Large public accounting firms have numerous international offices to service the foreign operations of their multinational corporate clients. A global competitor that effectively disperses its buyer-related activities can gain a service-based competitive edge in world markets over rivals whose buyer-related activities are more concentrated. Dispersing activities to many locations is also competitively advantageous when high transportation costs, diseconomies of large size, and trade barriers make it too expensive to operate from a central location. In addition, firms often disperse activities to hedge against fluctuating exchange rates, supply interruptions (due to strikes, mechanical failures, and transportation delays), and adverse political developments. Such risks are greater when activities are concentrated in a single location.

The classic reason for locating an activity in a particular country is lower costs.[15] Even though a global firm has strong reason to disperse buyer-related activities to many international locations, such activities as materials procurement, parts manufacture, finished goods assembly, technology research, and new product development can frequently be decoupled from buyer locations and performed wherever the best cost advantage lies. Components can be made in Mexico, technology research done in Frankfurt, new products developed and tested in Phoenix, and assembly plants located in Spain, Brazil, Taiwan, and Illinois. Capital can be raised wherever it is available on the best terms. Low cost is not the only locational consideration, however. A research unit may be located in a particular nation because of its pool of technically trained personnel. A customer service center or sales office may be located in a particular country to help develop strong relationships with pivotal customers. An assembly plant may be located in a country in return for the host government allowing freer import of components from centralized parts plants located elsewhere.

Coordinating Activities and Strategic Moves   By aligning and coordinating company activities in different countries, a firm can build sustainable competitive advantage in several different ways. If a firm learns how to assemble its product more efficiently at its Brazilian plant, the accumulated knowledge and expertise can be transferred to its assembly plant in Spain. Knowledge gained in marketing a company's product in Great Britain can be used to introduce the product in New Zealand and Australia. A company can shift production from one country to another to take advantage of exchange rate fluctuations, to enhance its leverage with host country governments, and to respond to changing wage rates, energy costs, or trade restrictions. A company can enhance its

---

[15]Ibid., p. 57.

brand reputation by consistently positioning its products with the same differentiating attributes on a worldwide basis. Honda's worldwide reputation for quality, first in motorcycles and then in automobiles, gave it competitive advantage in positioning its lawnmowers at the upper end of the market—the Honda name gave the company instant credibility with buyers. A global competitor can choose where and how to challenge rivals. It may decide to retaliate against aggressive rivals in the country market where the rival has its biggest sales volume or its best profit margins in order to reduce the rival's financial resources for competing in other countries. It may decide to wage a price-cutting offensive against weak rivals in their home markets, capturing greater market share and subsidizing any short-term losses with profits earned in other country markets.

A company that competes only in its home country has access to none of the competitive advantage opportunities associated with multinational location or coordination. By shifting from a domestic to a global strategy, a domestic company that finds itself at a competitive disadvantage to global companies can begin to restore its competitiveness.

Strategic Alliances

Strategic alliances are cooperative agreements between firms that go beyond normal company-to-company dealings but fall short of merger or full partnership.[16] An alliance can involve joint research efforts, technology-sharing, joint use of production facilities, marketing one another's products, or joining forces to manufacture components or assemble finished products. Strategic alliances are a means for firms in the same industry that are based in different countries to compete on a more global scale while still preserving their independence. Historically, export-minded firms in industrialized nations sought alliances with firms in less-developed countries to import and market their products locally—such arrangements were often necessary to gain access to the less-developed country's market. More recently, leading companies from different parts of the world have formed strategic alliances to strengthen their ability to serve whole continental areas and move toward more global market participation. Both Japanese and American companies have formed alliances with European companies in preparation for Europe 1992 and the opening of Eastern European markets.

Strategic alliances are a means for companies in globally competitive industries to strengthen their competitive positions while still preserving their independence.

Companies enter into alliances for several strategically beneficial reasons.[17] The three most important are to gain economies of scale in production and/or marketing, to fill gaps in their technical and manufacturing expertise, and to acquire market access. By joining forces in producing components, assembling models, and marketing their products, companies can realize cost savings not achievable with their own small volumes. Allies learn much from one another in performing joint research, sharing technological know-how, and studying one another's manufacturing methods. Alliances are often used by outsiders to

Competitive Strategy Principle
Strategic alliances are more effective in combating competitive disadvantage than in gaining competitive advantage.

---

[16]Ibid., p. 65. See, also, Kenichi Ohmae, "The Global Logic of Strategic Alliances," *Harvard Business Review* 89, no. 2 (March–April 1989), pp. 143–54.
[17]Porter, *The Competitive Advantage of Nations*, p. 66.

meet governmental requirements for local ownership, and allies can share distribution facilities and dealer networks, thus mutually strengthening their access to buyers. In addition, alliances affect competition; not only can alliances offset competitive disadvantages but they also can result in the allied companies directing their competitive energies more toward mutual rivals and less toward one another. Many runner-up companies, wanting to preserve their independence, have resorted to alliances rather than merger to try to close the competitive gap on leading companies.

Alliances have their pitfalls, however. Effective coordination between independent companies, each with different motives and perhaps conflicting objectives, is a challenging task requiring numerous meetings of numerous people over a period of time to iron out what is to be shared, what is to remain proprietary, and how the cooperative arrangements will work. Allies may have to overcome language and cultural barriers as well as suspicion and mistrust. After a promising start, relationships may cool, and the hoped-for benefits may never materialize. Most important, though, is the danger of depending on another company for essential expertise and capabilities over the long term. To be a serious contender, a company must ultimately develop its own capabilities in all areas important to strengthening its competitive position and building a sustainable competitive advantage. Where this is not feasible, merger is a better solution than strategic alliance. Strategic alliances are best used as a transitional way to combat competitive disadvantage in international markets; rarely if ever can they be relied on to create competitive advantage.

Strategic Intent, Profit Sanctuaries, and Cross-Subsidization

Competitors in international markets can be distinguished not only by their strategies but also by their long-term strategic objectives or strategic intent. Four types of competitors stand out:[18]

· · · · · · · · · · · ·

Competitors in international markets do not have the same strategic intent.

- Firms whose strategic intent is *global dominance* or, at least, high rank among the global market leaders; such firms pursue some form of global strategy.
- Firms whose primary strategic objective is *defending domestic dominance* in their home market, even though they derive some of their sales internationally (usually under 20 percent) and have operations in several or many foreign markets.
- Firms who aspire to a growing share of worldwide sales and whose primary strategic orientation is *host-country responsiveness*; such firms have a multicountry strategy and may already derive a large portion of their revenues from foreign operations.
- *Domestic-only firms* whose strategic intent does not extend beyond building a strong competitive position in their home country market; such firms base their competitive strategies on domestic market conditions and watch events in the international market only for their impact on domestic conditions.

---

[18]Prahalad and Doz, *The Multinational Mission*, p. 52.

The four types of firms are *not* equally well positioned to succeed in markets where they compete head-on. Consider the case of a purely domestic U.S. company in competition with a Japanese company operating in many country markets and aspiring to global dominance. The Japanese company can cut its prices in the U.S. market to gain market share at the expense of the U.S. company, subsidizing any losses with profits earned in its home sanctuary and in other foreign markets. The U.S. company has no effective way to retaliate. It is vulnerable even if it is the dominant domestic company. However, if the U.S. company is a multinational competitor and operates in Japan as well as elsewhere, it can counter Japanese pricing in the United States with retaliatory price cuts in its competitor's main profit sanctuary, Japan, and in other countries where it competes against the same Japanese company.

Profit Sanctuaries and Critical Markets   *Profit sanctuaries* are country markets where a company has a strong or protected market position and derives substantial profits. Japan, for example, is a profit sanctuary for most Japanese companies because trade barriers erected by the Japanese government effectively block foreign companies from competing for a large share of Japanese sales. Protected from the threat of foreign competition in their home market, Japanese companies can safely charge somewhat higher prices to their Japanese customers and thus earn attractively large profits at home. In most cases, a company's biggest and most strategically crucial profit sanctuary is its home market, but multinational companies also have profit sanctuaries in those country markets where they have strong competitive positions, big sales volumes, and attractive profit margins.

Profit sanctuaries are valuable competitive assets in global industries. Companies with large, protected profit sanctuaries have a competitive advantage over companies that don't have a dependable sanctuary. Companies with multiple profit sanctuaries are more favorably positioned than companies with a single sanctuary. Normally, a global competitor with multiple profit sanctuaries can successfully attack and beat a domestic competitor whose only profit sanctuary is its home market.

To defend against global competitors, firms don't have to compete in all or even most foreign markets, but they do have to compete in all critical markets; *critical markets* are markets in countries

- That are the profit sanctuaries of key competitors.
- That have big sales volumes.
- That contain prestigious customers whose business it is strategically important to have.
- That offer exceptionally good profit margins due to weak competitive pressures.[19]

The more critical markets a company participates in, the greater its ability to use cross-subsidization as a defense against competitors intent on global dominance.

• • • • • • • • • • • • •
Basic Concept
A nation becomes a company's profit sanctuary when a company, because of its strong competitive position or protective governmental trade policies, derives a substantial portion of its total profits from sales in that nation.

• • • • • • • • • • • • •
Competitive Strategy Principle
A global competitor with multiple profit sanctuaries can wage and generally win a competitive offensive against a domestic competitor whose only profit sanctuary is its home market.

---
[19]Ibid., p. 61.

As the chairman of British Aerospace recently observed, a strategic alliance with a foreign company is "one of the quickest and cheapest ways to develop a global strategy." AT&T has formed joint ventures with many of the world's largest telephone and electronics companies. Boeing, the world's premier manufacturer of commercial aircraft, has partnered with Kawasaki, Mitsubishi, and Fuji to produce a long-range, wide-body jet for delivery in 1995. General Electric and Snecma, a French maker of jet engines, have a 50-50 partnership to make jet engines to power aircraft made by Boeing, McDonnell-Douglas, and Airbus Industrie (the leading European maker of commercial aircraft and a company that was formed through an alliance among aerospace companies from Britain, Spain, Germany and France); the GE–Snecma alliance was regarded as a model because not only had it been in existence for 17 years but because it had also produced orders totaling $38 billion for 10,300 engines.

During the past 10 years, hundreds of strategic alliances have been formed in the motor vehicle industry as car and truck manufacturers and automotive parts suppliers moved aggressively to get in stronger position to compete globally. Not only have there been alliances between manufacturers strong in one region of the world and manufacturers strong in another region but there have also been strategic alliances between vehiclemakers and key parts suppliers (especially those with high-quality parts and strong technological capabilities).

General Motors and Toyota in 1984 formed a 50-50 partnership called New United Motor Manufacturing, Inc. (NUMMI) to produce cars for both companies at an old GM plant in Fremont, California. The strategic value of the GM–Toyota alliance was that Toyota would learn how to deal with suppliers and workers in the U.S. (as a prelude to building its own plants in the U.S.) while GM would learn about Toyota's approaches to manufacturing and management. Each company sent managers to the NUMMI plant to work for two to three years to learn and absorb all they could, then transferred their NUMMI "graduates" to jobs where they could be instrumental in helping their company apply what had been learned.

Gary Hamel, a professor at the London Business School, regards strategic alliances as a "race to learn" and gain the benefits of the partner's know-how and competitive capabilities. The partner that learns the fastest gains the most and, later, may turn such learning into a competitive edge. From this perspective, alliances become a new form of competition as well as a vehicle for globalizing company strategy. According to Hamel, Japanese managers and companies excel at learning from their allies and then exploiting the benefits. Toyota, for example, had moved quickly to capitalize on its experiences at NUMMI; by 1991 Toyota had opened two plants on its own in North America, was constructing a third plant, and was producing about 50 percent of the vehicles it sold

(continued)

The Competitive Power of Cross-Subsidization

Cross-subsidization is a powerful competitive weapon. It involves using profits earned in one or more country markets to support a competitive offensive against key rivals or to gain increased penetration of a critical market. Typically, a firm may match (or nearly match) rivals on product quality and service, then charge a low enough price to draw customers away from rivals. While price-cutting may entail lower profits (or even losses), the challenger still realizes acceptable overall profits when the above-average earnings from its profit sanctuaries are added in.

Cross-subsidization is most powerful when a global firm with multiple profit sanctuaries is aggressively intent on achieving global market dominance

ILLUSTRATION CAPSULE **14** *(concluded)*

in North America in its North American plants. While General Motors had incorporated much of its NUMMI learning into the management practices and manufacturing methods it was using at its newly opened Saturn plant in Tennessee, GM had moved more slowly than Toyota. American and European companies were generally regarded as less skilled than the Japanese in transferring the learning from strategic alliances into their own operations.

Consultants and business school professors who have studied company experiences with strategic alliances see four keys to making a strategic alliance work to good advantage:

- Picking a compatible partner, taking the time to build strong bridges of communication and trust, and not expecting immediate payoffs.
- Choosing an ally whose products and market strongholds *complement* rather than compete directly with the company's own products and customer base.
- Learning thoroughly and rapidly about a partner's technology and management.
- Being careful not to divulge competitively sensitive information to a partner.

Many alliances either fail or are terminated when one partner decides to acquire the other. A 1990 survey of 150 companies involved in terminated alliances found that three fourths of the alliances had been taken over by Japanese partners. A nine-year alliance between Fujitsu and International Computers, Ltd., a British manufacturer, ended when Fujitsu acquired 80 percent of ICL. According to one observer, Fujitsu deliberately maneuvered ICL into a position of having no better choice than to sell out to its partner; Fujitsu began as a supplier of components for ICL's mainframe computers, then expanded its role over the next nine years to the point where it was ICL's only source of new technology. When ICL's parent, a large British electronics firm, saw the mainframe computer business starting to decline and decided to sell, Fujitsu was the only buyer it could find.

There are several reasons why strategic alliances fail. Often, once the bloom is off the initial getting-together period, partners discover they have deep differences of opinion about how to proceed and conflicting objectives and strategies, such that tensions soon build up and cooperative working relationships never emerge. Another is the difficulty of collaborating effectively in competitively sensitive areas, thus raising questions about mutual trust and forthright exchanges of information and expertise. Perhaps the biggest reason is a clash of egos and company cultures—the key people upon whom success or failure depend turn out to be incompatible and incapable of working closely together on a partnership basis. On occasions, partners become suspicious about each other's motives and sometimes they are unwilling to share control and do things on the basis of consensus.

Source: Jeremy Main, "Making Global Alliances Work," *Fortune*, December 17, 1990, pp. 121–26.

over the long term. A domestic-only competitor and a multicountry competitor with no strategic coordination between its locally responsive country strategies are both vulnerable to competition from rivals intent on global dominance. A global strategy can defeat a domestic-only strategy because a one-country competitor cannot effectively defend its market share over the long term against a global competitor with cross-subsidization capability. The global company can use lower prices to siphon the domestic company's customers, all the while gaining market share, building market strength, and covering losses with profits earned in its other critical markets. When attacked in this manner, a domestic company's best short-term hope is to seek government

• • • • • • • • • • • •
Competitive Strategy Principle
To defend against aggressive international competitors intent on global dominance, a domestic-only competitor usually has to abandon its domestic focus, become a multinational competitor, and craft a multinational competitive strategy.

protection in the form of tariff barriers, import quotas, and antidumping penalties. In the long term, the domestic company must find ways to compete on a more equal footing—a difficult task when it must charge a price to cover average costs while the global competitor can charge a price only high enough to cover the incremental costs of selling in the domestic company's profit sanctuary. The best long-term strategic defenses for a domestic company are to enter into strategic alliances with foreign firms or adopt a global strategy and compete on an international scale. Competing only domestically is a perilous strategy in an industry populated with global competitors.

While a firm with a multicountry strategy has some cross-subsidy defense against a firm with a global strategy, it lacks competitive advantage and usually faces cost disadvantages. A global competitor with a big manufacturing share and state-of-the-art plants is typically a lower-cost producer than a multicountry strategist with many small plants and short production runs turning out specialized products country-by-country. Companies pursuing a multicountry strategy thus have to develop focusing and differentiation advantages keyed to local responsiveness to defend against a global competitor. Such a defense is adequate in industries with significant enough national differences to impede use of a global strategy. But if an international rival can accommodate necessary local needs within a global strategy and still retain a cost edge, then a global strategy can defeat a multicountry strategy. Illustration Capsule 15, which discusses how Nestlé became the world's number one food company, shows the power of a global strategy in today's markets.

STRATEGIES FOR INDUSTRY LEADERS

The competitive positions of industry leaders normally range from stronger than average to powerful. Leaders typically enjoy a well-known reputation, and strongly entrenched leaders have proven strategies (keyed either to low-cost leadership or differentiation). Some of the best-known industry leaders are Anheuser-Busch (beer), IBM (computers), McDonald's (fast food), Gillette (razor blades), Campbell Soup (canned soups), Gerber (baby food), AT&T (long-distance telephone service), and Levi Strauss (jeans). The main strategic concern for a leader revolves around how to sustain a leadership position, perhaps becoming the dominant leader as opposed to a leader. However, pursuit of industry leadership and large market share per se is primarily important because of the competitive advantage and profitability that accrues to leadership.

• • • • • • • • • • •
Industry leaders can strengthen their long-term competitive positions with strategies keyed to aggressive offense, aggressive defense, or muscling smaller rivals into a follow-the-leader role.

Three contrasting strategic postures are open to industry leaders and dominant firms:[20]

1. **Stay-on-the-offensive strategy**—This strategy rests on the principle that the best defense is a good offense. Offensive-minded leaders try to be "first-movers" to build a sustainable competitive advantage and a solid reputation as *the* leader. The key to staying on the offensive is relentless pursuit of continuous improvement and innovation. Striving

---

[20]Kotler, *Marketing Management*, chap. 23; Porter, *Competitive Advantage*, chap. 14; and Ian C. MacMillan, "Seizing Competitive Initiative," *The Journal of Business Strategy* 2, no. 4 (Spring 1982), pp. 43–57.

to become *the* source of new products, better performance features, quality enhancements, improved customer services, and ways to cut production costs not only helps a leader avoid complacency but it also keeps rivals on the defensive and scrambling to keep up. The array of offensive options also includes initiatives to expand overall industry demand—discovering new uses for the product, attracting new users, and promoting more frequent use. In addition, a clever offensive leader stays alert for ways to make it easier and less costly for potential customers to switch their purchases from runner-up firms over to its own products. Unless a leader's market share is already so dominant that it presents a threat of antitrust action (a market share under 60 percent is usually "safe"), then a stay-on-the-offensive strategy involves trying to grow *faster* than the industry as a whole and wrest market share from rivals. A leader whose growth does not equal or outpace the industry average is losing ground to competitors.

2. **Fortify and defend strategy**—The essence of "fortify and defend" is to make it harder for new firms to enter and for challengers to gain ground. The goals of a strong defense are to hold onto present market share, strengthen current market position, and protect whatever competitive advantage the firm has. Specific defensive actions can include:

   - Attempting to raise the competitive ante for challengers and new entrants via increased spending for advertising, customer service, and R&D.
   - Introducing more of the company's own brands to match the product attributes challenger brands have or could employ.
   - Figuring out ways to make it harder or more costly for customers to switch to rival products.
   - Broadening the product line to close off possible vacant niches for competitors to slip into.
   - Keeping prices reasonable and quality attractive.
   - Building new capacity ahead of market demand to try to block the market expansion potential of smaller competitors.
   - Investing enough to remain cost competitive and technologically progressive.
   - Patenting alternative technologies.
   - Signing exclusive contracts with the best suppliers and dealer/distributors.

   A fortify-and-defend strategy best suits firms that have already achieved industry dominance and don't wish to risk antitrust action. It is also well-suited to situations where a firm wishes to milk its present position for profits and cash flow because the industry's prospects for growth are low or because further gains in market share do not appear profitable enough to go after. But the fortify-and-defend theme always entails trying to grow as fast as the market as a whole (to stave off market share slippage) and reinvesting enough capital in the business to protect the leader's ability to compete.

ILLUSTRATION CAPSULE   15   NESTLÉ'S GLOBAL STRATEGY IN FOODS

Once a stodgy Swiss manufacturer of chocolate, Nestlé became one of the first multinational companies and then embarked on a global strategy during the 1980s. The themes of the Nestlé strategy were: acquire a wider lineup of name brands, achieve the economies of worldwide distribution and marketing, accept short-term losses to build a more profitable market share over the long term, and adapt products to local cultures when needed. In 1991 Nestlé ranked as the world's largest food company with over $33 billion in revenues, market penetration on all major continents, and plants in over 60 countries (see table below).

The Nestlé strategy was a response to two driving forces affecting the food industry in more and more nations around the globe: (1) changing consumer demographics, tastes, and cooking habits; and (2) the new cost-volume economics of increasingly "high-tech" food products like gourmet dinners, refrigerated foods, packaged mixes, and even coffee. In both industrialized and developing nations, the 1980s were characterized by growing numbers of relatively affluent single professionals and two-income couples with more cosmopolitan food tastes and less price-sensitive grocery budgets. Moreover, microwave ovens were fast becoming a standard household item, a development that not only affected weeknight and weekend food preparation methods but also changed the kinds of at-home food products people were buying. Products that appealed to this segment had tremendous growth potential. However, bringing such items to market was quickly turned into a high-risk, capital-intensive, R&D-oriented business that required millions of dollars of up-front capital for new product development and market testing, and millions more for advertising and promotional support to win shelf space in grocery chains. To get maximum mileage out of such investments, make up for the cost of product failures, and keep retail prices affordable began to take a larger and larger volume of sales, often more than could be generated from a single national market.

Nestlé management grasped early on that these driving forces would act to globalize the food industry and that companies with worldwide distribution capability, strong brand names, and the flexibility to adapt versions of the basic

Continent	1990 Sales	Major Products
Europe	$16.3 billion	Nescafé instant coffee, Vittel mineral water, Chambourcy yogurt, Findus and Lean Cuisine frozen foods, Herta cold cuts, Sundy cereal bars, chocolate candy, Buitoni pasta
North America	$ 8.3 billion	Nescafé instant coffee, Carnation CoffeeMate, Friskies pet foods, Stouffer frozen foods, Nestlé Crunch chocolate bars, Hills Bros. coffee
Asia	$ 3.6 billion	Nescafé instant coffee, Nido powdered milk, Maggi chili powder, infant cereals, and formulas
Latin America	$ 3.6 billion	Nescafé instant coffee, Nido powdered milk, infant cereal, Milo malt flavored beverages
Africa	$ 1.0 billion	Nescafé instant coffee, Maggi bouillon cubes, Nespray powdered milk, Nestlé chocolates, Milo malt-flavored beverages
Oceania (Australia, New Zealand)	$ 0.9 billion	Nescafé instant coffee, Findus frozen foods, Lean Cuisine frozen foods

(continued)

ILLUSTRATION CAPSULE 15 *(concluded)*

product to local tastes would gain significant competitive advantages. A series of acquisitions gave Nestlé a strong lineup of brands, some important new food products to push through its distribution channels, and a bigger presence in some key country markets. In 1985 Nestlé bought Carnation (Pet evaporated milk, Friskies pet foods, and CoffeeMate nondairy creamer) and Hills Bros. coffee (the number three coffee brand in the United States) to strengthen its North American presence. In 1988, Nestlé acquired Rountree, a British chocolate company whose leading candy bar is Kit Kat, and Buitoni, an Italian pastamaker. Shortly after the Rountree acquisition, Nestlé management shifted worldwide responsibility for mapping chocolate strategy and developing new candy products from Nestlé headquarters in Vevey, Switzerland, to Rountree's headquarters in York, England. Nestlé management believed this decentralization put the company's candy business in the hands of people "who think about chocolate 24 hours a day." As of 1989, almost everything Nestlé sold involved food products, and the company was the world's largest producer of coffee, powdered milk, candy, and frozen dinners.

The star performer in Nestlé's lineup was coffee, with 1990 sales of $5.2 billion and operating profits of $600 million. Nestlé's Nescafé brand was the leader in virtually every national market except the United States (Philip Morris's Maxwell House brand was the U.S. leader, but Nescafé was number two and Hills Bros., purchased by Nestlé in 1985, was number three). Nestlé produced 200 types of instant coffee, from lighter blends for the U.S. market to dark espressos for Latin America. Four coffee research labs spent a combined $50 million annually to experiment with new blends in aroma, flavor, and color. Although instant coffee sales were declining worldwide due to the comeback of new-style automatic coffeemakers, they were rising in two tea-drinking countries, Britain and Japan. As the cultural shift from tea to coffee took hold during the 1970s in Britain, Nestlé pushed its Nescafé brand hard, coming out with a market share of about 50 percent. In Japan, Nescafé was considered a luxury item; the company made it available in fancy containers suitable for gift-giving.

Another star performer has been the company's Lean Cuisine line of low-calorie frozen dinners produced by Stouffer, a company Nestlé acquired in the 1970s. Introduced in 1981 in the United States, the Lean Cuisine line has boosted Stouffer's U.S. market share in frozen dinners to 38 percent. To follow up on its U.S. success, Nestlé introduced Lean Cuisine into the British market. At the time, Nestlé products in British supermarkets were mostly low-margin items, from fish sticks to frozen hamburger patties. British managers proposed a bold upgrading to a line of more expensive, high-margin items led by Lean Cuisine. Nestlé headquarters endorsed the plan and indicated a willingness to absorb four years of losses to build market share and make Lean Cuisine a transatlantic hit. The Lean Cuisine line was introduced in Britain in 1985. By 1988 the Lean Cuisine line in Britain included 12 entrées tailored to British tastes, from cod with wine sauce to Kashmiri chicken curry. By 1989 Nestlé had a 33 percent share of the British market for frozen dinners. Sales exceeded $100 million in 1990, putting the Lean Cuisine brand into the black in Britain for the first time since its introduction to the British market. Lean Cuisine has recently been introduced in France.

Western Europe is Nestlé's top target for the early 1990s. The 1992 shift to free trade among the 12 member countries in the European Community will sweep away trade barriers which, according to a recent study, cost food companies over $1 billion in added distribution and marketing costs. With market unification in the 12-country EC, Nestlé sees major opportunities to gain wider distribution of its products, achieve economies, and exploit its skills in transferring products and marketing methods from one country and culture to another.

Source: The information in this capsule was drawn from Shawn Tully, "Nestlé Shows How to Gobble Markets," *Fortune*, January 16, 1989, pp. 74–78 and Nestlé's 1990 annual report.

3. **Follow-the-leader strategy**—The objective of this strategy is to enforce an unwritten tradition that smaller firms follow the industry leader in adjusting prices up or down and otherwise don't try to rock the boat. Assuming the role of industry policeman gives a leader added strategic flexibility and makes it risky for runner-up firms to mount an offensive attack on the leader's position. In effect, the leader uses its competitive muscle to thwart and discourage would-be challengers. The leader signals smaller rivals that any moves to cut into the leader's business will meet with strong retaliation. Specific "hardball" policing actions include quickly meeting all price cuts (with even larger cuts if necessary), countering with large-scale promotional campaigns when challengers make threatening moves to gain market share, and offering better deals to the major customers of next-in-line or "maverick" firms. Other measures that a leader can use to bully aggressive small rivals into playing follow-the-leader include pressuring distributors not to carry rivals' products, having salespeople bad-mouth the aggressor's products, and trying to hire away the better executives of firms that "get out of line."

STRATEGIES FOR RUNNER-UP FIRMS

Runner-up firms occupy weaker market positions than the industry leader(s). Some runner-ups play the role of *market challengers*, favoring offensive strategies to gain market share and a stronger market position. Others behave as *content followers*, willing to coast along in their current positions because profits are still adequate. Follower firms have no urgent strategic issue to confront beyond that of "What kinds of strategic changes are the leaders initiating and what do we need to do to follow?"

- - - - - - - - - - - -
Competitive Strategy Principle

Rarely can a runner-up firm successfully challenge an industry leader with an imitative strategy.

A challenger firm interested in improving its market standing needs a strategy aimed at building a competitive advantage of its own. *Rarely can a runner-up improve its competitive position by imitating the leading firm. A cardinal rule in offensive strategy is to avoid attacking a leader head-on with an imitative strategy, regardless of the resources and staying power an underdog may have.*[21] Moreover, if a challenger has a 5 percent market share and needs a 20 percent share to earn attractive returns, it needs a more creative approach to competing than just "try harder."

In cases where large size yields significantly lower unit costs and gives large-share firms an important cost advantage, small-share firms have only two viable strategic options: increase their market share or withdraw from the business (gradually or quickly). The competitive strategies most used to build market share are based on (1) becoming a lower-cost producer and using lower price to win customers from weak, higher-cost rivals and (2) using differentiation strategies based on quality, technological superiority, better customer service, best-cost, or innovation. Achieving low-cost leadership is usually open to an underdog only when one of the market leaders is not already solidly positioned as the industry's low-cost producer. But a small-share firm may still be able to reduce its cost disadvantage by merging with or acquiring smaller firms; the combined market shares may provide the needed access to size-related

---

[21]Porter, *Competitive Advantage*, p. 514.

economies. Other options include revamping the activity-cost chain to produce cost savings and finding ways to better control cost drivers.

In situations where scale economies or experience curve effects are small and a large market share produces no cost advantage, runner-up companies have more strategic flexibility and can consider any of the following six approaches:[22]

1. **Vacant niche strategy**—This version of a focus strategy involves concentrating on customer or end-use applications that major firms have bypassed or neglected. An "ideal" vacant niche is of sufficient size and scope to be profitable, has some growth potential, is well-suited to a firm's own capabilities and skills, and is outside the interest of leading firms. For example, regional commuter airlines serve cities with too few passengers to attract the interest of major airlines, and health food producers (like Health Valley, Hain, and Tree of Life) supply the growing number of local health food stores—a market segment traditionally ignored by Pillsbury, Kraft General Foods, Heinz, Nabisco, Campbell Soup, and other leading food products firms.

2. **Specialist strategy**—A specialist firm trains its competitive effort on one market segment: a single product, a particular end-use, or a special customer group. The aim is to build competitive advantage through product uniqueness, expertise in special-purpose products, or specialized customer services. Smaller companies that have successfully used a specialist type of focus strategy include Formby's (a specialist in stains and finishes for wood furniture, especially refinishing), Liquid Paper Co. (a leader in correction fluid for typists), Canada Dry (known for its ginger ale, tonic water, and carbonated soda water), and American Tobacco (a leader in chewing tobacco and snuff).

3. **"Ours-is-better-than-theirs strategy"**—This approach uses a combination focus-differentiation strategy keyed to product quality. Sales and marketing efforts focus on quality-conscious and performance-oriented buyers. Fine craftsmanship, prestige quality, frequent product innovations, and/or close contact with customers to develop a better product usually undergird this "superior product" type of approach. Some examples include Beefeater and Tanqueray in gin, Tiffany in diamonds and jewelry, Baccarat in fine crystal, Mazola in cooking oil and margarine, Bally in shoes, and Pennzoil in motor oil.

4. **Content follower strategy**—Follower firms deliberately refrain from initiating trend-setting strategic moves and from aggressive attempts to steal customers away from leaders. Followers prefer approaches that will not provoke competitive retaliation, often opting for focus and differentiation strategies that keep them out of the leaders' paths. They react and respond rather than initiate and attack. They prefer defense to offense. And they rarely get out of line with the leaders on price. Burroughs (in computers) and Union Camp (in paper products) have been successful market followers by consciously concentrating on

---

[22]For more details, see Kotler, *Marketing Management*, pp. 397-412; R. G. Hamermesh, M. J. Anderson, Jr., and J. E. Harris, "Strategies for Low Market Share Businesses," *Harvard Business Review* 56, no. 3 (May–June 1978), pp. 95–102; and Porter, *Competitive Advantage*, chap. 15.

selected product uses and applications for specific customer groups, focused R&D, profits rather than market share, and cautious but efficient management.

5. **Growth via acquisition strategy**—One way to strengthen a company's position is to merge with or acquire weaker rivals to form an enterprise that has more competitive strength and a larger share of the market. Commercial airline companies such as Northwest, US Air, and Delta owe their market share growth during the past decade to acquisition of smaller regional airlines. Likewise, public accounting firms have enhanced their national and international coverage by merging or forming alliances with smaller CPA firms at home and abroad.

6. **Distinctive image strategy**—Some runner-up companies try to stand out from competitors. They use a variety of strategic approaches: creating a reputation for the lowest prices, providing prestige quality at a good price, giving superior customer service, designing unique product attributes, being a leader in new product introduction, or devising unusually creative advertising. Examples include Dr Pepper's strategy of calling attention to its distinctive taste, Apple Computer's approach to making it easier and interesting for people to use a personal computer, and Honda's emphasis on the quality and dependability of its cars.

In industries where big size is definitely a key success factor, firms with low market shares have some obstacles to overcome: (1) less access to economies of scale in manufacturing, distribution, or sales promotion; (2) difficulty in gaining customer recognition; (3) an inability to afford mass media advertising on a grand scale; and (4) difficulty in funding capital requirements.[23] But *it is erroneous to view runner-up firms as inherently less profitable or unable to hold their own against the biggest firms.* Many firms with small market shares earn healthy profits and enjoy good reputations with customers. Often, the handicaps of smaller size can be surmounted and a profitable competitive position established by: (1) focusing on a few market segments where the company's strengths can yield a competitive edge; (2) developing technical expertise that will be highly valued by customers; (3) aggressively pursuing the development of new products for customers in the target market segments; and (4) using innovative, "dare-to-be different," "beat-the-odds" entrepreneurial approaches to outmanage stodgy, slow-to-change market leaders. Runner-up companies have a golden opportunity to gain market share if they make a leapfrog technological breakthrough, if the leaders stumble or become complacent, or if they have patience to nibble away at the leaders and build up their customer base over a long period of time.

STRATEGIES FOR WEAK BUSINESSES

A firm in an also-ran or declining competitive position has four basic strategic options. If it has the financial resources, it can launch a modest *strategic offensive* keyed either to low-cost production or "new" differentiation themes, pouring

---

[23]Hamermesh, Anderson, and Harris, "Strategies for Low Market Share Businesses," p. 102.

enough money and talent into the effort to move up a notch or two in the industry rankings. It can pursue *aggressive defense*, using variations of the present strategy and fighting hard to keep sales, market share, profitability, and competitive position at current levels. It can opt for an *immediate abandonment* strategy and get out of the business, either by selling out to another firm or by closing down operations if a buyer cannot be found. Or it can employ a *harvest strategy*, keeping reinvestment to a bare-bones minimum and maximizing short-term cash flows in preparation for an orderly exit. The gist of the first three options is self-explanatory. The fourth merits more discussion.

> *A competitively weak company can wage a modest offensive to improve its position, defend its present position, be acquired by another company, or employ a harvest strategy.*

A *harvest strategy* steers a middle course between preserving the status quo and exiting as soon as possible. Harvesting is a phasing down or endgame strategy where the game plan is to sacrifice market position any time short-term financial benefits can be realized. The overriding financial objective is to reap the greatest possible cash harvest to deploy to other business endeavors.

Harvesting actions are fairly standard. Firms cut their operating budgets to rock-bottom and pursue stringent internal cost control. Capital investment in new equipment is minimal or nonexistent depending on the current condition of fixed assets and whether the harvest is to be fast or slow. Firms may gradually raise prices and cut promotional expenses, reduce quality in not so visible ways, curtail nonessential customer services, decrease equipment maintenance, and the like. They understand that sales will shrink, but if they cut costs proportionately, profits will erode slowly.

Professor Kotler has suggested seven indicators of when a business should be harvested:[24]

1. When the industry's long-term prospects are unattractive.
2. When building up the business would be too costly or not profitable enough.
3. When the firm's market share is becoming increasingly costly to maintain or defend.
4. When reduced levels of competitive effort will not trigger an immediate falloff in sales.
5. When the enterprise can redeploy the freed resources in higher opportunity areas.
6. When the business is *not* a major component in a diversified corporation's portfolio of existing businesses.
7. When the business does not contribute other desired features (sales stability, prestige, a well-rounded product line) to a company's overall business portfolio.

The more of these seven conditions present, the more ideal the business is for harvesting.

Harvesting strategies make the most sense for diversified companies that have business units with respectable market shares in unattractive industries. In such situations, cash flows from harvesting unattractive business units can be reallocated to business units with greater profit potential in more attractive industries.

---

[24]Phillip Kotler, "Harvesting Strategies for Weak Products," *Business Horizons* 21, no. 5 (August 1978), pp. 17–18.

Crisis Turnarounds

Turnaround strategies are used when a business worth rescuing goes into crisis; the objective is to arrest and reverse the sources of competitive and financial weakness as quickly as possible. The first task is to diagnose the problem: What is causing the poor performance? Is it bad competitive strategy or poor implementation and execution of an otherwise workable strategy? Are the causes of distress beyond management control? Can the business be saved? To formulate a turnaround strategy, managers must find the problem and determine how serious it is.

Successful turnaround strategies depend on accurate diagnosis of a distressed company's situation and decisive action to resolve its problems.

Some of the most common causes of business trouble are: overly aggressive efforts to "buy" market share with profit-depressing price-cuts, heavy fixed costs due to underutilized plant capacity, ineffective R&D efforts, reliance on technological long-shots, inability to penetrate new markets, frequent changes in strategy (because the previous strategy didn't work out), and being overpowered by the competitive advantages of more successful rivals. There are five ways to pursue business turnaround:[25]

- Revise the existing strategy.
- Launch efforts to boost revenues.
- Pursue cost reduction.
- Sell off assets to raise cash to save the remaining part of the business.
- Use a combination of these efforts.

Strategy Revision   When weak performance is caused by "bad" strategy, the task of strategy overhaul can proceed along any of several paths: (1) shifting to a new competitive approach to rebuild the firm's market position, (2) overhauling internal operations and functional area strategies to better support the same overall business strategy, (3) merging with another firm in the industry and forging a new strategy keyed to the newly merged firm's strengths, and (4) retrenching into a reduced core of products and customers more closely matched to the firm's strengths. The most appealing path depends on prevailing industry conditions, the firm's particular strengths and weaknesses, and the severity of the crisis. "Situation analysis" of the industry, major competitors, the firm's own competitive position, and its skills and resources are prerequisites to action. As a rule, successful strategy revision must be tied directly to the ailing firm's strengths and near-term competitive capabilities and must focus narrowly on its best market opportunities.

Boosting Revenues   Revenue-increasing turnaround efforts aim at generating increased sales volume. There are a number of revenue-building options: price-cuts, increased promotion, a bigger sales force, added customer services, and quickly achieved product improvements. Attempts to increase revenues and sales volumes are necessary (1) when there is little or no room in the operating budget to cut expenses and still break even and (2) when the key

[25]For excellent discussions of the ins and outs of rescuing distressed firms, see Charles W. Hofer, "Turnaround Strategies," *Journal of Business Strategy* 1, no. 1 (Summer 1980), pp. 19–31; Donald F. Heany, " Businesses in Profit Trouble," *Journal of Business Strategy* 5, no. 4 (Spring 1985), pp. 4–13; and Eugene F. Finkin, "Company Turnaround," *Journal of Business Strategy* 5, no. 4 (Spring 1985), pp. 14–25.

to restoring profitability is increased utilization of existing capacity. In rare situations where buyer demand is not price sensitive, the quickest way to boost short-term revenues may be to raise prices rather than opt for volume-building price cuts.

Cutting Costs   Cost-reducing turnaround strategies work best when an ailing firm's cost structure is flexible enough to permit radical surgery, when operating inefficiencies are identifiable and readily correctable, and when the firm is relatively close to its break-even point. To complement a general belt-tightening, firms need to emphasize budgeting and cost control, eliminate jobs and stop hiring, modernize existing plant and equipment to gain greater productivity, and delay nonessential capital expenditures.

Selling Off Assets   Asset reduction/retrenchment strategies are essential when cash flow is a critical consideration and when the most practical way to generate cash is (1) through sale of some of the firm's assets (plant and equipment, land, patents, inventories, or profitable subsidiaries) and (2) through retrenchment (pruning marginal products from the product line, closing or selling older plants, reducing the work force, withdrawing from outlying markets, cutting back customer service, and the like). Sometimes firms sell their assets not so much to unload losing operations and stem cash drains as to raise funds to save and strengthen their remaining activities.

Combination Efforts   Combination turnaround strategies are usually essential in grim situations that require fast action on a broad front. Likewise, combination actions frequently come into play when a firm brings in new managers and gives them a free hand to make changes. The tougher the problems, the more likely the solutions will involve multiple strategic initiatives.

Turnaround efforts tend to be high-risk undertakings and often fail. A landmark study of 64 companies found no successful turnarounds among the most troubled companies in eight basic industries.[26] Many waited too long to begin a turnaround. Others found themselves short of both cash and entrepreneurial talent to compete in a slow-growth industry characterized by fierce battles for market share; better positioned rivals simply proved too strong to defeat.

THIRTEEN COMMANDMENTS FOR CRAFTING SUCCESSFUL BUSINESS STRATEGIES

Business experiences over the years prove over and over that disastrous courses of action can be avoided by adhering to certain strategy-making principles. The wisdom of these past experiences can be distilled into 13 commandments which, if faithfully observed, help strategists craft better strategic action plans.

1. *Always put top priority on crafting and executing strategic moves that enhance the company's competitive position for the long term and that*

---

[26]William K. Hall, "Survival Strategies in a Hostile Environment," *Harvard Business Review* 58, no. 5 (September–October 1980), pp. 75–85.

serve to establish it as an industry leader. In competitive markets, a strongly entrenched leadership position pays off year after year, but the glory of meeting one year's financial targets quickly passes. Shareholders are never well-served by managers who let short-term financial considerations override strategic initiatives that will bolster the company's long-term competitive position and strength.

2. *Understand that a clear, consistent competitive strategy, when well-crafted and well-executed, builds reputation and recognizable industry position; a strategy aimed solely at capturing momentary market opportunities yields fleeting benefits.* The pursuit of short-run financial opportunism without long-term strategic guidance tends to produce the worst kind of profits: one-shot rewards that are unrepeatable. Over the long haul, a company that has a well-conceived competitive strategy aimed at securing a strong market position will outperform and defeat a rival whose strategic decisions are driven by short-term financial expectations. In an ongoing enterprise, the game of competition ought to be played for the long term, not the short term.

3. *Try not to get "stuck back in the pack" with no coherent long-term strategy or distinctive competitive position, an "average" image, and little prospect of climbing into the ranks of the industry leaders.*

4. *Invest in creating a sustainable competitive advantage*—it is the single most dependable contributor to above-average profitability.

5. *Play aggressive offense to build competitive advantage and aggressive defense to protect it.*

6. *Avoid strategies capable of succeeding only in the best of circumstances*—competitors will react with countermeasures and market conditions are not always favorable.

7. *Be cautious in pursuing a rigidly prescribed or inflexible strategy—changing market conditions may render it quickly obsolete.* Any strategy, to perform satisfactorily, must be adaptable to fresh market circumstances. Strategic themes involving "top" quality or "lowest" cost should be interpreted as *relative to competitors* and/or *customer needs* rather than based on arbitrary management standards.

8. *Don't underestimate the reactions and the commitment of rivals*—especially when they are pushed into a corner and their well-being is threatened.

9. *Be wary of attacking strong, resourceful rivals without solid competitive advantage and ample financial strength.*

10. *Consider that attacking competitive weakness is usually more profitable than attacking competitive strength.*

11. *Take care not to cut prices without an established cost advantage*—only a low-cost producer can win at price-cutting over the long term.

12. *Be aware that aggressive moves to wrest market share away from rivals often provoke aggressive retaliation in the form of a marketing "arms race" and/or price wars—to the detriment of everyone's profits.* Aggressive moves to capture a bigger market share invite cutthroat competition particularly when the market is plagued with high inventories and excess production capacity.

13. *Employ bold strategic moves in pursuing differentiation strategies to open up meaningful gaps in quality, service, or performance features.* Tiny differences between rivals' competitive strategies and product offerings may not be visible or important to buyers.

KEY POINTS

Successful strategies fit a firm's *external* situation (industry and competitive conditions) and *internal* situation (strengths, weaknesses, opportunities, and threats). Table 6–2 provides a summary checklist of the most important situational considerations and strategic options. To match strategy to the situation, analysts must start with an overview of the industry environment and the firm's competitive standing in the industry (columns 1 and 2 in Table 6–2):

1. What type of industry environment does the company operate in (emerging, rapid growth, mature, fragmented, global, commodity product)? What strategic options and strategic postures are best suited for this environment?

2. What position does the firm have in the industry (strong vs. weak vs. crisis-ridden; leader vs. runner-up vs. also-ran)? How does the firm's standing influence its strategic options given the stage of the industry's development—in particular, which options have to be ruled out?

Next, strategists need to factor in the primary external and internal situational consideratons (column 3) and decide how all the factors add up. This should narrow the firm's basic market share and investment options (column 4) and strategic options (column 5).

The final step is to custom-tailor the chosen generic strategic approaches (columns 4 and 5) to fit *both* the industry environment and the firm's standing vis-à-vis competitors. Here it is important to be sure that (1) the customized aspects of the proposed strategy are well-matched to the firm's skills and capabilities and (2) the strategy addresses all strategic issues the firm confronts.

In screening out weak strategies and weighing the pros and cons of the most attractive ones, the answers to the following questions often indicate the way to go:

- What kind of competitive edge can the company realistically hope to have, and what strategic moves/approaches will it take to secure this edge?

- Does the company have the skills and resources to succeed in these moves and approaches—if not, can they be acquired?

- Once built, how can the competitive advantage be protected? What defensive strategies need to be employed? Will rivals counterattack? What will it take to blunt their efforts?

- Are any rivals particularly vulnerable? Should the firm mount an offensive to capitalize on these vulnerabilities? What offensive moves need to be employed?

- What additional strategic moves are needed to deal with driving forces in the industry, specific threats and weaknesses, and any other issues/problems unique to the firm?

T A B L E 6-2   Matching Strategy to the Situation   *(A checklist of optional strategies and generic situations)*

Industry Environments	Company Positions/Situations	Situational Considerations	Market Share and Investment Options	Strategy Options
• Young, emerging industry	• Dominant leader	• External	• Growth and build	• Competitive approach
• Rapid growth	– Global	– Driving forces	– Capture a bigger market share by growing faster than industry as a whole	– Overall low-cost leadership
• Consolidating to a smaller group of competitors	– National	– Competitive pressures	– Invest heavily to capture growth potential	– Differentiation
• Mature/slow growth	– Regional	– Anticipated moves of key rivals	• Fortify and defend	– Focus/specialization
• Aging/declining	– Local	– Key success factors	– Protect market share; grow at least as fast as whole industry	• Offensive initiatives
• Fragmented	• Leader	– Industry attractiveness	– Invest enough resources to maintain competitive strength and market position	– Attack
• International/global	• Aggressive challenger	• Internal	• Retrench and retreat	– End run
• Commodity product orientation	• Content follower	– Current company performance	– Surrender weakly held positions when forced to, but fight hard to defend core markets/customer base	– Guerrilla warfare
• High technology/rapid changes	• Weak/distressed candidate for turn-around or exit	– Strengths and weaknesses	– Maximize short-term cash flow	– Preemptive strikes
	• "Stuck in the middle"/no clear strategy or market image	– Opportunities and threats	– Minimize reinvestment of capital in the business	• Defensive initiatives
		– Cost position	• Overhaul and reposition	– Fortify/protect
		– Competitive strength	– Try to turn around	– Retaliatory
		– Strategic issues and problems	• Abandon/liquidate	– Harvest
			– Sell out	• International initiatives
			– Close down	– Licensing
				– Export
				– Multicountry
				– Global
				• Vertical integration initiatives
				– Forward
				– Backward

TABLE 6–3   Sample Format for a Strategic Action Plan

1. Basic long-term direction and mission

2. Key strategic and financial objectives

3. Overall business strategy

4. Specific functional strategies
   • Production
   • Marketing/sales
   • Finance
   • Personnel/human resources
   • Other

5. Recommended actions

As the choice of strategic initiatives is developed, there are several pitfalls to watch for:

- Designing an overly ambitious strategic plan—one that calls for a lot of different strategic moves and/or that overtaxes the company's resources and capabilities.
- Selecting a strategy that represents a radical departure from or abandonment of the cornerstones of the company's prior success—a radical strategy change need not be rejected automatically, but it should be pursued only after careful risk assessment.
- Choosing a strategy that goes against the grain of the organization's culture or that conflicts with the values and philosophies of senior executives.

Table 6–3 provides a format for presenting a strategic action plan for a single-business enterprise.

Bleeke, Joel A. "Strategic Choices for Newly Opened Markets." *Harvard Business Review* 68, no. 5 (September–October 1990), pp. 158–65.

Bolt, James F. "Global Competitors: Some Criteria for Success." *Business Horizons* 31, no. 1 (January–February 1988), pp. 34–41.

Carroll, Glenn R. "The Specialist Strategy." In *Strategy and Organization: A West Coast Perspective*, ed. Glenn Carroll and David Vogel. Boston: Pitman Publishing, 1984, pp. 117–28.

Feldman, Lawrence P., and Albert L. Page. "Harvesting: The Misunderstood Market Exit Strategy." *Journal of Business Strategy* 5, no. 4 (Spring 1985), pp. 79–85.

Finkin, Eugene F. "Company Turnaround." *Journal of Business Strategy* 5, no. 4 (Spring 1985), pp. 14–25.

SUGGESTED
READINGS

Hall, William K. "Survival Strategies in a Hostile Environment." *Harvard Business Review* 58, no. 5 (September–October 1980), pp. 75–85.

Hamermesh, R. G., and S. B. Silk. "How to Compete in Stagnant Industries." *Harvard Business Review* 57, no. 5 (September–October 1979), pp. 161–68.

Harrigan, Kathryn R. *Strategic Flexibility*. Lexington, Mass.: Lexington Books, 1985, chaps. 6 and 8.

Heany, Donald F. "Businesses in Profit Trouble." *Journal of Business Strategy* 5, no. 4 (Spring 1985), pp. 4–13.

Hofer, Charles W. "Turnaround Strategies." *Journal of Business Strategy* 1, no. 1 (Summer 1980), pp. 19–31.

Hout, Thomas, Michael E. Porter, and Eileen Rudden. "How Global Companies Win Out." *Harvard Business Review* 60, no. 5 (September–October 1982), pp. 98–108.

Kotler, Philip. *Marketing Management: Analysis, Planning, Control,* 5th ed. Englewood Cliffs, N.J.: Prentice Hall, 1984, chap. 11.

Lei, David. "Strategies for Global Competition." *Long Range Planning* 22, no. 1 (February 1989), pp. 102–9.

Mayer, Robert J. "Winning Strategies for Manufacturers in Mature Industries." *Journal of Business Strategy* 8, no. 2 (Fall 1987), pp. 23–31.

Ohmae, Kenichi. "The Global Logic of Strategic Alliances." *Harvard Business Review* 67, no. 2 (March–April 1989), pp. 143–54.

Porter, Michael E. *Competitive Strategy: Techniques for Analyzing Industries and Competitors*. New York: Free Press, 1980, chaps. 9–13.

Porter, Michael E. *The Competitive Advantage of Nations*. New York: Free Press, 1990, chap. 2.

Sugiura, Hideo, "How Honda Localizes Its Global Strategy." *Sloan Management Review* 33 (Fall 1990), pp. 77–82.

Thompson, Arthur A. "Strategies for Staying Cost Competitive." *Harvard Business Review* 62, no. 1 (January–February 1984), pp. 110–17.

Corporate Diversification Strategies

. . . to acquire or not to acquire: that is the question.
~Robert J. Terry

• • • • • • • •

Strategy is a deliberate search for a plan of action that will develop a business's competitive advantage and compound it.
~Bruce D. Henderson

In this chapter and the next, we move up one level in the strategy-making hierarchy. Attention shifts from formulating strategy for a single-business enterprise to formulating strategy for a diversified enterprise. Because a diversified company is a collection of individual businesses, corporate strategy-making is a bigger-picture exercise than crafting strategy for a single-business company. In a single-business enterprise, management only has to contend with one industry environment and how to compete successfully in it. But in a diversified company, corporate managers have to craft a multibusiness, multi-industry strategic action plan for a number of different business divisions competing in diverse industry environments. Managing a group of diverse businesses is usually so time-consuming and complex that corporate-level managers delegate lead responsibility for business-level strategy-making to the head of each business unit.

As explained in Chapter 2, a corporate strategy in a diversified company concentrates on:

1. Making moves to position the company in the industries chosen for diversification (the basic strategy options here are to acquire a company in the target industry, form a joint venture with another company to enter the target industry, or start a new company internally and try to grow it from the ground up).

2. Taking actions to improve the long-term performance of the corporation's portfolio of businesses once diversification has been

161

achieved (helping to strengthen the competitive positions of existing businesses, divesting businesses that no longer fit into management's long-range plans, and adding new businesses to the portfolio).

3. Trying to capture whatever strategic fit benefits exist within the portfolio of businesses and turn them into competitive advantage.

4. Evaluating the profit prospects of each business unit and steering corporate resources into the most attractive strategic opportunities.

In this chapter we survey the generic type of corporate diversification strategies and how competitive advantage can result from a company's diversification approach. In Chapter 8 we will examine how to assess the strategic attractiveness of a diversified company's business portfolio.

FROM SINGLE-BUSINESS CONCENTRATION TO DIVERSIFICATION

Most companies begin as small single-business enterprises serving a local or regional market. During a company's early years, its product line tends to be limited, its capital base thin, and its competitive position vulnerable. Usually, a young company's strategic emphasis is on increasing sales volume, boosting market share, and cultivating a loyal clientele. Profits are reinvested and new debt is taken on to grow the business as fast as conditions permit. Price, quality, service, and promotion are tailored more precisely to customer needs. As soon as practical, the product line is broadened to meet variations in customer wants and end-use applications.

Opportunities for geographical market expansion are normally pursued next. The natural sequence of geographic expansion proceeds from local to regional to national to international markets, though the degree of penetration may be uneven from area to area because of varying profit potentials. Geographic expansion may, of course, stop well short of global or even national proportions because of intense competition, lack of resources, or the unattractiveness of further market coverage.

Somewhere along the way the potential for vertical integration, either backward to sources of supply or forward to the ultimate consumer, may become a strategic consideration. Generally, vertical integration makes strategic sense only if it significantly enhances a company's profitability and competitive strength.

So long as the company has its hands full trying to capitalize on profitable growth opportunities in its present industry, there is no urgency to pursue diversification. But when company growth potential starts to wane, the strategic options are either to become more aggressive in taking market share away from rivals or diversify into other lines of businesses. A decision to diversify raises the question of "what kind and how much diversification?" The strategic possibilities are wide open. A company can diversify into closely related or totally unrelated businesses. It can diversify to a small extent (less than 10 percent of total revenues and profits) or to a large extent (up to 50 percent). It can move into one or two large new businesses or a greater number of small ones. And once it achieves diversification, the time may come when management has to consider divesting or liquidating businesses that are no longer attractive.

- - - - - - - - - - - - -
Strategic Management Principle

Diversification doesn't need to become a strategic priority until a company begins to run out of growth opportunities in its core business.

Why a Single-Business Strategy Is Attractive

Companies that concentrate on a single business can achieve enviable success over many decades without relying on diversification to sustain their growth. McDonald's, Delta Airlines, Coca-Cola, Domino's Pizza, Apple Computer, Wal-Mart, Federal Express, Timex, Campbell Soup, Anheuser-Busch, Xerox, Gerber, and Polaroid all won their reputations in a single business. In the nonprofit sector, continued emphasis on a single activity has proved beneficial for the Red Cross, Salvation Army, Christian Children's Fund, Girl Scouts, Phi Beta Kappa, and American Civil Liberties Union.

Concentrating on a single line of business (totally or with a small amount of diversification) has some useful organizational and managerial advantages. First, single-business concentration entails less ambiguity about "who we are and what we do." The energies of the *total* organization are directed down *one* business path. There is less chance that senior management's time or organizational resources will be stretched thinly over too many activities. Entrepreneurial efforts can focus exclusively on keeping the firm's business strategy and competitive approach responsive to industry change and fine-tuned to customer needs. All the firm's managers, especially top executives, can have hands-on contact with the core business and in-depth knowledge of operations. (Senior officers usually have risen through the ranks and possess first-hand experience in field operations—something hard to expect of corporate managers in broadly diversified enterprises.) Furthermore, concentrating on a single business carries a heftier built-in incentive for managers to come up with ways to strengthen the firm's long-term competitive position in the industry rather than pursuing the fleeting benefits of higher short-term profits. The company can use all its organizational resources to become better at what it does. Important competencies and competitive skills are more likely to emerge. With management's attention focused exclusively on just one business, the probability is higher that ideas will emerge on how to improve production technology, better meet customer needs with innovative new product features, or enhance efficiencies anywhere in the activity-cost chain. The more successful a single-business enterprise is, the more able it is to parlay its accumulated experience and distinctive expertise into a sustainable competitive advantage and a prominent leadership position in its industry.

There are important organizational and managerial advantages to concentrating on just one business.

The Risk of a Single-Business Strategy

The big risk of single-business concentration is putting all a firm's eggs in one industry basket. If the industry stagnates, declines, or otherwise becomes unattractive, a company's future outlook dims, its growth rate becomes tougher to sustain, and superior profit performance is much harder to achieve. At times, changing customer needs, technological innovation, or new substitute products can undermine or wipe out a single-business firm. Consider, for example, what word processing has done to the electric typewriter business and what compact disc players are doing to the market for cassette tapes and records. For this reason most single-business companies turn their strategic attention to diversification when their business starts to show signs of peaking.

When Diversification Starts to Make Sense

To better understand *when* a single-business company needs to consider diversification, consider Figure 7–1 where the variable of competitive position is plotted against various rates of market growth to create four distinct strategic situations that might be occupied by an undiversified company.[1] Firms that fall into the rapid market growth/strong competitive position box have several logical strategy options, the strongest of which in the near term may be continuing to pursue single-business concentration. Given the industry's high growth rate (and implicit long-term attractiveness), it makes sense for firms in this position to push hard to maintain or increase their market shares, further develop core competences, and make whatever capital investments are necessary to continue in a strong industry position. At some juncture, a company in this box may find it desirable to consider a vertical integration strategy to undergird its competitive strength. Later, when market growth starts to slow, prudence dictates looking into diversification as a means of spreading business risks and transferring the skills or expertise the company has built up into closely *related* businesses.

Firms in the rapid growth/weak position category should first consider their options for reformulating their present competitive strategy (given the high rate of market growth). Second they need to address the questions of (1) why their current approach has resulted in a weak competitive position and (2) what it will take to become an effective competitor. In a rapidly expanding market, even weak firms should be able to improve their performance and make headway in building a stronger market position. If a firm is young and struggling to develop, it usually has a better chance for survival in a growing market where plenty of new business is up for grabs than in a stable or declining industry. However, if a weakly positioned company in a rapid-growth market lacks the resources and skills to hold its own, its best option is to either merge with another company in the industry or merge with an outsider with the cash and resources to support the firm's development. Vertical integration—either forward, backward, or both—is an option for weakly positioned firms whenever it can materially strengthen the firm's competitive position. A third option is diversification into related or unrelated areas (if adequate financing can be found). If all else fails, abandonment—divestiture for a multibusiness firm or liquidation for a single-business firm—has to become an active strategic option. While abandonment may seem extreme because of the high growth potential, a company unable to make a profit in a booming market probably does not have the ability to make a profit at all—particularly if competition stiffens or industry conditions sour.

Companies with a weak competitive position in a relatively slow-growth market should look at (1) reformulating their present competitive strategy to turn their situation around and create a more attractive competitive position, (2) integrating forward or backward provided good profit improvement and competitive positioning opportunities exist, (3) diversifying into related or unrelated areas, (4) merger with another firm, (5) employing a harvest, then divest strategy, and (6) liquidating their position in the business by either selling out to another firm or closing down operations.

---

[1]Roland Christensen, Norman A. Berg, and Malcolm S. Salter, *Policy Formulation and Administration*, 7th ed. (Homewood, Ill: Richard D. Irwin, 1976), pp. 16–18.

F I G U R E 7–1   **Matching Corporate Strategy Alternatives to Fit an
Undiversifed Firm's Situation**

**COMPETITIVE
POSITION**

	WEAK	STRONG
RAPID	**STRATEGY OPTIONS** (in probable order of attractiveness) • Reformulate single-business concentration strategy (to achieve turnaround). • Acquire another firm in the same business (to strengthen competitive position). • Vertical integration (forward or backward if it strengthens competitive position). • Diversification. • Be acquired by/sell out to a stronger rival. • Abandonment (a last resort in the event all else fails).	**STRATEGY OPTIONS** (in probable order of attractiveness) • Continue single-business concentration –International expansion (if market opportunities exist). • Vertical integration (if it strengthens the firm's competitive position). • Related diversification (to transfer skills and expertise built up in the company's core business to adjacent businesses).
SLOW	**STRATEGY OPTIONS** (in probable order of attractiveness) • Reformulate single-business concentration strategy (to achieve turnaround). • Merger with a rival firm (to strengthen competitive position). • Vertical integration (only if it strengthens competitive position substantially). • Diversification. • Harvest/divest. • Liquidation (a last resort in the event all else fails).	**STRATEGY OPTIONS** (in probable order of attractiveness) • International expansion (if market opportunities exist). • Related diversification. • Unrelated diversification. • Joint ventures into new areas. • Vertical integration (if it strengthens competitive position). • Continue single-business concentration (achieve growth by taking market share from weaker rivals).

**MARKET
GROWTH RATE**

Companies that are strongly positioned in a slow-growth industry should consider using their excess cash to begin diversifying. Diversification into businesses where a firm can leverage its core competences and competitive strengths is usually the best strategy. But diversification into totally unrelated businesses has to be considered if none of the related business opportunities offer attractive profit prospects. Joint ventures with other organizations into

Companies that have strong competitive positions in slow-growth industries are prime candidates for diversifying into new businesses.

new fields are another logical possibility. Vertical integration should be a last resort (since it provides no escape from the industry's slow-growth condition) and makes strategic sense only if a firm can expect sizable profit gains. A strong company in a slow-growth industry usually needs to curtail new investment in its present facilities (unless it sees important growth *segments* within the industry) to free cash for new endeavors.

The decision on *when to diversify* is therefore partly a function of a firm's competitive position and partly a function of the remaining opportunities in its home-base industry. There really is no well-defined point at which companies in the same industry should diversify. Indeed, companies in the same industry can rationally choose different diversification approaches and launch them at different times.

BUILDING SHAREHOLDER VALUE: THE ULTIMATE JUSTIFICATION FOR DIVERSIFYING

Strategic Management Principle

To create value for shareholders, a diversifying company must get into businesses that can perform better under common management than they could perform operating as independent enterprises.

The underlying purpose of corporate diversification is to build shareholder value. For diversification to enhance shareholder value, corporate strategy must do more than simply diversify the company's business risk by investing in more than one industry. Shareholders can achieve the same risk diversification on their own by purchasing stock in companies in different industries. Strictly speaking, *diversification does not create shareholder value unless a group of businesses performs better under a single corporate umbrella than they would perform operating as independent, stand-alone businesses.* For example, if company A diversifies by purchasing company B and if A and B's consolidated profits in the years to come prove no greater than what each would have earned on its own, then A's diversification into business B has failed to provide shareholders with added value. Company A's shareholders could have achieved the same $2 + 2 = 4$ result on their own by purchasing stock in company B. Shareholder value is not *created* by diversification unless it produces a $2 + 2 = 5$ effect where sister businesses perform better together as part of the same firm than they could perform as independent companies.

Three Tests for Judging a Diversification Move

The problem with such a strict benchmark of whether diversification has enhanced shareholder value is that it requires speculative judgments about how well a diversified company's business would have performed on its own. Comparisons of actual performance against the hypothetical of what performance might have been under other circumstances are never very satisfactory and, besides, they represent after-the-fact assessments. Strategists have to base diversification decisions on future expectations. Attempts to gauge the impact of particular diversification moves on shareholder value do not have to be abandoned, however. Corporate strategists can make before-the-fact assessments of whether a particular diversification move is capable of increasing shareholder value by using three tests:[2]

---

[2]Michael E. Porter, "From Competitive Advantage to Corporate Strategy," *Harvard Business Review* 45, no. 3 (May–June 1987), pp. 46–49.

1. *The Attractiveness Test:* The industry chosen for diversification must be attractive enough to produce consistently good returns on investment. True industry attractiveness is defined by the presence of favorable competitive conditions and a market environment conducive to long-term profitability. Such simple indicators as rapid growth or a sexy product are unreliable proxies of attractiveness.

2. *The Cost of Entry Test:* The cost to enter the target industry must not be so high as to erode the potential for good profitability. A catch-22 situation can prevail here, however. The more attractive the industry, the more expensive it is to get into. Entry barriers for new start-up companies are nearly always high—were barriers low, a rush of new entrants would soon erode the potential for high profitability. And buying a company already in the business typically entails a high acquisition cost because of the industry's strong appeal. Costly entry undermines the potential for enhancing shareholder value.

3. *The Better-Off Test:* The diversifying company must bring some potential for competitive advantage to the new business it enters, or the new business must offer some potential for added competitive advantage to the company's other businesses. The opportunity to *create* sustainable competitive advantage where none existed before means there is also opportunity for added profitability and share-holder value.

> • • • • • • • • • • • • •
> *To build shareholder value via diversification, the industries and businesses a company targets must be capable of passing the attractiveness, cost-of-entry, and better-off tests.*

Diversification moves that satisfy all three tests have the greatest potential to build shareholder value over the long term. Diversification moves that can pass only one or two tests are highly suspect.

DIVERSIFICATION STRATEGIES

Once the decision is made to pursue diversification, any of several different paths can be taken. There is plenty of room for varied strategic approaches. We can get a better understanding of the strategic issues corporate managers face in creating and managing a diversified group of businesses by looking at six types of diversification strategies:

1. Strategies for entering new industries—acquisition, start-up, and joint ventures.
2. Related diversification strategies.
3. Unrelated diversification strategies.
4. Divestiture and liquidation strategies.
5. Corporate turnaround, retrenchment, and restructuring strategies.
6. Multinational diversification.

The first three involve ways to diversify; the last three involve strategies to strengthen the positions and performance of companies that have already diversified.

Strategies for Entering New Businesses

Entry into new businesses can take any of three forms: acquisition, internal start-up, and joint ventures. *Acquisition of an existing business* is probably the most popular means of diversifying into another industry and has the advantage of much quicker entry into the target market.[3] At the same time, it helps a diversifier overcome such entry barriers as technological inexperience, establishing supplier relationships, being big enough to match rivals' efficiency and unit costs, having to spend large sums on introductory advertising and promotion to gain market visibility and brand recognition, and getting adequate distribution. In many industries, going the internal start-up route and trying to develop the knowledge, resources, scale of operation, and market reputation necessary to become an effective competitor can take years and entails all the problems of getting a brand new company off the ground and operating. However, finding the right kind of company to acquire sometimes presents a challenge.[4] The big dilemma an acquisition-minded firm faces is whether to buy a successful company at a high price or a struggling company at a "bargain" price. If the buying firm has little knowledge of the industry but ample capital, it is often better off purchasing a capable, strongly positioned firm—unless the acquisition price is unreasonably high. On the other hand, when the acquirer sees promising ways to transform a weak firm into a strong one and has the money, know-how, and patience to do it, a struggling company can be the better long-term investment.

> One of the big stumbling blocks to entering attractive industries by acquisition is the difficulty of finding a well-positioned company at a price that satisfies the cost-of-entry test.

The cost-of-entry test requires that the expected profit stream of the acquired business provide an attractive return on the total acquisition cost and on any new capital investment needed to sustain or expand its operations. A high acquisition price can make earning an attractive return improbable or difficult. For instance, suppose that the price to purchase a company is $3 million and that the business is earning after-tax profits of $200,000 on an equity investment of $1 million (a 20 percent annual return). Simple arithmetic requires that the acquired busness's profits be tripled for the purchaser to earn the same 20 percent return on its $3 million acquisition price that the previous owners got on their $1 million equity investment. Building the acquired firm's earnings from $200,000 to $600,000 annually could take several years—and require additional investment on which the purchaser would also have to earn a 20 percent return. Since the owners of a successful and growing company usually demand a price that reflects their business's future profit prospects, it's easy for such an acquisition to flunk the cost-of-entry test. It's difficult to find a successful company in an appealing industry at a price that still permits attractive returns on investment.

> The biggest drawbacks to entering an industry by forming a start-up company internally are the costs of overcoming entry barriers and the extra time it takes to build a strong and profitable competitive position.

Diversification through *internal start-up* involves creating a new company under the corporate umbrella to compete in the desired industry. A newly formed organization not only has to overcome entry barriers, it also has to invest in new production capacity, develop sources of supply, hire and train employees, build distribution channels, grow a customer base, and so on. Generally, forming a start-up company to enter a new industry is more attractive when (1) there is ample time to launch the business from the ground up, (2) incumbent firms are likely to be slow or ineffective in responding to a

---

[3]In recent years, takeovers have become an increasingly used approach to acquisition. The term *takeover* refers to the attempt (often sprung as a surprise) of one firm to acquire ownership or control over another firm against the wishes of the latter's management (and perhaps some of its stockholders).

[4]Michael E. Porter, *Competitive Strategy: Techniques for Analyzing Industries and Competitors* (New York: Free Press, 1980), pp. 354–55.

new entrant's efforts to crack the market, (3) internal entry has lower costs than entry via acquisition, (4) the company already has most or all of the skills it needs to compete effectively, (5) adding new production capacity will not adversely impact the supply-demand balance in the industry, and (6) the targeted industry is populated with many relatively small firms so the new start-up does not have to compete head-to-head against larger, more powerful rivals.[5]

Joint ventures are a useful way to gain access to a new business in at least three types of situations.[6] First, a joint venture is a good device for doing something that is uneconomical or risky for an organization to do alone. Second, joint ventures make sense when pooling the resources and competences of two or more independent organizations produces an organization with more of the skills needed to be a strong competitor. In such cases, each partner brings special talents or resources that the other doesn't have and that are important for success. Third, joint ventures with foreign partners are sometimes the only or best way to surmount import quotas, tariffs, nationalistic political interests, and cultural roadblocks. The economic, competitive, and political realities of nationalism often require a foreign company to team up with a domestic partner in order to gain access to the national market in which the domestic partner is located. Domestic partners offer outside companies the benefits of local knowledge, managerial and marketing personnel, and access to distribution channels. However, such joint ventures often pose complicated questions about how to divide efforts among the partners and who has effective control.[7] Conflicts between foreign and domestic partners can arise over local sourcing of components, how much production to export, whether operating procedures should conform to the foreign company's standards or local preferences, and who should control cash flows and the disposition of profits.

RELATED DIVERSIFICATION STRATEGIES

In choosing which industries to diversify into, companies can pick industries either *related* or *unrelated* to the organization's core business. A related diversification strategy involves diversifying into businesses that possess some kind of "strategic fit." *Strategic fit* exists when different businesses have sufficiently related activity-cost chains that there are important opportunities for activity sharing in one business or another.[8] *A diversified firm that exploits these activity-cost chain interrelationships and captures the benefits of strategic fit achieves a consolidated performance greater than the sum of what the businesses can earn pursuing independent strategies.* The presence of strategic fit within a diversified firm's business portfolio, together with corporate management's skill in capturing the benefits of the interrelationships, makes related diversification a 2 + 2 = 5 phenomenon and becomes a basis for competitive advantage. The bigger

. . . .
Basic Concept
Related diversification involves diversifying into businesses whose activity-cost chains are related in ways that satisfy the better-off test.

---

[5]Ibid., pp. 344–45.

[6]Peter Drucker, *Management: Tasks, Responsibilities, Practices* (New York: Harper & Row, 1974), pp. 720–24.

[7]Porter, *Competitive Strategy*, p. 340.

[8]Michael E. Porter, *Competitive Advantage*, pp. 318–19 and 337–53; Kenichi Ohmae, *The Mind of the Strategist* (New York: Penguin Books, 1983), pp. 121–24; and Porter, "From Competitive Advantage to Corporate Strategy," pp. 53–57.

the strategic fit benefits, the bigger the competitive advantage of related diversification and the more that related diversification satisfies the better-off test for building shareholder value.

Strategic fit relationships can arise out of technology sharing, common labor skills and requirements, common suppliers and raw material sources, the potential for joint manufacture of parts and components, similar operating methods, similar kinds of managerial know-how, reliance on the same types of marketing and merchandising skills, ability to share a common sales force, ability to use the same wholesale distributors or retail dealers, or potential for combining after-sale service activities. The fit or relatedness can occur anywhere along the businesses' respective activity-cost chains. Strategic fit relationships are important because they represent opportunities for cost-saving efficiencies, technology or skills transfers, or other benefits of activity-sharing, all of which are avenues for gaining competitive advantages over rivals that have not diversified or that have not diversified in ways that give them access to such strategic fit benefits.

Some of the most commonly used approaches to related diversification are:

- Entering businesses where sales force, advertising, and distribution activities can be shared (a bread bakery buying a maker of crackers and salty snack foods).

- Exploiting closely related technologies (a maker of agricultural seeds and fertilizers diversifying into chemicals for insect and plant disease control).

- Transferring know-how and expertise from one business to another (a successful operator of hamburger outlets acquire a chain specializing in Mexican fast foods).

- Transferring the organization's brand name and reputation with consumers to a new product/service (a tire manufacturer diversifying into automotive repair centers).

- Acquiring new businesses that will uniquely help the firm's position in its existing businesses (a cable TV broadcaster purchasing a sports team and a movie production company to provide original programming).

Examples of related diversification abound. BIC Pen, which pioneered inexpensive disposable ballpoint pens, used its core competences in low-cost manufacturing and mass merchandising as its basis for diversifying into disposable cigarette lighters, disposable razors, and pantyhose—all three businesses required low-cost production know-how and skilled consumer marketing for competitive success. Tandy Corp. practiced related diversification when its chain of Radio Shack outlets, which originally handled mostly radio and stereo equipment, added telephones, intercoms, calculators, clocks, electronic and scientific toys, personal computers, and peripheral computer equipment. The Tandy strategy was to use the marketing access provided by its thousands of Radio Shack locations to become one of the world's leading retailers of electronic technology. Philip Morris, a leading cigarette manufacturer, employed a marketing-related diversification strategy when it purchased Miller Brewing, General Foods, and Kraft and transferred its skills in cigarette marketing to the marketing of beer and food products. Lockheed pursued a customer needs-based diversification strategy in creating business units to supply the Department of Defense with missiles, rocket engines, aircraft, electronic equipment,

---

ILLUSTRATION CAPSULE **16** **EXAMPLES OF COMPANIES WITH RELATED BUSINESS PORTFOLIOS**

Presented below are the business portfolios of four companies that have pursued some form of related diversification:

Gillette	PepsiCo

Gillette

- Blades and razors
- Toiletries (Right Guard, Silkience, Foamy, Dry Idea, Soft & Dry, Oral-B toothbrushes, White Rain, Toni)
- Writing instruments and stationery products (Paper Mate pens, Liquid Paper correction fluids, Waterman pens)
- Braun shavers, cordless curlers, coffeemakers, alarm clocks, and electric toothbrushes

PepsiCo

- Soft drinks (Pepsi, Mountain Dew, Slice)
- Kentucky Fried Chicken
- Pizza Hut
- Taco Bell
- Frito-Lay
- 7Up International (non-U.S. sales of 7Up)

Philip Morris Companies

- Cigarettes (Marlboro, Virginia Slims, Benson & Hedges, and Merit)
- Miller Brewing Company
- Kraft General Foods (Maxwell House, Sanka, Oscar Mayer, Kool-Aid, Jell-O, Post cereals, Birds-Eye frozen foods, Kraft cheeses, Sealtest dairy products, Breyer's ice cream)
- Mission Viejo Realty

Johnson & Johnson

- Baby products (powder, shampoo, oil, lotion)
- Disposable diapers
- Band-Aids and wound care products
- Stayfree, Carefree, Sure & Natural, and Modess feminine hygiene products
- Tylenol
- Prescription drugs
- Surgical and hospital products
- Dental products
- Oral contraceptives
- Veterinary and animal health products

Source: Company annual reports.

and ships, and contract R&D for weapons. Procter & Gamble's lineup of products includes Jif peanut butter, Duncan Hines cake mixes, Folger's coffee, Tide laundry detergent, Crisco vegetable oil, Crest toothpaste, Ivory soap, Charmin toilet tissue, and Head and Shoulders shampoo—all different businesses with different competitors and different production requirements. But P&G's products still represent related diversification because they all move through the same wholesale distribution systems, are sold in common retail settings to the same shoppers, are advertised and promoted in the same ways, and utilize the same marketing and merchandising skills. Illustration Capsule 16 shows the business portfolios of several companies that have pursued a strategy of related diversification.

Strategic fits among related businesses offer the competitive advantage potential of (a) lower costs or (b) efficient transfer of key skills, technological expertise, or managerial know-how.

Strategic Fit, Economies of Scope, and Competitive Advantage

A related diversification strategy has considerable appeal. It allows a firm to preserve a degree of unity in its business activities, reap the competitive advantages of skills transfer or lower costs, and still spread business risks over a broader base. A company that has developed valuable skills and competences in its original business can employ a related diversification strategy to exploit what it does best and *transfer* its competences and competitive skills to another business. Successful skills or technology transfers can lead to competitive advantage in the new business.

Diversifying into businesses where technology, facilities, functional activities, or distribution channels can also be shared can lead to lower costs because of economies of scope. *Economies of scope* exist whenever it is less costly for two or more businesses to be operated under centralized management than to function as independent businesses. The economies of operating over a wider range of businesses or product lines can arise from cost-saving opportunities anywhere along the respective activity-cost chains of the businesses. The greater the economies of scope associated with the particular businesses a company has diversified into, the greater the potential for creating a competitive advantage based on lower costs.

Both skills transfer and cost-sharing enable the diversifier to earn greater profits from its businesses than the businesses could earn operating independently. The key to cost-sharing and skills transfer opportunities is diversification into businesses with strategic fit. While strategic fit relationships can occur throughout the activity-cost chain, most fall into one of three broad categories.

Market-Related Fits When the activity-cost chains of different businesses overlap such that the products are used by the same customers, distributed through common dealers and retailers, or marketed and promoted in similar ways, then the businesses exhibit market-related strategic fit. A variety of cost-saving opportunities (or economies of scope) can arise from market related strategic fit: using a single sales force for all related products rather than separate sales forces for each business, advertising related products in the same ads and brochures, using the same brand names, coordinating delivery and shipping, combining after-sale service and repair organizations, coordinating order processing and billing, using common promotional tie-ins (cents-off couponing, free samples and trial offers, seasonal specials, and the like), and combining dealer networks. Such market-related strategic fits usually allow a firm to economize on its marketing, selling, and distribution costs.

In addition to economies of scope, market-related fit can generate opportunities to transfer selling skills, promotional skills, advertising skills, and product differentiation skills from one business to another. Moreover, a company's brand name and reputation in one product can often be transferred to other products. Honda's name in motorcycles and automobiles gave it instant credibility and recognition in the lawn mower business without spending large sums on advertising. Canon's reputation in photographic equipment was a competitive asset that facilitated the company's diversification into copying equipment. Panasonic's name in consumer electronics (radios, TVs) was readily transferred to microwave ovens, making it easier and cheaper for Panasonic to diversify into the microwave oven market.

Operating Fit Different businesses have *operating fit* when there is potential for cost-sharing or skills transfer in procuring materials, conducting R&D,

· · · · · · · · · · · · ·
Basic Concept
Economies of scope arise from the ability to reduce costs by operating two or more businesses under the same corporate umbrella; cost savings can stem from interrelationships anywhere along the businesses' activity-cost chains.

developing technology, manufacturing components, assembling finished goods, or performing administrative support functions. Sharing-related operating fits usually present cost-saving opportunities; some derive from the economies of combining activities into a larger-scale operation (*economies of scale*) and some derive from the ability to eliminate costs by doing things together rather than independently (*economies of scope*). The bigger the proportion of cost a shared activity represents, the more significant the shared cost savings become and the bigger the cost advantage that can result. The most important skills-transfer opportunities usually occur in situations where technological or manufacturing expertise in one business has beneficial applications in another.

Management Fit   This type of fit emerges when different business units have comparable types of entrepreneurial, administrative, or operating problems, thereby allowing managerial know-how in one line of business to be transferable to another business. Transfers of managerial expertise can occur anywhere in the activity-cost chain. Ford Motor Co. transferred its automobile financing and credit management know-how to the savings and loan industry when it acquired some failing S&Ls during the bailout of the crisis-ridden S&L industry. Emerson Electric transferred its skills in low-cost manufacture to its newly acquired Beaird-Poulan chain saw business division. The transfer of management know-how drove Beaird-Poulan's new strategy, changed the way its chain saws were designed and manufactured, and paved the way for new pricing and distribution emphasis.

Capturing Strategic Fit Benefits   It is one thing to diversify into industries with strategic fit and another to actually realize the benefits. To capture the benefits of sharing, related activities must be merged into a single functional unit and coordinated; then the cost-savings (or differentiation advantages) must be squeezed out. Merged functions and coordination can entail reorganization costs, and management must determine that the benefit of *some* centralized strategic control is great enough to warrant sacrifice of business-unit autonomy. Likewise, where skills transfer is the cornerstone of strategic fit, management must find a way to make the transfer effective without stripping too many skilled personnel from the business with the expertise. The more a company's diversification strategy is tied to skills transfer, the more it has to build and maintain a sufficient pool of specialized personnel. And it must not only supply new businesses with the skill but also see that they master the skill sufficiently to create competitive advantage.

UNRELATED DIVERSIFICATION STRATEGIES

Despite the strategic fit benefits associated with related diversification, a number of companies opt for unrelated diversification strategies. In unrelated diversification, the corporate strategy is to diversify into *any* industry where top management spots a good profit opportunity. There is no deliberate effort to seek out businesses where strategic fit exists. While firms pursuing unrelated diversification may try to ensure that their strategies meet the industry attractiveness and cost-of-entry tests, the conditions needed for the better-off test are either disregarded or relegated to secondary status. Decisions to diversify into one industry versus another are based on an opportunistic search for "good" companies to acquire—*the basic premise of unrelated diversification is that any company that can be acquired on good financial terms represents a good business to diversify into.* Much time and effort goes into finding and screening acquisition candidates. Typically, corporate strategists screen candidate companies using such criteria as:

- Whether the business can meet corporate targets for profitability and return on investment.
- Whether the new business will require substantial infusions of capital to replace fixed assets, fund expansion, and provide working capital.
- Whether the business is in an industry with significant growth potential.
- Whether the business is big enough to contribute significantly to the parent firm's bottom line.
- The potential for union difficulties or adverse government regulations concerning product safety or the environment.
- Industry vulnerability to recession, inflation, high interest rates, or shifts in government policy.

. . . .
Unrelated diversification is usually accomplished through acquisition; corporate strategists use a variety of criteria to identify suitable companies to acquire.

Sometimes, corporate strategy is directed at identifying companies that offer opportunities for financial gain because of their "special situation"; three types of companies make particularly attractive acquisition targets:

- *Companies whose assets are "undervalued"*—opportunities may exist to acquire such companies for less than full market value and make substantial capital gains by reselling their assets and businesses for more than their acquired costs.
- *Companies that are financially distressed*—such businesses can often be purchased at a bargain price, their operations turned around with the aid of the parent companies' financial resources and managerial know-how, and then either held as a long-term investment (because of their strong earnings potential) or sold at a profit, whichever is more attractive.
- *Companies that have bright growth prospects but are short on investment capital*—capital-poor, opportunity-rich companies are usually coveted diversification candidates for a financially strong firm.

Firms that pursue unrelated diversification nearly always enter new businesses by acquiring an established company rather than by forming a start-up subsidiary within its own corporate structure. Their premise is that growth by acquisition translates into enhanced shareholder value. Suspending application of the better-off test is seen as justifiable so long as unrelated diversification results in sustained growth in corporate revenues and earnings and none of the acquired businesses end up performing badly.

Illustration Capsule 17 shows the business portfolios of several companies that have pursued unrelated diversification. Such companies are frequently described as *conglomerates* because they follow no strategic theme in their diversification and because their business interests range broadly across diverse industries.

| **ILLUSTRATION CAPSULE** | **17** | DIVERSIFIED COMPANIES WITH UNRELATED BUSINESS PORTFOLIOS |

Union Pacific Corporation

- Railroad operations (Union Pacific Railroad Company)
- Oil and gas exploration
- Mining
- Microwave and fiber optic transportation information and control systems
- Hazardous waste management disposal
- Trucking (Overnite Transportation Company)
- Oil refining
- Real estate

United Technologies

- Pratt & Whitney aircraft engines
- Carrier heating and air-conditioning equipment
- Otis elevators
- Sikorsky helicopters
- Essex wire and cable products
- Norden defense systems
- Hamilton Standard controls
- Space transportation systems
- Automotive components

Westinghouse Electric Corp.

- Electric utility power generation equipment
- Nuclear fuel
- Electric transmission and distribution products
- Commercial and residential real estate financing
- Equipment leasing
- Receivables and fixed asset financing
- Radio and television broadcasting
- Longines-Wittnauer Watch Co.
- Beverage bottling
- Elevators and escalators
- Defense electronic systems (missile launch equipment, marine propulsion)
- Commercial furniture
- Community land development

Textron, Inc.

- Bell helicopters
- Paul Revere Insurance
- Missile reentry systems
- Lycoming gas turbine engines and jet propulsion systems
- E-Z-Go golf carts
- Homelite chain saws and lawn and garden equipment
- Davidson automotive parts and trims
- Specialty fasteners
- Avco Financial Services
- Jacobsen turf care equipment
- Tanks and armored vehicles

The Pros and Cons of Unrelated Diversification

Unrelated or conglomerate diversification has appeal from several financial angles:

1. Business risk is scattered over a variety of industries, making the company less dependent on any one business. While the same can be said for related diversification, unrelated diversification places no restraint on how risk is spread. An argument can be made that unrelated diversification is a superior way to diversify financial risk as compared to related diversification.

2. Capital resources can be invested in whatever industries offer the best profit prospects; cash from businesses with lower profit prospects can be diverted to acquiring and expanding businesses with higher growth

With unrelated diversification, a company can spread financial risks broadly, invest in whatever businesses promise financial gain, and try to stabilize earnings by diversifying into businesses with offsetting up- and-down cycles.

and profit potentials. Corporate financial resources are thus employed to maximum advantage.

3. Company profitability is somewhat more stable because hard times in one industry may be partially offset by good times in another—ideally, cyclical downswings in some of the company's businesses are counterbalanced by cyclical upswings in other businesses the company has diversified into.

4. To the extent that corporate managers are astute at spotting bargain-priced companies with big upside profit potential, shareholder wealth can be enhanced.

While entry into an unrelated business can often pass the attractiveness and cost-of-entry tests (and sometimes even the better-off test), unrelated diversification has drawbacks. The real Achilles' heel of conglomerate diversification is the big demand it places on corporate-level management to make sound decisions about fundamentally different businesses operating in fundamentally different industry and competitive environments. The greater the number of businesses a company is in and the more diverse they are, the harder it is for corporate managers to oversee each subsidiary and spot problems early, to become expert at evaluating the attractiveness of each business's industry and competitive environment, and to judge the caliber of strategic actions and plans proposed by business-level managers. As one president of a diversified firm expressed it:

> we've got to make sure that our core businesses are properly managed for solid, long-term earnings. We can't just sit back and watch the numbers. We've got to know what the real issues are out there in the profit centers. Otherwise, we're not even in a position to check out our managers on the big decisions.[9]

The two biggest drawbacks to unrelated diversification are the difficulties of managing broad diversification and the absence of strategic opportunities to turn diversification into competitive advantage.

With broad diversification, corporate managers have to be shrewd and talented enough to: (1) tell a good acquisition from a bad one, (2) select capable managers to run each business, (3) discern sound strategic proposals, and (4) know what to do if a business unit stumbles. Because every business encounters rough sledding, a good way to gauge the risk of diversifying is to ask, "If the new business got into trouble, would we know how to bail it out?" When the answer is no, unrelated diversification can pose significant financial risk, and the business's profit prospects are more chancy.[10] As the former chairman of a Fortune 500 company advised, "Never acquire a business you don't know how to run." It only takes one or two big strategic mistakes (misjudging industry attractiveness, encountering unexpected problems in a newly acquired business, or being too optimistic about the difficulty of turning a struggling subsidiary around) to cause a precipitous drop in corporate earnings and crash the company's stock price.

Second, without some kind of strategic fit and the added measure of competitive advantage it offers, the consolidated performance of a multibusiness port-

---

[9]Carter F. Bales, "Strategic Control: The President's Paradox," *Business Horizons* 20, no. 4 (August 1977), p. 17.

[10]Of course, some firms may be willing to risk that trouble won't strike before management has time to learn the business well enough to bail it out of almost any difficulty. See Peter Drucker, *Management: Tasks, Responsibilities, Practices* (New York: Harper & Row, 1974), p. 709.

folio tends to be no better than the sum of what the individual business units could achieve independently. And, to the extent that corporate managers meddle unwisely in business-unit operations or hamstring them with corporate policies, overall performance can even be worse. Except for the added financial backing from a cash-rich corporate parent, a strategy of unrelated diversification does nothing to enhance the competitive strength of individual business units. Each business is on its own in trying to build a competitive edge—the unrelated nature of sister businesses offers no basis for cost reduction, skills transfer, or technology sharing. In a widely diversified firm, the value added by corporate managers depends primarily on how good they are at deciding what new businesses to add, which ones to get rid of, how to use financial resources to build a higher-performing collection of businesses, and the quality of the decision-making guidance they give to general managers of their business subsidiaries.

Third, although in theory unrelated diversification offers the potential for greater sales-profit stability over the business cycle, in practice attempts at countercyclical diversification fall short of the mark. Few attractive businesses have opposite up-and-down cycles; most are similarly affected by cyclical economic conditions. There's no convincing evidence that the consolidated profits of broadly diversified firms are more stable or less subject to reversal in periods of recession and economic stress than the profits of less diversified firms.[11]

Despite these drawbacks, unrelated diversification can be a desirable corporate strategy. It certainly makes sense when a firm needs to diversify away from an unattractive industry and has no distinctive skills it can transfer to related businesses. Also, some owners prefer to invest in several unrelated businesses instead of a family of related ones. Otherwise, the advantages of unrelated diversification depend on the prospects for financial gain.

A key issue in unrelated diversification is how broad a net to cast in building the business portfolio. In other words, should the corporate portfolio contain few or many unrelated businesses? How much business diversity can corporate executives successfully manage? A reasonable way to resolve the problem is to answer two questions: What is the least diversification the firm needs to achieve acceptable growth and profitability? What is the most diversification the firm can manage given the complexity it adds?[12] The optimal answer usually lies between these two extremes.

Unrelated Diversification and Shareholder Value

Unrelated diversification is fundamentally a finance-driven approach to creating shareholder value whereas related diversification is fundamentally strategy-driven. *Related diversification represents a strategic approach to value creation* because it is predicated on exploiting the links between the activity-cost chains of different businesses to lower costs, transfer skills and technological

Unrelated diversification represents a financial approach to creating shareholder value; related diversification in contrast, represents a strategic approach.

---

[11]Ibid., p. 767. Research studies in the interval since 1974, when Drucker made his observation, uphold his conclusion—on the whole, broadly diversified firms do not outperform less diversified firms over the course of the business cycle.

[12]Ibid., pp. 692–93.

expertise, and gain benefit of other kinds of strategic fit. The objective is to convert the strategic fits among the firm's businesses into an extra measure of competitive advantage that goes beyond what business subsidiaries are able to achieve on their own. The competitive advantage a firm achieves through related diversification is the driver for building greater shareholder value.

In contrast, *unrelated diversification is principally a financial approach to diversification* where shareholder value accrues from astute deployment of corporate financial resources and from executive skill in spotting financially attractive business opportunities. For unrelated diversification to result in enhanced shareholder value (above the $2 + 2 = 4$ effect of what the subsidiary businesses could produce through independent operations and what shareholders could obtain by purchasing ownership interests in a variety of businesses to spread investment risk on their own behalf), corporate strategists must exhibit superior skills in creating and managing a portfolio of diversified business interests. This specifically means:

- Doing a superior job of diversifying into new businesses that can produce consistently good returns on investment (satisfying the attractiveness test).
- Doing an excellent job of negotiating favorable acquisition prices (satisfying the cost-of-entry test).
- Making astute moves to sell previously acquired business subsidiaries at their peak and getting premium prices (this requires skills in discerning when a business subsidiary is on the verge of confronting adverse industry and competitive conditions and probable declines in long-term profitability).
- Being shrewd in shifting corporate financial resources out of businesses where profit opportunities are dim and into businesses where rapid earnings growth and high returns on investment are occurring.
- Doing such a good job overseeing the firm's business subsidiaries and contributing to how they are managed (by providing expert problem-solving skills, creative strategy suggestions, and decision-making guidance to business-level managers) that the businesses perform at a higher level than they would otherwise be able to do (a possible way to satisfy the better-off test).

To the extent that corporate executives can craft and execute a strategy of unrelated diversification that produces enough of the above outcomes for the enterprise to consistently outperform other firms in generating dividends and capital gains for stockholders, then a case can be made that shareholder value has truly been enhanced.

DIVESTITURE AND LIQUIDATION STRATEGIES

Even a shrewd corporate diversification strategy can result in the acquisition of business units that, down the road, just do not work out. Misfits or partial fits cannot be completely avoided because it is impossible to predict precisely how getting into a new line of business will actually work out. In addition, long-term industry attractiveness changes with the times; what was once a good diversification move into an attractive industry may later turn sour. Subpar performance by some business units is bound to occur, thereby raising questions of whether to keep them or divest them. Other business units, despite adequate financial performance, may not mesh as well with the rest of the firm as was originally thought.

Sometimes, a business that seems sensible from a strategic fit standpoint turns out to lack the compatibility of values essential to a *cultural fit*.[13] Several pharmaceutical companies had just this experience. When they diversified into cosmetics and perfume, they discovered their personnel had little respect for the "frivolous" nature of such products compared to the far nobler task of developing miracle drugs to cure the ill. The absence of shared values and cultural compatibility between the medical research expertise of the pharmaceutical companies and the fashion-marketing orientation of the cosmetics business was the undoing of what otherwise was diversification into businesses with related chemical compounding expertise and distribution channels.

When a particular line of business loses its appeal, the most attractive solution usually is to sell it. Normally such businesses should be divested as fast as is practical, unless time is needed to get them in better shape to sell. The more business units in a diversified firm's portfolio, the more likely it will have to divest poor performers, "dogs," and misfits. A useful guide to determine if and when to divest a subsidiary is to ask the question, "If we were not in this business today, would we want to get into it now?"[14] When the answer is no or probably not, divestiture must be considered.

Divestiture can take either of two forms. The parent can spin off a business as a financially and managerially independent company in which the parent may or may not retain partial ownership. Or the parent may sell the unit outright, in which case a buyer needs to be found. As a rule, divestiture should not be approached from the angle of "Who can we pawn this business off on and what is the most we can get for it?"[15] Instead, it is wiser to ask "For what sort of organization would this business be a good fit, and under what conditions would it be viewed as a good deal?" Organizations for which the business is a good fit are likely to pay the highest price.

Of all the strategic alternatives, liquidation is the most unpleasant and painful, especially for a single-business enterprise where it means the organization ceases to exist. For a multi-industry, multibusiness firm to liquidate one of its lines of business is less traumatic. The hardships of layoffs, plant closings, and so on, while not to be minimized, still leave an ongoing organization that may be healthier after its pruning. In hopeless situations, an early liquidation usually serves owner-stockholder interests better than bankruptcy. Pursuing a lost cause exhausts an organization's resources and leaves less to liquidate; it can also mar reputations and ruin management careers. Unfortunately, it is seldom simple for management to differentiate between a lost cause and a potential for turnaround. This is particularly true when emotions and pride get mixed with sound managerial judgment—as often they do.

---

[13]Ibid., p. 709.
[14]Ibid., p. 94.
[15]Ibid., p. 719.

CORPORATE TURNAROUND, RETRENCHMENT, AND PORTFOLIO RESTRUCTURING STRATEGIES

Turnaround, retrenchment, and portfolio restructuring strategies come into play when corporate management has to restore an ailing business portfolio to good health. Poor performance can be caused by large losses in one or more business units that pull the corporation's overall financial performance down, a disproportionate number of businesses in unattractive industries, a bad economy adversely impacting many of the firm's business units, an excessive debt burden, or ill-chosen acquisitions that haven't lived up to expectations.

Corporate turnaround strategies focus on restoring money-losing businesses to profitability rather than divesting them. The intent is to get the whole company back in the black by curing the problems of the subsidiaries most responsible for pulling overall performance down. Turnaround strategies are most appropriate in situations where the reasons for poor performance are short-term, the ailing businesses are in attractive industries, and divesting the money-losers does not make long-term strategic sense.

Corporate retrenchment strategies focus on reducing the scope of diversification to a smaller number of businesses. Retrenchment is usually undertaken when corporate management concludes that the company is in too many businesses and needs to concentrate its efforts on a few core businesses. Sometimes diversified firms retrench because they can't make certain businesses profitable after several years of trying or because they lack funds to support the investment needs of all the businesses in their portfolios. Retrenchment is usually accomplished by divesting businesses that are too small to make a sizable contribution to earnings or that have little or no strategic fit with the company's core businesses. Divesting such businesses frees resources that can be used to reduce debt or support expansion of the corporation's core businesses.

. . . .

Portfolio restructuring involves bold strategic action to revamp the diversified company's business makeup through divestitures and acquisitions.

Portfolio restructuring strategies involve radical surgery on the mix and percentage makeup of the types of businesses in the portfolio. For instance, one company over a two-year period divested four business units, closed down four others, and added 25 new lines of business to its portfolio—16 through acquisition and 9 through internal start-up. Restructuring can be prompted by any of several conditions: (1) when a strategy review reveals that the firm's long-term performance prospects have become unattractive because the portfolio contains too many slow-growth, declining, or competitively weak businesses, (2) when one or more of the firm's core businesses fall prey to hard times, (3) when a new CEO takes over and decides to redirect where the company is headed, (4) when new technologies or products emerge and the portfolio needs changing to build a position in a potentially big new industry, (5) when the firm has a "unique opportunity" to make an acquisition so big that it has to sell several existing businesses to finance it, or (6) when major businesses in the portfolio have become more and more unattractive, forcing a shakeup in the portfolio in order to produce satisfactory long-term corporate performance.

Portfolio restructuring typically involves both divestitures and new acquisitions. Candidates for divestiture include not only weak or up- and-down performers or those in unattractive industries, but also those that no longer "fit" (even though they may be profitable and in attractive enough industries). Many broadly diversified corporations, disenchanted with how some of their acquisitions perform and unable to make successes out of so many unrelated business units, eventually restructure their portfolios. Business units incompatible with newly established related diversification criteria have been divested and the remaining units regrouped and aligned to capture more strategic fit benefits. Illustration Capsule 18 provides an example of corporate restructuring at Times Mirror Company.

The trend to demerge and deconglomerate has been driven by a growing preference to gear diversification toward creating strong competitive positions in a few, well-selected industries. Indeed, in response to investor disenchantment with the conglomerate approach to diversification (conglomerates often have *lower* price-earnings ratios than companies with related diversification strategies), some conglomerates have undertaken portfolio restructuring and retrenchment in a deliberate effort to escape being regarded as a conglomerate.

MULTINATIONAL DIVERSIFICATION STRATEGIES

The distinguishing characteristic of a multinational diversification strategy is a *diversity of businesses* and a *diversity of national markets*.[16] Here, corporate strategists must conceive and execute a substantial number of strategies—at least one for each industry, with as many multinational variations as is appropriate for the situation. At the same time, managers of diversified multinational corporations (DMNCs) need to be alert for beneficial ways to coordinate the firm's strategic actions across industries and countries. The goal of strategic coordination at the headquarters' level is to bring the full force of corporate resources and capabilities to the task of securing sustainable competitive advantages in each business and national market.[17]

The Emergence of Multinational Diversification

Until the 1960s, multinational companies (MNCs) operated fairly autonomous subsidiaries in each host country, each catering to the special requirements of its own national market.[18] Management tasks at company headquarters primarily involved finance functions, technology transfer, and export coordination. In pursuing a national responsiveness strategy, the primary competitive advantage of an MNC was grounded in its ability to transfer technology, manufacturing know-how, brand name identification, and marketing and management skills from country to country at costs lower than could be achieved by host-country competitors. Standardized administrative procedures helped minimize overhead costs, and once an initial organization for managing foreign subsidiaries was put in place, entry into additional national markets could be accomplished at low incremental costs. Frequently, an MNC's presence and market position in a country was negotiated with the host government rather than driven by international competition.

During the 1970s, however, multicountry strategies based on national responsiveness began to lose their effectiveness. Competition broke out on a global scale in more and more industries as Japanese, European, and U.S.

[16]C. K. Prahalad and Yves L. Doz, *The Multinational Mission* (New York: Free Press, 1987), p. 2.
[17]Ibid., p. 15.
[18]Yves L. Doz, *Strategic Management in Multinational Companies* (New York: Pergamon Press, 1985), p. 1.

| ILLUSTRATION CAPSULE | 18 | CORPORATE RESTRUCTURING AT TIMES MIRROR COMPANY |

Times Mirror is a $3.6 billion media and information company principally engaged in newspaper publishing, broadcast and cable television, and book and magazine publishing. During the 1983–90 period, the company engaged in corporate restructuring activities to revamp the content of its business portfolio. The table below summarizes the company's acquisition and divestiture moves:

		Dispositions	Acquisitions
1983	Dec.	New American Library	
1984	Feb.	Spotlight satellite programming	
	Dec.	Commerce Clearing House stock	*The Morning Call*
1985	June	Art and graphic products companies (3)	Learning International, Inc.
	August		Wolfe Publishing Limited
	Sept.	Hartford, Connecticut, Cable Television	
	Oct.	Long Beach, California, Cable Television	
1986	Feb.	80 percent of Publishers Paper Co.	
	May		*National Journal*
	June	Times Mirror Microwave Communications Co.	
		Television stations in Syracuse and Elmira, New York, and Harrisburg, Pennsylvania	
		Las Vegas, Nevada, Cable Television	
	July		*Bottlang Airfield Manual*
	Sept.	*Dallas Times Herald*	
	Oct.		The *Baltimore Sun* newspapers
	Dec.	Times Mirror Magazines book clubs	*Broadcasting* magazine
		Graphic Controls Corporation	60 percent of Rhode Island CATV (cable)
		The H.M. Goushã Company	CRC Press, Inc.
1987	Feb.		*Government Executive*
	Dec.	*The Denver Post*	*Field & Stream, Home Mechanix, Skiing, Yachting* magazines
	Throughout	Continuing timberland sales	
1988	Jan.	Times Mirror Press	
	Feb.		Richard D. Irwin, Inc.
	Throughout	Continuing timberland sales	

(continued)

companies expanded internationally in the wake of trade liberalization and the opening of market opportunities in both industrialized and less-developed countries.[19] The relevant market arena in many industries shifted from national to global principally because the strategies of global competitors, most

---

[19]Ibid., pp. 2–3.

ILLUSTRATION CAPSULE 18 *(concluded)*

	Dispositions	Acquisitions
1989 May		Zenger-Miller
June		Kaset International
1990 Jan.		Sun City Cable TV (California)
		Lewis Publishers
May		B. C. Decker
Oct.		Austin Cornish
Dec.		The Achieve Group
Total	Approximately $1 billion	Approximately $1 billion

This series of moves left Times Mirror with the following business portfolio as of 1991:

Newspaper publishing:
   Los Angeles Times, Newsday, the *Baltimore Sun* newspapers, *The Hartford Courant, The Morning Call, The (Stamford) Advocate,* and *Greenwich Time.*

Book publishing:
   Abrams art books; Matthew Bender law books; Mosby–Year Book medical books; CRC Press scientific books; Wolfe medical color atlases; Lewis Publishers; B. C. Decker; Austin Cornish nursing texts; and college texts by Richard D. Irwin, Inc.

Broadcast and cable television:
   CBS network affiliates KDFW-TV, Dallas, Texas, and KTBC-TV, Austin, Texas; ABC affiliate KTVI, St. Louis, Missouri; NBC affiliate WVTM-TV, Birmingham, Alabama; and cable TV operations in 13 states (Dimension Cable Services).

Magazine publishing:
   Popular Science, Outdoor Life, Golf Magazine, Ski Magazine, The Sporting News, The Sporting Goods DEALER, National Journal, Government Executive, Broadcasting, Sports inc., The Sports Business Weekly, Field & Stream, Home Mechanix, Skiing, and *Yachting.*

Other business/properties:
   Timberland; Jepperson Sanderson (producer of aeronautical charts and pilot training material); and Learning International, Zenger-Miller, and Kaset International (providers of professional training services).

Source: Company annual reports.

notably the Japanese companies, involved gaining a foothold in host-country markets by matching or beating the product quality of local companies and undercutting their prices. To fend off global competitors, traditional MNCs were driven to integrate their operations across national borders in a quest for better efficiencies and lower manufacturing costs. Instead of separately manufacturing a complete product range in each country, the plants of MNCs

ILLUSTRATION CAPSULE 19 HONDA'S COMPETITIVE ADVANTAGE
The Technology of Engines

At first blush anyone looking at Honda's lineup of products—cars, motorcycles, lawn mowers, power generators, outboard motors, snowmobiles, snowblowers, and garden tillers—might conclude that Honda has pursued unrelated diversification. But underlying the obvious product diversity is a common core: the technology of engines.

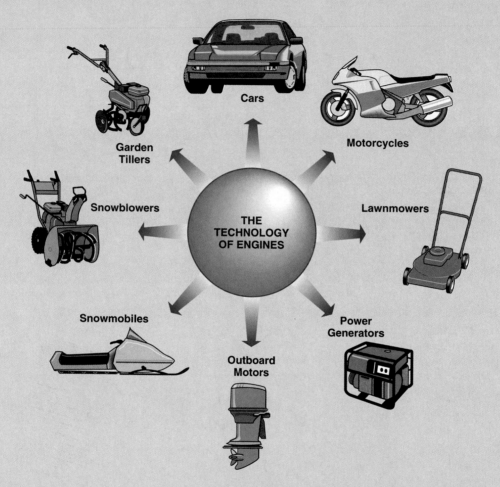

The basic Honda strategy is to exploit the company's expertise in engine technology and manufacturing and to capitalize on its brand recognition. One Honda ad teases consumers with the question, "How do you put six Hondas in a two-car garage?" It then shows a garage containing a Honda car, a Honda motorcycle, a Honda snowmobile, a Honda lawnmower, a Honda power generator, and a Honda outboard motor.

Source: Adapted from C. K. Prahalad and Yves L. Doz, *The Multinational Mission* (New York: Free Press, 1987), p. 62.

became more specialized in their production operations to gain the economies of longer production runs, permit use of faster automated equipment, and capture experience curve effects. Country subsidiaries obtained the rest of the product range they needed from sister plants in other countries. Gains in manufacturing efficiencies from converting to state-of-the-art, world-scale manufacturing plants more than offset increased international shipping costs, especially in light of the other advantages global strategies offered. With a global strategy, an MNC could locate plants in countries with low labor costs—a key consideration in industries whose products have high labor content. With a global strategy, an MNC could also exploit differences in tax rates, setting transfer prices in its integrated operations to produce higher profits in low-tax countries and lower profits in high-tax countries. Global strategic coordination also gave MNCs increased ability to take advantage of country-to-country differences in interest rates, exchange rates, credit terms, government subsidies, and export guarantees. As a consequence of these advantages, it became increasingly difficult for a company that produced and sold its product in only one country to succeed in an industry populated with aggressive competitors intent on achieving global dominance.

A multinational corporation can gain competitive advantage by diversifying into global industries with related technologies.

During the 1980s another source of competitive advantage began to emerge: using the strategic fit advantages of related diversification to build stronger competitive positions in several related global industries simultaneously. Being a diversified MNC (DMNC) became competitively superior to being a single-business MNC in cases where strategic fits existed across global industries. Related diversification is most capable of producing competitive advantage for a multinational company where expertise in a core technology can be applied to different industries (at least one of which is global) and where there are important economies of scope and brand name advantages to being in a family of related businesses.[20] Illustration Capsule 19 explains Honda's ability to exploit the technology of engines and its well-known name via its diversification into a variety of products with engines.

Sources of Competitive Advantage for a DMNC

When a multinational company has expertise in a core technology and has diversified into related products and businesses to exploit that core, a centralized R&D effort coordinated at the headquarters level holds real potential for competitive advantage. By channeling corporate resources into a strategically coordinated R&D/technology effort, as opposed to letting each business unit perform its own R&D function, the DMNC can launch a world-class, global-scale assault to advance the core technology, generate technology-based manufacturing economies within and across product/business lines, make across-the-board product improvements, and develop complementary products—all significant advantages in a globally competitive marketplace. In the absence of centralized coordination, R&D/technology investments are likely to be scaled down to match each business's product-market perspective, setting the stage for the strategic fit benefits of coordinated technology management to slip through the cracks and go uncaptured.[21]

A multinational corporation can also gain competitive advantage by diversifying into related global industries where strategic fits produce economies of scope and the benefits of brand name transfer.

[20]Prahalad and Doz, *The Multinational Mission*, pp. 62–63.
[21]Ibid.

The second source of competitive advantage for a DMNC concerns the distribution and brand name advantages that can accrue from diversifying into related global industries. Consider, for instance, the competitive strength of such Japanese DMNCs as Sanyo and Matsushita. Both have diversified into a range of globally competitive consumer goods industries—TVs, stereo equipment, radios, VCRs, small domestic appliances (microwave ovens, for example), and personal computers. By widening their scope of operations in products marketed through similar distribution channels, Sanyo and Matsushita have not only exploited related technologies but also built stronger distribution capabilities, captured logistical and distribution-related economies, and established greater brand awareness for their products.[22] Such competitive advantages are not available to a domestic-only company pursuing a single business. Moreover, with a well-diversified product line and a multinational market base, a DMNC can enter new country or product markets and gain market share with below-market pricing (and below-average cost pricing if need be), subsidizing the entry with earnings from one or more of its country market profit sanctuaries and/or earnings in other businesses.

· · · · · · · · · · · ·

Principle of Global Competition

A multinational corporation diversified into related global industries is well positioned to out-compete both a one-business domestic company and a one-business multinational company.

Both a one-business multinational company and a one-business domestic company are weakly positioned to defend their market positions against a determined DMNC willing to accept lower short-term profits in order to win a stronger long-term competitive position in a desirable new market. A one-business domestic company has only one profit sanctuary—its home market. A one-business multinational company may have profit sanctuaries in several country markets, but all are in the same business. Both are vulnerable to a DMNC that launches a major strategic offensive in their profit sanctuaries and lowballs its prices to win market share at their expense. A DMNC's ability to keep hammering away at competitors with lowball prices year after year may reflect either a cost advantage growing out of its related diversification strategy or a willingness to cross-subsidize low profits or even losses with earnings from its profit sanctuaries in other country markets and/or its earnings from other businesses. Sanyo, for example, by pursuing related diversification keyed to product-distribution-technology types of strategic fit and managing its product families on a global scale, can eventually encircle domestic companies like Zenith (TVs and small computer systems) and Maytag (home appliances) and put them under serious competitive pressure. Sanyo can peck away at Zenith's market share in TVs and in the process weaken retailers' loyalty to the Zenith brand. Sanyo can diversify into large home appliances (by acquiring an established appliance maker or manufacturing on its own) and cross-subsidize a low-priced market entry against Maytag and other less-diversified home appliance firms with earnings from its many other business and product lines. If Sanyo chooses, it can keep its prices low for several years to gain market share at the expense of domestic rivals, turning its attention to profits after the battle for market share and competitive position is won.[23]

The competitive principle is clear: A DMNC has a strategic arsenal capable of defeating both a single-business MNC and a single-business domestic company over the long term. The competitive advantages of a DMNC, however, depend on employing a related diversification strategy in industries that are

---

[22]Ibid., p. 64.
[23]Ibid.

already globally competitive or are on the verge of becoming so. Then the related businesses have to be managed so as to capture strategic fit benefits. DMNCs have the biggest potential for competitive advantage in industries with technology-sharing and technology-transfer opportunities and in those where there are important economies of scope and brand name benefits associated with competing in related product families.

A DMNC also has important cross-subsidization potential for winning its way into attractive new markets. However, a DMNC's cross-subsidization powers cannot be deployed in the extreme. It is one thing to use a *portion* of the profits and cash flows from existing businesses to cover "reasonable" short-term losses when entering a new business or country market; it is quite another to drain corporate profits indiscriminately (and thus impair overall company performance) to support either deep price discounting and quick market penetration in the short term or continuing losses over the longer term. At some juncture, every business and market entered has to make a profit contribution or become a candidate for abandonment. Moreover, the company has to wrest consistently acceptable performance from the whole business portfolio. So there are limits to cross-subsidization. As a general rule, cross-subsidization is justified only if there is a good chance short-term losses can be amply recouped in some way over the long term.

Illustration Capsule 20 provides examples of the business portfolios and global scope of several DMNCs.

> • • • • • • • • • • • • •
> *A DMNC's most potent advantages usually derive from technology-sharing, economies of scope, shared brand names, and its potential to employ cross-subsidization tactics.*

COMBINATION DIVERSIFICATION STRATEGIES

The six corporate diversification approaches described above are not mutually exclusive. They can be pursued in combination and in varying sequences, allowing ample room for companies to customize their diversification strategies to fit their own circumstances. The most common business portfolios created by corporate diversification strategies are:

- A "dominant-business" enterprise with sales concentrated in one major core business but with a modestly diversified portfolio of either related or unrelated businesses (amounting to one third or less of total corporatewide sales).
- A narrowly diversified enterprise having a *few* (two to five) *related core* business units.
- A broadly diversified enterprise made up of *many* mostly *related* business units.
- A narrowly diversified enterprise comprised of a *few* (two to five) *core* business units in *unrelated* industries.
- A broadly diversified enterprise having *many* business units in mostly *unrelated* industries.
- A multibusiness enterprise diversified into unrelated areas but with a portfolio of related businesses within each area—thus giving it *several unrelated groups of related businesses.*

In each case, the geographic markets of individual businesses within the portfolio can be local, regional, national, multinational, or global. Thus, a company can be competing locally in some businesses, nationally in others, and globally in others.

ILLUSTRATION CAPSULE   20 | THE GLOBAL SCOPE OF PROMINENT DIVERSIFIED
MULTINATIONAL CORPORATIONS

Company (headquarters base)	Major Lines of Business	Number of Employees	1990 Global Sales	Global Plant Locations
Unilever (Netherlands, Britain)	Vaseline products, Cutex, Prince Matchabelli products, Ragu sauces, Lipton teas and soups, laundry detergents, soaps, toothpaste and other personal care products, margarine, frozen foods, agribusiness, and chemicals	304,000	$40 billion in 75 different countries • Europe, 61% • North America, 18% • Rest of world, 21%	340 subsidiary companies in 30 different countries
Siemens (West Germany)	Electrical equipment, lighting, power plants, security systems, medical engineering, communications and information systems, telecommunications networks	373,000	$39 billion • Europe, 73% • North America, 10% • Asia and Australia, 9% • Latin America, 4% • Africa, 4%	28 countries
Philips (Netherlands)	Lighting, consumer electronics, domestic appliances, and telecommunications and data systems	273,000	$31 billion • Europe, 53% • North America, 29% • Asia and Australia, 10% • Latin America, 6% • Africa, 2%	60 countries
Nissan Motor Co. (Japan)	Automobiles, trucks, rockets, forklifts, boats, and textile machinery	130,000	$40.2 billion in 150 countries	15 countries
Toyota Motor Corp. (Japan)	Automobiles, trucks, buses, forklifts, power shovels, residential and commercial construction	97,000	$64.5 billion in 150 countries	11 plants in Japan 30 plants in 21 other countries
Hitachi (Japan)	Power plants, turbines, boilers, TV sets, VCRs, kitchen appliances, lighting fixtures, computers, word processors, fax machines, cranes, locomotives, machinery, wire and cable, chemicals, and steel products	291,000	$51 billion in 30 countries	7 countries
Dow Chemical Co. (United States)	Chemicals, plastics, hydrocarbons, pharmaceuticals, consumer products (1,800 different products in all)	62,000	$20 billion • Europe, 31% • U.S., 45% • Rest of world, 24%	120-plus plant locations in 32 countries
CPC International (United States)	Consumer foods (Hellman's, Mazola, Skippy, Knorr soups and sauces, margarine, English muffins, pasta) and corn refining products (corn starches, corn syrups, dextrose, animal feed ingredients)	35,300	$5.8 billion in 50 countries • North America, 46% • Europe, 36% • Latin America, 13% • Asia and Africa, 5%	28 countries

Diversification becomes an attractive strategy when a company runs out of profitable growth opportunities in its present business. There are two fundamental approaches to diversification—into related businesses and into unrelated businesses. The rationale for related diversification is *strategic*: diversify into businesses with strategic fit, capitalize on strategic fit relationships to gain competitive advantage, then use competitive advantage to achieve the desired $2 + 2 = 5$ impact on shareholder value. The reasons for diversifying into unrelated businesses hinge almost exclusively on opportunities for attractive financial gain—there is nothing *strategic* about unrelated diversification.

Figure 7–2 shows the paths an undiversified company can take on the road to managing a diversified business portfolio. Most companies have their strategic roots in single-business concentration. Vertical integration strategies may or may not be involved depending on the extent to which forward or backward integration strengthens a firm's competitive position or helps it secure a competitive advantage. When diversification becomes a serious strategic option, a company must choose to pursue related diversification, unrelated diversification, or some mix of both. There are advantages and disadvantages to all three options. Once diversification has been accomplished, management's task is to figure out how to manage the existing business portfolio. The six primary post-diversification alternatives are (1) make new acquisitions, (2) divest weak-performing business units or those that no longer fit, (3) restructure the makeup of the portfolio if overall performance is poor, (4) retrench to a narrower diversification base, (5) pursue multinational diversification, and (6) close down/liquidate money-losing business units that cannot be sold.

Ansoff, H. Igor. *Corporate Strategy.* New York: McGraw-Hill, 1965, chap. 7.

Bright, William M. "Alternative Strategies for Diversification." *Research Management* 12, no. 4 (July 1969), pp. 247–53.

Buzzell, Robert D. "Is Vertical Integration Profitable?" *Harvard Business Review* 61, no. 1 (January–February 1983), pp. 92–102.

Drucker, Peter. *Management: Tasks, Responsibilities, Practices.* New York: Harper & Row, 1974, chaps. 55, 56, 57, 58, 60, and 61.

Guth, William D. "Corporate Growth Strategies." *Journal of Business Strategy* 1, no. 2 (Fall 1980), pp. 56–62.

Hall, William K. "Survival Strategies in a Hostile Environment." *Harvard Business Review* 58, no. 5 (September–October 1980), pp. 75–85.

Harrigan, Kathryn R. "Matching Vertical Integration Strategies to Competitive Conditions." *Strategic Management Journal* 7, no. 6 (November–December 1986), pp. 535 –56.

———. "Formulating Vertical Integration Strategies." *Academy of Management Review* 9, no. 4 (October 1984), pp. 638–52.

———. *Strategic Flexibility.* Lexington, Mass.: Lexington Books, 1985, chap. 4 and Table A-8, p. 162.

Hax, Arnoldo, and Nicolas S. Majluf. *The Strategy Concept and Process.* Englewood Cliffs, N.J.: Prentice Hall, 1991, chaps. 9, 11, and 15.

Hofer, Charles W. "Turnaround Strategies." *Journal of Business Strategy* 1, no. 1 (Summer 1980), pp. 19–31.

Hoffman, Richard C. "Strategies for Corporate Turnarounds: What Do We Know About Them?" *Journal of General Management* 14, no. 3 (Spring 1989), pp. 46–66.

Kumpe, Ted, and Piet T. Bolwijn. "Manufacturing: The New Case for Vertical Integration." *Harvard Business Review* 88, no. 2 (March–April 1988), pp. 75–82.

FIGURE 7–2   **Checklist of Major Corporate Strategy Alternatives**

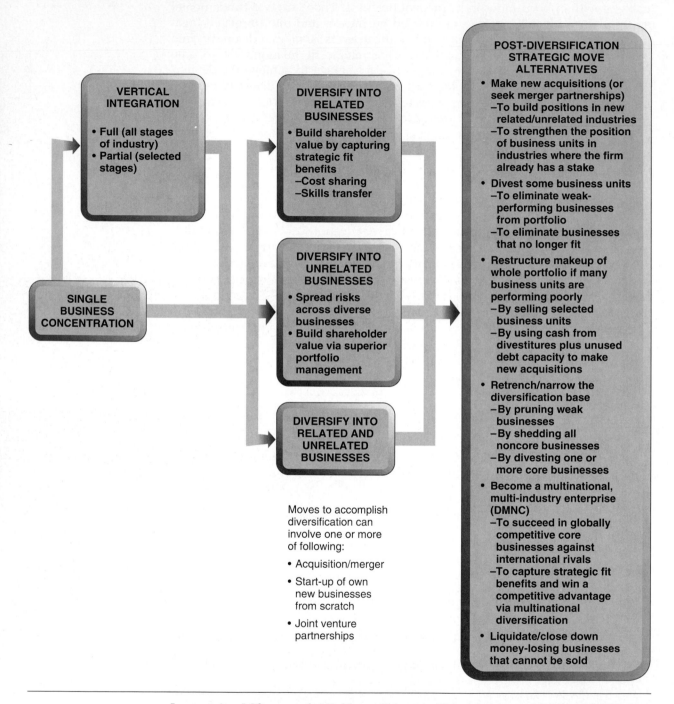

Lauenstein, Milton, and Wickham Skinner. "Formulating a Strategy of Superior Resources." *Journal of Business Strategy* 1, no. 1 (Summer 1980), pp. 4–10.

Ohmae, Kenichi. *The Mind of the Strategist.* New York: Penguin Books, 1983, chaps. 10 and 12.

Prahalad, C. K., and Yves L. Doz. *The Multinational Mission.* New York: Free Press, 1987, chaps. 1 and 2.

Techniques for Analyzing Diversified Companies

If we can know where we are and something about how we got there, we might see
where we are trending—and if the outcomes which lie naturally in our course are
unacceptable, to make timely change.
~Abraham Lincoln

• • • • • • •

No company can afford everything it would like to do. Resources have to be
allocated. The essence of strategic planning is to allocate resources to those
areas that have the greatest future potential.
~Reginald Jones

Once a company has diversified, three strategic issues continuously challenge corporate strategy-makers:

- How attractive is the group of businesses the company is in?
- Assuming the company sticks with its present lineup of businesses, how good is its performance outlook in the years ahead?
- If the previous two answers are not satisfactory, what should the company do in the way of getting out of some existing businesses, strengthening the positions of remaining businesses, and getting into new businesses to boost the performance prospects of its business portfolio?

The task of crafting and implementing action plans to improve the attractiveness and competitive strength of a company's business-unit portfolio is the heart of what corporate-level strategic management is all about.

Strategic analysis of diversified companies builds on the concepts and methods used for single-business companies. But there are also new factors to consider and additional analytical approaches to master. The procedure we will use to systematically evaluate the strategy of a diversified company, assess the caliber and potential of its businesses, and decide what strategic actions to take next consists of an eight-step process:

Strategic analysis in a
diversified company is an
eight-step process.

1. Identifying the present corporate strategy.
2. Constructing one or more business portfolio matrixes to reveal the character of the company's business portfolio.
3. Comparing the long-term attractiveness of each industry the company is in.
4. Comparing the competitive strength of the company's business units to see which ones are strong contenders in their respective industries.
5. Rating the business units on the basis of their historical performance and their prospects for the future.
6. Assessing each business unit's compatibility with corporate strategy and determining the value of any strategic fit relationships among existing business units.
7. Ranking the business units in terms of priority for new capital investment and deciding whether the general strategy and direction for each business unit should be aggressive expansion, fortify and defend, overhaul and reposition, or harvest/divest. (The task of initiating *specific* business-unit strategies to improve a subsidiary's competitive position is usually delegated to business-level managers, with corporate-level managers offering suggestions and having authority for final approval.)
8. Crafting new strategic moves to improve overall corporate performance—changing the makeup of the portfolio via acquisitions and divestitures, coordinating the activities of related business units to achieve cost-sharing and skills transfer benefits, and steering corporate resources into the areas of greatest opportunity.

The rest of this chapter describes this eight-step process and introduces the new analytical techniques needed to arrive at sound corporate strategy appraisals.

IDENTIFYING THE PRESENT CORPORATE STRATEGY

Evaluating a diversified firm's business portfolio needs to begin with clear identification of the firm's diversification strategy.

Strategic analysis of a diversified company starts by probing the organization's present strategy and business makeup. Recall from Figure 2–2 in Chapter 2 that a good overall perspective of a diversified company's corporate strategy comes from looking at:

- The extent to which the firm is diversified (as measured by the proportion of total sales and operating profits contributed by each business unit and by whether the diversification base is broad or narrow).
- Whether the firm's portfolio is keyed to related or unrelated diversification, or a mixture of both.
- Whether the scope of company operations is mostly domestic, increasingly multinational, or global.
- The nature of recent moves to boost performance of key business units and/or strengthen existing business positions.
- Any moves to add new businesses to the portfolio and build positions in new industries.

- Any moves to divest weak or unattractive business units.
- Corporate management efforts to pursue strategic fit relationships and use diversification to create competitive advantage.
- The proportion of capital expenditures going to each business unit.

Identifying the current corporate strategy lays the foundation for a thorough strategy analysis and, subsequently, for reformulating the strategy as it "should be."

MATRIX TECHNIQUES FOR EVALUATING DIVERSIFIED PORTFOLIOS

The most popular technique for assessing the quality of the businesses a company has diversified into is portfolio matrix analysis. *A business portfolio matrix is a two-dimensional display comparing the strategic positions of every business a diversified company is in.* Matrixes can be constructed using any pair of strategic position indicators. The most revealing indicators are industry growth rate, market share, long-term industry attractiveness, competitive strength, and stage of product/market evolution. Usually one dimension of the matrix relates to the attractiveness of the industry environment and the other to the strength of a business within its industry. Three types of business portfolio matrixes are used most frequently—the growth-share matrix developed by the Boston Consulting Group, the industry attractiveness–business strength matrix pioneered at General Electric, and the Hofer–A. D. Little industry life-cycle matrix.

> **Basic Concept**
> *A business portfolio matrix is a two-dimensional display comparing the strategic positions of every business a diversified company is in.*

The Growth-Share Matrix

The first business portfolio matrix to be widely used was a four-square grid devised by the Boston Consulting Group (BCG), a leading management consulting firm.[1] Figure 8–1 illustrates a BCG-type matrix. The matrix is formed using *industry growth rate* and *relative market share* as the axes. Each business unit appears as a "bubble" on the four-cell matrix, with the size of each bubble or circle scaled to the percent of revenues it represents in the overall corporate portfolio.

Early BCG methodology arbitrarily placed the dividing line between "high" and "low" industry growth rates at around twice the real GNP growth rate plus inflation, but the boundary percentage can be raised or lowered to suit individual preferences. A strong case can be made for placing the line so business units in industries growing faster than the economy as a whole end up in the "high-growth" cells and those in industries growing slower end up in "low-growth" cells ("low-growth" industries are those that can be described as mature, aging, stagnant, or declining).

Relative market share is the ratio of a business's market share to the market share held by the largest rival firm in the industry, with market share measured

> *The BCG portfolio matrix compares a diversified company's businesses on the basis of industry growth rate and relative market share.*

> **Basic Concept**
> *Relative market share is calculated by dividing a business's percentage share of total industry sales volume by the percentage share held by its largest rival.*

---

[1] The original presentation is Bruce D. Henderson, "The Experience Curve—Reviewed. IV. The Growth Share Matrix of the Product Portfolio" (Boston: The Boston Consulting Group, 1973), Perspectives No. 135. For an excellent chapter-length treatment of the use of the BCG growth-share matrix in strategic portfolio analysis, see Arnoldo C. Hax and Nicolas S. Majluf, *Strategic Management: An Integrative Perspective* (Englewood Cliffs, N. J.: Prentice Hall, 1984), chap. 7.

FIGURE 8–1   The BCG Growth- Share Business Portfolio Matrix

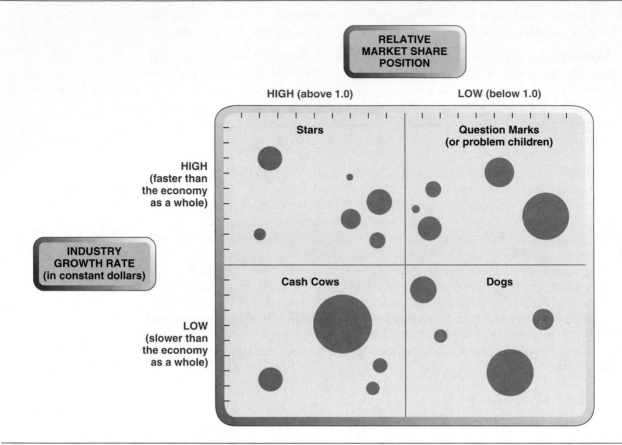

Note: *Relative* market share is defined by the ratio of one's own market share to the market share held by the largest *rival* firm. When the vertical dividing line is set at 1.0, the only way a firm can achieve a star or cash cow position in the growth-share matrix is to have the largest market share in the industry. Since this is a very stringent criterion, it may be "fairer" and more revealing to locate the vertical dividing line in the matrix at about 0.75 or 0.80.

in unit volume not dollars. For instance, if business A has a 15 percent share of the industry's total volume and A's largest rival has a 30 percent share, A's relative market share is 0.5. If business B has a market-leading share of 40 percent and its largest rival has 30 percent, B's relative market share is 1.33. Given this definition, only business units that are market-share leaders in their respective industries will have relative market share values greater than 1.0; business units that trail one or more rivals in market share will have ratios below 1.0.

BCG's original standard put the border between "high" and "low" relative market share at 1.0, as shown in Figure 8–1. When the boundary is set at 1.0, circles in the two left-side cells of the matrix represent businesses that are market-share leaders in their industry. Circles in the two right-side cells identify portfolio members that are in runner-up positions in their industry. The degree to which they trail is indicated by the size of the relative market share ratio. A ratio of .10 indicates the business has a market share only $1/_{10}$ that of the largest firm in the market; a ratio of .80 indicates a market share $4/_5$ or 80 percent as big as the leading firm's. Many portfolio analysts think that putting the boundary between high and low relative market share at 1.0 is unreasonably stringent because only businesses with the largest market share in their industry qualify for the two left-side cells of the matrix. They advocate putting the boundary at 0.75 or 0.80 so businesses to the left have *strong* or above-average market positions (even though they are not *the* leader) and businesses to the right are clearly in underdog or below-average positions.

Using *relative* market share instead of *actual* market share to construct the growth-share matrix is analytically superior because the former measure is a better indicator of comparative market strength and competitive position. A 10 percent market share is much stronger if the leader's share is 12 percent than if it is 50 percent; the use of relative market share captures this difference. Equally important, relative market share is likely to reflect relative cost based on experience and economies of large-scale production. Large businesses may be able to operate at lower unit costs than smaller ones because of technological and efficiency gains that attach to larger size. But the Boston Consulting Group accumulated evidence that the phenomenon of lower unit costs went beyond just the effects of scale economies; they found that, as the cumulative volume of production increased, the knowledge gained from the firm's growing production experience often led to the discovery of additional efficiencies and ways to reduce costs even further. BCG labeled the relationship between *cumulative production volume* and lower unit costs *the experience curve effect* (for more details, see Figure 3–1 in Chapter 3). A sizable experience curve effect in the industry's activity-cost chain places a strategic premium on market share: the competitor that gains the largest market share tends to realize important cost advantages which, in turn, can be used to lower prices and gain still additional customers, sales, market share, and profit. The stronger the experience curve in a business, the more dominant role in its strategy-making.[2]

With these features of the BCG growth-share matrix in mind, we are ready to explore the portfolio implications for businesses in each cell of the matrix in Figure 8–1.

> *Relative market share is a better indicator of a business's competitive strength and market position than a simple percentage measure of market share.*

Question Marks and Problem Children   Business units falling in the upper-right quadrant of the growth-share matrix were labeled by BCG as "question marks" or "problem children." Rapid market growth makes such businesses attractive from an industry standpoint. But their low relative market share (and thus reduced access to experience curve effects) raises a question about whether they can compete successfully against larger, more cost-efficient rivals—hence, the "question mark" or "problem child" designation. Question mark businesses, moreover, are typically "cash hogs"—so labeled because their cash needs are high (owing to the investment requirements of rapid growth and product development) and their internal cash generation is low (owing to low market share, less access to experience curve effects and scale economies, and consequently thinner profit margins). A question mark/cash hog business in a fast-growing industry may require large infusions of cash just to keep up with rapid market growth; it may need even bigger infusions to outgrow the

> ***Basic Concept***
> *A cash hog business is one whose internal cash flows are inadequate to fully fund its needs for working capital and new capital investment.*

---

[2]For two recent discussions of the strategic importance of the experience curve, see Pankoy Ghemawat, "Building Strategy on the Experience Curve," *Harvard Business Review* 64, no. 2 (March–April 1985), pp. 143–49 and Bruce D. Henderson, "The Application and Misapplication of the Experience Curve," *Journal of Business Strategy* 4, no. 3 (Winter 1984), pp. 3–9.

market and become an industry leader. The corporate parent of a cash hog business has to decide if it is worthwhile to fund the perhaps considerable investment requirements of a question mark division.

BCG has argued that the two best strategic options for a question mark business are: (1) an aggressive invest- and-expand strategy to capitalize on the industry's rapid-growth opportunities or (2) divestiture if the costs of expanding capacity and building market share outweigh the potential payoff and financial risk. Pursuit of a fast-growth strategy is imperative any time an attractive question mark business is in an industry with strong experience curve effects. In such cases, it takes major gains in market share to begin to match the lower costs of firms with greater cumulative production experience and bigger market shares. The stronger the experience curve effect, the more potent the cost advantages of rivals with larger relative market shares. Consequently, so the BCG thesis goes, unless a question mark/problem child business can successfully pursue a fast-growth strategy and win major market-share gains, it cannot hope to ever become cost competitive with large-volume firms that are further down the experience curve. Divestiture then becomes the only other viable long-run alternative. The corporate strategy prescriptions for managing question mark/problem child businesses are straightforward: divest those that are weaker and have less chance to catch the leaders on the experience curve; invest heavily in high-potential question marks and groom them to become tomorrow's "stars."

Stars   Businesses with high relative market share positions in high-growth markets rank as "stars" in the BCG grid because they offer excellent profit and growth opportunities. They are the business units an enterprise depends on to boost overall performance of the total portfolio.

Given their dominant market-share position and rapid growth environment, stars typically require large cash investments to expand production facilities and meet working capital needs. But they also tend to generate their own large internal cash flows due to the low-cost advantage of scale economies and cumulative production experience. Star businesses vary as to their cash hog status. Some can cover their investment needs with their own cash flows; others need funds from their corporate parents to stay abreast of rapid industry growth. Normally, strongly-positioned star businesses in industries where growth is beginning to slow tend to be self-sustaining in terms of cash flow and make little claim on the corporate parent's treasury. Young stars, however, typically require substantial investment capital *beyond what they can generate on their own* and are thus cash hogs.

Cash Cows   Businesses with a high relative market share in a low-growth market are designated "cash cows" in the BCG scheme. A *cash cow business* generates substantial cash surpluses over what it needs for reinvestment and growth. The reasons why a business in this cell of the matrix tends to be a cash cow are straightforward. Because of the business's high relative market share and industry leadership position, it has the sales volumes and reputation to earn attractive profits. Because it is in a slow-growth industry, it typically generates more cash from current operations than it needs to sustain its market position.

Many of today's cash cows are yesterday's stars, having dropped into the bottom cell as industry demand matured. Cash cows, though less attractive from a growth standpoint, are valuable businesses. Their cash flows can be used to cover dividend payments, finance acquisitions, and provide funds for investing in emerging stars and problem children being groomed as future stars. Every effort should be made to keep cash cow businesses in healthy condition to preserve their cash-generating capability over the long term. The goal should be to fortify and defend a cash cow's market position while efficiently generating dollars to reallocate to other business investments. Weakening cash cows, however, may become candidates for harvesting and eventual divestiture if industry maturity results in unattractive competitive conditions and dries up the cash flow surpluses.

A cash cow business is a valuable part of a diversified company's business portfolio because it generates cash for financing new acquisitions, funding cash hogs' requirements, and paying dividends.

Dogs   Businesses with a low relative market share in a slow-growth industry are called "dogs" because of their dim growth prospects, their trailing market position, and the squeeze that being behind the leaders on the experience curve puts on their profit margins. Weak dog businesses (those positioned in the lower right corner of the dog cell) are often unable to generate attractive cash flows on a long-term basis. Sometimes they cannot produce enough cash to support a rear-guard fortify-and-defend strategy—especially if competition is brutal and profit margins are chronically thin. Consequently, except in unusual cases, BCG prescribes that weaker-performing dog businesses be harvested, divested, or liquidated, depending on which alternative yields the most cash.

Weaker dog businesses should be harvested, divested, or liquidated; stronger dogs can be retained as long as their profits and cash flows remain acceptable.

Implications for Corporate Strategy   The chief contribution of the BCG growth-share matrix is the attention it draws to the cash flow and investment characteristics of various types of businesses and how corporate financial resources can be shifted between businesses to optimize the performance of the whole corporate portfolio. According to BCG analysis, a sound, long-term corporate strategy should utilize the excess cash generated by cash cow business units to finance market-share increases for cash hog businesses—the young stars unable to finance their own growth and problem children with the best potential to grow into stars. If successful, cash hogs eventually become self-supporting stars. Then, when stars' markets begin to mature and their growth slows, they become cash cows. The "success sequence" is thus problem child/question mark to young star (but perhaps still a cash hog) to self-supporting star to cash cow.

The BCG growth-share matrix highlights the cash flow, investment, and profitability characteristics of various businesses and the benefits of shifting financial resources between them to optimize the whole portfolio's performance.

Weaker, less-attractive question mark businesses unworthy of a long-term invest-and-expand strategy are often a liability to a diversified company because of the high-cost economics associated with their low relative market share and because they do not generate enough cash to keep pace with market growth. According to BCG prescriptions, these question marks should be prime divestiture candidates *unless* they can be kept profitable and viable with their own internally generated funds. Not every question mark business is a cash hog or a disadvantaged competitor, however. Those in industries with small capital requirements, few scale economies, and weak experience curve effects can often compete satisfactorily against larger industry leaders and contribute enough to corporate earnings to justify retention. Clearly, though, weaker question marks still have a low-priority claim on corporate resources and a dim future in the portfolio. Question mark businesses unable to become stars are destined to drift vertically downward in the matrix, becoming dogs, as their industry growth slows and market demand matures.

Dogs should be retained only as long as they contribute adequately to overall company performance. Strong dogs may produce a positive cash flow and show average profitability. But the further right and down a dog business is positioned in the BCG matrix, the more likely it is tying up assets that could be redeployed more profitably. BCG recommends a harvesting strategy for a weakening or already weak dog business. If a harvesting strategy is no longer attractive, a weak dog should be eliminated from the portfolio.

There are two "disaster sequences" in the BCG scheme of things: (1) when a star's position in the matrix erodes over time to that of a problem child and then is dragged by slowing industry growth down into the dog cell of the matrix and (2) when a cash cow loses market leadership to the point where it becomes a dog on the decline. Other strategic mistakes include overinvesting in a safe cash cow; underinvesting in a question mark so instead of becoming a star it tumbles into the dog category; and shotgunning resources over many question marks rather than concentrating on the best ones to boost their chances of becoming stars.

Strengths and Weaknesses in the Growth-Share Matrix Approach   The BCG business portfolio matrix makes a definite contribution to the strategist's tool kit when it comes to evaluating the portfolio's overall attractiveness and reaching broad prescriptions concerning the strategy and direction for each business unit. Viewing a diversified corporation as a collection of cash flows and cash requirements (present and future) is a major step forward in understanding the financial aspects of corporate strategy. The BCG matrix highlights the financial "interaction" within a corporate portfolio, shows the kinds of financial considerations that must be dealt with, and explains why priorities for corporate resource allocation can differ from business to business. It also provides good rationalizations for both invest-and-expand strategies and divestiture. Yet it has several legitimate shortcomings:

· · · · · · · · · · · ·

Despite the analytical insights it yields, the growth-share matrix has significant shortcomings.

1. A four-cell matrix based on high-low classifications hides the fact that many businesses (the majority?) are in markets with an "average" growth rate and have relative market shares that are neither high nor low but in-between or intermediate. In which cells do these average businesses belong?

2. While labeling businesses as stars, cash cows, dogs, or question marks does have communicative appeal, it is a misleading simplification to pigeonhole all businesses into one of four categories. Some market-share leaders have never really been stars in terms of profitability. All businesses with low relative market shares are not dogs or question marks—in many cases, runner-up firms have proven track records in terms of growth, profitability, and competitive ability, even gaining on the so-called leaders. Hence, a key characteristic to assess is the *trend* in a firm's relative market share. Is it gaining ground or losing ground and why? This weakness can be overcome by placing directional arrows on each of the circles in the matrix—see Figure 8–2.

FIGURE 8–2   **Present versus Future Positions in the Portfolio Matrix**

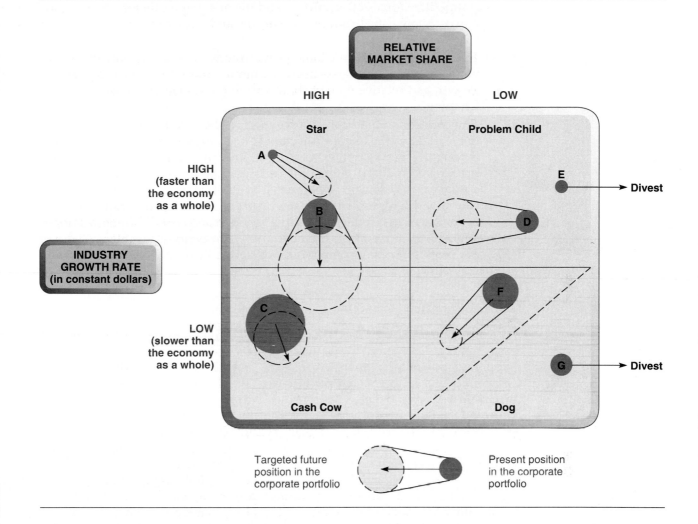

3. The BCG matrix is not a reliable indicator of relative investment opportunities across business units.[3] For example, investing in a star is not necessarily more attractive than investing in a lucrative cash cow. The matrix doesn't indicate if a question mark is a potential winner or a likely loser. It says nothing about whether shrewd investment can turn a strong dog into a cash cow.

4. Being a market leader in a slow-growth industry does not guarantee cash cow status because (a) the investment requirements of a fortify-and-defend strategy, given the impact of inflation on the costs of

---

[3]Derek F. Abell and John S. Hammond, *Strategic Market Planning* (Englewood Cliffs, N.J.: Prentice Hall, 1979), p. 212.

replacing worn-out facilities and equipment, can soak up much or all of the available internal cash flows and (*b*) as markets mature, competitive forces often stiffen, and the ensuing battle for volume and market share can shrink profit margins and wipe out any surplus cash flows.

5. To thoroughly assess the long-term attractiveness of the portfolio's business units, strategists need to examine more than just industry growth and relative market share variables—as we discussed in Chapter 3.

6. The connection between relative market share and profitability is not as tight as the experience curve effect implies. The importance of cumulative production experience in lowering unit costs varies from industry to industry. Sometimes a larger market share translates into a unit-cost advantage; sometimes it doesn't. Hence, it is wise to be cautious when prescribing strategy based on the assumption that experience curve effects are strong enough and cost differences among competitors big enough to totally drive competitive advantage (there are more sources of competitive advantage than just experience curve economics).

The Industry Attractiveness/Business Strength Matrix

In the attractiveness-strength matrix, each business is plotted using quantitative measures of long-term industry attractiveness and business strength/competitive position.

An alternative approach avoids some of the shortcomings of the BCG growth-share matrix. Pioneered by General Electric as a way to analyze its own diversified portfolio (with help from the consulting firm of McKinsey and Company), this nine-cell matrix is based on the two dimensions of long-term industry attractiveness and business strength/competitive position (see Figure 8–3).[4] Both dimensions of the matrix are a composite of *several* considerations as opposed to a single factor. The criteria for determining long-term industry attractiveness include market size and growth rate; technological requirements; the intensity of competition; entry and exit barriers; seasonality and cyclical influences; capital requirements; emerging industry threats and opportunities; historical and projected industry profitability; and social, environmental, and regulatory influences. To arrive at a formal, quantitative measure of long-term industry attractiveness, the chosen measures are assigned weights based on their importance to corporate management and their role in the diversification strategy. The sum of the weights must add up to 1.0. Weighted attractiveness ratings are calculated by multiplying the industry's rating on each factor (using a 1 to 5 or 1 to 10 rating scale) by the factor's weight. For example, a rating score of 8 times a weight of .25 gives a weighted rating of 2.0. The sum of weighted ratings for all the attractiveness factors yields the industry's long-term attractiveness. The procedure is shown on the next page:

---

[4]For an expanded treatment, see Michael G. Allen, "Diagramming G.E.'s Planning for What's WATT," in *Corporate Planning: Techniques and Applications*, ed. Robert J. Allio and Malcolm W. Pennington (New York: AMACOM, 1979); and Hax and Majluf, *Strategic Management: An Integrative Perspective*, chap. 8.

Industry/Attractiveness Factor	Weight	Rating	Weighted Industry Rating
Market size and projected growth	.15	5	0.75
Seasonality and cyclical influences	.10	8	0.80
Technological considerations	.10	1	0.10
Intensity of competition	.25	4	1.00
Emerging opportunities and threats	.15	1	0.15
Capital requirements	.05	2	0.10
Industry profitability	.10	3	0.30
Social, political, regulatory, and environmental factors	.10	7	0.70
	1.00		
Industry attractiveness rating			3.90

Attractiveness ratings are calculated for each industry represented in the corporate portfolio. Each industry's attractiveness score determines its position on the vertical scale in Figure 8–3.

To arrive at a quantitative measure of business strength/competitive position, each business in the corporate portfolio is rated using the same kind of approach as for industry attractiveness. The factors used to assess business strength/competitive position include such criteria as market share, relative cost position, ability to match rival firms on product quality and service, knowledge of customers and markets, possession of desirable core competences, adequacy of technological know-how, caliber of management, and profitability relative to competitors (as specified in the box in Figure 8–3). The analytical issue is whether to rate each business unit on the same generic factors (which strengthens the basis for interindustry comparisons) or on each unit's strength on the factors most pertinent to its own industry (which gives a sharper measure of competitive position). Each business's strength/position rating determines its position along the horizontal axis of the matrix—that is, whether it merits a strong, average, or weak designation.[5]

The industry attractiveness and business strength scores provide the basis for placing a business in one of the nine cells of the matrix. In the GE attractiveness-strength matrix, the area of the circles is proportional to the size of the industry, and the pie slices within the circle reflect the business's market share.

Corporate Strategy Implications   The most important strategic implications from the attractiveness-strength matrix concern the assignment of investment priorities to each of the company's business units. Businesses in the three cells at the upper left, where long-term industry attractiveness and business strength/competitive position are favorable, are accorded top investment priority. The strategic prescription for businesses falling in these three cells

---

[5]Essentially the same procedure is used in company situation analysis to do a competitive strength assessment (see Table 4–3 in Chapter 4). The only difference is that in the GE method the same set of competitive strength factors is used for every industry to provide a common benchmark for making comparisons across industries. In strategic analysis at the business level, the strength measures are *always* industry specific, never generic generalizations.

FIGURE 8–3   **General Electric's Industry Attractiveness/Business Strength Matrix**

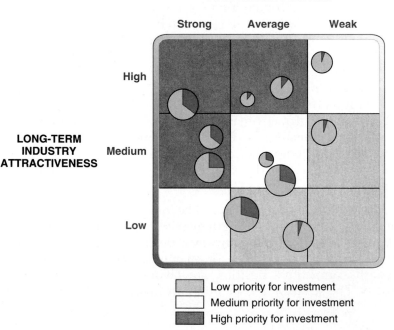

• Relative market share
• Possession of desirable core competencies
• Profit margins relative to competitors
• Ability to match or beat rivals on product quality and service
• Relative cost position
• Knowledge of customers and markets
• Technological capability
• Caliber of management

BUSINESS STRENGTH/ COMPETITIVE POSITION

• Market size and growth rate
• Industry profit margins (historical and projected)
• Intensity of competition
• Seasonality
• Cyclicality
• Technology and capital requirements
• Social, environ- mental, regulatory, and human impacts
• Emerging opportunities and threats
• Barriers to entry and exit

LONG-TERM INDUSTRY ATTRACTIVENESS

Strong   Average   Weak

High

Medium

Low

Low priority for investment
Medium priority for investment
High priority for investment

is "grow and build," with businesses in the high-strong cell having the highest claim on investment funds. Next in priority come businesses positioned in the three diagonal cells stretching from the lower left to the upper right. These businesses are usually given medium priority. They merit steady reinvestment to maintain and protect their industry positions; however, if a business in one of these three cells has an unusually attractive opportunity, it can win a higher investment priority and be given the go-ahead to employ a more aggressive strategic approach. The strategy prescription for businesses in the three cells in the lower right corner is typically harvest or divest (in exceptional cases where good turnaround potential exists, it can be "overhaul and reposition" using some type of turnaround approach).[6]

The nine-cell attractiveness-strength approach has three desirable attributes. One, it allows for intermediate rankings between high and low and between strong and weak. Two, it incorporates a much wider variety of strategically relevant variables. The BCG matrix is based totally on two considerations—industry growth rate and relative market share; the nine-cell GE matrix takes many factors into account to determine long-term industry attractiveness and business strength/competitive position. Three, and most important, it stresses the channeling of corporate resources to businesses with the greatest probability of achieving competitive advantage and superior performance. It is hard to argue against the logic of concentrating resources in those businesses that enjoy a higher degree of attractiveness and competitive strength, being very selective in making investments in businesses with "intermediate" positions, and withdrawing resources from businesses that are lower in attractiveness and strength unless they offer exceptional turnaround potential.

> The nine-cell attractiveness-strength matrix has a stronger conceptual basis than the four-cell growth-share matrix.

However, the nine-cell GE matrix, like the four-cell growth-share matrix, provides no real guidance on the *specifics* of business strategy; the most that can be concluded from the GE matrix analysis is what *general* strategic posture to take—aggressive expansion, fortify-and-defend, or harvest-divest. Such prescriptions, though valuable for overall portfolio management, don't address the issue of strategic coordination across related businesses and the specific competitive approaches and strategic actions to take at the business-unit level. Another weakness has been pointed out by Professors Hofer and Schendel: the GE method tends to obscure businesses that are about to become winners because their industries are entering the takeoff stage.[7]

The Life-Cycle Matrix

To better identify a *developing-winner* type of business, Hofer developed a 15-cell matrix. In this matrix businesses are plotted in terms of stage of industry

> The life-cycle matrix highlights whether a firm's businesses are evenly distributed across the stages of the industry life-cycle.

---

[6]At General Electric, each business actually ended up in one of five categories: (1) *high-growth potential* businesses deserving top investment priority; (2) *stable base* businesses that merit steady reinvestment to maintain position; (3) *support* businesses deserving periodic investment funding; (4) *selective pruning or rejuvenation* businesses deserving reduced investment; and (5) *venture* businesses meriting heavy R&D investment.

[7]Charles W. Hofer and Dan Schendel, *Strategy Formulation: Analytical Concepts* (St. Paul, Minn.: West Publishing, 1978), p. 33.

FIGURE 8–4   The Life-Cycle Portfolio Matrix

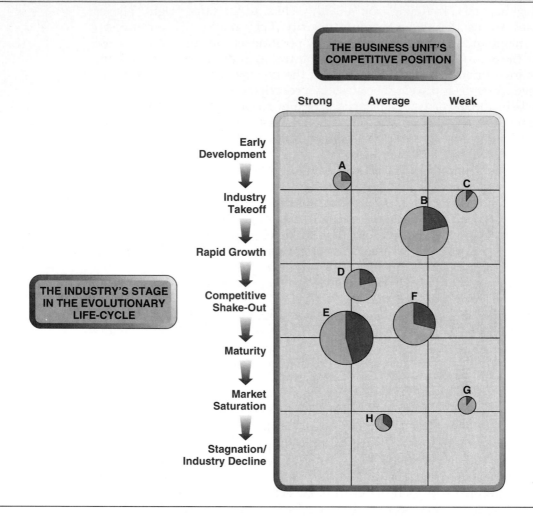

evolution and competitive position, as shown in Figure 8–4.[8] Again, the circles represent the sizes of the industries involved, and pie wedges denote the business's market share. In Figure 8–4, business A could be labeled a *developing winner*; business C a *potential loser*, business E an *established winner*, business F a cash cow, and business G a loser or dog. The power of the life-cycle matrix is the story it tells about the distribution of the firm's businesses across the stages of industry evolution.

Deciding Which Matrix to Construct

Restricting the analysis to just one type of portfolio matrix is unwise. Each matrix has its pros and cons, and each tells a different story about the

---

[8]Ibid., p. 34. This approach to business portfolio analysis was reportedly first used in practice by consultants at Arthur D. Little, Inc. For a full-scale review of this portfolio matrix approach, see Hax and Majluf, *Strategic Management: An Integrative Perspective*, chap. 9.

portfolio's strengths and weaknesses. Provided adequate data is available, all three matrixes should be constructed since it's best to assess the company's portfolio from different perspectives. The analytical objective is to understand the portfolio's mix of industries, the strategic position each business has in its industry, the portfolio's performance potential, and the kinds of financial and resource allocation considerations that have to be dealt with.

COMPARING INDUSTRY ATTRACTIVENESS

A central issue in evaluating a diversified company's strategy is judging the attractiveness of the industries it is in. Industry attractiveness has to be judged from three perspectives:

The attractiveness of the industries that a firm has diversified into needs to be evaluated from several angles.

1. *The attractiveness of each industry represented in the portfolio.* The relevant question is "Is this a good *industry* for the company to be in?" Ideally, each industry the firm has diversified into can pass the attractiveness test.
2. *Each industry's attractiveness relative to the others.* The question to answer here is "Which industries in the portfolio are the most attractive, and which are the least attractive?" Ranking the industries from most attractive to least attractive is a prerequisite to deciding how to allocate corporate resources.
3. *The attractiveness of all the industries as a group.* The question here is "How appealing is the *mix* of industries?" A company whose revenues and profits come chiefly from businesses in unattractive industries probably needs to consider restructuring its business portfolio.

All the industry attractiveness considerations discussed in Chapter 3 have application in this analytical phase.

An industry attractiveness/business strength portfolio matrix gives a strong, systematic basis for judging which business units are in the most attractive industries. If such a matrix has not been constructed, quantitative rankings of industry attractiveness can be developed using the same procedure described earlier for the nine-cell GE matrix. As a rule, all the industries represented in the business portfolio should, at minimum, be judged on the following attractiveness factors:

- *Market size and projected growth rate*—faster-growing industries tend to be more attractive than slow-growing industries, other things being equal.
- *The intensity of competition*—industries where competitive pressures are relatively weak are more attractive than industries with strong competitive pressures.
- *Technological and production skills required*—industries where the skill requirements are closely matched to company capabilities are more attractive than industries where the company's technical and/or manufacturing know-how is limited.
- *Capital requirements*—industries with low or attainable capital requirements are relatively more attractive than industries where investment requirements could strain corporate resources.

- *Seasonal and cyclical factors*—industries where demand is relatively stable and dependable are more attractive than industries where there are wide swings in buyer demand.
- *Industry profitability*—industries with healthy profit margins and high rates of return on investment are generally more attractive than industries where profits have historically been low or where the business risks are high.
- *Social, political, regulatory, and environmental factors*—industries with significant problems in these areas are less attractive than industries where such problems are no worse than most businesses encounter.
- *Strategic fits with other industries the firm has diversified into*—an industry can be attractive simply because it has valuable strategic fit relationships with other industries in the portfolio.

Strategic Management Principle

The more attractive the industries that a firm has diversified into, the better its performance prospects are likely to be.

Calculation of industry attractiveness ratings for all industries in the corporate portfolio provides a basis for ranking the industries from most to least attractive. If formal industry attractiveness ratings seem too cumbersome or tedious to calculate, analysts can rely on their knowledge of conditions in each industry to classify individual industries as having "high," "medium," or "low" attractiveness. However, the validity of such subjective assessments depends on whether analysts have studied industry conditions enough to make dependable judgments.

For a diversified company to be a strong performer, a substantial portion of its revenues and profits must come from business units in attractive industries. It is particularly important that core businesses be in industries with a good outlook for growth and above-average profitability. Businesses in the least attractive industries may be divestiture candidates, unless they are positioned strongly enough to overcome the adverse industry environment or they are a critical component of the portfolio.

COMPARING BUSINESS-UNIT STRENGTH

Assessments of how a firm's subsidiaries compare in competitive strength should be based on several factors.

Doing an appraisal of each business unit's strength and competitive position in its industry helps corporate managers judge a business unit's chances for success in its industry. The task here is to evaluate whether the business is well-positioned in its industry and the extent to which it already is or can become a strong market contender. The two most revealing techniques for evaluating a business's position in its industry are SWOT analysis and competitive strength assessment. Quantitative rankings of the strength/position of the portfolio's businesses can be calculated using either the attractiveness-strength matrix or the procedure presented in Chapter 4. Assessments of how a diversified company's subsidiaries compare in competitive strength should be based on such factors as:

- *Relative market share*—business units with higher relative market shares have greater competitive strength than business units with lower shares.
- *Ability to compete on price and/or quality*—business units that are cost competitive and/or that have established brand names and a reputation

for quality tend to be more strongly positioned than those struggling to establish a name or achieve cost parity with major rivals.

- *Technology and innovation capabilities*—business units recognized for their technological leadership and track record in innovation are usually strong competitors in their industry.
- *How well the business unit's skills and competences match industry key success factors*—the more a business unit's strengths match the industry's key success factors, the stronger its competitive position tends to be.
- *Profitability relative to competitors*—business units that consistently earn above-average returns on investment and have bigger profit margins than their rivals usually have stronger competitive positions than businesses with below-average profitability for their industry. Moreover, above-average profitability signals competitive advantage while below-average profitability usually denotes competitive disadvantage.

Other competitive strength indicators that can be employed include knowledge of customers and markets, production capabilities, marketing skills, reputation and brand name awareness, and the caliber of management.

Calculation of competitive strength ratings for each business unit provides a basis for judging which ones are in strong positions in their industries and which are in weak positions. If calculating competitive strength ratings is complicated by lack of sufficient data, analysts can rely on their knowledge of each business unit's competitive situation to classify each business unit as being in a "strong," "average," or "weak" competitive position. If trustworthy, such subjective judgments can substitute for quantitative measures.

Evaluating which businesses in the portfolio enjoy the strongest competitive positions adds further rationale for corporate resource allocation. A company may earn larger profits over the long term by investing in a business with a strong position in a moderately attractive industry than a weak business in a glamour industry. This is why a diversified company needs to consider *both* industry attractiveness and business strength in deciding where to steer resources.

Many diversified companies concentrate their resources on industries where they can be strong market contenders and divest businesses that are not good candidates for becoming leaders. At General Electric, the whole thrust of corporate strategy and resource allocation is aimed at putting GE's businesses into a number one or two position both in the United States and globally—see Illustration Capsule 21.

Strategic Management Principle
Shareholder interests are generally best served by concentrating corporate resources on businesses that can contend for market leadership in their industry.

COMPARING BUSINESS-UNIT PERFORMANCE

Once each subsidiary has been rated on the basis of industry attractiveness and competitive strength, the next step is to evaluate which businesses have the best performance prospects and which ones have the worst. The most important considerations in judging business-unit performance are sales growth, profit growth, contribution to company earnings, and the return on capital invested in the business; sometimes, cash flow generation is a big consideration, especially for cash cows or businesses with potential for harvesting.

Judgments about the expected future performance of each subsidiary indicate whether a firm's outlook for profitable growth with its current business lineup is bright or dim.

ILLUSTRATION CAPSULE | **21** | **PORTFOLIO MANAGEMENT AT GENERAL ELECTRIC**

When Jack Welch became CEO of General Electric in 1981, he launched a corporate strategy effort to reshape the company's diversified business portfolio. Early on he issued a challenge to GE's business-unit managers to become number one or number two in their industry; failing that, the business units either had to capture a decided technological advantage translatable into a competitive edge or face possible divestiture.

By 1989, GE was a different company. Under Welch's prodding, GE divested operations worth $9 billion—TV operations, small appliances, a mining business, and computer chips. It spent a

total of $24 billion acquiring new businesses, most notably RCA, Roper (a maker of major appliances whose biggest customer was Sears), and Kidder Peabody (a Wall Street investment banking firm). Internally, many of the company's smaller business operations were put under the direction of larger "strategic business units." But, most significantly, in 1989, 12 of GE's 14 strategic business units were market leaders in the United States and globally (the company's financial services and communications units served markets too fragmented to rank):

	Market Standing in the United States	Market Standing in the World
Aircraft engines	First	First
Broadcasting (NBC)	First	Not applicable
Circuit breakers	Tied for first with 2 others	Tied for first with 3 others
Defense electronics	Second	Second
Electric motors	First	First
Engineering plastics	First	First
Factory automation	Second	Third
Industrial and power systems	First	First
Lighting	First	Second
Locomotives	First	Tied for first
Major home appliances	First	Tied for second
Medical diagnostic imaging	First	First

In 1989, having divested most of the weak businesses and having built existing businesses into leading contenders, Welch launched a new initiative within GE to dramatically boost productivity and reduce the size of GE's bureaucracy. Welch argued that for GE to continue to be successful in

a global marketplace, the company had to press hard for continuous cost reduction in each of its businesses and cut through bureaucratic procedures to shorten response times to changing market conditions.

Source: Developed from information in Stratford P. Sherman, "Inside the Mind of Jack Welch," *Fortune,* March 27, 1989, pp. 39–50.

Information on a business's past performance can be gleaned from financial records. While past performance doesn't necessarily predict future performance, it does signal which businesses have been strong performers and which have not. Industry attractiveness/business strength evaluations should provide a solid basis for judging future prospects. Normally, strong business units in attractive industries have significantly better prospects than weak businesses in unattractive industries.

The growth and profit outlook for the company's core businesses generally determine whether the portfolio as a whole will turn in a strong or weak performance. Noncore businesses with subpar track records and little expectation for improvement are logical candidates for divestiture. Business subsidiaries with the brightest profit and growth prospects should have priority for having their capital investment requests funded.

STRATEGIC FIT ANALYSIS

The next analytical step is to determine how well each business unit fits into the company's overall business picture. Fit needs to be looked at from two angles: (1) whether a business unit has valuable strategic fit with other businesses the firm has diversified into (or has an opportunity to diversify into) and (2) whether the business unit meshes well with corporate strategy or adds a beneficial dimension to the corporate portfolio. A business is more attractive *strategically* when it has cost-sharing or skills transfer opportunities that can be translated into stronger competitive advantage and when it fits in with the firm's strategic direction. A business is more valuable *financially* when it can contribute heavily to corporate performance objectives (sales growth, profit growth, above-average return on investment, and so on) and materially enhance the company's overall worth. Just as businesses with poor profit prospects ought to become divestiture candidates so should businesses that don't fit strategically into the company's overall business picture. Firms that emphasize related diversification probably should divest businesses with little or no strategic fit unless such businesses are unusually good financial performers.

Strategic Management Principle
Business subsidiaries that don't fit strategically should be considered for divestiture unless their financial performance is outstanding.

RANKING THE BUSINESS UNITS ON INVESTMENT PRIORITY

Using the information and results of the preceding evaluation steps, corporate strategists can rank business units in terms of priority for new capital investment and develop a general strategic direction for each business unit. The task is to decide where the corporation should be investing its financial resources. Which business units should have top priority for new capital investment and financial support? Which business units should carry the lowest priority for new investment? Out of this ranking comes a clearer idea of what the basic strategic approach for each business unit should be—grow and build (aggressive expansion), fortify and defend (protect current position with new investments as needed), overhaul and reposition (try to move the business into a more desirable industry position and a better spot in the business portfolio matrix), or harvest/divest. In deciding whether to divest a business unit, strategists need to use a number of evaluating criteria: industry attractiveness, competitive strength, strategic fit with other businesses, performance potential (profit, return on capital employed, contribution to cash flow), compatibility with corporate priorities, capital requirements, and value to the overall portfolio.

As part of this evaluation step, consideration should be given to whether and how corporate resources and skills can be used to enhance the competitive

Improving the long-term financial performance of a diversified company entails giving priority to investments in businesses with good to excellent prospects and investing minimally, if at all, in businesses with subpar prospects.

standing of particular business units.[9] The potential for skills transfer and infusion of new capital become especially important when the firm has business units in less-than-desirable competitive positions and/or where improvement in some key success area could make a big difference to the unit's performance. It is also important when corporate strategy is predicated on strategic fit and the managerial game plan calls for transferring corporate skills and strengths to recently acquired business units in an effort to give them a competitive edge and bolster their market positions.[10]

CRAFTING A CORPORATE STRATEGY

The preceding analysis sets the stage for crafting strategic moves to improve a diversified company's overall performance. The basic issue of "what to do" hinges on the conclusions drawn about the overall *mix* of businesses in the portfolio.[11] Key considerations here are: Does the portfolio contain enough businesses in very attractive industries? Does the portfolio contain too many marginal businesses or question marks? Is the proportion of mature or declining businesses so great that corporate growth will be sluggish? Does the firm have enough cash cows to finance the stars and emerging winners? Do the company's core businesses generate dependable profits and/or cash flow? Is the portfolio overly vulnerable to seasonal or recessionary influences? Does the portfolio contain businesses that the company really doesn't need to be in? Is the firm burdened with too many businesses in average-to-weak competitive positions? Does the makeup of the business portfolio put the corporation in good position for the future? Answers to these questions indicate whether corporate strategists should consider divesting certain business, acquiring new ones, or restructuring the portfolio.

The Performance Test

. . . .

Corporate strategists can pursue any of five basic options to avoid a probable shortfall in financial performance.

A good test of the strategic and financial attractiveness of a firm's portfolio is whether the company can attain its performance objectives with its current lineup of businesses. If so, no major corporate strategy changes are indicated. However, if a performance shortfall is probable, corporate strategists can take any of several actions to close the gap:[12]

1. *Alter the strategic plans for some (or all) of the businesses.* This option involves renewed corporate efforts to get better performance out of its present business units. Corporate managers can push business-level managers for better business-unit performance. However, pursuing better short-term performance, if done too zealously, can impair a business's potential to perform better over the long term. Canceling expenditures that will bolster a business's long-term competitive position in order to squeeze out better short-term financial

---

[9]Hofer and Schendel, *Strategy Formulation: Analytical Concepts*, p. 80.

[10]Michael E. Porter, *Competitive Advantage* (New York: Free Press, 1985), chap. 9.

[11]Barry Hedley, "Strategy and the Business Portfolio," *Long Range Planning* 10, no. 1 (February 1977), p. 13; and Hofer and Schendel, *Strategy Formulation*, pp. 82–86.

[12]Hofer and Schendel, *Strategy Formulation*, pp. 93–100.

performance is a perilous strategy. In any case, there are limits as to how much extra performance can be squeezed out.

2. *Add new business units.* Boosting overall performance by making new acquisitions and/or starting new businesses internally raises some new strategy issues. Corporate managers must decide: (*a*) whether to acquire related or unrelated businesses, (*b*) what size acquisition(s) to make, (*c*) how the new units will fit into the present corporate structure, (*d*) what specific features to look for in an acquisition candidate, and (*e*) if acquisitions can be financed without shortchanging present business units in funding their investment requirements. Nonetheless, adding new businesses is a major strategic option, one frequently used by diversified companies to escape sluggish earnings performance.

3. *Divest weak-performing or money-losing businesses.* The most likely candidates for divestiture are businesses in a weak competitive position, in a relatively unattractive industry, or in an industry that does not "fit." Funds from divestitures can, of course, be used to finance new acquisitions, pay down corporate debt, or fund new strategic thrusts in the remaining businesses.

4. *Form alliances to try to alter conditions responsible for subpar performance potentials.* In some situations, alliances with domestic or foreign firms, trade associations, suppliers, customers, or special interest groups may help ameliorate adverse performance prospects.[13] Forming or supporting a political action group may be an effective way to lobby for solutions to import-export problems, tax disincentives, and onerous regulatory requirements.

5. *Lower corporate performance objectives.* Adverse market circumstances or declining fortunes in one or more core business units can render companywide performance targets unreachable. So can overly ambitious objective-setting. Closing the gap between actual and desired performance may then require revision of corporate objectives to bring them more in line with reality. Lowering performance objectives is usually a "last-resort" option, used only after other options have come up short.

Finding Additional Diversification Opportunities

One of the major corporate strategy-making concerns in a diversified company is whether to pursue further diversification and, if so, how to identify the "right" kinds of industries and businesses to get into. For firms pursuing unrelated diversification, the issue of where to diversify next is wide open—the search for acquisition candidates is based more on financial criteria than on industry or strategic criteria. Decisions to add unrelated businesses to the firm's portfolio are usually based on such considerations as whether the firm has the financial ability to make another acquisition, whether new acquisitions are needed to boost overall corporate performance, whether one or more acquisition opportunities have to be acted on before they are purchased

* * * * * * * * * * * *

In firms with unrelated diversification strategies, the problem of where to diversify next is addressed by hunting for businesses that offer attractive financial returns irrespective of what industry they're in.

---

[13]For an excellent discussion of the benefits of alliances among competitors in global industries, see Kenichi Ohmae, "The Global Logic of Strategic Alliances," *Harvard Business Review* 67, no. 2 (March–April 1989), pp. 143–54.

by other firms, and whether the timing is right for another acquisition (corporate management may have its hands full dealing with the current portfolio of businesses).

With a related diversification strategy, however, the search for new industries needs to be aimed at identifying those that have strategic fits with one or more of the firm's present businesses.[14] This means looking for industries whose activity-cost chains relate to the activity-cost chains of businesses already in the company's portfolio. The interrelationships can concern (1) product or process R&D, (2) opportunities for joint manufacturing and assembly, (3) marketing and distribution channel interrelationships, (4) customer overlaps, (5) opportunities for joint after-sale service, or (6) common managerial know-how requirements—essentially any area where market-related, operating, or management fits can occur.

Once strategic fit opportunities in other industries are identified, corporate strategists have to distinguish between opportunities where important competitive advantage potential exists (through cost-savings, skill transfers, and so on) and those where the strategic fit benefits are really very minor. The size of the competitive advantage potential depends on whether the strategic fit benefits are competitively significant, how much it will cost to capture the benefits, and how difficult it will be to merge and coordinate the business-unit interrelationships.[15] Analysis usually reveals that while there are many actual and potential interrelationships and linkages, only a few have enough strategic importance to generate meaningful competitive advantage.

Deploying Corporate Resources

To get ever-higher levels of performance out of a diversified company's business portfolio, corporate managers must also do an effective job of allocating corporate resources. Their strategy-making task is to steer resources out of low-opportunity areas into high-opportunity areas. Divesting marginal businesses serves this purpose by freeing unproductive assets for redeployment. Surplus funds from cash cows and harvested businesses also add to the corporate treasury. Options for allocating these funds include: (1) investing in the maintenance and expansion of existing businesses, (2) making acquisitions if needed, (3) funding long-range R&D ventures, (4) paying off existing long-term debt, (5) increasing dividends, and (6) repurchasing the company's stock. The first three are *strategic* actions; the last three, *financial* moves. Ideally, funds are available to serve both strategic and financial purposes. If not, strategic uses should take precedence over financial uses except in unusual and compelling circumstances.

GUIDELINES FOR MANAGING THE CORPORATE STRATEGY FORMATION PROCESS

Although formal analysis and entrepreneurial brainstorming are important factors in the corporate strategy-making process, there is more to where corporate strategy comes from and how it evolves. Rarely is there an all-inclusive for-

---

[14]Porter, *Competitive Advantage*, pp. 370–71.
[15]Ibid., pp. 371–72.

mulation of the total corporate strategy. Instead, corporate strategy in major enterprises emerges incrementally from the unfolding of many different internal and external events, the result of probing the future, experimenting, gathering more information, sensing problems, building awareness of the various options, developing ad hoc responses to unexpected "crises," communicating partial consensus as it emerges, and acquiring a "feel" for all the strategically relevant factors, their importance, and their interrelationships.[16]

Strategic analysis is not something the executives of diversified companies do all at once in comprehensive fashion. Such big reviews are sometimes scheduled, but studies indicate that major strategic decisions emerge gradually rather than from periodic, full-scale analysis followed by prompt decision. Typically, top executives approach major strategic decisions a step at a time, often starting from broad, intuitive conceptions and then embellishing, fine-tuning, and modifying their original thinking as more information is gathered, as formal analysis confirms or modifies emerging judgments, and as confidence and consensus build for what strategic moves need to be made. Often attention and resources are concentrated on a few critical strategic thrusts that illuminate and integrate corporate direction, objectives, and strategies.

KEY POINTS

Strategic analysis in diversified companies is an eight-step process. Step one is to identify the present corporate strategy. Step two is to construct business portfolio matrixes as needed to examine the overall composition of the present portfolio. Step three is to profile the industry and competitive environment of each business unit and draw conclusions about how attractive each industry in the portfolio is. Step four is to probe the competitive strength of the individual businesses and how well situated each is in its respective industry. Step five is to rank the different business units on the basis of their past performance record and future performance prospects. Step six is to determine how well each business unit fits in with corporate direction and strategy and whether it has important strategic fit relationships with other businesses in the portfolio. Step seven is to rank the business units from highest to lowest in investment priority, drawing conclusions about where the firm should be putting its money and what the general strategic direction of each business unit should be (invest-and-expand, fortify-and-defend, overhaul and reposition, harvest, or divest). Step eight is to use the preceding analysis to craft a series of moves to improve overall corporate performance. The primary corporate strategy moves involve:

- Making acquisitions, starting new businesses from within, and divesting marginal businesses or businesses that no longer match the corporate direction and strategy.
- Devising moves to strengthen the long-term competitive positions of the company's core businesses.
- Acting to create strategic fit opportunities and turn them into long-term competitive advantage.
- Steering corporate resources out of low-opportunity areas into high-opportunity areas.

---

[16]Ibid., pp. 58 and 196.

SUGGESTED
READINGS

Bettis, Richard A., and William K. Hall. "Strategic Portfolio Management in the Multi-business Firm." *California Management Review* 24 (Fall 1981), pp. 23–38.

————. "The Business Portfolio Approach—Where It Falls Down in Practice." *Long Range Planning* 16, no. 2 (April 1983), pp. 95–104.

Christensen, H. Kurt, Arnold C. Cooper, and Cornelius A. Dekluyuer. "The Dog Business: A Reexamination." *Business Horizons* 25, no. 6 (November–December 1982), pp. 12–18.

Hamermesh, Richard G. *Making Strategy Work* (New York: John Wiley & Sons, 1986), chaps. 1, 4, and 7.

Haspeslagh, Phillippe. "Portfolio Planning: Uses and Limits." *Harvard Business Review* 60, no. 1 (January–February 1982), pp. 58–73.

Hax, Arnoldo, and Nicolas S. Majluf. *Strategic Management: An Integrative Perspective.* Englewood Cliffs, N.J.: Prentice Hall, 1984, chaps. 7–9.

————. *The Strategy Concept and Process.* Englewood Cliffs, N.J.: Prentice Hall, 1991, chaps. 8–11 and 15.

Henderson, Bruce D. "The Application and Misapplication of the Experience Curve." *Journal of Business Strategy* 4, no. 3 (Winter 1984), pp. 3–9.

Naugle, David G., and Garret A. Davies. "Strategic-Skill Pools and Competitive Advantage." *Business Horizons* 30, no. 6 (November–December 1987), pp. 35–42.

Porter, Michael E. *Competitive Advantage.* New York: Free Press, 1985, chaps. 9–11.

————. "From Competitive Advantage to Corporate Strategy." *Harvard Business Review* 65, no. 3 (May–June 1987), pp. 43–59.

Implementing Strategy

Organization-Building, Budgets, and Support Systems

We strategize beautifully, we implement pathetically.
~An auto-parts firm executive

· · · · · · ·

Just being able to conceive bold new strategies is not enough. The general manager must also be able to translate his or her strategic vision into concrete steps that "get things done."
~Richard G. Hamermesh

· · · · · · ·

Organizing is what you do before you do something, so that when you do it, it is not all mixed up.
~A. A. Milne

Once the course of strategy has been charted, the manager's priorities swing to converting the strategic plan into actions and good results. Putting the strategy into effect and getting the organization moving in the chosen direction call for a different set of managerial tasks and skills. Whereas crafting strategy is largely an *entrepreneurial* activity, implementing strategy is largely an internal *administrative* activity. Whereas successful strategy formulation depends on business vision, market analysis, and entrepreneurial judgment, successful implementation depends on working through others, organizing, motivating, culture-building, and creating strong fits between strategy and how the organization does things. Ingrained behavior does not change just because a new strategy has been announced.

Implementing strategy is a tougher, more time-consuming challenge than crafting strategy. Practitioners emphatically agree that is is a whole lot easier to develop a sound strategic plan than it is to "make it happen."

THE STRATEGY IMPLEMENTATION FRAMEWORK

Strategy implementation entails *converting the strategic plan into action and then into results.* Implementation is successful if the company achieves its strategic objectives and targeted levels of financial performance. What makes the process so demanding is the wide sweep of managerial activities that have to be attended to, the many ways managers can tackle each activity, the skill it takes to get a variety of initiatives launched and moving, and the resistance to change that has to be overcome. Moreover, each strategy implementation situation is unique enough to require its own specific *action agenda.* Strategy should be implemented in a manner that fits that organization's situation. Managers have to take into account the nature of the strategy (implementing a strategy to become the low-cost producer is different from implementing a differentiation strategy keyed to superior quality and premium prices). And they must consider the amount of strategic change involved (shifting to a bold new strategy poses different implementation problems than making minor changes in an already existing strategy).

The Principal Tasks

While the details of strategy implementation are specific to every situation, certain administrative bases have to be covered no matter what the organization's situation. Figure 9–1 shows the principal administrative tasks that crop up repeatedly in the strategy implementation process. Depending on the organization's circumstances, some of these tasks will prove more significant and time-consuming than others. To devise an action agenda, managers have to determine what internal conditions are necessary to execute the strategy successfully and then create these conditions as rapidly as practical.

The keys to successful implementation are to unite the total organization behind the strategy and to see that every relevant activity and administrative task is done in a manner that tightly matches the requirements for first-rate strategy execution. The motivational and inspirational challenge is to build such determined commitment up and down the ranks that an enthusiastic organizationwide crusade emerges to carry out the strategy and meet performance targets. Along with enthusiasm and strategic commitment, however, must come a concerted managerial effort to create a series of strategy-supportive "fits." The internal organization structure must be matched to the strategy. The necessary organizational skills and capabilities must be developed. Resource and budget allocations must support the strategy, and departments must be given the people and budgets needed to carry out their assigned strategic roles. The company's reward structure, policies, information system, and operating practices all need to reinforce the push for effective strategy execution, as opposed to having a passive role or, even worse, acting as obstacles. Equally important, managers must do things in a manner and style that creates and nurtures a strategy-supportive work environment and corporate culture. The stronger the strategy-supportive fits created internally, the greater the chances of successful implementation.

Who Are the Strategy Implementers?

An organization's chief executive officer and the heads of major organizational units are the persons most responsible for seeing that strategy is implemented

---

FIGURE 9–1   **Implementing Strategy**   *(The principal tasks)*

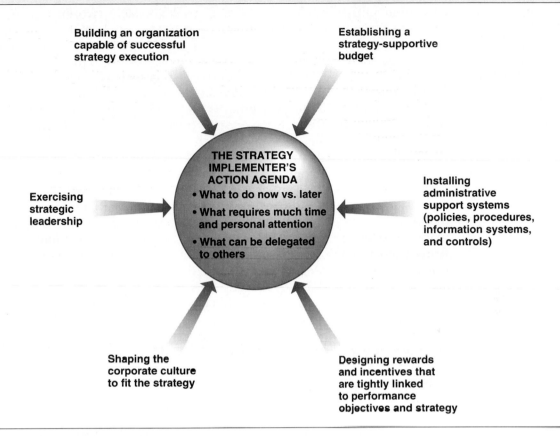

Building an organization capable of successful strategy execution

Establishing a strategy-supportive budget

Exercising strategic leadership

THE STRATEGY IMPLEMENTER'S ACTION AGENDA
• What to do now vs. later
• What requires much time and personal attention
• What can be delegated to others

Installing administrative support systems (policies, procedures, information systems, and controls)

Shaping the corporate culture to fit the strategy

Designing rewards and incentives that are tightly linked to performance objectives and strategy

---

successfully. However, implementing strategy is not a job just for senior managers; it is a job for the whole management team. Strategy implementation involves every organization unit, from the head office down to each operating department, asking "What do we have to do to implement our part of the strategic plan, and how can we best get it done?" In this sense, all managers become strategy implementers in their areas of authority and responsibility. Although major implementation initiatives have to be orchestrated by the CEO and other senior officers, top-level managers still have to rely on the active support and cooperation of lower-level managers to get things done. Lower-level managers are always active participants in the strategy implementation process. They not only initiate and supervise the implementation process in their areas of responsibility, they also are instrumental in seeing that the desired results and performance targets continue to be met day after day once the strategy is in place.

Every manager has an active role in the process of implementing and executing the firm's strategic plan.

Leading the Implementation Proess

One of the make-or-break determinants of successful strategy implementation is how well management leads the process. Implementers can exercise leadership in many ways. They can play an active, visible role or a low-key, behind-the-scenes one. They can make decisions authoritatively or on the basis of

· · · · · · · · · · · ·
*There is no one right
way to manage the
implementation process;
each firm's situation is
unique enough to require
custom actions and
managerial approaches.*

consensus, delegate much or little, be personally involved in the details or stand on the sidelines and coach others, proceed swiftly (launching implementation initiatives on many fronts) or deliberately (working for gradual progress over a long time frame). How managers lead the implementation task tends to be a function of: (1) their experience and accumulated knowledge about the business; (2) whether they are new to the job or seasoned incumbents; (3) their network of personal relationships with others in the organization; (4) their own diagnostic, administrative, interpersonal, and problem-solving skills; (5) the authority they've been given; (6) the leadership style they're comfortable with; and (7) their view of the role they need to play to get things done.

Another factor that affects a manager's approach to strategy implementation is the context of the organization's situation: the seriousness of the firm's strategic difficulties, the nature and extent of the strategic change involved, the type of strategy being implemented, the strength of any ingrained behavior that has to be changed, the financial and organizational resources available to work with, the configuration of personal and organization relationships in the firm's history, the pressures for quick results and improvements in near-term financial performance, and other such factors that make up the firm's "culture" and overall work climate. Each company's internal situation is unique enough that managers usually have to custom-tailor their action agenda to fit it. Successful strategy implementers carefully consider all the internal ramifications of implementing a new strategy and carefully diagnose the action priorities and the sequence in which things need to be done; then they get their organization moving and keep pushing it along.

In the remainder of this chapter and in Chapter 10, we survey the ins and outs of the manager's role as chief strategy implementer. For convenience, the discussion will be organized around the six administrative components of the strategy implementation process and the recurring administrative issues associated with each (see Figure 9–2). This chapter explores the management tasks of building an organization, establishing strategy-supportive budgets, and installing administrative support systems. Chapter 10 deals with linking rewards and incentives to performance objectives and strategy, building a strategy-supportive corporate culture, and exercising strategic leadership.

BUILDING A CAPABLE ORGANIZATION

Successful strategy execution depends greatly on good internal organization and competent personnel. Building a capable organization is always a top priority. Three types of organizational actions are paramount:

1. Developing an organizational structure that is conducive to successful strategy execution.
2. Seeing that the organization has the skills, core competencies, managerial talents, technical know-how, and competitive capabilities it needs.
3. Selecting the right people for key positions.

FIGURE 9–2   The Administrative Components of Strategy Implementation

BUILDING AN ORGANIZATION CAPABLE OF EXECUTING THE STRATEGY

Specific Tasks

- Creating a strategy-supportive organization structure.
- Developing the skills and core competencies needed to execute the strategy successfully.
- Selecting people for key positions.

ESTABLISHING A STRATEGY-SUPPORTIVE BUDGET

Specific Tasks

- Seeing that each organizational unit has a big enough budget to carry out its part of the strategic plan.
- Ensuring that resources are used efficiently to get "the biggest bang for the buck."

INSTALLING INTERNAL ADMINISTRATIVE SUPPORT SYSTEMS

Specific Tasks

- Establishing and administering strategy-facilitating policies and procedures.
- Developing administrative and operating systems to give the organization strategy-critical capabilities
- Generating the right strategic information on a timely basis.

DEVISING REWARDS AND INCENTIVES THAT ARE TIGHTLY LINKED TO OBJECTIVES AND STRATEGY

Specific Tasks

- Motivating organizational units and individuals to do their best to make the strategy work.
- Designing rewards and incentives that induce employees to do the very things needed for successful strategy execution.
- Promoting a results orientation.

SHAPING THE CORPORATE CULTURE TO FIT THE STRATEGY

Specific Tasks

- Establishing shared values.
- Setting ethical standards.
- Creating a strategy-supportive work environment.
- Building a spirit of high performance into the culture.

EXERCISING STRATEGIC LEADERSHIP

Specific Tasks

- Leading the process of shaping values, molding culture, and energizing strategy accomplishment.
- Keeping the organization innovative, responsive, and opportunistic.
- Dealing with the politics of strategy, coping with power struggles, and building consensus.
- Enforcing ethical standards and behavior.
- Initiating corrective actions to improve strategy execution.

Matching Organization Structure to Strategy

There are very few hard and fast rules for designing a strategy-supportive organization structure. Every firm's internal organization is somewhat idiosyncratic, the result of many organizational decisions and historical circumstances. Moreover, every strategy is grounded in its own set of key success factors and critical tasks. The only real imperative is to design the internal organization structure around the key success factors and critical tasks inherent in

Matching structure to strategy requires making strategy-critical activities and organizational units the main building blocks in the organization structure.

the firm's strategy. The following five-sequence procedure is a useful guide for fitting structure to strategy:[1]

1. Pinpoint the key functions and tasks necessary for successful strategy execution.
2. Reflect on how strategy-critical functions and organizational units relate to those that are routine and to those that provide staff support.
3. Make strategy-critical business units and functions the main organizational building blocks.
4. Determine the degrees of authority needed to manage each organizational unit bearing in mind both the benefits and costs of decentralized decision making.
5. Provide for coordination among the various organizational units.

Pinpointing the Strategy-Critical Activities   In any organization, some activities and skills are always more critical to strategic success than others. From a strategy perspective, much of an organization's total work is routine; it involves such administrative housekeeping as handling payrolls, managing cash flows, controlling inventories, processing grievances, warehousing and shipping, processing customer orders, and complying with regulations. Other activities are primarily support functions (data processing, accounting, training, public relations, market research, and purchasing). Yet there are usually certain crucial tasks and functions that have to be done exceedingly well for the strategy to be successful. For instance, tight cost control is essential for a firm trying to be the low-cost producer in a commodity business characterized by low margins and price cutting. For a luxury goods manufacturer, critical skills may be quality craftsmanship, distinctive design, and sophisticated promotional appeal. In high-tech industries, the critical activities tend to be R&D, product innovation, and getting newly developed products out of the lab and onto the market quickly. Strategy-critical activities vary according to the particulars of a firm's strategy and competitive requirements.

Two questions help identify what an organization's strategy-critical activities are: "What functions have to be performed extra well and in timely fashion for the strategy to succeed?" and "In what areas of the organization would malperformance seriously endanger strategic success?"[2] The answers generally show what activities and areas are crucial and where to concentrate organization-building efforts.

Understanding the Relationships among Activities   Before critical, supportive, and routine activities are grouped into organizational units, the strategic relationships among them need to be scrutinized thoughtfully. Activities can be related by the flow of material through the production process, the type of customer served, the distribution channels used, the technical skills and know-how needed to perform them, a strong need for coordination, the sequence in

---

[1]LaRue T. Hosmer, *Strategic Management: Text and Cases on Business Policy* (Englewood Cliffs, N.J.: Prentice Hall, 1982), chap. 10; and J. Thomas Cannon, *Business Strategy and Policy* (New York: Harcourt Brace Jovanovich, 1968), p. 316.

[2]Peter F. Drucker, *Management: Tasks, Responsibilities, Practices* (New York: Harper & Row, 1974), pp. 530, 535.

which tasks must be performed, and by geographic location, to mention a few. Such relationships are important because one (or more) of the interrelationships usually become the basis for grouping activities into organizational units. If strategic needs are to drive organization design, then the relationships to look for are those that link one piece of the strategy to another.

Grouping Activities into Organization Units   The chief guideline here is to make strategy-critical activities the main building blocks in the organization structure. The rationale is compelling: if activities crucial to strategic success are to get the attention and visibility they merit, they have to be a prominent part of the organizational scheme. When key business units and strategy-critical functions take a backseat to less important activities, they usually get fewer resources and end up with less clout in the organization's power structure than they deserve. On the other hand, when key units form the core of the whole organization structure, their role and power is highlighted and institutionalized. Senior executives seldom send a stronger signal about what is strategically important than by making key business units and critical functions the most prominent organizational building blocks and, further, giving the managers of these units a visible, influential position in the organization.

Determining the Degree of Authority and Independence to Give Each Unit   Companies must decide how much authority and decision-making latitude to give managers of each organization unit, especially the heads of business subsidiaries. Companies that are extremely centralized retain authority for big strategy and policy decisions at the corporate level and delegate only operating decisions to business-level managers. Those that are extremely decentralized give business units enough autonomy to function independently, with little direct authority exerted by corporate staff.

There are several guidelines for delegating authority to various units. Activities and organizational units with a key role in strategy execution should not be subordinate to routine and nonkey activities. Revenue-producing and results-producing activities should not be subordinate to internal support or staff functions. Decision-making authority should be decentralized (i.e., pushed down to managers closest to the scene of the action) whenever lower-level managers are in a position to make better, more informed, and more timely decisions than higher-level managers. However, decision-making authority should be centralized if higher-level managers are in the best decision-making position. With few exceptions, the authority to choose a strategy for an organizational unit and to decide how to implement it should be delegated to the manager in charge of the unit. Corporate-level authority over strategic and operating decisions at the business-unit level and below should be held to a minimum. The best approach is to select strong managers to head each organizational unit and give them enough authority to craft and execute an appropriate strategy; managers that consistently produce unsatisfactory results and have a poor track record in strategy-making and strategy-implementing should be weeded out.

One of the biggest exceptions to decentralizing strategy-related decisions arises in diversified companies with related businesses in their portfolios; in such cases, capturing strategic fit benefits is sometimes best done by centralizing decision-making authority. Suppose, for instance, that businesses with

As a rule, authority to make strategic decisions for an organizational unit should be delegated to the unit's manager.

Centralizing strategic decisions at the corporate level has merit when the related activities of related business units need to be tightly coordinated.

related process and product technologies are performing their own R&D. Merging each business's R&D activities into a single unit under the authority of a corporate officer may be both more cost efficient and more strategically effective.

Providing for Coordination among the Units   Coordinating the activities of organizational units is accomplished mainly through positioning them in the hierarchy of authority. Managers higher up in the pecking order generally have authority over more organizational units and thus the clout to coordinate, integrate, and arrange for the cooperation of units under their supervision. The chief executive officer, chief operating officer, and business-level managers are central points of coordination because of their positions of authority over the whole unit. Besides positioning organizational units according to managerial authority, strategic efforts can also be coordinated through project teams, special task forces, standing committees, formal strategy reviews, and annual strategic planning and budgeting cycles. Additionally, the formulation of the strategic plan itself serves a coordinating role. The process of setting objectives and strategies for each organizational unit and making sure related activities mesh helps coordinate operations across units.

On the other hand, when a firm is pursuing a related diversification strategy, coordination may be best accomplished by centralizing authority for a related activity under a corporate-level officer. Also, diversified companies with either related or unrelated diversification strategies commonly centralize such staff support functions as public relations, finance and accounting, employee benefits, and data processing at the corporate level.

The Structure-Follows-Strategy Thesis

The practice of *consciously* matching organization design and structure to the particular needs of strategy is a fairly recent—and research-based—management development. A landmark study by Alfred Chandler found that changes in an organization's strategy bring about new administrative problems which, in turn, require a new or refashioned structure for the new strategy to be successfully implemented.[3] His study of 70 large corporations revealed that structure tends to follow the growth strategy of the firm—but often not until inefficiency and internal operating problems provoke a structural adjustment. The experiences of these firms followed a consistent sequential pattern: new strategy creation, emergence of new administrative problems, decline in profitability and performance, a shift to a more appropriate organizational structure, and recovery to more profitable levels and improved strategy execution. Chandler found this sequence to be oft-repeated as firms grew and modified their corporate strategies. Chandler's research shows that the choice of organization structure *does make a difference* in how an organiza-

. . . .
Strategic Management Principle
Attempting to carry out a new strategy with an old organizational structure is usually unwise.

---

[3]Alfred Chandler, *Strategy and Structure* (Cambridge, Mass.: MIT Press, 1962). Although the stress here is on matching structure to strategy, structure can and does influence the choice of strategy. A "good" strategy must be doable. When an organization's present structure is so far out of line with the requirements of a particular strategy that the organization would have to be turned upside down to implement it, the strategy may not be doable and should not be given further consideration. In such cases, structure shapes the choice of strategy. The point here, however, is that once a strategy is chosen, structure must be modified to fit the strategy if an approximate fit does not already exist. Any influences of structures on strategy should come before the point of strategy selection rather than after it.

tion performs. A company's internal organization should be reassessed whenever strategy changes.[4] A new strategy is likely to entail new or different skills and key activities; if these go unrecognized, the resulting mismatch between strategy and structure can open the door for implementation and performance problems.

The *structure-follows-strategy* thesis is undergirded with powerful logic: how organizational activities are structured is a means to an end—not an end in itself. Structure is a managerial device for facilitating execution of the organization's strategy and helping to achieve performance targets. An organization's structural design is a tool for "harnessing" individual efforts and coordinating the performance of diverse tasks; a good design helps people do things efficiently and effectively. If activities and responsibilities are *deliberately* organized to link structure and strategy, it is easier to coordinate strategic moves across functional areas. Moreover, efforts to execute strategy on a day-to-day basis are less likely to result in frustration, finger-pointing when foul-ups occur, interdepartmental frictions, and inefficiency.[5]

How Structure Evolves as Strategy Evolves As firms expand from small, single-business enterprises to more complex strategic phases of vertical integration, geographic expansion, and line-of-business diversification, their organizational structures tend to evolve from one-person management to functional departments to divisions to decentralized business units. Single-business companies almost always have a centralized functional structure. Vertically integrated firms and companies with broad geographic coverage typically are organized into operating divisions. The basic building blocks of a diversified company are its individual businesses; the authority for most decisions is decentralized, and each business operates as an independent, stand-alone unit with corporate headquarters performing only minimal functions for the business.

The Strategic Advantages and Disadvantages of Different Organizational Structures

There are five strategy-driven approaches to organization: (1) functional specialization, (2) geographic organization, (3) decentralized business divisions, (4) strategic business units, and (5) matrix structures featuring dual lines of authority and strategic priority. Each form has its own strategic advantages and disadvantages.

The Functional Organization Structure A functional organization structure tends to be effective in single-business firms where key activities revolve around well-defined skills and areas of specialization. In such cases, in-depth specialization and focused concentration on performing functional tasks and activities can enhance both operating efficiency and the development of core competencies. Generally, organizing by functional specialties promotes

---

[4]For an excellent study documenting how companies have revised their internal organization to accommodate strategic change, see Raymond Corey and Steven H. Star, *Organizational Strategy: A Marketing Approach* (Boston: Harvard Business School, 1971), chap. 3.

[5]Drucker, *Management*, p. 523.

full utilization of the most up-to-date technical skills and helps a business capitalize on efficiency gains from using specialized manpower, facilities, and equipment. These are strategically important considerations for single-business companies, dominant-product companies, and vertically integrated firms and account for why they usually have some kind of centralized, functionally specialized structure.

However, just what form the functional specialization takes varies according to customer-product-technology considerations. For instance, a technical instruments manufacturer may be departmentalized into research and development, engineering, production, technical services, quality control, marketing, personnel, and finance and accounting. A municipal government, on the other hand, may be departmentalized according to purposeful function—fire, public safety, health services, water and sewer, streets, parks and recreation, and education. A university may divide its organizational units into academic affairs, student services, alumni relations, athletics, buildings and grounds, institutional services, and budget control. Two types of functional organizational approaches are diagrammed in Figure 9–3.

Functional departments develop strong functional mindsets and are prone to approach strategic issues more from a functional than a business perspective.

The Achilles' heel of a functional structure is the difficulty of getting and keeping tight strategic coordination across functional departments that don't "talk the same language" and that often don't adequately appreciate one another's strategic role and problems. Members of functional departments tend to have strong departmental loyalties and be protective of departmental interests, thus making it hard to achieve strategic and operating coordination across departmental lines. There's a natural tendency for each functional department to push for solutions and decisions that advance its own cause and give it more influence (despite the lip service given to cooperation and "what's best for the company").

Interdepartmental politics, attempts at functional empire-building, and conflicting functional viewpoints can impose a time-consuming administrative burden on the general manager, who is the only person with authority to resolve cross-functional differences and enforce cooperation. In a functional structure, much of a GM's time is spent opening lines of communication across departments, tempering departmental rivalries, and securing cooperation. In addition, a functionally dominated organization, because of strong preoccupation with developing functional expertise and improving functional performance, tends to have tunnel vision when it comes to promoting entrepreneurial venturesomeness, developing creative responses to major customer-market-technological changes, and pursuing opportunities beyond the industry's conventional boundaries.

A geographic organization structure is well suited for firms pursuing different strategies in different geographic regions.

Geographic Forms of Organization   Organizing on the basis of geographic areas or territories is a common structural form for enterprises operating in diverse geographic markets or serving an expansive geographic area. As indicated in Figure 9–4, geographic organization has its advantages and disadvantages, but the chief reason for its popularity is that it promotes improved performance.

In the private sector, a territorial structure is typically used by chain stores, power companies, cement firms, restaurant chains, and dairy products enterprises. In the public sector, such organizations as the Internal Revenue Service, the Social Security Administration, the federal courts, the U.S. Postal Service, state troopers, and the Red Cross have adopted territorial structures

FIGURE 9–3   Functional Organizational Structures

A. The Building Blocks of a "Typical" Functional Organizational Structure

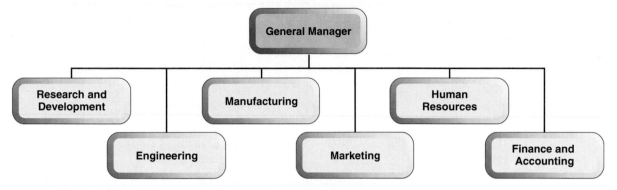

B. The Building Blocks of a Process-Oriented Functional Structure

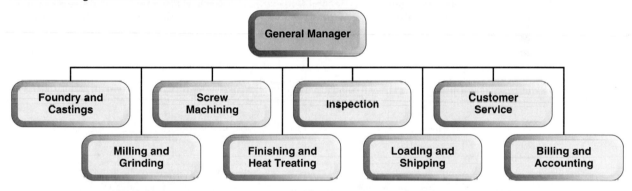

STRATEGIC ADVANTAGES	STRATEGIC DISADVANTAGES
• Permits centralized control of strategic results. • Very well suited for structuring a single business. • Structure is linked tightly to strategy by designating key activities as functional departments. • Promotes in-depth functional expertise. • Well suited to developing a functional-based distinctive competence. • Conducive to exploiting learning/experience curve effects associated with functional specialization. • Enhances operating efficiency where tasks are routine and repetitive.	• Poses problems of functional coordination. • Can lead to interfunctional rivalry and conflict, rather than cooperation—GM must referee functional politics. • May promote overspecialization and narrow management viewpoints. • Hinders development of managers with cross-functional experience because the ladder of advancement is up the ranks within the same functional area. • Forces profit responsibility to the top. • Functional specialists often attach more importance to what's best for the functional area than to what's best for the whole business—can lead to functional empire-building. • Functional myopia often works against creative entrepreneurship, adapting to change, and attempts to restructure the activity-cost chain.

to be directly accessible to geographically dispersed clienteles. Multinational enterprises use geographic structures to manage the diversity they encounter by operating across national boundaries.

Corey and Star cite Pfizer International as a good example of a company whose strategic requirements made geographic decentralization propitious:

FIGURE 9–4   A Geographic Organizational Structure

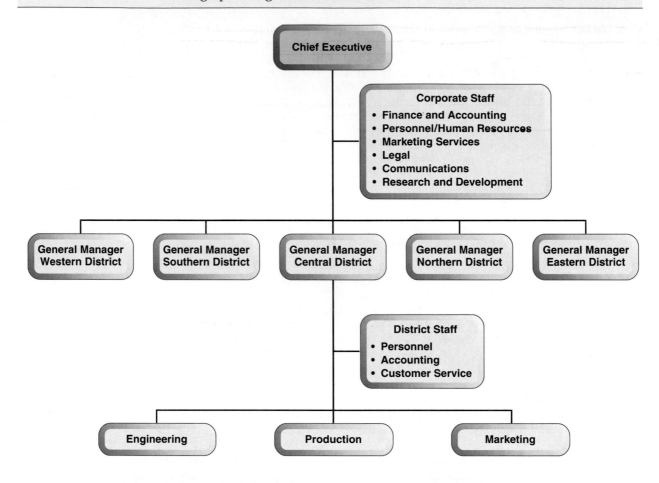

STRATEGIC ADVANTAGES

- Allows tailoring of strategy to needs of each geographical market.
- Delegates profit/loss responsibility to lowest strategic level.
- Improves functional coordination within the target market.
- Takes advantage of economies of local operations.
- Area units make an excellent training ground for higher-level general managers.

STRATEGIC DISADVANTAGES

- Poses a problem of how much geographic uniformity headquarters should impose versus how much geographic diversity should be allowed.
- Greater difficulty in maintaining consistent company image/reputation from area to area when area managers exercise much strategic freedom.
- Adds another layer of management to run the geographic units.
- Can result in duplication of staff services at headquarters and district levels, creating a relative-cost disadvantage.

Pfizer International operated plants in 27 countries and marketed in more than 100 countries. Its product lines included pharmaceuticals (antibiotics and other ethical prescription drugs), agriculture and veterinary products (such as animal feed supplements and vaccines and pesticides), chemicals (fine chemicals, bulk pharmaceuticals, petrochemicals, and plastics), and consumer products (cosmetics and toiletries).

Ten geographic Area Managers reported directly to the President of Pfizer International and exercised line supervision over Country Managers. According to a company position description, it was "the responsibility of each Area Manager to plan, develop, and carry out Pfizer International's business in the assigned foreign area in keeping with company policies and goals."

Country Managers had profit responsibility. In most cases a single Country Manager managed all Pfizer activities in his country. In some of the larger, well-developed countries of Europe there were separate Country Managers for pharmaceutical and agricultural products and for consumer lines.

Except for the fact that New York headquarters exercised control over the to-the-market prices of certain products, especially prices of widely used pharmaceuticals, Area and Country Managers had considerable autonomy in planning and managing the Pfizer International business in their respective geographic areas. This was appropriate because each area, and some countries within areas, provided unique market and regulatory environments. In the case of pharmaceuticals and agriculture and veterinary products (Pfizer International's most important lines), national laws affected formulations, dosages, labeling, distribution, and often price. Trade restrictions affected the flow of bulk pharmaceuticals and chemicals and packaged products, and sometimes required the establishment of manufacturing plants to supply local markets. Competition, too, varied significantly from area to area.[6]

Decentralized Business Units Grouping activities along business and product lines has been a trend among diversified enterprises for the past half century, beginning with the pioneering efforts of DuPont and General Motors in the 1920s. Separate business/product divisions emerged because diversification made a functionally specialized manager's job incredibly complex. Imagine the problems a manufacturing executive and his/her staff would have if put in charge of, say, 50 different plants using 20 different technologies to produce 30 different products in eight different businesses/industries. In a multibusiness enterprise, the needs of strategy virtually dictate that the organizational sequence be corporate to business to functional area within a business rather than corporate to functional area (aggregated for all businesses).

Thus while functional departments and geographic divisions are the standard organizational building blocks in a single-business enterprise, in a multibusiness corporation the basic building blocks are the businesses the firm has diversified into. Diversification is generally managed by decentralizing decision-making and delegating authority over each business unit to a business-level manager. The approach, very simply, is to put entrepreneurially oriented general managers in charge of each business unit, give them authority to formulate and implement a business strategy, motivate them with incentives, and hold them accountable for the results they produce. Each business unit then operates as a stand-alone profit center and is organized around

In a diversified firm, the basic organizational building blocks are its business units; each business is operated as a stand-alone profit center.

---

[6]Corey and Star, *Organization Strategy*, pp. 23–24.

Strategic Management Principle

A decentralized business-unit structure can block success of a related diversification strategy unless specific organizational arrangements are devised to coordinate the related activities of related businesses.

whatever functional departments and geographic units suit the business's strategy, key activities, and operating requirements.

Fully independent business units, however, pose a big problem to companies pursuing related diversification: *there is no mechanism for coordinating related activities across business units.* It can be tough to get autonomy-conscious business-unit managers to coordinate and share related activities; they are prone to argue about "turf" and about being held accountable for activities outside their control. To capture strategic fit benefits in a diversified company, corporate headquarters must devise some internal organizational means for achieving strategic coordination across related business-unit activities. One option is to centralize related functions at the corporate level. Examples include having a corporate R&D department if there are technology and product development fits to be managed, creating a corporate sales force to call on customers who purchase from several of the company's businesses, combining dealer networks and sales forces of closely related businesses, merging the order processing and shipping functions of businesses with common customers, and consolidating the production of related components and products into fewer, more efficient plants. Alternatively, corporate officers can develop bonus arrangements that give business-unit managers strong incentives to cooperate to achieve the full benefits of strategic fit. If the strategic fit relationships involve skills or technology transfers across businesses, corporate headquarters can set up interbusiness task forces, standing committees, or project teams to work out the specifics of transferring proprietary technology, managerial know-how, and related skills from one business to another.

A typical line-of-business organizational structure is shown in Figure 9–5, along with the strategy-related pros and cons of this type of organizational form.

Basic Concept

A strategic business unit (SBU) is a grouping of related businesses under the supervision of a senior executive.

Strategic Business Units In broadly diversified companies, the number of decentralized business units can be so great that the span of control is too much for a single chief executive. Then it may be useful to group related businesses and to delegate authority over them to a senior executive who reports directly to the chief executive officer. While this imposes a layer of management between business-level managers and the chief executive, it may nonetheless improve strategic planning and top-management coordination of diverse business interests. This explains both the popularity of the group vice president concept among multibusiness companies and the recent trend toward the formation of strategic business units.

A *strategic business unit* (SBU) is a grouping of business subsidiaries based on some important strategic elements common to each. The related elements could be an overlapping set of competitors, a closely related strategic mission, a common need to compete globally, an ability to accomplish integrated strategic planning, common key success factors, and technologically related growth opportunities. General Electric, a pioneer in the concept of SBUs, grouped 190 units into 43 SBUs and then aggregated them further into six "sectors."[7] At Union Carbide, 15 groups and divisions were decomposed into

---

[7]William K. Hall, "SBUs: Hot, New Topic in the Management of Diversification," *Business Horizons* 21, no. 1 (February 1978), p. 19. For an excellent discussion of the problems of implementing the SBU concept at 13 companies, see Richard A. Bettis and William K. Hall, "The Business Portfolio Approach—Where It Falls Down in Practice," *Long Range Planning* 16, no. 2 (April 1983), pp. 95–104.

FIGURE 9–5 **A Decentralized Line-of-Business Type of Organization Structure**

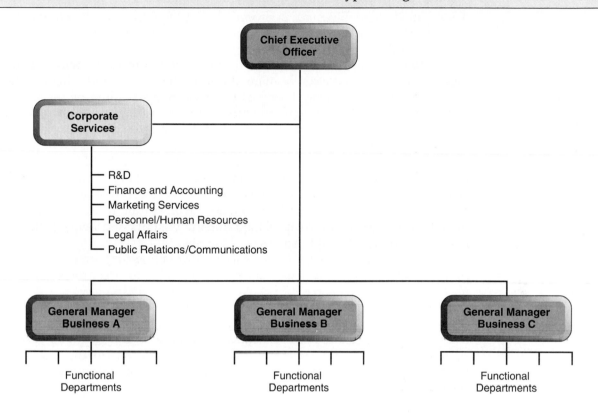

STRATEGIC ADVANTAGES

- Offers a logical and workable means of decentralizing responsibility and delegating authority in diversified organizations.

- Puts responsibility for business strategy in closer proximity to each business's unique environment.

- Allows each business unit to organize around its own set of key activities and functional requirements.

- Frees CEO to handle corporate strategy issues.

- Puts clear profit/loss accountability on shoulders of business-unit managers.

STRATEGIC DISADVANTAGES

- May lead to costly duplication of staff functions at corporate and business-unit levels, thus raising administrative overhead costs.

- Poses a problem of what decisions to centralize and what decisions to decentralize (business managers need enough authority to get the job done, but not so much that corporate management loses control of key business-level decisions).

- May lead to excessive division rivalry for corporate resources and attention.

- Business/division autonomy works against achieving coordination of related activities in different business units, thus blocking to some extent the capture of strategic fit benefits.

- Corporate management becomes heavily dependent on business-unit managers.

- Corporate managers can lose touch with business-unit situations, end up surprised when problems arise, and not know much about how to fix such problems.

150 "strategic planning units" and then regrouped and combined into 9 new "aggregate planning units." General Foods (now a division of Philip Morris) originally defined SBUs on a product-line basis but later redefined them according to menu segments (breakfast foods, beverages, main meal products, desserts, and pet foods).

The SBU concept provides broadly diversified companies with a way to rationalize the organization of many different businesses and a management arrangement for capturing strategic fit benefits and streamlining the strategic planning process. The strategic function of the group vice president is to provide the SBU with some cohesive direction and enforce strategic coordination across related businesses. The group vice president, as strategic coordinator for all businesses in the SBU, is in a position to organize the SBU in ways that facilitate sharing and skills transfers and to centralize "big" strategic decisions at the SBU level. The SBU, in effect, becomes a decision-making unit with broader strategic perspective than a single-business unit. It serves as the organizational mechanism for capturing strategic benefits and helps build competitive advantage for all businesses in the SBU.

SBUs also help reduce the complexity of dovetailing corporate strategy and business strategy and make it easier to "cross-pollinate" the growth opportunities in different industries. SBUs make headquarters' reviews of the strategies of lower-level units less imposing (there is no practical way for a CEO to review a hundred or more different businesses). A CEO can, however, effectively review the strategic plans of a lesser number of SBUs, leaving strategy reviews and direct supervision of individual businesses to the SBU heads. Figure 9–6 illustrates the SBU form of organization, along with its strategy-related pros and cons.

Matrix Forms of Organization   A matrix organization is a structure with two (or more) channels of command, two lines of budget authority, and two sources of performance and reward. The key feature of the matrix is that business (or product, project, or venture) and functional lines of authority are overlaid (to form a matrix or grid), and managerial authority over the activities in each unit/cell of the matrix is shared between the business/project/venture team manager and the functional manager, as shown in Figure 9–7. In a matrix structure, subordinates have a continuing dual assignment: to the business/product/project and to their home-base function.[8] The outcome is a compromise between functional specialization (engineering, R&D, manufacturing, marketing, finance) and specialization by product line, project, line-of-business, or special venture. All of the specialized talent needed for the product line/project/line-of-business/venture are assigned to the same divisional unit.

A matrix-type organization is a genuinely different structural form and represents a "new way of life." It breaks the unity-of-command principle; two reporting channels, two bosses, and shared authority create a new kind of organizational climate. In essence, the matrix is a conflict resolution system

---

[8]A more thorough treatment of matrix organizational forms can be found in Jay R. Galbraith, "Matrix Organizational Designs," *Business Horizons* 15, no. 1 (February 1971), pp. 29–40; and Christopher A. Bartlett and Sumantra Ghoshal, "Matrix Management: Not a Structure, a Frame of Mind," *Harvard Business Review* 68, no. 4 (July–August 1990), pp. 138–45.

FIGURE 9–6   An SBU Type of Organization Structure

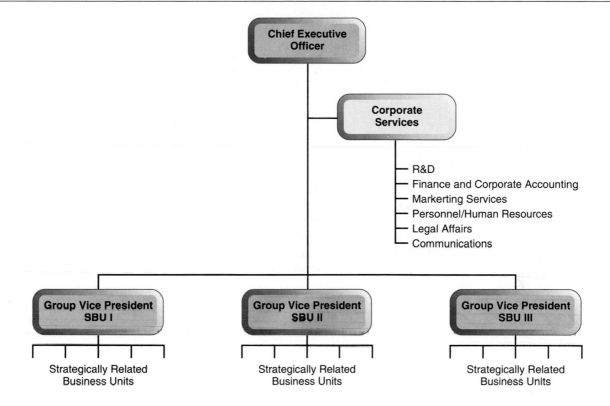

STRATEGIC ADVANTAGES

- **Provides a strategically relevant way to organize the business-unit portfolio of a broadly diversified company.**

- **Facilitates the coordination of related activities within an SBU, thus helping to capture the benefits of strategic fits in the SBU.**

- **Promotes more cohesiveness among the new initiatives of separate but related businesses.**

- **Allows strategic planning to be done at the most relevant level within the total enterprise.**

- **Makes the task of strategic review by top executives more objective and more effective.**

- **Helps allocate corporate resources to areas with greatest growth opportunities.**

STRATEGIC DISADVANTAGES

- **It is easy for the definition and grouping of businesses into SBUs to be so arbitrary that the SBU serves no other purpose than administrative convenience. If the criteria for defining SBUs are rationalizations and have little to do with the nitty-gritty of strategy coordination, then the groupings lose real strategic significance.**

- **The SBUs can still be myopic in charting their future direction.**

- **Adds another layer to top management.**

- **The roles and authority of the CEO, the group vice president, and the business-unit manager have to be carefully worked out or the group vice president gets trapped in the middle with ill-defined authority.**

- **Unless the SBU head is strong willed, very little strategy coordination is likely to occur across business units in the SBU.**

- **Performance recognition gets blurred; credit for successful business units tends to go to corporate CEO, then to business-unit head, last to group vice president.**

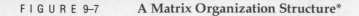

FIGURE 9–7   **A Matrix Organization Structure***

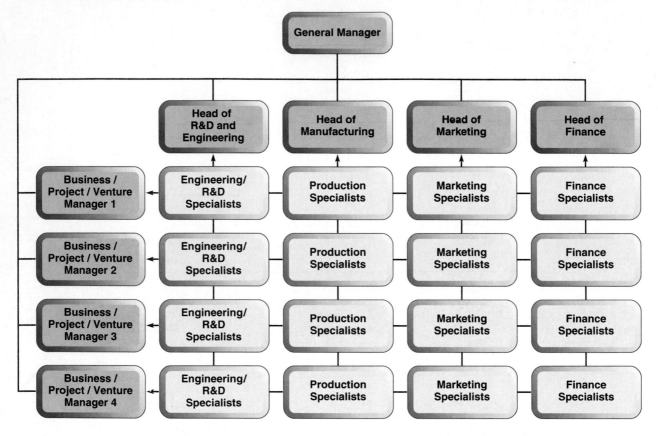

STRATEGIC ADVANTAGES

- Gives formal attention to each dimension of strategic priority.
- Creates checks and balances among competing viewpoints.
- Facilitates capture of functionally based strategic fits in diversified companies.
- Promotes making trade-off decisions on the basis of "what's best for the organization as a whole."
- Encourages cooperation, consensus-building, conflict resolution, and coordination of related activities.

STRATEGIC DISADVANTAGES

- Very complex to manage.
- Hard to maintain "balance" between the two lines of authority.
- So much shared authority can result in a transactions logjam and disproportionate amounts of time being spent on communications.
- It is hard to move quickly and decisively without getting clearance from many other people.
- Promotes an organizational bureaucracy and hamstrings creative entrepreneurship.

*Arrows indicate reporting channels

through which strategic and operating priorities are negotiated, power is shared, and resources are allocated internally on the basis of "strongest case for what is best overall for the unit."[9]

---

[9]For two excellent critiques of matrix organizations, see Stanley M. Davis and Paul R. Lawrence, "Problems of Matrix Organizations," *Harvard Business Review* 56, no. 3 (May–June 1978), pp. 131–42; and Erik W. Larson and David H. Gobeli, "Matrix Management: Contradictions and Insights," *California Management Review* 29, no. 4 (Summer 1987), pp. 126–38.

The impetus for matrix organizations stems from growing use of strategies that add new diversity (products, customer groups, technology, lines of business) to a firm's range of activities. Such diversity creates a need for product managers, functional managers, geographic area managers, new venture managers, and business-level managers—all of whom have important strategic responsibilities. When at least two of several variables (product, customer, technology, geography, functional area, and market segment) have roughly equal strategic priorities, a matrix organization can be an effective structural form. A matrix structure promotes internal checks and balances among competing viewpoints and perspectives, with separate managers for different dimensions of strategic initiative. A matrix arrangement thus allows each of several strategic considerations to be managed directly and to be formally represented in the organization structure. In this sense, it helps middle managers make trade-off decisions from an organizationwide perspective.[10] The other big advantage of matrix organization is that it can serve as a mechanism for capturing strategic fit. When the strategic fits in a diversified company are related to a specific functional area (R&D, technology, marketing), matrix organization can be a reasonable structural arrangement for coordinating sharing and skills transfer.

Companies using matrix structures include General Electric, Texas Instruments, Citibank, Shell Oil, TRW, Bechtel, Boeing, and Dow Chemical. Illustration Capsule 22 describes how one broadly diversified corporation with global strategies in each of its businesses has developed a matrix-type structure to manage its operations worldwide. However, most applications of matrix organization are limited to a portion of what the firm does (certain important functions) rather than spanning the whole of a large-scale diversified enterprise.

A number of companies shun matrix organization because of its chief weaknesses.[11] It is a complex structure to manage; people often end up confused over who to report to for what. Moreover, because the matrix signals that everything is important and, further, that everybody needs to communicate with everybody else, a "transactions logjam" can emerge. Action turns into paralysis since, with shared authority, it is hard to move decisively without first considering many points of view and getting clearance from many other people. Sizable transactions costs, communications inefficiency, and delays in responding can result. Even so, in some situations the benefits of conflict resolution and consensus-building outweigh these weaknesses.

Combination and Supplemental Methods of Organization   A single type of structural design is not always sufficient to meet the requirements of strategy. When this occurs, one option is to blend the basic organization forms, matching structure to strategy requirement by requirement and unit by unit. Another is to supplement a basic organization design with special-situation devices. Three of the most frequently used ones are:

[10]Ibid., p. 132.
[11]Thomas J. Peters and Robert H. Waterman, Jr., *In Search of Excellence* (New York: Harper & Row, 1982), pp. 306–7.

Asea Brown Boveri (ABB) is a diversified multi-national corporation headquartered in Zurich, Switzerland. ABB was formed in 1987 through the merger of Asea, one of Sweden's largest industrial enterprises, and Brown Boveri, a major Swiss company. Both companies manufactured electrical products and equipment. Following the merger, ABB acquired or took minority positions in 60 companies, mostly outside Europe. In 1991 ABB had annual revenues of $25 billion and employed 240,000 people around the world, including 150,000 in Western Europe, 40,000 in North America, 10,000 in South America, and 10,000 in India. The company was a world leader in the global markets for electrical products, electrical installations and service, and power-generation equipment and was the dominant European producer. European sales accounted for 60 percent of revenues, while North America accounted for 30 percent and Asia 15 percent.

To manage its global operations, ABB had devised a matrix organization that leveraged its core competencies in electrical-power technologies and its ability to achieve global economies of scale while, at the same time, maximizing its national market visibility and responsiveness. At the top of ABB's corporate organization structure was an executive committee composed of the CEO, Percy Barnevik, and 12 colleagues; the com-

mittee consisted of Swedes, Swiss, Germans, and Americans, several of whom were based outside Switzerland. The group, which met every three weeks at various locations around the world, was responsible for ABB's corporate strategy and performance.

Along one dimension of ABB's global matrix were 50 or so business areas (BAs), each representing a closely related set of products and services. The BAs were grouped into eight "business segments"; each segment was supervised by a different member of the executive committee. Each BA had a leader charged with responsibility for (1) devising and championing a global strategy, (2) setting quality and cost standards for the BA's factories worldwide, (3) deciding which factories would export to which country markets, (4) rotating people across borders to share technical expertise, create mixed-nationality teams to solve BA problems, and build a culture of trust and communication, and (5) pooling expertise and research funds for the benefit of the BA worldwide. BA leaders worked out of whatever world location made the most sense for their BA. For example, the BA leader for power transformers, who had responsibility for 25 factories in 16 countries, was a Swede who worked out of Mannheim, Germany; the BA leader for electric

(continued)

1. The *project team* or *project staff approach*, where a separate, largely self-sufficient work group is created to oversee the completion of a special activity (setting up a new technological process, bringing out a new product, starting up a new venture, consummating a merger with another company, seeing through the completion of a government contract, supervising the construction of a new plant). Project teams are a relatively popular means of handling one-of-a-kind situations with a finite life expectancy when the normal organization is ill-equipped to achieve the same results in addition to regular duties.

2. The *task force approach*, where a number of top-level executives and/or specialists are brought together to work on interdisciplinary assignments requiring specialized expertise from several parts of the organization. Special task forces provide increased opportunity for creativity, open communication across lines of authority, tight integration of specialized talents, expeditious conflict resolution, and common identification for coping with the problem at hand. One study showed that task forces were most effective when they had less than 10

ILLUSTRATION CAPSULE | 22 | *(concluded)*

metering was an American based in North Carolina.

Along the other dimension of the matrix was a group of national enterprises with presidents, boards of directors, financial statements, and career ladders. The presidents of ABB's national enterprises had responsibility for maximizing the performance and effectiveness of all ABB activities within their country's borders. Country presidents worked closely with the BA leaders to evaluate and improve what was happening in ABB's business areas in his/her country.

Inside the matrix were 1,200 "local" ABB companies with an average of 200 employees, each headed by a president. The local company president reported both to the national president in whose country the local company operated and to the leader of the BA to which its products/services were assigned. Each local company was a subsidiary of the ABB national enterprise where it was located. Thus, all of ABB's local companies in Norway were subsidiaries of ABB Norway, the national company for Norway; all ABB operations in Portugal were subsidiaries of ABB Portugal, and so on. The 1,200 presidents of ABB's local companies were expected to be excellent profit center managers, able to answer to two bosses effectively. The local president's global boss was the BA manager who established the local company's

role in ABB's global strategy and, also, the rules a local company had to observe in supporting this strategy. The local president's country boss was the national CEO, with whom it was necessary to cooperate on local issues.

ABB believed that its matrix structure allowed it to optimize its pursuit of global business strategies and, at the same time, maximize its performance in every country market where it operated. The matrix was a way of being global and big strategically, yet small and local operationally. Decision-making was decentralized (to BA leaders, country presidents, and local company presidents), but reporting and control was centralized (through the BA leaders, the country presidents, and the executive committee). ABB saw itself as a federation of national companies with a global coordination center.

Only 100 professionals were located in ABB's corporate headquarters in Zurich. A management information system collected data on all profit centers monthly, comparing actual performance against budgets and forecasts. Data was collected in local currencies but translated into U.S. dollars to allow for cross-border analysis. ABB's corporate financial statements were reported in U.S. dollars, and English was ABB's official language. All high-level meetings were conducted in English.

Source: Compiled from information in William Taylor, "The Logic of Global Business: An Interview with ABB's Percy Barnevik," *Harvard Business Review* 69, no. 2 (March–April 1991), pp. 90–105.

members, membership was voluntary, the seniority of the members was proportional to the importance of the problem, the task force moved swiftly to deal with its assignment, the task force was pulled together only on an as-needed basis, no staff was assigned, and documentation was scant.[12] In these companies, the prevailing philosophy about task forces is to use them to solve real problems, produce some solution efficiently, and then disband them. At the other extreme, Peters and Waterman report one instance where a company had formed 325 task forces, none of which had completed its charge in three years and none of which had been disbanded.

3. The *venture team approach*, whereby a group of individuals is formed for the purpose of bringing a specific product to market or a specific new business into being. Dow, General Mills, Westinghouse, General

---

[12]Peters and Waterman, *In Search of Excellence*, pp. 127–32.

Electric, and Monsanto have used the venture team approach to regenerate an entrepreneurial spirit. The difficulties with venture teams include deciding who the venture manager should report to; whether funding for ventures should come from corporate, business, or departmental budgets; how to keep the venture clear of bureaucratic and vested interests; and how to coordinate large numbers of different ventures.

Perspectives on the Methods of Organizing

The foregoing discussion brings out two points: (1) there is no perfect or ideal organization design and (2) there are no universally applicable rules for matching strategy and structure. All of the basic organizational forms have their strategy-related strengths and weaknesses. Moreover, two or more can be used simultaneously. Many organizations are large enough and diverse enough to have subunits organized by functional specialty, geographical area, market segment, line of business, SBU, and matrix principles. In a very real sense, *the best organizational arrangement is the one that best fits the firm's situation at the moment.* Judging from the frequency with which firms reorganize, every organizational arrangement outlives its usefulness—either an internal rearrangement becomes desirable or changes in the size and scope of customer-product-technology relationships make the firm's structure strategically obsolete. An organization's structure is dynamic, and changes are inevitable.

There is room to quibble over whether organization design should commence with a strategy-structure framework or with a pragmatic consideration of the situation at hand—the corporate culture, the personalities involved, and the way things have been done before. By and large, agonizing over where to begin is unnecessary; both considerations have to be taken into account. However, strategy-structure factors usually take precedence if structure is to be built around the organization's strategy-critical tasks, key success factors, and high-priority business units. Adapting structure to the peculiar circumstances of the organization's internal situation and personalities is usually done to modify the strategy-structure match in "minor" ways.

Drucker sums up the intricacies of organization design thusly:

> The simplest organization structure that will do the job is the best one. What makes an organization structure "good" are the problems it does not create. The simpler the structure, the less that can go wrong.
>
> Some design principles are more difficult and problematic than others. But none is without difficulties and problems. None is primarily people-focused rather than task-focused; none is more "creative," "free," or "more democratic." Design principles are tools; and tools are neither good nor bad in themselves. They can be used properly or improperly; and that is all. To obtain both the greatest possible simplicity and the greatest "fit," organization design has to start out with a clear focus on *key activities* needed to produce *key results*. They have to be structured and positioned in the simplest possible design. Above all, the architect of organization needs to keep in mind the purpose of the structure he is designing.[13]

---

[13]Drucker, *Management*, pp. 601–2.

Peters and Waterman, in their study of excellently managed companies, confirm what Drucker says; their organization prescription is "simple form, lean staff." Illustration Capsule 23 explains some of the organizational principles and approaches being used at these companies.

Building Core Competencies

A good match between structure and strategy is one key facet of organizational capability. But an equally dominant organization-building concern is that of staffing the structure with the requisite managerial talent, specialized skills, and technical expertise—and, most particularly, staffing in a manner calculated to give the firm a clear edge over rivals in performing one or more critical activities. *When it is difficult or impossible to outstrategize rivals (beat them with a superior strategy), the other main avenue to industry leadership is to outexecute them (beat them with superior strategy implementation).* Superior strategy execution is essential in situations where rivals have very similar strategies and can readily imitate one another's strategic maneuvers. Building core competencies and organizational capabilities that rivals can't match is one of the best ways to outexecute them. This is why one of top management's most important strategy-implementing tasks is to guide the building of core competencies in competitively important ways.[14] Core competencies can relate to any strategically relevant factor: greater proficiency in product development, better manufacturing know-how, the capability to provide customers better after-sale services, an ability to respond quickly to changing customer requirements, superior ability to minimize costs, an ability to re-engineer and redesign products more quickly than rivals, superior inventory management capabilities, better marketing and merchandising skills, or greater effectiveness in promoting union-management cooperation.

However, core competencies don't just appear naturally. They have to be deliberately developed and consciously nurtured. For core competencies to emerge from organization-building actions, strategy implementers have to build a critical mass of technical skills and capabilities in those subunits where superior performance of strategically critical tasks can mean greater strategic success. Usually, this means (1) giving above-average operating budgets to strategy-critical tasks and activities, (2) seeing that these areas are staffed with high-caliber managerial and technical talent, (3) insisting on high standards in performing these tasks/activities, backed up with a policy of rewarding people for outstanding results. In effect, strategy implementers must take actions to see that the organization is staffed with enough of the right kinds of people and that these people have the budgets, the administrative support, and the incentive rewards needed to generate the desired competencies and competitive capabilities.

Distinctive internal skills and capabilities are not easily duplicated by rivals; any competitive advantage that results is likely to be sustainable for some time, thus paving the way for above-average performance. Conscious management attention to building strategically relevant internal skills and strengths into the

• • • • • • • • • • • •

Strategic Management Principle

Building core competencies and organizational capabilities that rivals can't match is a sound basis for sustainable competitive advantage.

---

[14]C. K. Prahalad and Gary Hamel, "The Core Competence of the Corporation," *Harvard Business Review* 68 (May–June 1990), pp. 79–93.

ILLUSTRATION CAPSULE | 23 | ORGANIZATION LESSONS FROM THE "EXCELLENTLY MANAGED" COMPANIES

Peters and Waterman's study of America's best-managed corporations provides some important lessons in building a strategically capable organization:

- The organizational underpinning of most of the excellently managed companies is a fairly stable, unchanging form—usually a decentralized business/product division—that provides the structural building block which everyone in the enterprise understands and that serves as the base for approaching day-to-day issues and complexities.

- Beyond the crystal-clear primacy of this basic and simple organizational building block, the rest of the organization structure is deliberately kept fluid and flexible to permit response to changing environmental conditions. Much use is made of task forces, project teams, and the creation of new, small divisions to address emerging issues and opportunities.

- New divisions are created to pursue budding business opportunities, as opposed to letting them remain a part of the originating division. Often, there are established guidelines when a new product or product line automatically becomes an independent division.

- People and even products and product lines are frequently shifted from one division to another—to improve efficiency, promote shared costs, enhance competitive strength,

and adapt to changing market conditions.

- Many excellently managed companies have comparatively few people at the corporate level, and many of these are out in the field frequently, rather than in the home office all the time. Emerson Electric with 54,000 employees had a headquarters staff of fewer than 100 people. Dana Corporation employed 35,000 people and had a corporate staff numbering about 100. Schlumberger Ltd., a $56 billion diversified oil service company, ran its worldwide organization with a corporate staff of 90 people. At Intel (sales of over $1 billion), all staff assignments were temporary ones given to line officers. Rolm managed a $200 million business with about 15 people in corporate headquarters. In addition, corporate planners were few and far between. Hewlett-Packard Company, Johnson & Johnson, and 3M had no planners at the corporate level; Fluor Corporation ran a $6 billion operation with three corporate planners. At IBM, management rotated staff assignments every three years. Few IBM staff jobs were manned by "career staffers"; most were manned temporarily by managers with line jobs in the divisions who eventually rotate back to line jobs.

- Functional organization forms are efficient and get the basic activities performed well; yet they are not particularly creative or en-

(continued)

overall organizational scheme is therefore one of the central tasks of organization-building and effective strategy implementation.

Employee Training   Employee training and retraining are important parts of the strategy implementation process when a company shifts to a strategy requiring different skills, managerial approaches, and operating methods. Training is also strategically important in organizational efforts to build skills-based competencies. And it is a key activity in businesses where technical know-how is changing so rapidly that a company loses its ability to compete unless its skilled people are kept updated and maintain their cutting-edge expertise. Successful strategy implementers see that the training function is

ILLUSTRATION CAPSULE   23   (concluded)

trepreneurial, they do not adapt quickly, and they are apt to ignore important changes.

- The key to maintaining an entrepreneurial, adaptive organization is *small size*—and the way to keep units small is to spin off new or expanded activities into independent units. Division sizes often run no bigger than $50 to $100 million in sales, with a maximum of 1,000 or so employees. At Emerson Electric, plants rarely employed more than 600 workers, so that management could maintain personal contact with employees. (Emerson, by the way, has a good track record on efficiency; its strategy of being the low-cost producer has worked beautifully in chain saws and several other products.) At Blue Bell, a leading apparel firm, manufacturing units usually employ under 300 people. The lesson seems to be that small units are both more cost-effective and more innovative.

- To prevent "calcification" and stodginess, it helps to rely on such "habit-breaking" techniques as (a) reorganizing regularly; (b) putting top talent on project teams and giving them a "charter" to move quickly to solve a key problem or execute a central strategic thrust (i.e., the creation of the General Motors Project Center to lead the downsizing effort); (c) shifting products or product lines among divisions to take advantage of special management talents or the need for market realignments; (d) break-

ing up big, bureaucratic divisions into several new, smaller divisions; and (e) being flexible enough to try experimental organization approaches and support the pursuit of new opportunities.

- It is useful to adopt a simultaneous "loose-tight" structure that on the one hand fosters autonomy, entrepreneurship, and innovation from rank-and-file managers yet, on the other hand, allows for strong central direction from the top. Such things as regular reorganization, flexible form (the use of teams and task forces), lots of decentralized autonomy for lower-level general managers, and extensive experimentation all focus on the excitement of trying things out in a slightly "loose" fashion. Yet, regular communication, quick feedback, concise paperwork, strong adherence to a few core values, and self-discipline can impose "tight" central control so that nothing gets far out of line.

Application of these "principles" in the best-managed companies tends to produce an environment that fosters entrepreneurial pursuit of new opportunities and adaptation to change. A fluid, flexible structure is the norm—the basic form is stable, but there is frequent reorganization "around the edges." The aim is to keep structure matched to the changing needs of an evolving strategy and to avoid letting the current organization structure become so ingrained and political that it becomes a major obstacle to be hurdled.

Source: Drawn from Thomas J. Peters and Robert H. Waterman, Jr., *In Search of Excellence* (New York: Harper & Row, 1982), especially chaps. 11 and 12.

adequately funded and that effective training programs are in place. Normally, training should be near the top of the action agenda because it needs to be done early in the strategy implementation process.

Selecting People for Key Positions

Assembling a capable management team is also part of the strategy implementation task. Companies must decide what kind of core management team they need to carry out the strategy and find the right people to fill each slot.

. . . .
*A strong management
team with the right
personal chemistry and
mix of skills must be put
together early in the
implementation process.*

Sometimes the existing management team is suitable; sometimes it needs to be strengthened and/or expanded by promoting qualified people from within or by bringing in skilled managers from outside to help infuse fresh ideas and approaches. In turnaround and rapid-growth situations, and in instances where a company doesn't have the necessary type of management skills in-house, recruiting outsiders for key management slots is a fairly standard organization-building approach.

The important skill in assembling a core executive group is discerning what mix of backgrounds, experiences, know-how, values, beliefs, styles of managing, and personalities will contribute to successful strategy execution. As with any kind of team-building, it is important to put together a compatible group of skilled managers. The personal "chemistry" needs to be right, and the talent base needs to be appropriate for the chosen strategy. Molding a solid management team is an essential organization-building function—often the first strategy implementation step to take.[15] Until all the key slots are filled with the right people, it is hard for strategy implementation to proceed at full speed.

LINKING BUDGETS WITH STRATEGY

Keeping an organization on the strategy implementation path thrusts a manager squarely into the budgeting process. Not only must a strategy implementer oversee "who gets how much," but the budget must also be put together with an equal concern for "getting the biggest bang for the buck."

Obviously, organizational units need enough resources to carry out their part of the strategic plan. This includes having enough of the right kinds of people and sufficient operating funds for them to do their work successfully. Moreover, organizational units need to: (1) set up detailed, step-by-step action programs for putting each piece of the strategy into place, (2) establish schedules and deadlines for accomplishment, and (3) designate who is responsible for what by when.

. . . .
**Strategic Management
Principle**
*Depriving strategy-
critical organizational
units of the funds needed
to execute their part of the
strategic plan can
undermine the
implementation process.*

How well a strategy implementer links budget allocations to the needs of strategy can either promote or impede the implementation process. With too little funding, organizational units can't execute their part of the strategic plan proficiently. Too much funding wastes organizational resources and reduces financial performance. Both outcomes argue for the strategy implementer to be deeply involved in the budgeting process, closely reviewing the programs and budget proposals of strategy-critical subunits.

. . . .
*New strategies usually
call for significant budget
reallocations.*

Implementers must also be willing to shift resources when strategy changes. A change in strategy nearly always calls for budget reallocation. Units important in the old strategy may now be oversized and overfunded. Units that now have a bigger and more critical strategic role may need more people, new equipment, additional facilities, and above-average increases in their operating budgets. The strategy implementer must engineer reallocations, downsizing some areas, upsizing others, and steering ample resources into particularly

---

[15]For a fuller discussion of the top management team's strategic role, see Donald C. Hambrick, "The Top Management Team: Key to Strategic Success," *California Management Review* 30, no. 1 (Fall 1987), pp. 88–108.

critical activities. *Strategy must drive how budget allocations are made.* Underfunding organizational units essential for strategic success can defeat the whole implementation process.

Successful strategy implementers are good resource reallocators. For example, at Harris Corporation, one element of strategy is to diffuse research ideas into areas that are commercially viable. Top management regularly shifts groups of engineers out of government projects and moves them (as a group) into new commercial venture divisions. Boeing has a similar approach to reallocating ideas and talent; according to one Boeing officer, "We can do it [create a big new unit] in two weeks. We couldn't do it in two years at International Harvester."[16] A fluid, flexible approach to reorganization and reallocation of people and budgets is key to successful implementation of strategic change.

Fine-tuning existing strategy usually involves less reallocation and more extrapolation. Big movements of people and money from one area to another are seldom necessary. Fine-tuning can usually be accomplished by incrementally increasing or decreasing the budgets and staffing of existing organization units. The chief exception occurs where a prime strategy ingredient is to generate fresh, new products and business opportunities from within. Then, as attractive ventures "bubble up" from below, major decisions have to be made regarding budgets and staffing. Companies like 3M, GE, Boeing, IBM, and Digital Equipment shift resources and people from area to area on an "as-needed" basis to support budding ideas and ventures. They empower "product champions" and small groups of would-be entrepreneurs by giving them financial and technical support and by setting up organizational units and programs to help new ventures blossom more quickly.

PUTTING INTERNAL ADMINISTRATIVE SUPPORT SYSTEMS IN PLACE

A third key task of strategy implementation is to install internal administrative support systems that fit the needs of strategy. The specific considerations here are:

1. What kinds of strategy-facilitating policies and procedures to establish.
2. How to enhance organizational capabilities via the installation of new or enhanced administrative and operating systems.
3. How to get the right strategy-critical information on a timely basis.

Creating Strategy-Supportive Policies and Procedures

Changes in strategy generally call for some changes in how internal activities are conducted and administered. The process of changing from old ways to new has to be initiated and managed. Asking people to change their actions always "upsets" the internal order of things. It is normal for pockets of resistance to emerge and questions to be raised about the *hows* as well as the whys of change. The role of new and revised policies is to promulgate "standard

Successful strategy implementers are good at creating policies and procedures that make the strategy work better.

---

[16]Peters and Waterman, *In Search of Excellence*, p. 125.

operating procedures" that will (1) channel individual and group efforts in the right direction and (2) counteract any tendencies for parts of the organization to resist or reject the actions needed to make the strategy work. Policies and procedures help enforce strategy implementation in several ways:

1. Policy institutionalizes strategy-supportive practices and operating procedures throughout the organization, thus pushing day-to-day activities in the direction of efficient strategy execution.

2. Policy limits independent action and discretionary decisions and behavior. By stating procedures for how things are to be handled, policy communicates what is expected, guides strategy-related activities in particular directions, and restricts unwanted variations.

3. Policy helps align actions and behaviors with strategy, thereby minimizing zigzag decisions and conflicting practices and establishing more regularity, stability, and dependability in how the organization is attempting to make the strategy work.

4. Policy helps to shape the character of the working environment and to translate the corporate philosophy into how things are done, how people are treated, and what corporate beliefs and attitudes mean in terms of everyday activities. Policy operationalizes the corporate philosophy, helping establish a fit between corporate culture and strategy.

Managers need to be inventive in establishing policies to support a strategic plan. McDonald's policy manual, in an attempt to boost quality and service, spells out such detailed procedures as: "Cooks must turn, never flip, hamburgers. If they haven't been purchased, Big Macs must be discarded 10 minutes after being cooked and french fries 7 minutes. Cashiers must make eye contact with and smile at every customer." At Delta Airlines, it is corporate policy to test all applicants for flight attendants' positions for friendliness, cooperativeness, and teamwork. Caterpillar Tractor has a policy of guaranteeing 48-hour parts delivery anywhere in the world; if it fails to fulfill the promise, it supplies the part free. Hewlett-Packard requires R&D people to visit customers to learn about their problems, talk about new-product applications, and, in general, keep the company's R&D programs customer-oriented.

Thus there is a definite role for policies and procedures in the strategy implementation process. Wisely constructed policies and procedures help enforce strategy implementation by channeling actions, behavior, decisions, and practices in directions that promote effective strategy execution. When policies aren't strategy-supportive, they become obstacles and there is risk that people who disagree with the strategy will hide behind outdated policies to thwart the strategic plan. On the other hand, instituting policies that promote strategy-supportive behavior builds organization commitment to the strategic plan and creates a tighter fit between corporate culture and strategy.

None of this is meant to imply, however, that a huge manual full of policies is called for. Too much policy can be as stifling as wrong policy or as chaotic as no policy. Sometimes, the best policy for implementing strategy is a willingness to let subordinates do it any way they want if it makes sense and works. A little "structured chaos" can be a good thing when individual creativity is more essential to strategy than standardization and strict conformity. When Rene

McPherson became CEO at Dana Corp., he dramatically threw out $22\frac{1}{2}$ inches of policy manuals and replaced them with a one-page statement of philosophy focusing on "productive people."[17] Creating a strong supportive fit between strategy and policy can mean more policies, fewer policies, or different policies. It can mean policies that require things to be done a certain way or policies that give employees the autonomy to do the job the way they think best.

Installing Support Systems

Effective strategy execution typically involves developing a number of support systems. An airline, for example, cannot function without a computerized reservation system, a baggage handling system at every airport it serves, and a strong aircraft maintenance program. A supermarket that stocks 17,000 different items has to have systems for tracking inventories, maintaining shelf freshness, and allocating shelf space among fast-selling and slow-selling items. A company that manufactures many models and sizes of its product must have a sophisticated cost accounting system to price each item intelligently and know which items generate the biggest profit contribution. In businesses where large number of employees need cutting-edge technical know-how, companies have to install systems to train and retrain employees regularly and keep them supplied with up-to-date information. Fast-growing companies have to develop employee recruiting systems to attract and hire qualified employees in large numbers. Well-conceived, state-of-the-art support systems not only facilitate better strategy execution, they also can strengthen organizational capabilities enough to provide a competitive edge over rivals.

Strategic Management Principle
An innovative, state-of-the-art support system can be a basis for competitive advantage if it gives the firm capabilities that rivals can't match.

Strategy implementers must be alert to what specific support systems their company needs to execute its strategy successfully. A company with a strategy of superior quality, for example, must develop superior methods for quality control. A company whose strategy is to be a low-cost producer must develop systems to enforce tight cost containment. If the present administrative support and operating systems are inadequate, resources must be allocated to improve them. Illustration Capsule 24 describes the administrative support systems put in place at Mrs. Fields Cookies.

Instituting Formal Reporting of Strategic Information

Accurate information is an essential guide to action. Every organization needs a system for gathering and reporting strategy-critical information. Information is needed *before* actions are completed to steer them to successful conclusion in case the early steps don't produce the intended outcome and need to be modified. Monitoring the outcomes of the first round of implementation actions (1) allows early detection of need to adjust either the strategy or how it is being implemented and (2) provides some assurance that things are moving ahead as planned.[18] Early experiences are sometimes difficult to assess, but they yield the first hard data from the action front and should be closely scrutinized as a basis for corrective action.

Accurate, timely information allows strategists to monitor progress and take corrective actions promptly.

---

[17]Ibid., p. 65.
[18]Boris Yavitz and William H. Newman, *Strategy in Action* (New York: Free Press, 1982), pp. 209–10.

ILLUSTRATION CAPSULE **24** STRATEGY IMPLEMENTATION AT MRS. FIELDS COOKIES, INC.

In 1988 Mrs. Fields Cookies was one of the fastest growing specialty foods companies in the United States. Sales in 1987 were $150 million, up from $87 million in 1986. The company had over 400 Mrs. Fields outlets in operation and over 250 outlets retailing other bakery and cookie products. Debbi Fields, age 31, was the company's founder and CEO. Her business concept for Mrs. Fields Cookies was "to serve absolutely fresh, warm cookies as though you'd stopped by my house and caught me just taking a batch from the oven." Cookies not sold within two hours were removed from the case and given to charity. The company's major form of advertising was sampling; store employees walked around the shopping mall giving away cookie samples. People were hired for store crews on the basis of warmth, friendliness, and the ability to have a good time giving away samples, baking fresh batches, and talking to customers during the course of a sale.

To implement its strategy, the company developed several novel practices and a customized computer support system. One key practice was giving each store an *hourly* sales quota. Another was for Fields to make unannounced visits to her stores, where she masqueraded as a casual shopper to test the enthusiasm and sales techniques of store crews, sample the quality of the cookies they were baking, and observe customer reactions; she visited each outlet once or twice annually.

Debbi's husband Randy developed a software program that kept headquarters and stores in close contact. Via the computer network, each store manager receives a daily sales goal (broken down by the hour) based on the store's recent performance history and on such special factors as special promotions, mall activities, weekdays vs. weekends, holiday shopping patterns, and the

weather forecast. With the hourly sales quotas also comes a schedule of the number of cookies to bake and when to bake them. As the day progresses, store managers type in actual hourly sales figures and customer counts. If customer counts are up but sales are lagging, the computer is programmed to recommend more aggressive sampling or more suggestive selling. If it becomes obvious the day is going to be a bust for the store, the computer automatically revises the sales projections for the day, reducing hourly quotas and instructing how much to cut back cookie baking. To facilitate crew scheduling by the store manager, sales projections are also provided for two weeks in advance. All job applicants must sit at the store's terminal and answer a computerized set of questions as part of the interview process.

In addition, the computer software contains a menu giving store staff immediate access to company personnel policies, maintenance schedules for store equipment, and repair instructions. If a store manager has a specific problem, it can be entered on the system and routed to the appropriate person. Messages can be sent directly to Debbi Fields via the computer; even if she is on a store inspection trip, her promise is to respond to all inquiries within 48 hours.

The computerized information support system serves several objectives: (1) it gives store managers more time to work with their crews and achieve sales quotas as opposed to handling administrative chores and (2) it gives headquarters instantaneous information on store performance and a means of controlling store operations. Debbi Fields sees the system as a tool for projecting her influence and enthusiasm into more stores more frequently than she could otherwise reach.

Source: Developed from information in Mike Korologos, "Debbi Fields," *Sky Magazine*, July 1988, pp. 42–50.

Information systems need to be more comprehensive than just monitoring the first signs of progress. All key strategic performance indicators have to be tracked as often as practical. Many retail companies generate daily sales reports for each store and maintain up-to-the-minute inventory and sales records on each item. Manufacturing plants typically generate daily production reports and track labor productivity on every shift. Monthly profit-and-loss statements are common, as are monthly statistical summaries.

In designing formal reports to monitor strategic progress, five guidelines should be observed:[19]

1. Information and reporting systems should involve no more data and reporting than is needed to give a reliable picture of what is going on. The data gathered should emphasize strategically meaningful variables and symptoms of potentially significant developments. Temptations to supplement "what managers need to know" with other "interesting" but marginally useful information should be avoided.

2. Reports and statistical data-gathering have to be timely—not too late to take corrective action or so often as to overburden.

3. The flow of information and statistics should be kept simple. Complicated reports are likely to confound and obscure because of the attention that has to be paid to mechanics, procedures, and interpretive guidelines instead of measuring and reporting the really critical variables.

4. Information and reporting systems should aim at "no surprises" and generating "early-warnings signs" rather than just producing information. Reports don't necessarily need wide distribution, but they should always be provided to managers who are in a position to act when trouble signs appear.

5. Statistical reports should make it easy to flag big or unusual variances from plan, thus directing management attention to significant departures from targeted performance.

Statistical information gives the strategy implementer a feel for the numbers; reports and meetings provide a feel for new developments and problems; and personal contacts add a feel for the people dimension. All are good barometers of overall performance and good indicators of which things are on and off track. Identifying deviations from plan and the problem areas to be addressed are prerequisites for initiating any actions to either improve implementation or fine-tune strategy.

KEY POINTS

The job of strategy implementation is to translate plans into actions and achieve the intended results. The test of successful strategy implementation is whether actual organization performance matches or exceeds the targets spelled out in the strategic plan. Shortfalls in performance signal weak strategy, weak implementation, or both.

In deciding how to implement strategy, managers have to determine what internal conditions are needed to execute the strategic plan successfully. Then they must create these conditions as rapidly as practical. The process involves creating a series of tight fits:

- Between strategy and organization structure.
- Between strategy and the organization's skills and competencies.

---

[19]Drucker, *Management*, pp. 498–504; Harold Hoontz, "Management Control: A Suggested Formulation of Principles," *California Management Review* 2, no. 2 (Winter 1959), pp. 50–55; and William H. Sihler, "Toward Better Management Control Systems," *California Management Review* 14, no. 2 (Winter 1971), pp. 33–39.

- Between strategy and budget allocations.
- Between strategy and internal policies, procedures, and support systems.
- Between strategy and the reward structure.
- Between strategy and the corporate culture.

The tighter the fits, the more powerful strategy execution becomes and the more likely targeted performance can actually be achieved.

Implementing strategy is not just a top management function; it is a job for the whole management team. All managers function as strategy implementers in their respective areas of authority and responsibility. All managers have to consider what actions to take in their areas to achieve the intended results—they each need an *action agenda*.

The three major components of organization-building are (1) deciding how to organize and what the organization chart should look like, (2) developing the skills and competencies needed to execute the strategy successfully, and (3) filling key positions with the right people. All organization structures have strategic advantages and disadvantages; there is no one best way to organize. In choosing a structure, the guiding principles are to make strategy-critical activities the major building blocks, keep the design simple, and put decision-making authority in the hands of managers closest to the action. Functional and geographic organization structures are well suited to single-business companies. SBU structures are well suited to companies pursuing related diversification. Decentralized business-unit structures are well suited to companies pursuing unrelated diversification. Project teams, task forces, and new venture teams can also be useful organizational mechanisms to handle temporary or one-time strategic initiatives.

The other two aspects of organization-building—skills development and filling key positions—are just as important as matching structure to strategy. Taking action to develop strategy-supportive skills and create a distinctive competence not only strengthens execution but also helps build competitive advantage. Selecting the right people for key positions tends to be one of the earliest strategy implementation steps because it takes a full complement of capable managers to put the strategy into operation and make it work.

Reworking the budget to make it more strategy-supportive is a crucial part of the implementation process because every organization unit needs to have the people, equipment, facilities, and other resources to carry out its part of the strategic plan (but no *more* than what it really needs!). Strategy implementation often entails shifting resources from one area to another—downsizing units that are overstaffed and overfunded and upsizing those more critical to strategic success.

A third key implementation task is to install some necessary support systems—policies and procedures to establish desired types of behavior, information systems to provide strategy-critical information on a timely basis, and whatever inventory, materials management, customer service, cost accounting, and other administrative systems are needed to give the organization important strategy-executing capability.

In the next chapter, we examine the remaining three key tasks of the strategy implementation process: designing the reward system, creating a strategy-supportive corporate culture, and exercising strategic leadership.

Aaker, David A. "Managing Assets and Skills: The Key to a Sustainable Competitive Advantage." *California Management Review* 31 (Winter 1989), pp. 91–106.

Bartlett, Christopher A., and Sumantra Ghoshal. "Matrix Management: Not a Structure, a Frame of Mind." *Harvard Business Review* 68, no. 4 (July–August 1990), pp. 138–45.

Bettis, Richard A., and William K. Hall. "The Business Portfolio Approach—Where It Falls Down in Practice." *Long Range Planning* 16, no. 2 (April 1983), pp. 95–104.

Chandler, Alfred D. *Strategy and Structure.* Cambridge, Mass.: MIT Press, 1962.

Hall, William K. "SBUs: Hot, New Topic in the Management of Diversification." *Business Horizons* 21, no. 1 (February 1978), pp. 17–25.

Hambrick, Donald C. "The Top Management Team: Key to Strategic Success." *California Management Review* 30, no. 1 (Fall 1987), pp. 88–108.

Larson, Erik W., and David H. Gobeli. "Matrix Management: Contradictions and Insights." *California Management Review* 29, no. 4 (Summer 1987), pp. 126–27.

Leontiades, Milton. "Choosing the Right Manager to Fit the Strategy." *Journal of Business Strategy* 3, no. 2 (Fall 1981), pp. 58–69.

Mintzberg, Henry. "Organization Design: Fashion or Fit." *Harvard Business Review* 59, no. 1 (January–February 1981), pp. 103–16.

Paulson, Robert D. "Making It Happen: The Real Strategic Challenge." *The McKinsey Quarterly* Winter 1982, pp. 58–66.

Peters, Thomas J., and Robert H. Waterman, Jr. *In Search of Excellence.* New York: Harper & Row, 1982.

Powell, Walter W. "Hybrid Organizational Arrangements: New Form or Transitional Development?" *California Management Review* 30, no. 1 (Fall 1987), pp. 67–87.

Prahalad, C. K., and Gary Hamel. "The Core Competence of the Corporation." *Harvard Business Review* 68 (May–June 1990), pp. 79–93.

Waterman, Robert H.; Thomas J. Peters; and Julien R. Phillips. "Structure Is Not Organization." *Business Horizons* 23, no. 3 (June 1980), pp. 14–26.

SUGGESTED READINGS

CHAPTER 10

Implementing Strategy
Commitment, Culture, and Leadership

Weak leadership can wreck the soundest strategy; forceful execution of even a poor plan can often bring victory.
~Sun Zi

• • • • • • •

Effective leaders do not just reward achievement, they celebrate it.
~Shelley A. Kirkpatrick and Edwin A. Locke

• • • • • • •

Ethics is the moral courage to do what we know is right, and not to do what we know is wrong.
~C. J. Silas
CEO, Philips Petroleum

• • • • • • •

. . . a leader lives in the field with his troops.
~H. Ross Perot

In the previous chapter, we examined three of the strategy-implementer's tasks—building a capable organization, steering resources into strategy-critical programs and activities, and creating a series of internal support systems to enable better execution. In this chapter, we explore the three remaining implementation tasks: designing rewards and incentives for carrying out the strategy, creating a strategy-supportive corporate culture, and exercising strategic leadership.

DEVELOPING AN EFFECTIVE REWARD STRUCTURE

It is important for organizational subunits and individuals to be committed to implementing strategy and accomplishing strategic objectives. Companies typically try to solidify organizationwide commitment through motivation, incentives, and rewards for good performance. The range of options includes all the standard reward-punishment techniques—salary raises, bonuses, stock options, fringe benefits, promotions, fear of being "sidelined," praise, recognition, constructive criticism, tension, peer pressure, more (or less) responsibility, increased (or decreased) job control and decision-making autonomy, attractive geographic assignments, group acceptance, and opportunities for personal satisfaction. But rewards have to be used *creatively* and tightly linked to the factors necessary for good strategy execution.

The strategy-implementer's challenge is to design a reward structure that motivates people to do the things it takes to make the strategy work successfully.

Motivational Practices

Successful strategy-implementers are good at inspiring employees to do their best. They are skilled at getting employees to buy in to the strategy and commit to making it work. They work at devising strategy-supportive motivational approaches and using them effectively. Consider some actual examples:[1]

- At Mars, Inc. (best known for its candy bars), every employee, including the president, gets a weekly 10 percent bonus by coming to work on time each day that week. This on-time incentive is based on minimizing absenteeism and tardiness to boost worker productivity and to produce the greatest number of candy bars during each available minute of machine time.

- In a number of Japanese companies, employees meet regularly to hear inspirational speeches, sing company songs, and chant the corporate litany. In the United States, Tupperware conducts a weekly Monday night rally to honor, applaud, and fire up its salespeople who conduct Tupperware parties. Amway and Mary Kay Cosmetics hold similar inspirational get-togethers for their sales force organizations.

- A San Diego area company assembles its 2,000 employees at its six plants the first thing every workday to listen to a management talk about the state of the company. Then they engage in brisk calisthenics. This company's management believes "that by doing one thing together each day, it reinforces the unity of the company. It's also fun. It gets the blood up." Managers take turns making the presentations. Many of the speeches "are very personal and emotional, not approved beforehand or screened by anybody."

- Texas Instruments and Dana Corp. insist that teams and divisions set their own goals and have regular peer reviews.

- Procter & Gamble's brand managers are asked to compete fiercely against each other; the official policy is "a free-for-all among brands with no holds barred." P&G's system of purposeful internal competition breeds people who love to compete and excel. Those who "win" become corporate "heroes." Around them emerges a folklore of "war stories" of their valiant uphill struggles against great odds to make a market success out of their assigned brands.

Part of a strategy-implementer's job is to devise motivational techniques that build wholehearted commitment and winning attitudes among employees.

---

[1]The list that follows is abstracted from Thomas J. Peters and Robert H. Waterman, Jr., *In Search of Excellence* (New York: Harper & Row, 1982), pp. xx, 213–14, 276, and 285.

These motivational approaches accentuate the positive; others blend positive and negative features. Consider the way Harold Geneen, former president and chief executive officer of ITT, allegedly combined the use of money, tension, and fear:

> Geneen provides his managers with enough incentives to make them tolerate the system. Salaries all the way through ITT are higher than average—Geneen reckons 10 percent higher—so that few people can leave without taking a drop. As one employee put it: "We're all paid just a bit more than we think we're worth." At the very top, where the demands are greatest, the salaries and stock options are sufficient to compensate for the rigors. As some said, "He's got them by their limousines."
>
> Having bound his men to him with chains of gold, Geneen can induce the tension that drives the machine. "The key to the system," one of his men explains, "is the profit forecast. Once the forecast has been gone over, revised, and agreed on, the managing director has a personal commitment to Geneen to carry it out. That's how he produces the tension on which the success depends." The tension goes through the company, inducing ambition, perhaps exhilaration, but always with some sense of fear: what happens if the target is missed?[2]

If a strategy-implementer's use of rewards and punishments induces too much tension, anxiety, and job insecurity, the results can be counterproductive. Yet implementers should not completely eliminate tension, pressure for performance, and anxiety from the implementation process. There is, for example, no evidence that a no-pressure work environment leads to superior strategy execution. High-performing organizations need a cadre of ambitious people who relish the opportunity to succeed, love a challenge, thrive in a performance-oriented environment, and find some competition and pressure useful to satisfy their own drives for personal recognition, accomplishment, and self-satisfaction. There has to be some meaningful incentive and career consequences associated with implementation or few people will attach much significance to the strategic plan.

Rewards and Incentives

Positive motivational approaches generally work better than negative ones.

The conventional view is that a manager's plan for strategy implementation should incorporate more positive than negative motivational elements because when cooperation is positively enlisted and rewarded, people tend to respond with more enthusiasm and effort. Nevertheless, how much of which incentives to use depends on how hard the strategy implementation task will be. A manager has to do more than just talk to everyone about how important strategy implementation is to the organization's future well-being. Talk, no matter how inspiring, seldom commands people's best efforts for long. To get employees' sustained, energetic commitment, management almost always has to be resourceful in designing and using incentives. The more a manager understands what motivates subordinates and the more he or she relies on motivational incentives as a tool for implementing strategy, the greater will be employees' commitment to carrying out the strategic plan.

Linking Work Assignments to Performance Targets
The first step in creating a strategy-supportive system of rewards and incentives is to define

---

[2]Anthony Sampson, *The Sovereign State of ITT* (New York: Stein and Day, 1973), p. 132.

jobs and assignments in terms of the *results to be accomplished*, not the duties and functions to be performed. Training the job holder's attention and energy on what to *achieve* as opposed to what to do improves the chances of reaching the agreed-on objectives. It is flawed thinking to stress duties and activities in job descriptions in hopes that the by-products will be the desired kinds of accomplishment. In any job, performing activities is not equivalent to achieving objectives. Working hard, staying busy, and diligently attending to assigned duties do not guarantee results. As any student knows, just because an instructor teaches doesn't mean students are learning. Teaching and learning are different things—the first is an activity and the second is a result.

Emphasizing what to accomplish—i.e., performance targets for individual jobs, work groups, departments, businesses, and the entire company—makes the whole work environment results-oriented. Without target objectives, people and organizations can become so engrossed in doing their duties and performing assigned functions on schedule that they lose sight of what the tasks are intended to accomplish. By keeping the spotlight on achievement and targeted performance, strategy-implementers take proactive steps to make the right things happen rather than passively hoping they will happen (this, of course, is what "managing by objectives" is all about).

Creating a tight fit between work assignments and accomplishing the strategic plan thus goes straight to the objectives and performance targets spelled out in the strategic plan. If the details of strategy have been fleshed out thoroughly from the corporate level down to the operating level, performance targets exist for the whole company, for each business unit, for each functional department, and for each operating unit. These become the targets that strategy-implementers aim at achieving and the basis for deciding how many jobs and what skills, expertise, funding, and time frame it will take to achieve them.

Usually a number of performance measures are needed at each level; rarely does a single measure suffice. At the corporate and line-of-business levels, typical performance measures include profitability (measured in terms of total profit, return on equity investment, return on total assets, return on sales, operating profit, and so on), market share, growth rates in sales and profits, and hard evidence that competitive position and future prospects have improved. In the manufacturing area, strategy-relevant performance measures may focus on unit manufacturing costs, productivity increases, production and shipping schedules, quality control, the number and extent of work stoppages due to labor disagreements and equipment breakdowns, and so on. In the marketing area, measures may include unit selling costs, increases in dollar sales and unit volume, sales penetration of each target customer group, increases in market share, the success of newly introduced products, the severity of customer complaints, advertising effectiveness, and the number of new accounts acquired. While most performance measures are quantitative, several have elements of subjectivity—labor-management relations, employee morale, customer satisfaction, advertising success, and how far the firm is ahead or behind rivals on quality, service, and technological capability.

Rewarding Performance   The only dependable way to keep people focused on strategic objectives and to make achieving them "a way of life" throughout the organization is to reward individuals who achieve targets and deny rewards to those who don't. For strategy-implementers, "doing a good job" needs to

• • • • • • • • • • • • •
Job assignments should stress the results to be achieved rather than the duties and activities to be performed.

mean "achieving the agreed-on performance targets." Any other standard undermines implementation of the strategic plan and condones the diversion of time and energy into activities that don't matter much (if such activities are really important, they deserve a place in the strategic plan). The pressure to achieve the targeted strategic performance should be unrelenting. A "no excuses" standard has to prevail.[3]

But with pressure to perform must come ample rewards. Without a payoff, the system breaks down, and the strategy-implementer is left with the unworkable options of barking orders or pleading for compliance. Some of the most successful companies—Wal-Mart Stores, Nucor Steel, Lincoln Electric, Electronic Data Systems, Remington Products, and Mary Kay Cosmetics—owe much of their success to incentive and reward systems that induce people to do the very things needed to hit performance targets and execute strategy. Nucor's strategy was (and is) to be *the* low-cost producer of steel products. Because labor costs are a significant portion of total cost in the steel business, successful implementation of such a strategy required Nucor to achieve lower labor costs per ton of steel than competitors. To drive its labor costs per ton below rivals, Nucor management introduced production incentives that gave workers a bonus roughly equal to their regular wages provided their production teams met or exceeded weekly production targets; the regular wage scale was set at levels comparable to other manufacturing jobs in the local areas where Nucor had plants. Bonuses were paid every two weeks based on the prior weeks' actual production levels measured against the target. The results of Nucor's piece-rate incentive plan were impressive. Nucor's labor productivity (in output per worker) was more than double the average of the unionized work forces of the industry's major producers. Nucor enjoyed about a $100 per ton cost advantage over large, integrated steel producers like U.S. Steel and Bethlehem Steel (a substantial part of which came from its labor cost advantage), and Nucor workers were the highest paid workers in the steel industry. At Remington Products, only 65 percent of factory workers' paychecks is salary; the rest is based on piece-work incentives. The company inspects all products and counts rejected items against incentive pay for the responsible worker. Top-level managers earn more from bonuses than from their salaries. During the first four years of Remington's incentive program, productivity rose 17 percent.

These and other experiences demonstrate some important lessons about designing rewards and incentives:

1. *The performance payoff must be a major, not minor, piece of the total compensation package*—incentives that amount to 20 percent or more of total compensation are big attention-getters and are capable of driving individual effort.

2. *The incentive plan should extend to all managers and all workers*, not just be restricted to top management (why should all workers and managers work their tails off and hit performance targets so a few senior executives can get lucrative rewards?).

3. *The system must be administered with scrupulous care and fairness*—if performance standards are set unrealistically high or if individual

---

[3]Tom Peters and Nancy Austin, *A Passion for Excellence* (New York: Random House, 1985), p. xix.

performance evaluations are not accurate and well-documented, dissatisfaction and disgruntlement with the system will overcome any positive benefits.

4. *The incentives must be tightly linked to achieving only those performance targets spelled out in the strategic plan*—performance evaluations based on factors not related to the strategy signal that either the strategic plan is incomplete (because important performance targets were left out) or the real managerial action agenda is something other than what was stated in the strategic plan.

5. *The performance targets each individual is expected to achieve should involve outcomes that the individual can personally affect*—the role of incentives is to enhance individual commitment and channel behavior in beneficial directions. This role is not well-served when the performance measures an individual is judged by are outside his/her arena of influence.

Aside from these general guidelines it is hard to prescribe what kinds of incentives and rewards to develop except to say that the payoff must be directly attached to performance measures that indicate the strategy is working and implementation is on track. If the company's strategy is to be a low-cost producer, the incentive system must reward performance that lowers costs. If the company has a differentiation strategy predicated on superior quality and service, the incentive system must reward such outcomes as zero defects, infrequent need for product repair, low numbers of customer complaints, and speedy order processing and delivery. If a company's growth is predicated on a strategy of new-product introduction, incentives should be based on the percentages of revenues and profits coming from new products.

Why the Performance-Reward Link Is Important

The use of incentives and rewards is the single most powerful tool management has to win strong employee commitment to carrying out the strategic plan. Failure to use this tool wisely and powerfully weakens the entire implementation process. *Decisions on salary increases, incentive compensation, promotions, key assignments, and the ways and means of awarding praise and recognition are the strategy-implementer's foremost attention-getting, commitment-generating devices.* How a manager structures incentives and parcels out rewards signals what sort of behavior and performance management wants and who is doing a good job. Such matters seldom escape the scrutiny of every employee. The system of incentives and rewards thus ends up as the vehicle by which strategy is emotionally ratified in the form of real commitment. Incentives make it in employees' self-interest to do what is needed to achieve the performance targets spelled out in the strategic plan.

Using Performance Contracts

Creating a tight fit between strategy and the reward structure is generally best accomplished by agreeing on performance objectives, fixing responsibility and deadlines for achieving them, and treating their achievement as a *contract*. Next, the contracted-for strategic performance has to be the *real* basis for

• • • • • • • • • • •
Strategic Management Principle
The reward structure is management's most powerful strategy-implementing tool.

designing incentives, evaluating individual efforts, and handing out rewards. To prevent undermining the "managing-with-objectives" approach to strategy implementation, a manager must insist that actual performance be judged against the contracted-for target objectives. Any deviations must be fully explored to determine whether the causes are poor performance or circumstances beyond the individual's control. And all managers need to understand how their rewards have been calculated. In short, managers at all levels have to be held accountable for carrying out their part of the strategic plan, and they have to know their rewards are based on their strategic accomplishments (allowing for both the favorable and unfavorable impacts of uncontrollable, unforeseeable, and unknowable circumstances).

BUILDING A STRATEGY-SUPPORTIVE CORPORATE CULTURE

Basic Concept

Corporate culture refers to a company's inner values, beliefs, rituals, operating style, and political-social atmosphere.

Every organization is a unique culture. It has its own history, its own ways of approaching problems and conducting activities, its own mix of managerial personalities and styles, its own patterns of "how we do things around here," its own set of war stories and heroes, its own experiences of how changes have been instituted—in other words, its own atmosphere, folklore, and personality. A company's culture can be weak and fragmented in the sense that most people have no deeply felt sense of company purpose, view their jobs as simply a way to make money, and have divided loyalties—some to their department, some to their colleagues, some to the union, and some to their boss.[4] On the other hand, a company's culture can be strong and cohesive in the sense that most people understand the company's objectives and strategy, know what their individual roles are, and work conscientiously to do their part. A strong culture is a powerful lever for channeling behavior and helping employees do their jobs in a more strategy-supportive manner; this occurs in two ways:[5]

Strategic Management Principle

A strong culture and a tight strategy-culture fit are powerful levers for influencing people to do their jobs better.

- By knowing exactly what is expected of them, employees in strong-culture firms don't have to waste time figuring out what to do or how to do it—the culture provides a system of informal rules and peer pressures regarding how to behave most of the time. In a weak-culture company, the absence of strong company identity and a purposeful work climate results in substantial employee confusion and wasted effort.

- A strong culture turns a job into a way of life; it provides structure, standards, and a value system in which to operate; and it promotes strong company identification among employees. As a result, employees feel better about what they do, and more often than not, they work harder to help the company become more successful.

This says something important about the leadership task of strategy implementation: *to implement and execute a strategic plan, an organization's culture must be closely aligned with its strategy.* The optimal condition is a work environment

---

[4]Terrence E. Deal and Allen A. Kennedy, *Corporate Cultures* (Reading, Mass.: Addison-Wesley, 1982), p. 4.
[5]Ibid., pp. 15–16.

so in tune with strategy that strategy-critical activities are performed in superior fashion. As one observer noted:

> It has not been just strategy that led to big Japanese wins in the American auto market. It is a culture that enspirits workers to excel at fits and finishes, to produce moldings that match and doors that don't sag. It is a culture in which Toyota can use that most sophisticated of management tools, the suggestion box, and in two years increase the number of worker suggestions from under 10,000 to over 1 million with resultant savings of $250 million.[6]

What Is Corporate Culture?

The taproot of corporate culture is the organization's beliefs and philosophy about how its affairs ought to be conducted—the reasons why it does things the way it does. A company's philosophy and beliefs can be hard to pin down, even harder to characterize. In a sense they are intangible. They are manifest in the values and business principles that senior managers espouse, in the ethical standards they demand, in the policies they set, in the style with which things are done, in the traditions the organization maintains, in people's attitudes and feelings and in the stories they tell, in the peer pressures that exist, in the organization's politics, and in the "chemistry" that surrounds the work environment and defines the organization's culture. We are beginning to learn that an organization's culture is an important contributor (or obstacle) to successful strategy execution. A close culture-strategy match is crucial to managing a company's people resources with maximum effectiveness. A culture that energizes people all over the firm to do their jobs in a strategy-supportive manner adds significantly to the power and effectiveness of strategy execution. When a company's culture and strategy are out of sync, the culture has to be changed as rapidly as possible; a sizable and prolonged strategy-culture conflict weakens and may even defeat managerial efforts to make the strategy work.

Illustration Capsule 25 looks at some of the traits and characteristics of strong-culture companies to provide more insight into why the culture-strategy fit makes such a big difference. While the examples help demonstrate the contribution culture can make toward "keeping the herd moving roughly West" (as Professor Terry Deal puts it), the strategy-implementer's concern is with what actions to take to create a culture that facilitates strategy execution.

Creating the Fit between Strategy and Culture

It is the *strategy-maker's* responsibility to select a strategy compatible with the "sacred" or unchangeable parts of prevailing corporate culture. It is the *strategy-implementer's* task, once strategy is chosen, to bring corporate culture into close alignment with the strategy and keep it there.

Aligning culture with strategy presents a strong challenge. The first step is to diagnose which facets of the present culture are strategy-supportive and which are not. Then, there must be some innovative thinking about concrete actions management can take to modify the cultural environment and create a stronger fit with the strategy.

---

[6]Robert H. Waterman, Jr., "The Seven Elements of Strategic Fit," *Journal of Business Strategy* 2, no. 3 (Winter 1982), p. 70.

ILLUSTRATION CAPSULE 25 TRAITS AND CHARACTERISTICS OF STRONG-CULTURE COMPANIES

To better understand what corporate culture is and why it plays a role in successful strategy execution, consider the distinctive traits and themes of companies with strong cultures:

- At Frito-Lay, stories abound about potato chip route salesmen slogging through sleet, mud, hail, snow, and rain to uphold the 99.5 percent service level to customers in which the entire organization takes such great pride. At McDonald's the constant message from management is the overriding importance of quality, service, cleanliness, and value; employees are drilled over and over on the need for attention to detail and perfecting every fundamental of the business. At Delta Airlines, the culture is driven by "Delta's family feeling" that builds a team spirit and nurtures each employee's cooperative attitude toward others, cheerful outlook toward life, and pride in a job well done. At Johnson & Johnson, the credo is that customers come first, employees second, the community third, and shareholders fourth and last. At DuPont, there is a fixation on safety—a report of every accident must be on the chairman's desk within 24 hours (DuPont's safety record is 17 times better than the chemical industry average and 68 times better than the all-manufacturing average).

- Companies with strong cultures are unashamed collectors and tellers of stories, anecdotes, and legends in support of basic beliefs. L. L. Bean tells customer service stories. 3M tells innovation stories. P&G, Johnson & Johnson, Perdue Farms, and Maytag tell quality stories. From an organizational standpoint, such tales are very important because people in the organization take pride in identifying strongly with the stories, and they start to share in the traditions and values which the stories relate.

- The most typical values and beliefs that shape culture include (1) a belief in being the best (or at GE "better than the best"), (2) a belief in superior quality and service, (3) a belief in the importance of people as individuals and a faith in their ability to make a strong, positive contribution, (4) a belief in the importance of the details of execution, the nuts and bolts of doing the job well, (5) a belief that customers should reign supreme, (6) a belief in inspiring people, whatever their ability, (7) a belief in the importance of informality to enhance communication, and (8) a recognition that growth and profits are essential to a company's well-being. While the themes are common, however, every company implements them differently (to fit their particular situations), and every company's values are the articulated handiwork of one or two legendary figures in leadership positions. Accordingly, each company has its own distinct culture which, they believe, no one can copy successfully.

- In companies with strong cultures, managers and workers either "buy in" to the culture and accept its norms or they opt out and leave the company.

- The stronger the corporate culture and the more it is directed toward customers and markets, the less a company uses policy manuals, organization charts, and detailed rules and procedures to enforce discipline and norms. The reason is that the guiding values inherent in the culture convey in crystal-clear fashion what everybody is supposed to do in most situations. Often, poorly performing companies have strong cultures too. The difference is that their cultures are dysfunctional, being focused on internal politics or operating by the numbers as opposed to emphasizing customers and the people who make and sell the product.

Companies with strong cultures are clear on what they stand for, and they are serious about the tasks of establishing company values, winning employees over to these values, and causing employees to observe cultural norms religiously.

Source: Compiled from Thomas J. Peters and Robert H. Waterman, Jr., *In Search of Excellence* (New York: Harper & Row, 1982), pp. xxi, 75–77, and 280–85; and Thomas J. Peters and Nancy Austin, *A Passion for Excellence* (New York: Random House, 1985), pp. 282–83 and 334.

Symbolic Actions and Substantive Actions   Normally, managerial actions to tighten the culture-strategy fit are both symbolic and substantive. Symbolic actions are valuable for the signals they send about the kinds of behavior and performance strategy-implementers wish to encourage. The most common symbolic actions are events held to honor new kinds of heroes—people whose actions and performance serve as role models. Many universities give outstanding teacher awards each year to symbolize their commitment to and esteem for instructors who display exceptional classroom talents. Numerous businesses have employee-of-the-month awards. The military has a long-standing custom of awarding ribbons and medals for exemplary actions. Some football coaches award emblems to players to wear on their helmets as symbols of their exceptional performance.

Successful strategy-implementers are experts in the use of symbols to build and nurture the culture. They personally conduct ceremonial events, and they go out of their way to personally and publicly congratulate individuals who exhibit the desired traits. Individuals and groups that "get with the program" are singled out for special praise and visibly rewarded. Successful implementers use every ceremonial function and every conversation to implant values, send reinforcing signals, and praise good deeds.

In addition to being out front, personally leading the push for new attitudes and communicating the reasons for new approaches, the manager has to convince all those concerned that the effort is more than cosmetic. Talk and symbols have to be complemented by substance and real movement. The actions taken have to be credible, highly visible, and unmistakably indicative of management's commitment to a new culture and new ways of doing business. There are several ways to accomplish this. One is to engineer some quick successes in reorienting the way some things are done to highlight the value of the new order, thus making enthusiasm for the changes contagious. However, instant results are usually not as important as creating a solid, competent team psychologically committed to carrying out the strategy in a superior fashion. The strongest signs that management is committed to creating a new culture come from actions to replace traditional managers with "new breed" managers, changes in long-standing policies and operating practices, major reorganizational moves, big shifts in how raises and promotions are granted, and reallocations in the budget.

At the same time, chief strategy-implementers must be careful to *lead by example*. For instance, if the organization's strategy involves a drive to become the industry's low-cost producer, senior managers must be frugal in their own actions and decisions: spartan decorations in the executive suite, conservative expense accounts and entertainment allowances, a lean staff in the corporate office, and so on.

Implanting the needed culture-building values and behavior depends on a sincere, sustained commitment by the chief executive coupled with extraordinary persistence in reinforcing the culture through both word and deed. Neither charisma nor personal magnetism are essential. However, being highly visible around the organization is essential; culture-building cannot be done from an office. Moreover, creating and sustaining a strategy-supportive culture is a job for the whole management team. Senior officers have to keynote the values and shape the organization's philosophy. But for the effort to be successful, strategy-implementers must enlist the support of subordinate

Awards ceremonies, role models, and symbols are a fundamental part of a strategy-implementer's culture-shaping effort.

Strategic Management Principle
Senior executives must personally lead efforts to create a strategy-supportive culture.

T A B L E 10–1   Topics Generally Covered in Values Statements and Codes of Ethics

Topics Covered in Values Statements	Topics Covered in Codes of Ethics
• Importance of customers and customer service	• Honesty and observance of the law
• Commitment to quality	• Conflicts of interest
• Commitment to innovation	• Fairness in selling and marketing practices
• Respect for the individual employee and the duty the company has to employees	• Using inside information and securities trading
• Importance of honesty, integrity, and ethical standards	• Supplier relationships and purchasing practices
• Duty to stockholders	• Payments to obtain business/Foreign Corrupt Practices Act
• Duty to suppliers	• Acquiring and using information about others
• Corporate citizenship	• Political activities
• Importance of protecting the environment	• Use of company assets, resources, and property
	• Protection of proprietary information
	• Pricing, contracting, and billing

managers, getting them to instill values and establish culture norms at the lowest levels in the organization. Until a big majority of employees have joined the culture and share an emotional commitment to its basic values and beliefs, there's considerably more work to be done in both installing the culture and tightening the culture-strategy fit.

The task of making culture supportive of strategy is not a short-term exercise. It takes time for a new culture to emerge and prevail. The bigger the organization and the greater the cultural shift needed to produce a culture-strategy fit, the longer it takes. In large companies, changing the corporate culture in significant ways can take three to five years at minimum. In fact, it is usually tougher to reshape a deeply ingrained culture that is not strategy-supportive than it is to instill a strategy-supportive culture from scratch in a brand new organization.

Establishing Ethical Standards and Values

An ethical corporate culture has a positive impact on a company's long-term strategic success; an unethical culture can undermine it.

A strong corporate culture founded on ethical principles and sound values is a vital driving force behind continued strategic success. Many executives are convinced that a company must care about *how* it does business; otherwise it puts its reputation at risk and ultimately its performance. Corporate ethics and values programs are not window-dressing; they are undertaken to create an environment of strongly held values and convictions and to make ethical conduct a way of life. Strong values and high ethical standards nurture the corporate culture in a very positive way.

Companies establish values and ethical standards in a number of different ways.[7] Firms steeped in tradition with a rich folklore to draw on rely on word-of-mouth indoctrination and the power of tradition to instill values and enforce ethical conduct. But many companies today set forth their values and code of ethics in written documents. Table 10–1 shows the kinds of topics such statements cover. Written statements have the advantage of explicitly stating

---

[7]The Business Roundtable, *Corporate Ethics: A Prime Asset*, February 1988, pp. 4–10.

ILLUSTRATION CAPSULE | **26** | THE JOHNSON & JOHNSON CREDO

—We believe our first responsibility is to the doctors, nurses and patients, to mothers and all others who use our products and services.

—In meeting their needs everything we do must be of high quality.

—We must constantly strive to reduce our costs in order to maintain reasonable prices.

—Customers' orders must be serviced promptly and accurately.

—Our suppliers and distributors must have an opportunity to make a fair profit.

—We are responsible to our employees, the men and women who work with us throughout the world.

—Everyone must be considered as an individual.

—We must respect their dignity and recognize their merit.

—They must have a sense of security in their jobs.

—Compensation must be fair and adequate, and working conditions clean, orderly, and safe.

—Employees must feel free to make suggestions and complaints.

—There must be equal opportunity for employment, development and advancement for those qualified.

—We must provide competent management, and their actions must be just and ethical.

—We are responsible to the communities in which we live and work and to the world community as well.

—We must be good citizens—support good works and charities and bear our fair share of taxes.

—We must encourage civic improvements and better health and education.

—We must maintain in good order the property we are privileged to use, protecting the environment and natural resources.

—Our final responsibility is to our stockholders.

—Business must make a sound profit.

—We must experiment with new ideas.

—Research must be carried on, innovative programs developed and mistakes paid for.

—New equipment must be purchased, new facilities provided and new products launched.

—Reserves must be created to provide for adverse times.

—When we operate according to these principles, the stockholders should realize a fair return.

Source: 1982 Annual Report.

what the company intends and expects; and they serve as benchmarks for judging both company policies and actions and individual conduct. They put a stake in the ground and define the company's position. Value statements serve as a cornerstone for culture-building; a code of ethics serves as a cornerstone for creating a corporate conscience. Illustration Capsule 26 presents the Johnson & Johnson Credo, the most publicized and celebrated code of ethics and values among U.S. companies. J & J's CEO calls the credo "the unifying force for our corporation." Illustration Capsule 27 presents the pledge that Bristol-Myers Squibb makes to all of its stakeholders.

Once values and ethical standards have been formally set forth, they must be institutionalized and ingrained in the company's policies, practices, and actual conduct. Implementing the values and code of ethics entails several actions:

Values and ethical standards not only must be explicitly stated but they also must be deeply ingrained into the corporate culture.

- Incorporating the statement of values and the code of ethics into employee training and educational programs.
- Giving explicit attention to values and ethics in recruiting and hiring to screen out applicants who do not exhibit compatible character traits.
- Communicating the values and ethics codes to all employees and explaining compliance procedures.

ILLUSTRATION CAPSULE **27** THE BRISTOL-MYERS SQUIBB PLEDGE

To those who use our products . . .
We affirm Bristol-Myers Squibb's commitment to the highest standards of excellence, safety and reliability in everything we make. We pledge to offer products of the highest quality and to work diligently to keep improving them.

To our employees and those who may join us . . .
We pledge personal respect, fair compensation and equal treatment. We acknowledge our obligation to provide able and humane leadership throughout the organization, within a clean and safe working environment. To all who qualify for advancement, we will make every effort to provide opportunity.

To our suppliers and customers . . .
We pledge an open door, courteous, efficient and ethical dealing, and appreciation for their right to a fair profit.

To our shareholders . . .
We pledge a companywide dedication to contin-ued profitable growth, sustained by strong finances, a high level of research and development, and facilities second to none.

To the communities where we have plants and offices . . .
We pledge conscientious citizenship, a helping hand for worthwhile causes, and constructive action in support of civic and environmental progress.

To the countries where we do business . . .
We pledge ourselves to be a good citizen and to show full consideration for the rights of others while reserving the right to stand up for our own.

Above all, to the world we live in . . .
We pledge Bristol-Myers Squibb to policies and practices which fully embody the responsibility, integrity and decency required of free enterprise if it is to merit and maintain the confidence of our society.

Source: 1990 Annual Report.

- Management involvement and oversight, from the CEO to first-line supervisors.
- Strong endorsements by the CEO.
- Word-of-mouth indoctrination.

In the case of codes of ethics, special attention must be given to those sections of the company that are particularly sensitive and vulnerable—purchasing, sales, and political lobbying.[8] Employees who deal with external parties are in ethically sensitive positions and are often drawn into compromising situations. Procedures for enforcing ethical standards and handling potential violations have to be developed.

The implementation effort must permeate the company, extending into every organizational unit. The attitudes, character, and work history of prospective employees must be scrutinized. Every employee must receive adequate training. Line managers at all levels must give serious and continuous attention to the task of explaining how the values and ethical conduct apply in their areas. In addition, they must insist that company values and ethical standards become a way of life. In general, instilling values and insisting on ethical conduct must be viewed as a continuous culture-building, culture-nurturing exercise. Whether the effort succeeds or fails depends

---

[8]Ibid., p. 7.

largely on how well corporate values and ethical standards are visibly integrated into company policies, managerial practices, and actions at all levels.

Building a Spirit of High Performance into the Culture

An ability to instill strong individual commitment to strategic success and create constructive pressure to perform is one of the most valuable strategy-implementing skills. When an organization performs consistently at or near peak capability, the outcome is not only improved strategic success but also an organizational culture permeated with a spirit of high performance. This should not be confused with whether employees are "happy" or "satisfied," or "get along well together." An organization with a spirit of performance emphasizes achievement and excellence. Its culture is results-oriented, and its management pursues policies and practices that inspire people to do their best.

A results-oriented culture that inspires people to do their best is conducive to superior strategy execution.

Companies with a spirit of high performance typically are intensely people-oriented; and they reinforce this orientation at every conceivable occasion in every conceivable way to every employee. They treat employees with dignity and respect, train each employee thoroughly, encourage employees to use their own initiative and creativity in performing their work, set reasonable and clear performance expectations, utilize the full range of rewards and punishment to enforce high performance standards, hold managers at every level responsible for developing the people who report to them, and grant employees enough autonomy to stand out, excel, and contribute. To create a results-oriented organizational culture, a company must make champions out of the people who turn in winning performances:[9]

High-performance cultures make champions out of people who excel.

- At Boeing, IBM, General Electric, and 3M Corporation, top executives deliberately make "champions" out of individuals who believe so strongly in their ideas that they take it on themselves to hurdle the bureaucracy, maneuver their projects through the system, and turn them into improved services, new products, or even new businesses. In these companies, "product champions" are given high visibility, room to push their ideas, and strong executive support. Champions whose ideas prove out are usually handsomely rewarded; those whose ideas don't pan out still have secure jobs and are given chances to try again.

- The manager of a New York area sales office rented the Meadowlands Stadium (home field of the New York Giants) for an evening. After work, the salesmen were all assembled at the stadium and asked to run one at a time through the player's tunnel onto the field. As each one emerged, the electronic scoreboard flashed his name to those gathered in the stands—executives from corporate headquarters, employees from the office, family, and friends. Their role was to cheer loudly in honor of the individual's sales accomplishments. The company involved was IBM. The occasion for this action was to reaffirm IBM's commitment to satisfy an individual's need to be part of something great and to reiterate IBM's concern for championing individual accomplishment.

---

[9]Peters and Waterman, *In Search of Excellence*, pp. xviii, 240, and 269; and Peters and Austin, *A Passion for Excellence*, pp. 304–7.

- Some companies upgrade the importance and status of individual employees by referring to them as Cast members (Disney), Crew Members (McDonald's), or Associates (Wal-Mart and J. C. Penney). Companies like IBM, Tupperware, and McDonald's actively seek out reasons and opportunities to give pins, buttons, badges, and medals to good showings by average performers—the idea being to express appreciation and help give a boost to the "middle 60 percent" of the work force.

- McDonald's has a contest to determine the best hamburger cooker in its entire chain. It begins with a competition to determine the best hamburger cooker in each store. Store winners go on to compete in regional championships, and regional winners go on to the "All-American" contest. The winners get trophies and an All-American patch to wear on their shirts.

- Milliken & Co. holds Corporate Sharing Rallies once every three months; teams come from all over the company to swap success stories and ideas. A hundred or more teams make five-minute presentations over a two-day period. Each rally has a major theme—quality, cost reduction, and so on. No criticisms and negatives are allowed, and there is no such thing as a big idea or a small one. Quantitative measures of success are used to gauge improvement. All those present vote on the best presentation, and several ascending grades of awards are handed out. Everyone, however, receives a framed certificate for participating.

What makes a spirit of high performance come alive is a complex network of practices, words, symbols, styles, values, and policies pulling together to produce extraordinary results with ordinary people. The drivers of the system are a belief in the worth of the individual, strong company commitments to job security and promotion from within, managerial practices that encourage employees to exercise individual initiative and creativity, and pride in doing the "itty-bitty, teeny-tiny things" right. A company that treats its employees well benefits from increased teamwork, higher morale, and greater employee loyalty.

While emphasizing a spirit of high performance nearly always accentuates the positive, there are negative aspects too. Managers whose units consistently perform poorly have to be removed. Aside from the organizational benefits, weak performing managers should be reassigned for their own good—people who find themselves in a job they cannot handle are usually frustrated, anxiety ridden, harassed, and unhappy.[10] Moreover, subordinates have a right to be managed with competence, dedication, and achievement; unless their boss performs well, they themselves cannot perform well. Weak-performing workers and people who reject the cultural emphasis on dedication and high performance have to be weeded out. Recruitment practices need to aim at selecting highly motivated, ambitious applicants whose attitudes and work habits mesh well with a results-oriented culture.

Illustration Capsule 28 shows how one major company has linked its values and culture with its performance objectives.

---

[10]Peter Drucker, *Management: Tasks, Responsibilities, Practices* (New York: Harper & Row, 1974), p. 457.

Square D Company is a $1.7 billion producer of electrical equipment and electronic products. Below is the company's presentation of its vision, mission, principles, objectives, and actual performance against its long-term financial goals.

Vision

Dedicated to Growth
Committed to Quality

Mission

We are dedicated to growth for our customers, shareholders and employees through quality, innovation and profitable reinvestment.

Principles

As a company responsible to our customers, shareholders and employees, we will:

- Provide our customers with innovative, functional and reliable products and services at a cost and quality level consistent with their needs.
- Concentrate on enhancing long-term shareholder value.
- Actively pursue equal opportunity for all individuals and provide an environment which encourages open communications, personal growth and creativity.
- Expect integrity and professional conduct from our employees in every aspect of our business.
- Conduct our operations ethically and well within the framework of the law.

- Actively contribute to the communities and industries in which we participate.

Financial Objectives

We are committed to providing our shareholders with an attractive return on their investment, and our specific goals for doing so are to:

- Achieve a minimum after-tax return on capital of 14%.
- Leverage return on shareholders' equity through a capital structure which includes 25 to 35% debt.
- Achieve a minimum return on equity of 18%.
- Pay dividends equal to approximately 40% of earnings.
- Achieve average annual growth in earnings of at least 10%.

Operating Objectives

Market Leadership

- Have a leading market share position in our major markets.
- Be recognized as a leader in the application of technology to meet customer requirements.
- Be a "best-value" supplier throughout the world.
- Expand our international business to a level equaling 20 to 25% of company sales.
- Invest in research and development at a rate of 4% of sales as a means of achieving our market leadership objectives.

(continued)

Bonding the Fits: The Role of Shared Values

As emphasized earlier, "fits" with strategy need to be created internally as concerns structure, organizational skills and distinctive competence, budgets, support systems, rewards and incentives, policies and procedures, and culture. The better the "goodness of fit" among these administrative activities and characteristics, the more powerful strategy execution is likely to be.

McKinsey & Co., a leading consulting firm with wide-ranging experience in strategic analysis, has developed a framework for examining the fits in seven broad areas: (1) strategy, (2) structure, (3) shared values, attitudes, and philosophy, (4) approach to staffing the organization and its overall "people orientation," (5) administrative systems, practices, and procedures used to run the

* * * * * * * * * * * *
The values widely shared by managers and employees are the core of the corporate culture.

ILLUSTRATION CAPSULE   28   (concluded)

Employee Development
- Encourage initiative, innovation and productivity by appropriately recognizing and rewarding employee performance.
- Invest in employee training and development at a rate of 2% of payroll.
- Honestly and accurately appraise and evaluate the performance of each employee on at least an annual basis.
- Provide for the orderly succession of management.
- Maintain a positive affirmative action program and provide employees with the opportunity

for advancement commensurate with their abilities.

Social/Community Responsibility
- Maintain a safe, clean and healthy environment for our employees and the communities in which we operate.
- Invest 1.5% of net income in social, cultural, educational and charitable activities.
- Encourage appropriate employee involvement in community activities.

Performance against Financial Goals

Year Ended December 31	Long-Term Financial Goals	1988	1987	1986	1985	1984
After-tax return from continuing operations on average capital	14.0%	14.8%	13.5%	12.5%	13.9%	16.4%
Average total debt as a percentage of average capital	25.0–35.0	28.2	23.7	29.9	30.5	29.5
Return from continuing operations on average equity	18.0	18.1	15.7	15.5	17.7	20.6
Dividend payout percentage	40.0	45.7	48.6	53.9	60.9	49.7
Annual growth in earnings from continuing operations	10.0	8.1	11.2	(3.4)	(6.7)	65.0

Source: 1988 Annual Report.

organization on a day-to-day basis, including the reward structure, formal and informal policies, budgeting and programs, training, cost accounting, and financial controls, (6) the organization's skills, capabilities, and core competencies, and (7) style of top management (how they allocate their time and attention, symbolic actions, their leadership skills, the way the top management team comes across to the rest of the organization).[11] McKinsey has diagrammed these seven elements into what it calls the McKinsey 7-S framework

[11]For a more extended discussion, see Robert H. Waterman, Jr., Thomas J. Peters, and Julien R. Phillips, "Structure Is Not Organization," *Business Horizons* 23, no. 3 (June 1980), pp. 14–26; and Robert H. Waterman, Jr., "The Seven Elements of Strategic Fit," *Journal of Business Strategy* 2, no. 3 (Winter 1982), pp. 68–72.

FIGURE 10–1   **Bonding the Administrative Fits**   *(The McKinsey 7-S framework)*

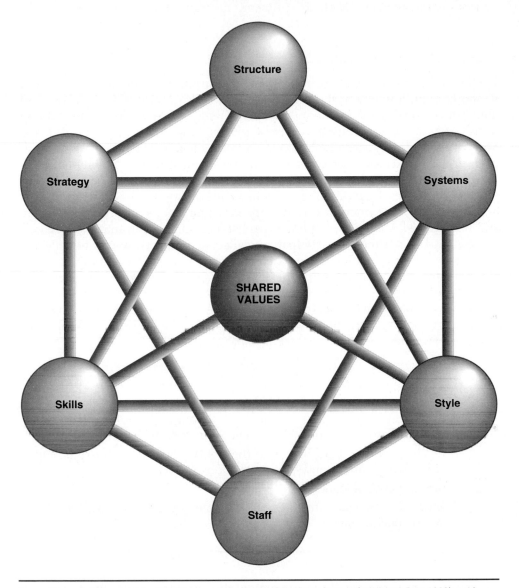

Source: Thomas J. Peters and Robert H. Waterman, Jr., *In Search of Excellence* (New York: Harper & Row, 1982), p. 10.

(the seven S's are strategy, structure, shared values, staff, systems, skills, and style—so labeled to promote recall) shown in Figure 10–1.

Shared values are the core of the 7-S framework because they are the heart-and-soul themes around which an organization rallies. They define its main beliefs and aspirations, its guiding concepts of "who we are, what we do, where we are headed, and what principles we will stand for in getting there." They bond the corporate culture and give it energy.

The McKinsey 7-S framework draws attention to some important organizational interconnections and why these interconnections are relevant in trying to effect change. In orchestrating a major shift in strategy and gathering momentum for implementation, the pace of change will be governed by all seven S's. The 7-S framework is a simple way to illustrate that the job of implementing strategy is one of creating fits and harmonizing the seven S's.

EXERTING STRATEGIC LEADERSHIP

The formula for good strategic management is simple enough: develop a sound strategic plan, implement it, execute it to the fullest, win! But it's easier said than done. Exerting take-charge leadership, being a "spark plug," ramrodding things through, and getting things done by coaching others are difficult tasks. Moreover, a strategy manager has many different leadership roles to play: chief entrepreneur and strategist, chief administrator and strategy-implementer, crisis solver, taskmaster, figurehead, spokesperson, resource allocator, negotiator, motivator, adviser, inspirationist, consensus builder, policymaker, mentor, and head cheerleader. Sometimes a strategy manager needs to be authoritarian and hard-nosed, sometimes a perceptive listener and compromising decision-maker. And sometimes a participative, collegial approach works best. Many occasions call for a highly visible role and extensive time commitments, while others entail a brief ceremonial performance with the details delegated to subordinates.

In general, the problem of strategic leadership is one of diagnosing the situation and choosing from any of several ways to handle it. Six leadership roles dominate the strategy-implementer's action agenda:

1. Staying on top of what is happening and how well things are going.
2. Promoting a culture in which the organization is "energized" to accomplish strategy and perform at a high level.
3. Keeping the organization responsive to changing conditions, alert for new opportunities, and bubbling with innovative ideas.
4. Building consensus, dealing with the politics of strategy formulation and implementation, and containing "power struggles."
5. Enforcing ethical standards.
6. Taking corrective actions to improve strategy execution and overall strategic performance.

Managing by Walking Around (MBWA)

To stay on top of how well the implementation process is going, a manager needs to develop a broad network of contacts and information sources, both formal and informal. The regular channels include talking with key subordinates, reading written reports and the latest operating results, getting feedback from customers, watching the competitive reactions of rivals, tapping into the grapevine, listening to rank-and-file employees, and observing the situation firsthand. However, some information is more reliable than the rest. Written reports can cover up or minimize bad news—or not report it at all. Sometimes subordinates delay reporting failures and problems, hoping that extra time will help them turn things around. As information flows up an organization, it tends to get "censored" and "sterilized" to the point that it may block or obscure strategy-critical information. Strategy managers must guard against surprises by making sure that they have accurate information and a "feel" for the situation. One way to do so is to visit "the field" regularly and talk with many different people at many different levels. The technique of *managing by walking around* (MBWA) is practiced in a variety of styles:[12]

- At Hewlett-Packard, there are weekly beer busts in each division, attended by both executives and employees, to create a regular opportunity to keep in touch. Tidbits of information flow freely between down-the-line employees and executives—facilitated in part because "the H-P Way" is for people at all ranks to be addressed by their first names. Bill Hewlett, one of HP's cofounders, had a companywide reputation for getting out of his office and "wandering around" the plant greeting people, listening to what was on their minds, and asking questions. He found this so valuable that he made MBWA a standard practice for all HP managers. Furthermore, ad hoc meetings of people from different departments spontaneously arise; they gather in rooms with blackboards and work out solutions informally.

- McDonald's founder Ray Kroc regularly visited store units and did his own personal inspection on Q.S.C.& V. (Quality, Service, Cleanliness, and Value)—the themes he preached regularly. There are stories of him pulling into a unit's parking lot, seeing litter lying on the pavement, getting out of his limousine to pick it up himself, and then lecturing the store staff at length on the subject of cleanliness.

- The CEO of a small manufacturing company spends much of his time riding around the factory in a golf cart, waving and joking with workers, listening to them, and calling all 2,000 employees by their first names. In addition, he spends a lot of time with union officials, inviting them to meetings and keeping them well informed about what is going on.

- Sam Walton, Wal-Mart's founder, insisted "The key is to get out into the store and listen to what the associates have to say. Our best ideas come from clerks and stockboys." Walton himself had a longstanding practice of spending two to three days every week visiting Wal-Mart's stores and talking with store managers and employees. On one occasion he flew the company plane to a Texas town, got out, and instructed the copilot to meet him 100 miles down the road. Then he flagged a Wal-Mart truck and rode the rest of the way to "chat with the driver—it seemed like so much fun." Walton made a practice of greeting store managers and their spouses by name at annual meetings and was known to go to the company's distribution centers at 2:00 A.M. (carrying boxes of doughnuts to share with all those on duty) to have a chance to find out what was on their minds.

- When Ed Carlson became CEO at United Airlines, he traveled some 200,000 miles a year talking with United's employees. He observed, "I wanted these people to identify me and to feel sufficiently comfortable to make suggestions or even argue with me if that's what they felt like doing. . . . Whenever I picked up some information, I would call the

MBWA is one of the techniques effective leaders use.

---

[12]Ibid., pp. xx, 15, 120–23, 191, 242–43, 246–47, 287–90. For an extensive report on the benefits of MBWA, see Thomas J. Peters and Nancy Austin, *A Passion for Excellence*, (New York: Random House, 1985), chaps. 2, 3, and 19.

senior officer of the division and say that I had just gotten back from visiting Oakland, Reno, and Las Vegas, and here is what I found."

- At Marriott Corp., Bill Marriott not only personally inspects all Marriott hotels at least once a year, but he also invites all Marriott guests to send him their evaluations of Marriott's facilities and services. He personally reads every customer complaint and has been known to telephone hotel managers about them.

Managers at many companies attach great importance to informal communication. They report that it is essential to have a "feel" for situations and to gain quick, easy access to information. When executives stay in their offices, they tend to become isolated and often surround themselves with people who are not likely to offer criticism or different perspectives; the information they get is secondhand, screened and filtered, and sometimes dated.

Fostering a Strategy- Supportive Climate and Culture

Strategy-implementers have to be "out front" in promoting a strategy-supportive organizational climate. When major strategic changes are being implemented, a manager's time is best spent personally leading the changes. When only strategic fine-tuning is being implemented, it takes less time and effort to bring values and culture into alignment with strategy, but there is still a lead role for the manager to play in pushing ahead and prodding for continuous improvements. Successful strategy leaders know it is their responsibility to convince people that the chosen strategy is right and that implementing it to the best of the organization's ability is "top priority."

Both words and deeds play a part. Words inspire people, infuse spirit and drive, define strategy-supportive cultural norms and values, articulate the reasons for strategic and organizational change, legitimize new viewpoints and new priorities, urge and reinforce commitment, and arouse confidence in the new strategy. Deeds add credibility to the words, create strategy-supportive symbols, set examples, give meaning and content to the language, and teach the organization what sort of behavior is needed and expected.

Highly visible symbols and imagery are needed to complement substantive actions. One General Motors manager explained the striking difference in performance between two large plants:[13]

> At the poorly performing plant, the plant manager probably ventured out on the floor once a week, always in a suit. His comments were distant and perfunctory. At South Gate, the better plant, the plant manager was on the floor all the time. He wore a baseball cap and a UAW jacket. By the way, whose plant do you think was spotless? Whose looked like a junkyard?

As a rule, the greater the degree of strategic change being implemented and/or the greater the shift in cultural norms needed to accommodate a new strategy, the more visible the strategy-implementer's words and deeds need to be. Lessons from well-managed companies show that what the strategy-leader says and does has a significant bearing on down-the-line strategy implementation and execution.[14] According to one view, "It is not so much the articula-

[13]As quoted in Peters and Waterman, *In Search of Excellence*, p. 262.
[14]Peters and Waterman, *In Search of Excellence*, chap. 9.

tion . . . about what an [organization] should be doing that creates new practice. It's the imagery that creates the understanding, the compelling moral necessity that the new way is right."[15] Moreover, the actions and images, both substantive and symbolic, have to be repeated regularly, not just at ceremonies and special occasions. This is where a high profile and "managing by walking around" comes into play. As a Hewlett-Packard official expresses it in the company publication *The HP Way*:

> Once a division or department has developed a plan of its own—a set of working objectives—it's important for managers and supervisors to keep it in operating condition. This is where observation, measurement, feedback, and guidance come in. It's our "management by wandering around." That's how you find out whether you're on track and heading at the right speed and in the right direction. If you don't constantly monitor how people are operating, not only will they tend to wander off track but also they will begin to believe you weren't serious about the plan in the first place. It has the extra benefit of getting you off your chair and moving around your area. By wandering around, I literally mean moving around and talking to people. It's all done on a very informal and spontaneous basis, but it's important in the course of time to cover the whole territory. You start out by being accessible and approachable, but the main thing is to realize you're there to listen. The second reason for MBWA is that it is vital to keep people informed about what's going on in the company, especially those things that are important to them. The third reason for doing this is because it is just plain fun.

Such contacts give the manager a feel for how things are progressing, and they provide opportunities to encourage employees, lift spirits, shift attention from the old to the new priorities, create some excitement, and project an atmosphere of informality and fun—all of which drive implementation in a positive fashion and intensify the organizational energy behind strategy execution. John Welch of General Electric sums up the hands-on role and motivational approach well: "I'm here every day, or out into a factory, smelling it, feeling it, touching it, challenging the people."[16]

Keeping the Internal Organization Responsive and Innovative

While formulating and implementing strategy is a manager's responsibility, the task of generating fresh ideas, identifying new opportunities, and responding to changing conditions cannot be accomplished by a single person. It is an organizationwide task, particularly in large corporations. Strategic leadership must result in a dependable supply of fresh ideas from the rank and file—managers and employees alike—and promote an entrepreneurial, opportunistic spirit that permits continuous adaptation to changing conditions. A flexible, responsive, innovative internal environment is critical in fast-moving high-technology industries, in businesses where products have short life cycles and growth depends on new-product innovation, in corporations with widely diversified business portfolios (where opportunities are varied and scattered), in industries where successful product differentiation is key, and in businesses where the strategy of being the low-cost producer hinges on productivity

One of the toughest strategic leadership tasks is keeping the organization innovative and responsive to changing conditions.

---

[15]Warren Bennis, *The Unconscious Conspiracy: Why Leaders Can't Lead* (New York: AMACOM, 1987), p. 93.
[16]As quoted in Ann M. Morrison, "Trying to Bring GE to Life," *Fortune*, January 25, 1982, p. 52.

improvement and cost reduction. Managers cannot mandate such an environment by simply exhorting people to be "creative."

One useful leadership approach is to take special pains to foster, nourish, and support people who are willing to champion new ideas, better services, new products and product applications, and who are eager for a chance to turn their ideas into new divisions, new businesses, and even new industries. When Texas Instruments reviewed some 50 or so successful and unsuccessful new-product introductions, one factor marked every failure: "Without exception we found we hadn't had a volunteer champion. There was someone we had cajoled into taking on the task. When we take a look at a product and decide whether to push it or not these days, we've got a new set of criteria. Number one is the presence of a zealous, volunteer champion. After that comes market potential and project economics in a distant second and third."[17] The rule seems to be an idea for something new or something different must either find a champion or die. And the champion needs to be someone who is persistent, competitive, tenacious, committed, and fanatic about the idea and seeing it through to success.

Empowering Champions   In order to promote an organizational climate where champions can blossom and thrive, strategy managers need to do several things. First, individuals and groups have to be encouraged to bring their ideas forward, be creative, and exercise initiative. Second, the champion's maverick style has to be tolerated and given room to operate. People's imaginations need to be encouraged to "fly in all directions." Freedom to experiment and informal brainstorming sessions need to become ingrained. Above all, people with creative ideas must not be looked on as disruptive or troublesome. Third, managers have to induce and promote lots of attempts and be willing to tolerate mistakes and failures. Most ideas don't pan out, but people learn from a good attempt even when it fails. Fourth, strategy managers should use all kinds of ad hoc organizational forms to support ideas and experimentation—venture teams, task forces, internal competition among different groups working on the same project (IBM calls the showdown between the competing approaches a "performance shootout"), informal "bootlegged" projects composed of volunteers, and so on. Fifth, strategy managers have to ensure that rewards for a successful champion are large and visible and that people who champion an unsuccessful idea are encouraged to try again rather than punished or shunted aside. In effect, the leadership task here is to devise internal support systems for entrepreneurial innovation.

Dealing with Company Politics

A manager can't formulate and implement strategy effectively without being perceptive about company politics and adept at political maneuvering.[18]

---

[17]As quoted in Peters and Waterman, *In Search of Excellence*, pp. 203–4.

[18]For further discussion of this point see Abraham Zaleznik, " Power and Politics in Organizational Life," *Harvard Business Review,* 48, no. 3 (May–June 1970), pp. 47–60; R. M. Cyert, H. A. Simon, and D. B. Trow, "Observation of a Business Decision," *Journal of Business*, October 1956, pp. 237–48; and James Brian Quinn, *Strategies for Change: Logical Incrementalism* (Homewood, Ill.: Richard D. Irwin, 1980).

Politics virtually always comes into play in formulating the strategic plan. Inevitably, key individuals and groups form coalitions, and each group presses the benefits and potential of its own ideas and vested interests. Politics can influence which objectives take precedence and which businesses in the portfolio have priority in resource allocation. Internal politics is a factor in building a consensus for one strategic option over another.

As a rule, politics has even more influence in strategy implementation. Typically, internal political considerations affect organization structure (whose areas of responsibility need to be reorganized, who reports to who, who has how much authority over subunits), staffing decisions (what individuals should fill key positions and head strategy-critical activities), and budget allocations (which organizational units will get the biggest increases). As a case in point, Quinn cites a situation where three strong managers who fought each other constantly formed a potent coalition to resist a reorganization scheme that would have coordinated the very things that caused their friction.[19]

In short, political considerations and the forming of individual and group alliances are integral parts of building organizationwide support for the strategic plan and gaining consensus on how to implement it. Political skills are a definite, maybe even necessary, asset for managers in orchestrating the whole strategic process.

A strategy manager must understand how an organization's power structure works, who wields influence in the executive ranks, which groups and individuals are "activists" and which are "defenders of the status quo," who can be helpful in a showdown on key decisions, and which direction the political winds are blowing on a given issue. When major decisions have to be made, strategy managers need to be especially sensitive to the politics of managing coalitions and reaching consensus. As the chairman of a major British corporation expressed it:

> I've never taken a major decision without consulting my colleagues. It would be unimaginable to me, unimaginable. First, they help me make a better decision in most cases. Second, if they know about it and agree with it, they'll back it. Otherwise, they might challenge it, not openly, but subconsciously.[20]

The politics of strategy centers chiefly around stimulating options, nurturing support for strong proposals and killing weak ones, guiding the formation of coalitions on particular issues, and achieving consensus and commitment. A recent study of strategy management in nine large corporations showed that successful executives used the following political tactics:[21]

- Letting weakly supported ideas and proposals die through inaction.
- Establishing additional hurdles or tests for strongly supported ideas that the manager views as unacceptable but that are best not opposed openly.
- Keeping a low political profile on unacceptable proposals by getting subordinate managers to say no.

Company politics presents strategy leaders with the challenge of building consensus for the strategy and how to implement it.

There are several political tactics managers should be adept in using.

---

[19]Quinn, *Strategies for Change*, p. 68.
[20]This statement was made by Sir Alastair Pilkington, Chairman, Pilkington Brothers, Ltd.; the quote appears in Quinn, *Strategies for Change*, p. 65.
[21]Quinn, *Strategies for Change*, pp. 128–45.

- Letting most negative decisions come from a group consensus that the manager merely confirms, thereby reserving personal veto for big issues and crucial moments.
- Leading the strategy but not dictating it—giving few orders, announcing few decisions, depending heavily on informal questioning and seeking to probe and clarify until a consensus emerges.
- Staying alert to the symbolic impact of one's actions and statements lest a false signal stimulate proposals and movements in unwanted directions.
- Ensuring that all major power bases within the organization have representation in or access to top management.
- Injecting new faces and new views into considerations of major changes to preclude those involved from coming to see the world the same way and then acting as systematic screens against other views.
- Minimizing political exposure on issues that are highly controversial and in circumstances where opposition from major power centers can trigger a "shootout."

The politics of strategy implementation is especially critical when attempting to introduce a new strategy against the support enjoyed by the old strategy. Except for crisis situations where the old strategy is plainly revealed as out-of-date, it is usually bad politics to push the new strategy through attacks on the old one.[22] Bad-mouthing old strategy can easily be interpreted as an attack on those who formulated it and those who supported it. The former strategy and the judgments behind it may have been well-suited to the organization's earlier circumstances, and the people who made these judgments may still be influential.

In addition, the new strategy and/or the plans for implementing it may not have been others' first choices, and lingering doubts may remain. Good arguments may exist for pursuing other actions. Consequently, in trying to surmount resistance, nothing is gained by "knocking" the arguments for alternative approaches. Such attacks often produce alienation instead of cooperation.

In short, to bring the full force of an organization behind a strategic plan, the strategy manager must assess and deal with the most important centers of potential support and opposition to new strategic thrusts.[23] He or she needs to secure the support of key people, co-opt or neutralize serious opposition and resistance, learn where the zones of indifference are, and build as much consensus as possible.

High ethical standards cannot be enforced without the open and unequivocal commitment of the chief executive.

Enforcing Ethical Behavior

For an organization to display consistently high ethical standards, the CEO and those around the CEO must be openly and unequivocally committed to ethical conduct.[24] In companies that strive hard to make high ethical standards a reality,

---

[22]Ibid., pp. 118–19.

[23]Ibid., p. 205.

[24]The Business Roundtable, *Corporate Ethics*, pp. 4–10.

top management communicates its commitment in a code of ethics, in speeches and company publications, in policies concerning the consequences of unethical behavior, in the deeds of senior executives, and in the actions taken to ensure compliance. Senior management iterates and reiterates to employees that it is not only their *duty* to observe ethical codes but also to report ethical violations. While such companies have provisions for disciplining violators, the main purpose of enforcement is to encourage compliance rather than administer punishment. Although the CEO leads the enforcement process, all managers are expected to contribute by stressing ethical conduct with their subordinates and by monitoring compliance. "Gray areas" must be identified and openly discussed with employees, and mechanisms provided for guidance and resolution. Managers can't assume activities are being conducted ethically or that employees understand they are expected to act with integrity.

There are several things managers can do to exercise ethics leadership.[25] First and foremost, they must set an excellent ethical example in their own behavior and establish a tradition of integrity. Company decisions have to be seen as ethical—"actions speak louder than words." Second, managers and employees have to be educated about what is ethical and what is not; ethics training programs may have to be established and "gray areas" identified and discussed. Everyone must be encouraged to raise ethical issues and discuss them. Third, top management should explicitly refer to the company's ethical code and take a strong stand on ethical issues. Fourth, top management must be prepared to act as the final arbiter on hard calls; this means removing people from a key position or terminating them when they are guilty of a violation. It also means reprimanding those who have been lax in monitoring and enforcing ethical compliance. Failure to act swiftly and decisively in pursuing ethical misconduct is interpreted as a lack of real commitment.

A well-developed program to ensure compliance with ethical standards typically includes: (1) an oversight committee of the board of directors, usually made up of outside directors; (2) a committee of senior managers to direct ongoing training, implementation, and compliance; (3) an annual audit of each manager's efforts and formal reports on managers' actions to remedy deficient conduct, and (4) periodically requiring people to sign documents certifying compliance with ethical standards.[26]

Leading the Process of Making Corrective Adjustments

No strategic plan and no scheme for strategy implementation can foresee all the events and problems that will arise. Making adjustments and "mid-course" corrections is a normal and necessary part of strategic management.

Corrective adjustments in the company's approach to strategy implementation should be made on an "as-needed" basis.

When responding to new conditions involving either the strategy or its implementation, management must first determine if immediate action needs to be taken. In a crisis, the typical approach is to push key subordinates to gather information and formulate recommendations, personally preside over extended discussions of the proposed responses, and try to build a quick consensus among members of the executive "inner circle." If no consensus

---

[25]Ibid.
[26]Ibid.

emerges or if several key subordinates remain divided, the burden falls on the strategy manager to choose the response and urge its support.

When time permits a full-fledged evaluation, strategy managers seem to prefer a process of incrementally solidifying commitment to a response.[27] The approach involves:

1. Staying flexible and keeping a number of options open.
2. Asking a lot of questions.
3. Gaining in-depth information from specialists.
4. Encouraging subordinates to participate in developing alternatives and proposing solutions.
5. Getting the reactions of many different people to proposed solutions to test their potential and political acceptability.
6. Seeking to build commitment to a response by gradually moving toward a consensus solution.

The governing principle seems to be to make a final decision as late as possible to: (1) bring as much information to bear as needed, (2) clarify the situation enough to know what to do, and (3) allow the various political constituencies and power bases to move toward a consensus solution. Executives are often wary of committing themselves to a major change too soon because it discourages others from asking questions that need to be raised.

• • • • • • • • • • • •

Strategy leaders should be proactive as well as reactive in reshaping strategy and how it is implemented.

Corrective adjustments to strategy need not be just reactive, however. Proactive adjustments can improve either the strategy or its implementation. The distinctive feature of a proactive adjustment is that it arises from management initiatives rather than forced reactions. Successful strategy managers employ a variety of proactive tactics.[28]

1. Commissioning studies to explore and amplify areas where they have a "gut feeling" or sense a need exists.
2. Shopping ideas among trusted colleagues and putting forth trial concepts.
3. Teaming people with different skills, interests, and experiences and letting them push and tug on interesting ideas to expand the variety of approaches considered.
4. Contacting a variety of people inside and outside the organization to sample viewpoints, probe, and listen, thereby trying to get early warning signals of impending problems/issues and deliberating short-circuiting all the careful screens of information flowing up from below.
5. Stimulating proposals for improvement from lower levels, encouraging the development of competing ideas and approaches, and letting the momentum for change come from below, with final choices postponed until it is apparent which option best matches the organization's situation.
6. Seeking options and solutions that go beyond extrapolations from the status quo.

---

[27]Quinn, *Strategies for Change*, pp. 20–22.
[28]Ibid., chap. 4.

7. Accepting and committing to partial steps forward as a way of building comfort levels before going ahead.
8. Managing the politics of change to promote managerial consensus and solidify management's commitment to whatever course of action is chosen.

The process leaders use to decide on adjusting actions is essentially the same for proactive as for reactive changes; they sense needs, gather information, amplify understanding and awareness, put forth trial concepts, develop options, explore the pros and cons, test proposals, generate partial solutions, empower champions, build a managerial consensus, and formally adopt an agreed-on course of action.[29] The ultimate managerial prescription may have been given by Rene McPherson, former CEO at Dana Corporation. In speaking to a class of students at Stanford, he said, " You just keep pushing. You just keep pushing. I made every mistake that could be made. But I just kept pushing."[30]

This points to a key feature of strategic management: the job of formulating and implementing strategy is not one of steering a clear-cut, linear course (i.e., carrying out an original strategy intact according to some preconceived and highly detailed implementation plan). Rather, it is one of creatively (1) adapting and reshaping strategy to unfolding events and (2) applying whatever managerial techniques are needed to align internal activities and attitudes with strategy. The process is iterative, with much looping and recycling to fine-tune and adjust in a continuously evolving process where the conceptually separate acts of strategy formulation and strategy implementation blur and join together.

KEY POINTS

The managerial tasks of designing rewards and incentives, creating a strategy-supportive corporate culture, and exercising strategic leadership are key facets of successful strategy implementation. The use of incentives is management's single most powerful tool in gaining employee buy-in and energetic commitment to carrying out the strategy. For incentives to work well (1) the monetary payoff should be a major percentage of the compensation package, (2) the incentive plan should extend to all managers and workers, (3) the system should be administered with care and fairness, (4) the incentives should be linked to performance targets spelled out in the strategic plan, and (5) each individual's performance targets should involve outcomes the person is able to affect personally.

Building a strategy-supportive corporate culture is important to successful implementation because it produces a work climate and organizational *esprit de corps* that thrives on meeting performance targets and being part of a winning effort. An organization's culture emerges from why and how it does things the way it does, the values and beliefs that senior managers espouse, the ethical standards expected, the tone and philosophy underlying key policies, and the traditions the organization maintains. Culture, thus, concerns the "atmosphere" and "feeling" a company has and the style in which it gets things done. Companies with strong cultures are clear on what they stand for, and they take the process

---

[29]Ibid., p. 146.
[30]As quoted in Peters and Waterman, *In Search of Excellence*, p. 319.

of getting people to "buy in" to the cultural norms very seriously. The stronger the fit between culture and strategy, the less managers have to depend on policies, rules, procedures, and supervision to enforce what people should and should not do; rather, cultural norms are so well observed that they automatically guide behavior.

Successful strategy-implementers also exercise an important leadership role. They stay on top of how well things are going by spending considerable time outside their offices, wandering around the organization, listening, coaching, cheer-leading, picking up important information, and keeping their fingers on the organization's pulse. They take pains to reinforce the corporate culture through the things they say and do. They encourage people to be creative and innovative in order to keep the organization responsive to changing conditions, alert to new opportunities, and anxious to pursue fresh initiatives. They support "champions" who are willing to stick their necks out and try something new. They work hard at building consensus on how to proceed, on what to change and what not to change. They enforce high ethical standards. And they push corrective action to improve strategy execution and overall strategic performance.

The action agenda for strategy implementation is expansive. It involves virtually every aspect of administrative and managerial work. However, each strategy implementation situation is unique to the organization and to its own circumstances. The strategy-implementer's action agenda, therefore, always depends on the current situation. Diagnosing the situation and devising actions to put strategy into place and achieve the desired results are major managerial challenges.

SUGGESTED READINGS

Bettinger, Cass. "Use Corporate Culture to Trigger High Performance." *Journal of Business Strategy* 10, no. 2 (March–April 1989), pp. 38–42.

Bower, Joseph L., and Martha W. Weinberg. "Statecraft, Strategy, and Corporate Leadership." *California Management Review* 30, no. 2 (Winter 1988), pp. 39–56.

Deal, Terence E., and Allen A. Kennedy. *Corporate Cultures*. Reading, Mass.: Addison-Wesley, 1982, especially chaps. 1 and 2.

Eccles, Robert G. "The Performance Measurement Manifesto." *Harvard Business Review* 69 (January–February 1991), pp. 131–37.

Freeman, R. Edward, and Daniel R. Gilbert, Jr. *Corporate Strategy and the Search for Ethics* (Englewood Cliffs, N.J.: Prentice Hall, 1988).

Gabarro, J. J. "When a New Manager Takes Charge." *Harvard Business Review* 64, no. 3 (May–June 1985), pp. 110–23.

Green, Sebastian. "Strategy, Organizational Culture, and Symbolism." *Long Range Planning* 21, no. 4 (August 1988), pp. 121–29.

Herzberg, Frederick. "One More Time: How Do You Motivate Employees?" *Harvard Business Review* 65, no. 4 (September–October 1987), pp. 109–20.

Kirkpatrick, Shelley A., and Edwin A. Locke. "Leadership: Do Traits Matter?" *Academy of Management Executive* 5, no. 2 (May 1991), pp. 48–60.

Kotter, John P. "What Leaders Really Do." *Harvard Business Review* 68 (May–June 1990), pp. 103–11.

O'Toole, James. "Employee Practices at the Best-Managed Companies." *California Management Review* 28, no. 1 (Fall 1985), pp. 35–66.

Pascale, Richard. "The Paradox of 'Corporate Culture': Reconciling Ourselves to Socialization." *California Management Review* 27, no. 2 (Winter 1985), pp. 26–41.

Peters, Thomas J., and Robert H. Waterman, Jr. *In Search of Excellence*. New York: Harper & Row, 1982, chaps. 4, 5, and 9.

Peters, Thomas J., and Nancy Austin. *A Passion for Excellence*. New York: Random House, 1985, especially chaps. 11, 12, 15–19.

Quinn, James Brian. *Strategies for Change: Logical Incrementalism*. Homewood, Ill.: Richard D. Irwin, 1980, chap. 4.

————. "Managing Innovation: Controlled Chaos." *Harvard Business Review* 64, no. 3 (May–June 1985), pp. 73–84.

Reimann, Bernard C., and Yoash Wiener. "Corporate Culture: Avoiding the Elitest Trap." *Business Horizons* 31, no. 2 (March–April 1988), pp. 36–44.

Scholz, Christian. "Corporate Culture and Strategy—The Problem of Strategic Fit." *Long Range Planning* 20 (August 1987), pp. 78–87.

Vancil, Richard F. *Implementing Strategy: The Role of Top Management*. Boston: Division of Research, Harvard Business School, 1985.

CASES IN STRATEGIC MANAGEMENT

A Guide to Case Analysis

I keep six honest serving men
(They taught me all I knew);
Their names are What and Why and When;
And How and Where and Who.
~Rudyard Kipling

In most courses in strategic management, students practice at being strategy managers via case analysis. A case sets forth, in a factual manner, the events and organizational circumstances surrounding a particular managerial situation. It puts readers at the scene of the action and familiarizes them with all the relevant circumstances. A case on strategic management can concern a whole industry, a single organization, or some part of an organization; the organization involved can be either profit seeking or not-for-profit. The essence of the student's role in case analysis is to *diagnose* and *size up* the situation described in the case and then to *recommend* appropriate action steps.

WHY USE CASES TO PRACTICE STRATEGIC MANAGEMENT

A student of business with tact
Absorbed many answers he lacked.
But acquiring a job,
He said with a sob,
"How does one fit answer to fact?"

The foregoing limerick was used some years ago by Professor Charles Gragg to characterize the plight of business students who had no exposure to cases.[1] Gragg observed that the mere act of listening to lectures and sound advice about managing does little for anyone's management skills and that the accumulated managerial wisdom cannot effectively be passed on by lectures and

---

[1]Charles I. Gragg, "Because Wisdom Can't Be Told," in *The Case Method at the Harvard Business School*, ed. M. P. McNair (New York: McGraw-Hill, 1954), p. 11.

assigned readings alone. Gragg suggested that if anything had been learned about the practice of management, it is that a storehouse of ready-made text-book answers does not exist. Each managerial situation has unique aspects, requiring its own diagnosis, judgment, and tailor-made actions. Cases provide would-be managers with a valuable way to practice wrestling with the actual problems of actual managers in actual companies.

The case approach to strategic analysis is, first and foremost, an exercise in learning by doing. Because cases provide you with detailed information about conditions and problems of different industries and companies, your task of analyzing company after company and situation after situation has the twin benefit of boosting your analytical skills and exposing you to the ways companies and managers actually do things. Most college students have limited managerial backgrounds and only fragmented knowledge about different companies and real-life strategic situations. Cases help substitute for actual on-the-job experience by (1) giving you broader exposure to a variety of industries, organizations, and strategic problems; (2) forcing you to assume a managerial role (as opposed to that of just an onlooker); (3) providing a test of how to apply the tools and techniques of strategic management; and (4) asking you to come up with pragmatic managerial action plans to deal with the issues at hand.

OBJECTIVES OF CASE ANALYSIS

Using cases to learn about the practice of strategic management is a powerful way for you to accomplish five things:[2]

1. Increase your understanding of what managers should and should not do in guiding a business to success.
2. Build your skills in conducting strategic analysis in a variety of industries, competitive situations, and company circumstances.
3. Get valuable practice in diagnosing strategic issues, evaluating strategic alternatives, and formulating workable plans of action.
4. Enhance your sense of business judgment, as opposed to uncritically accepting the authoritative crutch of the professor or "back-of-the-book" answers.
5. Gain in-depth exposure to different industries and companies, thereby gaining something close to actual business experience.

If you understand that these are the objectives of case analysis, you are less likely to be consumed with curiosity about "the answer to the case." Students who have grown comfortable with and accustomed to textbook statements of fact and definitive lecture notes are often frustrated when discussions about a case do not produce concrete answers. Usually, case discussions produce good arguments for more than one course of action. Differences of opinion nearly always exist. Thus, should a class discussion conclude without a strong, unambiguous consensus on what do to, don't grumble too much when you are *not* told what the answer is or what the company actually did. Just remember that

---

[2]Ibid., pp. 12–14; and D. R. Schoen and Philip A. Sprague, "What Is the Case Method?" in *The Case Method at the Harvard Business School*, ed. M. P. McNair, pp. 78–79.

in the business world answers don't come in conclusive black- and-white terms. There are nearly always several feasible courses of action and approaches, each of which may work out satisfactorily. Moreover, in the business world, when one elects a particular course of action, there is no peeking at the back of a book to see if you have chosen the best thing to do and no one to turn to for a provably correct answer. The only valid test of management action is *results*. If the results of an action turn out to be "good," the decision to take it may be presumed "right." If not, then the action chosen was "wrong" in the sense that it didn't work out.

Hence, the important thing for a student to understand in case analysis is that the managerial exercise of identifying, diagnosing, and recommending builds your skills; discovering the right answer or finding out what actually happened is no more than frosting on the cake. Even if you learn what the company did, you can't conclude that it was necessarily right or best. All that can be said is "here is what they did. . . ."

The point is this: *The purpose of giving you a case assignment is not to cause you to run to the library to look up what the company actually did but, rather, to enhance your skills in sizing up situations and developing your managerial judgment about what needs to be done and how to do it.* The aim of case analysis is for *you* to bear the strains of thinking actively, of offering your analysis, of proposing action plans, and of explaining and defending your assessments—this is how cases provide you with meaningful practice at being a manager.

PREPARING A CASE FOR CLASS DISCUSSION

If this is your first experience with the case method, you may have to re-orient your study habits. Unlike lecture courses where you can get by without preparing intensively for each class and where you have latitude to work assigned readings and reviews of lecture notes into your schedule, *a case assignment requires conscientious preparation before class.* You will not get much out of hearing the class discuss a case you haven't read, and you certainly won't be able to contribute anything yourself to the discussion. What you have got to do to get ready for class discussion of a case is to study the case, reflect carefully on the situation presented, and develop some reasoned thoughts. Your goal in preparing the case should be to end up with what you think is a sound, well-supported analysis of the situation and a sound, defensible set of recommendations about which managerial actions need to be taken.

To prepare a case for class discussion, we suggest the following approach:

1. *Read the case through rather quickly for familiarity.* The initial reading should give you the general flavor of the situation and indicate which issue or issues are involved. If your instructor has provided you with study questions for the case, now is the time to read them carefully.

2. *Read the case a second time.* On this reading, try to gain full command of the facts. Begin to develop some tentative answers to the study questions your instructor has provided. If your instructor has elected not to give you assignment questions, then start forming your own picture of the overall situation being described.

3. *Study all the exhibits carefully.* Often, the real story is in the numbers contained in the exhibits. Expect the information in the case exhibits to be crucial enough to materially affect your diagnosis of the situation.

4. *Decide what the strategic issues are.* Until you have identified the strategic issues and problems in the case, you don't know what to analyze, which tools and analytical techniques are called for, or otherwise how to proceed. At times the strategic issues are clear—either being stated in the case or else obvious from reading the case. At other times you will have to dig them out from all the information given.

5. *Start your analysis of the issues with some number crunching.* A big majority of strategy cases call for some kind of number crunching on your part. This means calculating assorted financial ratios to check out the company's financial condition and recent performance, calculating growth rates of sales or profits or unit volume, checking out profit margins and the makeup of the cost structure, and understanding whatever revenue-cost-profit relationships are present. See Table 1 for a summary of key financial ratios, how they are calculated, and what they show.

6. *Use whichever tools and techniques of strategic analysis are called for.* Strategic analysis is not just a collection of opinions; rather, it entails application of a growing number of powerful tools and techniques that cut beneath the surface and produce important insight and understanding of strategic situations. Every case assigned is strategy related and contains an opportunity to usefully apply the weapons of strategic analysis. Your instructor is looking for you to demonstrate that you know *how* and *when* to use the strategic management concepts presented earlier in the course. Furthermore, expect to have to draw regularly on what you have learned in your finance, economics, production, marketing, and human resources management courses.

7. *Check out conflicting opinions and make some judgments about the validity of all the data and information provided.* Many times cases report views and contradictory opinions (after all, people don't always agree on things, and different people see the same things in different ways). Forcing you to evaluate the data and information presented in the case helps you develop your powers of inference and judgment. Asking you to resolve conflicting information "comes with the territory" because a great many managerial situations entail opposing points of view, conflicting trends, and sketchy information.

8. *Support your diagnosis and opinions with reasons and evidence.* The most important things to prepare for are your answers to the question "Why?" For instance, if after studying the case you are of the opinion that the company's managers are doing a poor job, then it is your answer to "Why?" that establishes just how good your analysis of the situation is. If your instructor has provided you with specific study questions for the case, by all means prepare answers that include all the reasons and number-crunching evidence you can muster to support your diagnosis. *Generate at least two pages of notes!*

9. *Develop an appropriate action plan and set of recommendations.* Diagnosis divorced from corrective action is sterile. The test of a manager is always to

TABLE 1   A Summary of Key Financial Ratios, How They Are Calculated, and What They Show

Ratio	How Calculated	What It Shows
Profitability Ratios		
1. Gross profit margin	$$\frac{\text{Sales} - \text{Cost of goods sold}}{\text{Sales}}$$	An indication of the total margin available to cover operating expenses and yield a profit.
2. Operating profit margin (or return on sales)	$$\frac{\text{Profits before taxes and before interest}}{\text{Sales}}$$	An indication of the firm's profitability from current operations without regard to the interest charges accruing from the capital structure.
3. Net profit margin (or net return on sales)	$$\frac{\text{Profits after taxes}}{\text{Sales}}$$	Shows aftertax profits per dollar of sales. Subpar profit margins indicate that the firm's sales prices are relatively low or that its costs are relatively high, or both.
4. Return on total assets	$$\frac{\text{Profits after taxes}}{\text{Total assets}}$$ or $$\frac{\text{Profits after taxes} + \text{Interest}}{\text{Total assets}}$$	A measure of the return on total investment in the enterprise. It is sometimes desirable to add interest to aftertax profits to form the numerator of the ratio since total assets are financed by creditors as well as by stockholders; hence, it is accurate to measure the productivity of assets by the returns provided to both classes of investors.
5. Return on stockholders' equity (or return on net worth)	$$\frac{\text{Profits after taxes}}{\text{Total stockholders' equity}}$$	A measure of the rate of return on stockholders' investment in the enterprise.
6. Return on common equity	$$\frac{\text{Profits after taxes} - \text{Preferred stock dividends}}{\text{Total stockholders' equity} - \text{Par value of preferred stock}}$$	A measure of the rate of return on the investment which the owners of the common stock have made in the enterprise.
7. Earnings per share	$$\frac{\text{Profits after taxes} - \text{Preferred stock dividends}}{\text{Number of shares of common stock outstanding}}$$	Shows the earnings available to the owners of each share of common stock.
Liquidity Ratios		
1. Current ratio	$$\frac{\text{Current assets}}{\text{Current liabilities}}$$	Indicates the extent to which the claims of short-term creditors are covered by assets that are expected to be converted to cash in a period roughly corresponding to the maturity of the liabilities.
2. Quick ratio (or acid-test ratio)	$$\frac{\text{Current assets} - \text{Inventory}}{\text{Current liabilities}}$$	A measure of the firm's ability to pay off short-term obligations without relying on the sale of its inventories.
3. Inventory to net working capital	$$\frac{\text{Inventory}}{\text{Current assets} - \text{Current liabilities}}$$	A measure of the extent to which the firm's working capital is tied up in inventory.
Leverage Ratios		
1. Debt-to-assets ratio	$$\frac{\text{Total debt}}{\text{Total assets}}$$	Measures the extent to which borrowed funds have been used to finance the firm's operations.
2. Debt-to-equity ratio	$$\frac{\text{Total debt}}{\text{Total stockholders' equity}}$$	Provides another measure of the funds provided by creditors versus the funds provided by owners.

convert sound analysis into sound actions—actions that will produce the desired results. Hence, the final and most telling step in preparing a case is to develop an action agenda for management that lays out a set of specific

Ratio	How Calculated	What It Shows
3. Long-term debt-to-equity ratio	$\dfrac{\text{Long-term debt}}{\text{Total shareholders' equity}}$	A widely used measure of the balance between debt and equity in the firm's long-term capital structure.
4. Times-interest-earned (or coverage) ratio	$\dfrac{\text{Profits before interest and taxes}}{\text{Total interest charges}}$	Measures the extent to which earnings can decline without the firm becoming unable to meet its annual interest costs.
5. Fixed-charge coverage	$\dfrac{\text{Profits before taxes and interest} + \text{Lease obligations}}{\text{Total interest charges} + \text{Lease obligations}}$	A more inclusive indication of the firm's ability to meet all of its fixed-charge obligations.

Activity Ratios

Ratio	How Calculated	What It Shows
1. Inventory turnover	$\dfrac{\text{Sales}}{\text{Inventory of finished goods}}$	When compared to industry averages, it provides an indication of whether a company has excessive or perhaps inadequate finished goods inventory.
2. Fixed assets turnover	$\dfrac{\text{Sales}}{\text{Fixed Assets}}$	A measure of the sales productivity and utilization of plant and equipment.
3. Total assets turnover	$\dfrac{\text{Sales}}{\text{Total assets}}$	A measure of the utilization of all the firm's assets; a ratio below the industry average indicates the company is not generating a sufficient volume of business, given the size of its asset investment.
4. Accounts receivable turnover	$\dfrac{\text{Annual credit sales}}{\text{Accounts receivable}}$	A measure of the average length of time it takes the firm to collect the sales made on credit.
5. Average collection period	$\dfrac{\text{Accounts receivable}}{\text{Total sales} \div 365}$ or $\dfrac{\text{Accounts receivable}}{\text{Average daily sales}}$	Indicates the average length of time the firm must wait after making a sale before it receives payment.

Other Ratios

Ratio	How Calculated	What It Shows
1. Dividend yield on common stock	$\dfrac{\text{Annual dividends per share}}{\text{Current market price per share}}$	A measure of the return to owners received in the form of dividends.
2. Price-earnings ratio	$\dfrac{\text{Current market price per share}}{\text{Aftertax earnings per share}}$	Faster-growing or less-risky firms tend to have higher price-earnings ratios than slower-growing or more-risky firms.
3. Dividend payout ratio	$\dfrac{\text{Annual dividends per share}}{\text{Aftertax earnings per share}}$	Indicates the percentage of profits paid out as dividends.
4. Cash flow per share	$\dfrac{\text{Aftertax profits} + \text{Depreciation}}{\text{Number of common shares outstanding}}$	A measure of the discretionary funds over and above expenses that are available for use by the firm.

Note: Industry-average ratios against which a particular company's ratios may be judged are available in *Modern Industry* and *Dun's Reviews* published by Dun & Bradstreet (14 ratios for 125 lines of business activities), Robert Morris Associates' *Annual Statement Studies* (11 ratios for 156 lines of business), and the FTGSEC's *Quarterly Financial Report* for manufacturing corporations.

recommendations on what to do. Bear in mind that proposing realistic, workable solutions is far preferable to casually tossing out off-the-top-of-your-head suggestions. Be prepared to argue why your recommendations are more attractive than other courses of action that are open.

As long as you are conscientious in preparing your analysis and recommendations, and as long as you have ample reasons, evidence, and arguments to support your views, you shouldn't fret unduly about whether what you've prepared is the right answer to the case. In case analysis there is rarely just one right approach or one right set of recommendations. Managing companies and devising and implementing strategies are not such exact sciences that there exists a single provably correct analysis and action plan for each strategic situation. Of course, some analyses and action plans are better than others; but, in truth, there's nearly always more than one good way to analyze a situation and more than one good plan of action. So, if you have done a careful and thoughtful job of preparing the case, don't lose confidence in the correctness of your work and judgment.

PARTICIPATING IN CLASS DISCUSSION OF A CASE

Classroom discussions of cases are sharply different from attending a lecture class. In a case class students do most of the talking. The instructor's role is to solicit student participation, keep the discussion on track, ask "Why?" often, offer alternative views, play the devil's advocate (if no students jump in to offer opposing views), and otherwise lead the discussion. The students in the class carry the burden for analyzing the situation and for being prepared to present and defend their diagnoses and recommendations. Expect a classroom environment, therefore, that calls for *your* size-up of the situation, *your* analysis, what actions *you* would take, and why *you* would take them. Do not be dismayed if, as the class discussion unfolds, some insightful things are said by your fellow classmates that you did not think of. It is normal for views and analyses to differ and for the comments of others in the class to expand your own thinking about the case. As the old adage goes, "Two heads are better than one." So it is to be expected that the class as a whole will do a more penetrating and searching job of case analysis than will any one person working alone. This is the power of group effort, and its virtues are that it will help you see more analytical applications, let you test your analyses and judgments against those of your peers, and force you to wrestle with differences of opinion and approaches.

To orient you to the classroom environment on the days a case discussion is scheduled, we compiled the following list of things to expect:

1. Expect students to dominate the discussion and do most of the talking. The case method enlists a maximum of individual participation in class discussion. It is not enough to be present as a silent observer; if every student took this approach, there would be no discussion. (Thus, expect a portion of your grade to be based on your participation in case discussions.)

2. Expect the instructor to assume the role of extensive questioner and listener.

3. Be prepared for the instructor to probe for reasons and supporting analysis.

4. Expect and tolerate challenges to the views expressed. All students have to be willing to submit their conclusions for scrutiny and rebuttal. Each student needs to learn to state his or her views without fear of

disapproval and to overcome the hesitation of speaking out. Learning respect for the views and approaches of others is an integral part of case analysis exercises. But there are times when it is OK to swim against the tide of majority opinion. In the practice of management, there is always room for originality and unorthodox approaches. So while discussion of a case is a group process, there is no compulsion for you or anyone else to cave in and conform to group opinions and group consensus.

5. Don't be surprised if you change your mind about some things as the discussion unfolds. Be alert to how these changes affect your analysis and recommendations (in the event you get called on).

6. Expect to learn a lot from each case discussion; use what you learn to be better prepared for the next case discussion.

There are several things you can do on your own to be good and look good as a participant in class discussions:

- Although you should do your own independent work and independent thinking, don't hesitate before (and after) class to discuss the case with other students. In real life, managers often discuss the company's problems and situation with other people to refine their own thinking.

- In participating in the discussion, make a conscious effort to contribute, rather than just talk. There is a big difference between saying something that builds the discussion and offering a long-winded, off-the-cuff remark that leaves the class wondering what the point was.

- Avoid the use of "I think," "I believe," and "I feel"; instead, say, "My analysis shows . . . " and "The company should do . . . because. . . ." Always give supporting reasons and evidence for your views; then your instructor won't have to ask you "Why?" every time you make a comment.

- In making your points, assume that everyone has read the case and knows what it says; avoid reciting and rehashing information in the case—instead, use the data and information to explain your assessment of the situation and to support your position.

- Always prepare good notes (usually two or three pages' worth) for each case and use them extensively when you speak. There's no way you can remember everything off the top of your head—especially the results of your number crunching. To reel off the numbers or to present all five reasons why, instead of one, you will need good notes. When you have prepared good notes to the study questions and use them as the basis for your comments, *everybody* in the room will know you are well prepared, and your contribution to the case discussion will stand out.

PREPARING A WRITTEN CASE ANALYSIS

Preparing a written case analysis is much like preparing a case for class discussion, except that your analysis must be more complete and reduced to writing. Unfortunately, though, *there is no ironclad procedure for doing a written case analysis*. All we can offer are some general guidelines and words of wisdom—this is because company situations and management problems are so diverse that no one mechanical way to approach a written case assignment always works.

Your instructor may assign you a specific topic around which to prepare your written report. Or, alternatively, you may be asked to do a comprehensive written case analysis, where the expectation is that you will (1) *identify* all the pertinent issues that management needs to address, (2) perform whatever *analysis* and *evaluation* is appropriate, and (3) propose an *action plan* and set of *recommendations* addressing the issues you have identified. In going through the exercise of identify, evaluate, and recommend, keep the following pointers in mind.[3]

Identification   It is essential early on in your paper that you provide a sharply focused diagnosis of strategic issues and key problems and that you demonstrate a good grasp of the company's present situation. Make sure you can identify the firm's strategy (use the concepts and tools in Chapters 1–8 as diagnostic aids) and that you can pinpoint whatever strategy implementation issues may exist (again, consult the material in Chapters 9 and 10 for diagnostic help). Consult the key points we have provided at the end of each chapter for further diagnostic suggestions. Consider beginning your paper by sizing up the company's situation, its strategy, and the significant problems and issues that confront management. State problems/issues as clearly and precisely as you can. Unless it is necessary to do so for emphasis, avoid recounting facts and history about the company (assume your professor has read the case and is familiar with the organization).

Analysis and Evaluation   This is usually the hardest part of the report. Analysis is hard work! Check out the firm's financial ratios, its profit margins and rates of return, and its capital structure, and decide how strong the firm is financially. Table 1 contains a summary of various financial ratios and how they are calculated. Use it to assist in your financial diagnosis. Similarly, look at marketing, production, managerial competence, and other factors underlying the organization's strategic successes and failures. Decide whether the firm has core skills and competencies and, if so, whether it is capitalizing on them.

Check to see if the firm's strategy is producing satisfactory results and determine the reasons why or why not. Probe the nature and strength of the competitive forces confronting the company. Decide whether and why the firm's competitive position is getting stronger or weaker. Use the tools and concepts you have learned about to perform whatever analysis and evaluation is appropriate.

In writing your analysis and evaluation, bear in mind four things:

1. You are obliged to offer analysis and evidence to back up your conclusions. Do not rely on unsupported opinions, overgeneralizations, and platitudes as a substitute for tight, logical argument backed up with facts and figures.

---

[3]For some additional ideas and viewpoints, you may wish to consult Thomas J. Raymond, "Written Analysis of Cases," in *The Case Method at the Harvard Business School*, ed. M. P. McNair, pp. 139–63. Raymond's article includes an actual case, a sample analysis of the case, and a sample of a student's written report on the case.

2. If your analysis involves some important quantitative calculations, use tables and charts to present the calculations clearly and efficiently. Don't just tack the exhibits on at the end of your report and let the reader figure out what they mean and why they were included. Instead, in the body of your report cite some of the key numbers, highlight the conclusions to be drawn from the exhibits, and refer the reader to your charts and exhibits for more details.

3. Demonstrate that you have command of the strategic concepts and analytical tools to which you have been exposed. Use them in your report.

4. Your interpretation of the evidence should be reasonable and objective. Be wary of preparing a one-sided argument that omits all aspects not favorable to your conclusions. Likewise, try not to exaggerate or overdramatize. Endeavor to inject balance into your analysis and to avoid emotional rhetoric. Strike phrases such as "I think," "I feel," and "I believe" when you edit your first draft and write in "My analysis shows," instead.

Recommendations   The final section of the written case analysis should consist of a set of definite recommendations and a plan of action. Your set of recommendations should address all of the problems/issues you identified and analyzed. If the recommendations come as a surprise or do not follow logically from the analysis, the effect is to weaken greatly your suggestions of what to do. Obviously, your recommendations for actions should offer a reasonable prospect of success. High-risk, bet-the-company recommendations should be made with caution. State how your recommendations will solve the problems you identified. Be sure the company is financially able to carry out what you recommend; also check to see if your recommendations are workable in terms of acceptance by the persons involved, the organization's competence to implement them, and prevailing market and environmental constraints. Try not to hedge or weasel on the actions you believe should be taken.

By all means state your recommendations in sufficient detail to be meaningful—get down to some definite nitty-gritty specifics. Avoid such unhelpful statements as "the organization should do more planning" or "the company should be more aggressive in marketing its product." For instance, do not simply say "the firm should improve its market position" but state exactly how you think this should be done. Offer a definite agenda for action, stipulating a timetable and sequence for initiating actions, indicating priorities, and suggesting who should be responsible for doing what.

In proposing an action plan, remember there is a great deal of difference between being responsible, on the one hand, for a decision that may be costly if it proves in error and, on the other hand, casually suggesting courses of action that might be taken when you do not have to bear the responsibility for any of the consequences. A good rule to follow in making your recommendations is: *Avoid recommending anything you would not yourself be willing to do if you were in management's shoes.* The importance of learning to develop good judgment in a managerial situation is indicated by the fact that, even though the same information and operating data may be available to every manager or executive in an organization, the quality of the judgments about what the information means and which actions need to be taken does vary from person to person.[4]

It goes without saying that your report should be well organized and well written. Great ideas amount to little unless others can be convinced of their merit—this takes tight logic, the presentation of convincing evidence, and persuasively written arguments.

THE TEN COMMANDMENTS OF CASE ANALYSIS

As a way of summarizing our suggestions about how to approach the task of case analysis, we have compiled what we like to call "The Ten Commandments of Case Analysis." They are shown in Table 2. If you observe all or even most of these commandments faithfully as you prepare a case either for class discussion or for a written report, your chances of doing a good job on the assigned cases will be much improved. Hang in there, give it your best shot, and have some fun exploring what the real world of strategic management is all about.

---

[4]Gragg, "Because Wisdom Can't Be Told," p. 10.

TABLE 2   **The Ten Commandments of Case Analysis**

To be observed in written reports and oral presentations, and while participating in class discussions.

1. Read the case twice, once for an overview and once to gain full command of the facts; then take care to explore every one of the exhibits.
2. Make a list of the problems and issues that have to be confronted.
3. Do enough number crunching to discover the story told by the data presented in the case. (To help you comply with this commandment, consult Table 1 to guide your probing of a company's financial condition and financial performance.)
4. Look for opportunities to use the concepts and analytical tools you have learned earlier.
5. Be thorough in your diagnosis of the situation and make at least a one- or two-page outline of your assessment.
6. Support any and all opinions with well-reasoned arguments and numerical evidence; don't stop until you can purge "I think" and "I feel" from your assessment and, instead, are able to rely completely on "My analysis shows."
7. Develop charts, tables, and graphs to expose more clearly the main points of your analysis.
8. Prioritize your recommendations and make sure they can be carried out in an acceptable time frame with the available skills and financial resources.
9. Review your recommended action plan to see if it addresses all of the problems and issues you identified.
10. Avoid recommending any course of action that could have disastrous consequences if it doesn't work out as planned; therefore, be as alert to the downside risks of your recommendations as you are to their upside potential and appeal.

THE MANAGER AS CHIEF STRATEGY-MAKER AND CHIEF STRATEGY-IMPLEMENTER

THE FAITH MOUNTAIN COMPANY

James J. Dowd, Michael D. Atchison, and John H. Lindgren, Jr.,
University of Virginia*

Having passed the $5 million mark in annual sales, the Faith Mountain Company recorded its first profit in July 1991. According to industry norms, it was right on schedule, but it still came as something of a surprise to Cheri and Martin Woodard. It had been a remarkable year on several counts: the all-important catalog customer list had grown 31 percent, to 251,771 names; despite the recession, sales were up 41 percent; and, best of all, from a loss of $185,791 in fiscal year 1990, the company had posted a net profit of $161,476 for fiscal year 1991.

By December 1991, it was clear that Faith Mountain was on its way to another record-breaking year. When they stopped to reflect on the growth of their business, however, Cheri and Martin admitted they faced some tough questions. What next? Could they count on continued growth at this rate, and if so, could they manage it and remain profitable? Where should they grow, and how? What financial and human resources would be required, and would this small company in the Blue Ridge Mountains be able to attract and retain them?

In their first business plan, completed only last year in conjunction with a major effort to raise capital, they had set ambitious goals: by the year 1995, $10 million in sales from the Faith Mountain catalog, $5 million from the retail division, and an additional $10 million from acquisitions or development of another catalog company. Even as they struggled to keep pace with customer demand in their busiest time of the year, they knew they soon would have to find the time to review that plan, examine their goals, and renew their efforts to make them reality.

HISTORY OF THE FAITH MOUNTAIN COMPANY

Cheri Faith Woodard

Cheri Faith Woodard grew up, in her own words, "a product of the 70s—I wasn't a radical, but I had a vision of a better society, and a belief that things could be different." She left college before graduating, married, had a son, and helped found a cooperative natural foods store near College Park, Maryland. After a divorce in 1974, she moved to Sperryville, Virginia, a small town of about 500 people at the foot of the Blue Ridge Mountains. Only 69 miles from Washington, D.C., the natural beauty and very low cost of living in Rappahannock County attracted many young people to the area.

To support herself and her young son, Cheri worked in an antique shop. At the time, the best connecting route between two major state highways went

*This case was prepared for the 11th McIntire Commerce Invitational (MCI XI) held at the University of Virginia on February 13–15, 1992. The authors gratefully acknowledge the General Electric Foundation and the McIntire School of Commerce for their support.

through Sperryville, right around the corner from the antique shop. During vacation seasons, with heavy tourist traffic to and from the Shenandoah National Park, the shop did extremely good business. Cheri learned much about antiques and furniture restoration, and she enjoyed bargaining with customers.

Soon after arriving in Sperryville, Cheri met Florence Williamson, known throughout the area as "the herb lady." She knew how to grow all kinds of herbs and how to use them in recipes, medicines, and gardens. Many people, from local families to the directors of the National Herb Garden in Washington, D.C., sought her advice.

Cheri became interested in herbs while working at the natural foods store in Maryland, and she was eager to learn more. Mrs. Williamson was always busy, but as she approached 75, she decided she needed a helper, so she was willing to teach Cheri. The two began working together as teacher and apprentice.

In 1975, Cheri met Martin Woodard at a square dance. Martin had graduated from Vanderbilt University with a degree in sociology and history. He too was drawn to the quality of life in Rappahannock County and had established a successful masonry contracting business. In 1977, they were married.

Opening the Store

Meanwhile, Cheri began contemplating opening her own business. She had learned a great deal about herbs, and she sensed that more and more people were becoming interested in growing and using them. She also wanted to work at home to be near her son. She decided she would open a store to sell herbs, related products, and antiques. She discussed her ideas with Martin and Mrs. Williamson, and both gave their full support. Cheri remembered:

> Martin and I had faith in each other and in ourselves—we said, "We can do this!" And we were here in the Blue Ridge Mountains—so that's how we got our name. A business started on faith at the foot of the mountains: The Faith Mountain Herbs and Antique Shop.

The Woodards found a house for sale on Main Street in Sperryville, just a block down the street from the antique shop in which Cheri had worked. The front part of the house was built in 1790 and had been used as a doctor's office, a tavern, and a guest house. There was room in the backyard for an herb garden, and there were small outbuildings for storage or workshops. Even better, the house was big enough to serve as both home and store. With owner financing, the Woodards bought the house for $26,000, assumed a $200 monthly mortgage, and set about restoring the old house.

The family lived in the back of the house and used the four front rooms for the store. Cheri grew her own herbs in the backyard and bought others locally to sell in the store. The business grew slowly; herbs were inexpensive, and small amounts lasted a long time. Local businesspeople, suspicious of herbs and of the young couple, predicted the store would fail. With the full support of "the herb lady," however, Cheri began to establish a strong reputation as an "herb lady" in her own right, giving local talks and workshops on cooking with herbs, making wreaths of dried flowers, and the like.

Between 1977 and 1980, she slowly increased the variety of products offered, adding herb blends, dried flowers, simple garden supplies, books, kitchen tools, preserves, and handicrafts. She displayed the products on antique furniture she bought, restored, and offered for sale. Encouraged by praise from customers who had driven from Washington, D.C., for a day in the country, Cheri purchased her first ads in the *Washington Post* in 1979.

Birth of the Mail-Order Business

In 1980, construction was completed on Interstate 66, a highway connection eliminating most of the east-west traffic passing through Sperryville. Like the other businesses in Sperryville, Faith Mountain suffered, and its antique sales all but disappeared. Even though Cheri kept the store open all weekend to capture any possible business, she could not make the store profitable.

Faith Mountain was no longer merely an interesting way for Cheri to be able to work at home. She felt she deserved more reward for all her hard work, and she began to consider a mail-order catalog.

Tourists from around the country had stopped to shop at Faith Mountain on their way to Shenandoah National Park, so she knew her products appealed to a wide market. Further, more and more customers were writing to her, asking if she could send them a wreath or another product they remembered seeing in the store.

Confident that she had a market, she created the first Faith Mountain Herbs and Antiques catalog in the spring of 1980. The 12-page catalog offered mostly herbs and herbal products and featured simple line drawings and text. She was able to get the catalog printed and copied for free as a test of new machines by a friend who worked for Xerox Corporation. Her greatest difficulty was with the local post office, which had never worked with bulk mailings before. With advice from a cousin in the mail-order business, she obtained bulk rate permit No. 1 from the Sperryville post office and mailed her first 1,000 catalogs.

As the mail-order business began to grow, the Woodard family realized they had to move out of the house. They bought a local farm, grew more than 20 kinds of herbs and flowers, and dried them in their barn. Cheri hired part-time employees to help with the store and the catalog. In 1983, the first color photo catalog was mailed, with a press run of 110,000 copies.

Incorporation and Growth

Until that time, Martin Woodard had concentrated on his masonry business, helping out occasionally with the store and the catalog. Increasingly frustrated by problems with his employees and aware of the growing burden on Cheri, he began thinking about working with Faith Mountain full time.

By 1984, Faith Mountain's annual sales had reached $400,000. At a Direct Marketing Association meeting in Washington, D.C., the Woodards were referred to Don Press, director of the Smithsonian Museum Gift Catalog and part-time mail-order consultant. They asked him two questions: "Does our business have a future? If so, what is our next step?" Martin recalled what happened next:

> Don looked at everything, and then he told us: "Yes, you have something here. It's not going to be easy, but you do have a future with this business." So there was the validation, and I had to make a decision. I sold the masonry business and came on full time at Faith Mountain in the fall of 1984.

Martin became catalog director, with responsibility for merchandise selection, catalog production and marketing, and also for financial planning. Cheri retained responsibility for the store, for manufacturing and warehouse operations, customer service, and all personnel matters. Martin was very clear from the start he wanted no responsibility for people.

Working closely with their consultant, Cheri recalled, "We really started to get serious about the business and slowly put together a real company." They incorporated in 1985 and offered Don Press a seat on the board of directors. He referred them to more professional services for catalog production and helped them manage their finances by teaching them benchmark ratios for catalog operations' budgets and income statements. They bought some small buildings in 1985 to accommodate the growing business and rented additional space as needed.

In the same year, Cheri was elected to a three-year term as president of the Sperryville Business Council. She organized a Sperryville Spring Festival to correspond with the anniversary of the Faith Mountain Herbs and Antiques Store, and it became an annual event, drawing thousands to the town. That year, Faith Mountain printed 500,000 catalogs and annual sales exceeded $1.5 million.

By 1988, Faith Mountain was running out of room, and there was no more space to rent. Later that year, the Woodards' barn burned. It was clear that the company needed more space, and it would improve operations if all parts of the business, now scattered in several buildings throughout Sperryville, could be brought together under one big roof.

At the suggestion of their banker, the Woodards applied for funding from the U.S. Small Business Administration under a special loan program assisting small business expansions. With a "504 loan," the SBA would finance 40 percent of the expansion project, secured by a second deed of trust. A conventional lending institution would finance 50 percent of the project, with a first deed of trust, and the company would pay the remaining 10 percent.

The Woodards located a 1.75- acre site on Route 211 that would support construction of a 10,000-square-foot facility for offices, a warehouse, and possibly a retail outlet. The SBA loan package would include the land and the building, the warehouse equipment and shelves, the phone system, hardware and software improvements, and office furniture and partitions, for a total cost of $425,000. Cheri remembered:

> It was a *big leap* to spend that much money. We hadn't had much of a business plan, and now we had to show one to get the money. We had to get the site rezoned for commercial use, and then we just went ahead. In April 1989, we signed contracts to buy the land and contracts to begin construction on the building—this was before we had even gotten approval on the SBA loan! I remember Martin said, "We have to have faith." Almost a full month later, on May 10, we got the call from the SBA: We had the loan. Thank God—we had already spent it!

THE FAITH MOUNTAIN COMPANY IN 1991

Location

In 1991, the Faith Mountain Company operated out of that 10,000-square-foot site. The building had about 4,000 square feet of office space and 6,000 square feet of warehouse space. The company was then paying about $5,000 per month in principal and interest for the facility. The roof was constructed to permit addition of an mezzanine level, which would double the storage space in the warehouse area, and the entire building was designed to facilitate an addition of 10,000 to 15,000 square feet. The retail store still operated in its original location, about two miles away.

Organization and Staffing

As the company ended its 1991 fiscal year, it employed 39 people, 25 of those full time. The organization chart (Exhibit 1) shows that Cheri and Martin still shared responsibilities as they had in 1984.

As chief financial officer, Martin supervised Debbie Jenkins, the accounting supervisor. With one full-time clerk, Jenkins took care of day-to-day financial bookkeeping, including payables, receivables, and all internal financial reports. Payroll was handled by an outside firm. Martin was responsible for long-term financial planning. The current fiscal year (1992) was the first year in which monthly and year-to-date budget reports were created and used.

As catalog director, Martin was responsible for all aspects of the Faith Mountain Company catalogs. The past year was the first in which Faith Mountain had produced four different catalogs, one for each season; previously, the summer catalog had been essentially the spring catalog with sale prices. The 1991 spring catalog, featuring Easter gift items, was 40 pages and mailed at the end of December 1990. The summer catalog, at 32 pages, was mailed in mid-April. The 40-page fall catalog, featuring Halloween, Thanksgiving, and some Christmas items, was mailed at the end of June. And the Christmas catalog, at 48 pages their biggest ever, was mailed in mid-September.

Kim Baader, merchandising manager, was charged with selecting and promoting items for the catalogs. She and Martin went to gift, apparel, and other trade shows throughout the year, seeking vendors with quality products and a reputation for reliability in shipping. They brought potential catalog items back to the office, where Martin and Cheri, Baader and her assistant, and Margie Ellis, the store manager, would examine each piece and argue for or against offering it to Faith Mountain customers.

Having selected the catalog merchandise, under Martin's direction, Baader worked closely with a contract copywriter while Martin worked with the professional service firms contracted to design and produce the catalog, including layout, photography, and printing. Interviewing, inspecting, selecting, negotiating, and managing these vendors demanded so much time that in the summer of 1991, the former accounting clerk was promoted to catalog production manager to assume primary responsibility for these areas. Finally, before catalogs were mailed, Baader briefed the customer service and telemarketing staff on each catalog item, and she prepared summary product descriptions for easy reference on the automated entry system. By the time a catalog was mailed, work was already under way on the next.

As president, Cheri was responsible for overall direction of the company, and she was involved in all major decisions in all areas. Responsible for all aspects of human resource management in the firm, Cheri decided all personnel policies and practices and described them all in the Faith Mountain employee handbook. She had hired every employee in the company until

EXHIBIT 1   Organization Chart for the Faith Mountain Company, 1992

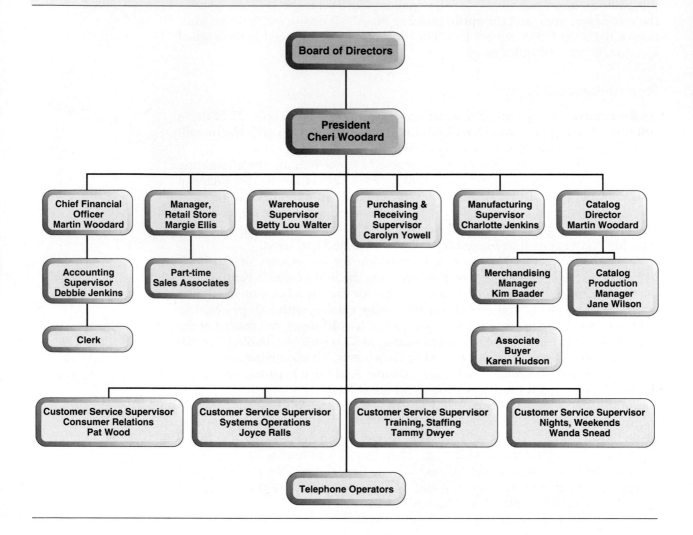

September 1991, when the store manager hired a part-time sales associate, with Cheri's knowledge, but without her prior approval. Cheri stated, "That was a funny feeling, and I'm not sure I like it."

As director of operations, Cheri supervised the following people and areas:

Margie Ellis, manager of the retail store, responsible for store sales, merchandising, staffing and customer service.

Betty Lou Walter, warehouse supervisor, responsible for product flow and shipping accuracy and timeliness.

Carolyn Yowell, purchasing and receiving supervisor, responsible for receiving merchandise, forecasting and managing back orders and overstocks.

Charlotte Jenkins, manufacturing supervisor, responsible for design and production of Faith Mountain products (wreaths, herb mixtures, etc.), including purchasing, scheduling, and inventory control.

In addition, Cheri supervised the customer service and telephone operations areas. Four customer service supervisors rotated primary responsibility for customer service calls each day, and each had her own special area of responsibility:

Pat Wood, customer service supervisor responsible for Wednesday and Friday, handled all customer correspondence (not including mail orders).

Joyce Ralls, customer service supervisor responsible for Tuesday, handled system hardware and software, including local maintenance and system planning.

Tammy Dwyer, customer service supervisor responsible for Monday and Thursday, was responsible for training and staffing of telephone operators.

Wanda Snead, customer service supervisor responsible for customer service in the evening (5–8:30) and on weekends generated day-end activity reports.

Finally, Cheri also directly supervised the telephone operators. Eight regular part-time employees (more part-timers were hired for peak season) were responsible for taking customer orders by phone, referring any customer complaints or problems to the customer service supervisor. The phone operators also opened and sorted mail orders each day, forwarding checks to the accounting department and verifying order forms for entry into the system.

Financial Position

Exhibits 2 and 3 provide information on the company's financial position in 1991. Other than the Small Business Administration loan described earlier, financing was primarily short term. R. R. Donnelley, the catalog printer, extended the firm $350,000 in credit with lenient terms. Inventory moved through the warehouse quickly, and trade payables to vendors were small. About 10 percent of catalog orders were handled as "drop shipments," where vendors shipped directly to the customer. Inventory financing was handled through a line of credit, recently increased from $350,000 to $500,000.

The Faith Mountain Mail-Order Strategy

In 1991, the Faith Mountain Company developed, manufactured, and marketed high-quality gifts, apparel, and home accessories, distributing them through its mail-order catalog and its retail store.

The company focused on the needs of women between ages 30 and 50 who owned their own homes and had family incomes of $40,000 to $60,000. Faith Mountain believed female homemakers sought traditional, nostalgic, whimsical, and romantic gifts, apparel, and home accessories to enhance the quality of their homes and family lives. Although increasing numbers of these women balanced their family responsibilities with work outside the home, they held traditional family values, and time spent at home with their families dominated their nonworking hours. Even as they sought products and gift items that reflected those values, they were reluctant to spend time driving through

EXHIBIT 2   **Balance Sheet of the Faith Mountain Company, 1987–91**   *(Fiscal years ending June 30; dollar amounts in thousands)*

	1987	1988	1989	1990	1991
Assets					
Cash	$ 3	$ 3	$ 15	$ 1	$ 48
Net accounts receivable	8	14	26	25	55
Inventories	114	176	183	320	410
Unamortized catalog costs	32	53	150	198	400
Total current assets	$157	$246	$374	$ 544	$ 913
Net property	35	69	203	511	489
Intangibles				10	9
Other noncurrent assets			3	2	4
	$192	$315	$580	$1,067	$1,415
Liabilities and Net Worth					
Bank loans—short-term (see Note 1)	$ 42	$ 46	$114	$ 212	$ 333
Current maturities of long-term debt				30	29
Other notes payable			135		
Accounts payable	60	84	113	321	304
Accruals	3	4	3	11	11
Advance from stockholder				15	
Total current liabilities	$105	$134	$365	$ 589	$ 677
Long-term bank debt (see Note 2)		42	28	417	399
Total liabilities	$105	$176	$393	$1,006	$1,076
Preferred stock	42				
Common stock (see Note 3)	92	264	310	370	518
Capital surplus					
Retained earnings	(47)	(125)	(123)	(309)	(179)
	$192	$315	$580	$1,067	$1,415

Note 1: Notes Payable, Bank

Notes payable, bank at June 30, 1991, consists of $333,000 drawn from an available line of credit of $350,000 with C&S/Sovran Bank.

The note is secured by a first security interest in all accounts receivables, inventory, and property and equipment and bears interest at C&S/Sovran Bank's prime rate plus $1\frac{1}{2}\%$ (10.0% at June 30, 1991). The note is payable on demand, with interest payable monthly. The line expires on October 30, 1991.

Under the requirements of the note agreement the company has agreed, among other things, to: (1) maintain its ratio of debt to net worth at no more than 5 to 1, measured at fiscal year end; (2) maintain all of its primary deposit relationships with C&S/Sovran as long as this commitment is outstanding; and (3) not incur any indebtedness so long as this commitment remains outstanding without the prior written consent of the bank. The note is guaranteed by Martin Woodard and Cheri Woodard, shareholders of the company.

congested urban or suburban areas to shop in "glitzy" commercialized malls. Instead, these women were increasingly likely to turn to mail-order catalogs, which offered the option of shopping at their own convenience, in their own homes, 24 hours a day.

Competition   The Woodards estimated approximately 50 catalog companies sold gifts, apparel, or home accessories. Within its own niche of "traditional" products in those categories, Faith Mountain had targeted four significant competitors. Based on knowledge they had gained from industry analysts and

EXHIBIT 2 *(concluded)*

Note 2: Long-Term Debt

A summary of the company's long-term debt, and collateral pledged thereon, consist of the following:

	June 30	
	1991	**1990**
C&S/Sovran Bank, note due in monthly installments of $456.00, including interest at 12.5% through January 1995, collateralized by truck	$ 15,903	$ 18,906
Signet Bank, capitalized lease obligation, discounted at a rate of 11.5% due in monthly installments of $1,034 to October 1993	24,356	24,163
Marathon Bank, note due in monthly installments of $944, plus interest at Marathon Bank's prime rate plus 1 through November 1999, collateralized by real estate	208,510	220,242
Virginia Asset Financing Corporation, note due in monthly installments of $1,741, including interest at 8.9% through January 2010, collateralized by the personal guarantees of Martin Woodard and Cheri Woodard, shareholders of the company, and a second deed of trust on real estate	179,439	183,110
Other	107	667
	$428,315	$447,088
Less current maturities	29,483	29,610
Long-term portion	$398,832	$417,478

Aggregate maturities required on long-term debt at June 30, 1991, are due in future fiscal years ending June 30 as follows:

1992	$29,483
1993	30,224
1994	24,933
1995	19,435
1996	16,580
Thereafter	307,660
	$428,315

Interest expense for the year ended June 30, 1991 and 1990, was $65,824 and $35,297, respectively.

Note 3: Stockholders' Equity

For year ended June 30, 1991, the company issued 1,150 units which comprised 1,150 shares of common stock and 1,150 warrants to purchase common stock. The gross proceeds of the issue was $115,000. Each warrant entitles the holder to purchase one share of common stock at a price of $90 per share, subject to certain conditions through June 30, 1992.

other sources, the Woodards described them in their 1990 business plan as follows:

Potpourri: Founded in the late 1960s and run by Bill and Sue Knowles and their two sons, the company is an institution in the industry. Industry sources estimate Potpourri prints 40 million catalogs per year, with annual sales in the $50 million range, and an average order size of $60. Bill and Sue are widely respected for their business sense and marketing/merchandising abilities, but as they approach their 70s, it is unclear whether the sons will be able to carry on their successful merchandising. We believe the quality of Potpourri's merchandise and customer service is inferior to Faith Mountain's.

EXHIBIT 3   **Income Statement for the Faith Mountain Company, 1987–91**   *(Fiscal years ending June 30; dollar amounts in thousands)*

	1987	1988	1989	1990	1991
Net sales	$1,234	$1,654	$2,429	$3,554	$5,025
Less: Cost of sales	496	780	1,249	1,936	2,900
Gross profit	$ 738	$ 874	$1,249	$1,936	$2,125
Percentage of net sales	59.81%	52.84%	51.42%	54.47%	57.71%
Less: Operating expenses	366	247	545	835	1,030
Catalog production and promotional expense	382	705	753	1,346	1,784
Depreciation		23	25	33	44
Operating profit	(10)	(101)	(74)	(278)	42
Other income	14	40	88	127	185
Less: Interest expense		11	12	35	66
Net profit before tax	4	(72)	2	(186)	161
Profit after tax	4	(72)	2	(186)	161
Net profit (loss)	$4	$(72)	$2	$(186)	$161
Net after dividends	4	(72)	2	(186)	161
Add: Beginning retained earnings	(51)	(47)	(125)	(123)	(340)
Less: Other		6			
Ending retained earnings	(47)	(125)	(123)	(309)	(179)

Charles Keath: With sales estimated in the $35 million range, this company is also widely respected for its excellent merchandising. It is owned by Charles Edmundson, who has built the company from the ashes of a failed catalog company. We believe Faith Mountain's catalog features higher-quality photographs and copywriting and we rate Faith Mountain's customer service more highly than that offered by Charles Keath.

W.M. Green: Only seven years old, the company is run by two sisters, Marianne Carson and Beth Everitt, and their brother, Mark Green, out of North Carolina. Annual sales are estimated at $4.5 million, with an average order size of about $110. Like Faith Mountain, this company features handmade traditional gifts, with some home accessories, but W.M. Green does not sell apparel. We respect the quality and customer service of W.M. Green but believe Faith Mountain's experience with a broader product line is a distinct advantage.

Sturbridge Yankee: Offering home accessories with a distinct American "country" flavor, this company has about $8 million in annual sales. It has opened three retail stores in New England, leading many to believe the company will emphasize retail stores over catalog operations. In any event, we believe the narrow focus on "Americana" will limit the company's growth.

For its own part, Faith Mountain adopted a mail-order strategy that focused on three key areas: merchandise, quality, and service.

Merchandise   Faith Mountain offered a broad range of high-quality products to its customers, united by "a lifestyle theme of traditional, cozy, and family-oriented life." In 1991, the company rotated over 500 products through its catalogs, including its own manufactured products, herbs and floral arrange-

| EXHIBIT 4 | Summary Descriptions of Faith Mountain's Major Product Lines |

Faith Mountain herb and floral arrangements, designed by Cheri Woodard and staff and created in the Sperryville studio, were the traditional core of the business. Faith Mountain was one of the original manufacturers of these products, and its creations were regularly copied for sale in other catalogs. Especially popular were the chain of flowers, eucalyptus arrangements, and the herb wreath, the best seller in every fall catalog since 1981.

Updated casual sportswear, including sweaters, skirts, dresses, and novelty items, appealed to women who sought high-quality classic designs with a stylish flair, suitable for entertaining, parties, church, and weekends, and to a limited extent, for work. Obtained from vendors such as Lanz, Susan Bristol, and The Eagle's Eye, these products were not exclusive to Faith Mountain, although the Woodards knew of no other catalog devoted to such "country fashions."

Unique jewelry, such as pins, earrings, belts, necklaces, and bracelets, sold well as impulse purchases. They were price blind and were easy to ship and warehouse.

Children's products, including puzzles, toys, and mazes, were selected to appeal to mothers, grandmothers, or other relatives who sought "wholesome, old-fashioned fun with educational value" as gifts for children age 2–8. In addition, the company sold lamps, rugs, and other accessories to bring a traditional or nostalgic appearance to children's bedrooms.

Seasonal decorative accessories, especially items for Halloween, Thanksgiving, Christmas, and Easter, were offered to help families decorate their homes for these holidays, according to old traditions and to create new ones. The line excluded "cheap plastic decorations, glitzy tinsel, or poorly constructed merchandise" to focus on long-lasting, high-quality items to keep and use every year, such as evergreen wreaths, advent calendars, and centerpieces.

Collectibles, limited edition series of handcrafted figurines, plates, dolls, cottages, and the like were increasingly popular among Faith Mountain customers. These items were created in series to inspire collecting every individual item in the set. Secondary markets sometimes developed for these items, which could bring prices far above the original purchase price. The items were ideal for catalogs because these generated repeated purchases, enhancing the responsiveness of the customer list, but manufacturers were selective in choosing catalog outlets.

Gifts, especially sentimental, inspirational, or symbolic items that reflect the customer's traditional values, were selected for the catalog. Faith Mountain did not offer "standard giftware" of silver, china, or glass, as these were easily available in many retail outlets. Instead, the catalog featured unusual items.

American crafts, or artistic handmade goods, were another way in which Faith Mountain could distinguish itself from ordinary retail outlets. To source and offer these goods, the company had to deal with artists, not vendors, and because the items were one of a kind, customers had to be educated about the use and value of these pieces. Because Faith Mountain was itself a small manufacturer, it was able to work effectively with artisans other outlets viewed as difficult or unreliable, and it offered these crafts as gifts and as decorative accessories.

Home and garden accessories, or items to decorate and personalize one's "living space," were sold to help customers create "comfortable, secure, cozy home environments." The vast array of items were available through manufacturers' representatives, trade shows, and personal contacts.

ments, sportswear, jewelry, gifts, and home and garden decorations. Exhibit 4 provides summary product line descriptions as contained in Faith Mountain's 1990 business plan.

Merchandise selection was a critical ingredient in the success of the company. The Woodards attributed their success in this area to the fact that they both "lived the lifestyle" of their customers and to the contacts they had developed in the gift industry over the past 14 years. They sought exclusive marketing rights for products and had begun to move more aggressively to private labeling. Finding and developing quality merchandise before the competition did was the driving force of the merchandising function at Faith Mountain.

Quality   The Woodards prided themselves on offering the best-quality herb and floral products in America, and they sought to offer only merchandise of the highest quality, representing the best value available. Because Faith Mountain manufactured approximately 20 percent of the merchandise it sold, it could personalize and customize products to individual customer needs. Cheri and Martin stressed the importance of doing a quality job in all aspects of the company, from producing the catalog through taking, packing, and shipping an order. Incentive plans for both warehouse and customer service employees rewarded error-free performance. Even more important, however, the Woodards believed their own dedication to quality in all phases of the company resulted in a highly motivated staff who took great pride in their jobs. The pride and quality, they believed, would show through to customers and make them believe they were dealing with a first-class organization.

Service   Finally, Faith Mountain set for itself the goal of quality customer service unsurpassed in the mail-order industry. The company had a toll-free telephone number for placing orders and for customer service inquiries and complaints. Its telephone system, a Siemens 20/40, could support 20 incoming lines and 40 phone sets and had automatic call distribution features and activity reporting capability. Order entry and product inquiry were handled on an ADDS minicomputer with the on-line Nashbar QOP system. Designed by a mail-order bicycle company, the system allowed for speedy order placement and easy access to product reference guides, so operators could answer questions with the customer still on the phone.

The phones in Sperryville were staffed from 8 A.M. to 8:30 P.M. seven days a week. After 8:30 P.M., calls were switched to a vendor who followed Faith Mountain protocol, took orders, and sent completed order forms to Sperryville by Federal Express the next morning. The average Faith Mountain order was about $75. Operators answered calls, "Faith Mountain; this is [first name]. May I help you?" They would place orders directly on the system, and if callers wanted customer service, they would transfer the call to the customer service supervisor on duty. The system was designed to answer 90 percent of all customer inquiries within two minutes, and customer service supervisors were authorized to do whatever was necessary to keep a customer happy.

From their research and experience in the industry, the Woodards knew the biggest obstacle to catalog shopping was the question of what to do with an order if the customer didn't like it. In such cases, after a customer service supervisor had talked with the customer, and if the customer was still dissatisfied, Faith Mountain would send United Parcel Service to the customer's home to retrieve the order at company expense. This policy was extremely rare in the industry and cost Faith Mountain approximately $8,000 in 1991. Other customer service policies included guaranteed lowest prices, optional Federal Express delivery, and extremely quick shipping from receipt of the order. Faith Mountain also enclosed coupons and the company history with every order.

The Faith Mountain Retail Store Strategy

Although small in comparison to the catalog business, Faith Mountain's retail store revenues totaled almost $300,000 in fiscal year 1991. The store was run by a full-time manager, Margie Ellis. She ordered merchandise for the store, hired, scheduled, and supervised the sales help, and made all the operating decisions at the store. The store employed two part-time women and three part-time high school girls, who worked on weekends. The store was open from 10 A.M. to 6 P.M. seven days a week.

The store had about 2,000 square feet of selling space on two floors. Its merchandise reflected the same product lines featured in the catalog, but not all items from the catalog were sold in the store, and about 20 percent of the store merchandise was not offered in the catalog. (There was some storage space in an attic and in a back room/office that the store manager rarely used.)

Customers walked in the front door of a very old house filled with antiques and the smell of herbs. The front room of the store was the "food room," with the herbs and oils, potpourri, and jewelry. Straight ahead to the right was the breezeway, where collectibles and dolls were kept. In the back and side room, customers found clothes, books, lotions, and products made in Virginia. Upstairs were two rooms—a year-round Christmas room and a room for children's products. One of the outbuildings on the property was used as an outlet for catalog overstocks, which were sold at a slightly lower price.

By 1991, the store had become an important part of the town. Where once Faith Mountain had hoped to capitalize on traffic drawn to the area, it had become a draw in its own right, and other businesses hoped to grow from the Faith Mountain traffic. Local people shopped at Faith Mountain, too. Margie Ellis described the store's community role in this way:

> There are lots of tourists in the fall—the peak weekend is in October, and then people might grumble a bit about the traffic, but there is no real resentment. This store is very important to the town. This is one of the few stores in the area you can *count on* being open. That doesn't mean much in some areas, but here it means a lot. A lot of local people know about it, depend on it for birthday presents, for clothes, for herbs.
>
> You know, in terms of volume or of profit margin, those herbs are nothing. I had moved them out of the front room back into the kitchen, and you should have seen the customers react! "How could you move them to the kitchen? You can't do that!" So now we know: in the front room we have to have the herbs.
>
> The biggest sellers are the clothes and gifts. For the most part, the clothes are bought by local people. Busy tourists coming through won't buy an outfit; they might buy a sweatshirt. For the local people to get this quality apparel, they would have to drive to a mall in Culpeper, or to Manassas, and they *do not* want to drive in northern Virginia traffic.

The Woodards believed the store served another valuable but intangible purpose—it gave Faith Mountain credibility and integrity. Customers who would not buy from the company by mail were able to drive to the store and see and touch products before ordering them; traffic in the store always surged after a catalog mailing. The location of the store—in Sperryville, in Rappahannock County, Virginia, at the foot of the Blue Ridge Mountains—gave an aura of authenticity to the products offered in the catalog. Being able to give directions to the store and to invite customers to visit was part of the company's image as a good, hardworking, honest family business. Many customers arrived and asked people to point out which of the Blue Ridge peaks was "Faith Mountain."

In September 1991, Margie Ellis and Martin Woodard developed the first annual budget for the retail store. Because the previous year had been so good, but the economy was not strong, they agreed to set the previous year's numbers

EXHIBIT 5   **Faith Mountain Company's Store Budget, 1992 Fiscal Year**

	First Quarter	Second Quarter	Third Quarter	Fourth Quarter	Total
Sales	$79,861	$99,284	$ 41,494	$77,059	$297,698
Cost of goods sold	35,770	44,469	18,586	34,515	133,340
Gross profit	44,091	54,815	22,908	42,544	164,358
Promotional costs:					
Retail advertising	1,650	2,300	1,650	1,500	7,100
Special events	250	2,000	200	1,400	3,850
Catalog costs	14,434	15,378	8,815	7,926	46,553
Total	16,334	19,678	10,665	10,826	57,503
Operating expense	4,114	6,303	3,275	2,481	16,173
General and administrative	18,653	21,741	20,114	20,148	80,656
Net income	$ 4,990	$ 7,093	$(11,146)	$ 9,089	$ 10,026

for the current year's targets. Margie reported directly to Cheri, but met monthly with Martin to review progress against the budget. Summary budget data appear in Exhibit 5.

THE MAIL-ORDER INDUSTRY

The Market in 1990

The July 1991 issue of *Direct Marketing* magazine reported highlights of the *1990 Guide to Mail Order Sales*, the 10th annual study by Arnold Fishman of Marketing Logistics. According to that study, the total mail-order sales in the United States in 1990 topped $200 billion, with consumer mail order at $98.2 billion, business mail order at $53.4 billion, and charitable contributions by mail at $49 billion. The consumer mail-order total was further defined as follows: $40.7 billion on services, $44.5 billion on products from specialty merchandisers, and $13 billion on products from general merchandisers.

According the the Fishman study, total mail-order sales for 1990 reflected 10.1 percent of general merchandise sales, 3.2 percent of retail sales, 2.1 percent of consumer services, and 1.8 percent of gross national product for the year. The following data on growth in the industry are excerpted from the same study:

- Overall growth for consumer mail order in 1990 is between 4 and 8 percent in money (current dollar) terms and –1 percent to +3 percent in real (adjusted for inflation) terms, somewhat higher than growth in overall retail or in department store chain sales.
- Among specific sales segments, growth was above average for sportswear (apparel), videocassettes (audio/video), libraries and schools supplies (business specialties), television and videotex (general merchandising), drugs/vitamins and physical fitness (health).
- Growth was below average for footwear (apparel), auto clubs, automotive/aviation, full line business supplies, consumer electronics

EXHIBIT 6   U.S. Mail Order Sales Growth, 1981–90

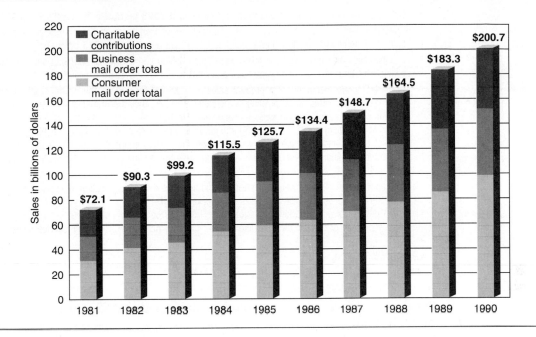

products, continuity cosmetics, crafts, catalog retailers (general merchandise), low end gifts, hardware/tools, fashion jewelry, photofinishing, photographic equipment, and apparel-oriented sporting goods.

- Among individual companies, major size companies with 20 percent growth included American Association of Retired Persons Insurance, Cabela's, Compu-Serve, J. Crew, Current Domestications, Frederick's, Hamilton Mint, Home Shopping Network, International Masters Publishers, Medco Containment, Prodigy, Tweeds, United Services Automobile Association, and Viking Office Products.
- Limited growth was experienced by L.L. Bean, Cincinnati Microwave, Collector's Guild, Cosmetique, GRI, Horchow, Quill, Reliable, Royal Silk, Sears, Roebuck & Company, Shopsmith, and Warshawsky.

Additional data from the *1990 Guide to Mail Order Sales* excerpted from the *Direct Marketing* article appear as Exhibits 6 through 8.

Trends for the Future

Over 100 years ago, Sears, Roebuck & Company set the industry standard for general merchandise marketing through catalogs. As Exhibit 6 shows, the continuing growth through the 1980s enticed many entrepreneurs to enter the industry. In addition, several retailers had responded to the mail-order threat by developing their own catalogs. In 1986, the U.S. Postal Service sent out 11.8 billion copies of 8,500 different catalogs. In the same year, the Direct Marketing

EXHIBIT 7   **Facts about the Mail-Order Catalog Business in the United States, 1990**

- On a per capita basis, Americans spent an average of $393 on mail-order purchases in 1990.
- Specialty mail-order vendors enjoy a substantially greater share of consumer mail-order product sales (77 percent) than do general merchandising mail-order vendors (23 percent).
- U.S. business mail-order sales in 1990 were $53.4 billion and charitable contributions were $45.9 billion. The total of U.S. mail order/sales and contributions was $200.3 billion.
- While U.S. consumer mail-order product sales may appear modest on the overall scale of gross national product, retail sales, or general merchandise sales, they are immense as a source of sales. Consumer mail-order product sales are equivalent to 82% of sales of the top 100 department stores ($70 billion), more than catalog showrooms, direct selling, and vending machines combined ($45.7 billion), and as much as any single consumer selling channel except mass general merchandisers and supermarkets. It is a leading consumer selling channel for specialty merchandise with prices under $1,000.
- U.S. consumer mail-order sales of products and services were $98.2 billion in 1990, $57.5 billion in products and $40.7 billion in services. This represents
    - 1.8 percent of gross national product.
    - 10.1 percent of general merchandise sales.
    - 3.2 percent of retail sales.
    - 2.1 percent of consumer service sales.

Source: *Direct Marketing*, July 1991.

Association surveyed these catalogers and found that 93 percent were increasing their mailings.

Some marketers argued the catalog industry was peaking. One 1984 study pointed to the fact that although the number of catalogs issued in the United States increased 68 percent in 1983, the customer base increased only 24 percent. It seemed unlikely that this customer group would increase its consumption sufficiently to support the additional catalogs entering the market and sustain the growth rates of current catalog companies.[1] In addition, a 1983 Stone-Adler market study had found that 43 percent of all U.S. households were against catalogs. Some experts expected this number to increase as mail-order companies continued to trade customer lists and a select number of people received an inordinate number of catalogs.

On the other hand, population projections for the United States (Exhibit 9) seemed to support those who predicted continued strong growth in the industry. Although many older people were not accustomed to credit card use, today's younger generations have been exposed to credit cards all their lives. As these generations grow older and their income increases, the ease of making credit card purchases through the mail would certainly improve the prospects of catalog purchasing. A 1989 study reported that 7 out of 10 families had no adult buyer home during the day to go shopping.[2] Jay Walker, chairman of Catalog Media Corporations, stated:

> Only 5 percent of retail sales are through catalogs. Now it is hard for you to tell me that a channel is mature at 5 percent penetration, when the underlying demographics of the population at large favor the channel. More working

---

[1]Maggie McComas, "Catalog Fallout," *Fortune*, January 20, 1986, pp. 63–64.
[2]Rayna Skolnik, "Selling Via Catalog," *Stores*, October 1989, pp. 47–50.

EXHIBIT 8   **Specialty Vendors of Consumer Products**

	Sales (Millions)	Number of Vendors	Percent of Sales
Animal care	$ 70	120	0
Apparel	4,250	570	10
Audio/video	630	370	1
Automotive aviation	620	540	1
Books	2,760	—	6
Collectibles	1,690	520	4
Consumer electronics/science	710	100	2
Cosmetic/toiletries	450	110	1
Crafts	840	780	2
Food	1,310	940	3
Gardening	850	700	2
Gifts	2,020	630	5
Hardware/tools	530	240	1
Health products	2,480	410	6
Home construction	310	490	1
Housewares	1,220	820	3
Jewelry	500	150	1
Magazines	6,020	5,000	14
Multiproducts	7,410	340	17
Newspapers	3,020	1,700	7
Photographic products	410	90	1
Records	780	—	2
Sporting goods	3,460	1,140	8
Stationery	440	80	1
Tobacco	30	30	0
Toys/games/children's products	710	380	2
Computer software	650	60+	1
Computer hardware	350	100+	1
Total	$44,520	16,410+	100%

Consumer products specialty vendor sales segments (vendors classified by major product category) fall into three tiers:

Top Size ($1 Billion+)	Middle Size ($.5 Billion–$1 Billion)	Moderate Size (Less Than $.5 Billion)
Multiproducts, gifts, collectibles, magazines, books, apparel, food, newspapers, housewares, health, sporting goods	Automotive/aviation, gardening, children's products, toys/games, records, computer software, jewelry, hardware/tools, audio/video, consumer electronics/science, crafts	Cosmetics/toiletries, computer hardware, stationery, tobacco, photographic products, home construction

Excluding books, magazines, newspapers, computer software, computer hardware and records, 9,520 businesses account for $30.9 billion in sales, or an average of $3.25 million in sales per business.

Source: *Direct Marketing*, July 1991.

women, less time, more credit cards, 800 numbers—all of these things favor the catalog industry continuing as a major growth trend.[3]

---

[3]Janice Steinberg, "Special Report: Direct Marketing," *Advertising Age*, October 26, 1987, pp. 51–51G.

EXHIBIT 9   **Actual and Projected Population of the United States, 1990, 1995, and 2000**

Male (in thousands)	1990	1995	2000
Under 5	9,426	9,118	8,661
5–17	23,377	24,787	25,027
18–24	13,216	12,290	12,770
25–34	22,078	20,579	18,662
35–44	18,785	21,104	21,945
45–54	12,406	15,292	18,296
55–64	10,103	10,149	11,557
65–74	8,171	8,476	8,242
Over 74	4,681	5,326	6,032
Total	122,243	127,121	131,192

Female (in thousands)	1990	1995	2000
Under 5	8,982	8,681	8,237
5–17	22,253	23,587	23,788
18–24	12,924	11,991	12,461
25–34	21,848	20,384	18,487
35–44	19,112	21,233	21,966
45–54	13,081	16,005	18,927
55–64	11,260	11,175	12,601
65–74	10,201	10,454	10,001
Over 74	8,505	9,507	10,607
Total	128,166	133,017	137,075

Total (in thousands)	1990	1995	2000
Under 5	18,408	17,799	16,898
5–17	45,630	48,374	48,815
18–24	26,140	24,281	25,231
25–34	43,926	40,963	37,149
35–44	37,897	42,337	43,911
45–54	25,487	31,297	37,223
55–64	21,363	21,324	24,158
65–74	18,372	18,930	18,243
Over 74	13,186	14,833	16,639
Total	250,409	260,138	268,267

"Specialogs"   One significant trend in the industry was the increasing use of "specialogs"—catalogs focused on a particular market segment. During the 1980s, many large, general merchandise catalog companies like Alden's and Montgomery Ward went out of business. In 1987 J.C. Penney began to provide catalogs targeted at petite women, extra-size women, tall women, big and tall men, nurses, brides, and other special groups. Advanced computer technology allows companies to identify, target, and track the purchases of their customers and then to develop special catalogs for groups sharing key characteristics. Then, highly sophisticated printing technology permits companies to prepare customized catalogs for particular clients. Some analysts predicted it would soon be common—and cost effective—for a mail-order company to send two different catalogs to neighboring households, depending on their past purchasing patterns.[4]

Credit Card Competition Increased competition between Visa USA and MasterCard for the mail-order market in 1991 resulted in new inducements to consumers who shop by mail. For example, Visa announced in June it would be offering a "Visa Catalog Collection": Consumers would be offered 40 catalogs at a nominal fee, and those who ordered catalogs through Visa would receive certificates good for up to 20 percent off their purchases. In response, MasterCard announced its "Forests for Our Future" green marketing approach: trees would be planted in the consumer's name for merchandise bought through certain catalogs. This promotion was designed to downplay the image of catalogers as tree killers. In essence, both companies were to provide free advertising for catalog companies, and the support of these two financial giants would likely boost sales.[5]

Government Regulations Catalogs remained vulnerable to the increasing costs of paper and postage. According to the *1990 Guide to Mail Order Sales*, a 1989 postage rate increase for third-class mail was still being felt in 1990. In addition, recent rulings from the Federal Trade Commission had increased legal risks for catalog companies. Previously, the FTC had held that manufacturers were liable for false product claims; in 1990, the FTC shifted that responsibility to the mail-order firms.[6]

On another front, mail-order firms awaited a decision from the U.S. Supreme Court concerning state taxes on mail-order goods. Targeting mail-order firms in particular, the state of North Dakota was attempting to collect sales taxes from any company that "regularly and continuously" solicited business in the state. Current practice, established by a 1967 Supreme Court case (*National Bellas Hess, Inc.* v. *Department of Revenue, 386 U.S. 753*), prohibited states from collecting taxes on companies without a physical presence in the state. The Direct Marketing Association and many mail-order firms had filed briefs arguing against the North Dakota standard, citing the excessive administrative burden such a change would impose on them. Oral arguments were scheduled for January 22, 1992.

Catalog Company Failures Even in a growing market, mail-order firms failed. A 1984 study of 35 failed catalog companies cited the following key contributing factors:

- Lack of market research; failure to evaluate the market and offer desired goods.
- Overusage of popular mailing lists.

---

[4]Ibid.

[5]Alison Fahey, "Credit Cards Tie in with Catalogs," *Advertising Age*, June 3, 1991. p. 50.

[6]Laurie Freeman and Janet Meyers, "FTC Gets Tough on Catalog Claims," *Advertising Age*, November 12, 1990, p. 73.

- Undercapitalization.
- Oversaturated marketplace.[7]

Most industry experts pointed to merchandise selection as the *sine qua non* of success in the mail-order business. Harold Schwartz, president of Hanover House Industries, noted that you cannot "fall in love with your catalog."[8] Mail-order firms had to be objective in determining what works and then be able to change their catalogs to meet new demands and to exit saturated markets.

THE FUTURE OF THE FAITH MOUNTAIN COMPANY

Confident that fundamental market forces were very positive for their company, Cheri and Martin Woodard believed the key strategic question for Faith Mountain was how to grow.

Overall Company Goals

The Faith Mountain Company intended to establish itself as the industry leader in quality, high-value gifts, apparel, and home accessories. To that end, top management had set for itself the overall goal of $25 million in annual sales by 1995, with $10 million from the Faith Mountain catalog, $5 million from the retail division, and an additional $10 million from the acquisition or development of another catalog company. The Woodards intended to achieve these targets and at the same time accomplish the following objectives:

- Grow as quickly as possible, yet maintain profitability.
- Grow at a rate that does not hurt product quality and customer service.
- Aggressively develop new products and exclusive vendor relationships.
- Stay close to our customers through surveys, the store, and personal contact.
- Provide the best quality and value in unique and unusual products.
- Be the best company to do business with.
- Provide a work environment that allows employees personal and professional growth, to insure the highest levels of motivation and knowledge among our people, and therefore the highest level of quality in all aspects of the company.

Growth for the Faith Mountain Catalog

Performance projections for the Faith Mountain catalog through 1995 appear in Exhibits 10 and 11. Martin estimated capital expenditures of $350,000 to $400,000 would be needed to increase catalog sales to $10 million.

The typical percentage breakdown of a catalog company's income statement in 1991 was as follows:

---

[7]New York University Advanced Catalog Seminar, "Successes and Failures Examined by Catalog Leaders," *Direct Marketing*, July 1984, pp. 98–101.
[8]Ibid.

EXHIBIT 10   Catalog Sales Forecast for Faith Mountain Company, Fiscal Years 1991–95

Season	Source of Names for Catalog Mailings	Quantity of Catalogs Mailed	Projected Sales
Fall 90	Rented lists	825,000	$ 990,000
	In-house	242,600	477,922
Holiday 90	Rented lists	980,000	1,244,600
	In-house	267,300	526,581
Spring 91	Rented lists	637,000	713,440
	In-house	295,750	553,052
Summer 91	Rented lists	300,000	276,000
	In-house	200,000	200,000
Totals	Rented lists	2,742,000	$ 3,224,000
	In-house	1,005,650	$ 1,757,555
1991 Total		3,747,650	$ 4,981,595
Fall 91	Rented lists	990,000	$ 1,188,000
	In-house	322,095	653,852
Holiday 91	Rented lists	1,080,000	1,371,600
	In-house	351,500	713,545
Spring 92	Rented lists	765,000	856,800
	In-house	385,500	744,015
Summer 92	Rented lists	360,000	331,200
	In-house	300,000	318,000
Totals	Rented lists	3,195,000	$ 3,747,600
	In-house	1,359,095	$ 2,429,412
1992 Total		4,554,095	$ 6,177,012
Fall 92	Rented lists	1,200,000	$ 1,584,000
	In-house	414,260	969,369
Holiday 92	Rented lists	1,300,000	1,820,000
	In-house	449,660	1,052,204
Spring 93	Rented lists	920,000	1,030,400
	In-house	490,560	995,836
Summer 93	Rented lists	300,000	276,00
	In-house	300,000	330,000
Totals	Rented lists	3,720,000	$ 4,710,400
	In-house	1,654,480	$ 3,347,409
1993 Total		5,374,480	$ 8,057,809

Net sales	100%
Cost of goods sold	45%
Gross margin	55%
Promotional costs	30%
Operating expenses	19%
Net profit	6%
Other income	1–3%

The relationship between net sales and promotional costs was the most important dynamic in the catalog business. Promotional costs include design and layout of the catalog, photography, color separations, printing and mailing, postage, list rental, and associated computer costs. Based on his experience,

EXHIBIT 10   *(concluded)*

Season	Source of Names for Catalog Mailings	Quantity of Catalogs Mailed	Projected Sales
Fall 93	Rented lists	1,400,000	$ 1,848,000
	In-house	519,000	1,245,600
Holiday 93	Rented lists	1,500,000	2,100,000
	In-house	566,400	1,359,360
Spring 94	Rented lists	1,020,000	1,142,400
	In-house	620,200	1,290,016
Summer 94	Rented lists	300,000	276,000
	In-house	450,000	513,000
Totals	Rented lists	4,220,000	$ 5,366,400
	In-house	2,155,600	$ 4,407,976
1994 Total		6,375,600	$ 9,774,376
Fall 94	Rented lists	1,400,000	$ 1,848,000
	In-house	651,000	1,562,400
Holiday 94	Rented lists	1,500,000	2,100,000
	In-house	698,286	1,675,887
Spring 95	Rented lists	1,020,000	1,142,400
	In-house	742,086	1,543,539
Summer 95	Rented lists	300,000	276,000
	In-house	500,000	570,000
Totals	Rented lists	4,220,000	$ 5,366,400
	In-house	2,591,372	$ 5,351,826
1995 Total		6,811,372	$10,718,226

Martin worked by rule of thumb requiring that increases in promotional costs increase sales by more than three times the additional cost.

Increasing the "House List"   Growth in the mail-order catalog industry was fueled by the company's customer list. An industry rule of thumb required a catalog company to mail 1,250,000 catalogs four times a year to reach critical mass and attain profitability. Accordingly, each mail-order company sought to build its "house list"—names and addresses of customers who had actually purchased product(s) from the catalog. Most smaller companies supplemented their house list by renting (for one-time use) outside lists, the house lists of other companies (through a broker), at an average price of $110 per thousand names. Any person from the rented list who purchased a product automatically went on the house list. Even the best outside list, however, was not as responsive to a mailing as the company's house list. When measured on a dollar-income-per-catalog-mailed basis, the response of the house list would be three to four times greater than any outside list.

The larger the house list, the less the company needed to rent other lists. Companies with larger lists exchange lists with each other rather than pay each other rental fees. Accordingly, as the house list grows, promotional costs decrease as net sales increase. (In addition, the company earns additional money from the rental of its own house list; in fiscal year 1991, Faith Mountain earned $130,000 in this way.)

The most marketable segment of any list was the group who had purchased product(s) within the previous six months. A key component of Faith Moun-

EXHIBIT 11   **Projected Income Statements, the Faith Mountain Company, Fiscal Years 1992–95**

	1992		1993		1994		1995	
	$	%	$	%	$	%	$	%
Gross sales	$6,433,012	107.5	$8,325,809	107.5	$10,056,616	107.5	$11,014,578	107.5
Returns and allowances	482,476	7.5	624,436	7.5	754,246	7.5	826,093	7.5
Net sales	5,950,536	100.0	7,701,373	100.0	9,302,370	100.0	10,188,485	100.0
Cost of goods sold	2,814,604	47.3	3,645,587	47.3	4,390,719	47.2	4,798,776	47.1
Gross profit	3,135,932	52.7	4,055,786	52.7	4,911,651	52.8	5,389,709	52.9
Promotional costs	1,951,776	32.8	2,502,946	32.5	2,995,363	32.2	3,250,127	31.9
Operating expense	720,015	12.1	931,866	12.1	1,125,587	12.1	1,232,807	12.1
General & administrative	410,000	6.9	475,000	6.2	565,000	6.1	615,000	6.0
Operating income	54,141	0.9	145,974	1.9	225,701	2.4	291,775	2.7
Other income	230,000	3.9	250,000	3.2	270,000	2.9	310,000	3.0
Net income	$ 284,141	4.8	$ 395,974	5.1	$ 495,701	5.3	$ 601,775	5.9

Includes catalog and the Sperryville retail store.

tain's growth strategy was to increase its six-month buyer list to 60,000 names. Martin explained the logic:

> We regularly exchange lists with approximately 15 other catalog companies. Assuming a mailing of 1 million catalogs and an entire house list of 150,000 names, we need to use 850,000 names from these other companies. A six-month buyer list of 56,700 names would allow us to incur no rental fees (850,000 names divided by 15 companies equals 56,700 names).
>
> Our six-month buyers typically respond with $4 in sales for every catalog mailed versus the outside response of approximately $1.10 per catalog mailed. In the most recent catalog promotion, we had approximately 20,000 six-month buyers. If this segment were tripled, we would see approximately $50,000 in savings due to exchanging lists rather than renting and $120,000 in increased sales from the larger number of responsive buyers. Assuming four such catalog promotions per year, Faith Mountain would realize $200,000 in savings and $480,000 in increased sales solely from the larger six-month-buyer house list.
>
> To increase the buyer list, we will have to increase the catalog circulation to approximately 7 million every 12 months. Working with our list brokers, we can develop mail plans—testing list segments by monitoring coded responses—to raise the rate of response and reduce the number of catalogs required for circulation.

Moving to Private-Label Sportswear   A second strategy for growth in the Faith Mountain catalog was to change the merchandise mix, particularly in the apparel lines, to reflect half Faith Mountain designs, with private labels, and half items from better manufacturers, to retain the quality brand name recognition. Martin gave an example of the benefits of this strategy:

> In general, the apparel industry has *no* flexibility on price, but smaller companies will do lots of deals if you are willing to commit to large quantities. For example, a vest: we paid $24 each and sold a *bunch*—somewhere between 750 and 1,000 of them—in last year's catalog for $49. The company we bought them from went out of business this year, taken down when the Sporting Life catalog went under. So Cheri called this guy, and he set her up with the factory in China where he

had bought them. Now they have our own label, and they cost us $12.50. It's not easy to do that—you have to take a substantial position—but on this vest, we were willing to, due to last year's sales.

Growth through Acquisition of Another Catalog

Demand for the gifts, home accessories, and apparel carried in the Faith Mountain catalog was seasonal. There were two peaks in the sales calendar: the first began in September and dropped off in late December, and the second began in January and ended in February. Although the company did significant business in the other months, this seasonality caused rapid shifts in demand on the company's staff and system capabilities and depressed overall operating earnings.

Cheri and Martin knew they could make more efficient use of company facilities, systems, and human resources if they could acquire or develop another business countercyclical to the existing catalog. Fixed costs would be amortized over a larger and more constant flow of business. Acquiring another catalog would be the quickest and safest method to realize these efficiencies. They believed the ideal acquisition would offer small, easy-to-handle products, whose sales would peak in the first half of the year.

Growth in the Retail Division

In 1991, the retail division consisted of the one original store on Main Street in Sperryville, but Cheri and Martin had discussed opening additional retail outlets. Martin favored active exploration of possible sites. Referring to Williams Sonoma, Eddie Bauer, The Sharper Image, and other retailers that had taken this route, he stressed the synergy between the catalog and retail outlets, especially as the mailings continued to increase. Cheri was slightly less sanguine about opening additional stores. Margie Ellis, the store manager in Sperryville, also had doubts:

> This store was really the birthplace of the company—here since 1790, here in the Civil War, right by the Blue Ridge Mountains—you can't re-create that. You can buy an old house somewhere and put herbs in it, but that won't be Faith Mountain.

Based on casual discussions with real estate specialists, the Woodards estimated the cost of building out a "high-end" store (gutting the inside) at approximately $18 a square foot. The average space in a shopping center mall was 1,600 to 2,000 square feet. Simply taking over an existing space and doing minor leasehold improvements might cost as little as $3,000, however; and in the 1991 market, many of these costs could be negotiated with landlords. For example, the Woodards had heard of one outlet chain that had recently spent $18,000 to open a store in Norfolk, Virginia, and the landlord reimbursed them $15,000.

Managing Projected Growth: Issues for Management

Financial Implications   The continuing economic recession in late 1991 seemed to have little effect on Faith Mountain sales, but in dealings with suppliers, Faith Mountain could feel the economic pinch. As Martin put it,

Companies that used to offer terms of 75 to 90 days now insist on 30 days net, but we still try to negotiate terms. It's really hard to get anyone to listen to you in the apparel industry—you have to be *golden* to get those guys to listen. The name of the game for survival in this business is *credit rating*. We can't be turned in, we can't be late, we can't be delinquent.

Achieving the sales goals would require additional capital, but it was not clear where this capital would be best obtained. In November 1991, Sovran Bank increased the company's line of credit to $500,000. To increase its equity capital, in the spring of 1991, the company had offered 1,500 shares and sold 1,150. The Woodard family retained 55 percent interest in the company, but Prime Capital Group, a venture capital firm, was now the largest shareholder outside the family. Cheri and Martin were aware that outside shareholders would place different pressures on them; already Martin sensed some pressure from stockholders to start paying dividends. Exhibit 12 describes the company's board of directors.

Support Systems Implications   Faith Mountain's current hardware configuration was capable of supporting 96 terminals with two simple upgrades—an additional 380 megabyte disc drive and a 4 megabyte RAM unit. The upgrade cost was $28,319 and was scheduled to occur in 1992. Additional workstations were available for $400. With these upgrades, the computer system could support projected growth through 1995. It appeared the Siemens phone system would be adequate through 1993. Finally, with the addition of a mezzanine level and with some new equipment and technical improvements in the warehouse, the current building would also support the projected $10 million in catalog sales by 1995.

Human Resources Implications   Cheri and Martin agreed that one of the greatest challenges facing Faith Mountain was in hiring, training, and managing the new people: operators, customer service supervisors, buyers, warehouse people, and managers necessary to achieve their goals. Even now, the two knew they were working at capacity. Martin described the situation this way:

> We need to identify the key positions and put good people in them. There are lots of little jobs that go begging now, but little things become much more important with size—if you can get .5 percent of sales with X change, that's a lot more significant at $10 million than at $500,000 in sales. For example, that might pay a salary—that person could add to the bottom line *and* carry his or her own weight. You have to think about who, and when, and how much more we can do of this before we can't do any more of it.
>
> I have people reporting to me now, but I still have a tendency to tell them what I want them to do and then expect them to go do it. Cheri has to tell people who work for me that they need to be self-starters, motivated people. I want to be able to tell them, "Go to the show and find me stuff that will sell"—not "Go find me six mugs and four blankets."

Cheri took her responsibility for all human resources matters very seriously. She had established the company's employee evaluation/self-evaluation process, initiated the training program, and prepared the company handbook of personnel policies. In 1991, she had started a new program for ongoing education and training through a local community college, and at year-end she was developing the company's first pension plan and an employee stock option

EXHIBIT 12   **Board of Directors and Supporting Professional Services**

Faith Mountain Board of Directors

Mr. Peter Elliman, a partner in Prime Capital, a private venture capital fund in Warrenton, Virginia, brought over 25 years of financial and corporate development experience to the board.

Mr. Don Press, past director of the Smithsonian Museum Gift Catalog, currently a catalog consultant, had helped the Woodards since 1984.

Ms. Joan Litle, a catalog consultant specializing in the creative and merchandising aspects of the industry.

Mr. James Jamieson, a member of the board of directors of several companies, had extensive experience in corporate finance and investment banking.

Ms. Linda Dietel, a local community activist with many business and community contacts.

Ms. Cheri Woodard, president of Faith Mountain.

Mr. Martin Woodard, secretary/treasurer of Faith Mountain.

Supporting Professional Services

Legal: Bill Sharp, senior partner of Kates and Sharp, in Front Royal, Virginia, sat in on all board meetings.

Accounting: Gary Lee, of Yount, Hyde and Barbour in Winchester, Virginia, assisted in monthly accounting and performed a year-end financial review.

Banking: Marathon Bank in Stephens City, Virginia, held company accounts in connection with the SBA loan, and Sovran Bank in Charlottesville, Virginia, extended the company a $500,000 line of credit.

Advertising: Forgit & White of New Hampshire designed the catalog, and Faith Mountain operated an in-house advertising agency named Telesis.

Printing: R.R. Donnelley, the largest commercial printer in the world, had printed the company's catalogs since 1988.

program. At the same time, however, she had misgivings about continuing to handle all aspects of human resource management as the company grew. She said:

> For a long time, people answered only to me—Martin didn't want to deal with them. Now he has people who report to him. There's a changing orientation now to *us*, not just to *me*. Martin made me the president. He said, "You're so good with people, with public relations—you be the figurehead." So *Working Woman* did a feature story on me, and there is just my picture in the catalog—we're selling to women, and he said they would relate better to me. And I've grown into that role, and now I like it, provided he gets the recognition he deserves in public— and that's *my* job.
>
> Martin is more the gambler, more of a risk taker, a visionary, while I'm more of a people person—I run the business; I see that the orders go out the door; I manage the order flow. But as we get ready to add more positions—add more people—I ask myself, what about initiation and indoctrination? I can't train them all—the management people need to be trained, too. How do you get that management time?

The Woodards had had their first serious personnel problem in 1991. In January 1991, they had hired an assistant buyer to work for the merchandising manager. In late August, they had to fire her. Martin explained:

> It just didn't work out. She was not working as hard as what we were used to, and she was more of a drain on people's time than a help. It wasn't clear to this person who her boss was—I should have told Kim, "Look, this is your assistant,

you tell her what to do," but she didn't want to have Kim for a boss, either. We also couldn't pay her what she thought she was worth—and even then what we did pay was too close to Kim's salary, and Kim wasn't happy about that because she was doing *far more*.

So we sat down with her, both Cheri and I, after three months, and we said we were having troubles. We talked things through with her, had her sign papers acknowledging the evaluation, and then we told Kim, "Look, you have to be the boss." Three months later, this person still wasn't coming around. We sat down with her again then and told her she had three more months, and if she hadn't improved by the end of October she'd have to leave. One month later I said, "Look, this isn't working, it's never going to work, let's get rid of her. We don't have that many people here, we might as well have the best." It was clear she was never going to be the best. We gave her four months' severance pay—so she ended up with a year's salary for eight months of work.

As Cheri and Martin considered adding staff in the company, Cheri emphasized the importance of strong human resources systems to train and support the new hires, while he stressed simply hiring the right people. They talked frequently about hiring an operations manager or a marketing manager to handle order taking, data processing, the warehouse, and human resources, including hiring, compensation, education, and morale. Cheri knew she would find it hard to give up responsibility for those areas. Martin described the requirements for such a person:

> They'd have to come in and work hard and fast. They'd have to have the entrepreneurial spirit and be willing to get out there and pack boxes with us on Saturdays, get their hands dirty. And they'd have to be willing to work for nothing, move out here in the middle of nowhere, and have an office in a corner in a warehouse.

Personal Implications   As they considered their own futures with Faith Mountain, both Martin and Cheri realized the projected growth of their business would have significant implications on their own lives. Martin described their work/family life together:

> I don't know what's work and what's not. We work a lot—we're in the building from 8 A.M. to 7 P.M. and on Saturday and Sunday. It's unusual for us to take an entire day off. Now that our son is away from home, half of our home conversation is about work. Who should we keep when we have to lay off the seasonal phone operators after Christmas? Should we do X or Y?
>
> Every now and then, Cheri and I take off an entire day, not coming in. And we try to take an extra day on business trips. And two times a year we get away for four to six days.
>
> In the long run, I'll still be involved with the business, but I'd like something without so much stress—there are times when cash is tight, people call and ask why they can't be paid right now—I'd like to avoid those pressures. I'd like to not be so hands-on, to be able to step back and know that the wheels won't fall off the wagon. We need some cushions, though—so we can ride through hard times. Right now we don't have the cushion. There is no margin for error, no room for major mistakes.
>
> I enjoy all this on a theoretical level, though. There's something about keeping score. What are your greatest strengths? What are your weaknesses? Adults can compete in the business world—that appeals to me—there's something about keeping score.

For her part, Cheri had many questions about the future.

> I see a goal for the business as making us a life—a lifestyle better than our parents'. But money is now what drives us. We want to avoid worries and be comfortable. But if we wanted money, we wouldn't have settled in Rappahannock County.
>
> What I really like is growing a business and feeling like I can make a difference in the lives of our employees and the lives of our customers. The challenge to me is building a corporate structure that allows the individual to excel and yet be part of the team. If we get very large, will we be able to have the same esprit de corps?

TURNER BROADCASTING SYSTEM IN 1992*

Arthur A. Thompson, Jr., University of Alabama

In this, the heyday of the large corporation that follows the morally and socially neutral judgments of committees of lawyers and accountants, Ted Turner is a character—in the best sense of that much misused word. He is in the great tradition of the individual entrepreneur who had a dream and backed it with his money and his sweat.

George N. Allen
Washington Journalism Review

Robert E. (Ted) Turner III was born in 1938 in Cincinnati, where his father, Ed, was in the outdoor advertising business. In the early 1940s, Ed Turner purchased a billboard firm in Savannah, Georgia, and moved his family there, where Ted got his first taste of the sea and sailing. Ted Turner's father was a stern, tough, self-made man who came from a poor, farm background in Mississippi. As a youngster, Ted was told to read a book every two days.[1] He was disciplined with a wire coat hanger. At 11, Ted was sent to McCallie Military School in Chattanooga, Tennessee; even though he professed dislike of the school, he completed six years at McCallie and graduated in the top 15 percent of his class as a company commander. (Later, he sent his own son, Robert Edward Turner IV, to McCallie.) At 17, he won the Tennessee State Debate Championship by redefining the basic question and taking an approach no one was prepared to debate.

During the summers of his high school years, he worked in the family business digging postholes and doing other manual labor tasks; one summer Turner worked a 40-hour week, was paid $50, and then was charged $25 a week to live at home. As Turner viewed it, "My father put the screws to me early. If he hadn't, I never would have survived. My father made me a man."

On graduation from McCallie, it was agreed by Turner and his father that he would enroll at Brown University in Providence, Rhode Island. When Turner informed his businessman father that he was planning to major in classics, his father wrote him a letter (which Ted had published in the school newspaper) describing Plato and Aristotle as "old bastards" and ending with the observation that "you are rapidly becoming a jackass, and the sooner you get out of that filthy atmosphere, the better. . . . You are in the hands of the Philistines, and dammit, I sent you there. I am sorry, Devotedly, Dad." Later Turner switched his major to economics.

Turner's college years at Brown were eventful. He shot a rifle from his dorm window and was thrown out of his fraternity for burning down its homecoming display. During his sophomore year, when his father refused to let him take a summer job at a Connecticut yacht club, he broke his agreement to refrain

---

*Prepared with the assistance of student researchers Miriam Aiken and Andrew White.

[1]Curry Kirkpatrick, "Going Real Strawwng," *Sports Illustrated*, October 14, 1977.

from drinking until he was 21 (for which he was to get a $5,000 reward), got drunk, and then got caught in a dorm room at Wheaton, a women's college in nearby Norton, Massachusetts; Brown University officials expelled him. Turner joined the Coast Guard for a short stint and then was readmitted to Brown. He became vice president of the debating union and commodore of the yacht club. But in his senior year he was expelled again when a Wheaton woman was caught in his dorm room.

Without a degree, Turner returned in 1960 to Georgia, where he went to work for his father and learned the business from the bottom up. His assigned tasks included posting the books and cutting weeds around billboards. A short time later, his father sent him to Macon to run the firm's branch office. In 1962, the elder Turner arranged to more than triple the size of his company and, with borrowed funds, he purchased billboard operations in Atlanta; Richmond, Virginia; and Roanoke, Virginia. Within a year, Turner's father had a breakdown and committed suicide.

THE FIRST CHALLENGE

Turner, at age 24, found himself in charge of a struggling business that was short of cash and $6 million in debt. The company's bankers advised Turner they didn't believe the business could survive under his unseasoned management and expressed reluctance at financing further operations. Turner was given an opportunity to sell out but refused and ended up persuading the lenders to stick with him a while. He then sold some assets to improve the company's cash position, arranged for some innovative financing, reworked contracts with customers, hired a sales force, and proceeded to turn things around. Within two years, the company was making its loan payments on time, and by 1969 the debt was paid off.

THE SECOND CHALLENGE

With the company now secure, Turner began to prospect for new growth opportunities. He believed the billboard business had only limited growth potential and was not challenging enough (it took only about half of his time to run things), so he elected to diversify into something more exciting. The first acquisitions were two radio stations in Chattanooga, a move that prompted Ted Turner to rename his company Turner Communications Corporation. Turner wanted to buy a radio outlet in Atlanta, but nothing attractive was available at the right price. In 1970, he settled for acquiring financially strapped WTCG-TV, Channel 17, a two-year-old, independent UHF station that was losing $50,000 per month trying to compete with Atlanta's three network affiliates, WSB-TV, WAGA-TV, and WXIA-TV. To finance the acquisition of Channel 17, Turner Communications Corporation went public, and its stock was traded in local over-the-counter markets; Ted Turner retained about 47 percent of the stock.

Turner's biggest problem in turning Channel 17's operations around was how to get Atlanta TV viewers to watch Channel 17 programs instead of the programs carried on the three major network stations. Writer Roger Vaughn, who knew Turner in college, has written two books about him, and has sailed with him, described Turner's efforts:

When Turner bought Channel 17, there was another independent in the Atlanta market. It belonged to United States Communications and was one of five stations in the country owned by that company, a subsidiary of the American Viscose conglomerate. It was a fact that the Atlanta market could not support two independents. "Ted knew this," one of the early Channel 17 employees says, "but I doubt if he realized how serious the situation was." Only one of the stations was going to survive, and it didn't look like it would be Channel 17, which was running a solid fifth out of five Atlanta stations.

The instability of the situation was reflected in the fact that in the first 22 months of Turner's ownership, the personnel of the station turned over twice. By the spring of 1971, every spare dollar Turner could find had been poured into the station. As Will Sanders recalls, the whole show was about to sink. Then overnight, without warning, the U.S. Communications station folded. It was a high stroke of luck for Turner, a lifeline for a drowning man.

In one day, Channel 17 went from fifth of five stations to fourth of four. As the only independent in Atlanta, the way ahead was clear for development, but the problems were still immense. UHF reception was terrible, for one thing. . . .

"I can remember going into an advertiser's office and asking him to buy time on Channel 17," Turner says. "The answer would be 'We don't buy UHF.' And I would tell them, 'Why not? It's coming, like FM radio. We're not asking you to pay for the future. We're just asking you to buy our audience at the same cost per thousand. Our audience isn't very big, but our viewers are way above the average viewers' mentality.'

"And they would say, 'How do you know that? How come!' and I would tell them, 'Because you have got to be smart to figure out how to tune in a UHF antenna in the first place. Dumb guys can't do it. Can you get Channel 17? No? Well, neither can I. We aren't smart enough. But my viewers are.'

"Then I would ask them if their commercials were in color. And they would say, 'Of course.' And I would tell them their commercials would stand out better on my station. Why? Because most of the programs were in black and white and when the commercial came on, it would have more shock value, it would catch the viewers' attention. They fell over. They hadn't thought of that.

"And finally I told them my audience was richer. Every set with UHF capability was color, which costs more. Don't you think that was a pretty good sales pitch?"

With the competition gone, Turner put more money into strengthening his signal. Then he got his second break. The Atlanta ABC affiliate was forced by the network to pick up the 6 P.M. news, which it had not been running. It is a television fact of life that roughly 25 percent of an audience will actively avoid the news. So Turner scheduled "Star Trek" at 6 P.M. and not only increased his rating at that hour but got a few more people acquainted with Channel 17's presence. In Turner's mind, a philosophy was beginning to take shape. As he told *Television/Radio Age* in 1974, "All three stations had big group-ownership money behind them. They all programmed pretty much alike. I felt the people of Atlanta were entitled to something different than a whole lot of police and crime shows with murders and rapes going on all over the place. I believe that people are tired of violence and psychological problems and all the negative things they see on TV every night."

Turner concentrated his energies on buying films, the titles of which he selected himself, and on composing a lineup of old shows that sounded like the sitcom hall of fame: "I Love Lucy," "Gilligan's Island," "Leave It to Beaver," "Petticoat Junction," "Father Knows Best," "Gomer Pyle," and "Andy Griffith." "We're essentially an escapist station," Turner announced to those who hadn't noticed. "As far as our news is concerned, we run the FCC minimum of forty minutes a day."

Having moved into the entertainment void left by ABC's commitment to news, Turner attacked the NBC affiliate (WSB-TV), Atlanta's number-one station. WSB had chosen not to air five network shows, which meant that those shows could be picked up by an independent in the area. Turner grabbed all five, and soon billboards (Turner's, of course) around Atlanta were announcing, "The NBC network moves to Channel 17," and listing the five shows.

"We didn't think we could take over as the number-one station in the market," Turner said at the time. "But we felt we could shake 'em up a bit, get 'em to think about us, let 'em know we were in the race." They were shook and started thinking. The move was splashed all over the newspapers, and if success could be measured in phone calls from NBC lawyers, it was a hit.

While WSB-TV was still fuming over its public embarrassment, Turner grabbed its rights to telecast Atlanta Braves games. At the time, the Braves were paying WSB to run 25 games a year. Turner made the Braves an offer they couldn't refuse, paying them $2.5 million for the TV rights to games for five years.

"The Braves games were the top-rated locally produced program in the Atlanta market," Gerry Hogan says. Hogan is general sales manager of Channel 17. He is a dapper, precise fellow with styled red hair and the office manner of a Park Avenue physician discussing a social disease of moderate seriousness. He left Chicago advertising in 1971 to take a chance with Turner.

"Signing the Braves did a lot for our image," Hogan says, "It changed our image from that of a kiddie station. It forced people to tune us in. We became a factor. Atlanta went from a three-station market plus WTCG to a four-station market. We were in it after the Braves signed with us."[2]

Atlanta-area residents were attracted by the new style of programming and began to tune in to Channel 17's programs more regularly. Viewers and advertising revenues increased steadily, and by 1972 Channel 17 had positive operating profits. While Channel 17 was still in the red, Turner acquired a second UHF station at a bankruptcy sale in Charlotte, North Carolina. It was purchased with Turner's personal funds because the directors of Turner Communications were not willing to risk corporate funds on the deal, given Channel 17's still unprofitable status and the high risk of trying to turn the Charlotte operation around. To help get the Charlotte station on track, Turner appeared on a series of televised "beg-a-thons" asking Charlotte viewers for financial support; he received more than 36,000 contributions ranging from 25 cents to $80. Turner collected $25,000 and used the proceeds to help finance the same movie-sports-rerun programming emphasis that he had pioneered in Atlanta. By 1975, the Charlotte station was breaking even, and Turner sold a controlling interest in the station to Turner Communications; later the station became an NBC affiliate.

THE EMERGENCE OF TURNER BROADCASTING SYSTEM

In 1975, the billboard advertising operations were spun off from Turner Communications and made a separate company, Turner Advertising, with Ted Turner as majority stockholder. Turner Advertising succeeded in becoming the

---

[2]Roger Vaughn, "Ted Turner's True Talent," *Esquire*, October 10, 1978, pp. 35–36. Quoted with permission.

largest billboard firm in the Atlanta and Chattanooga markets; the remaining branches were sold. Meanwhile, Turner Communications began repurchasing its stock on the open market, increasing Ted Turner's ownership percentage to about 85 percent of the shares outstanding.

Turner's 1972 bid to televise the Atlanta Braves baseball games on Channel 17 not only was the first step in the company's major sports involvement, but it also established a business relationship with the Braves owners, Chicago-based Atlanta LaSalle Corporation. In 1975, Atlanta LaSalle's management approached Ted Turner about buying the Braves club. Turner moved quickly, and in January, 1976 Turner Communications acquired the Braves through a newly formed, wholly owned subsidiary, Atlanta National League Baseball Club (ANLBC). The purchase price was $9.65 million, to be paid over 12 years at 6 percent interest.

In 1977, the company acquired, through Atlanta Hawks, Inc., a 95 percent limited partnership interest in Hawks, Ltd., owner of the Atlanta Hawks professional basketball team, which competed in the National Basketball Association. In 1978, Turner Communications acquired a limited partnership interest in Soccer, Ltd., the owner of the Atlanta Chiefs professional soccer team. Also in 1978, the company sold its radio stations in Chattanooga for $1,050,000 cash, realizing a pretax gain of $395,000.

Three important developments occurred in 1979. The company launched plans for the first 24-hour news programming network for cable television operators (to be called CNN); by the end of 1979, the company had invested $6.7 million in the CNN venture, acquired and begun renovations of a headquarters facility, hired key personnel, and obtained purchase commitments to provide the programming. The second development was to change the name of Turner Communications Corporation to Turner Broadcasting System, Inc., (TBS) and the letters of WTCG (Channel 17) to WTBS. The third involved an agreement to sell the Charlotte TV station for $20 million cash to help finance CNN's start-up.

Much managerial time and considerable company resources were invested in making a success of CNN. The challenge of this project was so big that Turner and TBS were unable to make any major new strategic moves between 1980 and 1985. But by early 1985, CNN was well on its way to earning its first profit, and the cash drain of CNN had eased considerably.

In April 1985, Turner announced he intended to purchase CBS, an organization 17 times the size of TBS. When his initial attempts to gain control of CBS by friendly means failed, Turner made a public tender offer to CBS shareholders. Turner planned to acquire 73 percent of the network's 30 million outstanding shares of stock. CBS's net worth was about $7.6 billion, or $254 per share; the face value of Turner's offer (composed of TBS stock, interest-bearing "junk bonds," and zero coupon bonds) was $175 a share, with estimates of the market value of the offer ranging between $130 and $155 a share.

CBS fought Turner's takeover attempt vigorously with a series of moves involving increased debt, stock repurchases, and a provision to place a ceiling on the amount of debt CBS could carry. Turner's court suit to halt the repurchase plan was denied; his lack of cash to compete with CBS's repurchase offer and lack of ability to wage a proxy battle ended the takeover attempt. Turner's abortive efforts to win control of CBS cost TBS $18.2 million in fees and expenses.

One week after his failed bid for CBS, Turner reached an agreement with MGM/United Artists Entertainment Company to purchase the movie company for $1.5 billion, about $29 a share. MGM's stock was trading at $24 at the time and had traded in the $13–$15 range in 1984. The 2,200-film library of MGM was the primary motivation for Turner's acquisition move. The acquisition was financed by the issue of $1.4 billion of high-yield, high-risk, junk bonds that were viewed with skepticism by many institutions. The acquisition was completed officially in March 1986.

A series of very complicated financing moves ensued to ease the extremely high debt burden TBS took on in the $1.5 billion buyout of MGM. MGM's moviemaking operations and various other assets were sold to pay some of the debt; all that was kept was the 2,200-film library. To ease the debt burden, in June 1986, TBS and Turner sold $568 million in TBS stock to a consortium of cable industry investors; these investors got 7 of the 15 seats on the company's board of directors. Proceeds of the stock sale went to pay down the debt.

In December 1987, TBS purchased rights to the RKO film and television library for approximately $30 million. The rights acquired included cable television rights and limited domestic free television rights not previously acquired when TBS purchased MGM/UA. Included in the RKO film library were approximately 750 feature-length theatrical motion pictures, 80 television productions, 50 short subjects, and in excess of 150 episodes of Abbot and Costello cartoons.

In October 1988, the company launched a new cable channel called TNT, or Turner Network Television, as a basic cable service for cable operators. Programming consisted principally of movies and other programming from the MGM library. Future programming plans included major sports and special events and original programming. Revenues were derived from the sale of advertising time and, beginning in 1989, the subscription sale of the service to cable operators. As an incentive to carry its programming, TNT provided four minutes per hour for local cable systems to sell their own advertising time.

In May 1990, TBS entered into a joint venture with three other companies to form SportSouth Network, a regional sports network serving the southeastern United States. TBS was a 44 percent owner of the partnership. SportSouth Network's programming included Braves baseball, Hawks basketball, college football, and various programs from Prime Network, a national service offering sports programming. As of January 1992, SportSouth Network was available via cable to 2.5 million U.S. households.

In December 1991, TBS acquired an ownership interest in and worldwide television distribution rights to the Hanna-Barbera cartoon library. In February 1992, the company announced plans to create a 24-hour-a-day cartoon network utilizing cartoons from the H-B library and the MGM/UA and RKO collections.

TBS'S BUSINESS IN 1992

As of 1992, Turner Broadcasting System was organized into five business groups: entertainment, news, syndication and licensing, sports, and real estate operations. The entertainment segment consisted of WTBS (often referred to as TBS SuperStation) and TNT, both carried on most cable TV systems across the United States. The news segment consisted of Cable News Network, which operated three 24-hour-a-day cable TV news services—CNN, Headline News, and CNN International. The syndication and licensing segment's principal activity was contracting with parties for use of films in the TBS libraries. The sports segment consisted of the Atlanta Braves, Atlanta Hawks, and SportSouth Network. The real estate operations included the company's ownership interest in the CNN Center building in Atlanta and operations associated with the Omni Coliseum where the Hawks' home games were played. Exhibit 1 provides financial information on the performance of TBS's business groups.

Overall, the company's revenues had grown at a brisk pace, but annual profits had a roller-coaster pattern:

Year	Revenues ($000)	Net Income ($000)
1976	$ 25,345	$ 648
1977	28,799	(1,232)
1978	33,843	1,203
1979	37,721	(1,496)
1980	54,610	(3,775)
1981	95,047	(13,423)
1982	165,641	(3,350)
1983	224,532	7,012
1984	281,732	10,062
1985	351,891	1,157
1986	556,917	(238,903)
1987	652,419	(131,208)
1988	806,626	(94,541)
1989	1,065,051	(70,647)
1990	1,393,521	4,662
1991	1,480,243	85,936

Exhibits 2 and 3 provide additional details on TBS's financial performance and current financial position.

TBS SUPERSTATION

A substantial portion of the company's entertainment segment was accounted for by TBS SuperStation. Although it operated as an independent UHF station broadcasting free over the air to the Atlanta market, its signal reached a far greater number of homes via cable TV systems in 50 states, Puerto Rico, and the Virgin Islands. According to A.C. Nielsen Co., TBS SuperStation was the fourth largest programming service available to cable systems (based on the number of households served) and the highest rated advertiser-supported programming service distributed to U.S. cable operators.

From the time Turner purchased WTBS-TV in 1970 to the fall of 1976, only 462,000 cable TV customers were added to the station's viewing audience. But two key events drastically changed the market potential for WTBS's signal. In 1975, the Federal Communications Commission determined that cable growth in many areas had been held back by FCC regulations forbidding cable operators from bringing in a more desirable distant signal over that of a local

E X H I B I T 1 Financial Information for TBS by Business Segment, 1978–91 (In thousands)

	1978	1980	1985	1986	1987	1988	1989	1990	1991
Revenues from unaffiliated customers									
Entertainment	$23,434	$35,495	$186,217	$204,378	$222,273	$266,570	$386,542	$662,932	$711,270
CNN cable operations	—	7,201	122,947	167,210	208,646	276,980	349,579	405,166	479,463
Program syndication and licensing	—	—	10,073	134,944	158,980	198,857	253,282	248,622	192,290
Professional sports	8,181	9,211	21,764	23,921	22,796	23,559	27,106	31,271	53,223
Real estate operations	2,228	2,703	8,072	23,479	38,026	43,277	42,109	42,632	39,885
Other	—	—	2,818	2,985	1,698	2,382	6,433	2,898	4,112
	$33,843	$54,610	$351,891	$556,917	$652,419	$806,626	$1,065,051	$1,393,521	$1,480,243
Operating profit (loss)									
Entertainment	$6,089	$10,166	$60,165	$12,532	$61,769	$53,553	$104,204	$75,471	$159,475
CNN cable operations	—	(16,024)	12,510	38,648	55,274	87,063	135,864	134,388	167,648
Program syndication and licensing	—	(4,461)	1,852	(6,652)	(10,014)	(123)	47,340	28,761	(5,473)
Professional sports	(1,688)	(2,905)	(6,480)	(12,158)	(6,699)	(9,212)	(7,405)	(16,168)	—
Equity in losses of limited partnership owning professional sports team	(1,225)	—	(2,707)	(1,675)	(21)	3,919	3,513	(1,051)	2,349
Real estate operations	418	15,689	(138)	(1,193)	1,552	2,225	665	3,428	511
Operating profit before interest and general corporate expenses	3,594	2,465	65,202	29,502	101,861	137,425	284,181	224,829	324,410
Interest expense	1,323	4,437	37,567	203,321	211,891	200,726	192,824	189,741	196,139
General corporate expenses	743	1,603	7,472	11,523	17,513	17,685	18,129	23,564	27,389
Dividends on minority interest	—	—	—	—	—	8,517	16,603	—	—
(Loss) profit before income taxes and extraordinary items	$1,528	$(3,575)	$20,163	$(185,342)	$(127,543)	$(89,503)	$56,625	$11,524	$100,982
Identifiable assets at end of year									
Entertainment	$19,942	$22,196	$125,480	$141,703	$160,793	$214,436	$325,775	$436,154	$491,490
CNN cable operations	—	12,257	57,638	58,549	73,821	82,021	116,459	195,369	219,377
Program syndication and licensing	—	—	10,226	1,439,211	1,367,855	1,327,574	1,311,514	1,238,991	1,282,077
Professional sports	6,974	5,894	17,808	28,354	24,599	—	—	—	—
Investment in limited partnership interests of professional sports team	—	—	1,181	981	917	29,097	36,420	53,391	55,546
Real estate operations	2,578	2,027	52,565	115,966	117,754	111,058	102,216	136,777	133,361
Corporate assets	904	11,644	91,660	119,219	92,612	94,795	222,379	91,840	215,376
	$30,398	$54,018	$356,558	$1,903,983	$1,838,351	$1,859,031	$2,114,763	$2,152,522	$2,397,227
Capital expenditures									
Entertainment	$2,532	$3,828	$2,123	$3,377	$2,090	$6,209	$6,623	$4,039	$6,357
CNN cable operations	—	9,731	6,168	3,237	8,274	4,730	15,524	9,539	13,561
Program syndication and licensing	—	—	—	3,520	1,176	315	3,460	477	1,816
Professional sports	77	180	273	172	231	229	164	841	684
Real estate operations	—	—	48,069	37,011	7,871	2,041	12,839	1,287	3,098
Other	—	—	1,021	6,233	7,001	2,665	23,498	10,055	10,395
	$2,609	$13,739	$57,654	$53,550	$26,643	$16,189	$62,108	$26,238	$35,911

Sources: 1980 Annual Report, 1985 10-K Report, 1987 10-K Report, and 1991 10-K Report.

EXHIBIT 2   **Consolidated Income Statement, Turner Broadcasting System, 1989–91**
(In thousands of dollars)

	1991	1990	1989
Revenues	$1,480,243	$1,393,521	$1,065,051
Cost of operations, exclusive of amortization			
and depreciation shown below	672,063	710,145	433,449
Selling, general and administrative	348,573	318,498	260,847
Amortization of film costs and other intangible assets	134,146	137,835	126,437
Depreciation of property, plant, and equipment	27,616	24,922	20,579
Interest expense, net of interest income	196,139	189,741	192,824
Settlement of pre-acquisition tax contingencies			(38,800)
Dividends on minority interest			16,603
	1,378,537	1,381,141	1,011,939
	101,706	12,380	53,112
Equity in income (loss) of unconsolidated investees	(724)	(856)	3,513
Income before provision for income taxes and extraordinary items	100,982	11,524	56,625
Provision for income taxes	58,046	27,102	28,993
Income (loss) before extraordinary items	42,936	(15,578)	27,632
Extraordinary items:			
Realization of operating loss carryforwards	43,000	20,200	
Loss on early extinguishment of debt, net of income tax benefit of $24,912			(98,279)
Net income (loss)	$ 85,936	$ 4,622	($ 70,647)

Source: *1991 Annual Report.*

independent; the FCC lifted its restrictions on "leapfrogging." Then, in December 1975, RCA launched its first communications satellite into orbit some 22,000 miles above the equator; a television signal could be beamed to the orbiting satellite and retransmitted to a receiving earth station antenna anywhere in the United States. Turner took full note of both changes. He quickly joined the cable operators' association and got to know the operators personally. And on seeing Home Box Office (a rival subscriber offering movies for home viewing on pay TV) unveil the first satellite broadcast to cable operators, Turner moved quickly. Satellite transmission of the WTBS signal began in December 1976, after being delayed six months by FCC proceedings. The number of cable subscribers receiving the WTBS signal soared:

Year	Subscribers
1977	1,350,000
1983	28,492,000
1987	43,100,000
1991	57,500,000

In 1979, the company began referring to WTBS as SuperStation; later, the station was officially designated as TBS SuperStation.

At year-end 1991, TBS SuperStation could be seen in 94 percent of U.S. homes with cable service and in 62 percent of U.S. homes with television. Much of the growth in the station's viewing audience was due to Turner's own entrepreneurial vision of the potential of cable and the personal sales job he did

EXHIBIT 3   **Consolidated Balance Sheets, Turner Broadcasting System, Inc., 1990 and 1991** *(In thousands of dollars)*

	1991	1990
Assets		
Current assets:		
Cash, including short-term investments of $60,407 and $34,032	$ 78,556	$ 43,733
Accounts receivable, less allowance of $14,994 and $11,767:		
Unaffiliated	264,765	249,125
Affiliated	81,352	70,336
Film costs	229,124	167,185
Installment contracts receivable, less allowance of $16,801 and $19,758	42,143	52,618
Prepaid expenses and other assets	79,527	31,053
Total current assets	775,467	614,050
Film costs and related intangibles, less current portion	1,162,862	1,217,799
Property, plant and equipment, less accumulated depreciation	218,950	210,146
Installment contracts receivable, less discount of $5,750 and $6,730	21,183	24,549
Other assets	218,765	86,073
Total assets	$2,397,227	$2,152,617
Liabilities and capital		
Current liabilities:		
Accounts payable and accrued expenses	$131,461	$131,834
Film contracts payable	27,639	42,097
Accrued interest	21,748	21,034
Accrued dividends	439	25,483
Participants' share and royalties payable	26,956	22,255
Current portion of long-term debt	67,292	54,537
Deferred income	40,079	33,764
Payable to affiliate	26,727	
Other	33,364	18,250
Total current liabilities	375,705	349,254
Long-term debt, less current portion	1,968,937	1,855,619
Other long-term liabilities	85,333	86,676
Total liabilities	2,429,975	2,291,549
Commitments and contingencies (Notes 2 and 6)		
Class B Cumulative Preferred Stock, par value $.125; authorized 12,600,000 shares; issued and outstanding 177,819 and 12,396,976 shares; aggregate redemption value of $5,483 and $382,240	4,855	334,160
Stockholders' deficit:		
Class C Convertible Preferred Stock, par value $.125; authorized 12,600,000 shares; issued and outstanding 12,396,976 shares	260,438	260,438
Class A Serial Preferred Stock, par value $.10; authorized 500,000 shares		
Class D Serial Preferred Stock, par value $.0625; authorized 100,000,000 shares		
Class A Common Stock, par value $.0625; authorized 75,000,000 shares; issued and outstanding 68,330,388 and 68,328,636 shares	4,328	4,328
Class B Common Stock, par value $.0625; authorized 300,000,000 shares; issued and outstanding 107,865,957 and 80,883,697 shares	6,798	5,112
Capital in excess of par value	496,455	120,066
Accumulated deficit	(805,622)	(863,036)
Total stockholders' deficit	(37,603)	(473,092)
	$2,397,227	$2,152,617

Source: *1991 Annual Report.*

promoting TBS SuperStation to cable operators. A rival executive observed, "You have to hand it to Turner. He surrounded himself with people who knew the cable industry, and he made friends. He had the timing, the ambition, the foresight, and the will to put his money where his mouth was."[3]

Programming   To fill the time slots for its 24-hour, seven-day-a-week broadcast schedule (8,760 hours per year), TBS relied on sports events (especially games of its sports affiliates), movies from its film libraries, program syndicators, and a limited amount of internal programming. Movies contributed the most-viewed segment of TBS programming; more than 40 movies were featured weekly along with a host of TV program reruns. Responding to critics who complained about using so many reruns and old movies instead of new programming, Turner quipped, "At least our shows were successful once."

In July 1985, TBS entered an agreement with the All-Union Association Soyuzsport and the U.S.S.R. State Committee for Television and Radio to organize a major international sports competition, known as the "Goodwill Games," to be held during 1986 in Moscow and during 1990 in the United States. Despite losing about $70 million on the 1986 and 1990 Goodwill Games, plans for the 1994 games in St. Petersburg, Russia (formerly Leningrad), were proceeding full steam.

Beginning in July 1981, programming at TBS was shifted to begin five minutes past the hour and at five minutes past the half hour. The rationale was explained by a WTBS executive:

> Ever since TV programming began, it has been scheduled on the hour and half hour. Since all stations program in this format, millions of viewers have to suffer through commercial clutter on all channels at the same time. Our trademark has been and continues to be innovation, and we're going to give viewers a chance to see something other than ads on those half-hour breaks. We're going to run programs when all other stations are running commercials. When dials are being flipped, we're going to provide an alternative for viewers. Once we have these viewers, we're going to keep them.

Advertising   Advertising revenues of TBS were largely a function of audience size. Because of its sizable, rapidly growing viewing audience, TBS was able to compete for national spot advertising and network advertising that otherwise would not be available to an independent station. In January 1979, TBS instituted substantially higher "SuperStation rates" for ads as a result of its greatly increased audience size. Even so, TBS ad rates were not up to what might be justified by its share of the national viewing audience. TBS management offered two reasons why this was so: (1) some national advertisers did not consider WTBS coverage and audience size large enough to shift some of their allocation of TV advertising away from the major networks, and (2) there was a significant time lag between documenting audience size and being able to establish rates on that basis. Still, scores of national advertisers ran ads on the SuperStation; total advertising revenues for TBS were $287 million in 1991, up from $276 million in 1990. According to the Nielsen ratings, TBS had an average of 793,000 viewing households in 1991 versus an average of 840,000 in 1990.

---

[3]Quoted in Vaughn, "Ted Turner's True Talent," p. 46.

Competition In the Atlanta market, TBS competed with affiliates of the three major television networks, three independent TV stations, and two affiliates of the Public Broadcasting Service in addition to other programming available to local cable subscribers. The PBS affiliates offered programming for educational or intellectual appeal; the three independents generally geared their programs to appeal to a variety of special audiences.

Competition for cable TV viewers came from several other large, independent stations that, like TBS, were "national" and offered an alternative to traditional network programming. Two of the biggest independents were WPIX-TV in New York and WGN-TV in Chicago. In 1981, the parent firm of WGN-TV in Chicago bought into the Chicago Cubs National League baseball team. Major competition also came from ESPN, a 24-hour sports network, and from pay TV operators, such as Home Box Office, Showtime, Cinemax, and the Movie Channel, which offered cable subscribers regular showing of movies, some of which were relatively new first- and second-run films. In addition, there were over 30 other cable channels, including the Disney Channel, the Nashville Network, MTV, Lifetime, the Discovery Channel, USA, Playboy, CNN, and C-Span. As of 1992, most cable TV subscribers could choose 10 to 40 channels in addition to the three major networks (ABC, NBC, and CBS), a PBS channel, and local independent TV stations (at least one independent TV station served virtually every metropolitan area). In mid-1990, the top choices of cable TV watchers were:

ESPN	57.0 million subscribers
TBS	55.2
CNN	56.5
USA	53.8
Nickelodeon	52.9

TURNER NETWORK TELEVISION (TNT)

Turner launched TNT as a 24-hour-a-day cable entertainment program service in October 1988. By year-end 1991, TNT was available in 55.6 million households, representing exposure to 93 percent of U.S. cable television homes and 60 percent of total U.S. television homes. Its average viewing audience was 509,000 households. Over 90 percent of TNT's programming came from about 7,000 films in the company's film libraries. In 1990, TNT initiated the telecast of 50 regular-season NBA professional basketball games and up to 30 playoff games per season. The contract ran for four seasons and cost TNT $275 million for the telecast rights. In 1990, TNT also paid $445 million for rights to telecast nine NFL games on Sunday nights during the next four seasons.

The company charged cable operators monthly subscription fees for providing TNT programming. In 1990, TNT earned $169 million in subscription fees, and, in 1991, subscription fees totaled $232 million. In addition, TNT generated domestic advertising revenues of $111 million in 1990 and $138 million in 1991.

As with TBS SuperStation, TNT competed with other cable TV programs available to cable subscribers, the three major TV networks, local over-the-air television stations, home video viewership (both owned and rented), movie theaters, and all other forms of audiovisual news, information, and entertainment sources.

In 1991, TNT expanded internationally by launching TNT Latin America, a 24-hour trilingual entertainment service distributed to cable operators in Latin America and the Caribbean (a total of 22 countries). At the end of 1991, TNT Latin America had 1.1 million subscribers and generated 1991 revenues of $2.4 million.

CABLE NEWS PRODUCTIONS

One of Ted Turner's most innovative ventures was the Cable News Network. Smelling an opportunity for an all-news network, Turner launched CNN on June 1, 1980, as a comprehensive, continuous, 24-hour-a-day programming service, consisting of world, national, and sports news; analysis; commentary; and special features. CNN was marketed by subscription to cable television systems nationwide and distributed by telecommunication satellite using the transmission services of a satellite common carrier. Like TBS and TNT, CNN also derived revenues from advertising.

At the June 1, 1980, sign-on date, CNN's signal was available to 1.7 million households; seven months later, CNN was providing programming to 663 cable systems having a total of 4.3 million households—a growth rate of 10,000 subscribers per day. At the end of 1991, CNN could be seen on cable in 57.9 million television households; CNN was also broadcast in the Caribbean, Australia, Japan, Europe, Asia, Africa, Latin America, and the Philippines—a total of 140 countries on six continents. By year-end 1991, cable news production was Turner Broadcasting's most profitable business unit, generating 1991 revenues of $480 million (32 percent of total corporate revenues) and operating earnings of $168 million (51 percent)—see Exhibit 1.

The first national telephone survey for CNN, conducted by a nationally known research firm in the early 1980s, showed that 77 percent of the respondents rated CNN's performance as above average or better relative to all services carried on their cable system; 31 percent ranked CNN as the best or one of the best channels offered. Management said "a significant number" of viewers who regularly viewed CNN considered it their primary source of national news. Ted Turner saw CNN as a no-frills network concerned with communicating the news, not exploiting it; according to Turner, "At CNN the news, not the anchor, is the star." CNN's biggest moment of world prominence came in 1991 when it broadcast live the commencement of the Gulf War from Baghdad; most of the world during that period relied on CNN as a major information source, and CNN captured many awards for its coverage.

CNN Programming and Personnel   The original CNN staff consisted of more than 400 journalists, reporters, executives, and technical personnel. The first president hired by Ted Turner to run CNN was Reese Schonfield, a 25-year veteran of television news. Schonfield had been founder and managing director of the Independent Television News Association (ITNA), which supplied a daily 90-minute news package to major independent television stations;

before running ITNA, Schonfield was with the United Press International Television News service for 17 years.

CNN operations were headquartered at Turner Broadcasting System facilities in Atlanta. Other domestic news bureaus were located in Washington, New York City, Chicago, Dallas, Detroit, Los Angeles, Miami, and San Francisco. CNN had foreign bureaus at 18 locations throughout the world and the capability to report live from virtually anywhere in the United States and around the world (using, where needed, local television news services and free-lance reporters and camera crews). CNN management believed its resource base gave it an unprecedented capability to go "live" anywhere in the world to cover major news breaking at any hour of the day or night. The aim at CNN was to report the news as it broke, not at midday, 6 P.M., or 11 P.M. as the network stations did.

CNN management saw an all-news channel as having several advantages in covering a breaking news story. First, interrupting normal programming for coverage of breaking news would enhance program content for most of the audience; for the network, the result would be an annoyed audience and a loss of revenue from commercials not aired. Second, CNN could stay with a developing news story without any time restraints. Third, when a network went live on a long-lasting event, it could not easily switch back to entertainment during the dull segments and then break off an entertainment program when the live action picked up; an all-news operation, however, could switch in and out of its normal programming, returning to the live event the moment it became more interesting. Fourth, CNN had the capability to go live whenever and wherever a good news story developed. Turner declared, "The majority of people now depend on TV for their basic news, and I don't think they're getting a straight story, only a few headlines about what bad has happened. That's pretty scary."[4]

The main weakness in CNN's "narrowcasting" approach was that its all-news format was not very appealing to viewers who watched TV for long stretches of time. Many of CNN's news events and stories were reported as many as 25 to 50 times each day. During normal viewing hours, CNN rewrote the script for the news every half hour to update and freshen its stories, but much of the film footage was still identical. Between 2 A.M. and 6 A.M., nearly everything shown was a repeat of material telecast earlier. CNN had an average viewing audience in the United States of 685,000 households versus 391,000 in 1990—the increase was chiefly due to the high audience levels during the Gulf War.

Advertising and Subscription Revenues   CNN sold 10 minutes of national advertising each hour, with an additional two minutes an hour to be sold by the local operators. Advertising revenues totaled $172 million during 1991, up from $151 million in 1990. Over 100 national advertisers chose to use CNN, including American Express, Bristol-Myers, General Motors, Campbell Soup, Eastern Airlines, Exxon, General Mills, General Foods, Goodyear, Holiday Inns, K mart, Kraft Foods, Merrill Lynch, Nestlé, Procter & Gamble, Quaker Oats, RCA, Schlitz, Sears, Toyota, and Xerox. Bristol-Myers' strategy in electing to advertise on CNN was to get TV exposure for some of its lesser-known

---

[4]As quoted in George N. Allen, "Ted Turner's Dream," *Washington Journalism Review,* September/October 1979, p. 32.

brands (Ammens powder and Congespirin cold remedy) whose sales were not large enough to justify paying the much higher ad rates charged by the three major networks. Joining the major advertisers on CNN were numerous mail-order houses, all using the same 800 toll-free number and Atlanta post office box; the mail-order products included records, jewelry, books and magazines, household items, and health and nutrition products. CNN received a commission on these sales of mail-order products bought by CNN viewers. CNN also had cable subscription revenues of $154 million in 1991, up from $142 million in 1990.

As had become a tradition in Turner ventures, during the start-up period at CNN, Turner appeared live and on tape on both CNN and WTBS to try to raise money for CNN. His ads promoting CNN urged people to send in their orders for bumper stickers, at $5 for a set of five, proclaiming "I Love CNN." Turner also donated a disk antenna to make CNN available to members of Congress at their Capitol offices.

Headline News   TBS launched CNN Headline News at the beginning of 1982. The goal of Headline News was to give viewers a concise, fast-paced update on current news headlines, business, weather, and sports every half hour. Headline News utilized the news-gathering resources of CNN. Carried by 5,500-plus cable systems in 1991, Headline News was seen in 48 million households. Total advertising revenues in 1991 for Headline News were $76 million, up from $69 million during the previous year. Subscription revenues for 1990 and 1991 were included in the totals for CNN. Headline News had an average viewing audience in 1991 of 182,000 U.S. households.

CNN International   International broadcasting of CNN-produced news programs began in the mid-1980s and expanded rapidly across the world. In 1988, CNN programs were available in 56 countries; in 1992, the total was 140 countries. CNN International generated $51.3 million in subscriber and advertising revenues in 1991, up from $24.8 million in 1990.

PROGRAM SYNDICATION AND LICENSING

In March 1986, TBS completed the acquisition of MGM/UA and subsequently sold essentially all of the nonfilm assets. Turner Entertainment Co., a wholly owned subsidiary of TBS, was formed to handle TBS's interests in the rental, licensing, and distribution of the 3,700 feature-length films and entertainment products in the MGM library. TEC was pursuing a variety of worldwide revenue sources, including the theatrical, home video, pay television, and syndication markets.

TBS's Film Libraries   MGM's film holdings represented one of the largest feature film libraries in the world and included approximately 2,200 MGM pictures, 750 pre-1950 Warner Bros. pictures, and 750 RKO pictures. Among the MGM pictures were such classics as *Gone with the Wind, Ben Hur, Gigi, 2001: A Space Odyssey, Mutiny on the Bounty, Dr. Zhivago,* and the *The Wizard of Oz,* as well as more recent releases such as *Poltergeist, Victor/Victoria,* and *2010.* The Warner Bros. films included *Casablanca, The Maltese Falcon, The Adventures of Robin Hood,* and *Yankee Doodle Dandy.* The RKO film holdings (to which the company acquired additional rights in December 1987) totaled 750 films and included *Citizen Kane, Gunga Din, Hunchback of Notre Dame*, and *King Kong.* The Hanna-Barbera library consisted of over 3,000 half hours of animated programming, including series on "The Flintstones," "Scooby Doo," "Yogi Bear," and "The Jetsons."

Licensing these films to broadcast television stations, networks, cable stations, pay television (Showtime and HBO), and other broadcasting sources around the world (called syndication) was an important source of current and expected revenues for TBS. In addition, the company had agreements to distribute some of the films to the home video rental market, to both movie theaters and nontheatrical exhibition outlets, and to merchandise outlets retailing home videos to consumers.

Colorization of Films   During the past several years, TBS initiated action to colorize some of the black-and-white films in its library. Agreements had been entered to colorize up to 250 motion pictures. Turner believed colorization would significantly enhance the potential revenues that could be derived from older films. Colorizing a black-and-white film cost anywhere from $225,000 to $300,000 per film, depending on its length. The colorization effect was considered a success, despite objections from numerous old-movie fans who believed colorization destroyed some of the artistic content of black-and-white pictures.

THE ATLANTA BRAVES BASEBALL CLUB

Ted Turner's purchase of the Atlanta Braves had several entrepreneurial pluses. Sports programming was a key feature of Channel 17, and Braves games had high audience ratings. By owning the Braves, Turner avoided contract disputes and renegotiations over broadcast rights and TV schedules, and the certainty of baseball programming enhanced Channel 17's appeal—especially to cable operators. Moreover, there was "fit" in another respect: Channel 17 could be used locally to promote attendance at Braves games; higher attendance meant more gate receipts, an ability to sign better players, and a better win-loss record. The improved record would attract more viewers to Channel 17. And with more viewers, Channel 17 could command higher advertising rates. These considerations, in conjunction with the acquisition terms (a purchase price of $9.65 million, payable $1 million in cash and the balance in quarterly installments over 12 years at 6 percent interest), were attractive to Turner despite the fact (1) there was little likelihood the Braves club would ever make much profit and (2) at the time of purchase, the Braves were doing poorly (some sportswriters labeled them a disaster).

Turner wasted little time in involving himself in the Braves activities. Bruce Galphin, in a feature article in a 1977 issue of *Atlanta* magazine, described some of what transpired:

> The Braves ended their first Turner season 32 games off the pennant pace, but attendance rose some 300,000 (to a still miserably unprofitable 830,000). Andy Messersmith was the new $1.5 million star on the field, but Ted Turner made the headlines. Before the season was out, everybody knew his name (and quite a few took it in vain).
>
> He turned somersaults for the fans. He vaulted his box-seat rail to congratulate home run-hitting Braves. (Cincinnati Reds' President Bob Howsam threat-

ened to have him arrested if Turner pulled that trick on his turf.) He put Channel 17 promotion on the back of Messersmith's uniform. He played poker with the players. Such varied maverick behavior drew rebukes from National League President Chub Feeney.

The Atlanta sports press was critical of the Braves in general and especially such deals as trading five players for Texas Ranger Jeff Burroughs. Turner retaliated by cutting off the press box's traditional free beer and sandwiches.

Bowie Kuhn fined the Braves $10,000 for making overtures to outfield Gary Matthews, then a San Francisco Giant, though soon to be a free agent. Blame that one not on Turner but on a now departed employee. But Turner did fly Matthews to Atlanta during the season for a cocktail bash and welcomed him with a Turner billboard at the airport.

That turned into one of Kuhn's charges in suspending Turner. Another was a drunken boasting match at the World Series with Bob Lurie, part owner of the Giants, about who would bid the most for Matthews. (Turner did: $1.75 million for a five-year contract. Kuhn at least left him that.)

"It's only my first year in baseball, OK?" says Turner. "I don't know that much about it, all right. I mean it's all complicated. When you get into a new kind of thing, there's a power structure that you're not really sure of, and there are unwritten rules as well as written rules. There's no book on how to be an owner."

Turner is proud, too, of bringing home run king Hank Aaron back to the Braves to take charge of the minor league teams and new-talent search. "His main thing is to go around and to fire up the young players and teach them how to hit the baseball."

He enjoys the company of his players. If he's forbidden to play poker with them, then he takes them hunting and generally treats them "like people." There are other owners who don't like this.

"They'd rather treat them like—well, like an owner–race horse relationship. My ballplayers aren't horses. They're my friends. I want them to be happy here."

In 1976, Ted Turner was suspended from all baseball activities for a year by Commissioner Bowie Kuhn for "conduct unbecoming to baseball." The Braves finished last in the Western Division of the National League the first four seasons under Turner's ownership. Early in the fifth season Turner remarked to a reporter, "I promised Atlanta that the Braves would be winners in five years; I still have one year to do it. Maybe there'll be a miracle. Besides, the Russians never make their five-year programs. They start new ones."[5] (The fifth year the Braves moved up to 4th place in their division, with a win-loss record of 81–80.)

The Atlanta Braves baseball team and associated activities were the principal component of the professional sports segment of Turner Broadcasting (Exhibit 4) and accounted for 9 percent of TBS's revenue in 1983, 5 percent in 1987, and 4 percent in 1991. Operating losses were incurred every year of Turner's ownership except for 1991 when the Braves won the National League pennant, went to the World Series, and caught the interest of sports enthusiasts.

Increased ticket prices were not expected to boost gate receipts substantially; ticket revenues were primarily a function of attendance, and attendance depended mainly on whether the team was a pennant contender.

---

[5]As quoted in Kim Chapin, "The Man Who Makes Waves," *Unlimited Mainliner*, May 1980, p. 86.

EXHIBIT 4   **Selected Statistics of Atlanta Braves Baseball Team
                   under Turner Ownership, 1976–91**

| | Win-Loss Record/Division Standing | | | | Season Attendance | | |
Year	Games Won	Games Lost	Games behind Division Leader	Final Rank in Division (Six Teams)	Atlanta Braves	All Major League Teams	Braves' Attendance Ranking (out of 26 Teams)
1976	70	92	32	6th	818,179	31,300,000	26th
1977	61	101	37	6th	872,464	38,700,000	26th
1978	69	93	26	6th	904,494	40,800,000	26th
1979	66	94	23½	6th	769,465	43,600,000	24th
1980	81	80	11½	4th	1,048,412	43,000,000	20th
1981†	50	56	8½	4th	535,418	26,450,000†	25th
1982	89	73	0	1st*	1,801,985	44,587,000	10th
1983	88	74	3	2nd	2,119,935	45,557,000	9th
1984	80	82	12	2nd (tie)	1,724,892	44,735,000	14th
1985	66	96	NA	5th	1,350,127	46,864,000	19th
1986	72	82	23½	6th	1,387,137	47,506,203	20th
1987	69	92	20½	5th	1,217,402	52,011,506	22nd
1988	54	106	39½	6th	848,089	52,998,904	22nd
1989	63	97	28	6th	944,930	55,173,095	22nd
1990‡	65	97	26	6th	980,129	54,823,768	22nd
1991	94	68	0	1st ·	2,140,217	56,813,159	16th

*Lost National League playoffs to St. Louis, three games to zero in the best-of-five series.
†Shortened season due to player's strike.
‡Shortened season due to lockout.

From 1978 to 1991, the operating expenses of the Braves increased rapidly because of escalating player salaries, travel costs, and preseason training costs. The only reason for the big jump in 1991 sports revenues over 1990 and 1991's small operating profit was that the Braves won the league championship, and attendance at Braves games reached record levels (see Exhibit 4).

The National League's baseball schedule called for 162 regular-season games—81 home games and 81 road, or away, games. The Braves home games were played in the Atlanta-Fulton County Stadium, seating capacity 52,194. In recent years, about 100 to 120 Braves games had been telecast by TBS. Beginning in 1991, SportSouth Network contracted to televise about 30 Braves games annually through 1993. The sales of broadcast rights for radio and television was the single biggest source of revenue for professional sports teams; the Braves franchise derived about $18 to $20 million in revenues annually from broadcast media sources.

In 1991, *Financial World* magazine estimated that the market value of the Braves team was about $75 million (this was before the pennant win).

THE ATLANTA HAWKS BASKETBALL TEAM

In 1976, Tom Cousins, an Atlanta real estate developer and principal owner of the Atlanta Hawks, approached Turner about buying the team. The Hawks team was in about the same condition as the Braves; the team had a poor win-

loss record, attendance was failing, and financial losses were sizable. The owners wanted out, even if it meant the franchise would be moved out of Atlanta.
When Turner's board of directors balked at acquiring the Hawks, Turner
acquired a 95 percent limited partnership interest himself. Turner's investment
was financed entirely by the company, however, through a $1 million secured
note receivable from Atlanta Hawks, Ltd., (AHL) and a $400,000 advance to
Turner. In addition, for a 2 percent partnership interest, Turner Advertising
advanced $742,000 to the Hawks on an unsecured basis. In 1977, the directors
of TBS agreed to let Turner transfer his 95 percent interest in the Hawks to the
company, at cost plus accrued interest. In 1979, the new general managing partner of AHL was granted a 1 percent ownership interest; in 1980, TBS acquired
the 2 percent limited partnership interest of Cousins for $41,000, bringing
TBS's share in AHL to 96 percent.

The Atlanta Hawks competed in the Central Division of the 22-team
National Basketball Association (NBA), the top professional basketball league
in the world. Like baseball team owners, basketball team owners received a pro
rata distribution of television revenues from telecasts by the national networks,
but unlike baseball team owners, they received none of the gate receipts from
away games (the home team retained the net gate receipts). Teams were subject
to rules and regulations promulgated by the NBA's commissioner of basketball.
Employment relationships with players were governed by a contract between
the NBA and the National Basketball Players Association.

During Turner's first year as owner of the Hawks, Curry Kirkpatrick
wrote:

> Turner's ignorance about both baseball and basketball is a matter of public record
> as well as the basis of many jokes he tells on himself. After two years as owner
> of the Braves, he thinks he finally knows what a balk is. But much of pro basket-
> ball has him stumped.
>
> He is forever calling NBA coaches managers and officials umpires. Although
> Turner knows his Hawks are "not too shabby" but rather "strawwwnnng" (two
> of the more annoying expressions in the terrific Turner lexicon someone once
> called "Southern bebop"), he does not seem to know their names or what posi-
> tions they play. For instance, former Hawk Ron Behagen was always "Berhagen"
> to Turner. When the hulking 6'7" forward, John Brown—whose name Turner
> appears to have less difficulty pronouncing—fouled out of a game, the owner
> jumped and yelped, "Golly! Now we've got only three guards left." Later in the
> same game, after the Hawks were warned for using the illegal zone defense,
> Turner was bewildered.
>
> "What the hell was that?" he said.
>
> "A zone warning," he was told.
>
> "Awww for Chrissakes, forget it," he concluded, angrily giving up.[6]

But what Turner lacked in knowledge, he substituted with energy, enthusiasm,
and a flair for promotion. In the 1979–80 season, the Hawks won the NBA Central Division Championship and compiled the best record of any Hawks team
since Atlanta obtained the franchise; the team set a new attendance record,
drawing 449,843 persons—an average of 10,792 fans per home game. The next
five seasons were disappointing however, and attendance fell off substantially.
Attendance during the 1988–89 season set a record for the team, averaging

---

[6]Kirkpatrick, "Going Real Strawwng," p. 76.

EXHIBIT 5   Selected Statistics of Atlanta Hawks Basketball Team, 1975–91

	Win-Loss Record/Division Standing				Season Attendance		
Year	Games Won	Games Lost	Games behind Division Leader	Final Rank in Division*	Atlanta Hawks	All NBA Teams	Hawks' Attendance Ranking (out of 22 teams)‡
1975–76	29	53	20	5th	n.a.	n.a.	n.a.
1976–77	31	51	18	6th	214,775	9,898,521	22nd
1977–78	41	41	11	4th	304,482	9,874,155	19th
1978–79	46	36	2	3rd	329,064	9,761,377	20th
1979–80	50	32	0	1st†	449,843	9,937,975	11th
1980–81	31	51	29	4th	362,702	9,449,340	16th
1981–82	42	40	13	2nd	308,899	9,964,919	20th
1982–83	43	39	8	2nd	292,673	9,637,614	20th
1983–84	40	42	10	3rd	292,690	10,014,543	20th
1984–85	34	48	25	5th	299,514	10,506,355	22nd
1985–86	50	32	7	2nd	377,678	11,214,888	19th
1986–87	57	25	0	1st	549,652	12,000,000	8th‡
1987–88	50	32	4	2nd	583,042	12,500,000	8th‡
1988–89	52	30	11	3rd	644,291	15,464,994	11th‡
1989–90	41	41	18	6th	573,731	17,368,659	19th‡
1990–91	43	39	18	4th	529,671	16,876,125	19th‡

n.a. = Not available

*There were six teams competing in the Hawks' division each year, except for 1975–76 when there were five teams.

†Hawks lost in first round of NBA playoffs.

‡The NBA expanded the number of teams to a total of 27 as of 1991.

14,219 per home game. The Hawks games were played at the Omni in downtown Atlanta (seating capacity 16,181); the lease agreement required payments to the Omni of 15 percent of gate receipts from each home game. Exhibit 5 details the Atlanta Hawks' performance under Turner ownership.

Ted Turner, using personal funds, and TBS routinely advanced the Hawks partnership the necessary funds to cover any losses and negative cash flows incurred. NBC had four-year rights to telecast NBA games beginning in 1990; for broadcast rights, NBC paid the NBA $600 million over four years. The Hawks' share of these fees amounted to about $22 million. In addition, TNT had broadcast rights for 50 regular-season and 30 playoff games; its fees to the NBA over four years amounted to $275 million, of which the Hawks received about $10 million. TBS SuperStation also televised about 25 Hawks games annually, and the SportSouth Network had recently negotiated an agreement to telecast up to 20 Hawks games each season through the 1993–94 season. *Financial World* in 1991 estimated the market value of the Atlanta Hawks team was $53.5 million; the franchise's 1990–91 operating performance was:

Total revenues	$19.1 million
Player salaries	10.0 million
Other operating expenses	7.1 million
Operating profit	1.2 million

REAL ESTATE OPERATIONS

The company got into real estate operations in a big way in 1985 when it acquired a 75 percent interest in a general partnership that owned the Omni International hotel and office complex in downtown Atlanta. The hotel contained 470 rooms and the complex had 830,000 square feet of office and retail shopping space. In 1986, the company acquired the remaining 25 percent ownership interest and renamed the office and shopping complex CNN Center; the corporate offices and operations of CNN and CNN Headline News were located in CNN Center. In later 1986, TBS created a wholly owned subsidiary called Turner Arena Production and Sales, Inc., to acquire and operate interests involving the Omni Coliseum. The subsidiary had contracts to operate the Omni Coliseum adjacent to CNN Center, was authorized to contract for major events held in the coliseum, and operated a computerized ticket sales agency specializing in sporting and entertainment events.

TED TURNER'S STYLE OF
ENTREPRENEURSHIP AND MANAGEMENT

Turner's approach to business and to dealing with people was both colorful and controversial. He was frequently interviewed by the media and seldom hesitated to say exactly what he thought. This delighted reporters, and when they printed his quotes a swirl of discussion often ensued. During the 1981 baseball strike, it was rumored and reported in the *Atlanta Constitution* that Turner, at one of the owner's meetings to discuss the strike situation, remarked that all the players should be drowned and the teams restaffed from scratch.

Over the years, writers and journalists used many labels to describe the personality and characteristics of Ted Turner: Captain Courageous, Captain Outrageous, Terrible Ted, the Mouth of the South, honest, petulant, childlike, loud, raucous, profane, impulsive, sentimental, egotistical, rebellious, ruthless, cold, money-grubbing, engrossing, multifaceted, flirtatious, hyperactive, sincere, outspoken, antiestablishment, likable, enjoyable, and chauvinistic. He had been called a humanist, a romantic, and the world's best-known sailor and had been accused of having basic racist tendencies, an elitist view of society, and a fascist ideology. Among his incongruous interests and activities, he had attended a state dinner at the White House, ridden in an ostrich race at Atlanta Stadium, read the Bible twice from cover to cover, permitted the screening of pornographic movies for his baseball players and their wives on a bus ride from Plains, Georgia, to Atlanta, nudged a baseball around the base paths with his nose, arrived drunk at a news conference following his victory in the world-famous America's Cup race, been named Yachtsman of the Year four times, appeared in ads for Cutty Sark Scotch, acquired a taste for Beechnut chewing tobacco, and quoted classical literature. In 1976, Turner was suspended from baseball, and in 1980 he was presented the Private Enterprise Examplar Medal by the Freedom Foundation at Valley Forge. In 1992, *Time* magazine saluted Turner as its 1991 Man of the year for his visionary role in creating CNN. He was also on *Forbes'* list of the 400 richest people in the world. In 1992 he married actress Jane Fonda.

Turner was highly motivated, energetic, and willing to do what it took to achieve his goals. He told one interviewer, "I have such a distaste for people who can't roll up their sleeves and get the job done. . . . My father always said to never set goals you can reach in your lifetime. After you accomplished them, there would be nothing left."[7] He valued and appreciated money—"Life is a game, but the way you keep score is money."[8] And he sought out success— "I've always been encouraged since I was a little kid to be a top competitor, and to be a worker, not a shirker"[9] Turner was known for being candid and honest with everyone. Honor, truth, and sincerity were his bywords.

Close associates described Turner as having a strong sense of what to do and when to do it. As one of his vice presidents expressed, "He's a good concept man. He's got a good eye for where profitable growth lies, where growth potential is. He has ability to put things together that make sense."[10]

Complementing Turner's sense of direction and sense of timing was a knack for picking capable managers to work under him. He delegated authority readily. Administrative matters and day-to-day operating details were left to his vice presidents and lower-echelon managers. He did not, as a rule, supervise them closely, preferring instead to let them do their jobs with a minimum of interference as long as things seemed to be progressing satisfactorily. The executives under Turner were regarded as devoted to him and seemed motivated by his leadership. A friend and sailing partner observed, "He is always winning, never losing, and he gives that same feeling to people sailing or working with him."

Turner's approach was to throw 100 percent of his energies into a project until he felt he could go on to something else. He got bored sitting still doing the same things over and over and handling routine matters. As one writer described it:

> When he approaches a project, he demonstrates great powers of positive thinking and an even greater innocence. ("It can't be done? Let's find out.") If things aren't going particularly well, Turner is capable of short temper tantrums and brief flurries of petulance. When a project bores him, Turner is quick to turn his back on it and move to something fresh, leaving to his corporate subalterns the job of seeing the project through—as well as the task of pouring oil on the inevitable troubled waters he has left in his wake.[11]

By Turner's own admission, the thing that turned him on was trying to win, the playing of the game, the competition, the matching of wits. He liked to turn losers into winners, in sports and in business. The general manager of WTBS-TV described his perception of Turner:

> He has a tremendous desire to win. He doesn't like to lose. If he does, he is one of the few people I know who benefits from the loss. He asks himself, "Why did I lose?" I don't know why he has to win so. It's a compulsion with him.
>
> One of my responsibilities is, if I know he is doing something wrong, to try and stop him. But did you every try to stop a speeding train?

---

[7] As quoted in Kirkpatrick, "Going Real Strawwng," p. 78.

[8] Ibid., p. 75.

[9] As quoted in Bruce Galphin, "Other Things to Do," *Atlanta*, Spring 1977, p. 40.

[10] As quoted in Wayne Minshew and DeWitt Rogers, "A Winner," *Atlanta Constitution*, January 8, 1977.

[11] As quoted in Chapin, "The Man Who Makes Waves," p. 85.

> If he wants something, he is going to get it. The problem is, he will pay more than it's worth. And the other guy knows it.[12]

However, Turner did not look at himself as a "win at all costs" practitioner:

> I don't think winning is everything. It's a big mistake when you say that. I think *trying* to win is what counts. Be kind and fair, and make the world a better place to live, that's what important. . . .
>
> I think the saddest people I've ever met were people with a lot of wealth. If you polled 90 percent of the people and asked them what they want most, most would want to be millionaires. I'll tell you, you've got to be one to know how unimportant it is.
>
> I'm blessed with some talents. I've made a lot of money, more than I ever thought I would. . . . But if I continue to be successful, I would like to serve my fellow man in some way other than doing a flip at third base. . . .
>
> People want leadership, somebody to rally around, and I want to be a leader.[13]

FUTURE OUTLOOK

In 1981, replying to questions from the casewriter, Ted Turner was confident and optimistic about the prospects for TBS:

> The future outlook is excellent. We have not peaked and I feel competition is always good; you continue to do better with competition.
>
> CNN's future is solid. . . .
>
> Moreover, we are currently doing well in competing both against the major networks and the other emerging alternatives.
>
> Five years from now, I expect TBS to be five times stronger.

Turner's 1981 assessment of TBS's prospects were pretty much on target. In 1981, TBS was a $95 million company; in 1986 it was a $557 million company; in 1991, the company's revenue was $1.48 billion, nearly three times the 1986 level, and the company earned record profits of $86 million. In the company's 1990 and 1991 annual reports, Turner observed:

> In 1970, we purchased WTCG, known today as TBS SuperStation. Since then, we have expanded from a staff of 50 in Atlanta to more than 3,800 employees in 25 cities throughout the world. A small UHF station has spawned four major networks cumulatively reaching millions of viewers on six continents. Revenues have climbed from approximately $1.5 million to $1.5 billion.
>
> We continue to build assets of long-lasting value. People everywhere want superior programming; that's what we provide. Advertisers, cable systems, and other customers want the programs that attract people; that's key to our revenue streams. Like everyone else, we've felt the recession, but we've kept growing anyway. Second, we have a stronger financial platform from which to grow those businesses. Not only can we service our near-term debt obligations out of our operations, but we can also generate free cash flow for reinvestment. We have much greater access to the capital markets. Third, we are closer to being the world's leading television provider of news, information, and entertainment programming. That's the goal; it hasn't changed. Fourth, international programming demand is vast, and we have only begun to serve it.

---

[12] As quoted in Minshew and Rogers, "A Winner."
[13] Ibid.

Looking ahead to our next 10 years, TBS has abundant opportunity to expand its position as a leading supplier of television programming. Three areas, in particular, will allow us to fulfill this goal. The first area concerns our foremost distribution base, the U.S. basic cable industry, which continues to be cable's fastest growing segment. The cable industry continues to experience growth on two fronts. Cable systems continue to expand their subscriber base, while cable programmers continue to claim an increasing market share of existing viewers.

An aggressive agenda of ongoing investments in programming through development and acquisition will enhance the growth of our asset base—the second area in our long-term expansion plan. This has been and will continue to be a major use of our cash reserves for several reasons. First, programming fuels the needs of our networks and positions them as industry leaders. Second, by accumulating valuable programming, the company can build software assets that are among the most sought-after commodities in the entertainment industry. Third, through syndication and licensing activities, the company can market its programming to all possible distribution and ancillary markets.

The global marketplace defines the third area of long-term growth for the company. In the years ahead, TBS will have the same opportunity to impact television programming abroad as we had domestically during the 80s. Continued privatization of television stations combined with development of expanded distribution technologies overseas present unlimited possibilities.[14]

---

[14]Compiled from the 1990 and 1991 *Annual Reports* of Turner Broadcasting System.

SONIC CORPORATION

Raymond E. Belford, Meinders School of Business
at Oklahoma City University

C. Stephen Lynn, chairman and chief executive officer of Sonic Corporation, was on top of the world as 1992 began. He had taken his company public in February 1991 in an initial public offering at $12.50 per share, paid down the majority of the debt owed by the company from two previous leveraged buyouts (LBO) in 1986 and 1988, and in so doing had established substantial wealth for himself. In October 1991, the company reported that net income more than doubled from the previous year. Lynn reported earnings of $3.1 million, or 49 cents per share, for the first fiscal year as a public company. Net income in 1990 was $940,600. At the end of 1991, the company's stock was trading on the NASDAQ National Market System at $31.25 per share (33 times earnings). In eight years, Lynn had substantially reversed the fortunes of the 1950s-style Sunbelt franchise drive-in hamburger chain he was brought in to run in 1983. The public offering had been oversubscribed. Sonic had significant cash reserves and a market value approaching $250 million by the end of December 1991—not bad for a company that was purchased six years earlier for about $10 million. Exhibit 1 highlights Sonic's operating results for the past five years. Exhibits 2 and 3 present Sonic's financial statements.

LYNN'S TURNAROUND STRATEGY

In the six years since the first LBO and leading up to the decision to go public, total revenues had grown from $29 million in 1985 to $53.9 million for the fiscal year ended August 31, 1991. Systemwide sales (which included sales of franchise units) had grown to $518 million from $292 million in 1985. Net income in 1991 was $3.1 million, compared with $514,900 in 1985. Even though the company had gone through restructuring, a second LBO in 1988, and the impact of changes in accounting principles, which caused a loss in 1989, Sonic now looked to be in excellent condition. The company, with approximately 1,100 outlet locations, was the fifth largest (up from seventh in 1987) chain in the hamburger segment of the fast-food industry, behind McDonald's, Burger King, Hardee's, and Wendy's.

During the past six years, Lynn had significantly reshaped the company after ridding it of board members and franchise holders who often seemed to make or approve decisions with a significant conflict of interest clouding their judgment. With the first LBO, the company shed itself of self-serving business practices and "good ol' boy" politics that previously permeated the organization. Lynn's professional team had begun to establish Sonic as a high-quality franchise-based organization. Growth in the number of franchises was restored—but with control. Unprofitable company operations continued to be sold to existing management or other franchise holders, and the remaining

EXHIBIT 1   Highlights of Sonic's Operating Results, 1987–91

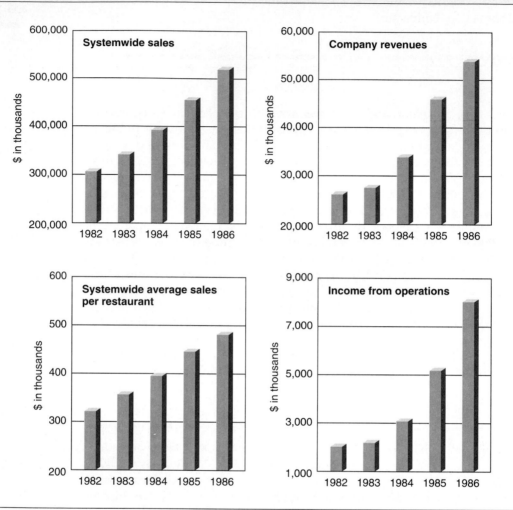

company-owned operations had become more profitable. The majority of the drive-in restaurants in the chain had purchased a "retrofit" package that upgraded store appearance and improved energy efficiency.

Advertising had grown from 330 participating stores and $880,000 spent on media production and purchases to approximately 1,000 participating stores and $8,980,000 spent on advertising and promotion (Exhibit 4). To enhance Sonic's 1950s nostalgia-based, drive-in service image, the company hired Frankie Avalon (a popular singer, actor, and teen idol from the late 1950s and early 1960s) to appear in commercials and promote the company and used special promotional sales programs such as the "Brown Bag Special" (two hamburgers, two french fries, and two soft drinks for a special price and delivered in a brown paper bag).

A cooperative food purchasing program had also been successful, with 95 percent of the restaurants participating by 1991 and the number of food-service

EXHIBIT 2   **Sonic Corp. Consolidated Statements of Operations, 1988–91**

	Company				Predecessor
	Year Ended August 31,			**Nine Months Ended August 31, 1989**	**Three Months Ended November 30, 1988**
	1991	**1990**	**Pro Forma 1989**		
Revenues:			(Unaudited)		
Sales by company-owned restaurants	$36,370,300	$30,573,500	$22,054,000	$17,185,000	$4,869,000
Franchised restaurants:					
Franchise fees and royalties	9,462,700	7,765,300	6,024,500	4,573,400	1,451,100
Equipment sales	6,832,900	6,418,800	4,750,600	3,673,000	1,077,600
Other	1,214,100	1,102,500	1,056,300	788,600	267,700
	$53,880,000	$45,860,100	$33,885,400	$26,220,000	$7,665,400
Costs and expenses:					
Company-owned restaurants	$28,436,700	$23,726,000	$17,355,800	$13,494,900	$3,860,900
Equipment cost of sales	5,750,800	5,397,600	4,034,700	3,110,700	924,000
Selling, general and administrative	7,529,000	7,539,600	6,245,200	4,787,000	1,433,200
Depreciation and amortization	1,802,000	1,792,800	1,583,800	1,175,200	262,400
Provision for restaurant closings and disposals	175,700	333,200	376,900	126,500	250,400
Minority interest in earnings of restaurant partnerships	2,168,500	1,888,500	1,212,500	963,700	248,800
	$45,862,700	$40,677,700	$30,808,900	$23,658,000	$6,979,700
Income from operations	$ 8,017,300	$ 5,182,400	$ 3,076,500	$ 2,562,000	$ 685,700
Other expenses (income):					
Interest expense:					
Related parties	327,600	627,500	619,800	470,600	—
Other	1,787,000	3,057,100	3,081,000	2,316,200	281,900
Interest income	(387,200)	(177,800)	(242,200)	(157,000)	(85,200)
Acquisition related expenses	—	—	2,197,600	—	2,197,600
Income (loss) before Income taxes and extraordinary expense	$ 6,289,900	$ 1,675,600	$ (2,579,700)	$ (67,800)	$ (1,708,600)
Provision (credit) for income taxes	2,568,500	735,000	(528,400)	242,800	(507,700)
Income (loss) before extraordinary expense	$ 3,721,400	$ 940,600	$ (2,051,300)	$ (310,600)	$ (1,200,900)
Extraordinary expense, net of tax benefit of $364,500	594,800	—	—	—	—
Net income (loss)	$ 3,126,600	$ 940,600	$ (2,051,300)	$ (310,600)	$(1,200,900)
Earnings per share:					
Income (loss) before extraordinary expense	$ .58	$.19	$(.41)	$(.06)	
Extraordinary expense	(.09)	—	—	—	
Net income (loss)	$ .49	$.19	$(.41)	$(.06)	
Weighted average shares outstanding	6,440,600	5,017,600	5,000,000	5,000,000	

Source: *1991 Annual Report*

suppliers reduced to 18. This program helped cut food costs systemwide and assure more uniform product quality from store outlet to store outlet. This, along with the installation of more automated cooking and order-filling equipment, helped stores offset most of the boost in labor costs associated with an increase in the federal minimum wage in April 1991.

Company-owned average sales per restaurant had grown from $302,000 in 1987 to $493,000 in 1991. Part of the increase was a result of price increases; however, improved store appearance and increased advertising were major

EXHIBIT 3   **Sonic Corp. Consolidated Balance Sheets, 1990–91**

	Fiscal Year Ending August 31	
	1991	**1990**
Assets		
Current assets:		
Cash and cash equivalents	$ 5,018,900	$ 2,549,600
Marketable securities	5,300,000	—
Accounts and notes receivable, net	2,136,000	1,934,100
Net investment in direct financing and sales-type leases	640,900	606,100
Inventories	1,278,400	1,121,600
Prepaid expenses and other	275,600	260,700
Total current assets	$14,649,800	$ 6,472,100
Net investment in direct financing and sales-type leases	2,642,500	2,809,400
Notes receivable, net	713,500	720,100
Property, equipment and capital leases, net	12,932,800	9,381,600
Intangibles and other assets	11,010,200	12,223,800
Total assets	$41,948,800	$31,607,000
Liabilities and Stockholders' Equity		
Current liabilities:		
Accounts payable	$ 786,700	$ 1,069,400
Deposits from franchisees	401,500	523,500
Accrued liabilities	2,548,800	2,659,900
Obligations under capital leases due within one year	527,500	486,200
Long-term debt due within one year	335,400	385,900
Total current liabilities	$ 4,599,900	$ 5,124,900
Obligations under capital leases due after one year	$ 4,779,200	$ 4,347,300
Long-term debt due after one year		
Related parties	—	5,229,500
Other	521,300	20,352,600
Other noncurrent liabilities	2,312,500	1,040,500
Deferred income taxes	615,100	698,400
Commitments and contingencies		
Stockholders' equity (deficit)		
Preferred stock, par value $.01; 1,000,000 shares authorized; none outstanding		
Common stock, par value $.01; 20,000,000 shares authorized; 7,785,000 shares issued and outstanding (4,812,000 at August 31, 1990)	77,800	48,100
Paid-in capital	33,595,700	2,839,400
Retained earnings	3,756,600	630,000
Carryover of predecessor basis	(8,269,300)	(8,269,300)
	$29,160,800	$ (4,751,800)
Notes receivable from treasury stock sales	—	(434,400)
Treasury stock, at cost; 2,500 shares	(40,000)	—
Total stockholders' equity (deficit)	29,120,800	(5,186,200)
Total liabilities and stockholders' equity	$41,948,800	$31,607,000

Source: *1991 Annual Report.*

EXHIBIT 4   **Trends in Sonic's Advertising and Promotional Efforts**

Fiscal Year	Number of Restaurants Participating	Percentage of Restaurants Participating	Funds Spent on Media Production and Advertising
1986	330	35	$ 880,000
1987	498	52	2,266,000
1988	682	70	4,018,000
1989	788	79	5,810,000
1990	870	84	7,937,000
1991	1,000	90	8,980,000

Source: Prospectus of Sonic Corporation February 28, 1991, and *1991 Annual Report.*

contributors to the improved performance. Systemwide, average sales per restaurant grew to $481,000 in 1991 compared with $321,000 in 1985.

The company was in the best shape it had been in for many years and had overcome many obstacles along the way.

COMPANY BACKGROUND

Sonic's roots began in 1953 when Troy Smith opened a drive-in restaurant featuring foot-long hot dogs, hamburgers, and french-fried onion rings under the name Top Hat in Shawnee, Oklahoma, a city of approximately 28,000 some 35 miles east of Oklahoma City. Smith did not have an extensive background in business but understood restaurant operations. In designing the Top Hat restaurant, Smith created a unique kitchen layout that resulted in fast and efficient service. The kitchen layout was very effective in everything from storage, inventory control, cooking efficiency, and order delivery. Smith had noted that some A&W Root Beer stands were using an intercom system for taking customer's orders, and he implemented the same type of system in his new restaurant. Before then, drive-ins relied on carhops who took orders from automobiles that drove up in front of the restaurant in much the same fashion as a waiter takes orders from tables. The new drive-in featured individual stalls for automobiles and each stall was equipped with a two-way intercom so the customer could place the order without waiting for a carhop to come to the automobile. Carhops were used to deliver the order to the car.

The Top Hat became a very popular gathering spot for families and young people. The growth in the number of automobiles, particularly among teenagers and singles in their early 20s, contributed to the popularity of the drive-in hamburger stand. Drive-in restaurants were just beginning to replace the local drugstore soda fountains as a favorite gathering spot for teens. The mid-1950s was the real beginning of the still-popular teen activity of "cruising."

Charles Pappe noted the popularity and success of the Top Hat and in the mid-50s asked for Smith's assistance in establishing a similar restaurant in the rural Oklahoma town of Woodward. Thus began a partnership between

Smith and Pappe. The two men constructed four additional restaurants in the state. The success of the operation led the two men to seek trademark protection for their enterprise, but they found the Top Hat name could not be trademarked. The Top Hat restaurants had been promoting their unique order system and fast delivery of freshly cooked products under the slogan "service with the speed of sound." Based on the success of the slogan and all the sonic booms in the 1950s with aircraft breaking one speed record after another, the two men came up with the name Sonic. In 1959, the original Top Hat restaurants were converted to Sonic Drive-ins. The first restaurant to bear the Sonic name was a new restaurant opened in Stillwater, Oklahoma.

Other individuals saw the success of the Sonic operations and began to ask Smith and Pappe to assist them in opening units. According to Lynn, it was a kind of "you've been successful, why don't you show me how to be successful" thing. These inquiries put Sonic on the road to franchising its fast-food concept.

SONIC'S INITIAL GROWTH STRATEGY

Smith and Pappe were not typical entrepreneurs in that they did not want to create a company to direct the franchise operations. They preferred to do things as simply as possible and avoid sophisticated accounting systems, legal agreements, and so on. Smith came up with the idea of collecting franchise royalties by talking a paper-goods supplier into adding a fee to each printed bag sold to a Sonic franchise holder. Franchise holders were then required to purchase their paper products from the supplier. This "bag royalty" system allowed Smith and Pappe to collect royalties from one source (the paper-goods wholesaler) rather than dealing directly with each individual franchise holder. The system allowed Sonic to collect royalties without having to audit the sales records of each franchise holder to verify royalties owed. The system was ruled to be legal and not a tying arrangement.

Individual franchise holders soon became successful in their own right and they, too, began getting inquiries from people interested in opening a new Sonic operation; what amounted to a pyramid-type selling arrangement evolved as franchisees found ways to make money getting other franchises started. Franchise holders also looked for opportunities to expand their territories. "A store manager might make friends with his bread man and recruit the bread man to be a manager in a new store," Lynn related. As a result, the original store manager might have a percentage not only of his store but also of the new operation the recruited friend would be managing. This led to multi-ownership of virtually all Sonic operations. In nearly all cases, each store manager was a part owner.

This system propelled Sonic forward, and growth was rapid. When Pappe died in 1967, 41 restaurants were operating under the Sonic name. The expansion continued under Smith's leadership, and by 1973 there were 130 Sonics. In June 1973, nine of the major multifranchise holders approached Smith about incorporating the company to provide additional leadership and create additional expansion. Smith was reluctant to incorporate, but agreed to if the nine would pay him for a share of the stock in a new corporation. Smith became the major stockholder in the new company, and, in 1974,

EXHIBIT 5   Growth in the Number of Sonic's Company-Owned and Franchised
Restaurant Units, 1974–91

Year	Company	Franchised Units	Total
1974	3	217	220
1975	8	291	299
1976	15	458	473
1977	45	737	782
1978	118	943	1061
1979	149	1033	1182
1980	126	997	1123
1981	115	931	1046
1982	114	886	1000
1983	96	879	975
1984	92	876	968
1985	85	885	970
1986	60	886	946
1987	46	909	955
1988	50	930	980
1989	64	932	996
1990	69	974	1043
1991	80	1032	1112

Source: Sonic annual reports and prospectus of February 1991.

Sonic Industries, Inc., purchased all rights, trade names, trademarks, and other company property from Smith. During the year, the new corporation also absorbed Sonic Supply, Inc., owned by Marvin D. Jirous and Matt M. Kinslow. When the purchase agreements were completed, Smith was elected chairman of the board, Jirous was named president, and Kinslow became vice president. Seven other multifranchise owners also became officers or directors and major stockholders in the new company: James L. Barrett; Ralph L. Mason; Ted V. Robertson; Troy N. Smith, Jr.; J. Dwight Van Dorn; James T. Williams; and James C. Winterringer.

The successful franchise formula continued to grow almost exponentially as the company expanded operations from 220 units in 1974 to 737 units in 1977 to 1,182 operating units in 1979 (Exhibit 5). This rapid growth was centered mainly in rural southern cities of around 15,000, and Sonic's name was in virtually all the Sunbelt states, with the exception of California. This period also saw Sonic assuming control of failed franchise units, helping drive the number of company-owned restaurants from 3 in 1974 to 149 in 1979.

TROUBLED TIMES

During this period, Sonic's net income also grew rapidly. In 1974, the company suffered a loss of $6,300. The following year, net income grew to $264,800 and in 1979, net income was $1,829,100. However, Smith began to worry because the 1979 income figure was down from 1978 and 1977 when earnings exceeded $2 million. This occurred despite sales growth from $246,700 in 1974 to $38,373,800 in 1979. (Sales represent only those accruing to Sonic Industries,

Inc., from franchise fees, royalties, and company operations. Total sales, including franchise operations, were more than $200 million.)

Sonic's rapid expansion appeared to be getting out of hand. Sonic drive-ins were being built almost overnight and placed wherever land could be located. In 1977 and 1978, new restaurant openings averaged almost one per day. The lack of planning, market analysis, and requirements for unit management resulted in numerous failures. In many cases, failed franchises were turned over to the company to be operated as company units. This led to some conflict of interest among the officers and board of directors. The board was controlled by multiunit franchise operators, and if a unit failed, they unloaded it on the company. In addition, when a quality manager candidate appeared, the franchise holders wasted no time in hiring the individual for their own operations, rather than recommending them for a company operation. The same kind of decisions were also being made with sites. The better sites were grabbed by one of the major franchise holders rather than designated as a company-owned site.

The tight board control also created an operation in which virtually no services were being provided to a franchise holder. The company's services were limited to selling a set of plans, the use of the name, and some troubleshooting assistance from time to time. There were no advertising cooperatives, no management training services, and no accounting services. In fact, one of the multiunit franchise holders/directors established a separate company to market accounting services to Sonic franchise holders.

The management of Sonic began to unravel. The franchise holder/directors who had been friends for years began to quarrel. In 1980, Sonic began closing some operations and posted a loss of $295,700 on $33,119,900 in revenues. Income rose to $538,400 in 1981 on $29,904,600 in sales; in 1982, Sonic earned $579,700 on $29,395,600 in sales; and in 1983 it earned $56,900 on $26,261,200 in sales. By 1983, the number of Sonic drive-ins in operation was down to 975.

The company continued to maintain low royalty and initial franchise fees. The board of directors seemed to be reluctant to raise franchise fees when it was apparent the company needed additional revenues. Raising royalties would directly affect the income and cash flow stream of the individual directors who held multiple franchises. This presented a conflict of interest. Most of these individuals had in excess of $1 million a year in cash flow from their franchise operations, in addition to the compensation they were receiving from Sonic Industries. Their franchise operations were their major source of income.

The company also had become a public company "by accident" due to the way stock was distributed in the multiownership system in the company. Sonic simply had too many shareholders and shares outstanding.

By the end of 1982, it became obvious to Smith that something had to be done. He was becoming more and more frustrated by the policies and actions of his board of directors and the internal squabbling. Smith had always been a reluctant leader who despised conflict and often felt uncomfortable in any kind of public meeting. He had been described as being uncomfortable in a meeting of only a few friends if he had to make a statement. Although generally well liked by everyone in the organization, he faced a major crisis in the company he had cultivated from that first Top Hat restaurant in Shawnee, Oklahoma, to the nation's 15th largest fast-food restaurant chain in units of operation.

NEW MANAGEMENT

As 1983 began to unfold and sales and profits continued to decline, Smith could no longer avoid the issues. He concluded the best option was to go outside the company and bring in a professional manager with no direct ties to any of the director/franchise holders and management staff of Sonic. In Smith's view, a housecleaning was in order and special management talent was needed.

On November 1, 1983, C. Stephen Lynn joined Sonic as president and chief executive officer. Smith continued as chairman of the board. Lynn was recruited from the Burston Corporation, a restaurant operator and franchisor, where he had served as executive vice president and chief operating officer. In view of the problems facing Sonic, Lynn seemed to be the ideal choice. In addition to his strong industry and marketing background, he also had a warm and outgoing personality and a very high level of energy and optimism. As one student who interviewed Lynn remarked, "His openness and candor catches you off guard. You don't usually expect a chief executive officer to be so open and honest about issues."

Lynn faced the additional challenge of attempting to correct Sonic's problems while still faced with the same director/franchise holders on the board. Even though Smith was able to recruit and hire Lynn, the chief executive did not always have the full support of the board, many of whom viewed him with skepticism. A new franchising agreement had been developed and was approved on the same day Lynn took over as chief executive officer. The new agreement was constructed more along the lines of traditional franchise agreements and phased out the "bag royalty" system.

Franchisees were also pressured to get past-due accounts current, and additional company-owned stores were closed. Lynn announced he would be restructuring Sonic's top management by recruiting outstanding individuals to provide new leadership and a professional team to lead Sonic's turnaround.

Larry L. Buckles was hired in February 1984 as executive vice president–administration and operations. Buckles was recruited from A. Copeland Enterprises, Inc. (Popeye's Famous Fried Chicken and Biscuits). In September, J. Vernon Stewart was brought in as senior vice president for marketing and corporate development. Stewart was in the consulting business and had served as a vice president in K-Bob's Steakhouse, Inc., and as senior director of development for Dunkin Donuts of America. Richard Roby joined the firm in July 1985 from Low Runkle Company, an Oklahoma City–based advertising and public relations firm, to fill the position of vice president of marketing communications, field marketing services, and assistant to the president. In March 1984, Jerry W. Grizzle was brought in as controller. Grizzle had been a territory sales manager for the Keebler Co. and had previously served as controller of the food service division of Scrivner, Inc.

With the majority of the new management team in place during 1984, Lynn began to embark on the quest to turn the company around and build comprehensive franchise and company store support programs.

The major problems facing the new management team were:

1. The company was not making any money.
2. Company-owned stores were losing money and were overstaffed.

3. No unit growth—units were declining.
4. Negative franchisee attitudes due to no "real" services being provided.
5. No management strategies, goals, or plans in place.
6. Traffic declining and market awareness very poor.
7. Image was old and faded.
8. No advertising.
9. Directors/franchise holders were bottom line oriented with nothing being reinvested in business.
10. Overselling of franchises had given Sonic a bad reputation and reduced quality of operations.
11. A political environment based on the power of the director/franchisee "gang of nine."

ACTIONS TAKEN BY LYNN AND SONIC'S NEW MANAGEMENT TEAM

To turn the organization around, Lynn and his management team embarked on a strategy that encompassed three points: (1) attack problems concerning franchisee attitude and Sonic's image; (2) improve purchasing; and (3) improve communications.

The key to attacking the attitude problem centered on marketing. To be successful, any plan depended on three critical issues: (1) the franchise owners and corporate owners had to "buy in" to it; (2) the plan had to be simple enough to be executed; and (3) it had to provide visible evidence of working by improving profit for the franchise owners.

To launch the marketing program, Lynn's group conducted several marketing studies. The studies revealed several significant points.

1. Sonic had high customer frequency with customer's averaging two visits per week.
2. There was a significant movement toward take-out orders versus eat-in orders.
3. Sonic had excellent quality with orders cooked and prepared from fresh products after the customer ordered.
4. The concept of using carhops had become unique since major competitors served customers over the counter and through drive-by windows.

Based on the studies, Sonic began to put together an organization to support the marketing effort with the creation of advertising and purchasing cooperatives, preparation of media ads, and updating of paper and styrofoam products.

Each franchise owner had been left pretty much alone when it came to purchasing food products. To reduce the food cost, efforts were begun to put together clusters of restaurants to purchase products in a co-op.

To overcome the poor relations with the franchise owners and improve communications, the company used the advertising and purchasing co-ops as a vehicle to communicate more frequently and freely with franchise owners. The company also established an advisory council and began holding annual conventions. In addition, efforts were begun to provide training for managers and a training facility with a test kitchen was established at the corporate offices in Oklahoma City.

In 1984, the company's 25th anniversary year, net income rebounded to $350,100 compared to $56,900 in 1983. Lynn's letter to the stockholders in 1984 stated:

> Building services and programs to move us forward is a high priority for your Sonic team. Our commitment to position Sonic as America's premier drive-in hamburger chain will require all of us to diligently work together in the most creative manner.
>
> During our 25th anniversary year, our priorities included:
>
> 1. Building the support programs that will allow our drive-ins to continue to succeed as we expand and as the so-called "majors" continue to come into our types of markets. This means that we will have to work together as a Sonic family—better than ever before. Working together, we will pool our purchasing leverage in foodstuff, advertising, sales, promotion, and supplies. We must do this, however, in a way that maintains our operationally based company concept.
> 2. Implementing of several major programs that began in 1984 and will be completed in 1985:
>
>   - Staffing additions at the senior level and the restructuring of the complete corporate staff, essentially completed during fiscal year 1984.
>   - Extensive market research on our customers, menu and building design.
>   - Formation of target marketing and purchasing cooperative groups at the local level—representing more than half of the Sonic drive-ins. . . .
>   - Development of a new building design and image for testing (scheduled to be completed in January 1985).
>   - Establishing centralized training as well as building a training facility and complete test kitchen within our corporate headquarters (scheduled to be completed December 24, 1984). . . .
>
> You can expect to see aggressive unit development based on research; however, we will be expanding carefully to ensure stable growth. We will not grow so quickly that it is at the expense of the progress already achieved.

At the beginning of 1985, the Franchise Sales and Services Division was formed under the direction of Stewart. The division pulled together various activities that previously had been handled by different parts of the organization with little or no coordination. The new division provided assistance for franchisees—from site selection and construction support to sales and profit improvement counseling.

Also in 1985, the Marketing Division focused on assembling 27 advertising cooperatives. Each co-op was funded by a percentage of sales from the participating drive-ins, with advertising support and production provided by Sonic. The co-op purchasing program was also further refined to create regional purchasing cooperatives with more buying leverage with suppliers. This soon led to systemwide purchasing to leverage the company's buying power even further and to improve the uniformity and quality of incoming supplies to all store outlets.

As the company was celebrating its 25th anniversary, many of the properties in the chain were beginning to show their age. The white buildings with red lettering looked out of place in the 1980s, and Lynn believed a face-lift was necessary if Sonic wanted to improve its image. The company developed a retrofit package that, when placed over existing structures, gave a modern, appealing effect, without losing the 1950s nostalgic feel. In addition, the retrofit reduced energy costs significantly. To encourage franchisees to purchase the retrofit package, Sonic demonstrated that the new design generated an average 20 percent increase in unit sales in addition to the overhead savings.

Not everything was doom and gloom as Lynn viewed the business. Individual franchise holders were, for the most part, making a profit. Much of the success of the franchise-owned operations, in Lynn's view, was due to making individual store managers part owners. Lynn stated, "I have always believed that owners make the best managers." In addition, Lynn viewed the drive-in concept as unique, and having no sit-down area in the typical restaurant saved on construction costs. Building costs ranged from $125,000 to $175,000 depending on location in 1986. The standard restaurant contained 24 individual parking spaces for automobiles with electronic ordering from each location. The standard lot size required for a restaurant unit was 100 feet by 160 feet. In studying the market, Lynn noted the trend in fast-food restaurant customers was growing in the take-out area: "More people were taking food out rather than eating it on the premises. This meant that we were already positioned to take advantage of this change and meant that new restaurants would not need to be built with sit-down areas which increase both investment costs and overhead." Lynn also had studies done that showed Sonic could provide faster service than the traditional industry leaders, such as McDonald's. According to Lynn:

> McDonald's has one drive-by window and one ordering point (unless you want to get out of your car). We have 24 ordering points and, in effect, 24 take-out windows. We discovered we can cook to order and deliver the product to the customer in almost half the average wait at McDonald's drive-by during peak periods.

Lynn also saw the standard menu as a strength. The basic menu included hamburgers, cheeseburgers, french fries, onion rings, hot dogs, chili dogs, fish, steak, and chicken sandwiches, malts and shakes, and soft drinks. Lynn emphasized two points with the menu: (1) "Menu proliferation increases costs," and (2) "People talk thin, but they eat fat." As a result, Lynn believed Sonic's limited hamburger and french-fry menu was on target.

Lynn continued to sell unprofitable company-owned units—often to the unit's existing manager with Sonic assisting with the financing. The majority of these former losers began producing a profit. Lynn believed this proved his point about owners managing better than employees.

Under Lynn's leadership the company was almost completely changed by the end of 1985. Profits increased to $514,900, and the drop in operating units stabilized. The metamorphosis was not complete, however, as Lynn still faced problems with a board dominated by franchise holders tied to the past. Company politics had prevented Lynn and his newly formed management team from making changes he believed were necessary for the company to grow into the Sonic he envisioned. He concluded that the conflicting interests of board members stood in the way of sound business decisions.

THE LEVERAGED BUYOUT

In late 1985, Lynn put his job on the line and approached the board of directors to propose a management buyout of the company. Lynn's initial proposal, prepared by Dean Witter, was to purchase all outstanding shares of the company for an average price of $4.50 per share. Book value per share was $5.12 in 1985, but the stock, which was not actively traded, was being offered at an ask price of $3.50 per share and was bid at $2.88 before the announcement. All investors with holdings of 5,000 shares or less would receive $4.50 in cash. Stockholders with more than 5,000 shares would receive $3 cash and a note for $1.50 per share. The offer was later amended to $4.50 cash for all shares. The board rejected the offer and countered with a proposed price of $4.75 cash per share. The offer was accepted by the purchasers, and the board approved the buyout in November 1985.

In April 1986, at a special stockholders' meeting, the buyout was approved. This placed the total value of the deal at slightly less than $10 million. Funds for the purchase were provided from direct investment, a term loan, and a $1.7 million subordinated loan from Equus Investments I, limited partnership. Besides management, the purchase group included Art Linkletter, famous television personality and author. Heller Financial, Inc., also participated in the purchase. Following the leveraged buyout, management owned 49 percent of the company; Equus Investments, 40 percent; Linkletter, 10 percent; and Larry Hartzog, 1 percent. The management group included founder Smith, who maintained 5 percent of the company.

THE SECOND LEVERAGED BUYOUT

In 1988, the company was recapitalized with Linkletter and the others bought out. A variety of issues brought about the recapitalization, which, in effect, was a second leveraged buyout. Sonic's management had met with a group of bankers in connection with an attempt by Sonic to acquire Western Sizzlin Steakhouses and later Church's Fried Chicken. Even though Sonic was unable to complete the deals, it developed a relationship with MAST Resources, Inc., a New York–based investment group. Lynn and other key members of management had an option from the 1986 LBO to purchase 50 percent of the common stock owned by Equus at $3 per share by the end of 1988. In addition, Linkletter wanted to be bought out, and the management group wanted to cash in on some of the value it had built in the company.

As a result, Sonic management exercised the option with Equus and negotiated the purchase of the balance of Equus's holdings. In the recapitalization, put together by MAST, Sonic Holdings Company was formed as a vehicle for completing the deal. Under the agreement, all shares of Sonic Industries, Inc., were transferred to the holding company at a value of $11 per share. Linkletter and other shareholders were bought out with cash and notes. Five members of management received cash, notes, and stock in the new company. The recapitalization was funded with $2 million from MAST and an $18.8 million loan obtained under a $24 million revolving credit agreement with First National Bank of Boston. The total debt following the transaction was approximately $25 million, and the company was valued at about $35 million. Following the recapitalization, management owned 47.5 percent of the company and investors in MAST owned 47.5 percent. The remaining 5 percent was owned by Smith. In the transaction, Sonic's management executives took approximately $8 million of their gain in cash and notes.

THE DECISION TO GO PUBLIC

At the April 1990 management retreat, the senior management of Sonic discussed taking the company public. Several reasons were given:

1. Relations with MAST were deteriorating and additional financial support from MAST was not forthcoming.
2. The MAST partnership was breaking up.
3. The high debt service on the LBO presented significant long-term risk for Sonic, and management feared debt service requirements if the economy went into a recession.
4. Management had no liquidity for its holdings and no market for its stock. Therefore, there was a desire to create liquidity and allow management to diversity some of its wealth.
5. The management team, with an average age of less than 50, viewed going public as presenting new challenges and additional experience.

At the conclusion of the meeting, Sonic decided to develop a plan to take the company public.

In the summer of 1990, Sonic invited six investment banking firms that had expressed interest in the offering to a "bake-off" (a competition where investment bankers attempt to sell their services to management). After the presentations, First Boston was chosen as the lead underwriter, but then Iraq invaded Kuwait and the stock market reacted with a major decline. The planned fall 1990 public offering was delayed.

In early February 1991, the market began to firm, and a prospectus was printed. In initial filings, the price was forecast to be between $10 and $12 per share. First Boston came to Sonic and requested the price be dropped to $9 to $11 per share. Management refused and maintained it wanted at least $10 per share and the original range remained. A "road show" was arranged for the underwriters and Sonic management to pitch the issue to institutional investors. Before the multicity road show was completed, the stock was oversubscribed by seven times. At the end of February, the stock was finally priced at $12.50 and the underwriting agreement completed. Even though Sonic was officially a public company at that point, its stock was not officially traded until the deal closed March 7. The stock began trading above the offering price and seemed to reach a barrier at $14 per share and took one dip to $12.25, but by early summer the stock broke through the $14 barrier and was trading at $19.50 in early August and reached a high of $24 before falling back to $22.50 at the end of October. After the public offering, management owned 27 percent of the outstanding shares; former MAST partners, 20 percent; and the balance of 53 percent was owned by the public.

SONIC'S BUSINESS IN 1992

Sonic drive-in restaurants were located in the Sunbelt, with the majority of the operations concentrated in the south central part of the United States. The company promoted itself as "America's Drive-In" and featured fast service and moderate prices with a menu dominated by hamburgers, hot dogs, chicken and fish sandwiches, french fries, onion rings, and soft drinks. The majority of the units were still run by individuals who owned a percentage of the restaurant they managed. Sonic prided itself on service and saw the carhop as a key to the service. According to Lynn, "The Sonic carhop looks at you, smiles at you, delivers your order promptly, and thanks you." The cooked-to-order food was delivered within an average of five minutes. Studies indicated Sonic had a greater frequency of return business and customer loyalty than many of its competitors.

Customers

Sonic's market research indicated its most typical customer was female, between the ages of 18 and 24, with an annual income between $10,000 and $14,999, and a member of a three-to-four-person family where both spouses were employed in blue-collar occupations. Forty-six percent of Sonic's business was done during the lunch hours and 44 percent during supper hours, with the remaining 10 percent derived from other periods. Sonic's average ticket price was $2.25 (compared to an industry average of $2.30 to $2.35).

Franchise Investment

The average cost to start a new Sonic franchise was approximately $370,000. With average first-year sales of $613,000 per unit, the ratio of first-year sales to capital costs was 1.7 to 1, which compared favorably with other similar franchises in the industry. However, the $370,000 initial investment cost was considerably less than Sonic's four larger competitors. The majority of the $370,000 was for land and building, which averaged $245,000. Equipment investment was about $85,000, working capital requirements averaged $25,000, and the initial franchise fee was $15,000.

Beginning in 1985, existing franchise owners were encouraged to purchase a "retrofit" package to update the appearance of their restaurants. By 1990, 71 percent of all units featured the new design. The retrofit package included a new exterior facade, vestibule, accent lighting, and neon signs and cost between $25,000 and $30,000. Based on energy costs savings and an average 20 percent increase in sales, the retrofit investment generated a very quick return.

Equipment Sales

Sonic sold restaurant equipment to existing and most new franchise operations. A complete package of equipment needed for a new restaurant could be provided by the company, with shipment and installation coordinated. The company sold its equipment sales business in 1987 but had to repossess it in 1988 when the purchaser defaulted.

Royalties and Signs

Each Sonic restaurant, including company-owned restaurants, operated under a franchise agreement that provided payments to Sonic on a graduated scale. Average royalties for units subject to 1984 franchise agreements were 1.75 percent of sales in 1990; average royalties for units operating under revised 1988 franchise agreements were 2.1 percent of sales. All restaurants were required to display the Sonic sign. Sonic owned the majority of its signs and leased them to the restaurants at monthly rental rates ranging from $76 to $150.

Locations

At the end of August 1991, 1,112 restaurants were operating. Growth in the company had mainly come from existing franchisees increasing the number of restaurants they operated. Sonic had developed multiple franchise agreements giving a franchisee an exclusive right to construct, own, and operate Sonic restaurants within a defined area. In exchange, the franchisee agreed to open a minimum number of restaurants within a prescribed time frame. Since 1984, Sonic had entered into 43 area development agreements. One such area development agreement was issued for the southern half of Florida that required the franchisee to open 150 new Sonic restaurants by 1996.

Operations

Sonic franchise holders operated with little direct supervision from Sonic Corporation. Sonic provided training in proper food preparation at corporate headquarters, but most training was done on the job by the owner-manager of the individual unit. A complete operating manual was provided for each location covering storage, preparation of menu items, order taking, cleaning, and maintaining of equipment. Sonic qualified food distributors and established specifications for supplying products to Sonic establishments. The company also provided training for managers and field service assistance when needed.

Outlook

In early 1992, Lynn reported to shareholders:

> We continue to focus our franchise expansion through single drive-in development with current franchisees and area development agreements with current and prospective franchisees. Area development agreements entered into in fiscal year 1991 totaled 24 and called for 350 drive-ins to be placed in operation over six years. The accompanying good news is that new drive-ins opened aside from exclusive territorial development agreements historically have outnumbered those opened under development agreements.
>
> Our plan? Doing more of the same on a more aggressive scale. . . .

REFERENCES   Sonic Industries, *1983 Annual Report*.
                 Sonic Industries, *1985 Annual Report*.
                 Sonic Industries, Form 10-K, 1985.
                 Sonic Industries, Proxy Statement, Special Meeting of Stockholders, April 24, 1986.

Sonic Corporation, Prospectus, February 28, 1991.

Sonic Corporation, *1991 Annual Report.*

Stephens, Inc., Research Paper prepared by Alison Bisno, CFA, March 26, 1991.

Interviews, speeches, guest lectures, of Sonic management between 1988 and 1991 including C. Stephen Lynn, J. Clifford Hudson, Jerry W. Grizzle, Larry L. Buckles, and J. Vernon Stewart.

"The Fast Food Industry," case prepared by Derrick E. Dsouza and Leslie R. Rue of Georgia State University, copyright 1988.

Some research on this case was done by students in Seminar in Business during the fall semester of 1988 in the Meinders School of Business. Contributing to the case were: Melanie Eisenhour, Colin Hill, Stephen Jackson, Kristin Johnson, Mark Murray, Janey Storvick, Samuel Enyim, Deny Setiawan, and Jackie Waddle.

Denton, Jon. "Sonic Soars in Best Net Income Year," *Daily Oklahoman.*

SIDETHRUSTERS, INC. (A)

Raymond M. Kinnunen, Northeastern University
John A. Seeger, Bentley College
Robert L. Goldberg, Northeastern University

I wanted to do something on my own. I wasn't sure what that was or how to do it. I had a little money put away so I started talking to people about a business to buy or become part owner of.

I saw a lot of crappy businesses. Then the president of the South Shore Chamber of Commerce said, "I know an inventor who has a neat new product. You might want to meet him."

Michael Bardlow described how he got into the business of producing and installing auxiliary motors for pleasure boats. His company, Sidethrusters, Inc., produced and installed devices (often called bow-thrusters) that helped large pleasure craft maneuver safely while approaching or leaving the dock.

Excited by his meeting with the inventor, Bardlow began investigating the prospects for starting a business. He called the Boston Coast Guard Center and learned about available data:

> I got a list of every registered vessel longer than 40 feet in the United States, not just in Boston. There were a ton of them, many more than I'd thought. I lose track of the zeros—it was 30,000.

> To get technical expertise, I called every major boat builder in the country and every naval architect I could find the name of. They were clearly in camps, which was not surprising. Nearly all the sail people were interested; they said, "Go for it." Powerboat people often said they didn't need the product, because their big boats had twin engines and were naturally maneuverable. And that's true, certainly, if you have a professional crew.

> So opinion was mixed, but I said, "All right. I'm going for it." I called a friend, a lawyer who's done this before, and we drafted an offering circular. He told me the rules, and we touched all the bases—product description, markets, competition, management, technical, financial. I was ready to go out and sell the idea.

During the three months after meeting the inventor, Bardlow drafted a business plan and raised $200,000 initial capital. The plan projected $357,000 total revenues for the first year with after-tax profits of $36,000. The total new boat market was estimated at approximately 17,000 vessels that might qualify for the product. After three years, the plan projected annual sales of more than $2 million with after-tax profits exceeding $350,000. (Exhibits 1 through 4 show the three-year projected financial statements taken from Bardlow's plan).

EXHIBIT 1   **Sidethrusters' Projected Balance Sheet (Year-end)**

	Year 1	Year 2	Year 3
Assets			
Cash, including short-term investment	$232,060	$463,604	$856,010
Inventory	$ 27,000	$ 72,000	$ 81,000
Patent	$ 5,000	$ 5,000	$ 5,000
Total assets	$264,060	$540,604	$942,010
Liabilities and capital			
Accrued expenses	$ 22,580	$ 87,046	$127,341
Capital stock, 1,000 shares outstanding	$ 1,000	$ 1,000	$ 1,000
Capital surplus	$199,550	$199,550	$199,550
Retained earnings	$ 40,930	$253,008	$614,119
Total liabilities and capital	$264,060	$540,604	$942,010

Source: Company financial records.

THE PRODUCT

The side-thruster was a motor-driven propeller, mounted in a tunnel that ran sideways through the hull of a boat—usually at the bow. The propeller could apply a sideways force on the hull, below the water line, either to the right or to the left. The idea was not new; for decades, bow-thrusters had been standard equipment on large craft such as ferryboats and tugs, which had to maneuver in constrained spaces. The application to small boats had not been practical until the inventor, Al Carella, adapted a hydraulic motor for the purpose. Bardlow described the need for his product:

> Say you've got a man 55 or 60 years old, coming into the town pilings at Edgartown with his wife. He's got a new $400,000 boat and he's petrified. Unless there's somebody on the dock, he goes back out and comes in again until there's somebody there he can yell to, "Catch us as we're coming in." This man is not a lifelong sailor, and he needs help.

Bardlow, in his patent and trademark applications and literature, called the product the "side-thruster" to draw attention to the advantages of having total side-motion power. He conceived the product as appropriate for both bow and stern installation, especially for longer pleasure craft and commercial fishing vessels, to provide the ultimate in safety and maneuverability. In vessels of greater tonnage, installation of the side-thruster in the bow, stern, and amidships would be highly feasible and desirable, he thought.

Sidethrusters, Inc., set out to establish its line of 6-inch, 8-inch, and 10-inch side-thrusters in the marketplace. The experience acquired through manufacturing, marketing, and selling these units would help the research and development of new products, Bardlow thought. The units were priced at $5,000 for the smallest unit, up to $15,000 for the largest. Additional installation costs varied depending on whether the work was done on a new boat during the manufacturing process or on an existing boat in dry dock. The business plan allowed for one trip to train each installing boat yard on the procedures to be followed.

EXHIBIT 2   Sidethrusters' Year 1 Projected Income and Cash Flow Statement

	Month												Totals
	1	2	3	4	5	6	7	8	9	10	11	12	
Units sold			2	4	6	8	8	9	10	10	14	16	87
Sales	$ 0	$ 0	$ 8,000	$17,000	$25,000	$33,000	$33,000	$36,500	$41,000	$41,000	$57,000	$66,000	$357,500
Less: COGS	2,317	2,317	6,117	9,917	13,717	17,517	17,517	19,417	21,317	21,317	28,917	32,717	193,104
Gross margin	($ 2,317)	($ 2,317)	$ 1,883	$ 7,083	$11,283	$15,483	$15,483	$17,083	$19,683	$19,683	$28,083	$33,283	$164,396
Other expenses													
MFB salary	$ 867	$ 867	$ 867	$ 867	$ 867	$ 867	$ 867	$ 867	$ 867	$ 867	$ 867	$ 867	$ 10,404
Secretarial	160	320	320	480	480	480	480	480	480	480	480	480	5,120
Advertising	1,000	1,000	1,000	1,000	1,000	1,000	1,000	1,000	1,000	1,000	1,000	1,000	12,000
Travel	0	0	560	1,190	3,750	4,810	2,310	6,055	2,870	2,870	7,490	4,620	36,525
Postage	200	200	200	300	300	300	300	300	300	300	400	400	3,500
Telephone	200	200	200	300	300	350	400	400	400	400	600	600	4,350
Operating supplies	200	200	200	200	200	200	200	200	200	200	200	200	2,400
Accounting*	420	420	420	420	420	420	420	420	420	420	420	420	5,040
Legal	4,000	0	0	0	0	0	0	0	0	0	0	0	4,000
Payroll taxes	224	224	234	245	245	245	245	245	245	245	245	245	2,887
Miscellaneous expenses	1,000	1,000	1,200	1,200	1,500	1,800	2,000	2,000	2,000	2,000	2,000	2,000	19,700
Research and development	5,000	0	0	0	0	0	0	0	0	0	0	0	5,000
Total other expenses	$13,271	$14,431	$ 5,201	$ 6,202	$ 9,062	$10,472	$ 8,222	$11,967	$ 8,782	$ 8,782	$13,702	$10,832	$110,926
Net income before taxes	($15,588)	($ 6,748)	($ 3,318)	$ 881	$ 2,221	$ 5,011	$ 7,261	$ 5,116	$10,901	$10,901	$14,381	$22,451	$ 53,470
Massachusetts tax*									1,074	1,090	1,438	2,245	5,847
Federal tax*									2,147	2,180	2,876	4,490	11,693
Net income	($15,588)	($ 6,748)	($ 3,318)	$ 881	$ 2,221	$ 5,011	$ 7,261	$ 5,116	$ 7,680	$ 7,631	$10,067	$15,716	$ 35,930
Add back noncash items	$ 420	$ 420	$ 420	$ 420	$ 420	$ 420	$ 420	$ 420	$ 3,641	$ 3,690	$ 4,734	$ 7,155	
Net cash before inventory	($15,168)	($ 6,328)	($ 2,898)	$ 1,301	$ 2,641	$ 5,431	$ 7,681	$ 5,536	$11,321	$11,321	$14,801	$22,871	
Additions to inventory	(27,000)	(3,600)	(3,600)	(7,200)	(10,800)	(14,400)	(14,400)	(16,200)	(18,000)	(18,000)	(25,200)	(28,800)	
Relief from inventory													
Cash payments of accruals	0	3,600	3,600	7,200	10,800	14,400	14,400	16,200	18,000	18,000	25,200	28,800	
Net cash monthly	($42,168)	($ 6,328)	($ 2,898)	$ 1,301	$ 2,641	$ 5,431	$ 7,681	$ 5,536	$11,321	$11,321	$14,801	$22,871	
Cumulative	$47,832	$41,504	$38,606	$39,907	$42,548	$47,979	$55,660	$61,196	$72,517	$83,838	$98,639	$121,510	
Earnings per share (1,000 shares outstanding)													$35.93

* Noncash items

EXHIBIT 3   Sidethrusters' Year 2 Projected Income and Cash Flow Statement

	Month												Totals
	1	2	3	4	5	6	7	8	9	10	11	12	
Units sold	20	22	24	26	28	30	30	32	32	34	36	40	354
Sales	$82,000	$90,000	$98,000	$107,000	$115,000	$123,000	$123,000	$131,000	$131,000	$139,000	$148,000	$164,000	$1,451,000
Less: COGS	41,183	44,983	48,783	52,583	56,383	60,183	60,183	63,983	63,983	67,783	71,583	79,183	710,786
Gross margin	$40,817	$45,017	$49,217	$54,417	$58,617	$62,817	$62,817	$67,017	$67,017	$71,217	$76,417	$84,817	$740,204
Other expenses													
MFB salary	$5,000	$5,000	$5,000	$5,000	$5,000	$5,000	$5,000	$5,000	$5,000	$5,000	$5,000	$5,000	$60,000
Secretarial	1,000	1,000	1,000	1,000	1,000	1,000	1,000	1,000	1,000	1,000	1,000	1,000	12,000
Advertising	1,000	1,000	1,000	1,000	1,000	1,000	1,000	1,000	1,000	1,000	1,000	1,000	12,000
Travel	5,740	6,300	6,860	7,490	10,050	11,110	8,610	12,670	9,170	9,730	13,860	11,480	113,070
Postage	450	500	500	500	600	600	700	700	750	800	850	900	7,850
Telephone	700	800	800	850	1,000	1,000	1,050	1,100	1,200	1,200	1,300	1,300	12,300
Operating supplies	300	400	400	450	500	600	600	600	650	700	700	700	6,600
Accounting*	500	500	500	500	500	500	500	500	500	500	500	500	6,000
Legal	0	0	0	0	0	0	0	0	0	0	0	0	0
Payroll taxes	632	632	632	632	632	632	632	632	632	632	632	632	7,584
Miscellaneous expenses	2,200	2,200	2,400	2,400	2,600	2,600	2,600	2,700	2,800	2,000	3,000	3,000	30,500
Total other expenses	$17,522	$18,332	$19,092	$19,822	$22,882	$24,042	$21,692	$25,902	$22,702	$23,562	$27,842	$25,512	$268,904
Net income before taxes	$23,295	$26,685	$30,125	$34,595	$35,735	$38,775	$41,125	$41,115	$44,315	$47,655	$48,575	$59,305	$471,300
Massachusetts tax*	2,330	2,669	3,013	3,460	3,574	3,878	4,113	4,112	4,432	4,766	4,858	5,931	47,136
Federal tax*	10,483	12,008	13,556	15,568	16,081	17,449	18,506	18,502	19,942	21,445	21,859	26,687	212,086
Net income	$10,482	$12,008	$13,556	$15,567	$16,080	$17,448	$18,506	$18,501	$19,941	$21,444	$21,858	$26,687	$212,078
Add back noncash items	$13,313	$15,177	$17,069	$19,528	$20,155	$21,827	$23,119	$23,114	$24,874	$26,711	$27,217	$33,118	
Net cash before inventory	$23,795	$27,185	$30,625	$35,095	$36,235	$39,275	$41,625	$41,615	$44,815	$48,155	$49,075	$59,805	
Additions to inventory	(45,000)	(39,600)	(43,200)	(46,800)	(50,400)	(54,000)	(90,000)	(57,600)	(57,600)	(61,200)	(64,800)	(72,000)	
Relief from inventory	36,000	39,600	43,200	46,800	50,400	54,000	54,000	57,600	57,600	61,200	64,800	72,000	
Cash payments of accruals	(22,580)			(45,559)			(61,510)			(71,107)			
Net cash monthly	($7,785)	$27,185	$30,625	($10,464)	$36,235	$39,275	($55,885)	$41,615	$44,815	($22,952)	$49,075	$59,805	
Cumulative	$113,725	$140,910	$171,535	$161,071	$197,306	$236,581	$180,696	$222,311	$267,126	$244,174	$293,249	$353,054	
Earnings per share (1,000 shares outstanding)													$212.08

*Noncash items

Sidethrusters' Year 3 Projected Income and Cash Flow Statement

						Month							
	1	2	3	4	5	6	7	8	9	10	11	12	Totals
Units sold	40	40	42	44	46	50	50	50	50	50	50	50	562
Sales	$164,000	$164,000	$172,000	$180,000	$189,000	$205,000	$215,000	$215,000	$215,000	$215,000	$215,000	$215,000	$2,364,000
Less: COGS	81,567	81,567	85,367	89,167	92,967	100,567	105,067	105,067	105,067	105,067	105,067	105,067	1,161,604
Gross margin	$ 82,433	$ 82,433	$ 86,633	$ 90,833	$ 96,033	$104,433	$109,933	$109,933	$109,933	$109,933	$109,933	$109,933	$1,202,396
Other expenses													
MFB salary	$ 5,417	$ 5,417	5,417	5,417	$ 5,417	5,417	5,417	$ 5,417	5,417	5,417	5,417	$ 5,417	$ 65,004
Secretarial	1,125	1,125	1,125	1,125	1,125	1,125	1,125	1,125	1,125	1,125	1,125	1,125	13,500
Advertising	1,000	1,000	1,000	1,000	1,000	1,000	2,000	2,000	2,000	2,000	2,000	2,000	18,000
Travel	11,480	11,480	12,040	12,600	15,230	16,850	15,050	18,550	15,050	15,050	18,550	15,050	176,980
Postage	1,000	1,050	1,100	1,200	1,200	1,300	1,300	1,400	1,400	1,500	1,500	1,500	15,450
Telephone	1,350	1,400	1,400	1,500	1,500	1,500	1,550	1,600	1,600	1,700	1,700	1,700	18,500
Operating supplies	750	800	800	850	900	900	950	1,000	1,000	1,000	1,000	1,000	10,950
Accounting *	700	700	700	700	700	700	700	700	700	700	700	700	8,400
Legal	0	0	0	0	0	5,000	0	0	0	0	0	0	5,000
Payroll taxes	837	837	837	837	837	837	837	837	837	837	837	837	10,044
Miscellaneous expenses	3,000	3,100	3,200	3,200	3,300	3,400	3,400	3,450	3,450	3,500	3,500	3,600	40,100
Research and development	3,000	3,000	3,000	3,000	3,000	3,000	0	0	0	0	0	0	18,000
Total other expenses	$ 29,659	$ 29,909	$ 30,619	$ 31,429	$ 34,209	$ 41,029	$ 32,329	$ 36,079	$ 32,579	$ 32,829	$ 36,329	$ 32,929	$ 399,928
Net income before taxes	$ 52,774	$ 52,524	$ 56,014	$ 59,404	$ 61,824	$ 63,404	$ 77,604	$ 73,854	$ 77,354	$ 77,104	$ 73,604	$ 77,004	$ 802,468
Massachusetts tax *	5,277	5,252	5,601	5,940	6,182	6,340	7,760	7,385	7,735	7,710	7,360	7,700	80,242
Federal tax *	23,749	23,636	25,207	26,732	27,821	28,532	34,922	33,235	34,810	34,697	33,122	34,652	361,115
Net income	$ 23,748	$ 23,636	$ 25,206	$ 26,732	$ 27,821	$ 28,532	$ 34,922	$ 33,234	$ 34,809	$ 34,697	$ 33,122	$ 34,652	$ 361,111
Add back noncash items	29,726	29,588	31,508	33,372	34,703	35,572	43,382	41,320	43,245	43,107	41,182	43,052	
Net cash before inventory	$ 53,474	$ 53,224	$ 56,714	$ 60,104	$ 62,524	$ 64,104	$ 78,304	$ 74,554	$ 78,054	$ 77,804	$ 74,304	$ 77,704	
Additions to inventory	(72,000)	(72,000)	(75,600)	(79,200)	(82,800)	(90,000)	(103,500)	(94,500)	(94,500)	(94,500)	(94,500)	(94,500)	
Relief from inventory	72,000	72,000	75,600	79,200	82,800	90,000	94,500	94,500	94,500	94,500	94,500	94,500	
Cash payments of accruals	(87,046)			(90,822)			(103,647)			(127,947)			
Net cash monthly	($ 33,572)	$ 53,224	$ 56,714	($ 30,718)	$ 62,524	$ 64,104	($ 34,343)	$ 74,554	$ 78,054	($ 50,143)	$ 74,304	$ 77,704	
Cumulative	$319,482	$372,706	$429,420	$398,702	$461,226	$525,330	$490,987	$565,541	$643,595	$593,452	$667,756	$745,460	
Earnings per share (1,000 shares outstanding)													$ 361.11

*Noncash items

FINANCING

Having completed his plan, Bardlow contacted a group of friends and associates who were interested in boating—doctors, lawyers, dentists, and other potential investors who might contribute start-up capital. They, in turn, called their associates and soon developed a network of potential investors.

Very quickly, $200,000 was raised from 16 investors. Two of the investors contributed $20,000, and one invested $30,000. Bardlow retained 35 percent of the company stock; his inventor/partner, 20 percent, and the investors had 45 percent ownership in the firm.

MANAGEMENT

Bardlow was a CPA and controller of Hayden Street Research and Management Company, an investment advisory firm. He had spent six years with Price Waterhouse before joining Hayden Street. He owned a 25-foot sailboat and was knowledgeable about the general marine industry. He intended to continue his work at Hayden Street during the start-up and to become the full-time president when Sidethrusters reached annual sales of 120 units. The CEO of Hayden Street Research supported Bardlow's plan, although he declined to become an investor in the new firm.

Bardlow's partner, Al Carella, became the company's vice president and only full-time employee. Carella had worked on propulsion systems with the Navy and Coast Guard over the past 20 years. He was the inventor of the side-thruster and assisted Bardlow in the sales effort. Carella had total responsibility for manufacturing, assembly, and shipping.

The first sale was to the Shannon Boat Company, which installed a unit in a 50-foot yacht at its Rhode Island boat yard. Bardlow recalled:

> One of the most nervous days in my life was watching a brand new, $350,000 boat sitting at the dock, with the president of Shannon next to me and my engineer standing in the cockpit saying, "OK, I'm ready." I'm saying to myself, "Please work. Please, please work." Al kicked it on.
>
> The bow went right away from the dock. The president said, "Wonderful. This is just what I want." The inventor is standing there smiling like a Cheshire cat. And I'm trying to remain cool and calm, as if I knew all along it would work. But we had never tested the thing. We assumed it would work, but we weren't sure. I was ecstatic. Shannon makes three to five 50-foot boats per year, and they gave us a blanket order.

In the first two years of company operations, approximately 110 sailboats in excess of 50 feet were built all over the world; side-thrusters were installed in 70 of those boats. Bardlow recognized early, however, that the growth he wanted called for more than just installations in new sailboats. It called for more than a part-time effort, as well. He left Hayden Street Research and decided to go to the aftermarket, retrofitting existing pleasure boats. "We decided to go after the powerboat market, because the ratio of power to sail is 25 boats to 1," said Bardlow. (Exhibit 5 shows approximate fleet sizes in the United States.)

An aggressive ad campaign featured quarter-page ads in industry magazines *Yachting* and a new publication called *Power and Motor Yacht*. "New

EXHIBIT 5   Statistics on Boat Sales and Boat Ownership, 1987–1988

New Boat Sales 1987

Inboard boats (cruisers)	13,100
Sailboats (auxiliary powered)	
30 feet and under	1,100
Over 30 feet	2,900
Total	17,100

Industry Estimate of Ownership 1987

Inboard boats owned (to include powered sailboats)	481,000

Registration by Boat Length 1988

	Inboard	Outboard	Total
Over 65 feet	1,855	1,257	3,112
40–65 feet	33,942	5,735	39,677
26–40 feet	245,835	54,921	300,756

Source: *A Statistical Report on America's Top Family Sport* (Chicago: National Marine Manufacturers Association, 1988).

Sidethruster maneuvers boats in tight spots!" shouted the headline, over a picture of a motor yacht swinging in to a crowded dock. "The first small thruster designed for boats 40' to 100' long!" The ads went on:

Sidethruster's new hydraulic thruster delivers big moving power in a small package. Installed in the bow, the six-inch model (less than half the size of a conventional thruster) can turn a 40-foot yacht nearly within its own length. A unique direct drive 7 hp motor delivers 260 lbs. of thrust in the 8-inch model and 230 lbs. for the 6-inch model.

Side-thrusters can be installed in one day. For more information on how to put some maneuvering power on your side, contact . . . .

THE RETROFIT MARKET

In the retrofit market, side-thrusters were installed on site at the boat owner's dry dock. Two oval holes were drilled on opposing sides of the fore section of the boat below the water line. Pressure hoses, a power take-off unit, and a precision machined brass pump unit were installed while the boat was in dry dock. All the materials were purchased from subcontractors; they were mostly assembled from readily available components.

To install the side-thruster, management had to hire its own work crew. Bardlow explained:

No boat yard would touch it. If a boat yard cuts two big holes in the hull and the boat happens to sink instead of moving sideways, that yard is liable to the tune of $250,000 to $500,000 (whatever the price of the boat was). I had to hire my own guys. We had never drilled a hole in the side of a boat—any boat.

The very first powerboat we did was a Grand Banks 36, owned by a doctor in New York. I personally led the three-man installation crew to the customer's yard. The guy doing the installation says, "I've worked on boats all my life; this is no problem." So we arrive and there's this gorgeous fiberglass boat waiting for us. To mark the site for the holes we ran tape from the bow along the side to locate the right height and length. Fortunately, we're doing this at 9 o'clock at night with flashlights, so no one can see us.

We drilled one hole. It is a six-inch unit, but a hull is shaped at an angle, so elliptically the hole comes out about 14 inches high. As my crew leader is drilling this thing I am saying, "Are you crazy? Look at the size of this thing." We drilled a little bit, then a little bigger. We finished the holes at 2 o'clock in the morning.

The boat owner came down the next morning at 9 o'clock, walked around the boat and the color drains from his face. No tunnel. Just two huge holes, one on either side of the hull, and fiberglass dust all over everything. We hadn't realized how much dust we created. The owner said, "You guys have this thing in my boat by this afternoon or tomorrow morning you're going to get sued!"

The next day they put the boat in the water. There was no leakage! It was perfectly dry and it worked. It worked really well!

Sidethrusters' installation crew flew to boat yards in Maryland, Florida, Texas, California, and Alaska to install units in owners' boats. Bardlow took the responsibility: Insurance coverage for product liability was prohibitively expensive, and if something went wrong the whole company would be at risk.

The retrofit market presented a great problem because every boat was different. No one boat in the powerboat market was standard. Even the same model boats were customized for individual buyers. Sidethrusters had installation agreements for half a dozen Grand Banks 42-foot cruisers, but Grand Banks offered three different engine configurations for its boats. Bardlow explained:

We did the first one, and we died putting it in, but we put it in. We get the second order, we say to ourselves, "We have already done one of these; it should be a lay-up." We cut all the hydraulic hoses based on our previous experience, went down to do the project, and the engines were in a different location. All our hoses were cut wrong. We had to airfreight new hoses in to complete the job.

I couldn't legitimately and accurately estimate how long it would take us to install a unit. Not even once.

EARLY RESULTS AND FUTURE PROSPECTS

Bardlow believed the market potential for the side-thruster was very large. During the first two years of operations, the company had sold over 80 side-thrusters; a number of those had been retrofits. Company revenues reached nearly $500,000, but Sidethrusters had not made a profit. Bardlow had not foreseen the travel expense for the installation crews as a factor when he put together the financial projections in his business plan. Because of the large potential market, however, he was confident the company would succeed.

CRAFTING STRATEGY IN SINGLE-BUSINESS COMPANIES

. . . .

MANNA GROCERY AND THE HEALTH-FOODS INDUSTRY

Barbara J. Allison, The University of Alabama*

In 1972, Richard Nixon was president, *The Godfather* was playing at theaters around the country, bell-bottom jeans were the rage, and American troops were returning home from Southeast Asia. That fall, in Tuscaloosa, Alabama, Bear Bryant was the head football coach at the University of Alabama (UA), the football team was undefeated and seeking its eighth national championship, and Earl Drennen opened Harmony Natural Foods on what UA students called "the strip."

Earl's father, a successful Tuscaloosa businessperson, suffered from poor health most of his life and died at the age of 65 after a 10-year bout with chronic illness. The circumstances surrounding his father's death disturbed Earl, and he began to research medical literature for the key to longevity and healthy living. In his readings, Earl became intrigued with the holistic approach to good health and decided to start practicing a holistic life-style. He began a daily regimen of exercise, modified his diet to include only natural and health foods, and began meditating for his mental and spiritual well-being. Earl stated:

> When I retire, I really want to be able to enjoy life. That is really the thrust that got me involved in the health-foods industry. Initially, I just started studying (the health-foods industry) and applying natural foods and holistic health to my personal life and, as a result, some positive changes occurred in my life.

Earl's improved health and physical well-being soon inspired him to open Harmony Natural Foods, the first retailer specializing in natural and organic foods in Tuscaloosa. Earl ran Harmony Foods until 1976.

> My brother had about 50 acres out in Boulder, Colorado, with four big log cabins and a big dining hall, that he shared with some other people. He called me up one day and he just said, "Won't you come on out and do something different?" So, we said, "OK," sold the business, and moved out there. Even some of the people that had worked with us moved out there. Frances and I thought that we had done all that we could do and had gone as far as we could go with the business. Both of us had a lot of energy and felt that we needed to express ourselves in other ways.

In 1979, the Drennens moved back to Tuscaloosa. There was no health-foods store in town that could adequately meet their dietary needs, so Earl and his wife, Frances, drove to Birmingham (about 60 miles northeast of Tuscaloosa) to do most of their grocery shopping. A carpentry accident that almost caused Earl to lose a hand prompted him to rethink what he wanted to do for a living:

---

*Prepared under the supervision of Professor Arthur A. Thompson, Jr. Copyright © 1991 by the author.

During the time I was out of work, I concluded I needed to get back into the original field that I had been in. I realized that there was so much more to learn and there was so much more I could do and so much more that (my wife and I) could offer the community. There was still a health-foods store where Harmony Natural Foods had been located, but it was totally inadequate. Frances and I believed that there was sufficient room in the Tuscaloosa market for an additional health-foods store. So, in January of 1980, we started the Manna Grocery, and I felt really good about doing that. I felt that I had upheld my moral and ethical obligations to the Tuscaloosa community.

In 1991, Manna Grocery was a thriving establishment with annual sales just under $700,000.

THE HEALTH-FOODS INDUSTRY

Throughout the 1980s, health and nutrition concerns captured the attention of the American public. Many individuals reevaluated their eating habits. The concept of a healthy diet penetrated the American psyche and contributed greatly to the increased consumption of health foods and the growth of the health-foods industry.

Health-conscious individuals started taking a closer look at what they ate and how they ate, reading food labels, checking for additives and sodium, monitoring the levels of saturated fat and cholesterol in their foods, counting calories, limiting their red meat intake (or deleting it), and eating foods that were high in fiber and complex carbohydrates. From 1970 to 1991, the health-foods industry grew from a $200 million industry to a $4 billion industry (see Exhibit 1), accounting for about 1.5 percent of food and vitamin sales in the United States.

History of the Health-Foods Industry

Traditional health-food stores emerged in the 1920s in California and in larger cities such as Chicago and New York. These stores attracted elite or eccentric groups of individuals such as socialites, performers, artists, and actors who believed that certain foods and nutrients could improve their health. Many of these individuals were also proponents of homeopathic medicine and frequented health-food stores for products that were believed to rejuvenate their bodies and minds.

By 1984, the Federal Trade Commission had deemed the term *health food* undefined/or undefinable and had prohibited the term from use in the advertising and labeling of any food. The term *health food* was usually used only when designating the name of a store. However, health food was also considered a generic term that covered all organic, natural, and special diet products. Natural foods were defined as products that contained no preservatives, emulsifiers, artificial colorings and flavorings, and or other additives. Organic food referred to produce grown without chemicals or synthetic pesticides and fertilizers and marketed without preservatives, dyes, or waxes; organic foods that were dried, canned, or boxed had no additives or preservatives, except for salt. With respect to beef and poultry, the term *organic* indicated the animal had been raised on organically grown feed and had not been given any antibiotics or hormones to enhance growth. Organically grown foods were usually cultivated in ways that minimized adverse impacts on the environment.

EXHIBIT 1   Growth of the Health-Food Industry

Year	Overall Sales
1971	$200 million
1979	$1.80 billion
1988	$3.55 billion
1989	$3.63 billion

Source: *Natural Foods Merchandiser,* June 1990, p. 34.

Increased consumer concerns regarding food quality surfaced soon after the formation of the Environmental Protection Agency (EPA) in 1970. Through the enactment of its various regulations, the EPA was instrumental in educating the public about food quality standards, food content, and potential food hazards and risks. As consumer knowledge about food increased, consumer attitudes toward food consumption changed in ways that paved the way for the modern natural-foods store. Until this time, most health-food stores operated in cramped quarters at out-of-the-way locations; merchandise selections were limited and unattractively displayed; and prices were well above regular food products. As the industry grew, proprietors began opening larger, better-lighted stores that were well kept and exhibited more up-to-date merchandising practices.

The nutritional interest generated in the early 1970s continued to build through the 1980s. The primary drivers were (1) publicity concerning the health benefits of natural foods; (2) the increased incidences of cancer, high blood pressure, and heart attacks, which required individuals to modify their dietary habits; and (3) greater concern for the environment.

Health-Food Stores

There were three types of health-food retailers in 1991: (1) supermarkets and other mass-merchandising outlets, (2) major health-food chains, and (3) independent natural and health-food stores. Exhibit 2 provides market share and sales data for these three segments.

Supermarkets and Mass-Merchandising Outlets   Sales of natural products by mass-market retailers reached $798 million in 1989, a 17.5 percent increase over 1988; this volume included only products merchandised in a distinct natural-food setting or supplied by natural-food enterprises. Much of the growth realized in the mass market during 1989 represented supermarket management's response to consumer concerns about cholesterol, additives, preservatives, and pesticide residues in food by stocking shelves with natural, cholesterol-free products, and organically grown produce. The merchandising and display of health food in supermarkets had been evolving since the late 1970s. In previous years, most stores employed formats in which each natural-food product was displayed beside competing brands of the same type item. To increase the visibility of their health-food merchandise, increasing numbers of supermarket retailers were segregating health-food products and creating health-food departments, sometimes reserving aisles just for natural products and hiring natural-foods experts to staff these specialized sections.

EXHIBIT 2   Types of Health and Natural-Food Retailers, 1989

Type of Store	Number of Stores	1989 Dollar Sales of Health Foods	Share of Industry Sales
Supermarkets and other mass-merchandising outlets	138,000	$798 million	20 %
Health-food chains	1,440	$503 million	13 %
Independent natural and health-food stores			
Small health-food stores	1,590	$708 million	18.0%
Medium health-food stores	2,160	$960 million	24.5
Small natural-food stores	540	$239 million	6.1
Medium natural-food stores	1,410	$626 million	16.0
Large natural-food store	220	$ 97 million	2.5
Independent store subtotal	5,920	$2.63 billion	67
Total	145,360	$3.93 billion	100 %

Source: *Natural Foods Merchandiser,* June 1990; pp. 34–35.

Kroger, the largest U.S. supermarket chain, built a high profile in natural foods by creating natural-foods sections in many of its stores; these stores had weekly sales averaging $375,000, of which between $4,500 and $9,500 represented natural foods. Among the other top 20 supermarket chains, only Ralphs and Vons in Los Angeles, Stop & Shop in Boston, and H. E. Butt in Texas were doing much in the marketing of natural foods. Midsized supermarket chains were more likely than large or small small-sized chains to stock natural products and to staff their natural-products sections.

Major Health-Food Chains   Major health-food chains (defined as retailers operating more than 40 stores) had 1,440 health-store outlets in 1989 and accounted for $500 million in sales. The five largest North American chains were General Nutrition Centers, Nature Food Centers, Great Earth International, Nutrition World, and Fred Meyer Nutrition. The health-food chain stores primarily marketed vitamins, food supplements, and a limited assortment of health-food products; they did not merchandise the full array of natural and health-food products that were on the market. A big fraction of the outlets of health-food chains were located in shopping malls.

Independent Natural and Health-Food Stores   Independent natural and health-food stores dominated the industry, accounting for 67 percent of industry sales. There was a distinction between health-food stores and natural-food stores. Health-food stores obtained more than 40 percent of their sales from vitamins, supplements, herbs, and personal care items, while natural-food stores derived less than 40 percent of their sales from these product categories (see Exhibit 3 for the various types of store formats). Virtually all of the 5,920 independent stores in operation in 1989 were owner-managed. One store operator observed, "Most of the new stores opening are coming from established, existing retailers. There's still room for the new entrepreneur, but even with these people, they have had a few years of experience working for another retailer." According to a major supplier of natural food products:

EXHIBIT 3   Types of Independent Health and Natural-Food Stores

Small Health-Food Store Format	Small Natural-Food Store Format	Medium Health-Food Store Format	Medium Natural-Food Store Format	Large Natural-Food Store Format
Vitamin-oriented outlets smaller than 1,000 square feet, these are typical "mom and pop" health-food stores. Their numbers are dwindling, primarily because the proliferation of natural grocery products is forcing them into larger sizes. Their marketing niche is deep product knowledge, health information, and customer service.	Food-oriented outlets smaller than 1,000 square feet, these stores are generally found in small towns or cramped inner-city spaces. About a fifth of them are co-ops. Some amazingly cram all sorts of departments into small spaces, but most eventually find larger quarters.	Vitamin-oriented stores larger than 1,000 square feet, these stores rely on supplements but pick up extra volume from food items. Many offer food service and some are transforming themselves into food-oriented outlets. This is the most likely format for multiple operation.	Food-oriented stores from 1,000 to 4,000 square feet, these are a diverse amalgam of natural-food stores. Many are smaller versions of natural supermarkets and may eventually expand into supermarket size as they seek to add departments and more products.	Food-oriented stores of more than 4,000 square feet, these stores emphasize perishable departments such as produce, deli, and meat. They attract many customers, but generally must be located in high-population areas. With high sales volumes, they seem to straddle the border between the natural products industry and conventional grocers.

Source: *Natural Foods Merchandiser,* June 1990, p. 35

EXHIBIT 4   Selected Operating Statistics for Independent Health-Food Stores, 1989

	Small Health-Food Stores	Small Natural-Food Stores	Medium Health-Food Stores	Medium Natural-Food Stores	Large Natural-Food Stores
Average cost of store	$ 75,000	$ 55,000	$140,000	$220,000	$ 652,000
Average retail size (sq. ft.)	757	821	1958	2212	7114
Customers per day	44	70	87	195	805
Average sale	$ 12.63	$ 8.80	$12.25	$ 11.05	$ 13.76
Average annual volume	$159,000	$210,000	$303,000	$654,000	$3,130,000
Sales per square foot	$ 210	$ 256	$ 155	$ 296	$ 440
% of stores offering food service	6.7%	23.0%	17.2%	25.2%	71.2%
Average retail space for food service*	100	170	516	925	665
Average seating	—	6	43	35	33
Average number of full-time employees	1.5	1.8	4.2	10.6	38.3
Average number of part-time employees	.9	2.9	4.4	9	26.5
Average hourly wage of full-time employees	$ 5.07	$ 4.98	$ 5.38	$ 5.50	$ 5.72
Average hourly wage of part-time employees	$ 4.86	$ 4.44	$ 4.74	$ 4.25	$ 4.91
Inventory value	$ 21,900	$ 18,000	$ 35,000	$ 40,500	$ 134,500
Annual inventory turns	4.7	7.9	5.6	11.3	16.3

*Square feet

Source: *Natural Foods Merchandiser,* June 1990, pp. 41–42, 44, 46, 51, 54

EXHIBIT 5   Operating Statements for Independent Health-Food Stores, 1989

	Small Health-Food Stores	Small Natural-Food Stores	Medium Health-Food Stores	Medium Natural-Food Stores	Large Natural-Food Stores
Gross volume ($)	$159,000	$210,000	$303,000	$654,000	$3,130,000
Cost of goods sold	62.3%	67.5%	63.4%	69.4%	66.3%
Gross profit margin	37.7	32.5	36.6	30.6	33.7
Payroll	18.1	19.5	19.3	16.8	18.1
Rent	5.2	3.6	5.7	2.7	2.5
Utilities	2	2.3	2.4	1.8	1.5
Advertising	1.8	1.9	2.5	1.2	1.6
Miscellaneous overhead	1.3	2.3	1.4	5	7.8
Pre-tax net profit	9.3%	2.9%	5.3%	3.1%	2.2%

Source: *Natural Foods Merchandiser,* June 1990, p. 41.

. . . (a) good, basic 3,000-square-foot store can be opened for a $105,000 total investment, including inventory, and can gross $15,000 a week if it's in the right location and merchandised properly.

Exhibit 4 provides representative operating statistics for the various types of independent stores. Exhibit 5 presents a percentage breakdown of the typical store's income statement.

Independent natural and health-food stores varied significantly regarding number of years in the business, market area population, and location (see Exhibit 6). One disadvantage of single-store ownership was the inability to exercise buying leverage with food manufacturers and distributors. Large

EXHIBIT 6   Selected Characteristics of Independent Health-Food Stores

	Small Health-Food Stores	Small Natural-Food Stores	Medium Health-Food Stores	Medium Natural-Food Stores	Large Natural-Food Stores
Ownership structure					
Sole proprietorship	51.1%	22.3%	31.3%	9.0%	4.3%
Partnership	14.7%	14.4%	6.3%	5.3%	13.2%
Private corporation	34.2%	44.5%	62.5%	67.9%	63.3%
Co-op	.0%	18.8%	.0%	17.8%	19.2%
Years in business					
Average age	8.4	9.4	11.9	12.2	13.2
Less than 2 years	2.1%	6.8%	9.9%	6.6%	4.8%
From 2 to 5 years	36.5%	23.1%	15.7%	16.1%	13.1%
From 6 to 10 years	32.9%	46.2%	19.2%	31.2%	30.3%
Greater than 10 years	28.5%	23.9%	55.2%	46.1%	51.8%
Oldest store in years	60	20	51	38	25
Market area population					
Rural (less than 50,000)	29.4%	54.3%	25.8%	16.7%	3.8%
Suburban (50,000 to 500,000)	52.9%	37.6%	45.2%	56.7%	57.7%
Urban (more than 500,000)	17.6%	8.1%	29.0%	26.7%	38.5%
Type of location					
Mall	5.5%	1.5%	19.5%	.0%	2.0%
Strip shopping center	37.8%	34.4%	45.2%	20.7%	32.7%
Business district	45.9%	42.6%	29.0%	41.4%	49.0%
Residential area	5.8%	8.3%	6.5%	27.6%	12.3%
Rural highway	5.0%	13.2%	.0%	10.3%	4.1%

Source: *Natural Foods Merchandiser*, June 1990, p. 48.

natural-food stores were sometimes referred to as *glamour stores*; examples included Mrs. Gooch's Natural Foods Ranch Markets, Whole Foods Markets, Sun Harvest Farms, Puget Consumers Co-op, Boney's Markets, and Squash Blossom. Their appeal was broad production selection and emphasis on fresh, organically grown produce. These stores had attractive layouts, utilized proactive merchandising practices, and appealed to a wider variety of food shoppers. For many of their customers, shopping at these trendy, upscale, glamour stores was the "in" thing to do.

Products

Products in health and natural-food stores differed notably from conventional food products—(see Exhibit 7 for examples). To the first-time or inexperienced shopper, many products on the shelves in a natural or health-food store appeared odd. There were bags of blue potato chips, cartons of nondairy beverages processed from rice and almonds, and supplements containing Spirulina, a blue-green algae. Unfamiliar items were not well understood and sometimes confusing to novice shoppers. Having a competent staff able to respond to the concerns and questions of newer shoppers was a key to broaden a store's customer base. Also, many products in the health-foods industry were packaged in recyclable materials.

EXHIBIT 7   Sample Comparisons of Conventional Products and Natural-Food Products

Mayonnaise
Hellman's real mayonnaise—conventional
    Ingredients: Soybean oil, partially hydrogenated soybean oil, whole eggs, vinegar, water, egg yolks, salt, sugar, lemon juice, and natural flavors. Calcium disodium edta used to protect freshness.
Hain eggless mayonnaise—natural
    Ingredients: 100% pure expeller pressed soy oil, water, honey, grain vinegar, lemon juice concentrate, spices, xanthan (vegetable gum), and onion powder. No cholesterol, preservatives, eggs, salt, or animal fats added.

Corn Chips
Frito-Lay corn chips—conventional
    Ingredients: Corn, vegetable oil (contains corn oil or partially hydrogenated sunflower oil), and salt. No preservatives.
Bearitos tortilla chips—natural
    Ingredients: Stoneground organic corn, high oleic sunflower or safflower oil, and/or unhydrogenated pure corn oil. No salt.

Ready-to-Eat Breakfast Cereal
Frosted Flakes—conventional
    Ingredients: Corn, sugar, malt, salt, flavoring, corn syrup. No artificial colors or flavors.
High Fiber cornflakes—natural
    Ingredients: Flaked, milled organic yellow corn,* corn bran,* unsweetened concentrated fruit juice (pineapple, peach, and pear), sprouted barley malt, and sea malt. No preservatives, refined sugar, or additives.

*Certified organically grown and processed in accordance with Section 26569.11 of the California Health & Safety Code.

Exhibits 8 and 9 depict the distinct departments found within most independent food stores along with their average contributions to overall store sales and the profit margins associated with these departments. Some of the best-selling products during 1989 and the early 1990s were organically grown foods, "green" products, oat bran, frozen health foods, and herbs.

Manufacturers and Suppliers of Health and Natural-Food Products

Some manufacturers specialized in only a few products while other companies were involved in the production of a large line of products. For example, Allegro specialized in the production of coffee, offering dozens of blends. Tree of Life offered a full line of juices, cereals, pasta, grains, jellies, and cheeses.

Retailers were served by five types of suppliers: natural-foods distributors, grocery distributors, local vendors, manufacturers, and brokers. About 183 distributors and wholesalers in 32 states serviced the industry in 1991. These suppliers, the majority of which were located in California, serviced anywhere from 30 to 5,000 accounts and had anywhere from 1 to 40 salespeople. Most served a multistate region, while a few large suppliers had nationwide coverage. Some specialized in supplying a few product lines; others carried a broad product line, although no supplier had the product line breadth to supply an

EXHIBIT 8   Percent of Overall Sales by Department for Independent
Health-Food Stores, 1989

Department	Small Health-Food Stores	Small Natural-Food Stores	Medium Health-Food Stores	Medium Natural-Food Stores	Large Natural-Food Stores
Vitamins/supplements	51 %	14.3%	42 %	10.3%	10 %
Personal care	7.1	5.6	5.0	4.9	4.8
Herbs	12.5	6.9	6.0	3.2	3.1
Grocery	14.7	29.1	21.1	27.9	25.6
Bulk foods	2.3	12.1	4.1	12.7	9.1
Produce	.6	11.3	2	13.8	17.2
Dairy/refrigerated	2.5	11.5	3	8.2	7.3
Frozen	3.5	2.9	3.5	4.7	4.2
Deli, juice bar	.4	2.3	1.9	5.5	7.2
Restaurant	0	.2	4.1	3.1	2.9
Meat, poultry, seafood	0	.1	0	.9	4.8
Bakery	0	.6	1	.6	.9
Books	2.9	2.2	3.6	1.8	1.5
Non-foods	2.5	.9	2.7	2.4	1.4
Total	100 %	100 %	100 %	100 %	100 %

Source: *Natural Foods Merchandiser*, June 1990, p. 35.

EXHIBIT 9   Profit Margins by Department and Overall for
Indepenent Health-Food Stores, 1989

Department	Small Health-Food Stores	Small Natural-Food Stores	Medium Health-Food Stores	Medium Natural-Food Stores	Large Natural-Food Stores
Vitamins/supplements	42.4%	43.3%	46.1%	40.0%	40.7%
Personal care	36.8	38.9	39.9	37.0	37.9
Herbs	40.2	50.2	43.4	43.3	49.3
Grocery	30.2	33.2	32.6	27.5	32.1
Bulk foods	30.0	40.4	38.2	34.2	34.9
Produce	25.0	32.2	34.0	30.4	30.5
Dairy/refrigerated	29.7	29.0	29.7	26.9	24.7
Frozen foods	26.2	35.3	28.7	31.1	28.7
Deli/juice bar	—	—	33.3	46.1	47.7
Restaurant	—	—	60.0	59.2	62.0
Meat, seafood, poultry	—	—	—	20.1	29.1
Bakery items	—	—	65.0	45.2	45.3
Books	31.8	36.7	36.2	34.8	33.2
Nonfoods	41.7	40.4	35.8	38.7	30.1
Gross profit margin (storewide)	37.7	32.5	36.6	30.6	33.7
Net profit margin (storewide)	9.3%	2.9%	5.3%	3.1%	2.2%

Source: *Natural Foods Merchandiser*, June 1990, pp. 35, 39.

entire store with its complete needs. Retailers could expect anywhere from a one- to seven-day delivery time on orders, depending on the supplier.

It was common for many of the larger distributors such as Tree of Life, Cornucopia Natural Foods, Inc., Stow Mills, and Nature's Best to have private-label items. Practically all of the distributors and wholesalers provided special services for retailers such as merchandising and promotional assistance, newsletters, volume discounts, free samples, and computerized ordering. Suppliers were reluctant to open accounts to serve stores in questionable locations or whose owners had no experience in natural-foods retailing. Suppliers liked to see a new retailer start out with a smaller store and expand from there.

Customers

The health-foods industry was catering to individuals from all walks of life in 1991. One industry survey found there were two basic consumer groups: primary shoppers and secondary shoppers. Primary shoppers were individuals who ate healthy foods for philosophical reasons, who chose natural-food stores because of an affinity in life-styles and values, and who spent the majority of their food dollars in natural-food stores. Secondary shoppers included people who ate health foods occasionally, who were eating healthy foods to treat a current health problem, who ate certain natural-food products on doctor's orders, but who spent the majority of their food budgets in supermarkets. Secondary shoppers were more price conscious than primary shoppers. Exhibit 10 provides information on the fundamental reasons people shopped at health-foods stores.

Industry reports suggested the average shopper was most likely to be an affluent white female, age 30 to 44, who had a college education. Over 60 percent of natural-foods shoppers had college degrees, and 73 percent were under 45 years old. The median income of natural-foods shoppers was $36,000 compared to $31,000 for all shoppers. About 40 percent of natural-food shoppers maintained vegetarian diets, compared to a national average of just 10 percent. Because surveys showed the majority of people wouldn't go out of their way to purchase a healthy product (even if a doctor advised them to), the most successful stores had visible locations and adequate parking. Strip-mall locations were generally considered optimal.

While most customers had frequented health and natural-food stores for a number of years, many were relatively new to the industry. To adequately service longtime shoppers familiar with most products, stores needed to provide only a modest level of product advice and customer assistance. However, new shoppers, many of whom had reservations about shopping at natural and health-food stores and were unfamiliar with most of the products, typically had many questions about products, and they needed to be given considerable personal attention to transform them into regular patrons.

In an effort to expand sales and customer bases, many retailers had begun store expansions and renovations. According to one owner, who recently opened a new store, "These (new customers) are not embracing my new store for the reasons that my old customers did. They are not into the philosophy of natural products. For them, the store is a popular upscale thing. That means our service must be excellent or they won't come back." Of the new stores that

EXHIBIT 10   **Fundamental Reasons People Shop at Health-Food Stores**

Reason	Percentage
To prevent future illness	50%
For spiritual or personal philosophy	20
To treat an existing health problem	10
To provide extra energy and stamina	10
Because healthy foods taste better	10
Total	100%

Source: *Natural Foods Merchandiser*, July 1990, p. 53.

opened in 1989, those having more floor space and wider product variety and selection were performing the best.

One store owner observed, "There's minimal consumer preference for one brand, or one variety over another. There are twice as many juices as there were five years ago, . . . (and) the number of varieties has outstripped demand." Another owner reported that many customers would go through his stores and buy nothing but specials: "New shoppers are more price conscious. They want to think they are getting a good deal—even though we generally preserve our margins on these specials."

Because many natural-foods products were different concerning ingredients, taste, and preparation, many people had to acquire a taste for certain health-food items and there was a great deal of buyer resistance to trying many items that health-foods stores stocked. This was especially true for secondary customers. A friend of the case writer once wrote in a Christmas letter:

> Jerry and I are doing what most Americans our age are doing—panicking about our past eating habits and trying to atone for our sins. I don't know about the rest of you, but I had a hard time this year planning amusing holiday treats out of fish and oat bran.

Competition

Competition varied according to geographic location. A health-food store operating in a city in Southern California was much more likely to have other health-food store competitors than a store operating in Tuscaloosa, Alabama (population 135,000). Competition was most often confined to a store's general locale; for example, a store in Tuscaloosa did not experience meaningful competition from stores in Birmingham, some 60 miles away. The biggest competitive threats for independent stores were:

- Supermarkets, which were beginning to merchandise their natural products in separate sections.
- Major food companies such as Del Monte, Kraft General Foods, and Campbell Soup, which typically sold through supermarket channels and were introducing new brands and reformulating existing products to more closely imitate the ingredients and nutritional content of health and natural-food products.

Recently, name-brand food companies had started using colors and patterns on their packages that were similar to the colors and patterns used by traditional health-food companies on their genuine health products. Also, they were using terms such as *nutritious*, *low fat*, and *natural* to describe their food items. Furthermore, supermarkets were not committed to natural products and health-food consumers in the way independent stores were. According to one industry analyst, "(Supermarkets) just want to sell what sells." An independent store owner noted, "The health foods stores that do their own marketing, that are proactive, are doing well. But many stores are still reactive." Another observed, "The growing stores are playing offense and the others are playing defense."

Customer Service   One way independent stores were able to gain a competitive advantage over their competitors in the mass market was by providing customers with knowledgeable and courteous staff members who would educate them on how to select and prepare natural and organic foods. Many owners of independent stores insisted that all their employees be able to assist customers who had certain health and dietary concerns, and that they be able to direct them to the products they needed.

Marketing   Many stores tried to improve their visibility by advertising actively in newspapers, on the radio, on billboards, on television, and by sending advertisements through the mail. Many store owners kept a mailing list of regular customers so they could be notified about such things as price specials and new products. Most store owners participated in promotions and specials sponsored by suppliers.

MANNA GROCERY

Harmony Natural Foods, Earl Drennen's first store, operated out of a 900-square-foot building that rented for $150 per month. Earl was able to acquire the location and purchase initial inventories with a $5,000 bank loan. Earl described the first store:

> The store was small, and we carried a limited number of products, mainly because, at that time, there just weren't that many products made available to us by the industry. We took the wood from a barn that had been torn down and used it to decorate the store. So, we had weathered wood on the walls, crude wooden shelves, and lots of earthtones throughout the store—it was very much in keeping with the times.

Harmony Natural Foods' store hours were 10 A.M. to 6 P.M. Monday through Saturday. Earl explained:

> I would go into work around 9 in the morning and work until about 3 in the afternoon. Then I would go home and do yard work, and Frances would come in from her morning job and work from 3 P.M. until around 7 at night.

In 1974, the Drennens, with the help of Scott Morrow and his wife, opened a small restaurant in the back of the store that sat approximately 12 people. Until this point, Earl and Frances had been the only Harmony employees. Scott and his wife worked at Manna for about a year and a half. The addition of the restaurant, which was open for lunch Monday through Saturday, raised the average number of customers patronizing Harmony per day from 65 to 150.

According to Earl, by the winter of 1975, they were beginning to outgrow their location:

> By 1975, the store was really catching on, and it began to get crowded. We acquired the building directly next door to the store; it had been a variety kind of gift shop called the Factory, which had gone out of business. We knocked a hole in the wall and obtained some more space.

The expansion, which provided approximately 500 more square feet, was financed with a $20,000 bank loan. With the $20,000 in working capital, Earl handled the added rental space, purchased additional inventories, and hired more employees.

Earl described the decision to sell Harmony in the summer of 1976:

> We had a number of people who wanted to buy the store, but we wanted to try to sell it to someone we felt would carry on the whole energy that we had put into the business up to that point. We really didn't want to leave the community or our employees (we had about eight employees at that time) high and dry. So, we ended up selling it to two friends, Malcolm LaBron and his wife, Debbie, and unfortunately they got burned by the business. I just don't think they realized how much work it was going to take to run the business. Unfortunately, most people think that you can just come in and open up at 10 A.M. and leave at 5 P.M., and that just isn't the case—you have to stay there as long as you need to. A business never grows up. It is always growing and changing; you can never take your success for granted. So, to make a long story short, the business went down, and the LaBrons ended up losing money and selling the business to someone else.

The LaBrons sold Harmony Natural Foods in 1978 to Carl Seigal, who owned a number of other businesses in the Tuscaloosa area. Seigal kept the store as a natural-food store and continued to operate the restaurant, but he renamed the enterprise Just Right Foods. Earl explained:

> Carl was single and led a real active life-style. He liked to water ski in the summer down in Florida, and, in the wintertime, he liked to go snow skiing in Colorado. He just didn't have the time necessary to run the business. In 1981, or 1982, he ended up selling it to someone who put in a pizza place, and then that went out of business.

A year after Earl and Frances returned to Tuscaloosa, they decided to open Manna Grocery. They took out a $35,000 loan with their original bank, acquired 2,000 square feet of strip mall rental space, purchased needed inventories and fixtures, and hired an employee. The rent was $500 per month. When Earl and Frances decided to open Manna, one of their major concerns was finding a good location for the business; they both felt fortunate in securing a location within 100 yards of the busiest intersection in Tuscaloosa. Manna Grocery's store hours were 10 A.M. until 6 P.M. Monday through Saturday. The interior of Manna Grocery was much different from the interior of Harmony Natural Foods. The decor consisted of lighter colors and natural woods, and much more refrigeration and freezer space was available.

Manna Grocery was successful for a few years but then ran into a cash flow squeeze that led Earl to sever the store's ties with its bank:

> In about 1983, we were really at a crucial point with the business because we just weren't making it. We needed to do something in relation to borrowing some

more money, and First Alabama Bank would not loan us the money. To this day, it is real obvious to me that the reason they didn't loan us the money was because they didn't have any vision, and they looked at our business as something that was weird and probably wasn't going to make it. Somehow, we got involved with Betty Kimbrough, who was a loan officer at AmSouth Bank, and she and the bank were just really positive about loaning us the money. They were positive about everything. It meant a lot to us that somebody believed in us.

In 1986, a run-in with local health department inspectors led to a decision to begin serving lunch items at Manna. According to Earl:

I really didn't want to get into the restaurant side of the business because it is just so demanding, and it is a lot of work. However, we were selling frozen yogurt, and the health department came in and said, "If you are going to sell frozen yogurt, you have to have a three compartment stainless steel sink." We told them that we had been selling the stuff for five years without a three compartment stainless steel sink, and we didn't see why we should have to get one now. But, they said, if we didn't put the sink in, we would have to stop selling frozen yogurt. So we asked the health department whether or not we could do more than sell yogurt if we got the sink, and they said yes. So since we were going to make the investment in the sink, we decided we would go ahead and make some sandwiches while we were at it.

Initially, a loan was not required to start the restaurant, but later, when a 200-square-foot kitchen was added, Earl took out a $10,000 loan with AmSouth. The restaurant provided seating for 24 people. By early 1989, Manna's store hours had been extended by one hour in the evenings, and the store was servicing approximately 200 customers a day, half of whom were patronizing the restaurant. In fact, the restaurant had become so successful that a bigger store with more parking was needed. Earl explained:

After a few years, the restaurant had become very popular, and the strip center that we were located in was not set up to handle the volume of business we were doing. We had a situation where a number of the other retail shops were frustrated because our customers were taking their parking spaces during lunch. So we were faced with the decision to either shut down the restaurant or move. While we were deliberating on what to do, we met Harmon Looney, who owned the building that we eventually moved into. Harmon was willing to work with us during our first year on our rent, $1,200 per month for the first year and $2,500 per month thereafter, to help us get established.

In early 1989, Earl negotiated a $200,000 bank loan with Hank Leonard, the head of commercial loans at AmSouth, and secured a sizable strip mall location on McFarland Boulevard, the busiest street in Tuscaloosa. Leonard had been eating at Manna Grocery, and, according to Earl, he was up on what was going on in the health-food industry and was willing to support Manna's expansion. Earl used the loan to bring in new inventory and to cover the cost of decorating and equipping the new store. Earl hired a friend, Tom McJenkin, who was a general contractor, to take care of the plumbing, wiring, air-conditioning units, the walk-in coolers, the freezers, and all of the kitchen equipment. Earl and Tom worked together on framing the walls, hanging the plasterboard, and building the tables, shelves, and counters:

We did most of the work ourselves out of necessity. In order to afford everything we wanted for the new store, we had to do as much of the work as we possibly

EXHIBIT 11   Operating Statements for Manna Grocery, 1986–90

	1990	1989	1988	1987	1986
Gross volume	$692,531	$556,118	$430,535	$319,280	$251,990
Cost of goods sold	54.9%	58.6%	60.0%	62.0%	65.0%
Gross profit margin	45.1%	41.4%	40.0%	38.0%	35.0%
Payroll	24.3%	24.2%	22.2%	21.5%	15.1%
Rent*	3.4%	2.5%	1.5%	2.0%	2.9%
Utilities	2.7%	2.9%	2.3%	2.3%	3.5%
Advertising	1.4%	.8%	.7%	.6%	1.1%
Miscellaneous overhead	6.3%	6.4%	4.8%	4.4%	4.8%
Pretax net profit	7.0%	7.5%	8.5%	7.2%	7.6%

* Includes rented equipment.
Source: Manna Grocery.

could by ourselves. When we first started working with the space, we really didn't have any clear plan as to how we were going to run the boards or how we were going to paint the walls; we just kind of got in here and, with each phase of the construction, we worked the details out together. Doing the remodeling ourselves meant putting in a lot of 16- and 18-hour days, but it was worth it because we really ended up with a beautiful store.

Earl and Frances were concerned that the move would cause them to lose some of their major customers because so many people had said the present store was small and charming. However, response to the new store was favorable; customers commented to Earl on how much easier it was to shop at the new location because the parking was better and the aisles were not so narrow and crowded. By early 1991, Manna was prospering (see Exhibit 11) and had between 150 and 200 customers per day in the restaurant and between 200 and 300 customers per day in the store. One customer told the case writer:

I'm really surprised at how big the store is and how clean and organized it is. I am also impressed with the diversity of products. It has a real light and refreshing atmosphere.

Manna's Product Line

When Earl opened Harmony Natural Foods, he carried mainly bulk foods such as grains, flour, and granola; the store also featured juices, freshly made peanut butter, and some vitamins. The best-selling items were peanut butter, yogurt, juices, whole wheat flour, and brown rice. The store stocked no produce or frozen foods. When Harmony's restaurant was opened, the menu consisted of 10 varieties of sandwiches, three kinds of salads, and a daily lunch special (usually some type of casserole served with homemade bread) priced at $1.50.

The product mix at the first Manna Grocery store included packaged health and natural-food products, bulk herbs and spices, frozen yogurt, a small assortment of organic produce, and a wide selection of cheeses and coffee. Two refrigerator cases held dairy products, juices, bottled water, and frozen foods. The most popular items at this location were rice cakes, oat bran cereal, frozen yogurt, and juices in quart containers. The restaurant menu consisted of seven

EXHIBIT 12   Manna Grocery's Estimated Sales and Profit Margins by Department

Department	Percentage of Sales	Gross Profit Margins
Vitamins/supplements	8%	40.0%
Personal care	5%	37.0%
Herbs	6%	43.3%
Grocery	20%	27.5%
Bulk foods	6%	34.2%
Produce	5%	30.4%
Dairy/refrigerated	7%	26.9%
Frozen	5%	31.1%
Deli, juice bar	4%	46.1%
Restaurant	28%	59.3%
Bakery	2%	45.2%
Books	2%	34.8%
Nonfoods	2%	38.7%

Source: Manna Grocery.

very popular sandwiches: avocado, cheese, tomato, and sprouts; cheese, tomato, and sprouts; cucumber, cream cheese, tomato, and sprouts; cream cheese, dates, and walnut; peanut butter, banana, and honey; tuna salad; and chicken salad. Manna Grocery gained much of its popularity from the quality of the sandwiches it served.

When Manna Grocery was moved to its second location, the product mix was expanded to include additional brands of those items that had been popular at the original Manna and an assortment of new products. Earl said the really popular items were foods that were easy to prepare such as frozen dinners, prepackaged dehydrated products (which took a maximum of 20 minutes to prepare), and ready-to-eat soups. Juices, peanut butter, jams, herbs, flours, and fresh-baked bread were also extremely popular. The restaurant menu was greatly expanded at the second location and included a number of sandwiches, vegetarian dishes, salads, soups, and casseroles. Exhibit 12 details the contribution to overall store sales by department and the profit margins by department within Manna Grocery in 1990. In 1990, Manna's inventory turned over approximately 16 times.

Suppliers

When Harmony Natural Foods opened, it had one supplier that made deliveries once a month; by the time the Drennens sold Harmony in 1976, the supplier was making deliveries twice a month.

When Earl opened Manna Grocery, he used three suppliers: Tree of Life, which supplied the store with all its major food items; First Colony, which supplied all the store's coffee; and Solgar, which supplied vitamins and supplements. Each supplier provided weekly delivery service. In 1989, when Earl decided to relocate the store, Manna was being serviced by 15 suppliers. At the start of 1991, Manna Grocery had 27 suppliers: seven natural-food distributors, three grocery distributors, eight local vendors, and nine direct distributors. According to Earl:

We have really strong relationships with our suppliers. Tree of Life is our main supplier, and we are considered by them to be a key account, or an A+ account. Being an A+ account means that we do a large volume of business with them, we have a very good credit rating with them, and we do a lot internally, in the store, to move the products that they supply us with. We are at a point now where we are big enough to have a say-so in the industry and, therefore, we have a lot of power insofar as our suppliers are concerned. However, we do have a few problems getting products from Indian Groceries every now and then—they are not always as responsive to our needs as I wish they would be.

Manna's Clientele

During the time Earl operated Harmony Natural Foods, approximately 80 percent of the store's customers were students and faculty members at the University of Alabama, and 20 percent of the store's customers were townspeople. Earl described the majority of Harmony's customers as being members of the counterculture and freethinkers. Later, when Earl opened Manna Grocery, the ratio of customers was almost the reverse (80 percent townspeople and 20 percent students and faculty). Also, Earl began to notice that more ethnic customers, especially people from India and the Middle East, were frequenting the store. The store's ethnic customers began asking him to carry certain special products, so he began using the services of such ethnic food suppliers as Indian Groceries and Sahadi Importing. Earl estimated that, in 1991, 15 percent of his customers were ethnic—some were UA students and some were local residents.

In 1991, the majority of Manna's customers were professionals from the Tuscaloosa community. Earl estimated that 75 percent of his customers were primarily health-conscious individuals, while 25 percent were primarily fitness-conscious individuals. Earl noted that Manna did the bulk of its business from September to April, with January through April being the best months. Business was significantly slower from May through August when the university operated at a reduced level and more locally grown fresh produce was available. Earl believed January through April tended to be stronger sales months because people coming into the store were trying to stick to their New Year's resolutions. In September and October, it was not uncommon for Manna to gain regular patronage from fitness-conscious students. In 1991, an estimated 10 percent of Manna's customers were 25 years old and younger, 15 percent were between the ages of 26 and 35, 25 percent were between the ages of 36 and 45, 25 percent were between the ages of 46 and 55, and 25 percent were 56 or older.

Manna Grocery's Competitors

Competition in Tuscaloosa's health-food market had evolved over the years. Earl explained:

Back in the early 70s, supermarkets just weren't carrying natural and health-food products; they were hardly carrying any of the products that we were. It just wasn't an issue for them. The only competition that we were getting, at that time, may have come from the local General Nutrition Center store, but I don't believe it affected our business.

In about 1986, an ethnic store called Jerusalem Grocery opened up, but they ended up going out of business in about six months. Then somebody else came in and started Middle Eastern Grocery, and they went out of business in nine

EXHIBIT 13   **Selected Price Comparisons for Manna Grocery, Two Nearby Supermarkets, and a General Nutrition Center Store**

| | Store | | |
Product	Manna	Bruno's	Kroger
Evian natural spring water, 50.7 fl. oz.	$1.85	$1.65	$1.65
Pacific Rice Products, Inc. Crispy Cakes, Raisins & Spice	$1.75	$1.76	$1.49
Dairy Fresh Vitamin D whole milk, 1 gallon	$2.89	$2.59	$2.65
Celestial Seasonings Tea, Country Peach	$2.59	$1.89	$2.49
Health Valley Oat Bran O's	$3.35	$3.03	NA
Nutella Spread, 13 oz.	$3.95	$4.08	NA
Hain eggless mayonnaise, 11 fl. oz.	$2.55	$2.56	$2.29
Nonorganic carrots, 1 lb.	.79	.59	.79
Health Valley blue corn flakes	$3.45	$3.13	NA

| | Store | |
Product	Manna	GNC
Twinlab Amino Fuel Chewable Wafers, 50 wafers	$13.95	$14.99
Twinlab Gainers Fuel, 3.95 lbs. vanilla flavored	$26.95 sale $24.50	$26.99
Bahamian Diet nutritional drink, 19 oz.	$23.65	$25.99 (sale $19.99)
Twinlab Phosfuel	$15.29	$16.99

months. They were selling their products considerably cheaper than I was selling mine.

In 1991, Earl did not believe supermarkets posed a competitive threat to Manna despite the fact that local supermarkets were stocking more natural and organic foods. Earl believed Manna was competitive with these other stores with respect to food prices (see Exhibit 13). Two of Tuscaloosa's most upscale and progressive supermarkets were a block away, one to either side; the two stores (Kroger and Bruno's) were both adding natural and health-food products, although neither had added a special department for such items.

Customer Service   Earl believed one of Manna's greatest strengths was its customer service. His philosophy about customer service had changed considerably over the years:

> When we opened Harmony, back in 1972, we were young, energetic, and free spirited, and the way we operated the business reflected that. We were never really rude to anybody, but I guess we just weren't very diplomatic, especially where older people were concerned. We just didn't care if the older people shopped with us. Like I said, we were young, we were real upfront with our life-style, and we just didn't have the awareness that we do today. So, when older people came into the store, we would talk to them, but that is really about it—we didn't have a store newsletter, or any other type of service. We would do special

orders and get something for somebody if they needed it, but the only real service that we provided was ourselves.

When Earl opened Manna Grocery, he made an effort to improve the store's level of customer service. He began providing a monthly in-store newsletter, and, in 1986, he began inserting information concerning food specials into the monthly newsletter. Earl also began training his employees more thoroughly. He insisted each employee be knowledgeable about products in the store, be able to assist customers with anything they needed, and be able to answer questions about nutrition and fitness.

When Manna Grocery was relocated, Earl began providing additional services for his customers. Informational brochures were provided to shoppers at checkout counters and at other locations in the store. Manna conducted a food-tasting day once a month where people could sample different products. Manna also began a small catering service. Earl commented on the catering service:

> Right now we are mainly catering student union programs. For instance, when Living Color did a concert at the university, we did the catering for them. We have catered a few other bands that have come through town as well. We also do a lot of catering for doctors' offices, graduations, and local businesses. We haven't been advertising our catering service; I think it has just caught on by word of mouth. But we really haven't done anything big with the catering yet, and I don't know if I want to get in it big. It just isn't a decision that we have made at this point. My feeling is that we probably will keep our catering service small; it is just easier to manage that way.

In September 1990, Manna began conducting monthly educational seminars that covered such topics as homeopathic medicine, medicinal herbs, and exercise (see Exhibit 14). The seminars were held at night after regular store hours (normal closing time was 7 P.M.) and were usually attended by 25 to 50 people, many of whom shopped for items after the lecture concluded.

Another way Earl ensured his customers received the proper service was by keeping the store adequately staffed. On an average day, Earl and four other salespeople were on the store floor ready to assist customers. Three other people worked in the restaurant area, taking customer orders and serving food. Earl commented that occasionally people mentioned he might have too many salespeople on the floor and he could save money by decreasing his sales staff. But Earl believed superior customer service was crucial to the store's long-term success, and he did not want customers to have to wait to get questions answered or pay their bill at the checkout counter.

Marketing and Advertising

When Earl operated the Harmony Natural Foods store, he had no marketing program; there was no radio, TV, or newspaper advertising and no point-of-sale displays in the store. When Earl opened Manna Grocery, a small marketing program was developed; it consisted of an in-store newsletter and several point-of-sale displays provided by various manufacturers and distributors. For about a year, in 1986, Manna conducted a radio advertising campaign; it ended when the radio station person responsible for writing and delivering the radio commercials moved:

EXHIBIT 14   **Seminar on Homeopathic Medicine Sponsored by Manna Grocery**

At 7 P.M. people slowly began gathering at Manna Grocery for the 7:30 P.M. seminar. The audience that assembled was a diverse group of individuals. There were young people, old people, couples, families, Asians, African-Americans, and Caucasians present. Above the faint trickle of a garden fountain, the various conversations of seminar attendants could be heard. A young lady offered an older woman an organic apple, a couple discussed how much they enjoyed the last seminar on herbal extracts, and a middle-aged man talked with friends about the lunch he had eaten at Manna Grocery earlier that day. At 7:36 P.M. Dr. Rebecca Koeppen, a tall woman with sandy blonde hair and an olive complexion, was introduced and the seminar began.

Dr. Koeppen began by defining the term *homeopathy.* She explained that it originated from the Greek words *homoios*, meaning similar, and *pathos*, meaning suffering, and therefore, homeopathy was defined as that which is similar ends suffering. Dr. Koeppen explained that it was Samuel Hahnemann, a late 18th and early 19th century German physician and medical writer, who pioneered the field of homeopathic medicine. Dr. Hahnemann found that by diluting an original curative substance, a homeopathic medicine, or remedy, could be created. Dr. Koeppen noted that based on a finding by French scientist Jacques Benveniste, at 23 dilutions there were a hundred trillion billion molecules of water to every molecule of the original curative substance. Interestingly enough, the more diluted a homeopathic remedy was (up to a point) the more effective it was.

Dr. Koeppen stated that homeopathic remedies were determined by a process called "proofing." During proofing, the remedies in question were administered to healthy individuals until the individuals developed the physical, emotional, and mental symptoms of an illness. It was then declared that whatever remedy caused an illness was the remedy that should be administered to the individual when the symptoms were present under normal conditions.

Dr. Koeppen explained that in order for homeopathic healing to take place two things were necessary: (1) the right remedy must be used, and (2) the person taking the remedy must have enough "vital force" or immune response to react. She mentioned that homeopathic physicians, as well as people treating their own illness, must know exactly how the person is feeling when they are ill in order to prescribe the correct remedy. A physician would need to know if the pain the patient felt was a throbbing, tearing, burning, constant, pulsating, shredding, or sharp pain. The physician would also need to know if the sick individual felt like being around people or being alone, being outside in the open air or being in a closed dark room. All these things helped the physician to prescribe the correct remedy. Dr. Koeppen mentioned that for sicknesses that come on quickly, accompanied by flush, hot skin and the person acting wildly (this is often experienced by small children) the remedy Belladonna is often prescribed. For individuals who are "weepy" and who express the need to be around people and to be "loved" during their illness, the remedy Pulsatilla is generally prescribed. Individuals seeking homeopathic cures must learn to get in touch with their bodies, to understand their pain and their emotions, and to pay attention to the signals that their bodies and minds are sending them both when they are sick and when they are well.

Dr. Koeppen ended the seminar by explaining that homeopathic medicine was a life philosophy—the belief that everything was always happening for the highest good of the whole. As a practitioner of homeopathic medicine, Dr. Koeppen noted that she must look at individuals in a holistic manner in order to successfully treat them—she looks at their body language, inquires about their past experiences, and asks how they are feeling emotionally and mentally as well as physically. Through this manner only is she able to heal the *whole* person.

The woman who was doing the commercials for us was just really into natural foods, and she had a real sense of what we were trying to do and the image that we were trying to convey. She ended up leaving, and we just never could find anybody to replace her. Everyone else thought we were weird, and we couldn't find anybody that could project the image that we were trying to convey.

When Manna relocated to its present site, Earl maintained the existing marketing program and began a radio advertising campaign announcing store specials, monthly seminar topics, and information about major products and services. The new store had attractive shelving and merchandise displays, a pleasant shopping ambience, and numerous hand-lettered signs and placards calling attention to specials and new products. The case writer, having patronized Manna Grocery for over five years, could see a growing sophistication and maturity in how Manna marketed and merchandised its product line to the public. A warm, personal touch was evident throughout the store as concerns merchandising practices, displays and product presentations, the restaurant menu, and the attentive, helpful nature of store personnel.

Employees

The quality of Earl's staff was one of his primary business concerns. Employee meetings were held weekly to solicit and discuss suggestions concerning the store and its operations. Monthly training seminars were conducted to keep employees abreast of industry trends and to present ways to provide better customer service. Employees were compensated for attending these meetings.

New employees went through a two-week training program where they were taught how to use checkout terminals and how to greet and assist customers; considerable time was spent teaching employees about products. All Manna employees, except for the kitchen and cleaning staff, were responsible for assisting customers in the store and restaurant. At the end of the training program, new employees met with Earl and the store manager for an interview, and their progress was assessed.

In 1991, Earl had 10 full-time employees and 18 part-time employees who earned an average $5.50 per hour and $4.50 per hour, respectively. Earl considered all of his employees to be extremely dedicated to the business, and, in turn, he was dedicated to them:

> Miriam Wright has worked with me since Manna Grocery opened, and she worked with me some at Harmony Natural Foods. We have two other people that have been with us for about five years in this business. These people are at a point where they really want to be with the business from here on out, and I feel really great about that. Because I am responsible for these people's life-styles and their incomes, I really want to see the business take off and be very strong, not just for me and my wife, but for everybody that works with us. I am into being very egalitarian, I guess, in terms of how I share the money. In fact, in the future, I hope to be able to provide a profit-sharing program for the employees. At this point that is just not possible because profits are not yet big enough to share. But down the road I would like to see that happen because it will build the employees up and make them feel more a part of the business.

Earl also felt very strong about his wife's contribution to the business:

> Frances does all of the bookkeeping; she always has. I don't really have a partner in the business, but you might say that Frances is my partner. She had been real instrumental in the success of the business, and I don't believe that I could have made it this far without her.

Earl Drennen

In response to the case writer's question about how many hours a week he was working at Manna and how hard he was working, Earl said:

I probably work about 60 hours a week. But I have a really high energy level; so working 60 hours a week is not very stressful for me. I also take a lot of time during the week to be with my wife and children. One of my sons plays baseball, and I go to practically all of his games. I find time during the week to work out as well; usually I lift weights and swim some laps in the pool. You know there are just so many people in this business that go through every day just so stressed out, so worried about how much money they're making or not making. They don't have time to enjoy life. And I just think they're really missing the point. But, at Manna, our bottom line is probably much different from the bottom line at other stores. (At Manna) the most important thing is how we are working together as a group of people. I get a lot more energy from the group dynamics, how we are working, communicating, and sharing with one another, than I do from a record sales day. I use meditation during the week, as do many of my employees, on a regular basis to relieve stress and to get in touch with my inner self. I still to this day am not possessed by the business, and I never will be. It is something that I enjoy doing, but it is not the most important thing in my life.

In response to the case writer's question about how he had changed over the years as a businessperson, Earl said:

There've been a lot of changes since 1972. Part of that change has been in marketing. Back in 1972, I didn't even need to know anything about marketing. Now, in 1991, marketing is one of the most important things. As well, I just didn't have the awareness about how to work with the community and my employees when I first got into the business like I do today. I think that the most important thing to me now is creating an atmosphere where people can come in and shop and be happy. I want a store environment where people can provide quality products and quality information to our customers. And I want to create an environment where the employees enjoy coming into work and working with one another, where there is an open dialogue between all the employees, and where everybody is treated equally and with respect. Even though I am the owner, or the president, of the business, I want everyone to know that they can come to me and say anything to me about the business and how we are operating it. I also like to see my employees take the initiative, use their own best judgment, and make a decision about what to do without feeling like they have to ask me first. Like the other day, I went into the kitchen and was going to help them prepare one of the dishes, and one of the restaurant staff stopped me and told me that we weren't making it the way we used to and hadn't been for some time. I had no idea that they had changed the recipe, but I didn't mind because it showed me that my employees knew I trusted them and respected their judgment. I hear so many horror stories about people who work in business that are intimidated by management and by the owner, and it doesn't have to be that way. Every day I am learning more and more about how to run the business. It is a continuous process and a very exciting process.

In response to a question about whether he could imagine having done anything else with his life and did he think he would have been as happy if he had chosen another career, Earl said:

Well, I will put it this way—there are a lot of things I can do; for whatever reason, I have been given a lot of talents. I used to do remodeling work and there is a part of me that would like to do that again. I am very good at landscaping. I enjoy being outside—having my hands in the dirt; I enjoy the physicalness of life. I would maybe like to learn how to play a musical instrument. If the business were to grow and prosper to the point that we were able to open another store, I would be happy to help make that happen. But, if it were going to take away from the things I want to do down the road, I wouldn't want to be a part of it. I enjoy this; I am not tired of it. But there are just so many things that I want to develop in my life. I just want to try to listen more internally and just take everything day by day. I just want more time to *be*.

REFERENCES

"1989 Market Overview," *Natural Foods Merchandiser*, June 1990, pp. 34–54.

Fishman, Stuart. "Pesticide Use Creates Challenges for Organic Trade: Growers are Searching for Safer Alternatives to Synthetics," *Organic Times*, Summer 1990, p. OT–10.

Johnson, Gil. "Who Is the Natural Products Consumer?" *Natural Foods Merchandiser*, July 1990, p. 52.

Nutrition Labeling and Education Act of 1989. Hearing before the Committee on Labor and Human Resources, United States Senate, 101st Congress, first session on S. 1425, November 13, 1990, p. 2.

Price, Charlene C. *Growth in the Health and Natural Foods Industry*, Washington, D.C.: United States Department of Agriculture, Economic Research Service, National Economics Division, 1984, p. 3.

Segal, Troy. "Just What Is 'Organic' Food—And Is It Good for You?" *Business Week*, September 25, 1989, p. 232.

Snyder, Tammy. "Homeopathy on the Rebound in U.S.," *Natural Foods Merchandiser*, December 1990, p. 14.

Walker, Jenepher. "Health Food Stores," *Small Business Reporter* 11, no. 2, (1973), p. 2.

KQED-TV SAN FRANCISCO

Ivy J. Millman, Stanford University
Jon Abbott, Stanford University
Robert R. Augsburger, Stanford University

"If the cable companies choose to drop our stations from their systems, how can we reach the public with quality television programs? We can't serve our communities if people can't find us." Anthony (Tony) Tiano, president of KQED, Inc., was increasingly concerned about the deregulation of the cable television industry and what it meant for his two public television stations. He needed a strategy to strengthen KQED's services in the era of cable broadcasting.

KQED'S BACKGROUND

KQED, Inc., was a publicly supported foundation, chartered under California law, operating two noncommercial, public television stations, KQED Channel 9 and KQEC Channel 32, as well as public radio station KQED-FM 88.5. KQED, Inc., also published the city magazine for the San Francisco Bay area, *San Francisco Focus Magazine*. The principal mission of KQED, Inc., was to broaden appreciation and understanding of the arts, sciences, and current affairs; to enlarge viewpoints and intellectual horizons; and to expand insight into human affairs and experiences. KQED had been broadcasting under VHF license since the mid-1950s and KQEC had a UHF license. There was a 27-member board of directors, each director elected by the members for up to two three-year terms.

KQED was among the most watched and supported stations in the public television system, attracting per capita viewership and financial support as high or higher than any station in the country. Although some public stations in other major cities had more viewers each week in absolute terms, KQED and Chicago's WTTW ranked highest in market penetration. In early 1986, KQED had a cumulative audience rating (percentage of unduplicated television households tuning in at least once per week) of 61 percent, second only to WTTW's 64 percent. By contrast, other bay area public television stations ranked much lower: KTEH San Jose at 16–18 percent, KCSM San Mateo at 12–16 percent. KQEC's penetration was 11 percent.

PROGRAMMING

KQED Channel 9 broadcast a balanced mix of quality programs covering a variety of subject areas during prime time each week, including alternative nature, science, history, current affairs, cultural, and performance fare. The finest available programs were broadcast for children on weekdays in the morning and in the after-school hours. Other weekday periods were used to "block feed" instructional television programs that high school districts tape for use in their curricula. Weekend daytime programming included high-quality children's fare (e.g., "Sesame Street" and "Mr. Roger's Neighborhood") in the mornings, and "how-to" cooking programs through the afternoon.

The primary programming approach for KQEC Channel 32 had been to establish series running in regular time slots, often called stripping. Programming blocks, which group programs of similar type, were implemented during the daytime hours. The strategy behind programming blocks was similar to that of radio station formats. Viewers could easily find programming of a certain type throughout the week for a set period, making this programming more accessible to interested viewers.

KQEC's prime-time schedule offered programs not provided on KQED Channel 9, as well as occasional repeats of some programs offered earlier in the week on KQED; the weekend daytime schedule offered high-quality children's programming. Weeknight airtime between 6 and 8 P.M. was devoted to adult learning and between 8 and 11 P.M. to current affairs programming.

While neither station broadcast 24 hours a day, the part-time broadcast schedule of KQEC (weekdays 5 P.M. to midnight and weekends 10 A.M. to midnight) was considered a problem by cable operators, who must program another service in place of 32 when the station was not broadcasting. There was the potential to split time with another channel or C-SPAN II, the cable-only service of U.S. Senate proceedings.

FUNDING

Like its sister stations in the public broadcasting system, KQED secured its operating funds from a number of sources. (See Exhibit 1 for KQED's Statement of Support, Revenue, and Expenses.) The station's Marketing Division was responsible for raising the majority of operating revenue each year. Led by Christopher Dann, vice president of marketing and development, the scope of the division's operations encompassed the development of individual, corporate, foundation, and government revenues by a variety of means, for both annual operations and capital resources. The division was divided into five revenue centers. Each of these departments differed in the approaches and initiatives it undertook for funding.

Membership   The goal of the Membership Department was to raise funds from individuals and families while strengthening members' ties to KQED and enhancing the community involvement that came from membership in KQED. Nearly two thirds of the operating support for the station came from individuals and families throughout northern California who made annual commitments of membership in the station.

With basic memberships starting at $35, KQED consistently ranked among the most successful stations in membership support when measured by revenue per member household and revenue per viewing household. Much of this success in recent years (Exhibit 2) could be attributed to the increasing volume and sophistication of the Membership Department's direct-mail efforts,

EXHIBIT 1   KQED, Inc., Statements of Support, Revenue, and Expenses, 1987–88

	Year Ended September 30	
	1988 Total All Funds	1987 Total All Funds
Support and revenue		
Contributions and membership	$14,116,835	$12,869,193
Programming and production	4,315,876	4,711,261
Auction and special events	2,004,262	2,059,962
San Francisco Focus	5,803,813	5,202,393
Community service grants	2,188,255	2,004,335
Facilities rental and ancillary merchandise	1,680,520	1,862,513
Instructional television	690,851	713,684
Other	632,343	316,461
Total support and revenue	$31,432,755	$29,739,802
Expenses		
Program services		
Programming and production		
Television		
Local	$ 6,980,797	$ 5,761,751
For distribution to public broadcasting entities	2,959,549	3,859,493
Broadcasting	2,346,949	2,395,622
FM production and broadcasting	1,241,385	1,437,205
Program information	1,471,988	1,469,702
San Francisco Focus	5,499,804	5,005,974
	$20,500,472	$19,929,747
Supporting services		
Fund-raising and membership development		
Auction and special events	$ 1,420,796	$1,189,427
Membership and pledges	4,026,988	3,465,712
	$ 5,447,784	$4,655,139
Facilities rental and ancillary merchandise	1,270,698	1,556,256
Program underwriting and grant solicitation	685,699	583,536
Management and general	2,825,386	2,468,787
	10,229,567	9,263,718
Total expenses	$30,730,039	$29,193,465
Excess of support and revenue over expenses before capital additions	$ 702,716	$ 546,337
Capital additions		
Contributions for capital improvements	$ 1,003,958	$ 229,164

which included renewal correspondence, additional gift appeals, and "acquisition" efforts to recruit new supporters.

The Membership Department was guardian of the station's most precious revenue resource: 240,000 member households who together in 1988 accounted for more than $14 million of KQED's revenue. In addition to direct mail, the department managed KQED's on-air pledge campaigns as well as successful telemarketing efforts.

As the station looked ahead, Chris Dann and Tony Tiano were both aware that the population of the bay area was growing to the north, east, and south

EXHIBIT 2   **KQED Members and Viewers**

Year	Number of Members	Member Dollars	February Viewers	Dollars per Viewer	Dollars per Member
1979	124,000	$ 3,651,000	936,000	$3.90	$29.44
1980	137,000	$ 4,200,000	1,001,000	$4.20	$30.66
1981	138,000	$ 5,100,000	1,053,000	$4.84	$36.96
1982	145,000	$ 5,900,000	1,200,000	$4.92	$40.69
1983	170,000	$ 7,870,000	1,322,000	$5.95	$46.29
1984	183,600	$ 8,435,000	1,274,000	$6.62	$45.94
1985	210,000	$10,733,000	1,453,000	$7.39	$50.70
1986	232,866	$11,040,000	1,456,000	$7.58	$47.31
1987	242,090	$12,653,000	1,536,000	$8.24	$52.37
1988	250,000	$13,971,000	1,589,000	$8.79	$55.88
1989	260,000	$14,614,000	1,536,000	$9.88	$58.41

EXHIBIT 3   **Distribution of Member Households by County**   *(Top 10 counties in 1988)*

Alameda	43,768
Santa Clara	40,556
San Francisco	35,002
San Mateo	29,421
Contra Costa	26,386
Marin	17,512
Sonoma	11,503
Monterey	7,168
Santa Cruz	6,748
Napa	3,704

of San Francisco (see Exhibit 3). "That's where our viewers and supporters are, and that's where our marketing challenge is in the years ahead. That is what I've told our staff," says Dann.

Underwriting   Among the many means of support on which public broadcasting relied was the support of corporations and foundations that underwrite or "sponsor" its programming. In return, the underwriter received many benefits, such as on- air acknowledgments; promotional opportunities tied to the program underwriting; specially designed announcement and display cards to distribute to customers and other constituencies; and acknowledgment in KQED's member program guide, *Fine Tuning*. The department was organized with account executives who managed relationships with area corporations and foundations.

Auction   KQED pioneered public television's auction nearly 30 years ago. The auction staff gathered donations of goods and services from area businesses each year in preparation for a televised auctioning of the items during 11 evenings in June.

Special Events This department raised funds through public participatory events held throughout the greater San Francisco Bay area. Among the annual events KQED offered each year were four "tastings" (the Wine & Food Festival, the International Beer & Food Festival, Old-Fashioned Ice Cream Social and Tasting, and Dessert Delight), as well as lectures and appearances by public television personalities. Concerned about the station's visibility in the East Bay, Peninsula, and South Bay communities where a high proportion of members reside, Chris Dann initiated plans for additional community events in these areas.

Dan cautioned that the station should not overlook the presence of the other smaller public television stations that might increase their marketing to viewers in overlapping broadcast areas. KTEH San Jose had begun to enhance its marketing throughout the bay area, especially on the Peninsula. "KQED's community is northern California. Our marketing and member outreach efforts need to reflect this." Dan planned to increase the number of events in outlying communities that were free to members, including a proposed balloon race in San Jose over the Independence Day weekend.

Capital Development The capital development staff managed personal and direct-mail solicitations to increase KQED's capital assets and endowments.

CABLE TELEVISION—AN EMERGING POWER

In the 1950s, cable was introduced by necessity, allowing areas where the intervening terrain was blocking signals from relatively nearby cities to receive commercial television signals. The growth in cable systems was welcomed by most television stations because they found cable distribution benefited viewership. The enhanced distribution provided by cable helped public television expand its audience across the United States, especially for the two thirds of public television stations whose weaker signals on the UHF band could now reach new communities. Today, for the most part, cable is still not viable in remote areas, and has achieved its largest penetration in urban, suburban, and "exurban" communities. Exhibits 4 and 5 present the demographics of cable and PBS subscribers.

Nationwide cable penetration had grown steadily and recently passed the critical milestone of 50 percent penetration (see Exhibit 6). In July 1987, the cable penetration into the more than 2.1 million television households in the San Francisco–Oakland Designated Market Area (DMA) reached 54.1 percent. Projections held that penetration might reach 57.5 percent by 1989. Cable networks were increasingly attracting the attention of national advertisers and had become viable competition for the three commercial networks' share of broadcast advertising budgets (see Exhibit 7 for the cable networks available in the San Francisco–Oakland DMA). As cable penetration increased, broadcasters, particularly the three networks, expressed concern over audience shifts to cable networks and pay services. Data presented in Exhibits 8–10 highlight this trend.

As cable began to emerge as big business, the Federal Communications Commission (FCC) had regulations that worked to protect local television stations. In 1972, the FCC issued an order requiring cable operators to carry

EXHIBIT 4   Demographics of Cable TV Subscribers—Indexed

	Total U.S.	Cable Subscribers	Noncable Subscribers
Household Income			
$50,000+	100	125	77
$40,000–49,999	100	111	99
$30,000–39,999	100	107	94
$20,000–29,999	100	99	101
$10,000–19,999	100	77	121
Under $10,000	100	66	132
Education			
College graduate	100	111	90
Attended college	100	116	86
High school graduate	100	99	101
Not high school graduate	100	82	117
Occupation			
Executive/managerial/administrative	100	125	76
Professional	100	111	90
Clerical/sales/technical	100	115	86
Other employed	100	94	106
Not employed	100	89	110
Household Size			
3+ Persons	100	106	95
2	100	99	75
1	100	75	123
Age			
18–34	100	101	99
35–54	100	107	94
55+	100	92	108

Example: Cable subscribers are 11% more likely to have household income between $40,000 and $49,999 than the U.S. population generally. Likewise noncable subscribers are 6% less likely than the U.S. population generally to have household income between $30,000 and $39,999.

Source: Cabletelevision Advertising Bureau, 1988.

signals from local television stations in the communities they serve. Also called "must carry," the regulation was to ensure "viewers' choices would not diminish." Under this order, cable operators were often required to carry two or more public television stations that largely duplicated each other's services. For years, duplicative public stations did not pose a problem except, coincidentally, in the San Francisco Bay area where there quickly developed, through unbridled proliferation of five public television stations, competition for carriage.

By the late 1970s, the cable industry had outgrown its infancy and mounted an assault on restrictive regulations. The FCC began removing itself from aspects of cable television regulation. In addition to a general trend of deregulation in broadcasting, this removal also reflected a change in the cable business itself. Cable systems began to be seen by the courts and the FCC as more like newspapers in their editorial role and their relative lack of need for federal regulation.

EXHIBIT 5   Demographics of Public TV Audience—Indexed

	Total U.S.	PTV Viewers Full Day	PTV Viewers Prime
Household Income			
$40,000 +	100 (24%)	117	129
$30,000–39,999	100 (15%)	107	100
$20,000–29,999	100 (19%)	105	100
$10,000–19,999	100 (23%)	87	83
<$10,000	100 (19%)	84	84
Education			
4+ years college	100 (21%)	114	129
Attended college	100 (17%)	106	100
High school graduate	100 (36%)	97	92
Not high school graduate	100 (26%)	88	88
Occupation			
Owner/managerial/professional	100 (26%)	108	119
Clerical and sales	100 (13%)	100	85
Skilled and semiskilled	100 (32%)	100	88
Not in labor force	100 (29%)	93	103
Age			
2–5	100 (6%)	167	89
6–11	100 (9%)	89	33
12–17	100 (9%)	67	56
18–34	100 (30%)	87	93
35–49	100 (19%)	100	121
50–64	100 (15%)	120	140
65+	100 (12%)	108	150

Source: NTI/NAC (January 1985) weekly cumulative persons.

EXHIBIT 6   National Cable Penetration Trends, 1970–87

Year	Cable Subscribers (000s)	Household Penetration	Pay Subscribers (000s)
1987	44,971	50.5%	27,600
1986	42,237	48.1%	23,706
1985	39,873	46.2%	24,165
1984	37,291	43.7%	22,375
1983	33,794	40.5%	21,151
1982	29,341	35.0%	17,311
1981	23,219	28.3%	11,842
1980	17,671	22.6%	7,599
1975	9,197	13.2%	NA
1970	4,498	7.5%	NA

Tony Tiano's concerns were fueled by recent court decisions and the FCC's response. In August 1986, the Supreme Court knocked out the rigid FCC order, citing violation of cable's First Amendment rights. The FCC, whose leadership under the Reagan administration had advocated deregulatory policy revisions,

EXHIBIT 7   **National Cable Stations Available on Cable Systems in San Francisco–Oakland DMA**

Arts & Entertainment (A&E)—Available on 2,400 systems nationwide, the network's 24-hour-a-day schedule mixes comedy, drama, documentaries, and the performing arts. 30 million subscribers.

BET (Black Entertainment Television)—24 hours of music videos, black college sports, news, classic movies, and family entertainment. 17.5 million subscribers.

CNN (Cable News Network)—24-hour coverage and analysis of major national and international events, and specialized daily reports on business, finance, sports, medicine, nutrition, science, fashion, entertainment, weather, and human interest. Comprehensive live coverage of breaking-news events from around the world. 42.9 million subscribers.

The Discovery Channel—Documentaries in the fields of science and technology, nature, history, world exploration, and human adventure. Cablecasts 9 A.M. to 3 A.M. EST. 26 million subscribers.

ESPN—24-hour schedule featuring professional, collegiate, and amateur sports along with sports news and information programs and a morning business news program. 45.2 million subscribers.

Financial News Network (FNN)—Live business and financial news and trends including reports on all major stock, commodity, and option exchanges. Interviews with economists and analysts. NYSE, AMEX, and exclusive NASDAQ ticker crawls. 20 million subscribers.

Lifetime—Television for "today's woman," with entertainment/information programming with an eye to relationships, health and fitness, parenting, fashion, and beauty. 35.4 million subscribers.

MTV: Music Television—The first 24-hour video music network.

Nickelodeon—Array of children's programming including cartoons, comedy, adventure, rock music, and magazine shows. Network includes "*Nick at Nite*," an entertainment service for young adults featuring hit series of the past. 36.8 million subscribers.

TBS SuperStation—Blend of family entertainment programming, original special presentations, sports, sitcoms, and motion pictures from a library of over 4,000 feature films, including selected MGM cinema classics. Sports coverage includes Atlanta Braves baseball, exclusive cable coverage of the NBA, and major college football. 42.5 million subscribers.

USA Network—24-hour broad-based entertainment network. 41 million subscribers.

VH-1: Video Hits One—First and only 24-hour music channel targeted at the 25 to 54-year-old audience. Interviews with celebrities, original productions, animated material, entertainment news. 24.4 million subscribers.

EXHIBIT 8   **National Growth/Decline in Household Average Audience, 1986–87 versus 1985–86**

	24 Hours	Prime Time	Daytime
Basic cable	+516,000	+ 906,000	+538,000
Pay cable	+101,000	+ 46,000	+ 15,000
Network affiliates	−581,000	−1,128,000	−963,000
Independents	+ 78,000	+ 414,000	−101,000

EXHIBIT 9   Signal Coverage

Percent of U.S. TV Households Able to Receive Service

Networks	99%
PBS	97%
ESPN	43%
WTBS (Atlanta)	42%
CNN	39%
USA	37%
MTV	34%
Nickelodeon	31%
Lifetime	29%
WGN (Chicago)	24%
A&E	23%
HBO	20%
BET	11%
Discovery	8%

Source: NTI (June–July 1986). Discovery Channel data from *Cable TV Programming* (June 16,1986), Paul Kagan Associates, Inc.

EXHIBIT 10   **Cable Subscriber Satisfaction with All Services Received**

Top 10 Services Percent "Very Satisfied"*

Disney Channel	83%
PBS	75%
CNN	64%
WTBS	64%
ESPN	63%
Weather Channel	62%
Nickelodeon	61%
Financial News Network	58%
MTV	56%
VH-1	56%

*Of those heads of households who watched "last week."
Source: ELRA Group, Inc., *Cablemark Probe* (first and second quarters 1986).

responded with a 54-page judgment that allowed cable systems to drop some local channels in favor of cable-only networks effective January 15, 1987.

REPEALING THE MUST-CARRY RULING

The regulations that were to go into effect January 15, 1987, included the following:

- Cable systems with 20 or fewer channels incur no must-carry obligation.
- Systems with 21 to 26 channels must devote seven channels to must-carry.
- Systems with channel capacity of 27 or more must devote 25 percent of their channel capacity to must-carry.

- Additionally, all operators with less 54 channels must include at least one noncommercial educational station. Systems with channel capacity of 54 or more must carry two such stations.

A "must-carry" station was defined as a television outlet located within 50 miles of the cable system with an average rating at points throughout the week of 2 percent (percentage of total television households). All stations less than one year old were considered must-carries regardless of their ratings status.

The rules were to be eliminated after five years, at which time the FCC would determine whether must-carry should be continued in isolated instances. Of the rulings, FCC Chairman Mark Fowler said, "Broadcasters will no longer be held hostage by the government and the government will no longer impinge on the cable's First Amendment rights."

James P. Mooney, president of the National Cable Television Association (NCTA), said the rule was "somewhat more stringent than cable bargained for. Yet, in the long-term sense, it is somewhat less permanent than the broadcasters bargained for." The National Association of Public Television Stations (NAPTS) objected to the rules, stating, "The FCC's action will serve to continue the trend of public stations being dropped."

The FCC's ruling, however, was stayed by the courts before its effective date as unconstitutional, leaving broadcasters without any regulatory guarantee of carriage. Local broadcasters, it seemed, would not be able to look to the FCC to require cable operators to carry local stations. Some suspected the courts preferred that broadcasters and cable operators reach some measure of compromise on their own.

In the new regulatory climate, stations had to convince cable operators that their broadcast services were worthy of carriage. For public television, this new climate was particularly challenging. Not only had the number of local public television stations increased, but so had the number of commercial program services competing for carriage on cable systems. The expansion of syndicated programming and newly available cable-only programming encouraged cable operators to make room on their available channels for new services.

Public television stations could not provide the financial incentives that the new cable channels could. First, cable-only services usually paid operators for carriage. Second, new cable-only services often would barter (i.e., trade) some portion of their advertising schedules that the local cable operator could turn around and sell to local advertisers, providing another stream of revenue beyond their subscriber fees. In addition, multiple system operators (MSOs) frequently held ownership stakes in the new cable-only programming services, providing further incentive to operators to make room for them on their systems.

Concerned about the impact of cable proliferation, PBS officials at the national level developed marketing materials for local stations to use in making their case with cable operators. PBS's research findings are displayed in Exhibits 11–14.

KQED AND CABLE

Eighty percent of the cable viewers in the San Francisco area were supplied by one of five multiple system operators: Viacom, Gill, United, Hearst, or Tele-

EXHIBIT 11   **General Information on Public Broadcast Stations**

- During an average week, public TV is watched by nearly 100 million people, 56% of the nation's TV households.
- Public TV viewers are 27% more likely to subscribe to cable than nonpublic TV viewers.
- Public TV viewers are more active in civic affairs—attending town meetings, signing petitions, writing legislators—than nonpublic TV viewers.
- 60% of all cable subscribers watch public TV each week.
- Cable subscribers try PBS first for science, performance, and quality children's programs—by a margin of more than two to one over similar specialized cable services.
- Viewers rate PBS programs first in program appeal, program impact, informational value, and desirability for repeat viewing, above the networks, HBO, Disney, Discovery, A&E, and other services.
- Two thirds of cable subscribers say one of the reasons they subscribe is for better reception of a PBS station or access to more than one PBS station.
- Among public TV viewers capable of receiving more than one PBS station or cable, an impressive 79% report watching more than one.

Sources: 1986–1987 Nielsen Television Index; Statistical Research Inc.; Roper Reports; Nielsen Homevideo Index, 4th quarter 1987; Television Audience Assessment, Inc.

EXHIBIT 12   **Main Reasons for Watching Public Television**

	All	Household Income $30,000+	Professionals, Owners, Managers	College Graduates
Specific programs mentioned	41%	47%	51%	53%
Quality of programs	19%	23%	29%	29%
Educational content of programs	12%	13%	14%	15%
No commercials	6%	8%	6%	8%

Source: R.H. Bruskin Associates, *Public Television Viewership Study* (November 1983).

Communications, Inc. (TCI). TCI, a Denver-based firm, was the largest operator in the country in terms of both subscribers and systems. Before the must-carry ruling, cable operators were required to carry all over-air television signals in their region. In the bay area, this meant some cable systems were forced to devote more than half their capacity to broadcast over-air stations instead of cable-only and satellite services (e.g., "superstations" from distant markets like WOR-TV New York and WTBS-TV Atlanta).

Some cable operators, eager to fill their channels with a station lineup that produced the highest viewership from their cable households and revenue from cable-only services, had taken full advantage of the revised must-carry ruling, dropping public and independent stations with weaker viewership. TCI had 90,000 subscribers in its six cable systems from Sunnyvale to Daly City and took bold moves in dropping many stations. In December 1986, TCI dropped San Jose's KTEH Channel 54 since its prime-time programming duplicated much of that on KQED's Channel 9. Tony Tiano could read the writing on the wall. The economics of broadcasting had changed, and cable operators were the new middlemen between television stations and their communities.

In developing a strategy, Tony Tiano knew deregulation posed other problems:

EXHIBIT 13   **Households Tuning in Public Television Each Week Nationally**

Season	Prime Time	Full Day
1977–78	13,559,000	27,410,000
1979–80	19,075,000	34,793,000
1981–82	25,347,000	41,484,000
1983–84	25,224,000	45,001,000
1985–86	28,261,000	47,846,000

Source: NTI October-March weekly cumulative households average.

EXHIBIT 14   **Audience Profiles of Selected PBS Programs**

	Ratings			Percent of Program's Total Audience					
	TA†	AA‡	POM*	$40k+ Annual Income	4+ Years College	Age 18–34	Age 35–49	Age 50+
"American Playhouse"	4.4	3.3	33	29	25	25	24	51
"Austin City Limits"	2.9	1.7	20	16	12	20	23	57
"Frontline"	5.0	3.2	34	36	30	25	33	42
"Great Performances:"								
Classical, opera	4.5	2.1	38	37	35	15	19	66
Dance	2.6	1.4	21	34	26	15	23	62
Drama	4.2	2.0	35	30	33	21	28	51
Biography	5.3	3.0	31	32	28	18	23	59
"MacNeil/Lehrer"	8.1	1.9	34	36	34	21	28	51
"Nature"	8.4	5.8	29	27	22	21	27	52
"NOVA"	7.9	5.3	34	31	27	25	28	47
"Smithsonian World"	6.9	4.8	36	33	31	19	30	51
"Wall Street Week"	4.2	3.5	28	32	34	9	22	69
"WonderWorks"	5.4	3.7	30	27	26	23	27	50
Total U.S. households			26	24	21	30	27	43

†TA = Total (i.e., cumulative) audience, the percentage of unduplicated television households in the United States that tune in to the program.
‡AA = Average audience.
*POM = Professionals/owners/managers.
Source: NTI surveys conducted October 1985 through April 1986. Percent distribution data are cumulative households categorized by head of household characteristics.

- Channel reassignment—Cable operators had discussed putting all independent stations (including public stations) in a "block" on the high end of the dial. This would pose particular problems for KQED. Broadcasting on Channel 9 since the mid-50s, the station was identified as "Channel 9" nearly as often as it was by its call letters, KQED. If the reassignment were made, only noncable homes would continue to receive KQED as an off-air signal on Channel 9. Cable homes might, for example, now find KQED on Channel 27 on their cable boxes at home.

- Cable channel integrity—Stations with shortened broadcast days were increasingly sharing their channel space with other services as operators scheduled services to make full-time use of channels when stations were off the air. Stations that shared channel carriage worried that their identity would be confused with that of the other service sharing the channel.

- Regulatory reporting requirement—Currently, cable operators could carry signals without prior consent of broadcasters as well as drop signals without notifying the broadcasters. The first notice that many stations had of being dropped was a viewer calling in and asking why he no longer could receive the station.

- Payment for carriage—Cable-only services paid operators for carriage. There was no exchange of payment by the public television stations for carriage or by the cable operators to carry off-air broadcasts. There was nothing in the rules preventing cable operators from charging public television for carriage in the future.

Tony Tiano brought Joe Camicia, a cable specialist familiar with local politics, on board as part of a proactive approach to the regulatory changes. Both Tiano and Camicia believed KQED was in a strong position to maintain carriage because of its large weekly viewership and reputation. At risk, however, was the smaller KQEC, which had already been dropped by some cable operators. Camicia noted early on that many operators saw KQEC as a duplication of the KQED service: "Operators with limited channel lineups are anxious to drop duplicate channels and independents in favor of more profitable satellite and premium (pay) services. To ensure as little erosion as possible for KQEC and to strengthen KQED for future changes, we need to make adjustments immediately."

CABLE OPERATORS: KQED'S CARRIAGE STRATEGIES

With the repeal of must-carry requirements, many cable operators began to argue that Channels 9 and 32 were near duplicate services and that 32's cable channel space might be given up to another service. In response, KQED began to promote the format blocks to cable operators to differentiate the station's two channels. Time blocks included children's (promoted as the "Electric Playground"), current affairs ("Electric Forum"), and adult instructional ("Electric Classroom") programming.

When KQEC Channel 32 was dropped by cable operator Televents in Contra Costa County, Tiano contacted more than 15,000 of the station's members in Televents service area, urging that they demand the station be reinstated on cable. It took some time, but letters of concern from a dedicated following in a retirement community got KQEC reinstated. Tiano and his staff felt, however, that confrontational grass-roots letter-writing campaigns were not adequate solutions for the long run.

Camicia believed KQED had something to offer cable operators, a positive public image and experience with responsive viewer service: As operators of monopoly franchises, local cable operators market to a public more than aware that they are the only game in town. If you don't like the service provided by the cable operator in your community, your only alternative is going back to off-air viewing, which inevitably means far fewer channel choices and very possibly bad reception. Like local public utilities, the

EXHIBIT 15   **Excerpts from a Speech by Chris Dann**

At the PBS Festival Conference on January 9, 1987, Chris Dann delivered a speech that made the following observations about cable:

> Cable and public television may both be in television, but are not in this business for the same reasons. Cable, like other private enterprise, is an industry with expectations of return on investment. By contrast, public television, born in an era of seemingly unbounded national prosperity and nurtured in one of government largess, was dedicated to service pro bono publico; founded and, for the most part to this day sustained, on tax-based not market-based economics. The cable operator—who wants us to forget his careful calculations of exceptional return on investment—will maintain that no one has the right to demand carriage on his system—the system for which he has made a substantial capital outlay. The public broadcaster, steeled by the righteousness of his position, retorts: "No cable operator has the right to deny me access to the public I am chartered and licensed to serve."

> The fact is—as governments demonstrate every day—enterprises founded and sustained on tax-based economics do not impose on themselves any obligation to define, with as much precision as market-based economics would demand, the nature, scope, or benefits of the services they are offering. Implicit in the fairly unbridled proliferation of public broadcasting stations, and in much of the programming on our channels, is the presumption that public television service should be regarded, *on face value*, as an acceptable and sustainable public service. Some 40 percent of public television stations are in duplicating service situations. We have depended upon must-carry regulations to perpetuate the otherwise indefensible practice of allowing stations to proliferate without attention to whether or not multiple stations were offering their markets genuinely expanded television services.

(continued)

cable operator with a monopoly franchise on television can attract the ire of community residents. Very often if an individual is upset with her cable service she'll call her city council representative at home. Needless to say local officials don't appreciate operators who are not customer responsive.

Tony Tiano reflected on the new climate:

> The economics have changed and we've got a new decision maker on the scene. Our challenge is to continue strengthening our services so cable operators see us as an important part of their channel lineups. Duplicate services on different public television stations are a problem. We're doing all we can to differentiate KQED 9's programming from KQEC 32's. Whether or not the new climate will support numerous local public television stations is an issue. There's not much reason for there to be a KQED and a KTEH if one station is different only in terms of when something is on, which is the case with KTEH. That's not a reason to spend an additional couple of million dollars every year.

> We've got to build bridges with the operators and let them know of our value as a community asset. KQED offers something that the national cable services can't, and that's local programming. We are our community's station. We produce current affairs programs and cultural presentations that showcase the issues and priorities of the greater bay area. In 1988 alone our television division spent nearly $7 million on local programming and production. If cable subscribers continue to see KQED as an invaluable local program service that cable operators offer for goodwill and community betterment then our carriage is nearly assured. That perception is a major part of public television's value to the cable operator.

EXHIBIT 15   *(concluded)*

I am certainly not the first to observe that the antidote to ill-fashioned regulation is not deregulation. So long as we recognize and honor the prospect, in any realm of commercial activity, of incidents when public interests and the interests of private entrepreneurs may not be congruent, we are obliged to accord public interests some protection. Regulation is the most appropriate means. Public broadcasting, as a public service in a field of enterprise so nearly overpowered by the interests of private practitioners, deserves and warrants some protective regulation. I hasten to note this corollary: it is incumbent upon the provider of the public service who seeks the protection of regulation to demonstrate that his public service is, in fact, in the public interest.

Both cable and public television will succeed or fail as a function of the quality of the television services we provide our markets, regardless of what becomes of federal or any other regulations. For cable operators, the amendment, even the elimination of must-carry regulations only adjusts the tilt of the playing field; it doesn't improve the teams or enhance the enjoyment of the spectators. Pay services that do not deliver on their promises will not engender new or renewed subscriptions. Systems that arbitrarily reassign established and well-known broadcast channel allocations, positioning immediate profit motives ahead of customer convenience, will find themselves stunting their prospects for growth.

For public broadcasters, the challenge is not to tilt the playing field back to where it was but, first, to face up to and deal with the challenge of market-based economics, and, second, do our best to see the playing field doesn't get tilted the other way through the total elimination of must-carry regulations.

CABLE PROGRAMMING: COMPETITION?

With new cable services like Arts & Entertainment, Discovery, and Nickelodeon appearing on local cable systems, Chris Dann was concerned about the impact on KQED's viewership and support. Excerpts from the speech he made at the PBS Festival Conference on January 9, 1987, are included in Exhibit 15. Some cable executives, realizing that many of these new services targeted niches served by public television, had begun to ask rhetorically why public television doesn't go back to doing "what is uniquely the element of public television . . . public affairs and local programming."

Chris Dann had a response, "Our viewers, in the focus groups we've conducted, stress that the unique characteristics of public television are its quality and diversity. So long as we can produce and present programs of high quality that the public appreciates and supports, there's a place for our service. We have not reached our levels of accomplishment by programming a single 'niche.' We offer the diversity of many 'niches,' all presented to the highest standards."

The cable networks had also made a substantial investment in their on-air "look." The Discovery Channel had positioned itself as the channel "that helps you discover the world." Dann recognized there was something to be said for image marketing and on-air positioning. PBS conducted focus groups to gather impressions of cable services. A PBS spokesperson said, "Participants with the Discovery Channel on the their cable system raved about the channel, and they loved it. Couple that with Nielsen data that shows these people don't watch very much and one possible conclusion is that Discovery's got a strong on-air positioning campaign. We need to be mindful of marketing ourselves in the same way. We've got the programming to be proud of. We can't afford to be bashful."

MOVING AHEAD

Tiano asked his colleagues to consider strategies for KQED in the new cable environment:

> Cable operators aren't going to work with KQED and KQEC unless it makes good business sense for them. The stronger our reputation for quality television and community service, the better our case with cable operators and the public-at-large.
>
> I had a lot of interesting conversations with board members who felt that non-commercial ought to mean no concern for who's out there watching, and whether or not they're going to support you, We provide a service. The level of support is an indication of the level of satisfaction with that service.

COMPETITIVE RIVALRY IN THE CHEERLEADER SUPPLY BUSINESS*

Barbara J. Allison, University of Alabama

The crowd looked on in amazement as the animal knifed through the tank of crystal blue water at 30 miles per hour and then hurled her body out of the water and into the bright, mid-April sky. Some 12 feet above the water, as she reached the apex of her ascent, the sunlight cast a halo around her sleek black-and-white body. With powerful grace, she rolled onto her side and reentered the water with a splash that sent a wall of water onto the front rows of the delighted audience! The animal that performed this aquatic feat was Shamu, a 7,000-pound female killer whale. Most days, Shamu was the feature attraction at San Antonio's Sea World. However, on that particular day, people were drawn to a pavilion at the southwest end of the aquatic amusement center where the Universal Cheerleaders Association was conducting its 11th annual National College Cheerleading and Dance Team Championship.

As park guests, cheerleading and dance enthusiasts, and friends and family members of the competitors assembled in the outdoor theater to observe the competition, they were greeted by an atmosphere of enthusiasm and nervous excitement. The pavilion was filled with music, movement, and an array of collegiate colors. Cheerleaders, outfitted in their schools' respective colors, could be seen parading through the open-air structure, practicing various partner stunts, or performing daring tumbling passes. Sequined dancers darted about, rehearsed street-smart dance moves, or perfected synchronized movements, and young college cheerleader and dancer "wanna-bees" shook multicolored pom-pons and chatted impatiently in restless anticipation of the championship finals.

With TV cameras rolling and hundreds of spectators looking on, the competition began as the Kentucky Wildcat cheerleading squad (three-time national champions) took the stage and the crowd fell silent. The squad's routine began as the fierce cry of an angry wildcat broke through the silence and simultaneously one of Kentucky's female cheerleaders was tossed into the air by two of her male teammates. The audience applauded as the young woman soared 18 feet into the air, performed a backward layout, and then landed with exacting precision in her teammates' cradled arms—a feat of which even Shamu herself would be proud.

The National College Cheerleading and Dance Team Championship was sponsored annually by Universal Cheerleaders Association (UCA), an affiliate of Universal Sports Camps, Inc.—one of the top two competitors in the cheerleader supply industry. The other leading competitor was National Cheerleaders Association (NCA), an affiliate of National Spirit Group, Inc., and a

---

*Prepared under the supervision of Professor Arthur A. Thompson, Jr.

subsidiary of Randy Best and Associates. The rivalry that existed between the two industry leaders was as fierce and deep as the heralded rivalries in collegiate football—Ohio State versus Michigan, Alabama versus Auburn, Texas versus Texas A&M; and Notre Dame versus . . . well, just about anybody.

Competition between UCA and NCA was particularly intense because of the strained relationship that existed between the presidents of the two companies. In 1972, Lawrence R. Herkimer, founder and president of NCA, hired a young and energetic Jeff Webb and began grooming him to be his successor. However, Webb decided to venture out on his own and formed UCA two years after joining NCA. Webb had this to say about his departure from NCA:

> At the time, I was vice president and general manager at NCA. And I had begun to realize that I had some real philosophical differences with Herkimer. It was extremely apparent to me that if I was going to continue on at NCA and make a career out of it, I was just not going to be happy. So, with $5,000 of my own money and $80,000 that I had borrowed from friends and family members, I decided to start my own cheerleading company, UCA.

In published interviews over the years, Webb indicated he did not think Herkimer was moving NCA or cheerleading in the right direction. Webb was passionate about cheerleading and was determined to have a personal impact in shaping cheerleading trends. He believed he had what it took to run a company effectively and make UCA the clear-cut industry leader.

THE CHEERLEADER SUPPLY INDUSTRY

In 1991, firms that supplied cheerleading groups with products and services were experiencing a lull in growth due to the recession and the financial plight of public and private educational institutions. The lull had occurred despite the increase in the number of individuals of prime cheerleading age (12–17). Also, companies had failed to capture the majority of the market with respect to the supply of instructional products. At the same time, the industry was experiencing a high degree of innovation in the areas of instructional products and services and apparel design and production. Responding to criticism about the risks of injury in performing cheerleading stunts, many of the major companies and participants had banned together to make the industry more safety conscious.

Although a number of companies were involved in the production and supply of apparel and spirit-related products, a cheerleader supply company was defined as an enterprise that was *primarily* involved in the supply of products and services, such as instructional camps, to cheerleading groups. There were approximately 15 national and regional companies in 1991. While most of the competition occurred among national and regional companies, a number of local companies and organizations posed a threat to these larger firms. Exhibit 1 displays basic industry information.

Companies catering to cheerleading groups were part of a much bigger industry referred to as the school spirit industry. The school spirit industry had sales of $200 million in 1991. It consisted of companies involved in the operation of cheerleader, dance team, drill, flag, and band camps; the sale of cheerleader, dance team, and band uniforms and accessories; and the sale of letter jackets and booster products.

EXHIBIT 1   Companies in the Cheerleader Supply Industry

Company	Primary Geographic Market	Instructional Camp Market Share*	
		Overall	Collegiate
Universal Cheerleaders Association (UCA)	National	38.4%	66%
National Cheerleaders Association (NCA)	National	36.8%	22%
United Spirit Association	Regional/West	10 %	11%
International Cheerleading Foundation	National	6 %	
Dynamic Cheerleaders Association	Regional-Midwest; Some national	2 %	
All-Star Cheerleader Camps	Midwest		
Ameri Cheer	Midwest-Ohio		
Champion Cheerleading	Southeast		
Cheer Michigan	Midwest-Michigan		
Cheerleaders of America	Midwest		
Eastern Cheerleaders Association	East		
Elite	Southeast		
Elite Cheerleading Organization	North		
Nation-wide Cheerleaders Association	North		
Power Cheerleading	Hawaii		
United States Cheerleading Association	Midwest-Michigan		
Local organizations	Local		

*Market share is based on the number of customers who attended instructional camps.

BUYERS OF CHEERLEADING PRODUCTS AND SUPPLIES

The customers served by cheerleading supply companies consisted of four major groups: (1) individuals trying to improve their cheerleading skills and squads of youths under 12, (2) junior high and senior high school (JH/SH) cheerleading squads and dance teams, (3) collegiate cheerleading squads and dance teams, and (4) coaches and advisors. The individual and youth squad population was mainly female cheerleaders, while the JH/SH and collegiate populations consisted of male and female cheerleaders and mascots and female dancers. Coaches and advisors were typically adults willing to manage and supervise the activities of cheerleading squads or dance teams. In 1991, approximately 750,000 to 1 million individuals were engaged in some form of cheerleading or dance squad activity in the United States. About one third of those participants at the JH/SH and collegiate levels attended instructional camps; the percentage was lower for individual and youth squad participants.

Squads included both regular and alternate members of a school, college, or university's cheerleading or dance groups. In addition, it was customary for a school to have one or more individuals functioning as costumed mascots; mascots were not counted as part of the cheerleading squad, but were included as a separate market segment because of their distinct costume and instructional requirements.

Jeff Webb, founder and president of UCA, mentioned that dance squads had gone through a number of different names over the years, but, in the early 1980s, dance participants had settled on the term *dance teams*.

Cheerleading squads were composed of as few as 3 members and as many as 24 or more. In 1991, there were all-girl, all-boy, and coed squads. All-girl squads were typically associated with the youth squad and JH/SH populations, but some all-girl collegiate squads still remained. Doug Brown, coordinator for athletic promotions and marketing and cheerleader advisor at the University of New Hampshire, detailed his school's all-female cheerleading squad:

> In the past, our squad got very little support and backing. Then in 1988, a former male cheerleader from Miami of Ohio came along and turned basically a bunch of arm-swinging girls into a very athletic and effective squad. We changed our tryout format as well. In the past, girls were eligible to try out at the end of their freshman year of college. Once a girl made the squad, she was allowed to remain on the squad for up to three years. We modified our tryouts so that each year the girls had to try out again—their being on the squad was no longer a sure bet; they had to work hard each year to ensure their place on the squad. This change made our squad more competitive and put our tryouts more in line with what other schools around the nation were doing with their tryouts.
>
> I believe that the changes since 1988 have also played a major role in our successes in national competitions. Over the last few years, we have qualified for both NCA's and UCA's national collegiate competitions. We had to stop attending NCA's competitions because the company did not cover our squad's traveling expenses like UCA did. We attend one of NCA's summer instructional camps, which is held at Boston University and is only a one-hour drive from our school. We would like to support UCA by attending one of its camps; however, the closest UCA camp is five hours away, and with squad funds being so tight, we really can't afford to do that.
>
> Over the years, our cheerleading squad has been composed of 16 female cheerleaders. A few years ago, we lowered that number to 14 in order to cut traveling and uniform expenses. Though our squad has traditionally been comprised of females, our tryouts are open to all individuals. I feel that there is still somewhat of a stigma attached to being a male cheerleader. What the University of New Hampshire needs to do is just get over that hump—get that first group of male cheerleaders in there; then I think that the stigma will begin to disappear.
>
> I realize though that a coed squad would bring with it new challenges and extreme changes. For starters, if we did have a coed squad, I don't know if we would have a 14-member squad made up of 7 males and 7 females, or 4 males and 10 females, or what! There definitely would be a lot of decisions to make. As well, I don't know how successful our squad would be at first. We have come so far in the past few years, the girls have made such a name for themselves it would be hard for them to have to start all over again. I don't really know just how my girls would react to guys being on the squad—some would be for it, some would be against it, and some would be like me—they just really wouldn't know how they felt. As well, we would have to get someone in here to teach us just how to be a coed squad. When you come right down to it, there really would be a lot of internal adjustments to make.

All-male squads were extremely rare in the 1990s. According to Tim Swiney, assistant director of student activities at Texas A&M and advisor for the university's all-male yell leader squad, all-male cheerleading squads could be traced back to military academies and the days when these institutions were open exclusively to males. Swiney had this to say about A&M yell leaders:

Traditionally, the yell leaders have been comprised exclusively of men. However, our elections are now open to all individuals—males and females—who will be juniors or seniors and who are in good academic standing. In the last three or four years, we have had a few of our female students compete for yell leader positions, and this year one of our young women came extremely close to winning. The school and the yell leaders would be highly amenable to having a woman be a part of the team, and I see it happening in the very near future.

Swiney also explained the basic activities of the yell leaders, how his five-member squad was selected, and the squad's various responsibilities:

We truly have a unique program here at Texas A&M. Our yell leaders perform various yells that have been handed down over the years. These yells are much different from the cheers and chants that you see being conducted today at sporting events for other colleges and universities. It is really hard to explain exactly what it is that our yell leaders do. But they have hand signals that go with each of the yells; so, the crowd knows exactly what yell is coming up next. As well, they do a lot of jumping up and down on one leg, and the yells are performed by the leaders bending over, placing their hands on their knees, and yelling as loud as they can. It may sound strange, or even funny, to those individuals who are not familiar with our school or our yell leaders, but basically everything we do is steeped in tradition, has some sort of meaning, and is symbolic of who we are.

In order to try out for the yell leaders, a candidate must present a petition of support with at least 100 names on it. Then on the day of tryouts, the competitors perform a number of yells. The candidates are subsequently voted on by the student body; this is much different than tryouts at most other schools where the candidates are selected by a panel of judges.

At Texas A&M, we have a very large ROTC program, probably the largest in the nation, and the majority of our yell leaders are members of the cadet corps. The cadets really support one another in their various endeavors, and this is especially true for those members competing for positions as yell leaders.

Our squad is responsible for conducting yells at football and basketball games, tennis matches, and women's volleyball matches. It is really hard to get all five members of the squad at every one of these athletic events, plus some of our yells do not lend themselves to sporting events other than football. As a result, our program is currently under review by the vice president's office.

Collegiate squads were typically coed, but since 1980 it had become more common for senior high schools to have coed cheerleading squads. Coed cheerleading squads tended to be larger than all-female or all-male squads; usually the squad had between 5 and 10 pairs (one male and one female) of cheerleaders, with the average number of members being 14. Many collegiate squads also had a "mike man" who was responsible for leading cheers and chants via public address systems. All-female squads were usually larger than all-male squads, with all-female squads having 10 to 12 members on average and all-male squads having an average of 5 to 7 members. Most squads had alternate members to fill in for sick or injured cheerleaders or members who had to leave the squad for whatever reason.

Dance teams were generally limited to JH/SH and collegiate populations and were almost exclusively female. Dance teams had between 6 and 24 members—with some having as many as 60 members.

At the senior high school and collegiate levels, it was not unusual for a school to have both varsity and junior varsity cheerleading and dance squads.

However, a school usually had only one dance team. Some senior high schools had two varsity cheerleading squads, one to cheer at football games and the other to cheer at basketball games. At the high school and collegiate levels, varsity cheerleading squads were composed of sophomores, juniors, and seniors or juniors and seniors, while junior varsity squads were typically made up of freshmen or freshmen and sophomores. At some schools, the varsity squad or team consisted of the top 50 percent of the candidates who made the cut, while the junior varsity squad or team consisted of the bottom 50 percent of the candidates who made the cut.

Cheerleaders, mascots, and dance teams performed their spirited duties at all types of sporting events, including football, basketball, wrestling, gymnastics, baseball, and soccer. Dance teams generally performed during halftime at football and basketball games.

Individuals and Youth Squads

Included in the market were a number of young girls generally between the ages of 4 and 16. They usually were not members of any given squad but were interested in developing their skills in preparation for future tryouts. Youth squads were typically associated with an elementary school or middle school or a city athletic league (little-league football). It was not clear how many of these youth squads there were in 1991; however, given the large number of youth sports programs in cities and schools, this market segment was thought to include several hundred thousand participants. Also, given the popularity of cheerleading, it could be argued that any young girl was a potential customer. In 1991, approximately 14 million girls attended kindergarten through seventh grade. While almost all individual and youth squad participants were females, an increasing number of young boys were becoming squad members.

Junior High and Senior High Market

The JH/SH market consisted of both boys (cheerleaders only) and girls generally between the ages of 12 and 18 who were members of squads or dance teams representing schools. This was the biggest market segment—composed of about 500,000 members.

Though both boys and girls were conducting cheers on the sidelines of American football fields, the great majority of these individuals were female.

Collegiate Market

The collegiate market contained about 12,000 individuals engaged in either cheerleading or dance activities. Virtually every junior college and university had at least one cheerleading squad. Many schools also had a mascot that required a custom-made outfit. At major universities whose sports teams appeared frequently on television, it was not uncommon for the cheerleading squads and dance teams to have several outfits and an array of equipment.

A few universities offered cheerleader scholarships. In the late 1980s, such scholarships had become increasingly popular but were not typical among most universities.

Coaches and Advisors

Coaches and advisors were typically adult faculty, staff, or administrative members of a school. Coaches were more thoroughly involved in the activities of their squads and teams than were advisors. Both coaches and advisors were responsible for supervising the general activities of their squads or teams, coordinating travel arrangements, and acting as liaisons between squads or teams and a school's business office (or what ever school entity was responsible for squad or team funds). According to Debbie Brown, cheerleader advisor at the University of Alabama and former Alabama cheerleader, coaches are generally more involved in the activities of their squads. In addition to the general responsibilities of both coaches and advisors, cheerleading coaches are also responsible for attending all squad practices; ensuring squad safety; maintaining squad progression with respect to tumbling, double stunts, and pyramids; and choreographing regular and competition routines. Brown also mentioned coaches were more likely than advisors to be paid for their contributions.

T. Lynn Williamson, administrator for personnel and cheerleading advisor at the University of Kentucky, was probably the most lauded advisor in collegiate cheerleading. He had the following to say about his role as cheerleading advisor and the U of K cheerleader program:

> In conjunction with my other duties at the University of Kentucky, I am the university's volunteer—nonpaid—cheerleading advisor. I was never a cheerleader myself; so I didn't feel that I should take on the role of coach—though I have learned a bit over the years and consider myself well-versed in the discipline of cheerleading. Along with myself, I have a four-member staff: one assistant advisor, two coaches, and one trainer. My assistant advisor and one of my coaches work on voluntary bases, while my other coach and trainer are graduate assistants and receive a stipend of about $8,000 each per academic year for their work with the squad. Actually, we have two squads here at the University of Kentucky—our Wildcat squad and Lady Cat squad.
>
> I believe very strongly in our cheerleading program and its ability to build a positive image for the university. In fact, in the last six years, our squad has placed either first or second in UCA's national collegiate cheerleading competition. We don't even try to attend NCA's competition because you have to pay your own way out to the competition, and it isn't even on TV—so what kind of deal is that? At any rate, UCA's competition plays on ESPN some eight times a year. Do you realize what kind of free exposure that is for the university? It would cost us thousands of dollars to generate that kind of positive publicity on our own.
>
> We offer scholarships to our cheerleaders. Each member receives the equivalent of one year's in-state tuition, or $1,700 per academic year. Also, we have an additional $2,500 in academic and athletic scholarship money which is granted to members who maintain a 3.0 grade point average and/or who are outstanding members of the squad.

Of Williamson's 14 years as the University of Kentucky's cheerleading advisor, he had the following to say:

> It is hard to put into words what this experience has meant to me—hard to say just how rewarding it has been. I put between 30 and 40 hours a week into our cheerleading program plus 30 to 40 hours into my regular job—some people might wonder if I'm not crazy. And maybe I am just a little off balance to spend so much time and energy on these kids. But there is one thing that I am sure of,

EXHIBIT 2   Number of Participants Attending Cheerleading Camps

	Cheerleader	Mascot	Cheer Advisor	Dancer	Dance Advisor	Totals
Individuals and youth squads	6,250+	NA	1,250	NA	NA	7,500
Junior high/senior high	173,975	6,500	18,000	33,274	1,751	233,500
College	6,924	344	382	1,282	68	9,000
Total	187,149	6,844	19,632	34,556	1,819	250,000

NA—not available or unknown

and that is the positive influence that this program has on each of the young people who are, and have been, a part of it. I work so hard at this job because I live with the conviction that when our young people leave this program, they leave as educated, independent, and mature adults. And that is worth every bit of the effort.

Advisors were generally associated with youth squad and JH/SH squads and teams, while coaches were normally associated with collegiate squads and teams.

CHEERLEADING PRODUCTS

Companies supplied three major categories of products: instruction in cheerleading and dance techniques, apparel items, and "spirit" items such as pompons, buttons, and ribbons.

Instructional Products

Instruction in cheerleading and dance techniques was provided at camps—three- to five-day sessions offered in the summer—and clinics—shorter, weekend sessions conducted year-round. Clinics were generally provided to squads and individuals on a communitywide basis. Clinics were usually held at smaller universities, high schools, or community centers; their role was to brief participants on such aspects of cheerleading as safety, technique, fund-raising, and crowd involvement. Cheerleading and mascot camps and dance camps were offered to each of the three major market segments: youth, JH/SH, and collegiate. Exhibit 2 shows attendance figures at instructional camps. Industry participants believed actual camp attendance wasn't higher than it was for a number of reasons, including that many squads believed instruction was not necessary, and many squads could not afford to attend these camps. Also, many private and public school administrators did not allow their squads and teams to participate at instructional camps.

Industry prices for instructional products ranged from $40 to $130 for commuting campers and $93 to $209 for resident campers. Prices were generally about $20 to $40 higher for collegiate camps than they were for youth and JH/SH camps.

According to Jeff Webb, it was not difficult to conduct instructional camps:

All one really needs is a few instructors and a flat piece of land and they have a camp. But, while it is easy to conduct a camp, it is extremely hard to maintain a camp or series of camps year after year. Such camps take a certain amount of dedication to the campers, creativity, and planning. Not every organization that is out there conducting camps possesses that dedication, creativity, and ability to plan.

These camps were staffed by various camp officials and instructors who were generally former or present high school and collegiate cheerleaders, mascots, and dancers. Most instructors worked for the various cheerleading industry companies only during the summer. Camp officials were often full-time employees.

Camp instructors were considered to be the cream of the crop in their areas of expertise. Most companies followed similar instructor-selection procedures. The usual way was for current instructors and camp officials to be on the look-out at the various JH/SH and collegiate camps for individuals who exhibited extraordinary leadership, communication, and cheerleading, mascot, or dance skills. As these individuals were discovered, they were invited to compete in tryouts for positions as instructors the following summer. These tryouts were generally held during the spring.

At these tryouts, the individuals were required to perform various routines related to their particular skills. For instance, individuals vying for female cheerleading-instructor positions were required to learn and perform—within three hours—one cheer, one chant, and one two-minute dance routine. Also, these young women were required to demonstrate their partner stunt and tumbling abilities. Males competing for cheerleading-instructor positions had the same tryout requirements as their female counterparts, less the dance routine requirement. In addition, a criterion for the selection of male instructors included the mastery of a standing back tuck. This selection process also included interviews with the candidates. On average, one third of the candidates for instructor positions were selected as instructors.

Pete Braughton had this to say about his experience as a UCA cheer-instructor:

> Being a UCA instructor has meant a great deal to me. I have made a lot of friends along the way and had some really great times with all of the other instructors. But I think the aspect of being an instructor that has meant the most to me has been the opportunity to share my experience and knowledge with others.
>
> I mean, when you take someone who doesn't know something—a stunt, a tumbling pass, or whatever—and you teach her how to do it, and then you look at her and her face is beaming with amazement and delight, it is just a wonderful feeling.
>
> Some people might think that cheering is just about cheers and jumps and things like that, but it is really so much more. It is about working together, accomplishing goals, and putting forth that extra effort at the point when many others might give up. When I work with a group of girls, and I see them really connect. See them connect with each other and with what they're doing—that lets me know that I have accomplished my major goals. And these goals are to expand the horizons, capabilities, and minds of these young people.

Karen Rosenstock, a former cheerleader at Forest Hill High School in Palm Beach, Florida, had the following observations to make about her three-year experience as an NCA instructor:

> The college squad that I am a member of attends a UCA camp, but in junior high and senior high school, my squads attended NCA's camps. All I have ever really known were NCA's camps—I just grew up with them and loved them.

I work as an NCA instructor because I enjoy working with the kids. It really doesn't matter to me which organization I work for, UCA, NCA, or whoever. All of these organizations really stand for the same thing. These organizations are all about helping individuals to reach their goals. At NCA, we instill in these young people a set of standards and values that I believe follow them throughout their lifetimes.

Tryouts were generally not held for individuals seeking positions as mascot instructors. Individuals recognized as possessing outstanding mascoting skills were usually selected as mascot instructors through informal agreements between themselves and a senior staff member at camp. Almost without exception, mascot instructors were people who were, or had been, collegiate mascots. Being a collegiate mascot, especially a mascot instructor, could prove lucrative; a number of mascot instructors went on to become professional mascots, earning as much as between $60,000 and $200,000 per year.

Instructors were paid generally between $195 and $250 per camp session. Instructors were usually qualified to teach at all levels (youth, JH/SH, or collegiate); however, the best and/or most experienced instructors were generally assigned to the collegiate camps.

Rookie instructors had to try out for positions as instructors each year for a predetermined number of years (usually between two and four). Once an individual had passed these tryouts for the predetermined number of years, he or she was considered a veteran instructor and no longer had to try out for positions as staff members. Veteran staff members were normally eligible to instruct at camps for as long as they wanted to. Instructors were asked to resign only if they exhibited poor conduct, poor instructional skills, or weakening athletic abilities.

Youth Cheerleading Camps   Youth cheerleading camps were generally one- to four-day camps conducted at high school or university facilities. These camps were strictly commuter camps. Attendees arrived about 8 A.M. and departed about 5 P.M.; a few camps had only half-day sessions.

Participants were instructed on the fundamentals of cheerleading—motions, voice control and projection, jumps, tumbling, partner stunts, and pyramids. Usually, the attendees were divided into groups based on age and skill level and then instructed in activities designed for their particular skill level.

Awards, ribbons, and trophies were passed out to outstanding camp participants. Often, trophies were awarded to the most outstanding all-around cheerleaders or the top two or three cheerleaders in various age groups. However, to keep enthusiasm high among all attendees, officials and instructors were careful to ensure that no youngster left camp empty-handed.

JH/SH Cheerleading and Mascot Camps   These camps normally began on Monday or Tuesday afternoon and ended on Friday afternoon. Occasionally, junior high and senior high school camps were conducted separately, and not all of the camps included mascot instruction. Primarily, JH/SH squads attended JH/SH cheerleading camps; however, it was not unusual for individual customers to attend such a camp. These camps were offered to both commuting campers and resident campers. The activities at JH/SH camps were generally much greater and much more involved than those at elementary camps.

For both cheerleaders and mascots, the days and evenings at camp were packed with learning new skills, practicing these skills, and exhibiting how well they had mastered these skills. Like the youth camps, the cheerleaders were exposed to the fundamentals of cheerleading; however, at the JH/SH camps, participants were encouraged to learn and perfect some of the more challenging jumps, partner stunts, tumbling moves, and pyramids. Also, JH/SH campers were taught advanced cheers, chants, fight songs, and dance routines.

The days of camps for mascots were filled with learning the role of a mascot, clowning techniques, crowd involvement, routines that combined all spirit groups, cheer motions, and stunting techniques.

During the day, campers learned, reviewed, and practiced new chants and cheers. In the evening, the various squads were broken down into groups of about four squads to perform before a group of judges (camp instructors) one cheer and one chant they had learned that day. This activity was designed to illustrate how quickly a squad could learn and master new skills. Many of the squads incorporated cheers, chants, pyramids, double stunts, and so on that they already knew into the routine of new cheers and chants. Later that evening, when all of the campers were assembled, the squads were awarded various ribbons based on how well they had performed their routines. Generally a blue ribbon represented a near-perfect routine, a red ribbon stood for a good routine, and a yellow ribbon symbolized a routine that needed more work. Also, every evening and on the last day of camp, squads that had exhibited extraordinary spirit and the ability to work well with others were awarded spirit sticks. Those squads awarded spirit sticks on the last day of camp were allowed to take them home to display in school trophy cases. The spirit stick was probably the most coveted of all awards presented at these camps (see Appendix).

On the last day of camp, or at some other designated time during camp, the best junior high and senior high squads were asked to perform a routine of cheers and chants so an all-around best junior high and senior high squad for the camp could be chosen. These routines also generally included tumbling, jumps, and various pyramids and partner stunts. Other awards also were given to camp participants.

Collegiate Cheerleading and Mascot Camps   Collegiate cheerleading and mascot camps were attended by various collegiate squads (generally varsity squads, as junior varsity squads had not been picked before the summer season of camps). These camps were very similar to JH/SH camps. The major difference was that college camps began later in the day and ended earlier in the evening so the young-adult campers could engage in various social activities such as camp dance parties and cookouts. Also, more advanced cheerleading skills were taught. The majority of the partner stunts taught at collegiate camps were coed stunts. However, highly difficult male/male partner stunts were being taught, and many of the young women had developed the strength necessary to perform traditional coed partner stunts.

Like elementary and JH/SH campers, collegiate campers were required to demonstrate their cheerleading abilities and were evaluated on a daily basis. As with their younger counterparts, the spirit stick was the ultimate symbol of accomplishment and a source of great squad pride. (See Exhibit 3 for details

EXHIBIT 3   **Skills Taught at Instructional Camps**

Jumps

Herkie   Russian toe-touch   Pike

Partner Stunts

Beginning   **Intermediate**

Rear thigh stand   Shoulder stand   Chair   Torch

Photographs courtesy of Richard Pospisil, Jr.

on the various jumps, partner stunts, and pyramids taught at youth, JH/SH, and collegiate cheer camps.)

JH/SH Dance Camps   JH/SH dance camps were attended by junior high and senior high school dance teams. At these camps, participants were taught various types of dance routines, including funk, high-kick, jazz, pom-pon, and prop (a routine that incorporates an apparatus, such as a ribbon, hula-hoop, or baton, and achieves a heightened visual impact). Generally, three new dance routines were taught each day. These routines varied in type and in difficulty. Usually one beginning, one intermediate, and one advanced-level dance routine were taught each day. Unlike cheer camps, the dancers did not learn their new skills as squads or as teams. The various dance teams broke into groups based on skill level and attended instructional sessions geared toward their

EXHIBIT 3   *(concluded)*

Pyramids

Liberty heel stretch

Cupie

Hand-to-hand

Beginning

Fan

High table top

Intermediate

Lucky seven chair

Two-one

Advanced

Photographs courtesy of Richard Pospisil, Jr.

individual aptitudes and interests. Through this process, a dance squad could take home as many as 12 new dance routines from one camp.

The individual squads were generally encouraged to bring a routine from home on which they were evaluated. The team with the best routine was generally awarded a trophy—this was probably the highest honor that could be received at one of these camps.

The last day of camp was a day of review, individual evaluations, and awards. Individuals were evaluated on their mastery of routines they had been taught during the week; most campers were evaluated on four routines. Like the cheerleaders, the dancers were presented ribbons that represented their mastery of a particular routine. Other awards were also given, including awards for the team that demonstrated the most improvement over the week and individual awards for outstanding achievement in dance. These honors were generally voted on by camp instructors.

Collegiate Dance Camps College dance teams attended collegiate dance camps. Collegiate dance camps were very similar to JH/SH dance camps. The major difference, like collegiate cheerleading camps, was that the camp day usually ended earlier and began later in the morning than did JH/SH camps. Also, more advanced dance routines were taught at the collegiate camps.

Coaches and Advisors At instructional camps, advisors attended various sessions on safety, fund-raising activities, how to conduct more effective practices, and their role in squad and team choreography.

Apparel Products

Apparel products consisted of the various garments and accessories worn by cheerleaders, mascots, and dancers while performing at athletic events or other related events (gamewear) and while attending camps (campwear).

There were numerous products for both male and female cheerleaders. For female cheerleaders, gamewear included: long-sleeved, short-sleeved, and sleeveless (shell top) sweaters, tops, and vests in V-, turtle-, and crew-necks; halter tops; midriff tops; straight skirts; knife-pleated skirts; and 4-, 6-, 8-, 12-, and 16-pleated skirts; jumpers; briefs; turtleneck bodysuits; socks; and shoes. Male gamewear consisted of long- and short-sleeved sweaters and tops in V-, turtle-, and crew-necks; pants; and shorts. These female and male products were available in a number of fabrics and weaves. Many of these products could be adorned with twill and chenille lettering and logos.

Female cheerleading accessories consisted of various jackets, cardigans, warmups, hair bows, jewelry, sports pins, duffel bags, megaphones, and pompons. Male cheerleading accessories generally included various jackets, cardigans, warmups, and megaphones. Various gamewear items and accessories were combined to create female and male cheerleading uniforms.

Mascot gamewear consisted almost exclusively of mascot costumes. The design of these costumes was dictated by a given school's mascot, be it a human character—pirate, Trojan, pioneer, or Viking; an animal—lion, alligator, bear, dolphin, or eagle; or a natural disaster—hurricane, tornado, tidal wave, or fire. Mascot campwear was generally the same as female and male campwear.

Dance gamewear generally consisted of any number of creative and original apparel ensembles. However, it was not uncommon for dance teams to wear female cheerleading gamewear. Dancewear included long-sleeved, short-sleeved, and sleeveless bodysuits; leotards; unitards; crop-tops; and dresses in V-, turtle-, and crew-necks; full- and capri-length pants; bike-length shorts; tights; socks; leggings; and jazz boots and shoes. These dance apparel products were available in fabrics such as Lycra®, cotton, and nylon. Like female and male cheerleading products, dance products could be embellished with lettering and logos.

Dance accessories included sequined belts, headbands, leg warmers, and cuffs; nylon belts and leg warmers; gloves; jewelry; duffel bags; and dance routine accessories, such as hula-hoops, colorful elastic bands, and pom-pons.

Campwear for cheerleaders, mascots, and dancers usually consisted of shorts and T-shirts embellished with the name of a squad's school or mascot, a creative slogan, or the wearer's name; socks; and shoes. Campwear for dancers often consisted of something a little more form fitting, such as Lycra® bike pants and crop-tops.

Orders for apparel products, especially gamewear products, were generally placed by squads and teams in the spring for delivery by the first football games in the middle of August or early September. Often, squads and teams would request that their orders arrive before they went to summer instructional camps. These camps began as early as the first week in June. As a consequence, the apparel side of the industry was very seasonal, just as the instructional side was.

The addition of dance gamewear, which often was not needed until basketball season began, had enabled many cheerleading industry and apparel companies to generate revenues during the fall and winter, thus reducing the seasonality of the business by a slight margin.

The average industry price for a complete cheerleader uniform ranged from $150 to $300, including shoes. A complete dancer uniform ranged from $100 to $200, and mascot costumes ranged from $500 to $2,000 or more.

Spirit Products

The number and types of spirit products available were practically endless. Spirit products consisted of spirit pins and ribbons, banners, and noise makers. Often, spirit paraphernalia, especially spirit pins and ribbons, were sold to fans by the cheerleaders or members of a spirit committee before a pep rally or athletic event. Customers received their spirit-related goods from local, regional, and national suppliers, with the majority of customers obtaining such supplies from local and regional vendors.

SUPPLIERS TO CHEERLEADING INDUSTRY

Universities and junior colleges allowed cheerleading industry companies to conduct instructional camps at their various facilities. These institutions provided meals and instructional facilities for commuting campers and meals, instructional facilities, and housing for resident campers. Companies paid these institutions based on the number and type of campers (resident or commuter) that attended each camp—upward of 60 percent of camper registration fees. Sometimes smaller companies used the facilities of high schools and community centers when conducting their instructional camps. Larger companies would often have these organizations sign contracts with them to ensure the long-term use of their facilities. According to Jeff Webb, many junior colleges and universities gladly welcomed camps at their facilities because the camps acted as great recruiting tools for these academic institutions. Roughly 90 percent of the individuals attending JH/SH camps indicated they were going to attend college after high school graduation.

Other suppliers to cheerleading industry companies consisted of various fabric supply companies, shoe companies, and spirit supply companies. Companies could source their manufacturing and operational supplies from a large number of vendors and manufacturers. This situation was also true for apparel and spirit companies. Apparel companies were usually involved strictly in the supply of gamewear and campwear—they did not provide instructional products. The composition of these companies differed greatly. Some were involved in the full manufacturing process of their products, while others operated strictly as suppliers. A large number of apparel companies were in operation in 1991. Spirit companies were those companies involved in the sale of spirit-related products. In 1991, there were numerous spirit supply companies. Many apparel and spirit companies lacked the capital, distribution systems, and management teams necessary to last within the industry.

SAFETY

Paralyzed cheerleader wins $2.1 million

Mobile (AP)—A high school cheerleader who was left paralyzed from the waist down when she fell on a concrete floor while attempting a difficult stunt will receive $2.1 million from the Mobile County school system, a teacher, and her former principal.

Attorneys for the 18-year-old Angie McAll and the defendants went before Mobile County Circuit Judge Braxton Kittrell Wednesday to say they had agreed to settle the lawsuit stemming from the June 1987 accident. . . .

In the early 1970s and mid-1980s, it had become very popular for cheerleading squads to incorporate minitrampolines into their crowd-motivating routines. At the height of their popularity, squads were utilizing minitrampolines to perform daredevil stunts. For example, trampolines were used by male cheerleaders to dive through perforations in pyramids or by female cheerleaders to catapult onto the tops of extremely high pyramids. In 1986, a Kentucky Wildcat cheerleader, Dale Baldwin, was paralyzed from the neck down after a miscue while performing a maneuver off a minitrampoline. According to close friends, Dale continued to support cheerleading after his accident, attending UCA's national competitions and staying in close contact with members of Kentucky's squad, and held little, if any, animosity toward the activity.

The injury to the high school cheerleader from Mobile, Alabama, occurred while the squad was performing a pyramid on a concrete surface. As a result of the young woman's injuries, she sued her school system, a teacher (her cheerleading sponsor), and her former principal. Many individuals believed the lawsuit was unjust because the members of the squad had been instructed not to perform that particular pyramid and never to perform any type of activity on a concrete surface. This incident led to massive cutbacks in the number of activities JH/SH squads in Alabama and other states were allowed to perform. Pyramids were limited to two-people high, and, in many cases, all partner stunts, tumbling, and even jumps were banned. By 1991, junior and senior high school administrators who had curtailed the activities that cheerleaders could perform had begun to relax their restrictions.

Though cheerleading was a relatively safe activity, a number of injuries inspired companies, coaches, advisors, and school administrators to take a closer look at the role of safety in cheerleading. In 1989, Jeff Webb, along with other industry members, produced a comprehensive guide to cheerleading safety. This guide, a cheerleading safety manual, provided state-of-the- art instruction in the areas of injury prevention, including instruction and information concerning stunt execution, dismounting, and spotting; strength-enhancing diets; stretching; and first aid.

Other safety-related issues included a training program offered by various companies to cheerleading coaches and advisors. During these programs, participants were trained in cardiopulmonary resuscitation, general first aid, and injury prevention. At the end of these training programs, individuals who had mastered all of the safety guidelines were awarded certificates. Such training served as protection against lawsuits, and the successful completion of such programs was a great accomplishment for coaches and advisors.

Cheerleaders, mascots, and dancers were often required to sign forms stating they would not bring suit against a school, member of a school's administration, coach, or advisor for injuries sustained while engaging in cheerleader, mascot, and dancer activities. Such forms were also signed by campers before participation in camps to relieve companies, camp officials, camp instructors, and camp site institutions of any liability related to camper injuries. Although the signing of such forms did not completely halt the lawsuits, it did heighten awareness of the dangers inherent in cheerleading and prompted coaches, advisors, camp officials and instructors, and other related parties to pay closer attention to the safety and supervision of cheerleaders, as well as mascots and dancers.

Also, it was not unusual for insurance companies to refuse to pay claims on injuries sustained while cheering, mascoting, or dancing.

MARKETING

Most cheerleading industry companies utilized promotional brochures, telemarketing, and newsletters to promote their products and services. Squads and teams placed instruction, apparel, and spirit paraphernalia orders with cheerleader suppy companies via mail-order forms contained in various promotional brochures or via telephone ordering services. According to industry participants, a strong telemarketing program was imperative for success.

Cheerleader and dance coaches and sponsors were bombarded with brochures advertising instructional camps, dance and cheer gamewear and camp-wear, and spirit paraphernalia. Some coaches and advisors received so many of these brochures that they discarded many of them after taking only a quick glance through their pages. Customers were not particular about where and from whom they ordered their uniforms and other supplies. According to one advisor:

> If the girls and I see something that we like, we will usually buy it, but it has to be the right price. I wouldn't say we buy the least expensive items, but I would say that we are extremely price conscious. I believe that many other squads share in our concern for keeping costs down.

Companies involved in the manufacture of apparel products and accessories marketed their products by affixing company logos and labels to their products. They also promoted their products and services through various special events, such as participating in parades, conducting national and regional championships, and contributing to charity events and organizations.

RECENT INDUSTRY DEVELOPMENTS

A number of trends were occurring in the industry in 1991, including innovative apparel designs; the development of new stunts and pyramids; and national companies providing campwear, private camp instruction, private coaching, and new instructional products. One of the more popular trends was the development of new designs and accents for cheerleading uniforms. Designs referred to the cut and style of tops, shirts, and pants, while accents pertained to the multi- or single-colored striping, logos, and insignia on uniforms. Most of these designs were generated through the use of recently developed computer graphics programs. Such technology allowed customers to virtually create their own unique uniforms. Another trend was the popularity of various accessories, especially personalized hair bows, socks, and jackets; spirit jewelry; bandannas tied around ankles, necks, and heads; and pom-pons made out of metallic, fluorescent, and opalescent materials.

Industry participants were continually developing new partner stunts, pyramids, cheers, chants, and dance moves. Along with new partner stunts and pyramids came innovations in the execution, including dismounts, and spotting of these feats. Also, rigorous male-male and female-female stunts had become increasingly popular. New dance moves were continually being created and modified to achieve the artistic expression necessary to establish elite cheerleading squads and dance teams. Such innovations passed freely between individuals, squads, and even companies.

In the early 1990s, companies began supplying specialized campwear especially suited for cheerleader activities. Until that time, local sporting goods companies and retailers had the market on these products. Campwear supplied by cheerleading companies was designed with the latest casual fashions in mind and adorned with catchy slogans, bright primary and neon colors, and bold wording.

Another trend in the early 1990s was that of private camp instruction. Across the country, a number of individuals were conducting their own private camp sessions. One conductor of private camps observed:

> This type of camp is extremely effective. Number one, when we—a friend and myself—conduct a camp, the instructor to camper ratio is 1 to 6—that is a much better ratio than what you see at larger camps where the ratio is 1 to 25 or

1 to 20. We are teaching the squads unique cheers and chants that few, if any, other squads will have—our campers really like that. Also, we are teaching them in their own environment; so we can modify our instruction to their particular needs and resources.

The price for one of our camps is $500, and that includes the squad's providing us with hotel accommodations, travel expenses, and meals. Our camps are three-day camps as compared to the four-day camps of larger companies, and our camps run from 9 A.M. to 3 P.M. with one-hour breaks for lunch. Many other camps keep their campers from 8 in the morning until 9 at night—and that, in my opinion, is just too long. The girls get so tired and worn out that they can barely function.

I think that private camps are a great alternative, not only to squads with limited resources, but to squads that are interested in an enhanced learning environment free of competition and other stresses inherent in larger camps.

In addition to private camp instruction, many squads were hiring individuals to choreograph and teach members competition routines. The price for this special instruction was generally between $100 and $325 per routine, with a few of the best private coaches charging as much as $2,000 to $4,000 per routine. Some squads were willing to pay those prices for special instruction.

A major issue in the industry in 1992 was that of fund-raising. Lawrence Herkimer, founder and president of NCA, was once quoted as saying:

> Cheerleading is wonderful, colorful—and depression-proof. Think about it. You're the parent of one of six little girls in the whole school chosen to be a cheerleader. No matter how bad times are, are you going to tell your little girl she can't have her sweater and pom-pons? Hell, you'll sell the boat before you have to tell her that.[1]

However, in 1991, companies were learning the hard way, through decreased camp attendance and apparel sales, that the business of cheerleading could be as vulnerable as any other company to recession.

As a result of decreased parental and school funds, some squads were conducting fund-raising activities to buy new uniforms and attend camps, competitions, and out-of-town athletic events. These fund-raising activities included car washes, candy-bar sales, cookie sales, and bake sales. Many companies provided fund-raising ideas in their newsletters and via coach/advisor sessions conducted at instructional camps.

In the late 1980s and 1990s, companies began offering instructional videos for use by both individuals and squads. The videos demonstrated partner stunts, cheers and chants, dancing, building pyramids, and cheering at athletic events such as basketball, wrestling, and soccer.

FOREIGN MARKETS

In the early and mid-1980s, foreign interest in American-style cheerleading was on the rise. Japan, Great Britain, New Zealand, and Australia were among the foreign countries having the most interest.

In 1986, Herkimer realized customer growth within the United States would soon peak and began exploring opportunities outside the United States. His

---

[1]A. Bagamery, "Go! Fight! Win!" *Forbes*, September 27, 1982, pp. 136–40.

search led him to Japan where he began building enthusiasm for cheerleading among the Japanese, whose cheerleaders had begun attending his camps in Hawaii. However, just when Herkimer had settled into his new market, the news came that UCA had signed a joint venture with Dentsu, a huge Japanese advertising agency; NHK, the Japanese broadcasting group; and several Japanese athletic equipment manufacturers. UCA's joint venture involved the sale of uniforms, royalties, and the training of cheerleaders for both schools and corporations such as Nissan. In 1991, UCA was the only cheerleader supply company that had any real presence in Japan.

SMALL REGIONAL AND LOCAL COMPETITORS

Along with national cheerleading industry apparel and spirit companies, other smaller companies competed for customers. These companies included regional companies and local organizations that conducted instructional camps, as well as local apparel companies and seamstresses. Cheer Michigan and Ameri Cheer were examples of companies that conducted instructional camps on a predominantly regional basis. These regional camps were usually three- to four-day commuter and resident camps and were offered to all cheerleading customers, as well as their coaches and advisors. Instruction at regional camps was generally not offered to dancers and their coaches and advisors. Local organizations operating instructional camps included senior high cheerleading squads, YMCAs, and youth clubs. These camps were usually one- to four-day commuter camps and were attended by individuals, youth squads, and junior high school squads. Some of these camps, especially the shorter camps, were very inexpensive, while others were moderately priced.

In some localities, sporting goods shops, uniform supply companies, and local seamstresses provided cheerleading, mascot, and dance uniforms and accessories. Usually, uniforms and accessories from local suppliers were slightly more expensive and less fashionable than those supplied by national apparel suppliers. However, local suppliers were better able than national suppliers to provide uniform repair and alteration services.

MAJOR COMPETITORS IN THE CHEERLEADING SUPPLY INDUSTRY

Dynamic Cheerleaders Association

Dynamic Cheerleaders Association (DCA) was begun in 1970 by Linda Ray Chappell. The company was primarily involved in the supply of cheer camps and campwear. According to Vicki Westhues, assistant to the president at DCA, the company had a very strong instructional program that focused exclusively on JH/SH squads. Westhues had the following observations to make about DCA's camps:

> We have a staff of 60 highly trained instructors—approximately 75 percent of our staff are veteran instructors—which is dedicated to providing our campers with a larger amount of new material in a fun, noncompetitive environment. We are not like other companies who focus on the competition aspect of cheerleading. Our philosophy is that our campers come to camp to learn, not to compete. We

do hold an annual, nontelevised national cheerleader competition, but again the focus here is still very much on learning, squad cooperation, and fun.

DCA conducted approximately 47 four-day instructional camps at 40 locations in 22 states. Each squad was given a Sunshine Book on the first day of camp; it contained pages on which squads could keep up with scheduled activities, record cheers and chants they had learned, track their progress, and record special events at camp. DCA held daily evaluations of material learned during camp and awarded ribbons based on spirit, leadership, cheering skill, improvement, and creativity. DCA's evaluation system was different from the systems of other companies in that it allowed squads to be judged in their area of strength instead of an overall evaluation. Other awards such as trophies and special ribbons were awarded on the final day of camp. In keeping with other camps, the company also awarded spirit sticks, or what DCA called DYNAMITE awards. Along with cheer camps, the company conducted six one-day cheerleading clinics and approximately five dance camps throughout the year. (See Exhibit 4 for camp prices.)

DCA did not have any exclusive contracts with camp site suppliers and utilized sites at the same institutions where other companies' camps were held. Westhues stated DCA did not have and did not strive to have exclusive contracts with institutions, noting that NCA sought to establish exclusive contracts with institutions and held the largest number of such contracts. Westhues indicated DCA was the first company to supply cheerleading campwear. According to her, the company had been involved in the supply of such products since 1976, much longer than most other companies, which were just beginning to explore that market:

> We have been supplying campwear accessories, or what we call fun stuff, for a number of years and have been very successful in it. It is the market where we make all of our money. We are really amazed that companies like NCA and UCA are just beginning to enter this market—and we *really* wish they would get out of it!

DCA supplied no gamewear. Campwear and accessories included shorts, T-shirts, shoes, hair bows, buttons and stationery, pencils, sunglasses, and picture frames embellished with cheerleading and dance slogans. In addition, the company was not involved in the manufacture of its products. DCA received its products from a number of different suppliers, including Artex and Champion.

In addition to supplying instructional and apparel products, the company offered customers instructional videos, manuals, and handbooks. DCA's president and staff had also worked hard to accommodate those squads that were not allowed to perform partner stunts and pyramids by providing instruction on creative alternatives, such as mini-stunts, hand-clap sequences, peel-offs, and body and arm spellouts.

DCA had a year-round mail-order business that company management believed was imperative to the successful promotion of a company's products and services and, thus, to a company's long-term success and profitability. DCA had six full-time employees and was located in Kansas City, Missouri.

International Cheerleader Federation

International Cheerleader Federation (ICF) was begun in 1964 and was the second oldest of the major cheerleader supply companies. It was headquartered in

EXHIBIT 4	Prices for JH/SH Camps and Collegiate Camps

Prices for JH/SH Camps

	DCA	ICF	USA	NCA	UCA
Resident Student					
Range	$125–160	$138–185	$130–208	$93–209	$125–195
Average	139	153	180	131	152
Most common	125	146	203	145	148
Resident Advisor					
Range	$105–135	$120–165	$80–158	$46–184	$40–138
Average	118	133	130	118	120
Most common	125	126	145	119	120
Commuting Student					
Range	$60–110	$65–113	$40–80	$40–143	$65–130
Average	77	85	79	88	88
Most common	75	85	80	89	88
Commuting Advisor					
Range	Free	$40 for		$15–145	Free
Average		each camp		40	
Most common				45	

Prices for Collegiate Camps

	NCA	UCA
Resident Student		
Range	$135–218	$115–170
Average	165	153
Most common	145	155
Resident Advisor		
Average	$137	Free
Commuting Student		
Range	$80–112	$80 for
Average	93	each camp
Most common	89	
Commuting Advisor		
Average	$62	Free

Shawnee-Mission, Kansas, and was positioned to compete almost directly with UCA and NCA in the JH/SH instructional and apparel markets.

According to Eric Denson, a former ICF Instructor, ICF differed from NCA and UCA in a number of fundamental areas:

> At ICF, we have many squads at our camps that probably wouldn't be able to get the more advanced ribbons or awards at one of UCA's or NCA's camps. Therefore, our ribbons and awards are based on various aspects of a squad's evaluated routine. For instance, our squads are judged in eight different categories, including entrance and exit, stunts and tumbling, smiling, and execution. We have different colored ribbons for the different categories.

So, if a squad can't jump or tumble real well but can really smile and turn on a crowd, they can still get a ribbon. This is much different from most other companies who judge squads on their overall execution of an evaluated routine—from jumping and tumbling, to smiling, to spirit. However, I do believe DCA's evaluations are a lot like ours.

ICF has a real strong program in my opinion. The only major drawback might be the rate of turnover among the instructional staff. Most of ICF's staffers are there for only a year and then move on to UCA or NCA where there is more prestige.

ICF conducted 122 JH/SH camps at 107 locations in 40 states, including Alaska. ICF did not conduct youth camps, JH/SH dance camps, or collegiate camps of any type. The company maintained an instructor-to-student ratio of 1 to 25 and emphasized learning, safety, personal attention, and politically free instruction (many squads were concerned that companies played favorites, paying special attention to select squads and teams). According to a member of the company's staff, ICF believed cheerleading industry companies were very similar, and that ICF did not differ from other companies with respect to the quality and focus of instruction. Lawrence Herkimer, president of NCA, made the following comment about competing with ICF:

> I tell you what, I love to compete against ICF. Its president, Randy Neil, is so involved in other projects, like film archives, that he can't afford to let his company get too big—if he did, he wouldn't be able to manage it. He keeps it just big enough and that's perfectly all right with me!

In the early 1990s, ICF broke into the professional football market by providing instruction to the coed Kansas City Chiefs cheerleaders. The company conducted clinics and events in South America, Canada, Ireland, Finland, and England. The company was also organizing its first nationally televised cheerleading championship—International Open Cheerleading Championships, to be televised on such stations as Prime Sports Northwest, Prime Ticket, and Home Team Sports.

ICF was involved in the supply of apparel products and accessories including uniforms, shoes, pom-pons, campwear, and books and videos. The company did not produce its apparel products and accessories; these responsibilities were carried out by ICF's sister company, Cheer Gear by Rally.

The company believed it had a strong telemarketing program and it held a solid position in the cheerleading industry. Though ICF had been involved in the youth and collegiate markets in the past, the JH/SH market was where the company thrived and had decided to remain. The high concentration of cheerleaders in the Midwest was at the root of the company's success.

United Spirit Association

United Spirit Association (USA), located in Mountain View, California, and headed by Michael Olmstead, catered to the different needs, outlooks, and programs of western schools. The company was a competitor in the much larger school spirit industry, of which the cheerleading industry was a part. USA's instructional products included JH/SH spirit camps, color guard and drum major camps, and a collegiate spirit and dance camp. The company's apparel products consisted of campwear for cheerleaders, dancers, flag teams, and other school groups involved in promoting school spirit.

USA's JH/SH spirit camps included cheer, dance, songleader/pom-pon, mascot, pep, flag, crowd leader, and stadium letter girl camps. These camps had an instructor-to-student ratio of approximately 1 to 25. The company held 69 camps per year at 35 locations in 11 states and Canada. The company held one collegiate spirit (cheer) and dance camp each year in Santa Barbara, California, at which the student-to-staff ratio was 20 to 1. The company was scheduled to begin a new type of camp, called "Elite Camps," in 1992, for qualifying advanced squads. Like other companies, USA provided its campers with progress evaluations; unity awards, trophies, and ribbons were awarded at various evaluation sessions. The company also offered junior one-day clinics for middle school and elementary school cheerleaders. In addition, USA was selected as a spirit consultant for the National Football League, produced major shows for professional sporting events, and produced and directed professional sporting events, and produced and directed professional dance teams for the San Francisco 49ers, San Diego Chargers, Golden State Warriors, Los Angeles Clippers, and Sacramento Kings.

Though the company was concerned with such industry issues and characteristics as safety, athleticism, and skills execution, at both the JH/SH and collegiate levels of instruction, USA's emphasis appeared to be on flash and glamour. The company billed itself as "America's most innovative choreographers (bringing) together the finest in spirit tradition with the energy of MTV."[2] Compared to other camps, such as NCA and UCA, United Spirit Association put less stress on collegiality (a characteristic that was indicative, and in many cases expected, of most cheerleading squads and dance teams across the nation) and, instead, promoted "squad unity." USA's emphasis on flash applied not only to the company's instructional products, but also to its campwear.

USA's president, Michael Olmstead, believed the company's regional basis was a strength rather than a weakness. He saw the company's regional focus as allowing the company to design its camps to more fully meet the special needs of its campers—or what it called "spirit leaders." USA claimed it offered more material and program diversity than any camp in America.

USA's apparel and accessory products consisted of multicolored tops and shorts, tennis shoes, and a large selection of metallic and iridescent pom-pons. USA was not involved in the production of its apparel products. The company had a strong mail-order business that included the distribution of instructional and apparel catalogs and a videotape that described the various products the company offered.

USA conducted a number of special events throughout the year, and in 1992 was slated to have its Fifth Annual USA Nationals Spirit Competition televised on ancillary cable stations throughout the nation.

National Spirit Group, Ltd./NCA

Though the company's formal name was National Spirit Group, Ltd., it was widely referred to as NCA. NCA was begun in 1953 by Lawrence R. Herkimer, some five years after Herkimer, the inventor of the famous "herkie jump," conducted his first cheerleading camp. According to Herkimer, he held his first camp in 1948 when he was a senior in college. He continued to teach summer

---

[2]USA's 1992 *Spirit Camp* location and price guide. *USA 1992 Spirit Camps Dare2 Dream.*

camps while he was working on his master's degree and, in the early 1950s, started conducting camps under the banner of the National Cheerleaders Association. Over the years, the company's stature had grown and, until recently, it was the recognized industry leader. Herkimer was generally regarded as the father of modern cheerleading.

In 1991, NCA provided instructional, apparel, and limited spirit products, such as booster ribbons and pins. Its instructional products consisted of youth, JH/SH, and collegiate cheer, dance, and mascot camps. NCA had two different types of dance camps—pom-pon and drill team—which it operated through its Superstar Dance and Drill affiliate. The primary reasoning behind this delineation was the belief that drill teams, which usually performed military-type, precision dance moves and were associated with bands, had different needs from pom-pon squads, which generally performed jazz, funk, and pom-pon routines. Like other companies, NCA held its dance camps in conjunction with its cheer camps; however, NCA and DCA, unlike other companies, held separate dance camps that were open strictly to dance teams. NCA's pom-pon and drill camps, or Superstar camps, were more expensive than its cheer camps. Herkimer noted that his company was the only cheerleading supply company to provide drill teams with the special instruction they required. Smaller companies such as American All Star Dance and Drill Team competed with NCA for drill team campers, but did not pose a substantial competitive threat to NCA. According to Herkimer, many of these smaller competitors were involved in other projects and businesses throughout the year and did not center their attention on camps and camp instruction.

Although NCA provided pom-pon and drill team instruction, its major emphasis was on the JH/SH cheer market, where the largest number of participants were. NCA had gone to greater lengths than other companies to generate interest and participation in its youth camps. Herkimer noted that the demand for little league football was on the rise; so, in about 1987, the company began focusing heavily on the youth market. The company had established an exclusive contract with Pop Warner, an organizer of little league football programs located in Philadelphia, Pennsylvania, to train its cheerleaders. NCA conducted 140 youth camps and trained between 7,500 and 8,000 youth campers in 1991. Camp prices for youth camps ranged from $45 to $60, depending on the length and location of a camp.

In 1991, the executive management of NCA decided to introduce two new instructional products—metro camps and dream camps. Metro camps were four- to five-day, half-day camps offered to JH/SH customers. Herkimer stated his company was very responsive to the needs of squads around the nation, and the company's sales representatives had observed the need for more affordable camps. Many school districts were under a money crunch and could not afford to pay $120 to $180 to send their cheerleaders to resident camps. Metro camps, which were conducted in larger metropolitan areas, were designed to attract schools with tighter purse strings (even schools that might be classified as disadvantaged); junior high squads, whose parents did not feel quite right about sending their children off to a big university for a week; and individual campers. Herkimer said:

> We encourage these young people to get two or three of their friends together and come to our camps. These camps are especially useful for kids who are thinking about trying out for cheerleader; it lets them see how much hard

work and dedication being a cheerleader takes and if they have the skills necessary to become a cheerleader. It let's them know if they *really* want to be a cheerleader.

These camps were expected to attract some 10,000 participants in 1992. NCA expected some decline in attendance at JH/SH camps due to the introduction of metro camps even though most metro attendees would be add-on, first-time camp participants. Prices for metro camps ranged between $50 and $70.

Herkimer said dream camps were the creation of the company's new owner, Randy Best, who wanted to experiment with some new high-end instructional products. According to Herkimer, while many squads were on a tight budget, others could afford almost anything they wanted; hence, the decision to introduce upper-end camps. Dream camps consisted of instructional classes incorporated into a vacation-type atmosphere. NCA planned to offer cruises to the Bahamas; London; Cancun, Mexico; Sydney, Australia; Paris; and Moscow. The prices for these camps ranged from $595 for the Cancun cruise to $1,759 for the cruise to Australia.

In 1982, NCA was the distinct leader in the industry with roughly two thirds of the country's JH/SH customers and one half of the country's collegiate customers attending its camps. In 1986, NCA was still the leader in instructional camps with 90,000 camp participants, 2,000 of whom were collegiate customers. However, in 1991, NCA had approximately 92,000 customers compared to UCA's 96,000 customers. NCA had approximately 2,000 to 4,000 collegiate campers in 1991. Herkimer noted:

> When Jeff first left NCA and began his own company, he really focused heavily on the collegiate market—and that was a smart move on his part. At that time we really weren't interested in that market because the numbers just weren't there. But in the last few years, we have really started to take an interest in the collegiate market, and we have made great strides and are now extremely competitive with UCA in the collegiate market.

NCA and UCA differed markedly in their approaches toward instruction. At NCA, the emphasis was reputed to be on flash and showmanship. As one industry member put it:

> At NCA, anything goes! The more the merrier. If you can build a pyramid four levels high—you build a pyramid four levels high. If you can do four back flips in a row—you do four back flips in a row. NCA really does focus on the performance aspect and visual appeal of cheerleading.
>
> This approach toward cheerleading really is quite different from that of UCA. At UCA, the focus is on involving the crowd. At UCA camps, campers learn shorter cheers and chants that the fans can learn quickly and enjoy doing. Even at UCA's competitions, the focus is on fan involvement; the emphasis on showmanship is still there—it is just more controlled.
>
> I wouldn't say that one approach is better than the other. But there is a tangible difference between NCA's and UCA's approach toward cheerleading. And I see NCA adopting many of UCA's philosophies in the very near future, especially with respect to crowd involvement.

Herkimer painted a much different picture of NCA's approach toward cheerleading although he did note the pendulum had begun to swing in a different direction, and the company's emphasis was more on safety, squad dynamics, building spirit, and learning:

Every camp has its hotdogs—those squads who can come in and do everything. But we realize that not all campers are like that—many of our squads are young squads that need to concentrate on learning the fundamentals, others are a bit more advanced and ready to try new and more difficult skills, and, like I said, others are just hotdogs—and we have classes for them too. We have adjusted our instructional programs to meet the varied needs of our squads. So we have classes where advanced skills are taught and beginning level courses for our rookie cheerleaders. We are really moving away from, or trying to cut back on, the competition aspect of cheerleading at our camps.

Our 120 or so salesmen are always out there gathering information about what our customers want. We do not have one set program—we have regionalized ourselves in order to meet the needs of different programs. We don't have a canned program. For instance, we have songleader programs for our western customers because there is a real interest for that sort of thing out there. Also, different parts of the country have different styles, and if we aren't responsive to that we will lose customers. I mean there are just some things you can't teach a cheerleader in the Bible belt that you *have* to teach to cheerleaders on the West Coast or they won't come to your camps—you know what I mean! "Soul Train" doesn't go over well at a camp in Mississippi, but it is a must in California.

Herkimer had a very definite philosophy about cheerleading instruction and what it took to make it in the cheerleading business:

I have been an educator most of my life, and that is the attitude that I take toward cheerleading—I am an educator of cheerleaders. At NCA, we are dedicated to the building of a cheerleader. And that means concentrating on building leadership skills in our campers. The individuals who attend our camps are ambassadors to their schools; so, the skills aspect of cheerleading really must take a backseat to other aspects such as building school spirit, being responsible, and being safety conscious. The jumping and cheering and pyramids are all important—but leadership, spirit, responsibility, and safety come first.

In order to make it in this business, you have to know your customer, deliver a quality product, and have competent service people who are well trained, dedicated, and know how to keep the customer happy. The way I see it, I get one chance to make a school mad—and that's it. I might lose them forever. And schools don't just come and go; they are there for a long time. At NCA, we are in it for the long haul—we think long term—so we will go out of our way to make a customer happy, even if it costs us upfront. That is as true for the instructional side of the business as it is for the apparel side; so, we are very liberal on our apparel return and repair policies as well as our camp refunds.

NCA maintained an instructor-to-camper ratio of about 1 to 25 at its collegiate and JH/SH camps. At youth camps, the company maintained a ratio of 1 to 10. Like other camps, NCA provided its campers with evaluation ribbons and trophies, as well as spirit sticks.

In 1991, NCA held 480 JH/SH camps at 267 locations in 46 states and Canada.

NCA was involved in a number of special events, including the Macy's Thanksgiving Day Parade, the Aloha Bowl halftime show (which it shared with its prior sister company, USA), the Cotton Bowl, and the St. Patrick's Day Parade. NCA periodically conducted special clinics in such countries as Brazil, Japan, New Zealand, and Australia.

Herkimer began the sale of apparel products and supplies in the late 1950s. Over the years, he had elected to purchase existing buildings to substantially lower costs and construction debt. In the early 1960s, Herkimer bought a knitting mill for $100,000; this purchase greatly enhanced his control over product quality and eliminated various subcontracting costs. In addition, Herkimer had purchased a milk-carton factory, which he used to produce plastic megaphones, drinking cups, buttons, and badges. According to Herkimer, when the company first began its accessories and apparel business, it contracted out its production requirements, but these contractors were not sensitive to Herkimer's needs.

> We would order specific sizes, like 25 size 5 uniforms, 30 size 7 uniforms and 10 size 9 uniforms and we'd get back 40 size five uniforms and 15 size seven uniforms. Our contractors just wouldn't give what we asked for. And the girls *really* wanted their uniforms to fit—you can understand that. So in order to get the quality, quantity, delivery, and service we required, we bought a cut and sew factory, a knitting mill, and began producing our own chenille. By the late 1960s, we were fully integrated.

Herkimer noted that his first venture into the apparel and accessories market began with his invention of the pom-pon and the supply of booster ribbons:

> At first we were just selling kits to the kids so that they could put together their own pom-pons—you know a little something to build school spirit, something we have always focused on here at NCA. When the demand for pom-pons became too great, we decided to start manufacturing them ourselves. That along with our booster ribbons, which said things like "Trample the Tigers," were really what got me involved in the apparel side of the business.
>
> All cheerleaders don't want to look alike; so you really have to be responsive to their needs—give them what they want as far as style, color, and size go. But the problem is that it is just so darn hard to supply products in this business. We have such a small order and production window. I mean you get one shot and that's it. If you aren't there for the customer when they are ordering during the months of April, May, and June, and then you can't deliver the product to them at least by the end of September, you're out of luck. It's sort of like selling Christmas trees; everybody wants one in December, but you can't give 'em away in January!
>
> We have really been blessed in this business in that we have not had any foreign competition, especially Asian competition. And that is due to our small ordering window. The way the Asians are set up, they need about a six-month lead time—and you just don't get that in our business.

NCA supplied cheerleader and dancer gamewear and mascot uniforms through its affiliate, Cheerleader Supply, Inc. In 1991, the company expanded its gamewear offerings to dancers and began supplying campwear to cheerleading industry customers. In 1987, NCA generated $19 million in revenue through the sale of its apparel items and accessories, compared to UCA's $4.6 million. NCA was still the dominant leader in uniform and accessories sales and production in 1991. NCA's apparel prices were in line with the industry average.

Like other companies, NCA was interested in cheerleader and dancer safety. Herkimer had contributed his thoughts and experiences concerning cheerleader safety to publications. The company also provided fund-raising ideas. Herkimer noted that at one time the company supplied its customers with fund-raising products such as candles, candy, and stuffed animals but got out of that side of the business because it did not prove cost effective.

In 1991, NCA had a number of very sophisticated promotional materials, including glossy brochures and catalogs advertising the company's instructional and apparel products. These brochures and catalogs were distributed to thousands of youth organizations and schools across the country. The products displayed in NCA's apparel catalogs resembled products displayed in fashion catalogs more than they did traditional cheerleading and dancer uniforms. NCA's approach to sales was much different compared to other companies in the cheerleading industry. NCA had approximately 200 telemarketing agents, 150 of which were field agents placed strategically throughout the United States. These 150 individuals were responsible for making face to face sales calls at junior and senior high schools. Most other companies did not have field agents.

In 1991, NCA had a number of very sophisticated promotional materials, including glossy brochures and catalogs advertising the company's instructional and apparel products. These brochures and catalogs were distributed to thousands of youth organizations and schools across the country. The products displayed in NCA's apparel catalogs resembled products displayed in fashion catalogs more than they did traditional cheerleading and dancer uniforms. NCA's approach to sales was much different compared to other companies in the cheerleading industry. NCA had approximately 200 telemarketing agents, 150 of which were field agents placed strategically throughout the United States. These 150 individuals were responsible for making face-to-face sales calls at junior and senior high schools. Most other companies did not have field agents.

In 1991, NCA had 35 full-time employees, approximately 750 individuals employed at its uniform and accessory production facilities, and 750 summer instructors.

Current NCA Situation   In 1986, a 61-year-old Herkimer realized he was fast approaching the day when he could no longer run his cheerleading empire on his own. Knowing this, he sold NCA to BSN of Dallas for $13 million cash and several million in deferred stock. BSN was an aggressive marketer of sports equipment. Along with NCA, BSN purchased USA, Teammates, and two sportswear factories. Teammates was a manufacturer of apparel items owned by Mark Alexander, who had left UCA in 1982 to start his own apparel supply business. BSN combined NCA's Cheerleader Supply Company with Teammates to form Cheerleader/Teammates. The new owners provided NCA with much stronger financial backing and more resources to counter the market inroads being made by UCA. However, NCA continued to lose ground to UCA. BSN organized the four companies with the intention of selling them as a package, which the company did some 18 months after purchasing NCA. The taker was Prospect Group, Inc., which bought the conglomerate for some $46 million, more than double the price BSN purchased it for, in March 1988 in a highly leveraged financial transaction. By the end of the year, Prospect Group, Inc., was failing financially, and NCA found itself in a very precarious financial position. According to Herkimer:

> Prospect Group's ultimate goal was to corner the cheerleading market. But the whole thing turned into just one big monster. They thought that the synergy between the companies would make it work, but it just never happened. The companies operated under different philosophies, were spread out all over the

country; it was just impossible to coordinate the activities of each of the four companies.

BSN's original owners attempted to buy back Prospect Group, Inc., but BSN's bank pulled its financing before the deal could go through. By the close of 1989, Prospect Group, Inc., was bankrupt. It began selling bits of the conglomerate. According to Herkimer:

> Prospect Group sold off USA and the two sportswear companies; so that left NCA and Cheerleader/Teammates. We were purchased by Randy Best and Associates in February 1991; they brought us out of Chapter 11 bankruptcy. NCA itself never went bankrupt; we always had a positive cash flow. It was just all the companies together—it just didn't work.

According to Herkimer, National Spirit Group, Ltd., along with its four affiliates, NCA, Superstar Dance and Drill, Cheerleader Supply Company, and Teammates, grossed $43 million in 1991, 75 percent of which was generated through the sale of apparel items and the remaining 25 percent through instructional camps. Herkimer knew Randy Best had saved his company, and if he had not come along when he did, the company would undoubtedly be operating under very different circumstances. Herkimer also knew that even though his company had remained successful, it had still been hurt by the events of the last few years. And he knew that if he did not do something in the near future, Jeff Webb and UCA would replace NCA at the top of the cheerleading industry.

Universal Sports Camps, Inc./UCA

UCA was an affiliate of Universal Sports Camps, Inc. The company had undergone enormous growth and change, including increased financial success and the development of four major affiliates. Between 1987 and 1991, UCA's revenues for camps and events had increased by 322 percent (see Exhibit 5). UCA was recapitalized in September 1989 by merging with a newly formed organization so former shareholders of UCA could realize the gains on their investment. Affiliates were UCA, Varsity Spirit Fashions and Supplies, Inc. (Varsity), Universal Dance Association (UDA), and American Association of Cheerleading Coaches and Advisors (AACCA). UCA was the company's first entity and was begun in 1974. Varsity, the company's uniform manufacturing and supply affiliate, and UDA were begun in 1979. AACCA, which was a nonprofit organization, followed in 1988. Each of these affiliates had trademarked names.

In 1991, the executive management of UCA was striving to achieve eight major strategic goals: (1) promotion of the cheerleading industry, (2) introduction of new product lines, (3) expansion of its sales efforts, (4) expansion of its camp sessions and locations, (5) increased use of its direct-marketing capabilities, (6) realization of heightened brand awareness, (7) larger information systems, and (8) expanded contract manufacturing.

In 1986, UCA served approximately 53,000 customers through its various instructional camps. By 1991, that number had grown to 96,000. Six thousand of these customers were collegiate customers, including cheerleaders, mascots, and dancers and their coaches and advisors. UCA had been the leader in the collegiate segment for several years, posting numbers considerably higher than its closest competitor, NCA. In 1986, UCA served 4,500 collegiate customers compared to NCA's 2,000; in 1991, UCA had widened its collegiate customer

E X H I B I T   5   UCA Financial Data, 1987–1991

| | Predecessor | | | | The Company | | | | |
| | Years Ended March 31, | | | April 1, 1989, to September 29, 1989 | Inception (September 29, 1989 to March 31, 1990) | Pro Forma Year Ended March 31, 1990 | Year Ended March 31, 1991 | Six Months ended September 30, | |
	1987	1988	1989					1990	1991
Income Statement Data									
Revenues									
Uniforms and accessories	$ 4,984	$ 6,572	$10,050	$ 9,828	$ 3,386	$13,214	$16,122	$12,955	$15,781
Camps and events	5,121	6,501	7,519	8,503	962	9,465	11,993	10,860	12,026
Total revenues	10,105	13,073	17,569	18,331	4,348	22,679	28,115	23,815	27,807
Cost of sales									
Uniforms and accessories	2,781	3,117	4,833	4,579	2,040	6,619	7,720	5,761	7,480
Camps and events	3,609	4,511	5,244	5,909	583	6,492	8,199	7,528	8,446
Total cost of sales	6,390	7,628	10,077	10,488	2,623	13,111	15,919	13,289	15,926
Gross profit	3,715	5,445	7,492	7,843	1,725	9,568	12,196	10,526	11,881
Selling, general, and administrative expenses	3,460	4,550	5,852	6,782	2,979	7,209	9,260	5,730	6,477
Operating income (loss)	255	895	1,640	1,061	(1,254)	2,359	2,936	4,796	5,404
Interest income (expense)	(71)	20	104	94	(745)	1,319	(1,278)	(688)	(622)
Other income (expense)	11	23	(17)	(36)	(46)	(132)	(545)	(432)	(264)
Income (loss) before income taxes	195	938	1,727	1,119	(2,045)	908	1,113	3,676	4,518
Income taxes (benefit)	90	362	650	691	(766)	391	490	1,443	1,760
Net income (loss)	$ 105	$ 576	$ 1,077	$ 428	$ (1,279)	$ 517	$ 623	$ 2,233	$ 2,758
Net income (loss) per share	$ —	$ —	$ 0.02		$ (0.64)	$ 0.26	$ 0.31	$ 1.12	$ 1.38
Cash dividends per share	$ —	$ —	$ —	$ —	$ —		$ —	$ —	$ —
Weighted average shares outstanding					2,000	2,000	2,000	2,000	2,000
Supplemental Information									
Net income							$ 1,459	$ 2,662	$ 3,168
Net income per share							$ 0.55	$ 1.00	$ 1.19
Weighted average shares outstanding							2,668	2,668	2,668
Balance Sheet Data (at period-end)									
Working capital	$ 817	$ 1,260	$ 1,617		$ (856)		$ (1,363)	$ 736	$ 688
Total assets	2,565	3,522	4,270		10,718		11,447	14,389	16,368
Long-term debt (excluding capital leases)	558	461	150		9,572		8,709	8,703	7,840
Shareholders' equity (capital deficit)	846	1,382	2,284		(3,237)		(2,614)	(1,048)	164

Source: UCA

EXHIBIT 5   *(concluded)*

	First Quarter	Second Quarter	Third Quarter	Fourth Quarter
Year ended March 31, 1990 (Pro forma)				
Total revenues	$6,532	$11,799	$2,674	$1,674
Operating income	715	2,899	(616)	(639)
Net income (loss)	234	1,562	(632)	(647)
Year ended March 31, 1991				
Total revenues	$9,375	$14,440	$2,728	$1,572
Operating income	1,471	3,325	(888)	(972)
Net income (loss)	652	1,581	(779)	(831)

margin by some 1,500 participants. Jeff Webb indicated he concentrated on increasing camper enrollment in UCA's collegiate camps because he believed the younger campers would soon follow:

> Young campers, especially junior high and senior high customers, really look up to—or actually idolize—their more mature, collegiate counterparts. If these younger campers are going to NCA's camps or ICF's camps and then they hear that a college squad attends one of our camps, well I just believe it won't be long before these kids come on over to our camps. And if you look at how our JH/SH camp numbers have increased over the years, you will see that is exactly what has happened.

UCA was dedicated to providing instruction at the youth level but did not concentrate too heavily on that market because youth leagues and cheerleading squads tended to come and go. The company was also very dedicated to its JH/SH and collegiate customers. According to Webb:

> We get in this room (referring to the executive conference room at UCA's headquarters), and we literally agonize over what we are going to teach these kids at camp each year—it is that important to us. It can get pretty emotional in here, and I have to admit there have been times when we have almost gotten into screaming fights about what we're going to teach at camp.
>
> We all get along real well, we understand one another and the philosophy behind our company, but we just want to get it right for these kids—and the result is a lot of emotion. I think it is great that we can be that open with one another, and in the end we come out the best for it because we end up with real quality material.

UCA operated some 423 cheerleader and dance team instructional camps in 1991, 6 of which were collegiate camps. These camps were held at 203 locations in 44 states (see Exhibit 6) and in Canada and Japan. UCA provided song leader instruction for JH/SH squads in California. UCA conducted youth, JH/SH, and collegiate camps. The company provided private camps and coaching to those individuals and squads requesting such services, but these services were not considered major activities of the company. In some cases, the camp fee was waived for advisors; this was true of other companies as well. UCA expected to conduct seven collegiate camps in 1992.

UCA's instructional revenues had grown from $5.1 million in 1987 to $12 million in 1991. Like other companies, UCA provided its participants with

---

EXHIBIT 6   **UCA 1991 Camp Locations**

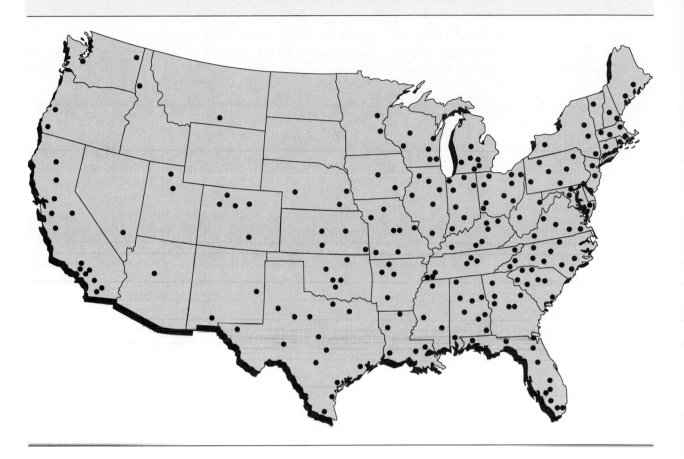

---

evaluation ribbons, trophies, and spirit sticks. A UCA mascot instructor described UCA's approach to the camp experience:

> I really enjoy working for this company, and I believe the company takes the optimal approach to cheer instruction. And that is an approach that is geared towards building strong, confident cheerleaders from the ground up, not like some other camps which expect the campers to come to camp prepared to compete and where the emphasis is on performance versus actual learning. Also, UCA caters to the needs of each individual. These campers come in with varying abilities and they leave with varying abilities—that's just the reality of the situation. To expect them all to come in the same just doesn't make good sense, at least not to me.
>
> I know that my sisters all went to NCA camps while they were growing up. And they would come home virtually in tears because they hadn't done well or weren't the best squad at camp. Doing well and winning were just that important to them, and I believe that NCA stresses that sense of competition among its campers. They decide at camp who goes to their national competitions. At UCA we don't do it that way; we hold qualifiers at the regional level and the collegiate squads submit videos of performances which are later judged.
>
> Basically, NCA's camps are regimented and competition-oriented. I disagree with this approach. After all, there can only be one first-place squad—and I don't

believe it's fair to the other squads for them to have to feel badly about not being number one.

Though NCA was the leader in uniform and accessory supply sales, Webb believed UCA offered customers the finest quality products and the best service in the industry. According to Webb, the timely delivery of uniforms and supplies was essential to the success of any company operating in the apparel side of the industry. He believed his company had acquired the computer and manufacturing systems and sales staff necessary to ensure his company's success in this aspect of the business.

In 1991, UCA began supplying campwear for cheerleaders and gamewear for dancers. UCA was not involved in the production or supply of mascot uniforms. UCA's apparel and accessory prices were commensurate with industry prices, with some articles priced somewhat below the industry average. In addition to UCA's instruction and apparel mail order program, cheerleaders and dancers who lived within 150 miles of Memphis could visit its corporate headquarters in order to select apparel items from the company's showroom.

Although UCA held a strong position in the apparel market, Webb realized NCA maintained a strong lead in this market. If UCA was going to become the leader in this lucrative side of the business, Webb knew it would be necessary to increase manufacturing capabilities and product recognition.

To achieve the first of these two objectives, Webb had planned to expand the company's use of its five contract manufacturers. Webb utilized contract manufacturers for the completion of uniforms and other products because it reduced UCA's fixed costs and allowed the company to adjust to the seasonal demand for apparel products. However, UCA was responsible for designing and providing construction and pattern specifications for its products. Webb was satisfied with the quality of the products produced by the company's contractors:

> We have five contractors that we work with. But before anything goes to the contractor, we have a computer system here at the main facility that produces the custom-designed patterns for each and every apparel item. This system has saved us a tremendous amount of money and has greatly improved the quality of our products. The way we are organized now, the patterns go straight to our contractors, and there is little room for error.
>
> We produce all of our knitted garments and do all of our lettering and insignia at the main facility. We don't contract this work out.

In an effort to achieve the second objective, UCA began affixing its company logo to the outside of uniforms and other apparel items. UCA's apparel sales had grown from $5 million in 1987 to $16.1 million in 1991.

UCA had a number of suppliers in 1991. A major supplier was Nike, which supplied the company with shoes it subsequently sold to cheerleaders and dancers. According to Webb, the majority of UCA's suppliers did not play a major role in the daily operations of the company. Their contributions were minimal, and they could be replaced with little difficulty and expense.

UCA was the industry leader in emphasizing safety in cheerleading. UCA had initiated the development of the *AACCA Cheerleading Safety Manual*. Other companies, such as NCA, ICF, and DCA, contributed to the publication of this manual.

UCA was also involved in providing its customers with fund-raising ideas. According to a UCA vice president:

> At one time, we supplied candy, cookies, and stuffed animals to our kids so they could sell them and help raise the money needed to buy uniforms and attend camp, but it just wasn't cost effective. We were knee deep in inventory all year round and found ourselves in a very competitive market that we did not want to spend a lot of energy in. Providing top-quality instruction and quality apparel items is our main focus, and there are just so many fund-raising companies out there it just didn't make good sense for us to remain in the business. So we got out of it, and I believe most other cheerleading companies have done the same thing.

UCA had numerous promotional programs in place in 1991. Heavy reliance was placed on monthly newsletters, videotapes of the company's various instructional camps, and promotional brochures describing the company's various instructional and apparel products. The company also cross-marketed its cheerleader and dance team camps and its uniforms and accessories. Other marketing tools included promoting special events, such as the company's National High School Cheerleading Championship, National Dance Team Championship, National College Cheerleading and Dance Team Championship, and ESPN's "Cheer for the Holidays." ESPN televised UCA's collegiate and high school cheerleading and dance team competitions numerous times throughout the year; UCA was the only company in 1991 to have its competitions televised on a strong national basis. Webb believed this national exposure provided his company with a distinctive promotional advantage over other companies:

> I can just see the other guys' faces when they turn on the television and see our competition on ESPN. I know it must just about drive them crazy to see UCA getting all of this national exposure, and I'd be willing to bet that they want to turn the TV off, but they don't because they want to see what we're up to.

Teams and squads competing in UCA's competitions did not have to attend its camps.

In addition, UCA participated in special events such as the Lord Mayor of Westminster's New Year's Day Parade held in London and Foley's Thanksgiving Day Parade, utilizing the company's "All Stars" (cheerleaders chosen at UCA camps who exhibited great talent and cheerleading skills) and "Dance Stars" (dancers chosen at the company's camps). The company was also involved in various philanthropic activities. In 1989, the company founded the UCA Children's Charities Foundation; this organization provided more than $150,000 per year to such organizations as the Muscular Dystrophy Association, LeBronheur Children's Hospital (pediatric cancer research), World Lens Project (pediatric eye surgery in Third World nations), and Duke University Medical Center (pediatric AIDS research).

Webb had managed to surround himself with very dedicated employees. The company employed 119 full-time employees, including 80 sales representatives, plus 48 part-time employees and had 750 summer camp instructors, trainers, and administrators.

Current UCA Situation   As Webb sat in his Memphis-based office, he reflected on UCA's future strategy. Webb planned to focus his company's attention on expanding product lines, strengthening its sales force, increasing its cheer-leader and dance team camp sessions, and promoting the school spirit industry through the company's nationally televised cheerleading and dance team championships. On the financial side, UCA's financial analysts predicted the company could continue to grow as much as 25 percent per year. Moreover, UCA had a low debt-to-equity ratio and robust cash flow. Given the popularity of cheerleading squads and dance teams, one of Webb's options was to take his company public. Webb had turned down an offer by BSN similar to the one NCA had accepted some six years prior; had he taken it, he would have been a multimillionaire.

Even if he decided against going public, Webb knew he was going to have to take on a new business role. He was going to have to delegate more of his current responsibilities to others. That was not going to be easy; he had been so closely involved in every aspect of UCA for so many years that he was not certain he could let go. And with his biggest rival making its way out of trouble, Jeff needed a strategy to propel UCA into a solid leadership position.

APPENDIX

The story behind the spirit stick is a very special one. According to Lawrence Herkimer:

> One summer during a camp, there was this squad, and it was just the most spirited squad you have ever seen. I mean the kids in this group were just wonderful! But they had no rhythm, no rhythm at all. And they had no beat; this group just really could not get it together. To be honest, they were just downright spastic. But they were so spirited, I just had to give them something, some type of award. So I broke a small branch off of a tree, and with a good bit of pomp and ceremony I gave it to them. I told them, "This is your spirit stick."
>
> Well before you know it, every squad is going around breaking the branches off of the trees and giving one another spirit sticks. Well, we couldn't have that; it was tearing up all the trees; so we had to start manufacturing the things.

The spirit stick was probably the most coveted award a cheerleading squad could receive. This award was usually a cylinder-shaped piece of wood that was 1 1/4 inch in diameter and 12 inches long. This piece of wood was generally adorned with multicolored stripping and spirited logos. The cost of one of these sticks to a cheerleading company was about $1, but to the campers, it was priceless!

The true value of a spirit stick could probably best be explained by the campers who received them. Honey Etter and Meg Vaden, captains for the Baylor School in Chattanooga, Tennessee, had the following comments to make about the value of a spirit stick.

Honey: Winning a spirit stick really boosts your squad's ego and self-confidence. Everyone just feels so proud; it's a great honor.

On the last night of camp, if you win a spirit stick, you get to keep it. Some squads get a spirit stick on the first or second night of camp, but then they stop trying and stop being spirited, and then they don't get to take one home. Being awarded a spirit stick on the last night means that the members of your squad gave it their best all week long.

Meg: A spirit stick is important because it represents how hard your squad *tries*—not how well your squad performs or what your squad can do. It's all about squad effort, being friendly, and showing school spirit.

Winning a spirit stick really is wonderful because it means your squad has spirit—and that is the single most important thing about being a cheerleader!

SUPRA BOATS AND THE COMPETITION SKI BOAT INDUSTRY

Aimee Hagedorn and A. J. Strickland, University of Alabama

In 1992, the competition ski boat industry was confronting several major strategic issues. Since early 1990, demand had fallen drastically in the United States as boat prices steadily increased and a severe recession virtually paralyzed the country's economy. At the same time, manufacturers had to respond to a widening array of user needs and preferences; it was becoming harder and harder to accommodate all the preferences of different buyers by offering just a few different boat models. Producers were trying to decide whether to broaden their product line or simply choose to differentiate their existing product line. To bolster sagging sales, some boat manufacturers had pursued related diversification, getting into the business of producing sportswear and other associated items to supplement their competition ski boat operations.

Supra Boats was a growing, dynamic company. Having entered the ski boat industry in the family segment and moved into the competition segment, Supra had a strong presence in both inboard ski boat markets with approximately the third largest market share. George Fowler, chief executive officer of Supra, wanted to take the company's present two-year plan and turn it into a five-year plan for making Supra the market share leader by the year 2000. Doing this would mean crafting a strategy to capture sales from and compete more effectively against the two current industry leaders, MasterCraft and Correct Craft.

HISTORY OF THE COMPETITION SKI BOAT INDUSTRY

Waterskiing dates back to 1922 when Ralph Samuelson became the first American to invent and ride a pair of water skis. The skis, simplistic by today's standards, were crude wooden boards with rubber footstraps and were roughly twice the length and width of today's skis. Throughout the 1920s and 30s, enthusiasm for waterskiing spread; in 1939, the American Water Ski Association (AWSA) was formed as a nonprofit organization to promote the sport. That same year, the first National Water Ski Championships were held. The towboat for this competition was an open wooden boat built of overlapping boards or strakes (similar to a wood johnboat) and powered by a four-cylinder outboard engine. The national championships were not held during World War II, and boat building was minimal during this time; after the war, however, the economy boomed as did interest and activity in the boating industry.

During the late 1940s and early 1950s, wooden inboard boats made by Chris Crafts, Century Resorters, and the Atom Skier by Correct Craft were favored by most skiers. These boats were the most powerful ski boat of the times, yet performance suffered due to the boats' large wakes. Outboards offered a smaller wake but did not have enough power—until the advent of the twin-rig concept in the early 1950s (see Exhibit 1).

EXHIBIT 1   **Types of Ski Boats**

Twin rig

Open-bow inboard

Closed-bow inboard

The twin-rig outboards quickly gained popularity among competition skiers and dominated the scene for the rest of the decade and into the 60s. Companies such as Mercury Marine, Evinrude, and Johnson recognized the potential market in waterskiing and invented the concept of promotional boats whereby manufacturers provided specially equipped boats for use in tournaments. Twin rigs, however, were difficult to set up and had high fuel consumption.

In search of the "perfect" ski boat, Leo Bentz, who operated a ski school in Florida, designed and built an inboard boat specifically for waterskiing. In the spring of 1960, the first Ski Nautique was displayed at the southern regionals in Birmingham, Alabama. It was the first inboard made of fiberglass and had a hull design that produced a smaller wake than its predecessors. Originally marketed and sold by Glass Craft Boat Company, the Ski Nautique concept was sold to Correct Craft the next year after Bentz approached the company's owners to sell them his mold. Correct Craft refined the Ski Nautique and the boat became a standard for others to emulate. The boat was highly successful, and boats with inboard motors made a resurgence in the sport.

In 1968, Rob Shirley, a competitive skier, noticed the growing market and absence of competition, so he designed and built his own ski boat, known as MasterCraft. Throughout the 1970s and early 1980s, Correct Craft and Master-Craft dominated the market and led the industry in innovations and technology. By the 1980s, inboards came to be used almost exclusively in AWSA-sanctioned tournaments, and many new start-up companies tried to compete with the two leaders. Yet, there still existed an opportunity for outboards as other water ski sport disciplines such as barefooting, kneeboarding, and show skiing were emerging.[1]

INDUSTRY STRUCTURE

In 1991, the National Marine Manufacturers Association (NMMA) estimated retail sales of all new and used boats and related products (including motors and engines, accessories and safety equipment, docking and storage, etc.) to be $10.5 billion, a 23 percent decrease from 1990. These results came on the heels of a similarly dismal 1990 when total industry sales dropped to $13.7 billion, down from $17.1 billion in 1989 and $17.9 billion in 1988.[2] Exhibit 2 presents estimated retail expenditures for recreational boating activities.

There were over 16.2 million recreational boats in use in 1991 (Exhibit 3) and 73.5 million people participating in recreational boating activities (Exhibit 4). The number of water-skiers grew only slightly in 1991 to 11.02 million, while the number of registered boats in the United States rose to nearly 11 million. Exhibit 4 presents additional statistics on recreational boating.

The Great Lakes region accounted for the greatest percentage of registered boats, with 28 percent of the U.S. total, followed by the Middle Atlantic, 20

[1]Drawn heavily from *WaterSki,* March 1991, and *The Water Skier,* April 1989.
[2]NMMA; *Boating Industry,* January 1992.

EXHIBIT 2   **Estimated Retail Expenditure on Boating***   *(in millions of $)*

Total Industry Dollars at Retail†

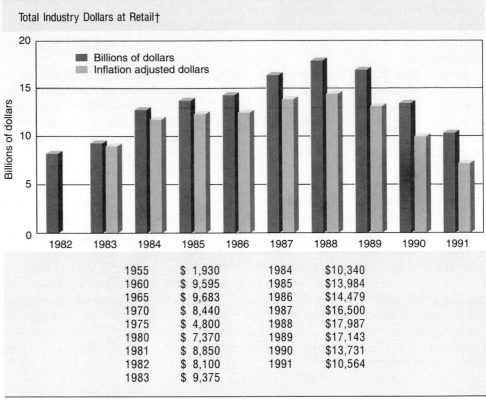

1955	$ 1,930	1984	$10,340
1960	$ 9,595	1985	$13,984
1965	$ 9,683	1986	$14,479
1970	$ 8,440	1987	$16,500
1975	$ 4,800	1988	$17,987
1980	$ 7,370	1989	$17,143
1981	$ 8,850	1990	$13,731
1982	$ 8,100	1991	$10,564
1983	$ 9,375		

Source: *National Marine Manufacturers' Association, *Boating 1991*.
       †*Boating Industry*, January 1992.

EXHIBIT 3   **Estimated Number of Recreational Boats Owned, 1982–91**

1982	12,820,000
1983	13,041,000
1984	13,455,000
1985	13,778,000
1986	14,318,000
1987	14,515,000
1988	15,093,000
1989	15,658,000
1990	15,987,000
1991	16,248,000

Source: National Marine Manufacturers' Association, *Boating 1991*.

percent; Gulf Coast, 18 percent; West coast, 11 percent; Midwestern Mountains,
10 percent; East Central, 8 percent; and New England, 5 percent. The United
States was the largest boating/waterskiing nation in the world, followed by
Australia and Canada.

EXHIBIT 4   Selected Boating Statistics, 1990 and 1991

	1991	1990
People participating in recreational boating	73,480,000	73,370,000
Water-skiers	11,022,000	11,006,000
All boats in use	16,248,000	15,987,000
Outboard boats owned	7,992,000	7,885,000
Inboard boats owned (includes auxiliary-powered sailboats)	558,000	555,000
Nonpowered sailboats (excluding sailboards)	1,298,000	1,298,000
Inboard/outdrive boats	1,721,000	1,659,000

Source: National Marine Manufacturers' Association, *Boating*, 1990 and 1991 issues.

Segment Sales

The $4.3 billion pleasure and ski boat market had three main segments: inboards, outboards, and stern drives (inboard/outboards). Inboards were further classified as either runabouts or cruisers, and runabouts could have an open or closed bow (see Exhibit 1). Outboards, stern drives, and inboard runabouts were generally 16 to 25 feet long, while cruisers were anywhere from 30 to 50 feet long. Traditionally, outboards were the biggest sellers, followed by stern drives and inboards, although outboard and stern-drive manufacturers had always outnumbered inboard manufacturers. Over the past 20 years, sales for each segment had fluctuated, with each segment experiencing intermittent periods of increasing and decreasing sales (Exhibit 5).

During the recessions of both the early 1980s and 1990s, the inboard and stern-drive markets were the most affected. In the early 1980s, both suffered an average 36 percent initial drop in sales, while outboard sales fell only 10 percent. In both 1990 and 1991, sales fell drastically—30 and 35 percent for inboards, 27 and 25 percent for stern drives, compared to 22 and 14 percent for outboards. However, both the inboard and stern-drive segments recovered nicely from the early 1980s recession with sales picking up by 35 to 40 percent on average, respectively. The inboard market sustained its sales growth through 1989, while stern-drive sales peaked in 1988. Exhibit 6 presents additional sales statistics.

Although sales of competition ski boats in the international market were negligible, exports of pleasure boats had risen sharply the past few years (Exhibit 7). For the first time since 1980, exports had exceeded imports by approximately $225 million in 1989. In 1990, that figure more than doubled to nearly $528 million. The trend was a direct result of a decline in the value of the U.S. dollar against foreign currencies, making foreign purchases of U.S.-made boats more attractive.

Boat Shows

For both boat manufacturers and retail dealers, boat shows were an occasion to compare competitive products and test buyer response. Based on the amount of consumer interest generated at national and regional shows, manufacturers

EXHIBIT 5   **Estimated Number of Pleasure and Ski Boats Sold at Retail, 1971–1991**

Calendar Year	Outboard Boats Sold	Inboard Boats Sold	Inboard/ Outdrive Boats Sold
1971	278,000	22,500	44,000
1972	375,000	23,000	63,000
1973	448,000	12,000	78,000
1974	425,000	11,000	70,000
1975	328,000	10,200	70,000
1976	341,000	11,000	80,000
1977	336,000	11,500	84,000
1978	331,000	12,100	90,000
1979	322,000	12,600	89,000
1980	290,000	8,200	56,000
1981	281,000	8,400	51,000
1982	236,000	8,395	55,000
1983	273,000	11,385	79,000
1984	317,000	15,280	108,000
1985	305,000	16,700	115,000
1986	314,000	18,000	120,000
1987	342,000	19,700	144,000
1988	355,000	20,900	148,000
1989	291,000	21,400	133,000
1990	227,000	15,000	97,000
1991	195,000	9,800	73,000

Source: National Marine Manufacturers' Association, *Boating*, 1990 and 1991 issues.

EXHIBIT 6   **Retail Sales Statistics for the Boating Market, 1986–1991**

	1986	**1987**	**1988**	**1989**	**1990**	**1991**
Outboard Boats						
Total units sold	314,000	342,000	355,000	291,000	227,000	195,000
Retail value	$834,600,000	$1,001,003,000	$1,224,750,000	$1,134,027,000	$978,143,000	$871,260,000
Average unit cost	$2,658	2,927	$3,450	$3,897	$4,309	$4,468
Inboard Boats-Runabouts						
Total units sold	5,300	6,600	7,400	9,100	7,500	6,200
Retail value	$85,473,000	$107,382,000	$130,610,000	$179,152,000	$139,600,000	$116,442,000
Average unit cost	$16,127	$16,270	$17,650	$19,687	$17,684	$18,781
Inboard Boats-Cruisers						
Total units sold	12,700	13,100	13,500	12,300	7,500	3,600
Retail value	$1,421,130,000	$1,665,860,000	$1,884,600,000	$1,908,960,000	$1,383,015,000	$668,412,000
Average unit cost	$111,900	$127,165	$139,600	$155,200	$184,402	$185,670
Inboard/Outdrive Boats						
Total units sold	120,000	144,000	148,000	133,000	97,000	73,000
Retail value	$1,860,960,000	$2,450,160,000	$2,584,672,000	$2,354,100,000	$1,794,306,000	$1,292,903,000
Average unit cost	$15,508	$17,015	$17,464	$17,700	$18,498	$17,711

Source: National Marine Manufacturers' Association, *Boating*, 1988 and 1991 issues.

EXHIBIT 7   Trends in U.S. Export-Import of Pleasure Boats, 1985–1990

	Dollar Volume					
	1985	**1986**	**1987**	**1988**	**1989**	**1990**
Exports	$60,596,000	$110,984,000	$219,871,000	$414,467,000	$616,469,000	$792,716,000
Imports	$367,935,000	$370,890,000	$397,519,000	$509,701,000	$409,965,000	$265,160,000

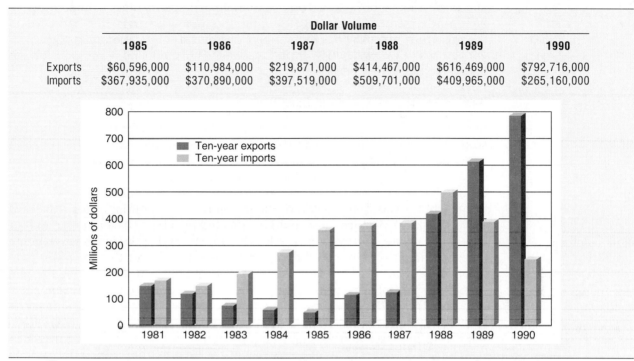

Sources: National Marine Manufacturers' Association, *Boating*, 1988 and 1990; and *Boating Industry*, January 1992.

would decide how many of each model boat to manufacture for the upcoming year, how best to market each product, and where to focus advertising efforts. Dealers would also base their orders on the consumer interest indicated at regional and local shows. Interest level was gauged by the percentage of people coming through a dealer's or manufacturer's booth at a show and expressing an interest to buy as well as by the number of boats sold at the show.

Also of interest to competition ski boat manufacturers was the Waterski Expo, a new trade show for the water-ski industry, held in September 1991. While the ski boat industry and the water-ski industry in general tended to get overlooked at the large marine trade shows such as IMTEC (International Marine Trades Exhibit and Convention), the Waterski Expo focused on these two industries. Manufacturers were able to network and introduce their new products to dealers and retailers without getting lost in the crowd.

Entry Barriers and Manufacturing Costs

Entry into boat manufacture required a company to meet several financial hurdles. For inboard boats, the cost to produce just one prototype was over $100,000. A plug (shape) had to be built and then a mold. According to industry sources, a plug and mold both cost $3,000 to $40,000 or more, and a design could cost thousands more, as well. Once a company had the necessary tooling and equipment and had begun production, economies of scale became critical.

Construction time for one boat was approximately 10 to 13 days, depending on the model being built. Because of the capital requirements and manufacturing and design know-how, actual and potential participants in the competition ski boat market were usually large existing boat manufacturers that had tracked the growth of the ski boat market and decided to enter the arena. One new entrant was Sea Ray, which introduced its own model of a competition ski boat—the Ski Ray—in 1991.

Demographics and Economic Conditions

In a 1990 National Sporting Goods Association (NSGA) sports participation study, fishing was America's fourth most popular pastime, while motorboating and waterskiing ranked 8th and 29th, respectively. It was estimated that interest in waterskiing would double if competition skiing became an Olympic event. It was first on the list of new sports to be admitted to the Olympic Games, but it was being delayed due to a serious influential factor—the boat driver. A skier's performance could be affected by a boat driver's error and/or bias. The "cruise control" concept for the throttle and speedometer was being tested in hopes of eliminated driver error (driving slower than or faster than actual speed), and videotaping the driver's boat path had already been implemented to control bias (moving the boat to either help or hurt the skier).

Before the 1991 recession, the rising popularity of waterskiing and recreational boating was attributed in part to the growing number of baby boomers who were buying lakefront homes and adopting outdoor-oriented life-styles. Statistics indicated a dramatic increase in the boat buying population among the baby boomers, who had reached prime boat buying age. According to sales data of the NMMA, the typical boat buyer was between the ages of 25 and 54. In the NSGA study, for both boating and skiing, the greatest number of participants had a threshold income greater than or equal to $50,000 and lived in highly populated areas.

Because boats were luxury items, the boating industry suffered during periods of economic decline. The ski boat industry had escaped a 10 percent luxury tax enacted by Congress for boats costing over $100,000. Still, new federal user fees required boaters using certain bodies of water to pay from $25 for 16- to 19-foot boats up to $100 for boats over 40 feet.

In the wake of the Persian Gulf War, the United States experienced its worst economic recession in a decade. Consumer confidence dipped to its lowest level since 1982, while sales of new cars and trucks reached their lowest level since 1983. Although housing starts were the lowest since 1945 and unemployment was an alarming 7.1 percent, inflation was only 3.1 percent. To help revive the economy and prompt consumers to spend again, the Federal Reserve pursued easy money policies that drove down banks' prime rate from 10 percent before the recession to 6.5 percent in the first quarter of 1992.

Leading Factors in Choosing a Ski Boat

For the majority of consumers, the quality of a ski boat was judged according to several factors: reliability and durability, wake and spray characteristics, and performance (tracking and turning ability, speed control, and engine power).

A market tracking study conducted by the Water Sports Industry Association (WSIA) revealed price and quality were the most important factors in the brand selection of boats and water-ski products for the general population of water-skiers; quality and brand reputation were more important for experienced skiers. Of the households that responded to the survey, about 82 percent owned a boat at the time, with the family runabout being the most popular. If they were to replace a boat soon, most indicated a shift from the runabout to a more special-purpose boat. Fifty-eight percent of those who responded owned an outboard; for skiing, however, stern-drive and inboard engines were preferred, especially among experienced skiers. Eight percent of the respondents said they would buy a tournament ski boat, double the level of existing ownership.

Mergers, Acquisitions, and Industry Consolidation

By 1991, a number of manufacturers had either been acquired by or had merged with another company. In 1984, MasterCraft was bought by the Coleman Company; in 1989, Ski Supreme was acquired by Genmar, Inc.; in 1989, Malibu Boats purchased Flightcraft, an Australian ski boat manufacturer; and in 1991, American Skier was purchased by WESMAR Marine Holdings. Also, in 1990, Supra Boats merged with Marine Sports, Inc. In 1991, Supra/Marine Sports created the Moomba Boat Company as a subsidiary.

Regulatory Developments

As the number of boating and waterskiing participants grew, the nation's waterways became increasingly crowded. Safety, courtesy, and environmental issues became more prevalent, sometimes drawing debate and controversy. Speed limit laws, noise limits, and environmental laws to protect against erosion by regulating boat wakes had been imposed on boaters/skiers by virtually every state. In 1991, Florida's Department of Natural Resources proposed legislation to establish a statewide boating speed limit of 30 mph for *all* waters. The boating industry feared that if such a bill was passed, other states might follow suit.

In response to such actions, the American Water Ski Association (AWSA) created a Waterways Education Committee focused on educating skiers about legislation and teaching them how to organize to fight adverse legislation and burdensome regulations. The committee compiled a data base of each states' laws and regulations concerning use of the waterways, produced a manual on how to lobby legislatures, and explored the development of a lawyer/lobby referral service made up of AWSA members.

SUBSTITUTES

Personal watercraft (PWC) were an economic and fun alternative for water sports enthusiasts. Also known as "jet skis" and "waverunners," PWCs were originally introduced as standup models. Manufacturers soon introduced sitdown models to appeal to a larger group of potential customers. Sitdown models proved immensely successful as sales quickly overtook sales of standup models (Exhibit 8).

Initially, PWCs were thought of as water toys for the young, but as models became larger and more accommodating for the entire family, their appeal

EXHIBIT 8   Sales of Personal Watercraft, Standup and Sitdown Models, 1988–1991

	Total	Standup	Percent	Sitdown	Percent	Retail Value	Average Unit Cost
1988	50,000	30,000	60	20,000	40	NA	NA
1989	80,000	35,200	44	44,800	56	NA	NA
1990	72,000	22,320	31	49,680	69	NA	NA
1991	68,000	16,320	24	51,680	76	$355,104,000	$4,928

Source: *Boating Industry,* January 1991 and 1992 issues.

spread. A few new models could carry up to three people, while one manufacturer even had a model where two people could ride side by side. Some of the larger PWCs could even pull skiers.[3]

PWCs were popular not just for personal use but for rental use also. Many lakes, resorts, and tourist areas had PWC rentals available. Even some police departments had begun to use the vehicles to patrol coastal waterways and other bodies of water.

By 1990, over 200,000 PWCs were in use, and it was a $250 million industry. Although the popularity of the PWC exploded in the late 1980s, sales fell 10 percent in 1990 and 5.5 percent in 1991.[4] Retail prices ranged from $2,300 to $8,000, depending on the model. In 1991, 39 models were produced by 11 companies, including the "big three"—Kawasaki, Yamaha, and Bombardier.[5] Seventy to 80 percent of PWCs were sold through motorcycle dealers, but the number of marine dealers increased slightly with the introduction of the sitdown models.

Apparently still in the growth stage, the PWC market seemed ripe for new entrants. Despite the 10 percent decline in 1990 sales, Polaris Industries LP, a major snowmobile manufacturer, introduced a model late in 1991, while Brunswick Corporation's U.S. Marine division was also eyeing the market. John Flowers, director of product planning and development for U.S. Marine, commented that whenever a segment competing with pleasure boats achieved sales volume, the market was enticing. Another industry source saw PWCs' greatest growth potential in the traditional boating market via marine dealers.

Yet, the PWC market was being challenged by the new, untested miniboat segment. Miniboats were hybrids of PWCs and small boats. Although Kawasaki (the only one of the big three with a miniboat product) and a few other smaller companies manufactured miniboats, the majority of competitors discounted the miniboat market.

The use of the PWC was being challenged also. Because of numerous accidents (mostly from lack of product use education), many regulations had been imposed on the vehicles. Also, because of the rowdy manner in which some PWCs were operated, the vehicles had earned a bad reputation among boaters and skiers alike for being extremely annoying. This resulted in the enactment of additional restrictive legislation.[6]

---

[3] *WaterSki,* September–October 1991.

[4] *Boating Industry,* January 1992.

[5] *1992 ABOS Marine Blue Book.*

[6] *Boating Industry,* June 1991.

SUPPLIERS

The major suppliers to the inboard boat industry were engine manufacturers. Engines were offered in a variety of models based on General Motors, Ford, and Chrysler blocks and components (to date, no foreign manufacturers produced inboard engines); 250 to 285 horsepower engines with separate hydraulic transmissions were most common among the competition inboards. The big three automakers' marine divisions built the base engines (same engines as for cars), and marine engine manufacturers marinized (treated for marine use) and customized the engines to suit their needs.

In the mid-1980s, automakers were challenged by legislation requiring that auto engines be made to tighter fuel efficiency and pollution control standards. This affected marinized engines because pollution control devices entailed a slight decrease in power. One solution to this problem was found in geared-drive transmission (rather than direct drive), thus allowing the engine to churn the prop at a rate just faster than one revolution per second. Yet another solution was presented when, in 1991, Ford introduced its new 5.8-liter 351 HO (high output) block with 285 horsepower, a 20 percent increase in power over the standard 351.

In the early 1990s, three marine engine companies dominated the inboard market: Indmar, MerCruiser, and Pleasurecraft Marine (PCM). According to industry sources, inboard engines comprised roughly 98 percent of both Indmar and PCM's production volumes and only about 2 percent of MerCruiser's. Both Indmar and PCM specialized in inboards, while MerCruiser concentrated primarily on stern drives and produced a much larger quantity of engines than the other two manufacturers.

Indmar was one of the first to utilize Ford's new engine, adding features such as electronic ignition and an oversized exhaust manifold to make it the best inboard power product of all the company's small-block (351 or less cubic inches) engines. Indmar also used engines built by GM, and in 1991, Indmar agreed to marinize Chrysler's marine engines exclusively under the name Tri Power Indmar. In addition, Indmar built private-label versions of its engines for use by boat manufacturers. By producing both small- and big-block (454 or more cubic inches) models based on Ford and GM engines, Indmar had one of the broadest product lines of any inboard marinizer; its agreement with Chrysler virtually assured Indmar of having the most comprehensive line of inboard power products in the industry.

Although MerCruiser's speciality was in outdrive power, the company began stepping up its production of inboard engines. MerCruiser's inboard line included both small- and big-block GM engines, with two 5.7-liter 350 ci models specifically for use in competition inboards. The Competition Ski engine offered 250 horsepower, while the new Magnum Tournament Ski engine produced 265 horsepower. Both products were equipped with MerCruiser's Thunderbolt IV High-Energy ignition system and the PowerPlus exhaust system with oversized manifolds, among other features.

PCM was well known for its leadership and innovation in marine engine technology. With the introduction of its Pro Boss engine, based on the new Ford 351 HO, the company boasted of having the only electronic management system (EMS) in the inboard power industry. Pro Tec, PCM's name for the system, controlled spark advance, corrected engine knock, and monitored all vital engine functions including oil pressure, temperature, and engine revving. It could detect problems and would lower engine revolutions to protect the engine from potential damage. Like Indmar and MerCruiser's competition ski boat engines, the Pro Boss had larger exhaust system manifolds than standard, which PCM called the Pro Flo system. In addition, the Power Plus transmission system featured a 1.23:1 geared-drive ratio to further boost power. Like the other manufacturers, PCM had a well-rounded product line with both small- and big-block engines suitable for all types of inboard ski boats.

Of the 15 inboard boat manufacturers whose boats were reviewed in *Water-Ski* magazine's 1992 Boat Buyer's Guide, four powered their products with PCM engines, five with Indmar, and six with MerCruiser.[7]

TECHNOLOGY AND CHARACTERISTICS OF THE SKI BOAT SEGMENTS

All boats were constructed in a somewhat similar manner. They all had a hull, deck, floor, console, seats, and engine. They were all built from a mold from the outside in, and virtually all were made from fiberglass, a material far superior than wood for strength and reliability. Yet, both the other materials used and the methods of construction varied widely among manufacturers according to the type of boat being built.

One of the most distinctive and important differences in the construction of ski boats had to do with hull configuration. Basically, there were two types of hull designs for inboard ski boats: a deep V and a modified V. A deep V hull was one in which the degree of dead rise (usually 15 to 35 degrees) from bow to stern remained the same. With a deep V design, less hull was actually in the water, thereby causing a boat to ride higher and better in rough water, yet also have a somewhat larger wake. The modified V configuration was a hull having more than 15 degrees of dead rise at the bow and less than 15 degrees at the stern. In effect, it was a deep V that tapered off to a shallow V, resulting in more surface area on top of the water, a smaller wake, and generally better tracking.

Another fundamental element of the hull was the chine, or the point where the bottom and sides came together. A boat's turning, handling, stability, planning, tracking, and spray control characteristics were all affected by the degree of angle to the chine.[8]

Outboards

Perhaps the greatest advantage of outboards was that they had excellent maneuverability, especially at low speeds. Also, with the trim function, they had the ability to cruise through shallow waters with little difficulty. Outboards generally had good power at top speeds and relatively low noise levels. Power steering was offered on some models, with power trimming usually a standard feature. Engines could be easily upgraded. Outboards were roomy, as well, with plenty of walk-around and storage room.

However, outboards did not make very good ski boats for several reasons. First, they had turbulent wakes and a rough table (the flat part in between

---

[7]*WaterSki*, January 1992.
[8]*World Waterskiing*, June 1984.

wakes); second, they had marginal handling ability in ski sites with tight dimensions; and third, their controls lacked the smoothness and precision needed for skiing. They were not as naturally balanced as inboards, and they had no platform on the back of the boat for the convenience and ease of putting on skis.

Another disadvantage of outboards was that they required a specially trained mechanic for tune-ups, adjustments, and repairs. Typically, outboards did not come "packaged" from the manufacturer; that is, the controls for steering, throttle, shift, and trim had to be set by a mechanic, although some manufacturers had begun prepackaging their products. One of the greatest complaints of outboard owners concerned having to mix the oil with the gas; however, automatic mixing had increasingly become a standard feature.[9]

Closed-Bow, Tournament Inboards

These 19- to 20-foot-long boats were excellent performers, designed with the serious skier's needs and demands in mind. When riding in one, its most noticeable aspects were its "sports car" feel and "fingertip" control. Competition inboards had quick and easy handling in tight dimensions, excellent tracking ability, and low steering effort and play, resulting in easy operator effort. Standard features on inboards included two precise speedometers and a tachometer, a large dash-mounted mirror, platform, and ski pylon (an upright steel bar mounted in front of the engine to which ski ropes can be attached).

Engine installation for inboards was simpler than for outboards and stern drives and was easily built into the overall design of the boat. Inboard engines were mounted in the center of the boat and therefore were easily serviceable. Inboards had tremendous "get up" and adequate "go" acceleration. The traditional direct-drive ratio for gear transmissions was 1:1, although some models were offered with an optional 1.23:1 or 1.5:1 ratio, providing additional power and increased propeller efficiency. The propeller was fixed; therefore there was no trimming function. Wakes were defined at lower speeds and small at higher speeds, making them suitable (and desirable) for slalom, tricking, and jumping, while spray coming from the back of the boat was minimal.

The greatest drawbacks of inboards included less than adequate slow-speed handling (because only the rudder was being turned), high interior and drive-by noise level, less interior and storage space due to the centrally mounted engine, and high retail prices. Yet, the resale value of inboards in general, whether open or closed bow, was the highest of all the markets. This could be attributed to the high quality, durability, and long life of inboards, as well as to the fact that the inboard market was the smallest of the three segments.[10]

Open-Bow, Family/Pleasure Inboards

These boats began appearing in the early 1980s in response to demand from both recreational and serious skiers who had growing families but also wanted a quality water ski boat with more room and luxury features. Open-bow inboards were nearly comparable to their closed-bow counterparts in

---

[9] WaterSki, May 1988 and 1989.
[10] WaterSki, March 1989.

performance and standard features, yet they were longer (20 to 24 feet) and wider than the closed bow, thus offering increased roominess and comfort. Because of differing demands, the family inboards usually came in a variety of models and styles. Perhaps the only complaint of the open bow was that the ride in the front of the boat was not as smooth as in the back of the boat, resulting in a sometimes "wet ride." Many new buyers of family inboards included those who, after skiing behind an inboard, decided to convert from a stern-drive boat.[11]

Stern Drives (Inboard/Outboards)

Stern drives combines attributes of both inboards and outboards. There was the runabout-sized boat ranging in length from 17 to 20 feet and family-sized boat at lengths of 20 to 23 feet. These boats had historically been aimed at recreational boaters and skiers by not providing such "serious" skier necessities as a rearview mirror, ski pylon, platform, and precise speedometers and steering/tracking ability. In 1991, however, many stern-drive manufacturers were making serious inroads toward "skier-izing" their products.

Like the outboard, stern-drive boats had excellent maneuverability and low-speed control, as well as power steering and the trimming function to aid in speed, tracking and acceleration control, and shallow water operations. They were also relatively quiet and roomy, with plenty of walk-about room and storage capacity. As in inboards, stern drives had automotive, marinized engines allowing for easy serviceability. The bow usually stayed dry, yet it had a high planing attitude, thereby impairing visibility at the start of the ride. Such planing attitude resulted in a well-defined wake for tricking but turbulent wakes for slalom.[12]

TRENDS IN COMPETITION INBOARDS

Year after year, the pursuit of the "ultimate" tournament ski boat was relentless. Manufacturers were constantly striving to improve their products and differentiate themselves mainly through innovation and price. In the early 1990s, the most common industrywide trends were in hull design, interior styling and design, drivability, and ski-ability.[13]

Hull Design   There were several noticeable trends in hull design. The first was that hulls were becoming longer and wider. Correct Craft was the first to initiate this move in its 1990 Ski Nautique (it was the first hull design change since the inception of the 2001 model in 1982). The company abandoned the old industry standards of 18 to 18.5 feet in length and 80-inch beam (width) to produce a 19.5-foot model with 91-inch beam. Since then, virtually all companies had followed suit with 19-to-20-foot by 85-to-92-inch beam models. MasterCraft's 1991 model incorporated the company's first hull design change since 1977.

---

[11]*WaterSki,* June 1990.
[12]*WaterSki,* April 1989.
[13]*WaterSki,* March 1991.

Second, hulls were being designed so as to drastically reduce the amount of spray from the boat. In 1991, there were more "deep short-line" slalom skiers than ever before, and spray from the back of the boat could hurt a skier's performance. The manufacturers' goal was to produce a model with little or no spray. Once again, Correct Craft, with its 1990 Ski Nautique models, led the industry in seriously (and successfully) attacking this problem. Slim tunnels (or spray chines) in the rear of the hull helped displace the water so there was virtually no spray. Other manufacturers had made significant improvements in their models, as well. Several companies re-created their hull designs for 1992 and obtained patents for their new designs. Most of the shapes were modifications and refinements of the existing hull designs, although a few innovative concepts were introduced.

Yet another trend had to do with hull warranties; they were becoming longer and more comprehensive. Many companies now offered a limited lifetime warranty on the hull, deck, and structural components of some or all of their products. This was a welcome addition for the consumer, not just for product liability but also for peace of mind.

Styling and Design   For both hulls and interiors, different types of styling and decor were cropping up. For instance, California and European styling were gaining popularity. The California style incorporated multicolor graphics and upholstery for a sleeker, racier appearance, while the European style created a more contemporary look through flowing, aesthetic lines. There was also more foot and hip room, a direct result of the increased length and width. And, industrywide, there was a general increase in the quality of workmanship in interior features such as upholstery, dash, storage, and engine compartments.

Drivability   Tournament inboards were beginning to follow some automotive trends such as adjustable, more supportive seats (a few companies even offered lumbar support) and foot wells. Tilt steering, once unheard of, was practically an industry standard by 1991. Perhaps the best new feature was better instrumentation. Malibu Boats invented MEMS (Malibu Electronic Management System), a high-tech system control center at the driver's fingertips. And some engines, such as PCM, implemented electronic controls to improve performance and help prevent damage. All companies, in one way or another, were considering ergonomics in their seating and control layout.

Ski-ability   The biggest performance improvement was found in straight-line tracking ability. For a world record in slalom to be accepted, the boat path could not deviate more than eight inches from the center line of its course. The shorter the slalom line gets, the more force a skier exerts, and therefore the more important tracking becomes.

Another seemingly small, yet significant improvement was made in the tops of ski pylons, thanks to a MasterCraft innovation. New antichafing designs where the ski rope is attached reduced wear and tear for longer rope life. Platforms had been enhanced, also, by making them a more integral part of the overall design of the boat.

Overall, the trend in recreational boats was toward better ski-ability and instrumentation. In tournament boats, the trend was toward greater comfort, luxury touches, and improved ski-ability. A fine line existed between family and tournament ski boats, but it seemed as though manufacturers were trying to reach two markets with essentially the same basic design.

THE AMERICAN WATER SKI ASSOCIATION

The American Water Ski Association was the nation's governing body of the sport of waterskiing. As a nonprofit organization, its purpose was "to organize, develop, and promote the sport, coordinate and sanction local and national competitions and clinics, select national and world teams, and train and certify coaches and officials." In 1990, some 640 tournaments were held. Additionally, AWSA was a member of the International Water Ski Federation, the world governing body of waterskiing, and an Affiliated Sports Organization member of the United States Olympic Committee.

As of 1990, there were 24,400 AWSA members. In 1991, membership increased 16.8 percent, largely because of a new membership approach and the hiring of a director of membership development. There were over 28,500 members (of which only one third were competitive skiers) in 1991 in six official sport divisions: traditional three-event waterskiing, the American Barefoot Club (ABC), the American Kneeboard Association (AKA), the National Collegiate Water Ski Association (NCWSA), the National Show Ski Association (NSSA), and the National Speedboat and Water Ski Association (NSWSA). In addition, a National Disabled Skiers' Committee was formed, and the AWSA sanctioned three-event competitions for this group.

The backbone of AWSA was the numerous water-ski clubs that existed nationwide. In 1991, there were over 550 affiliated active clubs in the United States. It was mainly through the clubs that AWSA continued its growth. Clubs put on ski shows, hosted tournaments, and held clinics for water-ski instruction, as well as instruction for tournament officials.

Yet another supporting branch of AWSA was the American Water Ski Educational Foundation (AWSEF). This entity maintained the Water Ski Museum/ Hall of Fame, supervised college scholarship programs, and helped support U.S. water-ski teams in recognized international competitions.

To compete in AWSA-sanctioned tournaments, one had to be an active AWSA member. Active membership was $35 per year and included $100,000 secondary medical accident insurance during club skiing activities (including practice), tournaments, and ski shows; a subscription to *The Water Skier* magazine (published seven times a year); and eligibility for special offers and programs sponsored by AWSA, such as legislative/regulatory assistance concerning the waterways, water-ski instructor certification, and towboat insurance. A $20 per year supporting membership included only a subscription to *The Water Skier* and eligibility for special offers and programs.

For traditional three-event water skiing, the largest of AWSA's sport divisions, skiers competed in one of five regions based on where they lived or skied: the West, Midwest, South, South Central, or East. Based on numbers of AWSA members, the Midwest was the largest region, with 8,338 members in 10 states. The western region, by far the largest in land mass, had 7,150 members in 15 states (including Alaska and Hawaii). The southern region had 5,415 members in 7 states, the eastern region had 4,020 members in 13 states, and the

South Central region had 3,584 members in 5 states. Only seven states had over 1,000 AWSA members: California (3,700), Florida (2,532), Texas (2,450), Wisconsin (1,911), Illinois (1,306), Michigan (1,118), and Washington (1,021). Ten states had under 100 members, six of which had fewer than 50 (New Mexico, North and South Dakota, Montana, Wyoming, and Rhode Island).[14]

BOAT TESTS

In 1983, AWSA began testing ski boats to encourage manufacturers to strive for continuous improvement in their products and to certify towboats for use in AWSA-sanctioned tournaments, including traditional three-event, kneeboard, barefoot, show ski, collegiate, and disabled tournaments. Tests were conducted under the supervision of AWSA and U.S. Olympic Committee officials, and boats were tested on the following characteristics:

- Distance required to pull a skier out of the water to 36 mph.
- Amount of spray in the slalom course.
- Wake characteristics for slalom and trick.
- Straightness of boat path in the slalom and jump courses; deviation from center line.
- Handling and maneuverability.
- Human engineering—how well the boat was functionally designed.

To receive certification, each boat had to pass AWSA standards. One of three rankings was given to each boat passing the evaluations: eligible towboat, approved towboat, or national tournament towboat. Each one was eligible to participate in AWSA-sanctioned tournaments and programs. In addition, an approved towboat had participated in 20 plus AWSA sponsored events the previous year, while a national tournament towboat had pulled four out of the five (prior-year) regional championships for three-event skiing, as well as the national championships.

In 1982, only four towboats were in use at competitions. Since the inception of the boat tests in 1983, the number of manufacturers participating in the tests and the number of boats tested has steadily increased (see Exhibit 9). For 1992, 29 boats from 14 manufacturers were tested; 25 passed as eligible towboats. Of these, 22 were inboards, and only one boat was dually certified for use in traditional and barefoot tournaments. There were 15 approved towboats and 3 national tournament towboats.[15]

COMPETITIVE RIVALRY

Rivalry in the competition ski boat industry was almost purely national. One industry expert noted, "As long as our (boat-building) technology stays within the U.S., competition will remain on the national level. No one else has the

---

[14]Drawn heavily from *The Water Skier*, April 1989, March–April 1991, June 1991, and the AWSA membership pamphlet.
[15]*The Water Skier*, May 1983 and January–February 1984–1992.

EXHIBIT 9   **Participation and Results of ASWA Testing of Competition Ski Boats, 1983–92**

Year	Number of Participating Manufacturers	Number of Boats Tested	Number of Boats Passing
1983	6	8	6
1984	11	16	11
1985	12	18	15
1986	12	18	15
1987	15	22	21
1988	11	19	18
1989	16	25	22
1990	16	26	25
1991	14	26	23
1992	14	29	25

capabilities we do—not even Japan." Competition was not likely to go global until after the turn of the century. Before U.S. companies could take advantage of the cheap labor available in foreign countries and produce abroad, technological advances and manufacturing capabilities still needed further development. Furthermore, companies needed to grow and strengthen their financial condition to be able to operate efficiently in a global marketplace.

Competition in inboard ski boats centered mainly around differentiation, innovation, and quality, while some companies also relied on their tenure in the industry and others competed on the basis of lower prices. As of 1991, there had been no price wars, but it remained a possibility as the industry matured. The battle for market share was fierce, and many companies simply expanded their product line to fulfill the varied demands of consumers.

Manufacturers sold their products to retail dealers who in turn sold to the general public. *Boating Industry* surveys revealed that in 1991, the average dealer grossed slightly under $1 million with 60 percent of sales in boats, motors, and trailers (compared to 70 percent in 1990); 12 percent in parts and accessories; 11 percent in service; 14 percent in used boats (compared to just 5 percent in 1990); and 3 percent in financing and insurance. The decline in new boat sales was attributed mainly to the deepening recession.[16]

In 1990, a marketing research firm surveyed ski boat dealers from all over the United States. Results indicated no one brand was carried by more than 6 percent of the dealers and the average dealer carried 1.5 lines of ski boats. When dealers were asked which ski boat manufacturers came to mind first, MasterCraft ranked first with 26 percent, Correct Craft second with 25 percent, and Supra third with 11 percent. This measure, called unaided awareness, was important because studies had shown that as unaided awareness increased, so did market share and "favorable predisposition" (which brands of boats dealers would either most prefer to carry or would consider carrying). The survey showed that MasterCraft ranked first in favorable predisposition with 33 percent, followed by WellCraft (28 percent), Four Winns (27 percent), Correct Craft (26 percent), and Sea Ray (25 percent).

---

[16]*Boating Industry,* January 1992.

The dealers surveyed were categorized into one of three positions according to the quality and value of the product(s) they carried: Position I for low quality/moderate value, position II for high quality/high value, and position III for moderate quality/low value. Twenty-seven percent of the dealers were in position I and favored Four Winns, Bayliner, and WellCraft; 29 percent were in position II and favored Supra, Malibu, and Cobalt; the remaining 44 percent were in position III and favored MasterCraft, Correct Craft and Sea Ray. Exhibit 10 displays these results in matrix form. When deciding which ski boats to carry, the most influential characteristics included having a nationally known brand, multiple-use models, and wide product line; company's size and length of time in business were also important.[17]

Most companies did the majority of their advertising in boating and water-skiing magazines, and they promoted their products at boat shows, major pro tournaments, and amateur tournaments. Many also had a promotional boat program in which the company chose certain interested individuals with some degree of influence in their skiing community to use its product as a "promo" boat and take it to local and regional tournaments for use and exposure. A promo person received a new boat each year at a discounted price under an agreement to use it in a specified number of tournaments within his or her region. The skier was reimbursed for charges incurred to transport the boat and also received a stipend for each tournament in which the boat participated. However, the user was usually responsible for the sale of the boat at the end of the competition season.

MASTERCRAFT

MasterCraft, along with Correct Craft, dominated the competition ski boat industry during the 1970s and early 1980s. In 1984, the company was acquired by the Coleman Company and became part of Coleman's water recreation operations division. Although MasterCraft had eight models for 1992, most advertising and promotional efforts went toward the ProStar 190 model, its best-selling, top-of-the-line competition inboard. The ProStar 190 came standard with an Indmar engine having a 1:1 gear ratio or with an optional 1.5:1 ratio called a Power Slot. (MasterCraft was the first in the industry to introduce such an option.) The other models included the ProStar and ProSport 205 (both open-bow versions of the ProStar 190); the Barefoot 200, an outboard ski boat for barefooting; two versions (open and closed bow) of a more spacious family boat called the MariStar 210; and two versions of a 25-foot cruiser (one with a cabin and the other one open bow with room for 11 people) called the MariStar 240. In 1991, the open-bow Maristar 210 received *Powerboat* magazine's Award for Product Excellence by being voted the 1991 Ski Boat of the Year. Both versions of the ProStar 190 (the 1:1 and the Power Slot) and the ProStar 205 and Barefoot 200 were AWSA- approved towboats for 1992, and the ProStar 190 was one of only three boats to be used to pull the 1991 National Water Ski Championships and U.S. Open. In addition, MasterCraft was the sole towboat sponsor of Cypress Gardens in Winter Haven, Florida, and the Professional Water Ski Tour.

---

[17]Strength and Weakness Analysis for Supra Sports by Message Factors, Inc., June 1990.

EXHIBIT 10   **Quality-Value Perceptions of Competition Ski Boat Manufacturers, Dealer Survey Results, 1990**

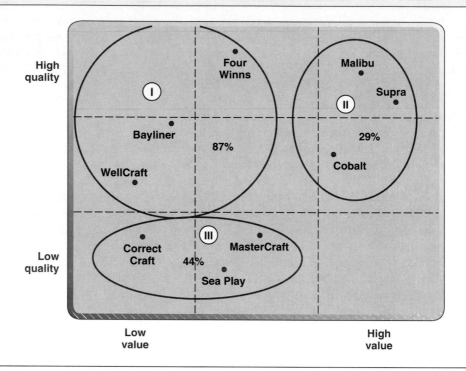

MasterCraft entered the industry in the competition ski boat market, going mainly after the family segment during the 1980s. By 1989, MasterCraft was the market share leader in competition ski boats with approximately 26.6 percent. For years, MasterCraft boasted of having the only 10-year hull and engine warranty in the industry. But after negotiating with Mobil Oil Company, MasterCraft upgraded its warranty in 1991 to a limited lifetime warranty. The hull warranty was covered by MasterCraft while all lubricated engine parts were covered by Mobil as long as Mobil 1 engine oil was used in the care and maintenance of the engine.

MasterCraft had the strongest and most extensive promo boat program in the industry, according to industry experts. The company had an estimated 105 dealers nationwide, as well as 10 distributors abroad. MasterCraft products were endorsed by 17 professional water-skiers who formed the official "MasterCraft Pro Ski Team."

Retail prices for the MasterCraft line ranged from $23,000 to $35,800 (including trailer), while resale values after one year of use ranged from $17,700 to $27,500.

In a 1989 study of magazine expenditures for 16 ski boat manufacturers, MasterCraft spent more than any other company (17 percent of expenditures for all 16 companies) and was the only company to advertise in all eight magazines reviewed (six boating, two waterskiing). MasterCraft was the only major competition ski boat manufacturer to advertise in *Boating* magazine, where it spent the greatest percentage of its magazine advertising dollars. *WaterSki* magazine was allotted the next largest sum in MasterCraft's advertising budget. By heavily advertising the fact that the ProStar 190 held more world records than all other ski boats combined, MasterCraft advertisements consistently focused on quality and superiority over its competition. Exhibit 11 contains sample MasterCraft ads.

CORRECT CRAFT

Correct Craft was owned by the fourth generation of the original founding family. "On the waters of the world since 1925" as their slogan went, Correct Craft was the oldest of the competition ski boat companies. Correct Craft had always concentrated on having a quality image, yet before 1990, skiers complained that the company's Ski Nautique models had a larger wake than other ski boats. In 1990, Correct Craft solved this problem with new models having a new hull design. The new Ski Nautique all but revolutionized the industry with its radically longer and wider hull and virtually "no spray" characteristic.

In 1992, Correct Craft offered buyers five models: the closed-bow tournament Ski Nautique (in which a PCM Power Plus engine with 1.23:1 gear ratio was standard) and an open-bow version (both AWSA approved for 1992); the family-oriented Sport Nautique with walk-through bowrider; and both an open- and closed-bow version of its barefoot boat, the Nautique Excel (also called the Barefoot Nautique). The Excel was different from the other models (and all other inboard ski boats) in that the engine was placed astern to maximize seating and storage capacity. Also new for the Excel was a deep V hull configuration designed for boating in larger bodies of water and for barefooting; the closed-bow Excel was also AWSA approved.

All Correct Craft hulls were covered by a limited lifetime warranty and a transferable limited five-year warranty for those who frequently sold boats to buy a new one. Engine parts were covered by the engine manufacturer.

In 1989, Correct Craft still occupied the second position in market share with an estimated 22.2 percent, but it had slipped from 28 percent in 1985. Like most major ski boat companies, Correct Craft had a promotional program, although it tended to be more selective than others. There were approximately 100 Correct Craft dealers in the United States and several distributors abroad. About one third of Correct Craft's sales were overseas. Retail prices ranged from $23,900 to $26,800, and, like MasterCraft, Correct Craft products had high resale value after one year ($18,400 to $20,600). The company also had a pro ski team comprising 10 world-class professional skiers to endorse its products.

Correct Craft had contracts with a couple of notable ski show and tournament sites to use Ski Nautiques exclusively. The Masters at Callaway Gardens, the most prestigious ski tournament in the United States, had never used any boat other than Ski Nautique; likewise for Sea World of Orlando. In addition, the Ski Nautique was another of the three towboats used to pull the 1991 Nationals and U.S. Open.

In magazine expenditures, Correct Craft spent approximately 8 percent of expenditures for all 16 companies in the previously mentioned study—less than half what MasterCraft spent—and advertised in only one boating

EXHIBIT 11   **Sample MasterCraft Ad**

magazine and both water-ski magazines. Basically, Correct Craft advertise-ments were similar to those of MasterCraft, focusing on quality and competi-tive superiority (see Exhibit 12).

MALIBU

Malibu Boats were formed in 1982 by an ex-plant manager of the Ski Centurion boat company, Robert Alkema. Alkema's philosophy was to manufacture a higher value boat to meet the beginning-to-advanced skier's needs and budget. In 10 years, the company went from being a small upstart venture to being a recognized player in the inboard ski boat industry. Malibu's sales were boosted in 1989 when it purchased Flightcraft, an Australian ski boat company. By 1991, the company was battling it out with Supra Boats for the number three position in market share.

In 1992, Malibu had eight models in its product line—six Malibu and two Flightcraft models, all equipped with MerCruiser's Competition Ski engine. The Malibu line consisted of both a European and California series. There were four European models: the closed-bow Malibu Skier Euro-f3, now the company's premiere tournament ski boat; the open-bow Malibu Sunsetter Euro-f3; and the Mystere 215 (closed bow)/Mystere 215LX (open bow) Euro-f3. The California series included the closed-bow Malibu Skier, formerly the company's traditional top-rated competition ski boat, and the open-bow Malibu Sunsetter. The Australian series comprised the two closed-bow Flightcraft models: the 18XLT inboard and the 20XLOB (outboard) for barefooting. Both of these boats, as well as the Skier and Sunsetter Euro-f3, were AWSA approved for 1992. In 1989 and 1991, the Skier Euro-f3 was named Tournament Ski Boat of the Year by *Hotboat* magazine, while the Malibu Skier (California series) was voted Best Value Boat of the Year by *Powerboat* magazine in 1989.

Malibu boats had more standard features than other boats in the industry, and its models sold for a relatively lower price. Malibu did not engage in exten-sive marketing efforts; rather, the company concentrated on developing a superb dealer network and word-of-mouth advertising from satisfied users. Malibu spent only 7 percent of the total expenditures for the 16 companies in the 1989 advertising study, placing almost 70 percent of its advertisements in the two waterskiing publications and the rest in two boating magazines. In its ad, Malibu emphasized the high value of its products, as well as quality (see Exhibit 13 for sample ads).

Malibu was known for its innovativeness. The company's latest models had several new and different features—most notably the Malibu Electronic Man-agement System (MEMS). MEMS was a control center that housed 18 monitor-ing and actuating functions within the driver's reach. The company had also developed a pivoting ski pylon to reduce rope wear and was one of the first to have introduced an air cushion system in the driver's seat for contour and lum-bar support.

One characteristic that distinguished Malibu from its competitors was its employee stock ownership program; in 1989, employees were awarded stock equal to 10 percent of their annual salary. Malibu operated with a worker-oriented environment in order to promote quality workmanship, reduce defects and warranty costs, and instill greater pride and job satisfaction.

EXHIBIT 12   **Sample Correct Craft Ad**

World Record Holders Ski Nautique

Capturing a world record doesn't come easy. It's definitely hard work. Putting in a few hours at a tournament is a mere drop in the bucket compared to the years of practice it takes to get there.

Home is where the real work gets done - practice, evaluation, perfection. For every world record set at a tournament, it is exceeded *tenfold* on the home course.

CURRENT WORLD RECORD HOLDERS*

MEN SLALOM Andy Mapple	**BAREFOOT WOMEN SLALOM** Jennifer Calleri
WOMEN SLALOM Deena Mapple	
MEN TRICKS Tory Baggiano	**BAREFOOT MEN TRICKS** Rick Powell
WOMEN JUMP Deena Mapple	**BAREFOOT WOMEN TRICKS** Jennifer Calleri
FREESTYLE Dave Reinhart	*As of 4/1/91

More world records are set by skiers using Correct Crafts than all other manufacturers combined. These skiers count on Correct Craft for strong, consistent world record pulls, day after day.

During a tournament, it wouldn't matter if these pros were pulled by a milk truck. They've done their homework.

They practice behind the best and it shows.

Given a *choice*, world record holders chose a Nautique.

CORRECT CRAFT. INC
on the waters of the world since 1925

6100 South Orange Avenue
Orlando, FL 32809
407/855-4141

For the name of your
local dealer,
call: 1-800-346-2092

EXHIBIT 13   **Sample Malibu Ad**

Malibu had 120 dealers nationwide, two distributors in Europe, approximately 100 promo boaters, and four world-class water-skiers endorsing its products. Also, Malibu was the only manufacturer with two production facilities—one in California and one in Tennessee. Malibu offered a lifetime limited warranty on all its products and a lower retail price than its competitors. Retail prices for the Malibu and Flightcraft lines were $17,700 to $22,000, while resale values after one-year's use were $13,600 to $16,900.

SUPRA BOATS

George Fowler had been general manager of MasterCraft for six years and then founded, and subsequently sold, Supreme Industries (manufacturer of Ski Supreme inboards). Fowler was one of the first people in the inboard ski boat industry to recognize the market opportunities of a roomier, more luxurious family/pleasure boat with tournament ski boat performance. He founded Supra Boats in 1980 and decided to establish the company in the family ski boat market before moving into the competition ski boat segment. Fowler's expertise and experience in the boating industry were instrumental in positioning Supra as a viable market leader and innovator.

In 1982, Supra introduced the industry's first open-bow inboard, and by 1985, the company had a 10 percent share of the market. By 1989, Supra's market share had increased to 18.3 percent—the third largest in the industry. From 1984 to 1989, Supra enjoyed a 29.5 percent annual growth rate with sales increasing from $7.4 million to $26.9 million. In 1990, the company was acquired by Marine Sports, Inc., a publicly held company. With Marine Sports' added financial strength, Supra planned to add new models, acquire additional subsidiary companies, and explore the possibility of building a new state-of-the-art manufacturing facility.

Supra likened its boats to Porsche and Mercedes-Benz automobiles, and it targeted the discriminating, upscale buyer who sought both quality and performance in a ski boat. In 1992, the company had 11 models, one of the most comprehensive product lines in the industry. Eight of the 1992 models were carried over from 1991 with only slight changes. The open-bow Saltare and closed-bow, cuddy cabin Pirata were the biggest family boats, holding up to 10 people in their 23-foot-long, 99-inch-wide frames; these models offered special amenities such as a double bucket driver's seat and a bar complete with glasses. The open-bow Mariah and closed-bow (cuddy cabin) Bravura held up to eight people and were 21 feet long by 95 inches wide. The open-bow SunSport and closed-bow Marauder also had eight-person capacity and were 20 feet long, 96 inches wide. The rest of the original line included the 19.5-foot-by-85.5-inch open-bow Conbrio and closed-bow Comp ts6m, both of which held six people. The latter was Supra's tournament skiing model, AWSA approved and twice heralded Ski Boat of the Year by *Powerboat* magazine. The Comp had been the exclusive towboat for the 1987 World Waterskiing Championships and the 1986, 1988, and 1990 World Cup. The PCM Power Plus engine (1.23:1 gear transmission) was standard in these eight models, and retail prices ranged from $22,900 to $30,400, while one-year resale values started at $17,600 and topped out at $23,300.

New for 1992 was a lower-priced line, comprising three models, called the 3000 Series. This line was created for those who wanted the same ride and luxuries as in the original Supra line, but a more competitive price. The closed-bow, AWSA-approved Impulse and open-bow Espirit both had the same dimensions and capacity as the Comp and Conbrio, while the Spirit had the SunSport/Marauder specifications. Other than the warranty and the engine (a PCM with 1:1 transmission), the 3000 Series offered basically the same standard features and options as did the higher priced line. Whereas all Supra products were backed by a limited lifetime warranty for the hull and deck), the 3000 Series had only a 6-year/600-hour limited warranty. Past annual warranty costs for Supra were approximately 2.19 percent of sales.

In addition to the 3000 Series, Supra had another, even lower priced product by its sister company, Moomba Sports. Using a hull design licensed from an Australian boat company, the Moomba Boomerang retailed for $15,000 and targeted first-time ski boat buyers. It was a bare-bones type of ski boat that offered a decent ski pull and ride for a modest price.

One of the factors contributing to Supra's success was its technology. According to one issue of *Powerboat* magazine, "The company is an industry leader when it comes to building strong, sturdy hulls." Supra boats featured a unique hull design. The SupraTrac™ hull design incorporated a semimodified V-shape at the bow that tapered to a flat planing surface near the middle of the hull. Supra applied technology developed for the aerospace industry and used the highest quality construction materials such as Kevlar, Coremat, and biaxial fiberglass bonded with AME 4000 resin to produce the strongest possible hulls.

Supra had approximately 175 dealers worldwide and 50 promotional boats. With the majority of promotional programs, the boat owner was responsible for selling the boat each year before obtaining a new promo boat, but with Supra's program, a Supra dealer was responsible for finding a buyer. Unlike the other top companies, Supra chose not to have professional skiers endorse its products because of the added cost. Since Supra's strongest presence was in the family market, the company preferred to invest more in the quality of its products and in advertising. Of the 16 major competitors, Supra was fourth in advertising expenditures according to the 1989 advertising study. One third of Supra's advertising funds were for ads in *WaterSki* magazine while the rest were for AWSA's publication and various boating magazines. Supra's ads focused on the high quality and luxuriousness of its products (Exhibit 14).

Management's immediate priority was to develop a strategic plan for becoming the industry's market share leader by the year 2000. George Fowler, Supra's CEO, wondered what strategic approach made the most sense.

EXHIBIT 14   **Sample Supra Ad**

COMPETITION IN THE U.S. FROZEN DAIRY DESSERT INDUSTRY

Arthur A. Thompson, Jr., University of Alabama
Tracy R. Kramer, University of Alabama

Production of frozen dairy desserts in the United States was essentially flat throughout the 1970–90 period. Underneath this calm surface of leveling sales volume, however, were several highly competitive, lucrative industry segments, each vying for an increasing share of a mature market. Trying to capitalize on the trail blazed by Häagen-Dazs, many local and national ice cream companies had launched new superpremium ice cream brands and aggressively pursued ways to gain wider distribution. TCBY had fueled industry interest in frozen yogurt, and other yogurt manufacturers and ice cream makers were scrambling to tap into that market. Makers of ice milk products were trying to reposition themselves to capitalize on consumers' increased attention to health and nutrition. And ice cream novelty manufacturers were playing on the "urge to splurge" concept heightened by the superpremium players. Companies in each segment of the frozen dairy dessert industry were striving to capture the interest of consumers with a stream of new ice cream–related and/or frozen yogurt–related products. The end result was a very competitive market.

HISTORY OF THE ICE CREAM INDUSTRY

Ice cream evolved from chilled wines and other iced beverages. The earliest known commercial venture was in 1660 in Paris where water ices and possibly cream ices were manufactured and sold. The date of ice cream's arrival in America is uncertain, but in 1700, guests of Maryland's governor were treated to an ice-creamlike delicacy. George Washington and Thomas Jefferson both enjoyed ice cream; Dolley Madison greatly increased the popularity of ice cream, serving it as a dessert at her husband's second inauguration in 1812. An American, Nancy Johnson, invented the hand-cranked salt-and-ice freezer in 1846. The first commercial ice cream plant in this country was established in 1851, and Bassett's Ice Cream, introduced in 1861 in Philadelphia, ranked as the oldest brand still on the U.S. market in 1992. The first ice cream sodas were created by a Philadelphia businessman who added carbonated beverages to ice cream. When these concoctions were banned from sale on Sunday, a syrup was substituted for the carbonation, and the sundae came into being. The ice cream cone was first made and sold at the St. Louis World's Fair in 1904 when rolled waffles were used as "dishes" for ice cream.

The commercial production of ice cream was facilitated by a number of mechanical and technical advances: the homogenizer (which gave ice cream its smooth texture), freezers, mechanical refrigeration, electric motors, sophisticated test equipment, packaging machines, insulation methods, and the motorized delivery van. Dramatic boosts in production resulted—from 5 million gallons in 1899 to 30 million gallons in 1909 to 150 million gallons in 1991.

Other products such as ice cream on sticks, bars, and other forms of ice cream, ice milk, and sherbet (known as novelties) originated in the 1920s. By 1922, a million Eskimo Pie ice cream bars were being sold each day. The Good Humor bar on a stick followed, and in 1924, the Individual Drinking Cup Company began manufacturing its Dixie Cup containers for individual servings of ice cream. The banana split also came into popularity. By the 1920s, ice cream was a typical American food, sold everywhere from corner drugstores to the best restaurants. Ice cream gained in popularity during the Prohibition as people joked that the "cold stuff" was a substitute for the "hard stuff."

Rationing of milk and sugar during World War II curtailed ice cream production, but production snapped back quickly in 1946, and sales of all kinds of ice cream products averaged over 16 quarts per capita by 1950. Consumption of ice cream alone remained around the 15-quart per capita level from 1955 to 1987 (see Exhibit 1), with total production tracking population growth. When drugstores began replacing their soda fountains with more profitable drug and cosmetic products in the 1950s, the bulk of ice cream sales shifted to custard stands, mom- and-pop stores, fast-food outlets, and supermarkets. By 1960, half of all ice cream sales were through supermarkets. Most supermarket chains wasted little time in introducing their own private-label brands of ice cream, most of which were lower in butterfat, artificially flavored, higher in air content, and cheaper.

MARKET SIZE AND GROWTH

The retail value of ice cream and related products in 1990 was about $5 billion. Production of ice cream alone in 1990 was estimated at 816 million gallons. Increases in ice cream production had slowed significantly over the past five decades:

Period	Average Annual Growth Rate
1940–49	7.5%
1950–59	2.6%
1960–69	.9%
1970–79	.3%
1980–85	2.1%
1986	1.6%
1987	1.4%
1988	−1.0%
1989	3.4%
1990	.7%

Source: *The Latest Scoop*, 1990, p. 9.

ICE CREAM INDUSTRY STRUCTURE

The ice cream industry in the United States had historically been composed of a multitude of regional and local producers. For a century, commercial ice cream was made in local dairies, neighborhood stores, or restaurants for limited distribution in the immediate area. As improvements in refrigeration

EXHIBIT 1   Total U.S. Production of Ice Cream and Related Products for Selected Years, 1909–90

Year	Total Frozen Products		Ice Cream	
	Total Gallons (000s)	Per Capita Quarts	Total Gallons (000s)	Per Capita Quarts
1909	29,637	1.31	29,637	1.31
1919	152,982	5.86	152,982	5.86
1920	171,248	6.43	171,248	6.43
1930	255,439	8.30	255,439	8.30
1940	339,544	10.29	318,088	9.64
1950	634,768	16.79	554,351	14.66
1955	819,934	19.96	628,525	15.30
1960	969,004	21.54	699,605	15.55
1965	1,130,215	23.36	757,000	15.65
1970	1,193,144	23.42	761,732	14.95
1975	1,263,213	23.45	836,552	15.53
1980	1,225,223	21.58	829,798	14.61
1985	1,360,974	22.88	901,449	15.16
1986	1,382,329	23.02	923,597	15.38
1987	1,401,848	23.15	928,356	15.33
1988	1,388,429	22.70	882,079	14.43
1989	1,435,274	23.26	831,159	13.47
1990	1,445,315	23.18	816,077	13.09

Source: *The Latest Scoop*, 1990, p. 9.

techniques made it possible to transport the product long distances, larger dairy corporations and bigger ice cream producers began squeezing out or absorbing the smaller companies; about 1,700 ice cream plants closed between 1957 and 1970. Most dairy producers viewed ice cream as a sideline of selling milk.

In 1970, 1,628 plants were producing ice cream in the United States; by 1990 the number had declined to 709 (see Exhibit 2). Many of these were small local operations, but major producers operated large fully equipped plants. In early 1983, Dreyer's Grand Ice Cream installed $2.5 million worth of new equipment in its Los Angeles plant, making this facility capable of producing more than 5 million gallons of ice cream per year. Ben & Jerry's had a 23,000-square-foot facility that could process up to 820 gallons of ice cream an hour. Some manufacturers preferred to operate relatively small, geographically scattered plants, believing it allowed stricter quality control and delivery of a fresher product to surrounding localities. It was not uncommon for a major name-brand marketer of ice cream to contract with local dairy producers to make and distribute its brand locally to cut down on steep transportation charges from its own more distant plants.

HÄAGEN-DAZS AND THE SUPERPREMIUM PHENOMENON

Reuben Mattus of the Senator Ice Cream Company in the Bronx, New York, viewed the increasing market share of the best-selling brands with alarm as he watched his company's products being edged out in the supermarkets.

EXHIBIT 2   **Employees, Plants, and Capital Expenditures in
the Frozen Dessert Industry, 1970–90**

Year	Thousands of Employees	Plants Producing Ice Cream and Related Products	Capital Expenditures for New Plants and Equipment (Millions of dollars)
1970	24.1	1,628	$ 43.7
1971	22.6	1,520	28.0
1972	21.1	1,451	35.8
1973	21.3	1,330	29.2
1974	21.3	1,239	27.8
1975	20.2	1,167	37.2
1976	20.3	1,124	43.2
1977	19.1	1,095	56.8
1978	18.5	1,062	56.4
1979	19.9	990	46.3
1980	19.6	949	46.8
1981	20.1	895	41.8
1982	17.8	884	79.9
1983	17.7	862	75.5
1984	20.0	853	84.0
1985	18.9	865	NA
1986	18.2	845	105.4
1987	20.3	829	137.1
1988	21.2	765	158.5
1989	21.0	729	140.3
1990	20.6	709	142.3

Source: *The Latest Scoop,* 1990, pp. 4–7.

In response, he developed a high butterfat ice cream with all natural ingredients and began to market it in 1961 under the name Häagen-Dazs. Although Mattus was soon able to sell all the ice cream he could make, the initial success of the Häagen-Dazs brand produced no overnight move to superpremium quality on the part of either consumers or producers. However, the 1960s did bring a proliferation of ice cream shops featuring high-quality products. Many were local businesses, while others, such as Baskin-Robbins, expanded across the nation.

Consumer enthusiasm for superpremium ice cream products spurted dramatically in the 1980s. By 1990, superpremium brands accounted for about 13 percent of the $5 billion in annual retail sales of ice cream. Despite the market penetration efforts of such major manufacturers as Kraft General Foods and Borden, no brand of ice cream commanded more than 14 percent of the market in 1989. Regional manufacturers were still a prominent factor, and many had established very respectable niches in local and regional markets (see Exhibit 3).

THE ICE CREAM MANUFACTURING PROCESS

Ice cream consisted largely of cream and milk combined with sweeteners and flavorings. Depending on the variety and brand, ice cream ingredients could include fresh or frozen cream, whole milk, skim milk, buttermilk, butter,

EXHIBIT 3   **Major Ice Cream Producers, Brands Produced, and Geographic Areas of Sales Strength**

Company	Brand of Ice Cream	Area of Sales Strength
Kraft General Foods	Frusen Glädjé	New York, New England, California
	Breyers	Eastern United States
	Sealtest	Eastern United States
Borden	Lady Borden	Southeast, Southwest
	Borden	Southeast, Southwest
(distributor for)	Gelare	West Coast, New York
Ben & Jerry's Homemade, Inc.	Ben & Jerry's Homemade	New England
Integrated Resources	Steve's	Massachusetts, New England, Mid-Atlantic
	Swensen's	South Florida, Texas, Arizona, California, New England
Grand Metropolitan, Ltd.	Häagen-Dazs	New England, Mid-Atlantic, California
Friendly Restaurants	Friendly's	New England, Mid-Atlantic, Midwest
Bluebell Dairies	Bluebell	Texas
Dreyer's Grand Ice Cream	Dreyer's/Edy's	Midwest, western United States
Schrafft's Ice Cream Company	Schrafft's	New York
Larry's Ice Cream	Larry's	Florida, Georgia, South Carolina, California
Allied-Lyons North America	Baskin-Robbins	Nationwide
Pet, Inc.	Great Ice Creams of the South	Florida, Georgia, North Carolina, South Carolina, Tennessee, Virginia, West Virginia
Mayfield Dairies	Mayfield's	Georgia, Tennessee
Bassett's Ice Cream Company	Bassett's	Pennsylvania, New York

powdered milk products, sugar, honey, corn sweeteners, sucrose, dextrose, fructose, fresh eggs, frozen or powdered eggs, salt, colorings, and flavorings; fruit and nuts were added to some varieties. Many manufacturers included additives such as stabilizers and emulsifiers. Stabilizers were used to prevent the formation of ice crystals in the product; emulsifiers produced a smooth, creamy texture. Many types and brands of ice cream were made with all natural ingredients, however.

The ingredients were blended in a mixing tank. The mix then went to a pasteurizer where it was heated and held at a predetermined temperature for a specified period. Homogenization was the next step in the process; under pressure of 2,000 to 2,500 pounds per square inch, the milk fat globules were broken into still smaller particles to make the ice cream smooth. The mix was then quickly cooled to a temperature of about 40 degrees Fahrenheit.

The actual freezing of the mix could be done in a continuous freezer, which used a steady flow of mix, or in a batch freezer, which made a single quantity of ice cream at a time. While it was being frozen, the ice cream was whipped and aerated by blades (called dashers) in the freezers. The aeration, known as overrun, was controlled in all states by requirements regarding the weight and content of total food solids of all products labeled as ice cream. Overrun, stated as a percentage of two times the actual air content, could be as great as 100 percent, meaning the product would actually be 50 percent air. Too little overrun resulted in a rock-hard frozen mass, while too much made ice cream thin and foamy.

Federal standards required that ice cream contain a minimum of 10 percent milk fat and weigh not less than 4.5 pounds per gallon. Ice cream that contained at least 1.4 percent egg yolks could be labeled as french ice cream or frozen custard.

If a continuous freezer were used, ingredients such as fruit and nuts could be added after the freezing stage by a mechanical flavor feeder. Otherwise they were added along with the liquid flavors to the mix before freezing. In the filling operation, the ice cream was packaged in gallon, half-gallon, quart, or pint containers or was used to fill molds to make ice cream bars or other novelties. Ice cream was stored at subzero temperatures to further harden the product. From the hardening room, it was loaded into refrigerated trucks for distribution. Production levels varied throughout the year, with May, June, July, and August being peak production months.

The costs of manufacturing ice cream varied greatly according to the quality of ingredients, the amount of air incorporated, and the size and efficiency of facilities. On the average, ingredients cost the ice cream processor 53.2 percent of revenues; processing and packaging, 31.5 percent; distribution expense, 9.5 percent; administrative expense, 2.8 percent; and pretax profit margins averaged 3.0 percent of revenue.

TYPES OF ICE CREAM

The difference between ice creams was directly related to the quality, richness, and freshness of the ingredients and the way they were blended and treated. The economy brands used a higher proportion of dried products, air, stabilizers, and emulsifiers and had a lower milk fat content. High-quality ice creams contained fresh whole products, less air, as much as 20 percent milk fat, and a minimum of additives.

Butterfat and overrun were commonly used as criteria to classify ice creams as ordinary, premium, or superpremium. Typical supermarket brands contained the minimum 10 to 12 percent of butterfat and 80 to 100 percent overrun. Premium brands had 12 to 16 percent butterfat and 40 to 60 percent overrun, while the superpremium varieties included 16 to 20 percent butterfat and less than 40 percent overrun. Many premium and superpremium brands used no additives or artificial flavors or colors. A four-ounce scoop of superpremium vanilla contained about 260 calories; the same scoop of premium had only 180, while an economy brand had 150 or fewer calories. As of 1990, there was little industry standardization in the classification and labeling of various types of ice cream; producers that wanted to promote their brands as premium or superpremium could ignore the butterfat and overrun criteria observed by most sellers. However, the U.S. Food and Drug Administration established standards that would require food manufacturers to label foods as "light," "low

EXHIBIT 4   Total and Per Capita Production of Ice Cream Products

	1990	Percent Change from 1989
Total, ice cream & related frozen desserts	1,445,315,000 gals.	+ 0.7
Per capita production	23.18 qts.	− 0.3
Ice cream (hard & soft)	816,077,000 gals.	− 1.8
Per capita production	13.09 qts.	− 2.8
Ice milk (hard & soft)	348,800,000 gals.	− 7.4
Per capita production	5.59 qts.	− 8.4
Frozen yogurt (hard & soft)	118,644,000 gals.	+43.9
Per capita production	1.90 qts.	+41.8
Sherbet (hard & soft)	50,278,000 gals.	− 4.5
Per capita production	0.81 qts.	− 5.5
Water ices	50,704,000 gals.	+ 3.1
Per capita production	0.81 qts.	+ 2.0
Other frozen dairy products	60,812,000 gals.	+40.4
Per capita production	0.98 qts.	+39.4

Source: *The Latest Scoop*, 1990, p. 4.

fat," "nonfat," or "reduced calories" according to the number of fat grams and calories per a specified serving size.

Ice milk was similar to ice cream except that it contained 2 to 7 percent milk fat. Sherbet had to include 1 to 2 percent milk fat and weigh not less than six pounds per gallon. The best-known sherbets were those flavored with fruit, but other flavors of sherbet appeared in the 1970s. Frozen yogurt and tofu desserts were similar to ice milk, but the milk fat was replaced, in part or in whole, with vegetable fat. Gelato had less butterfat and overrun than ice cream and carried a much stronger flavor impact. Exhibit 4 shows total and per capita production figures for ice cream and related products for 1990.

From a pricing perspective, the ice creams available in the United States in 1990 could be characterized as luxury priced, superpremium, premium, standard priced, and economy priced. The luxury-priced ice creams included such specialty brands as Godiva ($3.69 per pint). In the superpremium group (the leaders being Häagen-Dazs, Frusen Glädjé, Ben & Jerry's Homemade), prices ranged from $1.89 per pint to $2.29. Most of the best-selling ice creams (Breyers, Dreyer's/Edy's, Sealtest) fit into the premium category and retailed from $2.89 up to $3.29 per half gallon in 1992. Luxury-priced and superpremium ice creams were almost always sold in round pint cartons, while premium and lower priced types were usually sold by half gallons; 65 percent of all packaged ice cream sold was in half-gallon containers. Standard-priced ice creams (usually produced by local dairies) carried prices of $1.99 to $2.49 and included some premium-quality products at the lower price. The economy-priced category consisted of store brands and inexpensive local ice creams and were priced from $1.49 to $1.89. It was not uncommon for some premium-quality products (based on butterfat and overrun criteria) to be sold at superpremium prices; a few premium ice creams were marketed at popular prices. Light, fat-free, and sugar-free frozen desserts and "ice creams" were usually marketed as superpremium products and retailed at around $4 per half gallon.

DISTRIBUTION

While the majority of ice cream was sold in supermarkets, consumer desires for elaborate ice cream desserts and a variety of unusual flavors spawned numerous parlor franchise outlets and dipping stores that featured cones, sundaes, sodas, milk shakes, ice cream dessert specialties, and hand-packed ice cream. As of 1990, 31 franchisors were operating almost 7,000 retail ice cream outlets. The total sales of ice cream and related products in commercial eating places were distributed as follows:

Establishment	Store Sales 1990 (Millions of dollars)
Restaurants, lunchrooms	$ 75,927.0
Limited menu restaurants (Fast foods)	69,800.5
Commercial cafeterias	4,374.4
Social caterers	2,239.8
Ice cream & frozen custard stands	2,003.7
Total eating places	$154,345.4

Source: *The Latest Scoop,* 1990, p. 25.

Most ice cream companies that contracted out the manufacture of their brands to local dairies also relied on them to deliver their products to supermarkets and keep the freezer cases stocked with the most popular flavors. Other companies that produced their own ice cream, such as Ben & Jerry's and Häagen-Dazs, maintained a network of regional distributors to deliver their products to supermarkets. However, Dreyer's Grand Ice Cream operated its own plant-to-store delivery system in an effort to attain better control over product freshness and to secure better space in supermarket freezer displays.

SOFT-SERVE ICE CREAM

Soft-serve ice cream was a partially frozen, but not hardened, dessert. The soft, creamy texture was easy to consume and provided instant gratification. Children, who made up 50 percent of the customer base for soft-serve products, enjoyed licking the products.

Soft ice cream was particularly popular during the 1930s in neighborhood drug and candy stores. Sales surged after World War II, and over the next 30 years soft-serve and frozen custard stands, such as Dairy Queen and Tastee Freeze, dotted highways and street corners throughout the United States. Interest in soft ice cream began to wane until it reached an all-time low in the mid-1980s when premium ice creams gained the public's attention. However, by the late 1980s, consumption of soft ice cream picked back up with the introduction of blended desserts and mix-ins such as Dairy Queen's Blizzard—a milk shake-like product blended with pieces of candy.

Soft *ice cream* was a term used for convenience that usually referred to an ice milk product that contained less than 10 percent butterfat. Frozen custards, also a soft-serve "ice cream" product, contained 1.4 percent egg yolk solids by weight. Both soft ice cream and frozen custard had a fat content of 3 to 10 percent. In terms of flavor, the soft state allowed a fuller flavor, so the lower fat

EXHIBIT 5   Soft-Serve Production—Total and Per Capita Ice Cream and
Related Products, 1970–90

Year	Ice Cream		Ice Milk		Sherbet		Other Frozen Products		Total Products	
	Total Gallons (000s)	Per Capita Quarts	Total Gallons (000s)	Per Capita Quarts	Total Gallons (000s)	Per Capita Quarts	Total Gallons (000s)	Per Capita Quarts	Total Gallons (000s)	Per Capita Quarts
1970	24,991	0.49	152,423	2.99	1,244	0.02	11,103	0.22	189,761	3.72
1975	33,058	0.61	182,180	3.38	2,546	0.05	6,314	0.12	224,098	4.16
1980	27,922	0.49	209,800	3.70	1,442	0.03	3,263	0.06	242,427	4.28
1985	39,683	0.67	239,327	4.03	2,272	0.04	1,619	0.03	282,901	4.76
1986	36,895	0.61	246,940	4.11	2,448	0.04	870	0.01	287,153	4.77
1987	41,791	0.69	253,499	4.19	3,172	0.05	2,319	0.04	300,781	4.97
1988	38,087	0.62	259,745	4.25	2,995	0.05	1,646	0.03	302,473	4.95
1989	42,226	0.68	256,241	4.15	3,686	0.06	65,522	1.06	367,675	5.96
1990	49,125	0.79	230,411	3.69	3,133	0.05	128,756	2.06	411,425	6.60

Source: *The Latest Scoop*, 1990, p. 21.

content was difficult to distinguish. However, the lower fat content also contributed to the tendency for the product to be coarse and icy. Soft ice cream also contained 11 to 14 percent milk solids, 12 to 15 percent sugar, .25 to .60 percent stabilizers and emulsifiers, and 30 to 35 percent total solids. The keys to a smooth, creamy finished product were: (1) reducing the sugar content of the mix by 2 to 3 percent of that used for a hard ice cream product, and (2) reducing the freezing point for drawing out the product to 10 to 22 degrees Fahrenheit. Less sugar was required for soft ice cream because the additional chilling of the blast freezer required for hard products dissipated the sweetness of sugar. The lower temperature produced a stiffer product that was immediately available for consumption.

About 24 percent of ice cream and ice milk was produced in a soft-serve form; in 1990, this amounted to 279 million gallons. The vast majority of soft-serve desserts were actually ice milk. In 1990, the total production of soft-serve products, including ice cream, ice milk, sherbet, and yogurt, was 411 million gallons, 230 million gallons of which were ice milk (see Exhibit 5). Dairy Queen and Tastee Freeze were the leading marketers of soft-serve products.

FROZEN YOGURT

Yogurt was an accidental discovery by desert nomads traveling over the vast expanses of southwest Asia. They carried their milk in bags made of sheep's stomachs. The hot sun and joggling on the backs of pack animals fermented the milk and yielded a dairy product with a semisolid consistency. This fermentation and solidification process was caused by bacteria from the sheep's stomach. Centuries later, Ilya Metchnikoff identified the specific kinds of lactobacilli (milk bacteria) that differentiated yogurt from clabber or fermented milk. The Russian-born French bacteriologist was convinced that yogurt contained bacilli that could kill unfriendly bacteria in the intestines.

Through his experiments at the Pasteur Institute, he succeeded in identifying two types of friendly bacteria in yogurt—a discovery that helped make him co-winner of the Nobel Prize in 1908. He named one bacteria *Lactobacillus bulgaricus* in honor of the Bulgarian octogenarians who had inspired his interest. This bacteria caused an acid action in milk that caused the coagulation. The second bacteria, *Streptococcus thermophilus,* fermented the milk sugar into lactic acid, which gave yogurt its flavor and aroma.

Once the milk bacteria were isolated, it became possible to produce yogurt on a large scale. Metchnikoff championed yogurt as a "miracle milk" that killed the putrefying bacteria and promoted a healthy intestinal system. One of Metchnikoff's followers, Isaac Carasso, began making and selling yogurt in Barcelona but moved his business to Paris during World War I. He opened a yogurt plant in 1929 and named his product Danone for his son Daniel. By the mid-1950s, the company opened the world's largest yogurt factory, catering to French and European tastes. Carasso also opened a yogurt plant in New York City following the outbreak of World War II that catered primarily to the ethnic groups in the area. By the mid-1960s, Carasso and a partner, Joseph Metzger, were reasonably successful in familiarizing the American public with yogurt.

The yogurt that was popular in the United States was considerably different from the Middle Eastern yogurts. Rather than using whole milk or goat's milk, American yogurt was generally made from partially skimmed pasteurized milk (about 1.7 percent milk fat), enriched with milk solids, and contained significantly fewer calories. One cup of plain yogurt had from 120 to 125 calories. In the United States, yogurt was generally eaten as a snack or dessert and was sweetened with either fruit or a sugar base or flavored with vanilla, coffee, or chocolate to remove the tart taste of plain yogurt.

There were no official industry standards for the production of frozen yogurt, but many large dairies and manufacturers were pushing for industry standards. In 1989, the leading frozen yogurt manufacturers developed a proposal for frozen yogurt standards that was submitted to the FDA. The proposed standards required that frozen yogurt:

- Be frozen under agitation.
- Contain "safe and suitable" ingredients, including pasteurized or ultrapasteurized dairy ingredients.
- Contain live culture bacteria *Lactobacillus bulgaricus* and *Streptococcus thermophilus.*
- Have a titratable acidity (TA) of at least 0.3 percent in the mix before adding flavorings, or the TA of uncultured ingredients must increase at least 0.15 percent due to bacterial action.
- Not contain food grade acids added for the purpose of meeting the minimum TA level.
- Not undergo any chemical preservation treatment that reduced the live culture fermentation.
- Contain at least 3.25 percent milk fat, 8.25 percent milk solids, 1.3 pounds of total solids per gallon, and weigh at least 4 pounds per gallon.
- Contain between 0.5 and 2 percent milk fat to be called "low fat" frozen yogurt.
- Contain less than 0.5 percent milk fat to be called "nonfat" frozen yogurt.

Manufacturing Process for Soft-Serve Frozen Yogurt

Frozen yogurt was prepared by freezing while stirring a pasteurized mix, containing one or more of the following ingredients: whole milk, partially defatted milk, skim milk, other milk products, and with or without fruit, nuts, flavoring materials, sweeteners, stabilizers, emulsifiers, and any other safe or suitable ingredient. This pasteurized mix was cultured by one or more strains of *Lactobacillus bulgaricus* and *Streptococcus thermophilus*. These bacteria multiplied and reacted with lactose (milk sugar) and continued to live in the mix and finished products even after the freezing process. After being inoculated with culture, the mixture incubated between $2\frac{3}{4}$ and 3 hours until an acidity of 0.75 percent was achieved.

The prepared frozen yogurt mix was then added by point-of-sale vendors to soft-serve freezers that were similar in operation to batch freezers. The mix was poured into the feeding chamber where it froze on contact with the cylinder wall, creating fine crystals. A rotating beater, or auger, in the cylinder continuously scraped the frozen product from the wall, producing a smooth, creamy product.

Two basic types of soft-serve freezers were pressurized and gravity fed. Pressurized freezers used a pump to force the mix into the dispensing barrel. The ratio of air and mix could be adjusted to expand the volume (overrun) and increase the yield. In gravity-fed freezers, the mix was refrigerated in a tank located directly above the freezing chamber. This freezer used gravity to allow mix and air to flow into the freezing chamber. The ratio of mix to air was not controllable and was blended by the rotating action of the auger. While gravity-fed freezers were the easiest to operate, the overrun fluctuated between 35 and 50 percent. These freezers could also be used for soft-serve ice cream and ice milk products.

Soft-serve machines were available in many sizes and capacities. The cost of the equipment started at $5,000 for a countertop unit and $8,000 for a floor-standing unit. The models also were available in single-flavor or two-flavor twist units. The twist was a desirable feature since a third flavor could be created by combining two flavors. The units varied greatly in size and required relatively low maintenance. Consequently, it was a simple procedure for almost any establishment to add a soft-serve product. The combination of limited investment requirements, limited space requirements, and easy access to frozen yogurt mixes from manufacturers such as Colombo and Honey Hill Farms all contributed to an abundance of supply in the industry.

The Frozen Yogurt Market Size and Structure

Although frozen yogurt had been around for many years, it began gaining momentum in the early 1980s, and between 1985 and 1990 the compound annual growth rate of the market was 57.6 percent, or a 516 percent increase of 1990 sales over 1985 sales.[1] Industry analysts attributed this phenomenal growth to two factors: an increase in the number of outlets offering frozen yogurt and an increase in average store sales of frozen yogurt. However, increased consumer attention to health and nutrition and a smoother, creamier

---

[1] *The National Dipper*, December 1989–January 1990, p. 26.

yogurt that contained fewer live cultures so the product tasted less tart facilitated acceptance of the product.

Six major types of companies competed in the frozen yogurt industry. Frozen yogurt franchises, ice cream franchises, independently owned frozen yogurt shops, and other food-service operators participated in the retail end of the industry. Frozen yogurt and/or frozen yogurt mix manufacturers and companies that sold frozen yogurt equipment were in the manufacturing side of the industry. Franchises were the largest force in the industry in 1990, but industry analysts predicted fast-food chains could easily dominate the industry. The five leading producers of frozen yogurt mix in the United States were Colombo, Honey Hill Farms, Hawthorn Mellody, International Yogurt, and TCBY. The leading hard-pack producers of frozen yogurt in half-gallon containers were Dreyer's and Borden, while Dreyer's and Kraft General Foods dominated in the quart containers.

The average price of a half gallon of hard-pack frozen yogurt was $2.09. Average annual sales for a frozen yogurt shop were estimated at $150,000.[2] In some markets, the figure was as high as $400,000, while Everything Yogurt's midtown Manhattan outlet grossed $1 million annually.

FROZEN DESSERT CONSUMERS

Nine out of 10 households purchased ice cream, and 83 percent of the country's households bought it for home consumption. New Englanders consumed 26.9 quarts of ice cream and related products per person in 1990, while the rest of the nation averaged about 23.2 quarts per capita.

The maturation of the baby boom generation resulted in a large adult population that was both self-indulgent and health conscious. On one hand, ice cream seemed to be the perfect snack or dessert. Adults ate three times as much ice cream as children, and men consumed more than women. Adults were more prone to purchase premium and superpremium brands, frequently equating price with quality and taking the superiority of higher priced items for granted. The pint and single-serving containers were very popular with one- and two-person households.

The 1980s was also a decade of increased health consciousness, a trend that spawned the introduction of hundreds of low-fat and fat-free products. Gelatins and/or a chemical breakthrough called Simplesse replaced fats in ice cream and yogurt, and the sugar substitute NutraSweet was often used—both products reduced the calories and total fat content of the frozen dairy product. Frozen yogurt, which might contain little or no sugar, butterfat, or cholesterol, substantially increased in popularity during the 1980s.

Despite the apparent contradiction, many health-conscious people did not exclude rich ice cream from their diets. People might exercise more and eat more nutritiously, but they also tended to splurge more. With desserts, instant gratification was often the goal; calories and cholesterol didn't count. Also, because of ice cream's wholesome image, some people viewed it as an appropriate reward for exercise or dieting.

---

[2]*The National Dipper*, December 1989–January 1990, p. 27.

EXHIBIT 6   Most Popular Ice Cream and Frozen Yogurt Flavors in the United States

Flavors	Ice Cream Percent of Total Sales	Soft-Serve Frozen Yogurt Percent of Volume
1. Vanilla	31.0%	30%
2. Chocolate	8.8%	26%
3. Neopolitan	6.2%	NA
4. Vanilla fudge	4.2%	NA
5. Cookies 'n cream	3.9%	NA
6. Butter pecan	3.8%	NA
7. Chocolate chip	3.6%	NA
8. Strawberry	3.5%	10%
9. Rocky road	1.3%	NA
10. All others	33.7%	34%

It was also hypothesized that an ailing economy made people turn to small luxuries such as frozen dairy desserts. Purchases of premium and super-premium ice cream crossed economic and cultural lines, and there was little data on the makeup of these buyers or on brand loyalty. Foreign mystique was readily available by purchasing Frusen Glädjé (Swedish for "frozen delight"), Alpen Zauber (German for "alpine magic"), or Häagen-Dazs (meaningless words in English or Danish), all of which were headquartered in New York.

Consumer willingness to try new flavors and ice cream creations often seemed unlimited. However, vanilla was still the preferred flavor of more than 30 percent of consumers. Vanilla was the most popular flavor of frozen yogurt, possibly due to the popularity of mix-ins and toppings associated with the product. The most popular flavors of both ice cream and frozen yogurt are shown in Exhibit 6. Pralines 'N Cream (vanilla laced with praline-covered pecans and caramel) was voted all-time favorite among Baskin-Robbins' more than 500 flavors. Variations of chocolate were in the 2nd through 10th positions. Several companies, including Dreyer's and Baskin-Robbins, had developed new chocolate and chocolate-combination flavors.

SUBSTITUTES AND ICE CREAM NOVELTIES

Ice milk and sherbet were relatively well-established substitutes for ice cream and had stable consumption patterns. While frozen yogurt producers considered their products as competitors in the ice cream industry, some considered yogurt a substitute. Tofu-based dessert products gained recognition in the early 1980s. The best known of the tofu mixtures was Tofutti, a nondairy, bean curd–based dessert made by the Brooklyn-based company Tofu Time. Tofutti had no butterfat or cholesterol, contained no dairy products (which made it suitable for the 30 million lactose-intolerant Americans), and had only half the calories of ice cream. To gain acceptance in supermarkets for Tofutti, Tofu Time had entered into an agreement for Häagen-Dazs to act as distributor for its hard-serve product in the grocery segment. Tofutti retailed for about $2.50 per pint, and its packaging cultivated the same superpremium image as Häagen-

Dazs. Tofu Time had opened its own dipping stores in New York, and Tofutti was also sold in soft-serve form through more than 30 Häagen-Dazs franchise stores.

A relative newcomer to the ice cream market was sorbet, a low-calorie frozen dessert with an intense fruit flavor and a creamier texture than regular sherbet. Castle & Cooke's Dole Fruit Sorbet and Häagen Dazs' Le Sorbet were both introduced in 1984. Both companies emphasized the French origins of sorbet and the all-natural compositions of their products. The round pint containers were similar to those of superpremium ice cream, and each pint sold for about $1.99. Sorbet contained no dairy products; Le Sorbet contained only fruit, water, and sugar and was available in flavors such as raspberry, mango, lemon, strawberry, cantaloupe, and passion fruit.

A multitude of new pudding and juice bars from companies such as General Foods, Castle & Cooke, and Welch's had appeared in the late 1980s to compete with Eskimos Pies, Good Humor bars, and Popsicles. Many of the new products bore labels proclaiming "all natural" and describing the nutrients contained in the bars. Popsicle, Good Humor, and other companies known for ice cream novelties responded with new shapes and flavors of their own. The pudding bars and juice bars typically carried a higher price than traditional ice-cream-on- a-stick products.

ICE CREAM NOVELTIES

The ice cream novelty category included bars, sticks, cones, sandwiches, and parfaits made from ice cream, ice milk, and sherbet. Novelties typically accounted for between 20 and 25 percent of total ice cream sales.

In trying to capture more of the adult market, many manufacturers had begun to make high-quality, richer novelties. Often targeted at one- or two-person households, the premium or superpremium novelties were made smaller and were sold in packages of fewer units. Typical of this trend was ice cream Bon Bons (small morsels of chocolate-covered ice cream), which sold for about $2.79. Also popular were ice cream versions of favorite candy bars, such as Snickers, 3 Musketeers, Milky Way, and Nestle's Crunch. A 12-pack retailed in grocery stores for about $3. Dove Bar International offered a six-ounce ice cream bar with four ounces of superpremium ice cream hand-dipped in dark bittersweet chocolate. Created by a candy maker, the Dove Bar was described by one ice cream expert as two ounces of "very fine candy—the ice cream is really the chaser." In 1990, Dove began experimenting with different flavors of ice cream in its product. A four-bar variety pack retailed for $2.29.

COMPETITIVE RIVALRY

In the early 1980s, competition in the frozen dessert industry was primarily in the superpremium ice cream segment. By the early 1990s, however, competition for customers and for market share was still strong in the superpremium segment but was intensified as yogurt and ice milk manufacturers entered the fray. Marc Cooper, a franchisee of Herrell's, a small Boston-area chain, said that over the last several years "seven of my closest competitors have gone out of business. . . . Frozen yogurt has made a dent and pushed some under and the availability of superpremiums in supermarkets has hurt."[3]

Howard Waxman, editor of *Ice Cream Reporter,* said of the superpremium market: "It's been a hot industry through the 1980s, but we're on the brink of significant changes. Superpremium is slowing down, in large part because of competition from other products taking (market) share from it."[4] Len Tokey, of Summer's Sweet Memories, Inc., in Toronto, said: "Sales of premium ice cream will level off in North America in the 1990s. Public concern with fat, cholesterol, and calories will be the main reason. New products made with sugar substitutes and non-fat products that taste like 'rich' ice cream will take market share as will frozen yogurt."[5] However, Mark Stevens, Häagen-Dazs president, believed superpremium ice creams will remain popular because "people want to make every calorie count—they want wonderful food."[6]

As for the future of premium and superpremium ice creams, Dick Gradwohl of MG's Ice Cream Parlor in Kent, Washington, predicted new product innovations would be the key to future successes:

> Every industry goes through life cycles. Products and services within industries also progress through the process—birth, growth, maturity, and decline. The ice cream industry has been in the maturity stage for quite some time. Because the market is ready for change, new products will come into this industry very strong. Change means opportunity for those who can create products that cause change or ride new trends. In the past two years, we have developed six new waffle cone flavors and colors that have caused a positive change in the consumer's mind with the result of increased sales and profits. We now have on the drawing board 20 additional new product ideas. Some of these will go by the wayside, but you don't know which ones. We are constantly brainstorming to come up with new profitable products—fun, fun, fun.[7]

Over the last several years, the significant gains in overall frozen dairy dessert sales had been led by increases in frozen yogurt sales. However, most industry analysts predicted sales would level off, if not actually decline, for several reasons. First, there was overexpansion in the industry—units opened faster than demand warranted. The FIND/SVP market research company predicted many independent operators would be forced to close as a result of an industry shakeout in the early 1990s. This, in turn, would cause increased competition and declining profits as competition for customers would prevent outlets from raising prices enough to cover the rising costs of labor and rent.[8]

A second problem in the yogurt industry was that frozen yogurt had become a commodity. The product was no longer limited to yogurt stands but was widespread. Yogurt franchisors had expanded their distribution channels to include grocery and convenience stores, and ice cream franchisors had turned to frozen yogurt for growth. By 1988, Baskin-Robbins had changed its name to Baskin-Robbins Ice Cream & Yogurt and had installed yogurt machines in over

---

[3]*The Wall Street Journal,* December 21, 1988, p. B1.
[4]Ibid., p. B1.
[5]*The National Dipper,* December 1989–January 1990, p. 14.
[6]*The Wall Street Journal,* December 21, 1988, p. B1.
[7]*The National Dipper,* December 1989–January 1990, p. 18.
[8]Ibid., p. 26.

20 percent of its 2,500 U.S. shops. International Dairy Queen (IDQ), with 1990 sales of $2.2 billion, offered yogurt in 65 percent of its 4,622 units and realized a 6 percent sales increase in those stores offering yogurt compared to 2 percent increases overall. IDQ's vice president of marketing, Gary See, said, "There has been some cannibalization (of ice cream sales), and there will continue to be, but not as much as one might think because we're reaching a new base of customers."[9]

McDonald's began offering frozen yogurt in its 9,000 units, a move some predicted would cause a significant shakeup in the industry. Mimi Hurst, vice president of TCBY (the largest frozen yogurt franchisor), was optimistic about McDonald's entry: "I think McDonald's and Dairy Queen will expand awareness of frozen yogurt. We won't have to educate customers about frozen yogurt anymore. Now we can narrow our focus and work on differentiating TCBY's yogurt from everybody else's."[10] Zack White of Zack's Famous Frozen Yogurt did not see McDonald's entry into the field as positive: "In the very real world, David doesn't slay Goliath very often."[11]

Independent ice cream shop owners were also offering yogurt. Albert Fitz of Magic Fountain in Clifton, New Jersey, said: "We sell frozen yogurt at our store for several reasons. First, because all the competitors do; second, the healthier reasons; and third, low-fat and nonfat frozen yogurts taste as good as, if not better than, some ice creams. Frozen yogurt adds to our sales in regards to new customers who would never purchase ice cream, but it detracts from our normal ice cream customers, who would buy ice cream instead, if this was their only choice."[12] Gary Daniels of Sweet Retreat in San Jose, California, offered frozen yogurt for different reasons: "Yes, we offer frozen yogurt in addition to ice cream. Eating out is usually a shared experience, so we wanted to provide the consumer with enough diversity to insure that our store would be selected to share that experience. Currently, frozen yogurt is 19 percent of our total sales, while ice cream is 46 percent; however, frozen yogurt was 14 percent and ice cream 51 percent in 1989. Since our sales have increased 24 percent this year, both products have shown growth, but frozen yogurt is growing at a faster rate."[13]

As for the future of frozen yogurt sales, FIND/SVP predicted new frozen yogurt-based novelties would continue to be developed to take advantage of the current popularity of frozen yogurt. A wider variety of novelty products could include frozen yogurt-based bon bons, prepackaged frozen yogurt cones coated with chocolate and nuts, and bars and sandwiches made with frozen yogurt.[14] Additionally, new products that incorporated NutraSweet as a sugar substitute were expected to do well in the future.

Competition was also heating up in the premium ice milk category. Traditionally, ice milk was an economy product targeted at families on a budget. John Harrison, manager of product development at Dreyer's, said of the usual product: "Ice milk had a bad rap, and rightly so, for years. It had a dense, gummy,

---

[9]*Restaurant Business*, May 1, 1992, p. 230.

[10]Ibid.

[11]Ibid.

[12]*The National Dipper*, December 1990–January 1991, p. 15.

[13]Ibid.

[14]*The National Dipper*, December 1989–January 1990, p. 26.

stringy, coarse texture."[15] However, ice milk manufacturers such as Kraft General Foods and Dreyer's Grand Ice Cream, Inc., were seeking government approval to call their gourmet versions of ice milk "light ice cream." Peter Allen of FIND/SVP said, "These products are designed to offer, at a premium price, a much sought after combination of features of today's consumers: high quality and lower fat. But under current standards of identity, the product must be labeled 'ice milk,' a term often associated with thrift. Marketers would prefer labels like 'reduced fat ice cream' or 'low-fat ice cream.'"[16]

Superpremium ice cream manufacturer Häagen-Dazs did not see ice milk as a competitive threat, however. Mark Stevens said the company had no plans to compete in this market, stating: "Ice milk is a failure, so (makers of the product) are trying to reposition it as light ice cream. Häagen-Dazs stands for the highest possible standards of quality and ingredients. Trying to dress up ice milk isn't the proper answer."[17]

Regarding the future of the overall frozen dessert industry: "What you see is further segmentation of the market," said Carol Kirby, vice president of marketing at Baskin-Robbins.[18] Analysts were predicting new product innovations, new distribution outlets, and product repositioning in every segment.

KRAFT GENERAL FOODS

In 1988, Philip Morris Companies, Inc., successfully moved from a cigarette company to a consumer foods producer with the purchase of Kraft. With the subsequent merger of Kraft and General Foods, Philip Morris (PM) became the largest food manufacturer in the United States and second in the world. PM's 1990 total revenues were $51.2 billion, of which $26.1 million (or 51 percent) was contributed by KGF. PM's chairman and CEO, Michael Miles, said: "Philip Morris will be aggressively seeking to expand its worldwide food operations in the years ahead."[19] Miles also said KGF would grow operating revenues by 7 to 9 percent and operating income by 14 to 16 percent.

KGF's growth projections were substantiated by several factors: most KGF brands had significantly greater market share than competitive brands; it was the leader in all three major retail channels of distribution—dry, refrigeration, and frozen—and was second in food-service distribution; it had a strong international presence; and its research and development in food technology was the cutting edge in the industry.

Ice cream accounted for less than 5 percent of the sales of KGF's Food Products Division. Kraft's ice cream products were marketed under the brand names Sealtest, Breyers, and Frusen Glädjé. Sealtest and Breyers were widely available in states east of the Mississippi River. Breyers was one of the best-selling premium ice creams in the country, and KGF continued to extend the market coverage for this brand by initiating distribution in some western and midwestern areas. Breyers was promoted as all natural and was positioned as a top-of-the line brand in the premium ice cream segment. KGF was a licensee

---

[15]*The Wall Street Journal*, December 21, 1988, p. B1.
[16]*The National Dipper*, December 1990–January 1991, p. 13.
[17]*The Wall Street Journal*, December 21, 1988, p. B1.
[18]Ibid.
[19]*Dairy Foods*, April 1990, p. 36.

of Simplesse, a fat substitute used in its Sealtest Free nonfat ice cream—a product developed and marketed to be responsive to consumer desires for a lower calorie ice cream that still had rich ice cream "mouth feel." Frusen Glädjé was the No. 2 selling superpremium in the United States behind Häagen Dazs. It was sold through Frusen Glädjé's approximately 60 dipping stores as well as through supermarkets.

GRAND METROPOLITAN/HÄAGEN-DAZS

The Grand Metropolitan Company was a London-based international food and restaurant conglomerate with 1990 sales of $14.8 billion and net income $1.8 billion. The conglomerate had three primary divisions: food, drinks, and retailing. Included in the Retailing Group were Pearle Vision Centers and Burger King, Inc. fast-food restaurants. In the Food Group were the Pillsbury Company, Alpo Pets, and the nearly 400 Häagen-Dazs Shoppes.

Grand Met operated approximately 260 shops in 20 states in the United States. Some of these shops were dipping stores, while others were larger dessert shop operations. Häagen-Dazs was also sold through grocery and other retail stores. Häagen-Dazs' shops contributed only 8 percent of total Häagen-Dazs sales. Vice President of Marketing Yves Coleon said the shops were the major component in building Häagen-Dazs' brand image and reaching the customer.

In 1990, Häagen-Dazs was the brand leader of superpremium ice cream and was distributing its product through supermarkets as well as its dipping stores. It was also the national distributor for Tofutti and Le Sorbet and was available in Japanese and Tokyo markets through joint ventures formed with Suntory of Japan. Häagen-Dazs had recently introduced a superpremium frozen yogurt available in both its shops and through supermarkets. It came in five flavors—vanilla, chocolate, strawberry, peach, and vanilla-almond crunch—was 96 percent fat-free, and contained all-natural ingredients without stabilizers or gums. Häagen-Dazs frozen yogurt bars in several flavors were also available.

BORDEN, INC.

Borden, Inc., operated in two major industry segments: food and chemicals. Its food operations were divided into three divisions: grocery and specialty products, snacks and international consumer products, and dairy. Net sales in 1990 were $6.7 billion; the Dairy Division accounted for 23 percent of sales and 10 percent of operating income in 1990.

Lady Borden was the company's premium brand of ice cream. Lady Borden had been a market leader in the premium category for many years and remained a strong contender. The Dairy Division also experienced strong sales gains when it began production of a superpremium version of Lady Borden targeted at capturing market share at the high end of the market.

BASKIN-ROBBINS

The Baskin-Robbins ice cream business was founded in 1946 by Burton Baskin and Irvine Robbins and was engaged in the development and manufacture of ice cream products, operation of retail ice cream stores, and granting of franchises for such stores. Allied-Lyons North America Corporation owned 100 percent of the shares of stock of Baskin-Robbins in 1992.

Baskin-Robbins operated over 2,400 dipping stores in the United States and 1,000 stores outside the United States, including Moscow. The company also had five overseas plants—in London; Brisbane, Australia; Peterborough, Ontario; Seoul; and Tokyo. Over half of the U.S. dipping stores were company owned. All store supplies and materials, from ice cream to napkins, were purchased from one of Baskin-Robbins' network of licensed distributors.

In 1985, Baskin-Robbins began to restructure the company—from its product line to its interiors to its name—in an effort to attract more adult customers without alienating its base of children. According to Carol Kirby, Baskin-Robbins' marketing director, "We were out of touch and needed new dessert lines that were in step with the times. There was no way we were going to abandon our '31 flavors' concept. That's what set us apart. Nor did I want to get into the butterfat wars and come out with an ice cream that was even richer than what was already out there. Instead, I thought we should expand into the segment that the superpremiums had failed to address: frozen yogurt and other health-oriented desserts."[20] The company was also the first store to carry a 100 percent aspartame-sweetened dairy dessert when it launched Low, Light & Luscious in April 1989. By 1990, there were five sugar-free flavors.

The company took great pride in flavor development. It offered over 500 flavors on a rotating basis. Additionally, it created flavors native to the different parts of the world in which it operated. For example, it offered durian in the Far East—a local fruit with a strong odor not appetizing to most Americans— and ube from a purple yamlike fruit with an earthy taste. In 1991, Baskin-Robbins was concentrating efforts on Chinese, Indian, and European markets and was test marketing a frozen yogurt in its Japanese stores.

STEVE'S HOMEMADE ICE CREAM

Steve's Homemade Ice Cream gained fame for its mix-in concept, whereby chunks of fruit, nuts, cookies, and candies were mixed into its superpremium ice cream. The company distributed mixed-in ice cream in prepackaged pints to supermarkets, grocery stores, gourmet shops, delicatessens, and convenience stores. It also franchised Steve's Ice Cream Shops to independent owners who purchased ice cream from the company in 2½-gallon containers for distribution to the public. In the mid-1980s Steve's was acquired by Integrated Resources.

In August 1988, Integrated Resources acquired 100 percent interest in Swensen's Inc., which owned, operated, developed, and franchised ice cream shops and limited menu restaurants featuring Swensen's premium ice cream. By 1990, 249 Swensen's and 100 Steve's ice cream shops were in operation. In February 1989, Integrated Resources acquired 86 percent interest in Heidi's Frozen Yogurt Shoppes, which added another 56 outlets. Steve's net sales in 1990 were $19.1 million (excluding franchise income of $6.7 million) with net income of $252,000 (due in part to acquisition expenses).

---

[20]*Dairy Foods*, April 1990, p. 47.

In 1990, Integrated Resources was offering a Triple Trademark franchise concept to existing and potential new franchisees. The concept would allow an entrepreneur to offer each of its branded lines (Steve's, Swensen's, and Heidi's) plus, through a special arrangement, David's Cookies, in one store for the price of a single franchise. The store would be split into three sections with independent counter designs, signs, and products.

The company also owned 60 percent of American Glacé, Inc., which marketed a no-cholesterol, no-fat, low-calorie soft-serve frozen dessert mix to yogurt and ice cream stores and sold prepackaged pints to supermarkets, convenience stores, and delicatessens primarily in New Jersey, Connecticut, California, Florida, and Canada. Steve's Homemade became the first superpremium maker to venture into the reduced-calorie market when it introduced six flavors of Steve's Gourmet Light in 1989. By 1990, there were 12 flavors and more on the drawing board. David Smith, Steve's director of marketing, said, "Public reaction has been phenomenal. We're dominating the category."[21]

TCBY ENTERPRISES (THE COUNTRY'S BEST YOGURT)

TCBY began as an retirement project by Frank D. Hickingbotham in 1981 in Little Rock, Arkansas. The first store was a success, and soon Hickingbotham opened two more stores managed by his sons and brother-in-law. In the spring of 1982, he hired a consultant to determine if anyone was attempting to build a national chain of yogurt franchises. "Our thrust was to position it as an ice cream parlor. The soothsayers said it couldn't be done—that we wouldn't survive the winter."[22] By the end of 1990, TCBY had 1,847 franchised, licensed, or company-owned stores in every state in the United States and in six other countries, making it the largest yogurt franchisor with over 35 percent of the market. Sales and franchising revenues in 1990 exceeded $151.3 million with net income of nearly $20 million. Some analysts questioned whether TCBY merely capitalized on the growth of frozen yogurt or whether it actually fueled the growth.[23]

Hickingbotham did not consider other yogurt distributors as TCBY's competition: "We are really competing against the ice cream chains."[24] TCBY Enterprises was vertically integrated, with a separate subsidiary for each phase of the business. Each subsidiary had its own president and board and Hickingbotham's son, Herren, was president of TCBY Systems, the franchise subsidiary.

In 1988, Hickingbotham claimed there were no problems with franchisees, stating that 65 percent of new franchises were opened by existing franchisees. The company offered franchisees a strong brand image, joint advertising, and low debt. The cost to open a new store was only $140,000 in 1990, depending on location, and Hickingbotham often allowed TCBY stores to open in areas with light travel in order to keep costs down. But through 1990, the company continued to grow by adding new outlets while same-store sales were faltering.

---

[21]*Dairy Foods*, April 1990, p. 43.

[22]*Venture*, May 1989, p. 16.

[23]*Dairy Foods*, April 1990, p. 46.

[24]*Venture*, May 1989, p. 16.

Previously, the company's primary source of revenues was new franchises; by late 1989, the bulk of its business came from selling yogurt to franchisees for about $7 a gallon versus a $5 a gallon price paid by competitors. Franchisees began to rumble, particularly when the largest store, operated in the Chicago area, filed for bankruptcy. Many franchisees formed an association to present a list of grievances to Hickingbotham, including a request for a 15 to 20 percent decrease in the wholesale price of yogurt. One of the complaints against Hickingbotham concerned his $1.7 million compensation, plus his Rolls-Royce and use of a corporate jet—often accompanied by his dog.

BEN & JERRY'S HOMEMADE, INC.

In May 1978, Ben Cohen and Jerry Greenfield, best friends since the seventh grade, opened an ice cream parlor in Burlington, Vermont, in a renovated gas station, using the skills they had learned in a $5 correspondence course. They planned to get the business going and then sell it. By 1990, Ben & Jerry's was posting sales of over $77 million and was still growing. Net income for 1990 was $2.6 million.

Ironically, the founders were not initially happy with the success of their venture. They believed the cash-based morality of corporations was distasteful. They found that as the company grew, they no longer knew all of the employees, could no longer share decision making, and could no longer ensure that everyone was as liberal as Ben and Jerry. Cohen said, "I think it would be a mistake for a right-of-center person to work at a left-of-center company."[25] It was no longer fun for the founders. Greenfield left the company in 1982, choosing a less stressful life in Arizona (although he returned in 1985). Cohen found a way to ease his conscience and justify further growth—he decided to make the company into a force for social change. He regarded Ben & Jerry's as an entity held in trust for the community, and 7.5 percent of pretax profits went to charities or to fund social issues Cohen and/or Greenfield felt strongly about.

Ben & Jerry's was an experiment in alternate ways to manage business and growth. Fred Lager, Ben & Jerry's chief operating officer, said, "(Ben) is looking to show other people that you can run a business differently from the way most businesses are run, that you can share your prosperity with your employees, rewrite the book on executive salaries, rewrite the book in terms of how a company interacts with the community—and you can still play the game according to the rules of Wall Street. You can still raise money, still go to the banks, still have shareholders who are getting a good return on their investment."[26]

Much of Ben & Jerry's corporate culture reflected on the alternative lifestyles of its founders. There was not a corporate dress code; T-shirts and jeans were the norm. Executive salaries were capped at seven times the lowest paying job. Annual meetings were reminiscent of Woodstock with dozens of live rock bands and the accounting manager skydiving into the meeting. Jerry Greenfield was the "Undersecretary of Joy," charged with putting more joy into the workday. And, of course, there were the social programs.

---

[25] *Forbes*, November 13, 1989, p. 64.
[26] *INC.*, July 1988, p. 52.

Ben & Jerry's used its ice cream products to fund social and community issues. It used proceeds from its Peace Pop product to fund a foundation called 1% Peace, which lobbied Congress for cuts in the U.S. defense budget. Proceeds from its Rain Forest Crunch ice cream went to save the Amazon. The peanut brittle candy used in the ice cream was purchased from a company called Community Products, Inc. (CPI). CPI was a satellite firm Cohen formed in response to restrictions placed on a publicly owned company. Through Ben & Jerry's, Cohen could give only 7.5 percent; through CPI, he gave 60 percent. CPI made the peanut brittle with nuts from the Brazilian rain forest, and 40 percent of total candy sales went to rain forest–based preservation organizations and international environmental projects. Ben & Jerry's sales director, Rick Brown, predicted Cohen's reform efforts were going to win him a Nobel Prize: "For peace. We think he's going to win the Nobel Peace Prize."[27] Both the Peace Pop and Rain Forest Crunch ice cream were priced significantly higher than standard products.

Ben & Jerry's commissioned a Washington research firm to perform an audit of the firm's social performance. The auditors commended the company on its charitable contributions, but criticized the company's lack of nutritional labeling and its high-fat, high-cholesterol ice cream without offering alternatives to the health conscious. In response, the company introduced Ben & Jerry's Light and Ben & Jerry's frozen yogurt in 1989.

Ben & Jerry's marketing emphasized the ice cream's high quality and natural ingredients and projected a "down-home" Vermont image. Packages and advertising carried pictures of Cohen and Greenfield, paintings of cows, and hand lettering. The company relied primarily on word-of-mouth advertising and capitalized on the free media attention given to Ben & Jerry's social programs.

On the serious side of Ben & Jerry's there was concern that the company's growth was undirected. Cohen preferred to slow or stop growth, but responsibilities to shareholders required growth to survive. The company lacked systems and controls to handle further growth. According to Cohen, "We didn't have good systems or standard operating systems. So every time we had to do something that was pretty much a repetitive process, it would get started from the beginning—instead of just pulling out the procedure and following it. I had this image of these molecules jiggling, going back and forth . . . instead of going in a straight line. Eventually we'd get the job done, but it took a whole lot more energy."[28] On one occasion, when the company was short 300 pallets of ice cream, Lager called all hands into production and Greenfield called in a masseuse to give workers massages during their breaks. After this episode, the company decided it was time for professional management and by 1990, Cohen and Greenfield were much less involved in the day-to-day operations. The company slowed the sales of new franchises in 1989, stating that future efforts would concentrate on existing stores and new product development.

---

[27]*Forbes*, November 13, 1989, p. 64.
[28]*INC.*, July 1988, p. 56.

COLOMBO, INC.

In 1991, Colombo, Inc., was the oldest yogurt dairy in the United States. It was founded by Rose and Sarkis Colombosian in 1929 and was purchased by Bongrain SA of France. As a privately held company, financial figures were not available. The company called itself "the leading player in the global frozen yogurt market." Its product was available in over 1,600 grocery and convenience stores. Approximately two thirds of all yogurt sold by independent frozen yogurt shops was supplied by Colombo and sold under the Colombo brand.

Colombo offered three product lines: Regular, Colombo Lite, and Nonfat Colombo. Colombo distributed 21 flavors of regular and nonfat yogurt prepackaged to grocery stores and food service operations. The company began the Grocery Advantage program in 1990, targeted at placing fully branded, self-serve cabinets with two-flavor twist machines in more than 600 grocery stores. A national field operations staff served each location to maintain quality control. To its independent shops and grocery stores participating in the program, Colombo offered its Special Flavor program, in which 60 flavors rotated onto the shelves. Like ice cream makers, Colombo hoped that the variety would create consumer enthusiasm and that favorite flavors would become a standard offering.

Colombo's latest product innovations were Diet Colombo and Colombo Gourmet. Hard-pack Colombo Gourmet was available in eight flavors in 6.5-ounce cups or 2.5 gallons for food service operations. Colombo supported its products with point-of-sale merchandising material, including T-shirts, aprons, caps, flavor boards, table tents, counter cards, nutritional information handouts, and ad slicks. It also opened a training facility called Colombo University in Atlanta, Georgia, where yogurt shopowners gained classroom and hands-on experience during a three-day session.

HONEY HILL FARMS

Honey Hill Farms was founded in 1977 as a soft-serve frozen yogurt supplier to retail frozen yogurt shops. Later, the company supplied mix to supermarkets that placed the company's self-serve cabinets in their aisles. Honey Hill Farms posted sales of $50 million in 1989 and $70 million (estimated) in 1990. The company's recent product innovation, and basis for future growth, was its line of hard-packed premium frozen yogurt.

The hard-packed premium frozen yogurt was priced at $2.29 per pint and was marketed in cartons illustrated with close-up photos of each flavor's ingredients. The line boasted creative product varieties such as Cookie Jar (with chunks of Oreo cookies); Caramel Pecan Wave; Massive Mocha; Strawberry Avalanche; White Almond Chocolate (with white chocolate-coated almonds); Peach Orchard; Vanilla Chocolate Hunk; Chocolate Thunder; Vanilla Velvet; and Raspberry Rush.

Honey Hill Farms claimed that its hard-pack frozen yogurt line outsold "all other pint frozen yogurts west of the Rockies by 2 to 1." The company also claimed to have a 66 percent market share in those markets in which it sold. Honey Hill Farms supported both its hard-pack and soft-serve lines with point-of-purchase materials and print ads. Its media package also included instructions on how to capitalize on the advertising materials provided by the company.

In 1990, Honey Hill Farms' greatest problems concerned defeating takeover raiders. According to its president, Fred Di Cosola, the company was the target of several takeover and acquisition attempts and/or inquiries in 1989 and 1990; he insisted the company was not for sale.

INTERNATIONAL DAIRY QUEEN

The International Dairy Queen (IDQ) was a purveyor of fast food and desserts in the United States and other nations. In 1991, the company had over 5,300 Dairy Queen franchises—3,721 direct franchises and 1,587 territorial-operator franchises. The company also had 59 Golden Skillet franchises, 562 Orange Julius franchises that it acquired in 1987, and 126 Karmelkorn Shoppes franchises that it acquired in 1986. IDQ posted revenues of $289 million in 1991 with net profits of $28 million. Seventy-seven percent of the 1991 revenues were from supplies to franchisees, and 16 percent were from service fees, which were royalties of approximately 4 percent of the franchisees' revenues.

While IDQ was attempting to restructure and grow, the company's net expansion in terms of new franchisees was flat—IDQ was opening hundreds of new high-volume stores, but it was closing just as many underperforming units. To improve the corporate and franchisee image, IDQ instituted a program called Image. Through Image, IDQ loaned funds to franchisees for the purpose of remodeling and updating their stores. Newly updated units tended to generate improved sales, which, in turn, increased IDQ's royalties.

IDQ claimed that its Dairy Queen units were well positioned against its competitors due to its dessert-oriented menu and predominantly small-town presence. It did not believe it was a threat to or threatened by fast-food chains. The company was in good standing from a cash position since all but 5 of its 6,000-plus units were franchised, and franchisees were responsible for all capital improvements. IDQ's capital expenditure budget was minimal.

GILLETTE AND THE MEN'S WET-SHAVING MARKET

Lew G. Brown, University of North Carolina at Greensboro
Jennifer M. Hart, University of North Carolina at Greensboro

SAN FRANCISCO

On a spring morning in 1989, Michael Johnson dried himself and stepped from the shower in his Marina district condominium. He moved to the sink and started to slide open his drawer in the cabinet beneath the sink. Then he remembered he had thrown away his last Atra blade yesterday. He heard his wife, Susan, walk past the bathroom.

"Hey, Susan, did you remember to pick up some blades for me yesterday?"

"Yes, I think I put them in your drawer."

"Oh, OK, here they are." Michael saw the bottom of the blade package and pulled the drawer open.

"Oh, no! These are Trac II blades, Susan. I use an Atra."

"I'm sorry. I looked at all the packages at the drugstore, but I couldn't remember which type of razor you have. Can't you use the Trac II blades on your razor?"

"No. They don't fit."

"Well, I bought some disposable razors. Just use one of those."

"Well, where are they?"

"Look below the sink. They're in a big bag."

"I see them. Wow, 10 razors for $1.97! Must have been on sale."

"I guess so. I usually look for the best deal. Seems to me that all those razors are the same, and the drugstore usually has one brand or another on sale."

"Why don't you buy some of those shavers made for women?"

"I've tried those, but it seems that they're just like the ones made for men, only they've died the plastic pink or some pastel color. Why should I pay more for color?

"Why don't you just use disposables?" Susan continued. "They are simpler to buy, and you just throw them away. And, you can't beat the price."

"Well, the few times I've tried them they didn't seem to shave as well as a regular razor. Perhaps they've improved. Do they work for you?"

"Yes, they work fine. And they sure are better than the heavy razors if you drop one on your foot while you're in the shower!"

"Never thought about that. I see your point. Well, I'll give the disposable a try."

HISTORY OF SHAVING

Anthropologists do not know exactly when or even why men began to shave. Researchers do know that prehistoric cave drawings clearly present men who were beardless. Apparently these men shaved with clamshells or sharpened animal teeth. As society developed, primitive men learned to sharpen flint implements. Members of the early Egyptian dynasties as far back as 7,000 years ago shaved their faces and heads, probably to deny their enemies anything to grab during hand-to-hand combat. Egyptians later fashioned copper razors and, in time, bronze blades. Craftsmen formed these early razors as crescent-shaped knife blades, like hatchets or meat cleavers, or even as circular blades with a handle extending from the center. By the Iron Age, craftsmen were able to fashion blades that were considerably more efficient than the early flint, copper, and bronze versions.

Before the introduction of the safety razor, men used a straight-edged, hook-type razor and found shaving a tedious, difficult, and time-consuming task. The typical man struggled through shaving twice a week at most. The shaver had to sharpen the blade (a process called *stropping*) before each use and had to have an expert cutler hone the blade each month. As a result, men often cut themselves while shaving; and few men had the patience and acquired the necessary skill to become good shavers. Most men in the 1800s agreed with the old Russian proverb: "It is easier to bear a child once a year than to shave every day." Only the rich could afford a daily barber shave, which also often had its disadvantages because many barbers were unclean. Another proverb observed, "Barbers learn to shave by shaving fools."

Before King C. Gillette of Boston invented the safety razor in 1895, he tinkered with other inventions in pursuit of a product that once used would be thrown away. The customer would have to buy more, and the business would build a long-term stream of sales and profits with each new customer.

"On one particular morning when I started to shave," wrote Gillette about the dawn of his invention, "I found my razor dull, and it was not only dull but beyond the point of successful stropping and it needed honing, for which it must be taken to a barber or cutler. As I stood there with the razor in my hand, my eyes resting on it as lightly as a bird settling down on its nest, the Gillette razor was born." Gillette immediately wrote to his wife who was visiting relatives, "I've got it; our fortune is made."

Gillette had envisioned a "permanent" razor handle onto which the shaver placed a thin, razor "blade" with two sharpened edges. The shaver would place a top over the blade and attach it to the handle so only the sharpened edges of the blade were exposed, thus producing a "safe" shave. A man would shave with the blade until it became dull and then would simply throw the used blade away and replace it. Gillette knew his concept would revolutionize shaving; however, he had no idea his creation would permanently change men's shaving habits.

THE SHAVING INDUSTRY IN THE 1980s

After the invention of the safety razor, the U.S. men's shaving industry grew slowly but surely through World War I. A period of rapid growth followed, and the industry saw many product innovations. By 1989, U.S. domestic razor and blade sales (the wet-shave market) had grown to a $770 million industry. A man could use three types of wet shavers to remove facial hair. Most men used the disposable razor, a cheap, plastic-handled razor that lasted for 8 to 10 shaves on average. Permanent razors, called blade and razor systems, were also popular. These razors required new blades every 11 to 14 shaves. Customers could purchase razor handles and blade cartridges together, or they could purchase packages of blade cartridges as refills. The third category of wet shavers included injector and double-edge razors and accounted for a small share of the razor market. Between 1980 and 1988, disposable razors had risen from a 22 percent to a 41.5 percent market share of dollar sales, while cartridge systems had fallen from 50 percent to 45.8 percent, and injector and other had fallen from 28 percent to 12.7 percent. In addition, the development of the electric razor had spawned the dry-shave market, which accounted for about $250 million in sales by 1988.

Despite the popularity of disposable razors, manufacturers found the razors were expensive to make and generated little profit. Some industry analysts estimated that, by 1988, manufacturers earned three times more on a razor and blade system than on a disposable razor. Also, retailers preferred to sell razor systems because they took up less room on display racks and the retailers made more money on refill sales. However, retailers liked to promote disposable razors to generate traffic. As a result, U.S. retailers allocated 55 percent of their blade and razor stock to disposable razors, 40 percent to systems, and 5 percent to double-edge razors.

Electric razors also posed a threat to razor- and-blade systems. Unit sales of electric razors jumped from 6.2 million in 1981 to 8.8 million in 1987. Low-priced imports from the Far East drove demand for electric razors up and prices down during this period. Nonetheless, less than 30 percent of men used electric razors, and most of these men also used wet-shaving systems.

Industry analysts predicted personal-care products manufacturers' sales would continue to grow, but the slowing of the overall U.S. economy in the late 1980s mean sales increases resulting from an expanding market would be minimal and companies would have to fight for market share to continue to increase sales.

The Gillette Company dominated the wet-shave market in 1988 with a 60 percent share of worldwide razor market revenue and a 61.9 percent share of the $770 million U.S. market. The other players in the wet-shave market were Schick with 16.2 percent of market revenues, BIC with 9.3 percent, and others, including Wilkinson Sword, made up the remaining 12.6 percent.

The Gillette Company

King Gillette took eight years to perfect his safety razor. In 1903, the first year of marketing, the American Safety Razor Company sold 51 razors and 168 blades. Gillette promoted the safety razor as a saver of both time and money. Early ads proclaimed the razor would save $52 and 15 days shaving time each year and the blades required no stropping or honing. During its second year, Gillette sold 90,884 razors and 123,648 blades. By its third year, razor sales were rising at a rate of 400 percent per year, and blade sales were booming at an annual rate of 1,000 percent. In that year, the company opened its first overseas branch in London.

Such success attracted much attention, and competition quickly developed. By 1906, consumers had at least a dozen safety razors from which to choose. Some, like the Zinn razor made by the Gem Cutlery Company, sold for $5 as did the Gillette razor. Others, such as the Ever Ready, Gem Junior, and Enders sold for as little as $1.

With the benefit of a 17-year patent, Gillette found himself in a very advantageous position. However, it was not until World War I that the safety razor gained wide consumer acceptance. One day in 1917, King Gillette had a visionary idea: have the government present a Gillette razor to every soldier, sailor, and marine. In this way, millions of men just entering the shaving age would adopt the self-shaving habit. By March 1918, Gillette had booked orders from the U.S. military for 519,750 razors, more than it had sold in any single *year* in its history. During WWI, the government bought 4,180,000 Gillette razors as well as smaller quantities of competitive models.

Although King Gillette believed in the quality of his product, he realized that marketing, especially distribution and advertising, would be the key to success. From the beginning, Gillette set aside $.25 per razor for advertising and by 1905 had increased the amount to $.50. Over the years, Gillette used cartoon ads, radio shows, musical slogans and theme songs, prizes, contests, and cross-promotions to push its products. Older males best remembered Gillette for its Cavalcade of Sports programs that began in 1939 with the company's sponsorship of the World Series. Millions of men soon came to know Sharpie the parrot and the tag line, "Look Sharp, Feel Sharp, Be Sharp!"

Because company founder King Gillette invented the first safety razor, Gillette had always been an industry innovator. In 1932, Gillette introduced the Gillette Blue Blade, which was the premier men's razor for many years. In 1938, the company introduced the Gillette Thin Blade; in 1946, it introduced the first blade dispenser that eliminated the need to unwrap individual blades; in 1959, it introduced the first silicone-coated blade, the Super Blue Blade. The success of the Super Blue Blade caused Gillette to close 1961 with a commanding 70 percent share of the overall razor and blade market and a 90 percent share of the double-edged market, the only market in which it competed.

In 1948, Gillette began to diversify into new markets through acquisition. The company purchased the Toni Company to extend its reach into the women's grooming-aid market. In 1954, the company bought Paper Mate, a leading maker of writing instruments. In 1962, Gillette acquired the Sterilon Corporation, which manufactured disposable hospital supplies. As a result of these moves, a marketing survey found that the public associated Gillette with personal grooming as much as, or more than, with blades and razors.

In 1989, the Gillette Company was a leading producer of men's and women's grooming aids. Exhibit 1 lists the company's major divisions, and Exhibit 2 shows the percentages and dollar volumes of net sales and profits from operations for each of the company's major business segments from 1986 to 1988. Exhibit 3 presents income statement and balance sheet information for 1986–88.

Despite its diversification, Gillette continued to realize the importance of blade and razor sales to the company's overall health. Gillette had a strong foothold in the razor and blade market, and it intended to use this dominance to help it achieve the company's goal—"sustained profitable growth." To reach this goal, Gillette's mission statement indicated the company should pursue "strong technical and marketing efforts to assure vitality in major existing product lines; selective diversification, both internally and through acquisition; the elimination of product and business areas with low growth or limited profit potential; and strict control over product costs, overhead expenses, and working capital."

EXHIBIT 1   **Gillette 1988 Product Lines by Company Division**

Safety Razor
Trac II
Atra
Good News

Toiletries and Cosmetics
Adorn
Toni
Right Guard
Silkience
Soft and Dri
Foamy

Dry Look
Dry Idea
White Rain
Lustrasilk
Aapri Skin Care Products

Stationery Products
Paper Mate
Liquid Paper
Flair
Waterman
Write Bros.

Oral Care
Oral B toothbrushes

Braun Products
Electric razors
Lady Elegance
Clocks
Coffee grinders and makers

EXHIBIT 2   **Gillette's Sales and Operating Profits by Product Line, 1986–88**   *(In millions)*

	1988		**1987**		**1986**	
	Sales	Profits	Sales	Profits	Sales	Profits
Blades and razors	$1,147	$406	$1,031	$334	$ 903	$274
Toiletries and cosmetics	1,019	79	926	99	854	69
Writing instruments and office products	385	56	320	34	298	11
Braun products	824	85	703	72	657	63
Oral-B	202	18	183	7	148	8
Other	5	(.1)	4	2	48	(1)
Totals	$3,582	$644	$3,167	$548	$2,908	$424

Gillette's Net Sales and Profit by Business Line

	Blades and Razors		**Toiletries and Cosmetics**		**Stationery Products**		**Braun Products**		**Oral B Products**	
	Sales	Profits	Sales	Profits	Sales	Profits	Sales	Profits	Sales	Profits
1988	32%	61%	28%	14%	11%	9%	23%	13%	6%	3%
1987	33%	61%	29%	18%	10%	6%	22%	13%	6%	2%
1986	32%	64%	30%	16%	11%	3%	20%	15%	5%	2%
1985	33%	68%	31%	15%	11%	2%	17%	13%	6%	3%
1984	34%	69%	30%	15%	12%	3%	17%	12%	3%	2%

Gillette introduced a number of innovative shaving systems in the 1970s and 1980s as part of its strategy to sustain growth. Gillette claimed that Trac II, the first twin-blade shaver, represented the most revolutionary shaving advance ever. The development of the twin-blade razor derived from shaving researchers' discovery of the hysteresis process—the phenomenon of whiskers being lifted out of the follicle during shaving and, after a time, receding. Gillette invented the twin-blade system so the first blade would cut the whisker and the second blade would cut it again before it receded. This system produced a

EXHIBIT 3   Gillette's Income Statement and Balance Sheet Data, 1986–88   *(In millions)*

	1988	1987	1986
Net sales	$3,581.2	$3,166.8	$2,818.3
Cost of sales	1,487.4	1,342.3	1,183.8
Other expenses	1,479.8	1,301.3	1,412.0
Operating income	614.0	523.2	222.5
Other income	37.2	30.9	38.2
Earnings before interest and taxes	651.2	554.1	260.7
Interest expenses	138.3	112.5	85.2
Nonoperating expenses	64.3	50.1	124.0
Earnings before taxes	448.6	391.5	51.5
Income taxes	180.1	161.6	35.7
Earnings after taxes	268.5	229.9	15.8
Retained earnings	1,261.6	1,083.8	944.3
Earnings per share	$ 2.45	$ 2.00	$ .12
Average common shares outstanding (thousands)	109,559	115,072	127,344
Dividends paid/share	$ 0.86	$ 0.785	$ 0.68
Stock price range			
High	$ 49	$ 457/8	$ 341/2
Low	291/8	175/8	171/8
Assets			
Cash	$ 156.4	$ 119.1	$ 94.8
Receivables	729.1	680.1	608.8
Inventories	653.4	594.5	603.1
Other current assets	200.8	184.5	183.0
Total current assets	$1,739.7	$1,578.2	$1,489.7
Fixed assets, net	683.1	664.4	637.3
Other assets	445.1	448.6	412.5
Total assets	$2,867.9	$2,691.2	$2,539.5
Liabilities and Equity			
Current liabilities*	$ 964.4	$ 960.5	$ 900.7
Current portion long-term debt	9.6	41.0	7.6
Long-term debt	1,675.2	839.6	915.2
Equity	$ (84.6)	$ 599.4	$ 460.8

*Includes current portion of long-term debt

Source: *Gillette Company Annual Report,* 1985–88.

closer shave than a traditional one-blade system. Gillette also developed a clog-free, dual-blade cartridge for the Trac II system.

Because consumer test data showed a 9-to-1 preference for Trac II over panelists' current razors, Gillette raced to get the product to market. Gillette supported Trac II's 1971 introduction, the largest new product introduction in shaving history, with a $10 million advertising and promotion budget. Gillette cut its advertising budgets for its other brands drastically to support Trac II. The double-edge portion of the advertising budget decreased from 47 percent in 1971 to 11 percent in 1972. Gillette reasoned that growth must come at the expense of other brands. Thus, it concentrated its advertising and promotion on its newest shaving product and reduced support for its established lines.

Gillette launched Trac II during a World Series promotion and made it the most frequently advertised shaving system in America during its introductory period. Trac II users turned out to be predominantly young, college-educated men who lived in metropolitan and suburban areas and earned higher incomes. As the fastest growing shaving product on the market for five years, Trac II drove the switch to twin blades. The brand reached its peak in 1976 when consumers purchased 485 million blades and 7 million razors.

Late in 1976, Gillette, apparently in response to BIC's pending entrance into the U.S. market, launched Good News!, the first disposable razor for men sold in the United States. In 1975, BIC had introduced the first disposable shaver in Europe; and by 1976, BIC began to sell disposable razors in Canada. Gillette realized that BIC would move its disposable razor into the United States after its Canadian introduction, so it promptly brought out a new, blue plastic, disposable shaver with a twin-blade head. By year's end, Gillette also introduced Good News! in Austria, Canada, France, Italy, Switzerland, Belgium, Greece, Germany, and Spain.

Unfortunately for Gillette, Good News! was really bad news. The disposable shaver delivered lower profit margins than razor and blade systems, and it undercut sales of other Gillette products. Good News! sold for much less than the retail price of a Trac II cartridge. Gillette marketed Good News! on price and convenience, not performance; but the company envisioned the product as a step-up item leading to its traditional high-quality shaving systems.

This contain-and-switch strategy did not succeed. Consumers liked the price and the convenience of disposable razors, and millions of Trac II razors began to gather dust in medicine chests across the country. Many Trac II users figured out that for as little as 25 cents, they could get the same cartridge mounted on a plastic handle that they had been buying for 56 cents to put on their Trac II handle. Further, disposable razors created an opening for competitors in a category that Gillette had long dominated.

Gillette felt sure, however, that disposable razors would never gain more than a 7 percent share of the market. The disposable razor market share soon soared past 10 percent, forcing Gillette into continual upward revisions of its estimates. In terms of units sold, disposable razors reached a 22 percent market share by 1980 and a 50 percent share by 1988.

BIC and Gillette's successful introduction of the disposable razor represented a watershed event in commoditization. Status, quality, and perceived value had always played primary roles in marketing of personal care products. But consumers were now showing they would forgo performance and prestige in a shaving product—about as close and personal as one can get.

In 1977, Gillette introduced a new blade-and-razor system at the expense of Trac II. It launched Atra with a $7 million advertising campaign and over 50 million $2-rebate coupons. Atra (which stands for Automatic Tracking Razor Action) was the first twin-blade shaving cartridge with a pivoting head. Engineers had designed the head to follow a man's facial contours for a closer shave. Researchers began developing the product in Gillette's United Kingdom research and development lab in 1970. They had established a goal of improving the high performance standards of twin-blade shaving and enhancing the Trac II effect. The company's scientists discovered that instead of moving the hand and face to produce the best blade shaving angle, the razor head itself could produce a better shave if it could pivot so as to maintain the most effective shaving angle. Marketers selected the name Atra after two years of extensive consumer testing.

Atra quickly achieved a 7 percent share of the blade market and about one third of the razor market. The company introduced Atra in Europe a year later under the brand name Contour. Although Atra increased Gillette's share of the razor market, 40 percent of Trac II users switched to Atra in the first year.

In the early 1980s, Gillette introduced more new disposable razors and product enhancements. Both Swivel (launched in 1980) and Good News! Pivot (1984) were disposable razors featuring movable heads. Gillette announced Atra Plus (the first razor with the patented Lubra-smooth lubricating strip) in 1985 just as BIC began to move into the United States from Canada with the BIC shaver for sensitive skin. A few months later, Gillette ushered in MicroTrac— the first disposable razor with an ultra-slim head. Gillette priced the MicroTrac lower than any other Gillette disposable razor.

The company claimed to have designed a "state-of-the-art" manufacturing process for MicroTrac. The process required less plastic, thus minimizing bulk and reducing manufacturing costs. Analysts claimed Gillette was trying to bracket the market with Atra Plus (with a retail price of $3.99 to $4.95) and MicroTrac ($.99) and protect its market share with products on both ends of the price and usage scale. Gillette also teased Wall Street with hints that, by the end of 1986, it would be introducing a "state-of-the-art" shaving system that could revolutionize the shaving business.

Despite these product innovations and introductions in the early 1980s, Gillette primarily focused its energies on its global markets and strategies. By 1985, Gillette marketed 800 products in more than 200 countries. The company felt a need at this time to coordinate its marketing efforts regionally and then globally. Unfortunately for Gillette's management team, others noticed its strong international capabilities. Ronald Perelman, chairman of the Revlon Group, attempted an unfriendly takeover in November 1986. To fend off the takeover, Gillette bought back 9.2 million shares of its stock from Perelman and saddled itself with additional long-term debt to finance the stock repurchase. Gillette's payment to Perelman increased the company's debt load from $827 million to $1.1 billion and put its debt-to-equity ratio at 70 percent. Gillette and Perelman signed an agreement preventing Perelman from attempting another takeover until 1996.

In 1988, just as Gillette returned its attention to new product development and global marketing, Coniston Partners, after obtaining 6 percent of Gillette's stock, engaged the company in a proxy battle for four seats on its 12-person board. Coniston's interest had been piqued by the Gillette-Perelman $549 million stock buyback and its payment of $9 million in expenses to Perelman. Coniston and some shareholders believed Gillette's board and management had repeatedly taken actions that had prohibited its stockholders from realizing their shares' full value. When the balloting concluded, Gillette's management won by a narrow margin—52 to 48 percent. Coniston made $13 million in the stock buyback program that Gillette offered to all shareholders, but Coniston agreed not to make another run at Gillette until 1991. This second takeover attempted forced Gillette to increase its debt load to $2 billion and pushed its total equity to negative $84.6 million.

More importantly, both takeover battles forced Gillette to wake up. Gillette closed or sold its Jafra Cosmetics operations in 11 countries and jettisoned weak operations such as Misco, Inc. (a computer supplies business), and S.T. Dupont (a luxury lighter, clock, and watch maker). The company also thinned

EXHIBIT 4   **Warner-Lambert's Product Lines by Company Division, 1988**

Ethical Pharmaceuticals	Gums and Mints	Other Products
Parke-Davis drug	Dentyne	Schick razors
Nonprescription Products	Sticklets	Ultrex razors
Benadryl	Beemans	Personal Touch
Caladryl	Trident	Tetra Aquarium
Rolaids	Freshen-up	
Sinutab	Bubblicious	
Listerex	Chiclets	
Lubraderm	Clorets	
Anusol	Certs	
Tucks	Dynamints	
Halls	Junior Mints	
Benylin	Sugar Daddy	
Listerine	Sugar Babies	
Listermint	Charleston Chew	
Efferdent	Rascals	
Effergrip		

its work force in many divisions, such as its 15 percent staff reduction at the Paper Mate pen unit. Despite this pruning, Gillette's sales for 1988 grew 13 percent to $3.6 billion, and profits soared 17 percent to $268 million.

Even though Gillette concentrated on fending off these takeover attempts, it continued to enhance its razor and blade products. In 1986, Gillette introduced the Contour Plus in its first pan-European razor launch. The company marketed Contour Plus with one identity and one strategy. In 1988, the company introduced Trac II Plus, Good News! Pivot Plus, and Daisy Plus—versions of its existing products with the Lubra-smooth lubricating strip.

Schick

Warner-Lambert's Schick division was the second major competitor in the wet-shaving business. Warner-Lambert, incorporated in 1920 under the name William R. Warner & Company, manufactured chemicals and pharmaceuticals. Numerous mergers and acquisitions over the past 70 years resulted in Warner-Lambert's involvement in developing, manufacturing, and marketing a widely diversified line of beauty, health, and well-being products. The company also became a major producer of mints and chewing gums, such as Dentyne, Sticklets, and Trident. Exhibit 4 presents a list of Warner-Lambert's products by division as of 1988.

Warner-Lambert entered the wet-shave business through a merger with Eversharp in 1970. Eversharp, a long-time competitor in the wet-shave industry, owned the Schick trademark and had owned the Paper Mate Pen Company before selling it to Gillette in 1954. Schick's razors and blades produced $180 million in revenue in 1987, or 5.2 percent of Warner-Lambert's worldwide sales. Refer to Exhibit 5 for operating results by division and Exhibit 6 for income statement and balance sheet data.

In 1989, Schick held approximately a 16.2 percent U.S. market share, down from its 1980 share of 23.8 percent. Schick's market share was broken down as

EXHIBIT 5   **Warner-Lambert's Net Sales and Operating Profit by Division, 1985–88**
             (In millions)

	Net Sales				Operating Profit (Loss)			
	1988	**1987**	**1986**	**1985**	**1988**	**1987**	**1986**	**1985**
Health care								
Ethical products	$1,213	$1,093	$ 964	$ 880	$420	$351	$246	$224
Nonprescription products	1,296	1,195	1,077	992	305	256	176	177
Total health care	$2,509	$2,288	$2,041	$1,872	$725	$607	$422	$401
Gums and mints	918	777	678	626	187	173	122	138
Other products*	481	420	384	334	92	86	61	72
Divested businesses								(464)
R&D					(259)	(232)	(202)	(208)
Net sales and operating profits	$3,908	$3,485	$3,103	$2,832	$745	$634	$599	$ (61)

*Other products includes Schick razors, which accounted for $180 million in revenue in 1987.
Source: *Warner-Lambert Company Annual Report,* 1987, and *Moody's Industrial Manual.*

follows: blade systems, 8.8 percent; disposable razors, 4.1 percent; and double-edged and injectors. 3.3 percent.

Schick's loss of market share in the 1980s occurred for two reasons. First, even though Schick pioneered the injector razor system (it controlled 80 percent of this market by 1979), it did not market a disposable razor until mid-1984—eight years after the first disposable razors appeared. Second, for years, Warner-Lambert had been channeling Schick's cash flow to its research and development in drugs.

In 1986, the company changed its philosophy; it allocated $70 million to Schick for three years and granted Schick its own sales force. Despite Schick's loss of market share, company executives believed they had "room to play catch up, especially by exploiting new technologies." In late 1988, Schick revealed it planned to conduct "guerrilla warfare" by throwing its marketing resources and efforts into new technological advances in disposable razors. As a result, Warner-Lambert planned to allocate the bulk of its $8 million razor advertising budget to marketing its narrow-headed disposable razor, Slim Twin, which it introduced in August 1988.

Schick believed the U.S. unit demand for disposable razors would increase to 55 percent of the market by the early 1990s from its 50 percent share in 1988. Schick executives based this belief on their feeling that men would rather pay 30 cents for a disposable razor than 75 cents for a refill blade. In 1988, Schick held an estimated 9.9 percent share of dollar sales in the disposable razor market.

Schick generated approximately 67 percent of its revenues overseas. Also, Schick earned higher profit margins on its nondomestic sales—20 percent versus its 15 percent domestic margin. Europe and Japan represented the bulk of Schick's international business, accounting for 38 percent and 52 percent, respectively, of 1988's overseas sales. Schick's European business consisted of 70 percent systems and 29 percent disposable razors, but Gillette's systems and disposable razor sales were 4.5 and 6 times larger than Schick's respective European sales.

EXHIBIT 6   **Warner-Lambert Income Statement and Balance Sheet Data, 1986–88**
(In thousands)

	1988	1987	1986
Net sales	$3,908,400	$3,484,700	$3,102,918
Cost of sales	1,351,700	1,169,700	1,052,781
Other expenses	2,012,100	1,819,800	1,616,323
Operating income	544,600	495,200	433,814
Other income	61,900	58,500	69,611
Earnings before taxes and interest	606,500	553,700	503,425
Interest expenses	68,200	60,900	66,544
Earnings before taxes	538,300	492,800	436,881
Income taxes	198,000	197,000	136,297
Nonrecurring item	—	—	8,400
Earnings after taxes	340,000	295,800	308,984
Retained earnings	1,577,400	1,384,100	1,023,218
Earnings per share	$ 5.00	$ 4.15	$ 4.18
Average common shares outstanding (in thousands)	68,035	71,355	73,985
Dividends paid/share	$ 2.16	$ 1.77	$ 1.59
Stock price range			
High	$ 79½	$ 87½	$ 63⅛
Low	59⅞	48¼	45
Assets			
Cash	$ 176,000	$ 24,100	$ 26,791
Receivables	525,200	469,900	445,743
Inventories	381,400	379,000	317,212
Other current assets	181,300	379,600	720,322
Total current assets	$1,263,900	$1,252,600	$1,510,068
Fixed assets, net	1,053,000	959,800	819,291
Other assets	385,300	263,500	186,564
Total assets	$2,702,800	$2,476,900	$2,515,923
Liabilities and Equity			
Current liabilities*	$1,025,200	$ 974,300	$ 969,806
Current portion long-term debt	7,100	4,200	143,259
Long-term debt	318,200	293,800	352,112
Equity	$ 998,600	$ 874,400	$ 907,322

*Includes current portion of long-term debt.
Source: *Moody's Industrial Manual.*

However, Schick dominated in Japan. Warner-Lambert held over 60 percent of Japan's wet-shave market. Although Japan had typically been an electric shaver market (55 percent of Japanese shavers use electric razors), Schick achieved an excellent record and reputation in Japan. Both Schick and Gillette entered the Japanese market in 1962; and their vigorous competition eventually drove Japanese competitors from the industry, which by 1988 generated $190 million in sales. Gillette's attempt to crack the market flopped because it tried to sell razors using its own salespeople, a strategy that failed because Gillette did not have the distribution network available to Japanese companies. Schick, meanwhile, chose to leave the distribution to Seiko Corporation. Seiko imported razors from the United States and then sold them to wholesalers nationwide. By 1988, Schick generated roughly 40 percent of its sales and 35 percent of its profits in Japan. Disposable razors accounted for almost 80 percent of those figures.

BIC Corporation

Marcel Bich founded the BIC Corporation in the United States in 1958, but its roots grew from France. In 1945, Bich, who had been the production manager for a French ink manufacturer, bought a factory outside Paris to produce parts for fountain pens and mechanical lead pencils. In his new business, Bich became one of the first manufacturers to purchase presses to work with plastics. With his knowledge of inks and experience with plastics and molding machines, Bich set himself up to become the largest pen manufacturer in the world. In 1949, Bich introduced his version of the modern ballpoint pen, originally invented in 1939, which he called BIC, a shortened, easy-to-remember version of his own name. He supported the pen with memorable, effective advertising; and its sales surpassed even his own expectations.

Realizing that a mass-produced, disposable ballpoint pen had universal appeal, Bich turned his attention to the United States. In 1958, he purchased the Waterman-Pen Company of Connecticut and then incorporated as Waterman-BIC Pen Corporation. The company changed its name to BIC Pen in 1971 and finally adopted the name BIC Corporation for the publicly owned corporation in 1982.

After establishing itself as the country's largest pen maker, BIC attacked another market—the disposable lighter market. When BIC introduced its lighter in 1973, the total disposable lighter market stood at only 50 million units. By 1984, BIC had become so successful at manufacturing and marketing its disposable lighters that Gillette, its primary competitor, abandoned the lighter market. Gillette sold its Cricket division to Swedish Match, Stockholm, manufacturer of Wilkinson razors. By 1989, the disposable lighter market had grown to nearly 500 million units, and BIC lighters accounted for 60 percent of the market.

Not just content to compete in the writing and lighting markets, BIC decided to enter the U.S. shaving market in 1976. A year earlier, the company had launched the BIC Shaver in Europe and Canada. BIC's entrance into the U.S. razor market started an intense rivalry with Gillette. The companies were not strangers to each other—for years they had competed for market share in the pen and lighter industries. However, razors were Gillette's primary business and an area where the company had no intention of relinquishing market share. But BIC established a niche in the U.S. disposable razor market.

BIC, like Gillette, frequently introduced new razor products and product enhancements. In January 1985, following a successful Canadian test in 1984, BIC announced the BIC Shaver for Sensitive Skin. BIC claimed 42 percent of the men surveyed reported they had sensitive skin, while 51 percent of those who had heavy beards reported they had sensitive skin. Thus, BIC believed there was a clear need for a shaver that addressed this special shaving problem. The $10 million ad campaign for the BIC Shaver for Sensitive Skin featured John McEnroe, a highly ranked and well-known tennis professional, discussing good and bad backhands and normal and sensitive skin. BIC repositioned the original BIC white shaver and the shaver men with normal skin should use, while it promoted the new BIC Orange as the razor for sensitive skin.

EXHIBIT 7   BIC's Net Sales and Income Before Taxes, 1986–88   *(In millions)*

	1988	1987	1986
Net sales			
Writing instruments	$118.5	$106.7	$ 91.7
Lighters	113.9	120.0	115.0
Shavers	51.9	47.1	49.6
Sport	10.6	16.8	11.3
Total	$294.9	$290.6	$267.6
Income (loss) before taxes			
Writing instruments	$ 16.7	$ 17.5	$ 15.0
Lighters	22.9	28.2	28.5
Shavers	9.4	8.5	8.0
Sport	(4.7)	(3.5)	(3.6)
Totals	$ 44.3	$ 50.7	$ 47.9

Source: *BIC Annual Report*, 1988 and 1989.

BIC also tried its commodity strategy on sailboards, car-top carriers, and perfume. In 1982, BIC introduced a sailboard model at about half the price of existing products. The product generated nothing but red ink. In April 1989, the company launched BIC perfumes with $15 million in advertising support. BIC's foray into fragrances was as disappointing as its sailboard commoditization attempt. Throughout the year, Parfum BIC lost money, forcing management to concentrate its efforts on reformulating its selling theme, advertising, packaging, and price points. Many retailers rejected the product, sticking BIC with expensive manufacturing facilities in Europe. BIC found that consumers' perceptions of commodities did not translate equally into every category. For example, many women cut corners elsewhere just to spend lavishly on their perfume. The last thing they wanted to see was their favorite scent being hawked to the masses.

Despite these failures, BIC Corporation was the undisputed king of the commoditizers. BIC's success with pens and razors demonstrated the upside potential of commoditization, while its failures with sailboards and perfumes illustrated the limitations. BIC concentrated its efforts on designing, manufacturing, and delivering the "best" quality products at the lowest possible prices. And although the company produced large quantities of disposable products (i.e., over 1 million pens a day), it claimed each product was invested with the BIC philosophy: "maximum service, minimum price."

One of BIC's greatest assets was its distribution and its strength in retail. The high profile the company enjoyed at supermarkets and drugstores enabled it to win locations in the aisles and display space at the checkout—the best positioning.

Even though BIC controlled only the No. 3 spot in the wet-shaving market by 1989, it had exerted quite an influence since its razors first entered the U.S. market in 1976. In 1988, BIC's razors generated $52 million in sales with a net income of $9.4 million and held a 22.4 percent share of the disposable razor market. Exhibits 7 and 8 present operating data by product line and income statement and balance sheet data.

EXHIBIT 8   BIC Corporation's Income Statement and Balance Sheet Data, 1986–88
                   (In thousands)

	1988	1987	1986
Net sales	$294,878	$290,616	$267,624
Cost of sales	172,542	165,705	147,602
Other expenses	81,023	73,785	67,697
Operating income	41,313	51,126	52,325
Other income	4,119	1,836	7,534
Earnings before taxes and interest	45,432	52,962	59,859
Interest expenses	1,097	2,301	11,982
Earnings before taxes	44,335	50,661	47,877
Income taxes	17,573	21,944	24,170
Extraordinary credit	—	—	2,486*
Utilization of operating loss			
Carry forward	2,800	—	—
Earnings after taxes	29,562	28,717	26,193
Retained earnings	159,942	142,501	121,784
Earnings per share	$ 2.44	$ 2.37	$ 2.16
Average common shares outstanding			
(in thousands)	12,121	12,121	12,121
Dividends paid/share	$ 0.75	$ 0.66	$ 0.48
Stock price range			
High	$ 30 3/8	$ 34 7/8	$ 35
Low	24 3/8	16 1/2	23 1/4
Assets			
Cash	$ 5,314	$ 4,673	$ 5,047
Certificates of deposit	3,117	803	6,401
Receivables, net	43,629	41,704	32,960
Inventories	70,930	59,779	50,058
Other current assets	37,603	47,385	34,898
Deferred income taxes	7,939	6,691	5,622
Total current assets	$168,532	$161,035	$134,986
Fixed assets, net	74,973	62,797	58,385
Total assets	$243,505	$223,832	$193,371
Liabilities and equity			
Current liabilities	$ 55,031	$ 54,034	$ 45,104
Current portion long-term debt	157	247	287
Long-term debt	1,521	1,511	1,789
Equity	$181,194	$164,068	$142,848

*Gain from elimination of debt.

Source: *Moody's Industrial Manual* and *BIC Annual Report.*

The introduction of the disposable razor revolutionized the industry and cut into system razor profits. However, despite the low profit margins in disposable razors and the fact that the industry leader, Gillette, emphasized razor-and-blade systems, BIC remained bullish on the disposable razor market. In 1988, BIC held a 22.4 percent share of the dollar sales in the disposable razor market. In 1989, a spokesperson for BIC claimed BIC "was going to stick to what consumers liked." The company planned to continue marketing only single-blade disposable shavers. BIC also stated that it planned to maintain its strategy of underpricing competitors, but it would also introduce improve-

EXHIBIT 9   **Swedish Match AB's Income Statement and Balance Sheet Data, 1986–88**
(In thousands of U.S. dollars)

	1988	1987	1986
Net sales	$2,814,662	$2,505,047	$1,529,704
Cost of sales	NA	NA	NA
Operating expenses	2,541,128	2,291,023	1,387,360
Other expenses	108,206	95,420	48,711
Earnings before taxes and interest	165,328	118,604	93,633
Interest expenses	5,386	19,084	21,618
Earnings before taxes	159,942	99,520	72,015
Income taxes	57,612	29,996	39,165
Earnings after taxes	102,330	69,524	32,850
Dividends paid/share	$ 0.53	$ 0.51	$ 1.75
Stock price range			
High	$ 22.53	$ 19.65	$ 66.75
Low	15.00	11.06	22.00
Assets			
Cash and securities	$ 159,616	$ 117,027	$ 323,993
Receivables	611,372	561,479	297,321
Inventories	421,563	415,116	258,858
Total current assets	$1,192,551	$1,093,622	$ 880,172
Fixed assets, net	707,664	671,409	397,411
Other assets	161,085	132,799	93,211
Total assets	$2,061,300	$1,897,830	$1,370,794
Liabilities and equity			
Current liabilities	$ 996,214	$ 905,778	$ 576,534
Current portion long-term debt			
Long-term debt	$ 298,505	$ 316,542	$ 244,118
Equity			

Source: *Moody's International Manual.*

ments such as the patented metal guard in its BIC Metal Shaver. Research revealed the BIC Metal Shaver provided some incremental, rather than substitute, sales for its shaver product line. BIC executives believed the BIC Metal Shaver would reach a 5 to 8 percent market share by 1990.

Wilkinson Sword

Swedish Match Holding Incorporated's subsidiary, Wilkinson Sword, came in as the fourth player in the U. S. market. Swedish Match Holding was a wholly owned subsidiary of Swedish Match AB, Stockholm. The parent company owned subsidiaries in the United States that imported and sold doors, produced resilient and wood flooring, and manufactured branded razors, blades, self-sharpening scissors, and gourmet kitchen knives. (Exhibit 9 presents income statement and balance sheet data for Swedish Match AB).

A group of sword smiths founded Wilkinson in 1772, and soldiers used the company's swords at Waterloo, in the charge of the Light Brigade, and in the Boer War. However, as the sword declined as a combat weapon, Wilkinson retreated to producing presentation and ceremonial swords. By 1890, Wilkinson's cutlers had begun to produce straight razors, and by 1898, it was producing safety razors similar to King Gillette's. When Gillette's blade became popular in England, Wilkinson made stroppers to resharpen used blades. Wilkinson failed in the razor market, however, and dropped out during World War II.

By 1954, Wilkinson decided to look again at the shaving market. Manufacturers used carbon steel to make most razor blades at that time, and such blades lost their serviceability rapidly due to mechanical and chemical damage. Gillette and other firms had experimented with stainless steel blades, but they had found that despite their longer-lasting nature, the blades did not sharpen well. But some men liked the durability; and a few small companies produced stainless steel blades.

Wilkinson purchased one such small German company and put Wilkinson Sword blades on the market in 1956. Wilkinson developed a coating for the stainless steel blades (in the same fashion that Gillette had coated the Super Blue Blade) that masked their rough edges, allowing the blades to give a comfortable shave and to last two to five times longer than conventional blades. Wilkinson called the new blade the Super Sword-Edge. Wilkinson introduced the blades in England in 1961 and in the United States in 1962, and they became a phenomenon. Schick and American Safety Razor followed a year later with their own stainless steel blades, the Krona-Plus and Personna. Gillette finally responded by late 1963 with its own stainless steel blade; and by early 1964, Gillette's blades were outselling Wilkinson, Schick, and Personna combined. Wilkinson, however, had forever changed the nature of the razor blade.

In 1988, Wilkinson Sword claimed to have a 4 percent share of the U.S. wet-shave market; and it was predicting a 6 percent share by mid-1990. Industry analysts, however, did not confirm even the 4 percent share; they projected Wilkinson's share to be closer to 1 percent. Wilkinson introduced many new products over the years, but they generally proved to be short-lived. The company never really developed its U.S. franchise.

However, in late 1988, Wilkinson boasted it was going to challenge the wet-shave category leader by introducing Ultra-Glide, its first lubricating shaving system. Wilkinson designed Ultra-Glide to go head-to-head with Gillette's Atra Plus and Schick's Super II Plus and Ultrex Plus. Wilkinson claimed Ultra-Glide represented a breakthrough in shaving technology because of an ingredient, hydromer, in its patented lubricating strip. According to Wilkinson, the Ultra-Glide strip left less residue on the face and provided a smoother, more comfortable shave by creating a cushion of moisture between the razor and the skin.

Wilkinson introduced Ultra-Glide in March 1989 and supported it with a $5 million advertising and promotional campaign (versus Atra Plus's $80 million multimedia investment in the United States only). Wilkinson priced Ultra-Glide 5 to 8 percent less than Atra Plus. Wilkinson was undaunted by Gillette's heavier advertising investment, and it expected to cash in on its rival's strong marketing muscle. Wilkinson did not expect to overtake Gillette but believed its drive should help it capture a double-digit U.S. market share within two to three years.

Many were skeptical about Wilkinson's self-predicted market share growth. One industry analyst stated, "Gillette dominates this business. Some upstart won't do anything." One Gillette official claimed his company was unfazed by Wilkinson. He was quoted as saying in late 1988, "They (Wilkinson) don't have a business in the U.S.; they don't exist."

EXHIBIT 10   **Gillette Shaving Evaluation Card**

INSTRUCTIONS: Please check one box in each column

Overall Evaluation of Shave	Freedom from Nicks and Cuts	Caution	Closeness	Smoothness	Comfort
☐ Excellent	☐ Excellent	☐ Exceptionally Safe	☐ Exceptionally Safe	☐ Exceptionally Smooth	☐ Exceptionally Comfortable
☐ Very Good	☐ Very Good	☐ Unusually Safe	☐ Very Close	☐ Very Smooth	☐ Very Comfortable
☐ Good	☐ Good	☐ Average	☐ Average	☐ Average Smoothness	☐ Average Comfort
☐ Fair	☐ Fair	☐ Slight Caution Needed	☐ Fair	☐ Slight Pull	☐ Slight Irritation
☐ Poor	☐ Poor	☐ Excessive Caution Needed	☐ Poor	☐ Excessive Pull	☐ Excessive Irritation

Source: The Gillette Company

Nonetheless, Gillette became enraged and filed legal challenges when Wilkinson's television ads for Ultra-Glide broke in May 1989. The ads stated Ultra-Glide's lubricating strip was six times smoother than Gillette's strip and that men preferred it to the industry leader's. All three major television networks had reservations about continuing to air the comparison commercials. CBS and NBC stated they were going to delay airing the company's ads until Wilkinson responded to questions they had about its ad claims. In an 11th-hour counterattack, Wilkinson accused Gillette of false advertising and of trying to monopolize the wet-shave market.

GILLETTE'S SOUTH BOSTON PLANT

Robert Squires left his workstation in the facilities engineering section of Gillette's South Boston manufacturing facility and headed for the shave test lab. He entered the lab area and walked down a narrow hall. On his right were a series of small cubicles Gillette had designed to resemble the sink area of a typical bathroom. Robert opened the door of his assigned cubicle precisely at his scheduled 10 A.M. time. He removed his dress shirt and tie, hanging them on a hook beside the sink. Sliding the mirror up as one would a window, Robert looked into the lab area. Rose McCluskey, a lab assistant, greeted him.

"Morning, Robert. I've got your things all ready for you." Rose reached into a recessed area on her side of the cubicle's wall and handed Robert his razor, shave cream, after-shave lotion, and a clean towel.

"Thanks. Anything new you've got me trying today?"

"You know I can't tell you that. It might spoil your objectivity. Here's your card." Rose handed Robert a shaving evaluation card (see Exhibit 10).

Robert had been shaving at the South Boston plant off and on for all of his 25 years with Gillette. He was one of 200 men who shaved every workday at the plant. Gillette used these shavers to compare its products' effectiveness with competitors' products. The shavers also conducted R&D testing of new products and quality control testing for manufacturing. An additional seven to eight panels of 250 men each shaved every day in their homes around the country, primarily conducting R&D shave testing.

Like Robert, each shaver completed a shave evaluation card following every shave. Lab assistants like Rose entered data from the evaluations to allow Gillette researchers to analyze the performance of each shaving device. If a product passed R&D hurdles, it became the responsibility of the marketing research staff to conduct consumer-use testing. Such consumer testing employed 2,000 to 3,000 men who tested products in their homes.

From its research, Gillette had learned that the average man had 30,000 whiskers on his face that grew at the rate of $1/2$ inch per month. He shaved 5.8 times a week and spent three or four minutes shaving each time. A man with a life span of 70 years would shave more than 20,000 times, spending 3,350 hours (130 days) removing $27 1/2$ feet of facial hair. Yet, despite all the time and effort involved in shaving, surveys found that if a cream were available that would eliminate facial hair and shaving, most men would not use it.

Robert finished shaving, marked his evaluation card, and slid it across the counter to Rose.

William Mazeroski, manager of the South Boston shave test lab, walked into the lab area carrying computer printouts with the statistical analysis of last week's shave test data.

Noticing Robert, William stopped. "Morning, Robert. How was your shave?"

"Pretty good. What am I using?"

"Robert, you are always trying to get me to tell you what we're testing! We have control groups and experimental groups. I can't tell you which you are in, but I was just looking at last week's results, and I can tell you that it looks like we are making progress. We've been testing versions since 1979, and I think we're about to get it right. Of course, I don't know if we'll introduce it or even if we can make it in large quantities, but it looks good."

PLANNING SESSION

Paul Hankins had called a meeting in his 37th-floor office in Boston's Prudential Center office building. Attending the meeting were Sarah Kale, vice president of marketing research; Brian Mullins, vice president, marketing, shaving and personal care group; and Scott Friedman, business director, blades and razors.

"The purpose of this meeting," Paul began, "is to begin formulating a new strategy for Gillette North Atlantic, specifically for our shaving products. I'm interested in your general thoughts and analysis. I want to begin to identify options and select a strategy to pursue."

Scott began by distributing copies of market share data (see Exhibits 11 and 12). He said "These are our U.S. share numbers through 1988. As you can see, Atra blades seem to have leveled off and Trac II blades are declining. Disposable razors now account for over 41 percent of the market in dollars and for over 50 percent of the market in terms of units. In fact, our projections would indicate that disposable razors will approach 100 percent of the market

EXHIBIT 11   Gillette Market Share of Dollar Sales, 1981–88

Product or Category	1981	1982	1983	1984	1985	1986	1987	1988
Atra blades	15.4%	17.3%	19.4%	18.7%	20.2%	20.9%	20.0%	20.5%
Trac II blades	17.5%	16.4%	15.2%	14.6%	14.1%	13.5%	11.8%	11.4%
Gillette blades	47.3%	48.9%	52.1%	54.2%	55.8%	57.1%	54.1%	56.0%
Gillette disposables	14.3%	15.4%	17.4%	20.0%	21.1%	22.7%	22.2%	24.0%
All disposables	23.0%	23.2%	27.0%	30.6%	32.7%	34.9%	38.5%	41.4%
Gillette disposables as percent all disposables	67.9%	66.9%	64.7%	65.7%	64.6%	64.2%	57.6%	58.4%
Gillette razors	50.3%	52.5%	54.9%	58.8%	62.2%	67.6%	64.1%	61.0%

Source: Prudential-Bache Securities.

EXHIBIT 12   Gillette System Cartridges   *(Dollar share of U.S. blade market)*

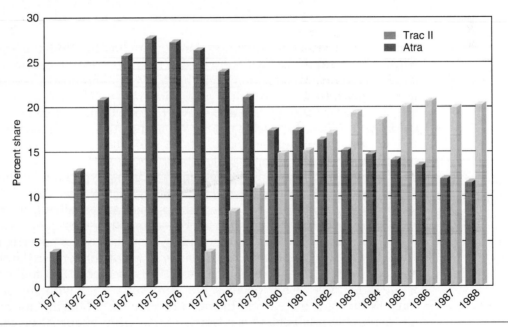

Source: The Gillette Company and Prudential-Bache Securities.

by the mid- to late 1990s given current trends. Although we have 56 percent of the blade market and 58 percent of the disposable razor market, our share of the disposable razor market has fallen. Further, you are aware that every 1 percent switch from our system razors to our disposable razors represents a loss of $10 million on the bottom line."

Sarah Kale observed that Gillette had contributed to this problem: "Well, as market leader, we never believed that the use of disposable razors would grow as it has. We went along with the trend, but we kept prices low on our disposable razors, which made profitability worse for both us and our competition because they had to take our price into consideration in setting their prices.

EXHIBIT 13   **Blade and Razor Media Spending—United States**

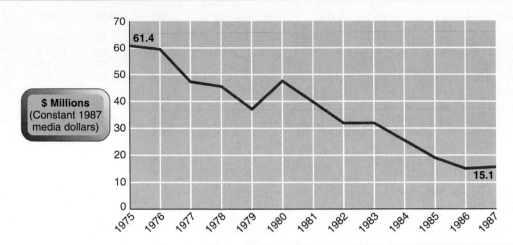

Source: The Gillette Company.

Then, to compensate for the impact on our profitability from the growth of the disposable razor market, we were raising the prices on our system razors. This made disposable razors even more attractive for more price-sensitive users and further fueled the growth of disposable razors. This has occurred despite the fact that our market research shows that men rate system shavers significantly better than disposable razors. We find that the weight and balance contributed by the permanent handle used with the cartridge contributes to a better shave."

"There's one other thing we've done," Scott added. "Look at this graph of our advertising expenditures in the U.S. over the 1980s (see Exhibit 13). In fact, in constant 1987 dollars, our advertising spending has fallen from $61 million in 1975 to about $15 million in 1987. We seem to have just spent what was left over on advertising. We are now spending about half of our advertising on Atra and half on Good News! Tentative plans call for us to increase the share going to Good News! Our media budget for 1988 was about $43 million. Further, we've tried three or four themes, but we haven't stuck with any one for very long. We're using the current theme, 'The Essence of Shaving' for both system ad disposable products. Our advertising has been about 90 percent product based and 10 percent image based."

"Well, Scott's right," Sarah noted, "but although share of voice is important, share of mind is what counts. Our most recent research shows a significant difference in how we are perceived by male consumers based on their age. Men over 40 still remember Gillette, despite our reduced advertising, from their youth. Younger men's views can be summed up simply—twin-blade, blue, and plastic."

"We have a 'steel' man and a 'plastic' man. In fact, for males between 15 and 19, BIC is better known than Gillette with respect to shaving. Younger men in general, those under 30, these 'plastic' men, feel all shavers are the same. Older men and system users feel there is a difference."

"We've always had a male focus and women identify the Gillette name with men and shaving, even those who use our products marketed to women. You know that there are more women wet shavers than men in the U.S. market, about 62 million versus 55 million. However, due to seasonality and lower frequency of women's shaving, the unit volume used by women is only about one third that of the volume used by men. Women use about 8 to 12 blades a year versus 25 to 30 for men. It is still very consistent for us to focus on men."

"Well, we've got plenty of problems on the marketing side, but we also have to remember that we are part of a larger corporation with its own set of problems," Brian suggested. "We're only 30 percent or so of sales, but we are 60 percent of profits. And, given the takeover battles, there is going to be increased pressure on the company to maintain and improve profitability. That pressure has always been on us, but now it will be more intense. If we want to develop some bold, new strategy, we are going to have to figure out where to get the money to finance it. I'm sure the rest of the corporation will continue to look to us to throw off cash to support diversification."

"We've got to come up with a new strategy. What do you think our options are, Scott?" Paul asked.

"Well, I think we're agreed that the 'do nothing' option is out. If we simply continue to do business as usual, we will see the erosion of the shaving market's profitability as disposable razors take more and more share. We could accept the transition to disposable razors and begin to try to segment the disposable razor market based on performance. You might call this the 'give-up' strategy. We would be admitting that disposable razors are the wave of the future. There will obviously continue to be shavers who buy only based on price, but there will also be shavers who will pay more for disposable razors with additional benefits, such as lubricating strips or movable heads. In other words, we could try to protect the category's profitability by segmenting the market and offering value to those segments willing to pay for it. We would de-emphasize system razors."

"Or, we could try to turn the whole thing around. We could develop a strategy to slow the growth of disposable razors and to reinvigorate the system razor market."

"How does the new razor system fit into all this?" Paul asked.

"I'm pleased that we have continued to invest in R&D despite our problems and the takeover battles," Brian answered. "Reports from R&D indicate that the new shaver is doing well in tests. But it will be expensive to take to market and to support with advertising. Further, it doesn't make any sense to launch it unless it fits in with the broader strategy. For example, if we decide to focus on disposable razors, it makes no sense to launch a new system razor and devote resources to that."

"What's the consumer testing indicating?" asked Scott.

"We're still conducting tests," Sarah answered, "but so far the results are very positive. Men rate the shave superior to both Atra or Trac II and superior to our competition. In fact, I think we'll see that consumers rate the new shaver as much as 25 percent better on average. The independently spring-mounted twin blades deliver a better shave, but you know we've never introduced a product until it was clearly superior in consumer testing on every dimension."

"OK. Here's what I'd like to do," Paul concluded. "I'd like for each of us to devote some time to developing a broad outline of a strategy to present at our next meeting. We'll try to identify and shape a broad strategy then that we can begin to develop in detail over the next several months. Let's get together in a week, same time. Thanks for your time."

REFERENCES Adams, Russell B., Jr. *King Gillette: The Man and His Wonderful Shaving Device*. Boston: Little, Brown and Company, 1978.

Bic Annual Report, 1989.

Caminiti, Susan. "Gillette Gets Sharp," *Fortune*, May 8, 1989, p. 84.

Dewhurst, Peter. "BICH=BIC," *Made in France International*, Spring 1981, pp. 38–41.

Dunkin, A., L. Baum and L. Therrein. "This Takeover Artist Wants to be a Makeover Artist, Too," *Business Week*, December 1, 1986, pp. 106, 110.

Dun's Million Dollar Directory, 1989.

Fahey, Alison, and Pat Sloan. "Gillette: $80M to Rebuild Image," *Advertising Age*, October 31, 1988, pp. 1, 62.

———. "Kiam Gets Some Help: Grey Sharpens Remington Ads," *Advertising Age*, November 13, 1989, p. 94.

———. "Wilkinson Cuts In," *Advertising Age*, November 28, 1988, p. 48.

Gillette Annual Corporate Reports, 1985–1988.

Hammonds, Keith. "At Gillette Disposable Is a Dirty Word," *Business Week*, May 29, 1989, pp. 54–55.

———. "How Ron Perelman Scared Gillette into Shape," *Business Week*, October 12, 1987, pp. 40–41.

Jervey, Gay. "Gillette and BIC Spots Taking on Sensitive Subject," *Advertising Age*, March 18, 1985, p. 53.

———. "Gillette, Wilkinson Heat up Disposable Duel," *Advertising Age*, June 10, 1985, p. 12.

———. "New Blade Weapons for Gillette-BIC War," *Advertising Age*, November 5, 1984, pp. 1, 96.

Kiam, Victor. "Remington's Marketing and Manufacturing Strategies," *Management Review*, February 1987, pp. 43–45.

———. "Growth Strategies at Remington," *Journal of Business Strategy*, January–February 1989, pp. 22–26.

Kummel, C. M., and J. E. Klompmaker. "The Gillette Company—Safety Razor Division." In *Strategic Marketing: Cases and Applications*, ed. D. W. Cravens and C. W. Lamb. Homewood, Ill.: Richard D. Irwin, 1980, pp. 324–45.

McGeehan, Patrick. "Gillette Sharpens its Global Strategy," *Advertising Age*, April 25, 1988, pp. 2, 93.

Newport, John Paul. "The Stalking of Gillette," *Fortune*, May 23, 1988, pp. 99–101.

North American Philips Corporation Annual Report, 1987.

Pereira, Joseph. "Gillette's Next-Generation Blade to Seek New Edge in Flat Market," *The Wall Street Journal*, April 7, 1988, p. 34.

Shore, Andrew. *Gillette Report*. New York: Shearson Lehman Hutton, October 19, 1989.

———. *Gillette Company Update*. New York: Prudential-Bache Securities, May 18, 1990.

Raissman, Robert. "Gillette Pitches New Throwaway," *Advertising Age*, July 9, 1984, p. 12.

"Razors and Blades," *Consumer Reports*, May 1989, pp. 300–4.

Rothman, Andrea. "Gillette, in a Shift, to Emphasize Cartridge Blades over Disposables," *The Wall Street Journal*, November 18, 1988, p. B6.

Sacharow, Stanley. *Symbols of Trade*. New York: Art Direction Book Company, 1982.

Sloan, Pat, "Marschalk Brains Land Braun," *Advertising Age*, March 18, 1985, p. 53.

———. "Remington Gets the Edge on Gillette," *Advertising Age*, May 16, 1988, pp. 3, 89.

Sutor, Ruthanne. "Household Personal Care Products," *Financial World*, December 27, 1988.

The Europa World Year Book 1990, vol. II.

Trachtenberg, Jeffrey A. "Styling for the Masses," *Forbes*, March 10, 1986, pp. 152–53.

Warner-Lambert Annual Corporate Report, 1987.

Weiss, Gary. "Razor Sharp: Gillette to Snap Back from a Dull Stretch," *Barron's*, August 25, 1986, pp. 15, 37.

EASTMAN KODAK VERSUS FUJI PHOTO FILM CO., LTD.

H. Donald Hopkins, Temple University

"I wonder how Fuji will react," mused Frank Harris, analyst for Morris Stinson Brokers and a specialist on Eastman Kodak stock. He was referring to the planned introduction of Eastman Kodak's photo compact disc due out in March 1992. Kodak's photo CD was a system of electronic photography allowing prints to be stored on a compact disc and shown on a television or a computer. Fuji and Kodak were very sensitive to each other's competitive moves, particularly since Fuji had started to gain headway in the U.S. market with its distinctive bright green boxes of film, and Kodak had started to gain inroads into the Japanese market long dominated by Fuji. Eastman Kodak, a U.S.-based company, had sales of over $19 billion and was the world's largest maker of film and photography products. Fuji Photo was an $8 billion company and Japan's leading producer of film and camera products.

THE KODAK-FUJI RIVALRY

When Fuji Photo Film Co. began selling film in the United States, Kodak did not take its new rival seriously. Kodak believed Fuji's film colors were unrealistically bright, and the Fuji name was not well known by film buyers. Even so, by 1990, Fuji had a 10 percent share of the U.S. market for camera film. Two of the most fascinating episodes of rivalry between these now archrivals were referred to as the "Battle of the MBAs" and the "Battle of the Blimps."

Battle of the MBAs

The University of Rochester is located in Kodak's headquarters' city of Rochester, New York. The university had received a significant portion of its endowment from George Eastman, Kodak's founder. In the 1980s and early 1990s, Kodak donated $5 million to the university, the majority of which was designated for support of the William E. Simon School of Business. Over the years, Kodak had paid for scores of its employees to enroll in the school's MBA program. In 1987, to the consternation of Eastman Kodak officials, the Simon school accepted a student named Tsuneo Sakai for its MBA class starting in September; Sakai was the planner of new imaging products for Fuji Photo Film Company.

According to news reports, Eastman Kodak officials pressured the university to rescind its acceptance of Sakai. To try to smooth the situation, the university arranged for Sakai to attend the Massachusetts Institute of Technology's business school. University of Rochester officials were said to be concerned Kodak would withdraw "a significant number of students" from its MBA program if Sakai enrolled. Word got out, however, and reacting to criticism of its decision, the university decided to readmit Sakai. Kodak's CEO in a letter to university trustees said, "Our actions were seen by some as an infringement upon academic integrity, which was certainly not our intent."[1] Kodak officials supposedly were concerned that confidential information about Kodak's products and plans might be disclosed to Sakai during class discussions. Following the university's readmission decision, a Kodak spokesman said the company respected the university's decision and would wait to see if Sakai enrolled before deciding on any action.

In 1988, Fuji funded an endowed scholarship at the Rochester Institute of Technology (RIT) for photography students. Kodak was a large contributor to RIT, having donated some $4 to $8 million over 10 years. The Fuji scholarship was to be devoted solely to photography, the first of its kind at the school. A Fuji spokeswoman said RIT was picked "because of its reputation, not because it was in Rochester."

Battle of the Blimps

On several summer days in 1987, Tokyo residents could see two large blimps, one Fuji bright green and the other traditional Kodak yellow, hovering over downtown Tokyo. The mock battle for "air supremacy" symbolized the mounting competitive rivalry and marketing war between the world's two largest film companies. Kodak, piqued from observing the green Fuji blimp flying over sporting events in the United States and Europe, decided to give Fuji a taste of its own promotional tactics in Japan and fly its blimp within sight of Fuji's Tokyo headquarters. In August 1986, Kodak leased the only available blimp in Japan, decorated it in Kodak's traditional yellow emblazoned with Kodak's name and trademarks, and flew it within sight of Fuji headquarters in Tokyo. According to a securities analyst who happened to be talking on the telephone to people in Fuji's finance department when the first sighting occurred, "They were furious."

What ensued could be described as "blimp dogfights." Fuji retaliated by flying its European blimp to Japan to do "battle" with Kodak's blimp. Several months later, in November 1986, the Fuji and Kodak blimps had a "dogfight" over nearby sporting events. Fuji was sponsoring a baseball series between American and Japanese all-stars while Kodak was sponsoring a judo tournament a short distance away. The manager of Fuji's advertising department, Hidenobu Miyata, complained that the Kodak blimp was seriously near Fuji's blimp. He claimed the yellow aircraft refused to comply with requests to retreat. Miyata said, "I think they were being a little too aggressive not to back off. We felt like Kodak was up for a fight."[2]

Kodak, on the other hand, accused Fuji of intentionally scheduling its blimp's flight over the baseball series to compete with Kodak's blimp. Toshio Nakano, manager of public relations for Kodak Japan, said, "So why did they wait until now? I don't call it a gentleman's act. It's nasty. It seems to me this is a hit-and-run operation on their part."[3] On numerous occasions in 1987, Tokyo pedestrians could see both blimps hovering in the skies over Tokyo. In January 1987, Kodak Japan sent out its customary Japanese New Year's greeting

---

[1]*The Wall Street Journal*, September 14, 1987, p. 16.

[2]*The Wall Street Journal*, December 30, 1986, p. A1.

[3]Ibid.

cards; the scene chosen for the card was a Kodak blimp with Mt. Fuji in the background.

The blimp battle had its roots in 1984 when Fuji outbid Kodak and spent $7 million to become the official film of the 1984 Los Angeles Olympics. The Fuji blimp was flown over the Olympic grounds. Kodak responded by buying over 100 TV ads on the network that telecast the games. "If you watched the Olympics on American TV, you never saw the Fuji blimp," said William Reyea, a securities analyst in Tokyo. "It was part of the contract when they bought 102 ads."[4] To this, a Kodak spokesman replied, "Absolute nonsense. We respect the right of TV producers to cover any event as they see fit." Kodak was the official film for the 1988 Olympics in Seoul, paying a reported $8 million for the rights, and stationed its blimp overhead during scheduled sporting events.

ME-TOO TACTICS

Regardless of what set off the "Battle of the Blimps," the Fuji surprise at the 1984 Los Angeles Olympics caused Kodak to start scrutinizing Fuji's actions. Fuji had increased its market share in the United States from 2 percent to 10 percent in photographic film and paper, although much of the increase came at the expense of weaker firms, such as 3M and Agfa-film, which Fuji targeted to avoid making Kodak feel threatened. Researchers in Rochester painstakingly analyzed Fuji's films to understand their attributes. "It's me-too technology," said one Kodak technical analyst. "We do what Fuji does. We're obsessed with Fuji."[5] Supersaturated colors were one attribute of Fuji film for years. Kodak thought the colors were unrealistically bright. However, when Kodak market researchers learned some customers liked Fuji's film, Kodak introduced its VR-G series that offered colors just as bright.

When researching Fuji's productivity, Kodak discovered Fuji's sales per employee were nearly four times higher than Kodak's.[6] To close the gap, Kodak launched a major internal effort to train workers in problem-solving, Japanese-style quality control, and how to improve production methods. It further studied other aspects of Fuji's performance and began benchmarking Kodak performance against Fuji performance. Wherever Fuji's performance was better, Kodak began efforts to match Fuji. A Fuji Photo USA official, commenting on Kodak's scrutiny of Fuji's moves and performance, said, "I'd just as soon they go back to not paying attention to us. I don't need that kind of flattery."[7]

BATTLE OF THE THROWAWAYS

Kodak and Fuji announced in February 1987 plans to introduce throwaway cameras. Kodak beat Fuji to the punch by announcing its camera one day before Fuji had scheduled a news conference for the same purpose. Kodak's camera was called the Fling, while Fuji's was called the Fujicolor Quick Snap.

---

[4]Ibid., p. A12.

[5]*Business Week*, February 23, 1987, p. 138.

[6]Ibid.

[7]Ibid.

With both versions, the entire camera was sent to a photo finisher instead of just the film. In a previous episode of one-upmanship (or being quicker on the draw) in 1983, Fuji had stolen Kodak's thunder by introducing a new series of films immediately before Kodak did likewise.

MOVE AND COUNTERMOVE

Following Fuji's entry into the U.S. market, Kodak decided in 1984 to stake out a strategic position in the $1.5 billion Japanese market for film and paper. While Kodak had sold its products in Japan for many years, it had never given the Japanese market much attention. From 1984 to 1990, Kodak spent an estimated $500 million building its base in the Japanese photographic film and papers markets. The company created a new subsidiary for Japan (Kodak Japan) and increased its Japan-based work force from 12 to 4,500. Kodak had to contend with Fuji's entrenched market position and dominant technical process. Fuji's strategy in Japan was to match Kodak on quality, surpass Kodak in high-speed color films, and capitalize on its dominant position in major Japanese film-processing labs. Fuji controlled about 250 labs to Kodak's less than 150 in 1985. These labs were the main customers for photographic paper.

One element of Kodak's drive into Japan was to stay on top of Japanese R&D in photographic technology by entering into joint ventures with a variety of Japanese partners, developing its own R&D center, and opening a technical assistance center to help customers. For example, Kodak bought 10 percent of a 35mm Japanese camera manufacturer and Kodak's Verbatim floppy disk subsidiary operated a joint venture with Mitsubishi Chemical Industries.

A second element of Kodak's strategy in Japan was to gain greater control over the distribution of its own products. Kodak bought Kusuda Business Machines, which had been marketing Kodak's micrograph and business imaging systems in Japan. Film sales in Japan had been handled by a Japanese firm, Nagase & Co.; in 1986, Kodak increased its control over distribution and marketing by forming a new joint venture company called Kodak-Nagase. As a result, Kodak got shelf space and displays in the 30,000 to 60,000 camera stores that sold most of Japan's film. However, Kodak was largely stymied in getting into the "mom- and-pop" stores that stocked only one brand of film; those stores overwhelmingly preferred to stock the best-selling Fuji film.

A third element of Kodak's strategy in Japan was its willingness to trim its prices to match (or sometimes beat) Fuji's price. In the United States, Kodak film always sold at a premium over Fuji film.

The Japanese rail network (which was served by thousands of small kiosks that mostly sold only Fuji film) was especially hard for Kodak to crack. To get its products into these kiosks, Kodak had to work with up to four agents, including the kiosk operator, real estate agent, and wholesaler. Usually, regardless of Kodak's pitch, Fuji was given a chance to match or beat any offer Kodak made.

One of Kodak's new products introduced in Japan to combat Fuji's lead in film processing and paper sales was the minilab. These were intended to chip away at Fuji's 100-plus advantage in large labs. Fuji fought back by offering bigger enlargement sizes than the minilabs. Recently, Fuji had started to introduce its own minilabs. On two occasions, Kodak Japan had been able to deny shelf space to Fuji because it had products that Fuji did not have—disposable and panoramic disposable cameras. Except for these two occasions, retailers in Japan always devoted more shelf space to displaying Fuji products than Kodak products.

Kodak apparently had the technology for the panoramic cameras for years but didn't see a market for it. Kodak Japan pushed the product since the Japanese liked to take pictures of large groups. William Jack, vice president of Kodak Japan, noted, "When the Japanese have golf outings, they often want everyone lined up for a group picture, and getting everyone in with a conventional camera is quite difficult."[8] The waterproof disposable had been a hit with Japanese youth who liked to snorkel; disposable cameras were the central thrust of Kodak's youth-oriented advertising in Japan.

On the promotional front, Kodak Japan had taken on Fuji in a "battle of who has the biggest neon signs." Kodak won by constructing a gigantic yellow sign that took several years to complete; the sign was located in downtown Tokyo at the Japanese equivalent of Times Square.

Kodak claimed its market share had gone up in the amateur color film market in Japan. The *Japan Economic Journal (JEJ)*, however, published data showing Kodak with 10 percent of the color film market in 1989 versus 13 percent in 1987. *JEJ* also said Fuji had gone from 71 percent to 73 percent and Konica from 16 percent to 17 percent during the same period. Kodak's sales of all products in Japan had increased 600 percent to about $1.3 billion during the 1987–89 period.

THE U.S. PHOTOGRAPHIC MARKET

Overall market growth for photographic products in the United States had been sluggish and was expected to remain slow for the foreseeable future:[9]

	1984	1985	1986	1987	1988
Still camera unit sales (in millions)	17.0	17.8	16.4	18.7	17.8
Film sales (millions of rolls)	610	667	694	781	811
Photofinishing (in millions)	$3,500	$3,700	$4,000	$4,400	$4,800

In 1990, *Standard & Poor's Industry Surveys* offered the following description of the U.S. photographic industry:[10]

> About 17.8 million cameras were sold to U.S. dealers in 1988 (latest available) down 4.8 percent from the year before. Demand continued to be strong for lens-shutter 35mm cameras, which accounted for more than half of industry dollar volume. . . . Gains for lens-shutter cameras have come largely at the expense of higher-end 35mm single-lens reflex (SLRs) and lower-end disc cameras. Unit

---

[8]*The Wall Street Journal*, December 7, 1990, p. B7.
[9]Ibid.
[10]*Standard & Poor's Industry Surveys*, March 15, 1990, p. 49.

sales of the sophisticated and expensive SLRs fell about 6 percent in 1988, to approximately 1.5 million, accounting for only 8.4 percent of industry unit volume, versus 14.7 percent of that volume four years earlier. However, SLRs represented 23.6 percent of the dollar value of industry camera sales in 1988, reflecting their higher price. The rate of decline in SLR unit sales slowed in 1988, after a 16 percent drop in 1987.

The market share, in units, of disc cameras plunged to just 5.6 percent in 1988 from 27.1 percent in 1984, when 1.0 million of the pocket-size cameras were sold to dealers. Due to their lower price, these cameras accounted for only 1.9 percent of the dollar value of cameras sold. Weak prospects for disc cameras were indicated by Eastman Kodak's announcement in early 1988 that it was suspending production of this type of camera.

Sales of instant cameras have also been fading. In 1988, according to PMA (Photo Marketing Association International), about 2.1 million instant cameras were sold to U.S. dealers, down from 2.7 million the year before. Instant cameras represented 11.8 percent of industry unit volume and 7.8 percent of dollar value. As recently as 1983, about 4 million instant cameras were sold, at a time when Eastman Kodak and Polaroid were both in the market. Eastman Kodak withdrew from this segment in early 1986 following a court ruling that the company had infringed upon Polaroid patents. . . .

Meanwhile, cartridge camera sales totaled about 5.6 million units, down about 7 percent from the year before. Cartridge cameras accounted for 31 percent of industry unit volume, but only about 4.8 percent of dollar volume.

According to PMA, 811 million rolls of film were purchased in the United States during 1988, up about 4 percent from the year before. Film for 35mm cameras was the most popular format (61 percent), followed by cartridge (16 percent), instant (11 percent), and disc (11 percent). Not surprisingly, 35mm film also provided the bulk of the industry's processing volume, accounting for 75 percent of the 15.43 billion conventional exposures processed in 1988. In comparison, prior to the fast sales of "point and shoot" cameras, 35mm film represented just 34 percent of processing volume in 1980 and 12.4 percent in 1975, according to PMA. Cartridge film represented 15 percent of processing volume in 1987 followed by disc film at 7 percent. The PMA estimates that color print developing accounted for 93 percent of the 15.4 billion conventional exposures processed in 1988, followed by slide (4.5 percent) and black-and-white print developing (2.6 percent). (Note: Some of PMA's numbers may be only for the amateur photography market, excluding professional activity.)

Stand-alone minilabs accounted for an estimated 28.9 percent of the retail dollars spent on photo processing in 1988, down slightly from 1987's 29.4 percent. Another 22.6 percent of photo-processing sales were made through drugstores, followed by discounter/mass merchandisers (15.4 percent), camera stores (13.5 percent), and a variety of others (19.6 percent), according to the PMA.

Along with slow growth rates, great overcapacity had put pressure on prices. Fuji added film production lines to its large paper factory in Tilburg, Netherlands, and built its first U.S. manufacturing plant in South Carolina in 1990 (though this plant was initially scheduled to produce sensitized plates for offset printing, not film or paper, it was expected to add these if Fuji's U.S. sales warranted). Fuji was not the first Japanese photographic firm to build a plant in the United States; Konica had built a manufacturing plant for photographic paper in Greensboro, North Carolina, in 1988. In addition, Polaroid had increased the fight for shelf space with its entry in 1989 into conventional photography with a film called One-Film; this film was an all-purpose film that eliminated the need for consumers to choose between the vast array of film types available. Even though it had been well received by large U.S. retail chains, neither Kodak nor Fuji had responded.

Other film competitors in the United States included Fotomat, a subsidiary of Konishiroko; 3M's Scotch Brand; Agfa-film of West Germany; and several private-label brands. GAF withdrew in the late 1980s due to declining margins. Kodak commanded about 80 percent of the U.S. film market and Fuji about 10 percent.

A PROFILE OF EASTMAN KODAK

Kodak has been described as large, lumbering, elephantine, and bureaucratic. Because of its traditionally paternalistic employment practices, it was sometimes called the "Great Yellow Father." Kodak, along with Xerox, was a major employer in the upstate New York city of Rochester, where its headquarters and plants spread over 3,000 acres. The company ranked 18th on the 1991 *Fortune 500* list, with sales of $19.4 billion and 133,200 employees worldwide. Exhibit 1 contains a five-year summary of Eastman Kodak's operating performance.

The company had business interests in four areas: (1) photographic imaging (film, cameras, and photographic papers); (2) chemicals; (3) information products (microfilm, copiers, printers, and graphic arts products); and (4) healthcare products (X-ray film, medical imaging, and diagnostic testing devices such as blood analyzers). Nearly 40 percent of total sales came from the company's core business in photographic imaging.

Eastman Kodak's most exciting new photographic product was its photo CD system scheduled for introduction in 1992. Photo CD combined the best attributes of photography (an unmatched ability to capture images using affordable cameras and film) with the best attributes of electronics (efficient storage, ready manipulation, and ease of transmission). The photo CD system allowed users to have their 35mm negatives transferred to compact discs by photofinishers and then shown on home television by using a special photo CD player that could also play audio CDs; the photo CD players started at prices under $400. The company's strategy for the 1990s was to set the standards and lead the way in film-based digital imaging. Eastman Kodak management believed there were vast opportunities to take the same features and technologies used in its photo CD system and apply them to products and systems in medicine, education, manufacturing, and commercial businesses.

Company History

George Eastman, Kodak's founder, sold his first camera in 1883. Kodak was the first fully integrated photographic company in the world. Its motto was, "You press the button and we do the rest." From the 1880s until the 1930s, Kodak pioneered in the creation of markets for black- and-white films and papers. In the 1930s, Kodak introduced color film and then over the next 50 years marketed every conceivable application of color imaging to customers around the world.

Though Kodak's share of the film market was about 80 percent in 1990, its share of film processing was only about 15 percent because of a 1954 Justice Department consent decree that required the company to unbundle the sale of

EXHIBIT 1   **Highlights of Eastman Kodak 's Financial and**
                   Operating Performance, 1986–90   *(Dollars in millions)*

	1990	1989	1988	1987	1986
Income Statement Data					
Sales	$18,908	$18,398	$17,034	$13,305	$11,550
Earnings before income taxes	1,257	925	2,236	1,984	598
Net earnings	703	529	1,397	1,178	374
Return on sales	3.7%	2.9%	8.2%	8.9%	3.2%
Return on stockholders' equity	10.5%	7.9%	21.8%	19.0%	5.9%
Balance Sheet Data					
Current assets	$ 8,608	$ 8,591	$ 8,684	$ 6,791	$ 5,857
Properties at cost	17,648	16,774	15,667	13,789	12,919
Accumulated depreciation	8,670	8,146	7,654	7,126	6,643
Total assets	24,125	23,652	22,964	14,698	12,994
Current liabilities	7,163	6,573	5,850	4,140	3,811
Long-term borrowings	6,989	7,376	7,779	2,382	981
Shareholders' equity	6,737	6,642	6,780	6,013	6,388
Supplemental Information					
Sales					
Imaging	$ 7,128	$ 6,998	$ 6,642	$ 6,206	$ 8,352
Information	4,140	4,200	3,937	3,494	
Chemicals	3,588	3,522	3,123	2,635	2,378
Health	4,349	4,009	3,597	1,206	1,056
R&D expenditures	1,329	1,253	1,147	992	1,059
Employees in U.S.	80,350	82,850	87,900	81,800	83,600
Employees worldwide	134,450	137,750	145,300	124,400	121,450

Notes: 1990 earnings before taxes reflects $888 million for litigation judgment that reduced net earnings by $564. 1989 earnings reflect restructuring costs of $875 million that reduced net earnings by $549 million.
Source: *Eastman Kodak*, 1990.

film and film development. Previously, when a customer bought Kodak film, the price of development was part of the price of the film; when a roll of film was finished it would be sent by the customer to a Kodak processing lab at no extra cost. As a result of the consent decree, Kodak lost its monopoly grip on film processing. Other companies began marketing photographic papers, processing equipment, and chemicals for film processing to the host of film developing operations that quickly sprang up after the consent decree. In the early 1990s, Kodak's share of the total market for all types of film and photographic supplies (not including cameras) was close to 50 percent.

Kodak's dominant industry position stemmed from its leadership in film technology. Of all its photographic products, film was its premier profit maker. Only recently had a broad-scope competitor such as Fuji been able to challenge it in this area. Previously, Kodak had almost total mastery of the photographic industry and had kept ahead of every other competitor in virtually every dimension of photography except instant photography, where Polaroid was the leader. Part of the reason for this was that Kodak's bundling of film sales and film processing before the 1954 consent decree posed a huge entry barrier and discouraged potential competitors from pursuing innovations in color film technology.

Since the consent decree, Kodak had preserved its dominant leadership position by holding new innovations in reserve. When a competitor attempted entry against Kodak with a better product it had spent large sums to develop, Kodak would quickly incorporate the technological improvements and product innovations it had been holding in reserve to outmatch the competitor's new product offering. In the early 1960s, a joint venture between Du Pont and Bell & Howell to develop a color film research program failed because in every instance where the partnership was able to improve its film, Kodak would use its reservoir of product improvements and superior technological skills to promptly incorporate into its own products essentially the same features that Du Pont/Bell & Howell came up with. In 1961, when the joint venture partners decided to introduce a new film based on tens of millions of dollars of research, Kodak retaliated with Kodachrome II, a far better quality film. The Du Pont/Bell & Howell film was withdrawn from production before it even reached the market.

Frequently, competitors tried to compete with Kodak by charging lower prices. However, price-cutting strategies met with only limited success because most consumers were unwilling to accept films that might be of lower quality. Fuji was able to overcome this perception somewhat by stressing a quality brand image while charging slightly lower prices. In 1991, the other competitors in the industry were mostly niche players focusing on a small customer group wishing to avoid supersaturated colors, very high resolution, or Kodak. Polaroid's niche was instant photography, and Fotomat's niche was speedy film processing.

Kodak's Systems Approach

Kodak's product development and marketing strategy in the photographic market relied on a "systems approach" whereby each Kodak camera utilized a unique film format packaged in a cartridge or magazine compatible with and designed specifically for that camera system. Kodak's systems approach got Kodak camera buyers to use the entire array of Kodak products in the system and made it harder to combine use of rivals' products with Kodak's products. Rival film makers that wanted to compete for the film business of Kodak camera owners had to make a film and package it in a cartridge or magazine that matched what each Kodak camera required.

Several of Kodak's systems had been major market successes. The Instamatic sold 10 million cameras in the first 26 months after introduction in 1963. In 1972, Kodak introduced a smaller version of the Instamatic called the Pocket Instamatic. It was estimated that by 1975 Kodak had sold 60 million Instamatics, while competitors had sold just 10 million clones. The company sustained its dominant industry position by making surprise changes in camera design and film requirements. Unsuspecting rivals were then forced, on short notice, to invest in retooling complex production equipment and redesigning their products to keep pace. Kodak rarely announced product developments ahead of time, preferring to surprise competitors and capture a lead of several months or a year or more in the marketplace. Kodak's competitors typically found themselves playing catch-up.

To deflect criticism and possible antitrust action, Kodak licensed its camera systems to rivals. However, probably the main motive for licensing was that it increased the number of cameras that could use Kodak's films (the company's most profitable product).

Not all of Kodak's products and systems were successful in the marketplace, however. Its instant photography system, its disc system, and its 8mm camcorder all encountered problems. Kodak's disc camera, introduced in 1982, was a source of customer dissatisfaction because of the graininess of the photographs it produced. The disc camera sold poorly in Europe and Japan where photographers were used to the high resolution of 35mm photos. It seemed unlikely that the disc system would generate an 8-to-10-year life cycle of healthy sales like the Instamatic, making it doubtful that Kodak would recover its estimated $300 million in development costs. In 1988, Kodak announced it was suspending production of the disc camera.

Kodak's run at the camcorder video market was also a disappointment. In 1984, Kodak teamed up with Japan's Matsushita Electric to market an 8mm video camera. It was billed as the "world's first commercial 8mm camcorder." It was lighter and more compact than camcorders already on the market and used a new narrower tape developed by Kodak. The product ultimately failed because of outdated camera designs supplied by Matsushita, according to some analysts.

Then there was Kodak's instant camera system, which Kodak spent millions to develop in a decade-long effort to invent around Polaroid's patent monopoly on instant-developing film. Kodak announced on April 20, 1976, that its new instant camera would go on sale in Canada in May and in the United States in July. Kodak's system was billed as "completely new" compared to what Polaroid offered. It required many more components to manufacture than Polaroid's cameras. Polaroid filed a patent infringement suit at 4:59 P.M. April 26, 1976. Polaroid ultimately prevailed in its lawsuit against Kodak, and Kodak was required to pay an $873.2 million fine to Polaroid and withdraw from the instant photography business. Kodak was also required to give the buyers of its instant cameras a refund since film would no longer be available. In the period before the judgment, however, Kodak had become disenchanted with its foray into instant photography because its sales proved much smaller than anticipated—what some observers had touted as an eventual replacement for conventional photography proved to be a novelty or niche product.

Kodak's strategic objective in 1991 was to be the "world's best" in both conventional and electronic imaging. According to Kodak's top management, the company had in place (1) the strategic architecture for managing the alliance of chemical-based and electronic imaging, (2) technology centers for development of core products platforms, and (3) an international organization providing a fully global reach. Yet, in recent years, the company's net earnings had been dismal because of a series of writeoffs for "restructuring," the fine paid to Polaroid for patent infringement, and the effects of economic recession (see Exhibit 1).

When Kodak moved into information products, it began competing in areas where it was not the leader, did not have technical advantage, and did not have cost leadership. In some of these areas, it competed with its archrival Fuji. Fuji sold copiers, videotapes, and floppy computer disks. Kodak sold floppy disks through its Verbatim floppy disk subsidiary, and it also sold copiers. In 1988, Kodak lodged an unfair trading complaint with the International Trade Commission alleging that Fuji, Sony, and Hitachi charged 40 percent to 60 percent less for floppy disks in the United States than they did in Japan.

Current Chairman Kay Whitmore, who became Kodak's CEO on June 1, 1990, was enthused about the prospects for Kodak's photo CD. Photo CD was a reaction to Sony's Mavica camera introduced in 1982; the Mavica was a "filmless" video still camera whose pictures could be displayed immediately on TV. Canon, Toshiba, and Fuji came out with a similar product, though Toshiba's and Fuji's used a "memory card" rather than a floppy disk. Kodak's initial response to these products, according to one Kodak manager, was, "Holy cow, let's circle the wagons." The second reaction was photo CD. To avoid the bureaucracy of Kodak, the photo CD unit was set up to function as an independent business. With photo CD, users would use film to snap pictures (unlike Sony's filmless Mavica). But when the film was submitted for processing, they could opt to store their photos on a CD. Viewing what was on the CD required a TV and a special player made for Kodak by NV Philips. With the system, picture takers could also enlarge or crop their photos and return edited photos to the lab to get prints.

Kodak, in uncharacteristic style, announced photo CD long before its actual introduction. This early announcement was intended to signal rival firms that might be developing electronic photographic products. Kodak, which frequently set the standard in photographic products, considered it was important to let rivals know Kodak was developing an electronic camera with high resolution that used film. The fact that Kodak's product used film while the first venture into electronic photography, Sony's Mavica, didn't let rivals, especially Fuji, know the product development path Kodak was pursuing was one that would not undermine film sales over the long term.

A PROFILE OF FUJI PHOTO FILM CO.

Founded in 1936, Fuji was a leading international manufacturer and marketer of photographic film, photographic papers, cameras, video cameras, videotapes, audiocassette tapes, floppy disks, color scanners, medical imaging products, and computer output microfilming devices. Headquartered in Japan, Fuji had 1990 sales of $8.6 billion, of which 62 percent was domestic and 38 percent foreign. About 50 percent of Fuji's sales came from consumer photographic products, another 10 percent from magnetic tape products, and the remainder from its commercial products for printing, medical, office, and industrial users.

The company described its strategy as "globalization through localization." Toward this end, Fuji was expanding its presence into additional countries; the strategy in each country was to produce products locally whenever feasible and to adapt Fuji products and marketing to host country conditions as needed. Fuji in 1991 was forging ahead with plans to establish additional production bases in Europe and to reinforce its presence in North America; already Fuji had 15 manufacturing plants (including joint ventures) in 12 countries outside Japan. Fuji had publicly stated it was committed to becoming an integral part of the host nations and communities where it had business interests, with the aim of contributing "not only to the regional economy but also to the fabric of local society." The company described itself as being "ecologically concerned" and claimed credit for consistently taking a progressive posture on environmental protection.

Fuji saw the industry environment as becoming increasingly difficult due to growing price competition both in Japan and in its overseas markets, an intensifying race with rivals to develop new products, an unstable international situation, fluctuating foreign exchange rates, and increasing trade frictions. To deal with this environment, Fuji was aggressively developing and introducing new products in all of its operating divisions, increasing its sales and promotion efforts to boost demand, and adding more production and operating bases overseas to widen its international presence.

Like Eastman Kodak, Fuji emphasized combining its expertise in photographic chemicals and optical technologies with advanced electronics technologies to create new products and open new markets. Fuji, too, was well aware that it mattered a great deal whether the next era in photography (which advanced electronics technologies seemed about to spawn) involved filmless products or whether film would continue to be an integral part of the photographic process.

Background

Fuji first entered the United States in 1964 as a supplier of private-label film. In the mid-1960s, Fuji spent millions of dollars to design a new 8mm home movie system; just when it was all set to introduce its new system in the United States in 1967, Kodak announced the release of its Super 8 movie camera having a larger film format that couldn't use Fuji film. Fuji abandoned its product. At this point, Fuji concluded it made more strategic sense to follow Kodak's lead, avoid attracting Kodak's attention, and do nothing to provoke retaliation from Kodak. For many years thereafter, Fuji concentrated on building its U.S. base gradually, using strategies aimed at taking market share away from weaker U.S. competitors rather than Kodak. Starting in 1972, Fuji began selling film under its own name in camera stores; to help gain market recognition in the United States, Fuji provided the purchasers of Japanese cameras with several boxes of free Fuji film. In 1978, distribution of Fuji film was expanded to include drugstores, supermarkets, and discount chains.

In 1977, Fuji cut the price of its print paper to a level under Kodak; Kodak retaliated by matching Fuji's price and boosting its marketing efforts for print paper. In 1983, Fuji brought out a new high-resolution film in two speeds; Kodak responded by introducing a similar film and offering it in four speeds.

Fuji concluded from experiences such as these that it would be unable to outcompete Kodak in the way other Japanese firms had beaten American firms in automobiles, TVs, radios, stereo equipment, and microwave ovens. But, like other Japanese firms, it could subsidize its market share attack on Kodak in the United States using funds from its chief profit sanctuary in Japan where it had a commanding 70 to 75 percent market share. Fuji believed that by continuing to build Fuji's reputation for quality products and underpricing Kodak film products, it could win a 15 percent market share in the United States over the long term.

Essential to Fuji's strategy was the need to ensure that Fuji's film products were 100 percent compatible with Kodak cameras and Kodak film, thereby allowing price-conscious consumers to substitute Fuji film for Kodak film. Such a strategy effectively meant Fuji had to follow Kodak's lead on technology; when Kodak introduced technologically improved products, Fuji had to follow quickly with imitative improvements of its own. Fuji became skilled over the years in being a prompt follower of Kodak's lead in technology. For

EXHIBIT 2   Fuji Photo Film Company Financial and
                 Operating Highlights, 1986–90   *(In millions of dollars)*

	1986	1987	1988	1989	1990
Income Statement Data					
Net sales					
Domestic	$2,905.0	$3,633.4	$4,459.1	$4,416.2	$ 4,528.5
Overseas	1,602.5	2,002.2	2,379.3	2,312.3	2,815.7
Total	$4,507.5	$5,635.6	$6,838.4	$6,728.5	$ 7,344.3
Cost of goods sold	2,530.7	3,067.8	3,740.0	3,577.5	3,862.6
Operating Expenses					
Selling, general and administrative	$ 937.7	$1,232.0	$1,531.2	$1,615.1	$ 1,845.8
R&D	263.3	346.8	429.4	411.5	410.6
Interest and dividend income	121.1	144.4	176.0	198.5	268.4
Interest expense	58.0	63.6	75.7	89.4	136.9
Net income	369.3	497.8	640.0	603.6	622.6
Balance Sheet Data					
Total assets	$5,631.9	$7,234.0	$9,140.1	$9,683.7	$10,547.8
Long-term debt	205.2	192.9	357.4	503.1	691.5
Total liabilities	2,328.4	2,872.5	3,529.2	3,749.7	4,244.2
Shareholders' equity	3,303.5	4,361.5	5,610.9	5,934.0	6,303.7
Supplemental Information					
Number of employees	17,180	17,703	18,195	19,677	21,946
Exchange rate (yen/dollar)	168	145	128	138	145

Source: *1990 Annual Report.*

instance, Fuji was the first Kodak rival to market a film compatible with Kodak's disk system; Fuji researchers and engineers came up with an imitative film and got it on the market just eight months after Kodak's introduction.

Recent Events and Operating Results

Fuji relied heavily on its Japanese-based research and development unit to provide a steady stream of new products and to keep it in a position to match Kodak on technology. Annual R&D expenditures were around $400 million, equal to 5 to 6 percent of corporate revenues (see Exhibit 2). Until the past five years, Fuji had profit margins (net earnings as a percent of sales) of about 10 percent, among the largest of any of the major Japanese companies. Market maturity in Japan together with the previously mentioned troubles in the global market environment had pulled Fuji's profit margins down considerably—to just 3.2 percent in 1990. Fuji ranked 163 on the 1991 Fortune Global 500 list (Kodak ranked 55).

Fuji operated one of the lowest cost videotape plants in the world in Odawara, Japan; its first videotape plant in the United States (in South Carolina) began production in 1991. In Japan, Fuji had a flexible, mobile work force; employees moved freely from one plant to another, making different products as needed to keep a balance between production and changes in demand. Such mobility was possible because of the proximity of Fuji's plants in Japan.

In 1990 and 1991, Fuji had a variety of new product debuts: new films in the Fujicolor Super HG and Fujichrome Velvia lines, new Fujicolor Quicksnap camera models, new compact and instant cameras, and innovative electronic imaging products. Fuji continued to express its desire to avoid provoking or threatening Kodak. As Fuji's president commented some years earlier: "We are a piquant but small Japanese pepper. If I were Kodak, I wouldn't worry about us at all."[11]

---

[11]As quoted in *Fortune*, August 22, 1983, p. 122.

KENTUCKY FRIED CHICKEN CORP.

Jeffrey A. Krug and W. Harvey Hegarty, Indiana University

During the 1960s and 1970s, Kentucky Fried Chicken Corp. (KFC) pursued an aggressive strategy to expand the number of its restaurant outlets, quickly establishing itself as one of the largest fast-food restaurant chains in the United States (see Exhibit 1). KFC was also one of the first U.S. fast-food restaurant chains to expand overseas. By 1990, restaurants located outside of the United States were generating over 50 percent of KFC's total sales. KFC operated in 58 countries and was the largest fast-food restaurant chain outside of the United States.

Japan, Australia, and the United Kingdom accounted for the greatest share of KFC's international expansion during the 1970s and 1980s. However, as KFC entered the 1990s, a number of other international markets offered significant opportunities for growth. China, with a population of over 1 billion, and Europe, with a population roughly equal to the United States, offered such opportunities. Latin America also offered a unique opportunity because of the size of its markets, its common language and culture, and its geographical proximity to the United States. KFC had already established successful subsidiaries in Mexico and Puerto Rico and operated franchises in 20 other Latin American countries.

As Mexico continued to struggle with economic and currency problems, a debate ensued within KFC management regarding further expansion in Mexico. Bob Briggs, vice president of international finance, opposed further expansion in Mexico until economic stability could be established in that country. Instead, Briggs supported expansion in other areas of the world. But Guillermo Heredia, vice president of Latin America, believed KFC had an opportunity to make significant market share gains in Mexico by expanding now. Heredia argued strongly that another competitor—McDonald's—was expanding in Mexico, and KFC's past market share gains could easily be lost if it failed to follow through with its planned growth strategy in Mexico.

COMPANY HISTORY

Fast-food franchising was still in its infancy in 1954 when 64-year-old Harland Sanders began his travels across the United States to speak with prospective franchisees about his "Colonel Sanders Recipe Kentucky Fried Chicken." By 1960, Colonel Sanders had granted KFC franchises to over 200 take-home retail outlets and restaurants across the United States. He had also established a number of franchises in Canada. By 1963, the number of KFC franchises had risen to over 300 and revenues had reached $500,000.

In 1964, at the age of 74, the Colonel had tired of running the day-to-day operations of his business, so he sought out potential buyers, eventually deciding to sell the business to two Louisville businessmen—Jack Massey and John Young Brown Jr.—for $2 million. Massey was named chairman of the board,

EXHIBIT 1   Leading U.S. Fast-Food Chains, 1988 and 1989

Chain	Parent	U.S. Sales (millions of dollars) 1988	1989	1989 Units
McDonald's	McDonald's	$11,380	$12,012	8,270
Burger King	Grand Metropolitan	4,840	5,110	5,361
Pizza Hut	PepsiCo	2,800	3,100	6,050
Hardee's	Imasco Ltd.	2,810	3,040	3,327
KFC	PepsiCo	2,900	3,000	4,997
Wendy's	Wendy's International	2,720	2,830	3,490
Domino's Pizza	Domino's Pizza	2,300	2,600	5,008
Dairy Queen	Dairy Queen	1,859	2,068	4,700
Taco Bell	PepsiCo	1,600	1,840	3,080
Denny's	TW Holdings	1,227	1,300	1,300
Arby's	DWG Corp.	1,100	1,300	2,158
Red Lobster	General Mills	1,050	1,200	1,000
Little Caesar's	Little Caesar's	908	1,200	2,747
Big Boy	Elias Bros.	1,030	1,040	1,030
Dunkin' Donuts	Allied-Lyons	880	1,014	1,925
Jack in the Box	Foodmaker Inc.	775	875	1,031
Shoney's	Shoney's Inc.	779	860	704
Subway	Doctors Associates	583	855	3,440
Sizzler	Collins Foods	749	846	628
Long John Silver's	Jerrico Inc.	753	785	1,525
Ponderosa	Metromedia Co.	696	710	720
Roy Rogers	Imasco Ltd.	575	620	660
Bonanza	Metromedia Co.	571	620	652
Friendly	Tennessee Restaurants	564	590	848
Popeye's	Biscuit Investment	447	590	1,030
Baskin-Robbins	Allied-Lyons	502	524	2,600
Western Sizzlin'	Western Sizzlin'	488	500	550
Carl's Jr.	Carl Karcher	399	481	482
Golden Corral	Investors Management	456	465	501
Bennigan's	S&A Restaurant Corp.	455	459	222
Perkins	Tennessee Restaurants	375	450	370
Chi-Chi's	Foodmaker Inc.	431	422	203
Total		$49,002	$53,256	70,609

Source: *S&P's 1990 Industry Surveys.*

and Brown, who would later become governor of Kentucky, was named president. The Colonel stayed on as a public relations man and goodwill ambassador for the company.

During the next five years, Massey and Brown concentrated on expanding KFC's franchise system across the United States. In 1966, they took KFC public and the company was listed on the New York Stock Exchange. By the late 1960s, a strong foothold had been established in the United States, and Massey and Brown turned their attention to international markets. In 1969, a joint venture was signed with Mitsuoishi Shoji Kaisha, Ltd., in Japan, and the rights to operate 14 existing KFC franchises in England were acquired. Subsidiaries were also established in Hong Kong, South Africa, Australia, New Zealand, and Mexico. By 1971, KFC had 2,450 franchises and 600 company-owned restaurants worldwide and was operating in 48 countries.

Heublein, Inc.

In 1971, KFC entered negotiations with Heublein, Inc., to discuss being acquired. The decision was partially driven by Brown's desire to pursue other interests, including a political career (Brown was elected governor of Kentucky in 1977). On April 10, Heublein announced an agreement had been reached. Shareholders approved the acquisition on May 27, and KFC became a subsidiary of Heublein.

Heublein produced vodka, mixed cocktails, dry gin, cordials, beer, and other alcoholic beverages. It was also the exclusive distributor of a variety of imported alcoholic beverages. Heublein had little experience in the restaurant business. Conflicts quickly erupted between Colonel Sanders, who continued to act in a public relations capacity, and Heublein management. In particular, Colonel Sanders became increasingly distraught over quality control issues and restaurant cleanliness. By 1977, new store openings had slowed to about 20 per year (in 1989, KFC opened a new restaurant on average every two days). Stores were not being remodeled and service quality was declining.

In 1977, Heublein sent in a new management team to redirect KFC's strategy. Richard P. Mayer, who later became chairman and chief executive officer, was part of this team. (Mayer remained with KFC until 1989, when he left to become president of General Foods USA.) A back-to-basics strategy was immediately implemented. New unit construction was discontinued until existing stores could be upgraded and operating problems eliminated. Stores were refurbished, cleanliness and service were emphasized, marginal products were eliminated, and product consistency was reestablished. By 1982, KFC had established a successful strategic focus and was again aggressively building new units.

R.J. Reynolds Industries, Inc.

On October 12, 1982, R.J. Reynolds Industries, Inc., (RJR) announced it would acquire Heublein and operate it as a wholly owned subsidiary. The merger with Heublein represented part of RJR's overall corporate strategy of diversifying into unrelated businesses. RJR's objective was to reduce its dependence on the tobacco industry, which had driven RJR sales since its founding in North Carolina in 1875. Sales of cigarettes and tobacco products, while profitable, were declining because of the increased awareness among Americans of the negative health consequences of smoking.

RJR's diversification strategy included the acquisition of a variety of companies in the energy, transportation, and food and restaurant industries. RJR had no more experience in the restaurant business than did Heublein when Heublein purchased KFC in 1971. However, RJR decided to take a hands-off approach to managing KFC. Whereas Heublein had installed its own top management at KFC headquarters, RJR left KFC management largely intact, believing existing KFC managers were better qualified to operate KFC's businesses than were its own managers. By doing so, RJR avoided many of the operating problems that Heublein had experienced during its management of KFC. This strategy paid off for RJR, as KFC continued to expand aggressively and profitably under RJR's ownership.

In 1985, RJR acquired Nabisco Corporation for $4.9 billion. Nabisco sold a variety of well-known cookies, crackers, cereals, confectioneries, snacks, and other grocery products. In October 1986, Kentucky Fried Chicken was sold to PepsiCo, Inc.

PEPSICO, INC.

Corporate Strategy

PepsiCo, Inc., (PepsiCo) was first incorporated in Delaware in 1919 as Loft, Inc. In 1938, Loft acquired the Pepsi-Cola Co., a manufacturer of soft drinks and soft-drink concentrates. Pepsi-Cola's traditional business had been the sale of its soft-drink concentrates to licensed independent and company-owned bottlers, which manufacture, sell, and distribute Pepsi-Cola soft drinks. Pepsi-Cola's best known trademarks were Pepsi-Cola, Diet Pepsi, Mountain Dew, and Slice. Shortly after its acquisition of Pepsi-Cola, Loft changed its name to Pepsi-Cola Co. On June 30, 1965, Pepsi-Cola Co. acquired Frito-Lay Inc. for 3 million shares, thereby creating one of the largest consumer companies in the United States. At that time, the present name of PepsiCo, Inc., was adopted. Frito-Lay manufactured and sold a variety of snack foods. Its best known trademarks were Fritos brand corn chips, Lay's and Ruffles brand potato chips, Doritos and Tostitos chips, and Chee•tos brand cheese-flavored snacks. In 1989, 66 percent of PepsiCo's net sales were generated by its soft-drink and snack-food businesses.

Beginning in the late 1960s, PepsiCo began an aggressive acquisition program as an outlet for the large cash flows generated by its soft-drink and snack-food businesses. Initially, PepsiCo pursued an acquisition strategy similar to that pursued by R.J. Reynolds during the 1980s, buying a number of companies in areas unrelated to its major businesses. For example, North American Van Lines was acquired in June 1968. Wilson Sporting Goods was merged into the company in 1972, and Lee Way Motor Freight was acquired in 1976. However, success in operating these businesses failed to live up to expectations, mainly because the management skills required to operate these businesses lay outside of PepsiCo's area of expertise.

In 1984, then-Chairman and Chief Executive Officer Don Kendall decided to restructure PepsiCo's operations. Most importantly, PepsiCo would divest those businesses that did not support PepsiCo's consumer-product orientation. PepsiCo sold Lee Way Motor Freight in 1984. In 1985, Wilson Sporting Goods and North American Van Lines were sold. Additionally, PepsiCo's foreign bottling operations were sold to local businesspeople who better understood the cultural and business conditions operating in their respective countries. Lastly, Kendall reorganized PepsiCo along three lines: soft drinks, snack foods, and restaurants (see Exhibit 2). PepsiCo's corporate strategy was to direct all future investments at strengthening PepsiCo's performance in these three related areas.

Restaurant Business and Acquisition of Kentucky Fried Chicken

The 1984 reorganization was important in that it eliminated a number of unrelated and unsuccessful businesses that had diverted management attention away from PepsiCo's more successful consumer businesses. The reorganization

EXHIBIT 2   PepsiCo, Inc.—Principal Divisions, 1990

Executive offices: Purchase, New York

Soft-Drink Segment	Snack-Food Segment	Restaurants
PepsiCo Worldwide Beverages Sommers, New York	PepsiCo Worldwide Foods Plano, Texas	Kentucky Fried Chicken Louisville, Kentucky
Pepsi-Cola Co. Sommers, New York	Frito-Lay, Inc. Dallas, Texas	Pizza Hut, Inc. Wichita, Kansas
Pepsi-Cola International Sommers, New York	PepsiCo Foods International Dallas, Texas	Taco Bell Corporation Irvine, California
		PepsiCo Food Service Purchase, New York

into soft-drink, snack-food, and restaurant groups helped to redirect management time and resources back to these major businesses.

PepsiCo entered the restaurant business in 1977 when it acquired Pizza Hut's 3,200-unit restaurant system. Taco Bell was merged into a division of PepsiCo in 1978. The restaurant business complemented PepsiCo's consumer-product orientation. The restaurant business of fast food followed much of the same patterns as the marketing of soft drinks and snack foods. Therefore, PepsiCo's management skills could easily be transferred among its three business segments. This was compatible with PepsiCo's practice of frequently moving managers among its business units as a way of developing future top executives.

PepsiCo's restaurant chains also provided an additional outlet for the sale of Pepsi soft-drink products. In addition, Pepsi soft-drink and fast-food products could be marketed together in the same television and radio segments, thereby providing higher returns for each advertising dollar.

To complete its diversification into the restaurant segment, PepsiCo purchased Kentucky Fried Chicken from RJR Nabisco in 1986 for $841 million. The acquisition of KFC gave PepsiCo the leading market share in three of the four largest and fastest growing segments within the U.S. quick-service industry. At the end of 1989, Pizza Hut held a 32 percent share of the $10 billion U.S. pizza segment, Taco Bell held 54 percent of the $3.7 billion Mexican food segment, and KFC held 51 percent of the $5.9 billion U.S. chicken segment. In an analysis of PepsiCo's restaurant business in 1989, Shearson Lehman Hutton analyst Caroline Levy commented, "On balance, PepsiCo's restaurants are clearly outperforming the industry and most of the major chains." See Exhibits 3 and 4 for business segment financial data and restaurant count.

PepsiCo's success during the last decade can be seen by its upward trend in *Fortune* magazine's annual survey of "America's Most Admired Corporations." For the 1990 survey, *Fortune* polled 8,000 executives, directors, and financial analysts, who were asked to rate the largest companies in their industry. The survey covered 305 companies in 32 industry groups. PepsiCo was labeled the sixth most admired corporation overall, rising from seventh in 1989. In particular, PepsiCo was ranked high in value as a long-term investment, innovativeness, wise use of corporate assets, quality of management, and quality of

EXHIBIT 3 **PepsiCo, Inc. Operating Results, 1989** *(In millions of dollars)*

	Soft Drinks	Snack Foods	Restaurants	Total
Net sales	$5,776.7	$4,215.0	$5,250.7	$15,242.4
Operating profit	690.1	820.9	421.2	1,932.2
Percent of net sales	11.9%	19.5%	8.0%	12.7%
Assets	$6,241.9	$3,366.4	$3,095.2	$12,703.5
Capital spending	267.8	257.9	424.6	959.5*

*Includes corporate spending of $9.2 million.

EXHIBIT 4 **Number of PepsiCo, Inc. Units Worldwide, 1984–1989**

Year	KFC	Pizza Hut	Taco Bell	Total
1984	6,175	4,208	1,833	12,216
1985	6,396	4,482	2,173	13,051
1986	6,575	5,017	2,409	14,001
1987	7,522	5,394	2,696	15,612
1988	7,761	5,707	2,878	16,346
1989	7,948	6,205	3,067	17,220
Five-year compound annual growth rate	5.2%	8.1%	10.8%	7.1%

products/services offered. PepsiCo's rise is dramatic when compared with its place in past *Fortune* rankings of the most admired companies:

	PepsiCo Ranking
1990	6
1989	7
1988	14
1987	24
1986	25

FAST-FOOD INDUSTRY

According to the National Restaurant Association (NRA), 1989 food-service sales topped $227.2 billion for the approximately 400,000 restaurants and other food outlets making up the U.S. restaurant industry. Fast-food sales, which represented the fastest growing segment within the restaurant industry, reached $65.5 billion. The NRA estimated that sales of the over 86,000 fast-food restaurants would grow by 7.4 percent to approximately $70.4 billion in the United States in 1990. The U.S. restaurant industry as a whole was projected to grow by 6 percent. Approximately 50 percent of the growth in the fast-food segment was expected to come from new unit openings. Another 40 percent would result from higher prices, while the remaining growth would come from improved volume at existing outlets.

EXHIBIT 5   U.S. Fast-Food Sales by Business Segment, 1987–1989   *(In millions of dollars)*

Business Segment	1987	1988	1989
Hamburgers and roast beef	$27,257	$30,386	$33,880
Steak	9,811	10,724	11,954
Pizza	8,126	9,087	10,225
Chicken	4,822	5,345	5,912
Mexican	3,079	3,317	3,673
Seafood	1,480	1,666	1,841
Pancakes and waffles	1,309	1,435	1,553
Sandwiches and other	956	1,185	1,386
Total fast-food sales	$56,840	$63,145	$70,424

Source: U.S. Department of Commerce, *Restaurant Business* magazine, *S&P's Industry Surveys*.

Major Business Segments

Eight major business segments made up the fast-food segment of the food-service industry; Exhibit 5 shows sales for each of these segments for 1987 through 1989. Hamburgers, hot dogs, and roast beef represented the largest segment of the U.S. market, reaching $33.9 billion in sales in 1989. The largest competitors were McDonald's, Burger King, Hardee's, and Wendy's. McDonald's market share within this segment was 35 percent, compared to a 15 percent share for Burger King, its nearest competitor.

The second largest fast-food segment was steak, which was largely dominated by Denny's and Big Boy. The pizza segment, the third largest fast-food segment, was the industry's fastest growing. Pizza Hut dominated this segment, with Domino's Pizza and Little Caesar's following close behind. Domino's targeted the home delivery market, while Little Caesar's concentrated mainly on take-out sales. Pizza Hut, while traditionally a dine-in restaurant concept, had successfully implemented a home delivery and take-out system.

Kentucky Fried Chicken, more than any other business segment leader, had dominated its business segment, accounting for over 50 percent of total sales within the chicken segment in 1989. KFC's nearest competitors were Church's Fried Chicken and Popeye's Famous Fried Chicken. Other chicken chains included Bojangles, Chick-fil-a, and Grandy's.

Industry Consolidation

Although the restaurant industry had outpaced the overall economy in recent years, there were indications that the U.S. market was slowly becoming saturated. Monthly sales of U.S. eating and drinking establishments were up only 1.1 to 3.8 percent from those of the prior year in the last half of 1989. Following a period of rapid expansion and intense restaurant building during the 1970s and 1980s, the fast-food industry had begun to consolidate. In January 1990, Grand Metropolitan, a British company, purchased Pillsbury Co. for $5.7 billion. Included in the purchase was Pillsbury's Burger King chain. Grand Met moved to strengthen the franchise by upgrading existing restaurants and eliminating several levels of management to cut costs.

Within the chicken segment, a number of acquisitions had intensified competition behind Kentucky Fried Chicken. In particular, the second largest chicken segment restaurant chain, Church's, was acquired by Al Copeland Enterprises in 1989 for $392 million. Copeland also owned Popeye's Famous Fried Chicken, the third largest chicken chain. Following the Church's acquisition, Copeland converted 303 of Church's 1,368 restaurants into Popeye's franchises, bringing the Popeye's restaurant system to a total of 1,030. This made Popeye's the second largest chicken chain in the United States. Several hundred Church's units were scheduled to be sold to raise cash to pay for the acquisition. Although the acquisition enlarged the competitive base controlled by Copeland, the Copeland restaurant system was still dwarfed by KFC's 4,997 U.S. restaurants.

Perhaps more important to Kentucky Fried Chicken was Hardee's acquisition of 600 Roy Rogers restaurants from Marriott Corporation in early 1990. Hardee's immediately began to convert these restaurants to Hardee's units and had introduced "Roy Rogers" fried chicken to its menu.

Demographic Trends

Intense marketing by the leading fast-food chains was expected to stimulate demand for fast food in the United States during the 1990s. In addition, demographic changes were contributing to the increased popularity of fast food. One change was the rise in single-person households from 17 percent of all U.S. households in 1970 to approximately 25 percent in 1990. Single people were more inclined to eat out than larger households. In addition, disposable household income was expected to increase, mainly because more women were working. Career couples, faced with less time for cooking and other household activities, were eating out more often. According to *Standard & Poor's Industry Surveys*, Americans spent 38 percent of their food dollars at restaurants in 1988, up 25 percent from 1970. Most of this rise came from increased consumption, while the balance came mainly from higher prices. The National Restaurant Association estimated that Americans ate out on average 3.7 times per week and spent an average of $3.52 per meal in 1988.

While these demographic trends were helping to boost demand for fast food in the United States, a number of societal changes partially offset these trends. For example, microwaves had been introduced into approximately 70 percent of all U.S. homes. This had resulted in a variety of products that could be quickly and easily prepared. In addition, there was a tendency for people to forgo fast food for more upscale restaurants.

International Quick-Service Market

Because of the aggressive pace of new restaurant construction in the United States during the 1970s and 1980s, future growth resulting from new restaurant construction in the United States was limited. In any case, the cost of finding prime locations was rising, increasing the pressure on restaurant chains to increase per-store sales to cover higher initial investment costs. One alternative to continued investment in the U.S. market was expansion into international markets, offering large customer bases and comparatively little competition. However, few U.S. restaurant chains had yet defined aggressive strategies for penetrating international markets.

EXHIBIT 6   The World's 20 Largest Fast-Food Chains, 1989

	Franchise	Location	Units	Countries
1	McDonald's	Oakbrook, Ill.	11,162	52
2	Kentucky Fried Chicken	Louisville, Ky.	7,948	58
3	Burger King	Miami, Fla.	6,041	34
4	Subway Sandwiches	Milford, Conn.	4,000	5
5	Wendy's	Dublin, Ohio	3,755	23
6	Hardee's	Rocky Mount, N.C.	3,291	9
7	Taco Bell	Irvine, Calif.	3,125	9
8	Kozo Sushi	Osaka, Japan	2,347	3
9	Arby's	Atlanta, Ga.	2,224	8
10	Long John Silver's	Lexington, Ky.	1,500	3
11	Church's Fried Chicken	Jefferson, La.	1,111	9
12	Big Boy	Warren, Mich.	1,000	3
13	Popeye's	Jefferson, La.	750	6
14	Loteria	Tokyo, Japan	702	3
15	A&W Restaurants	Livonia, Mich.	599	9
16	Taco Time	Eugene, Ore.	321	7
17	Country Kitchen	Minneapolis, Minn.	265	2
18	White Castle	Columbus, Ohio	244	2
19	Wimpy	London, England	220	21
20	Flunch	Villeneuve d'Ascq. France	118	3

Source: *Hotels & Restaurants International,* May 1990.

Two restaurant chains that had established successful international strategies were McDonald's and Kentucky Fried Chicken. While McDonald's had the most restaurants in the U.S. market, Kentucky Fried Chicken operated the greatest number of units outside of the United States, opening its 3,000th restaurant abroad in 1989. However, in terms of sales, McDonald's remained the world's largest restaurant chain. In 1989, McDonald's foreign sales were $5.3 billion, about twice that of KFC, which had foreign sales of $2.4 billion. In early 1990, McDonald's was operating 2,900 restaurants in 52 countries. Exhibit 6 shows *Hotels and Restaurants International's* 1990 list of the world's 20 largest fast-food restaurant chains.

There were a number of possible explanations for the relative scarcity of fast-food restaurant chains outside the United States. First, the United States represented the largest consumer market in the world, accounting for almost one fourth of the world's gross national product. The United States had traditionally been the strategic focus of the largest restaurant chains. In addition, Americans had been more quick to accept the fast-food concept. Many other cultures had strong culinary traditions that were not easy to break down. The Europeans, for example, had long histories of frequenting more midscale restaurants, where they might spend several hours in a formal setting enjoying native dishes and beverages. While Kentucky Fried Chicken was building restaurants in Germany, it previously failed to penetrate the German market because Germans were not accustomed to take-out food or to ordering food over the counter. McDonald's had greater success penetrating the German market because it made a number of changes in its menu and operating procedures to better appeal to the German culture. For example, German beer was served in all of McDonald's German restaurants. KFC had more success in Asia, where chicken was a traditional dish.

Aside from cultural factors, international operations carried risks not present in the U.S. market. Long distances between headquarters and foreign franchises often made it difficult to control the quality of individual franchises. Large distances could also cause servicing and support problems. Transportation and other resource costs could also be higher than in the domestic market. In addition, time, cultural, and language differences posed communication and operational problems.

KENTUCKY FRIED CHICKEN CORP.

One of PepsiCo's greatest challenges when it acquired Kentucky Fried Chicken in 1986 was how to mold two distinct corporate cultures. When R.J. Reynolds acquired KFC in 1982, it realized it knew little about the fast-food business and decided to rely on existing KFC management to continue managing the company. As a result, there was little need for mixing the cultures of the two companies. However, one of PepsiCo's major concerns when considering the purchase of KFC was whether it had the management skills required to successfully operate KFC using PepsiCo managers. PepsiCo had already acquired considerable experience managing fast-food businesses through Pizza Hut and Taco Bell operations. It was eager to pursue strategic changes within KFC that would improve performance.

PepsiCo's corporate culture had long been based heavily on a "fast-track" New York approach to management. It hired the country's top business and engineering graduates and promoted them based on performance. As a result, top performers expected to move up through the ranks quickly and to be paid well for their efforts.

The corporate culture at Kentucky Fried Chicken in 1986 contrasted sharply with that at PepsiCo. KFC's culture was built largely on Colonel Sanders' laid-back approach to management. Also, employees enjoyed relatively good employment stability and security. Over the years, a strong loyalty had been created among KFC employees and franchisees, mainly because of the efforts of Colonel Sanders to provide for his employees' benefits, pension, and other nonincome needs. In addition, there was a friendly, relaxed atmosphere at KFC's corporate offices. This corporate culture was left essentially unchanged during the Heublein years.

When PepsiCo acquired KFC, it began to restructure the KFC organization, replacing more of KFC's top managers with its own. By the summer of 1990, all of KFC's top positions were occupied by PepsiCo executives. In July 1989, KFC's president and chief executive officer, Richard P. Mayer, left KFC to become president of General Foods USA. Mayer had been at KFC since 1977, when KFC was still owned by Heublein. PepsiCo replaced Mayer with John Cranor III, the former president of PepsiCo East, a Pepsi-Cola unit. In November 1989, Martin Redgrave moved from PepsiCo to become KFC's new chief financial officer. In the summer of 1990, Bill McDonald, a Pizza Hut and Frito-Lay marketing executive, was named senior vice president of marketing. Two months before, PepsiCo had named Kyle Craig, a former Pillsbury executive, as president of KFC's USA operations.

Most of PepsiCo's initial management changes in 1987 focused on KFC's corporate offices and USA operations. In 1988, attention was turned to KFC's

EXHIBIT 7   **KFC Organizational Chart, 1990**

KFC Corporate Offices
John Cranor III (12 months)*
President and chief executive officer

Martin Redgrave (8 months)
Chief financial officer

Bill McDonald (1 month)
Senior vice president, marketing

KFC USA	**KFC International**
Kyle Craig (5 months)	Allan Huston (3 months)
President	President
Guillermo Heredia	Robert Briggs (13 months)
Vice president-Latin America	Vice president-International finance

*Number of months with KFC as of August 1, 1990.

international division. PepsiCo replaced KFC International's top managers with its own. First, it lured Don Pierce away from Burger King and made Pierce president of KFC International. However, Pierce left KFC in early 1990; Pierce commented he wished to change jobs partly to decrease the amount of time he spent traveling. PepsiCo replaced Pierce with Allan Huston, who was formerly senior vice president of operations at Pizza Hut. In late 1988, PepsiCo also brought in Robert Briggs, former director of finance at Pepsi-Cola International, as vice president of international finance. See Exhibit 7 for a current organizational chart.

An example of the type of conflict faced by PepsiCo in attempting to implement changes within KFC occurred in August 1989. A month after becoming president and chief executive officer, Cranor addressed KFC's franchisees to explain the details of a new franchisee contract. This was the first contract change in 13 years. The new contract gave PepsiCo management greater power to take over weak franchises, to relocate new stores, and to make changes in existing restaurants. In addition, existing stores would no longer be protected from competition from new KFC restaurants. The contract also gave management the right to raise royalty fees on existing restaurants as contracts came up for renewal. After Cranor finished his address, there was an uproar among the attending franchisees, who jumped to their feet to protest the changes. The franchisees had long been accustomed to relatively little interference from management in their day-to-day operations. This type of interference, of course, was a strong part of PepsiCo's philosophy of demanding change.

Operating Results

KFC's recent operating results are shown in Exhibit 8. Despite KFC's continued dominance of its industry segment, it experienced a 14 percent decline in worldwide profits in 1989 to $100 million, down from $117 million in 1988. This resulted mainly from lower volumes in U.S. stores, partially the result of higher pricing in 1989. Also, intense competition within the United States continued to affect sales. In contrast to the U.S. market, KFC continued to profit from its international units. In particular, international sales in 1989 were

EXHIBIT 8   **KFC Operating Results, 1984–1989**

	Worldwide Sales (Billions of Dollars)	KFC Corp. Sales (Billions of Dollars)	KFC Corp* Profit (Millions of Dollars)	Percent of Sales
1984	$2.9			
1985	3.1			
1986	3.5			
1987	4.1	1.1	90.0	8.3%
1988	5.0	1.2	116.5	9.6%
1989	5.4	1.3	100.0	7.5%
CAGR%	13.2%			

*KFC corporate figures include company stores and franchisee fees. Data before 1987 consolidated within R.J. Reynolds.
Source: PepsiCo annual reports for 1986, 1987, 1988, and 1989.

strongest in Australia, New Zealand, and Canada, where additional units, increased prices, and volume increases helped to significantly increase profits over 1988.

KFC's Marketing Survey

As KFC entered 1990, it focused its marketing strategy on three issues: pricing, new product introductions, and improved distribution. Pricing was of special significance. In 1989, KFC had undertaken a series of price increases, partially to offset higher chicken costs. However, higher prices had cut into sales by the fourth quarter of 1989. In an interview with *Nation's Restaurant News* in February 1990, Smith Barney analyst Joseph Doyle estimated that 3 percent of the 5 percent decline in KFC's fourth-quarter 1990 sales came from price hikes. The unexpected decline in KFC sales demonstrated the importance consumers placed on price and perceived value. As a result, KFC entered 1990 determined to create a better consumer image regarding the value of its products. In early 1990, KFC lowered prices on a number of menu items to make them more competitive. Some prices were planned to be rolled back to 1979 levels. In addition, a number of promotions were planned to offer customers special pricing on double buckets of chicken and other food combinations.

Much of the competitive pressure felt by KFC was the result of KFC's traditional slowness in introducing new products to its menu. The popularity of its original recipe fried chicken allowed KFC to expand through most of the 1980s without significant competition from other chicken competitors. As a result, new product introductions were never an important part of KFC strategy. However, the introduction of chicken sandwiches by hamburger chains had changed the list of KFC's competitors. McDonald's introduced its McChicken sandwich in the United States in 1989 while KFC was still testing its new sandwich. KFC introduced its chicken sandwich several months later. By beating KFC into the market, McDonald's was able to develop a strong consumer awareness for its sandwich. The increased popularity of healthier foods was also creating a need for new products. To capitalize on this trend, KFC was testing grilled chicken on the bone in Louisville and Las Vegas. A grilled chicken fillet sandwich was also being tested and two new products—Hot

Wings, a spicy chicken wing, and Hot & Spicy Chicken—were introduced in early 1990.

A third marketing strategy of increasing importance was distribution. KFC had traditionally catered to the take-out and dine-in market. However, the successful implementation of home delivery systems by pizza chains such as Domino's and Pizza Hut had created a new outlet for fast-food sales. Most of the growth in the pizza segment during the past three years had come from home delivery. In early 1990, KFC began testing home delivery in Louisville, Columbus, and several Chicago suburbs. Other locations that offered significant growth opportunities were shopping malls, airports, hospitals, and universities.

Operating Efficiencies

In 1989, KFC reorganized its U.S. operations to eliminate overhead costs and to increase efficiency. Included in this reorganization was a revision of KFC's crew training programs and operating standards. A renewed emphasis was placed on improving customer service, cleaner stores, faster and friendlier service, and continued high-quality products. In 1987, computer-controlled fryers were introduced to improve quality and to reduce costs. Computer fryers cooked at an even temperature, resulted in less waste of oil and product, and required less labor.

Restaurant Expansion and International Operations

KFC opened its 3,000th restaurant outside the United States in 1989. While U.S. operations showed a decline in operating profits in 1989 as the result of declining customer counts and higher chicken and labor costs, KFC's international operations continued to improve on all criteria. KFC management expected that international operations would be called on to provide an increasing percentage of KFC's overall sales and profit growth as the U.S. market continued to be saturated.

MEXICO

KFC was one of the first restaurant chains to recognize the importance of international markets. By 1971, KFC was operating in 48 countries. In Latin America, KFC operated subsidiaries in Mexico and Puerto Rico and was operating 94 franchises in 19 countries in the Caribbean at the end of 1989. KFC planned to open new units in several South American countries in the near future. In the summer of 1990, a franchise was opened in Chile, increasing the number of countries in which KFC operated to 59. Other countries considered to be promising markets were Argentina and Brazil, whose large populations and market sizes offered significant opportunities for growth.

Franchising

In Mexico, KFC had traditionally relied on the operation of company-owned stores. At the end of 1989, KFC was operating 57 restaurants, all company-

EXHIBIT 9   **Fast-Food Industry in Mexico, 1989**

	1989 Units	Market Share
KFC	57	9.5%
McDonald's	8	1.3%
Burger Boy	48	8.0%
Pollo Loco	110	18.3%
Church's	13	2.2%
Pizza Hut	19	3.2%
VIPs	52	8.7%
Sanborn's	41	6.8%
Other	252	42.0%
Total	600	100.0%

owned (see Exhibit 9). Franchising was still in its infancy in Mexico. Until the end of 1989, franchises were difficult to operate because of government restrictions on the payment of royalties and lack of legal protection for the transfer of technology and trade secrets. As a result, it had been more advantageous to operate company-owned stores, which allowed KFC to maximize control over assets and technology. However, a new franchise law was passed in 1989, opening the way for franchising in Mexico. The new legislation eliminated much of the discretionary power of the Secretariat of Industry and Commerce to regulate foreign franchising in Mexico and allowed parties to a franchising agreement to establish their own terms and conditions. KFC planned to use franchising to drive growth in Mexico and planned to open its first franchises in 1990.

At the end of 1989, KFC was operating restaurants in three regions; Mexico City, Guadalajara, and Monterey. By limiting operations to these three regions, KFC had been able to better coordinate operations and minimize distribution costs. With the passing of new franchise legislation, however, KFC was able to more easily expand its store base to other regions, where responsibility for management could be handled by individual franchisees. Arby's, McDonald's, and Baskin-Robbins had already signed new franchise agreements by July 1990. This increased the pressure on KFC to quickly expand its own franchises in Mexico or risk losing market share, most importantly to McDonald's.

Economic and Political Environment

Many factors made Mexico a potentially profitable location for U.S. direct investment and trade. Mexico's population of 85 million people was approximately one third as large as the United States. Because of its geographical proximity to the United States, transportation costs were minimal. This increased the competitiveness of U.S. goods in comparison with European and Asian goods, which had to be transported at substantial cost across the Atlantic or Pacific Ocean. The United States was Mexico's largest trading partner. Almost 75 percent of Mexico's imports came from the United States, while 72 percent of Mexico's exports were to the U.S. market (see Exhibit 10). In addition, low wage rates made Mexico an attractive location for production.

EXHIBIT 10   **Mexico's Major Trading Partners, 1988**

	Percent of Total Exports	Percent of Total Imports
United States	72.9	74.9
Japan	4.9	6.4
West Germany	1.3	3.5
France	1.8	2.0
Rest of world	19.1	13.2

Source: *Business International*, 1990.

The lack of U.S. investment in and trade with Mexico during this century was mainly the result of Mexico's long history of restricting trade and foreign direct investment in Mexico. The Institutional Revolutionary Party (PRI), which came to power in Mexico during the 1930s, had traditionally pursued protectionist economic policies to shield its people and economy from foreign firms and goods. Industries had been predominantly government-owned or controlled and production had been pursued for the domestic market only. High tariffs and other trade barriers had restricted imports into Mexico and foreign ownership of assets in Mexico had been largely prohibited or heavily restricted.

In addition, a dictatorial and entrenched government bureaucracy, corrupt labor unions, and a long tradition of anti-Americanism among many government officials and intellectuals had reduced the motivation of U.S. firms to invest in Mexico. Also, the 1982 nationalization of Mexico's banks resulted in higher real interest rates and destroyed investor confidence. Since then, the Mexican government had battled high inflation, high interest rates, labor unrest, and lost consumer purchasing power (see Exhibit 11). Total foreign debt, which stood at $95.1 billion at the end of 1989, remained a problem.

Investor confidence in Mexico, however, had improved since December 1988, when Carlos Salinas de Gortari was elected president. Salinas embarked on an ambitious restructuring of the Mexican economy, initiating policies to strengthen the free-market components of the economy. Top marginal tax rates were lowered to 36 percent in 1990, down from 60 percent in 1986, and new legislation had eliminated many restrictions on foreign investment. Foreign firms were allowed to buy up to 100 percent equity in many Mexican firms. Previously, foreign ownership of Mexican firms was limited to 49 percent. Many government-owned companies were sold to private investors to eliminate government bureaucracy and improve efficiency. Government spending had been reduced, and price and wage controls had been implemented. In addition, many tariff and nontrade barriers were eliminated.

Privatization

The privatization of government-owned companies had come to symbolize the restructuring of Mexico's economy. Over 700 government-owned companies had been sold, including Mexicana and AeroMexico, the two largest airlines in Mexico. On May 14, 1990, legislation was passed to privatize all banks.

EXHIBIT 11   **Economic Data for Mexico, 1986–1989**

	1986	1987	1988	1989
Population (millions)	79.6	81.2	83.3	85.0
GDP (billion pesos)	77.8	193.0	398.0	500.0e
Real GDP growth (%)	(3.6)	1.6	1.4	2.9
Exchange rate (average) pesos/$	611.8	1,378.2	2,273.1	2,453.5
Inflation (%)	86.2	131.8	114.2	20.0
Current account ($ billion)	(1.7)	3.9	(2.4)	(5.4)
Reserves (excluding gold, $ billion)	5.7	12.5	5.3	7.3
External debt ($ billion)	100.9	109.3	100.4	95.1
Debt service ratio (%)	50.7	37.3	43.1	–

e—estimated.
Source: *Business International*, 1990.

However, 400 companies remained under government ownership, representing 90 percent of the assets owned by the state at the start of 1988.

Prices, Wages, and Foreign Exchange

A two-tiered exchange rate system had been in force in Mexico since December 1982. Under this system, a controlled rate was used for imports, foreign debt payments, and conversion of export proceeds. A free-market rate was used for other transactions. In January 1988, the Mexican government announced the Pact for Stabilization and Economic Growth (PECE), which replaced the government's December 1987 regulation on prices and wages. The PECE was designed to limit increases in prices and wages, as well as drastic changes in value of the peso against the dollar. On January 1, 1989, Salinas announced the peso would be allowed to depreciate against the dollar by one peso per day. This applied to exports, imports, foreign debt, and royalty payments. The result had been a grossly overvalued peso, which lowered the price of imports. This led to an increase in imports of over 23 percent in 1989.

While the PECE had slowed the rate of inflation and lowered interest rates, it had also resulted in lost purchasing power, as wage increases failed to keep up with inflation. This had increased labor unrest.

Labor Concerns

One of KFC's primary concerns was the stability of Mexico's labor markets. Labor was relatively plentiful and cheap in Mexico, though much of the work force was still relatively unskilled. While KFC benefited from lower labor costs, it encountered significant problems with labor unrest, job retention, absenteeism, and punctuality. A good part of the problem with absenteeism and punctuality was cultural. However, problems with worker retention and labor unrest were mainly the result of workers' frustration over the loss of their purchasing power due to inflation and government controls of wage increases. *Business Latin America* estimated purchasing power fell by 35 percent in Mexico between January 1988 and June 1990. Though absenteeism was on the decline due to job security fears, it was still about 8 to 14 percent. Turnover of production line personnel was running at 5 to 12 percent per month.

Risks and Opportunities

Managers in KFC Mexico were hopeful that the government's new economic policies would bring inflation under control and promote growth in Mexico's economy. They also hoped that greater economic stability would help to eliminate much of the labor unrest. Of greatest concern to Guillermo Heredia, KFC's vice president of Latin America, was KFC's market share in Mexico. Heredia expected McDonald's and Arby's to begin aggressive building programs in Mexico, since both had signed franchise agreements in early 1990. If KFC failed to grow at least as quickly as these and other competitors, it could easily lose its No. 1 market share in Mexico. In fact, KFC planned to counter McDonald's by expanding its franchise base in Mexico and relying less heavily on company-owned restaurants than it had in the past. However, this strategy had significant risk. The franchising law was new. As a result, KFC could only hope that its technology and trade secrets would be protected under the new law, which had not yet been tested in the courts.

In addition to the risks surrounding the new franchise law, KFC worried that the Mexican government might be unable to correct the severe problems in Mexico's economy. It was also questionable whether the PRI would maintain its power in the future. The PRI faced serious challenges from the opposition Party of the Democratic Revolution (PRD) in 1991 elections for the Senate and Chamber of Deputies. If the PRI were to lose power to the PRD in the near future, the PRD, which favored more government control in the economy, could overturn the more free-market policies recently implemented by the PRI.

KFC's alternative, one favored by many at PepsiCo, was to approach investment in Mexico more conservatively, until greater economic and political stability could be achieved. Meanwhile, resources could be directed at other investment areas with less risk, such as Japan, Australia, China, and Europe. However, PepsiCo's commitments to these other markets were unlikely to be affected by its investment decisions in Mexico, as PepsiCo's large annual cash flows could satisfy the investment needs of KFC's other international subsidiaries, regardless of its investments in Mexico. However, the danger in taking a conservative approach in Mexico was the potential loss of market share in a large market where Kentucky Fried Chicken enjoyed enormous popularity.

COMPETITION IN THE WORLD SHORT-HAUL AIRCRAFT INDUSTRY

William C. Schulz, Oglethorpe University

Short-haul commercial aircraft have had an important role in providing fast transportation between points less than 300 miles apart. Before World War II, flying short distances was essential since the range and reliability of airplanes was limited. Intercontinental travel in both the United States and Europe, the birthplaces of commercial aviation, involved "hopscotching across the country" and appealed to the hearty and adventurous.

In the late 1930s, Douglas Aircraft Co. designed and built the DC-3, which became the first commercial aircraft to offer reasonable speed, safety, and comfort for coast-to-coast travel. This aeronautical innovation enabled the U.S. airline industry to make long-distance travel attractive to passengers. The length of the average flight started to climb, and air travel routes began to segment into short- and long-haul markets. Meanwhile, the airlines in Europe lagged behind the U.S. airlines in terms of size, technology, and service.

After World War II, an abundance of U.S. government surplus aircraft combined with a large supply of pilots enabled many new small, short-haul airlines to form. The U.S. government, which had originally regulated the "trunk" or major airlines in 1938, took steps to regulate a new group of airlines, called *feeder* or *local service* carriers. Between 1945 and 1951, the Civil Aeronautics Board certified 19 local carriers having average trip lengths less than 70 miles.[1]

THE TURBOPROP ERA

The short-haul market for commercial air travel was largely ignored by aircraft manufacturers during the 1950s; local service carriers utilized whatever aircraft they could get from the major airlines that met the federal payload weight limitation standard of 12,500 pounds or less. The choices were few, and the quality low. It was not until 1964, when the lightweight, high-horsepower turboprop engine was invented, that the design of a true short-haul commercial aircraft became feasible. The turboprop made it possible to design a plane that could carry up to 18 passengers while still meeting the federal payload weight limits. The first planes provided specifically for the U.S. short-haul airline market, such as the Beechcraft 99 and the De Havilland DHC-6 Twin Otter, were unpressurized, loud, and relatively uncomfortable; but they filled a market niche, and the short-haul aircraft industry was born.

---

[1]This history paraphrased from James Malloy, Jr., *The U.S. Commuter Airline Industry: Policy Alternatives* (Lexington, Mass: Lexington Books, 1985), pp. 1–20.

Another early and major player in the industry was Netherlands-based Fokker Aircraft, which had established itself as a premier airplane manufacturer during World War I and before World War II. The Fokker F-27, with English-made Rolls-Royce Dart engines, became an industry standard for pressurized, 50-seat aircraft. The more comfortable F-27 was an ideal size for European airline operators, which were not subject to the same weight limitations as the U.S. feeder airlines.

A fourth major player emerged in the international short-haul market in 1973, from an unlikely source—Brazil. The Embraer company, a state-controlled business with private backing, introduced the Bandeirante airplane and began to export them as early as 1975. The Bandeirante was fuel efficient and more quiet than the earlier Beechcraft and De Havilland models and was reliable and affordable. By 1982, over 200 of these planes had been sold.

AIRLINE DEREGULATION

The takeoff in demand for, and subsequent international supply of, short-haul aircraft began in the late 1970s when it became apparent the U.S. government was going to deregulate the major airlines, allowing them to abandon smaller markets that could not generate enough passenger traffic to support flights using large jet aircraft. In September 1978, the Airline Deregulation Act was signed into law, and a new interest in short-haul aircraft took hold. The act had the following major points:

- Subsidy payments for "essential air service" could be made to commuter airlines.
- Commuter airlines were eligible for FAA equipment loan guarantees for the first time.
- Commuter airlines were included in the uniform methods that established joint fares between airlines.
- Restrictions on the payload weights were raised to 18,000 pounds and 60 seats.

This law gave new carriers access to funds critical in starting a highly capital-intensive business such as an airline and formalized the manner in which commuter airlines could price and link their product to major air carriers. It also opened many markets the major airlines had vacated. The opportunity for growth was evident as 257 startup airlines formed between January 1978 and June 1980. The added competition created a tremendous need for aircraft, but the uncertainty of carrier survival made aircraft sales a potentially risky business—during the same period 240 commuter airlines went bankrupt.

Despite the financial risks in the commuter airline market in the United States, which represented the largest single market for short-haul aircraft, the commuter segment began to grow and resegment. Both larger carriers with larger aircraft and the traditional low-density feeder carriers prospered. These customer factors prompted aircraft manufacturers to attempt to meet the varied needs of the short-haul operators; demand ranged from a 19-seat, unpressurized plane to a four-engine "quiet jet" made by British Aerospace.

EXHIBIT 1   **Designs and Forecasted Demand for Short-Haul Aircraft, 1980–2000**

	Seat Size of Aircraft		
FAA Forecast of Unit Sales	**15–19 Seats**	**20–40 Seats**	**41–60 Seats**
Number of designs as of 1983	10	7	4
Total sales, 1980–2000	2,187	1,996	1,215
Sales per year, 1980–2000	109	100	61
Annual sales per design	10.9	14.3	15.3

Source: James Malloy, Jr., *The U.S. Commuter Airline Industry: Policy Alternatives* (Lexington, Mass.: Lexington Books, 1985), p. 120.

DIVERSE CUSTOMERS AND PRODUCTS

Airplane manufacturers had to work closely with airline executives, military personnel, and government officials to meet both customer needs and flight safety regulations. The particular needs of a segment of customers were generally made clear when the airline issued its specifications; manufacturers then reacted to these specifications by designing or modifying a plane to fit the stated need. The short-haul market was particularly difficult to accommodate, from the manufacturer's perspective, because of its varied and fragmented nature. A single airline might need planes that held as few as 10 to 20 passengers or as many as 110, while at the same time needing fleet commonality (in terms of having airplanes that used the same basic engines and spare parts) to help control maintenance costs.

The majority of short-haul aircraft carried between 10 and 20 people. The limit at 20 was more related to legal constraints than technology since U.S. law required that a flight attendant be aboard flights with more than 19 passengers. The 19-passenger designs dominated both the U.S. and European markets, though many manufacturers believed that the trend was changing. Exhibit 1 shows the number of designs, by seat class, and the Federal Aviation Administration's forecasts for future sales. Exhibit 2 shows Fokker Aircraft's forecasted demand for small commercial planes to the year 2000.

THE GLOBAL ARENA

Deregulation of the U.S. airline industry, and the subsequent growth of the global airline system, had attracted new entrants into all arenas of aircraft manufacture. In the medium-to-long and ultra-long-range markets, Airbus Industries, a consortium of European and North American aerospace firms, had challenged McDonnell Douglas for the second position behind Boeing Aircraft. In the short-haul markets, there had been an impressive entry into the marketplace by new competitors, many of which were either state-owned enterprises (SOEs) or joint ventures. Entrants since 1978 included Embraer, from Brazil; Bombardier and Canadair, from Canada; Aerospatiale/Alenia from France and Italy; Saab, from Sweden; Casa/Nurtanio, from Spain and Indonesia; MPC, a Germany–China joint venture; British Aerospace, from the United Kingdom; Allison, Bromon, Commuter Air Transports, and Skytrader,

EXHIBIT 2   **Forecasted Demand for Commuter Aircraft, by Size of Plane, 1988–2000**

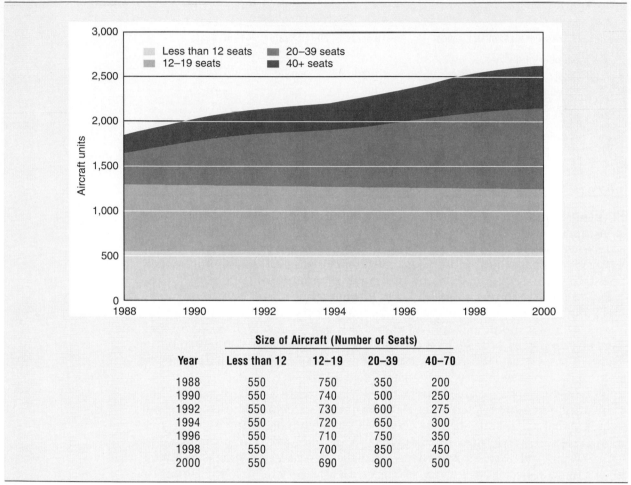

	Size of Aircraft (Number of Seats)			
Year	Less than 12	12–19	20–39	40–70
1988	550	750	350	200
1990	550	740	500	250
1992	550	730	600	275
1994	550	720	650	300
1996	550	710	750	350
1998	550	700	850	450
2000	550	690	900	500

Source: Fokker Aircraft USA.

all from the United States; and a 1990 entrant from Eastern Europe, Czechoslovakia's LET company.

The rush of new players into the short-haul business had occurred predominantly in Europe, though the single most successful new entrant, in terms of aircraft sales, had been the Brazilian company, Embraer. The Europeans and Embraer had made significant advances in small aircraft technology and were eroding the market share of Fairchild, the only U.S. manufacturer with any clout in the market. Bromon, a new U.S. entrant, was planning to release a 46-passenger airplane in 1990 and would become the first new U.S. participant in the larger markets. Exhibit 3 lists the aircraft in production or design as of 1990. Exhibit 4 shows the most popular models in service in 1988.

As of 1989 the two largest markets, in terms of available aircraft, were the 10-to-19-seat category and the 31-to-50-seat category. The Embraer Brasilia dominated the 20-to-30-seat market so thoroughly through the 1980s that no effective competition existed. However, new aircraft were being designed in 1990

EXHIBIT 3 — Comparison of the Types of Short-Haul Commercial Aircraft Available, 1990

Aircraft Manufacturer	Model	Price (Million)	Seating Capacity	Aircraft Type	Country(s) of Manufacture	Comments
10–19 Seats						
Dornier	228–101	$ 1.7	15	Turboprop	Germany	Not pressurized
British Aerospace	Jetstream 31	3.6	18	Turboprop	Great Britain	Larger version in design
Beechcraft	1900	3.5	19	Turboprop	United States	
Beechcraft	1900–D (Design)	NA	19	Turboprop	United States	Standup cabin
Dornier	228–202	3.3	19	Turboprop	Germany	
Embraer	CBA-123 (Design)	NA	19	Pusher-prop	Brazil	Fast and fuel efficient
Embraer	EMB-110P1/41	2.4	19	Turboprop	Brazil	
Fairchild	MetroIII Heavy	3.6	19	Turboprop	United States	
Fairchild	Metro III	3.5	19	Turboprop	United States	Market share leader
20–30 Seats						
De Havilland/Short	NRA-90-B (Design)	NA	25	Pusher-prop	Canada-Ireland	
Casa	C -212	4	26	Turboprop	Spain	
Dornier	DO.328 (Design)	NA	30	Turboprop	Germany	Pressurized
Embraer	EMB-120 Brasilia	6.2	30	Turboprop	Brazil	Market leader
IPTN	N-250	NA	30	Turboprop	Indonesia	
Short	330	3.9	30	Turboprop	Ireland	
31–50 Seats						
Saab-Scandia	SF-340	6.9	35	Turboprop	Sweden	
Short	360-300	4.6	36	Turboprop	Ireland	
De Havilland	Dash 8-100	8	37	Turboprop	Canada	
LET-Czech	LET-CT7-9 (Design)	5.5	40	Turboprop	Czechoslovakia	
Embraer	EMB-145 (Design)	NA	40	Jet	Brazil	New jet design
US Aircraft	DC3-TP	1.5	42	Turboprop	United States	Refurbished 1950s aircraft
CASA/IPTN	CN-235 (Design)	8.7	44	Turboprop	Spain-Indonesia	
British Aerospace	Super 784	6	48	Turboprop	Great Britain	
Canadair	CL-601RJ (Design)	13	48	Jet	Canada	
ATR	ATR 42-300	8.4	50	Turboprop	France-Italy	
Allison	CV 580A	5.4	50	Turboprop	United States	Refurbished 1950s aircraft
De Havilland	Dash 7	8	50	Turboprop	Canada	
De Havilland	Dash 8-300	10	50	Turboprop	Canada	
Fokker	F-50	10	50	Turboprop	Holland	
Saab	2000 (Design)	NA	50	Turboprop	Sweden	
51–99 Seats						
British Aerospace	ATP	11.5	64	Turboprop	Great Britain	
ATR	ATR 72	10.5	66	Turboprop	France-Italy	
British Aerospace	146-100	16.8	82	Jet	Great Britain	Quiet jet
Fokker	F-28	11	85	Jet	Holland	
Over 99 Seats						
ATR	ATR-92 (Design)	NA	100	Jet	France-Italy	
British Aerospace	146-200	17.8	100	Jet	Great Britain	
Mbb-Catic-Short	MPG-175 (Design)	NA	100	Jet	Germany-Ireland-China	
Fokker	F-100	20	107	Jet	Holland	Fokker considering expansion
British Aerospace	146-300	18.5	108	Jet	Great Britain	

EXHIBIT 4   Leading Models of Small Commercial Aircraft in Service, 1988

Rank	Manufacturer	Model	Number of Aircraft in Commercial Service	Total Seats	Percent of Total Seating Capacity	1988 Fleet Flying Hours
1	Fairchild	Metro	254	4,826	13.1%	528,746
2	Short	360	75	2,700	7.3	187,156
3	British Aerospace	Jetstream 31	136	2,584	7.0	278,779
4	British Aerospace	Jet.146	28	2,520	6.8	65,222
5	Aerospatiale	ATR42	49	2,254	6.1	168,901
6	Saab	340	70	2,240	6.1	168,901
7	Embraer	Brasilia	64	1,920	5.2	160,463
8	Beech Aircraft	1900	84	1,596	4.3	190,202
9	De Havilland	Dash 7	31	1,550	4.2	77,053
10	De Havilland	Twin Otter	77	1,463	4.0	122,161
11	De Havilland	Dash 8	41	1,312	3.5	96,061
12	Embraer	Bandeirante	69	1,242	3.4	146,076
13	Fokker	F27	24	1,080	2.9	62,400
14	Convair	580	20	960	2.6	24,254
15	Cessna	402	119	952	2.6	129,541
16	Piper	Navajo	109	872	2.4	106,694
17	Beech Aircraft	99	56	840	2.3	130,625
	Total top 17 aircraft		1,306	30,911	83.8	2,643,235
	All others in service		495	6,065	16.2	514,333
	Industry total		1,801	36,976	100.0%	3,157,568

Source: RAA, 1990.

that would compete with the Brasilia in the 30-seat market and in the other markets. These newer designs incorporated integrated electronic cockpits, such as those found on the new large jets; new materials, including advanced metal composites and plastics; new propulsion systems; and interior characteristics that allowed for standup headroom and quiet travel.

JOINT VENTURE ARRANGEMENTS

The modern short-haul airplane was almost as sophisticated as the large commercial jet aircraft manufactured by Boeing, McDonnell Douglas, and Airbus. To build commercial aircraft of any size required that a manufacturer possess capabilities in advanced structures, metal forming, advanced electronics, systems integration and testing, aerodynamic testing and theory, materials management, and engineering management. The risks of the business were high, as new designs of short-haul aircraft could cost between $40 million and $500 million. The pressures to have a high degree of competence in many technical areas and to develop a broad access to markets had driven short-haul manufacturers to form alliances when designing and building new commuter aircraft.

The Fokker F-100 Project

The Fokker F-100, a 110-seat jet, was typical of the joint venture arrangements being made in developing new aircraft designs. Fokker was responsible for the design and integration of components of the aircraft and subcontracted the

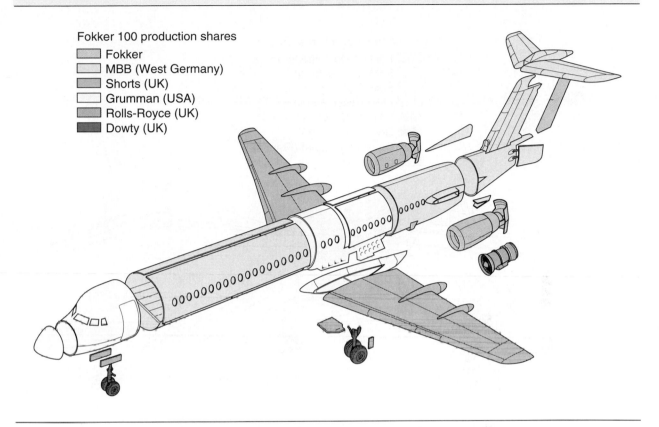

Fokker 100 production shares

- Fokker
- MBB (West Germany)
- Shorts (UK)
- Grumman (USA)
- Rolls-Royce (UK)
- Dowty (UK)

major components to other manufacturers in the industry. Several other major players were providing components for the F-100 and F-50, chosen on the basis of their expertise in a particular area and their willingness to accept production and sales risks (see Exhibit 5).

Other International Joint Ventures

Spain's Construcciones Aeronauticas (CASA) and P.T. Nurtanio of Indonesia had combined to build a 44-seat regional turboprop, at two locations.[2] Aeritalia from Italy and Aerospatiale of France had collaborated to build 50-seat and 60-seat turboprop models, to be assembled at Aerospatiale's Toulouse, France, manufacturing site (also the assembly site for a jumbo-jet product line).

These joint ventures allowed participants to spread risk and expand markets as well as to reduce costs by sharing design and engineering tasks that would have taxed the staff of any one company acting alone. While joint ventures had the disadvantages of sharing proprietary information, loss of

---

[2]The discussion on joint ventures draws heavily from David M. North, "Commuter, Corporate Manufacturers Spread Risks, Costs of New Designs," *Aviation Week & Space Technology,* June 3, 1985, pp. 275–82.

EXHIBIT 5	*(concluded)*

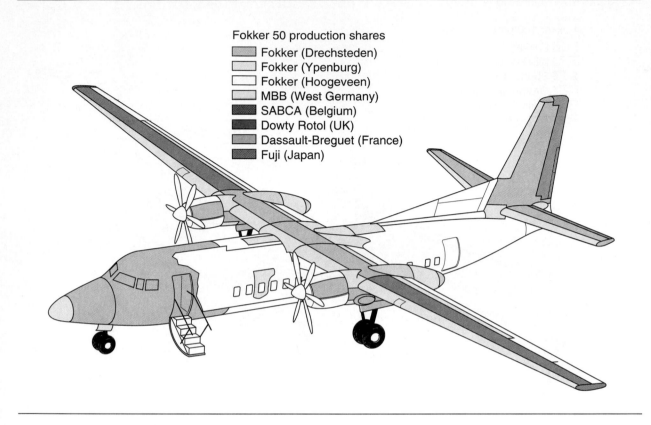

Fokker 50 production shares
- Fokker (Drechsteden)
- Fokker (Ypenburg)
- Fokker (Hoogeveen)
- MBB (West Germany)
- SABCA (Belgium)
- Dowty Rotol (UK)
- Dassault-Breguet (France)
- Fuji (Japan)

managerial autonomy and flexibility, and problems in insuring equity in both risk and gain, as long as the objectives of the partners were compatible, joint venture arrangements were regarded as a desirable vehicle for gaining greater global market access.[3]

However, international joint ventures in aerospace could prove hazardous, as Embraer had discovered. In 1987, Embraer announced the new Argentinian firm, Fabrica Argentina de Materiel Aerospacial (FAMA), would be a risk-sharing partner in the development of an advanced-technology 19-seater called the CBA-123. Edvaldo Pereira Lima, of *Air Transport World*, explained:

> The capital for FAMA was to come from the Argentina government and outside investors. According to the agreement with Embraer, FAMA would have to invest $100 million on the CBA-123 program . . . economic and political turmoil in Argentina prevented any effective move toward these goals. FAMA failed to attract international investors, while local capitalists went through uncertain times of their own. At the same time, in mid-1989, there was a dramatic change of administration in Argentina, which meant that the top management at FAMA

[3]Moxon, Roehl, Truitt, "International Cooperative Ventures in the Commercial Aircraft Industry: Gains, Sure, But What's My Share?" in *Cooperative Strategies in International Business*.

also was changed and the new leaders needed time to get the agreement going again.[4]

As of 1990, the FAMA-Embraer partnership was strained, and the costs to build and test the development aircraft continued to climb as the schedule was set back further.

STRUCTURE OF THE BUYING SIDE OF THE MARKET

Commercial aircraft manufacturers sold to five broad classes of customers: (1) the world's airlines, (2) governments and military organizations, (3) cargo operators, (4) leasing companies, and (5) private companies and individuals. The buying characteristics of the different customers varied, both between and within groups.

Since deregulation, one major structural characteristic had dominated the decisions of what type of aircraft fleet regional airlines should or could own: the relationship to a major airline or government. Both in the United States and Europe, many commuter airlines were either affiliated with a major airline or were owned in part by a government or a major carrier. Functioning as a feeder airline pressured regional carriers into offering services comparable to what passengers got when they boarded the major carriers' flights. Short-haul airlines serving major carriers tended to acquire aircraft that were pressurized, had a wide and quiet cabin, were larger than 19 seats, and were fast. The added cost of such planes was sometimes underwritten by the major carriers, spreading the risk. Feeder airlines typically shared resources for ticketing, computer reservations and flight scheduling, and baggage connections with the major airline partner they fed passengers to.

These affiliations between regional and major airlines were not necessarily a panacea for the regional carriers, however. Fare wars among the major airlines often spilled over to affect the local and regional carriers, putting tremendous pressures on margins. Also, when a major carrier, such as Eastern Air Lines, filed bankruptcy, its feeder carriers were virtually grounded.

A number of short-haul airlines operated, however, without direct affiliation with a major carrier. Such independents sometimes found that access to major airports was either limited or costly, due to congested airspace and a lack of boarding gates at busy airports. In Europe, the 19-passenger regional airliners had been squeezed out of the largest hubs, such as Frankfurt, London, and Paris, due to high landing and parking fees and the political favoritism shown major national carriers.

The small independent airlines' response had been to offer direct city-pair service, bypassing the hub-and-spoke system and offering passengers the quickest flight between two points not served by major airports. This market was ideal for the 19-seat aircraft, as the flight lengths were on the average longer than the average hub-based lengths (105 nautical miles in the United States and 183 nautical miles in Europe) and could provide seat/mile returns to justify the small aircraft size. Using smaller craft enabled independents to schedule more flights per day, a key success factor in dense markets. One

---

[4]E. P. Lima, "Getting Pushy," *Air Transport World*, September 1990, pp. 167–69.

industry executive noted, "What kills an airline is buying equipment that's too big . . . a commuter is no good without frequency, especially . . . where you have competition from the automobile."[5]

Another problem nonaffiliated airlines faced was that they often did not have the financial resources to buy the most appropriate aircraft—the fleet choice hinged on whatever financing terms could be arranged, even if the plane was too large or otherwise did not properly fit operating conditions. Fokker Aircraft, for example, had self-financed up to $30 million in contingent debt as a result of financing independent airlines that otherwise could not have financed the purchase of Fokker's planes.

Governments also participated in defining the airlines' choices of aircraft by subsidizing selected routes and carriers. In the United States, the government had supported "essential air carrier" (EAS) services since 1978 and had awarded direct subsidies under regulation for all airlines. The EAS subsidies attempted to ensure that local air service was available to all cities certified for EAS as of October 1978. These subsidies had ranged from a high of $122 million in 1981 to a low of $24 million in 1988. In Brazil, the four regional carriers were subsidized and a 3 percent surcharge was placed on all long-range travel. These government programs allowed carriers to acquire aircraft that they could not afford otherwise.

Despite the uncertainty and narrow margins, short-haul airlines had experienced significant growth (see Exhibit 6). Exhibit 7 shows the aircraft fleets of selected commuter airlines.

STRUCTURE OF THE PRODUCING SIDE OF THE MARKET

Modern aircraft manufacturers were more assembly firms than manufacturing enterprises. Many of the key parts and components were obtained from outside suppliers and manufacturing specialists. Since the 1970s, there had been complex interdependencies among the various airframe makers in terms of joint ventures and subcontracting, with some aircraft having 80 percent of the major structural components built by "competitors." This type of complexity also existed in the aircraft component industries such as avionics, radar, hydraulics and fuel delivery systems, wiring, power plants, landing gear, cabin interiors, and simulators.

Like the aircraft producers, the major aerospace equipment suppliers were becoming globally active and interconnected. The commercial equipment sector had been quite stable in the United States, though it had been affected by the consolidation and mergers that were leading to its domination by fewer, more powerful companies. Typifying the modern U.S. aerospace firm was Allied-Signal Aerospace Co., which had businesses in primary and auxiliary power units (Garrett), wheels and brakes (Bendix), fluid systems (AiResearch), and many various electronics fields. Allied-Signal had an asset base of $11.2 billion, with yearly sales near $12 billion and operating margins of 11 percent, making it a strong force in the marketplace.[6] Exhibit 8 illustrates the entry and

---

[5]From an interview with *Interavia*, October 1985.
[6]From "Shark Eat Shark: Call it Consolidation," *Interavia*, July 1988, p. 658.

EXHIBIT 6   Selected Statistics on Regional Airline Operations, 1970–89

Year	Enplaned Passengers	Number of Aircraft Operated	Carriers in Operation	Airports Served	Average Trip Length (Miles)	Average Seat Capacity/Aircraft	Average Annual Utilization (Hours/Plane)
1970	4,270	687					
1971	4,698	782					
1972	5,262	791					
1973	5,688	885			Not available		
1974	6,842	997					
1975	7,243	1,073					
1976	7,914	1,009					
1977	9,185	1,119					
1978	11,026	1,047	228	681	121	11.9	1,080
1979	13,972	1,265	227	746	123	12.5	1,193
1980	14,810	1,339	214	732	129	13.9	1,299
1981	15,400	1,463	246	766	136	15.1	1,363
1982	18,550	1,573	215	817	141	15.6	1,373
1983	21,820	1,545	196	854	149	18.1	1,563
1984	26,000	1,747	203	853	160	18.4	1,582
1985	27,000	1,745	179	854	173	19.2	1,635
1986	28,360	1,806	179	824	158	18.4	1,622
1987	31,787	1,841	169	834	158	19.7	1,598
1988	35,188	1,801	163	861	173	20.5	1,709
1989	37,359	1,907	n/a	n/a	181	21.8	1,712

EXHIBIT 7   Aircraft Fleets of Selected Commuter Airlines, 1987

Airline (Affiliate)	Fleet Size	Manufacturer/Model
Aspen Airways (United)	10	Convair 580 (Re-engined 1950s propeller plane)
	4	BAe 146–100A
Britt Airways (Continental)	12	Beech 99
	19	Fairchild Metro III
	2	BAC -111 (Older 80-passenger jets)
	2	Embraer Brasilia
Presidential Airways	10	Boeing 737–200 (130-seat jets)
	15	BAe 146–200
Westair (United)	5	Short 360
	33	Embraer EMB-110
	12	Embraer EMB-120
	6	BAe 146–200
On order	28	Embraer EMB-120
On option	10	Embraer EMB-120

EXHIBIT 8   **Entry and Exit in Selected Sectors of the U.S. Aero Equipment Industry, 1985–88**

Sector	Entry	Exit
Avionics	Collins Aviation	General Aviation
	Garrett Canada	
	Honeywell/Sperry	
	LaPoint Industries	
	Mentor Radio Co.	
	Tracor Aerospace	
Flight performance/management systems		
Firms in 1988: 13	Teledyne Avionics	Garrett
Firms in 1985: 11	Trendkey	
	Universal Nav. Corp.	
Seats and cabin furnishing		
Firms in 1988: 14	AiResearch Aviation	American Safety Flight Systems
Firms in 1985: 12	Hayes International	AMI Industries
	Sabreliner Corp.	BAS, Inc
	SOCEA/Aerospatiale	
	Weber Aircraft	

exit that occurred in selected areas of the U.S. equipment industry between 1985 and 1988.

GLOBAL COMPETITION AMONG SUPPLIERS

Competition between the European and Japanese equipment makers for large and small aircraft contracts was increasing. The European equipment sector had undergone major changes that would affect its competitiveness in the marketplace into the next century; four major forces were at work. First, the weak U.S. dollar during the late 1980s created opportunity for the purchase of U.S. companies (Dowty Group of the United Kingdom purchased a former Boeing subsidiary, Hydraulic Units Inc., based in Duarte, California; and Smith Industries of the United Kingdom purchased Lear Siegler's Avionics Systems operations at Grand Rapids, Michigan). This had opened U.S. markets to European suppliers and had created extra capacity in Europe. Second, many European companies had shed unprofitable subsidiaries. Thompson-CSF, the largest equipment manufacturer in France, for example, had sold its Thompson-Lucas operations. According to a Thompson-CSF official:

> The sale of Thompson-Lucas is a question of investment priorities. We're in the process of acquiring companies that are more directly related to our main area of work, and we want to sell off some of our operations that no longer meet the company's current goals. This is an effort to concentrate more on our primary business strategy.

The third force that had reshaped the European equipment industry was that equipment manufacturers had begun to team up to secure international contracts, similar to the way the U.S. firms pooled their resources and competencies. And, fourth, the defense budgets of the European nations had been rapidly shrinking, forcing the suppliers to look for commercial business outside national boundaries. The most dramatic example was the turnaround of the French equipment industry during the 1980s; the French suppliers had transformed themselves from stodgy firms, dependent on national markets, into globally competitive firms active in advanced research, development, and technology programs and operating with streamlined corporate structures.[7]

Tension had begun to build in the 1990s in the form of increased competition between U.S. firms and their European counterparts for the business of the smaller aircraft manufacturers. This competition was exacerbated by the entrance of the Japanese, who had also bid for major contracts. In September 1986, the European consortium ATR awarded the landing gear contract for the ATR72 to the French supplier Messier-Hispano-Bugatti after it agreed to match contractual conditions proposed by the Sumitomo Company of Japan. The European reaction was critical of the Japanese bid. According to one ATR manager:

> The price offered by Sumitomo to produce the ATR72 landing gear was well below what Messier originally had bid. This was despite the fact that Messier was responsible for the current ATR42 landing gear, and that its ATR72 design was derived from the gear now in production for the ATR42. We in Europe have to ask ourselves whether the Sumitomo bid on the ATR72 landing gear should be considered dumping.

One Messier-Hispano-Bugatti official said:

> We were forced to make a financial sacrifice on our response to the Sumitomo bid with the hope that the ATR72 production ultimately will reach several hundred aircraft . . . if the ATR72 production stops at 100 aircraft, then we will have made a very bad decision. Only after the production reaches a level of a couple hundred will we start breathing a little easier.

This level of intense competition among the global suppliers was not expected to recede as Europe prepared to form a common market in 1992 and the Japanese became more focused in their efforts to be world leaders in aerospace.

PROFILES OF SELECTED MANUFACTURERS

A brief description of the producers of small commercial aircraft follows. Exhibit 9 contains performance summaries for selected major competitors.

Aerospatiale/Alenia (France/Italy)

This international consortium of aircraft companies from France and Italy had become a strong force in the larger turboprop market and had been competing head-on with Fokker Aircraft of the Netherlands. The companies had collaborated in an effort to establish manufacturing capability, market penetration and access, profits, and national prestige. Both of the primary firms in the

---

[7]From "French Aerospace Equipment Manufacturers," *Aviation Week & Space Technology,* August 22, 1988, p. 67.

EXHIBIT 9   Comparative Financial and Operating Performance of Selected Commuter Aircraft Manufacturers, 1985–90

Company	1990	1989	1988	1987	1986	1985
Aerospatiale (Millions of French francs–Fr)						
Net sales	35,237	33,903	32,121	31,360	33,854	34,257
Operating income	(5,925)	(2,189)	3,482	n/a	(4,564)	(2,664)
Net income after tax	(396)	129	(63)	136	303	543
Inventories	20,041	16,469	22,782	n/a	17,874	19,599
Total current assets	38,633	34,997	45,019	n/a	42,659	43,342
Total assets	47,897	42,883	52,096	n/a	54,841	54,262
Current ratio	1.12	1.19	1.54	1.45	1.64	1.56
Total current liabilities	34,363	29,486	29,281	n/a	26,036	27,708
Long-term debt	4,249	3,757	8,229	n/a	16,577	13,998
Capital expenditures	2,401	2,184	1,667	n/a	1,092	921
Employees	32,154	30,183	32,638	33,717	35,113	43,219
R&D	n/a	2,700	8,100	n/a	6,900	6,800
Bombardier Inc. (Canadair/Short) (Millions of Canadian dollars–$)						
Net sales	2,093	1,396	1,389	989	548	400
Operating income	119	97	n/a	n/a	n/a	n/a
Net income after tax	92	68	67	46	16	10
Inventories	583	220	n/a	n/a	n/a	n/a
Total current assets	1,104	554	485	433	277	274
Total assets	1,525	871	753	668	420	427
Total current liabilities	769	339	303	261	170	114
Long-term debt	147	71	65	35	40	n/a
Employees	22,500	n/a	n/a	n/a	n/a	n/a
British Aerospace PLC (Millions of pounds–£)						
Net sales	10,540	9,085	5,643	4,075	3,137	2,647
Operating income	220	441	74	n/a	188	183
Net income after tax	239	212	156	(110)	84	127
Inventories	2,830	2,362	2,039	1,537	1,175	1,090
Total current assets	5,901	6,109	3,839	715	2,611	2,123
Total assets	9,291	9,176	6,499	4,709	3,277	2,741
Current ratio	1.280	1.320	1.303	1.370	1.727	2.024
Total current liabilities	4,625	4,619	2,947	2,553	1,512	1,049
Long-term debt	925	994	318	306	236	265
Capital expenditures	834	860	490	n/a	98	98
Employees	127,900	127,499	133,605	86,802	75,480	75,645
R&D	635	575	76	n/a	62	54

n/a—not available

consortium were state-owned enterprises (SOEs), as were most of the non-U.S. short-haul firms. Professor Ravi Sarathy, an industry expert, noted:

Given the dubious profitability of the various competing aircraft ventures, it is useful to ask whether profits are the paramount objective. Of the five manufacturers, four are SOEs. Their objectives could give precedence to sales maximization, employment creation, technological advancement, and foreign exchange earnings, with losses being willingly borne and subsidized by the state treasury. Examples abound with SOEs in aerospace: Aerospatiale's attempts to sell the Airbus in rivalry with Boeing, the subsidies already given to De Havilland,

EXHIBIT 9   *(continued)*

Company	1990	1989	1988	1987	1986	1985
De Havilland of Canada						
(Millions of Canadian dollars)						
Net sales					299	204
Operating income					19	11
Net income after tax					(94)	(40)
Inventories					237	144
Total current assets					303	181
Total assets		Subsidiary of Boeing, USA			345	226
Current ratio		(Separate data, not available)			1.515	1.199
Total current liabilities					200	151
Long-term debt					18	54
Capital expenditures					2	1
Employees						3,500
R&D						49
Dornier GMBH (Subsidiary of Daimler-Benz)						
(Millions of Deutsche marks)						
Net sales	2,826	2,203	1,919	1,608	2,122	2,117
Operating income	(247)	(217)	122	n/a	173	264
Net income after tax	(36)	(88)	(5)	15	42	24
Inventories	1,459	1,872	1,916	n/a	731	688
Total current assets	3,075	3,324	2,854	n/a	2,592	2,325
Total assets	3,675	3,950	3,695	n/a	2,762	2,471
Current ratio	1.85	1.77	1.63	1.34	1.160	1.165
Total current liabilities	1,976	1,747	1,064	n/a	2,234	1,995
Long-term debt	150	150	150	n/a	0	0
Capital expenditures	157	201	164	n/a	78	73
Employees	10,583	10,036	9,785	9,683	9,557	8,772
R&D	1,287	924	653	n/a		
Embraer Aircraft						
(Millions of U.S. dollars)						
Net sales	582	701	523	474	378	
Operating income	(277)	n/a	n/a	n/a	n/a	
Net income after tax	126	416	178	157	145	
Inventories	399	n/a	n/a	n/a	n/a	
Total current assets	574	n/a	n/a	n/a	n/a	
Total assets	1,109	n/a	n/a	n/a	n/a	
Total current liabilities	850	n/a	n/a	n/a	n/a	
Current loans	509	n/a	n/a	n/a	n/a	
Long-term debt	129	n/a	n/a	n/a	n/a	
Capital expenditures	21	14	17	28	24	
Employees	9,007	12,607	12,069	10,157	8,592	
R&D	127	107	53	43	29	

Embraer's attempts to gain market share in the United States when selling the Bandeirante. Given the previous history of SOEs in the aerospace industry, it is unlikely that market share can be won from them except by also sustaining losses.[8]

---

[8]Ravi Sarathy, "Prospects of New Generation Turboprop Aircraft," *Transportation Journal*, Summer 1985, p. 84.

EXHIBIT 9   *(concluded)*

Company	1990	1989	1988	1987	1986	1985
Fokker N.V.						
(Millions of Dutch guilders)						
Net sales	3,202	2,799	2,054	1,055	1,403	1,339
Operating income	50	34	(6)	n/a	(251)	(273)
Net income after tax	83	42	13	(107)	19	33
Inventories	2,528	1,632	1,595	n/a	733	212
Total current assets	3,038	2,444	1,943	n/a	1,082	908
Total assets	4,501	3,861	3,318	n/a	1,486	1,277
Current ratio	2.11	2.08	2.10	1.74	2.63	3.33
Total current liabilities	1,440	1,175	927	n/a	412	273
Long-term debt	1,892	1,565	1,259	n/a	289	263
Capital expenditures	181	111	98	n/a	67	92
Employees	13,561	12,925	11,690	11,709	10,860	10,053
R&D	n/a	n/a	n/a	n/a	n/a	n/a
SAAB-Scania AB						
(Millions of Swedish kronors)						
Net sales	29,035	44,905	42,488	41,403	35,222	31,840
Operating income	2,081	818	2,528	n/a	2,796	2,508
Net income after tax	352	1,008	1,561	1,445	1,306	695
Inventories	5,375	9,219	9,294	n/a	8,767	7,789
Total current assets	25,793	25,286	23,245	n/a	19,345	17,495
Total assets	43,146	46,527	40,747	n/a	31,463	27,010
Current ratio	1.56	1.32	1.59	1.63	1.70	1.64
Total current liabilities	16,549	19,094	11,575	n/a	11,406	10,644
Long-term debt	4,016	4,712	4,524	n/a	3,047	1,820
Capital expenditures	3,410	4,572	3,255	n/a	2,403	1,872
Employees	50,011	53,408	51,892	49,412	47,407	45,181
R&D	2,453	3,191	3,204		2,611	2,401

Sources: Worldscope Industrial Company Profiles, 1987, and Compact Disclosure (1990), Europe.

Between 1981 and 1986, ATR operations lost a cumulative 7 million French francs; the largest operating loss was posted in 1986. As of 1990, with the French government's active promotion of activities in orbital satellite delivery, the European Space Plane Project, assorted jumbo-jet products, and the ATR consortium, it seemed improbable that ATR would do anything other than take an aggressive strategic position in the industry despite its lack of operating profits. The fuel-efficient ATR42 and ATR72 had sold well in the United States, and the proposed ATR92 jet signaled an intention to challenge Fokker and British Aerospace for the honor of becoming the fourth major aircraft producer, behind Boeing, McDonnell Douglas, and Airbus Industries. ATR was establishing itself as a good prime contractor, with access to plenty of capital, and with the potential to establish strong ties to the North American market.

As of October 1990, ATR was negotiating with Boeing on a possible acquisition of Boeing's Canadian subsidiary, De Havilland Aircraft. The De Havilland division had not been able to meet the expectations Boeing had when it bought the Canadian company in 1986. If consummated, the arrangement would strengthen the hand of the European consortium in the commuter transport field and would allow Boeing to unload a marginal operation that had drained resources when they were most needed. De Havilland built the Dash 8 Series 100 and the Series 300, high-wing, turboprop transports that are not unlike the ATR42 and 72. The sale would have to be reviewed by Investment Canada, a federal agency that regulated foreign investment in the country. The European companies intended to create a grouping of the ATR consortium and De Havilland capabilities to satisfy a worldwide, growing commuter aircraft market.[9]

Allison Industries (United States)

Allison Industries was a subsidiary of General Motors and was primarily a manufacturer of large turboprop engines, such as those that powered the Lockheed C-130 Hercules, and advanced technology Ultra-high Bypass jet engines. Since 1985, it had assembled a team of former Convair engineers and undertaken a joint venture with Flight Trails in Carlsbad, California, to renovate Convair 580s for commuter and executive operations.

The Convair Super 580 and Flagship renovations provided airlines a low upfront cost, large aircraft with speed and comfort. Operating costs were higher than the competitors' and were fuel-price sensitive.

Beech Aircraft (a Raytheon Subsidiary, United States)

Beech Aircraft had been producing private-owner aircraft since 1932 in the United States, corporate executive aircraft since 1937, and short-haul aircraft since 1968. Beech had an excellent reputation for quality but had never been a cost-efficient producer. In 1980, Beech Aircraft was acquired by the U.S. electronics firm Raytheon Co. and continued to produce in the general, corporate, and short-haul markets. The $790 million purchase of Beech by Raytheon coincided with the start of a decline in corporate airplane sales that continued into 1987. Despite the sales slump, Raytheon had allowed Beech to proceed with a $250 million investment in an all-new aircraft, the Starship, an innovative turboprop.

The new plane seated 10 people, burned 35 percent less fuel than a comparable jet, and was roomier, quieter, and faster than any small turboprop built as of 1990. Its unique design included an airframe made of high-strength plastic composites. Deliveries were expected to begin by late 1990. Critics said the plane's profit potential was in doubt because of its high price—$3.7 million— and a lack of demand. It also had to compete with Italian planemaker Rinaldo Piaggio whose 7- to 9-passenger Avanti advanced turboprop was lighter, 15 percent faster, and needed only one pilot compared with two for the Starship.[10]

U.S. general aircraft manufacturers, including Beech, had been slow to recognize the growth market for commuter aircraft. Only Beech, the world's largest manufacturer of turboprops, had any significant commuter sales. Since the late 1980s, Beech had focused on the 19-seat market and offered the Model 1900. In 1990, Beech introduced a standup cabin version of the 1900, the 1900-D. Chester Schickling, Beech's 1990 international marketing sales manager, in an interview with *Air Transport World* explained his firm's strategy:

---

[9]*Aviation Week & Space Technology,* July 30, 1990, p. 87.
[10]Mark Ivey, "Will Breaking the Plastic Barrier Be Enough for Beech?" *Business Week*, December 28, 1987–January 4, 1988, p. 78B.

We do not dispel (the notion) that there is a 30-passenger-plus dominance; but there will always be a market for a 19-passenger aircraft. Before the economic changes occur in Europe in 1993, we want to establish ourselves as a premier manufacturer of regional airliners.[11]

As of mid-1990, Beech had not locked in a firm sale of the 1990-D. Beech believed it could serve the needs of the world markets, relying on its parent company for needed support, and offering in-house financial services that would enable it to cut competitive deals for its customers. However, it was not clear that Beechcraft had a clear strategic direction. The company, which was devoting more attention to corporate aircraft, announced in 1990 a $1 billion contract with the U.S. Air Force to sell the Beechjet as a trainer. This, combined with Beech's commitment to the Starship program, left little room for further penetration in the commuter markets without putting its production facilities under great strain.[12]

Boeing/De Havilland (Canada)

The De Havilland division of Boeing (the world's largest aircraft producer with headquarters in Seattle) had been a manufacturer of turboprop aircraft since the introduction of the Twin-Otter in the 1960s. The product line as of 1990 included many high-wing designs that served a wide range of markets. Boeing's De Havilland models were quite competitive in the 35-to-50-seat short-haul markets and the 37-seat Dash 8-100 was particularly fuel efficient and fast. As of 1989, De Havilland's Dash 7 and 8 were among the top 11 commuter aircraft.

The financial and operating performance of De Havilland had not met Boeing's expectations. Boeing acquired De Havilland from the Canadian government for about $130 million in 1986. Since then, Boeing had invested $450 million in R&D and plant modernization. Despite all the improvements in 1990, Boeing was losing approximately $700,000 on every Dash-8 built, even though there had been high market demand for the Dash-8 models. In mid-1990, Boeing entered negotiations to sell De Havilland to the European Aerospatiale/Alenia consortium.

Bombardier (Canada, Parent of Canadair and Shorts Aircraft Companies)

Bombardier was a Canadian-based company engaged in design, development, manufacturing, and marketing activities in the fields of mass transit and railway equipment, aircraft, snowmobiles, and military products. Bombardier's aerospace business grew out of its acquisition of Canadair in 1986 and of Shorts of Northern Ireland in 1989. It was Canada's leading aerospace firm. Bombardier operated plants in Canada, the United States, Austria, Belgium, France, the United Kingdom, Finland, and Sweden. Over 85 percent of its sales were made outside Canada.[13]

---

[11]R. W. Moorman, "Raising the Roof," *Air Transport World*, July 1990, p. 137.
[12]Rita Koselka, "Ready for Takeoff," *Forbes*, June 25, 1990, pp. 122–24.
[13]*Bombardier Annual Report*, 1990, p. 1.

In 1990, Bombardier doubled in size for the second time in three years. The company internationalized its aerospace operations by acquiring Ireland's Short Brothers PLC and announcing a new, high-technology commuter jet. Bombardier said its acquisition of Shorts:

> . . . Establishes our presence more solidly and securely in the world aerospace and defense markets. It also gives us more direct access to governmental and institutional customers in the United Kingdom and other European countries while strengthening our technological capacity.
>
> As was the case with Canadair, we have begun a reorganization of Shorts that is in line with our policies of decentralization and multidivisional management. The reorganization is well underway and is concurrent with an intensive program to modernize the facilities and equipment of our new Belfast subsidiary.[14]

As of 1990, Canadair produced the Challenger twin-engine business jet, more than 200 of which were being used in 15 countries. Canadair's new-generation 50-seat regional jet was scheduled for delivery starting in 1992; the regional jet market was estimated to be near 1,000 aircraft by the year 2000. Canadair planned to sell more than 400 of its small commuter jets by the end of the decade. Canadair was also a supplier of structural components to Boeing, McDonnell Douglas, Lockheed, Aerospatiale, and British Aerospace.

British Aerospace (United Kingdom)

British Aerospace (BAe) was the leader of the United Kingdom's $12 billion aerospace industry, which has become ever more important to the country's economic performance. As of 1990, British Aerospace offered a wide array of products, including a 19-seat commuter jet, a 64-seat turboprop (which was a market disappointment), and a large "quiet neighbor" jet. BAe supported all its products with "one channel support" for repairs and spare parts. Its planes were noted for their interior comfort, room, and overall reliability. British Aerospace had built its strategy around total support of the North American market. Brian Thomas, executive vice president for civil aircraft marketing, commented in 1988:

> We have 500 people at Dulles (northern Virginia)—75 percent of them assigned to customer support—eclipsing the volume and quality of all the other European manufacturers' North American support put together . . . we see the U.S.A. continuing to be a major market opportunity for the next 10 years . . . we have to be ready to respond to whatever happens.[15]

British Aerospace executives believed that future airport congestion would lead to demand for larger aircraft; Thomas said:

> I would be a very worried man if we were only in the 19-seater business. [Congestion] must push up aircraft size, unless more runways are laid . . . perhaps the (19-seat) category of aircraft will disappear from major hubs in the latter part of the 1990s, to be replaced by 30-seaters, which will be forced out in their turn and replaced by 60-seaters and so on.[16]

---

[14]Ibid., p. 3.
[15]Bron Rek, "BAe Tightens Grip on North American Civil Market," *Interavia*, August 1988, p. 755.
[16]Ibid.

British Aerospace's commitment to larger aircraft was in line with rival European companies. Fokker, ATR, and Saab were all proceeding with plans to build large turboprop and jet designs, leaving Embraer/FAMA's new fuel-efficient, pusher-prop design (the CBA-123) a great opportunity to exploit the 19-seat market if it did not decline.

Dornier/Mbb (Germany, a Division of Daimler-Benz)

Dornier, a division of Daimler-Benz, one of Germany's most prestigious companies (and the maker of Mercedes-Benz cars and trucks), produced two 15-to-19-seat planes. The Do228–101 and 202 had been popular, unpressurized aircraft, with over 119 built, 52 on order, and another 150 being built by Hindustan Aeronautics. Dornier had been a fine financial performer, with excellent operating margins.

The new Do328, a 30-seat pressurized, high-technology aircraft scheduled to be rolled out in 1991, reflected Dornier's strategy of attempting to use every technical feature that could increase the competitiveness of its airplanes. The Do328 combined a large cabin volume with high-technology composites to create a fast, efficient, and quiet airplane. Dornier believed that between 1,200 and 1,400 planes in the Do328 category could be sold worldwide by the year 2005. Plans included building a 40-passenger stretch version of the Do328.[17] Dornier hoped to rely on its strong design skills and the fact that it could tap into the resources of Daimler-Benz as needed to launch new, high-tech products. However, development of the Do328 had been rocky; there had been a bitter battle over funding between Dornier and Daimler-Benz. Some industry observers claimed, "Dornier was chained with the reputation of producing an aircraft that would be obsolete when it arrived."[18]

Embraer (Brazil)

In the early 1970s, a group of enterprising engineers and government officials created a Brazilian state-owned aircraft company known as Empresa Brasileira De Aeronautica S.A. (Embraer). Six years later, Embraer made Brazil the sixth largest aircraft-producing nation in the world. Its first all-Brazilian product was the EMB-110 Bandeirante, which was a no-frills, unpressurized 19-seater that was an affordable bridge aircraft between the older Beechcraft and De Havilland planes and the advanced-generation turboprops. Sales were brisk, and Embraer was exporting nearly $40 million worth of aircraft by 1978, when U.S. deregulation occurred. After U.S. deregulation, export sales nearly doubled, and Embraer began to build an advanced replacement aircraft for the Bandeirante.[19]

Embraer wanted to be the world leader in small aircraft and had developed the capability to build a world-class plane, the EMB-120 Brasilia—a 30-seat, pressurized, fast, efficient, comfortable aircraft that had no peers as of 1990. Embraer's export sales had climbed from $74 million in 1984 to $327 million in 1987. In 1990, Embraer was attempting to enter the future 19-seat market with

---

[17]Information provided by Peter Pletschacher in *Interavia*, July 1987, pp. 711–13.

[18]Robert W. Moorman, *Air Transport World*, December 1991, p. 82.

[19]For an interesting case featuring the details of Embraer's birth, see Ramamurt & Austin's Harvard Business School Case 9–393–090, "Embraer."

an advanced-technology aircraft, the CBA-123, that it hoped would dominate like the Brasilia did. The CBA-123 was a "pusher-prop"—fast, quiet, and nearly 40 percent more fuel efficient than earlier designs. Embraer had not bet the company on the 19-seat market solely, however; it had also begun to build a regional jet airliner that would seat up to 40 passengers and cruise at over 450 miles per hour.

Embraer had problems, however. In 1990, Brazil was experiencing inflation rates as high as 73 percent per month, and Brazilian President Fernando Collor de Mello had launched an anti-inflation and government austerity plan to privatize 188 state-owned or operated companies, including Embraer. Since 1970, when the Brazilian government owned 82 percent of Embraer, the government had sold nearly 70 percent of its holdings.

In October 1990, the company laid off about 4,000 employees in an attempt to save about $125 million a year in operating expenses. The company estimated it would lose $165 million in 1990 due to aircraft delivery delays and $65 million due to unexercised options by airline customers to purchase new planes for their fleets. All this was in addition to the turmoil Embraer faced with its joint venture partner on the CBA-123, FAMA of Argentina. Due to economic conditions worse than Brazil's, FAMA had reduced its commitment to the airplane's development, leaving Embraer alone in bearing the development risks. Despite being an acknowledged world leader in short-haul aircraft, some observers predicted Embraer would have trouble surviving without renewed government support.

Fairchild Aircraft (United States)

Fairchild Aircraft had been a major player in providing short-haul commuter aircraft since deregulation. Its 19-seat Metro III had almost double the total available seats in the market than its nearest rival, yet Fairchild had a rocky time during the 1980s. Fairchild was the only U.S. manufacturer to attempt to build commuter planes larger than 19-seaters, having entered into a joint venture with Saab to coproduce the 34-seat Saab/Fairchild 340. Saab assumed primary production responsibilities, and Fairchild's financial woes forced it to withdraw from the joint venture before it had a chance to show profits.

Fairchild was based in San Antonio, Texas, and in 1990 was being bought by Gene Morgan Financial Investments (GMFI) of Los Angeles, California. The sale to GMFI was expected to end Fairchild's struggle for survival and set the stage for growth and development as an independent, privately owned aviation services enterprise. Company President Thomas J. Smith expected Fairchild's primary business to remain the design and manufacturing of 19-passenger twin turboprop Metro aircraft for regional airlines. By the end of 1990, Fairchild expected to have 52 commuter airlines worldwide using its Metro models, with a total of 384 in scheduled service.[20]

When Fairchild emerged from Chapter 11 bankruptcy, it planned to recall enough employees to be able to produce 24 aircraft annually; demand for its 19-passenger planes had been solid, despite the company's financial difficulties. The Metro III was one of the first advanced turboprops to come on the market; it was pressurized and fast and competitive in all other areas. Fairchild Aircraft

---

[20]Carole A. Shifrin, "Sale Will Enable Fairchild to End Uncertainty, Pursue Growth," *Aviation Week & Space Technology,* December 14, 1987, pp. 105–11.

had plans to build an advanced Metro IV and V series, but it was unclear if the necessary financial resources would be available.

Fokker Aircraft (The Netherlands)

Fokker Aircraft was one of the first firms to pursue the short-haul market, well before the United States deregulated its airline industry. With its F-27 Mk 500, and more recently the F-50, Fokker had set the standard for 50-seat, turboprop commuters. Fokker was turning its attention to larger short-haul jet aircraft, selling the 100-seat F-100, and had made overtures to coproduce a 150-seat jet with McDonnell Douglas.

Fokker's joint development of the F-50 and F-100 had put a financial strain on the company; design and manufacturing investment for the Fokker 50 was $65 million and for the Fokker 100, $112 million. At the same time, Fokker had also suffered managerial problems due to the retirement of a number of experienced executives. A reorganization plan was implemented in 1987 in an attempt to shorten lines of communication.

Although Fokker Aircraft lost $25 million in 1987 and had to be refinanced in 1988, it had sold over 150 new, quiet, and fuel-efficient 50-seat Fokker 50 turboprops and 100-seat Fokker 100 jets to such airlines as USAir and American, establishing itself as a major player in the jet aircraft manufacturing arena. As of 1990, Fokker had fallen behind on its flood of orders for the F-100. Although production of the Fokker 50 was right on schedule at about 34 planes a year, the company had more than 370 orders and options for the Fokker 100 and was struggling to double its production to 60 to 70 planes annually. The first Fokker 100 customer, Swissair, had already imposed penalties for late delivery. Some observers believed Fokker might have to seek out a joint venture or a merger to meet its production targets; Fokker was rumored to be talking with Rockwell International, which was looking for new opportunities to offset cutbacks in the U.S. defense budget.[21]

Fokker believed short-haul routes would soon require larger aircraft and was aggressively seeking orders in all parts of the world. Between 1990 and 2000, passenger air traffic in the Asia-Pacific region was expected to double, generating an estimated $100 billion market for commercial jet aircraft. Fokker Aircraft officials believed the company was well positioned in the Asia-Pacific Rim market; Ansett Airlines was the largest operator of the new Fokker offerings. British Aerospace had predicted the overall turboprop fleet in the Pacific Basin would increase to about 785 aircraft in 2005. British Aerospace and Fokker also predicted growing retirements of aging aircraft in the 40- to 50-seat range, and both companies expected to establish strong resale capabilities in Asia.[22] In October 1990, Fokker announced it intended to stretch its 100-seat F-100 into at least a 130-seat airplane and offer the plane for delivery in 1996; a Fokker official commented:

> We presented the concept to a number of potential customers and the response was more positive than we anticipated . . . the policy behind the launch of the (stretched airplane) is to increase the scale of the company and achieve greater economies of scale; Fokker is playing in a major league field and we have to grow to a larger size.

---

[21]Jefferson Grigsby, "The Red Baron Flies Again," *Financial World*, September 19, 1989, pp. 30–34.

[22]*Aviation Week & Space Technology,* February 12, 1990, pp. 62–69.

Saab (Sweden)

Saab Aircraft was formed in 1937 to produce military and commercial aircraft for the Swedish government. It had produced top-of-the-line jet fighter aircraft such as the Viggen. Historically, Saab Aircraft had been dominated by its military aircraft orientation, and in 1979, the Saab-Scania (the parent company of Saab Aircraft, and a producer of automobiles) board of directors decided to invest heavily in commercial aircraft development to achieve a better balance between military and commercial markets. It formed a joint venture with Fairchild to share development risks. The two partners codeveloped the Saab/Fairchild 340, a 34-seat turboprop commuter aircraft. Saab invested over 200 million Swedish kroner to build a new 270,000-square-foot factory and assumed aircraft integration and final assembly responsibility, with Fairchild building the wings and empennage (tail section).[23]

When Fairchild began to have financial difficulties and withdrew from the joint venture in 1987, Saab proceeded on its own. Its 1990 backlog for the 340B was nearly 350 aircraft and the large demand had enabled Saab to enlarge its production facilities.

Saab had also begun initial production of the new model 2000. Product definition work on the 50-seat Saab 2000 regional turboprop transport had been finished, and the selection of major system suppliers was nearly complete. Spain's Construcciones Aeronauticas SA had been picked to design and manufacture the complete wing for the Saab 2000. Finland's Valmet Corp. Flygplansindustri was selected to produce the empennage for the new aircraft. Advanced negotiations were under way with a U.S. firm for a 6-tube avionics package and with a U.K. firm for the aircraft's propellers. Saab was close to selecting companies outside of Sweden to build part of the fuselage and to produce the landing gear. In January 1990, the manufacture of three test aircraft began, and the first flight was scheduled for early 1992.[24]

Like Fokker and British Aerospace, Saab believed the marketplace for short-haul aircraft was truly global. Saab-Scania's automobiles and heavy trucks were popular in Asia, and recently the company began offering its short-to-medium-haul turboprop airplanes to Asia's regional airlines. In April 1990, Japan Air System (JAS) ordered eight of Saab-Scania's 340B turboprops for a total of $100 million. This was a tremendous breakthrough for Saab-Scania, which had been attempting to compete in the Japanese market for six years. The firm's new, larger airplane, scheduled for debut in 1992, was thought to be very suitable for flights in Southeast Asia, where most of the routes were operated with larger aircraft.[25]

Short Brothers Aircraft (Ireland, a Division of Canada's Bombardier)

Short Brothers Aircraft, based in Belfast, Ireland, had been producing aircraft since 1900 and some claimed the three brothers who formed the company were the first manufacturers of aircraft in the world. The company had contributed

[23]The early history of the Saab/Fairchild 340 has been paraphrased from Hans G. Anderson's *Saab Aircraft Since 1937*, 1990, pp. 56–60.

[24]Carole A. Shifrin, "Saab Completes Definition Work, Selects Contractors for Saab 2000," *Aviation Week & Space Technology*, October 23, 1989, pp. 72–73.

[25]*Asian Finance (Hong Kong)*, July 15, 1990, p. 24.

to both military and commercial aviation history since its founding. In the 1960s, Short offered a rugged, practical, and versatile freighter aircraft, dubbed the Skyvan, which was fuel efficient and had good short-field capabilities. The company then designed a nonpressurized commercial, short-haul derivative of the Skyvan, which became the SD-30; it had sold well throughout the world. The SD-30 Skyvan had been used by commuter airlines since the early 1970s and was famous for its box-shaped square fuselage.

In 1989, the company was acquired by Canada's Bombardier and became a wholly owned subsidiary. As of 1990, Short sold dependable 30-to-35-seat air-craft, with good seat utilization, at competitive prices. Short had participated in a handful of jet aircraft supplier roles, including providing manufacturing support for the Fokker F-100 and Boeing 757, and had actively been involved in joint venture activities.

In 1990, Short Brothers entered into a joint venture with Germany's Messer-schmitt-Boelkow-Blohm Transport Aircraft Group and the People's Republic of China's Aero-Technology Import and Export Corp. to design and manufacture a twin-engine transport capable of high-speed operations that would bridge the gap between today's larger turboprops and smaller jet transports. Delivery of the first transports was scheduled for 1995.[26]

---

[26] *Aviation Week & Space Technology,* May 16, 1988, pp. 67, 69.

COMPETITION IN THE
WORLD TIRE INDUSTRY, 1992

Arthur A. Thompson, Jr., University of Alabama*

Tire manufacturing became an important industry in the first half of the 20th century as motor vehicles increasingly became the dominant mode of transportation. The demand for original equipment tires was directly related to the number of new motor vehicles currently produced, while the demand for replacement tires depended on such factors as the number of vehicles in service, the average number of miles driven per vehicle, and tire tread durability. In 1992, the replacement market was roughly four times as big as the original equipment segment; a vehicle during its useful life could require anywhere between two and six sets of replacement tires. Replacement tire sales generated much bigger profit margins for manufacturers than original equipment sales because tiremakers could command higher prices on the replacement sales through wholesale and retail channels than they could on selling tires in mass quantities to the hard-bargaining car and truck manufacturers.

World tire production in 1991 was approximately 850 million tires, with the following geographic breakdown:

Production Location	Units Shipped	Percent of Total
North America	247 million	29%
Asia	236	28%
Western Europe	194	23%
Eastern Europe and Russian republics	109	13%
South America	45	5%
All others	19	2%
	850 million	10%

During the late 1980s, the industry went through a major consolidation, resulting in the acquisition of five leading U.S. producers and the leading British producer and in a reshaping of the industry's competitive structure:

Date	Deal	Purchase Price
December 1986	Sumitomo Rubber Industries (Japan) acquired control of Dunlop Tire (Great Britain)	$80 million
October 1987	Continental (the leading German producer) purchased General Tire (the fourth largest U.S. tiremaker)	$628 million
May 1988	Bridgestone Corp. (the largest Japanese-based tire manufacturer) acquired Firestone Tire and Rubber Co. (the third largest U.S.-based tiremaker)	$2.6 billion

*Prepared with the research assistance of Ken Tucker, Jennifer Lowry, and Andrew White, University of Alabama. Copyright © 1992 by Arthur A. Thompson, Jr.

Date	Deal	Purchase Price
May 1988	Pirelli (the leading Italian producer) acquired Armstrong Tire (the fifth largest U.S. producer)	$197 million
January 1989	Sumitomo Rubber Industries (Japan) purchased the U.S. operations of Dunlop Tire Corp. (two plants, sales of $500 million)	unknown
October 1989	Yokohama Rubber (Japan) acquired Mohawk Rubber (the seventh largest U.S. producer)	$150 million
November 1990	Groupe Michelin (a French-based producer with the biggest market share of any European tiremaker) acquired Uniroyal Goodrich Tire Co. (the second largest U.S. producer) to make Michelin the world's largest producer of tires	$1.5 billion

Whereas U.S.-based companies had dominated the world tire industry before 1986, accounting for about 35 percent of the world's tire production (well above the 20 to 25 percent share of Japanese-based producers), in 1992 only two major U.S.-based producers of tires remained in market contention: Goodyear Tire (the world's largest tiremaker since the 1920s, until the acquisition by Michelin dropped it to second place) and Cooper Tire and Rubber. No other of the five U.S.-based tire producers had as much as $100 million in sales annually. All had market shares under 1 percent and competed only in very small and restricted market niches.

The world's 10 largest tire manufacturers accounted for 75 percent of world-wide tire production (see Exhibit 1). In addition to the major producers, there were between 100 and 120 other producers of tires, each with one or more plants serving mainly a national or continental market.

For the past 15 years, tire companies had been plagued with chronic over-capacity caused by a shift in demand from low-mileage, bias-ply tires to much longer lasting radial tires and maturing demand for motor vehicles. All the tire companies had invested in R&D and technological advances to improve tire performance, traction, and tread wear under a variety of road conditions, resulting in increases in the number of miles driven before tires had to be replaced. This, coupled with a worldwide leveling off in the production of new motor vehicles, had caused the sales of both original equipment and replacement tires to flatten, making the industry mature and cyclical.

Competition for market share had become intense, creating downward pressure on prices. To preserve profit margins, manufacturers had been forced to cut costs, close marginally efficient plants, and modernize the plants kept open. Most of the plants that were shut, however, had made old-style bias-ply or bias-belted tires. Mature demand, fierce rivalry, and the globalizing of competition were the drivers behind industry consolidation.

In 1992, market conditions in North America were particularly severe. Tire capacity exceeded annual shipments by about 20 percent. In the mid-1980s, the major U.S. tire companies (Goodyear, Uniroyal-Goodrich, Firestone, and General) had programs to phase out their older, relatively high-cost plants to bring production capacity into closer balance with demand, but the rash of takeovers of the U.S. companies by foreign producers changed the competitive picture. The new owners halted the scheduled factory closings and launched extensive capital investment programs to modernize the plants they had acquired and make them cost-effective producers; their goal was to dramatically expand their share of the North American tire market. The result was a glut of tiremaking capacity in a market where tire shipments were flat.

EXHIBIT 1 **Sales and Market Share of the World's 10 Largest Tire Producers, 1990**

Company (Headquarters Country)	Major Brands	1990 Tire Sales (Billions of Dollars)	Market Share (by Volume)
1. Groupe Michelin (France)	Michelin, Uniroyal, BF Goodrich	$10.1	19.0%
2. Goodyear (U.S.)	Goodyear, Kelly-Springfield, Lee, Douglas	8.2	16.8%
3. Bridgestone Corp. (Japan)	Bridgestone, Firestone	8.3	14.6%
4. Continental (Germany)	Continental, General, Uniroyal Englebert, Semperit	3.6	6.2%
5. Pirelli Group (Italy)	Pirelli, Armstrong	3.2	5.3%
6. Sumitomo (Japan)	Sumitomo, Dunlop	3.0	5.3%
7. Yokohama (Japan)	Yokohama, Mohawk	2.0	4.0%
8. Toyo Tire (Japan)	Toyo	1.1	1.8%
9. Cooper Tire and Rubber (U.S.)	Cooper, Falls	0.9	1.3%
10. Hankook (Korea)	Hankook	0.6	1.0%
			75.3%

Source: Compiled from a variety of sources, including *Modern Tire Dealer, Tire Business,* and *The Economist.*

THE ORIGINAL EQUIPMENT MARKET SEGMENT

All original equipment (OE) tires were sold by the tire manufacturers directly to the car and truck manufacturers. Vehicle manufacturers bought all of their tires from the tire manufacturers; none had integrated backward into tire manufacturing as they had into other component vehicle parts. OE tire demand was rigidly fixed by the number of vehicles being produced—each new automobile, for example, was equipped with five tires (four on the ground and a spare). Exhibit 2 shows world production of motor vehicles.

Since tires were such a small cost item in the overall price of new vehicles, changes in OE tire prices had virtually zero effect on total OE tire demand. However, while overall OE tire demand was highly price inelastic, the demand facing an individual tire manufacturer was considered highly elastic due to the ease with which motor vehicle manufacturers could switch to other tire manufacturers' brands.

Competition among the tire manufacturers to supply tires to the automobile and truck manufacturers was fierce. All the major tiremakers were eager to have new vehicles equipped with their own brand of tires to enhance replacement sales, the belief being that vehicle owners satisfied with their OE tires would be more likely to choose the same brand when replacement time came. The sale of OE tires was thus seen as strategically important, not only as a way to strengthen sales in the more profitable replacement segment but also to achieve volume-related scale economies in manufacturing. At the same time, the car and truck manufacturers were sophisticated buyers and devoted considerable time and effort to tire purchasing and to their relationships with tire manufacturers. The tire purchasing strategies of the Japanese and U.S. automakers were in sharp contrast.

EXHIBIT 2   **World Motor Vehicle Production, 1950–1990**   (*In thousands*)

Year	United States	Canada	United States and Canada Total	Europe	Japan	Other	World Total
1990	9,780	1,896	11,676	18,614	13,487	4,336	48,113
1989	10,874	1,934	12,808	18,946	13,026	4,216	48,996
1988	11,214	1,949	13,163	18,213	12,700	4,134	48,210
1987	10,925	1,635	12,560	17,518	12,249	3,576	45,903
1986	11,335	1,854	13,189	16,701	12,260	3,147	45,297
1985	11,653	1,933	13,586	15,959	12,271	2,995	44,811
1984	10,939	1,829	12,768	15,293	11,465	2,532	42,058
1983	9,205	1,524	10,729	15,708	11,112	2,206	39,755
1982	6,986	1,276	8,262	14,808	10,732	2,311	36,113
1981	7,943	1,323	9,266	14,440	11,180	2,344	37,230
1980	8,010	1,374	9,384	15,446	11,043	2,641	38,514
1979	11,480	1,632	13,112	16,293	9,636	2,478	41,519
1978	12,899	1,818	14,717	16,118	9,269	2,195	42,299
1977	12,703	1,775	14,478	15,885	8,515	2,069	40,947
1976	11,498	1,640	13,138	15,207	7,841	2,155	38,341
1975	8,987	1,424	10,411	13,473	6,942	2,172	32,998
1970	8,284	1,160	9,444	13,243	5,289	1,427	29,403
1965	11,138	847	11,985	9,571	1,876	835	24,267
1960	7,905	398	8,303	6,830	482	873	16,488
1955	9,204	452	9,656	3,738	68	166	13,628
1950	8,006	388	8,394	1,991	32	160	10,577

Source: Compiled by the Motor Vehicle Manufacturers Association of the U.S., Inc., from various sources.

Tire Purchasing Practices of the U.S. Automakers

All the U.S. auto and truck manufacturers (General Motors, Ford, Chrysler, Navistar, and PACCAR) set detailed tire specifications for each of their car and truck models that would-be tire suppliers had to meet for their tires to be considered as original equipment. In 1990, tiremakers had to meet as many as 50 specifications on a given tire, as opposed to just 10 or so in 1960.

It was typical for U.S. auto/truck manufacturers to establish higher quality standards and stricter specifications for the OE tires they purchased than was the case for the usually available kinds of replacement tires. Some automobile manufacturers regularly inspected the plants of their tire suppliers to make sure quality standards were being met, and it was not unusual for them to ask for data on costs to compare against their own independently made estimates of what it cost their tire supplier to make tires to their specifications. Different size cars and trucks were equipped with different size tires. The smallest cars had 13-inch wheelbases and required narrower treads; large luxury cars had 14-inch and 15-inch wheelbases and required wider treads. Tires for heavy-duty trucks and tractor-trailer rigs were equipped with still bigger and stronger tires, capable of withstanding heavier loads.

Vehicle manufacturers typically contracted out their tire requirements annually on a model-by-model basis, normally using several tire suppliers to equip their full lineup of models (see Exhibits 3, 4, and 5). Using their bargaining leverage, U.S. automobile manufacturers over the years had negotiated an average price for OE tires that was several dollars per tire below what wholesale

EXHIBIT 3 **Estimated Brand Market Share for Original Equipment Passenger Tires in the United States, 1991**

Original Equipment Buyer	Tire Company						
	Goodyear	Firestone	Michelin	Uniroyal Goodrich	General Tire	Dunlop	Bridgestone
General Motors	33.5%	1.5%	14.5%	32.5%	18.0%	0.0%	0.0%
Ford	26.0	39.0	23.5	0.0	11.5	0.0	0.0
Chrysler	83.0	0.0	0.0	0.0	17.0	0.0	0.0
Mazda	15.0	50.0	0.0	0.0	0.0	0.0	35.0
Honda of U.S.	30.0	0.0	47.0	0.0	0.0	16.0	7.0
Toyota	15.0	40.0	0.0	0.0	3.0	42.0	0.0
Diamond Star	100.0	0.0	0.0	0.0	0.0	0.0	0.0
Nissan	0.0	35.0	22.0	0.0	35.0	8.0	0.0
Nummi (GM-Toyota)	50.0	50.0	0.0	0.0	0.0	0.0	0.0
Volvo	0.0	0.0	100.0	0.0	0.0	0.0	0.0
Saturn	0.0	100.0	0.0	0.0	0.0	0.0	0.0
Isuzu	15.0	35.0	0.0	50.0	0.0	0.0	0.0
Subaru	0.0	0.0	100.0	0.0	0.0	0.0	0.0
Hyundai	35.0	0.0	65.0	0.0	0.0	0.0	0.0
Overall OE market share	38.0%	16.0%	16.0%	14.0%	11.5%	2.75%	1.25%

Source: *Modern Tire Dealer*, January 1991, p. 27.

EXHIBIT 4 **Trends in Tire Brand Market Shares for OE Passenger Car Tires, 1978–91**

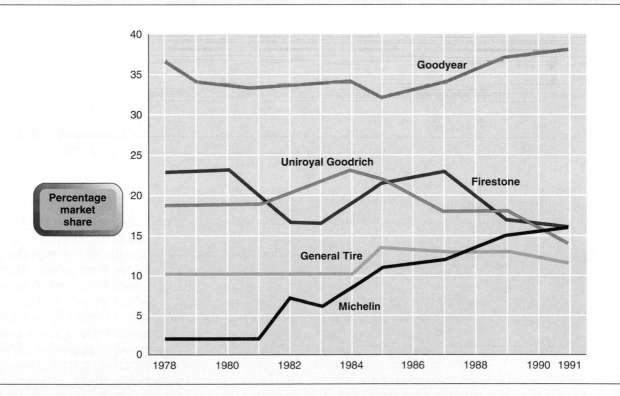

EXHIBIT 5   **Major Suppliers of Original Equipment Tires to Motor Vehicle Producers in Western Europe and Asia**

Motor Vehicle Producers	Major Tire Supplier(s)
Western Europe	
General Motors	Continental
Ford Motor Co.	Continental, Goodyear, one other
Honda	Continental
Toyota	Continental
Mazda	Continental
Nissan	Continental
Peugeot-Citroen	Continental, Michelin, Pirelli
Volvo	Goodyear, Continental
Mercedes-Benz	Michelin, Continental, Goodyear
BMW	Michelin, Continental
Volkswagen-Audi	Michelin, Goodyear, Continental, one other
Renault	Continental, Sumitomo, Pirelli
Saab	Michelin, Continental
Fiat	Pirelli, Continental, Michelin, Goodyear
Porsche	Pirelli, Goodyear, Michelin
Asia	
Honda	Bridgestone, Sumitomo, Yokohama, and one other
Toyota	Bridgestone, Sumitomo, Toyo, Yokohama, Goodyear, Michelin, and one other
Mazada	Bridgestone, Sumitomo, Toyo, Yokohama, Goodyear, and one other
Nissan	Bridgestone, Sumitomo, Toyo, Yokohama, Goodyear, Michelin, Continental/General, and two others
Isuzu	Sumitomo, Toyo, Yokohama, Goodyear, Michelin, and one other
Mitsubishi	Bridgestone, Sumitomo, Toyo, Yokohama, Michelin, and one other
Daihatsu	Sumitomo, and one other
Hyundai (Korea)	Hankook, Kumho

distributors paid tiremakers for somewhat lower quality replacement tires. In effect, the automobile companies bought OE tires for roughly half the retail price commanded by replacement tires.

Tire Purchasing Practices of the Japanese Automakers

In Japan, the major Japanese vehicle manufacturers usually obtained the bulk of their tires from a single supplier, utilizing a long-term partnership arrangement. Each vehicle manufacturer worked very closely with its tire suppliers, emphasizing the importance of a mutually beneficial long-term relationship. Seldom did Japanese vehicle makers request price bids from rival tiremakers to supply the tires needed at their Japanese-based assembly plants. When the vehicle maker's principal tire supplier did not have the capability to provide competitively priced tires of the desired size and quality for a particular model, then the automaker obtained the tires from another tiremaker. This occurred frequently enough that Japanese automakers, despite relying heavily on one primary tire supplier, used several tire suppliers to round out their total tire needs at their Japan-based plants.

The leading suppliers of the 66 million OE tires purchased by the Japanese vehicle manufacturers for cars and trucks made in Japan were as follows:

Bridgestone Tires	39%
Yokohama Rubber	21%
Sumitomo Rubber	17%
Toyo Tire	10%
Michelin	7%
All others	6%
	100%

The Japanese automakers placed less stress on explicit tire specifications and were less price oriented in comparison to the U.S. automakers. They did, however, work diligently with their tire suppliers to hold down tire costs and improve tire quality, and they emphasized timely delivery and other facets of the "just-in-time" inventory and logistics systems they used extensively with all auto components suppliers to control purchasing, materials handling, and warehousing costs. In Japan, all of the Japanese tire manufacturing plants were located within a few miles of the assembly plants of the Japanese automakers.

However, when the Japanese automakers constructed car and truck assembly plants outside Japan (in the United States, Europe, and other parts of Asia), they tended to establish supply relationships with more than one tiremaker (see Exhibits 3 and 5) and then work gradually toward choosing a principal supplier for each plant location based on their experiences with each tiremaker. Normally, it was not cost-effective for them to import Japanese-made tires from their principal tire supplier in Japan. In 1992, the Japanese automakers were beginning to source a growing portion of the tires needed at their U.S.-based assembly plants from Japanese-owned tire companies. More and more models of Japanese cars and trucks made in the United States were being equipped with Firestone and Dunlop tires (see Exhibit 3).

THE REPLACEMENT TIRE MARKET

Replacement tires accounted for 70 to 75 percent of tiremaking production. Unit shipments had been flat since the 1970s; see Exhibit 6 for volume trends in the United States by segment. Weak demand during the late 1970s and early 1980s was partly a function of sharply higher gasoline prices, which reduced the average number of miles driven annually per vehicle. In the United States, the average had dropped to 9,500 miles in 1983 versus about 10,800 before the gasoline shortage era. Recently, stable gasoline prices had contributed to a rise in annual mileage driven per vehicle. Every 100-mile change in the average number of miles traveled per vehicle produced a 1 million unit change in the size of the replacement market, assuming average treadwear life of 25,000 to 30,000 miles per tire.

Tire manufacturers produced a large variety of grades and lines of tires for distribution under both manufacturers' brand names and private labels. Branded replacement tires were made to the tiremaker's own specifications, usually less rigid than required by vehicle manufacturers for OE tires. Some private-label tires supplied to wholesale distributors and large chain retailers were made to the buyer's specifications rather than to the manufacturer's standards.

EXHIBIT 6   **Trends in U.S. Tire Shipments, 1986–1991**   *(In millions)*

	1986	1987	1988	1989	1990	1991
Passenger						
Replacement	144.3	151.9	153.2	151.6	152.3	152.0*
OE	54.4	52.9	54.4	51.2	47.2	42.3*
Retread	18.0	16.5	15.1	11.5	10.0	8.5*
	216.7	221.3	222.7	214.3	209.5	202.8*
Truck, light truck, bus						
Replacement	31.8	34.5	33.8	33.3	36.6	32.3*
OE	6.8	7.8	8.6	8.1	7.0	6.0*
Retread	20.0	20.5	21.8	21.9	22.2	22.3*
	58.6	62.8	64.2	63.3	65.8	60.6*
Farm (front and rear)						
Replacement	2.498	2.778	2.749	2.742	2.550	2.200*
OE	.512	.595	.753	.890	.955	.800*
	3.010	3.373	3.502	3.632	3.505	3.000*
Large Over-the-Road						
Replacement	.113	.124	.131	.130	.132	.138*
OE	.050	.056	.070	.069	.060	.050*
	.163	.180	.201	.199	.192	.188*
Industrial pneumatic and utility						
Replacement	4.300	5.200	5.400	4.900	5.115	5.200*
OE	8.700	10.200	10.400	9.600	10.693	10.300*
	13.000	15.400	15.800	14.500	15.808	15.500*
Total	291.473	303.053	306.403	295.931	294.805	282.088*

*Estimated

Sources: Rubber Manufacturers Association, *Tire Retreading/Repair Journal*, General Tire, Goodyear, others.

To those untrained in tiremaking techniques or unfamiliar with tiremaking practices, replacement tires appeared to be comparable to OE tires. But there were often subtle differences in tread depth, grades of rubber, and component construction such that many, if not the majority of, replacement tires on the market were not equal to the quality and durability of OE tires. As a consequence, replacement tires tended to have a somewhat shorter life cycle than did OE tires. Low-grade replacement tires had a tread life of 10,000 to 20,000 miles compared to 30,000 to 45,000 (or longer) for OE tires. In 1992, most manufacturers provided guaranteed mileage warranties to the buyers of replacement tires; moreover, nearly all branded replacement tires carried lifetime warranties against manufacturing defects, and all tires met certain specified safety standards regarding traction and resistance against heat buildup.

As the business of motor vehicle manufacturing developed into a major industry worldwide, the major brand-name tiremakers capitalized on their reputation and experience as suppliers of OE tires by building strong wholesale and retail dealer networks through which to market replacement tires to vehicle owners. The major tire producers often used network TV campaigns to promote their brands, introduce new types of tires, and pull customers to their retail dealer outlets. Their network TV ad budgets commonly ran from $10 million to $30 million, and their budgets for cooperative ads with dealers were from $20 million to $100 million. Several tire companies sponsored auto racing events to promote the performance capabilities of their tires.

EXHIBIT 7   **Share of Replacement Tire Sales in the United States, by Type of Retail Outlet, 1982 versus 1992**

Type of Retail Outlet	1982	1992*
Traditional multibrand independent dealers	44%	44%
Discount multibrand independent dealers	7%	15%
Chain stores, department stores	20%	14%
Tire company stores	10%	9%
Service stations	11%	8%
Warehouse clubs	—	6%
Other	8%	4%
	100%	100%

*Estimate
Source: Goodyear Tire and Rubber Company.

Replacement tires were marketed to vehicle owners through a variety of retail channels: independent tire dealers, service stations, manufacturer-owned retail tire stores, major department stores with auto centers, retail chains (such as Wal-Mart, Sears, K mart, and Montgomery Ward), automobile dealerships, warehouse clubs, and assorted other outlets (see Exhibit 7). In the United States alone, there were approximately 42,000 tire, battery, and accessory dealers in 1992.

Independent tire dealers usually carried the brands of several different major manufacturers and a discount-priced private-label brand so as to give replacement buyers a full assortment of qualities, brands, and price ranges to choose from. Service stations affiliated with Exxon, Chevron, and Amoco marketed Atlas brand tires; other service stations, especially those that really pushed tire sales, stocked one or two manufacturers' brand tires and maybe a private-label brand. Retail tire outlets that were owned or franchised by the manufacturers (i.e., Goodyear Tire Stores and Firestone Auto Master Care Centers) carried only the manufacturer's name brands and perhaps a private-label or lesser-known, discount-priced line made by the manufacturer. Department stores and the major retail chains occasionally carried manufacturers' label tires but usually marketed only their own private-label brands. Exhibit 8 shows market shares of the various brands in the U.S. replacement market for 1991.

To provide tires suitable for many different types of vehicles driven under a variety of road and weather conditions, manufacturers found it advantageous to have a broad product line to appeal to most buyer segments. When vehicle owners went to a tire dealer to shop for replacement tires, they had a variety of tread designs, tread widths, tread durabilities, performance characteristics, and price categories to choose from. Car and light-truck owners were often confused by the number of choices they had; few buyers were really knowledgeable about tires. Many ended up choosing on the basis of price, while others followed the recommendation of the local dealer whom they regularly patronized. The retail prices of replacement tires ranged from retreaded (or recapped) tires selling for under $20 to $35 each to top-of-the-line tires going for $125 to $175 each. Tire dealers ran frequent price promotion ads in the local newspapers, making it easy for price-sensitive buyers to watch for sales and buy at off-list prices. In recent years, consumers had become more price conscious and less brand loyal (thus eroding the importance of securing

EXHIBIT 8   **Estimated Brand Shares of Replacement Market for Tires, United States, 1991**

Passenger Car Tires		Light-Truck Tires		Highway Truck Tires	
Goodyear	15.0%	Goodyear	11.0%	Goodyear	23.0%
Michelin	8.5	B.F. Goodrich	10.0	Michelin	15.0
Firestone	7.5	Firestone	5.0	Bridgestone	11.0
Sears	5.5	Michelin	6.0	General Tire	7.0
General	4.5	Cooper/Falls	5.0	Firestone	6.0
BF Goodrich	3.5	Kelly-Springfield	5.0	Kelly-Springfield	6.0
Bridgestone	3.5	Armstrong	4.0	Dunlop	6.0
Cooper	3.5	General Tire	4.0	Yokohama	5.0
Kelly	3.0	Bridgestone	3.0	Cooper	4.0
Multi-Mile	3.0	Dunlop	2.0	Toyo	3.0
Sentry	2.5	Remington	2.0	Armstrong	2.0
Uniroyal	2.5	Uniroyal	2.0	Hankook	2.0
Cordovan	2.0	Dayton	1.0	Kumho	2.0
Dayton	2.0	Kumho	1.0	Others	8.0
Dunlop	2.0	Yokohama	1.0	Total	100.0%
Pirelli	2.0	Toyo	1.0		
Armstrong	1.5	Others	36.0		
Falls Mastercraft	1.5	Total	100.0%		
Hercules	1.5				
Monarch	1.5				
Montgomery Ward	1.5				
Remington	1.5				
Summit	1.5				
Yokohama	1.5				
Atlas	1.0				
Centennial	1.0				
Cornell	1.0				
Delta	1.0				
Jetzon	1.0				
Laramie	1.0				
Lee	1.0				
Mohawk	1.0				
National	1.0				
Regal	1.0				
Sigma	1.0				
Spartan	1.0				
Star	1.0				
Stratton	1.0				
Toyo	1.0				
Others	2.5				
Total	100.0%				

Source: *Modern Tire Dealer*, January 1991, p. 27; *Market Data Book 1991; Tire Business*, January 1992, p. 13.

replacement sales through OE sales to vehicle manufacturers). However, it was hard for car owners to comparison shop on the basis of tire quality and tread durability because of the proliferation of brands, lines, grades, and performance features. Manufacturers had resisted the development of standardized specifications for replacement tires and there was a general lack of common terminology in describing tire grades and construction features.

In most communities, the retail tire market was intensely competitive. Sellers advertised extensively in newspapers, on outdoor billboards, and occasionally on local TV to establish and maintain their market shares. Price was the dominant competitive variable. Many dealers featured and pushed their private-label "off-brand" tires because they could obtain higher margins on them than they could selling the name-brand tires of major manufacturers. Dealer-sponsored private-label tires accounted for 15 to 20 percent of total replacement tire sales in the United States in 1991. Surveys showed dealers were able to influence a car owner's choice of replacement tires, both as to brand and type of tire. Most replacement tire buyers did not have strong tire brand preferences, making it fairly easy for tire salespeople to switch customers to tire brands and grades with the highest dealer margins. Normal dealer margins on replacement tires were in the 35 to 40 percent range, but many dealers shaved margins to win incremental sales.

Since the mid-1970s, tire retailers' profit margins had been under competitive pressure, partly because of stagnant growth in tire sales and partly because of declining retail prices since 1980 (see Exhibit 9). To bolster profitability, tire dealers had expanded into auto repair services (engine tuneups, shock-absorber and muffler replacement, and brake repair), retreading, and automobile accessories. Some tire retailers were experimenting with becoming "total car care centers." Auto service work was very attractive because gross profit margins were bigger than the margins earned on replacement tire sales. The fastest growing tire dealers were using a strategy of opening multiple locations, providing quick tire change turnaround, employing extensive advertising, buying large quantities of tires from wholesale distributors at favorable prices, and using a high-volume/low-margin pricing strategy based on high inventory turnover, fuller utilization of facilities and tire-changing/mounting personnel, and related volume-based economies.

TYPES OF TIRES

In 1992, virtually all car and truck tires were of radial construction. Bias-ply and bias-belted tires, once the dominant types of tire, had rapidly faded from the scene during the past 15 years. Bias-ply tires were the cheapest to manufacture and used tiremaking technology that had been around for decades. In bias-ply tires, the tire casing consisted of many thin sheets of rubberized fabric, called plies, which were alternately layered crisscross with their grains diagonal or on a bias. Except for retreads, bias-ply tires were the cheapest and lowest grade replacement tires on the market.

Bias-belted tires represented an improvement in bias-ply tire construction and offered better mileage, strength, and safety; they were produced with technology and equipment well known by all tire manufacturers. In bias-belted tires, the casing was formed using thicker, diagonal layers of belted rubberized fabric plies, reinforced with steel in the case of steel-belted tires. In 1992, bias-belted tires were also considered low grade and were bought mainly by the most budget-constrained vehicle owners.

Radial tires were much harder and more expensive to manufacture than bias tires. In 1992, only Michelin, Goodyear, Bridgestone, and a few other tiremakers had truly mastered radial tire technology to the point where they could manufacture a radial tire of superior quality for all sizes of cars and trucks. All the remaining manufacturers were working hard to improve their radial tiremaking skills; while their radial tires were of acceptable quality,

EXHIBIT 9   **Median Retail Prices of Passenger Car Tires in the U.S. Market, 1971–1990**

Year	Median retail prices			
	Bias-Ply	Bias-Belted	Radial	Overall
1990	$39.98	$39.94	$52.50	NA
1989	38.57	39.17	54.96	NA
1988	38.00	38.40	52.85	NA
1987	35.50	37.90	51.80	NA
1986	35.00	38.00	53.80	50.84
1985	36.63	39.95	54.60	51.81
1984	37.15	39.00	55.50	51.74
1983	39.93	43.66	60.00	55.03
1982	39.00	44.00	65.00	58.93
1981	37.95	44.41	72.13	59.50
1980				60.59
1979				54.05
1978				49.31
1977				45.13
1976				42.26
1975				40.95
1974				37.28
1973				34.22
1972				31.93
1971				31.34

Source: National Tire Dealers and Retreaders Association, information supplied by telephone.

they were generally unable to match the industry leaders when it came to making top-quality radial tires for larger cars and trucks. It had taken Goodyear until the mid-1980s to make its radial tire quality approach Michelin's. Michelin had pioneered radial tire technology and its steel-belted radial tires were generally regarded by European and U.S. consumers as the best on the market. Just recently had Bridgestone gotten to the point where it could nearly match Michelin on tire quality.

Michelin's strength as a competitor stemmed from its development and mastery of radial tire technology. The company began marketing radial tires in 1948 and was the only European radial tire manufacturer until 1963. Radial tires were first marketed in Japan in the early 1950s. Radial tires became so popular in Europe and Japan that by the mid-1960s they were the dominant-selling tire. In 1972, Michelin became the first foreign manufacturer to build a tire plant in the United States; it had sought to avoid locating a plant in the United States because of the higher wage rates, but European market saturation coupled with U.S. tariffs on tire imports made a U.S. plant the most feasible way to penetrate the U.S. tire market. In its first year, Michelin sold 35 percent of all radials sold in the United States.

Michelin's dramatic success in steel-belted radial tires started a pronounced market trend away from bias tires during the 1960s in Europe and during the 1970s in the United States. Radial tires emerged as the fastest growing segment of the industry. Radials appealed to consumers because of their improved safety and puncture resistance, better skid and traction performance, their contribution to better gas mileage (due to less friction with road surfaces), and longer service life. A set of better quality radials could last 40,000 to 60,000 miles, and even the 25,000 to 35,000 mileage life for lower grade radials represented a big improvement over the 10,000 to 20,000 mileage life of bias tires. Although more expensive than bias-ply and bias-belted tires (see Exhibit 9), radial tires still delivered substantially more miles of service per dollar of cost than bias tires.

A conscious decision by U.S. tiremakers during the 1960s and early 1970s to go slow on radial tire manufacturing opened the door for foreign firms to enter the American tire market. U.S. tiremakers saw the U.S. market eventually converting over to radials, but a number of obstacles turned them away from promoting rapid conversion. Use of radial tires as original equipment first required motor vehicle manufacturers to modify vehicle suspension systems at a small but not insignificant cost. Meanwhile, tiremakers ran up against an array of quality control problems and technical difficulties in making radials for larger American cars. Radial manufacturing required different-style production equipment; the cost of industrywide conversion to radial production in 1965 was estimated at over $700 million. In light of these barriers, U.S. tiremakers chose to introduce a bias-belted "transition" tire in the United States that allowed the industry to pursue a slower, phased-in conversion to radials, which would be completed in the 1980s.

Demand for radials in the United States took off quicker than expected, however, and U.S. makers were caught with too much bias tire capacity, too little radial tire capacity, and a host of radial tire production problems. All this coincided with the major European and Japanese markets for radials beginning to level off. Moreover, because of their early efforts in leading the conversion to radials, Michelin and the Japanese producers had confronted the technical difficulties of larger-sized radial tire construction sooner, providing them with a technological lead and a quality differential over U.S. producers. Despite a price disadvantage, foreign tiremakers, especially Michelin, made inroads into the U.S. market, then used this foothold to build their U.S. market shares steadily over the next decade. Until price competition intensified in the 1980s, Michelin sold its radials at a 30 percent premium over rival brands.

During the 1980s, radial tires virtually took over the world tire market. By 1982, all new automobiles in the United States came with radial tires as standard equipment, and by 1986, 83 percent of the tires sold in the passenger tire replacement market were radials. In 1992, over 99 percent of passenger tire sales in the United States were of radial construction and less than 4 percent of all tires sold in the United States (for all types of vehicles) were of bias-ply or bias-belt construction.

High-Performance Tires

In 1980, Goodyear introduced "high-performance" radial tires and created one of the industry's fastest growing segments. High-performance tires were of superior construction, provided more safety under a variety of hazardous road conditions, and were designed for sportier high-horsepower cars that had rack and pinion steering; they retailed for as much as $30 to $40 per tire more than other premium-quality tires. In 1992, high-performance radials accounted for about 30 percent of the OE market and 32 percent of replacement purchases. Industry estimates were that 35 percent of the new vehicles produced in 1995 would be equipped with high-performance radials. While other tiremakers had recently begun offering their versions of high-performance radials, Goodyear in 1992 was the clear leader with about 50 percent of the OE market for high-performance tires; Goodyear's share of replacement sales of high-performance radials was much smaller, however.

All-Season Tires

The most popular category of tires in 1992 was the all-season tire. All-season tires were of radial construction and were designed to deliver superior traction in both rain and snow—a popular feature with drivers in the "snow belt," many of whom were used to putting snow tires on their vehicles for the winter. Sales of all-season passenger tires in the United States had grown from 1 million units in 1977 to 70 million units in 1986 to over 145 million units in 1991. All-season tread designs constituted about 80 percent of the replacement tires sold in the U.S. market in 1992 (versus 17 percent in 1982), and 70 percent of new vehicles in 1992 were equipped with all-season tires. Insofar as all-season tread designs were concerned, the makeup of the U.S. replacement market in 1991, including retreaded tires, was 121 million all-season tires, 6.3 million snow tires, and 32 million conventional tires.

Private-Label Tires

Private-label tires were usually manufactured to specifications below those carrying manufacturers' brands. The leading manufacturers made tires for private labeling to utilize otherwise idle excess capacity; lesser known manufacturers were often big private-label producers. Some private-label production was sold directly to major chain retailers; these were typically made to the retailer's own specifications and carried a private-label brand specified by the retailer. Other private-label brands were sold in mass quantities to wholesale distributors, which in turn marketed them to retailers. The largest distributors of private-label tires contracted to purchase enough volume (sometimes as many as several million tires annually) to win a significant price break from manufacturers and passed through some of the savings to retailers. Private-label tires sold at a discount to name-brand tires and were mainly attractive to the most price-conscious buyers.

Truck Tires

Truck tires and tires for specialty vehicles (motor homes, boat trailers, motorcycles, tractors, farm implements, buses, and off-the-road construction vehicles) represented a relatively small portion of industry volume (under 15 percent) but accounted for over one fourth of industry revenues. The median price of truck tires in 1991 ranged from a low of $60 for a bias tire to over $500 for a large-size steel-belted radial. Tires for tractors and for heavy-duty earthmoving equipment ranged in price from several hundred dollars to over $5,000 per tire. Tires for earth-moving equipment had large ribbed treads for added traction and often were 6 to 10 feet in diameter. Only a limited number of tiremakers made tires for heavy trucks and other specialty vehicles. Goodyear produced tires for virtually every type of vehicle; in the United States and

Europe, Michelin dominated heavy-duty truck tire replacement with market shares in excess of 40 percent.

Retreaded Tires

Retreaded tires were made from tires with wornout treads. New treads, suitable for retreading, could be obtained from tire manufacturers or from tread manufacturers that specialized in retreading. Retreading equipment was available from several suppliers, and a small retread shop could be set up by a local dealer for an investment of less than $250,000. In the United States, about 1,500 retread plants were operating. Most cities of 50,000 or more had at least one retread shop that served the local market for passenger car and light-truck retreads in competition with retreads available from wholesalers and manufacturers. Tire retreading for heavy-duty trucks was usually done by a manufacturer of retreads rather than by a local retread shop; in the United States, the leading maker of truck retreads was Bandag, with a 70 percent market share. Virtually all retailers sold replacement tires at "trade-in" prices; those wornout tires suitable for retreading were collected and sold to retreaders.

In 1992, the retreaded tire segment was small and declining partly because buyers could put on a new set of tires for about $100 more than the cost of retreads and partly because of safety concerns. There were instances when the tread on a retreaded tire separated from the tire casing; the hazards of retreads increased with speed, heat, and rough road conditions. The trucking industry was the biggest user of retreaded tires. In 1992, U.S. truck retread sales were 23 million units, equal to $1.5 billion in sales revenues. The outlook for truck tire retreads was optimistic, with unit sales expected to remain steady or even increase slightly. Radial truck tires were retreaded an average of three times, and freight companies were retreading over 80 percent of the radial tires on their trailer trucks and delivery vehicles. The size of the U.S. passenger car retread market in 1991 was 7 million units, accounting for $250 million in sales; projections were that unit volume would decline steadily. Radials were over 90 percent of the retread market and the percentage was increasing. Retread buyers were very price conscious. The average price for passenger car retreads in 1992 was about $35, compared to an average price of $60 for new passenger car tires. Truck retreads averaged $75 per tire. Radial retreads were more expensive than bias tire retreads. Dealer margins on retreads were in the 40 to 45 percent range, compared to margins of 35 to 40 percent on new tires.

Tire Grading Practices

An article in the April 1983 issue of *Consumer Reports* began with the observation:

> There are few products more mystifying to buy than a tire for your car. How can you judge which tire will last longer? Are you really getting a better tire by paying a premium price?[1]

---

[1] "U.S. Punctures Tire Grading," *Consumer Reports*, April 1983, p. 166.

To help U.S. consumers answer such questions, in 1980, the National Highway Traffic Safety Administration (NHTSA) acting under a congressional mandate instituted a comparative grading system for all tires sold in the United States; tiremakers were ordered to test their tires and report the grades assigned to them in three performance areas—traction, heat resistance, and tread life. The *Consumer Reports* article commented on the value of the grading system to consumers:

> Traction and heat resistance are important safety factors, but their labeling has not provided consumers with a meaningful way to choose among tires. For traction, almost all tires are rated either A or B, the two top grades. The difference between the two grades has little practical meaning. As for heat resistance, every tire sold in the U.S. must pass a Department of Transportation heat-resistance test, so even a tire carrying the lowest heat-resistance grade, a C, is safe.
>
> The tread-life factor, on the other hand, is an indicator of how long the tire will last before becoming hazardously bald. It thus has significant economic as well as safety relevance. The grade is represented by a number, each point of which represents 300 miles of life. Thus, a grade of 150 means a tread life of 45,000 miles under the ideal test-track conditions. (In real-world driving, you might achieve considerably less, depending on how you drive and on the materials used in your state's highways.)[2]

In February 1983, NHTSA suspended indefinitely the requirement for grading tires on the basis of tread wear, citing the statistical variability in tread-life test results and the likelihood of disseminating "potentially misleading information." Much of the statistical variability stemmed from giving tiremakers the latitude to set different confidence intervals in their testing procedures; inexactness in manufacturing resulted in not all samples of a particular tire performing the same in road-track tests. Some manufacturers assigned tread-wear grades based on a 95 percent confidence interval (95 percent of all tires sold would meet the assigned grade), whereas others adopted a more stringent 99 percent confidence interval.

Manufacturers were well aware that tread-life grading could significantly affect the purchases of replacement tire buyers. Both Michelin and Goodyear vigorously opposed the tread-life grades. A Goodyear official said the standard served only to "confuse customers" and that it "led to misuse and misinterpretation." Michelin opposed tread-wear grading on grounds that it would trigger a "grading war" among tire manufacturers, arguing that "designing tires merely to achieve high tread-wear grades may result in tires of inferior quality because of the compromises that will have to be made in safety-related performance characteristics." As of 1992, the NHTSA had not reinstituted requirements for tread-wear grading.

Insofar as the world market was concerned, the recent improvements in tire-making and tread life had been driven more by competitive pressures than by government regulations. Motor vehicle manufacturers in the United States and Europe had increased their demands on tiremakers for improved mileage and performance on OE tires (and at the same time they shopped hard on price). The battle for market share in the replacement tire market, given slack demand and an excess of tiremaking capacity, was forcing rival tire manufacturers to

---

[2]Ibid., p. 166.

attract replacement tire purchasers on the basis of quality and performance as well as on price.

MANUFACTURING

Tires consisted of four basic components: (1) the casing or carcass that formed the skeleton of the tire, (2) the tread (made from compounded rubber), (3) the sidewall, also made of compounded rubber, that sheathed the casing and protected it from damage, and (4) high-tensile steel bead wire that was formed into stiff loops and then embedded in parts of the sidewall and casing to give the tire added strength and to prevent the edges of the tire from stretching. Tire manufacturing was a three-stage process that included materials processing, fabrication of the component tire parts, and tire assembly.

Materials Processing

Over 200 raw materials were used in manufacturing tires, the most important of which were natural rubber, synthetic rubber, fabric and fabric cord (nylon, rayon, polyester, and/or fiberglass), polyvinyl alcohol, sulfur, crude oil, carbon black, and high-carbon steel bead wire. Crude oil was the single largest raw material cost; about 10 gallons of crude oil was consumed in making an average-size passenger car radial tire. Raw material costs for a typical passenger car radial tire were about $16 in 1992.

Virtually all of the raw materials were commodities, available in bulk form from a variety of sources. Several manufacturers had integrated backward into rubber plantations, rubber manufacturing, and tire textiles (fabrics used in tiremaking) and supplied all or part of their production needs for these materials. The principal functions during materials processing involved cutting the rubber, mixing the needed rubber compounds and making sheet rubber, and putting adhesive on the cord and then heat-setting the fabric.

Fabrication of Components

During this phase, several activities occurred. The bead wire was rubber coated and formed into loops. Rolls of cord fabric were treated to facilitate bonding, then cut on an angle and spliced into a continuous sheet in preparation for making the casing. Some sheet rubber stock was milled to the desired width and thickness, forced through an extruder to form tread slabs of exact dimensions and design, cooled, and the "green" treads stored until time for assembly. Other sheet rubber stock was warmed and rolled into thin sheets. Sheeted gum stocks, used for tubeless innerliner and special reinforcement, were cut to various widths in readiness for tire assembly. Belts of fabric, or steel reinforced fabric, were rubber coated, cut into appropriate shapes, and then spliced into rolls.

Tire Assembly

This multistage process first involved assembling tire casing and sidewall components on a rotating collapsible drum called a building drum. At the next step, several workers using a tire-building machine added belts and the tread to produce a green tire. Green tires were sprayed with mold release lubricants, painted, inspected, and moved to the curing press. Tires assumed their final shape through the use of high pressure and high temperature in the molding press (referred to as the vulcanization process). Cured, or vulcanized, tires were next moved to the buffing and trimming areas where excess molding material was trimmed and white raised letters or whitewall stripes buffed out. The completed tire was electronically tested, visually inspected, and stacked for shipment.

The materials processing and tire component fabrication stages were very similar for both bias tire and radial tire production, though more labor time was involved for radials. Tire building required substantially more labor time for radial tires than did bias production. A tire builder could build only 100 radials in the time required to build 150 bias tires. In addition, quality control and inspection of radials was more labor intensive than for bias tires. It was not unusual for U.S. tiremakers to have the percentage of scrap or defective radial tires run two to three times higher than bias tire production, a reflection of the complexity of radial tiremaking technology and the difficulty that workers encountered in making defect-free tires 100 percent of the time.

Most tire plants operated by U.S. and European companies were laid out according to process, with each process having its own section of the plant and each activity having its own assigned area. The manufacturing flow was from materials processing to component fabrication to tire assembly with items stocked and stored at each end of the three processes as they awaited the next stage. Materials handling was considerable and components could travel long distances between steps.

Japanese tire plants, in contrast, were organized with more emphasis on integrating the process and creating a series of production lines, with each line doing some of its materials processing and all of its own component fabrication and tire assembly. Materials processing was centralized for those few functions where economies of scale were sizable and it was too expensive to have separate pieces of equipment for each workstation. This made the production process continuous within each workstation and minimized materials handling and the distance traveled by each part. Such arrangements utilized one third less space, reduced changeover costs from tire model to tire model, and shortened the lead times for production scheduling from 12 weeks to 1 week. The Japanese arranged for just-in-time shipments of raw materials from suppliers to cut back sharply on space requirements for storing inventory as well as working capital for inventory stocks. They also worked closely with suppliers of raw materials specifications to eliminate the need for materials checking and testing when raw materials arrived. Insofar as possible, incoming raw materials were moved directly into the manufacturing flow and stocked at the workstation where they were needed.

Labor Costs

Although tire manufacturing was relatively capital intensive (a new plant of minimum efficient size could cost as much as $250 million, and plant modernization costs of $50 million to $200 million per plant were common), there was significant labor content. Labor costs ran from a low of about 15 percent to a high of about 40 percent of total costs, depending on wage rates and labor efficiency; the U.S. average was about 25 percent. Some parts of the radial tire manufacturing process required 25 percent more labor time than for bias tire assembly. In 1992, hourly wage and fringe benefit costs varied widely among countries:

Country	Estimated Average Wage and Fringe Benefit Costs per Hour
United States (as per contracts with United Rubber Workers Union)	$23.00
Europe	18.00
Japan	18.00
Canada	17.00
Taiwan	3.00
Mexico	2.60
Korea	2.00
Brazil	1.80

Industry observers were predicting increased worldwide sourcing of tires from countries having the lowest labor costs, with Korea, Mexico, and Brazil becoming increasingly attractive production locations. Several major tire manufacturers were said to be considering plant locations in low-wage countries. Shipping costs for tires made in foreign countries and then marketed in the United States were approximately $1 per tire in 1992.

Manufacturers with tire plants in high-wage locations were working hard to reduce the labor-cost content of their tires to enable them to be more cost competitive. The average manufacturing costs of passenger car tires made in Korea and Brazil were estimated to be between $20 and $25 in 1992; Japanese-made tires were thought to entail manufacturing costs in the $25 to $30 range for an average size tire.

For the most part, the high-cost producers of tires in 1992 were U.S. plants formerly owned by Firestone, Uniroyal-Goodrich, General Tire, and Dunlop; their manufacturing costs averaged $30 to $36 for passenger car radials. Uniroyal-Goodrich and Firestone were said to have the highest costs; labor costs were an estimated 40 percent of total production costs at some Goodrich tire plants. Korean producers, especially Kumho, were thought to be the world's overall low-cost leaders in 1992, but Korean-made tires had not yet won buyer recognition for quality as had the tires of Michelin, Goodyear, Bridgestone, and several other leading producers.

Efforts to reduce labor costs at U.S. plants focused mainly on unionized plants and generally took the form of boosting worker productivity through both automation and the elimination of costly work rules. Tiremakers' relations with the United Rubber Workers Union had historically been stormy. The URW over the years had won, sometimes after long strikes, an excellent wage and fringe benefit package—one comparable to what the United Auto Workers union had negotiated with the major automakers. Each local union had also negotiated plant work rules that in many cases held down labor productivity. Labor militancy was a fact of life in unionized plants; grievance filings and arbitration of disputes were frequent occurrences.

By the mid-1980s, the pressure to reduce labor costs was so great that industrywide pattern bargaining had given way to bargaining on a plant-by-plant basis, even within the same company. "Distressed plants" often had special contract provisions that resulted in cost savings big enough to stave off a plant shutdown. In a few cases, companies thrust their plant managers into a "survival of the fittest" contest to see who could achieve the biggest overall cost reductions (but with emphasis on winning the biggest labor cost concessions since these represented a major variable cost item); the winner's plant was kept open and the loser's was either closed or scheduled for layoffs and scaled-down production. In many instances, tire production was shifted from unionized plants with high labor costs to nonunion plants with lower labor costs. Eight of the nine tire plants built in the United States since 1970 were nonunion and had been located in states and communities where the threat of union organization was weak. All U.S. tire plants closed since 1970 had been unionized plants. Exhibit 10 shows the North American plants of the various tiremakers, their unionized status, their tiremaking capacities, and the types of tires produced at each plant.

COST-CUTTING EFFORTS

Falling tire prices, mature demand conditions, and overcapacity industrywide during the 1980s had given a clear competitive edge to low-cost tiremakers. Manufacturers, especially those with the highest production costs, were scrambling hard to cut costs across the board and to eliminate inefficient production. No part of the cost structure was being ignored. Efforts were under way to try to automate more of the radial tire-building process, particularly those activities with high labor content. Most manufacturers were investing heavily in new equipment to boost productivity levels; aging equipment was being scheduled for earlier than usual replacement; and in some plants, the layout of production activities was being reconfigured to achieve a more economical manufacturing flow. The costs of plant renovation efforts commonly ran into the tens of millions of dollars per plant, particularly in the case of plants more than 10 years old.

Companies were also concentrating on ways to improve their radial tiremaking practices. Radial tire quality was a big factor with both OE and replacement buyers since the worst made radial tires provided a harder and bumpier ride, tended to wear unevenly, got out of balance easier, sometimes did not maintain the proper inflation and tire pressure for long periods, and consequently had a shorter tread life—characteristics that created owner dissatisfaction and complaints. Virtually all of the radial tire manufacturers were under competitive pressure to improve the performance of their radial tires at the same time they were struggling to reduce production costs.

The closing of nearly 30 tire plants in North America since 1975 had eliminated about 23 percent of North American tiremaking capacity; most of these plants were outmoded facilities that made bias-ply and bias-belted tires. Total U.S. tiremaking capacity had fallen from a high of just over 1 million tires per day in 1975 to 830,000 per day in 1992 (see Exhibit 10). Over 75 percent of this capacity was in passenger car tires. Only seven U.S.-headquartered tiremakers were in business in 1992, down from 12 in 1986, 14 in 1965, 23 in 1945, and 178 in 1921. Of these seven, five were one-plant operations with total sales under

EXHIBIT 10 **Plants and Estimated Production Capabilities of Major Tire Producers in North America, 1991**

Company/Plant Location	Year Opened	Unionized Plant	Employees	Tire Types	Estimated Capacity
United States					
Goodyear					
Akron, Ohio	1983	Yes	600	9	2,000 u/d
Danville, Virginia	1966	Yes	2,150	3, 6, 8	12,000 u/d
Gadsden, Alabama	1929/78	Yes	2,100	1, 3, 4	33,000 u/d
Topeka, Kansas	1944	Yes	2,000	2, 4, 6	8,100 u/d
Union City, Tennessee	1968	Yes	3,000	1, 2	50,000 u/d
Madisonville, Kentucky	1966	Yes	300	2, 4, 7	11,000 u/d
Lawton, Oklahoma	1978	No	2,250	1	53,000 u/d
Kelly-Springfield (Goodyear)					
Freeport, Illinois	1964	Yes	1,515	2, 4	24,000 u/d
Tyler, Texas	1962/85	Yes	1,450	1	32,000 u/d
Fayetteville, North Carolina	1969	Yes	2,900	1,2	55,000 u/d
Bridgestone/Firestone					
Decatur, Illinois	1963	Yes	1,970	1, 2	25,000 u/d
Des Moines, Iowa	1945	Yes	1,795	1, 3, 4, 6	14,000 u/d
Wilson, North Carolina	1973	No	1,990	1	28,000 u/d
Oklahoma City, Oklahoma	1969	Yes	1,770	1, 2	30,000 u/d
La Vergne, Tennessee	1972/83	Yes	1,700	1, 2, 3	12,000 u/d
Warren Co., Tennessee	1990	Yes	750	3	4,000 u/d
Michelin Tire					
Greenville, South Carolina	1975	No	2,500	1	23,000 u/d
Spartanburg, South Carolina	1978	No	1,550	3	5,000 u/d
Lexington, South Carolina	1981	No	1,250	1	15,000 u/d
Dothan, Alabama	1979	No	900	2	4,500 u/m
Norwood, North Carolina	1987	No	400	8	12,600 u/d
General Tire (Continental)					
Charlotte, North Carolina	1967	Yes	1,264	1	27,000 u/d
Bryan, Ohio	1967	Yes	389	4, 6, 7	260 u/d
Mayfield, Kentucky	1960	Yes	1,618	1, 2, 3, 4	23,810 u/d
Mount Vernon, Illinois	1974	No	1,549	1, 3, 9	21,800 u/d
Uniroyal-Goodrich Tire Co. (Michelin)					
Opelika, Alabama	1963	Yes	1,200	1, 2	26,000 u/d
Ardmore, Oklahoma	1969	No	1,900	1	32,000 u/d
Tuscaloosa, Alabama	1946	Yes	2,000	1, 2	30,000 u/d
Fort Wayne, Indiana	1961	Yes	1,400	1, 2	29,000 u/d
Pirelli Armstrong Tire					
Des Moines, Iowa	1943/88	Yes	1,000	1,2,3,5	8,835 u/d
Hanford, California	1962/88	Yes	600	1	17,000 u/d
Nashville, Tennessee	1973/88	Yes	650	1	16,000 u/d
Cooper Tire*					
Findlay, Ohio	1919	Yes	1,000	1, 2, 3	19,000 u/d
Texarkana, Arkansas	1964/85	Yes	1,550	1, 2	34,500 u/d
Tupelo, Mississippi	1959/84	No	950	1	25,500 u/d
Albany, Georgia	1991	No	—	2, 3	7,000 u/d *projected
Dunlop Tire (Sumitomo)					
Buffalo, New York†	1923/86	Yes	1,080	1, 2, 3, 5	8,835 u/d
Huntsville, Alabama	1969	Yes	1,321	1, 2	28,120 u/d

EXHIBIT 10   (*concluded*)

Company/Plant Location	Year Opened	Unionized Plant	Employees	Tire Types	Estimated Capacity
Mexico					
Goodyear					
Mexico City	1941	—	2,150	1, 2, 3, 4	16,000 u/d
Bridgestone/Firestone de Mexico‡					
Mexico City	1958/88	Yes	450	2, 3	1,900 u/d
Cuernavaca	1977/88	Yes	550	1, 2, 3	2,800 u/d
Hulera Euzkadi§					
Mexico City	1936	Yes	767	1, 2, 3, 4, 6	3,457 u/d
Guadalajara	1972	Yes	820	1, 2, 3	8,858 u/d
Uniroyal-Goodrich (Michelin)					
Tacuba	1945	Yes	400	1, 2, 3	3,200 u/d
Queretaro	1977	Yes	350	1, 2	4,500 u/d
General Tire (Continental)					
Mexico City	1924/88	Yes	609	2, 3	2,100 u/d
San Luis Potosi	1975/88	Yes	604	1, 2	3,600 u/d
Canada					
Goodyear					
Medicine Hat, Alberta	1960	Yes	230	1, 4	7,200 u/d
Valleyfield, Quebec	1964	Yes	850	1	21,000 u/d
Napanee, Ontario#	1990	No	400	1	6,000 u/d
Bridgestone/Firestone					
Joliette, Quebec	1965	Yes	880	1	12,500 u/d
Michelin					
New Glasgow, Nova Scotia	1971	No	2,000	1, 2	9,000 u/d
Waterville (Granton), Nova Scotia	1982	No	1,000	3, 6	2,000 u/d
Bridgewater, Nova Scotia	1971	No	1,300	1, 2	11,000 u/d
Uniroyal-Goodrich Tire Co.					
Kitchener, Ontario South	1962	Yes	700	1, 2	12,000 u/d

*Cooper in 1990 purchased the Albany, Ga. tire plant closed by Firestone four years earlier and plans to resume production of passenger tires in the second half of 1991. Securities analysts speculate that the plant ultimately will be used to produce radial truck tires, which Cooper presently has built for it by other manufacturers.

†The Buffalo plant capacity figure includes the expansion of Dunlop's truck tire line.

‡Formerly Hulera el Centenario.

§Uniroyal-Goodrich owns 35 percent of the company.

#Goodyear's Napanee plant began partial production in May 1990 and is expected to have a capacity of 3 million tires per year (14,800 u/d) by the end of 1991.

Tire types: 1-Auto; 2-Light truck; 3-Truck/bus; 4-Agricultural; 5-Motorcycle; 6-Earthmover/OTR; 7-Industrial; 8-Aircraft; 9-Racing. Depending on information supplied by manufacturer, plant capacities are expressed either as "u" (units) or "t" (tons) per (/) "d" (day).

Source: *Market Data Book 1991, Tire Business*, January 1992, p. 37.

$100 million annually, and three of these five small producers made car and truck tires.

COMPETITION

In 1992, competition centered around the variables of price and tire performance. The retail prices of tires of all types were trending downward in most world markets (see Exhibit 9 for the price trends in the United States).

EXHIBIT 11   Number of Retail Outlets Carrying Selected Tire Brands, 1991

Tire Brand (Parent Company)	Number of Retail Points of Sale
Armstrong (Pirelli)	978
Bridgestone (Bridgestone Corp.)	5,960
Cooper (Cooper Tire and Rubber)	1,518
Dunlop (Sumitomo)	2,046
Firestone (Bridgestone)	4,208
General (Continental A.G.)	2,107
Goodrich (Michelin)	4,215
Goodyear (Goodyear Tire and Rubber)	7,964
Kelly-Springfield (Goodyear)	2,421
Michelin (Groupe Michelin)	7,169
Pirelli (Pirelli Group)	2,133
Uniroyal (Michelin)	2,321

Source: *Market Data Book 1991*, *Tire Business*, January 1992, p. 14.

Tiremakers had emphasized performance characteristics such as traction, handling, and braking. Overall tire quality and tire performance were on the upswing. Increased tread life on OE and replacement tires threatened to cut deeply into the number of sets of replacement tires needed per vehicle in service. Moreover, competition among the tiremakers was increasingly global.

In the U.S. market, the tires of foreign-headquartered companies had become more visible and better known. In 1992, roughly 25 percent of all new passenger cars sold in the United States were made at plants in Europe and Japan; virtually all came equipped with foreign-made tires. Many European car imports came equipped with Michelin, Pirelli, or Continental tires, and most Japanese car imports were equipped with Bridgestone tires.

Bridgestone was the first Japanese tire company to produce tires in the United States; it began manufacturing truck tires in the United States in 1984, acquiring a truck tire plant from Firestone. Between 1984 and 1988, Bridgestone worked hard to expand its network of retail dealers to provide better access to replacement tire buyers. Its 1988 acquisition of Firestone gave it a six-plant production base in North America and a network of some 4,000 retail tire outlets and auto care centers.

Michelin had built a nationwide network of U.S. dealers years earlier and was represented by over 7,000 dealers in all cities and most towns; a substantial number of dealers carried the Michelin brand as their primary line. Exhibit 11 shows the number of retail dealers handling the major brands of replacement tires in the United States. The Michelin name was well known and widely advertised in the United States, Europe, and parts of Asia. Michelin's market share in replacement tires was much lower than for OE tires because of its premium pricing strategy. The top-dollar prices charged by Michelin dealers scared off some would-be buyers and usually resulted in the dealer switching the buyer to another brand in the store, often a brand carrying as big or bigger dealer percentage margin as the Michelin brand. The name-brand replacement tires of the leading U.S. manufacturers typically carried lower dealer margins than most Asian and European brands.

Michelin, Pirelli, Bridgestone, Sumitomo, Yokohama, Toyo, and the Korean tire producers (Hankook and Kumho) were all trying to increase their shares of the U.S. market. Recent declines in the value of the dollar against the Japanese yen were one of the factors prompting the Japanese to acquire tiremaking facilities in the United States to support their strategic objective of increasing sales and market share in the United States. The Japanese and Korean tiremakers dominated the tire market in the Pacific and Southeast Asia, except for New Zealand and Australia; Goodyear had a strong presence in New Zealand and Australia.

Japanese efforts to penetrate the European market had not met with as much success as in the United States. Japanese cars accounted for between 10 and 12 percent of new car sales in Europe and for just less than 10 percent of total car registrations, making it harder for the Japanese tiremakers to enter the replacement tire segment just on the basis of selling Japanese-made replacement tires for Japanese-made cars. In terms of overall new car-truck production in Europe, U.S. manufacturers (Ford and GM) had about a 23 percent market share, the Japanese about an 11 percent share, and the European manufacturers a 66 percent share. In Europe, the market leaders in tires were Michelin, Goodyear, Continental, Pirelli, and Dunlop (a British brand tire that had recently been acquired by Sumitomo). Sumitomo's acquisition of Dunlop's troubled and unprofitable European operations was seen as a signal of Japanese intent to use the well-known Dunlop brand name to increase its penetration of the European tire market. Distribution channels for replacement tires in Europe functioned in much the same manner as in the United States, with the competitive focus on price, performance, and strong dealer networks.

In recent years, the European tire market had been characterized by a fierce price war. Between 1988 and 1991, European producers had cut prices on some tire models as much as 40 percent to win OE orders from automotive manufacturers. In 1990 alone, prices on OE tires had fallen 17 percent. Continental's CEO observed, "We are only a handful of players. In spite of that, we are fighting each other like hell."[3]

RESTRUCTURING AND DIVERSIFICATION

Slowdowns in unit volume growth, a stiffening of competitive pressures brought on by market diversity, and declining profit prospects in tires during the 1970s had prompted the leading U.S. tire manufacturers to take a hard look at their dependence on tires and to consider what their future course should be. Goodyear, Firestone, Goodrich, General Tire, and Uniroyal all concluded market maturity in tires called for diversification into other businesses to open new avenues for growth and profitability. Each began to make acquisitions.

By the early 1980s, their business portfolios included investments in plastics, aerospace, flooring, footwear, rubberized roofing, petroleum production and transportation, chemicals, packaging film, and a variety of industrial products. By the mid-1980s, however, most U.S. tire manufacturers were retreating from their forays into diversification and were in a restructuring/retrenchment mode.

---

[3]As quoted in *Business Week*, February 27, 1990, p. 63.

Diversification had proved more or less disastrous, siphoning off funds needed to strengthen their core tire business and leaving them vulnerable to competition from foreign tire producers. In many instances, diversification had not proved to be as profitable as the tire business.

In the mid-1980s, GenCorp Inc., parent of General Tire, announced the sale of some of its television stations, the closing of a bias-ply tire plant, and a significant stock repurchase program. Firestone's diversified businesses, which accounted for 25 percent of sales in 1979, made up less than 5 percent by year-end 1986. Businesses that were divested included plastic resins, beer kegs, automotive seat belts, polyurethane foam, and wheels for trucks, tractors, and construction machinery. Uniroyal in the mid-1980s divested all of its nontire operations and then merged its entire tire business with the tire division of B.F. Goodrich to form Uniroyal-Goodrich Tire Company; two years later, it was acquired by Groupe Michelin.

PROFILES OF THE LEADING COMPETITORS

In 1992, the world tire industry was struggling to emerge from a fierce price war and a global battle for market share. Excess production capacity, made worse by slack demand for new motor vehicles throughout 1991, had created a tough business climate. Many of the leading tiremakers posted significant losses or else lower profits in 1991 (see Exhibit 12).

Late in 1991, tire manufacturers took steps to end their price war. Continental led the way by announcing a 7.5 percent across-the-board price increase on its line of General tires sold in the United States; 10 other North American producers followed Continental's lead with announcements of price increases ranging between 2 and 8 percent. Going into 1992, it remained to be seen whether the price increases would stick, since most U.S. tire plants were operating at less than 85 percent of capacity and supply capability was expected to exceed demand until 1995 or later.

Profiles for the various tire companies follow.

Goodyear Tire and Rubber Co.

Goodyear's principal business was the development, manufacture, distribution, and sale of tires throughout the world. Tires and tubes represented 83 percent of Goodyear's corporate sales of $10.9 billion in 1991; other products and businesses included an oil and gas production and pipeline subsidiary and the manufacture of nontire automotive products, synthetic rubber, chemicals, and high-technology items for aerospace, defense, and other applications. Until the merger-consolidation wave in 1986–88, Goodyear had been both the world's largest tire producer and the world's largest rubber manufacturer. It had held this ranking since the 1920s.

The company operated 44 tire products plants in 28 countries and had seven rubber plantations. Its major tiremaking locations outside the United States were in Canada (three plants), Germany (two plants), Luxembourg, Britain, Mexico, and Brazil (two plants). In addition to Goodyear tires, the company owned Kelly-Springfield Tire Co. and Lee Tire and Rubber Co.; both Kelly-Springfield and Lee made private-label tires in addition to their own branded

EXHIBIT 12   **Comparative Statistics on the 10 Largest Tire Manufacturers, 1984–90**
(Dollars in millions)

Company	Year	Sales	Net Income (Loss)	Assets	Stockholders' Equity	Number of Employees
Goodyear	1984	$10,241	$ 411.0	$ 6,194	$3,171	133,271
	1989	11,044	206.8	8,406	2,144	111,469
	1990	11,453	(38.3)	8,964	2,098	107,671
	1991	10,907	96.6	8,511	2,731	99,952
Michelin	1984	8,141	(411.4)	9,801	1,285	120,000
	1989	10,154	450.2	13,842	3,505	124,408
	1990	11,522	(1,088.5)	14,914	2,173	140,826
	1991	12,325	(945.1)	14,943	2,177	140,826
Bridgestone	1984	5,527	106.6	4,665	1,687	33,577
	1989	11,787	64.9	10,863	2,910	93,193
	1990	12,395	29.4	12,883	3,247	95,276
	1991	13,131	33.1	12,872	3,297	95,276
Firestone	1984	3,758	102.0	2,571	1,236	59,900
	1985	3,602	3.0	2,528	1,163	54,700
	1986	3,501	85.0	2,593	1,167	55,000
	1987	3,867	145.0	2,921	1,179	53,000
	1988	Acquired by Bridgestone				
Pirelli	1984	5,126	105.8	5,333	NA	62,000
	1989	8,637	199.7	10,472	2,700	69,329
	1990	8,463	116.4	10,476	2,739	68,703
	1991	9,024	124.1	10,513	2,449	68,703
Continental	1984	2,184	25.3	1,097	285	26,401
	1989	5,185	140.9	3,723	1,102	47,495
	1990	5,310	362.0	7,167	2,892	27,000
	1991					
General Tire	1984	2,727	7.2	2,037	910	27,800
	1985	3,021	75.2	2,073	951	27,000
	1986	3,099	130.0	2,119	1,048	26,700
	1987	Acquired by Continental				
Sumitomo	1984	1,602	11.5	1,335	108	6,900
	1989	3,315	45.7	2,960	332	20,000
	1990	3,788	8.1	3,713	384	21,000
	1991	4,019	9.3	3,710	411	4,870
Yokohama	1984	1,932	6.9	1,574	126	10,675
	1989	2,502	61.2	2,566	378	11,073
	1990	2,963	67.3	3,004	481	12,722
	1991	3,129	72.3	2,988	466	6,589
Cooper Tire and Rubber	1984	555	24.6	280	161	4,805
	1989	867	58.2	520	310	6,041
	1990	896	66.5	616	369	6,225
	1991	1,001	79.4	671	440	6,545
Toyo Tire	1986	1,284	15.1	956	115	3,611
	1989	1,635	23.2	1,419	214	NA
	1990	1,757	20.0	1,711	334	NA
	1991	1,867	9.0	1,937	354	4,012

Note: All foreign financial figures are adjusted to reflect 1990 exchange rates.

Sources: Compiled by the case researchers from *Fortune*, various issues; company annual reports; *Diamond's Japan Business Directory*, 1987, p. 422; *Japan Company Handbook: First Section 1992*, p. 424; and Dow Jones News/Retrieval.

tires. In 1985, Goodyear and Toyo Tire formed a joint venture to produce tires for large-scale vehicles and off-the-road equipment; Nippon Giant Tire Co., the joint venture, operated one plant in Japan (annual tire sales of $55 million in 1990). Goodyear in 1992 controlled about 37 percent of the tiremaking capacity in the United States and about 20 to 25 percent of the world's tiremaking capacity. Foreign sales accounted for about 42 percent of revenues. About 40 percent of Goodyear's tire sales were to the OE market and 60 percent to the replacement market.

The Goodyear brand was the leader in both the North American market (the world's largest) and in Latin America. The company ranked No. 2 in market share everywhere in the Asian market outside of Japan (behind Bridgestone). In Europe, Goodyear was challenging Pirelli and Continental for the No. 2 ranking behind Michelin; going into 1992, Goodyear had the third largest share in Europe.

In addition, Goodyear was aggressively pursuing cost reduction and plant modernization programs at all of its tire plants. The company invested $4 billion in tire plant modernization during the 1980s, and plant productivity had improved substantially worldwide. Since 1985, output per labor-hour in North American plants had risen 52 percent. On the average, Goodyear's production costs for tires were below average worldwide. Goodyear's goal was to become a still lower cost producer. Goodyear's corporatewide budget for R&D was about $250 million to $300 million. Its reputation for tire quality was good to excellent, generally on a par with Michelin and slightly ahead of Bridgestone. Goodyear was the clear quality leader in high-performance radial tires. The company's Goodyear Eagle line of tires was noted for being top quality. Goodyear had the broadest line of tire products of any manufacturer.

Goodyear was active in purchasing multioutlet retailers, and its sales force was striving to convert independent tire dealers to the Goodyear brand and to a lesser extent to win new accounts for Kelly-Springfield and Lee tires. Goodyear's strategy in acquiring large-volume independent dealers that typically carried three or four brands was to increase the share of Goodyear tires being sold in these outlets; Goodyear had nearly 8,000 retail dealers in the United States. Late in 1991, Wal-Mart agreed to market Douglas brand radial car and light-truck tires made by Goodyear's Kelly-Springfield subsidiary. Goodyear saw the replacement market as holding the biggest potential for increasing its market share. Goodyear's share of the U.S. replacement market was only 15.5 percent, well below its 38 percent share of the U.S. OE segment.

The company in 1991 was among the top 50 leading national advertisers. It had maintained a high profile in auto racing for over 20 years to stress the high-performance capabilities of its tires. Goodyear promoted its tires with the slogan, "The best tires in the world have Goodyear written all around them." The name Goodyear was one of the best known brand names in the world, and in the United States, Goodyear blimps had become a prominent advertising symbol.

In early 1991, Goodyear reported a $38 million loss on its 1990 operations, the company's first money-losing year since the Depression. In June 1991, Goodyear's board of directors in a surprise move decided to replace the company's CEO; chosen as new CEO was Stanley G. Gault, who only two months earlier had retired as CEO of Rubbermaid Corporation. Gault had joined Goodyear's board in 1989 and was regarded as a very effective chief executive with a talent for innovation and aggressive marketing. Gault immediately elevated the already high emphasis on Goodyear's companywide program to become a low-cost producer, setting a goal of reducing costs by $350 million within three years.

In addition, Gault set programs in motion to boost sales by introducing new types of tires. In early 1992, Goodyear introduced the Aquatred line with a tread design that prevented hydroplaning and a new Invicta tire designed to produce less friction and boost fuel economy by 4 percent. Goodyear also recruited Sears to sell seven lines of Goodyear tires at Sears' 850 auto centers; Goodyear's research showed that some 2 million Goodyear tires a year were being replaced by tires bought at Sears.

Within a year of Gault's appointment, Goodyear's stock had risen by 130 percent. Goodyear, after losing $38 million in 1990, made an impressive turnaround in the second half of 1991, earning $97 million in 1991 and was expected to show strong profits in 1992.

Groupe Michelin

Groupe Michelin was a French company with about $10.1 billion in worldwide tire sales in 1991 and total sales of $11.5 billion. Michelin's acquisition of Uniroyal-Goodrich propelled it past Goodyear to be the global market share leader. Michelin operated 70 tire plants in 15 countries. Michelin was strongest in Europe (where it had a market share of approximately 30 percent) and the United States (where its overall market share was about 15 percent). Michelin's market share in heavy-duty truck tires was much bigger than its share of the passenger tire market. In North America, Michelin had 12 tire plants, representing about 23 percent of the total tiremaking capacity; 7 plants (all nonunion) made Michelin brand tires and 5 plants (1 nonunion) made Uniroyal and Goodrich brand tires.

Michelin was the acknowledged leader in radial tire technology (through its competitive edge was shrinking rapidly), and its reputation for radial tire quality was the best in the industry. The company was extremely secretive about its tiremaking practices, but its plants were reputed to be among the most highly automated in the industry. Michelin tires were generally premium priced and appealed mainly to quality-sensitive buyers who drove relatively expensive cars. Truck owners were attracted to Michelin brand tires because of their perceived tread wear and longer life cycle (in terms of being retreadable). Michelin drummed the theme to OE and replacement tire buyers that its tires deserved a price premium because they were unmatched in terms of quality and performance.

In fall 1992, Michelin introduced the Michelin XH4 line of tires guaranteed to deliver 80,000 miles of tread wear. Industry observers believed if tires with a tread wear life of 80,000 miles worked their way into the OE market, the repercussions on the replacement market would be far reaching. According to one official, if new vehicles came equipped with 80,000-mile tires, "by the time the owner replaces the OE tires, he won't be planning to keep the car much longer, and he won't be looking at first-line replacement tires."[4] In early 1992,

---

[4]As quoted in *Tire Business*, January 13, 1992, p. 13.

Michelin introduced an XFE tire line, incorporating new tread designs and tread compounds that reduced rolling resistance by 15 to 20 percent and improved a vehicle's fuel economy by 3 percent.

In 1990, Michelin reported losses of nearly $1 billion on total sales of $11.5 billion; the company lost $124 million in 1991 on corporatewide sales of $12 billion. Michelin had debt of almost $6 billion, nearly three times its total equity. The company had plans to downsize its work force by 16,000 people (out of a total of 140,000) by year-end 1992 and to cut 1992 investment spending by 75 percent. However, Michelin was not cutting back on R&D spending.

Michelin's problems stemmed primarily from the price war in the European OE tire segment and from its Uniroyal-Goodrich acquisition. Uniroyal-Goodrich was a high-cost producer, had older and less efficient plants, and was losing U.S. market share. As of 1992, Michelin had moved slowly to introduce its technology and management approaches at Uniroyal-Goodrich. Further, Michelin had opted to maintain separate sales forces and distribution facilities for each of its three flag brands—Michelin, Uniroyal, and BF Goodrich.

Michelin had positioned the Michelin brand as the top-quality, premium-priced radial in both the OE and replacement markets in the United States (and elsewhere). The BF Goodrich brand was being positioned to focus on the performance and light-truck segments in the U.S. replacement market. Uniroyal brands were being aimed at the OE segment (where Uniroyal had long had a presence, chiefly as a supplier to General Motors) and at the middle of the replacement segment for vehicle owners seeking a medium-grade tire at a medium or average price. Michelin's marketing goal was to minimize competition and overlap among the three brands and to cover as wide a portion of the total U.S. market as feasible. In 1991, 7,200 U.S. dealers carried the Michelin brand, 4,200 carried the BF Goodrich lines, and 2,300 carried Uniroyal lines (see Exhibit 11).

During the early 1980s, Uniroyal had sold all of its European operations to Continental; as of 1992, Continental was continuing to market Uniroyal's brands in Europe. Before the merger of Uniroyal and Goodrich in 1986, both companies had divested all their company-owned tire stores. Goodrich had withdrawn from the sale of OE tires in 1981.

Bridgestone Tire

Bridgestone was the Goodyear of Japan, with a dominant 50 percent share of the Japanese passenger tire market and strength in truck tires as well. It was the third largest producer worldwide, and it was normally the most profitable of the four leading Japanese tiremakers. Bridgestone had become the dominant Japanese producer following World War II using technology licensed from Goodyear. The company had made substantial technology investments of its own in recent years and was an accomplished manufacturer of radial tires.

Bridgestone had moved aggressively in 1988 to acquire Firestone when it appeared that Pirelli was seriously interested in buying Firestone. To block Pirelli's bid, Bridgestone offered a stunning $2.6 billion for Firestone, an amount most observers believed far exceeded Firestone's value. Following the acquisition, Bridgestone announced a three-year, $1.5 billion program to modernize Firestone's operations and to construct a new $350 million radial truck tire plant near Bridgestone's existing plant outside Nashville (acquired from

Firestone in 1984). Bridgestone also renamed its Firestone unit Bridgestone/Firestone Inc. (BFS).

In 1990, BFS suffered $350 million in losses, bringing Bridgestone's overall profits down to just $33 million on sales of $13.2 billion. In mid-1991, Bridgestone replaced BFS Chairman George Aucott with Yichiro Kaizaki, a Bridgestone executive vice president and top aide to Bridgestone's CEO. In 1991, Bridgestone's subsidiaries in the United States (BFS), Latin America, and Europe (Bridgestone/Firestone Europe) posted losses of $500 million. Going into 1992, only three of Bridgestone's geographic divisions were operating at a profit—its Japanese operation and its units in Thailand and Indonesia. While Bridgestone said its U.S. and European units would reach break-even during the second half of 1992, knowledgeable observers were skeptical.

So far, the Bridgestone brand was not a big factor in the European market, although sales were growing along with the sales of Japanese cars in Europe. However, the acquisition of Firestone had given Bridgestone a seven-plant manufacturing base and more distribution outlets in Europe, putting it in position to be a major player. Bridgestone's areas of market strength outside Japan and the United States were in Asia, the Pacific, and South America, where Japanese cars and trucks were being heavily marketed. The company had strong market share momentum, was spending heavily on innovation and improved facilities, and was viewed as the only company in the industry capable of challenging Goodyear and Michelin on a truly global scale.

At the time of its acquisition by Bridgestone, Firestone had tire and related products facilities in Argentina, Brazil, Canada, France, Italy, Portugal, Spain, Venezuela, and New Zealand and had minority interests in tire operations in Mexico, South Africa, Thailand, Kenya, and the Philippines; the plant in Spain was the largest of Firestone's foreign operations. Additionally, Firestone owned a rubber plantation in Liberia and manufactured a major part of its requirements for synthetic rubber, rayon polyester, and nylon cord.

The company produced and marketed a broad line of tires for automobiles, trucks, trailers, buses, construction vehicles, agricultural machinery, off-the-road vehicles, and other vehicles for both the OE and replacement markets. Besides Firestone brand tires, the company marketed tires under the Dayton and Road King names.

In 1983, Firestone had acquired JCPenney automotive centers. As of 1988, Firestone owned and operated approximately 1,500 retail automotive centers that offered a wide range of maintenance and repair services under the "MasterCare by Firestone" program and doubled as retail tire outlets. Firestone tires were also sold through independent dealers and some service stations. Bridgestone viewed Firestone's existing distribution channels as a major asset in being able to secure a greater U.S. market share for its Bridgestone and Firestone brands.

The Pirelli Group

Pirelli was seen as astute at picking good market niches. Pirelli had beat out Michelin for the leadership position in the European high-performance tire segment. Substantial numbers of European sports cars came equipped with Pirelli tires made at its Italian plants. In 1992, Pirelli operated 29 tire plants in nine countries.

When Pirelli failed at acquiring Firestone, it immediately bought Armstrong Tire and Rubber, which operated three tire plants in the United States and had sales of about $700 million. Armstrong competed only in the replacement tire market and was a major supplier of private-label tires—its biggest private-label customer was Sears.

Pirelli quickly launched a four-year, $200 million program to upgrade Armstrong's plants and changed the company name to Pirelli Armstrong. Pirelli also took immediate steps to boost the sale of its Pirelli brand in the United States by combining the sales forces and distribution efforts of the Pirelli and Armstrong brands and offering Armstrong's nearly 1,000 retail dealers a broader range of products with little overlap. The Pirelli brand was positioned at the high-performance and premium-priced end of the market (giving dealers a brand to compete against Goodyear and Michelin), while the Armstrong brand, which was strongest in the farm market, was promoted as a medium-range tires for price-conscious buyers.

In early 1992, Pirelli was developing plans to convert Armstrong's newly modernized Hanford plant, where Pirelli tire-building equipment had been installed, from producing mostly Armstrong and private-label tires over to 100 percent Pirelli-brand production by 1995. Pirelli had just introduced its first all-season tire designed for the North American market; the tire was priced for the middle segment of the market but carried a longer-than-average tread wear warranty.

Pirelli's biggest strategic move had been to seek a merger with Continental and create an $8.4 billion tire company with a 16 percent market share. Extensive negotiations were held with reluctant Continental officials over several months in 1991, ending in a failure to agree. Pirelli had argued that its Brazilian operations would complement Continental's Mexican plant and that Pirelli's market strength in Italy and southern Europe was an ideal match with Continental's strength in Germany and northern Europe. Together, argued Pirelli, they could mount a more effective attack on the eastern Europe and U.S. markets.

Although Pirelli was regarded as a low-cost producer, the price war in Europe had eroded its margins. In 1991, Pirelli posted a net loss of $125 million on total sales of about $3.5 billion.

Continental AG

Continental was Germany's largest tire producer and the No. 2 company, behind Michelin, in Europe. Worldwide, Continental was the fourth largest manufacturer of radial truck tires and the fifth largest maker of radial passenger tires. Its acquisition of General Tire made it the world's fourth largest producer (up from sixth in 1986). Continental supplied OE tires to Mercedes-Benz, BMW, Volvo, Audi, Volkswagen, and Porsche. Continental was committed to product development and research. Its tires were viewed as premium quality, and it offered independent tire dealers attractive profit margins. In 1992, Continental had 24 tire plants in 16 countries.

In 1987, when Continental acquired General Tire, it said the relationships between Continental and General brands in the United States would be patterned after its European approach where its flag brands (Continental, Uniroyal Englebert, and Semperit) all competed with each other for market share.

However, in 1991, Continental decided to merge its sales force for the Continental and General brands under General Tire management at the subsidiary's Akron headquarters.[5] The plan was to position General tires in the mainstream portion of the market and target Continental brands for the upscale and high-performance segments, thus ending brand overlap and offering dealers more models to better cover the price-quality spectrum. Continental believed this approach would encourage more dealers to carry both brands; as of 1992, only 20 percent of the combined dealer network carried both brands. The new program also offered dealers the advantages of combined delivery, common purchase terms, the ability to avoid duplicating inventories on sizes and models, and more economical co-op advertising packages.

Following the 1987 acquisition of General Tire, Continental launched a five-year, $670 million program to modernize General's U.S. and Canadian plants. It also entered into a joint venture with Japan's Yokohama Tire and Toyo Tire to construct a $200 million truck tire plant in Mount Vernon, Illinois.

In recent years, Continental had strengthened its access to the replacement market by buying a 400-unit retail chain in Great Britain and buying minority interests in 400 additional retail outlets in Germany, Scotland, Canada, and the United States. Continental believed the best way to gain market share was by acquiring more dealers rather than through a merger of producers. It had turned down Pirelli's merger overtures for this reason. One Continental official noted:[6]

> Now all the players, including Japan's Sumitomo, Pirelli and us, are of the size and the state of the art that a merger wouldn't provide any synergies or strategic matches. We've ruled out there being any elephant mergers again.

Sumitomo Rubber Industries

Sumitomo was the third largest Japanese tiremaker and the world's sixth largest. Following World War II, Sumitomo had acquired tiremaking technology under an ongoing licensing agreement with Uniroyal. In 1986, Sumitomo acquired the European tire business of Dunlop Tire, making it the first Japanese producer to establish a major European base. A few years later, Sumitomo purchased Dunlop's two U.S. tire plants in Buffalo, New York, and Huntsville, Alabama; in the United States, Dunlop supplied some OE tires and had a 2.5 percent share of the replacement market. Going into 1992, Sumitomo operated 18 tire plants in seven countries.

Sumitomo was trying to increase its U.S. share in OE tires via its Dunlop brand and was marketing both its Sumitomo and Dunlop brands in the replacement tire segment. It sold replacement tires through wholesale distributors in the United States, which in turn marketed them to independent tire dealers as a second or third line. In 1992, Sumitomo radials retailed for a price virtually equal to name-brand U.S. radials, but cost the dealer $5 to $15 less per tire, depending on size. Sumitomo provided buyers of its replacement tires with a written, 60,000-mile guarantee, something few other tiremakers were willing to do. In recent years, Sumitomo had invested over $250 million to modernize the Dunlop tire plants in the United States and Europe and to boost labor

---

[5]*Tire Business*, November 4, 1991, p. 12.
[6]As quoted in Anthony Baldo, "The Big Skid," *Financial World*, October 16, 1990, p. 31.

productivity. In 1990, output per worker at the two U.S. Dunlop plants was only 60 percent of that at Sumitomo's plants in Japan.

Yokohama Tire Corporation

Yokohama was the second largest tire company in Japan and the seventh largest in the world. In 1992, Yokohama operated six tire plants in Japan and one in the United States (the Mohawk tire plant in Salem, Virginia, acquired in 1989). It was also in a joint venture with Toyo and General in a truck tire plant in Illinois. Years ago, Yokohama had entered into a technology licensing agreement with BF Goodrich; in exchange for its technology, BFG received a minority ownership position in Yokohama Tire. Yokohama's strategic objective was to become the world's fifth largest manufacturer. Yokohama was concentrating its R&D efforts on advanced designs, better engineering, and innovation. In 1986, it introduced a new-style asymmetrical tire for the high-performance tire segment, and it offered truck tires that delivered proven fuel savings, retreadability, and long tread life.

In the United States, Yokohama was one of the suppliers of tires to the newly emerging "price club" and "warehouse club" retail outlets. These outlets were estimated to sell about 10 million passenger tires in 1992 (about 10 percent of the replacement market). Observers were predicting fast growth for price clubs and warehouse clubs, mainly at the expense of mass-merchandise chains.

Cooper Tire and Rubber Co.

Based on tiremaking capacity, Cooper was the fourth largest of 13 tire producers in North America and the ninth largest tire marketer in the world. The company had total sales of $1 billion in 1991, tire sales of $750 million, and four tire plants, all in the United States. In 1990 and 1991, Cooper Tire had the biggest overall net profit margins on tire sales (net income as percentage of total sales) of any major tire manufacturer. The company's sales had more than tripled since 1980.

Cooper marketed only through replacement tire channels. Its two brands, Cooper and Falls Mastercraft, were distributed through independent tire stores. It also sold private-label tires to oil companies, mass-merchandise retailers, and independent buying groups. Cooper's 10 largest customers accounted for 53 percent of sales. In recent years, Cooper had begun exporting tires to Canada and countries in Latin America, Western Europe, the Middle East, Asia, Africa, and Oceania; in 1992, tire exports accounted for 5 percent of Cooper's sales. The company had 15 lines of passenger car tires, 9 lines of light-truck tires, and 10 lines of medium-truck tires. The company planned to introduce seven new tire lines in 1992.

All Cooper Tire employees were on an incentive plan. Workers could more than double their base rate through incentives, and manager incentives were tied to the return on assets managers were able to achieve in their assigned area of responsibility. Cooper spent about $14 million annually on R&D and recently had been spending about $100 million annually to install advanced technology in its plants. Cooper's management was committed to improving manufacturing methods, expanding its tiremaking capacity, and continuing its excellent reputation for customer service.

Korean Tire Producers

The two leading Korean tire manufacturers were Hankook and Kumho; both companies had two plants located in Korea and were the dominant suppliers of OE tires to the growing and ambitious Korean auto producers. Kumho had one of the world's 10 largest tire manufacturing plants, and it was outfitted with the most advanced equipment and systems available. Kumho supplied over 100 countries with a full line of bias and steel radial tires for everything from small passenger cars to off-the-road earth-moving equipment. The company was diversified into petrochemicals, rubber, electrical products, lubricants, and finance; it had total sales of about $750 million, about $585 million of which was tires. Hankook had total sales of $640 million, 100 percent of which came from tires.

Both Hankook and Kumho had built capacity aggressively on the expectation that the Korean car export business would grow rapidly. However, U.S. sales of the Hyundai (the leading Korean car), Daewoo's joint venture with General Motors, and Kia's relationship with Ford had not as yet produced a boom in Korean car exports to the United States. The Korean tire producers had excess capacity in 1992 and were using their low-cost producer position to gain volume on the basis of the low prices at which they were willing to supply replacement tires to wholesale distributors and tire dealers in the United States.

DCM-TOYOTA LTD. OF INDIA

Madhav S. Shriram, DCM Shriram Industries, Ltd.
Alan G. Robinson, University of Massachusetts at Amherst
Dean M. Schroeder, Valparaiso University

CASE 15

In the five years since the start of the joint venture between DCM Limited of India and the Toyota Motor Company of Japan to produce light commercial vehicles (LCVs), a great deal of progress had been made. The DCM-Toyota Ltd. (DTL) plant in Surajpur was now building a world-class vehicle, one that Mr. Awasthi, the company's executive director, believed to be by far the best of its kind manufactured in India. The DTL LCV, called the Dyna, was equipped with an engine that was more powerful, rugged, and fuel efficient than its competitors. It had a sturdy construction, and its plush interior and exterior finish were superior to those of most Indian-built cars. The Dyna embodied the latest in LCV technology from Japan; in fact, certain components had been improved and strengthened for the harsh Indian driving conditions.

The DTL plant was modern, well-engineered and -managed, and operated under the Toyota production system. The employees were highly motivated, well educated, and thoroughly trained. Even Toyota was impressed with the plant and with the high productivity of its Indian workers. And yet the company had been slow to make a profit. The strong yen and stiff competition were making things difficult. In 1984, when DTL was in the planning phase, the exchange rate was 21 yen to the rupee. In February 1989, the rupee bought only 8.25 yen. Critical LCV components imported from Japan, and priced in yen, were now costing two and a half times more than planned. Consequently, in fiscal year 1988, DTL lost Rs 57,133,420[1] on Rs 904,902,313 in total sales. The company's performance continued to improve gradually, however; it reported a modest profit of Rs 3 million in the first quarter of 1989. This profitability was attributed largely to a new marketing strategy of price increases that broke ranks with the competition. Unfortunately, this strategy also resulted in a loss of eight percentage points of market share and dropped DTL from first place in vehicle sales volume to last among the top three 3.5-tonne[2] LCV manufacturers.

It was unclear what the long-term effects would be of the shift in marketing strategy from price competition to competing on the basis of superior quality. Many Indian buyers were unfamiliar with the high technology in the DTL vehicles, nor were they accustomed to the level of quality they represented. Furthermore, it was not clear that the nation's infrastructure could support such a high-technology and quality vehicle. There was no nationwide network with the necessary skills and technology to fully service the vehicle. Furthermore, Indian law put DTL on a strict schedule to increase the domestic content of its

[1]The February 1989 exchange rate for rupees (Rs) was approximately 15 rupees per U.S. dollar.

[2]A tonne, or metric ton, is equal to approximately 1.13 tons.

LCV to 90 percent, and it was uncertain whether domestic manufacturers could meet the required high standards critical to retaining the DTL vehicle's exceptional quality.

BACKGROUND

DCM Ltd.

In 1989, DCM Ltd. was the 14th largest multiproduct manufacturing company in India. Its product line included textiles, sugar, both industrial and potable alcohol, fertilizers, edible oils, business machines, cement, polyvinylchloride (PVC), and foundry products. In 1989, its sales were approximately Rs 6.5 billion and it employed 25,000 people.

DCM was founded in 1889 as Delhi Cloth Mills Ltd., largely through the efforts of Gopal Rai, the company's first secretary (i.e., top manager). The venture, which produced textiles, was so successful it paid its first dividend to investors only six months later. When Gopal Rai's health failed in 1906, his younger brother, Madan Mohan Lal, took over as secretary. Shortly thereafter, the company began to falter, primarily because of the high prices it had to pay for raw cotton. The poor performance persisted until Shri Ram, son of Madan Mohan Lal, became actively involved in the company. Shri Ram was the dominant figure in the growth of DCM into a successful conglomerate.

When he was in high school, Shri Ram got a job selling cloth as a shop assistant. Although it was then standard practice to stretch the cloth on the measuring table and shortchange customers by two inches per yard, Shri Ram gave his customers not only the full yard, but an extra two inches as well. The shop owner was furious when he found out, but soon realized that customers kept coming back, and his volume of business was growing quite rapidly. Shri Ram would later bring to DCM this philosophy of treating people fairly.

When Shri Ram first came to work at DCM, the firm was losing money. Shri Ram persuaded his father to appoint him head of ginning, which had the worst record of all the departments. By introducing a system of worker incentives (a radical idea at that time in India), Shri Ram turned the department around in short order. The sudden increase in production and profits persuaded an initially reluctant board of directors to approve the companywide implementation of these incentives. After this success, Shri Ram was able to talk the board into giving him control of the other departments as well. Within three years of his joining the company, Shri Ram became the de facto secretary of DCM and his father a mere figurehead.

World War I brought the company an important break. The British, who had previously repressed the Indian textile industry to protect their domestic manufacturers, now encouraged it to produce as much as possible. Through the manufacture of canvas tents for troops, DCM grew rapidly and was able to lay down a financial base from which to continue its growth. During World War II, DCM started to manufacture hurricane lamps and to diversify into agricultural products such as sugar and fertilizers. These moves were very natural, for two reasons. First, the economy of India was largely based in agriculture (which, even in 1989, accounted for 80 percent of GNP). Second, the government, which wished to increase domestic production to reduce imports, was encouraging all companies to diversify as much as possible. By the time India became independent from Great Britain in 1947, DCM had grown into one of the five largest business houses in India. Since Shri Ram's death in 1965, the firm had remained under the control of the Shriram family. In 1985, Bansi Dhar, a grandson of Shri Ram, was appointed chairman and managing director. Throughout all of DCM's divisions, the company always strove to deliver the high quality and extra value implicit in Shri Ram's "2 extra inches." For example, the company's two sugar plants adhered to the rigid international quality standards for crystal size, purity, opacity, evenness of grain, and speed of dissolution in water, rather than the much less stringent Indian standards.

The Business Climate

In 1989, India, a nation of over 800 million people, was the largest democracy in the world. It was an "emerging" nation with a wide gap between rich and poor. While the average Indian worker earned less than Rs 15 ($1) per day, India boasted a world-class scientific community, excellent academic institutions (including five Institutes of Technology and the world-famous Tata Institute), as well as the ability to produce nuclear weapons and loft satellites into geosynchronous orbit. India had a tightly regulated and mixed economy. Although the private sector was very active, most of the "core" industries—such as mining and extraction (of coal, iron ore, and gold), steel, banking, electric power, airlines, shipping, railways, communications, and the postal service—were nationalized. Some industries had been taken over by the state owing to fears of exploitation by foreigners or monopolies, others because of their immense capital requirements or the desire to subsidize their products and services for the general public. By and large, these state-run industries were inefficient and poorly managed. For example, in 1989, the world price of steel was half of what it cost to produce it in India.

India's infrastructure could make industrial business operations quite challenging. The absence of reliable electric power provided a good example. Because it was subject to frequent outages and disruptions, most medium-to-large firms had captive power generation plants to avoid the problems that an interruption in the power supply of even a fraction of a second could cause to equipment and instrumentation. An infrastructural issue of special concern to DTL was the quality of the Indian road system. Many of the roads had been built shortly after independence from Britain and were designed to last for only five years. In March 1989, *India Today* called attention to the poor condition of these roads, and to the poor management that compounded the problem:

> Though India ranks fourth in the world, after the U.S., Brazil, and the Soviet Union in road length, the quality of the road network would embarrass many small African countries. And the World Bank has categorized India as a country where both the road network and road-building technology are obsolete. . . .
>
> The fact that many officials connected with the road sector have been busy feathering their own nest has further added to the collapse of the system. The states' Public Works Departments (PWDs), which are responsible for both okaying road-building contracts and approving the work, are notorious for corruption. . . . Senior officials estimate that often as much as half the money allocated for the construction of roads may disappear into the pockets of corrupt officials and private contractors. There have been instances of roads being built only on paper in remote areas—all the money having been creamed off.

It has not helped matters that other officials connected with the road sector are equally corrupt. Overloaded trucks are a major cause of road deterioration, yet truckers defy the law with impunity by bribing the highway police. All-India Motor Transport Congress Secretary-General Chitaranjan Das points out that bribing the police is now such an established practice that even trucks which are not overloaded have to fork over money. The Income Department even accepts these payments as legitimate expenses incurred by truck operations.[3]

Poor road conditions, in their turn, inflicted heavy damage on the nation's vehicles—an estimated Rs 20 billion annually in excess wear and tear.

In 1947, India inherited a comprehensive system of licensing from the departing British. The system had been set up during World War II to ensure the efficient and equitable allocation of scarce resources such as power, coal, steel, cement, foreign exchange, petroleum products, and rail capacity. Although the system worked well initially, it gradually became more bureaucratic and complex. Nothing could be done until all the appropriate officials had approved and granted licenses. Typical business operations required clearances from the government for foreign exchange, power usage, raw materials, imports, and loans.

In 1980, however, Indira Gandhi was elected prime minister and began liberalizing the private sector. She also encouraged joint ventures with foreign companies, not only for technology transfer, but to open export markets as well. Licenses for joint ventures with foreign companies could now be obtained with greater speed and ease, and hundreds of foreign joint ventures were formed. In the motor vehicle industry, they were begun with such companies as Toyota, Mitsubishi, Mazda, Nissan, Honda, and Suzuki.

In 1984, Mrs. Gandhi was assassinated, and her son, Rajiv Gandhi, became the new prime minister. He continued to improve the Indian business climate: marginal income tax rates were reduced from as high as 97.75 percent down to 50 percent, quotas on imports of many capital goods and raw materials were abolished, and tariffs were lowered. These moves resulted in the rapid growth of exports and foreign investment in India. Industrial investment jumped 50 percent in the first year of the new policies.[4] The stock market rose to over 250 percent above its 1980 level and hit new highs throughout fiscal year 1986, and interest rates declined dramatically. New capital raised in the market by the private sector rose from almost none in 1980 to Rs 10.6 billion in fiscal year 1985, and again to Rs 24.3 billion in fiscal year 1987. Capital raised in the 1990 market was expected to set a new record. Other signs of increasing sophistication in the private financial markets—as reported in 1989 by *The Economist Intelligence Unit*—included a rapidly growing number of institutional investors, and new opportunities for foreign investors through mutual fund portfolios of Indian stocks.[5]

Although the business climate had improved considerably since 1980, many problems remained. Business leaders were calling for increased privatization of government-controlled firms to increase the quality and efficiency of the country's infrastructure as well as to help lower the national debt. Nevertheless, moves in these directions met with considerable resistance, since privati-

---

[3]*India Today,* March 18, 1989, pp. 78–79.
[4]*The Economist,* February 25, 1989, pp. 75–76.
[5]*The Economist Intelligence Unit,* Country Report No. 1, India (1989).

zation was heresy to many powerful special interest groups in India.[6] Another factor with the potential to slow India's future growth was a projected shortage of electric power brought on by the increased economic activity. Scheduled hydroelectric projects, which required long lead times under the best conditions, were being slowed by environmental concerns, as were new coal-burning power plants. Current government policy was shifting toward generating electric power with natural gas, to make use of some recent major natural gas discoveries in India, and because the plants were cleaner and could be brought online quickly. Unfortunately, because of severe limitations on the capital available to make the needed improvements in the electric power infrastructure, power shortages remained a threat to continued rapid industrial development.

THE LCV MARKET

Although the alternatives available for transportation in India included ox carts, river barges, railways, and airplanes, in 1989, the road system was providing most of the extra transportation capacity required by India's rapidly growing economy. In 1951, only 11 percent of Indian goods were being transported by road; the rest moved by rail or water. By 1986, this figure had grown to 50 percent; it was projected to reach 62 percent by the year 2001. The government-controlled railroads were usually slow. Oddly enough, airfreight was not much faster, owing to a national policy requiring it to be thoroughly searched and to sit on the ground for at least 24 hours, as a precaution against terrorist bombings. Consequently, the demand for commercial vehicles had been rising. Yet until 1980, there was a large gap in the product range of trucks available. The only trucks on the market were either small pickup trucks of less than 1 tonne capacity, or full-sized trucks with a capacity of 7 tonnes or greater. Very few LCVs—trucks with capacity ranging from 2 to 6 tonnes—were manufactured in India. (Exhibit 1 provides a picture of the DTL LCV in various configurations and lists body options and configurations.) The government projected a national market of 24,000 LCVs annually by 1985, which it expected to grow to 47,000 by 1991. Exhibit 2 gives the annual sales of LCVs since 1984 and the projections through 1991 made by DTL's marketing staff.

Over the previous decade, eight companies, four of them joint ventures with Japanese firms, began producing LCVs in India. The Indo-Japanese joint ventures were those of DCM and Toyota, Eicher Motors and Mitsubishi, Swaraj and Mazda, and Allwyn and Nissan. Exhibit 3 gives product volume and market share information for all eight firms. In 1989, five of them manufactured LCVs rated at 2 tonnes; the others produced 3.5-tonne LCVs. The market for 2-tonne trucks was dominated by two domestic companies, Bajaj and the Tata Engineering and Locomotive Company (TELCO). Bajaj was known in India for its (relatively small) three-wheeled delivery vehicles, while TELCO held a hefty 75 percent of the full-size truck market. Mahindra, Standard, and Allwyn-Nissan (the only Indo-Japanese joint venture that produced a 2-tonne vehicle) all had relatively small market shares. All three of the 3.5-tonne LCV manufacturers were Indo-Japanese joint ventures and produced very similar

---

[6]Ibid.

DCM-Toyota range: Body options and configurations for specific jobs.

- Fixed-side deck
- Drop-side deck
- High-side deck
- Tipper/Dumper
- Bottle carrier
- Garbage compactor
- Troop carrier
- Aluminum closed van
- Aluminum high-side deck
- Personnel carrier
- Standard bus
- Deluxe bus
- Mobile clinic
- Others

The DYNA 600 is on the short list of the UNDP (United Nations Development Programme) for supply of factory-made configurations to UN organisations worldwide.

Body Options

Bottle carrier

High-side deck

Bus (super-long wheel-base)

Troop carrier

Aluminum closed van

Mobile clinic

Tipper/Dumper

EXHIBIT 2   **Sales of Light Commercial Vehicles**   *(Number of vehicles sold and projected sales on April–March basis)*

Class	1984–85	1985–86	1986–87	1987–88	1988–89	1989–90	1990–91
LCV (2T)	23,409	22,881	23,918	30,569	30,651	32,000	34,000
LCV (3.5T)		2,653	5,287	8,375	10,997	12,000	13,000

Source: DTL market research from government documents.

EXHIBIT 3   **Number of Vehicles Sold and Market Share for Light Commercial Vehicles in 1987–88 and 1988–89**

Manufacturers	1987–88 July-June	Market Share (Percent)	1988–89 July-March	Market Share (Percent)
LCVs (2-tonne class)				
Bajaj	12,663	42	9,513	40
Mahindra	5,276	17	3,567	15
Standard	1,689	6	857	4
TELCO 407/608	8,680	28	8,013	34
Allwyn-Nissan	2,132	7	1,632	7
Total (LCV—2T)	30,440	100	23,582	100
LCVs (3.5-tonne class)				
DCM-Toyota	3,417	37	2,439	29
Eicher-Mitsubishi	3,373	36	3,496	41
Swaraj-Mazda	2,498	27	2,529	30
Total (LCV—3.5T)	9,288	100	8,464	100

Source: DTL market research from government documents.

vehicles. DTL was the first of these companies to begin production; Eicher-Mitsubishi and Swaraj-Mazda followed less than a year behind.

All the Indo-Japanese joint ventures suffered from the rapid rise in the yen. Eicher-Mitsubishi, for example, experienced a production cost increase, attributable entirely to the stronger yen, of Rs 24,000 per vehicle from May to November 1988.

TELCO

TELCO had been manufacturing large trucks in India since 1964; the LCV was the smallest vehicle it had ever produced. Most of TELCO's truck manufacturing technology was derived from former commercial ties with Daimler-Benz of West Germany in the 1960s. In 1989, TELCO was an entirely Indian company that relied exclusively on Indian design and engineering technology. TELCO produced two kinds of LCV: Models 407 and 608. The Model 608, a 3-tonner, had yet to be successfully launched into the market. It had been introduced several times but had been pulled back because of technical problems with the gearbox and other components. The Model 407, priced at Rs 174,000, was much less expensive than the Indo-Japanese joint-venture LCVs, all of which were priced around Rs 230,000. In addition, the 407 was simple and rugged in design. Although rated for loads of up to only 1.5 tonnes, it was capable of carrying up to 4 tonnes. Its technology was older and common. When a 407 broke down, which happened frequently, it could be fixed in almost any village shop. The 407 got relatively poor gas mileage of 8 to 10 km/litre, whereas all of the Indo-Japanese joint venture vehicles delivered approximately 12 km/litre. Its dominance of the LCV market was credited to its low cost, rugged construction, ease of repair, and to TELCO's name recognition—the company's full-sized trucks were the most common on India's highways.

Bajaj

Bajaj manufactured two-wheeled scooters and three-wheeled delivery vehicles. Scooters were the primary mode of transportation for a large percentage of the population of India. Bajaj entered the 2-tonne LCV market by purchasing the Matador line from the Firodia family. The Bajaj LCV came in two standard configurations: a small bus or delivery van, and a fixed-sided truck. The company's strategy was to pursue market share by maintaining the very low price of Rs 100,000. Although the Matador had front-wheel drive and a fairly fuel-efficient engine, DTL executives did not regard it as state of the art and reported that the vehicles often developed severe maintenance problems after about three years.

Mahindra

Mahindra manufactured four-wheel drive vehicles, including jeeps, which it supplied to the Indian armed forces. The military was also a primary market for Mahindra's LCV. However, the company was doing poorly in the civilian LCV market. It had recently entered into a technical collaboration with Peugeot to produce an efficient diesel engine and had just purchased Allwyn-Nissan.

Allwyn-Nissan

Allwyn-Nissan's vehicle was rated at 2 tonnes, which put it in more direct competition with the TELCO 407 than with the products of the other Indo-Japanese joint ventures. Allwyn was a state-owned company; the joint venture was also run by the government, which provided most of its business. Sales were reported to be very low. Rumor had it that workers were called in to manufacture trucks only after the company received orders. Up until 1989, Allwyn-Nissan had not been much of a factor in the LCV market.

Standard

Standard was an automobile manufacturer based in Madras in southern India. It sold primarily in the south, and was not a major player in the LCV market. In fact, its LCV operation was now virtually shut down.

Eicher-Mitsubishi

Eicher-Mitsubishi was the last to enter the field, beginning production in July 1986, and was so far the most successful of the four Indo-Japanese joint ventures. Eicher was one of the finest tractor manufacturers in India. By avoiding such expensive capital purchases as air-conditioning, conveyor belts, automated equipment, and a modern new plant, great short-term savings and a low break-even point were made possible. Its 3.5-tonne vehicle was almost identical to the DTL Dyna and had been, until recently, sold for the same price. (Unlike the Dyna, however, its trucks were not undercoated or painted electrostatically.) Much of the credit for Eicher-Mitsubishi's success was given to its chairman and managing director, Vikram Lal, who had been described as a "human dynamo." Another factor was the company's dealership network; its trucks were sold through its tractor dealerships, which were well-established throughout India. Not surprisingly, the company made many individual sales of trucks to farmers and independent truckers.

Swaraj-Mazda

Swaraj-Mazda was a government-owned tractor manufacturer in the state of Punjab, a rich agricultural region of northern India. The company, which dominated the Punjab tractor market, was intending to anchor its LCV market there as well. It began producing LCVs in October 1985. Although these trucks were almost identical to the Dyna, DTL had nevertheless managed to be quite successful in Punjab, primarily because of an aggressive local DTL dealer.

THE DCM-TOYOTA JOINT VENTURE

History

In 1980, DCM Ltd. proposed to Toyota a joint venture to manufacture LCVs in India. The two companies were well matched in several respects. Both had similar backgrounds in textiles from which each had diversified, and each had a long tradition of high-quality manufacturing and providing excellent value to the customer.

Established in 1937, the Toyota Motor Corporation was by 1989 the largest automobile manufacturer in Japan and the second largest in the world. Interestingly, its parent company, Toyoda Automatic Loom Works, once sold textile manufacturing machinery to Delhi Cloth Mills in 1930. In addition to 11 plants in Japan, the company had 30 plants in 15 other countries. It employed over 86,000 people and sold its vehicles in 140 countries. Non-Japanese sales accounted for almost half of its total production.

After the partners verified the high market potential with their own extensive surveys, DCM-Toyota Ltd. (DTL) was incorporated on August 1, 1983, with its registered offices at the DCM building in New Delhi. Toyota took 26 percent of the equity and DCM 33 percent; the remaining 41 percent was raised in the Indian stock market, where it was oversubscribed sevenfold. The new company built a facility designed to manufacture 15,000 (18,000 with overtime) LCVs per year. It was sited in Surajpur, a town of approximately 20,000 people, located about 35 kilometers[7] southwest of New Delhi. Because it was in an area targeted for economic development by the government, DTL

---

[7]A kilometer is approximately six tenths of a mile.

benefited from considerable tax breaks. All research and development costs were 100 percent deductible in perpetuity, 25 percent of DTL's profits were tax exempt for 7 years after plant startup, and 20 percent of the profits derived from the LCV business were exempt from taxes for 10 years after the first LCV was sold.

The Plant, Technology, and Training

Of all the LCV producers, DTL had the most modern plant and production system. Its plant had nine production lines: chassis and final assembly, frame assembly, hub and drum machining, axle assembly, engine assembly, and the welding, painting, trim, and deck lines. A diagram of the plant illustrating the process flow is given in Exhibit 4.

The latest production technologies, although rare in India, were used in the manufacture of the Dyna. On the paint line, for example, phosphate undercoating was deposited through electrolysis in a dip tank for complete coverage, electrostatic spray painting was employed for uniformity, and painted components were baked to harden the finish. On the hub and drum line, advanced five-axis computer-controlled machining centers assured high precision in parts. Engines were assembled in a specially controlled clean room.

The plant operated on the Toyota production system (TPS), a "pull" system that was the original just-in-time (JIT) system. All operations were pulled on, ultimately, by the final assembly line; the other lines had only to keep small buffers of their finished products full. Instruction sheets fed in at the beginning of each of the trim, deck, and chassis and final assembly lines assured they were all synchronized. All work-in-process movement was on dollies custom-designed for each specific operation.

To learn the TPS, foremen and managers from all levels in DTL had been sent to Toyota City in Japan for training. During their absence, the personnel department had carefully selected workers from the local area who fitted desired profiles. TPS selection guidelines required all workers to have a high school education or an ITT (a technical school) diploma. They were required to be under 23 years of age, since older applicants were considered too inflexible and fixed in their thinking. Local villagers were preferred and constituted some 120 of the 143 production workers. In addition to undergoing tests of intelligence, aptitude, and dexterity, applicants were also given a complete medical examination, including psychological screening to assess whether each applicant was a "good person in heart and mind."

The workers were trained in the Toyota style, beginning with talks and video shows about Toyota. They were taught the aims and values of the TPS, which were rooted in the motto "good thinking, good product." They learned about quality circles, *kaizen* (continuous improvement), *muda* (waste), *poka-yoke* (mistake-proof devices), *kanban* (control cards), and all the other tools of the TPS, and they also received training on truck assembly and the DTL plant. The goal of this training was to instill a strong sense of responsibility for high quality in the workers, who were taught to stop the assembly line if any quality problems arose. Not only were no penalties incurred for interrupting production, but stopping the line was encouraged, since it exposed problems that could be solved once and for all. Because the TPS made all workers responsible for quality control (QC), DTL kept only a skeleton QC department of six people. Great care was taken to demonstrate to the workers their vital importance

EXHIBIT 4   DTL's Surajpur Plant

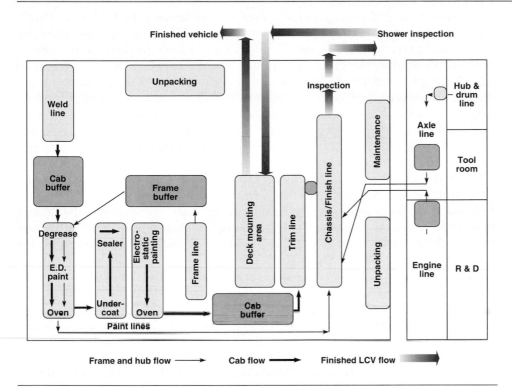

to the organization. To emphasize this, all personnel and guests ate together in DTL's one cafeteria.

The meticulous training paid off. In the planning stage, it was expected that the productivity of DTL's Indian workers would be only 20 to 35 percent of that of the workers in Toyota City. It soon became clear that this had been a gross underestimate; the Indian workers were 65 percent as productive as their Japanese counterparts and continued to improve. This figure was quite impressive since the Japanese plants were more highly automated than DTL's. Interestingly, DTL's target of zero defects before shipment was actually achieved on some days. As in Japan, the line and office workers were all strongly committed to the company; they frequently stayed after hours (without pay) for quality circles or when additional production was needed. If the company needed extra workers on the line in peak periods, instead of the normal Indian practice of hiring temporaries, clerical staff was assigned there to help. Even Toyota executives were impressed by the productivity and high-quality output of the Surajpur plant.

The Dyna Truck

The DTL vehicle, the Dyna, came in two basic models—the Dyna-1 and the Dyna-3. The Dyna-3 was a complete truck with a standard cab and deck. The Dyna-1, a mechanically complete truck without the cab or deck, was for customers who wanted to finish it for their own special purposes. Both models are shown in Exhibit 5, together with their technical specifications. Production information for the Dyna models for fiscal year 1988 and the first three quarters of 1989 are given in Exhibit 6.

Approximately 20 percent of the vehicles manufactured by DTL were Dyna-1 models. The Dyna-1 customer could either have DTL custom-finish the vehicle or could take it to a private "body builder" to be finished inexpensively with wood or other materials. The Dyna-1 trucks finished by DTL were sold mainly to government agencies or institutional buyers with special requirements. Custom cabs and decks were built by DTL to conform to both customer specifications and Toyota's quality standards. Examples of these special purpose vehicles (SPVs) were delivery vehicles for soft-drink distributors, armored vehicles for the police and security forces, ambulances for emergency services, and buses. A variety of SPV configurations can be seen in Exhibit 1. SPV sales could be very seasonal for certain markets, such as soft-drink manufacturers, which had high summer demand, and for which it was very hard to build inventories because of planning uncertainty. For example, the factory of Campa Cola, the largest soft-drink manufacturer in northern India, was burned during demonstrations following Mrs. Gandhi's assassination. This led to a slump in demand for Dyna bottle carriers.

The capacity of the Dyna was 3.5 tonnes, but the truck was actually designed for up to 6 tonnes and had been operated with loads as high as 10.5 tonnes. It was built for low-fuel-cost transport of goods, possibly perishable, which needed to travel quickly. One advantage of a medium-size truck like the Dyna was that it could travel city streets 24 hours a day, whereas bigger trucks could not because of laws against their daytime use in certain populated areas.

Experience quickly showed that the Dynas took a lot more punishment than was originally anticipated. They were often overloaded by 100 to 150 percent and driven at great speed over bad roads. The resulting burst tires, broken axles, fractured leaf springs, bent frames, and completely stripped gears meant that, early in the venture, a lot of the parts needed to be upgraded. Also, the vehicles were frequently involved in high-speed accidents and were often dented owing to aggressive driving, since many drivers were unaccustomed to the speeds and acceleration the Dyna could attain. The upgraded Dyna was a far more rugged vehicle than its Japanese counterpart. In fact, when riding with Indian drivers testing it under normal Indian road conditions, Japanese engineers never failed to express amazement at the punishment the Dyna could take.

Suppliers

In early 1989, 25 percent by value of the component parts of DTL's vehicles were still imported from Japan. This was either because, like the engine components and transmission gears, they required precision and high quality, or because, like the large frame and cab members, they had to be stamped using dies and presses larger than those commonly available in India. DTL began with 42 percent local content, reached 75 percent local content by the end of 1988, and had to attain 90 percent by the end of 1991 or face severe penalties from the government. The problem DTL was encountering in its indigenization efforts was to develop a base of domestic suppliers with the technology and inclination to produce certain high-quality components. Some of the major challenges in this regard were as follows.

EXHIBIT 5	Dyna Standard Configuration

Technical Specifications

Engine

Model	: 14B
Type	: 4-cylinder in line DI diesel engine.
Bore & Stroke (mm)	: 102 x 112
Piston Displacement (cc)	: 3660
Comp. Ratio	: 18
Max. Power (DIN)	: 94 HP at 3400 rpm.
Max. Torque (DIN)	: 24 kgm at 1800 rpm.
Air Cleaner	: Oil bath type with pre-cleaner.
Fuel System	: Bosch type, rotary distribution pump with centrifugal mechanical governor and automatic timer.

Transmission

Clutch	: Hydraulically operated single dry plate with diaphragm spring.
Gear Box	: 5 forward-speed all synchromesh.
Final Drive	: 12-inch Crown Wheel.

Steering
Recirculating Ball Nut type with variable ratio of 30:1 to 34:1.

Front axle
Reverse Elliot I-Beam.

Rear axle
Full-floating in Banjo type housing.

Suspension
Semi-elliptic laminated leaf springs with auxiliary leaf springs at the rear and double-acting hydraulic telescopic shock absorbers on all four wheels.

Brakes

Service Brake	: Hydraulically operated drum brakes with tandem master cylinder and vacuum booster.
Parking Brake	: Internal expanding at rear of gear box.
Exhaust Brake	: Vacuum-assisted with ON-OFF operating lever.

Electrical
Battery: 12V, 70AH
Alternator: 12V-45A

Frame
Ladder-type with reinforced C-channel section.

Tires
Front: 2, Rear: 4, Spare Tire: 1
Size: 7.50 x 16 — 12 PR.

Dimensions

	Cab & Chassis with Optional Rear Deck LWB	Cowl & Chassis Version for Bus Applicator SLWB
Wheel base (mm)	3290	3785
Overall length (mm)	6000	6440
Overall width (mm)	1995	1995
Overall height (mm)	2215	2025
Deck (Internal LxWxH)		
Drop-side (mm)	4350x2030x610	N.A.
Fixed-side (mm)	4350x1850x530	N.A.
High-side (mm)	4350x1850x1175	N.A.
Min. Turning Radius (m)	6.1	6.9
Ground Clearance (mm)	210	210
GVW (kg)	5990	5990

Standard Configurations

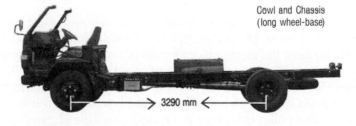

Cowl and Chassis (long wheel-base)

3290 mm

Fixed-side deck

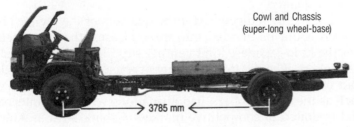

Cowl and Chassis (super-long wheel-base)

3785 mm

Cabin and chassis

EXHIBIT 6   **DCM-Toyota Limited LCV Sales by Model During 1988–89**
                 (Including exports)

Models	1987–88 July–June	1988–89 July–March
-1 Based models		
-1 (cowl and chassis)	297	191
Bus	193	141
SPV (special purpose vehicle)	32	13
Total	522	345
-3 Based models		
-3 (cabin and chassis)	397	205
High-side deck	1,069	710
Drop-side deck	415	359
Fixed-side deck	917	772
SPV	230	164
Total	3,028	2,210
Grand total	3,550	2,555

Source: DTL marketing staff.

- Large, high-quality metal stampings and plastic-molded components were not readily available in India because of a shortage of presses and molding machines capable of handling the sizes of dies required.
- The technology to bond rubber to metal—which was necessary for engine mounts, alternator mounts, and other critical components—was in its infancy in India.
- The precision required for some parts to meet Japanese standards was not achievable in India, where much of the technology in use was very old.

Fortunately, DTL had one advantage over the other Indo-Japanese joint ventures: the company's Indian parent, DCM Ltd., operated a world-class foundry. Plans were in the works to have the engine blocks manufactured there. Pistons might be supplied by Shriram Pistons and Rings Ltd., another firm controlled by the Shriram family. DTL was also considering redesigning the dashboard to be manufactured in six parts instead of one. This would have allowed it to be produced domestically with smaller machines but raised concerns of increased assembly costs and lower quality.

To date, DTL had successfully indigenized three quarters of the Dyna. The domestic suppliers used could be divided into three classes: the large well-established suppliers, the Indo-Japanese joint venture suppliers, and the small, local, independent suppliers. The big manufacturers typically produced high-quality products, had excellent delivery, and were very responsive. Some of these companies, such as the tire suppliers, had affiliations with large international companies and operated in competitive markets. Others, such as Automotive Axles Ltd., which manufactured axle housings and gears, were near-monopolies because no other Indian companies could match their technology. The Indo-Japanese joint venture suppliers fell into two categories: (1) those established to serve DTL, and (2) those established to serve the Indian government's joint venture with Suzuki to produce automobiles. The former delivered to DTL on a JIT basis and had excellent quality, though they tended to be high priced. DCM and Toyota established a collaboration, independent of DTL, and located two kilometers from the Surajpur plant, to supply wiper motors, starters, and alternators. The joint ventures set up to serve Suzuki did not always deliver reliably, largely because DTL was such a small customer (relative to Suzuki). The small local manufacturers supplied various special nuts, bolts, and small metal and plastic components. Delivery was usually not problematic, but quality could be. These suppliers made extensive use of DTL's ancillary development department (ADD) to improve their quality.

Parts supplied by all vendors were handled initially by the ADD, whose major tasks were to help indigenize the DTL vehicle, to integrate suppliers into the firm as JIT "partners," and to provide suppliers with advice on techniques to improve their quality. Sometimes suppliers genuinely did not understand why higher quality was needed. For example, DTL had to work hard to persuade its bus body builders that the vehicle needed to be watertight, should have no sharp edges, and should not rattle. One of them was quoted as saying: "This is a bus, not a car."

DTL Marketing

The DTL sales department was staffed with 20 people in the head office and 5 salespeople stationed in regional offices around the country. Customers for LCVs ranged from large institutions operating entire fleets of vehicles to individuals who may have owned farms or small businesses. To reach them, the sales staff was divided into two groups: international/institutional and domestic. Institutional customers included large companies and state and local governments. (DTL was waiting for clearance to sell to the national government and armed forces, potentially a very large market.) Institutional selling was done directly to the institutions involved. The orders were generally for fleets of vehicles and often for customized Dyna-1 models such as buses, armored vehicles, or bottle trucks. DTL was traditionally strong in this market. Competitors could not match the quality and engineering of the special purpose Dyna-1's. DTL also exported to Bangladesh, Nepal, Sri Lanka, Bhutan, Mauritius, and Pakistan and was trying to gain business in countries in the Middle East. The Indian government provided financial support and other export-related assistance to all LCV manufacturers. DTL's export potential was somewhat limited because Toyota did not want the Dyna exported to nations that it was serving already.

Trucks were sold domestically through DTL's network of 53 main dealerships and 57 subdealers or branches. These were also supported by an additional 33 authorized service centers. Dealership status was granted only to those who could meet Toyota's rigorous standards, which required that facilities be staffed with factory-trained technicians with the knowledge and tools to do all required service and repairs to LCVs. Dealers also had to maintain large inventories of spare parts. (Subdealers were those who were not yet fully qualified dealers.) The entire dealership network, established from scratch starting in 1985, included some dealers that sold exclusively DTL products and some that sold other complementary products as well. DTL provided free training to service technicians and helped dealers import service equipment. The dealer's profit on a typical LCV sale was about Rs 5,000. The normal procedure was for a dealer to get a customer order and forward it to the factory; delivery usually occurred within a month.

Until mid-1988, DTL competed on the basis of price with Eicher-Mitsubishi and Swaraj-Mazda, its two major rivals in the 3.5-tonne LCV market. All three companies produced vehicles of similar sizes and capacities. Even though DTL executives viewed their vehicle as superior to the others in quality, engineering, and performance, price was still used as the basis for competition. As a result, DTL held a slightly higher market share than either of the other two companies. In mid-1988, the marketing manager was transferred to another post in DCM, and the marketing staff was restructured. The new marketing management initiated a different strategy that called for disengagement from the "price wars" and the marketing of the Dyna based on its superior quality. The Dyna was then priced about Rs 10,000 higher than its competitors. Eight points of market share were lost over the next nine months. However, the strategy shift resulted in one significant benefit: unlike its rivals, DTL was now profitable for the first time in its history. Vikram Lal, chairman of Eicher-Mitsubishi, then the market leader in the 3.5-tonne LCV class, was quoted as stating that his company would lose "about Rs 3 Crore [30 million] this year."[8]

The Dyna's Fit with the Market

Of the three Indo-Japanese joint ventures, DTL alone used a JIT manufacturing system and conveyorized assembly lines. In addition, DTL had more modern painting facilities, with electrodeposition of primer and electrolytically deposited paint. While this provided DTL a competitive advantage in manufacturing technology and product quality, it was uncertain whether the added expense was justified, for three reasons.

First, consumers were wary of the new technology in the Dyna trucks, particularly with the unfamiliar Toyota name on them. The new truck came with a higher price tag than people expected and was built to much higher standards than customers were accustomed to. The Dyna did not break down every few days, and problems common to older designs of LCVs—ruptured fuel lines and broken fan belts, for example—had, by and large, been eliminated. Tire wear was one of the major costs of truck ownership, because tires were very expensive in India. Unlike the older truck designs, including TELCO's, the Dyna was designed to have its wheels aligned and tires balanced on computerized equipment, which greatly reduced tire wear. Quite apart from the generally high standards to which the entire vehicle was manufactured, this reduced tire wear alone made the Dyna a less expensive vehicle to operate in the long term than the other LCVs.

The second reason for concern was that service for the Dyna was not available in many parts of the country. India is vast, and the number of dealers capable of providing full service for the vehicle was relatively limited. The DTL dealership network was new, having been established only in the last four years, whereas competitors had been able to take advantage of long-standing truck or tractor dealership networks spread throughout India. Consequently,

---

[8]*India Today,* March 31, 1989, p. 80.

DTL had been less successful than the other LCV manufacturers in selling to individual buyers.

The third concern for DTL was that its high standards made indigenization of components quite difficult. Since there were only a handful of suppliers in India capable of manufacturing certain necessary components to DTL's quality standards, DTL's ability to negotiate price concessions was limited. For some components, there were no domestic manufacturers that could meet the quality standards.

Despite these challenges, in June 1989, S. G. Awasthi, DTL's executive director, remained a steadfast supporter of his company's current strategy:

> The management policy adopted by DTL so far has paid rich dividends and this policy is likely to yield even richer dividends in the future. I am confident that the corporate strategy adopted by DTL would be a model for other automobile manufacturers in the years to come.

Vivek Bharat Ram, grandson of Shri Ram and the current managing director of DTL, shared this view of the company's future:

> The basic principle on which DTL has always operated is that of following the customer-first philosophy. This is the policy I intend to firmly adhere to in the future also.

While DTL was clearly committed to developing and implementing strategies that offered the equivalent of Shri Ram's "2 extra inches" to the LCV market, there was concern about market acceptance of such a product. The shift in strategies from one of matching the pricing moves of competitors to one of value pricing based on the Dyna's higher quality led to the company's first profitable quarter, but it also resulted in a loss of eight points of market share. DTL moved from first in market share among the three 3.5-tonne LCV manufacturers to last (see Exhibit 4) as a result of breaking ranks on pricing. Concerns focused on whether the market share could, or should, be regained and what the longer term consequences of a shift in market position would mean.

Singh, K., and A. Joshi. *Shri Ram: A Biography.* London: Asia Publishing House, 1968. *The Economist,* March 4, 1989, p. 34.   REFERENCES

CHEMICAL ADDITIVES CORPORATION—SPECIALTY PRODUCTS GROUP

Charles Hoffheiser and Lester A. Neidell, University of Tulsa

Nick Williamson, general manager, Specialty Products Group (SPG), gazed out his window and sighed. It was August 1990 and the atmosphere inside his office was as unpleasant as the 100-degree weather of the Fort Smith, Arkansas, headquarters of SPG. He swiveled back to face his management team, and said, "OK, I've heard your arguments about positioning and pricing 'R&D 601, 602, and 603.' I wish there were some way to get a consensus from you guys. I'll consider our options over the weekend."

The decisions facing Williamson would have substantial impact on the future of SPG. A strategy of moving away from large-volume commodity wax markets toward becoming a premier supplier of specialty chemical additives to niche markets was not going as smoothly as anticipated. Three newly developed products might well be the catalyst to hasten that shift. These new products, known by their experimental designations R&D 601, 602, and 603, were corrosion inhibitors used during the transport and storage of liquid urea ammonium nitrate (UAN) fertilizer.

LIQUID FERTILIZERS

Liquid fertilizers had numerous advantages over the traditional solid fertilizers principally used in U.S. agriculture: (1) excellent performance under a variety of weather conditions; (2) reduced toxicity; (3) ability to be easily blended with other nutrients, insecticides, and herbicides; and (4) milder environmental impact (but not benign; a spill or leak of undiluted UAN could still kill wildlife and vegetation).

Unfortunately, UAN liquids corroded the steel tanks, pipelines, railcars, and barges used for storage and transport, resulting in repair costs that could exceed $1 million per incident for the typical UAN producer. The industry had tried a variety of corrosion inhibitors (chemicals that were added in small dosages to UAN after production) to reduce the rate at which the UAN ate away a metal surface. Inhibitors did not prevent corrosion; they slowed the chemical reaction of metal dissolving into UAN. An excellent inhibitor might increase the average life of a typical $20 million storage system from as little as 3 years to longer than 20 years.

Leaks and spills also created liabilities for EPA fines. If a tank failure resulted in massive environmental damage, federal lawsuits could potentially bankrupt a producer. Corrosion inhibitor suppliers might also be liable for leaks and environmental damages.

633

Manufacturers produced UAN fertilizer in continuous-process facilities with typical minimum capacities of 10,000 tons a year. They then added corrosion inhibitors and stored the inhibited UAN in tanks to await shipment. Producers shipped UAN through a distributor/dealer network that delivered the product to the right farmer, at the right time, and with appropriate other agricultural chemicals added as necessary. Some larger dealers provided custom-application services to apply UAN blends to fields and crops. The same distribution system also handled the solid fertilizers UAN was slowly replacing.

SPG designed these experimental products to replace SPG's earlier entries into this market, as well as to regain business previously lost to a widely used, foreign-sourced material, Corblok 105-B. The sales and marketing managers each strongly argued contrary marketing tactics. Vice President of Sales Ron White reasoned that despite any performance advantages of the new SPG products, market conditions in the U.S. fertilizer industry required that SPG price the new products as low as possible using only the mandatory minimum corporate markup over standard cost. White had always operated with the objective of keeping company plants operating close to capacity to minimize standard costs. Price leadership and volume were, in his eyes, the key to SPG's success.

Jim Walker, newly hired as director of marketing (a new position at SPG), vehemently favored a value-based pricing approach, recognizing both product performance and competitive conditions. The technical director regularly reminded these two managers that the three products performed differently in different producers' UANs and added, "You guys better start selling some of this stuff soon to pay off our investment of over four man years of technical effort!"

CHEMICAL ADDITIVES CORPORATION

SPG was one of four divisions of the Chemical Additives Corporation (CAC), a multinational company providing solutions to production problems in oil fields, refineries, chemical plants, and other industrial applications. The corporate mission statement was:

> to produce and market specialty chemical products and the technical services and equipment necessary to utilize CAC's products effectively.

CAC pursued a strategy of developing customized equipment and chemical treatment programs to add value to customers' operations through optimization of operating efficiency or increased reliability. CAC's strengths included expertise in organic phosphate ester chemistry (the key to advanced technology corrosion inhibitors) and in the mixing of incompatible fluids (e.g., oil and water). It considered itself to be the worldwide leader in oil industry corrosion control and had developed and patented much of the technology historically used in these applications. However, over the past 10 years, competitors found it increasingly easy to design products outside patent coverages, particularly as R&D departments began to use advanced computer modeling techniques. Computer modeling made it much easier to design new families of chemical products.

CAC organized its operations into four operating groups—Oil Field Chemicals, Refinery Chemicals, Instrument Group, and Specialty Products. Each group maintained its own sales, marketing, and product development functions. A central research department conducted long-range, basic chemical research for all divisions.

The Oil Field Chemicals Group was the world's largest supplier of oil field production chemicals, including corrosion inhibitors and drilling aids. Since its products went "down the hole," appearance, odor, and handling characteristics, such as foaming, were often not of concern to customers. The sales force's requests for customer-specific products drove product development. This division had over 4,000 products in its line. The group justified this product line breadth in two ways: (1) no two oil deposits were identical in chemical makeup, and (2) as wells aged, increasing amounts of exotic chemicals were needed to enhance oil production.

Refinery Chemicals marketed process efficiency aids for the production side of refineries. It also sold fuel additives such as fuel-injector cleaners to refiners and to wholesalers of gasoline and truck diesel fuel.

The Instrument Group designed and marketed filtration and purification systems that solved a variety of water and oil-related process problems in refineries. Customers often used this equipment in conjunction with CAC's chemical treatment programs. This group also sold a complete line of premium-quality corrosion monitoring instruments.

Specialty Products Group had two major product groups: (1) about 100 types of commodity petroleum waxes (similar but not identical to the types used in candles) that were separated from crude oil and (2) synthetic polymers based on a chemical called propylene. Common examples of polymers are plastic food wrap or vinyl siding for houses. SPG's synthetics, however, were not the type used in plastic film, cups, or containers. Customers often called them *synthetic waxes* because they had properties similar to commodity petroleum waxes. Nick Williamson tried to alter this perception by extensive trade advertising and by instructing division personnel to refer to all division products as "specialty polymers." SPG's products had hundreds of applications, ranging from shoe polish to chewing gum to cardboard box sealing adhesives. Various SPG products had also found modest use as antidust and anticaking additives for solid fertilizers, and as a result, SPG conducted all of CAC's business in the worldwide fertilizer industry.

Exhibit 1 contains selected CAC and divisional financial data; Exhibit 2 shows the distribution of SPG revenue and profit by end-use market.

SPG's Competitors

Each division had its own set of specialized competitors as well as competition from various divisions of large chemical companies such as Du Pont, Dow, Witco, and Shell. The 1980s ushered in a new era in the chemical industry—worldwide competition. (Corblok, principal competitor to SPG's UAN anticorrosion additives, was an example of this.) Foreign suppliers also directly affected other SPG markets. These included Mitsui, BASF, Hoechst, and Dead Sea Works, an Israeli-government-owned coal gasification plant that produced waxes as by-products of gasoline production. Except for Dead Sea, all competitors were much larger than SPG (and CAC) and were reputed to be among the most efficient chemical companies in the world.

SPG found itself with a key disadvantage versus major chemical firms because its synthetic process required liquid polypropylene, a product form

EXHIBIT 1   **Chemical Additives Corporation Financial Data, 1985–89**
                    (In thousands of dollars)

	1985	1986	1987	1988	1989
Income Statement Data					
Net sales	$253,841	$297,208	$302,567	$287,931	$294,068
COGS	160,268	189,498	181,531	174,919	171,769
Gross profit	93,573	107,710	121,036	113,012	122,299
Selling expense	33,623	41,532	49,746	53,235	56,292
R&D expense	6,370	7,520	9,487	11,537	12,065
G&A expense	10,860	12,470	14,107	14,614	15,455
Operating profit	42,720	46,188	47,696	33,626	38,487
Investment income	774	2,500	2,139	2,533	3,722
Interest expense	(2,089)	(1,893)	(1,552)	(1,384)	(1,191)
Other net	623	1,136	203	585	1,782
EBIT	42,028	47,931	48,486	35,360	42,800
Income tax	17,143	20,174	19,190	13,310	17,000
Net earnings	$ 24,885	$ 27,757	$ 29,296	$ 22,050	$ 25,800
Balance Sheet Data					
Cash	$ 16,581	$ 12,478	$ 3,018	$ 37,201	$ 43,461
Accounts receivable	45,127	61,981	55,836	51,055	56,896
Inventory	39,639	43,751	39,785	38,976	41,296
Other current assets	64,466	77,768	77,711	91,869	104,175
Total current assets	175,544	197,782	200,318	209,105	221,514
Current liabilities	44,468	48,579	39,957	39,808	45,675
Long-term debt	12,500	11,250	10,000	8,750	7,500
Stockholders' equity	112,999	132,989	145,159	153,042	164,148
Other Financial Information					
Shares (000)	5,972	11,864	11,864	11,865	11,715
Dividends per share	$1.20	$0.76	$0.95	$1.00	$1.03
CAC Revenue by Division					
Oil Field Chemicals	$158,048	$181,614	$201,378	$199,498	$211,804
Refinery Chemicals	33,069	32,524	32,117	30,342	32,499
Specialty Products	41,554	46,410	41,483	36,969	40,041
Instruments	21,170	36,660	27,589	21,122	9,724

supplied by only one company. The majors often had captive suppliers and used much larger volumes of less expensive gaseous polypropylene, available from many suppliers.

SPG's Marketing

Before 1980, SPG sold its products only through distributors. Galaxy Wax and Schmidt Associates, both of which maintained regional warehouses, served the U.S. market for SPG. The Leveque Group, headquartered in Brussels, Belgium, was responsible for sales to Europe, Africa, and the Middle East. Leveque also served as principal distributor of wax products manufactured by BASF and Hoechst, both headquartered in West Germany. A joint venture between CAC and Nissan Trading Company (Japan) sold into the Far East.

In 1979, in an attempt to capture the distributor margin for SPG, Williamson hired Ron White to establish a direct sales force. By 1990, SPG had two regional managers and nine salespeople in the United States:

EXHIBIT 2　　　SPG End-Use Segments in 1989

End-Use Market	Percent of Total SPG Sales in Dollars	Percent of Total Pretax Profits	Product Life Cycle
Plastics	5%	12%	Late growth, Maturity
Coatings	10%	18%	Late growth, Maturity
Sealants	25%	25%	Mature
Food additives	5%	3%	Mature
Laminating wax	25%	15%	Decline
Others	30%	27%	Mostly mature

Philadelphia	East regional sales office, 1 sales representative
Atlanta	1 sales representative
Boston	1 sales representative
Cleveland	1 sales representative
Chicago	2 sales representatives
Fort Smith	1 sales representative
Houston	1 sales representative
Los Angeles	West regional sales office, 1 sales representative

But even after 11 years of direct selling, there were still situations in which SPG lost business to wax distributors on price, delivery, and, in some cases, technical service.

Annual salary and benefit costs for each sales representative were about $80,000, while the two regional managers were paid about 20 percent more. These figures included a company car, but not travel and other sales expenses, which averaged an additional 10 percent of sales revenue. These numbers did not include a profit bonus plan, which typically added 2 percent of sales revenue to selling costs. An annual "salesperson of the year" award, usually based on exceeding forecast poundage figures, provided a further bonus of 5 percent of the $50,000 base to one salesperson. Salespeople developed an annual territorial sales forecast to help plan production runs and order raw materials. The sales force devoted little effort to prospecting because White kept a "sales efficiency" log for each representative that did not adjust for this sales task. Sales efficiency was calculated by dividing sales calls that yielded an order by total sales calls.

THE UAN CORROSION INHIBITOR OPPORTUNITY

In February 1985, the general manager of the Refinery Chemicals Group (RCG) sent Nick Williamson a memo suggesting that certain CAC products might be useful in solving corrosion problems encountered by the Jackson Pipeline Company (JPL) of Fort Smith, Arkansas. One of the refinery group's (and CAC's) largest customers, JPL was a major U.S. pipeline company, active in the transport of crude oil, gasoline, diesel and jet fuels, chemicals, and natural gas. The memo noted that, as a result of the oil bust of 1980–83, JPL attempted to build its transportation volume of other products and began shipping UAN produced by JPL's wholly owned fertilizer company, Fertex Chemicals (also with its main plant in Fort Smith). Additional UAN shipments were procured from Farm Products (Kansas City, Missouri) and Agriproducts (Sioux Falls, South Dakota). JPL's pipeline system extended to Texas, Arkansas, Oklahoma, Missouri, Kansas, Iowa, the Dakotas, Illinois, and Indiana.

Historically, UAN was shipped by (in order of increasing cost) barge, rail tank cars, and tank truck. To use JPL's pipeline system, UAN producers were required to incorporate a corrosion inhibitor approved by JPL. However, unexpected corrosion problems with UAN severely hurt profitability of JPL's fertilizer shipping business.

The RCG memo was timely; SPG, too, had suffered from the petrochemical industry recession of 1981–83. Also, Williamson was being pushed by CAC's executive committee to move away from commodity wax products into chemical specialties that could provide protection against the price wars affecting chemical commodity markets.

Initial Entry into the UAN Corrosion Control Market

In late 1986, SPG introduced Stealth 3660, an oil field corrosion inhibitor, for use in transporting liquid UAN. SPG's choice of Stealth 3660 was based on its proven success in the oil field and the assumption that corrosion control was a similar phenomenon regardless of end-use environment. After testing, JPL recommended 3660 to its Fertex subsidiary and to its two other customers, Farm Products and Agriproducts. SPG priced 3660 at its standard markup, 100 percent above its standard cost. At this price, 3660 cost fertilizer producers 50 percent less than the previously approved Corblok 105-B inhibitor. All three UAN manufacturers soon switched to 3660.

However, Fertex detected toxic fumes exceeding Occupational Safety and Health Administration (OSHA) defined lethal concentrations at the top hatch of trucks used to deliver the product from CAC's Chicago plant. In 1987, Fertex reverted to using Corblok.

Unwilling to lose this market, Williamson instructed R&D to select another product from the oil field corrosion inhibitor line. In mid-1987, SPG introduced Stealth 3662 to JPL and its three customers. The toxicity problem appeared to be solved, while the usage cost was the same as 3660. By late 1987, all three fertilizer companies were buying 3662 in tank-truck quantities. As mid-1988 approached, word of mouth in the fertilizer industry persuaded firms such as Iowa Fertilizer, Ferticon, Nitrogen Industries, Marathon Chemical, and others to use 3662.

Like Stealth 3660, SPG priced 3662 at 100 percent markup over standard cost. Tank-trunk (40,000 pounds) quantities sold for $0.80 per pound, and 55-gallon drums for $0.83 per pound, with costs of $0.40 per pound and $0.415 per pound, respectively. According to CAC policy, if a product were not priced at least 100 percent above cost, it was not defined as a "specialty chemical" and did not qualify for recognition as supporting the corporate mission of becoming a specialty chemical firm. SPG's goal was to derive at least 30 percent of its gross sales revenue from specialties by 1990.

In late 1988, Fertex reported to SPG that its UAN was causing severe foaming problems when mixed with other fertilizer components such as pesticides and herbicides, a practice that was typical at the fertilizer dealer level. By

EXHIBIT 3   SPG's Organization Chart

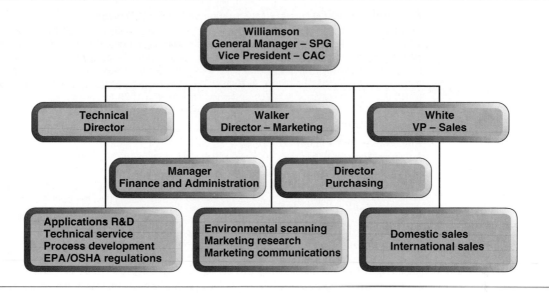

spring 1989, Fertex switched back to Corblok. As a result of the foaming incidents, SPG became aware that UAN passed through a dealer/distributor network before farmers applied it to fields and crops. SPG salespeople had typically called on fertilizer producers and not on other channel members.

Worried about SPG's ability to compete effectively in the UAN corrosion control market, Williamson directed Ron White to hire a sales engineer or product manager to get the UAN corrosion inhibitor program on track. In August 1989, Bob Brown joined SPG in this capacity. Williamson also hired a director of marketing, Jim Walker, in October 1989 and charged him with changing the culture of SPG from a sales/manufacturing/technology-driven business to a market-driven business.

SPG's 1989 organizational chart is shown in Exhibit 3, while Exhibit 4 contains background information on SPG's key personnel.

Corrosion Inhibitor Technology

Corrosion results from a complex chemical reaction that changes steel to useless iron oxide. UAN producers used two basic types of corrosion inhibitors: passivators and film-formers. Passivators formed a protective coating by chemically reacting with the steel surfaces they were supposed to protect. Although some people believed them to be effective, researchers found that corrosive materials could penetrate the coating, resulting in rapid formation of deep pits. Typical repair cost for a storage tank exceeded $1 million, and customers had even reported one or two complete tank failures.

Film-formers left a microscopic layer of inhibitor on the steel surface by incompletely dissolving in the corrosive liquid UAN. This new technology was considered by the National Association of Corrosion Engineers (NACE) to be a sound alternative to designing tanks and piping using expensive, exotic steel alloys or plastics.

EXHIBIT 4   Key SPG Personnel

Nick Williamson—Executive Vice President and General Manager

With a degree in chemical engineering, Williamson joined SPG in 1966 as a process engineer and worked his way through the production and process engineering ranks to his current position in 1982. He had no sales, marketing, or finance experience. Along the way, he completed his master's degree in chemical engineering and developed a process to make synthetic wax. He persuaded corporate management to invest $10 million in 1975 to build a plant for these products, and it came on stream in 1976. First commercial sale of any significance occurred in 1979 to a hot melt adhesive manufacturer, a mature industry at the time. His management philosophy was to be involved in every detail of the SPG operation.

Ron White—Vice President of Sales

A personal friend of Williamson's, he was hired in 1980. A former Air Force KC -135 tanker pilot, he had for years been a member of the leading country club in Fort Smith and was a 3 handicap golfer. Before his employment at SPG, he was the sole U.S. distributor of potassium permanganate, a commodity reagent widely used as a catalyst and in research laboratories. His college degree was in chemistry.

Jim Walker—Director of Marketing

With a chemical engineering degree, he joined American Cyanamid in 1970 as a process engineer. He moved to sales and marketing in 1974, responsible for contract sales of sulfuric acid and alum and became marketing manager for specialty urethane catalysts at Dow in 1978. By this time, he had earned his MBA in chemical marketing from Fairleigh Dickinson. He was appointed director of marketing for Corn Products Corp. in 1984.

Bob Brown—Sales Engineer

He graduated from Carnegie Mellon University with a chemistry degree in 1978 and was first employed by Firestone's Chemical division concentrating in specialty urethane adhesives sales. Three years later, he became a water management chemicals and services specialist at Western Corporation. He was a highly successful salesman, with specific training in consultative needs satisfaction selling and technical service.

All SPG's UAN products were of the film-forming variety. This technology and the related one of solubility control were basic and very strong technologies for CAC and were the source of numerous patents.

Corrosion Inhibitor Use in the U.S. Market

The 1980s were traumatic for U.S. farmers and the industries that supplied them. By 1988, the fertilizer industry (including UAN producers) experienced a shakeout that reduced industry capacity by 20 percent. One UAN plant with book assets of over $40 million netted just $3.5 million at auction. Although U.S. farmers detected improved prospects by the end of 1988, fertilizer producers faced stiff, low-cost foreign competition on their largest volume solid products, sometimes losing money on every ton sold. The cost of liquid UAN ocean shipment kept imports from attacking the North American market, but domestic producers, in a competitive frenzy, cut UAN prices such that they sometimes made only $1 per ton pretax. The shakeout led many to believe the situation would soon return to a more "normal" $30 per ton.

Corrosion control was necessary once UAN entered the distribution system. A number of different products were used over the years to reduce corrosion. Some UAN producers tried unsuccessfully to differentiate their product based

EXHIBIT 5   Competitive Inhibitors—1990

Product	Supplier	Type*	Price ($/lb.)	Treat Cost ($/Ton)†
Ammonia	Many	P	0	0
Borax	Many	P	.14–.17	.28–.35
Chromate	Many	F	.47	.28
Corblok	IWC	F	1.87	.47
DAP	Many	P	.082	.20–.25
Stealth 3662	SPG	F	.80	.24
RG 2064	Western	F	1.90	.19–.38
OA-5	Tennessee	F	.375	.30

*P = passivating; F = film-former
†Treatment cost is per ton of UAN

on the presence of a corrosion inhibitor. Dealers and farmers were more concerned with the cost per acre of fertilized land and on-time, fast delivery, especially during the hectic spring planting and fall harvest. Processing problems, such as incompatibility with other agricultural chemicals and foaming, were not tolerated. There was little dealer loyalty among farmers when they needed to plant or harvest.

Manufacturers produced UAN liquids as 28 percent and 32 percent blends in water. Dealers diluted UAN with additional water before it was suitable for crop application. As a rule, the more dilute the UAN, the more corrosive it was to steel. Once a fertilizer manufacturer added a corrosion inhibitor such as Corblok 105-B or Stealth 3662 at the proper dosage at the plant, corrosion control was effective through the entire distribution network.

Competitive Products

The following inhibitors were in use in January 1989 as SPG began its program to develop a replacement for Stealth 3662. Except for borax, all were liquid materials (also see Exhibit 5):

Ammonia   A toxic gas used as a fertilizer, ammonia was the cheapest source of nitrogen, the same nutrient provided by UAN. Some producers believed corrosion could be eliminated simply by neutralizing acids from the production process by adding ammonia. It was one of the raw materials in the manufacture of UAN. Instances of rapid pitting corrosion in 1970 led many producers to try other inhibitors. Principal advantage was that it was virtually free.

Borax   Classified as "acceptable" by the Tennessee Valley Authority (TVA), borax was used by only one manufacturer. Several other UAN manufacturers had found it to be unacceptable.

Sodium Chromate   Why a material considered by the Environmental Protection Agency (EPA) to be a primary pollutant was allowed in fertilizer points out the strange regulatory environment typically faced by the chemical industry. This product was an excellent corrosion inhibitor but was also toxic to fish and wildlife. Only one plant used it. It was a film-former.

Corblok This phosphate ester film-former was produced in Germany by Servo, a well-respected chemical firm; supplied to North American markets by IWC, a Dutch company; and sold through M. Joseph & Co. of Philadelphia. Corblok was shipped to Houston via ocean freight. Storage facilities were leased at the port of Houston. This product did not foam, was difficult to dissolve in UAN, but provided excellent corrosion protection. Technical service was the responsibility of a corrosion engineer based in Holland. The Leveque Group confirmed claims of many European customers regarding the effectiveness of this product.

DAP Also a fertilizer (only at 100 percent strength), DAP was made by several UAN producers and tested "effective" by TVA. Jackson Pipeline had tried it, found that it left deposits that interfered with pipeline pumps, and that there was pitting corrosion beneath the deposits. Still, DAP enjoyed a 30 percent market share and was sold by direct sales reps or distributors, depending on location. The nutrient content that it imparted to UAN was negligible, but it enjoyed a psychological benefit of "providing crop nutrients."

Stealth 3662 Similar in chemistry to Corblok but easily soluble in UAN, Stealth 3662 was an excellent inhibitor but, as noted previously, created foaming problems. It was produced in Chicago and Galveston, Texas, using the same process equipment as many other CAC products.

OA-5 Tennessee Chemical produced this material in Knoxville. SPG's own tests proved it to be effective. But it was extremely difficult to dissolve in UAN, sometimes merely floating to the surface of the UAN storage tank, even after plant operators were sure they had mixed it properly. Several plants also reported foaming problems when attempting to mix OA-5 with their UAN. This foaming was of a different type than that reported for Stealth 3662. Sold by a direct sales force, this film-former was different in composition from Corblok or Stealth 3662.

RG-2064 and Equivalents Although neither Consolidated nor Western had promoted any products specifically for UAN transport and storage, both were strong in organic phosphate ester chemistry, but they had applied it to water treatment applications, a market much larger than UAN. Both companies employed many more sales reps than SPG and CAC and were already selling water treatment chemicals to UAN plants, for boiler, cooling, and waste-water treatment applications. These operations were run by the same people that ran the UAN process equipment. These companies also were attacking CAC's oil field business and achieving significant success, even though their products were more expensive to use than CAC's. Consolidated's revenue was equal to CAC's, but its profit rate was 20 percent higher than CAC. Western had sales and profits double those of CAC.

Exhibit 6 contains the 1989 capacities of all North American UAN producers and indicates the brand(s) of inhibitor used in mid-1988 and mid-1989.

EXHIBIT 6   **UAN Corrosion Inhibitor Market, 1989 Capacities**   *(0.25 Lb./Ton Dosage)*

Company*	City*	Capacity (000 Tons)	Potential SPG Volume (000 Lbs.)	Mid-1988 Inhibitors	Mid-1989 Inhibitors	Needs Easy Mix Product	SPG Advantage
Farm Products	Kansas City, Kan.	250	63	3662	3662	No	—
Nitron, Inc.	St. Petersburg, Fla.	10	3	3662	3662	Yes	—
Can-Am Corp.	Edmonton, Alberta	15	4	3662	3662	Yes	—
Can-Am Corp.	Lincoln, Neb.	80	20	3662	3662	Yes	—
Agriproducts	Sioux Falls, S.D.	238	60	3662	3662	No	—
Iowa Fertilizer	Dubuque, Iowa	230	58	3662	Corblok	No	Service/Cost
Marathon	Toledo, Ohio	180	45	3662	Corblok	No	Service/Cost
Ferticon	New Orleans	510	128	3662	Corblok	No	Service/Cost
Iowa Fertilizer	Santa Fe	10	3	3662	Corblok	Yes	—
Fertex	Fort Smith, Ark.	1,400	350	3662	Corblok	No	Service/Cost
Nitrogen Inds.	Spokane, Wash.	160	40	3662	Corblok	No	Service/Cost
Iowa Fertilizer	Miami	51	13	3662	RG-2064	Yes	?
Nitro Products	Pensacola, Fla.	65	16	Ammonia	Ammonia	No	Performance
RJS Inc.	Idaho Falls, Idaho	230	58	Ammonia	Ammonia	No	Performance
Georgia Chemical	Savannah, Ga.	680	170	Ammonia	Ammonia	No	Performance
Jackson Chemical	Jackson, Miss.	500	125	Ammonia	Ammonia	No	Performance
Illini Fertilizer	Marietta, Ga.	329	82	Ammonia	Ammonia	No	Performance
NC Fertilizer	Jacksonville, N.C.	230	58	Borax	Borax	No	Service/Pits
RJS Inc.	Fresno, Calif.	129	32	Chromate	Chromate	No	Cost/Safe
Novatec	Windsor, Ontario	175	44	Corblok	Corblok	No	Service/Cost
Eagle Industries	Bettendorf, Ia.	175	44	Corblok	Corblok	No	Service/Cost
RJS Inc.	Winnipeg, Manitoba	210	53	Corblok	Corblok	No	Service/Cost
Edsel Chemical	Sacramento	90	23	Corblok	Corblok	No	Service/Cost
Edsel Chemical	Portland, Ore.	55	14	Corblok	Corblok	Yes	Service/Cost
Edsel Chemical	Spokane, Wash.	200	50	Corblok	Corblok	No	Service/Cost
Comanche Powder	Tucson, Ariz.	20	5	Corblok	Corblok	No	Service/Cost
Illini Fertilizer	Cincinnati	150	38	DAP	DAP	No	Service/Pits
Nutricorp	Council Bluffs, Iowa	500	125	DAP	DAP	No	Service/Pits
Ferticon	Evansville, Ind.	80	20	DAP	DAP	No	Service/Pits
US Industries	Cherokee, Ala.	65	16	DAP	DAP	No	Service/Pits
Illini Fertilizer	Dalton, Ga.	100	25	DAP	DAP	Yes	Service/Pits
Illini Fertilizer	La Salle, Ill.	300	75	DAP	DAP	No	Service/Pits
Farm Products	Hays, Kan.	250	63	DAP	DAP	No	Service/Pits
Nitrotech	Kingston, Ontario	25	6	DAP	DAP	Yes	Service/Pits
Cherokee Nitrogen	Enid, Okla.	270	68	DAP	DAP	No	Service/Pits
Nutricorp	Baton Rouge, La.	1,000	250	DAP	DAP	No	Service/Pits
Nitrogen Inds.	Lincoln, Neb.	158	40	DAP	DAP	Yes	Service/Pits
Canadian Nitrogen	Niagara Falls, Ontario	120	30	OA-5	OA-5	No	Service/Foam
Fertilex	Stockton, Calif.	200	50	OA-5	OA-5	No	Service/Foam
Fertilex	Compton, Calif.	100	25	OA-5	OA-5	No	Service/Foam
Edsel Chemical	Burlington, Iowa	200	50	OA-5	OA-5	No	Service/Foam
Total		9,740	2,435				

*Names and locations changed to protect confidentiality

Product Development

In 1988, after the foaming problems with Stealth 3662, SPG initiated an R&D program to develop a product specifically designed for UAN corrosion control. SPG's technical director estimated four labor years of technical effort over two years was required. The typical cost per labor year was $100,000, including salary and benefits, the use of all group and corporate laboratory facilities, and the cost to build corrosion test apparatus. Jim Walker believed a one labor year marketing effort at $80,000 per year was needed to understand market needs adequately and to develop literature and marketing communications programs. Hosting a hospitality suite at the Ammonium Nitrate Producers Study Group (ANPSG) meeting held each fall would increase annual marketing expenses by $5,000.

White felt confident that his department could sell any product, given a good price; the technical director was confident in the success of the development effort. Two sales efforts were possible (1) 100 percent of Brown's time at $80,000 per year (salary, benefits, car) plus 2 percent of revenue for travel and entertainment costs (T&E), or (2) 5 percent of the entire sales force's time (including regional managers) plus the same T&E.

Williamson considered these costs and alternative sales efforts and reviewed the following data:

- Tax rate 33 percent.
- Corporate cost of capital 8 percent.
- Corporate mandate for 30 percent present value after tax ROI.
- SPG requirement that new businesses generate $2 million in sales and/ or $800,000 gross profit within three years of market entry.

He then instructed his technical director to develop a direct replacement for Corblok.

Early in 1989, Brown arranged a trip with a Fertex sales representative to several fertilizer dealers. His objective was to obtain extensive information about how UAN was used at the dealer level—other nutrients added, mixing techniques, blending with pesticides and herbicides, and so on. Of particular interest to Brown was the extent to which dealers were affected by the foaming problem that had precipitated SPG's new R&D efforts. He was surprised when dealers responded negatively to his questions about foaming. Despite using Fertex UAN containing Stealth 3662, they had not experienced this condition. Brown began to wonder if only certain blends and ingredients foamed, and if these blends were used only in certain regions of the country.

He also learned that a considerable amount of UAN "trading" occurred in the industry. For example, if Fertex had a customer in North Dakota, it would receive the sales revenue, but Agriproducts' Sioux Falls plant would actually supply the UAN. Fertex would return the favor if Agriproducts had a customer in Arkansas. Computerized accounting systems kept track of the trades, and the companies settled accounts quarterly.

In addition to these market factors, the technical director's staff, after running hundreds of corrosion and foaming tests with several producers' UANs, discovered three factors that influenced the interaction between UAN and steel surfaces: (1) higher temperature; (2) higher UAN velocity, especially in a pipeline environment; and (3) presence of impurities. The technical department also found that different producers' UANs, though identical in nutrient content, required different dosages of *any* corrosion inhibitor for effective corrosion control. Other inhibitor suppliers (including IWC/Corblok) recommended the same dosage throughout the industry. SPG's technical director suggested using an industrywide inhibitor dosage rate of 1.5 to 2.0 pounds per ton of UAN so even the most drastic conditions would not cause corrosion problems.

While the three newly developed products were similar, each had slightly different performance characteristics. 601 worked well in Fertex UAN but

EXHIBIT 7   SPG Inhibitor Costs Per Pound, Tank-Car Lots   *(October 1989)*

Product	Fixed	Variable	Total
Stealth 3662	$0.100	$0.300	$0.400
R&D 601	0.160	0.480	0.640
R&D 602	0.160	0.480	0.640
R&D 603	0.160	0.480	0.640

Notes:
1. R&D 601 for "easy to treat" UAN such as Fertex.
2. R&D 602 for "hard to treat" UAN such as Agriproducts.
3. R&D 603 for easy dispersion, all UAN's but very slight foam.
4. Add $0.015 to variable costs for 55-gallon drums, net weight 473 lbs. (215 Kg).
5. Add $0.06 to variable costs for 300-gallon returnable tote tanks, net weight 2,580 lbs. (1173 Kg).
6. Billing terms net 30, freight collect, FOB CAC plant.

would not function in several others. 601 was easier to disperse than 602, while the latter was effective in all UAN brands. Most UAN plants used high-speed pumps to move the UAN through their systems. For this reason, it was believed there would be few problems dispersing SPG's R&D 601 and 602 products into the UAN. Once dispersed, no separation occurred. 603 was easiest to disperse (though not quite as easy as the existing 3662 product), but it exhibited a slight foaming tendency (not believed to be as severe as that of 3662). 603 was effective in all UANs.

All three products were deliverable in tank-truck (40,000-pound) quantities. Also, in response to increased state and local regulations on the disposal of empty drums, SPG planned to offer all three products in 300-gallon returnable and reusable tote tanks, each costing $1,200. Between 30 and 40 round-trips were obtainable before the tanks had to be refurbished at a cost of $300 each. Exhibit 7 shows the cost structure of SPG's products.

Sales (White) and marketing (Walker) continually debated the UAN corrosion inhibitor marketing program as fall 1990 approached. The planned October 1990 rollout would give SPG a strategic window of approximately three months as UAN producers went to high production rates to prepare for spring fertilizer consumption. Failure to obtain business by February would effectively close the window until July, when another production push would occur for fall fertilizer consumption.

Market Segmentation Possibilities

Jim Walker and Bob Brown debated the possibility that different customers had different needs. It might be advantageous to offer multiple products, each with a distinct communication and pricing program. Superior performance characteristics, such as foaming control and ease of dispersion, could command a premium price from certain customers. Other customers and potential customers were less concerned with performance (as their use of low corrosion performance inhibitors indicated) than with price.

Walker and Brown identified three possible performance segments: (1) premium—requiring extensive corrosion control; (2) average—requiring moderate corrosion control; and (3) low—requiring minimal corrosion control. In addition, corrosion-oriented segments might be further stratified by dispersion needs and/or price. Segmentation strategies were among the issues raised at an earlier management meeting.

DECISIONS, DECISIONS, DECISIONS

As Nick Williamson shuffled the papers on his desk he listed the decisions he had to make. The discussion earlier in the afternoon focused on pricing of the new products, but he realized pricing was only one of the factors that had to be resolved.

THE GREAT WESTERN BREWING COMPANY LIMITED (A)*

Brooke Dobni and Rein Lepnurm, University of Saskatchewan

It was a chilly afternoon in November 1991. Peter McCann, president of Great Western Brewing Company, was gazing out the window at the snow drifting across the street of downtown Saskatoon, Saskatchewan. The release of the company's third brand, Great Western Gold, was only days away, and he wondered if the next few months would produce the planned gains in market share.

He knew the long-term viability of the new operation depended on a lot of cooperation between people and events and a little bit of good luck. Since the employee takeover deal of one year ago, it had been a roller-coaster ride for everyone at the brewery. The young company had gone from a stunning 22 percent of Saskatchewan market share one month after start-up to the present low of 10 percent. McCann knew the work required to keep the operation solvent was just beginning. The novelty of the original brand launches was wearing off, and Great Western was going to have to hold its own against its major competitors, Labatt Breweries and Molson Breweries.

BACKGROUND

In recent years, the brewing industry had seen a shift toward increasingly efficient use of resources. Mergers were being used to achieve increased efficiency and strengthen corporate competitiveness necessary to tap the vast U.S. beer market. It was as a result of this situation that the Great Western Brewing Company was born.

On January 18, 1989, the merger of Molson Breweries of Canada and the North American operations of Elders IXL, an Australian company that owned Carling O'Keefe, was announced. The implications of this announcement were significant—1,400 jobs were to be cut and seven plants closed across Canada over three years. After the merger, the new corporation would have assets of $2.3 billion and annual production capacity of 12.6 million hectoliters (hLs) of beer.[1] The Carling O'Keefe facility in Saskatoon was one of the seven Canadian breweries scheduled to be closed.

For the employees of the Saskatoon Carling O'Keefe brewery, the announcement came as a shock. Their only comfort was the package of special early retirement programs, enhanced severance benefits, and career counseling to minimize the impacts of the merger. Approximately 40 of the 70 Saskatoon workers were going to be laid off when Molson moved all of its Saskatchewan production to Regina.

---

* Prepared with the assistance of MBA students B. Allen, R. Maguire, S. Oliver, C. Yeung, and Y. Zhu. Some of the data in this case, financial or other, has been disguised to protect the confidentiality of the business.

[1] A hectoliter (hL) = 100 litres = 22 imperial gallons = 24.4 dozen 12-ounce cans of beer.

With an uncertain future, a group of employees considered the idea of buying the brewery from Carling and operating it themselves. Greg Kitz, a 14-year employee with the plant, prepared a package to solicit investor interest in buying the facility. This effort was unsuccessful, so the employees were left with only one option, an employee buyout.

The buyout was a high-risk venture, and the employees who were committed to the project must have considered their other options. They could try to find another job and start over. This would probably be the most difficult option with approximately 1,000 people per month leaving Saskatchewan to look for better opportunities elsewhere. Several employees took jobs at Molson's Regina brewery. But a few brave, committed employees took the severance packages, worth on average $20,000, and the chance of a lifetime.

An employee association was formed with 23 of the approximately 70 full-time employees from the Carling O'Keefe plant. The goal of the association was to, upon consummation of a deal with Carling O'Keefe, buy out the brewery and go into the brewing industry. In the end, only 15 of those 23 would remain with the project.

The 15 workers needed a leader to champion their cause and bring expertise and credibility to the venture. Peter McCann was attracted by the challenge. McCann had spent his entire career, over 30 years, in the brewing industry working in breweries and malt plants throughout the world. He held a bachelor's degree in brewing science from Heriot-Watt University in Edinburgh, Scotland, as well as management diplomas from England and the University of Western Ontario. In the months that followed, the Carling facility was sold to 16 investors and the Great Western Brewing Company was formed. McCann assumed the position of chief operating officer, in addition to becoming the 16th shareholder.

The group of 16 now formed a cohesive unit determined to turn the plant into a successful regional brewery. Each person invested what was, for most, their life savings, between $50,000 and $100,000 each. Their commitment amounted to 25 percent of the purchase price of approximately $5 million. The Saskatchewan Economic Diversification Corporation (SEDCO) invested the other 75 percent of the initial investment price. A chartered bank provided an operating loan of $250,000.

STRATEGY

Peter McCann never had to dwell on what strategy to follow in the marketplace. The beer industry had become an intuitive part of McCann's career as a brewmaster. Great Western's strategy was to position itself as the "Saskatchewan" brewer, by maximizing Saskatchewan content and having a high community profile. It was projected that if Great Western could get 10 percent of the Saskatchewan market share within the first year, it would break even.

The Canadian brewing industry had a number of highly successful and competent brewing companies. Each brewer was capable of producing a high-quality beer, but the key to success in the industry was to create product differentiation at competitive prices. The Great Western product line was no different from its competition. The launch of regular and light products gave Great Western differentiated mainstream products to compete against the industry leaders. What Great Western had was a product that appealed to the internal values of people in Saskatchewan. The success of Great Western's product line hinged on the loyalty of the Saskatchewan consumer to locally produced products.

In the early period of Great Western's oeprations, McCann had become convinced the survival of Great Western would be linked to the success of its marketing initiatives. Great Western would have to build its product line and promote its beer as a product for people who were committed to the province and who wanted to share in the success of an underdog in its fight against the big breweries with their huge plants in the east. It would be essential for consumers to forsake their traditional brands to try Great Western. Once they tried Great Western, it was equally important to keep them buying.

According to Doug Sargeant, vice president of marketing of Great Western Brewery, the Saskatoon media were very supportive at the time of the new brewery's launch. They helped sell the company to the people of Saskatchewan. Everyone in the province seemed to be trying Great Western, and the brewery had to struggle to keep adequate supplies of beer in the liquor stores. Even the local restaurants and bars, which had been cautious about stocking Great Western, were placing orders after a few weeks as the public in Regina and Saskatoon demanded a Great Western product with their meals.

Now, almost two years after Great Western hit the market, people were still drinking "Saskatechewan's Own," but sales were down. The honeymoon was over and the local press was not providing its liberal doses of Great Western promotion. The company was at an important crossroad in ensuring its survival. With a reduced but stable market share, Great Western had carved out its niche in the Saskatchwan marketplace. In the future, Great Western had to decide whether or not it should be content as a regional brewery or it it should expand its horizons and carve out similar niches in the neighboring provinces of Alberta and Manitoba. Moreover, given the present underutilized plant capacity,[2] the American market was also an attractive opportunity.

McCann knew the introduction of Great Western Gold marked a change in strategy of the company. Great Western's first two brands were positioned head-to-head with the market share leaders, Labatt's Blue and Molson Canadian. Great Western had to establish a presence in this segment to survive. Having done this, the brewery could now look at niche opportunities, either by introducing brands that were not available in Saskatchewan or by attacking the weakly defended, low market share brands of other brewers. It was anticipated by McCann that the major breweries would not be likely to react strongly to the latter strategy as the brands targeted offered very low margins. The incremental sales achieved by Great Western, on the other hand, would significantly improve its financial position by allowing the company to allocate fixed costs over a larger production base.

CANADIAN BREWING INDUSTRY—MARKET OVERVIEW

The Canadian brewing industry was characterized by comprehensive regulation and declining beer consumption. From 1975 to 1988, the Canadian adult population grew by about 25 percent, while beer sales increased only by 10

---

[2]Even at 10 percent of Saskatchewan market share, Great Western was producing 55,000 hLs annually. Total annual capacity of Great Western was 262,000 hLs.

EXHIBIT 1   **Consumption of Beer, Spirits, and Wine in Canada, 1975–1990**
                   (Liters per capita)

Selected	Liters per Capita		
Years	Beer	Spirits	Wine
1975	85.92	7.82	5.90
1979*	84.00	8.32	8.22
1980*	86.79	8.03	8.41
1981*	86.09	8.35	8.98
1982	85.34	8.12	9.19
1983	83.54	7.64	9.43
1984	83.50	7.05	9.45
1985	82.52	6.72	9.78
1986†	82.13	6.55	10.20
1987	81.87	6.34	9.97
1988	83.11	6.30	10.31
1989	81.83	6.13	9.87
1990	80.62	5.82	9.47

* Consumption figures reflect the effect of strikes in the brewing industry in western Canada.
†Consumption figures reflect the effect of strikes in the brewing industry in Alberta, Ontario, and Newfoundland.
Source: Brewers Association of Canada, *Annual Statistical Bulletin*, 1990.

percent. This resulted in a per capita consumption erosion of approximately 11 percent (see Exhibit 1). This shift in consumer demand away from beer products was prompted by several factors, including increased health and safety consciousness, changing age demographics, and greater taxation of beer in relation to other beverages. By 1989, there was no indication of any significant reversal in these trends. In fact, volume was expected to remain static or to decline slightly over the next five years.

Brand loyalty toward beer products had generally weakened over the past 10 years, and brewers in Canada had been forced to also sell beer on the basis of image and fashion. This was partially attributable to the U.S. marketing campaigns that infiltrated the Canadian airways through U.S. cable TV. Further, a number of marketing and licensing agreements between Canadian and U.S. breweries were entered into during this period.

As an example of this consumer fickleness toward brand loyalty, in 1983, when Carling O'Keefe broke with tradition and introduced Miller High Life and Miller Lite in tall bottles, it was able to capture an incremental 9 percent of the total Canadian market. This share came at the expense of other Canadian brands and cannibalized some of Carling's traditional brands. Later, the twist-off cap introduced by Labatt in 1984 was said to have added about 1.5 to 3 percent to its total market share.

Domestic beer sales in Canada in 1990 totaled 20,092,150 hectoliters. Despite stagnant unit volume, price increases had caused the value of beer shipments to increase 13.7 percent. The value of beer sold in the fiscal year 1990 was $8.9 billion.[3] Saskatchewan, however, was estimated to have only 549,200 hectoliters of sales.

---

[3]Consumer expenditure includes purchase of beer for home and on-premise consumption; see Brewers Association of Canada, *1990 Annual Statistical Bulletin*, p. 36.

Competitive threats to the Canadian beer industry included foreign imports, impending trade agreements that could open Canadian markets even more, interprovincial trade barriers, continued consumer movement toward healthier life-styles, sin taxes imposed by the federal government, and "the share of belly" concept. The belly concept held that each person consumed only a finite quantity of liquid and, unless the population increased, the market size would be stagnant. Beer producers, therefore, had to compete with all other beverages.

Among brewery products, bottled beer was the biggest seller with 79.2 percent of total value of beer shipments. In Canada in 1988, bottled beer sales increased by 22.1 percent. Canned beer had 13.6 percent of the total value of beer shipments and saw a strong increase of 26 percent in 1988. Import beers accounted for 2.2 percent of total beer sales in 1988. However, import sales activity was expected to increase over the long term under the terms and conditions of the proposed North American Free Trade Agreement (NAFTA).[4]

The threat of free trade and abolishment of interprovincial beer sale regulations were real concerns for Canadian brewers. Yet it was not regarded as much of a threat to Great Western as it was to Labatt and Molson. "If interprovincial barriers come down, we can see lots of brewing plants being shut down," Sargeant said. When asked whether such shutdowns could create more employee takeovers like the Great Western, Sargeant said it would probably never happen again: "Molson obviously underestimated the threat Great Western could pose to them when they sold their Saskatoon plant to its employees. This oversight must have been costly to Molson."

In an effort to improve the competitive advantages of Canadian brewers in an increasingly global marketplace, interprovincial trade barriers were being reviewed and reciprocal sales agreements were being negotiated between provinces to give Canadian brewers access to new markets.

THE SASKATCHEWAN SITUATION

Beer consumption in Saskatchewan had been declining moderately since 1982. Parallel consumption patterns had been observed across Canada. At present, Saskatchewan had the lowest per capita beer consumption of any province (see Exhibit 2).

Within Saskatchewan, the Saskatchewan Liquor Board regulated retail distribution and sale of beer in the province. All other Canadian provinces had similar liquor boards and liquor authorities that controlled retail liquor stores and the licensing of off-sale establishments. These organizations enjoyed considerable power over the retailing of beer through supply management of sales establishments. Pricing authority also ensured continued provincial revenues and controlled competition within the industry.

American beer had been licensed for sale in Canada for many years. Prices were established by liquor boards in each province. In 1990, Saskatchewan became one of the first provinces to be "totally GATT fair." Under the General Agreement on Tariffs and Trade (GATT), Saskatchewan was required to open its borders to foreign brew. Saskatchewan's Liquor Board argued its prices were in accordance with GATT insofar as U.S. products had access to the market.

---

[4]Beverage and Tobacco Products Industries, Statistics Canada, *Catalogue 32-251 Annual*, 1988.

EXHIBIT 2   **Sales of Beer by Province and per Capita Consumption, 1990**   *(In hectoliters)*

Month	Manitoba	Saskatchewan	Alberta	Total
January	50,168	34,910	93,694	178,722
February	58,130	34,022	101,086	193,238
March	41,656	40,715	123,769	206,140
April	59,549	42,540	124,738	226,827
May	66,991	50,825	154,991	272,807
June	69,637	61,168	155,899	286,704
July	77,824	63,851	163,971	305,646
August	70,170	57,262	164,256	291,688
September	50,553	39,445	113,598	203,596
October	56,620	42,914	122,284	221,818
November	52,207	39,506	116,216	207,929
December	62,969	42,045	126,504	231,518
Total	716,474	549,203	1,561,006	2,286,683
Per Capita Consumption	.710	.549	.634	

Source: The Brewers Association of Canada, *Annual Report*, 1990.

Pricing differences were attributed to differing distribution costs incurred by the Liquor Board (see Exhibit 3).

Molson and Labatt distributed their products through their own distribution company, the Saskatchewan Brewers' Association (SBA). Great Western had a contract with SBA for beer distribution on a fee-for-service basis, exactly the same as Molson and Labatt. Other brewers, such as U.S. brewers, either had to negotiate a deal with the Saskatchewan Brewers' Association, pay the Liquor Board handling charges, or establish their own distribution channel in the province. With the tight control over distribution, Saskatchewan Brewers felt less threatened about the implications of GATT and free trade in the brewing industry.

NATIONAL AND INTERNATIONAL PRESSURES FOR DEREGULATION

National pressures for deregulation had been increasing since a 1987 conference in Toronto, where an endorsement in principle was made to achieve a general reduction or elimination of interprovincial trade barriers, including those relating to beer. In response to this, an interprovincial panel on liquor board marketing practices was appointed, but as of yet, the panel had not reached a consensus on action.

The international pressures were evolving from two sources. In 1987, a GATT panel sided with the European Community (EC) ruling that Canada's listing, marketing, and pricing practices for alcoholic beverages violated its obligations as a GATT member. Intense negotiation around this issue resulted in an agreement that required Canada to open its market to beer imported from EC member states and to remove discriminatory pricing practices.

Second, when the Canada-U.S. Free Trade Agreement (FTA) talks began in the mid-1980s, the Canadian brewers lobbied for an exemption. In October 1987, these efforts paid off as both the Canadian and U.S. negotiators recognized the industry needed time to readjust. The exemption allowed Canada to

EXHIBIT 3   **Saskatchewan Beer Prices, Select Brands, 1990**

Beer Prices (per dozen including deposit where applicable)				
	Saskatchewan	**Alberta**	**British Columbia**	**Manitoba**
Milwaukee's Best (I) (cans)	$16.00	$10.10	NA	$13.40
Old Milwaukee (I) (cans)	16.40	10.20	9.30	13.30
Pabst Blue Ribbon (I) (cans)	16.40	NA	13.40	13.70
Michelob (I) (bottles)	18.70	14.40	14.00	18.00
Labatt's Blue (D) (cans)	13.80	13.50	12.05	13.80

Source: *Saskatoon Star-Phoenix*, October 12, 1990.

Notes:

1. (I) = Import

   (D) = Domestic

2. Labatt's Blue is considered a good proxy for domestic beer in terms of domestic beer prices due to its substantial market share.

3. Prices effective in October 1990.

continue to limit access by U.S. brands to distribution channels with quotas and higher taxes on U.S. beer.

The exclusion from the FTA and the Canadian government's willingness to agree to industry adjustment was seen by industry analysts as a window of opportunity for Canadian brewers to accomplish three things: (1) satisfy GATT that the Canadian beer market would be opened, (2) provide Canadians with more competitive and possibly lower priced beer products, and (3) give the industry time to gear up for the inevitable competition with U.S. firms 5 to 10 years down the road.[5]

MAJOR COMPETITORS

Until the merger of Molson with Carling O'Keefe Breweries of Canada Limited (Carling), the Canadian brewing industry was dominated by three firms— Labatt with a 42 percent market share, Molson at 31.6 percent of market, and Carling with a 19.6 percent share.

Since the brewing industry was capital intensive and economies of scale were critical for profitability, the barriers to entry were high. This had led to a concentration of sales, and by 1990, two players dominated the Canadian beer industry. These conventional brewers were John Labatt Breweries of Canada (Labatt) and Molson Breweries of Canada Limited (Molson), with combined estimated brewing capacities of 14 million hLs and 12 million hLs, respectively.

Great Western had identified Molson and Labatt as its primary competition in Canada. Great Western had launched brands that competed head-to-head with Molson Canadian and Labatt Blue products.

Molson Breweries of Canada

Molson Breweries was founded by John Molson in 1786 and in 1989 was North America's oldest continuing brewer. Until 1955, Molson was primarily a

---

[5]*Toronto Globe and Mail*, November 12, 1987.

regional brewer serving the Quebec market. By the early 1960s, the company had expanded its brewing business and had plants in most Canadian provinces. By the late 1980s, Molson Breweries was part of TCLM, a diversified Canadian multinational corporation with more than 11,000 employees and revenues of $2.4 billion.

In 1988, Elders IXL, based in Australia and recent acquiree of Carling O'Keefe, approached TCML about a possible merger of their respective Canadian brewing operations. Further negotiations laid the groundwork for an eventual 50-50 partnership. The merged entity was seen by Molson as an important factor in a North American strategy that would require a strong and efficient infrastructure to battle the mammoth U.S. brewers, primarily Anheuser-Busch, Miller Brewing Company, the Stroh Brewing Company, G. Heileman Brewing Company, and Adolph Coors Company.

The merged entity was called Molson Breweries with the stronger Molson products as the core brands, therefore ensuring preservation of the Molson name.

Labatt Breweries of Canada

Labatt's brewing operation was part of John Labatt Ltd., a diversified food and beverage company with business in three main sectors—brewing, agriculture, and packaged foods.

Labatt's dominant market share could be traced back to several events that occurred over the past decade. In 1979, after realizing that profitability could be sustained only through market share improvement and not overall market growth, Labatt made the first move to the so-called brand and packaging wars that characterized the 1980s. In 1989, Labatt produced 31 different brands, operated 12 breweries in nine provinces, and spent over $36 million in advertising. Labatt's leading brand, Blue, was sold in all provinces and had an estimated 18 percent national share.

Labatt had close marketing and licensing agreement ties with Anheuser-Busch and, like the U.S. firm, focused its brand development through sports and community events. Labatt also owned 45 percent of the Toronto Blue Jays Major League Baseball team.

Regional Brewers

During the late 1970s and throughout the 1980s, Amstel, Northern Breweries, and most recently the Great Western Brewing Company emerged as regional brewers. Regional brewers produced over 25,000 hLs but considerably under 1 million hLs. The product was generally targeted for a local market or region.

Great Western, as a regional brewer with production levels of over 55,000 hLs, was sandwiched between microbrewers and the megabrewers of Labatt and Molson, with competition coming from both sides. Most recently, the regional brewers had become aggressive in their marketing strategies in efforts to capture market share. The establishment of minimum price levels by regulation had helped this cause by eliminating any efforts of price wars. Great Western had had to carefully position itself to maintain a steady pressure on mainstream markets and develop desired niches not in the mainstream market.

EXHIBIT 4   Production of Canadian Microbrewers, 1988

Company Name	City, Province	Production (hLs)
The Upper Canada Brewing Co. Ltd.	Toronto, Ontario	20,603
Big Rock Brewing Ltd.	Calgary, Alberta	17,618
Horseshoe Bay Brewery & Troller Pub	Horseshoe Bay, B.C.	15,500
Okanagan Spring Brewery	Vernon, B.C.	11,443
Connors Brewing Co. Ltd. No. 1	Missisauga, Ontario	10,000
Island Pacific Brewing Co.	Victoria, B.C.	10,000
Granville Island Brewing Co.	Vancouver, B.C.	9,800
Highland Breweries Ltd.	Sydney, N.S.	6,700
Creemore Springs Brewery	Creemore, Ontario	4,685
G.M.T. Brewery	Montreal, Quebec	4,000
Bavarian Specialities (Canada) Ltd.	Riverview, N.B.	3,000
Massawippi Brewing Co. Inc.	Lennoxville, Quebec	3,000
Shaftebury Brewing Co. Ltd.	Vancouver, B.C.	3,000
Wellington County Brewery Ltd.	Guelph, Ontario	2,260
Canadian Heritage Brewing Co. Ltd.	Richmond, B.C.	2,045
The Ottawa Valley Brewing Co., Inc.	Nepean, Ontario	2,000
Halton County Brewery	Burlington, Ontario	1,818
Great Lakes Brewing Co.	Brampton, Ontario	500
Sculler Brewing Co. Ltd.	St. Catherines, Ontario	195
Golden Lion Brewing Co.	Lennoxvllle, Quebec	N/A
G.A. Miller Brewing Co.	Thunder Bay, Ontario	N/A
Nanton Interbrew Ltd.	Nanton, Alberta	N/A
Les Brasseurs du Nord	St. Jerome, Quebec	N/A
Conners Brewing Co. (Don Valley)	North York, Ontario	N/A
Island Brewery Ltd.	Charlottetown, P.E.I.	N/A
The Simcoe Brewing Co.	Newmarket, Ontario	N/A
Wheatley Brewery	Wheatley, Ontario	N/A
York Brewery	Brampton, Ontario	N/A

Microbrewers, Brew Pubs, and Home Brewers

Microbrewers were local companies producing under 25,000 hLs for their immediate markets; the best known were Brick, Upper Canada, Connors, and Big Rock. Exhibit 4 indicates the growing number of microbrewers in the Canadian market; none, however, were based in Saskatchewan.

Two new sectors emerged in the 1980s, brew pubs and home brewers. Brew pubs were licensed establishments that brewed their own products for on-premise consumption. The last 10 years in Canada had seen the emergence of brew pubs. Like English pubs, they provided a place for community gathering and socialization. Beer was brewed and consumed on premise, and the capacity for production was very limited. These establishments were an increasingly popular alternative to the bar scene.

Home brewers made beer from a prepackaged kit for personal consumption. This segment had been growing dramatically in recent years as evidenced by the increasing number of brewing supply retailers locating in small to large centers. While little formal research had been gathered to quantify the size of this market, it was estimated that 1 percent of the adult beer drinking population had entered the home brewing industry. Home brewers universally indicated they brewed their own beer to save money.[6] Those who were involved in home brewing also indicated they enjoyed the taste of their beer and would continue their personal brewing efforts.

THE GREAT WEATERN BREWING COMPANY—OPERATIONS OVERVIEW

Marketing

The key success factors for Great Western beer in Saskatchewan, identified by Sargeant, were its image of being a local brewer using Saskatchewan-produced grain as its main raw material and supporting community events. This successful local image gave Great Western its initial 22 percent of the Saskatchewan beer market share. And the phenomenal success at the beginning gave Great Western much publicity in the local media. The coverage provided Great Western with free advertising. Sargeant noted, "The media was very kind to us, generally reporting the success side of the company. At times, such reports could be misleading; the public could overestimate the success of the company."

Sargeant believed there were two groups of people with differing perceptions of the company. One group thought the company was now strong enough to stand on its own feet. People in this group had been influenced by the media to overestimate the success of the company. The company risked losing the support of these people because they no longer perceived it as a fledgling local brewer that needed continued support from Saskatchewan consumers. The other group consisted of people who understood the real situation at Great Western. The initial break-even sales target was projected to be 5 to 6 percent of the market with 26 employees. The phenomenal success brought the employment level at Great Western up to 45 people. The company needed at least 8 percent of the market to break even, while its actual market share fluctuated between 9 and 11 percent.

Contrary to the industry norm of heavy television advertising and sponsorship, Great Western had never spent any money on television advertising. Ninety-nine percent of its advertising was done through radio and the rest through newspapers and magazines. Great Western got the lower local rate rather than the national rate on radio commercials—about $2,000 for a three-week program consisting of 35 to 45 commercial spots. The commercials alternated between stations to improve the hit ratio, catching more people's attention. One quarter page in the local newspaper, the *Saskatoon Star Phoenix*, cost $1,000. "Radio is the best medium for advertising," Sargeant argued, "because when people hear commercials on radio it does not bother them or force them to switch channels as television commercials do. It has the best retention rate on people who listen to radio regularly. People reading newspapers may simply skip over the ad, but people listening to radio just cannot do so unless they shut off the radio." Total marketing cost for a brand of beer at Great Western was about $1 per dozen beers. About half of that cost was spent on media advertising.

---

[6]Approximately 53 cents of every dollar in beer sales was taxes.

EXHIBIT 5   Saskatchewan Liquor Board Retail Prices and Brands Available, 1991

Product	Price
Regular and lite brands (bottles)	
6 pack	$6.60 including $0.60 deposit
12 pack	$12.70 including $1.20 deposit
24 pack	$24.80 including $2.40 deposit
Price or generic brands (bottles)	
12 pack	$12.45 including $1.20 deposit
Canned beer (all brands)	
6 pack	$6.90 including $0.30 deposit
12 pack	$13.80 including $0.60 deposit
24 pack	$27.60 including $1.20 deposit

Competing Brands Available in Saskatchewan

Labatt	Carling	Molson	Great Western
Blue	Fosters Lager	Canadian	Regular
50 Ale	Colt 45*	Coors	Light
Budweiser	Miller High Life	Coors Lite	Gold
Bud Lite	Miller Lite	Bohemian*	
Schooner	Old Vienna	Molson Golden	
Labatt's Lite	Old Vienna Lite	Molson Light	
Guiness	Trilight	Pilsner	
Labatt Dry	Extra Old Stock		
Beer*	Calgary Lager		

*Low price brand

At present, Great Western had only two brands on the market, regular and light. The company planned to push out two more brands after the release of Great Western Gold. Another light beer with a very low (3.2 percent) alcohol content and a malt beer were in the planning stages. As Sargeant explained, "We are only producing at one third of our capacity now and any increase of production will reduce our unit cost. New brands usually attract new segments of the market and bring in extra sales, while the cost of launching a new brand is minimal apart from its start-up costs." Such setup costs were usually low except for draft beer.

The pricing of beer was restricted by regulations set by the Saskatchewan Liquor Board. Different brands of the same type of beer were set at basically the same price, so profit margins were a function of production costs. Regulation forced brewers to compete on the basis of product differentiation, supporting marketing efforts aimed at brand loyalty. Exhibit 5 gives the Saskatchewan Liquor Board regulated beer prices in 1990 and brands available. Exhibit 6 provides market share data.

Great Western Gold was not intended to be just another brand to be added to the existing line of Great Western brands. It carried the hopes of the company to regain its lost market share. Gold was a malt liquor with 6.5 percent alcohol content. According to Sargeant,

E X H I B I T   6   Comparative Markets Shares of Canadian Beer Producers, 1972–1988

	1972	1973	1974	1975	1976	1977	1978	1979	1980	1981	1982	1983	1984	1985	1986	1987	1988
Labatt	33.9%	36.9%	35.9%	36.6%	37.6%	38.4%	38.6%	36.6%	36.5%	34.9%	36.7%	36.3%	34.6%	38.0%	39.1%	40.3%	41.9%
MBC	29.2	30.5	31.6	33.5	33.6	33.9	34.1	36.2	35.9	35.1	35.8	34.7	31.5	30.6	29.8	31.5	31.6
Carling	30.6	28.3	26.1	25.3	24.9	24.1	23.2	22.7	23.2	22.8	23.1	24.3	28.2	25.0	22.8	22.0	19.6
Other	5.3	4.0	6.1	4.2	3.3	2.9	3.2	3.5	3.5	3.8	2.9	3.6	4.2	4.8	4.5	4.7	4.7
Imports	0.3	0.3	0.3	0.4	0.6	0.7	0.9	1.0	0.9	3.4	1.5	1.1	1.5	1.6	3.8	1.5	2.2
Total	100.0%	100.0%	100.0%	100.0%	100.0%	100.0%	100.0%	100.0%	100.0%	100.0%	100.0%	100.0%	100.0%	100.0%	100.0%	100.0%	100.0%

Source: TMCL, Brewers Association of Canada, and Statistics Canada.

Provincial Market Share Data of November 30, 1989

	Percentage Share			Percentage of Canada Sales
	Molson	Carling	Labatt	
Newfoundland	19%	28%	53%	2.3%
Nova Scotia	—	—	82	3.0
Prince Edward Island	2	—	53	0.4
New Brunswick	—	—	43	2.3
Quebec	33	31	36	26.1
Ontario	40	15	41	39.6
Manitoba	14	29	57	3.9
Saskatchewan	40	23	37	2.9
Alberta	42	20	29	8.2
British Columbia	26	22	44	10.9
NWT/Yukon	—	—	—	0.3
				100.0%

Source: Molson, Labatt Breweries.

Unfortunately, alcohol still sells beer. There are still a lot of people who are very sensitive to what they get for their money. Since prices for Gold and regular beers are much the same, many price-conscious beer drinkers would prefer to have Gold simply for its extra alcohol content. In the current market, there is only one brand, the O'Keefe Extra Old Stock, that has alcohol content higher than the regular 5 percent. It has 6 percent alcohol and 2 percent of the market share. It will be significant to us if we can get half of that.

Great Western also wanted to use Gold to target the younger adult drinkers. These younger drinkers were more price conscious and did not care as much about supporting locals as their elders did. Great Western wanted to focus on these younger drinkers because brand loyalty for beer was believed to develop around the age of 25.

To effectively reach these markets, the company had launched its promotions for the Gold brand to get quick results. Heavy advertising had been used on both radio and newspapers; however, television advertising was still avoided. Direct mail, end-of-aisle displays, posters, and enter-and-win sweepstake draws had also been used. There was even a sweepstake draw for three pieces of real gold worth over $500 each as the prizes. Sales representatives went to bars and restaurants to promote the new brand with special promotional packages.

Great Western had seven sales representatives throughout the province. The segment that needed the most personal selling attention and promotions was the local pubs and bars. "We just can't leave our beer to the pubs and hope it will sell by itself. Today's beer drinkers at the pubs do not have much loyalty to any brands of beer. It's up to the reps to push our beer to the bartenders and managers," Sargeant asserted. The "value-added" promotional strategies the company had used regularly included scratch-and-win cards, free tickets to sports events and concerts, and free key chains put in each case of beer.

The subject of social responsibility for brewers was a sensitive issue. Great Western spent a lot of time promoting responsible drinking and reinforcing in people not to "drink and drive." "It's contradictory to our interest in promoting our sales," Sargeant admitted, "but we also want people to be safe and healthy so that they can drink more of our beer. We are certainly not telling them not to drink at all. We are simply telling them not to drink and drive at the same time."

Demand for beer was seasonal and greatly affected by the weather. The summer months of May to August were the peak periods, with over 40 percent of annual sales occurring during the period. Sales dropped sharply in September and did not begin to pick up until February. Sargeant recognized that he had only 32 days, 16 summer weekends, to really push the company's products.

While its priority was still the Saskatchewan market, Great Western was also constantly searching for new market opportunities. With the newly installed canning line facility, Sargeant wondered if it was feasible to ship canned beers to the neighboring provinces of Manitoba and Alberta, since transportation costs for canned beer were less than for bottled beer. The Manitoba and Alberta markets combined were more than four times the Saskatchewan market. If Great Western could get 1 percent of these markets, it would be equivalent to increasing its Saskatchewan market share by 4 percent.

The U.S. market had been another natural target for Great Western. Great Western had made efforts to obtain the licensing rights to produce a Chinese brand beer, Qingdao (pronounced *chingdow*). Qingdao was a well-known

Chinese beer that had achieved significant market acceptance in the United States with its direct imports from China. The Chinese brewing company had shown great interest in the deal, and the two sides had discussed the matter in detail and exchanged plant visits at the senior management level. However, problems still existed since a U.S. company currently held the exclusive distribution rights for the Qingdao brand in the United States. Further, Great Western would also have to provide several employment positions for its Chinese counterpart as part of the attempted agreement. Sargeant was aware the Qingdao beer was well known for drawing mineral water directly from the Laoshan Mountain spring, a key success factor for the brand name. It was questionable how the market (especially the ethnic Chinese market) would react once they discovered that the beer was no longer directly imported from China, but brewed under license in Canada.

Employee Ownership

According to one of Great Western's employee owners, "People are the key. Our people are willing to work for a little less money and are always eager to help out wherever there is work to be done. It allows us to operate at a lower cost and to react quickly to changes." Each of the 16 people who came together to reopen the brewery had a large stake in the operation both personally and financially. The distribution of shareholdings ranged from 2.3 to 9.9 percent; no one person controlled more than 10 percent of shares outstanding.

The commitment of the group and their experience were significant assets to the project. Among the 16 people, they had combined brewing experience of over 300 years. However, their experience was mainly in production and operations, not management of a brewery.

To keep costs low, the group was willing to take voluntary pay and benefits cuts of approximately 25 to 30 percent. The impact of the labor cost reduction on operating costs was significant, providing the brewery with an advantage over the national brewers.

Peter McCann and representatives of the United Food and Commercial Workers Union had negotiated a two-year contract under which all full-time employees would receive $15.50 per hour. This represented approximately 80 percent of the wage paid by Carling O'Keefe and other major competitors. A part-time employee and workers on a 130-day probation would receive $7.75 per hour. Employee benefits were also reduced from the Carling O'Keefe level of 25 percent of base pay to 15 percent of base pay. The specific benefits to be allocated were to be agreed on by the employees.

Initial staffing requirements of 26 people were based on market share estimates of 5 to 10 percent and production requirements of 30,000 to 50,000 hLs in the first year of operation. However, the early success of the company allowed Great Western to expand to its current total staff level of 45 people, including the 16 shareholders.

Having 15 shareholders who were also unionized members of the bargaining unit had a tremendous impact on business operations. John O'Connor was a shareholder, head of the Brewery Workers Local Union, and a shipping clerk or "whatever position needs to be filled on any particular day." O'Connor claimed he did not have a conflict of interest in the dual roles he played. "Negotiations," he stated, "were relaxed and informal. McCann and I sat down for two days, discussed the situation, and came to an agreement. It's as simple as that. We treat our employees fairly. They have a vested interest in the success of this company. In return, we get their loyalty. Since we began operations, there has not been one sick day taken. I think that says a lot."

Great Western's organizational structure was innovative and nontraditional in the sense that the organization was hierarchical in design but functioned on bottom-up approvals. Employees, owners, and management gathered weekly to discuss issues related to weekly and monthly market positions, in addition to planning upcoming promotional activities. Through common interests, shared focus, and cooperation, the employees, owners, and management approached problems in a coordinated manner in which consensus was reached before an organizational commitment. Problems were brought into the open before they became serious and resolutions were reached as a result of negotiations. This process was not always easy or expedient, but decisions reached were understood by all and implemented.

Twenty-nine of the 45 employees were, however, nonshareholders and their interests and morale were affected by different factors. Great Western prided itself in providing a dynamic work environment. The family atmosphere and approach extended to the nonshareholders. Everyone was on a first-name basis and it was not uncommon for part-time positions to be filled by family members of the investors. An open-door policy was maintained, and management regularly solicited the advice of all employees for promotion and product launch recommendations.

Facilities

The Great Western building opened in 1928 under the name Hub City Brewing Co. A large portion of the original equipment was still in use at the brewery; however, the equipment had been upgraded to keep pace with new technology, and new buildings had been added as required.

The plant occupied a city block (approximately 11,000 square meters or 2.6 acres) in downtown Saskatoon. The brewery's buildings took up about 65 percent of the site, with the remainder used for parking, building access roads, and a private garden area. The older buildings, which housed the office, brewing equipment, aging cellars, and bottling plant, were constructed from brick. The newer buildings, which included the warehouse and cold storage cellar, were insulated steel frame construction with steel cladding. All of the buildings were in good repair and had been projected to serve the needs of the new operation for at least 20 years.

Production

McCann claimed: "Production operations at Great Western is one of the company's strong points. Our people have the experience required to make a quality beer." Although the brewery was old, it was well equipped with the tools required to produce high-quality beer. The actual brewing equipment was constructed mainly from stainless steel and included a malt and corn storage area, malt mill, brewing syrup tank, cereal cooker, mash mixer, lauder tun, brew kettle, wort cooler, 27 fermentation tanks, beer filters, 18 primary storage tanks, 14 secondary storage tanks, and 6 packaging tanks.

As was typical of breweries, Great Western brewed beer in batches. A batch was 180 hLs, or 4,300 dozen bottles, and took about 28 days from start to finish, including aging time. Several brews could be prepared in parallel since most of the 28 days was spent in fermentation and aging tanks. Up to 34 brews could be produced in a five-day period, which made the present capacity of the brewery about 260,000 hLs per year. Under the management of one of the previous owners, equipment for diluting beer with water before final packaging was installed and used to increase capacity by another 20 percent. It was unlikely this technique would ever be used by Great Western because doing so would violate the company's commitment to quality.

The smallest batch that could be produced using the present brewing equipment was 140 hLs (3,300 dozen). This batch size was suitable for small-scale test marketing of new brands.

The brewery had both a bottling line and a canning line. The bottling line was capable of filling 350 bottles per minute. The maximum bottling capacity was roughly 350,000 hLs per year, based on three shifts and allowing for downtime. Some of the equipment was quite old and downtime was increasing. To complicate matters, replacement parts were no longer stocked and had to be manufactured in-house by resident millwrights.

The canning line, which was installed in the summer of 1990, could operate at a maximum of 400 cans per minute, a limitation imposed by the capacity of the pasteurizer. The equipment was purchased used but had been reconditioned by brewery mechanics and was expected to last for several years.

Great Western was not presently equipped to handle draught beer. In early 1988, the Saskatchewan brewing industry switched from "Peerless" kegs to new "Sankey" kegs. Peerless and Sankey were both brand names for beer kegging systems. Beer sold unpasteurized in bulk containers, usually 12 gallons, was called draft beer and sold "on tap" in bars and restaurants from kegs. The Peerless keg was the industry standard for many years. Recently, the improved design of the Sankey keg had almost replaced the Peerless keg because there was less wasted product left in the keg when emptied and because it was better suited to automatic washing and filling. Gib Henderson, vice president of operations, estimated it would cost $500,000 to install the equipment required to process Sankey kegs, including the cost of the kegs.

Great Western normally maintained five working days of stock, with warehousing done on site. The warehouse had sufficient storage for finished product ready to ship, as well as for empty bottles, cartons, and pallets. The working capacity of the warehouse was 250,000 dozen bottles.

Raw materials were stored in various locations on the site. Malt barley was stored in tanks and silos near the brew-house. Other brewing materials, such as hops, did not require much space and were stored near their point of consumption in quantities sufficient for six months to one year of production. The brewery had a secure supply of high-quality raw materials. Most raw materials were bought from local Saskatchewan suppliers. Hops were imported from British Columbia, Washington, or England. Historically, there had been no problem with hop supplies. The majority of the raw material cost was driven by commodity products. As such, Great Western did not pay a penalty relative to its competitors for low-volume purchases.

An abundant supply of water was critical for any brewery. Not only was it used in the product itself, but it was also required to carry out the rigorous cleaning program required to ensure sterility during brewing. Great Western used the City of Saskatoon water supply. Water consumed in making the beer was triple filtered to remove all traces of chlorine and bacteria and was treated to adjust the chemical balance to make it suitable for brewing.

Quality Control

Quality control in the brewing industry was critical. In the case of a small regional brewery, it took on even more importance because a single batch of "off" beer could cost the company a significant percentage of its market share. Great Western emphasized quality control. Foremost in the quality control program was the pride employees had in their product. The company had a very strong culture to produce only the best it could. Careful attention was paid to the choice of raw materials, and a careful "hand-crafted" brewing process was used. No compromises were made in the interest of saving costs at the expense of quality. Great Western had a well-equipped quality control lab staffed by an experienced chemist to ensure the finished product met both Great Western and regulatory specifications throughout the process.

Great Western used traditional European brewing methods that placed the emphasis of the operation on the quality and taste of the finished product rather than on the most efficient and cost-effective method. This resulted in a better beer, but it was being sold to an unappreciative market because Saskatchewan consumers did not understand or appreciate the difference in the taste, quality, or tradition associated with European methods of brewing beer. "Beer is beer" was the attitude of most consumers; that explained the industry norm of heavy advertising to influence consumer preference by establishing preferable images.

Production Scheduling

Since Great Western usually operated well below one third of capacity, creative scheduling was used to make the most of time and people. Changeover from bottles to cans or between bottle sizes was time consuming and was normally done only during scheduled downtime between production runs. In any single seven-hour shift, it was not practical to package more than four brands, which meant the minimum economic quantity for packaging was about 3,000 dozen.

Bottling runs were scheduled to allow the line to run for full shifts to minimize setup times. The bottling line ran two to five days a week, as needed to meet demand. The rest of the time was used for equipment maintenance, housekeeping duties, or operation upgrades. As an example, the canning line was installed during downtime with the help of the packaging line workers. This allowed the line to be quickly installed, kept the crew busy, and provided first-hand training that allowed those individuals to operate and troubleshoot the line once it was operational.

Scales of Operation and Overhead

One of the problems Great Western had to address was underutilization of capacity. Great Western's total annual capacity was 262,000 hLs, well above the 1990 production of 55,000 hLs. According to Gil Henderson:

The brewery is capable of producing enough beer to supply 50 percent of the demand in the Saskatchewan market. This underutilization leads to inefficient operations with frequent setup changes and low labor utilization. When you are operating at just above break even, incremental sales are critical. It allows you to reduce the impact of overhead costs. We also need to find other products to allow us to use some of our capacity. Our overhead costs are disproportionately high.

Several options had been explored by Great Western, including producing bottled water, packaging juices or carbonated drinks, leasing out warehouse space, and others, but as yet none of these options had been aggressively pursued. The focus of the effort had been on survival in the beer market.

One other problem had been the stability of demand for the product. It had proved difficult to manage the operation when demand for the product fluctuated widely. The estimated cost structure for production at Great Western is detailed in Exhibit 7.

Production Support for Differentiated and Niche Products

The flexibility of the labor force, the low-cost marketing program, and the ability of the equipment to handle small batch sizes allowed Great Western's operations to quickly and easily accommodate small-run niche products. This production flexibility allowed the company to experiment with new brands and to pursue opportunities with a small window such as "seasonal" brews released to coincide with special occasions. However, Great Western could not package more than six different brands on the same shift. It was not uncommon for some brewers to package several brands from one type of brew. Beer was brewed overstrength. High-alcohol beer was customarily packaged first, then the brew was progressively "cut" with water to produce regular and low-alcohol brands. Since Great Western did not "cut" its beer, it was restricted to 6 brands rather than 12, 18, or more brands by the limited availability of packaging tank space.

Distribution

All beer brewed in the province was distributed by the Saskatchewan Brewers' Association (SBA), a company jointly owned by Labatt and Molson. SBA had warehouses in seven centers across the province. The warehouses received bulk loads from the breweries. Local distribution was done daily from the warehouses to retailers on an order basis. The warehouses also managed the return of empties to the breweries. Beer was distributed to over 1,600 licensed outlets in Saskatchewan, including liquor board stores, bars and nightclubs, restaurants, and special occasion events.

Orders were placed from the warehouse to breweries by computer. Stock levels were usually kept at about two weeks' supply but fluctuated with unexpected demand. Both stock level and sales by brand were reported to the brewery weekly. The breweries were also provided with weekly gross sales quantities, by brewery, for the province; this provided quick and accurate market feedback.

SBA operated on a user-pay, not-for-profit basis. Distribution costs were approximately $1 per dozen. Great Western, however, had to pay a markup since it was provided with full goods distributions and sorting returns on a fee-for-services basis. The rates charged were higher than rates charged to Molson and Labatt.

EXHIBIT 7   Great Western Brewing Company's Estimated
             Cost of Production ($) Per hL (24.4 dozen= 1 hL)

Brewing costs:	
Wages/salaries	$ 3.52
Benefits	0.53
Vacation pay	0.21
Malt	5.00
Hops	0.45
Adjunct	1.50
Supplies	1.60
Total brewed costs	$12.81
Bottling/can costs:	
Wages/salaries	$ 8.11
Benefits	1.22
Vacation pay	0.49
Cost of cans	16.88
Cost of bottle loss	0.60
Crowns	1.20
Labels	1.20
Cartons	8.00
Supplies	1.00
Bottle amortization	1.13
Total packaging cost	$39.83
Total cost of production	$52.64 = 2.16/dozen

Finance

The Great Western Brewing Company Limited had earned $250,000 for the first 10 months ending October 31, 1990. Its products were priced competitively with Labatt and Molson even though Great Western did not share similar economies of scale. From January to March, the company had been getting started and was heavily involved in product development and quality testing.

The finance department at Great Western consisted of the manager of finance, an accounting graduate from the University of Saskatchewan, and an accounting clerk. A computerized financial control system was in use and performance was monitored on a daily basis. A standard costing system was used to manage variances.

Great Western was highly leveraged; over 75 percent of assets were financed by debt. The major creditor was Saskatchewan Economic Development Corporation, owned by the Government of Saskatchewan. Two types of loans were provided by SEDCO. One was a $300,000 participating loan that had no scheduled principal and interst payments; repayments were based on the profitability of Great Western. Twenty-five percent of net cash flow had to be repaid every year to retire the participating loans. Second, a mortgage loan had a five-year maturity and a fixed 12.5 percent interest rate with scheduled principal and interest payments.

The remaining 25 percent of Great Western's assets were financed through equity. The 16 shareholders chose a structure that could take advantage of provincial investment tax credits for personal income tax purposes. Exhibits 8, 9, and 10 present comparative financial performance data for Great Western and its two major Canadian competitors, Labatt and Molson.

EXHIBIT 8   **Comparative Income Statements for Labatt, Molson, and Great Western, 1990**
                   (In thousands of Canadian dollars)

	Labatt	Molson	Great Western
Gross sales	$5,274,000	$2,549,957	$8,306
Operating costs and expenses			
Cost of sales, selling and administration	4,876,000	2,300,030	7,454
Depreciation and amortization	134,000	56,847	295
Net interest expense	33,000	25,784	283
Operating income before income taxes	231,000	167,296	274
Income taxes	72,000	59,809	43
Net income	$ 169,000	$ 107,487	$ 231

Notes:

1. Labatt's fiscal year-end is April 30; Molson's is March 31; and Great Western's, is December 31.
2. Only 32.15% of Labatt's gross revenue but 75.32% of operating income before income taxes were from brewing activities.
3. 53.83% of Molson's gross revenue and 77.31% of operating income before income taxes were from brewing activities.
4. Information regarding Labatt and Molson is from the 1990 annual reports of the respective companies.

EXHIBIT 9   **Comparative Balance Sheets for Labatt, Molson, and Great Western, 1990**
                   (In thousands of Canadian dollars)

	Labatt	Molson	Great Western
Assets			
Current assets			
Cash and accounts receivable	$ 718,000	$ 691,996	$ 910
Inventories	397,000	255,025	1,064
Other current assets	69,000	65,131	61
Total current assets	1,184,000	707,711	2,036
Noncurrent assets			
Property, plant and equipment	1,181,000	538,749	4,787
Other noncurrent assets	581,000	595,453	0
Total noncurrent assets	1,762,000	1,134,202	4,787
Total assets	$2,946,000	$1,841,913	$6,823
Liabilities and Shareholders' Equity			
Current liabilities			
Accounts payable and accrued liabilities	$ 557,000	$ 305,267	$1,194
Current portion of long-term debt	26,000	37,996	394
Other current liabilities	45,000	49,202	0
Total current liabilities	628,000	592,465	1,588
Long-term liabilities			
Long-term debt	544,000	252,960	3,741
Other long-term liabilities	130,000	270,749	0
Total long-term liabilities	674,000	523,709	3,741
Total liabilities	$1,302,000	$1,116,174	$5,329
Shareholders' equity			
Convertible debentures	277,000	0	0
Share capital	595,000	145,907	1,263
Retained earnings	801,000	601,641	231
Cumulative translation adjustment	(29,000)	(21,809)	0
Total shareholders' equity	$1,644,000	$ 725,739	$1,494
Total liabilities and shareholders' equity	$2,946,000	$1,841,913	$6,823

Source: Company annual reports.

EXHIBIT 10   **Comparative Performance Measures for Labatt, Molson, and Great Western, 1990**

	Molson	Labatt	Great Western
Net sales ($000)	$2,549,957	$5,274,000	$ 8,306†
Net income ($000)	$ 117,911	$ 169,000	$ 231†
Number of employees	13,900	16,000	45
Net sales per employee	$ 183,450	$ 339,000	$184,578
Pre-tax profit per employee	$ 12,036	$ 14,438	$ 6,089
Total assets per employee	$ 132,512	$ 184,125	$151,622

†Great Western's net sales and net income are estimates.

Source: From the 1990 annual reports of the respective companies.

THE CROSSROADS

Peter McCann believed Great Western was now at a crossroads. He did not have all the answers regarding the future. One thing was certain, however. Some tough decisions were required if Great Western was to remain competitive. McCann believed the key success factors for a regional brewer were tight control of production costs, broad public product acceptance, flexible operations to respond to changing consumer needs, brand association, and the maintenance of close associations with local markets. Exhibit 11 presents Great Western's sales and profit projections for 1991–94.

McCann walked into the hospitality room of Great Western where the shareholders had assembled for their Friday morning meeting. The conversation settled down as he cleared his throat. "The monthly figures are in, and Gold seems to be stealing market share, about 1 percent of the total market," he announced. Applause broke out as the room basked in the achievement of the launch. McCann continued, "We think that 2 percent market share is achievable. The bad news is our total market share continues to erode for our other brands. I am open for suggestions on where we go from here."

EXHIBIT 11   **Projected Income Statements for Great Western Brewing Company, 1991–94**

	1991	1992	1993	1994
Sales	$8,306	$10,902	$11,446	$12,019
Cost of goods sold	4,074	5,339	5,543	5,753
Distribution and freight	934	1,375	1,589	1,825
Total cost of goods sold	5,008	6,714	7,132	7,577
Gross profit	$3,298	$ 4,188	$ 4,314	$ 4,441
Overhead expenses				
Engineering	$ 415	$ 561	$ 572	$ 584
Brewing	80	108	116	122
Marketing	651	880	943	990
Quality control	28	38	41	43
Administration	430	564	576	587
Salaries and benefits	1,288	1,327	1,353	1,380
Interest	283	243	209	180
Out of Province marketing	0	250	268	281
Total overhead expenses	$3,175	$ 3,971	$ 4,077	$ 4,166
Net operating income	123	216	237	275
Other income	151	70	72	75
Net income before taxes	274	286	309	350
Income taxes	79	84	93	109
Net income	$ 195	$ 203	$ 217	$ 242

Assumptions:

1. 5 percent growth in sales every year.

2. 1991 sales figures have been adjusted by 27.5 percent over 1990 figures to reflect 12 months' operations and inflation.

3. 3 percent inflation in 1991, and 2 percent thereafter.

4. 1.5 percent decrease in COGS each year because of increasing utilization of plant.

5. 1 percent increase in distribution and freight each year because of increasing out-of-province distribution.

6. Interest payment decreases because of amortization of loan.

7. 25 percent tax rate for the first $200,000 profit, and 39 percent on the additional profits.

CRAFTING STRATEGY IN DIVERSIFIED COMPANIES

PEPSICO, INC.

Richard C. Hoffman, University of Delaware*

A quarter of a century has passed since Pepsi-Cola and Frito-Lay merged to form PepsiCo. We've seen dramatic changes, many of which we initiated. . . . Our long-term objective is simple, yet ambitious. We want to be the best consumer products company in the world.

These were part of PepsiCo Chairman and CEO Wayne Calloway's opening remarks to shareholders and employees in early 1990. The company's recent performance indicated it had made progress toward its goal during the previous year. PepsiCo was a diversified company with sales exceeding $15 billion, up 22 percent from the previous year, and net income of $901 million, up 18 percent. These results helped boost the company's stock price 62 percent. During the past five years, PepsiCo's profits had grown at a 26 percent average annual compound rate.

PepsiCo's portfolio included businesses in three different consumer segments: soft drinks (Pepsi-Cola), restaurants (Taco Bell, Kentucky Fried Chicken, and Pizza Hut) and snack foods (e.g., Frito-Lay). PepsiCo competed aggressively in each of its industries by embracing change and striving to make its products synonymous with quality. PepsiCo's management emphasized the following three strategic themes to build a competitive advantage in each consumer segment.

- Major brands with leadership position in large, growing markets.
- Sophisticated, yet efficient, operating systems.
- Improved cash flow for low-risk, high-return investments in each industry segment.

These strategic themes reflected PepsiCo's well-known marketing skills and lesser known operations and distribution capabilities. As one industry analyst noted, "PepsiCo's strength is that they have the ability to manufacture and distribute billions of little things increasingly efficiently."

Each of PepsiCo's consumer businesses had somewhat different industry environments and presented varying opportunities and threats for the firm. Moreover, there were differences in the competitive positions of each business unit in their respective industries. These and other issues concerning each of PepsiCo's business units are described in the following sections.

SOFT-DRINK SEGMENT

The soft-drink segment was the oldest and largest business in PepsiCo's portfolio. The Pepsi-Cola Company manufactured and marketed soft-drink concentrates including Pepsi-Cola, Mountain Dew, and Slice, as well as other

*Copyright © 1991 Richard C. Hoffman. The assistance of Karyn Hodge in the preparation of this case is gratefully acknowledged.

brands worldwide. The Pepsi-Cola unit also operated soft-drink bottling companies in the United States. It was the second largest soft-drink producer in the world (behind Coca-Cola). Pepsi-Cola products were popular with consumers and contributed heavily to PepsiCo's bottom line.

The Industry

In 1990, the soft-drink industry consisted of firms that produced and distributed nonalcoholic, flavored carbonated beverages. Among nonalcoholic substitutes, coffee and tea were lagging in the market; coffee consumption had declined nearly 33 percent in the past 20 years. Soft drinks, however, had been one of the best beverage performers, posting a sales increase of 5.6 percent, to $38.7 billion or 31 percent of all beverage sales. In the United States, soft drinks accounted for one quarter of all beverage consumption; this market had grown at a rate of 2.5 percent, with a projected 4.5 percent growth over the next five years. In 1988, U.S. consumption of soft drinks increased for the 13th consecutive year, rising to 50.8 billion gallons (see Exhibit 1). This was nearly two 12-ounce cans per day for every man, woman, and child in America.

Much of the increase was attributable to higher per capita consumption, which had been rising 3.5 percent annually. Experts expected total volume growth in the United States to slow to 3 to 4 percent for 1989 because of higher prices charged to cover rising costs for raw materials and packaging.

Much of the volume and per capita growth over the past seven years had resulted from new product introductions. New products were increasingly becoming a key success factor in the face of changing consumer preferences. New products introduced since 1981 accounted for 15 percent of the industry's volume in 1987. The only notable new products that had lost momentum during this period were juice-added soft drinks. In 1987, the market share of all juice-added soft drinks declined to 4.5 percent from 4.9 percent in 1986. Although a plethora of new flavors had been introduced in the market, the cola flavor category was still the American favorite, accounting for 69.3 percent of U.S. consumption in 1989. Other popular flavors included orange, lemon-lime, root beer, and cherry-cola.

Demographic changes in the United States had helped to create new segments. As the baby boomers aged and became more health conscious, so did their tastes in soft drinks. These trends created an increasing demand for diet, low-calorie, and caffeine-free soft drinks. The unit growth for these increasingly popular beverages were in the double digits versus the lackluster 2 to 4 percent volume growth for the regular sugar-flavored colas. The compounded annual volume growth rate for diet soft drinks had been running at 10 percent. In 1989, diet soft drinks accounted for 28 percent of the U.S. market, up from 23 percent just five years ago.

The structure of the soft-drink industry consisted of two key value activities that had traditionally been performed by different groups of firms. The production of the concentrated syrup base for soft drinks was produced by the well-known firms in the industry such as Coca-Cola, Pepsi-Cola, and Royal Crown. The bottling and distribution of soft drinks was handled by independent bottlers, many of which were franchisees of the large concentrate producers. In the past three years, the industry had become increasingly consolidated as concentrate producers such as Pepsi-Cola and Coca-Cola

EXHIBIT 1   Per Capita U.S. Liquid Consumption   *(In gallons)*

Beverage	1970	1975	1980	1985	1987	1988
Soft drinks	27.4	32.4	40.7	46.8	49.2	50.8
Coffee	33.5	29.5	26.9	25.5	23.6	22.4
Milk	26.9	24.9	21.5	20.6	20.2	20.2
Tea	5.7	6.4	7.1	6.5	6.0	5.9
Juices	7.2	8.5	9.8	10.3	10.6	10.8
Beer*	30.7	34.7	37.0	34.6	34.4	34.0
Wine*	2.2	2.7	3.2	3.0	2.7	2.6
Distilled spirits*	3.0	3.3	3.0	2.6	2.3	2.2
Subtotal	136.5	142.4	149.2	149.9	149.1	149.0
Assumed water consumption	58.5	53.4	49.7	46.9	46.1	46.1
Total	195.0	195.8	198.9	196.8	195.2	195.2

*Based on population age 21 years and over.
Source: *S&P Industry Surveys.*

acquired their bottlers' distribution business to gain distribution economies of scale.

Coca-Cola was still the leader in the industry with a market share of 40.5 percent. It was the market share leader in all but one of the primary distribution channels through which soft drinks were sold. In food stores, which accounted for an estimated 40.6 percent of total industry volume, Coca-Cola Company led PepsiCo by 32.4 to 30.6 percent. However, Pepsi-Cola remained the leading soft drink in supermarkets with a 14.8 percent share in 1988 versus Classic Coke's 14.3 percent. Exhibits 2, 3, and 4 show the relevant competitors in the U.S. industry, their total market shares, the market shares of various brands, and the market shares by distribution channel.

Growing consolidation and relatively slow market growth had contributed to increased competitive intensity in the soft-drink industry. This resulted in fierce competition for market share among the major concentrate producers. Advertising, promotion, and new product introductions became keys to competitive success by the end of the decade. However, price competition to gain market share was also used with increased frequency during the 1980s. In general, competitors were finding it difficult to differentiate their products and maintain brand loyalty in such an environment.

The international soft-drink markets were very promising. The international industry volume was 13 billion cases in 1989, about 70 percent larger than the U.S. market. Although per capita consumption was relatively low, it was expected to increase as soft drinks became more available and widely promoted abroad. International volume was forecast to grow at 9 to 11 percent over 1990–91 and to exceed that rate during 1992–93.

Coca-Cola had been the leading soft-drink producer worldwide since the end of World War II. Its international sales topped $4.7 billion in 1989, up 5.4 percent from the previous year; this represented 65 percent of its total soft-drink sales. PepsiCo was a distant second in international markets but was also less dependent on international sales.

EXHIBIT 2   **U.S. Soft-Drink Corporate Market Shares, 1986–1990**   *(In percent)*

Company	1986	1987	1988	1989	1990
Coca-Cola Co.	39.9%	40.3%	40.5%	40.0%	40.4%
PepsiCo	29.8%	30.2%	30.7%	31.7%	31.8%
Dr Pepper	5.3%	5.4%	5.6%	5.6%	5.8%
Seven-Up	5.1%	5.3%	4.9%	4.3%	4.8%
Cadbury Schweppes	4.2%	3.7%	3.5%	3.1%	3.2%
Royal Crown Cos.	3.1%	2.9%	2.7%	2.8%	2.6%
A&W Brands	1.2%	1.6%	2.0%	2.2%	NA

Source: *S&P Industry Surveys.*

EXHIBIT 3   **Leading U.S. Soft-Drink Brands, 1986–1990**

Brand	Market Share in Percent				
	1986	1987	1988	1989	1990
Coca-Cola Co. Classic	18.9%	19.8%	20.1%	19.5%	19.4%
Pepsi-Cola	18.5%	18.8%	18.7%	17.8%	17.3%
Diet Coke	7.1%	7.7%	8.2%	8.8%	9.1%
Diet Pepsi	4.3%	4.8%	5.2%	5.7%	6.2%
Dr Pepper	4.1%	4.3%	4.5%	4.6%	4.8%
Sprite	3.6%	3.5%	3.6%	3.6%	3.6%
Mountain Dew	2.6%	2.9%	3.2%	3.6%	3.8%
7UP	3.5%	3.4%	3.1%	3.0%	2.9%
Caffeine Free Diet Coke	1.4%	1.7%	2.0%	2.4%	2.6%
RC Cola	1.7%	1.6%	1.4%	1.6%	1.4%
New Coke	2.3%	1.6%	1.4%	1.4%	1.4%
Caffeine Free Diet Pepsi	1.3%	1.3%	1.4%	1.2%	1.4%

Source: *S&P Industry Surveys.*

EXHIBIT 4   **U.S. Market Shares by Distribution Channel, 1990**

Channel (Percent of Market Share)	Coca-Cola	PepsiCo	Dr Pepper	7-Up	Royal Crown	Other
Food stores (40.6%)	32.4%	30.6%	3.6%	6.5%	3.6%	23.3%
Convenience stores (3.8%)	36.3%	38.8%	5.2%	5.3%	2.7%	11.7%
Drugstores (1.7%)	48.0%	30.3%	3.0%	5.8%	2.2%	10.7%
Mass merchandisers (1.3%)	42.1%	42.0%	3.1%	4.1%	4.1%	4.6%
Fountain (22.1%)	59.8%	26.2%	6.1%	2.9%	1.7%	3.3%
Vending (12.2%)	45.4%	34.0%	7.5%	4.1%	2.1%	6.9%
Other (18.3%)	33.4%	40.0%	7.2%	6.0%	2.8%	10.6%
Overall (100%)	40.3%	30.2%	5.4%	5.3%	2.9%	15.9%

Source: *S&P Industry Surveys.*

The Pepsi-Cola Company

Pepsi-Cola brands accounted for about $14 billion in U.S. retail sales, or about one third of the $43 billion U.S. retail sales of soft drinks in 1989. These were impressive figures for a firm that began in 1903 when Caleb D. Bradham, a pharmacist, started to market his invention in North Carolina. In 1990, Pepsi-Cola was the second largest soft-drink producer in the world and was ranked 10th among the most recognized brand names in the world (4th in the United States) among 6,000 brands surveyed by Lander Associates, a San Francisco consulting firm. In 1990, Pepsi-Cola Company's sales had grown 3.5 percent versus 2.5 percent for the industry as a whole, while its international sales growth exceeded 4 percent.

Pepsi-Cola brands and their respective shares of worldwide retail sales included: Pepsi ($13.4 billion), Diet Pepsi ($3.3 billion), Mountain Dew ($1.8 billion) and 7UP ($1.1 billion). All of these brands were available in 150 countries and together accounted for a 15 percent market share outside the United States.

PepsiCo believed in building sales and setting the standard for consumer excitement in the soft-drink industry by continuously fine-tuning its advertising, distribution, and marketing to improve performance. Four key strategies were used to increase sales. Pepsi tried to create market excitement by being identified with youth, refreshment, and enjoyment. One of its most popular advertising programs that reflected this theme was the "Pepsi—a new generation" campaign. Pepsi's second strategy had been to sharpen its focus on Diet Pepsi and capitalize on the expanding diet soft-drink market. PepsiCo was also trying to expand the market for Mountain Dew, the seventh largest soft-drink brand in the United States. For the past two decades, Pepsi had been trying to develop a unique taste and image for this product. Pepsi's fourth strategy was to expand sales by developing new product categories and serving different consumer groups. New products included a reformulation of Diet Pepsi, Diet Mountain Dew, H2oh! (to compete with seltzers), Pepsi-AM (a morning soft drink), and Mountain Dew Sport.

Pepsi-Cola had one of the largest distribution networks for its soft drinks, with more than 900 company-operated and franchised bottling plants worldwide. By acquiring 29 domestic bottling franchises in 1989, Pepsi owned operations that distributed 48.5 percent of its U.S. volume. In addition, Pepsi had equity interests in 77 other franchises, representing another 20 percent of its bottling business. Pepsi continued to consolidate its distribution systems to improve operating efficiency and better serve soft-drink retailers. Moreover, this large distribution network provided a competitive advantage in introducing new products quickly to the marketplace.

To further improve operating efficiencies, Pepsi had developed long-term relationships with suppliers and introduced new manufacturing and warehousing techniques. Pepsi expected to save an estimated $25 million by cutting costs and improving operating efficiencies in these areas. Furthermore, in 1989, Pepsi-Cola decentralized its domestic soft-drink operations into four geographic divisions, which were united by a national marketing program. The international division was also reorganized into six divisions to improve response to local opportunities.

THE RESTAURANT BUSINESS GROUP

The restaurant group was comprised of three worldwide franchise systems: Pizza Hut, Taco Bell, and Kentucky Fried Chicken. By combining popular foods with quick service, the three restaurant chains had provided a major source of growth. In 1989, the combined sales growth of PepsiCo's restaurant segment in the United States was 14 percent, twice the industry average.

The Fast-Food Industry

Over the past 20 years, Americans had been spending a rising portion of their food dollars at restaurants. Demographic factors, such as more two-income families, more women in the work force, and a decrease in the number of children to feed at home, had made eating out an attractive option. In 1989, U.S. consumers spent about $167 billion at roughly 400,000 restaurants; this was a 6.6 percent increase over 1988. Americans spent about 44 percent of their food dollars at restaurants in 1990, up from 33 percent in 1980. According to the National Restaurant Association (NRA), Americans eat out an average of 3.7 times per week, with an average per person check of $3.53.

For the past several years, the restaurant industry had been suffering from internal difficulties including market saturation, high labor expenses, and encroachments from grocery store deli counters and microwavable products. After a decade or more of rapid growth, some of the large chains were beginning to show signs of retrenchment and were scaling down their operations. By 1990, 20 of the 100 largest U.S. restaurant chains had fewer outlets than two years before.

New products, home delivery, and cost-cutting measures had been implemented to offset some of these industry trends and to increase sales among fast-food restaurants. Salads and buffets were among the important new products many fast-food restaurants had added in recent years to increase sales. Future menu options were likely to be targeted toward the increased health consciousness of an aging population.

Improving service, quality, and customer convenience were key factors for maintaining a competitive edge in the restaurant industry. An increasing portion of meals purchased at restaurants were for off-premise consumption. This reflected both hurried life-styles and a desire to avoid food preparation at home. According to the NRA, restaurant traffic for carryout food rose 28 percent between 1982 and 1987, compared with only a 5 percent rise in traffic for on-premise eating. Off-premise business accounted for 45 percent of restaurant traffic in 1988, up from 34 percent in 1984. This trend had important implications for fast-food restaurants. Many catered to this quick service preference by emphasizing take-out service and home delivery. Drive-through windows had become very common, and this trend had opened a sizable market for products that could be distributed through a home-delivery service.

Controlling food and labor costs represented a significant part of operating efficiency in restaurants. Food and beverage costs accounted for 33 percent of each sales dollar at restaurants, excluding tips. Payroll expenses represented about 26 percent of each sales dollar and roughly 2 percent more went for employee benefits. Federal legislation regarding the minimum wage and

EXHIBIT 5   Franchise Restaurant Chain Sales in United States by Menu Type
                 (In millions of dollars)

Major Sales Activity	1987	1988	1989	1990*
Chicken	$ 4,822	$ 4,946	$ 5,147	$ 5,666
Burgers/franks/roast beef, etc.	27,257	31,986	34,443	37,570
Pizza	8,126	9,607	10,278	11,488
Mexican	3,079	2,976	3,101	4,003
Seafood	NA	723	754	837
Pancakes/waffles	1,309	1,263	1,405	1,563
Steak/full menu	9,811	11,338	12,183	13,687
Sandwich/other	956	1,442	1,782	2,315
Total	$55,360	$64,281	$69,093	$77,129

*Estimates

Source: *Franchising in the Economy* (International Franchising Association, Educational Foundation/Horwath International, 1990).

employee health benefits affected these operating costs substantially. Fixed costs in the restaurant industry represented sizable expense items—rent, utilities, and advertising. The restaurant industry netted an average of 7 percent return on sales. Profitability levels varied depending on the level of sales and the efficiency of each restaurant outlet.

Distribution was an increasingly important competitive factor in the restaurant industry. Franchising had become an important vehicle for growth in restaurant sales. About 40 percent of U.S. restaurant sales were by franchise chains. By offering restaurant franchises, companies could rapidly expand a brand and a new concept without bearing the full costs of acquiring land, buildings, and equipment. In a franchising relationship, these costs were generally borne by the franchisee, who paid a royalty of about 3 to 5 percent of sales to the parent company and also contributed about 4 percent toward advertising. In return, the franchisee received brand-name recognition, training, and marketing support. Data on restaurant chains was reported three ways: (1) company-owned, data on units directly owned by the parent company; (2) franchisee, data on units owned by franchisees only; or (3) system-wide, data on both company-owned and franchised units.

In 1989, franchise restaurant chains produced $69.1 billion in U.S. sales, up 7.5 percent from 1988. This represented 41 percent of industry sales. The number of franchise chain restaurants had tripled since the 1970s, and currently, there were over 94,000 outlets in the United States. During this same time period, the population only increased by 12 percent. It was, therefore, easy to understand why many less profitable firms in the industry had been forced to close. Exhibit 5 summarizes franchise restaurant chain sales by type of menu (e.g., burgers, chicken, etc.).

Fast-food restaurants were projected to have sales of $77.1 billion during 1990. The four biggest fast-food segments by menu offering were hamburger, pizza, chicken, and Mexican restaurants. Chains emphasizing hamburgers, hot dogs, or roast beef remained the largest part of the U.S. franchise restaurant industry. Within this segment, McDonald's market share was 36 percent compared to 15 percent for runner-up Burger King and 8 percent and 9 percent for Hardee's and Wendy's, respectively. In 1989, McDonald's 8,027 outlets accounted for 17.4 percent of all sales by U.S. franchise restaurant chains and 7.2 percent of total restaurant spending.

Pizza franchise chains had about 20,275 outlets with estimated sales of about $10.2 billion in 1989. This figure was up about 26 percent from two years earlier. The leading chains—Pizza Hut, Domino's, and privately owned Little Caesar's—accounted for more than 50 percent of segment sales. This segment grew at a compounded annual rate of 10.7 percent during 1984–89. Exhibit 6 gives systemwide sales figures for the major competitors in this segment.

The chicken segment, with estimated total sales over $5 billion in 1989, was led by Kentucky Fried Chicken. Kentucky Fried Chicken's combined company-owned and franchised domestic sales represented 50 percent of the chicken segment. The second and third largest chains, Church's Fried Chicken and Popeye's Famous Fried Chicken, merged in 1989. Their combined systemwide U.S. sales were over $1 billion. Other sizable chicken chains appear in Exhibit 6. The chicken restaurant segment grew at a compounded annual rate of 4.2 percent during 1984–89.

The Mexican food segment grew at a compounded annual rate of 11.6 percent as people looked for an alternative to the traditional products offered by other chains during 1984–89. This segment produced roughly $3 billion in sales for 1989. Mexican chains were expanding, and there were many regional chains (see Exhibit 6).

Differentiation in fast foods was created mainly through new products, advertising, and promotion. McDonald's was by far the largest U.S. television advertiser among restaurant chains, spending more than twice as much as runners-up Burger King and Kentucky Fried Chicken.

As the U.S. market became more competitive, franchised restaurants continued to expand into international markets. Thirteen percent of all U.S. franchisers had locations abroad, totaling almost 7,000 units by the beginning of 1990. The most popular international markets in terms of number of units were: Japan (1,872), Europe (1,498), and Canada (1,338). International expansion was expected to be a major source of growth for the industry in the 1990s. International markets for fast food grew about 13 percent during 1989 and were projected to grow twice as fast as the U.S. market over the next two years. Fast-food markets outside the United States were not highly segmented. All of the leading international competitors in each menu segment were the leading U.S.-based firms. McDonald's, Kentucky Fried Chicken, and Pizza Hut had the largest international operations. In 1989, McDonald's 2,892 international outlets produced sales of $5.5 billion.

PepsiCo's Restaurants

PepsiCo was the largest restaurant conglomerate in the world in 1990. Its three chains combined, Kentucky Fried Chicken (KFC), Pizza Hut, and Taco Bell, had over 18,000 units with worldwide system sales of $11.5 billion in 1989. All three restaurant chains were ranked among the top 12 chains, which contributed 70 percent of the industry's growth in recent years. A summary of operating results for PepsiCo's company-owned restaurants is provided in Exhibit 7.

EXHIBIT 6   Fast-Food Restaurant Sales, Units, Ranking: Industry, Industry Leaders, and Leaders in the Chicken, Pizza, and Mexican Segments, 1988 and 1989

| | Sales (in millions) Systemwide | | | Establishments Systemwide | | | |
| | Franchisees | | Company-Owned Worldwide | Franchised | | Company-Owned Worldwide | Industry Sales Rank |
	United States	International		United States	International		
Industry							
1989	$69,094	NA	$23,439	94,285	7,206*	27,761	
1988	64,280	NA	22,277	90,345	6,996	27,305	
Industry Leaders							
McDonald's							
1989	12,012	5,523	4,637	2,800	2,850	8,320	1
1988	11,385	4,678	4,196	2,600	2,607	7,913	
Burger King							
1989	5,035	664	969	5,387	655	873	2
1988	4,942	531	826	5,210	263	818	
Chicken Segment							
Kentucky Fried Chicken							
1989	$ 3,000	$2,400	$ 1,331	4,961	3,000	2,112	4
1988	2,900	2,100	1,209	4,897	2,862	1,571	
Church's							
1989	530	40*	322	1,111	102	807	26
1988	559	30*	324	1,281	87	990	
Popeye's							
1989	525	—	85	739	—	114	27
1988	485	—	70	715	—	102	
Chick-Fil-A							
1989	264	9*	NA	411	NA	NA	56
1988	232	8*	NA	386	NA	NA	
Chicken Segment							
Grandy's							
1989	$ 181	—	NA	195	—	107	72
1988	175	—	NA	189	—	NA	
Pizza Segment							
Pizza Hut							
1989	$ 3,300	$ 785*	$ 2,454	6,243	1,167	3,232	3
1988	2,800	583*	2,014	5,707	955	2,984	
Domino's Pizza							
1989	2,500	15*	588	5,185	NA	1,382	7
1988	2,300	7*	623	4,597	298	1,370	
Little Caesar's							
1989	1,130	70	300	2,632	115	687	13
1988	908	92	243	2,124	251	578	

*Estimated; NA = not available.

Kentucky Fried Chicken, which PepsiCo acquired in October 1986, had domestic system sales of about $3 billion in 1989 and accounted for 50 percent of the U.S. chicken market. With almost 8,000 units, it had more than three times as many U.S. restaurants as the next largest chicken chain. The company and its franchisees operated in 57 countries with international sales of $2.3 billion. During 1989, KFC opened its 3,000th unit abroad, making it the largest U.S. franchised restaurant chain abroad in terms of units.

EXHIBIT 6   (*concluded*)

| | Sales (in millions) Systemwide | | | Establishments Systemwide | | | |
| | Franchisees | | Company-Owned Worldwide | Franchised | | Company-Owned Worldwide | Industry Sales Rank |
	United States	International		United States	International		
Round Table							
1989	$ 295	—	—	540	—	—	48
1988	267	—	—	535	—	—	
Showbiz Pizza							
1989	263	NA	NA	248	NA	130	58
1988	261	NA	NA	258	NA	NA	
Pizza Inn							
1989	260	NA	NA	468	NA	225	59
1988	295	NA	NA	666	NA	NA	
Mexican Segment							
Taco Bell							
1989	$2,000	$35*	$1,466	3,082	43	1,784	8
1988	1,600	37*	1,157	2,878	52	1,716	
Chi Chi's							
1989	431	61*	323	191	NA	NA	32
1988	423	18*	299	187	NA	122	
El Torito							
1989	379	NA	NA	181	NA	NA	37
1988	415	NA	NA	188	NA	NA	
Chili's							
1989	369	—	266	193	—	138	39
1988	298	—	218	159	—	NA	
Del Taco/Nangles							
1989	200	12*	NA	350	NA	NA	66
1988	210	10*	NA	380	NA	NA	

*Estimated; NA = not available; — = not relevant.

Sources: *PepsiCo Annual Report; Restaurant Business*, March 20 and November 20, 1989 and 1990; and T. Dixon, *The 1990 Franchise Annual* (Info Press Inc.).

EXHIBIT 7   **PepsiCo's Restaurants—Operating Results, 1988 and 1989**

	Kentucky Fried Chicken	Pizza Hut	Taco Bell
Sales (millions)*			
1989	$1,331	$2,454	$1,466
1988	1,209	2,014	1,157
Operating profits (millions)			
1989	$100	$209	$113
1988	117	153	82

*Worldwide sales (company-owned outlets only).

Source: *PepsiCo Annual Report*.

Pizza Hut, acquired in 1977, was the leading pizza chain in the world and had a 32 percent market share of the $10 billion U.S. franchised pizza market. For 1984–89, Pizza Hut had been the fastest growing major international franchise restaurant with compounded annual growth of 25 percent in units and 30 percent in sales. In that period, Pizza Hut entered 27 countries, including 5 in 1989. It operated internationally in 54 countries and was the leading pizza chain in 46 of these markets. Pizza Hut was expected to continue rapid international expansion.

Taco Bell, acquired in 1978, was the leading chain in the Mexican food segment, with only a few regional competitors. Its systemwide domestic sales of $2 billion represented 64 percent of the $3.1 billion Mexican fast-food industry segment. Although Taco Bell operated only 43 units in seven international markets systemwide, PepsiCo was trying to expand Taco Bell internationally through continuous investment. Company-owned restaurants of Pizza Hut and Taco Bell produced $820 million in international sales in 1989.

PepsiCo used several competitive weapons to improve its position in the restaurant industry. To keep abreast of the fast-food industry and the trends toward healthier food and take-out service, PepsiCo began providing consumers with value-oriented menus. Taco Bell's value menu, introduced in 1988, helped to increase sales and profits. Second, PepsiCo emphasized new varieties of existing brands (e.g., meat lovers' pizza) and new products (e.g., KFC's hot wings) to help stimulate sales. Advertising also played an important part in this strategy. During 1986–87, PepsiCo spent $70 million on a national advertising campaign for Taco Bell titled "the cure for the common meal."

Expanding distribution by using innovative methods for reaching new consumers in different locations was also part of PepsiCo's strategy to increase sales and market share. Pizza Hut had been expanding its home-delivery segment and profits from delivery units have doubled. Its U.S. delivery share grew 13 percent, and by 1990, Pizza Hut had 2,600 points of distribution, which PepsiCo wished to double over the next four years. In addition, Pizza Hut Express Kiosks, which could be located in cafeterias, airports, schools, and stadiums, were being test-marketed with fairly good results. Finally, PepsiCo added 1,130 new restaurants both in the United States and abroad during 1989.

PepsiCo's marketing and distribution strategies for each of its three chains were driven by the perspective that competition existed not only in a company's own segment but also in every other alternative prepared food from the grocery store delis to home cooking. The company's goal was to make PepsiCo restaurant food as widely available as possible.

SNACK-FOOD SEGMENT

PepsiCo's snack-food segment primarily manufactured and marketed snack chips under the Frito-Lay brand in the United States and other brands abroad.

The Industry

Snack foods was a $35 billion industry in the United States and included candy, chips, cookies, and crackers. Americans' annual consumption of potato, corn, and tortilla chips, cheese puffs, pretzels, nuts, and ready-to-eat popcorn exceeded 13 pounds in 1989 compared to 9 pounds in 1979. Retail sales of these snacks climbed to $9.6 billion. The U.S. snack-food industry had an annual growth rate of 5 percent compared to an 8 percent growth rate internationally. International snack chip retail sales totaled $9.5 billion with an annual per capita consumption of less than 11 pounds. This was bound to increase due to market growth and promotional efforts by U.S. snack companies that were expanding into this growing segment. Industry profit margins averaged 4.6 percent.

Frito-Lay, Borden Inc., and Procter & Gamble were the leading national marketers of salty snacks in the United States. Exhibit 8 shows the relative U.S. market shares of the competitors in this segment. The national companies faced about 100 to 150 local competitors throughout the United States. Frito-Lay was clearly the leader in the salty snack-food segment, with Borden achieving only one third of Frito-Lay's $3.2 billion in sales.

Packaging, distribution, advertising, and new product introductions were the keys to success in this industry. Consumer tastes were constantly changing, and companies had to keep up with changing preferences to maintain a profitable level of sales and sustain market share. In addition, companies had to satisfy many regional preferences; for example, hot and spicy products were in greater demand in the southwestern United States. Health trends had made light products (i.e., with less oil) more appealing. Packaging was of great importance because of the perishable nature of the product. It was also used to increase sales by redesigning a maturing product's package or developing innovative ways to seal packages for freshness.

Internationally, snack foods was a small but growing market. Frito-Lay and Borden were the only two key international players in an industry dominated by local firms. The bulk of the salty snack market outside the United States was in Europe. Both competitors had entered several European markets. Borden was strong in Spain, had entered the United Kingdom in 1988 via acquisition of Sooner Snacks, and held the No. 1 position in sweet snacks in West Germany. Borden also had operations in Canada, Asia, and Latin America. In 1989, Borden's international snack-food sales totaled $222.2 million, up from $187 million the previous year. The 1989 figure represented 18.5 percent of the firm's total snack-food sales of $1.2 billion.

PepsiCo's Snack Businesses

PepsiCo merged with Frito-Lay in 1965. Frito-Lay was PepsiCo's most profitable division, accounting for 35 percent of company sales and 42 percent of its profits in 1989. Frito-Lay had the largest share of sales in the $7 billion salty snack-food market. It was four times the size of its largest competitor, Borden Inc. In 1989, Frito-Lay's pound volume grew 7 percent and sales of U.S. products grew 9 percent.

Frito-Lay's worldwide products included Doritos, Ruffles, Lay's, Fritos, and Chee-tos. Its product line also included Tostitos and a ready-to-eat popcorn, recently acquired from Smartfoods. Doritos was Frito-Lay's largest brand with estimated worldwide retail sales of $1.2 billion for 1989. This brand faced no single large competitor but did have competition from many regional brands,

EXHIBIT 8   U.S. Salty Snack Market, 1986–1988

	1986	1987	1988
Total sales (000,000)	$2.20	$2.23	$2.30
Market share			
Frito-Lay	40%	40.0%	37.5%
Borden	11%	11.0%	14.6%
Procter & Gamble	7%	8.8%	9.0%
All other brands	42%	40.2%	38.9%

Source: *Business Week*, May 22, 1989.

EXHIBIT 9   Retail Sales of Frito-Lay's Worldwide Snack Brands, 1990

Lay's Potato Chips	$700 million
Ruffles	$1 billion
Fritos	$600 million
Chee-tos	$500 million
Doritos	$1.2 billion

Source: *PepsiCo Annual Report*, 1990.

especially on price. Doritos accounted for one half of the $2 billion corn chip market. Eight of the top 10 selling snack chips in the United States were made by Frito-Lay. Frito-Lay's worldwide brands and estimated worldwide retail sales are presented in Exhibit 9.

Frito-Lay's international snack-food businesses operated in 19 countries and held a 25 percent market share of the total international snack-chip market. In 1989, PepsiCo acquired Smiths Crisps Ltd. and Walker Crisps Ltd. in the United Kingdom for $1.34 billion. These acquisitions made PepsiCo the leading snack-food company in Europe.

PepsiCo had implemented three strategies to keep sales growing in this segment. Product line extensions were developed by introducing new flavors of existing brands. These line extensions were profitable because they basically involved seasoning changes that were adjusted to satisfy consumer preferences in different regions. Each line extension was then promoted not merely as a new flavor but as a new product. Another strategy was creating new products and new snack segments to meet evolving consumer needs. Frito-Lay recently introduced a new line of light snacks with one third less oil than regular brands. Frito-Lay also planned to introduce multigrain products made from whole wheat, corn, and other natural grains. Due to the company's reputation, these products could easily be distributed to stores that were willing to create the additional shelf space to feature the new products. The third strategy PepsiCo had created for this segment was to open new markets through packaging and distribution. An example of this was packaging chips in canisters, which were sold predominantly through drugstores.

Marketing programs were national in scope but were executed locally to respond quickly to area opportunities and develop customized marketing approaches. Advertising was important for competing in the snack-food industry. Frito-Lay spent $60.2 million on advertising in 1985 and the figure had increased substantially since then.

Frito-Lay was continuously trying to improve the way it managed operations. During 1989, it decentralized U.S. operations into four geographic units to improve overall efficiency and to increase local impact. Technology had also helped to improve competitiveness. Frito-Lay was one of the first companies to introduce handheld computers for its sales force. This enabled the sales force to generate specific sales data on a particular store or city daily. The market data were also entered into the company computer system. This allowed sales managers to spot problems and react quickly to competitive conditions.

Frito-Lay had developed a competitive advantage through its distribution network and its exceptional 10,000-person sales force. Frito-Lay delivered direct from its manufacturing plants to individual stores, eliminating the cost of warehousing operations.

FUTURE AREAS OF EMPHASIS

PepsiCo entered the 1990s a vigorous competitor in each of its consumer segments. Each of its businesses was a major player in its respective industry. The recent financial performance of PepsiCo's business groups as well as of the corporation as a whole appear in Exhibits 10 and 11.

In recent years, the firm had emphasized the transfer of skills and ideas from one consumer segment to another to obtain the best from each segment. For example, distribution know-how derived from both the soft-drink and snack segments were used in the restaurant segment to attempt to make chicken, pizza, and tacos as readily available as Doritos and Pepsi. Pepsi-Cola's efforts to integrate forward into bottling and distribution had been stimulated, in part, by Frito-Lay's success in selling directly to supermarkets. Moreover, PepsiCo planned to use its growing snack-food distribution system in Europe to increase soft-drink sales in the region. Wayne Calloway had fostered these linkages between segments by transferring managers back and forth among them. For example, John Cranor, the former head of Pepsi's eastern U.S. soft-drink business, was transferred to run Kentucky Fried Chicken, while Frito-Lay's new chief, Roger Enrico, had transferred to that position from Pepsi Worldwide Beverage Division.

PepsiCo's consumer businesses each faced increased domestic competition, especially in soft drinks and restaurants. Nevertheless, all three segments had growing international opportunities. The location of PepsiCo's major international subsidiaries (wholly owned or joint ventures) is depicted in Exhibit 12. These subsidiaries were responsible for coordinating activities and issuing franchises in their respective regions. Although PepsiCo had both company-owned and franchised bottling companies and restaurants in many more countries, these units reported to one of the subsidiaries depicted in the exhibit. The proper location of the international subsidiaries was important to the execution and stability of PepsiCo's international strategy.

EXHIBIT 10 **Financial Performance of PepsiCo's Consumer Segments, 1987–1989**
(In millions)

	Soft Drinks	Restaurants	Snack Food	Corporate
Domestic sales				
1989	$4,623.3	$4,684.8	$3,211.3	
1988	3,667.0	3,950.3	2,933.3	
1987	3,112.9	3,499.5	2,782.8	
Foreign sales				
1989	$1,153.4	$ 565.9	$1,003.7	
1988	971.2	430.4	581.0	
1987	862.7	341.0	419.2	
Operating domestic profits				
1989	$ 586.9	$ 361.8	$ 668.3	
1988	409.5	307.0	587.3	
1987	363.1	281.6	520.0	
Operating foreign profits				
1989	$ 103.2	$ 59.4	$ 152.6	
1988	53.4	44.4	49.0	
1987	46.5	37.8	27.6	
Assets				
1989	$6,241.9	$3,095.2	$3,366.4	$2,423.2
1988	4,074.4	3,105.1	1,641.2	2,314.6
1987	2,779.8	2,782.9	1,632.5	1,827.5
Depreciation				
1989	$ 306.3	$ 269.9	$ 189.3	$ 6.5
1988	195.7	271.3	156.8	5.5
1987	166.5	237.1	154.1	5.3
Capital expenditures				
1989	$ 267.8	$ 424.6	$ 257.9	$ 9.2
1988	198.4	344.2	172.6	14.9
1987	202.0	370.8	195.6	6.6

Source: *PepsiCo Annual Report.*

As Wayne Calloway pondered the corporate goal of becoming the best consumer products company in the world, he could not help but think the only certainty in the company's markets was change. In particular, consumer interests and tastes changed rapidly. In such an environment, management had to make investments that would keep the firm on the cutting edge. Allocating the firm's finite resources to achieve the overall corporate goal was not easy. The firm's differing growth opportunities in each industry had to be balanced against those available in the domestic versus international markets. As Exhibit 12 indicates, the choice of international markets involved additional trade-offs between growth and country risk. Moreover, Calloway recognized that substantial resources would be required simply to maintain the strong positions the firm had achieved in each industry.

EXHIBIT 11   **Financial Summary for PepsiCo and Subsidiaries, 1984–1989**   *(In millions except per share; shareholder and employee amounts, unaudited)*

	Compounded Growth Rates 5 Year 1984–89	1989	1988	1987	1986	1985	1984
Summary of Operations							
Net sales	16.6%	$15,242.4	$12,533.2	$11,018.1	$9,017.1	$7,584.5	$7,058.6
Sales and operating expenses		13,459.5	11,184.0	9,890.5	8,187.9	6,802.4	6,479.3
Interest expenses		609.6	344.2	294.6	261.4	195.2	204.9
Interest income		(177.2)	(122.2)	(112.6)	(122.7)	(96.4)	(86.1)
Income from operations before taxes		1,350.5	1,127.2	945.6	690.5	683.3	460.5
Income taxes		449.1	365.0	340.5	226.7	256.7	180.5
Income from operations	26.3%	$901.4	$762.2	$605.1	$463.8	$426.6	$280.0
Net income	33.5%	901.4	762.2	594.8	457.8	543.7	212.5
Income per share from operations	28.0%	$3.40	$2.90	$2.30	$1.77	$1.53	$0.99
Net income per share	35.3%	3.40	2.90	2.26	1.75	1.94	0.75
Cash dividends per share	11.6%	0.960	0.800	0.670	0.628	0.585	0.555
Average shares outstanding		265.3	263.5	263.1	262.2	280.7	287.5
Cash Flow Data							
Net cash from operations	14.0%	$1,885.9	$1,894.5	$1,334.5	$1,212.2	$817.3	$981.5
Investments for cash*		3,296.6	1,415.5	371.5	1,679.9	160.0	—
Purchases of fixed assets	11.2%	943.8	725.8	770.5	858.5	770.3	555.8
Cash dividends paid	9.4%	241.9	199.0	172.0	160.4	161.1	154.6
Year-End Position							
Total assets		15,126.7	11,135.3	9,022.7	8,027.1	5,889.3	4,876.9
Total debt		6,942.8	4,107.0	3,225.0	2,865.3	1,506.1	948.9
Shareholders' equity		3,891.1	3,161.0	2,508.6	2,059.1	1,837.7	1,853.4
Per share	17.5%	14.76	12.03	9.63	7.91	6.98	6.58
Market price per share	35.5%	$64	$39 1/2	$33 7/8	$26 1/4	$23 3/4	$14
Shares outstanding		263.7	262.8	260.4	260.3	263.1	281.7
Employees		266,000	235,000	225,000	214,000	150,000	150,000
Shareholders of record		95,000	94,000	92,000	87,000	72,000	62,000
Statistics							
Return on average equity		25.6%	26.9%	26.5%	23.8%	23.1%	15.4%
Return on net sales		5.9%	6.1%	5.5%	5.1%	5.6%	3.9%
Net debt ratio		51%	37%	35%	40%	24%	11%

*For acquisitions and equity.

Source: *PepsiCo Annual Report.*

EXHIBIT 12   **PepsiCo's Major Foreign Subsidiaries by Segment, Regional Growth, and Risk**

Nation/Region	Segments and Number of Subsidiaries	Average Annual Growth(%) 1980–88*	Projected Growth (%) 1990*	Country Risk Index†
Canada	Pepsi, 5; KFC, 1; Frito-Lay, 1	3.3	1.6	86.3
Latin America				
Argentina	Pepsi, 1; 7-Up, 1	−0.2	2.7	34
Chile	Pepsi, 1	1.9	4.3	54.7
Mexico	Pepsi, 1	0.5	3.3	57.1
Uruguay	Pepsi, 1	−0.4	−0.1	60.1
South Atlantic/Caribbean				
Bermuda	Pepsi, 2	—	1.0	65.2
Netherlands Antilles	Pepsi, 8; Frito-Lay, 1	8.4‡	1.3‡	55.3‡
Puerto Rico	7-Up, 1; Frito-Lay, 1	—	—	NA
France	Pepsi, 1	1.8	3.1	91.1
West Germany	Pepsi, 2	1.8	4.0	94.1
Ireland	Pepsi, 3; 7-Up, 1; KFC, 1	1.7	3.5	86.3
Italy	Pepsi, 1	2.2	3.2	84.6
Spain	Pepsi, 2	2.5	4.1	82.5
Turkey	Pepsi, 1	5.3	4.6	66.6
United Kingdom	Pepsi, 1; 7-Up, 1; Pizza Hut, 1; Snacks, 3	2.8	1.6	84.5
USSR	Pizza Hut, 1	1.9	−1.9	54.5
Pacific Basin				
Australia	Pepsi, 1; KFC, 1; Pizza Hut, 1	3.3	1.3	76.4
Japan	KFC, 1	3.9	4.4	93.4
New Zealand	KFC, 1	2.2	1.9	74.5
Philippines	Pepsi, 1; 7-Up, 1	0.1	4.7	42.4

*Growth in gross domestic product (excludes foreign earnings). 1980–88 median growth = 2.39%; 1990 projected median growth = 3.2%.

†Risk based on political risk, payment record, trade finance, and access to bond and loan markets. Median index = 47.6; top quartile (100–76), bottom quartile (27–1).

‡Estimated.

Sources: *PepsiCo Annual Report; Who Owns Whom* (New York: Dun & Bradstreet, 1990), and *Euromoney,* September 1990.

THE HORN & HARDART COMPANY

Louis R. Oliker, Syracuse University

The Horn & Hardart Company was engaged in two principal lines of business: direct marketing and restaurant operations. The company's wholly owned subsidiary, the Hanover Companies, was one of the largest direct-mail marketers in the United States. The parent company also had two major restaurant operations, owning and/or operating almost 300 restaurant units through its wholly owned subsidiaries Horn & Hardart Restaurant Corporation (HHRC) and International King's Table Inc. (IKING).

Rising operating costs, declining profit margins in its restaurant businesses, increased leverage, and several unfortunate acquisitions had reduced the company's financial position to a historically low level. Management and the board of directors were contemplating a number of strategic options, including potential merger partners, equity participants, asset dispositions, and corporate restructuring.

THE EARLY YEARS

Horn & Hardart's name was generally associated with its reputation as a restaurant company. It had its birth in 1888 in Philadelphia when Joseph R. Horn, eager to become a restaurateur, advertised for an experienced partner. He received only one positive reply, from Frank Hardart. With money borrowed from the former's family, they opened a 15-stool lunchroom in downtown Philadelphia. Its success led to expanding to include several other locations in the city, using a central commissary where most of the cooking and baking were done to keep costs as low as possible. The food was delivered several times a day to all the local outlets.

Ten years later, the two partners incorporated the business as the Horn & Hardart Baking Company. In 1900, Hardart, while touring Europe, purchased equipment from Berlin's celebrated "waiterless restaurant." Once installed in one of its Philadelphia outlets in 1902, this Automat "seemed to offer a solution to the contamination scares that had swept American cities for decades. Its advanced food-handling techniques were appealing to the growing number of city dwellers who needed low-cost meals away from home but were skeptical, often for good reason, of the food at corner lunchstands."[1]

By 1932, the Horn & Hardart central commissary was producing 2 million meals each year. Its highly secret coffee formula, quality controls (for both taste and safety), and low prices had catapulted it into financial success. However, what really raised the company to renown was its 1912 opening on Manhattan's Times Square. "For H&H, the site on Broadway at 46th Street was a dream

---

[1]Daniel Cohen, "For Food Both Cold and Hot, Put Your Nickels in the Slot," *Smithsonian Magazine*, January 1986, p. 52.

location. The subway disgorged 200,000 people each day onto the streets of the Great White Way. Sensing its big chance, the Philadelphia firm launched a sister Horn & Hardart Company to run its New York outlets."[2]

The first two decades of the Automat restaurant concept were successful in both of H&H's urban locations. The concept's most financially productive era was initiated by the Great Depression. The company increased its sales revenues by 50 percent in the first two years after the stock market crash of 1929. It truly became a countercyclical operation, as its profits, stock price, and employment rose sharply. Happy just to have a job during this period, the company's employees resisted numerous attempts to unionize.

Broadway plays, films, columnists, cartoonists, and the general public gave the New York City Automat restaurants a storied luster that soon spread to every part of the country and eventually, to most of Europe. Radio programs set many of their humorous scenarios in Automat locations—with Jack Benny leading the way. The company's success continued unabated throughout World War II and into the 1950s.

The cultural changes that characterized the post-war prosperity period did not work to Horn & Hardart's financial advantage. Its low-cost image lost its appeal for a younger generation that sought less standardized and more elegant dining experiences. The luster slowly disappeared from this once innovative restaurant concept. Management did not pick up on this environmental shift and opened itself to its first operating losses (1965), unionism (1966), and the eventual bankruptcy of the Philadelphia H&H (1971).[3]

The New York company was unsuccessful in its efforts to resuscitate the Automat concept. It survived by transforming all but one of its restaurant locations—most of which were in Manhattan's finest locations—to a variety of fast-food franchises. This move brought a resurgence of success to the company's New York City operations and set the stage for the emergence of the present-day company.

DIVERSIFICATION AND GROWTH

Restaurant Operations

Horn & Hardart's conversion of its restaurants in the 1960s and 1970s from cafeterias and Automats was a strategic effort to keep up with changing times. Burger King, Arby's, Tony Roma's, and the 1980s version of the Automat, the Dine-O-Mat, replaced the old concepts (except for a sole Automat at 42nd Street). The company also acquired a restaurant chain in the Carolinas, which added over 150 Bojangles units to its restaurant portfolio. Its Arby's franchises expanded to a number of Florida locations to become an integral part of HHRC operations.

Late in 1987, the management of H&H became interested in International Kings Table, a chain of 89 buffet-style restaurants. With a dominant presence in California, Oregon, Washington, and other western states, it provided access to a new marketplace. Its acquisition was completed in early 1988, becoming the

---

[2]Ibid., p. 54.
[3]Ibid., pp. 58–61.

company's second wholly owned restaurant subsidiary (along with HHRC). The combined restaurant businesses made up the total restaurant group.

Direct Marketing

As restaurant operations struggled to increase their profit margins, management decided to diversify to other businesses. In 1972, the company acquired Hanover House Industries, then a direct-response merchandiser. For the next few years, H&H operated the new acquisition in much the same fashion as had the previous owners. In 1978, the Hanover Companies (its new name) invoked a new growth strategy—creating new catalogs differentiated by product line, as opposed to prospecting for new customers for existing catalogs. A number of new catalogs were added to the firm's portfolio, each targeted to a market niche (see Exhibit 1).

As it became one of the largest direct marketers in the country over the next decade, Hanover offered over 22,000 items through its 22 catalogs, each designed to appeal to individuals of various ages, life-styles, and income levels. It also offered some of its most popular items through advertising in newspapers and magazines. By 1987, the direct-marketing subsidiary, which accounted for some $317 million or nearly 75 percent of the company's revenues, continued its growth in terms of both sales revenues and earnings (see Exhibit 2).

Revenues in 1987 rose more than 24 percent, outpacing the direct-marketing industry as a whole. Profit for this subsidiary increased 48 percent over 1986, to $20.9 million. Unfortunately, a complacent management allowed Hanover to lose its cutting edge during the next year, prompting the board of directors to replace its executive leadership in early 1988.

The diversification into the direct-mail business had returned the parent company to profitability. From the mid-1970s, Hanover's profits more than offset the losses accrued by the restaurant business (then consisting only of HHRC). As the decade waned, management began to understand more clearly what a valuable asset it had acquired. By the mid-1908s, Hanover had become the dominant (core) business for H&H.

Profit margins for the direct-mail business were, on the average, well above those in the restaurant business. The former business was less labor intensive than the latter and more responsive to the operating controls established by corporate management. Competition was keen in both industries. However, the diversity provided by 22 catalogs, which by the late 1980s, had been increasingly well positioned, had allowed Hanover management to successfully differentiate its market strategy.

Hanover owed much of its success to a continued demonstration of operations expertise, marketing skill, a detailed knowledge of its prospective markets, and superior customer service. Its approach to the direct-mail market had been to function as a series of specialty shops, each selling a particular type of merchandise to a carefully defined group of potential customers. In this way, each catalog emulated specialty boutiques found in shopping malls.

Hanover controlled its own subsidiary units, two of which enabled it to provide the creative catalog development activities and customer contact operations that were featured so prominently in its turnaround. The Levitt Advertising Agency played a significant role in the firm's innovative market

EXHIBIT 1   **Horn & Hardart Company's Direct-Marketing Business**

The company conducted its direct-marketing operations through the Hanover Companies (name changed to Hanover Direct, Inc., effective January 1, 1990). Its revenue was derived from sales generated by 22 catalogs, which were treated as separate strategic business units.

Catalog	Items Offered	Year First Published by Hanover Direct
Hanover House	Novelties and housewares	1966
Lakeland Nurseries	Horticultural products	1968
Old Village Shop	Gifts and gadgets	1977
Les Premiere Editions	Moderate-price women's fashions	1978
Chelsea Collection	Sophisticated, moderate-price women's fashions	1980
Night'N Day Intimates	Lingerie	1981
Sync	Electronics equipment	1982
Fashion Galaxy	Discount women's fashions	1982
Mature Wisdom	Senior citizen merchandise	1982
Hall of Hanover	Higher price women's fashions	1983
Domestications	Sheets, towels, household items	1984
Tapestry	Decorative home products	1984
Colonial Kitchen	Kitchen and cookware items	1985
Essence	Contemporary women's fashions	1984
Silhouettes	Contemporary apparel for larger women	1986
International Male	Contemporary apparel for men	1986
Undergear	Men's activewear and fashion underwear	1986
Simply Tops	Blouses, tops, and accessories	1987
Men America	Contemporary men's fashions	1987
Career Guild	Career women's clothing	1988
Favorites	Collection of best-selling items from other catalogs	1988
Outtakes	Discount men's fashions	1988

EXHIBIT 2   **Consolidated Statement of Operations for Horn & Hardart Company**
(Years ended December 26, 1987, and December 31, 1988, in thousands)

	1987	1988
Revenues		
Direct marketing	$317,077	$316,832
Restaurant group	106,196	175,380
Other revenues	2,658	6,825
Total revenues	$425,931	$499,037
Costs and expenses		
Cost of sales/operating expenses	$358,552	$435,753
Provision for restructuring	—	17,000
General/administration/advertising expenses	49,470	61,036
Interest expense	13,676	21,920
Interest and dividend income	(5,863)	(3,761)
Total cost and expenses	$415,835	$531,948
Income (loss) before income taxes and extraordinary items	$ 10,096	$(32,911)
Income taxes (benefit)	4,238	(410)
Income (loss) before extraordinary item	$ 5,858	$(32,501)
Extraordinary item: use of net operating loss	3,838	—
Net income (loss)	$ 9,696	$(32,501)

EXHIBIT 3   Horn & Hardart's 1989 Organization Chart

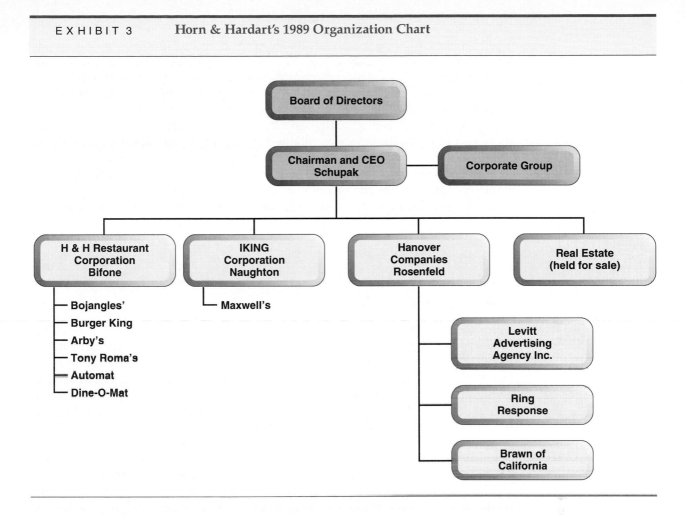

approach, and the Ring Response unit serviced the telephone traffic that transmitted customer orders to the various fulfillment centers from which product shipments were made. (See Exhibit 3 for an organization chart.)

Hanover even segmented its markets by income level within product categories, although the number and composition of this catalog mix changed rapidly, according to the benefits anticipated from evolving market conditions. Hanover maintained a vigilant posture regarding its own acquisition policy. It was continually evaluating new catalog opportunities to fill its gaps and broaden its specialized coverage of the market. Five of its current catalogs were businesses acquired with this segmentation concept in mind.

However, by late 1989, Hanover, despite the renewed efforts of a different style of management, was unable to pursue any further acquisitions. Cash conservation was necessary to meet day-to-day operating costs and interest obligations. The U.S. Postal Service had announced considerable increases in the postage rate for catalogs. Management was aware that some smaller catalog owners might suffer major problems in factoring these new costs into their financial plans. Some would be unable to do so and still show a profit. While they might become takeover candidates, Hanover management was realizing the frustration of being unable to take advantage of such growth opportunities.

Hotel-Casino

The company operated, through its Royal Center subsidiary, a casino in Las Vegas known as the Paddlewheel. This hotel-casino complex was acquired in 1979 and operated as a concessionaire under a 20-year agreement with a limited partnership that owned the facility. This partnership included the then-chairman and CEO of H&H, Barry Floresque, and its vice chairman, Donald Schupak. While never a particularly profitable venture, and even less so in more recent years, the company retained ownership of an adjacent piece of real estate that was considered a valuable asset.

H&H was incorporated under the laws of the state of New York in 1912 and reincorporated in Nevada in 1960. Its principal executive offices were located in Las Vegas. However, its main operating center had always been in New York City.

INDUSTRY ENVIRONMENTS

Direct Marketing

The direct-mail business was the fastest growing segment within a retailing industry that experienced a dramatic decline during 1990–91. According to the Direct Mail Association, direct-marketing sales had risen approximately 15 percent in the 1970s, 10 percent in the 1980s, and should continue at near double-digit levels during the 1990s. Industry revenues for 1989 approached $38 billion. It is estimated that about 50 percent of U.S. households ordered by mail in 1989. The direct-mail business had become an accepted medium for shopping, primarily because of the convenience it offered for dual-income families. The growing use of toll-free telephone calls, credit cards, computers, overnight package delivery, and fax machines had helped increase popularity.

The Direct Marketing Association estimated more than 5,000 firms are involved in the mail-order business in the United States, and yet the top 10 firms accounted for slightly more than 30 percent of total industry revenues. Thus, even in years of poor economic expansion, larger, better capitalized companies might take market share from their smaller, less aggressive competitors.

During recessionary environments like early 1991, direct-mail companies substantially outperform traditional retailers. Once the economy begins showing signs of faltering, it is not unusual for direct-mail companies to cut back their mailings and to concentrate on customers who show the highest persistency rates (greatest frequency of sales) and the highest dollar amounts ordered per mailing. Consequently, mailing costs may be kept to a minimum and margins improved, producing greater operating results (albeit at lower revenue levels).

The Restaurant Industry

The trend toward eating out has grown steadiy since the early 1960s, as the proportion of working wives has increased. The fast-food and dinner house segments of the restaurant industry flourished as the frequency of eating out increased. However, a recent industry study found that nearly all the real growth in "eating places" revenue had been attributable to off-premises eating (take-out or home delivery). Moreover, consumer surveys found that most customers *did not* intend to eat out more frequently. These factors suggested the U.S. market was at a peak and would grow in real terms only as the population increased.

The general environment for eating out was strong and likely to remain so. The industry was plagued, however, with overcapacity in some of its most important markets because new building continued for about two years after the eating-out market had leveled off. Partly as a result of this factor, competition had intensified. In such an environment, some of the best-performing chains attributed their success to providing a special level of service to the customer. For moderately upscale customers, this factor is more important than any other.

In both the direct-marketing and restaurant group segments, the company normally experienced increased cost of sales and operating expenses as a result of the general rate of inflation in the economy. Operating margins were generally maintained through selective price increases where market conditions permitted. In the restaurant group, due to the high number of part-time hourly workers, legislative changes in the minimum hourly wage have had a direct impact on operations. Due to competitive pressures, such changes could not always be offset by price increases.

Most of the company's inventory was mail-order merchandise, which undergoes sufficiently high turnover so cost of goods sold approximates replacement costs. Because direct-marketing sales are not contingent on a particular supplier or product brand, the company could adjust its product mix to mitigate the effects of inflation on its overall merchandise base.

RECENT OPERATIONS AND ISSUES

In 1988, Horn & Hardart suffered some striking financial setbacks. The Hanover Companies lost money in the first quarter of 1989, while launching what was to become a successful effort to reverse those losses before the year was over. The company's stock price (which trades on the American Stock Exchange under the symbol HOR) dropped alarmingly, as market analysts expressed their uncertainty about the firm's ability to maintain the momentum necessary to regain its competitive edge. H&H's slow turnaround did not begin until the fourth quarter of 1989.

IKING had performed poorly from the day of its acquisition, and imprudent changes in its operation, made in the summer of 1988, had a near disastrous impact on its bottom line. The Bojangles restaurant chain continued to accumulate losses—$47.6 million in 1987 and another $19 million in 1988. An attempt to unload this chain was unsuccessful. In addition, H&H's New York City restaurants were not producing adequate returns. The hotel-casino lost money, and general and administrative costs were rising sharply. Long-term debt had doubled since 1986 (see Exhibit 4). This highly leveraged position created cash flow problems for the company.

Barry Floresque, then chairman and CEO of H&H, had acquired 4 percent of the company's common stock in 1977 and took control the following year via a tough proxy battle. He had moved quickly to sell as many failing restaurant locations as possible to strengthen the firm's balance sheet. He experienced

EXHIBIT 4   **Business Segment Performance for Horn & Hardart Company, 1986–89**
                   (In thousands for each year)

	1986	1987	1988	1989
Revenues				
Direct marketing	$255,995	$317,077	$316,832	$382,637
Restaurant group:				
IKING	—	—	78,113	85,205
HHRC	147,230	107,306	97,267	66,406
Corporate and other	1,730	1,548	6,825	3,468
Total revenues	$404,955	$425,931	$499,037	$537,716
Operating income (loss)				
Direct marketing	$ 14,085	$ 20,857	$ 6,824	$ 19,030
Restaurant group:				
IKING	—	—	4,133	26
HHRC	(28,976)	6,567	(16,518)	1,459
Corporate and other	(6,215)	(9,515)	(9,191)	(8,083)
Total operating iincome (loss)	$(21,106)	$ 17,909	$(14,752)	$ 12,432
Interest expense	$ 12,650	$ 13,676	$ 21,920	$ 25,329
Extraordinary items	(4,090)	3,838	—	—
Net income (loss)	$(28,439)	$ 9,696	$(32,501)	$ (8,959)
Year-end total assets	280,792	340,761	363,328	396,698
Long-term obligations	91,015	157,174	196,294	230,664

early success with this approach. The company's stock price, adjusted for splits, climbed from about $2 in the late 1970s to $29 by 1983. Shares outstanding had grown from 700,000 to 14.8 million during this same period. "Panting for expansion money and eager to show profits on this greatly swollen capitalization, Floresque sold the company's valuable real estate, most of it in Manhattan. These real estate sales contributed $23 million to reported profits over the past three years (1985–87)."[4]

Claiming he had washed his hands of operations, Floresque started on a deal-making, acquisition spree that netted the company its hotel-casino complex, Bojangles, and IKING. During this period, he was drawing a huge salary from the company. He personally owned another company, in partnership with H&H's vice chairman, Donald Schupak, that received $1.2 million from the company over a three-year period (1985–87) for the use of two corporate jets. He also got the company to buy a number of disastrous Bojangles operations, which he personally owned along with Schupak. This latter deal resulted in a shareholders' lawsuit, and the firm ended up assuming the considerable debt associated with these failed operations (although it paid only $1 as the total purchase price!).

In July 1988, a subsidiary of the company purchased Maxwell's Restaurant in San Francisco, an operation controlled by Schupak. The sale price was $1.45 million. That unit then lost more than $300,000 the year after the acquisition. The residual assets of Maxwell's have since been sold by the company, at a loss.[5]

---

[4]Burr Leonard, "Why Didn't They Pay Him to Stay Home?" *Forbes,* June 15, 1987, p. 120.

[5]Mark A. Boyer, "Update: Horn & Hardart," *Asset Analysis Focus,* October 31, 1989, p. 279.

The proxy statements of the company had included a section on a number of "Certain Transactions" over Floresque's tenure as CEO. These notations continued into the current decade and reflected questionable payments and loans by the company to a variety of businesses owned and/or operated by Floresque and Schupak. When the sale of the Paddlewheel operation was being considered, a very real conflict of interest arose relative to Schupak's involvement, since he represented *both* the buyer and the seller in such a transaction.

Floresque then turned his hand in an attempt to launch Value Television, a home shopping television venture designed to sell high-end merchandise from Hanover House catalogs. This effort in the late 1980s cost the firm more than $5 million when it failed in infancy.[6]

The combination of all these financial machinations finally caught up with Floresque. The board of directors accepted his resignation in September 1988. He received a very generous severance package—close to $6 million. The only thing the company's management got in return was the proxy rights to vote his 1 million plus shares of stock. Donald Schupak was promoted from vice chairman to chairman/CEO and immediately initiated a strategy designed to get the company on a profitable footing.

Under 'New' Management

The new CEO's efforts were too late to reverse the negative trend already apparent for 1988. H&H reported a $32.5 million loss for that year, compared to a small profit of $9 million the previous year (see Exhibit 2). This loss included a $17 million write-off associated with the restructuring of the restaurant group (both HHRC and IKING). Corporate revenues for 1988 had risen to almost $500 million, a 17 percent gain from the previous year's $426 million. However, most of this gain had been derived from the acquisition of the IKING chain, which added $78 million in revenues, while producing a significant operating loss.

The Hanover Companies

The revised strategy for Hanover had the goal of converting a merchandise- and operations-driven company to one characterized as a market- and consumer-driven company. Hanover's new president, Jack Rosenfeld, swiftly initiated this new course, reversing the downward trend the firm had been experiencing. Under his control, Hanover entered 1989 as a company well positioned to take full advantage of its new focus.

A merchandise-driven business utilizes direct mail simply as a means to sell products by buying them in bulk and then searching for customers through direct mail and advertisements. This approach worked well for Hanover for a number of years. But in the changing global marketplace comprised of tightly focused marketing companies, ever more discriminating consumers, and rising costs of operations, it lost its viability. This was true for a number of other direct-marketing firms as well.

---

[6]Leonard, "Why Didn't They Pay Him," pp. 124–25.

The market-driven approach uses a different order of decision making. Both emphasis and priorities are changed. A marketing department was added to Hanover's creative capability (a unit that did not even exist until mid-1988). Hanover's marketing research activities were combined with sophisticated circulation improvements:[7]

- Refining the data base management program.
- Improving catalog presentation and format.
- Expanding fulfillment operations (thus reducing delivery time).
- Adding professional marketing personnel to perform in-house a number of functions previously contracted to outside organizations.

New facilities were developed for Hanover's administrative operations. The Weehawken, New Jersey, location also greatly reduced the firm's occupancy cost relative to its previous Manhattan location. Combined with the aggressive leadership Rosenfeld brought to Hanover, these changes initiated the firm's resurgence during the 1989 fiscal period.

Rosenfeld's strategic goals for Hanover over the next five years involved activities designed to:

- Continue building large—$50 million plus—franchise catalogs, with one in each of the following areas: home furnishings, women's apparel, men's apparel, and gifts.
- Continue to build support systems and customer service to top-of-the-line standards, consistent with achieving reasonable profit goals.
- Increase the firm's ability to use and leverage 15 million customer names and the data base that drives the customer-contact system.
- Retain the ability, by publishing catalogs in multiple markets, to enter quickly any new merchandise or market niche that becomes hot. Also, be prepared just as quickly to abandon any niche that has ceased to be viable.
- Continue an aggressive search for acquisition candidates to further the development of a specific franchise, or to gain a running start in a new market niche.
- Research alternate media for selling directly to customers in their homes and expand outbound telemarketing to a significant percentage of total sales using noncatalog printed mailings.

He believed that by 1995 Hanover could be one of the few large direct-to-home marketers selling consumer products to multiple markets through various media. By that time, it would have several franchises, and those franchises would be extended globally. It would have state-of-the-art data systems and fulfillment/delivery capabilities in a number of strategic locations.

The Restaurant Group

The Horn & Hardart Restaurant Corporation (HHRC) relocated its headquarters to Charlotte, North Carolina, home base of the Bojangles subsidiary and midway between its operating group in New York City and the south Florida group. Its first and most important objective was to stabilize the rapidly dete-

---

[7]Alison Fahey, "Hanover Orders up New Catalog Looks," *Advertising Age*, February 20, 1980, p. 27.

riorating operating results at Bojangles. A new management team replaced the former management in early 1989 (Exhibit 3).[8]

Following a period of evaluation, marketing changes were introduced that phased out certain price-cutting techniques that had lowered the public's perceived value of HHRC's restaurant image and products. A new public relations campaign was launched in an effort to directly address the image problem. Intensive negotiations were undertaken to restore franchisee confidence, settle franchisee claims, and stimulate new investment by franchisors in upgraded operations, marketing, and new restaurant development.

HHRC's New York operations, Burger King and Tony Roma's in particular, were still performing at a loss during the first half of 1989. These poor results were principally attributable to uncertainty concerning the company's future commitment to its New York City operations and a lack of clarity concerning H&H's status as a franchisee for the Burger King Corporation. A poor marketing effort on the part of this latter corporation had increased local unit marketing expense, hurting sales and profitability. Takeover rumors and threats, together with corporate management's stated intention of rationalizing its New York City assets, resulted in high management turnover in many of the New York locations and, as a result, delayed capital spending.

IKING, which had performed poorly since its acquisition, got a new management team, which proceeded with its own turnaround strategy. One of its basic problems was its highly leveraged financial position. The aggregate purchase price of IKING had been approximately $65 million, of which $22 million had been provided from H&H's scarce working capital. The balance was in the form of a $53 million credit facility consisting of an eight-year term loan, which was nonrecourse to H&H. Approximately $38.9 million of excess of cost over net assets acquired was recorded for the acquisition (making one wonder why H&H acquired IKING).

During 1989, IKING's new management team tried to stabilize the firm's operations and reduce the high customer attrition rate. A situation analysis revealed the chain's low-quality image, its use of old-fashioned menus, lack of consumer sensitivity, inadequate personnel training, and its public perception as a low-income/senior-user franchise. In response to these findings, management developed a series of remedial programs aimed at reversing these negative trends and improving profit margins. These programs were based on the market- and-customer-driven strategy formulated by corporate management in New York.

Operating Results

Total revenues for 1989 (see Exhibits 2 and 4) improved significantly from the previous year, up $38.7 million or 8 percent, to $538 million. This increase was due primarily to Hanover's improved operations and, to a lesser degree, to the inclusion of IKING's operating results for the entire year. However, these increased revenues were offset to a great degree by the 32 percent decline in HHRC revenues. This latter unit was being downsized as failing restaurants were removed from HHRC's portfolio and placed in an accounting category as "property held for sale."

---

[8]Cassandra Poteat, "Bojangles' Parent Picks Charlotte as New Base," *Charlotte Observer*, February 5, 1989, Sec. D, p. 3.

Under its new management, Hanover had improved the overall quality of its operations. This improvement was particularly attributable to the efforts of the new marketing department. The creative output of that unit had upgraded circulation by targeting new catalog markets, initiating new product testing programs, and increasing pages and merchandise categories in carefully selected catalogs. In addition, the enhanced use of telemarketing and higher quality customer service had a positive impact on revenues. Operating income for the year had risen above $19 million, up from $6.8 million the year before.

The reverse was true for both IKING and HHRC. The former had increased its revenue production, but its operating income had declined to a paltry $26,000, down from $4 million in 1988. Costs were rising at a faster rate than revenues. The latter business experienced a revenue decline of over $31 million. While its net income experienced an $18 million swing from 1988 to 1989, this improved performance had more to do with the sale of assets than from the implementation of successful operating programs.

Interest expense, which had doubled since 1987, exceeded $25 million in 1989 (Exhibit 5). The consolidated operating profits for H&H of $12.4 million were wiped out by interest expense, and the company experienced a loss of $9 million for the period. However, even this red ink was a major improvement over the $32.5 million loss of the year before (see Exhibits 4 and 5). Exhibit 6 shows the structure of the company's long-term debt obligations.

ORGANIZATIONAL REACTIONS TO TAKEOVER RUMORS

In early April 1989, the company became aware of rumors it would become subject to a proxy contest in connection with its annual meeting. On April 12, a shareholder transmitted a letter to the company stating that he planned to nominate Theodore H. Kruttschnitt, J. David Hackman, and Edmund R. Manwell for election to the board of directors at the annual meeting.

In response to this notification, the board approved a new apointment to fill an existing vacancy and bring the board to a total of eight members. The board also initiated discussions with Kruttschnitt, Hackman, and Manwell in an effort to settle what could have turned out to be a bitter proxy battle. On May 5, 1989, the board agreed to appoint all three men as members, thus expanding the board to 11 seats. In exchange for this agreement, the three new appointees agreed they would not attempt to acquire the company or solicit proxies in opposition to current management for two years.

Kruttschnitt was the beneficial owner of 2,725,300 shares of H&H's common stock. This 19.14 percent of the company's total capitalization made him the largest personal shareholder. He had become increasingly alarmed about the company's future as its losses had piled up over 1988 and 1989, its credit position worsened, and its stock price depreciated. (His personal loss was estimated to exceed $20 million.) His acceptance of three positions on the board was a concession to avoid a costly proxy fight and to provide an opportunity for him to bring his managerial expertise to bear. He expressed initial concern about the potential effectiveness of the five-year plan introduced by Schupak early in 1989.

Schupak's plan included:

- Expanding IKING.

EXHIBIT 5   **Consolidated Balance Sheets for Horn & Hardart Company, 1987–89**
(In thousands)

	1987	1988	1989
Assets			
Current assets			
Cash and cash equivalents	$ 49,630	$ 13,951	$ 35,978
Marketable securities	14,601	6,664	—
Accounts, notes receivable	41,509	40,794	25,427
Inventories	45,636	30,640	42,240
Assets held for sale	—	4,732	18,894
Other current assets	22,412	24,312	31,858
Total current assets	$173,788	$121,093	$154,397
Mortgage note receivable	$ 28,594	$ 10,788	$ 10,788
Property at cost			
Land	7,378	4,301	3,318
Buildings and improvements	16,312	14,592	11,647
Lease rights and improvements	28,403	44,992	28,248
Furniture and equipment	44,975	39,380	26,304
Assets held by capital lease	7,881	3,411	3,330
Assets leased to others	20,123	24,753	15,778
Total	$125,072	$131,429	$88,625
Accumulated depreciation and amortization	(42,800)	(37,397)	(22,259)
Net property	82,272	94,032	66,366
Assets (property) held for sale	8,071	63,598	105,621
Excess of cost over net assets of acquired businesses	21,025	58,598	45,238
Other assets	27,011	15,219	14,288
Total assets	$340,761	$363,328	$396,698
Liabilities and Shareholders' Equity			
Current liabilities			
Current portion of long-term debt and obligations under capital leases	$ 6,548	$ 11,338	$ 14,772
Accounts payable	56,819	47,234	66,491
Accrued liabilities	14,626	37,737	30,958
Total current liabilities	$ 77,993	$ 96,309	$112,221
Noncurrent liabilities			
Long-term debt	$148,812	$182,246	$216,246
Obligations under capital leases	6,541	11,512	11,487
Other	1,821	2,536	2,931
Total noncurrent liabilities	$157,174	$196,294	$230,664
Total liabilities	$235,167	$292,603	$342,885
Common and other shareholders' equity			
Class A preferred stock	—	—	—
Common stock, $.66 2/3 par value	$ 9,851	$ 9,874	$ 9,874
Capital in excess of par value	126,450	123,660	123,862
Accumulated deficit	(22,979)	(55,480)	(64,439)
Treasury stock, at cost	(5,993)	(5,008)	(6,025)
Deferred compensation	—	—	(7,900)
Notes receivable from sale of common stock	(380)	(2,321)	(1,559)
Unrealized loss on marketable securities	(1,355)	—	—
Total Common and other shareholders' equity	$105,594	$ 70,725	$ 53,813
Total liabilities and shareholders' equity	$340,761	$363,328	$396,698

EXHIBIT 6   **Horn & Hardart Company's Long-Term Debt Structure, 1988 and 1989**
                   (In thousands)

Long-Term Debt Obligations	Dec. 31, 1988	Dec. 30, 1989
Senior secured increasing rate notes (due 10/91)*	$ —	$ 50,000
Guarantee of employee stock ownership indebtedness	—	5,500
Term loan (12.3 % interest)	42,250	37,798
Revolving credit facilities (Interest from 11.5% to 12.3%)	18,569	9,438
Industrial revenue bonds (interest from 5.4% to 11.9%)	12,176	11,735
Mortgage notes payable (interest from 7.1% to 13.8%)	22,173	18,505
Collateral loans (equipment secured) (interest from 7.5% to 17.3%)	1,399	443
14% senior subordinated debentures (due in 1997)	50,000	50,000
11% subordinated notes (due 1991)	15,876	16,408
7 1/2 % convertible subordinated debentures (due 10/91)	30,000	30,000
Other	685	724
Total	$193,128	$230,551
Less current portion	10,882	14,305
Noncurrent portion	$182,246	$216,246

*These notes, issued through a private placement in 1989, represent a two-year bridge loan, secured by Hanover's common stock and certain New York City properties. The notes were to be repaid before maturity from the proceeds of "assets held for sale." They require, as a binding loan covenant, a positive net worth on the part of the company equal to or above $50 million.

- Downsizing the Bojangles chain.
- Converting the Florida Arby's to Hardee franchises with some expansion involved.
- Reducing debt.
- Reinvesting the proceeds of the sale of the company's New York City real estate in a new high-performance restaurant chain that had yet to be identified.

The New York City properties had been placed in a pool, along with closed Bojangles locations, to be divested as quickly as possible. This divestiture plan was part of a restructuring program approved by the board in late 1988. In early 1989, the Las Vegas hotel-casino was placed into the pool.

The above plan was predicated on Hanover being able to generate at least 60 percent of the projected operating earnings necessary to finance its implementation. Asset sales were alleged to provide another 25 to 30 percent of the plan's capital requirements, with the remainder derived from restaurant operations.

Arthur D. Little Inc. had been called in to consult with corporate management and review the above plan. Its assessment, dated January 10, 1989, concluded the plan was doable, but conditioned that possible success on a number of qualifications concerning its problem-solving potential.[9]

However, with the financial picture for 1989 in mind, the board began to consider alternatives, one of which was to withdraw from the restaurant and hospitality business. This would radically change the business definition of the

---

[9]*The Feasibility of Horn & Hardart's Five Year Outlook: 1989–1993* (New York: Arthur D. Little, Inc., 1989) pp. 12–22.

parent company and downsize the corporation to include only its major profit center. The Hanover Companies would then become *the* business and the sole future source of both growth and earnings.[10]

STRATEGIC ALTERNATIVES

At its annual meeting in June 1990, the board of directors met with H&H management to outline a strategy that would include one or more of the following alternatives:

1. Seek a merger partner whose financial resources were capable of meeting H&H's debt obligations and increase Hanover to its real potential.
2. Seek the equity participation of a number of possible investment candidates, either corporate or individual.
3. Divest all property assets, as well as total restaurant operations.
4. Make changes in a number of the senior management positions, as a clear demonstration to both the marketplace and shareholders that the company's problem set was being comprehensively addressed.
5. Refinance the company's debt structure, designed to improve its cash flow and provide breathing room to fully implement one or more of these options.

The board resolved to implement a *new* plan that was strategically oriented. Although they were discussed, it did not want to incorporate any additional cash conservation measures that would hurt the long-term value of the Hanover Companies, now renamed Hanover Direct, Inc. Such measures could include, but would not be limited to:

- Eliminating most of Hanover's marketing research activities.
- Delaying any new catalog development.
- Backlogging virtually all catalog growth plans.
- Passing up the possible catalog acquisition opportunities that would develop in response to the sharp postal rate increases.
- Intentionally delaying both customer shipments and payments to creditors.

These actions were considered to be the final steps, which would be taken only under financial duress. They were commonly associated with a pre-bankruptcy action. The board, however, believed the company's cash flow crunch was a manageable problem, but *not* within its present cash-creation capability. This was the reason for a sense of urgency in either restructuring current debt or finding new sources of capital to relieve the rising pressures on the firm's operating capital.

It was with these issues in mind that the board deliberated a new strategic direction at its 1990 annual meeting.

---

[10]Gene G. Marcial, "Horn & Hardart: In a Hurry to Get Out of Fast Food," *Business Week*, July 12, 1990, p. 60.

THE BLACK & DECKER CORPORATION

Arthur A. Thompson and John Gamble, University of Alabama

In 1992, the Black & Decker Corporation was a diversified global manufacturer and marketer of household, commercial, and industrial products. The company operated 61 manufacturing plants, 32 in the United States and 29 in 14 other countries; its products were marketed in over 100 countries. Black & Decker was the world's largest producer of power tools, power tool accessories, and security hardware. Its small-appliance business was the U.S. leader, and the company was among the leaders in the global market for small household appliances. B&D's plumbing subsidiary was the fastest growing maker of kitchen and the bathroom faucets in the United States. Black & Decker was also the worldwide leader in golf club shafts and glass container-making equipment and was among the major global suppliers of fastening systems.

Surveys showed Black & Decker was the seventh most powerful consumer brand name in the United States (behind Coca-Cola and Kodak but ahead of Levi's and Hershey's) and was in the top 20 in Europe. The company's brand names were recognized worldwide, and it enjoyed a reputation for quality, design, innovation, and value. The company had paid a dividend on its common stock every quarter of every year since 1937.

COMPANY BACKGROUND

Black & Decker was incorporated in 1910. Over the next 70 years, the company established itself as the dominant name in power tools and accessories, first in the United States and then across a broad global front but particularly in Europe. Growth was achieved by adding to its lineup of power tools and accessories and by increasing its penetration of more and more foreign markets.

Diversification into Small Household Appliances

Black & Decker began to pursue diversification because of growing maturity of its core power tools business. In 1984, Black & Decker acquired General Electric's housewares business for $300 million. GE's brands had about a 25 percent share of the small-appliance market and generated annual revenues of about $500 million. GE sold its small-appliance division, despite its No. 1 market position, because of the division's low profitability. GE's strong suit was in irons and toaster ovens where its share was close to 50 percent; sales of GE irons totaled about $250 million. Among the other 150 GE products acquired by Black & Decker were coffee makers, hair dryers and hair curlers, food mixers and processors, toasters, electric skillets, can openers, waffle irons, and blenders.

25% market share

Also in 1984, Black & Decker purchased three European tool manufacturers to fill in product gaps and strengthen its manufacturing base; the acquisition involved a Swiss manufacturer of portable electric woodworking tools for professional users, the leading European manufacturer of drill bits, and a German producer of hobby and precision power tools.

The acquisition of GE's housewares division launched Black & Decker on a course to transform the company from a power tools manufacturer into a consumer products company. In early 1985, the firm changed its name from Black & Decker Manufacturing Co. to Black & Decker Corp. to reflect its new emphasis on "being more marketing driven" rather than being merely engaged in manufacturing.

Failed Acquisition Attempts

In early 1988, Black & Decker began an unsolicited takeover bid for American Standard Inc., a diversified manufacturer of bathroom fixtures, air-conditioning products, and braking systems for rail and automotive vehicles. American Standard had revenues of $3.4 billion and earnings of $127 million in 1987 (compared to revenues of $1.9 billion and earnings of almost $70 million for Black & Decker). After several months of negotiations, the takeover effort failed and B&D withdrew from the battle to win control of American Standard.

In January 1989, Black & Decker negotiated a deal with Allegheny International to purchase its Sunbeam/Oster Appliance division for about $260 million. Sunbeam/Oster was a leading manufacturer and marketer of small household appliances—blenders, can openers, food mixers, electric skillets, steam irons, and other kitchen items. However, in February, Allegheny International backed out of the sale and merged with another company.

The Emhart Acquisition

A month later, in March 1989, Black & Decker agreed to acquire Emhart Corporation for $2.8 billion, rescuing the firm from a hostile takeover bid. Emhart had 1988 sales of $2.8 billion, earnings of $127 million, assets of $2.4 billion, and shareholders' equity of $971 million. Emhart was a diversified manufacturer of industrial products (1988 sales of $1.6 billion), information and electronic systems (1988 sales of $654 million), and consumer products (1988 sales of $547 million). Approximately 40 percent of Emhart's sales and earnings came from foreign operations, the majority of which were concentrated in Europe. Exhibit 1 provides a profile of Emhart's business portfolio. Exhibit 2 provides data on the financial performance of Emhart's business units in the years preceding its acquisition by B&D.

In the days after the announcement of Black & Decker's friendly plan to acquire Emhart, B&D's stock price dropped about 15 percent. There was considerable skepticism over the wisdom of the acquisition, both from the standpoint of whether Emhart's businesses had attractive strategic fit with B&D's businesses and whether Black & Decker could handle the financial strain of making such a large acquisition. Emhart was significantly larger than Black & Decker:

1988 Financials	Emhart Corp.	Black & Decker Corp.
Sales revenues	$ 2.76 billion	$ 2.28 billion
Net earnings	$126.60 million	$ 97.10 million
Assets	$ 2.43 billion	$ 1.83 billion
Stockholders' equity	$970.90 million	$724.90 million
Long-term debt	$674.30 million	$277.10 million

The acquisition agreement called for Black & Decker to purchase 59.5 million shares (95 percent) of Emhart Corp. common stock at $40 per share—almost three times book value per share ($14.32). Black & Decker had to secure $2.7 billion in financing to acquire Emhart. To come up with the funds, Black & Decker entered into a credit agreement with a group of banks that consisted of

EXHIBIT 1   **Emhart Corporation's Business Portfolio in 1989**   *(At the time of the company's acquisition by Black & Decker)*

Business and Product Categories	Trademarks/Names	Primary Markets/Customers
Industrial Businesses (1988 sales of $1.6 billion)		
Capacitors, audible signal devices	Emhart, Mallory, Sonalert, Arcotronica	Telecommunications, computer, automotive, and electronic components industries
Electromechanical devices, solid-state control systems, hydrocarbon leak detection systems	Emhart, Mallory, Pollulert	Appliance, automotive, and environmental controls manufacturers
Commercial door hardware, electronic locking systems	Emhart, Carbin, Russwin	Commercial, institutional building construction, and original equipment manufacturers
Footwear materials (insoles, toe puffs, shanks, eyelets, tacks, and nails)	Emhart, Texon, Aquiline	Manufacturers of footwear
Fastening systems (rivets, locknuts, screw anchors, adhesive systems, sealants, and grouts)	Emhart, Molly, Warren, Gripco, Bostik, Kelox, Dodge, Heli-Coil, POP	Appliance, construction, electronics, furniture/woodwork, packaging, automotive, and other transportation industries
Glass container machinery	Emhart, Hartford, Powers, Sundsvalls	Producers of glass containers for beverage, food, household, and pharmaceutical products
Printed circuit board assembling machinery	Emhart, Dynapert	Electronics industry
Information and Electronic Systems (1988 sales of $654 million)		
Technology-based systems and services (including computer-based systems), scientific research services, program management	Emhart, PRC, Planning Research Corp., PRC System Services, PRC Environmental Management, PRC Medic Computer Systems, Nova, Stellar	Governmental units and agencies, real estate multiple listing services, group medical practices, and public utilities
Consumer Products Businesses (1988 sales of $547 million)		
Door hardware, including lock sets, high-security locks, and locking devices	Emhart, Kwikset	Residential construction
Nonpowered lawn and garden equipment, landscape lighting	Garden America, True Temper	Do-it-yourself homeowners
Underground sprinkling and watering systems	Lawn Genie, Drip Mist, Irri-trol	Landscape specialists, do-it-yourself consumers
Golf club shafts, bicycle-frame tubing	True Temper, Dynamic Gold, Black Gold	Golf club manufacturers
Bathroom and kitchen faucets	Price Pfister, The Pfabulous Pfaucet with the Pfunny Name	Residential and commercial construction
Adhesive, sealants	Bostik, Thermogrip	Residential and commercial construction, do-it-yourself consumers
Fasteners, staplers, nailers	Blue-Tack, POP, Molly	Residential and commercial construction

EXHIBIT 2   **Financial Performance of Emhart's Business Groups, 1986–88**
                   (In millions of dollars)

	1988	1987			1986
Revenues					
Industrial					
Components	$ 641.8	$ 671.9			$ 653.9
Fastening systems	640.5	638.8			576.3
Machinery	279.0	291.1			419.2
	$1,561.3	$1,601.8			$1,649.4
Information and electronic systems	653.7	438.3			39.3
Consumer	547.5	414.4			405.6
Total	$2,762.5	$2,454.5			$2,094.3
Operating Income (Loss)				*	
Industrial					
Components	$ 63.8	$ 65.7	$ 48.2	$ (5.4)	
Fastening systems	74.8	78.7	68.3	24.8	
Machinery	42.7	34.1	44.4	3.9	
	$ 181.3	$ 178.5	$160.9	$ 23.3	
Information and electronic systems	37.2	22.3	2.0	2.0	
Consumer	84.8	68.3	60.4	51.7	
	$ 303.3	$ 269.1	$223.3	$ 77.0	
Corporate expense	(35.0)	(32.9)	(30.3)	(34.0)	
Total	$ 268.3	$ 236.2	$193.0	$ 43.0	
Identifiable Assets					
Industrial					
Components	$ 457.8	$ 472.0			$ 400.3
Fastening systems	428.4	428.2			409.7
Machinery	167.8	164.8			297.2
	$1,054.0	$1,065.0			$1,107.2
Information and Electronic systems	546.7	361.3			334.5
Consumer	702.7	225.1			266.1
	$2,303.4	$1,651.4			$1,707.8
Corporate	123.2	378.5			148.9
Total	$2,426.6	$2,029.9			$1,856.7

* 1986 before provision for restructuring.
Source: *Emhart 1988 Annual Report.*

term loans due in 1992 through 1997 and a revolving credit loan of up to $575 million. The loans carried an interest rate of 1/4 percent above whatever the prevailing prime rate was. Scheduled principal payments on the term loans were as follows:

1992	$201,217,000
1993	274,287,000
1994	275,221,000
1995	743,923,000
1996	401,318,000

The credit agreement included covenants that required Black & Decker to achieve certain minimum levels of cash flow coverage of its interest obligations and not to exceed specified leverage (debt to equity) ratios during the term of the loan:

Fiscal Year	Maximum Leverage Ratio	Minimum Cash Flow Coverage Ratio
1992	3.25	1.35
1993	2.75	1.50
1994	2.25	1.55
1995 & Thereafter	1.50	1.60

Note: The leverage ratio was calculated by dividing indebtedness, as defined by the credit agreement, by consolidated net stockholders' equity. The cash flow coverage ratio was calculated by dividing earnings before interest, taxes, depreciation, and amortization of goodwill minus capital expenditures by net interest expense plus cash income tax payments and dividends declared.

Other covenants in the credit agreement limited Black & Decker's ability to incur additional indebtedness and to acquire new businesses or sell assets.

Black & Decker recorded the excess amount of its purchase price for Emhart over the book value of Emhart's net assets as goodwill to be amortized on a straight-line basis over 40 years. This resulted in Black & Decker having increased depreciation and amortization charges of about $45 million annually.

Divestitures

Senior management at Black & Decker realized early that as much as $1 billion of Emhart's business assets would have to be sold to reduce B&D's interest expenses and debt obligations and enable it to meet its covenant agreements. According to accounting rules, these assets had to be sold within a year or be consolidated with the rest of B&D's assets—a move that could cause B&D to fail to meet its maximum leverage covenant. The Emhart businesses that were identified for sale within one year from the acquisition date included footwear materials, printed circuit board assembly equipment (Dynapert), capacitors, chemical adhesives (Bostik), and the entire information and electronic systems business unit (PRC).

During 1989 and early 1990, Black & Decker sold the Bostik chemical adhesives division to a French company for $345 million, the footwear materials business to the United Machinery Group for approximately $125 million, and its Arcotronics capacitors business to Nissei Electric of Tokyo for about $80 million; the net proceeds from these sales were used to reduce debt. In early 1990, when the one-year period expired, Black & Decker was forced to consolidate about $566 million of the unsold assets, boosting the goodwill on its balance sheet by $560 million and raising annual amortization charges by $14 million. To keep from violating the maximum debt/equity ratio allowed under its credit schedule, Black & Decker was forced to issue $150 million in new preferred stock, $47 million of which was purchased with money from its 401(k) employee thrift plan when no other buyers came forward.

Throughout 1991, Black & Decker continued to struggle to meet its covenant agreements. The company divested Emhart's Garden America business unit and the Mallory Controls operations in North America and Brazil for a combined total of about $140 million. The company also sold its True Temper Hardware unit, its PRC Medic unit, and its U.S. capacitors business for a combined total of nearly $110 million. The prices that B&D got for the Emhart businesses it sold were generally below management's expectations, partly because oncoming recessionary effects reduced what buyers were willing to pay.

Nonetheless, these divestitures (described by B&D management as "nonstrategic assets") and the sale of $150 million in preferred stock allowed Black & Decker to reduce its total debt from a peak of $4 billion following the Emhart acquisition in April 1989 to $2.9 billion at year-end 1991. Even so, Black & Decker was still hard pressed to generate enough cash to meet its debt repayment schedule, a problem compounded by the 1990-91 recession, which hit the company's tool and household goods businesses fairly hard. The company's stock price fell from the mid-20s at the time of the Emhart acquisition to a low of $11 to $12 in early 1991—many observers believed the fundamental cause of B&D's financial plight was that it had paid too much for Emhart. There was also concern whether there was enough strategic fit between Emhart and B&D. By early 1992, Black & Decker's stock price had recovered to the low 20s, partly because a decline in the prime rate from 10 percent to 6.5 percent had lowered B&D's interest burden substantially.

Exhibit 3 provides a 10-year summary of Black & Decker's financial and operating performance.

BLACK & DECKER'S CEO—NOLAN D. ARCHIBALD

The chief architect of Black & Decker's foray into diversification was Nolan D. Archibald. Black & Decker hired Archibald as president and chief operating officer in 1985, soon after the acquisition of GE's small household appliance business. Before joining Black & Decker, Archibald was president of the $1.7 billion consumer durables group at Beatrice Companies, where he was responsible for such business units as Samsonite luggage, Culligan water treatment products, Del Mar window coverings, Stiffel lamps, and Aristocraft kitchen cabinets.

At the time he was hired, Archibald was 42; he was chosen from a pool of some 50 candidates for the position and turned down offers to be president at two other companies to take the B&D job. Archibald had been at Beatrice since 1977 and was successful in engineering turnarounds in three of Beatrice's businesses. Before that, he had headed a turnaround of Conroy Inc.'s Sno-Jet Snowmobile business. Archibald spent two years of his youth winning converts as a Mormon missionary, was an All-American basketball player at Utah's Dixie College, became a standout player at Weber State College in Utah, earned his MBA degree at Harvard Business School, and tried out (unsuccessfully) for the Chicago Bulls professional basketball team. Corporate headhunters rated Archibald as a good strategic thinker who was personable, versatile, and sensitive to people.

According to one Black & Decker dealer, before Archibald took over as president in September 1985, "Black & Decker had been coasting along for quite a few years like a ship without a captain."[1] Archibald wasted little time in reorganizing Black & Decker's worldwide manufacturing operations. Within three months, Archibald initiated a restructuring plan to close older, inefficient plants and boost factory utilization rates by consolidating production within

---

[1] As quoted in *Business Week*, July 13, 1987, p. 90.

B&D's newest and biggest plants. Approximately 3,000 jobs were eliminated, including a number of high-level managerial positions. In 1985, B&D took a $215 million write-off for plant shutdowns and other cost-saving reorganization efforts.

Before 1985, the company had pursued a decentralized, multicountry strategy. Each geographic area of the world had its own production facilities, its own product-design centers, and its own marketing and sales organizations to better cater to local market conditions. Over the years, this had resulted in short production runs at scattered production sites, reduced overall manufacturing efficiency, and prevented achievement of scale economies—for example, there were about 100 motor sizes in B&D's product line. Archibald set the company on a more globalized approach to product design and manufacturing, with much greater communication and coordination between geographic operating units. Production at plants was organized around motor sizes, the number of product variations reduced, and production runs lengthened. From 1984 to 1989, seven plants were closed. Archibald also insisted more emphasis be put on quality control—during the early 1980s, B&D's reputation in power tools had been tarnished by shoddy product quality.

Meanwhile, Archibald put additional resources into new product development and redesign of the company's power tools and small-appliance lines. The company introduced a line of men's hair blowers, toasters with wider slots, a line of cordless power tools, and a heavy-duty power saw with a blade that moved back and forth for tasks such as cutting through plaster walls. Archibald set a goal for the tool division to come up with more than a dozen new products each year—more than B&D had introduced in the five years before his arrival. To help get new product ideas, Archibald created 10 panels of dealers and end-users to provide suggestions. Work on a new line of cordless kitchen appliances was accelerated.

Archibald's biggest marketing challenge was transferring consumers' brand loyalty for GE small appliances over to Black & Decker. Some observers believed Black & Decker would have trouble because B&D's traditional customers were men, and buyers of houseware products were usually women—as a *Wall Street Journal* article headline put it, "Would You Buy a Toaster from a Drillmaker?"

B&D executives believed, however, many women were familiar with the Black & Decker name because they bought power tools as gifts for men and because B&D had pioneered the development of household appliances powered by rechargeable batteries. Black & Decker's handheld Dustbuster vacuum cleaner was the market leader with a 45 percent share. B&D also had been marketing a cordless rotary scrub brush, a cordless rechargeable shoe shiner, and a rechargeable flashlight. Even before acquiring GE's houseware's business, B&D had planned to introduce a line of cordless kitchen appliances, but gaining ample retail shelf space was often a hit-and-miss proposition. What made the GE acquisition attractive to B&D was the extra clout that offering retailers a full line of housewares would have in competing for shelf space.

Black & Decker's competitors in small appliances saw the brand name transition from GE to Black & Decker as an opportunity to gain market share that once was GE's. Sunbeam Appliance quadrupled its 1985 ad budget to $42 million because it wanted to replace GE as the best-known brand in small appliances. Norelco launched a new line of irons and a handheld can

EXHIBIT 3   Summary of Black & Decker's Financial and Operating Performance, 1982–91   *(In thousands of dollars except for per common share data)*

	1991	1990	1989(g)	1988(f)	1987	1986	1985(e)	1984(d)	1983	1982
Summary of Operations										
Total revenues	$4,636,954	$4,832,264	$3,172,540	$2,280,923	$1,934,799	$1,791,194	$1,732,278	$1,532,883	$1,167,752	$1,160,233
% change	(4.0)	52.3	39.1	17.9	8.0	3.4	13.0	31.3	.6	(6.8)
Operating income	$ 401,414	$ 486,394	$ 259,170	$ 159,115	$ 112,473	$ 55,325	$ 93,287	$ 150,428	$ 91,781	$ 84,958
% of total revenues	8.7	10.1	8.2	7.0	5.8	3.1	5.4	9.8	7.9	7.3
% change	(17.5)	87.7	62.9	41.5	103.3	(40.7)	(38.0)	63.9	8.0	(37.4)
Earnings (loss) from continuing operations before income taxes and extraordinary item	$ 107,531	$ 123,495	$ 62,926	$ 125,695	$ 69,766	$ 34,743	$ (159,825)	$ 140,804	$ 38,451	$ 55,481
% of total revenues	2.3	2.6	2.0	5.5	3.6	1.9	(9.2)	9.2	3.3	4.8
% change	(12.9)	96.3	(49.9)	80.2	100.8	—	—	266.2	(30.7)	(44.1)
Income taxes (benefits)	$ 54,500	$ 72,400	$ 32,900	$ 28,600	$ 14,200	$ 7,200	$ (1,400)	$ 45,400	$ 10,300	$ 14,800
Effective tax (benefit) rate	50.7%	58.6%	52.3%	22.8%	20.4%	20.7%	(.9)%	32.2%	26.8%	26.7%
Earnings (loss) from continuing operations before extraordinary item	$ 53,031	$ 51,095	$ 30,026	$ 97,095	$ 55,566	$ 27,543	$ (158,425)	$ 95,404	$ 28,151	$ 40,681
% change	3.8	70.2	(69.1)	74.7	101.8	—	—	238.9	(30.8)	(44.3)
Earnings (loss) from discontinued operations	—	—	—	—	—	—	—	—	16,000	$ (117,283)
Net earnings (loss) before extraordinary item	$ 53,031	$ 51,095	$ 30,026	$ 97,095	$ 55,566	$ 27,543	$ (158,425)	$ 95,404	$ 44,151	$ (76,602)
% change	3.8	70.2	(69.1)	74.7	101.8	—	—	116.1	—	—
Extraordinary item	—	—	—	—	—	$ (21,239)	—	—	—	—
Net earnings (loss)	$ 53,031	$ 51,095	$ 30,026	$ 97,095	$ 55,566	$ 6,304	$ (158,425)	$ 95,404	$ 44,151	$ (76,602)
% change	3.8	70.2	(69.1)	74.7	781.4	—	—	116.1	—	—
Per Common Share Data(a)										
Earnings (loss):										
Continuing operations	$0.81	$0.84	$0.51	$1.65	$0.95	$0.49	$(3.11)	$1.95	$0.65	$0.97
Discontinued operations	—	—	—	—	—	—	—	—	.37	(2.79)
Extraordinary item	—	—	—	—	—	(.38)	—	—	—	—
Total	.81	.84	.51	1.65	.95	.11	(3.11)	1.95	1.02	(1.82)
Cash dividends	.40	.40	.40	.40	.40	.58	.64	.58	.52	.76
Stockholders' equity	14.18	14.94	12.24	12.38	11.12	10.61	9.94	13.58	11.79	10.70

Other Data[b]	1991	1990	1989[g]	1988[f]	1987	1986	1985[e]	1984[d]	1983	1982
Number of employees	38,600	43,400	38,600	20,800	19,700	21,700	22,400	23,000	14,500	15,700
Total assets	$5,532,769	$5,889,534	$6,258,089	$1,825,109	$1,668,045	$1,580,571	$1,452,146	$1,473,448	$985,358	$995,329
Long-term debt	$2,625,833	$2,755,634	$2,629,718	$ 277,091	$ 250,578	$ 195,544	$ 334,501	$ 279,540	$159,108	$263,864
Total debt	$2,870,365	$3,268,345	$4,057,473	$ 492,574	$ 478,536	$ 407,426	$ 371,983	$ 303,763	$179,515	$306,239
Stockholders' equity	$1,027,163	$ 920,693	$ 720,721	$ 724,868	$ 649,114	$ 616,659	$ 504,848	$ 683,507	$554,416	$450,419
Capital expenditures	$ 107,667	$ 112,968	$ 112,103	$ 98,404	$ 58,766	$ 82,375	$ 118,299	$ 91,835	$ 75,759	$ 80,837
Depreciation and amortization	$ 202,324	$ 210,063	$ 130,978	$ 93,488	$ 99,036	$ 107,370	$ 93,338	$ 66,211	$ 51,973	$ 48,444
Working capital	$ 356,045	$ 221,146	$ 679,596	$ 555,786	$ 450,650	$ 355,128	$ 344,684	$ 461,545	$423,809	$406,542
Current ratio	1.3	1.1	1.3	1.7	1.6	1.5	1.7	2.2	2.8	2.8
Total revenues to average total assets	.81	.80	.78	1.31	1.19	1.18	1.18	1.25	1.18	1.09
% return on average stockholders' equity[c]	5.4	6.3	4.2	14.1	8.8	1.1	(26.7)	15.4	5.2	8.1

(a) Based on the average number of shares of common stock outstanding during each year, except stockholders' equity, which is based on stockholders' equity, excluding preferred equity, divided by common shares outstanding at year-end.

(b) Number of employees, capital expenditures, and depreciation and amortization relate to continuing operations of the corporation.

(c) Calculated on total stockholders' equity on an "as reported" basis for 1984 through 1991. For years 1982 and 1983, a pro forma basis was used with earnings from continuing operations and stockholders' equity adjusted to exclude portions allocable to operations sold.

(d) Includes housewares operations acquired on April 27, 1984.

(e) Operating results for 1985 include a restructuring charge of $215,000 before tax ($205,000 after tax).

(f) The corporation adopted Statement of Financial Accounting Standard No. 96 in 1988. Accordingly, tax benefits recorded since 1988 as a result of utilizing net operating loss carryforwards are included as a reduction of income tax expense rather than as an extraordinary item.

(g) Includes Emhart operations acquired on April 27, 1989.

opener powered by rechargeable batteries to wrest share away from GE/ Black & Decker. Hamilton Beach introduced a battery-operated carving knife. Nearly all small-appliance producers were rumored to be trying to develop cordless adaptations of irons, coffee makers, handheld mixers, and electric carving knives.

Archibald responded to the brand transfer challenge with a series of actions. Since Black & Decker had until 1987 to put its own name on all the GE products it acquired, it led off the transfer process by first putting its name on GE's innovative, expensive, high-margin Spacemaker products that were mounted under kitchen cabinets—a line that was not as strongly identified with the GE name. Then B&D introduced a new iron (invented by GE) that shut off automatically when it sat too long or was tipped over; B&D's TV ads for the iron showed an elephant walking away from an iron that had been left on, with a tag line: "Even elephants forget." The brand transfer was accomplished product by product, in each case accompanied by heavy advertising. Under Archibald, Black & Decker spent approximately $100 million during the 1985–87 period to promote the brand transition. The company also organized a large team of brand transition assistants to hang paper tags on display models of newly rebranded products in about 10,000 retail stores across the United States—the tags stated GE previously sold products now made by Black & Decker. Most analysts regarded Archibald's brand transfer program as successful; a Harvard Business School professor stated, "It is almost a textbook example of how to manage a brand transition."[2]

By year-end 1988, Archibald was widely credited with engineering another impressive turnaround, having boosted Black & Decker's profits to $97.1 million—up sharply from the loss of $158.4 million posted in 1985 (see Exhibit 3). Archibald was promoted to chairman, president, and chief executive officer in 1986.

BLACK & DECKER'S BUSINESS PORTFOLIO IN 1992

In 1992, Black & Decker Corp. was a diversified multinational enterprise; its business portfolio consisted of:

- Power tools and power tool accessories for both do-it-yourselfers and professional tradespeople.
- Household appliance products.
- Consumer-use fastening products.
- Security hardware for both residential and commercial use.
- Lawn and garden care products.
- Outdoor recreational products.
- Plumbing products.
- Commercial fastening products.
- Machinery for making glass containers.
- Machinery for manufacturing printed circuit boards.
- Information systems and services.

---

[2]Ibid.

Exhibit 4 provides a more detailed listing of the products produced and marketed by each of these businesses. Exhibit 5 provides financial performance data by business group and by geographic area. A brief description of each business group follows.

Power Tools and Accessories

Black & Decker was the world's largest manufacturer, marketer, and servicer of power tools and accessories. In 1991 alone, the power tools division introduced 50 new products; over the past five years, B&D had introduced more than 200 new and redesigned power tool products. B&D's approach to product development and manufacturing reflected a global outlook, although global strategies were modified to local country requirements as needed. B&D had formed "global business teams" to achieve worldwide coordination in power tool design, manufacturing, and marketing and to bring new power tool products to market quickly and efficiently. More than 200 companies had visited Black & Decker's power tools plant in Great Britain; the plant had won the Queen's Award for high standards and practices in quality, design, technology, and production. Most of the company's products carried a two-year warranty.

Industry Growth and Competition   Demand for power tools and accessories was regarded as mature and cyclical. Volume was influenced by residential and commercial construction activity, by consumer expenditures for home improvement, and by the overall level of manufacturing activity (a number of manufacturers used power tools in performing certain production tasks—automotive and aerospace firms, for example, were heavy users of power tools). The 1990–92 recession in the United States had produced a slump in power tool sales. However, rising demand for cordless tools was a significant sales plus. During the 1992–97 period, the power tool industry in the U.S. was expected to grow at a compound annual rate of 1.5 percent in constant dollars. Demand in Europe was expected to grow faster due to sales opportunities to users in the newly democratic countries in Eastern Europe. Worldwide, the biggest percentage growth was projected to occur in developing countries where use of power tools was still rather limited. Worldwide sales of power tools and accessories were an estimated $6 billion in 1991.

Market Segments   There were two distinct groups of buyers for power tools: professional users and do-it-yourselfers. Professional users included construction workers, electricians, plumbers, repair and maintenance workers, auto mechanics, and manufacturing workers. Professional users were very quality conscious and features conscious; they tended to buy only tools that were durable, functional, dependable, and precision capable. They tended to be very knowledgeable and informed as compared to do-it-yourselfers, many of whom were first-time buyers and used power tools infrequently.

Because the needs of professional users and do-it-yourself consumers tended to be sharply different, some manufacturers had a heavy-duty professional line and a consumer/do-it-yourselfer line while others catered to just one segment. Professional users tended to purchase their tools through jobbers, contractor supply firms, industrial supply houses, and some building supply centers. Tools for the consumer segment were sold at home

EXHIBIT 4   **Black & Decker's Business Portfolio in 1992**

Consumer and Home Improvement Products Group

Power tools (1991 sales: $1.095 billion)
- Drills
- Screwdrivers
- Saws
- Sanders
- Grinders
- Car care and automotive products
- Workmate workcenters

Power tool accessories (1991 sales: $32 million)
- Drill bits
- Screwdriver bits
- Saw blades

Consumer-use fastening products (1991 sales: $185 million)
- Blind fasteners
- Wall anchors
- Rivets and rivet guns
- Staple and glue guns

Security hardware (1991 sales: $454 million)
- Lock sets
- Deadbolts
- Door closers
- Exit devices
- High security locks
- Master keying systems

Plumbing products (1991 sales: $148 million)
- Faucets and fixtures
- Valves
- Fittings

Household products (1991 sales: $723 million)
- Cordless vacuum cleaners
- Cordless flashlights
- Cordless scrub brushes
- Cordless shoe shiners
- Irons
- Toasters
- Toaster ovens
- Coffee makers
- Can openers
- Food mixers
- Food processors and choppers
- Blenders

Lawn and garden care products (1991 sales: $198 million)
- Hedge and lawn trimmers
- Edgers
- Electric lawn mowers
- Blowers and vacuums
- Thatchers
- Shredders
- Electric chain saws

Outdoor recreational products (1991 sales: $100 million)
- Golf club shafts
- Tubing for bicycle frames
- Kayak paddles

Commercial and Industrial Products Groups

Fastening systems (1991 sales: $371 million)
- Rivets and riveting tools
- Threaded inserts
- Stud welding fastening systems
- Lock nuts
- Self-drilling screws
- Construction anchors

Glass container-making machinery
  (1991 sales: about $180 million)

Assembly equipment for making printed circuit boards
  (1991 sales: about $180 million)

Information Systems and Services Group

This group consisted entirely of the business of PRC, Inc. (1991 sales: $684 million), an information technology firm that contracted with customers to provide the following:

    Systems integration
    Software development and computer services
    Data network development
    Engineering and management services
    Scientific research services
    Environmental engineering and consulting services
    Real estate multiple listing services
    Computer-aided emergency dispatch systems

EXHIBIT 5   Black & Decker's Financial Performance by Business Segment and
Geographic Area, 1989–91

Business Segments

1991	Consumer and Home Improvement Products	Commercial and Industrial Products	Information System and Services
Sales to unaffiliated customers	$3,224,372	$ 728,206	$684,376
Operating income before goodwill amortization	307,232	113,278	35,432
Goodwill amortization	53,089	17,698	3,125
Operating income	254,143	95,580	32,307
Identifiable assets	4,605,945	1,574,051	380,563
Capital expenditures	80,096	12,816	12,708
Depreciation	92,577	16,155	12,098
1990			
Sales to unaffiliated customers	$3,425,703	$ 887,509	$519,052
Operating income before goodwill amortization	355,533	143,463	28,279
Goodwill amortization	48,918	17,062	2,344
Operating income	306,615	126,401	25,935
Identifiable assets	4,792,075	1,532,318	327,839
Capital expenditures	85,455	16,413	9,891
Depreciation	102,067	21,959	9,894
1989			
Sales to unaffiliated customers	$2,856,599	$ 315,941	$ —
Operating income before goodwill amortization	236,594	43,408	—
Goodwill amortization	20,261	5,111	—
Operating income	216,333	38,297	—
Identifiable assets	4,567,007	1,045,510	—
Capital expenditures	101,082	7,444	—
Depreciation	85,873	8,212	—

Geographic Areas

1991	United States	Europe	Other
Sales to unaffiliated customers	$2,599,436	$1,409,478	$628,040
Sales and transfers between geographic areas	223,022	143,630	164,310
Total sales	$2,822,458	$1,553,108	$792,350
Operating income	$ 188,427	$ 163,968	$ 27,868
Identifiable assets	3,479,143	2,391,445	595,472
1990			
Sales to unaffiliated customers	$2,785,980	$1,371,585	$674,699
Sales and transfers between geographic areas	213,860	150,283	187,330
Total sales	$2,999,840	$1,521,868	$862,029
Operating income	$ 249,932	$ 166,184	$ 45,771
Identifiable assets	3,583,638	2,296,307	782,687
1989			
Sales to unaffiliated customers	$1,734,525	$ 935,560	$502,455
Sales and transfers between geographic areas	112,317	73,494	233,594
Total sales	$1,846,842	$1,009,054	$736,049
Operating income	$ 114,119	$ 92,837	$ 47,674
Identifiable assets	3,259,304	1,654,185	698,428

Source: *1991 Annual Report.*

improvement centers (such as Home Depot and Lowe's), building materials centers, mass merchandisers (Sears), discount chains (Wal-Mart, Kmart), and hardware stores.

Until the late 1980s, the consumer tool segment was growing at a faster clip than the professional segment. But narrowing price differentials and a rising interest on the part of gung-ho do-it-yourselfers in professional quality tools had, in the U.S. market, spurred demand for heavy-duty professional tools. The professional tool segment in the United States was a $400 million market, compared to $1.5 billion to $ 1.6 billion for the consumer tools segment. B&D believed sales of power tools and power tool accessories to professional users in North America (Canada, Mexico, and the United States) represented a $1 billion market.

Competition   Power tool manufacturers competed on such variables as price, quality, product design, product innovation, brand-name reputation, size and strength of retail dealer networks, and after-sale service. All makers were working to bring out new products that were lightweight, compact, cordless, less noisy, prone to less vibration, strong, and fit easily and comfortably in users' hands. The major manufacturers had sales forces whose main task was to expand and strengthen the network of retail dealers carrying their line of tools. Salespeople signed on new dealers and called on major accounts—wholesale distributors, discount chains, home improvement centers, and other mass merchandisers—to win better access to shelf space in their retail outlets, help with promotion and display activities, and upgrade dealers' product knowledge and sales skills. Some manufacturers offered training seminars and provided training videos to dealers/distributors. Manufacturers that concentrated on the professional segment engaged in limited advertising and promotion activities, spending their dollars for trade magazine ads, trade shows, and in-store displays. Those that concentrated on the consumer segment, like Black & Decker, spent comparatively heavy for TV and magazine ads and also for co-op ad programs with dealers.

Black & Decker's Competitive Position   In 1992, Black & Decker was the overall world leader in the world power tool industry, followed by Japanese-maker Makita and Germany's Robert Bosch Power Tools, a division of Robert Bosch Corp.—one of Germany's leading companies (1991 sales of $20 billion) and a major global supplier of automotive components, electronics products, and small household appliances. Black & Decker's strength was in the consumer tools segment (see Exhibit 6); it was the market leader in the United States, Europe (where it had had a presence since the 1920s), and many other countries outside Europe. No other manufacturer came close to matching B&D's global distribution capabilities in the do-it-yourself segment. Makita, along with Ryobi, were the leaders in Japan and several other Asian countries. Bosch was strongest in Europe. In late 1991, Bosch announced that Robert Bosch Tools would merge with Skil, a subsidiary of Emerson Electric, to form a 50-50 joint venture to manufacture and market power tools.

In consumer tools, Black & Decker's strongest U.S. competitor was Sears, which marketed tools under the Sears Craftsman label. Sears' longtime supplier of tools was Singer; Singer's tool manufacturing operations had recently been acquired by Japan's Ryobi. Singer/Ryobi supplied Sears with 80 to 90 percent of its tool requirements. Skil's strength was in power saws; its joint

EXHIBIT 6   Estimated U.S. Sales and Market Shares of Power Tool Manufacturers, 1979 and 1991   *(Dollar values in millions)*

| | Consumer Tools | | | | Professional Tools | | | | Total Tools | | | | Accessories | |
| | 1979 | | 1991 | | 1979 | | 1991 | | 1979 | | 1991 | | 1991 | |
Company	Dollar Sales	Percent Share	Dollar Sales	Percent Share	Dollar Sales	Percent Share	Dollar Sales	Percent Share	Dollar Sales	Percent Share	Dollar Sales	Percent Share	Dollar Sales	Percent Share
Black & Decker	$169	44.5%	$325	39.7%	$205	42.1%	$125	17.9%	$374	43.1%	$ 450	29.6%	$ 110	10.0%
Sears/Ryobi	107	28.2	280	34.0	9	1.8	50	7.1	116	13.4	330	21.7	20	1.8
Makita	2	0.5	43	5.2	22	4.5	160	22.9	24	2.8	203	13.4	157	14.3
Milwaukee	6	1.5	4	0.5	89	18.2	145	20.7	95	10.9	149	9.8	146	13.3
Skil	52	13.7	82	10.0	54	11.1	40	5.7	106	12.2	122	8.0	128	11.6
Porter Cable	—	—	—	—	NA	NA	50	7.1	NA	NA	50	3.3	50	4.5
Delta	—	—	—	—	NA	NA	40	5.7	NA	NA	40	2.6	50	4.5
Bosch	—	—	—	—	25	5.1	30	4.3	25	2.9	30	2.0	—	—
Hitachi	—	—	—	—	NA	NA	20	2.9	NA	NA	20	1.3	5	0.5
Others	44	11.6	86	10.6	84	17.2	40	5.7	128	14.7	126	8.3	434	39.5
Total	$380	100.0%	$820	100.0%	$488	100.0%	$700	100.0%	$868	100.0%	$1,520	100.0%	$1,100	100.0%

NA = not available

Sources: Compiled by the case researchers from a variety of sources, including telephone interviews with company personnel; data for 1979 is based on information in Skil Corporation, Harvard Business School, case #9-389-005.

venture with Robert Bosch Power Tools was expected to give the two partners more clout in gaining shelf space and greater global coverage capabilities.

Although surveys showed consumers associated the Black & Decker name with durable power tools, trade professionals viewed B&D tools as products for do-it-yourselfers. The company's charcoal-gray professional line was not seen by professional users as sufficiently differentiated from B&D's traditional black line of consumer tools. Professionals preferred tools made by Makita, Skil, and Milwaukee (a U.S. tool manufacturer with a reputation for quality, heavy-duty tools). However, no toolmaker currently held the largest share in every tool category. During the 1970s and 1980s, Makita had steadily increased its share of the professional segment and as of 1992 was the brand most used by professionals.

In 1991, B&D executives formed a team, headed by the president of B&D's power tools division, to come up with a new strategy for the professional market. The team elected to create a new line of industrial-grade tools for professional users under the DeWalt brand, a name borrowed from a 65-year-old maker of high-quality stationary saws acquired by B&D in 1960. The team changed the tool's color from gray to industrial yellow because it was easy to see, signaled safety, and was a color pros liked. Every product in B&D's professional line was redesigned based on input from professionals, dealers, and B&D engineers. The redesigned versions were all tested by professional users; every item had to meet or beat Makita's tools in user tests before going into production.

The new DeWalt line was introduced in March 1992. As part of the introduction, B&D created a fleet of demonstration booth vans, which were parked near major retailers or construction sites. The company also instituted a policy of offering professional users the loan of a DeWalt power tool when waiting for their equipment to be fixed at any of the company's 117 U.S. service centers. There were also DeWalt demonstration booths at each of the service centers. Initial response to the DeWalt line was excellent. B&D officials expected DeWalt to be a $100 million to $200 million brand and have a 25 to 50 percent market share in the United States within three years. Archibald's goal was for DeWalt's revenues to equal or exceed Makita's revenues in the U.S. market by 1996.

In addition to its 117 service and repair centers in the United States, Black & Decker had 123 foreign service centers, primarily in Canada, Mexico, Europe, Latin America, and Australia. Although recessionary influences caused a drop in 1991 power tool sales in the United States, Australia, and Brazil, B&D had record sales and operating profits in Europe in 1991.

To gain distribution for its products in Japan and begin to challenge Makita and Ryobi in their home market, B&D had recently entered into a joint venture with a Japanese distributor of power tools. B&D had more than doubled its sales of power tool accessories (particularly drill bits, screwdriver bits, and saw blades) in North America over the past five years. The company had a just-in-time procurement, inventory management, and distribution program to shorten the cycle of supplying customers; this "quick response" system received sales data electronically from the top retailers and processed orders automatically.

In 1991, B&D was named Vendor of the Year by Lowe's, a large North American home center chain; it also received the Partners in Progress award from

Sears (Sears began selling Black & Decker products when it implemented its "brand central" theme of stocking many name-brand items as well as traditional Sears' brands).

Household Products

As of 1992, Black & Decker's household products business had established itself as a worldwide leader in products used for home cleaning, garment care, cooking, and food and beverage preparation. It had the largest market share of any full-line producer of household appliance products in the United States, Canada, Mexico, and Australia and a growing presence in Europe, Southeast Asia, and Latin America. The household products division was using the worldwide distribution network and brand-name recognition that had been established by the tools division to gain greater global penetration in household appliances. In 1992, B&D's irons and Dustbuster cordless vacuums were being marketed in more than 100 countries. To accelerate international expansion, B&D had formed global business teams to focus the corporation's technical expertise and marketing capabilities on (1) launching new houseware products in foreign countries where B&D already had a presence and (2) expanding into new countries.

Industry Growth and Competition Like power tools, the market for small household appliances was both mature and cyclical. Growth opportunities existed mainly in the form of creating innovative new products and in increasing market penetration in the countries of Eastern Europe and other developing nations where household appliance saturation rates were low. Sales of small household appliances in the United States had fluctuated between $2.2 billion and $2.7 billion for the past five years, with no evident trend. Exhibit 7 shows the makeup and size of the market for small household appliances in the United States. The global market for small appliances (excluding electric fans and vacuum cleaners) was approximately $6 billion to $8 billion. Industry experts projected growth of 1.5 to 2.5 percent (in constant dollars) during the 1992–96 period, with potential for a bigger near-term rebound since recessionary influences in the United States and Australia had produced a sales downturn in 1992. Sales of household appliances tended to be greatest during the Christmas shopping period.

Black & Decker's Competitive Position Black & Decker was the market leader in most product categories in the U.S. market (see Exhibit 8 for market shares of the major competitors by product category). *Consumer Reports* gave Black & Decker products generally high ratings for various household appliances. Black & Decker confronted different competitors in different product categories and in different areas of the world. In irons, for example, B&D's strongest U.S. competitors were Wear-Ever/Proctor-Silex and Sunbeam, but in Europe, its strongest competitor was German-maker Rowenta. In food processors, B&D's strongest competitor in the United States was Hamilton Beach, but its strongest U.S. competitor in can openers was Rival. B&D's brand awareness in the United States and Canada was twice that of its nearest competitor in small appliances.

EXHIBIT 7   Size and Makeup of the Small Household Appliance Market
in the United States, 1990

	1990 Sales of Small Household Appliances in the United States			1990 Estimated Unit Volume of Small Household Appliances	
	Dollar Sales (Millions)	Percent Share		Units (Thousands)	Percent Share
Electric housewares	$5,065	80.29%	Clocks	40,530	22.80%
Vacuum cleaners	1,680	26.63	Coffee makers	17,740	9.98
Household fans	1,075	17.04	Irons	16,950	9.54
Food processors	500	7.93	Electric grills/skillets/fryers	11,100	6.25
Coffee makers	450	7.13	Vacuum cleaners, nonhandheld	10,960	6.17
Cookware	450	7.13	Smoke detectors	10,000	5.63
Irons	225	3.57	Toasters	8,900	5.00
Toasters	220	3.48	Can openers	6,200	3.49
Can openers	100	1.59	Timers	5,850	3.29
Corn poppers	30	.48	Blenders	5,600	3,15
Other housewares	335	5.31	Vacuums, handheld rechargeable	5,000	2.81
Other appliances	1,243	19.71	Food processors	4,760	2.68
Total	$6,308	100.00%	Hand mixers	4,400	2.48
			Slow cookers	4,160	2.34
			Air purifiers	3,800	2.14
			Corn poppers	2,900	1.63
			Toaster ovens	2,800	1.58
			Vacuums, hand-held electric	2,500	1.41
			Ice cream makers	1,530	0.86
			Electric knives	1,420	0.80
			Bag sealers	1,400	0.79
			Mixers, stand type	1,100	0.62
			Coffee grinders	800	0.45
			Intrusion systems	800	0.45
			Juicers	410	0.23
			Floor polishers	175	0.10
			Convection ovens	125	0.07
			Bread makers	105	0.06
			Other small appliances	5,755	3.20
			Total	177,770	100.00%

Sources: Compiled by the case researchers from data presented in *American Metals Market*, September 30, 1991, p. 4, and *Appliance*, April 1991, p. 27.

Black & Decker was using its quick response system to good advantage in household appliances as well as power tools. B&D had electronic point-of-sale linkage with many of its retail customers to speed order processing, manage inventories, and plan its own production more efficiently. It also supplied modular in-store displays for retailers to use in showcasing the features of B&D's new household appliance products. In 1992, B&D received Vendor of the Year awards from its two most important customers, Wal-Mart and Target. Survey data showed B&D's household products were ranked ahead of all other brands that retailers preferred to sell.

Security Hardware

B&D's security hardware business was the world leader in door hardware for homes and businesses. Its Kwikset brand was the best-selling U.S. brand of

EXHIBIT 8   Market Shares of Major Small Appliance Competitors, 1990

Company	Blenders	Can Openers	Coffee Makers	Food Processors	Hand Mixers	Irons	Smoke Detectors	Toaster Ovens	Toasters	Vacuum Cleaners	Handheld Vacuums
Black & Decker	9%	26%	20%	25%	34%	50%	—	57%	16%	—	45%
Wear-Ever	—	6	16	—	—	21	—	19	35	—	—
Sunbeam	—	8	—	13	25	17	—	—	6	—	—
Mr. Coffee	—	—	28	—	—	—	—	—	—	—	—
Hamilton Beach	27	7	3	21	14	3	—	—	—	—	—
Toastmaster	—	2	—	—	—	—	—	13	27	—	—
Rival	—	33	—	—	12	—	—	—	—	—	—
Braun	17	—	9	3	—	—	—	—	—	—	—
Oster	35	3	—	5	—	—	—	—	—	—	—
Hoover	—	—	—	—	—	—	—	—	—	34%	5
Eureka	—	—	—	—	—	—	—	—	—	23	3
Singer	—	—	—	—	—	—	—	—	—	11	—
Royal	—	—	—	—	—	—	—	—	—	3	37
Pittway	—	—	—	—	—	—	60%	—	—	—	—
Jameson	—	—	—	—	—	—	25	—	—	—	—
Others	12	15	24	33	15	9	15	11	16	29	10
Total	100%	100%	100%	100%	100%	100%	100%	100%	100%	100%	100%

Source: Compiled by the case researchers from data presented in *Appliance*, April 1991.

residential door locks and hardware. The Kwikset brand was particularly favored by do-it-yourselfers; B&D had boosted Kwikset's sales by providing retailers with a videotape that took the mystery out of changing locks for do-it-yourselfers. In Europe, B&D had recently introduced new lines of garage door locks, fire-resistant locks, and high-security key cylinders for the German, Dutch, and Italian markets.

This business, acquired from Emhart, had achieved significant cost savings by integrating its purchasing, distribution, and marketing activities with B&D's other consumer products businesses. B&D's worldwide distribution network was also providing the hardware group wider geographic sales opportunities. In many instances, door hardware was sold in the same retail channels as B&D's power tools and accessories.

Plumbing Products

B&D's plumbing products business, Price Pfister, had gained market share since the Emhart acquisition, though it trailed the market leaders in kitchen and bathroom faucets. Price Pfister had benefited from access to B&D's retail distribution network and its corporate support systems (quick response), gaining more shelf space in home improvement centers. Price Pfister had also introduced fashionable, but affordably-priced, new designs and new lines that had become popular with plumbing wholesalers and plumbing contractors. Price Pfister had increased its brand recognition with TV ads, using the theme "The Pfabulous Pfaucet with the Pfunny Name." Price Pfister's major competitors were American Standard, Kohler, and Delta, all of which had bigger market shares of the approximately $1.5 billion U.S. market for sink, tub, shower, and lavatory plumbing hardware.

Recreational Outdoor Products

B&D's True Temper Sports business unit was the leading global producer of golf club shafts, supplying major golf club manufacturers around the world. Nine out of 10 golf professionals used clubs with True Temper shafts. The sales of this unit had declined significantly in 1991 as recessionary influences in several major markets produced a general slowdown in golf equipment sales. However, the golf industry had enjoyed record growth during the 1986–90 period, and demographic trends pointed to renewed expansion since golf was growing in popularity among the increasingly populous 45 to 75 age group in the United States, Europe, and Japan. Golfers were also upgrading their golf equipment in response to manufacturers' introduction of high-tech golf clubs with graphite, boron, and titanium shafts; the new shafts had much bigger profit margins than conventional steel shafts.

The 1992 Olympic Summer Games marked the third consecutive Olympics at which U.S. cyclists competed on True Temper bicycle frames. Olympic kayakers also used True Temper paddles (three 1988 gold medalists had used True Temper paddles).

Lawn and Garden Equipment

Black & Decker's lawn and garden products unit introduced nine new products in 1991. This business unit also utilized the same distribution channels as the power tools business, and the buyers of B&D's lawn and garden equipment could get items repaired at B&D's 240 company-owned service centers worldwide and several hundred other authorized service centers operated by independent owners. It was also employing the quick response system. Where feasible, B&D's lawn and garden products had a global design.

Fastening Systems

This business unit marketed 11 brands of fastening products. To link their identities, B&D in 1991 began marketing them under the banner of Emhart Fastening Teknologies. Management believed this would leverage its brand names and enhance the unit's ability to market to industrial users on a more global scale. Joining the marketing activities of these brands under a single banner to create more of a full line of fastening products was considered vital to get the business of industrial customers, which preferred to deal with a limited number of suppliers. Recently, the fasteners unit had introduced new stud welding and assembly systems that boosted its sales to automotive manufacturers worldwide by 25 percent. A "total quality" initiative had been launched throughout the Emhart Fasteners Teknologies group. The Warren division was selected by Honda of America from among 300 suppliers for Honda's 1991 Quality Performance Award and 1991 Delivery Performance Award—Warren achieved 100 percent on-time delivery and zero rejections per million pieces. The Gripco division received Ford's Q1 Award, Chrysler's QE Award, and GM's Mark of Excellence award in 1991.

The fasteners unit had seven U.S. plants and two European plants and marketed to customers in the United States, Europe, and the Far East. Principal customers were automotive, electronics, aerospace, machine tool, and appliance companies. Products were sold directly to users and also through distributors and manufacturer's representatives. Competition centered around product quality, performance, reliability, price, delivery, and ability to provide customers with technical and engineering services. Competition came from many manufacturers in several countries. B&D management believed the Emhart Fasteners Teknologies group was among the global leaders in the fasteners industry.

Glass Container-Making Machinery

Several U.S. manufacturers and a number of foreign firms competed with B&D's glass container-making machinery business. However, B&D's Emhart Glass/Powers division was considered the global leader and offered the world's most complete line of glass container-making equipment. Important competitive factors were price, technological and machine performance features, product reliability, and technical and engineering services. An increasing worldwide preference for recyclable glass packaging was expected to produce steady growth in demand for glass container-making equipment. Glass container-making equipment was in 24-hour use in virtually all plants worldwide, creating a predictable need for servicing and rebuilding; over two thirds of the unit's revenues came from rebuilding and repair services and technology upgrades. The business reported sales and profit gains in 1991 and entered 1992 with a substantial order backlog.

Dynapert

The Dynapert business unit provided automated equipment for assembling printed circuit boards to electronics customers around the world. The equipment was among the most complex computer-controlled machinery being used in any industrial application. Dynapert had two manufacturing plants (one in the United States and one in England) and sales and service facilities throughout the world. The unit had launched a "total quality" program and implemented just-in-time manufacturing techniques.

Sales were made directly to users by an employee sales force and independent sales representatives. Dynapert faced competition from both U.S. and foreign manufacturers. Competition centered around technological and machine performance features, price, delivery terms, and provision of technical services. The Dynapert division, which generated annual sales of about $180 million, had been put on the market for sale shortly after the Emhart acquisition, but so far a buyer willing to pay an acceptable price had not been found.

Information Systems and Services

This segment consisted of a single business unit known as PRC, Inc., headquartered in McLean, Virginia. PRC and its predecessors had been in business since the mid-1970s. A majority of PRC's business came from contracts with various agencies and units of the federal government. Approximately 40 percent of PRC's 1991 revenues were from contracts with the Department of Defense. In addition, PRC was the leading provider of on-line printed residential real estate multiple listing systems and computer-aided emergency dispatch systems.

The types of services PRC provided were highly competitive, and strategic defense expenditures were expected to decline given the end of the Cold War. Many of PRC's competitors were large defense contractors with significantly greater financial resources. As the Department of Defense's expenditures for weapons programs continued to decline, these large contractors were expected to bid more aggressively for the types of contract work done by PRC.

PRC had also been put on the market for sale after the Emhart acquisition. In 1991, PRC had sales of $684 million and pretax operating earnings of $32.3 million. In mid-1991, B&D appointed a new person to head PRC; shortly thereafter, PRC launched an initiative to pursue new markets. The objective was to shift PRC's business mix so that half came from U.S. customers and half from overseas customers.

BLACK & DECKER'S FUTURE OUTLOOK

Black & Decker outperformed competitors and gained market share in most of its major businesses in 1991—even in businesses where difficult economic conditions resulted in sales declines. Nolan Archibald believed the company was in position to prosper when market conditions improved. Archibald's two top objectives were to reduce B&D's debt still further, selling nonstrategic assets if necessary, and to increase net income 20 percent annually over the next several years.

SIFCO INDUSTRIES, INC., IN CHINA

Liming Zhao, University of Alabama

One afternoon in June 1989, Kevin O'Donnell, CEO of SIFCO Industries, Inc., sat in his Cleveland, Ohio office, contemplating SIFCO's joint venture project in China. Through numerous discussions over the past two and a half years in both China and the United States, the three parties involved in the venture were ready to submit the formally signed joint venture contract, article of association, and technology transfer agreement to the SIFCO board for approval. However, the June 4 occupation of Tiananmen Square by the Chinese army cast heavy clouds over this project, and Kevin O'Donnell was wondering whether the board would or should approve the project.

SIFCO HISTORY

SIFCO was founded in Cleveland in 1913 by five men who were dedicated to applying relatively new scientific principles to improving physical properties of metals, specifically by the use of thermal cycles. While the art of heat-treating was ancient, the body of knowledge that would turn an art into a science was just beginning to accumulate. In 1916, this company merged with The Forest City Machine Company, a manufacturer of metal poles. Since the major manufacturing process for this product was forging, the merger added forging capability to the heat-treating company and the company was renamed the Steel Improvement and Forge Company (SIFCO).

At the time SIFCO was formed, Cleveland was one of the centers of the rapidly growing automobile and steel industries, and the city became a leader in the volume of steel forgings produced. The economies and practices of the auto industry made it difficult for forging suppliers that depended on that industry for most of their business to earn a consistent profit. So SIFCO found applications for forged products in other industries. SIFCO served many industrial markets including oil and petrochemical, aerospace, nuclear power generation, transportation, ordnance, mining, and off-highway. SIFCO was a medium-sized firm with annual sales over $60 million. Exhibit 1 highlights SIFCO's financial position.

Charles H. Smith Jr., son of the former president, became SIFCO's CEO in 1943 just after he completed his thesis at MIT on the forging of austenitic stainless steels for turbo-supercharger applications. He became chairman of the board in 1983 when Kevin O'Donnell was named president and CEO. An MBA graduate of Harvard Business School, with years of experience in SIFCO, O'Donnell had also served in the Navy, Booz Allen, Atlas Alloys of Canada, and the Peace Corps in Korea and at the Washington, DC, headquarters.

EXHIBIT 1 **Selected Financial Data for SIFCO Industries, Inc., 1983–87**

	1987	1986	1985	1984	1983
Net sales	$63,112	$61,323	$59,255	$56,008	$54,959
Operating income (loss)	2,619	886	(2,404)	(1,320)	105
Equity in net earnings (loss) of SIFCO, S.A.	—	—	501	646	(2,188)
Net gain on disposal of capital assets and investments	815	1,403	—	—	—
Income (loss) before income taxes	3,434	2,289	(1,903)	(674)	(2,083)
Provision (benefit) for income taxes	1,374	505	(1,048)	(229)	(536)
Income (loss) before cumulative effect of change in accounting method	2,060	1,784	(855)	(445)	(1,547)
Cumulative effect on prior years of change in accounting method	—	736	—	—	—
Net income (loss)	2,060	2,520	(855)	(445)	(1,547)
Net income (loss) per share before cumulative effect of change in accounting method	$ 0.95	$ 0.83	$ (.40)	$ (.21)	$ (.72)
Cumulative effect on prior years of change in accounting method	—	.34	—	—	—
Net income (loss) per share	.95	1.17	(.40)	(.21)	(.72)
Cash dividends per share	.15	.10	.10	.20	.20
Shareholders' equity	$29,693	$27,898	$25,512	$27,561	$28,583
Shareholders' equity per share at year-end	$ 13.77	$ 12.96	$ 11.87	$ 12.83	$ 13.32
Return on beginning shareholders' equity	7.4%	9.9%	(3.1%)	(1.6%)	(5.0%)
Long-term debt	$ 6,935	$10,188	$11,400	$12,856	$ 9,931
Long-term debt-equity percent	23.4%	36.5%	44.7%	46.6%	34.7%
Interest coverage	4.5	3.6*	—	—	—
Working Capital	12,171	14,471	10,519	11,203	12,945
Current ratio	1.8	2.3	1.8	2.0	2.5
Net plant and equipment	$19,416	$21,623	$20,006	$20,916	$17,633
Total assets	$55,369	$54,655	$54,806	$55,853	$50,319
Shares outstanding at year-end	2,157	2,152	2,150	2,148	2,146

Stock Prices by Quarters

	1987		1986	
	High	**Low**	**High**	**Low**
First quarter	8⅝	6¾	5¼	4⅜
Second quarter	11⅛	7⅜	7⅛	4⅞
Third quarter	9⅞	8⅜	7¾	6
Fourth quarter	9⅝	8⅞	7½	5¾

FORGING TECHNOLOGY

The forging process involved the use of closed-impression dies and forging hammers, forging machines, and forging presses to work hot steel into intricate shapes. Forging kneaded the hot metal, concentrating on the grain structure and fiber formation at points of greatest shock and stress (the basis of strength and toughness in forgings was the fiberlike structure inherent in the steel) to obtain maximum impact strength, toughness, and high fatigue resistance. The maximum refinement and improvement of the physical properties of metal were obtained only by the forging process.

The forging of hot metal began some 4,000 years ago on the similar principle used today—the blow of a hammer to a billet of hot metal to form a tool or weapon. Over the years, technology had improved the power and precision of the hammer, but individual forgings were alike. A process developed in the 1850s by Elisha K. Root and C. E. Billings, at the Colt Arms Company in Connecticut, proved to be a technological breakthrough in the art of forging; their innovation permitted the design of precision forging dies for making interchangeable parts at greater speed and eliminated a great deal of handwork (filing and grinding) to finish the parts.

Modern technologies, such as computer-aided design and computer-aided manufacturing, automatic temperature control, induction heating, and so on, found great application in the forging industry. Modern forging was an incorporation of ancient ideas with the newest discoveries of space age metallurgy. Warm and cold forge technologies were developed and utilized to meet different requirements. Today's forged component offered greater strength, maximum weight/strength relationship, greater fatigue resistance, elimination of porosity, dimensional conformity, a refined crystalline structure, orientation of grain flow, faster and easier machining, lower scrap rates, and tremendous reliability.

SIFCO FORGE GROUP

The Forge Group was headed by Vice President and Group General Manager Edwin Schmidt, a graduate of Yale (BS) and the Wharton School of Business at the University of Pennsylvania (MBA).

The Forge Group had three divisions: Steel Improvement & Forge Division, Coldforge Division, and International Forging Sales. It manufactured hot, warm, and cold forgings for commercial and high-technology markets. The Forge Group had 11 sales offices in different states with general sales offices in Cleveland.

The Forge Group's die forgings of complex shapes covered the range of carbon, alloy, high-temperature, and titanium metals. High-volume commercial forgings from 1 to 500 pounds and cold and warm forgings in low and medium carbon steels and alloys from 2 to 50 pounds were typical. Titanium weights ranged up to 90 pounds. The group provided complex forgings like airframe, engine component, crankshaft, landing gear, connecting rods, and other complex forgings and component assemblies. Some of the companies that specified SIFCO forgings included Alco, Armco, Avco Lycoming, Bell Helicopter, Boeing, Caterpillar, Chrysler, John Deere, Ford, General Motors, McDonnell Douglas, General Electric, International Harvester, Westinghouse, Pratt and Whitney, and Lockheed.

International Operations

SIFCO Forge Group's move into international business ventures and the transfer of forging technology and management to other countries began in 1951. The first program was in Canada and involved building and managing a plant for aircraft engine forgings. By 1990, SIFCO had business ties with Argentina,

Brazil, India, Japan, France, Ireland, Korea, and England. These included an agreement to manage a government-owned facility; joint ventures partly owned by SIFCO; the transfer of managerial expertise, technology, and production assistance for a fixed fee; contracts for sales representation; and marketing orientation and development of products in the United States under licenses from abroad.

SIFCO's involvement in Argentina and Brazil was in the form of joint ventures and, in India, in the form of a technical assistance agreement. In each instance, the recipients not only became major concerns but also significant exporters. Charles H. Smith Jr. once said:

> With steel improvement-related forge plants in both Argentina and Brazil, the company was asked to consider almost every new forging project proposed in any developing country. Unfortunately, few such projects met the basic criteria the company management considered essential for success. Even where these criteria were met, the company lacked the resources to invest in every developing country's quest for industrialization.

CHINA PROJECT

In September 1986, through Kowin Development Corporation, a trading company based in Los Angeles, SIFCO learned that Shanghai Heavy Die Forging Plant (SHD), which was owned by Shanghai Mechanical & Electrical Industrial Investment Corporation (SMEIIC), had been seeking a foreign joint venture partner that could provide advanced forging technology and an export channel.

SIFCO's management viewed this as a good opportunity to enter China's market. Through the assistance of the Kowin Development Corporation, SIFCO and SMEIIC began correspondence. Within a few months, both parties had expressed a strong interest and in late 1986, SIFCO was invited to visit Shanghai.

After receiving SHD's invitation, SIFCO top management reviewed the strategic considerations that would affect any decision to enter China. Several issues were identified:

1. China had 25 percent of the world's population and was vastly underdeveloped. China represented the largest potential market in Asia for SIFCO Forge Group's products. Since forging parts had applications in a variety of industries, market demand for quality forgings in China would be great for a long time.

2. China had embarked on a grand modernization program in 1979 and had been developing rapidly. Forging was basic to the development of a country's infrastructure and its industries. SIFCO's forging technology represented a great improvement over what was current in China. And, SIFCO had unique experience and capability in transferring forging technology to developing countries.

3. A major constraint in China's development plans was the hard currency to finance imports of badly needed foreign technology and capital equipment. Consequently, government policy encouraged investments with export or import substitution potential. SIFCO management expected strong demand for SIFCO forgings from Chinese manufacturers that were currently importing quality forgings from Japan, Germany, and other western countries.

4. The manufacture of forging parts was highly labor and overhead intensive. With the lowest wage rates in the world, China could prove to be an excellent low-cost supply base for the world market. SIFCO had concentrated on the higher end of the U.S. forging market because of formidable competition from commercial forging manufacturers in Korea, Italy, Taiwan, and other countries. As part of an overall strategy, SIFCO could sell SIFCO-China joint venture products in U.S. commercial forging markets.

5. Since the goal was to establish a long-term relationship, a joint venture would be suitable. SIFCO could become a minority partner in a solid company. Management believed this was an opportunity for SIFCO to parlay its forging manufacturing and marketing expertise into significant increased earnings despite a flat U.S. forging market.

CHINA'S ECONOMIC OUTLOOK

China had a long-term target of quadrupling per capita national income between 1980 and 2000 and becoming a midlevel developed economy by 2050. Efforts to stabilize aggregate domestic demand and control imports, investment, inflation, and foreign exchange had dominated China's economic policy in recent years.

China's current economic reform began in 1978 to reduce inefficiencies in the economy, speed development, and raise consumer living standards. (See Exhibit 2 for the key statistics for China's economy from 1970 to 1986.) China was a relative newcomer to the international world of foreign direct investment, only opening the country to such activity in 1978. Beijing had subsequently put into place laws, regulations, incentives, and policies aimed at encouraging foreign investment. Beijing was interested in directing foreign investment to manufacturing, rather than service industries, and into industries that were export oriented and involved technologies new to China.

The Joint Venture Law

China promulgated the Law of the People's Republic of China on Joint Ventures Using Chinese and Foreign Investment (see Exhibit 3) in July 1979 and Regulations for the Implementation of the Law of the People's Republic of China on Joint Venture Using Chinese and Foreign Investment in September 1983. These were intended to enable China to absorb capital and technology from abroad while conserving foreign exchange.

Several key features of the law and regulation were the following:

1. The law prescribed no upper limit to the proportion of foreign investment in a joint venture (Article 4). This was in contrast to the laws of most developing countries, which generally stipulated an upper limit of 49 percent. There was a lower limit of 25 percent, apparently to ensure the foreign participant would have sufficient commitment to the venture.

Also in contrast to the laws of other developing countries, the Chinese law did not define preferred industries for joint ventures but preserved for the government the flexibility to direct investment funds through supplementary measures according to current needs.

EXHIBIT 2   China's Key Economic Statistics, 1970–86   *(Estimates)**

	1970	1975	1980	1981	1982	1983	1984	1985	1986
Industrial Production Index									
(1970 = 100)	100	159	240	250	269	297	339	400	437
Production									
Coal (MT millions)	327.4	473.0	620.0	620.0	666.0	715.0	789.0	830.0	870.0
Crude oil (bpd millions)	0.6	1.34	2.12	2.0	2.04	2.2	2.3	2.5	2.5
Electric power (kWh billions)	107.0	187.0	300.6	309.3	327.7	351.4	377.0	407.0	445.0
Steel (MT millions)	17.8	24.0	37.1	35.6	35.5	39.9	43.4	46.6	52.1
Cotton (MT millions)	2.0	2.4	2.7	3.0	3.6	4.6	6.2	4.14	3.34
Cotton cloth (Meter billions)	5.5	9.7	13.5	14.3	15.4	14.9	13.7	14.3	13.8
Grain (MT millions)	243.0	234.0	321.0	325.0	353.4	337.2	407.1	378.9	391.1
GNP (1985 $billions)	130.2	169.9	223.0	239.1	259.0	232.5	316.4	354.3	379.0
Real GNP per capita									
Growth (yearly %)	5.5	3.3	4.7	3.5	6.7	8.1	10.3	10.3	3.3
Total foreign trade									
Current $billions	4.4	13.9	38.2	39.6	39.2	42.2	53.1	70.7	78.8
Exports (fob $billions)	2.2	7.1	18.9	21.6	22.4	23.7	27.6	31.3	30.9
Imports (cif $billions)	2.2	6.8	19.3	18.0	16.3	18.3	25.5	39.4	42.9
U.S.–P.R.C. Trade†									
U.S. exports ($millions)‡	—	303.0	3,754.0	3,603.0	2,912.0	2,173.0	3,004.0	3,856.0	3,106.0
U.S. imports ($millions)	—	170.0	1,161.0	2,062.0	2,502.0	2,477.0	3,381.0	4,224.0	5,240.0

*Source: CIA estimates as of September 1986
MT=metric tons.
†Source: U.S. Department of Commerce
‡Blank indicates data not available

U.S.-China Trade, January–September 1987   *(Millions U.S. dollars)*

	September 1987	September 1986	August 1987	January–September 1987	January–September 1986
U.S. exports	$ 304.0	$ 216.5	$ 278.2	$ 2,373.3	$2,421.7
U.S. imports	602.7	456.3	656.7	5,269.6	3,830.9
Total	906.7	672.8	934.9	7.642.9	6,252.6
Balance	$−298.7	$−239.8	$−378.5	$−2,896.3	$−1,409.2

Composition of Trade with China   *(Millions U.S. dollars)*

	January–September 1987	January–September 1986
U.S. exports		
Agricultural	$ 230.6	$ 52.9
Nonagricultural	2,142.7	2,368.5
U.S. imports		
Agricultural	207.9	164.3
Nonagricultural	5,061.7	3,666.6

EXHIBIT 3   **Joint Venture Law of the People's Republic of China**   *(Adopted by the Second Session of the Fifth National People's Congress on July 1, 1979)*

Article 1.   With a view to expanding international economic cooperation and technological exchange, the People's Republic of China permits foreign companies, enterprises, other economic entities or individuals (hereinafter referred to as foreign participants) to incorporate themselves, within the territory of the People's Republic of China, into joint ventures with Chinese companies, enterprises or other economic entities (hereinafter referred to as Chinese participants) on the principle of equality and mutual benefit and subject to authorization by the Chinese government.

Article 2.   The Chinese government protects, by the legislation in force, the resources invested by a foreign participant in a joint venture and the profits due him pursuant to the agreements, contracts and articles of association authorized by the Chinese government as well as his other lawful rights and interests.

All the activities of a joint venture shall be governed by by the laws, decrees and pertinent rules and regulations of the People's Republic of China.

Article 3.   A joint venture shall apply to the Foreign Investment Commission of the People's Republic of China for authorization of the agreements and contracts concluded between the parties to the venture and the articles of association of the venture formulated by them, and the commission shall authorize or reject these documents within three months. When authorized, the joint venture shall register with the General Administration for Industry and Commerce of the People's Republic of China and start operations under license.

Article 4.   A joint venture shall take the form of a limited liability company.

In the registered capital of a joint venture, the proportion of the investment contributed by the foreign participant(s) shall in general not be less than 25 percent.

The profits, risks and losses of a joint venture shall be shared by the parties to the venture in proportion to their contributions to the registered capital.

The transfer of one party's share in the registered capital shall be affected only with the consent of the other parties to the venture.

Article 5.   Each party to a joint venture may contribute cash, capital goods, industrial property rights, etc. as its investment in the venture.

The technology or equipment contributed by any foreign participant as investment shall be truly advanced and appropriate to China's needs. In cases of losses caused by deception through the intentional provision of outdated equipment or technology, compensation shall be paid for the losses.

The investment contributed by the Chinese participant may include the right to the use of a site provided for the joint venture during the period of its operation. In case such a contribution does not constitute a part of the investment from the Chinese participant, the joint venture shall pay the Chinese government for its use.

The various contributions referred to in the present article shall be specified in the contracts concerning the joint venture or in its article of association and the value of each contribution (excluding that of the site) shall be ascertained by the parties to the venture through joint assessment.

Article 6.   A joint venture shall have a board of directors with a composition stipulated in the contracts and the articles of association after consultation between the parties to the venture, and each director shall be appointed or removed by his own side. The board of directors shall have a chairman appointed by the Chinese participant and one or two vice chairmen appointed by the foreign participant(s). In handling an important problem, the board of directors shall reach decision through consultation by the participants on the principle of equality and mutual benefit.

The board of directors is empowered to discuss and take action on, pursuant to the provisions of the articles of association of the joint venture, all fundamental issues concerning the venture, namely, expansion projects, production and business programs, the budget, distribution of profits, plans concerning manpower and pay scales, the termination of business, the appointment or hiring of the president, the vice president(s), the chief engineer, the treasurer and the auditors as well as their functions and powers and their remuneration, etc. The president and vice president(s) (or the general manager and assistant general manager(s) in a factory) shall be chosen from various parties to the joint venture.

Procedures covering the employment and discharge of the workers and staff members of a joint venture shall be stipulated according to law in the agreement or contract concluded between the parties to the venture.

EXHIBIT 3   *(concluded)*

Article 7.   The net profit of a joint venture shall be distributed between the parties to the venture in proportion to their respective shares in the registered capital after the payment of a joint venture income tax on its gross profit pursuant to the tax laws of the People's Republic of China and after the deduction therefrom as stipulated in the articles of association of the venture for the reserve funds, the bonus and welfare funds for the workers and staff members and the expansion funds of the venture.

A joint venture equipped with up-to-date technology by world standards may apply for a reduction of or exemption from income tax for the first two or three profit-making years.

A foreign participant who re-invests any part of his share of the net profit within Chinese territory may apply for the restitution of a part of the income taxes paid.

Article 8.   A joint venture shall open an account with the Bank of China or a bank approved by the Bank of China.

A joint venture shall conduct its foreign exchange transactions in accordance with the foreign exchange regulations of the People's Republic of China.

A joint venture may, in its business operations, obtain funds from foreign banks directly.

The insurance appropriate to a joint venture shall be furnished by Chinese insurance companies.

Article 9.   The production and business programs of a joint venture shall be filed with the authorities concerned and shall be implemented through business contracts.

In its purchase of required raw and semiprocessed materials, fuels, auxiliary equipment, etc., a joint venture should give first priority to Chinese sources. It may also acquire them directly from the world market with its own foreign-exchange funds.

A joint venture is encouraged to market its products outside China. It may distribute its export products on foreign markets through direct channels or its associated agencies or China's foreign trade establishments. Its products may also be distributed on the Chinese market.

Whenever necessary, a joint venture may set up affiliated agencies outside China.

Article 10.   The net profit a foreign participant receives as his share after executing his obligations under the pertinent laws and agreements and contracts, the funds he receives at the time when the joint venture terminates or winds up its operations, and his other funds may be remitted abroad through the Bank of China in accordance with the foregoing exchange regulations and in the currency or currencies specified in the contracts concerning the joint venture.

A foreign participant shall receive encouragements for depositing in the Bank of China any part of the foreign exchange he is entitled to remit abroad.

Article 11.   The wages, salaries or other legitimate income earned by a foreign worker or staff member of a joint venture, after payment of the personal income tax under the tax laws of the People's Republic of China, may be remitted abroad through the Bank of China in accordance with the foreign exchange regulations.

Article 12.   The contract period of a joint venture may be agreed upon between the parties to the venture according to its particular line of business and circumstances. The period may be extended upon expiration through agreement between the parties, subject to authorization by the Foreign Investment Commission of the People's Republic of China. Any application for such extension shall be made six months before the expiration of the contract.

Article 13.   In cases of heavy losses, the failure of any party to a joint venture to execute its obligations under the contracts or the articles of association of the venture, *force majeure*, etc., prior to the expiration of the contract period of a joint venture, the contract may be terminated before the date of expiration by consultation and agreement between the parties and through authorization by the Foreign Investment Commission of the People's Republic of China and registration wit the General Administration for Industry and Commerce. In case of losses caused by breach of the contract(s) by a party to the venture, the financial responsibility shall be borne by the said party.

Article 14.   Disputes arising between the parties to a joint venture which the board of directors fails to settle through consultation may be settled through conciliation or arbitration by an arbitral body of China or through arbitration by an arbitral body agreed upon by the parties.

Article 15.   The present law comes into force on the date of its promulgation. The power of amendment is vested in the National People's Congress.

2. The law provided for a tax holiday to cover the first two to three profit-making years (Article 7). This provision could take the form of either a reduction or an exemption and applied in particular to a joint venture "equipped with up-to-date technology by world standards."

3. The law was quite liberal with regard to marketing. The provisions of Article 9, which stated the joint venture was encouraged to export while being permitted to distribute products within China, sought to balance China's desire to take advantage of a foreign participant's marketing network with the foreign partner's desire to penetrate the Chinese market.

4. The law seemed designed to protect China against exploitation and reflected China's experience with Soviet technical assistance in the late 1950s, which often involved outdated technologies. Article 5 provided that the "technology or equipment contributed by any foreign participant as investment must be truly advanced and appropriate to China's needs."

5. The regulation identified six categories of industries permitted for joint ventures (Article 3):

   a. Energy development, building material, chemical and metallurgical industries.
   b. Machine manufacturing, instrument and meter industries and offshore oil exploitation equipment manufacturing.
   c. Electronics and computer industries and communication equipment manufacturing.
   d. Light, textile, foodstuffs, medicine, medical apparatus and packing industries.
   e. Agriculture, animal husbandry and agriculture.
   f. Tourism and service trades.

O'Donnell once commented: "If you look at what the Chinese are trying to do with their five-year plan, even if you consider just a few sectors like energy, transportation, and food production (farm equipment), every one of those areas will require a tremendous number of forgings."

6. A joint venture had the right to hire and discharge its workers and staff.

China's State Council, the administrative body of the Chinese central government, issued policies to encourage foreign investment from foreign countries (Exhibit 4). The Shanghai municipal government issued special policies to give more favorable treatment to Sino-foreign joint venture firms with advanced technology, export-oriented business (Exhibit 5).

Under the joint venture law, a growing number of foreign firms had invested in joint ventures in China. Exhibit 6 lists the major U.S. investments in China.

INDUSTRIAL ORGANIZATION IN SHANGHAI

Located at the mouth of Yangtze River at the Pacific Ocean, Shanghai was the largest city in terms of both population and industrial output in China. The total population in the Shanghai metropolitan area was about 12 million. Historically, Shanghai had been China's leading technological and industrial base, providing a substantial percentage of industrial revenue to the nation and spearheading China's growing exports into foreign markets.

EXHIBIT 4 **Provisions of the State Council of the People's Republic of China for the Encouragement of Foreign Investment** *(Promulgated on October 11, 1986)*

Article 1. These provisions are hereby formulated in order to improve the investment environment, facilitate the absorption of foreign investment, introduce advanced technology, improve product quality, expand exports in order to generate foreign exchange and develop the national economy.

Article 2. The State encourages foreign companies, enterprises and other economic entities or individuals (hereinafter referred to as "foreign investors") to establish Chinese-foreign equity joint ventures, Chinese-foreign cooperative ventures and wholly foreign-owned enterprises (hereinafter referred to as "enterprises with foreign investment") within the territory of China.

The State grants special preferences to the enterprises with foreign investment listed below:

(1) Production enterprises whose products are mainly for export, which have a foreign exchange surplus after deducting from their total annual foreign exchange revenues the annual foreign exchange expenditures incurred in production and operation and the foreign exchange needed for the remittance abroad of the profits earned by foreign investors (hereinafter referred to as "export enterprises").

(2) Production enterprises possessing advanced technology supplied by foreign investors which are engaged in developing new products, and upgrading and replacing products in order to increase foreign exchange generated by exports or for import substitution (hereinafter referred to as "technologically advanced enterprises").

Article 3. Export enterprises and technologically advanced enterprises shall be exempt from payment to the State of all subsidies to staff and workers, except for the payment of or allocation of funds for labor insurance, welfare costs and housing subsidies for Chinese staff and workers in accordance with the provisions of the State.

Article 4. The site use fees for export enterprises and technologically advanced enterprises, except for those allocated in busy urban sectors of large cities, shall be computed and charged according to the following standards:

(1) Five to 20 RMB yuan per square meter per year in areas where the development fee and the site use fee are computed and charged together;

(2) Not more than three RMB yuan per square meter per year in site areas where the development fee is computed and charged on a one-time basis or areas which are developed by the above-mentioned enterprises themselves.

Exemptions for specified periods of time from the fees provided in the foregoing provision may be granted at the discretion of local people's governments.

Article 5. Export enterprises and technologically advanced enterprises shall be given priority in obtaining water, electricity and transportation services, and communication facilities needed for their production and operation. Fees shall be computed and charged in accordance with the standards for local state enterprises.

Article 6. Export enterprises and technologically advanced enterprises, after examination by the Bank of China, shall be given priority in receiving loans for short-term revolving funds needed for production and distribution, as well as for other needed credit.

Article 7. When foreign investors in export enterprises and technologically advanced enterprises remit abroad profits distributed to them by such enterprises, the amount remitted shall be exempt from income tax.

Article 8. After the expiration of the period for the reduction or exemption of enterprise income tax in accordance with the provisions of the State, export enterprises whose value of export products in that year amounts to 70 percent or more of the value of their products for that year, may pay enterprise income tax at one half the rate of the present tax.

Export enterprises in the special economic zones and in the economic and technological development zones and other export enterprises that already pay enterprise income tax at a tax rate of 15 percent and that comply with the foregoing conditions, shall pay enterprise income tax at a rate of 10 percent.

Article 9. After the expiration of the period of reduction or exemption of enterprise income tax in accordance with the provisions of the State, technologically advanced enterprises may extend for three years the payment of enterprise income tax at a rate reduced by one half.

Article 10. Foreign investors who reinvest the profits distributed to them by their enterprises in order to establish or expand export enterprises or technologically advanced enterprises for a period of operation of not less than five years, after application to and approval by the tax authorities, shall be refunded the total amount of enterprise income tax already paid on the reinvested portion. If the investment is withdrawn before the period of operation reaches five years, the amount of enterprise income tax refunded shall be repaid.

Article 11. Export products of enterprises with foreign investment, except crude oil, finished oil and other products subject to special State provisions, shall be exempt from the consolidated industrial and commercial tax.

Article 12. Enterprises with foreign investment may arrange the export of their products directly or may also export by consignment to agents in accordance with State provisions. For products that require an export license, in accordance with the annual export plan of the enterprise, an application for an export license may be made every six months.

EXHIBIT 4 *(concluded)*

Article 13. Machinery and equipment, vehicles used in production, raw materials, fuel, bulk parts, spare parts, machine component parts and fittings (including imports restricted by the State), which enterprises with foreign investment need to import in order to carry out their export contracts do not require further applications for examination and approval and are exempt from the requirement for import licenses. The customs department shall exercise supervision and control, and shall inspect and release such imports on the basis of the enterprise contract or the export contract.

The imported materials and items mentioned above are restricted to use by the enterprise and may not be sold on the domestic market. If they are used in products to be sold domestically, import procedures shall be handled in accordance with provisions and the taxes shall be made up according to the governing sections.

Article 14. Under the supervision of the foreign exchange control departments, enterprises with foreign investment may mutually adjust their foreign exchange surpluses and deficiencies among each other.

The Bank of China and other banks designated by the People's Bank of China may provide cash security services and may grant loans in renminbi to enterprises with foreign investment.

Article 15. The people's governments at all levels and relevant departments in charge shall guarantee the right of autonomy of enterprises with foreign investment and shall support enterprises with foreign investment in managing themselves in accordance with international advanced scientific methods.

With the scope of their approved contracts, enterprises with foreign investment have the right to determine by themselves production and operation plans, to raise funds, to use funds, to purchase production materials and to sell products; and to determine by themselves the wage levels, the forms of wages and bonuses and the allowance system.

Enterprises with foreign investment may, in accordance with their production and operation requirements, determine by themselves their organizational structure and personnel system, employ or dismiss senior management personnel, increase or dismiss staff and workers. They may recruit and employ technical personnel, managerial personnel and workers in their locality. The unit to which such employed personnel belong shall provide its support and shall permit their transfer. Staff and workers who violate the rules and regulations, and thereby cause certain bad consequences may, in accordance with the seriousness of the case, be given differing sanctions, up to that of discharge. Enterprises with foreign investment that recruit, employ, dismiss or discharge staff and workers, shall file a report with the local labor and personnel department.

Article 16. All districts and departments must implement the "Circular of the State Council Concerning Firmly Curbing the Indiscriminate Levy of Charges on Enterprises." The people's governments at the provincial level shall formulate specific methods and strengthen supervision and administration.

Enterprises with foreign investment that encounter unreasonable charges may refuse to pay and may also appeal to the local economic committees up to the State Economic Commission.

Article 17. The people's governments at all levels and relevant departments in charge shall strengthen the coordination of their work, improve efficiency in handling matters and shall promptly examine and approve matters reported by enterprises with foreign investment that require response and resolution. The agreement, contract and articles of association of an enterprise with foreign investment shall be examined and approved by the departments in charge under the State Council. The examination and approval authority must within three months from the date of receipt of all documents decide to approve or not to approve them.

Article 18. Export enterprises and technologically advanced enterprises mentioned in these provisions shall be confirmed jointly as such by the foreign economic relations and trade departments where such enterprises are located and the relevant departments in accordance with the enterprise contract, and certification shall be issued.

If the actual results of the annual exports of an export enterprise are unable to realize the goal of the surplus in the foreign exchange balance that is stipulated in the enterprise contract, the taxes and fees which have already been reduced or exempted in the previous year shall be made up in the following year.

Article 19. Except where these provisions expressly provide that they are to be applicable to export enterprises or technologically advanced enterprises, other articles shall be applicable to all enterprises with foreign investment.

These provisions apply from the date of implementation to those enterprises with foreign investment that have obtained approval for establishment before the date of implementation of these provisions and that qualify for the preferential terms of these provisions.

Article 20. For enterprises invested in and established by companies, enterprises and other economic organizations or individuals from Hong Kong, Macao, or Taiwan, matters shall be handled by reference to these provisions.

Article 21. The Ministry of Foreign Economic Relations and Trade shall be responsible for interpreting these provisions.

Article 22. These provisions shall go into effect on the date of issue.

EXHIBIT 5   **Provisions of the Shanghai Municipality for the Encouragement of Foreign Investment**   *(Promulgated on October 23, 1986)*

Article 1.   In order to take further steps to facilitate the absorption of foreign investment, introduce advanced technology, expand exports to generate foreign exchange and quicken Shanghai's economic development, various districts and departments within the City of Shanghai must seriously implement these provisions apart from the firm implementation of the "Provisions of the State Council of the People's Republic of China for the Encouragement of Foreign Investment."

Article 2.   All export enterprises and technologically advanced enterprises shall be exempt from local income tax during the period for the exemption of enterprise income tax in accordance with the provisions of the State. After the expiration of the period, those enterprises shall be exempt from local income tax for three years, and afterwards, they shall pay the tax at a rate reduced by one half for another three years.

Article 3.   After the expiration of the period of the exemption of local income tax in accordance with the foregoing provision, export enterprises whose value of export products in that year amounts to 70 percent or more of the value of their products for that year shall still be exempt from the local income tax.

Article 4.   Except for those located in busy urban sectors, export enterprises and technologically advanced enterprises shall be exempt from land use fees for three years after their establishment. Beginning from the fourth year, the fees shall be paid at a 50 percent rate of the minimum level prescribed in concerned regulations, but they shall not be higher than 2.50 RMB yuan per square meter per year.

Article 5.   Enterprises with foreign investment shall be exempt from the housing subsidies, which would otherwise be paid to the State, in accordance with the number of Chinese staff and workers. The enterprises can retain the money as the fund to improve the housing conditions of their Chinese staff and workers.

Article 6.   Enterprises with foreign investment may employ and recruit technical personnel, managerial personnel and workers within the territory of Shanghai. These enterprises may also employ or borrow the above-mentioned personnel from other provinces and cities under the guidance of the labor and personnel department. If they are dismissed, they shall return to where they come from.

Article 7.   Export enterprises and technologically advanced enterprises shall be given priority in obtaining water, electricity, gas, transportation services and communication facilities needed for their production and operation. Fees shall be computed and charged in accordance with the standards for local state enterprises.

Article 8.   Export enterprises and technologically advanced enterprises, after examination by banks with which they open accounts or other financial institutions, shall be given priority in receiving loans for short-term revolving funds needed for production and distribution, as well as for other needed credit.

Article 9.   Under the Shanghai Municipal Foreign Investment Administration, a foreign investment service will be established. It is designed to offer administrative service for foreign investors.

Article 10.   Under the supervision of the foreign exchange control department, a foreign exchange adjustment agency will be established to help enterprises with foreign investment mutually adjust their foreign exchange surpluses and deficiencies.

Article 11.   In order to facilitate the supply of raw materials for enterprises with foreign investment, a commodities service agency for enterprises with foreign investment will be established.

Article 12.   Economic and technological development zones will be given greater autonomy and enterprises with foreign investment established there will be given more preferences. The concrete measures will be promulgated separately.

Article 13.   For enterprises with foreign investment subject to examination and approval by Shanghai Municipality, the competent authorities shall give official replies to their project proposals within 30 days from the date of receipt of the documents. The same time limit shall apply to feasibility study report, contract, and articles of association. Approval certificate shall be issued within 10 days after the necessary documents are produced.

Article 14.   For enterprises invested and established by companies, enterprises and other economic organizations or individuals from Hong Kong, Macao or Taiwan, matters shall be handled by reference to these provisions.

Article 15.   The Shanghai Municipal Foreign Economic Relations and Trade Commission shall be responsible for interpreting these provisions.

Article 16.   These provisions shall go into effect on November 1, 1986.

EXHIBIT 6   List of Major U.S. Foreign Investments in China

Company Names	Project Investment (in millions)
Occidental Petroleum's PingShuo coal mine	$650
ARCO/CNOOC South China Sea gas field development	170
Beatrice Foods/CITIC	100
Seacliff Group/Shanghai Exhibition Group	175
E.I. Pacific Development/CITS	72
AMC/Beijing Jeep	51
Transworld Group/Xinjiang Textile Industrial Co.	40
Warner Lambert Co./Suzhou Pharmaceutical Co.	18
R.J. Reynolds Inc./Xiamen cigarette factory	20
Babcox & Wilcox/Beijing Boiler Factory	12
Foxboro Co./Shanghai Instrument Industry Co.	10
Hewlett Packard/Beijing Computer Industry Corp.	10
E.R. Squibb	10
Otis Elevator Co./CITIC & Tianjin Lift Co.	5

Shanghai was one of the three municipalities (Beijing, Shanghai, and Tianjin) that were subordinated to the central government directly. Because of its strategic position in China's economic development, the Shanghai municipal government was delegated greater authority to do international business and approve joint venture projects. The governmental structure of Shanghai municipality included a party secretary, who set policy, and a mayor and seven deputy mayors, who carried out the administrative functions. One deputy mayor was in charge of all economic activity within the municipality.

Reporting to the mayor were a number of commissions and bureaus. Municipal commissions were generally higher than the bureaus in the hierarchy. The bureaus were responsible for all goods and services produced within Shanghai. All economic activity within Shanghai was effectively controlled at the municipal level.

There were six commissions in Shanghai, all making policies and plans and approving key projects. These six commissions were as follows:

- Planning Commission.
- Economic Commission.
- Foreign Investment Commission.
- Foreign Economic Relation and Trade Commission.
- Science and Technology Commission.
- Education Commission.

There were 30 bureaus in Shanghai, 10 making industrial products and 20 providing services. The 10 industrial bureaus, which reported to the Economic Commission, were as follows:

- Chemical Industry (rubber, fertilizers, insecticides).
- Electronic Industry (electronic element, device, instrument, computer).
- Power Industry (power generation).
- Petrochemical Industry (gasoline, oils).

- Light Industry (bicycles, watches, shoes, sewing machines, flasks, arts and handicrafts).
- Agricultural machinery (tractors, diesel engines, farm implements).
- Textile Industry (textiles and textile machinery).
- Mechanical & Electrical Industry (machine tools, trucks, bearings, elevator, electrical devices).
- Metallurgical Industry (iron, steel, rare metals).
- Construction (and construction equipment).

Functional responsibility for the management of SHD belonged to the Shanghai Mechanical & Electrical Industry Bureau (SMEIB). There were 14 divisions in SMEIB, overseeing the planning, technology, production, marketing, financing, personnel, import & export, and foreign investment associated with all facets of 80 plants including SHD. SMEIIC was in charge of forming joint ventures with foreign firms. This administrative structure was extremely hierarchical. However, many officials participated in several organizations (see Exhibit 7). These multiple roles provided a means for intraorganizational communication not inherent in the structure itself.

Labor Practices

China did not have a free labor market. Workers were first recommended by the municipal office in charge of the plant needing additional workers. To achieve full employment, new workers often were assigned to a plant that did not need additional workers. Workers were trained by the factory at which they were employed, and plant discipline was maintained through social and incentive pressure. It was extremely rare for a worker, once hired, to be discharged.

Chinese workers in a forging plant earned an average wage of RMB240 (equivalent to $60) per month for six eight-hour days. In addition to a bonus, the workers also received such benefits as rent for housing, free medical care and medication, a food allowance, children's educational allowance, a transportation subsidy, paid sick leave, 30 days' paid leave to visit a spouse (married) or parents (unmarried) if a worker lived in a different city from the spouse/parents. A cap on wages had been removed, and foreign-invested firms had freedom to set wages and offer differential wages. Some wages, however, were not set commensurate with productivity.

The total number of employees at a Chinese plant was far greater than at its U.S. counterpart because a Chinese plant had to operate its own cafeteria, nursery and kindergarten, cleaning fleet, security, intercity shipping, and other services.

Shanghai's Heavy Die Forging Plant

Company Background

Located in Shanghai, China's largest city, SHD specialized in manufacturing general-purpose commercial forgings. As one of the key forging manufacturers in Shanghai, SHD directly reported to Shanghai Mechanical & Electrical Industrial Bureau (SMEIB) (see Exhibit 7). In creating a joint venture, SMEIIC represented SMEIB as the owner.

EXHIBIT 7 Shanghai Organizational Chart

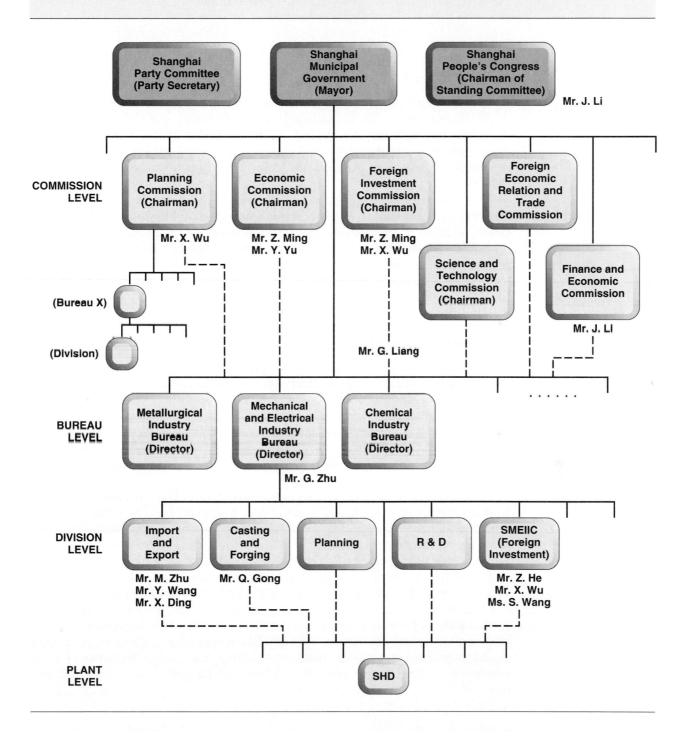

Both the Register of Shipping of China and the American Bureau of Shipping (ABS) issued documents indicating SHD was capable of producing marine forgings in accordance with the rules of the register and the bureau.

With more than 1,050 employees, including about 100 engineers and technicians, the plant had annual sales of RMB 22 million yuan (about $7 million), and the growth rate of earnings before taxes had been 6 percent for the past five years. SHD provided open forgings and certain closed die forgings to domestic markets; export was rare.

Industry Analysis

China's forging technology lagged about 10 years behind the world level. Most of the manufacturers in this industry used a hammer and hydropress to produce free forgings and die forgings with the quality below world standards. Mass production with mechanical presses was rare. Forging dies were made manually. High-quality forgings, particularly forgings made by press, had to be imported from abroad.

There were 15 forging plants or workshops in Shanghai under various bureaus, each producing to the needs of its respective bureau. There was little rationalization of production. Marketing across bureau lines, cities, or provinces was allowed. However, because of "protectionism," these kinds of selling needed greater efforts.

In 1984, the government established that, within four years, all forging firms in China would purchase materials and sell their forgings on the market freely. Competition was getting tense among the forging firms.

Initiation of the Project

With the development of the open-door policy, Shanghai was given special permission to introduce foreign technology, absorb foreign capital, and export. On top of the Provisions of the State Council of the People's Republic of China for the Encouragement of Foreign Investment, Shanghai issued the Provisions of the Shanghai Municipality for the Encouragement of Foreign Investment in 1986, offering more favorable terms for foreign investors. SHD was one of the firms in Shanghai to be encouraged to acquire advanced technology and utilize foreign capital.

Mr. Z. He (pronounced "Ha"), general manager of SMEIIC, said "I used to be the director of SHD for 10 years. I feel that SHD has the potential to be improved considerably and become competitive in the world market if more advanced technology is acquired."

Since late 1985, SHD had been actively looking for a joint venture partner that was able to provide capital and technology and was willing to sell joint venture products in the world market through its own marketing channel.

Once in a private discussion, a deputy director of SHD said: "If we can form a joint venture with a foreign partner, according to the government regulations, we would enjoy more benefits like technology advancement, greater decision-making autonomy, handsome salary and wage increases for all employees, better fringe benefits, addition of company cars. . . . You just name it!"[1]

---

[1]China discourages companies from owning company cars. Each Chinese company in Shanghai has a quota for the number of cars it can own. However, a foreign-Chinese joint venture can own more cars.

MERGER NEGOTIATIONS

Initial Shanghai Round

After a couple of months of correspondence, SMEIIC invited SIFCO to visit. In December 1986, O'Donnell visited Shanghai and started a joint venture discussion with SMEIIC and SHD. The general manager of SMEIIC was present at all the discussions. This visit ended with a memorandum of understanding. In this memo, both parties expressed the intent of forming a joint forging business venture in Shanghai and agreed to further explore the economic viability of the project. At the meeting, the Chinese side asked SIFCO to take the responsibility of selling forgings to the world market. During this visit, Mr. Yu, deputy director of SMEIB, expressed his support for such a joint venture. Mr. Chen, the president of China Forging Industry Association, also voiced his support and discussed other cooperative possibilities with O'Donnell.

Later, O'Donnell recalled: "I think SHD demonstrated the capability of absorbing our technology. . . . I felt very comfortable dealing with SHD people. They were honest and sincere in venturing to reach an agreement."

In February 1987, a SIFCO Forge Group team headed by Ed Schmidt visited Shanghai to assess SHD's background and technological capability. The meetings further confirmed the technical and economic viability of the venture. Another memorandum of understanding was signed. SIFCO agreed in principle to transfer hammer forging technology to SHD and to sell the joint venture forgings to the U.S. market. The Chinese side agreed to provide land, building, labor, and cash. Schmidt later commented:

> SHD is ideally positioned for absorption of technical assistance and for rapid expansion to meet China's demand for forged product. With the basic core equipment of 6,000-pound to 20,000-pound closed die forging steam hammers and up to 1,000-ton hydraulic presses for open die forging already in place, we can plan a sharp increase in productive capacity through improved manufacturing methods and additions of selective forging and support equipment.

Cleveland Round

In May 1987, the SMEIIC team headed by He visited SIFCO in Cleveland. The purpose of the meeting was to discuss the major issues in a feasibility study for the joint venture. SIFCO hired a Chinese national, currently studying business in the United States, to be involved in the project.

During the meeting, the technology and export issues were discussed. The development plan was set, and SIFCO agreed to sell the forgings in the U.S. market to a total of $20 million in eight years starting from the third year after the venture was established. Differences continued around the following key issues:

1. *SIFCO's equity contribution:* The focus was on the estimation of SIFCO's technology value—$2.06 million for technical know-how, technical assistance, and CAD/CAM hardware and software. SIFCO wanted to reinvest a substantial part of this amount in the venture as its equity contribution and use the remaining to cover training and technical assistance expenses. The Chinese kept questioning how SIFCO could put that value on its technology and insisted on a breakdown of the grand total.

2. *Financial data from SHD:* SIFCO provided SHD with all its financial data. However, SHD had not provided any data to show its profitability for the past five years. The only information the Chinese team gave was: "Believe us, we've been making money for the past 10 years." The SIFCO team asked: "How could we know we want to put money there without seeing your financial data?" At last the Chinese team told SIFCO it could not provide the information without getting permission from the Shanghai municipal government. The team promised to talk to the government and provide the financial data later somehow.

3. *Press technology:* SHD initially wanted SIFCO to provide press equipment and technology from the first year. SIFCO suggested it introduce press technology in the third or fourth year since China's market was not ready for press forging parts.

Both parties agreed to meet again soon, but then SIFCO did not hear anything from SHD for about two and a half months after the Chinese team left. So SIFCO telexed SMEIIC, saying: "Let us be honest with one another and in the spirit of cooperation and friendship that we have all displayed thus far, quickly decide if further JV study is worthwhile for SHD and SIFCO." Fifteen days later, SMEIIC telexed back, saying, "We wholeheartedly hope to keep on making arrangements for our joint venture; we are speeding up our work to send you the financial information enthusiastically." It took about three months for SMEIIC to report to the government and to get the go-ahead.

Before long, SIFCO received SHD's information related to the feasibility study, but the financial data were sparse. SHD also sent SIFCO its five-year projection of joint venture sales, cost of goods sold (COGS), earnings before taxes (EBT), and exports. SIFCO was surprised to find out that materials accounted for about 86 percent of COGS. SHD also included a request for introduction of press equipment and technology in the first year to enable it to bid on potential orders from the Shanghai Volkswagen Automobile Company.

Second Shanghai Round

In November 1987, O'Donnell visited Shanghai again for further discussions. The terms of technology transfer and joint venture were discussed in full. O'Donnell faced between 8 and 12 people in all the meetings. The heated discussions were centered on profitability, equity contribution by each party, the value of SIFCO's technology, and work force considerations:

1. *Profitability of the joint venture:* When asked why the material cost was so high and EBT was so low in the projection, the SHD team said the highest market prices of materials were used so the projection was prudent and reliable and both sides would be happier when the actual profits exceeded the "conservative profitability projection." The team felt by doing so it showed its sincerity and commitment. O'Donnell said: "I am your partner. But you treat me like your customer." When asked about the income statement, balance sheet, and other financial data, SHD said it could provide statistical data only as references. The SIFCO team said: "You never gave us your annual profit for the most recent five years. Our explanation is that the projection reflects your low profitability. We don't think SIFCO will invest under this situation."

2. *Equity contribution:* SIFCO wanted to have a smaller venture since it did not have that much money for the initial investment. SMEIIC insisted the whole existing plant and employees be included and SIFCO's equity contribution could not be below 25 percent, which is the minimum share the government set for foreign partners.

Neither side could reach agreement on these two issues. During the deadlock, the Chinese asked the accompanying Chinese student to explain the American business philosophy behind the projection. Then the Chinese promised to give SIFCO the financial data verbally since they could not get permission from the government agency concerned. Mr. He also said: "We started understanding him (O'Donnell). His questioning and argument showed his commitment to this joint venture. The American wouldn't put the money into water."

When negotiations resumed, the chief accountant of SHD provided the financial data, showing SHD's profitability was close to the top among all the forge shops in China. Then the past 11 months' average material cost was used as the average market price of materials in the projection. The projected profitability of the venture turned out to be very attractive.

3. *Value of SIFCO's technology:* SIFCO asked for $2.06 million for its technology, of which $860,000 would be an up-front payment. The remaining $1.2 million would be paid equally in four years to cover the expense of SIFCO's technical assistance and training of engineers and managers. SIFCO estimated the total time needed would be about 2,400 worker-days in four years. The Chinese thought the figures were too high to accept.

4. *Work force:* To reduce initial capital investment requirements, both parties agreed to use SHD's existing building and facilities. However, SHD wanted the joint venture to take the existing work force of 1,050. SIFCO suggested a joint venture with a maximum work force of 450. O'Donnell questioned: "We are competing with Korea, Japan, the U.S., and Canada in the world market. Currently, SHD produces 180 pound forgings per day per person while the figure in SIFCO is more than triple that amount. What are we going to do with these people?" SHD insisted all employees be included, making a number of arguments:

- Serious tension would be created among the existing employees if only part of the work force would be involved because of the great difference of wages and benefits.
- SHD had the social responsibility to keep its employees.
- Though the pound/person ratio was low in SHD, the projected cost of forging parts was only 60 percent of SIFCO's equivalents because of the low wages in China.

Mr. Yu, deputy chief of SMEIB, met and entertained the SIFCO team. He seemed appreciative of this project and supportive of SMEIIC and SHD's positions.

The preliminary agreement reached from this negotiation included a two-phase investment plan suggested by SHD. In the first phase, SIFCO invested $1.5 million and the Chinese side $4.5 million. At the end of the second year, SIFCO would reinvest $500,000 of the dividends it would earn and SHD would invest its remaining fixed assets of $1.5 million. The equity of the joint venture would be in a ratio of 62.5 percent by SHD, 25 percent by SIFCO, and 12.5 percent by the China Investment and Development Bank. SHD would contribute building, land, and machinery. SIFCO would contribute cash and equipment. The bank would contribute cash.

Also, SIFCO agreed to transfer press technology together with hammer technology beginning the first year. SIFCO also agreed to act as the venture's export sales agent and be responsible for selling the forgings in the U.S. market for $20 million over eight years. SIFCO would receive advance commissions of $100,000 per year for four years starting from the first year. However, the Chinese did not agree to the 10 percent commission rate. The preliminary agreement also stated the duration of the joint venture contract would be 15 years with optional extensions at expiration.

Both parties agreed the feasibility study would be completed by SHD with the assistance of SIFCO. SIFCO would list the detailed content of technology that it was to transfer. The commission rate was temporarily set at 10 percent for the feasibility purpose. Prepared information would be exchanged on January 20, 1988. However, the Chinese still insisted the 1,050 employees be included and that SIFCO reduce its fees for technology transfer and the commission rate. The expected date for the discussion of the feasibility study and the pending issues was April 1989.

Back in Cleveland, SIFCO started working on the potential export of the venture's products. Some drawings of potential export products were sent to SHD and quotes were asked.

Early in 1988, SMEIIC informed SIFCO it had contacted a Hong Kong investment company, JF China Investment Ltd., which showed interest in the project. JF China's visits to Shanghai and the follow-up correspondence resulted in the understanding that SIFCO would provide technology and equipment as its equity share, SMEIIC would contribute SHD's existing equipment and building, and JF China would contribute cash. Both SIFCO and SMEIIC were happy with JF China's participation. The venture would not only solve the "two-phase investment" problem but also get some hard currency working capital. JF China also indicated it would like to be a "silent" partner, that is, not involved in management.

The Third Shanghai Round

Before making another visit to Shanghai, SIFCO made careful preparations. First, O'Donnell contacted the Chinese Embassy in Washington and learned the new Chinese government policy allowed the foreign-Chinese joint venture to determine the proper number of employees before business started and it became the responsibility of the Chinese supervising bureau of the Chinese partner (i.e., SMEIB) to assign new jobs to those not hired.

Second, SIFCO contacted the potential customers for the forgings. It found that there was a good chance of selling the forgings at 65 percent of the prevailing U.S. market prices.

Also, the China Forging Industry Association invited SIFCO to give a seminar on contemporary forging technology at its annual meeting in Sichuan, China, in early May. SIFCO saw this as a good opportunity to gain more publicity in the Chinese forging industry and to contact more Chinese forging manufacturers. Though SIFCO had received a couple of invitations from Chinese firms to discuss creating a joint venture, it still believed SHD was the proper partner.

In late April, SIFCO's team visited Shanghai again. The negotiations were divided into two sessions and, in between, the SIFCO team attended the seminar in Sichuan. JF China was not present at the negotiations because of a scheduling problem. The tense and lengthy discussions were around the following issues:

1. *Value of SIFCO's technology:* SMEIIC and SHD still questioned the $860,000 technology transfer fee and $1.2 million expense. The Chinese said they were willing to pay SIFCO's experts' technical assistance and training on an actual expenditure basis. SIFCO argued that, by paying this amount, all of SIFCO's commercial forging technologies including the ones developed during the term of the joint venture contract would be accessible by the venture, and a lot more costs, including opportunity cost and replacement cost, were involved in SIFCO's human resource costs. Additionally, SIFCO firmly stated a technology transfer fee and expenses were the "keystone" for the joint venture deal.

2. *Work force:* Lengthy discussions occurred on this issue. At times, officials from SMEIB and the Foreign Economic Relation and Trade Commission participated in the meetings. SIFCO argued the joint venture was not designed to be an employment vehicle for people but was to be a profit-making operation for its partners who then employed the people. However, it was not until the negotiators met with Mr. Ming, vice chairman of the Shanghai Economic Commission, who confirmed the government policy, that the Chinese relaxed a bit on this issue.

3. *Export price:* The Chinese argued the export pricing was too low and insisted that SIFCO raise it to 75 to 80 percent of the prevailing U.S. market prices. SIFCO tried to explain that (1) the higher the selling price, the more commission SIFCO would get; (2) it was the customer, not SIFCO, that decided the price; and (3) when the customer accepted the forgings, price could be set higher than the entry price.

SIFCO's team was also told that foreign partners could bring their dividends out of China only at a hard currency ratio of RMB 3.72 if the venture had hard currency available. Otherwise the dividends could stay as an investment or be brought out at a soft currency ratio of RMB 6 to 1.

SIFCO and SMEIIC decided to start working on the design and manufacture of a flange for export in 1989.

A new memorandum of understanding contained the following agreement:

1. Technology transfer fee and expense were accepted. To save foreign exchange for the joint venture, up to $220,000 of the expense would be paid by local currency RMB (renminbi).
2. The total number of employees should be substantially reduced. The exact number would be decided by the venture's start-up office.
3. Export price was set at 65 percent of the U.S. market price. It could be raised as the exports increased.
4. SMEIIC would appoint a general manager and SIFCO a deputy general manager.
5. To earn hard currency at the earliest possible date, both parties would work together diligently to make sample forgings for the U.S. oil market.
6. The commission rate was set at 8 percent of selling price.

New Partner

JF China suddenly decided not to invest in the JV project in August 1988. The excuse was that JF China did not think its investment could be paid back as quickly as the feasibility study indicated. A new partner had to be found.

By the end of August, both SIFCO and SMEIIC had contacted Ek Chor Investment Co., Ltd., a subsidiary of Chia Tai Group of Companies headquartered in Thailand. Chia Tai had invested in 11 joint ventures in China. One of the joint ventures was Shanghai–Ek Chor Motorcycle Co., Ltd., which was importing quality forging parts from Japan. In September, three senior managers from Chia Tai's president's office visited SMEIIC and SHD. They disclosed that Chia Tai was considering investing in an automotive joint venture in China. In late October, Ek Chor's president and vice president visited SMEIIC and SHD, showed great interest, and agreed to invest. Ek Chor wanted the venture to be the supplier of forging parts for the existing motorcycle and potential automotive subsidiaries in China. The three parties decided to discuss and finalize the arrangements in early December 1988.

The Fourth Shanghai Round

The new agreement reached in Shanghai by the three parties added the following:

1. Chia Tai would invest $1.5 million in cash. The equity share among SMEIIC, SIFCO, and Chia Tai would be 69.2 percent, 15.4 percent, and 15.4 percent respectively.
2. The joint venture would give priority to the production of the forgings for Shanghai–Ek Chor Motorcycle Co., Ltd.
3. A controller would be appointed by Chia Tai.
4. The feasibility study, joint venture contract, article of association, and technology transfer agreement would be revised accordingly.
5. The Chinese partners and Chia Tai could earn commissions if they exported forgings through their own channels.

Final Memo and the Signing of the Contract

In early March 1989, all the three partners gathered again to discuss the pending issues, particularly the work force. The final and binding memo signed included the following:

1. At the establishment of the joint venture, the total manning would be 850. Workers displaced by establishing this level would be the responsibility of the Chinese partner. The 850 workers would be under contract for employment for one year. At the end of that year, any additional workers declared surplus to the needs of the company would be handled by the Chinese authority concerned.
2. Chia Tai's equity share was allowed to increase up to 30 percent in the future.
3. Official signing of the documents was set for May 1989.

The official signing ceremony for the three documents was held May 16, 1989, in Shanghai. It was reported that this was the first foreign-Chinese joint venture in the forging industry in China.

O'Donnell commented:

> This opportunity to enter the exciting Chinese market under the conditions we have been able to negotiate coordinates nicely with SIFCO's asset redeployment strategy. We are able to realize value for our 75 years of forging experience, both in up-front payments and through the continuing participation as an equity partner and sales agent in this newly created joint venture.

The *Plain Dealer* newspaper, PR Newswire, and Chinese local newspapers all reported this news.

According to the agreement, the three documents were subject to the approval of the competent authorities, which would be the boards of directors for SIFCO and Chia Tai and government agencies (SMEIB and Shanghai Foreign Investment Commission) for SMEIIC. In addition, SIFCO had to obtain an export license for technology transfer to a communist country.

SUDDEN CHANGE

On June 4, the Chinese army occupied Tiananmen Square. The whole world reacted. All media sources were full of news of China. European countries decided to establish economic sanctions against China. President Bush suspended arms and high-tech selling to China, and the U.S. State Department advised U.S. citizens not to travel to China. Exhibit 8 details U.S.-China venture policies before and after the Tiananmen Square incident. Many American firms backed out of China.

SIFCO's board meeting was scheduled for mid-July. There were so many questions to be answered and decisions to be made. SIFCO executives wondered what steps should be taken. There were many views of what was in the long-run interests of the people of China as well as of SIFCO.

EXHIBIT 8   **U.S.-China Venture Development Consortium Newsletter**

Part I: Changes or Events before June 4 Incident

Tax Exemptions

The government has offered preferential treatment to 235 enterprises manufacturing high-tech products.

The enterprises cover integrated circuits, electronic computers, software, and computerized telephone exchanges.

The preferential treatment, which went into effect on January 1, 1987, includes exemption of product value-added tax and business taxes for a predetermined period, reduction of income taxes by 54 percent and deduction of less than 10 percent of their sales volume, to promote research on development of new products.

Distribution Channel

Informed Chinese domestic sources reported that 72 industrial products are still under the mandatory direction of the central government for distribution and allocation.* Fifty-eight industrial products are under the control of State Planning Commission and Ministry of Material Administration. These include: coal, crude oil, heavy oil, diesel oil, gasoline, chemical products, power equipment and measurement tools, kerosene, lubricants, steel, timber, cement, copper, aluminum, lead, zinc, tin, copper material, aluminum material, iron, sulfuric acid, sodium carbonate, rubber, tire, automobiles, transistors, nickel, magnesium, sheet glass, diamonds, coke, asphalt, sulfuric iron ore, 17 chemical raw materials, latex materials, newsprint, letter press paper, packaging paper, various vehicles, wire and cable.

Export Risk Fund

Export risk funding management systems are being set up to promote international trade and raise funding for export. In Shanghai, for example, municipal government recently approved the "Measurement for the Management of Export Risk Funds" worked out by the Financial Bureau and Foreign Economic Relations and Trade Commission. The measures cover three points: Export-oriented enterprises can get 2 to 4 RMB fen (cent in Chinese currency) from every one U.S. dollar sale; half of the foreign exchange income retained by the local government will be used as export risk funds; when enterprises and goods supply units adjust their retained foreign exchange on the foreign exchange adjustment center, 20 percent of their income in RMB will be used as risk funds.

Sino-U.S. Tax Seminar

Some 48 American experts gathered on May 23 in Beijing for a two-day seminar on taxation and accounting. The experts are hoping to obtain from the seminar a better understanding of China's taxation and accounting systems. This seminar is emphasizing taxation, accounting and auditing problems in foreign-invested enterprise in China, and ways to deal with such problems in the United States.

Technology

China will set up a network to coordinate national efforts to promote broader acceptance of new industrial technology. The network aims, on a nationwide scale, to develop technological cooperation, conduct technological consultations and human resource exchanges, and promote the commercialization of scientific and technological achievements.

Funds Shortage

The Agricultural Bank of China has urgently called on local governments to help raise money for the purchase of summer grain from farmers. The People's Bank of China, the country's central bank, was urged to work together with local financial departments in making enterprises pay outstanding accounts and their arrears on loans.

Water Tax

Many Chinese big cities have water shortages. For the first time in history, Beijing is going to impose heavy charges on new consumers of scarce water in the capital. This tax will amount to between 20 and 100 times the government-fixed water price. New businesses and other organizations should be aware of the additional costs.

---

*This means each year the central government will set up planned production quotas for these product categories. Those *Chinese firms* that receive the government orders will be guaranteed raw material supply at the government-fixed prices. The firms, however, have to sell these products through government-controlled distribution channels at the government-fixed prices to the designated buyers. Production and marketing of these categories at market price in excess of the central production quota are allowed, but producers have to purchase raw materials at market prices, almost always higher than government-fixed prices.

The Chinese central government generally does not give any mandatory plans to *joint venture companies*. However, Sino-foreign joint ventures or foreign subsidiaries in China can enter this central planning system through their Chinese partners, if their products fall into the above-mentioned categories. Joint venture companies as well as Chinese domestic companies have free choice to compete for the product categories not covered in the central planning system.

EXHIBIT 8   *(continued)*

Banking Services

The Bank of European Union of France has opened an office in Beijing. This is the 85th foreign bank representative office opened in China.

China continues to modernize its banking systems. The introduction of the credit card has updated traditional methods of settling accounts at Chinese banks. A total of 900 million yuan in transactions have been made since 1986 when the first Great Wall card was issued in China. 200 million yuan transactions took place this year. About 70,000 people currently hold Great Wall cards. China how has over 30 teller machines.

Private Business

China has started to impose new restrictions on private business. According to stipulations worked out by Shanghai Municipal Industrial and Commercial Bureau, private businesses are not allowed to do wholesaling or retailing of the following 26 commodities: petroleum including crude oil, heavy oil and oil products; metal materials including ferrous and nonferrous metals, rare metals, pig iron and steel ingots and blanks; timber; cement; chemicals, paints, dyes, rubber tires and raw materials for light industry; coal, coke and coal products; motor vehicles and main parts; tractors and main parts; machine tools and electric motors; fertilizers; pesticides; protective plastic film for agricultural use; cotton; wool; newsprint and printing paper; color TVs and black-and-white TVs; refrigerators; washing machines; bicycles including storage battery-driven bicycles; rice and flour; edible oil; sugar and salt. Violators will be prosecuted.

Communications

China has been working on improving the communication system, another bottleneck of modernization advancement. Residents of Dalian, Liaoning Province, can now use credit cards for 130 computer-controlled public telephones. The cards are on sale in four denominations and save callers the trouble of having to find enough coins for public telephone booths.

Part II: Political and Economic Situation after June 4 Event

Political Situation

1. The 13th Central Committee of the Chinese Communist Party of China (CPC) dismissed Zhao Ziyang and several of his followers from their leading positions and named Jiang Zemin, former party secretary of Shanghai, as the new party general secretary.

2. The party and the government are going to focus on the following tasks:
   - To continue the crackdown of the "counterrevolutionary rebellion"; carry out ideological and political education and oppose bourgeois liberalization.
   - To enhance party building, democracy and legality; eliminate government corruption.
   - To continue focusing on economic construction and adhere to the policies of carrying out reform and opening to the outside world.
   - To stabilize market prices; continue to cut down capital construction and maintain current consumption level so as to seek a sustained, steady and coordinated economic development.

3. In order to get foreign investment and technology back to China again, the party and government leaders, Deng Xiaoping, Jianzemin, Yang Shangkun, Li Peng made a number of speeches at various occasions reaffirming the following points:
   - China will not change its policy for economic reform and opening to the outside world.
   - China will not change its policies regarding Taiwan, Macao, and Hong Kong.
   - China will not change its foreign policies.
   - China will not change its policies regarding minority, religions and overseas-Chinese affairs.

A systematic and careful review has been made on *China Daily, People's Daily, Beijing Review, China Reconstructs* and other publications available from June 4 up till July 17. No change of tones from the Chinese government regarding its open-door policies has been found. No changes of government regulations and any specific actions taken by the government have taken place that might affect the current and future operations of foreign firms and international joint ventures in China.

EXHIBIT 8   *(concluded)*

This review seems to indicate that although Chinese government has been acting very strongly on domestic political issues, it seems determined to keep the economic and open-door policies unchanged.

Economic Brief

Domestic Economy

- Total national industrial output reaches 639.6 billion yuan for the first two quarters of 1989, an increase of 10.8% as compared to the same period of 1988.
- Capital construction has slowed down. The total investment realized in capital projects is 44.2 billion yuan for the first five months, a decrease of 7.1% as compared to the same period of 1988.
- Total price level of retail goods has increased by 25.5% for the first five months.
- Total retail value reaches 410 billion yuan, an increase of 20% compared to the same period.
- Total import and export reaches $50.3 billion for the first two seasons, an increase of 16.9% compared to the same period of last year.
- A total of 2,569 new foreign investment projects have been approved by the central government during the first five months, an increase of 66.7% compared to the same period last year. Total foreign investment is $3.76 billion, an increase of 32.7%.

International Trade and Cooperation

According to Chinese official news media, several large U.S. companies are ready to resume business as usual in China. U.S. companies have invested about $3 billion in China, some $350 million in direct equity investment and the rest is in bank loans, technology transfer arrangements, and oil exploration payments.

In Shanghai, businessmen from West Germany, Australia, the United States, and Japan expressed their intentions to invest more in the city.

The leaders of the 48 Group of British traders have telegraphed messages to governors of Shando and Hubei provinces assuring them of their determinations to develop trade with their Chinese counterparts.

A U.S. bank executive commented: "Business is nonpolitical. Once the door is open, you are in or all your competitors will be."

Robin Hood*

Joseph Lampel, New York University

It was in the spring of the second year of his insurrection against the High Sheriff of Nottingham that Robin Hood took a walk in Sherwood forest. As he walked he pondered the progress of the campaign, the disposition of his forces, the Sheriff's recent moves, and the options that confronted him.

The revolt against the Sheriff had begun as a personal crusade. It erupted out of Robin's conflict with the Sheriff and his administration. However, alone Robin Hood could do little. He therefore sought allies, men with grievances and a deep sense of justice. Later he welcomed all who came, asking few questions and demanding only a willingness to serve. Strength, he believed, lay in numbers.

He spent the first year forging the group into a disciplined band, united in enmity against the Sheriff, and willing to live outside the law. The band's organization was simple. Robin ruled supreme, making all important decisions. He delegated specific tasks to his lieutenants. Will Scarlett was in charge of intelligence and scouting. His main job was to shadow the Sheriff and his men, always alert to their next move. He also collected information on the travel plans of rich merchants and tax collectors. Little John kept discipline among the men and saw to it that their archery was at the high peak that their profession demanded. Scarlock took care of the finances, converting loot to cash, paying shares of the take, and finding suitable hiding places for the surplus. Finally, Much the Miller's son had the difficult task of provisioning the ever-increasing band of Merrymen.

The increasing size of the band was a source of satisfaction for Robin, but also a source of concern. The fame of his Merrymen was spreading, and new recruits poured in from every corner of England. As the band grew larger, their small bivouac became a major encampment. Between raids the men milled about, talking and playing games. Vigilance was in decline, and discipline was becoming harder to enforce. "Why," Robin reflected, "I don't know half the men I run into these days."

The growing band was also beginning to exceed the food capacity of the forest. Game was becoming scarce, and supplies had to be obtained from outlying villages. The cost of buying food was beginning to drain the band's financial reserves at the very moment when revenues were in decline. Travelers, especially those with the most to lose, were now giving the forest a wide birth. This was costly and inconvenient to them, but it was preferable to having all their goods confiscated.

Robin believed that the time had come for the Merrymen to change their policy of outright confiscation of goods to one of a fixed transit tax. His lieutenants strongly resisted this idea. They were proud of the Merrymen's famous motto: "Rob the rich to give to the poor." "The farmers and the townspeople,"

---

they argued, "are our most important allies." "How can we tax them, and still hope for their help in our fight against the Sheriff?"

Robin wondered how long the Merrymen could keep to the ways and methods of their early days. The Sheriff was growing stronger and becoming better organized. He now had the money and the men and was beginning to harass the band, probing for its weaknesses. The tide of events was beginning to turn against the Merrymen. Robin felt the campaign must be decisively concluded before the Sheriff had a chance to deliver a mortal blow. "But how," he wondered, "could this be done?"

Robin had often entertained the possibility of killing the Sheriff, but the chances for this seemed increasingly remote. Besides, killing the Sheriff might satisfy his personal thirst for revenge, but it would not improve the situation. Robin had hoped that the perpetual state of unrest, and the Sheriff's failure to collect taxes, would lead to his removal from office. Instead, the Sheriff used his political connections to obtain reinforcement. He had powerful friends at court and was well regarded by the regent, Prince John.

Prince John was vicious and volatile. He was consumed by his unpopularity among the people, who wanted the imprisoned King Richard back. He also lived in constant fear of the barons, who had first given him the regency but were now beginning to dispute his claim to the throne. Several of these barons had set out to collect the ransom that would release King Richard the Lionheart from his jail in Austria. Robin was invited to join the conspiracy in return for future amnesty. It was a dangerous proposition. Provincial banditry was one thing, court intrigue another. Prince John had spies everywhere, and he was known for his vindictiveness. If the conspirators' plan failed, the pursuit would be relentless and retributions swift.

The sound of the supper horn startled Robin from his thoughts. There was the smell of roasting venison in the air. Nothing was resolved or settled. Robin headed for camp promising himself that he would give these problems his utmost attention after tomorrow's raid.

DELTA AIR LINES INC.

Paul M. Swiercz, George Washington University

In the postderegulation era of air travel, Delta Air Lines had continued its transformation from a regional domestic air carrier into a powerful international competitor. In 1978, Delta ranked fifth in the industry, transporting 3.3 million passengers and earning total revenues of $2.05 billion. By 1990, it moved up to No. 3, transporting 67.2 million passengers and generating total revenues of $8.58 billion.

Delta's success as the most consistently profitable airline in the United States was attributed to many factors, but the company's CEO, Ron Allen, believed one factor outranked the others. "We simply have the best work force in the industry, and we are committed to maintaining our reputation as a great place to work."

Delta's strategy, as revealed over its 60-year history, stood out from those of other major corporations on two counts: simplicity and unyielding consistency. C. E. Woolman, Delta's first CEO and still its guiding spirit, set the course: "to be the best air carrier in the business." All of Delta's top executives since Woolman had come up through the ranks of the Delta family and mirrored Woolman's vision of the firm as an outstanding passenger airline. Exhibit 1 provides a brief profile of Delta CEOs.

But until deregulation, Delta was viewed as a regional carrier, confining most of its operations to the Southeast and building its reputation as a premier carrier with an excellent reputation for service. From its Atlanta headquarters, management focused on finding better ways to serve passengers the large doses of southern hospitality for which Delta had become famous. A primary objective was to create the "Delta family feeling," principally within the firm, but also between the company and its passengers.

Ron Allen joined Delta in 1963 fresh out of the industrial engineering program at Georgia Tech. In 1987, at age 45, he was promoted from his position as president and chief operating officer to chairman and chief executive officer, succeeding his mentor Tom Beebe. Allen soon announced the objective of making Delta the "most respected airline in the world."

By the end of 1990, the company had successfully made the transition from a large regional to a global carrier. Nonetheless, the international competitive arena was still up for grabs, and the bankruptcy of its long-term competitor, Eastern, signaled new challenges in the domestic market. As Allen reflected on his tenure, three events stood out in his mind. The first was the result of the National Transportation Safety Board's investigation of the August 1988 crash of Flight 1114 in Dallas-Forth Worth. The crash killed 12 passengers and two crew members. The board accused Delta of lax training procedures, and a headline in the industry's major trade publication read, "Probe Finds Fault with Captain's Approach to Cockpit Discipline."[1]

---

[1] *Aviation Week and Space Technology*, April 2, 1990, pp. 62–65. The investigatory report stated in part, "In light of this discussion the safety board finds the slow implementation of procedural modifications by Delta Air Lines was a contributory factor in this accident."

EXHIBIT 1   Delta Chief Executives

C. E. Woolman—Graduated from the University of Illinois in 1912 with a bachelor's degree in agriculture. In 1925, he joined Huff Daland Dusters, Inc., following a brief career as an agricultural extension agent. In 1934, he became general manager of Delta and reigned as the company's most powerful executive until his death on September 11, 1966.

Charles H. Dolson—Began his airline career as a pilot for American Airlines. He joined Delta in 1934 and helped organize Chapter 44 of the Airline Pilots Association two years later. After a steady series of promotions, he became chief executive officer following Woolman's death. He introduced team management at Delta and retired in 1972.

W. T. Beebe—A veteran personnel official who joined Chicago & Southern in 1947. He entered Delta with the merger in 1953 and quickly rose to the rank of senior vice president for administration. In November 1971, he became chairman of the board and chief executive officer.

David C. Garret, Jr.—A Delta employee since 1946, he played a key role in helping the airline enter the jet age. With Dolson's promotion to president in 1965, he became vice president of operations. In 1972, he was appointed president and in 1978 chief executive officer.

Ron Allen—Graduated from Georgia Tech in 1963 and immediately began working for Delta. As a protégé of Tom Beebe, he quickly moved up the organization. In 1967, he was appointed assistant vice president for administration. From 1970–79, he served as senior vice president for personnel. He was appointed president and chief operating officer in 1983 and chairman and CEO in 1987.

The second arose out of recent contract negotiations with the pilots. A contract had been signed, and the pilots had retained their position as the highest paid in the industry. But the 20 months of negotiations had been difficult, more rancorous than any in the company's modern history.[2]

And third, on August 10, 1990, President and Chief Operating Officer Hollis L. Harris announced he was leaving Delta to become CEO of Continental Airlines Holdings Inc. At age 58, Harris had spent his entire 36-year career at Delta. He was the highest ranking executive in the company's history to jump ship and was described by industry insiders as the "quintessential Delta man."

These difficulties, in the larger scheme, seemed modest. Delta, while strongly disagreeing with the safety board's conclusion, moved to tighten training procedures. The labor contract was settled, and both parties were satisfied with the terms of the agreement. And the departure of Harris was moderated by the depth of managerial talent from which to draw his replacement.

Nonetheless, as Allen reflected on these events and the competitive battles ahead, a simple question demanding a complex answer drew his attention: "How can we maintain the family spirit and competitive vigor of a regional carrier and simultaneously compete in a deregulated global market?" He decided to take this question to the executive committee.

COMPANY HISTORY

Delta was formed in 1928 in Monroe, Louisiana, by C. E. Woolman and a group of investors; like numerous others, they were caught up in the enthusiasm for

---

[2]Delta signed a contract on September 4, 1990. It called for a weighted average wage increase over its 54-month life span of 10.3 percent. The contract was made retroactive to March 1989.

air travel flowing from Charles Lindberg's trans-Atlantic flight in April of the previous year. Organized under the name Delta Air Services Inc., the company set its sights on the passenger air market. Over the next two years, Woolman and his associates scrambled to prepare the company for its future. In 1930, they reorganized again, this time changing the name to the Delta Air Corporation and making application for an all-important airmail contract. Optimism was running high, the company was well capitalized, and the company had the latest equipment and some of the best pilots in the business. They had put together a route network running Charleston, South Carolina, to Fort Worth, Texas, via Columbia, Augusta, Atlanta, Birmingham, Meridian, Jackson, Monroe, Shreveport, and Dallas. But to make things work, they needed to be awarded the airmail contract from the U.S. Post Office. In January, the celebration they had planned was turned into a wake by what they saw as a corrupt Post Office contracting system. The company was forced to sell many of its assets and return to its crop-dusting roots just as the Great Depression tightened its stranglehold on the national economy; the company struggled to remain solvent. Fortuitously, congressional action by aggressive New Deal legislators renewed the chances for the postal contract, and in 1934 the company got the airmail contract it needed to backstop its passenger travel business. The first passengers boarded the new Delta on August 5, 1934, for a flight from Atlanta to Dallas.

In 1941, the company moved its base of operations to Atlanta; the city provided not only facilities at the Atlanta Airport but also business travelers. In 1953, Delta acquired struggling Chicago and Southern Airways, opening up access to the industrial Midwest and making it the sixth-ranking domestic carrier. In 1972, Delta purchased Northeastern Airlines to give it routes along the heavily traveled eastern shore corridor.

Delta enjoyed steady growth right up until deregulation traumatized the industry in 1978. A vocal opponent of deregulation, Delta struggled to adjust to the new world of competitive air travel as new low-cost carriers entered the industry. The 1981–82 recession hit the weakened industry hard, and Delta reported its first money-losing year in four decades. Belt-tightening and an overall improvement in the economy returned the company to profitability in 1983.

Delta's conservative business practices, its highly dedicated well-paid work force, and its strong market position combined to make it a solid performer throughout the following seven years of economic prosperity. In 1986, it purchased Western Airlines, acquiring important hubs in Los Angeles and Salt Lake City. In 1991, Delta had four major hubs and four minor hubs (Exhibit 2) and operated 2,446 daily departures to 150 domestic and 27 international cities. Delta's four commuter partners (Atlantic Southeast, Comair, Business Express, and Skywest, all 20 percent owned by Delta) had an additional 1,800 daily flights, most of which connected to Delta flights at the eight hubs.

DELTA'S STRATEGY, 1934–90

As depicted in Exhibit 3, certain strategic elements stood out to distinguish Delta from its competitors. These elements included the following:

EXHIBIT 2   **A Summary of Delta Hubs, 1991**

Hub	Departures	Share %/Position	Gates
Atlanta	430	70/1	62
Cincinnati	145	85/1	25
Dallas/Fort Worth	254	29/2	31
Salt Lake City	159	84/1	33
Orlando	70	34/1	24
Los Angeles	106	17/1	17
Boston	54	20/1	13
Portland	30	30/1	9

Source: H. Becker, *Delta Airlines Inc.* (Hulton, NY: Shearson Lehman Brothers, October 10, 1991), CIRR, SLBC -91 (90-1883).F.

EXHIBIT 3   **Key Elements of Delta's Strategy, 1934–90**

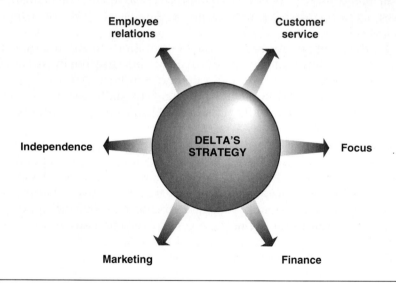

Independence   For many years observers described the airline industry as an oligopoly. (In economics, an oligopoly is a market condition in which sellers are so few that the actions of any one have a measurable impact on competitors). Oligopoly in the airline industry had been a fact of life for most of its history. At different times, it had either been directly encouraged or at least tolerated by regulatory authorities; large carriers, over the years, developed ways to avoid fierce competition in the industry. Delta was unique among the major airlines in that it had always positioned itself an arm's length away from its fellow carriers.

Part of this reluctance to join the inner circle dated back to Woolman's experience with the cost of collusion in the firm's formative years. In 1930, Woolman attended, but did not participate in, the infamous "spoils conference" where Eastern and other major carriers received valuable route concessions; the meeting raised a storm of public controversy and led to President Roosevelt's six-month nationalization of airmail delivery. To ensure that the company would not be tainted by the experience when the contracts were again opened for competitive bidding, Woolman on May 22, 1934, stepped down as an officer and director to assume the role of general manager.

Employee Relations   Delta's reputation for being a model employer was legendary within the business community. One tangible product of the "Delta family feeling" came in 1982 when Delta employees presented management with the gift of a new $30 million Boeing 767, christened "The Spirit of Delta." The level of employee commitment at Delta was partly an outgrowth of management's practice of routinely calling public attention to the accomplishments and contributions of Delta employees. Good words and an egalitarian culture were key elements in Delta's human resource strategy. Delta, despite the almost total absence of unions,[3] had a high-profile personnel department and it paid the highest wages in the industry (see Exhibit 4).

From its earliest days the company had worked toward providing solid job security; its promote-from-within policy had allowed employees to explore wide-ranging job opportunities. So strong was the company's commitment to the recognition of personnel as a critical strategic variable that two of its CEOs, W. T. Beebe and Ron Allen, had been promoted to top executive status from jobs in the personnel department, a rare occurrence in most companies. (Exhibit 5 summarizes Delta's key personnel practices.)

Customer Service   Delta had consistently sought a competitive advantage based on superior service. Elements of quality and service in the airline industry included in-flight service amenities (wider seats, better meals, free beverage service), convenient flight times and greater flight frequency, fewer delays and flight cancellations, superior baggage handling, better safety records, and more frequent-flyer bonus points. Delta routinely ranked as No. 1 in the industry for fewest customer complaints. For the past several years, the company's tag line on all advertising and promotional activities had been "We love to fly and it shows."

Focus   In its early years, Delta was a two-product company. For the first eight years of its existence, the crop-dusting division subsidized the passenger services division. It wasn't until 1938 that the passenger division showed its first profit. Since then, Delta's devotion to passenger air service had become a company hallmark; in contrast with many of its competitors, Delta had never experimented with diversification. Delta executives concentrated solely on the problem of moving passengers from point A to B in the safest, most cost-efficient manner possible. Ron Allen had stated, "We're not striving to be the biggest in the world, just the most profitable."[4]

---

[3]Only its pilots, members of ALPA, and its flight dispatchers, members of the independent Professional Airline Flight Control Association, were unionized.

[4]"If Delta's Going to Make a Move, 'It's Now or Never,'" *Business Week*, June 3, 1991, p. 95.

EXHIBIT 4   **Comparative Personnel Expenses per Employee, 1990**

Company	Expenses per Employee
Delta	$56,077
Northwest	50,880
United	47,192
TWA	46,346
American	46,174
Pan Am	45,536
U.S. Air	44,240
Southwest	42,844
Continental	36,424
America West	28,738

Source: Helane Becker, *Pan Am* (Hulton, N.Y.: Shearson Lehman Brothers, October 11, 1990).

EXHIBIT 5   **Personnel Practices at Delta**

Compensation
Consistently a market leader in both direct and indirect compensation. Executive compensation was modest relative to firms of similar size. Free air travel was an important benefit.

Recruitment and Selection
Each day Delta received between 1,000 and 2,000 unsolicited applications. The vast majority of employees started out at one of four entry-level jobs. Individuals without previous industry experience were preferred. There was just one employment office staffed by a dozen personnel representatives.

Promotions and Transfers
The personnel office posted all approved openings on bulletin boards with job titles, salaries, locations, and descriptions. Anyone in the company could apply. Employees were expected to actively seek out opportunities.

Problem Solving
There was an official open-door policy; anyone with a problem who couldn't resolve it through the normal chain of command could go see anyone in the hierarchy without worrying about it reflecting badly on them.

Training
Regulations required that certain employee groups—pilots, mechanics, and flight attendants—receive continuous training. Delta's open transfer and promotion policies dictated that a large portion of the nonregulated work force undergo continuous training.

Job Security
The company was committed to full employment. Whereas other carriers frequently resorted to work force reductions to lower payroll costs, Delta pursued a no-layoff policy despite ups and downs in air travel. No early retirement programs had been offered. Delta voluntarily extended job offers to all nonofficer full-time permanent Western Airlines employees.

Culture
Managers encouraged employees to address them on a first-name basis. "Customer service" was a central theme. Loyalty to the company was expected. Economy was preached daily; executive offices were spartan and paper clips were used until they wore out.

Communication
Management went to great lengths to keep in touch with employees. Small groups of workers met at least every 18 months with the senior management of their department.

Finance   Profitability was a cherished concept at Delta. Throughout its history as a public corporation, Delta had been a consistent profit performer. Delta's financial strategies were restrained, conservative, and devoid of experimentation. The company had a history of undertaking major financial investments out of sync with the industry. In the early 1950s, when getting to the market first was viewed as all important, Delta held back. Eastern, its main competitor, purchased a fleet of MD DC-6 propeller planes. Delta decided to wait and purchase the first generation of jets. Delta did the same in the 1970s, when it chose once again to forgo route expansion and instead purchase more fuel-efficient planes. When deregulation and volatile fuel prices arrived, Delta had the newest, most fuel-efficient fleet in the industry. Delta executives believed that market share came second to operational efficiency and people skills.

Conservatism was also observed in a number of other financial areas. In accounting, the company depreciated its equipment over a 10-year period versus the 15-year period typical of the other airlines. It also amortized investment tax credits over the tax life of the property rather than deducting it the year the equipment was put into service.

Marketing   Delta's primary marketing thrust was word-of-mouth advertising, supported by a focused effort to nurture customer loyalty. Delta had used the same advertising agency for the past 40 years. In that period, it had launched a series of advertising campaigns designed to promote its service image. Its two most recent campaigns—"Delta: We're ready when you are" and "We love to fly and it shows" were consistent with this long-term strategy.

In 1981, American Airlines introduced the first frequent-flyer program. Other carriers followed in rapid succession. These programs soon became recognized as a big hit with business travelers, Delta's primary customer base; Delta's frequent-flyer program was considered one of the industry's best. Many business travelers flying routes served by Delta often made a special point by scheduling Delta flights because of the frequent-flyer bonuses that Medallion level members (those flying 40,000 or more miles on Delta annually) earned.

PROBLEMS AND ISSUES IN THE 1990s

Delta's current strategy called for it to continue disciplined expansion, especially into the international market. It had filed applications for an additional 14 international destinations (Exhibit 6). Currently, 13 percent of Delta's available seat miles were international, but by 1994 this percentage was expected to increase to 20 percent. Delta management was planning for a 6 percent annual growth in capacity through the remainder of the 1990s. To meet this goal, the company expected to spend nearly $22 billion to acquire new equipment and terminal facilities. Total employment was expected to grow by 5 percent; in 1991, Delta employed 63,439 people, of which 56,907 were domestic permanent employees, 5,107 were temporary, and 1,423 were in the international division.

Overall growth was expected to occur along two distinct paths. First, the company was prepared to acquire troubled carriers if favorable prices could be negotiated. (Pan Am, TWA, Continental, and Midway were all operating under

EXHIBIT 6   **International Route Applications**

Atlantic	Pacific
Atlanta to Manchester	Portland to Hong Kong
Moscow	Los Angeles to Tokyo
Leningrad	Seoul
Tbilsi (Soviet Georgia)	Nagoya
Rome/Milan	Taipei
Barcelona	Bangkok
Madrid	
Berlin	

bankruptcy protection and each had assets that could complement Delta's route system.) The second path involved further use of strategic global alliances. Delta, Singapore Airlines, and Swissair were collaborating on a range of activities—from simple marketing agreements to complex operations exchanges. Thus far, they had agreed the goal of the alliance was cost-sharing and greater mutual profitability rather than market share or growth for growth's sake.

Potential Threats

Public concern over the negative effects of deregulation had expressed itself in a profusion of proposals to re-regulate fares and routes; this was despite Transportation Department insistence that competition was working.[5] A study prepared by the House Public Works and Transportation Committee reported 94 airline-related bills pending in the 101st Congress. Highest among the lawmaker concerns was the industry's continuing concentration. A 1990 study by the Transportation Department revealed that 9 of the 29 carriers that flew large aircraft accounted for 90 percent of all revenue passenger miles. At six of the largest hubs, (those handling 4 million or more passengers annually), three fourths or more of all departing flights were made by a single carrier. In Atlanta, for example, Delta commanded 82.6 percent of the market.[6]

Some legislators claimed the largest airlines would move to stifle competition even further by coupling their power over airport gates and landing slots with such marketing tools as computerized reservation systems,[7] frequent-flyer bonus programs, and inducements to travel agents. America West's CEO, Edward R. Beauvais, was among those calling for a reexamination of public policy; America West Airlines had prospered in the new deregulated environment until recently. Beauvais claimed restrictive access to airports and abuse of computerized reservation systems, among other things, had been major impediments to continued expansion by carriers such as America West.[8]

---

[5]James Ott, "Competition Study Identifies Few Problems in the U.S. System," February 19, 1990, *Aviation Week and Space Technology*, pp. 74–75.

[6]Airlines Gradually Filling Eastern's Void," *Atlanta Journal Constitution*, May 18, 1991, p. B3.

[7]Paul Desmond, "Justice Department Probes Legality of Airline Network," *Network World*, July 16, 1990, pp. 13–14.

[8]Michael Mecham, "Regulation Bills Prompt Carriers to Counterattack," *Aviation Week and Space Technology*, November 13, 1989, pp. 70–71.

Gate and landing slot access at major airports had been a problem for years. To control congestion in 1969, the Federal Aviation Administration (FAA) allocated takeoff and landing slots at four high-density airports: Chicago's O'Hare, Washington National, and New York's LaGuardia and JFK. In 1986, it initiated a rule that permitted carriers with those slots to sell them to other bidders. Because of their value, most carriers had chosen to retain ownership and lease them to noncompeting carriers. At 55 airports, including 15 of the 27 largest, incumbent carriers could exercise veto control over the construction of new gates. Delta exercised such control at Atlanta, Chattanooga, Cincinnati, and Lexington.

Global Competition

In 1991, the battle for competitive advantage in international air markets was well under way. Spurred by the consolidation of the European Community, the collapse of regimes in Eastern Europe, and the growing importance of Asian and Latin American economies, all the world's major airlines were maneuvering to secure footholds in the key North American, Asian, and European markets. The North American market accounted for 40 percent of world air traffic and was expected to grow at about 6 percent annually through the 1990s. The Far Eastern market, driven by the fast economic growth of Japan, Korea, Taiwan, and Singapore, was expected to grow at more than 9 percent annually during the decade.

Carriers such as British Airways, Air France, Lufthansa, and JAL were entrenched leaders in the international travel market, due partly to their legacy as government-owned carriers and the preferential treatment they enjoyed as a consequence. In the United States, Pan Am and Transworld Airlines (TWA) as late as 1978 together controlled 64.2 percent of the United States international passenger traffic; however, both had fallen on hard times and in early 1991 had less than one third of their former market share. Industry observers viewed American Airlines as the best positioned U.S. carrier for becoming a dominant international competitor. Profit margins on long-distance international flights were generally higher than on short-distance, higher cost domestic flights.

Crowded Major Airports

Major airports around the world were becoming overburdened by increases in air traffic. In the United States, 22 airports consistently had serious traffic delays and that number was expected to double by the end of the 1990s. Studies indicated the situation was similar in Europe and worse in Asia.[9]

Two airport options were attracting increasing attention. Satellite airports (usually neglected, older airports) were continuing to receive attention as alternatives to using major airports. Southwest Airlines had established a foothold at the old, almost forgotten, Detroit City Airport, which was twice as close to General Motors and Chrysler headquarters as Detroit's newer main airport. In California, United Airlines had bolstered its flight offerings to and from satellite

---

[9]Robert J. Hannan, "Airport Work Takes Wing," *ENR*, September 6, 1990, pp. 76–77.

airports at Ontario (an alternative to the Los Angeles airport) and Oakland (an alternative to the San Francisco airport).[10]

A second option was the development of new airports designed to accommodate short takeoff and landing aircraft (STOL). Aircraft designed to take full advantage of these airports (vertiports), such as the Bell/Boeing V-22 tilt-rotor, were not yet in production, but technology appeared promising. In 1987, London opened the first STOL port in Europe.[11] The airport's objective was to tap the city's business traveler market by offering a fast and easy route to Europe that would get passengers to Paris in less time than it took them to get to the regional airport at Heathrow. In Atlanta, municipal airports northeast and west of the main Hartsfield Atlanta International Airport had become economically significant due to their ability to accommodate corporate aircraft.

Trains, until the emergence of jet engines in the 1950s, were strong airline competitors. New train technologies held out the promise of reviving this competition once again. High-speed ground transportation (HSGT) had already proved itself in Japan and Europe. HSGT was potentially superior to both airplanes and automobiles for trips between 100 and 600 miles.[12] A trip from Paris to Geneva, for example, took 3½ hours by train versus 65 minutes by plane; the one-way, first-class train ticket cost $89 while a one-way unrestricted plane ticket sold for $277. By train, it took four hours to travel from Milan to Rome compared to 65 minutes by plane; a first-class, one-way train ticket was priced at $70 while a one-way plane fare was $153. Recently a Texas consortium had announced plans for a route connecting Dallas, Houston, and San Antonio, scheduled to begin operation in 1988.

---

[10]Jim Ellis, "When a 'Satellite' Airport May Be Just the Ticket," *Business Week* (Industrial/Technology Edition), July 16, 1991, pp. 170–71.

[11]Marion Cotter, "Where the Sky's the Limit for Profits," *Marketing*, October 22, 1987, pp. 27–28.

[12]Richard A. Uher, "Levitating Trains: Hope for Gridlocked Transportation," *Futurist*, September–October 1990, pp. 28–32.

Financial Statistics for Delta Airlines, 1986–1990

Five-Year Summary

Date	Sales ($000)	Net Income	EPS
1990	$8,582,231	$302,783	$5.28
1989	8,089,484	460,918	9.37
1988	6,915,377	306,826	6.30
1987	5,318,172	263,729	5.90
1986	4,460,062	47,286	1.18
Average Annual Growth Rate	17.7%	59.0%	45.4%

1990 Operating Expenses *(In millions of dollars)*

Salaries and related	$3,426.0
Aircraft fuel*	1,232.6
Aircraft maintenance and repairs	241.0
Aircraft rent	325.8
Other rent	219.7
Landing fees	137.3
Passenger service	367.4
Passenger commissions	813.8
Other cash costs	939.9
Depreciation and amortization	459.2
Total operating expenses	$8,162.7

*Delta used 2 billion gallons of jet fuel annually.
A one-cent change equals $20 million, pretax.

Key Financial Ratios

	6/30/90	6/30/89	6/30/81
Quick ratio	0.43	0.73	1.05
Current ratio	0.56	0.84	1.19
Net sales/total assets	1.19	1.25	1.20
Net sales/employee	$139,153	$137,614	$125,917
Total liabilities/total assets	0.64	0.60	0.62
Current debt/equity	0.01	0.00	0.00
Long-term debt/equity	0.56	0.21	0.25
Total debt/equity	0.57	0.21	0.26
Total assets/equity	3.41	2.48	2.60
Net income/net sales	0.04	0.06	0.04

CROWLEY INN

Arthur Sharplin, McNeese State University

Crowley, Louisiana, hometown of colorful Louisiana governor Edwin "Fast Eddie" Edwards, is in the heart of Cajun country 60 miles west of Baton Rouge. Crowley Inn, which has 59 rooms, a restaurant, and a bar, is at the intersection of Louisiana Highway 13, the main north-south route through Crowley, and Interstate Highway 10. Also at that intersection are a Texaco and an Exxon station, a Kentucky Fried Chicken store, and a Burger King restaurant. Many townspeople took special interest in the inn. Mayor Bob Istre said, "Crowley Inn is the first business you see, the only one out there that calls itself 'Crowley' anything." Inn manager Shirley Miller explained, "*C'est pour du monde de la village au Crowley* (It is for the people of the village of Crowley)."

The inn was completed in 1973. The owner defaulted on his $800,000 loan in 1986, resulting in seizure by the lender, a savings and loan company. The S&L was taken over by the Resolution Trust Corporation (RTC) in 1990. Then, on May 21, 1991, the RTC sold the inn to Art and Kathy Sharplin, of Lake Charles, 45 miles west of Crowley. Art taught business at McNeese State University in Lake Charles.

They formed Crowley Motel, Inc., (CMI) to hold the property and assigned Art's associate, Debbie King, to manage the investment with the help of an onsite manager. Debbie, 35, had been one of Art's MBA students, and he had employed her part time after she dropped out of the program. At various times, Debbie had worked for the regional Baby Bell telephone company and had managed a parcel delivery service and two credit and collection agencies.

The RTC's manager, Pam Potts, quit without notice in June. Debbie had been preparing to terminate Pam anyway, with a month's pay, and she immediately promoted Shirley Miller, the daytime front-desk clerk, to manager. Shirley was high school educated, active in local society, and was in her 40s.

The bar, called Martin's Tavern, had been rented to Burnell Martin, a local barber, and CMI assumed that lease, which was to expire at the end of 1992. The tavern had become a popular night spot for Crowleyites, frequented by the mayor, the sheriff, and other leading citizens, as well as by rice farmers, crawfishers, and oil-field hands. A true Cajun, Burnell had talked of setting up an off-track betting parlor and then arranged to get two of Louisiana's first video poker machines, which were to be legal beginning in June 1992.

In February 1992, famous Cajun chef Roy Lyons agreed to lease the restaurant for two years, naming it Chef Roy's Cafe Acadie. Debbie breathed a sigh of relief. She remarked, "The restaurant has been one big headache. It required more employees than the motel, took most of our management time, ate us alive with repairs, and lost money every month." Art had helped his brother build and operate several other motels years earlier and knew motel restaurants typically lose money.

The Sharplins had intended to sell the inn after fixing it up, and that remained a possibility. But Art had asked Debbie and Shirley to assume a

10-year holding period in management decisions. Given that time horizon, the managers were looking for ways to improve motel operations and to implement a marketing plan. And the idea of getting a national franchise, such as Best Western or Red Carpet, was only temporarily on hold.

FACILITIES

The physical plant had presented a challenge to Debbie, who said she knew "less than nothing about running a motel, let alone fixing one." Most rooms were distinctly substandard—sagging and stained bedding, broken furniture, 20-year-old TVs and room air conditioners, ceilings discolored by leaks, faded curtains hanging loose at one end, plumbing fixtures pitted and coated with white scum, washroom counters spotted with cigarette burns, mouse holes in walls, and tacky traps behind credenzas, each holding a grisly menagerie of dehydrated bugs and roaches. It all seemed even worse in the dim hue cast by the cheap, old incandescent lamps with their yellowed and tattered shades.

Outside, water seeped through cracked pavement from a broken underground pipe, nurturing a patch of green slime. The clack, clack, clack of the sewer plant blower gave notice of imminent failure in that vital system. From the sewer plant, it was possible to see into the small equipment room, where an aging water heater had piled clumps of damp rust on the floor. And past the dumpster, overflowing with customer and trespasser refuse, a pothole in the truck parking area had grown to become a muddy pond.

The lobby building was little better. Art discovered the air-conditioning system heated and cooled the void above the hung ceilings, in addition to the usable space. And one of the two main condenser units had been inoperative for months. Someone had poured tar on leaks in the roof overhang, and the black goo hung in stringy drops from the pegboard soffit and the shrubs beneath. In the restaurant kitchen, only one of the overhead exhaust systems worked; an oven door was tied shut with a stocking; cold air leaked from the walk-in freezer; and a long-disabled deep fryer still held its last charge of grease.

But the inn had originally been well built—and it was still attractive. The guest room building was made of concrete blocks and steel-reinforced slabs, with front and back walls of grooved wood paneling over pine studs. Piping was copper and cast iron, not plastic. One wall in each room was latex enameled and the others had vinyl wall covering, torn and unglued in a few places, but of good quality. The lobby building, of brick veneer, was shrouded by 90-year-old live oaks and much younger pines. And the neat gray and blue decor added a subdued welcomeness.

From May 1991 to February 1992, Crowley Inn's cash flow was applied to upgrading the property. Art and Kathy bought 60 rooms of used furniture, drapes, lamps, and bedspreads from the refurbishment contractor for a Holiday Inn in Beaumont, Texas. Debbie purchased 60 each of new RCA TVs with remote controls, GE clock radios, and chrome clothes racks with hangers. She also got new shower rods and curtains, bed linens, pillows, and a full complement of new beds and foundations. Kathy modified and helped install the drapes, advised on aesthetics, and livened the lobby with greenery and artwork. Shirley arranged for several local men—unemployed artisans she could hire for minimum wage—to help as needed. As each shipment arrived, they would come in to take out the old and install the new. They did much more—sanding the cigarette burns off the bathroom counters, painting, plugging mice holes, patching concrete, and so on. An air-conditioning contractor replaced or repaired 20 room air conditioners, renovated the lobby building heating, ventilating, and air-conditioning system, and worked long hours on the restaurant coolers and freezers. A roofer replaced the leaky third of the motel roof and put proper patches on the lobby building. Total cost of the renovations was about $130,000.

Two prospective franchisors were asked to inspect the property. Best Western identified about $100,000 in needed improvements—more modern room lights and furniture, new carpeting, covering the concrete block walls with vinyl, and so on—but seemed eager to do the deal. Red Carpet Inns was ready to franchise immediately, suggesting only minor changes. Debbie concluded the inn was then essentially up to standard for low-end franchises, such as Day's Inns, Comfort Inns, Scottish Inns, and Red Carpet, but not for lower midrange ones, like Best Western and Quality Inns. Front-desk clerk Josie Forrestier put it differently: "Crowley Inn used to be just a dump. Now, it is *une bonne place pour rester* (a good place to stay)."

PERSONNEL AND ORGANIZATION

When the RTC's manager resigned, the motel employed six housekeepers plus a supervisor, a maintenance man, and five front-desk clerks, all at minimum wage. There was no written job description for any jobs. The RTC had balked at paying overtime, and it had become standard practice to show eight-hour shifts on time cards, although employees often worked more or less. A housekeeper explained, "Pam gave us more than we could do. So we had to punch out and then go back and finish the work." In fact, most time cards for that period show handwritten checkout times, with no indication of who had made the entries. This was allegedly done because Pam could not keep the time clock working properly. The industry standard for room cleaning time was about a half hour per room, including laundering. Expensive hotels allowed more, and inexpensive ones less.

However much time the housekeepers actually spent, the rooms stayed dirty. Two large dogs, or maybe camels, had been left alone for a time in room 112. Pale spots in the soiled mauve carpet marked where they had done their "business," and the odors gushed out to greet new guests. One guest, a nurse from Florida, chose another room. In July 1991, she wrote Mayor Istre,

> I am writing to express my concern re the deplorable condition of the Crowley Inn. The mattresses and springs in our room would probably have been rejected by the worst flophouse in the country. The mattresses had a permanent swag, not to mention, sir, a URINE STAIN about 36 inches in length. The tub has mildew all around the caulking. The drapes and spreads haven't seen a laundry in years, it appears. The carpet has stains. The pillows also are stained, not to mention lumpy. Neither mattresses nor pillows have protective covers that can be wiped down between customers. The swimming pool looked cloudy and green our entire stay, and though the desk clerk assured us it was OK, we declined.

No housekeeper, not even the head one, had worked at any other motel. Each was left to decide the best way to clean rooms. And there was no regular inspection by any manager. During June and July 1991, two or three people a night refused to stay after seeing their rooms.

Inspecting the motel after receiving a copy of the nurse's letter, Art and Debbie agreed with her assessment. Many of the problems, Art believed, reflected the discouragement of the employees. In one room, toilet paper came off the bottom of the roll; in another, off the top. Here was a bed with a small, flowered pillow and a large, white one; next door, an identical set. In room 124, a double bedspread was stretched to half cover a king-size bed, while a king-size spread in room 122 fell in clumps around a double bed. In this room, five tiny bars of soap; in that one, none. Waste baskets of various sizes and one, two, or none per guest room; pint freezer boxes for ice buckets; shower curtains loose from hanger rings; a stiff washcloth behind a commode; another hung on a shower curtain rod; a KFC box, with dehydrated chicken parts, peeping from under a bed all contributed to a feeling of neglect. And the furniture, old, cheap, and stained though it was, need not have been so misdistributed. Chair counts ranged from four to none. An orange sled chair was paired with a puce over-stuffed one. And some rooms had chairs with no tables or tables with no chairs.

Wallace Mayer, the maintenance man, was responsible for cleaning the parking areas, mowing the lawn, taking waste to the dumpster, making bank deposits, moving heavy items, adding chlorine to the sewer plant, maintaining the swimming pool, and fixing anything that broke. Wallace, 67 but physically strong and good-natured, went about his tasks with consistency, if not speed. Housekeepers often stacked bulging bags of refuse in the vending machine areas until Wallace could take them to the dumpster, 50 feet away. It was just as well; the bags hid the gray-matted residue next to the machines and the cans and candy wrappers cast behind them. Wallace kept the lawn and shrubs trimmed, but dairy cups and flattened cans were often left for another day. And six-packs of defeated soldiers could sometimes be seen standing at the parking lot curb in mute, noontime tribute to Bacchus, whom Cajuns place just above Zeus.

The province of neither housekeeping nor maintenance, room windows and screens suffered neglect. Rain splatter had formed rivulets on the dusty panes, and layers of ancient cobwebs gave the half screens a fuzzy translucence.

As the renovation progressed, Debbie and Shirley began frequent, though sporadic, inspections. Art decreed, "No employee walks past a piece of trash. Nobody!" Cards saying "It was my pleasure to clean your room" were given to housekeepers to sign and leave on credenzas. Debbie obtained videos on proper bed making and room cleaning. She asked the head housekeeper to train her charges and to inspect all guest rooms daily. Of the six housekeepers, only Sandra Guillotte adapted—and survived. The head housekeeper soon decided she, too, could not meet Shirley's and Debbie's escalating demands. The new one, Carol Hoffpauir, promised she could. In February 1992, Shirley told of the improvement:

> We're getting compliments. We used to be afraid to ask if a guest enjoyed their stay. But today, at least five people commented on how nice the rooms were. Carol checks every room every day, and I do twice a week. We set a new record last week, a whole week without a complaint. The housekeepers still miss things—a bath cloth, or something left in a drawer—but they are doing so much better.

EXHIBIT 1   Crowley Inn Organization and Employees

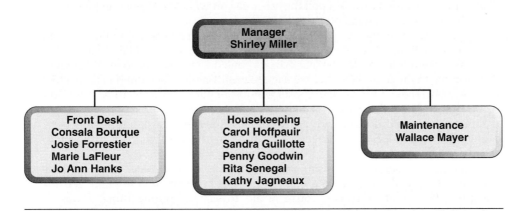

Art asked Shirley, "Why are the housekeepers doing better?" "Because we keep demanding more," she replied, "If we didn't demand it, they wouldn't do it." Carol Hoffpauir agreed, adding,

> I write them up every day, which rooms they clean and what they do wrong. We talk, and they can all read my notes on the clipboard, which I leave on the desk. If they do good, I tell them and I tell Shirley.
>
> I wish I could find five workers who take pride in cleaning the way I do. Two of the girls do, but the others seem to just tolerate it. I can hire and fire; I just have to tell Shirley my reasons. But I would rather get them out of their old routine.

Art asked, "Doesn't the improved situation here inspire them?" "I reckon so," Carol replied. "But you have to tell them when they mess up." Debbie added, "We know that new surroundings don't motivate."

Exhibit 1 shows the organization and employees at the end of February 1992. The desk clerks and Wallace were paid $5 an hour; the housekeepers, minimum wage; Shirley, $300 a week; and Carol, $200. Art had instituted paid one-week vacations, but there was no company medical insurance and no retirement plan. Shirley talked about her job:

> I have a little problem supervising these people. You see, going from house-keeper, to the front desk, to being a manager—I was one of them; I can't come out and fuss at them. It was really hard at first. I called them together and told them it was business for eight hours. After that, we can go have a beer together. I told them, "I don't demand respect—don't call me 'Ma'am' or screen my calls. But when I say I want this done, I want it done. I don't want to stay on your butt." They are not kids. And I'm not running an old folks home, or a community center.
>
> Everybody is from Crowley or Church Point, all Cajun. They take things very lightly. They are all struggling. But they leave their problems at home, unless they get too big. Sometimes, you just need to talk. I listen. I cried when I had to fire Joanne (the former head housekeeper). She's happier though, drinking and trying to get unemployment. Marie works in the restaurant after she finishes here, because she needs the money. Her mother is sick—over 90 percent stoppage in her heart. I could go on and on. This is a second home, for all of us.

Mr. Wallace is part of the furniture. He has been here six, seven, maybe eight years. He does not want 40 hours—says it will cut his Social Security. Takes off Friday noon. He is good; you just have to point it out. He loves his job, and we all depend on him. We took a poll the other day on what Mr. Wallace enjoys most; we think he likes blowing off the parking lot best.

You get to know the customers. We talk, give them a little Cajun flavor: "Oh, you're from Texas. Well, we went to San Antonio last year . . . blah, blah, blah." It makes them come back. The truck drivers and oil-field hands holler at us when they come in the door. Whether we use the right English they don't care. It's like being a bartender. Our regular guests will just about tell you their life story. You even get to know the ones who come here for a couple of hours. They trust us; park their girlfriend right here in front. Some men leave women behind here. The other day, one stood on the interstate an hour with her thumb up, until somebody stopped.

Cajuns may seem a little standoffish at first. Not at the front desk; this is *our* territory, and we feel secure. The girls always have a smile and gab for a guest. But at other places, you're afraid to say the wrong thing. I was in Wisconsin with Byron (her son, a priest) last year and I told someone, "Catch me a Coke." They kidded me about it. Byron took me aside and said, "Mom, you don't *catch* a Coke; you just get one." He used to bring his priest friends home. I would beg him, "Byron, don't bring these educated people here." But once I got to know them I get the biggest kick when they come. And I can't get them out of the house. We shouldn't be ashamed of our language, anyway. Listen to Governor Edwards: "Dis, dat, and dem." And he's a lawyer, definitely an educated man.

Jo Ann and Josie were at the front desk, just outside Shirley's office, and stepped to the door to listen. Jo Ann said, "All the improvements make us proud and we want to do better—makes me smile more. We bring a problem to Shirley and it gets taken care of, immediately. If it is a big one, Shirley gets on the phone with Debbie and it gets solved." Josie added, "It's exciting. Every day, I look forward to coming to work." Jo Ann's shift was over, and she excused herself; Josie continued,

Customers like to hear us talk. They can't get over how friendly we are. Some say they expected to see a mean type of people. They think Cajuns are ignorant, uneducated, barefooted people with web toes. We are different. But we're Americans—Texas is over here and Mississippi is over there. I tell customers everybody around here is friendly. I make people feel welcome. I want them to feel they are getting their money's worth. I want them to know I am their friend and to think of this as a home away from home. I say, "It's a quiet little place," except on Saturday night, when the band gets too loud and some of the people are—what's a nice way of putting it?—highly intoxicated.

The other night, a guy had invited two girls to his room and the second one showed up early. They were fighting and screaming, disturbing the other guests. So I called the sheriff. The one in the room reached right over the deputy and, Pow! laid the other one out. The deputy brought her up here in handcuffs and threw her in the car.

The inn is like my home, too. When Kenny and the Jokers (a Lafayette, Louisiana, band) play in the bar, I come about an hour early to hear them. And my kids (17, 15, 14, and 13 years old) love to come here, sometimes to go swimming. There is nowhere else to do that. We eat in the restaurant sometimes. When I worked in housekeeping, I would come by sometimes just to visit. I always try to be here 30 minutes early, and I usually hang around that long after my shift.

During the annual rodeo and the monthly horse show, the inn's regular guests merged with equestrians. Drowsy tourists' senses were jostled by the jangle of spurs on concrete stairs and the too-earthy aroma of a dozen horse trailers. Wide-brimmed hats were worn everywhere—at restaurant tables, on the crowded dance floor in the tavern, even in the bathroom. One inebriated October cowboy thought his bed a dance floor, until it collapsed. Another, dispirited by lost love, tried to aim at his head but blew just his palm away, spraying scraps of flesh and bone into a new mattress. And a famous Cajun musician, held hostage during drug withdrawal by two burly friends, broke a table and ripped a towel rack from the wall.

Mostly, though, Crowley Inn was, as Josie said, a quiet little place, a place where Texaco could house visiting executives and straying locals could enjoy secret liaisons. And it seemed so much a part of the employees' and towns-people's lives that Art wondered if he and Kathy were really the sole owners of the inn.

Ninety-two-year-old retired Catholic priest Msgr. Jules O. Daigle, of nearby Welsh, Louisiana, would agree with Shirley that Cajuns should not be ashamed of the way they talk. He insisted that Cajun was a true language, saying, "To call Cajun bad French is to call French and Italian bad Latin." Daigle fought for years to preserve the Cajun language and culture. In the preface to his Cajun-language dictionary, he wrote:

> Historically, the Cajuns are the descendants of the French people who colonized the general area of ancient Acadia, now known as Nova Scotia, beginning in 1604. . . . In 1755, the British began a cruel, systematic program of deportation of our ancestors. . . . Penniless, ill-clad and, worst of all, being both French and Catholics, nothing but scorn and hatred awaited them in the colonies. . . . After serving their indenture to the British colonists, some of them made their way back to Acadia or to Canada. Others found refuge in the French islands of Martinique, Guadaloupe, St. Dominque, etc. In the meanwhile, many of the Acadians who had evaded capture by the British sought refuge in the forests among the friendly Indians of the north. Of all the Acadians deported by the British, a considerable number were brought to England as prisoners: eventually, most of these found their way into France. . . . It was from all the above groups that many of the Acadians came to Louisiana, beginning in the early 1760s. Free at last, they had to begin a totally new and different kind of life, in a strange land. . . . The Acadians had to invent a new vocabulary, find new types of foods, develop a new cuisine and a whole new way of life. Thus was born the Cajun language and Cajun culture. . . .
>
> To some, a Cajun is a crude, ignorant, backward person who speaks little or no English. . . . His principal interest in life is boozing, eating and having a good time. To be sure, there are such Cajuns, but they are an infinitesimal minority and are in no way characteristic of the Cajun people.[1]

Daigle added that the Cajuns are bishops, judges, lawyers, contractors, professors, beauticians, bricklayers, farmers, teachers, and so forth. He concluded, "Yes, and sure enough some of them are lazy, ignorant bums and drunks: all in about the same proportion as the rest of the American population."

---

[1] Jules O. Daigle, *A Dictionary of the Cajun Language* (Ann Arbor, Mich.: Edwards Brothers, 1984), pp. viii–x.

MARKETING

Art and Kathy had initially been inclined to seek a franchise; Best Western was the leading candidate and Quality Inns a close second. In February 1992, they were continuing to discuss the matter. Debbie and Shirley expressed ambivalence about franchising, but they were both excited about promotion and other aspects of marketing.

Crowley Best Western?

Most motels are franchised. Franchisors typically provide a reservation system, advice on pricing, national advertising, a franchisee directory showing locations and amenities, quality control standards, yearly inspections, training, informational services, design help, and an approved-supplier catalog. Best Western's charge for Crowley Inn would be about $21,000 up front and that much each year. Other franchisors get a certain percentage of room revenue. For example, Red Carpet quoted 4.5 percent for Crowley Inn, with no initial fee. Holiday Inns was collecting as much as 7 percent.

Art believed Crowley Inn could qualify for a Best Western franchise within six months by making the following expenditures (in addition to paying the annual fee):

Initial franchise fee	$ 21,000
Best Western signs	12,000
Reservation and accounting system	15,000
Required renovations	96,000
Total	$144,000

Debbie, Shirley, and Art reached consensus that this would allow hiking the average daily rate (ADR) by $4 or increasing average occupancy by 15 percent, or some combination of the two. Art concluded, "Assuming 64 percent occupancy, which I think is about the industry average, the added revenue would be $56,000 a year, a good return on $144,000." Debbie objected:

> Well, 68 percent has been about our average. Even that should jump this year with or without a franchise. We have really improved this property since last summer, when we ran 76 percent. Besides, some of the renovations Best Western requires won't improve customer service—things like covering the concrete-block wall with vinyl and replacing the two-by-four ceiling tiles in the baths and lobby with two-by-two squares. I'll bet we could do the worthwhile renovations, which would cost maybe $60,000 and raise ADR by $3 without a franchise.

"What about Red Carpet?" asked Art, "We can have their sign up in a month."

"I don't think they add a thing," replied Debbie. Shirley agreed.

Art said, "OK, but you know there has been talk of a Day's Inn just seven miles away, in Rayne. If we were Best Western, no one would dare do that."

After a few more minutes of discussion, they all agreed to defer the decision on franchising for at least six months. "We haven't taken a cent out of this thing," said Art, "and I would like for you to produce some cash before we reinvest any more big chunks."

The Marketing Plan

Art asked Debbie to help prepare a marketing plan. "What should be our main objective," she asked. "What's wrong with 'maximize shareholder wealth'?" he replied. A few days later Debbie brought Art her rough draft. The final version is presented in the Appendix.

Debbie and Shirley were in essential agreement about each element of the marketing plan. During the last week of February 1992, they met to discuss both the process and the time frame for implementing it.

FINANCE

Art and Kathy paid the RTC $475,000 cash for the inn. They advanced another $21,000 to Crowley Motel, Inc., then and more later for working capital. CMI gave the Sharplins demand notes earning 10 percent interest for all but $1,000 of their investment and issued common stock for that. Exhibits 2 and 3 provide financial reports for CMI.

The Bank Loan

After buying Crowley Inn, Art and Kathy applied for a $380,000 loan from Evangeline Bank, in Crowley, to partly reimburse themselves and to fund improvements. The bank offered a half percent under bank prime (then 10.5 percent) for a 7-year loan with 15-year amortization. But the bank's attorney delayed approving the title, noting the inn sign and the sewer plant encroached over the adjacent property and 10 guest rooms had been built over an existing right-of-way (for a road to property behind the inn). Art knew this when he bought the inn and thought it a small matter, since the problem had existed without complaint for 20 years. However, he suggested the loan amount be cut to $200,000 in view of the title problems.

The bank continued to delay closing and after a few weeks Art and Kathy resolved not to bother with the loan. Art explained:

> We might be happier taking 8,000 or 10,000 a month in interest, principal, and fees than we would getting, say, $380,000 at once. I never have believed this "optimum debt ratio" stuff anyway. Of course, having the inn financed might make it easier to sell. But we will cross that bridge if we come to it.

Besides, Art acknowledged, there was no certainty they could get the loan anyway.

Cost Structure

The motel business typically involves high fixed costs, partly because of the capital required. For example, Holiday Inns claimed its costs for a new motel averaged $65,000 per room. And Art's brother Jerry said a new 60-room Best Western would cost about $22,000 a room, including land cost.

The problem was not severe for CMI. Its debt was held by its owners, and interest charges had been accrued rather than paid. But Art directed Shirley to pay interest out, along with half the cash flow (which would be treated as payment of principal), beginning in April 1992.

EXHIBIT 2   **Recent Income Statements for Crowley Inn**

	May–December 1991	January 1992
Revenue		
Room revenue*	$272,011	$48,770
Telephone revenue	7,351	1,334
Restaurant revenue†	136,977	18,085
Rental income‡	5,400	1,120
Miscellaneous revenue	9,218	637
Total revenue	$430,957	$69,946
Expenses		
Food purchases	$ 45,994	$ 5,857
Telephone	11,789	1,224
Salaries and wages	128,029	16,101
Payroll tax expense	14,478	3,085
Operating supplies	11,147	2,376
Office supplies	4,209	127
Taxes, licenses, and fees	6,755	1,709
Credit card fees	1,348	715
Professional fees	14,529	1,520
Travel and entertainment	1,199	0
Advertising	12,223	4,984
Repairs and maintenance	14,707	7,447
Miscellaneous	1,358	440
Utilities	36,285	6,655
Cable television	1,307	148
Insurance	15,293	2,002
Interest	31,487	6,344
Depreciation	23,100	3,300
Total expenses	$375,237	$64,034
Income before taxes	$ 55,720	$ 5,912
Income taxes (22%)	12,258	1,301
Net income	$ 43,462	$ 4,611

*Monthly room revenue for May 21, 1991, through December 1991 was as follows: May, $16,648; June, $30,941; July, $42,720; August, $46,303; September, $36,240; October, $40,221; November $36,738; and December, $22,200.

†The restaurant was leased beginning February 1, 1992, for $2,300 a month, including utilities (estimated at $600 a month). Up to that point, it had accounted for about 60 percent of salaries and wages, food purchases, and shares of several other expense items.

‡This includes $900 a month for the bar. The remainder is for rental of the banquet room.

Debbie calculated the variable cost per room-night at Crowley Inn as follows:

Housekeeping labor	$3.21
Supplies	2.61
Laundry	.80
Avoidable utilities and telephone	1.70
Total	$8.32

Debbie had been keeping close tabs on room cleaning costs, supplies, and other variable items. After studying CMI's cost structure, she decided to concentrate more on marketing. Debbie explained:

EXHIBIT 3   Recent Balance Sheets for Crowley Inn

	May 21, 1991	December 31, 1991	January 31, 1992
Assets			
Cash	$ 7,745	$ 12,007	$ 9,389
Accounts receivable		17,274	12,277
Land	40,000	40,000	40,000
Improvements	358,728	438,962	441,963
Furniture and fixtures	75,647	132,269	133,069
Accumulated depreciation		(23,100)	(26,400)
Security deposits	11,930	11,930	11,930
Total assets	$494,050	$629,344	$622,228
Liabilities and Equity			
Note payable, A&K Sharplin	$493,051	$570,969	$555,700
Accrued & withheld tax		13,913	17,455
Total liabilities	$493,051	$584,882	$573,155
Common stock	$ 1,000	$ 1,000	$ 1,000
Retained earnings		43,462	48,073
Total equity	$ 1,000	$ 44,462	$ 49,073
Total liabilities and equity	$494,051	$629,344	$622,228

At a $32.50 ADR, each extra room-night produces $24.18 for fixed costs and profit. That's $725 per month, about $8,700 a year, almost enough to pay for two billboards on I-10. If we raise prices, rather than let occupancy rise, the result may be even better. At 72 percent occupancy, we sell about 1,275 room-nights a month. So anything that lets us raise rates by $1 produces $15,000 a year.

To Art's chagrin, Shirley also became less tightfisted. On February 21, 1992, Debbie called from Crowley to say she was excited about all the nice improvements Shirley was making. "The oak trees have been pruned and fertilized, she got someone to edge the lawn, and there is new paint all around," said Debbie. Later that day, Kathy told Art she had learned Shirley wanted to paint the entire motel and lobby building.

Possible Sale of the Inn

In February 1992, Art was approached by two prospective buyers, Mahesh Patel, who owned an Econo-Lodge motel in Huntsville, Texas, and Fred Gossen, Jr., a businessman from Rayne, Louisiana, seven miles east of Crowley. The Patel name was familiar to Art. It was the surname used by thousands of émigrés from western India, many of whom invested in low-end motels and convenience stores in the United States. Art believed Patels owned half the economy motels in Louisiana and adjoining states.

Art convinced Kathy they should offer to sell the inn real estate, chattels, and leases to Gossen for $800,000, with $200,000 down and seller financing of the remainder at 12 percent for seven years, with 180-month amortization. They made a similar offer to Patel, but at $900,000 with $250,000 down and a five-year balloon.

Kathy had changed her mind by the next day. "Why don't we take out, say, $10,000 a month for a couple of years," she said, "We can probably still sell the motel for $800,000."

Art called Debbie to meet them at his campus office. "If we refuse an $800,000 offer," he began, "it is as if we just bought the inn for that amount." Debbie and Kathy agreed.

"Assuming Kathy is right," Art continued, "what discount rate should we use to settle the question?"

After a moment's thought, Debbie said, "This is effectively an equity investment in an entrepreneurial business. So I would suggest something like 40 percent."

"But can't we treat the project as a normally financed one; that is, say, $600,000 in 12 percent debt and $200,000 in equity?" Art asked, "If you stick with your 40 percent for equity, that gives a discount rate of 19 percent."

Kathy interjected, "I don't understand this discount rate stuff, Art. But if we get $200,000 in cash, we will have to put it in the Merrill Lynch account at about 5 percent. That's a far cry from 19."

"Instead of doing that, we could pay off the 11 percent debt on the Pepsi building [a building Art and Kathy owned in Pineville, Louisiana]," said Art.

After a few minutes more discussion, Art promised to fax a note to Gossen withdrawing the offer. "What about Patel?" asked Kathy. "That offer is not in writing," replied Art, "Besides, there is zero chance a Patel is going to accept without negotiating. And when he makes the first counter, the law deems my offer withdrawn. Besides, real estate deals have to be in writing to be enforceable."

"By the way," Debbie asked, "why did you quote $100,000 higher to Patel?"

"Three reasons: I think Fred will treat our people better, I would not be as confident of getting paid, and a broker is involved on that deal," answered Art.

The next day, Art asked Shirley, "What do you think about the sale idea?"

She replied, "It's your decision, but $800,000 is a lot of money." Art knew Shirley hoped he would not sell. She had often said she loved her job; a sale would put it at risk.

He asked, "Do you know that if I put $800,000 in the bank at 6 percent it would only draw $4,000 a month?" "Is that all?" exclaimed Shirley. "Debbie and I can get you a lot more than that without selling."

Art stopped by to see Chef Roy and get his input about a possible sale. Roy said, "I personally hope you keep the motel. But I can't advise you to turn down a profitable deal."

When Art saw Burnell Martin, the lounge operator, Burnell volunteered, "I hear you are thinking about selling. Art, keep this place. It's a gold mine."

APPENDIX: THE MARKETING PLAN

Mission

The mission of Crowley Inn is to maximize return on invested capital by providing quality lodging and related services delivered by competent and enthusiastic employees operating a clean, well-maintained facility—at prices fully reflecting the quality of service.

Marketing Objective

The objective of the marketing plan is to maximize motel revenue while keeping expenses low. Revenue targets for 1992 are:

Room revenue ($33.00 ADR; 72% occupancy)	$512,000
Telephone revenue (1991 rate + 10%)	24,453

Target Market

Our current guests are mostly blue-collar persons on business travel, about 20 percent from Louisiana and the rest from all regions of the country. About 45 percent pay with cash or check; 36 percent use credit cards; and 19 percent have us bill a third party. Here is data taken from 247 folios [forms guests fill out upon check-in] completed in February 1992:

Purpose of Travel		Home Address		Payment	
Work crew	48	Louisiana	52	Employer	47
Truck driver	38	Northeast	27	Credit card	89
Local	15	Southeast	17	Cash	111
Tourist	10	Northwest	13		
Business	38	Southwest	21		
Military	2	Foreign	11		
Cannot tell	96	Cannot tell	106		

(Marie LaFleur, who knew most regular inn guests, sorted the folios by purpose of travel. The "local" category, she said, mainly involved romantic liaisons.)

With average occupancy of 41 rooms, we serve a tiny percentage of those who pass our door. Daily traffic counts near the inn during 1990 were as follows (provided by the Louisiana Department of Transportation):

I-10 east of Crowley (both directions)	29,530
I-10 west of Crowley (both directions)	26,600
Hwy 13 north of I-10 (both directions)	7,570
Hwy 13 south of I-10 (both directions)	18,430

Visitors to families and businesses in Crowley (1990 population was 14,038) and surrounding Acadia Parish (1990 population was 55,882) may also be potential new customers. The Cajun tradition of fais-dodo (a country dance, usually involving staying overnight) and family togetherness in general, pull many who leave the area back to it frequently.

In addition to our present customer base, we will seek to attract more upscale guests, including (1) white-collar business travelers, (2) tourists, and (3) sojourners in the local area.

Product

Our main product is a room-night, which includes the elements listed below.

1. An attractive, comfortable, secure room—well-supplied, clean, and with all amenities in good order.

2. Attractive, functional vending machines.

3. Attractive, clean, neat grounds and paved areas.

4. Easy access to good food, drink, and entertainment.

5. Daily servicing of room by attractive, well-dressed personnel to exceed standards set by Best Western or comparable franchisors.

6. Guest services provided by enthusiastic, competent, attractive, articulate, well-dressed personnel who reflect the local culture.

A room-night is more perishable than a bruised tomato. We accept delivery of 59 room-nights every day, and unsold ones spoil sometime around midnight.

Shirley and Debbie plan to enhance the value and salability of room-nights in 1992 by:

1. Aggressive training and supervision of housekeepers.

2. Aggressive training of front-desk clerks, including role-playing of common types of guest contacts.

3. Inspections of all rooms daily by the head housekeeper.

4. Aggressive training and supervision of the maintenance person.

5. Inspection of all rooms and facilities at least weekly by Shirley, and at least monthly by Debbie.

6. Setting up control systems to assure creative compliance with vital policies.

7. Upgrading of the work team, through training, supervision, and/or replacement of employees.

Price

Current prices at Crowley Inn are shown below. Pricing of room-nights is done by front-desk clerks, who have a list of "approved" commercial customers.

1. Basic room night $31.00 ($29 commercial)
2. Each guest above one/room $4.00/night
3. Local telephone calls $0.50
4. Long-distance calls   AT&T rates plus 40%
5. Facsimile transmissions $2.00/page
6. Rollaway bed or crib $5.00/night

Members of the American Association of Retired Persons and others over 65 are eligible for commercial rates. ADR has been about $32.50 since a $2 per room-night price increase in July 1991. Two factors tend to pull ADR down. First, few customers are charged the $4 per extra guest. In fact, only about 1 in 20 (based on a check of February 1991 folios) completes the "No of persons in room" blocks on the folio. Second, front-desk clerks give commercial rates to most who ask for a discount. Shirley says pricing policies are clear and understood by all front-desk clerks, but they do not follow policies well.

Shirley and Debbie plan to:

1. Review pricing policies and change them or enforce them.
2. Set up control systems to identify and correct improper pricing practices.
3. Insure that telephone billing equipment and practices are correct.
4. Price room-nights at no less than the double-occupancy rate during special events, when the inn normally fills up.
5. Price room-nights at no less than the double-occupancy rate whenever as many as 40 rooms are reserved.
6. Review pricing frequently and quickly implement justified changes, as when occupancy moves reliably above 75 percent.

Promotion

Crowley Inn relies primarily on billboards for advertising. For eastbound traffic there are two signs, on the left 16 miles out and on the right 4 miles out. For westbound traffic, signs are on the left at 13 miles and on the right at 7. The signs carry the slogan, "Comfort you can afford," and have a large inset saying, "24 hr Grill." They are yellow and white on a black background.

Debbie is developing an image, involving a slogan, a logo, and sign designs. A consultant is helping. The new slogan is "Comfortable, caring, and Cajun." This is intended to suggest comfortable lodging supplied by caring personnel with a Cajun flair. The logo is a large C containing a rice design, used alone or in spelling "Crowley Inn."

Debbie plans to rent two additional billboards on I-10, one in each direction, and have all billboards repainted. Chef Roy agreed to pay a fifth of the cost, and a fifth of the sign space will be devoted to advertising Cafe Acadie. A "board" across the bottom of each sign will announce special features such as HBO-Showtime, Martin's Tavern, and live entertainment. Each billboard costs about $400 to repaint and about $400 per month.

She also plans to place two signs along Highway 13 a few miles on either side of the inn. Each of these is expected to cost about $300 to paint and $200 per month.

Debbie just purchased space on electronic bulletin boards at the Tourist Information Centers at the east and west I-10 entry points to Louisiana. Users will dial a two-digit code that will connect them to the front desk at the inn.

Crowley Inn will join the Louisiana Travel Promotion Association (LTPA). LTPA publishes the *Louisiana Tour Guide* annually and helps members with advertising, printing, and the like.

Though the inn is right beside I-10, an informal survey suggests many people pass without noticing it. So Kathy and Shirley plan to have the guest-room doors painted a noticeable color, such as burgundy, and to use bright colors elsewhere to make the inn more conspicuous.

Shirley and Debbie plan to start making sales calls on present and prospective direct-bill customers and sending them direct-mail advertisements from time to time. They also are seeking ways to entice tour groups to the inn.

Place

Crowley Inn is 16 miles east of its nearest competitor, a TraveLodge in Jennings. The Jennings Holiday Inn is three miles further west. East of Crowley, the larger town of Lafayette has a Holiday Inn, a La Quinta Inn, a Motel 6, and several other motels and hotels.

Crowley is home to the Louisiana Rice Festival, held annually in May, and nearby towns sponsor festivals celebrating crawfish, frogs, ducks, and other animals and plants. During the days surrounding each festival, the inn normally is booked solid. The inn also fills up during the monthly horse show in Crowley and during the annual rodeo.

Crowley is the seat of Acadia Parish (county), and Art suggested this makes it the "Capital of Acadiana" (Cajun country is often called Acadiana). A famous Cajun restaurant, Belizaires', is a half mile south of the Crowley Inn, and its signs attract many visitors. Debbie and Shirley plan to feature the "Capital of Acadiana" theme in ads and signs and to encourage the Crowley Chamber of Commerce to do so. Mayor Istre thought this was a good idea.

W. L. GORE & ASSOCIATES, INC.

Frank Shipper, Salisbury State University
Charles C. Manz, Arizona State University

"To make money and have fun."
W. L. Gore

On July 26, 1976, Jack Dougherty, a newly minted MBA from the College of William and Mary bursting with resolve, dressed in a dark blue suit, reported for his first day at W. L. Gore & Associates. He presented himself to Bill Gore, shook hands firmly, looked him in the eye, and said he was ready for anything.

What happened next was one thing for which Jack was not ready. Gore replied, "That's fine, Jack, fine. Why don't you look around and find something you'd like to do." Three frustrating weeks later he found that something, dressed in jeans, loading fabric into the mouth of a machine that laminated the company's patented Gore-Tex membrane to fabric. By 1982, Jack had become responsible for all advertising and marketing in the fabrics group. This story was part of the folklore that was heard over and over about W. L. Gore. By 1991, the process was slightly more structured. New associates took a journey through the business before settling into their own positions, regardless of the position for which they were hired. A new sales associate in the Fabric Division might spend six weeks rotating through different areas before concentrating on sales and marketing. Among other things, he or she might learn how Gore-Tex fabric was made, what it could and could not do, how Gore handled customer complaints, and how it made investment decisions.

Anita McBride related her early experience at W. L. Gore & Associates this way:

> Before I came to Gore, I had worked for a structured organization. I came here, and for the first month it was fairly structured because I was going through training and this is what we do and this is how Gore is and all of that, and I went to Flagstaff for that training. After a month I came down to Phoenix, and my sponsor said, "Well, here's your office, and here's your desk," and walked away. And I thought, "Now what do I do," you know? I was waiting for a memo or something, or a job description. Finally after another month I was so frustrated, I felt, "What have I gotten myself into?" And so I went to my sponsor and I said, "What the heck do you want from me? I need something from you." And he said, "If you don't know what you're supposed to do, examine your commitment, and opportunities."

BACKGROUND

W. L Gore & Associates evolved from the late Wilbert L. Gore's experiences personally, organizationally, and technically. He was born in Meridian, Idaho, near Boise in 1912. By age six, he claimed he had become an avid hiker in the Wasatch Mountain Range in Utah. In those mountains, at a church camp, he met Genevieve (called Vieve by everyone), his future wife. In 1935, they got married, which was, in their eyes, a partnership—a partnership that lasted a lifetime.

He received both a bachelor of science degree in chemical engineering in 1933 and a master of science in physical chemistry in 1935 from the University of Utah. He began his professional career at American Smelting and Refining in 1936; moved to Remington Arms Company in 1941; and moved once again to E. I. du Pont de Nemours in 1945 where he held positions of research supervisor and head of operations research. While at Du Pont, he worked on a team to develop applications for polytetraflurothylene, frequently referred to as PTFE in the scientific community and known as Teflon by consumers. On this team, Wilbert Gore, called Bill by everyone, felt a sense of excited commitment, personal fulfillment, and self-direction. He followed the development of computers and transistors and believed that PTFE had the ideal insulating characteristics for use with such equipment.

He tried a number of ways to make a PTFE-coated ribbon cable without success. A breakthrough came in his home basement laboratory. He was explaining the problem to his son, Bob. Bob saw some PTFE sealant tape made by 3M and asked his father, "Why don't you try this tape?" His father then explained to his son, "Everyone knows you can not bond PTFE to itself." So, Bob went on to bed.

Bill Gore remained in his basement lab and proceeded to try what everyone knew would not work. About 4 A.M., he woke his son waving a small piece of cable around, saying excitedly, "It works, it works." The following night father and son returned to the basement lab to make ribbon cable coated with PTFE.

For the next four months, Bill Gore tried to persuade Du Pont to make a new product—PTFE-coated ribbon cable. By this time in his career, Bill Gore knew some of the decision makers at Du Pont. After talking to a number of decision makers, it became clear that Du Pont wanted to remain a supplier of raw materials and not a fabricator.

Bill began to discuss with his wife the possibility of starting their own insulated wire and cable business. On January 1, 1958, their wedding anniversary, they founded W. L. Gore & Associates, which they viewed as another partnership. The basement of their home served as their first facility. After finishing dinner on their anniversary, Vieve turned to her husband of 23 years and said, "Well, let's clear up the dishes, go downstairs, and get to work."

Bill Gore was 45 years old with five children to support when he left Du Pont. He left behind a career of 17 years and a good and secure salary. To finance the first two years of the business, they mortgaged their house and took $4,000 from savings. All of their friends cautioned them against taking the risk.

The first few years were rough. In lieu of salary, some of their employees accepted room and board in the Gore home. At one point, 11 employees were living and working under one roof. Then came the order from the City of Denver's water department that put the company on a profitable footing. One afternoon, Vieve answered a phone call while sifting PTFE powder. The caller indicated he was interested in the ribbon cable, but wanted to ask some technical questions and asked for the product manager. But Bill was out running some errands, so Vieve explained that he was out at the moment. Next he asked for the sales manager and, finally, the president. Vieve explained that they were also out. The caller became outraged and hollered, "What kind of company is this anyway?" With a little diplomacy, the Gores eventually secured an order for $100,000. This order put the company over the hump and it began to take off.

W. L. Gore & Associates continued to grow and develop new products primarily derived from PTFE, including its best-known product, Gore-Tex. In 1986, Bill Gore died while backpacking in the Wind River Mountains of Wyoming. Before he died, however, he had become chairman and his son, Bob, president. Vieve remained as the only other officer, secretary-treasurer.

THE OPERATING COMPANY

W. L. Gore & Associates was a company without titles, hierarchy, or any of the conventional structures associated with enterprises of its size. The titles of president and secretary-treasurer were used only because they were required by the laws of incorporation. In addition, Gore did not have a corporate-wide mission or code of ethics statement, neither did Gore require nor prohibit business units from developing such statements for themselves. Thus, the associates of some business units who felt a need for such statements had developed them. The majority of business units within Gore did not have such statements. When questioned about this issue, one associate stated, "The company belief is that (1) its four basic operating principles cover ethical practices required of people in business and (2) it will not tolerate illegal practices." Gore's management style was often referred to as unmanagement. The organization had been guided by Bill's experiences on teams at Du Pont and has evolved as needed.

For example, in 1965, W. L. Gore & Associates was a thriving and growing company with a facility on Paper Mill Road in Newark, Delaware, with about 200 employees. One warm Monday morning in the summer, Bill Gore was taking his usual walk through the plant. All of a sudden he realized he did not know everyone in the plant. The team had become too big. As a result, the company established a policy that no facility would have over 150 to 200 employees. Thus was born the expansion policy of "Get big by staying small." The purpose of maintaining small plants was to accentuate a close-knit and interpersonal atmosphere.

By 1991, W. L. Gore & Associates consisted of 44 plants worldwide with over 5,300 associates. In some cases, the plants were clustered together on the same site as in Flagstaff, Arizona, with four plants on the same site. Twenty-seven of those plants were in the United States and 17 were overseas. Gore's overseas plants were located in Scotland, Germany, France, Japan, and India.

PRODUCTS

The products that W. L. Gore made were organized into eight divisions—electronic, medical, waterproofing fabrics, fibers, industrial filtration, industrial seals, coatings, and microfiltration.

The electronic products division produced wire and cable for various demanding applications in aerospace, defense, computers, and telecommunications. The wire and cable products had a reputation for unequaled reliability. Most of the wire and cable was used where conventional cables could not operate. For example, Gore wire and cable assemblies were used in the space shuttle

Columbia because they would stand the heat of ignition and the cold of space. Gore wire was used in the moon vehicle shuttle that scooped up samples of moon rocks, and Gore's microwave coaxial assemblies opened new horizons in microwave technology. On earth, the electrical wire products helped make the world's fastest computers possible because electrical signals could travel through them at up to 90 percent of the speed of light. Because of the physical properties of the Gore-Tex material used in their construction, the electronic products were used extensively in defense systems, electronic switching for telephone systems, scientific and industrial instrumentation, microwave communications, and industrial robotics. Reliability was a watchword for all Gore products.

In medical products, reliability was literally a matter of life and death. Gore-Tex expanded PTFE was an ideal material used to combat cardiovascular disease. When human arteries were seriously damaged or plugged with deposits that interrupt the flow of blood, the diseased portions could often be replaced with Gore-Tex artificial arteries. Gore-Tex arteries and patches were not rejected by the body because the patient's own tissues grew into the grafts' open porous spaces. Gore-Tex vascular grafts came in many sizes to restore circulation to all areas of the body. They had saved limbs from amputation and saved lives. Some of the tiniest grafts relieved pulmonary problems in newborns. Gore-Tex was also used to help people with kidney disease. Associates were developing a variety of surgical reinforcing membranes, known as Gore-Tex cardiovascular patches, which could literally mend broken hearts, by patching holes and repairing aneurysms.

Through the waterproof fabrics division, Gore technology had traveled to the top of the world on the backs of renowned mountaineers. Gore-Tex fabric was waterproof and windproof, yet breathable. Those features had qualified Gore-Tex fabric as essential gear for mountaineers and adventurers facing extremely harsh environments. The PTFE membrane blocked wind and water but allowed sweat to escape. That made Gore-Tex fabric ideal for anyone who worked or played hard in foul weather. Backpackers had discovered that a single lightweight Gore-Tex fabric shell would replace a poplin jacket and a rain suit and dramatically outperform both. Skiers, sailors, runners, bicyclists, hunters, fishermen, and other outdoor enthusiasts had also become big customers of garments made of Gore-Tex fabric. General sportswear and women's fashion footwear and handwear of Gore-Tex fabric were as functional as they were beautiful. Boots and gloves, both for work and recreation, were waterproof thanks to Gore-Tex liners. Gore-Tex was even becoming government issue for many military personnel. Wet suits, parkas, pants, headgear, gloves, and boots kept the troops warm and dry in foul-weather missions. Other demanding jobs also required the protection of Gore-Tex fabric because of its unique combination of chemical and physical properties.

The Gore-Tex fibers products, like the fabrics, ended up in some tough places. The outer protective layer of NASA's spacesuit was woven from Gore-Tex fibers. Gore-Tex fibers were in many ways the ultimate in synthetic fibers. They were impervious to sunlight, chemicals, heat, and cold. They were strong and uniquely resistant to abrasion.

Industrial filtration products, such as Gore-Tex filter bags, reduced air pollution and recovered valuable solids from gases and liquids more completely than alternatives; they also did it more economically. They could make coal-burning plants smoke free, contributing to a cleaner environment.

The industrial seals division produced joint sealant, a flexible cord of porous PTFE that could be applied as a gasket to the most complex shapes, sealing them to prevent leakage of corrosive chemicals, even at extreme temperature and pressure. Steam valves packed with Gore-Tex valve stempacking never leaked and never needed to be repacked.

The coatings division applied layers of PTFE to steel castings and other metal articles by a patented process. Called Fluoroshield protective coatings, this fluorocarbon polymer protected processing vessels in the production of corrosive chemicals.

Gore-Tex microfiltration products were used in medical devices, pharmaceutical manufacturing, and chemical processing. These membranes removed bacteria and other microorganisms from air or liquids, making them sterile.

FINANCIAL INFORMATION

W. L. Gore was a closely held private corporation. Financial information was as closely guarded as proprietary information on products and processes. Eighty percent of the stock was held by the Gore family and veteran associates, 10 percent by current associates, and 10 percent by others.

According to Shanti Mehta, an associate, Gore's return on assets and equity ranked it among the top 5 percent of major companies. According to another source, W. L. Gore & Associates was working just fine by any financial measure. It had had 27 straight years of profitability and positive return on equity. The compounded growth rate for revenues at W. L. Gore over the past 20 years had been over 18 percent discounted for inflation.[1] In 1969, total sales were $6 million; in 1982, $125 million; in 1983, $160 million; in 1985, $250 million; in 1987, $400 million; in 1988, $426 million; and in 1989, $600 million. This growth had largely been financed without debt.

ORGANIZATIONAL STRUCTURE

Bill Gore wanted to avoid smothering the company in thick layers of formal "management." He believed they stifled individual creativity. As the company grew, he knew a way had to be devised to assist new people to get started and to follow their progress. This was seen as particularly important when it came to compensation. W. L. Gore & Associates developed what it called the "sponsor" program to meet these needs. When people applied to W. L. Gore, they were initially screened by personnel specialists as in most companies. For those who met the basic criteria, there were interviews with other associates. Before anyone was hired, an associate must have agreed to be that person's sponsor. The sponsor was to take a personal interest in the new associate's contributions, problems, and goals. The sponsor was both a coach and an advocate. The sponsor tracked the new associate's progress, helping and encouraging, dealing with weaknesses and concentrating on strengths. Sponsoring was not a short-term commitment. All associates had sponsors and many had more than one. When individuals were hired, they had a sponsor in their immediate

---

[1] In comparison, only 11 of the 200 largest companies in the Fortune 500 have had positive ROE each year from 1970–88 and only two other companies missed only one year. The revenue growth rate for these 13 companies was 5.4 percent compared to 2.5 percent for the entire Fortune 500.

work area. If they moved to another area, they also had a sponsor in that work area. As associates' responsibilities grew, they could acquire additional sponsors.

Because the sponsoring program looked beyond conventional views of what made a good associate, some anomalies occurred in the hiring practices. Bill Gore proudly told the story of "a very young man" of 84 who walked in, applied, and spent five very good years with the company. The individual had 30 years of experience in the industry before joining Gore. His other associates had no problems accepting him, but the personnel computer did. It insisted his age was 48.

An internal memo by Bill Gore described three kinds of sponsorship and how they might work as follows:

1. The sponsor who helps a new associate *get started* on the job. Also, the sponsor who helps a present associate get started on a new job (starting sponsor).
2. The sponsor who sees to it the associate being sponsored *gets credit* and recognition for contributions and accomplishments (advocate sponsor).
3. The sponsor who sees to it that the associate being sponsored is *fairly paid* for contributions to the success of the enterprise (compensation sponsor).

A single sponsor could perform any one or all three kinds of sponsorship. A sponsor was a friend and an associate. All the supportive aspects of the friendship were also present. Often (perhaps usually) two associates sponsored each other as advocates.

W. L. Gore & Associates had not only been described as unmanaged, but also as unstructured. Bill Gore referred to the structure as a lattice organization. A lattice structure is portrayed in Exhibit 1. The characteristics of this structure were:

1. Lines of communication are direct—person to person—with no intermediary.
2. No fixed or assigned authority.
3. Sponsors, not bosses.
4. Natural leadership defined by followership.
5. Objectives are set by those who must "make them happen."
6. Tasks and functions organized through commitments.

The structure within the lattice was described by the people at Gore as complex and had evolved from interpersonal interactions, self-commitment to group-known responsibilities, natural leadership, and group-imposed discipline.

Bill Gore once explained this structure by saying, "Every successful organization has an underground lattice. It's where the news spreads like lightning, where people can go around the organization to get things done." Another description of what was occurring within the lattice structure was constant cross- area teams—the equivalent of quality circles going on all the time. When a puzzled interviewer told Bill he was having trouble understanding how planning and accountability worked, Bill replied with a grin, "So am I. You ask me how it works, every which way."

The lattice structure did have some similarities to traditional management structures. For instance, a group of 30 to 40 associates who made up an advi-

EXHIBIT 1　　　The Lattice Structure

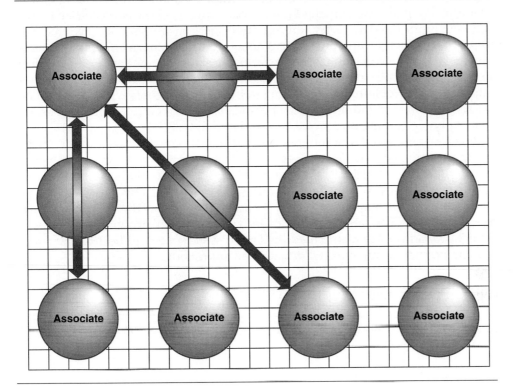

sory group met every six months to review marketing, sales, and production plans. As Bill Gore has conceded, "The abdication of titles and rankings can never be 100 percent."

The lattice structure was not without its critics. As Bill Gore stated, "I'm told from time to time that a lattice organization can't meet a crisis well because it takes too long to reach a consensus when there are no bosses. But this isn't true. Actually, a lattice, by its very nature, works particularly well in a crisis. A lot of useless effort is avoided because there is no rigid management hierarchy to conquer before you can attack a problem."

The lattice had been put to the test on a number of occasions. For example, in 1975, Dr. Charles Campbell, the University of Pittsburgh's senior resident, reported a Gore-Tex arterial graft had developed an aneurysm. An aneurysm is a bubble-like protrusion that is life-threatening. If it continued to expand, it would explode. Obviously, this kind of problem had to be solved quickly and permanently.

Within only a few days of Dr. Campbell's first report, he flew to Newark to present his findings to Bill and Bob Gore and a few other associates. The meeting lasted two hours. Bill Hubis, a former policeman who had joined Gore to develop new production methods, had an idea before the meeting was over. He returned to his work area to try some different production techniques. After only three hours and 12 tries, he had developed a permanent solution. In other words, in three hours, a potentially damaging problem to both patients and the company was resolved. Furthermore, Hubis's redesigned graft went on to win widespread acceptance in the medical community. By 1991, it dominated the market with a 70 percent share.

One critic, Eric Reynolds, founder of Marmot Mountain Works Ltd. of Grand Junction, Colorado, and a major Gore customer, said, "I think the lattice has its problems with the day-to-day nitty-gritty of getting things done on time and out the door. I don't think Bill realizes how the lattice system affects customers. I mean after you've established a relationship with someone about product quality, you can call up one day and suddenly find that someone new to you is handling your problem. It's frustrating to find a lack of continuity." He went on to say, "But I have to admit that I've personally seen at Gore remarkable examples of people coming out of nowhere and excelling."

Bill Gore was asked a number of times if the lattice structure could be used by other companies. His answer was, "No. For example, established companies would find it very difficult to use the lattice. Too many hierarchies would be destroyed. When you remove titles and positions and allow people to follow who they want, it may very well be someone other than the person who has been in charge. The lattice works for us, but it's always evolving. You have to expect problems." He maintained the lattice system worked best when put in place in start-up companies by dynamic entrepreneurs.

ORGANIZATIONAL CULTURE

In addition to the sponsor program, Gore associates were asked to follow four guiding principles:

1. Try to be fair.
2. Use your freedom to grow.
3. Make your own commitments, and keep them.
4. Consult with other associates before any action that may hurt the reputation or financial stability of the company.

The four principles were often referred to as fairness, freedom, commitment, and discretion. The last principle was also often referred to as the waterline principle. The terminology was drawn from an analogy to ships. If someone poked a hole in a boat above the waterline, the boat would be in relatively little real danger. But if someone poked a hole below the waterline, the boat would be in immediate danger of sinking.

In practice, the fourth principle provided associates with a great deal of discretion. For example, W. L. Gore had no travel policy, no request for travel forms, no prohibition against first-class travel, and no expense reports. The associate called an internal travel consultant and gave the individual his or her requirements. All tickets issued to Gore travelers were accompanied by a note that stated, "The normal coach fare is X, you've saved Y." Upon return, the associate could file a travel investment report and be reimbursed for his or her savings investment.

According to Debbie Sharp, "Very few people take advantage of this. It's only the infrequent travelers who sometimes get carried away. If we see expenses that stand out, we'll call the traveler and ask him to be more careful next time. But no one ever pays money back on an investment report."

The travel consultant also had a high amount of discretion. For example, W. L. Gore had been doing business with three different rental car companies when one became more expensive. The travel consultant dropped that firm and picked up another without checking with anyone else.

The operating principles were put to a test in 1978. By this time, the word about the qualities of Gore-Tex were being spread throughout the recreational and outdoor markets. Production and shipment had begun in volume. At first, a few complaints were heard. Next, some of the clothing started coming back. Finally, a great deal of the clothing was being returned. The trouble was that the Gore-Tex was leaking. Waterproof fabric was one of the two major properties responsible for Gore-Tex's success. The company's reputation and credibility were on the line.

Peter W. Gilson, who led Gore's fabric division, said, "It was an incredible crisis for us at that point. We were really starting to attract attention, we were taking off—and then this." Peter and a number of his associates in the next few months made a number of those below-the-waterline decisions. First, the researchers determined certain oils in human sweat were clogging the pores in Gore-Tex and altering the surface tension of the membrane. Thus, water could pass through. They also discovered a good washing could restore the waterproof property. At first this solution, known as the "Ivory Snow Solution," was accepted.

A single letter from "Butch," a mountain guide in the Sierras, changed the company's position. Butch wrote how he had been leading a group and, "My parka leaked and my life was in danger." As Gilson said, "That scared the hell out of us. Clearly our solution was no solution at all to someone on a mountaintop." All of the products were recalled. As Gilson said, "We bought back, at our own expense, a fortune in pipeline material. Anything that was in store, at the manufacturers, or anywhere else in the pipeline."

In the meantime, Bob Gore and other associates set out to develop a permanent fix. One month later, a second generation Gore-Tex had been developed. Gilson told dealers that if at any time a customer returned a leaky parka, they should replace it and bill the company. The replacement program cost Gore roughly $4 million.

One thing that might strike an outsider in the meetings and the other places in the Gore organization was the informality and amount of humor. One of the most common words often heard in meetings was "Bullshit!" In contrast, other commonly heard words were "responsibilities" and "commitments." This was an organization that seemed to take what it did very seriously, but its members did not take themselves too seriously.

Gore, for a company of its size, had a very short organizational pyramid. The pyramid consisted of Bob Gore, the late Bill Gore's son, as president, and Vieve, Bill Gore's widow, as secretary-treasurer. All the other members of the Gore organization were referred to as associates. Words such as employees, subordinates, and managers were taboo in the Gore culture.

Gore did not have any managers, but it did have many leaders. Bill Gore described in an internal memo the kinds of leadership and the role of leadership as follows:

1. The associate who is recognized by a team as having a special knowledge or experience (for example, this could be a chemist, computer expert, machine operator, salesman, engineer, lawyer). This kind of leader gives the team *guidance in a special area.*
2. The associate the team looks to for coordination of individual activities to achieve the agreed-on objectives of the team. The role of this leader is to

persuade team members to *make the commitments* necessary for success (commitment seeker).

3. The associate who proposes necessary objectives and activities and seeks agreement and team *consensus on objectives.* This leader is perceived by the team membership as having a good grasp of how the objectives of the team fit in with the broad objective of the enterprise. This kind of leader is often also the "commitment seeking" leader.

4. The leader who evaluates relative contribution of team members (in consultation with other sponsors) and reports these contribution evaluations to a compensation committee. This leader may also participate in the compensation committee on relative contribution and pay and *reports changes in compensation* to individual associates. This leader is then also a compensation sponsor.

5. The leader who coordinates the research, manufacturing, and marketing of one product type within a business, interacting with team leaders and individual associates who have commitments regarding the product type. These leaders are usually called *product specialists.* They are respected for their knowledge and dedication to their products.

6. *Plant leaders* who help coordinate activities of people within a plant.

7. *Business leaders* who help coordinate activities of people in a business.

8. *Functional leaders* who help coordinate activities of people in a "functional" area.

9. *Corporate leaders* who help coordinate activities of people in different businesses and functions and who try to promote communication and cooperation among all associates.

10. *Intrapreneuring associates* who *organize new teams* for new businesses, new products, new processes, new devices, new marketing efforts, new or better methods of all kinds. These leaders invite other associates to "sign up" for their project. It is clear that leadership is widespread in our lattice organization and that it is continually changing and evolving. The situation that leaders are frequently *also* sponsors should not confuse that these are different activities and responsibilities. Leaders are not authoritarians, managers of people, or supervisors who tell us what to do or forbid us doing things; nor are they "parents" to whom we transfer our own self-responsibility. However, they do often advise us of the consequences of actions we have done or propose to do. Our actions result in contributions, or lack of contribution, to the success of our enterprise. Our pay depends on the magnitude of our contributions. This is the basic discipline of our lattice organization.

Many other aspects were arranged along egalitarian lines. The parking lot did not have any reserved parking spaces except for customers and the handicapped. There was only one area in each plant in which to eat. The lunchroom in each new plant was designed to be a focal point for employee interaction. As Dave McCarter of Phoenix explained, "The design is no accident. The lunchroom in Flagstaff has a fireplace in the middle. We want people to like to be here." The location of the plant was also no accident. Sites were selected based on transportation access, a nearby university, beautiful surroundings, and climate appeal. Land cost was never a primary consideration. McCarter justified the selection by stating, "Expanding is not costly in the long run. The loss of money is what you make happen by stymying people into a box."

Not all people functioned well under such a system, especially initially. For those accustomed to a more structured work environment, there were adjustment problems. As Bill Gore said, "All our lives most of us have been told what to do, and some people don't know how to respond when asked to do something—and have the very real option of saying no—on their job. It's the new associate's responsibility to find out what he or she can do for the good of the operation." The vast majority of the new associates, after some initial floundering, adapted quickly.

For those who required more structured working conditions and could not adapt, Gore's flexible workplace was not for them. According to Bill, for those few, "It's an unhappy situation, both for the associate and the sponsor. If there is no contribution, there is no paycheck."

As Anita McBride, an associate in Phoenix, said, "It's not for everybody. People ask me do we have turnover, and yes we do have turnover. What you're seeing looks like utopia, but it also looks extreme. If you finally figure the system, it can be real exciting. If you can't handle it, you've got to go. Probably by your own choice, because you're going to be so frustrated."

Associates had also encountered criticism from outsiders who had problems with the idea of no titles. Sarah Clifton, an associate at the Flagstaff facility, was being pressed by some outsiders as to what her title was. She made one up and had it printed on some business cards—SUPREME COMMANDER. When Bill Gore learned what she did, he loved it and recounted the story to others.

In rare cases, an associate "is trying to be unfair," in Bill's own words. In one case, the problem was chronic absenteeism and in the other the individual was caught stealing. "When that happens, all hell breaks loose," said Bill Gore. "We can get damned authoritarian when we have to."

Over the years, Gore & Associates faced a number of unionization drives. The company neither tried to dissuade an associate from attending an organizational meeting nor retaliated when fliers were passed out. Each attempt was unsuccessful. None of the plants had been organized to date. Bill believed no need existed for third-party representation under the lattice structure. He asked the question, "Why would associates join a union when they own the company? It seems rather absurd."

Overall, the associates appeared to have responded positively to the Gore system of unmanagement and unstructure. Bill estimated the year before he died that, "The profit per associate is double" that of Du Pont.

ASSOCIATE DEVELOPMENT

Ron Hill, an associate in Newark, said W. L. Gore "will work with associates who want to advance themselves." Associates were offered many in-house training opportunities. Most were technical and engineering focused because of the type of organization W. L. Gore was, but the company also offered in-house programs in leadership development. In addition, the company had cooperative programs with associates to obtain training through universities and other outside providers in which Gore picked up most of the educational costs for the associates. The emphasis in employee development, as in many parts of W. L. Gore, was that the associate must take the initiative.

COMPENSATION

Compensation at W. L. Gore & Associates took three forms—salary, bonus, and an Associates' Stock Option Program (ASOP).[2] Entry-level salary was in the middle of the range for comparable jobs. According to Sally Gore, daughter-in-law of the founder, "We do not feel we need to be the highest paid. We never try to steal people away from other companies with salary. We want them to come here because of the opportunities for growth and the unique work environment." Associates' salaries were reviewed at least once a year and more commonly twice a year. The reviews were conducted by a compensation team for most workers in the facility in which they work. The sponsors for all associates acted as their advocate during this review process. Before meeting with the compensation committee, the sponsor checked with customers or whoever used the results of the person's work to find out what contribution had been made. In addition, the evaluation team considered the associate's leadership ability and willingness to help others to develop to their fullest.

Besides salaries, W. L. Gore had a bonus and ASOP profit-sharing plan for all associates. The bonus consisted of 15 percent of the company's profits distributed among all associates twice a year. In addition, the firm bought company stock equivalent to 15 percent of the associates' annual income and placed it in an (ASOP) retirement fund. Thus, an associate became a stockholder after being at Gore for one year. Bill wanted every associate to feel they were the owners.

The principle of commitment was seen as a two-way street. W. L. Gore & Associates tried to avoid layoffs. Instead of cutting pay, which was seen at Gore as disastrous to morale, the company had used a system of temporary transfers within a plant or cluster of plants and voluntary layoffs.

RESEARCH AND DEVELOPMENT

Research and development, like everything else at Gore, were unstructured. There was no formal research and development department. Yet the company held over 150 patents, although most inventions were held as proprietary or trade secrets. Any associate could ask for a piece of raw PTFE, known as a silly worm, with which to experiment. Bill Gore believed all people had it within themselves to be creative.

The best way to understand how research and development worked was to see how inventiveness had previously occurred at Gore. By 1969, the wire and cable division was facing increased competition. Bill Gore began to look for a way to straighten out the PTFE molecules. As he said, "I figured out that if we ever could unfold those molecules, get them to stretch out straight, we'd have a tremendous new kind of material." He thought that if PTFE could be stretched, air could be introduced into its molecular structure. The result would be greater volume per pound of raw material without affecting performance. Thus, fabricating costs would be reduced and the profit margins would be increased. Going about this search in a scientific manner with his son, Bob, the Gores heated rods of PTFE to various temperatures and then

---

[2]Gore's ASOP is similar legally to an ESOP (Employee Stock Option Plan). Gore simply does not use the word *employee* in any of its documentation.

slowly stretched them. Regardless of the temperature or how carefully they stretched them, the rods broke.

Working alone late one night in 1969 after countless failures, Bob, in frustration, yanked at one of the rods violently. To his surprise, it did not break. He tried it again and again with the same results.

The next morning, Bob demonstrated his breakthrough to his father, but not without some drama. As Bill Gore recalled, "Bob wanted to surprise me so he took a rod and stretched it slowly. Naturally, it broke. Then he pretended to get mad. He grabbed another rod and said, 'Oh the hell with this,' and gave it a pull. It didn't break—he'd done it." The new arrangement of molecules changed not only the wire and cable division, but also led to the development of Gore-Tex and what is now the largest division at Gore plus a host of other products.

Initial field-testing of Gore-Tex was conducted by Bill and Vieve in the summer of 1970. Vieve made a hand-sewn tent out of patches of Gore-Tex. They took it on their annual camping trip to the Wind River Mountains in Wyoming. The very first night in the wilderness, they encountered a hail storm. The hail tore holes in the top of the tent, but the bottom filled up like a bathtub from the rain. As Bill Gore stated, "At least we knew from all the water that the tent was waterproof. We just needed to make it stronger, so it could withstand hail."

The second largest division began on the ski slopes of Colorado. Bill was skiing with his friend Dr. Ben Eiseman of the Denver General Hospital. As Bill Gore told the story, "We were just to start a run when I absentmindedly pulled a small tubular section of Gore-Tex out of my pocket and looked at it. 'What is that stuff?' Ben asked. So I told him about its properties. 'Feels great,' he said, 'What do you use it for?' 'Got no idea,' I said. 'Well give it to me,' he said, 'and I'll try it in a vascular graft on a pig.' Two weeks later, he called me up. Ben was pretty excited. 'Bill,' he said 'I put it in a pig and it works. What do I do now?' I told him to get together with Pete Cooper in our Flagstaff plant, and let them figure it out." Now hundreds of thousands of people throughout the world walk around with Gore-Tex vascular grafts.

Every associate was encouraged to think, experiment, and follow a potentially profitable idea to its conclusion. For example, at a plant in Newark, Delaware, a machine that wrapped thousands of yards of wire a day was designed by Fred L. Eldreth, an associate with a third-grade education. The design was done over a weekend. Many other associates had contributed their ideas through both product and process breakthroughs.

Even without a research and development department, innovations and creativity worked very well at Gore & Associates. The year before he died, Bill Gore claimed, "The creativity, the number of patent applications and innovative products is triple" that of Du Pont.

MARKETING STRATEGY

Gore's marketing strategy was based on making the determination that it could offer the best valued products to a marketplace, that people in that marketplace appreciated what it manufactured, and that Gore could become a leader in that area of expertise. The operating procedures used to implement the strategy followed the same principles as other functions at Gore.

First, the marketing of a product revolved around a leader who was referred to as a product champion. According to Dave McCarter, "You marry your technology with the interests of your champions as you've got to have champions for all these things no matter what. And that's the key element within our company. Without a product champion you can't do much anyway, so it is individually driven. If you get a person interested in a particular market or a particular product for the marketplace, then there is no stopping them."

Second, a product champion was responsible for marketing the product through commitments with sales representatives. Again according to McCarter, "We have no quota system. Our marketing and our salespeople make their own commitments as to what their forecasts are. There is no person sitting around telling them that that is not high enough, you have to increase it by 10 percent, or whatever somebody feels is necessary. You are expected to meet your commitment, which is your forecast, but nobody is going to tell you to change it. . . . There is no order of command, no chain involved. These are groups of independent people who come together to make unified commitments to do something and sometimes when they can't make those agreements . . . you may pass up a marketplace, . . . but that's OK because there's much more advantage when the team decides to do something."

Third, the sales representatives were on salary. They were not on commission. They participated in the profit sharing and ASOP plans in which all other associates participated.

As in other areas of Gore, the individual success stories came from diverse backgrounds. McCarter related one of these success stories as follows:

> I interviewed Sam one day. I didn't even know why I was interviewing him actually. Sam was retired from AT&T. After 25 years, he took the golden parachute and went down to Sun Lakes to play golf. He played golf a few months and got tired of that. He was selling life insurance.
>
> I sat reading the application; his technical background interested me. . . . He had managed an engineering department with 600 people. He'd managed manufacturing plants for AT&T and had a great wealth of experience at AT&T. He said, "I'm retired. I like to play golf, but I just can't do it everyday so I want to do something else. Do you have something around here I can do?" I was thinking to myself, this is one of these guys I would sure like to hire, but I don't know what I would do with him.
>
> The thing that triggered me was the fact that he said he sold insurance and here is a guy with a high degree of technical background selling insurance. He had marketing experience, international marketing experience. So the bell went off in my head that we were trying to introduce a new product into the marketplace that was a hydrocarbon leak protection cable. You can bury it in the ground and in a matter of seconds it could detect a hydrocarbon (gasoline, etc.). I had a couple of other guys working on it who hadn't been very successful with marketing it. We were having a hard time finding a customer.
>
> Well, I thought that kind of a product would be like selling insurance. If you think about it, why should you protect your tanks? It's an insurance policy that things are not leaking into the environment. That has implications, big-time monetary. So, actually, I said, "Why don't you come back Monday? I have just the thing for you." So he did. We hired him; he went to work, a very energetic guy. Certainly a champion of the product, he picked right up on it, ran with it single-handed. . . . Now it's a growing business. It certainly is a valuable one too for the environment.

In the implementation of its marketing strategy, Gore relied on cooperative and word-of-mouth advertising. Cooperative advertising was especially used to promote Gore-Tex fabric products, which were sold through a number of clothing manufacturers and distributors, including Apparel Technologies, Lands' End, Austin Reed, Timberland, Woolrich, North Face, Grandoe, and Michelle Jaffe. Gore engaged in cooperative advertising because the associates believed positive experiences with any one product would carry over to purchases of other and more Gore-Tex fabric products. Apparently, this strategy was paying off. Richard Zuckerwar, president of the Grandoe Corporation, said about his company's introduction of Gore-Tex gloves, "Sports activists have had the benefit of Gore-Tex gloves to protect their hands from the elements. . . . With this handsome collection of gloves . . . you can have warm, dry hands without sacrificing style."

The power of informal marketing techniques extended beyond consumer products. According to McCarter, "In the technical end of the business, company reputation probably is most important. You have to have a good reputation with your company." He went on to say that without a good reputation, a company's products would not be considered seriously by many industrial customers. In other words, the sale was often made before the representative called. Gore had been very successful using its marketing strategies to secure a market leadership position in a number of areas ranging from waterproof outdoor clothing to vascular grafts.

ACKNOWLEDGMENTS

A number of sources were especially helpful in providing background material for this case. The most important sources were the W. L. Gore associates who generously shared their time and viewpoints about the company. We especially appreciate the input received from Anita McBride, who spent hours with us sharing her personal experiences as well as providing many resources including internal documents and videotapes. In addition, Trish Hearn and Dave McCarter also added much to this case through sharing their personal experiences as well as ensuring that the case accurately reflected the Gore company and culture.

REFERENCES

Aburdene, Patricia, and John Nasbitt. *Reinventing the Corporation.* New York: Warner Books, 1985.

Angrist, S. W. "Classless Capitalists," *Forbes*, May 9, 1983, pp. 123–24.

Franlesca, L. "Dry and Cool," *Forbes*, August 27, 1984, p. 126.

Hoerr, J. "A Company Where Everybody Is the Boss," *Business Week*, April 15, 1985, p. 98.

Levering, Robert. *The 100 Best Companies to Work for in America.*

McKendrick, Joseph. "The Employees as Entrepreneur," *Management World*, January 1985, pp. 12–13.

Milne, M. J. "The Gorey Details," *Management Review,* March 1985, pp. 16–17.

Posner, B. G. "The First Day on the Job," *Inc.*, June 1986, pp. 73–75.

Price, Kathy. "Firm Thrives without Boss," *AZ Republic*, February 2, 1986.

Rhodes, Lucien. "The Un-manager," *Inc.*, August 1982, p. 34.

Simmons, J. "People Managing Themselves: Un-management at W. L. Gore Inc." *Journal for Quality and Participation*, December 1987, pp. 14–19.

"The Future Workplace," *Management Review,* July 1986, pp. 22–23.

Trachtenberg, J. A. "Give Them Stormy Weather," *Forbes*, March 24, 1986, pp. 172–74.

Ward, Alex. "An All-Weather Idea," *The New York Times Magazine*, November 10, 1985, sec. 6.

Weber, Joseph. "No Bosses. And Even 'Leaders' Can't Give Orders," *Business Week*, December 10, 1990, pp. 196–97.

"Wilbert L. Gore," *Industry Week*, October 17, 1983, pp. 48–49.

THE HOME DEPOT, INC.

Paul M. Swiercz, George Washington University

Less than 12 years after its first store opened in Atlanta in 1979, the Home Depot had become America's largest home center retailer and one of the nation's 30 largest retailers. The Home Depot's meteoric rise stemmed from its innovativeness in combining the economies of scale inherent in a warehouse format with a high level of customer service. Home Depot stores were approximately 100,000 square feet in size, with an additional 10,000 to 20,000 square feet of outside selling area. The stores stocked about 30,000 kinds of building materials, home improvement supplies, and lawn and garden products. Sales volume in the 1980–91 period had increased from a modest $22 million (4 stores) to $5.1 billion (174 stores).

The company was noted for its progressive corporate culture and workplace practices. At Home Depot, management believed its people really did make a difference. The company paid above-average wages to its employees, approximately 90 percent of whom were full time (a rarity in the retail business). Salespeople had a reputation for being knowledgeable and prepared to answer even the most naive questions of would-be do-it-yourselfers (DIYs).

Corporate culture was promulgated through a variety of communication techniques and an intensive training program. For example, Bernard Marcus, chairman, and Arthur Blank, president, had personally trained each of the company store managers, all of whom were promoted from within. Training was such an important issue at Home Depot that Marcus believed Home Depot employees became ill-suited to work anywhere else. He says, "Where do we find these people? Nowhere. We make them. We tell our people to make it here because they won't be able to make it at another organization. They'd be misfits."[1]

Individualism, an entrepreneurial spirit, and decentralized management were prized at Home Depot. "We teach from the top down," Marcus said. "We give employees the tools to do the job, then let them do it. At every level, they are not afraid to make decisions."[2]

The challenge for Home Depot in the 1990s and beyond was to balance continued growth and retain its entrepreneurial spirit without sacrificing the values that had set it apart from other retailers. In 1979, Marcus predicted Home Depot would become "the Sears Roebuck of this industry."[3] Those who have witnessed the difficulties faced by Sears as it attempted to adjust to changing business conditions will recognize the irony in Marcus's words. Exhibit 1 contains a 10-year review of Home Depot's financial and operating performance.

---

[1]Bill Saporito, "The Fix Is In at Home Depot," *Fortune*, December 29, 1988, p. 79.
[2]*St. Petersburg Times*, December 24, 1990, p. 11.
[3]Saporito, "The Fix Is In," December 29, 1988, p. 79.

EXHIBIT 1   **The Home Depot's Financial and Operating Highlights, 1982–91**

	5-Year Annual Compound Growth Rate	10-Year Annual Compound Growth Rate	1982	1983
Statement of Earnings Data				
Net sales	38.4%	58.4%	$117,645	$256,184
Earnings before taxes	53.1	70.0	$ 9,870	$ 18,986
Net earnings	59.8	70.3	$ 5,315	$ 10,261
Net earnings per share ($)†	46.1	61.4	$ 0.05	$ .08
Weighted average number of shares (000s)†	9.1	6.9	112,557	125,724
Gross margin—% to sales	—	—	28.4	27.3
Store selling and operating expenses as a % of sales	—	—	16.5	17.0
Pre-opening expenses as a % of sales	—	—	.4	.9
General and administrative expenses as a % of sales	—	—	3.3	2.9
Net interest income (expense) as a % of sales	—	—	.2	.9
Earnings before taxes as a % of sales	—	—	8.4	7.4
Net earnings as a % of sales	—	—	4.5	4.0
Balance Sheet Data and Financial Ratios				
Total assets	44.8%	64.9%	$ 33,014	$105,230
Working capital	46.9	60.5	$ 12,901	$ 49,318
Merchandise inventories	31.7	50.3	$ 17,575	$ 58,712
Net property and equipment	49.3	80.1	$ 5,954	$ 21,129
Long-term debt	18.3	53.4	$ 236	$ 4,384
Stockholders' equity	59.7	78.3	$ 18,354	$ 65,278
Book value per share ($)†	47.9	66.1	$ 0.32	$ .52
Long-term debt to equity—%	—	—	1.3	6.7
Current ratio	—	—	1.92:1	2.43:1
Inventory turnover	—	—	5.8x	4.9x
Return on average equity—%	—	—	45.1	24.5
Statement of Cash Flows Data				
Depreciation and amortization	43.2%	76.7%	$ 389	$ 903
Capital expenditures	52.5	67.5	$ 2,883	$ 16,081
Cash dividends per share ($)†	—	—	—	—
Customer and Store Data				
Number of states	16.5%	22.3%	2	4
Number of stores	23.7	36.1	10	19
Square footage at year-end	27.8	41.6	696	1,449
Change in square footage—%	—	—	37.3	108.2
Average square footage per store	—	—	70	76
Number of customer transactions	33.9	54.3	4,164	8,479
Average sale per transaction ($)	3.4	2.7	$ 28.25	$ 30.21
Number of employees	33.5	45.7	1,100	2,400
Other Data				
Net sales increase—%	—	—	128.3	117.8
Average total company weekly sales	38.4%	58.4%	$ 2,262	$ 4,927
Weighted average weekly sales per operating store	12.3	13.0	$ 281	$ 360
Comparable store sales increase—%‡	—	—	47	31
Weighted average sales per square foot ($)‡	8.6	8.6	210	245
Advertising expense as a % of sales	—	—	2.6	2.9

*Fiscal years 1990 and 1984 consisted of 53 weeks, all other years reported consisted of 52 weeks.
†All per share and share data have been adjusted for a three-for-two stock split effected in the form of a dividend in June 1991.
‡Adjusted to reflect the first 52 weeks of the 53-week fiscal year in 1990.

EXHIBIT 1   *(concluded)*

1984*	1985	1986	1987	1988	1989	1990*	1991
$432,779	$700,729	$1,011,462	$1,453,657	$1,999,514	$2,758,535	$3,815,356	$5,136,674
$ 26,252	$ 11,619	$ 47,073	$ 95,586	$ 125,833	$ 182,015	$ 259,828	$ 396,120
$ 14,122	$ 8,219	$ 23,873	$ 54,086	$ 76,753	$ 111,954	$ 163,428	$ 249,150
$ .11	$ .06	$ .18	$ .33	$ .44	$ .63	$ .90	$ 1.20
128,093	127,817	134,562	161,981	172,988	177,705	181,253	207,999
26.4	25.9	27.5	27.8	27.0	27.8	27.9	28.1
17.2	19.2	18.7	18.1	17.8	18.3	18.2	18.1
.4	1.1	.3	.3	.4	.3	.4	.3
3.0	2.9	2.7	2.6	2.4	2.5	2.4	2.3
.3	(1.2)	(1.1)	(.2)	(.1)	(.1)	(.1)	.3
6.1	1.7	4.7	6.6	6.3	6.6	6.8	7.7
3.3	1.2	2.4	3.7	3.8	4.1	4.3	4.8
$249,364	$380,193	$ 394,741	$ 528,270	$ 699,179	$1,117,534	$1,639,503	$2,510,292
$100,110	$106,451	$ 91,076	$ 110,621	$ 142,806	$ 273,851	$ 300,867	$ 623,937
$ 84,046	$152,700	$ 167,115	$ 211,421	$ 294,274	$ 381,452	$ 509,022	$ 662,257
$ 73,577	$160,816	$ 168,981	$ 244,503	$ 332,416	$ 514,440	$ 878,730	$1,254,774
$117,942	$199,943	$ 116,907	$ 52,298	$ 107,508	$ 302,901	$ 530,774	$ 270,575
$ 80,214	$ 89,092	$ 163,042	$ 320,559	$ 382,938	$ 512,129	$ 683,402	$1,691,212
$ .63	$ .70	$ 1.13	$ 1.93	$ 2.26	$ 2.97	$ 3.86	$ 8.01
147.0	224.0	71.7	16.3	28.1	59.1	77.7	16.0
3.22:1	2.27:1	1.85:1	1.75:1	1.74:1	1.94:1	1.73:1	2.17:1
4.2x	4.1x	4.6x	5.4x	5.8x	5.9x	6.0x	6.1x
19.3	9.7	20.3	21.1	21.6	25.2	27.6	18.5
$ 2,368	$ 5,193	$ 8,697	$ 10,646	$ 14,673	$ 21,107	$ 34,358	$ 52,283
$ 50,769	$ 99,767	$ 52,363	$ 89,235	$ 105,123	$ 204,972	$ 400,205	$ 432,198
—	—	—	$ 0.02	$ 0.03	$ 0.05	$ 0.07	$ 0.11
6	7	7	8	10	12	12	15
31	50	60	75	96	118	145	174
2,381	4,001	4,828	6,161	8,216	10,424	13,278	16,480
64.3	68.0	20.6	27.6	33.4	26.9	27.4	24.1
77	80	80	82	86	88	92	95
14,256	23,324	34,020	48,073	64,227	84,494	112,464	146,221
$ 30.36	$ 30.04	$ 29.73	$ 30.24	$ 31.13	$ 32.65	$ 33.92	$ 35.13
4,000	5,400	6,600	9,100	13,000	17,500	21,500	28,000
68.9	61.9	44.3	43.7	37.6	38.0	38.3	34.6
$ 8,166	$ 13,476	$ 19,451	$ 27,955	$ 38,452	$ 53,049	$ 71,988	$ 98,782
$ 366	$ 343	$ 355	$ 418	$ 464	$ 515	$ 566	$ 633
14	2	7	18	13	13	10	11
247	223	230	265	282	303	322	348
2.5	3.2	2.4	2.0	1.5	1.1	.9	.7

COMPANY HISTORY

In June 1979, Home Depot opened its first stores in Atlanta, Georgia, with 180 employees. Twelve years later, the company had 174 full-service warehouse stores in 34 markets in 15 states (mainly Georgia, Florida, Texas, Arizona, California, and the Northeast). Home Depot had over 28,000 employees in early 1992 and was regarded as one of the fastest growing companies in the United States. Between 1987 and 1991, its sales revenues had grown at an average annual compound rate of 38 percent. Even so, the company had plenty of opportunity to continue rapid growth since its $5.1 billion in sales represented only about a 5 percent share of the estimated $105 billion market for home-improvement supplies in just the United States.

Home Depot's CEO Bernard Marcus began his career in the retail industry in a small pharmacy in Milburn, New Jersey. He later joined Two Guys Discount Chain to manage its drug and cosmetic departments and eventually became the vice president of merchandising and advertising for the parent company, Vornado, Inc. In 1972, he moved into the do-it-yourself home-improvement sector as president of Handy Dan/Handy City, a subsidiary of Daylin, Inc. Sanford Sigoloff, Daylin's CEO, and Marcus had a strong difference of opinion over control, and at 5 P.M. one Friday in 1978, Marcus and two other Handy Dan top executives were discharged.

That weekend, Home Depot was born when the three men—Marcus, Arthur Blank (now president of Home Depot), and Ronald Brill (now chief financial officer)—laid out the plans for the do-it-yourself chain. Venture capital was provided by investment firms that included Invemed of New York as well as private investors. Two key investors were Joseph Flom, a prominent lawyer who specialized in takeovers, and Frank Borman, then chairman of Eastern Airlines.

When the first stores opened near Atlanta in 1979, the company leased space in three former Treasury Discount Stores with 60,000 square feet each. All three were suburban locations north of the city. Industry experts gave Home Depot 10-to-1 odds it would fail.

In 1980, a fourth Atlanta store opened, and the company had annual sales of $22.3 million. The next year, Home Depot ventured beyond Atlanta to open four stores in south Florida and also had its first public stock offering at $12 a share. The company was voted the Retailer of the Year in the home center industry in 1982. By early 1990, its stock had soared by 7,019 percent and split seven times.

By 1983, Marcus was a nationally recognized leader in the do-it-yourself industry. New Orleans was a strong market with many homeowners and young people, so Home Depot moved in with three stores. Other additions were in Arizona and Florida. Two stores opened in Orlando, in the backyard of the Winter Haven–based Scotty's, and one more in south Florida. Home Depot's strong drawing power became evident as 1983 sales per share approached $15 million, equal to about 500,000 transactions per store.

In 1984, Home Depot's common stock was listed on the New York Stock Exchange. Marcus believed the only restraint Home Depot faced that year was its ability to recruit and train new staff fast enough. However, Home Depot was soon to face other problems. In December, things briefly turned sour when Home Depot bought the nine-store Bowater Warehouse chain with stores in

Texas, Louisiana, and Alabama. Bowater had a dismal reputation, its merchandise didn't match Home Depot's, and nearly all employees had to be dismissed because they were unable to fit the company's strong customer service orientation.

Of the 22 stores opened in 1985, most were in eight new markets, including the less-hospitable terrain of Houston and Detroit. The company lost money with promotional pricing and advertising costs. This rapid growth into unknown territories also took management attention from the other stores. The media quickly noted Home Depot was having problems and suggested its troubles could be related to rapid expansion into the crowded home center business. Home Depot's earnings dropped 40 percent in 1985.

Marcus had to regroup in 1986. He slowed Home Depot's growth to 10 stores in existing markets, including the first super-size store with 140,000 square feet. Home Depot withdrew from the Detroit market, selling its five new stores.

In 1987, six California stores and two Tennessee stores were opened, and the company had annual sales of $1 billion. That same year, Home Depot introduced an advanced inventory management system; as a result, inventory was turned 5.4 times a year instead of 4.5 times. It also awarded its first quarterly dividend.

In 1988, 21 new stores opened; most were in California. For the second time, Home Depot was voted the Retailer of the Year in the home center industry.

Home Depot expanded its market beyond the Sunbelt in early 1989 by opening two stores in the Northeast—East Hanover, New Jersey, and North Haven, Connecticut. By the end of 1989, there were five stores in the Northeast. The year was also a benchmark year for technological developments. All stores began using UPC (universal product code) scanning systems to speed checkout time. The company's satellite data communications network installation improved management communications and training. Sales for the year totaled $2.76 billion, and plans were made to open a 135,000-square-foot store in Los Angeles. In 1989, the company made its initial contribution of $6 million to the employee stock ownership plan. On its 10th anniversary, Home Depot opened its 100th store (in Atlanta) and by year's end had parlayed its three-part marketing philosophy of everyday low prices, a large merchandise assortment, and excellent customer service into the position of being the nation's largest home center chain.

Thirty stores opened in 1990, bringing the total to 147. The largest store—140,000 square feet—was in San Diego. Sales for 1990 were $3.8 billion. During 1991, Home Depot opened 30 stores, closed 1 store, and relocated four others. Revenues were $5.1 billion.

Forty new stores were planned for 1992, including further penetration in the Northeast (18 stores) where the company had long-term goals to operate 150 stores. Home Depot was scheduled to open its first stores in Washington, Nevada, and North Carolina. Management anticipated opening 10 new stores in the Southeast and 12 in the West.

By 1995, the company was projecting a total of 350 stores and annual sales of $10 billion. By the end of 1996, Home Depot hoped to be operating over 500 stores. The company believed its potential for stores in the United States was well in excess of 1,000; in addition, management saw opportunities to expand elsewhere in the world.

CORPORATE CULTURE

The culture at Home Depot was characterized by a strong emphasis on individuality, informality, nonconformity, growth, and pride. These traits mirrored those of the founders of the company, who, within hours of being fired, were busily planning the Home Depot stores to go into competition with the company from which they had just been dismissed. According to Arthur Blank, Home Depot's culture was "really a reflection of Bernie and me. We're not formal, stuffy folks. We hang pretty loose. We've got a lot of young people. We want them to feel comfortable."[4]

The importance of the individual to the success of the whole venture was consistently emphasized at Home Depot. Marcus's statements bear this out: "We still are first-generation entrepreneurs. . . . We are hands-on managers. . . . We're individuals. People here think for themselves. . . . Their dreams and desires can carry them wherever they want to go." While emphasizing the opportunities for advancement at Home Depot, Marcus had little regard for the kind of "cradle-to-grave" job that used to be prevalent in America and was still the norm in Japan. To him, this was "a kind of serfdom."[5]

Informality was always in order at Home Depot—"spitballs fly at board meetings" and there was always someone around to make sure that ties got properly trimmed. When executives visited stores, they went alone, not with an entourage of assistants and subordinates. Most had worked on the floors in the beginning and knew the business from the ground up. They were approachable and employees frequently came forward with ideas and suggestions.

Nonconformity was evident in many different areas of the company, from the initial warehouse concept to the size and variety of merchandise to human resources practices. Both Marcus and Blank "flout conventional corporate rules that foil innovation." Management viewed training employees at all levels as one of the most powerful means of transmitting corporate culture, and Home Depot used it extensively. One analyst noted that Home Depot (in a reverse of the "top to bottom" training sequence in most organizations) trained the carry-out people first. "The logic is that the guy who helps you to your car is the last employee you come into contact with, and they want that contact to be positive."[6]

ORGANIZATIONAL STRUCTURE

The official organizational structure (see Exhibit 2) of Home Depot was much like that of other retail organizations, but according to a human resources spokesperson, the environment was so relaxed and casual you felt like you could report to anyone. Marcus and Blank were supported by four senior vice presidents, including the chief financial officer, the senior vice president of corporate development, and the senior vice president of merchandising for the eastern division. There were 10 vice presidents—merchandising for the Northeast, merchandising for the West, human resources, legal, finance, advertising

---

[4]*St. Petersburg Times*, December 24, 1990, p. 11.
[5]*Business Atlanta*, November 11, 1988.
[6]*Chain Store Executive*, April 1983, pp. 9–11.

EXHIBIT 2   Home Depot's Organization Structure, 1990

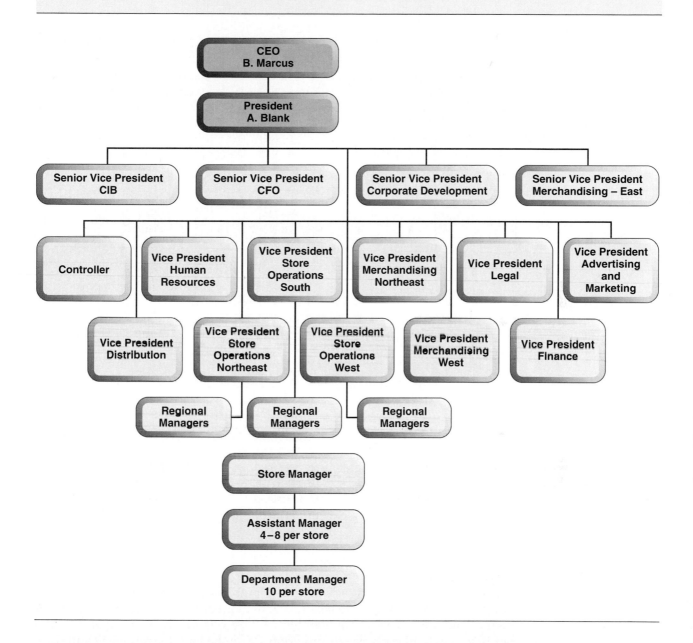

and marketing, distribution, three vice presidents of store operations—and the controller.

The three operational vice presidents were responsible for the Northeast, South, and West. Under each vice president was a group of regional managers. There were approximately 20 regional managers companywide. Each regional manager was responsible for six to eight stores.

Store layout and merchandise displays were very similar from store to store (see Exhibit 3). The company's corporate headquarters was responsible for store "look," but individual managers could change a display or order more or

EXHIBIT 3   **Layout of a Typical Home Depot Store**

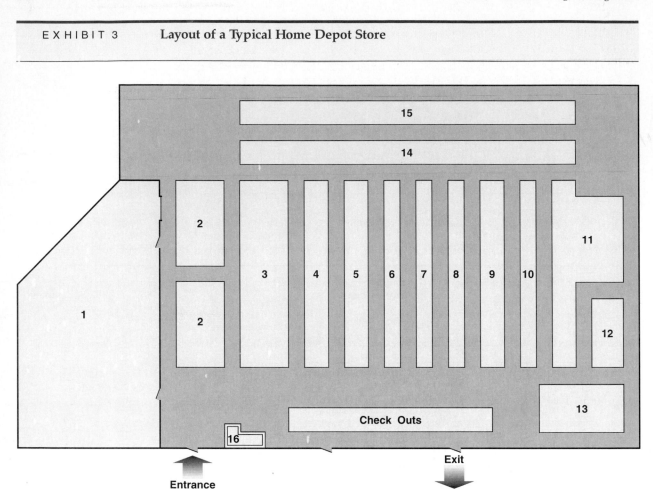

1 **Shrubs/outside garden**   5 **Flooring/paneling**   9 **Hardware**   13 **Lighting/fan center**
2 **Lawn and garden**   6 **Carpet/vinyl center**   10 **Electrical**   14 **Building materials**
3 **Paints/wallpaper/blinds**   7 **Ceramic tile**   11 **Plumbing**   15 **Lumber**
4 **Furniture**   8 **1X boards**   12 **Kitchen center**   16 **Service desk**

less of a product if they could justify the change. The managers within individual stores made decisions regarding their employees, such as firing and hiring, but they looked to corporate headquarters in areas such as training, merchandising, and advertising. One manager of a store in Georgia said that if he did not like a particular display or promotion, then he had discretionary authority to change it or drop it. The manager went on to say he and other store managers worked hand in hand with corporate headquarters and that if he wished to make "major" changes or had a significant store or personnel problem, he would deal with corporate.

At the store level, Home Depot was set up much as would be expected, with managers, assistant managers, and department managers. The average Home Depot store had one store manager whose primary responsibility was to be the master delegator. There were usually four to six assistant managers who presided over the store's 10 departments. Each assistant manager was responsible for one to three departments. One assistant manager was responsible for receiving and the "back end" (stock storage area) in addition to his or her departments. One assistant manager acted as an administrative assistant in the "front end" (phones, customer service area, time clock) in addition to his or her departments. The assistant managers were supported by department managers who were each responsible for one department. The department managers reported directly to the assistant managers and had no firing/hiring capabilities. Assistant managers normally handled ordering and work schedules; department managers handled questions from employees and job assignments.

OPERATIONS

Operating efficiency was seen as crucial to Home Depot's strategy of charging everyday low prices while still offering a high level of customer service. From installing computerized checkout systems that eliminated item pricing to implementation of satellite communications systems in most of its stores, the company had shown innovativeness in its operating strategy.

By the end of 1989, every Home Depot store was using the UPC scanning system, which replaced most keying by the cashier; this resulted in faster customer checkout and greater accuracy. Home Depot's attitude of complete customer satisfaction led the company to stock the shelves after hours in order to free clerks to help with customers during the day. In an effort to ease customer crowding and preserve the company's competitive lead in providing excellent customer service, new stores had sometimes deliberately been located very close to existing ones to cannibalize customers away. Management believed its cannibalization strategy made sense because if a new store was properly located on the periphery of two trade areas (one served by the older store), customer traffic was relieved at the older location and a new base of customers was attracted to the new location.

A money-saving device had been an in-house, two-way TV network that allowed Home Depot top executives to get instant feedback from local managers. This addition had increased employee motivation and saved many dollars due to timely information.[7] The network gave the company the capability to communicate its operating philosophies and policies more effectively because information presented by top management could be delivered personally and go out to all store employees simultaneously.

Home Depot was firmly committed to energy conservation and had installed reflectors to lower the amount of lighting needed in a store. The reflectors darkened the ceiling but saved thousands of dollars a year in energy bills. Further, it had purchased a computerized system to maintain comfortable temperatures, a challenge because of the stores' concrete floors, exposed ceilings, and open oversized doors for forklift deliveries. The system also had an automated feedback capability that could be used for equipment maintenance.

The adoption of the point-of-sale (POS) technology (computerized registers that recorded sales transactions and types, method of payment, etc.) had improved each store's ability to identify and adapt to trends quickly. The

---

[7]Chuck Hawkins, "Will Home Depot Be 'The Wal-Mart' of the '90s," *Business Week,* March 19, 1990, p. 124.

information provided by the POS technology was transferred to computer centers in Atlanta and Fullerton, California, where consumer buying trends were analyzed. This allowed Home Depot to adjust its merchandising mix and track both buying trends and inventory. Electronic data interchange with major vendors to further streamline inventory replenishment, purchase orders, and invoice processing was set to begin in 1992.

Home Depot and its employees continuously looked for avenues to cut costs while maintaining quality. For example, the point-of-sale coordinator discovered that leased phone/credit approval lines shared by many stores could be great money savers. Because the connection on the lines was continuous with no dialing required, authorizations could be obtained in far less time than with conventional dial-ups—4 to 8 seconds compared to 45 to 90 seconds.

In 1987, the company introduced an advanced inventory management system that allowed it to increase inventory turns significantly (from 4.2 in 1984 to 5.8 in 1989), carry a smaller inventory, and tie up less working capital to finance it. Home Depot management believed the store efficiencies were big enough to give the company a cost structure significantly lower than the competition.

FINANCE

In 1992, Home Depot executives believed the company's financial position had never been stronger and the company had sufficient capital to continue expanding for a number of years (see Exhibit 1.)

Home Depot had encouraged employees to participate in and benefit from the company's success, as evidenced by the employee stock purchase plan, under which the company could grant eligible employees options to purchase shares of common stock at a price equal to 85 percent of the stock's fair market value at the date of grant. Top management believed broad-based employee stock ownership had been an important strategic factor in encouraging employees to build and sustain strong relationships with customers.

In 1989, the company made an initial $6 million contribution to the Home Depot employee stock ownership plan (ESOP). The ESOP was established to provide additional retirement security for the employees, while simultaneously reducing taxable income and discouraging hostile takeover attempts.

MERCHANDISING

In keeping with Home Depot's philosophy, "if you don't make dust, you eat dust," the company had made thousands of changes in its merchandising and service mix. According to Marcus, "We could sell them anything . . . but we don't. We don't want the customer to think we're a discounter, a food store, a toy store, or anything else, because it would confuse (them)."[8] Although Home Depot was conceived as a DIY warehouse, in 1992, the company was committed to serving the do-it-yourself and professional markets equally well.

---

[8]Susan Caminiti, "The New Champs of Retailing," *Fortune*, September 24, 1990, p. 2.

Advertising

The company maintained an aggressive advertising campaign using various media for both price and institutional publicity. Print advertising, usually emphasizing price, was prepared by an in-house staff to keep control of content, layout, media placement, and cost. Broadcast media advertisements were generally institutional and promoted Home Depot the company, not just pricing and specials. Advertisements stressed the "you'll feel right at home" slogan, name recognition, and the value of Home Depot's customer service.

Customer Target Market

The warehousing DIY market had gained impetus from the baby boomers. The typical do-it-yourselfer was a married male homeowner, age 25 to 54, with a high school diploma or some college education, and an annual income of $20,000 to $40,000.[9] Projections indicated households headed by 25- to 35-year olds with earnings over $30,000 would increase by 34 to 38 percent through 1995. The 45-to-54 age group earning over $30,000 was expected to increase by 40 percent.[10] Home Depot believed these consumers would be spending more time at home and would most likely spend proportionately more money making their homes bigger and better.

Industry estimates showed DIY sales were growing at an average of 10 percent per year and projected a 9 percent growth rate over the next five years.[11] These estimates were supported by the results of an independent survey[12] reporting that the self-proclaimed do-it-yourselfer population had expanded by 6.7 percent since 1986. While Home Depot's primary customers were do-it-yourselfers, the company was intent on increasing its appeal to home remodeling contractors, building maintenance professionals, and other professional customers.

Economics

The DIY industry exhibited a demand pattern that was largely recession proof. Since only 15 percent of Home Depot's business came from contractors, a downturn in home construction had only a modest impact on Home Depot sales. In addition, analysts pointed out that during hard times, consumers couldn't afford to buy new or bigger homes and instead maintained or upgraded their existing homes. Given that a home was often a household's primary financial asset, homeowners tended to protect the value of that asset. Home improvement spending had declined in only one recession during the past 20 years. Furthermore, because of the severity of the 1990–92 recession, the company had attracted many unemployed construction contractors to work in its stores, further enhancing the expert guidance provided to customers.

---

[9]"Do It Yourself," *American Demographics* 10 (March 1988), p. 21.

[10]*Population Bulletin* 21 (February 1989), pp. 17–34.

[11]"Retail Do-It-Yourself Market Profile," *Do-It-Yourself Retailing,* September 1989, pp. 53–65.

[12]Richard L. Carter et al., "D-I-Y Activity, Hardlines Patronage on the Rise," *Hardware Age,* October 1989.

Merchandising Strategy

Home Depot's 1989 annual report stated, "We are in the business of selling products, of investing to maximize sales, gross-margins and inventory turns." To meet customers' growing desire to upgrade their homes' value, Home Depot was bringing in better product lines that were previously unavailable from a mass-merchandising retailer. Management recognized that success depended on the firm's ability to act and react with speed, spot changes, and catch trends early.[13] Consequently, the merchandise mix was always being revised to include the latest and most innovative products.

The company's merchandising unit was staffed with people who had prior experience in marketing products carried by Home Depot. Each merchandiser was assigned at least two product categories, and their responsibilities involved monitoring sales volume, discontinuing items whose sales were trending downward, searching for new lines, negotiating with vendors, coordinating with store operations to resolve product problems, and training store employees on new products.

The merchandising strategy of Home Depot was predicated on (1) excellent customer service, (2) everyday low pricing, and (3) broad product selection. The company was experimenting with a 30,000-square-foot garden center/greenhouse prototype and was increasing the amount of environmentally safe "green" merchandise on its shelves.

Customer Service

Customer service was the single biggest factor that differentiated Home Depot from its competitors. Home Depot's stress on highly qualified, helpful employees, professional clinics, and in-store displays had evolved into a customer service approach that management referred to as "customer cultivation." The intent was to give DIY customers the support and confidence that no home project was beyond their capabilities with Home Depot personnel close at hand.

Home Depot's store clerks went beyond simply recommending appropriate products, tools, and materials. Sales personnel cultivated the customer by demonstrating methods and techniques of performing a job safely and efficiently. Management believed that providing excellent customer service was the key element in Home Depot's strategy because it was the most difficult to execute and the most difficult for competitors to copy.

All of the stores offered hands-on workshops on projects such as kitchen remodeling, basic plumbing, ceramic tile installation, and other activities that customers expressed an interest in. Offered mainly on weekends, they varied in length depending on complexity. Only the most experienced staff members, many of them former skilled craftsmen, taught at these workshops. Promotion of the workshops was done through direct-mail advertising and in-store promotion.

Pricing Strategy

Home Depot stressed its commitment to "everyday low pricing." At Home Depot, this concept meant across-the-board lower prices and few cut-price sales and specials. Home Depot employed professional shoppers to regularly

---

[13]Ralph D. Shipp, *Retail Merchandising Principles and Applications* (Boston: Houghton Mifflin, 1976), p. 3.

check competitors' prices and make sure Home Depot charged less. The company's 1989 gross margin was 27.0 percent compared to the home center composite gross margin of 26.87 percent.[14]

One of the major reasons Home Depot was able to undercut competitors' prices (sometimes by as much as 25 percent) was its bargaining power and its close relationship with suppliers. The company purchased from approximately 1,900 vendors, the majority of which were manufacturers. A confidential survey of manufacturers conducted by Shapiro and Associates found that Home Depot was "far and away the most demanding" of customers.[15] Shipping dates were the main area where Home Depot was most vocal. However, manufacturers agreed that the concessions made to Home Depot were offset by its large and fast-growing sales volume.

Products and Services

A typical Home Depot store stocked approximately 30,000 products, including variations in color and size. Each store carried a wide selection of quality and nationally advertised brand-name merchandise. Sales were divided among the various product categories as follows:

Product Group	Percent of 1990 Sales Revenues
Building materials, lumber, floor and wall coverings	31.0%
Plumbing, heating, and electrical supplies	29.0%
Seasonal and specialty items	14.6%
Paint and furniture	13.2%
Hardware and tools	12.2%
	100.0%

A typical store layout is shown in Exhibit 3. A list of services provided to customers is shown in Exhibit 4.

Average Store Profile

According to Bob Evans in the store planning division of Home Depot, all stores were company-owned, not franchised, and most were "free standing, built to current Home Depot standards." Home Depot owned close to 40 percent of its buildings, leasing the remainder. While the company preferred locations surrounded by shopping centers, Home Depot executives were not interested in having stores that were attached to a shopping center or mall.

Construction time depended on site conditions, local requirements, and related factors and could take up to a year. Current store sizes ranged from 67,000 to 140,000 square feet, with an additional 10,000 to 20,000 square feet of outside (garden) selling space. Store sizes varied since it was company policy to "make the store fit the land" and since many of the original stores were located in leased strip-center space.

---

[14]Christopher Jensen, "Bar-Coding—A Status Report on Industry Standards," *Do-It-Yourself Retailing*, March 1989, pp. 199–205.

[15]"Study: Vendors Call Depot Toughest Negotiator," *National Home Center News*, December 15, 1986.

EXHIBIT 4

Most new stores were in the 100,000-square-foot range. In some cases, Home Depot had 25,000 to 30,000 people walking through a store per week. Because of the heavy store traffic, older stores were being gradually remodeled or replaced with new ones to add room for new merchandise, increase selling space, widen aisles, and provide more parking spaces.

The Home Depot store "look" featured warehouse-style shelves, wide cement-floored aisles, end-displays pushing sale items, and the ever-present orange banners indicating the store's departments. Most stores had banners on each aisle to help customers locate what they're looking for. Regional purchasing and distribution centers were employed to keep the stores well stocked; regionalization was preferred to a single strong corporate department "since home improvement materials needed in the Southwest would differ somewhat from those needed in the Northeast."

HUMAN RESOURCES

Home Depot was noted for its progressive human resources policies emphasizing the importance of the individual to the success of the whole company's operations.

Recruitment/Selection

Having the right number of people, in the right jobs, at the right time was recognized by management as critical. Employee population varied greatly among stores depending on store size, sales volume, and the season. In the winter, a store might have fewer than 75 employees and in the spring add another 25 to 40 employees. Some of the larger northeastern stores had as many as 280 employees. Full-time employees filled approximately 90 percent of the positions.

When a store first opened, it attracted applicants through advertisements in local newspapers and trade journals such as *Home Center News*. A new store would usually receive several thousand applications. When seasonal workers and replacements were needed, help-wanted signs were displayed at store entrances. Walk-in candidates were another source—applications were available at the customer service desk at all times. There was no formal program to encourage employees to refer their friends for employment. At the assistant store manager level, direct recruitment contact was made with potential candidates who worked for Home Depot's competitors.

Interviews were scheduled one day per week; however, if someone with trade experience applied, an on-the-spot interview might be conducted. The company tended to look for older people who could bring a high level of knowledge and maturity to the position. In addition to related experience, Home Depot looked for people who had a stable work history, a positive attitude, an outgoing personality, excitement, and a willingness to work hard.

The selection process included pre-employment tests (honesty, math, drugs). Stores displayed signs in the windows that anyone who used drugs need not apply. Interviews were conducted with three or four people—an initial qualifier, the administrative assistant in operations, an assistant store manager, and the store manager. Reference checks were completed before a job offer was made. More in-depth background checks (financial, criminal) were conducted on management-level candidates.

Starting salaries typically ranged from $7 to $11 per hour. In the Atlanta job market, salaries averaged about $8.60 per hour. A cashier with minimal experience started at $5.50, and a highly experienced tradesperson could be paid $15 or more. Managers did not hire anyone at minimum wage. Ronald Brill, CFO, explained why: "People earning minimum wage don't have the commitment to the customer and the level of service we expect."[16]

Retention

Employee turnover varied from store to store. In the first year of a store's operation, turnover could run as high as 60 to 70 percent; it then fell to about 30 percent in succeeding years. The company's goal was to reduce turnover to below 20 percent. The major causes of turnover were students who returned to school, employees who were terminated for poor performance, and tradespeople who considered Home Depot an interim position (they often returned to positions in their trades paying as much as $50,000 per year). Few people left the organization looking for "greener pastures" in the retail industry.

Home Depot employees could expect merit increases every six months; earnings could increase 10 to 11 percent per year. Store managers earned $45,000 base salary plus potentially lucrative stock options. Stock was also important to other employees in the organization—assistant managers earned stock options, and all employees could purchase Home Depot stock at a 15 percent discount through payroll deductions. One employee hired in 1979 invested $750 in stock; in 1991, that stock was valued at over $250,000. The ESOP provided full vesting within seven years.

Career development was formally addressed during semiannual performance reviews, with goals and development plans mutually set by employees and managers. The company was committed to promotions from within and had a formal job posting program. Vacancy lists were prepared at the regional level and distributed to the stores. Store managers were promoted from within the ranks of assistant managers. Affirmative action plans were in place to increase female and minority representation.

Home Depot had periodic programs to recognize employees for good customer service, increased sales, safety, cost savings, and length of service. Badges, cash awards, and other prizes were distributed in monthly group meetings.

Home Depot executives worked hard to create an environment in which employees could be happy and where they could feel productive and secure. The company stressed to employees their role in Home Depot's success. The company environment avoided bureaucracy, was informal yet intense, and encouraged honesty and risk-taking. Each store manager maintained an open-door policy with employees, and a manager might spend two or three hours discussing a concern with an employee.

---

[16]*New Jersey Star-Ledger*, February 5, 1989.

Top executives maintained their access to employees through frequent visits to the stores. An in-house TV broadcast, "Breakfast with Bernie and Arthur," was held quarterly. Impromptu questions were solicited from the employees. One recent broadcast addressed a 20 percent slip in Home Depot's stock when the Gulf crisis began and reassured employees of the chain's strength, predicting the stock market would rebound.[17] Department managers met with employees weekly to provide new information and solicit feedback. Worker opinions also mattered at the top. When the company planned to open on New Year's Day, the employees voted to close and prevailed. When the company wrote a checkout training manual, a store cashier from Jacksonville helped write it. Internal sales charts were posted on bulletin boards so employees would know how their store compared with others in the area.

Training

Home Depot believed knowledgeable salespeople were a key success factor and spent much time training them to "bleed orange." Training, from the new employees' weeklong orientation session to regularly scheduled training classes, was a priority for top management, usually costing around $400,000 for every new store. Corporate executives spent a sizable fraction of their time in the stores, training employees. "We teach from the top down, and those who can't teach don't become executives," said Marcus, who, along with Blank, had personally taught every store manager and assistant manager to take care of the customer first, then stock the shelves.[18]

Regular employees went through both formal and on-the-job training. Classes were held on product knowledge (to give the employee "total product knowledge . . . , including all the skills a tradesperson might have"), merchandising concepts and salesmanship, time management, personnel matters, safety and security, and how to interpret the company's various internally generated reports.

New employees averaged four weeks of training before they were allowed to work on their own. Even then, when there were no other customers in the department, newer employees were expected to watch more experienced employees deal with customers so they could pick up more pointers about products, sales, and customer service. Employees were cross-trained to work in various departments, and even the cashiers learned how to work the sales floor.

Recently, the company had established the "Home Depot Television Network," allowing, via satellite link, live Sunday morning broadcasts to every store. Topics included company policies and philosophies, product upgrades, and new developments. That the programs were broadcast live, with telephone call-ins, enhanced their effectiveness. Marcus believed Home Depot employees gave 105 percent and stuck with Home Depot because "we train our people, listen to them, respond to them, acknowledge their efforts, and offer them opportunity."[19]

---

[17] *Atlanta Journal-Constitution,* September 8, 1990.
[18] *Business Month*, September 1989, p. 39.
[19] *Business Atlanta*, November 11, 1988.

As Home Depot's vice president for human resources stated in the 1991 annual report:

> We believe that our people are the most important difference between ourselves and our competitors. . . . Much effort goes into developing our people. Beyond providing excellent wages and benefits including stock ownership opportunities, we provide a psychologically enlightened workplace environment which is conducive to a satisfying and stimulating career. We can't expect our employees to bond with their customers if we don't have good relationships with our own people.

BAMA PIE, LIMITED

Raymond E. Belford, Oklahoma City University

Bama Pie, Limited's phenomenal growth over the past 24 years of its 65-year history was due directly to the growth of its major customer, McDonald's, and a fanatical commitment to quality. As the single-source supplier of pies to McDonald's U.S. operations, Bama was testimony to how a small, aggressive, and creative company could succeed competing with much larger organizations. By providing top-quality pie products and "never missing an order," Bama had been able to expand its core pie business by landing 50 percent of McDonald's oven-ready, prebaked frozen biscuit needs. Its new role as a supplier of McDonald's breakfast biscuit requirements was expected to allow Bama to increase total sales to approximately $100 million in 1992. Bama Pie's actual financial information was closely guarded since it was a privately held, family-owned limited partnership; the company's CEO was 38-year-old Paula Marshall-Chapman, who had succeeded her father and grandfather as head of the business.

Bama Pie produced more than 1 million pies per day from facilities in Tulsa, Oklahoma, for McDonald's. In 1968, the firm was producing only 500 pies per day. In 1991, the company completed a $38 million facility in Tulsa to produce the biscuits for McDonald's, arranging the bank financing within about six weeks. The new facility, in early 1992, was producing more than 120,000 biscuits per hour.

Other major customers included Pizza Hut (for which Bama was producing approximately 25 percent of its bread stick requirements), TCBY, and Braum's (an Oklahoma-based ice cream chain).

The company, in an effort to lessen its dependence on McDonald's, had begun seeking business with other major fast-food and convenience food companies. In 1992, more than 70 percent of Bama's business was with McDonald's. Less than 10 percent of the company's revenues came from products carrying the Bama Pie brand, the best-known of which was a 3-inch pecan pie. Of the McDonald's business, about 4 percent was exported to McDonald's operations in Hong Kong and Taiwan. In early 1992, Bama was working toward establishing a joint venture in Hong Kong to provide pies to McDonald's in Hong Kong, the People's Republic of China, and Taiwan. Bama also had a licensing arrangement in Canada with a Canadian baker that provided pies to McDonald's Canadian operations.

The firm considered itself responsible for McDonald's pies worldwide. Marshall-Chapman's father, Paul Marshall, began providing technical assistance to McDonald's in the early days as he, Ray Kroc (McDonald's founder), and Fred Turner (early president of McDonald's) worked together. The technical assistance in helping establish local bakeries in McDonald's global enterprise had always been provided at no cost to McDonald's. "We see it as part of our service," said Marshall-Chapman.

In 1991, Bama competed in the national Baldrige awards for quality and made the fourth cut. The companies that reached the fifth cut were chosen for the prestigious award. The company was under consideration in 1992 for the award. Marshall-Chapman was named Quality Fanatic of the Year in 1989 by Philip Crosby of the Quality College.

The word most often heard around Bama Pie headquarters in Tulsa was *quality*. Marshall-Chapman had attended numerous quality conferences and had spoken to international groups about commitment to quality. The company had dropped the traditional mission statement (see Exhibit 1) for "Bama's Quality Circle." According to Marshall-Chapman, "We had a very nice mission statement of a traditional nature—very wordy, very flowery, like most progressive companies. If you've read most mission statements, they tend to be written for Wall Street or people outside the organization. We felt the mission should be written for our employees. Our Quality Circle is very simple and keeps us focused." (See Exhibit 2 for a description of the Quality Circle.)

The company also had a values statement (Exhibit 3) that reinforced "quality as a way of life," at Bama. The company's quality statement was read before every meeting held in the company. "It helps keep us focused," Marshall-Chapman explained.

COMPANY HISTORY

The history of Bama Pies dates to 1927 when Henry C. Marshall decided to utilize the pie-baking talents of his wife, Cornelia Alabama Marshall (who went by the name Bama), to provide employment for himself after a lengthy period of being out of work. Bama Marshall began baking pies for the lunch counter at the Woolworth's in Dallas. Her talents created a market for her pies that topped 75 per day (including take-home purchases), and the local owner of Woolworth's expanded his lunch counter to 75 stools to handle customer volume.

Bama was soon baking up to 300 pies per day for Woolworth's, and business at the lunch counter was booming. Bama was spending so much time at her work, Henry began to think she was being unfaithful to him and was "carrying on" with the owner of the Woolworth's. He sent his son, Paul, down to "spy" on Bama. When Paul reported back that the reason the owner "liked Mama so much is because of the pies she was making," Henry came up with an idea.

The following passage from *A Piece of the Pie* by Paul Marshall describes the event.[1]

> I heard Papa ask Mama something that made me cringe.
> "Blanchie, how are things at Woolworth's?"
> That question sounded innocent enough, but I knew Papa was fishing for an answer that would drive him into the rage which he had been holding in for weeks. (Paul still thought his father believed his mother was having an affair.) I looked over at Mama and saw her relaxed manner. She had no idea what was happening with Papa.
> "I'm working harder these days, that's for sure. A man from the head office came down this week."
> She stopped talking there. I guess she wanted to see if Papa was interested in her news or just making conversation.
> Papa looked over at Mama and said, "So?"

---

[1]Paul Marshall with Brian and Sandy Miller, *A Piece of the Pie* (Tulsa: Walsworth Press Co., Inc., 1987).

EXHIBIT 1   **Bama Pie, Ltd., Mission Statement**

Bama Pie, Ltd., is an international company in business to develop, produce, and market fresh, frozen, and ready-to-prepare food products generally described as convenience foods, snacks, and other bakery items. We shall serve our products to food service and retail customers and are dedicated to developing new markets as well as serving our major customer, McDonald's. All our products will conform to specific requirements which will ensure our name represents QUALITY to ourselves, our customers, and our suppliers. This will provide continued growth and a fair return to the partners on their investment.

We shall continue to operate as a privately held and fiscally responsible company, and shall be oriented to serving our customer's needs.

In support of this, we are committed to:

- Being flexible and responsive to our customers.
- Ensuring that product requirements are adhered to throughout our processes.
- Maintaining a high degree of employee motivation by providing an environment of equal opportunity, fair treatment, and growth opportunities. This includes fair and equitable compensation, involvement, recognition, and rewards.
- Operating and establishing "partnership relationships" with our suppliers.
- Providing management with information and controls which empowers the planning and decision-making process.
- Being a "Corporate Good Citizen" by active and responsible involvement in our community.

EXHIBIT 2

BUZZINGS

The Busy B's • Bama Pie Ltd • BTC • Bama Pallet • Base Inc • Bama Sweets • Bama Foods • January 1992

BAMA'S QUALITY CIRCLE

OUR QUALITY FUTURE

1991 was a transition year for our Quality culture. You may have not been aware it was because "Quality" is a way of life at Bama—but subtle changes have been occurring. As a company, in our sixth year involved with the Quality Process, our needs are very different. We have matured with Crosby's principles and now is the time to adopt our own values. In 1992 we will be building a solid quality foundation based on these principles.

- People
- Products
- Services
- Profits
- Continuous Improvement

Our mission is to consistently strive to improve all processes, through continuous improvement, to ensure total customer satisfaction.

—Paula Marshall-Chapman

EXHIBIT 3   The Bama Values Statement

Customers
Bama will provide our customers with products and services that conform to their requirements and deliver them on time, at a competitive price.

Suppliers
Bama will encourage open and honest communication with our "partners" and reward those who have adopted and demonstrated use of the continuous improvement process. We will also encourage the sharing of ideas.

Passion
Bama will conduct our business with the integrity, professionalism and with a strategy of continuous improvement. This will provide increased profits and create worldwide awareness of our products. We will continue to focus on being a "Corporate Good Citizen" by being active in our community.

Products and Services
Product quality and product safety will be the responsibility of every employee. We will sell quality products and services at a fair value. We will anticipate and react to our customers' needs. We will take pride in all products and services which we perform.

People
Bama will attract result-oriented people, provide a safe work environment, operate as an equal opportunity employer, focus on employee development and retention, develop mutual trust and respect for each other, and support promotion from within. We will inspire new ideas and innovation by creating the environment whereby we create employee satisfaction.

Quality
Through continuous improvement our name will represent QUALITY to our customers, our suppliers, and ourselves. We believe that if we live by these values we will establish the Bama Companies as world class and will achieve our long-range objectives.

"So he told me what a good job I was doing and how he wished more employees worked as well as I did. Then he asked me if I would be willing to move to Amarillo and be in charge of the lunch counter at the new store there."

I got even more worried right then. Papa didn't say anything right at first. I must have held my breath for at least 10 minutes waiting for Papa to blow.

But he never did. When he finally broke the silence, he spoke in a soft voice. "Blanchie, if you can make pies for Mr. Tanner to sell, why can't you make pies for me to sell?"

Mama looked over at him, surprised like.

"What do you mean?" she asked.

"Just that. If Mr. Tanner can make money on your pies, why can't we? I've been thinking about this for weeks now. I'm not talking foolishness. You make some pies and I'll carry them around the area here and sell them."

Mama just rolled her head back, shut her eyes, and moaned a sigh. It was more like she was tired than anything else.

Papa didn't pay her any mind. He just kept on talking. "I've been looking at those Hubig pies in the stores. They make the smaller seven-inch pies thin so they look larger. They could cost a quarter of what the big nine-inch family pies cost," Papa's voice was getting stronger. He wasn't looking at Mama anymore, but looking out above the rooftops across the street.

"I've checked on prices. Dried fruit runs about 5 cents a pound and that's the most expensive part of the pie. How many pies could you make with a pound of dried fruit?"

Mama didn't answer. Papa didn't seem to be expecting an answer, either, because he just kept talking and even started gesturing with his arms, swinging this way and that.

"Your pies taste a hundred times better than Hubig's. Why, before long we'll be selling pies all over Dallas, then the whole country."

Papa stopped suddenly and turned to Mama who was wilted next to him. I think she must have been wishing he'd calm down and start talking about the smell of fresh cut grass or something.

"I've even come up with a name for the company." It was too dark to tell, but his voice sounded like there must have been a gleam in his eyes.

"Now you know I've always called you Blanchie because I didn't like Cornelia Alabama, or even 'Bama' like your family called you. But for a company, 'Bama' is just fine. In fact, I like it real good. 'The Bama Pie Company,' how does that sound Blanchie?"

I couldn't see Mama right then, but hearing the swing squeaking, I figured she sat up in her seat before she answered Papa.

"Well, I . . ."

I think Mama was surprised at how excited Papa was at the idea of starting a business selling her pies. From hearing her hesitate, I knew Papa would be selling Mama's pies before long.

"The idea sounds all right. But we don't have much of a place to make pies or enough pans and equipment. We . . ."

"Don't worry about a thing, Blanchie. Tell me what you need and I'll get it for you."

"Well, I'll have to think about it for a while. I . . ."

"Fine," Papa said. "We'll start tomorrow."

Thus, the Bama Pie Company was born, according to Paul Marshall's recounting of the event. The next day, Henry took $1.67 and went out to obtain what was needed. He talked a bakery goods supplier into granting credit with the $1.67 paid down on an order that totaled more than $25. He obtained the rest of what was needed on credit from the grocery store where the family had shopped and was known. That evening, the family pitched in to make pies, and the following day, Henry set out to sell the first Bama Pies. The first day's sales far exceeded expectations, and the company began to grow.

Soon the sales route had expanded to the delivery of two baskets of pies per day. When sales were slow, Henry Marshall would walk further and extend the route until all the pies were sold each day. One day, as evening was approaching and he had a few pies left, he spotted a grocery store across the street from where he was. He approached the grocer and asked if he could leave the pies on consignment, promising to service the store daily with fresh products. The grocer agreed and thus began a new phase; Bama Pie became a wholesale distributor.

Soon a car was purchased and modified to carry the pies; and the company established routes in the Dallas area. All the Marshall children became involved in the business, including Paul. The company tried to expand into Waco in 1931, but was unsuccessful because of the Depression.

In the mid-1930s, Paul Marshall observed the operation of Bama's major competitor, Hubig Pies. He was overwhelmed with the modern, high-volume, machine-aided production. Seeing the operation made him aware of how small and old-fashioned Bama was. He attempted to convince his father of the need to purchase new equipment, but to no avail. The company continued to produce pies in a highly labor-intensive process. Paul's dream had become bigger than his father's; he saw the need to change to high-volume, machine-production methods as the way to expand the company. This conflict became a source of disagreement over the years between Paul and his father.

During the next few years, the older Marshall children opened other Bama Pie operations, including one in Oklahoma City started by Paul's sister Grace and her husband. In a move for independence, Paul moved to Oklahoma City and began working for his sister as a route salesman. It was in Oklahoma City that Paul met and eventually married Lilah Drake, who worked in the kitchen of the pie company. Both had the dream of opening their own Bama Pie shop and looked toward Tulsa as a potential market; they began saving for the future.

In the meantime, Paul's brother, Henry, who had reopened the Bama Pie store in Waco, decided to leave the Waco operation and move to Tulsa. While Paul understood his dad's rule that whoever established a territory first had rights to it, he was disappointed that Tulsa would be taken. When Paul and Lilah discovered Henry was simply going to walk away from the Waco business, they decided to take over the Waco operation. Within a year, Waco was profitable and expanding. In January 1937, Paul's father told him his brother would like to return to Waco, which was closer to his wife's family. Paul and his brother agreed to trade operations, and on February 6, 1937, Paul and Lilah, with their new son, John, arrived in Tulsa.

The company struggled through 1937, and a decision to buy a large quantity of new "soft wheat flour" from General Mills nearly did the company in. The new flour was developed for pies, but the formula worked best with baked pies, not the fried pies that made up the bulk of Bama's sales. After discovering the problem and restoring lost customer confidence, the company had grown to six drivers and 14 women assisting Lilah in the bakery by the spring of 1938.

The company continued to prosper as the United States entered World War II, and Paul was given a draft classification of 4-F (which exempted him from being called to duty) since the company was a major supplier to the military.

In December 1943, the owner of Mrs. Marshall's Pies offered to sell his company to Paul Marshall. Paul recounted the meeting in his book:

> "Paul, I just wanted to meet another damned fool named Marshall who was in the pie business."
>
> I laughed and decided I like Archie Marshall.
>
> We talked shop for a while, then Archie asked, "Would you like to buy my business?"
>
> My eyes popped wide open. Who did he think I was, Rockefeller or something? I was almost embarrassed to answer him. But I wanted him to know who he was dealing with from the beginning. I wasn't going to play the high roller. "Archie," I said, "I couldn't buy the spare tire off of your Cadillac."
>
> Archie didn't look at me right then. He just swung his feet back and forth under the table and stared out the window for a few seconds. Then he turned to me and said, "I didn't ask you if you *could* buy my business. I asked you if you would *like* to buy my business."
>
> Well, it was a fact that I would love to have his business, but I didn't understand what he was talking about. "Sure, Archie, I'd like to have your business, but I don't have the kind of money you're looking for. I can tell you that right now."
>
> "I'll work that out," (Archie said.)

They did work out a deal, and Bama Pie Company acquired Mrs. Marshall's Pies. One of the major contributions of the acquisition was an understanding of quality. Paul Marshall said, "The most valuable asset we acquired was a 10-cent calendar advertising Karo syrup. On that calendar was a phrase that became our slogan, 'Keep your eye on the key to success, QUALITY.'"

By the end of 1945, Bama Pies was a well-established and profitable operation. But over the next few years, the company was beset with major union organizing problems that left Paul Marshall with a bitter resentment of unions.

He fought the union's attempt to unionize his company despite threats on his life and the members of of his family. He endured beatings of his drivers, threatening calls at 2 A.M., stink bombs that ruined products, smashed pies in the grocery stores, boycotts, and other forms of harassment.

He called national attention to his plight when he had a welder friend create a rotating track with a department store manikin fitted to it to put on the front of his bakery as a "counter-picket." He dressed the manikin in a suit and placed an American flag in its hands. The manikin moved continuously back and forth on a track above the street while the union's live picket walked back and forth below. Since the bakery was on heavily traveled U.S. Route 66, the counter-picket attracted national attention with photos appearing in *Life* and other magazines. One day a group of kids who had gathered to watch Duke (as the manikin was called) started calling the live union picket a "dummy." The union picket picked up a rock and threw it at one of the kids. This brought a barrage of rocks from the kids and he was driven off. That ended the picketing, but not the harassment.

As the union eroded Bama Pie's markets among grocery stores and hotel restaurants, Paul Marshal began to look for new markets immune from union pressures. At a Chicago bakery equipment auction in 1951, he encountered a refrigerated truck carrying frozen pies. In May 1953, he got into the frozen pie business when he contracted to provide pies for five new Howard Johnson's restaurants being constructed on the new Turner Turnpike linking Tulsa with Oklahoma City. Once in the frozen pie business, he quickly saw that the future of Bama Pies was in frozen pies—with frozen pies there were no stale pies to pick up, no more waste.

Bama supplied the Howard Johnson's restaurants until mid-1955, when Marshall was informed by the head office that Howard Johnson's was going to begin making its own pies. Bama Pies moved to large supermarkets. By the late 1950s, the company was working on a frozen turnover fried pie that could be sold in restaurants. By the beginning of 1960, all the other Bama Pie operations owned and operated by Paul's brothers and sisters had gone out of business, leaving only the Tulsa operation.

Another major turning point for Bama Pies occurred in 1965 when Paul Marshall landed the account of Sandy's restaurant chain (later purchased by Hardee's). In his book, Paul describes the event as follows:

> I couldn't wait to get back to Tulsa so I could tell our employees about the orders we'd have coming in.
>
> For 30 miles I nearly broke my arm patting myself on the back for landing the Sandy's account. I thought over what we had said in our meeting and grinned to myself. Then suddenly the sobering truth of our agreement hit home.
>
> During my chat with Mr. Andres (president of Sandy's) he had pointed out all of the Sandy's locations on a wall map. And like some dunce, I was only thinking of the pies we would be selling to all those locations. The little red pins on the map were spread out over the midwest, from Arizona to Ohio. But I only saw inches between pins.
>
> The reality of what those pins meant hadn't registered on me at the time, but now it was hitting me full force. Our trucks would have to drive 100 to 500 miles between stops! There wouldn't be any way my company could survive with shipping costs gobbling our profits.
>
> By the time I was on the outskirts of Bloomington, I had come up with a plan to make it all work. I decided the only way to justify delivering pies to such

spread-out markets was to acquire more fast-food customers and establish distribution points. The thought never occurred to me to call off the deal with Sandy's.

It was 11 o'clock when I reached Bloomington. The McDonald's hamburger store had just opened so, after I parked in their lot, I grabbed one of our sample frozen pies out of the dry-ice cooler in the trunk and then walked in and ordered coffee.

"You got any pie?" I asked the manager as he served my coffee.

"No, but I wish we did," he said.

Marshall discovered that individual McDonald's units were not allowed to make menu decisions and was told he needed to go to McDonald's headquarters in Chicago. He decided to make a cold call immediately and headed his car toward Chicago with his remaining frozen pies. Surprisingly, he was able to see the frozen-food buyer and arranged to leave some samples for a dinner of McDonald's executives that evening. He then headed back to Tulsa.

When he called to see how the pies fared, he was told they weren't bad, but were not what McDonald's was looking for. He convinced Al Bernardin, the McDonald's buyer, to allow him to attempt to develop a pie that McDonald's would want.

Bernardin told Marshall, "Well, Paul, we'd be willing to work with you on developing a good pie. But I'm certainly not going to promise anything. And I'll warn you, if you work for 10 years trying to come up with a pie that fits our needs, you still might not get the order."

The next attempt to make a pie that McDonald's would accept brought an unexpected response. The quality wasn't good enough. He was told the crust needed to be lighter and the apples needed to be sliced, rather than chipped.

"We want a quality product, not a cheap one. I promise you that we will pay the price for quality," Bernardin told him. Marshall was surprised that a low-priced, high-volume restaurant chain would be more interested in quality than price, but he was happy for the opportunity to develop the high-quality product McDonald's demanded.

For more than a year, Marshall traveled almost weekly between Tulsa and Chicago until he finally produced a product that McDonald's was satisfied with.

The pies were test-marketed in Joplin and Springfield, Missouri, and soon amounted to nearly 7 percent of each store's sales. Soon, Marshall was called to Chicago to meet with the top executives of McDonald's. To supply McDonald's more than 600 restaurants on a national basis would require a significant investment for Bama Pies, and Marshall was concerned about coming up with the $250,000 he estimated would be needed.

When Fred Turner, McDonald's president, asked him if he was ready to begin supplying McDonald's on a national basis, Marshall had to tell the truth and admit he probably couldn't.

In his book, he describes the event:

"How much money would you need to get ready to supply McDonald's?" (Turner asked.)

I was glad I had done some figuring on that question already. "It would cost us $250,000 to build a line that would produce 20,000 pies an hour."

"Can you get that kind of money?" he asked, his eyes never wavering from mine.

Mr. Turner was questioning me like a judge who wanted to know if I was guilty or not—there was no discussion called for.

"I don't know," I said, feeling weak in the pit of my stomach. I figured Mr. Turner was wondering why we Oklahoma hicks were wasting his time. I had hoped our meeting would be real casual, just friends sitting down to talk over what would be needed to make McDonald's pies. I wasn't prepared for the rapid-fire questions and piercing eyes of Mr. Turner.

"How long have you been doing business at your bank?" Mr. Turner asked.

"Probably 25 years or so," I replied, hoping he wasn't going to ask our credit limit.

"Do you owe them anything?"

"Not much. Our mortgage is paid down quite a bit."

"Fine," he said. "I'll send a couple of men down to Tulsa to talk with your banker and see if we can make this pie business work."

"Thank you, sir."

"What kind of contract would you like?" Mr. Turner asked.

"If we can't give you the quality and service you need, Mr. Turner, a contract won't help either of us. But if we can, we won't need one."

"I like your way of thinking, Paul," Mr. Turner said. He reached out and shook my hand, then Johnny's hand and marched out the door.

A couple of days later, two McDonald's executives visited Marshall's bank, and the next day the bank called and said, "Paul, I understand you could use a quarter of a million dollars?"

Thus began a long-term relationship with McDonald's that allowed Bama Pies to grow as McDonald's has grown. During the 1970s and 1980s, Paul and Lilah traveled worldwide with McDonald's officials as consultants to assist local bakers that would be supplying pies for McDonald's far-flung global enterprise. In 1987, Bama Pies received an award for being a 20-year vendor to McDonald's.

PAULA MARSHALL-CHAPMAN

Paula Marshall-Chapman succeeded her father in 1985 as chief executive officer of the company and immediately assumed quality as a focus. "To be honest, we almost lost the account in the mid-80s because we had let our quality fall a bit as we struggled to keep up with our growth," Marshall-Chapman said. She said her father was ready to retire and was almost becoming a problem. "Someone would call from McDonald's about a problem, and he might tell them just what they could do with it. He really didn't relate to the younger technical staff that McDonald's was sending around. He might tell one of them that they didn't know anything about the pie business and that he was 'buddies with Ray Kroc and had been making pies since before they were in diapers.'"

"When I took over, I spent a lot of time just listening," she said.

Taking over the company was not an automatic thing for Marshall-Chapman—she had to earn her way to the top. Paula first joined the company in 1970; she recalled: "My ideas of going off to college were sidetracked when I was a senior in high school. I got pregnant. I first went to work in the thrift stores (Bama Pie's retail operation for picked up and damaged products) and began learning about the business. I learned how to meet and talk to customers, how to display merchandise, how I could increase sales by providing samples, and I also learned how much poor quality costs. We were selling pies for a nickel in the thrift store that could be sold for 50 cents if the product had not been damaged."

After a few years, Paula moved to the central office and learned how to manage the company's fleet of 35 trailer trucks. (The company now runs more than 90 trucks through Bama Pie Trucking, a subsidiary.) She said that job provided a learning experience in areas of government regulation, fuel costs, record keeping, and generally broadened her view of the company.

In the mid-1970s, Bama decided to computerize, and Paula was selected to make the purchase. As a result, she was the person trained to run the new system, and in that capacity she learned the value of training people and helping people solve problems. Since she also had to set up the company's systems on the computer, she learned about costs, payables, invoicing, and again broadened her view of the company. "In my position, I got to be known as Bama's problem solver," she recalled.

Her father noticed her management talents but had been grooming her older brother, Johnny, to take over the company. Paula remembered, "Dad began to say things to me like: 'You really like this business, don't you?' 'Why don't you want to do more.' 'Women probably don't need to be in a CEO role.' Like most kids, when a parent says you can't do something, that's what you decide you want to do just to show them they are wrong."

Paula began her college education during this time, attending Tulsa Junior College and working full time. In 1982, her older brother had a serious illness and her other brother "got into a fight" with her father, so her father came to her and said, "You're going to have to be the one, or we're going to have to sell the company."

For the next three years, she traveled with her father everywhere. She said when her father first presented her as the future CEO to some of the McDonald's officials, they laughed. "During that time I learned a lot," she says. Some of the best advice her father gave her included: "Always have a good work ethic. Be committed to what you are doing. Commitment is what gets through hard times and there will always be hard times."

In 1985, Paul Marshall handed over the reins of the company to Paula and retired to Naples, Florida. According to other Bama executives, when he left, he left. He let her run the company and stayed out of the way. The company, which had been incorporated, was reorganized as a partnership in 1985 to allow Paula's parents to cash out their equity. Paula then became a general partner.

Between 1985 and 1992, Paula reshaped the company. She recruited a young, professional executive staff. She also completed a bachelor's degree through Oklahoma City University's Competency Based Degree Program and was recognized as a distinguished alumna of that program in 1989.

Employees described Paula as a "unique chief executive." One marketing representative who had previously worked for Pizza Hut in the PepsiCo organization was asked to compare what it was like at Pizza Hut and Bama. He said:

> At PepsiCo, everything was numbers driven. You either made the numbers, or you were gone. You didn't feel like you were treated as a person. Big companies are like that. You worked for an organization. Here you work for a human being who treats you as a human being. Paula is more concerned about long term. She doesn't look for someone to blame when a problem arises, she only wants to look for what caused the problem and find a way to fix the problem. I've never seen her blame anyone for anything.

MANAGEMENT IN 1992

Marshall-Chapman reshaped the management team significantly after she took control of the company and assembled a highly professional staff with an average age under 40.

John Davsko, 45, was vice president of operations. He joined Bama Pie in 1989 after 19 years of high-level operations management with Pillsbury. A graduate of St. Louis University in 1968, he also had a brief career as a major league baseball pitcher with the St. Louis Cardinals and Cincinnati Reds.

William L. Chew, 35, vice president of finance, joined the firm in 1987 after two years as controller of a real estate management and development company and seven years with Price Waterhouse in Chicago. He was a 1978 graduate of the University of Illinois and a certified public accountant.

Kay White, 46, vice president of human resources, joined Bama Pie in 1976 as a line worker in production. She was promoted to supervisor and then plant manager and served 2½ years as operations director.

Brenda Rice, 31, vice president for quality assurance systems, joined the company in 1989. She previously was employed in McDonald's R & D Division and worked with Bama Pies in developing the biscuit for McDonald's. She also worked as product development technologist with Magic Pantry Foods (Canada). She received an associate degree in food science from Humber College, Toronto, Canada, in 1981.

With more than 70 percent of the company's business coming from McDonald's, Bama had never developed a fully functioning marketing department. During 1991, the company began establishing a marketing strategy and hired Lynn Dickson, previously associated with Pizza Hut, to begin developing a professional marketing function within the company. Exhibit 4 presents an organization chart for the company.

PRODUCTS

The products Bama Pies produced included 3-ounce pies and 3-inch biscuits for McDonald's, bread sticks for Pizza Hut, 9-inch graham cracker pie shells, 3-inch and 9-inch pecan pies, and soft cookies.

The 3-ounce pies supplied to McDonald's were provided frozen as either ready to fry or bake, with the bulk of the volume having apple or cherry fillings. The company could also produce pies with lemon, peach, and apricot fillings. The original pies supplied to McDonald's were fried turnovers. The baked product was an optional choice in the restaurants in the McDonald's organization and had been increasing in popularity.

The 3-inch biscuit was processed in the new 135,000-square-foot facility in Tulsa and was prebaked to a ready-to-bake stage, frozen, and then baked off in the individual restaurant. The product took several years to develop, with McDonald's, Bama Pies, and Quaker Oats (the other 50 percent supplier) jointly working on the project. Currently, Bama supplied operations west of the Mississippi, and Quaker supplied restaurants east of the Mississippi. During the development of the product, the group experimented with more than 200 recipes.

According to Marshall-Chapman, the reason McDonald's wanted a ready-to-bake product was to ensure a consistent product at all its units. When biscuits

EXHIBIT 4   Bama Pie, Ltd., Corporate Organization as of September 1990

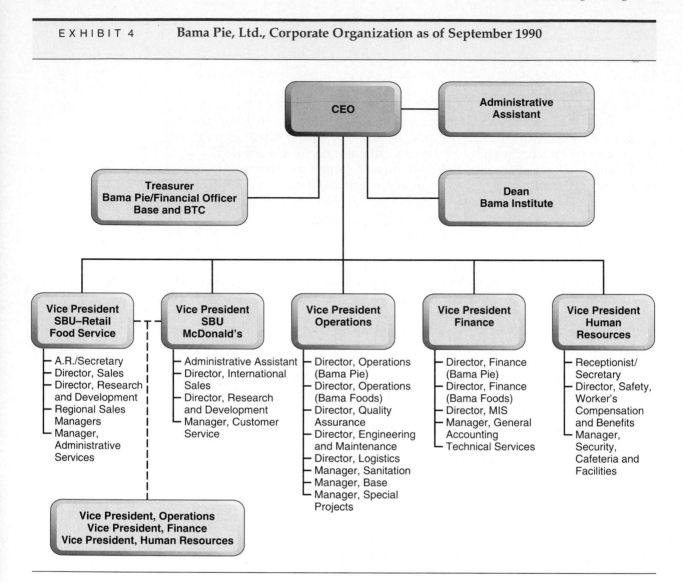

first began appearing in restaurants, they were made from mixes. "Our customer has 8,000 domestic restaurants and, thus, 8,000 biscuit bakers. That means a lot of variation is possible," Marshall-Chapman said.

The long development time resulted from McDonald's insistence that the frozen product be equal in quality to fresh-baked, made-from-scratch products. To provide the product, a carefully controlled process was developed. The biscuits were essentially 90 percent baked, frozen, and then shipped to distribution centers for delivery to the restaurants. The product, packaged in a baking bag, was then finished off in convection ovens at the local restaurant to give that "just baked" appearance, taste, and texture.

The bread sticks were produced in the 11th Street plant of Bama Pies and were a frozen dough product, made under a confidential agreement with

Pizza Hut with the recipe kept secret. The dough was processed, rolled to a specific thickness, and shipped frozen in flat pieces about 9 inches by 12 inches. The dough was thawed and the sticks cut at the restaurant before baking.

The 3-inch and 9-inch pecan pies were a mainstay of Bama Pies and had been produced for almost the entire 65 years of operation. The recipe was virtually unchanged from the original developed by Marshall-Chapman's grandmother. The pies were fully baked, packaged in single wraps, and then boxed in a variety of quantities. Customers included Wal-Mart and Sam's Wholesale Clubs.

The 9-inch graham cracker shells were produced for retail sale and were also provided to TCBY and Braum's. The shells came in a metal pie pan ready to be filled with a customer's own filling. The shells were often used for cheesecake and ice box pies or could be filled with ice cream or yogurt to provide an ice cream pie product.

The cookies were soft products that competed directly with the large soft cookies produced under the Grandma's label by Frito-Lay, a PepsiCo subsidiary. The cookies were packaged individually and boxed for retail sale. See Exhibit 5 for a comparison of the ingredients used in these products.

OPERATIONS

McDonald's Pies

The 3-ounce pies for McDonald's were processed in the 11th Street plant. Ingredients were mixed in two different areas. The dough was prepared in large mixers that fed a moving conveyor system that rolled the dough out on two separate belts approximately 24 inches wide. The filling was prepared in large, heated mixing bowls with real fruit added. This mixture was pumped through seven separate hoses that streamed filling on the bottom conveyor of dough. The top layer was then placed on top of the filling, and the pies were then cut and sealed in a two-step operation. The pies were sent to a spiral freezer where they were frozen. The process was basically the same whether the pie was a fried product or a baked product. The dough mixture was different for each product, and the baked product had slits cut in the top of each pie.

After freezing, the pies were processed slightly differently. The fried product was dipped in a liquid that immediately froze to the pie and caused the finished pie to have a bubbly, flaky texture. The pies were then hand-packed 12 to a tray, with six trays then boxed in an automated operation. Four boxes were packaged with shrink-wrap before moving into the storage freezer. The baked pies were processed similarly, but instead of being dipped when exiting the freezer, they were sprayed with water and dusted with cinnamon before packaging.

Each hour, samples were taken from the production process to the test kitchen where the same ovens and fryers used by McDonald's were installed. The product was finished off and tested to assure specifications were being met. Each line was capable of producing 40,000 pies per hour, and more than 1 million pies were produced daily at the plant.

EXHIBIT 5   Bama Pie's Use of Ingredients in Its Products, 1984 versus 1991

Description	1984 Pounds (in millions)	1991 Pounds (in millions)
Frozen apples	3.5	9.2
Frozen cherries	3.0	1.6
Flour	2.0	11.0
Shelled pecans	2.0	.3
Shortening	1.5	4.2
Sugar	1.0	2.6
Shelled eggs	.9	.4

Note: Reduction in cherries is because the cherry pie is now optional at McDonald's restaurants. In 1984, it was a required menu item. Reduction in pecans and eggs is due to reduced number of pecan pies being sold, an outcome attributed to increased weight and health concerns.

McDonald's Biscuits

The McDonald's biscuit was produced in a new facility that *Baking & Snack* magazine called "world class."[2] The facility contained two parallel production lines that included 250-foot ovens. The dough was mixed and laid down on a flour-dusted conveyor belt that transferred the dough through a series of rollers until it was a 50-inch-wide sheet. The dough was then cut and passed through a metal detector before dropping into the baking pans. The biscuit pans passed three wide through the oven where modular construction and nine heating zones transformed the dough into a biscuit ready for freezing in about 15 minutes. The highly automated line removed the pans, cleaned them, re-oiled them, and returned them for reuse. The biscuits were then cartoned and put through a spiral freezer after cooling to 90 degrees. After freezing, the biscuits were wrapped and passed through another metal detector before being boxed for shipment and moved into the storage freezer.

Graham Shells

The graham shells were produced on a highly automated line that was installed in 1991 and put into operation in early 1992. The graham meal was mixed and fed into a hopper that dumped an exact measurement of meal into an aluminum pie pan and was then automatically pressed and formed. The shell moved through a process where the clear plastic cover was pressed into place and sealed to the pan. Next, the shells were automatically stacked and boxed for shipment.

Pizza Hut Bread Sticks

Using the secret recipe from Pizza Hut, the dough was mixed and fed onto a conveyor belt into a series of rollers that reduced the sheet of dough to the proper thickness and width. The dough was then run through a cutter that produced sheets of dough approximately 9 inches by 12 inches. These sheets were

---

[2]Laurie Gorton, "World Class: Bama Creates a Flexible Plant Dedicated to Making Ready-to-Bake Biscuits," *Baking & Snack*, November 1991.

then frozen in a spiral freezer before packaging and boxing. The bread stick line was located in the 11th Street plant.

Pecan Pies

The 3-inch and 9-inch pecan pies were also produced in the 11th Street plant. The dough was prepared and rolled and fed onto a conveyor line where it was cut and dropped into the aluminum pie shell. The dough was then automatically formed inside the shell. The pies continued on and were filled with pecans and pie filling before entering an oven approximately 200 feet long. Once the pies were baked, they were conveyed back to packaging by passing through a cooling tunnel where they went through automated packaging machines and were hand-packed and boxed.

Cookies

The soft-batch cookies were processed in much the same manner as the pecan pies. The batter was measured and dropped onto a conveyor belt that took the cookies through the oven and returned them through a cooling tunnel for packaging.

THE MCDONALD'S RELATIONSHIP

The relationship with McDonald's was unusual in that Bama had been the single-source supplier of pies for 24 years and had never had a contract. Moreover, Bama did not sell directly to McDonald's. McDonald's selected and approved suppliers, but the actual sales were made to independently owned distribution centers that supplied the McDonald's restaurants around the country.

The company did not have a contract for the biscuit product either. "When a couple of banks heard we wanted to borrow $40 million to build a biscuit plant and didn't have a contract to even buy one biscuit, they ran away," Marshall-Chapman said. McDonald's put the company in touch with Texas Commerce Bank in Houston, and Bama found a bank that was actively seeking to develop a business relationship with McDonald's. In fact, the bank had formed a special group of McDonald's specialists. The bank understood that McDonald's developed "partnership arrangements" with suppliers and that contracts were not a part of the business. "They (both the bank and McDonald's) were eager to help, and we completed the deal at extremely favorable rates," Marshall-Chapman said.

COMMITMENT TO QUALITY AND STAYING PRIVATE

Favorable lending rates were extremely important to Bama Pies, since the company and Marshall-Chapman were committed to remaining private. Marshall-Chapman believed going public would ruin the company: "Public companies have to run the business for Wall Street. They have to think quarterly. I want to run our business for my customers and my employees. I want to concentrate on developing the business, not worrying about what is happening to my stock price."

Decisions were made based on what the management team thought was best. A commitment to quality was evident in everything the company did. Marshall-Chapman believed that not having to answer to stockholders allowed the company to focus on quality; she indicated the company was ahead of the people who were teaching total quality management: "They (the Quality College and others) are now calling us and asking us what we've done new and what we're currently working on."

Bama insisted on quality from its suppliers. Suppliers were expected to ship random samples of product runs due for Bama in advance so they could be pretested. "We want to know if there is a problem before the shipment leaves their plant," Marshall-Chapman said. Vendors were willing to cooperate because it was much less expensive to provide the samples and get preapproval for shipment than to risk having a whole order rejected after shipment and returned.

The company had instilled a total quality management discipline within its approximately 600 employees through various training programs and educational opportunities. Getting the employees involved in all aspects of quality was evidenced in everything, including internal record keeping. Within a year's time, inventory adjustments based on physical counts dropped from between $50,000 and $70,000 per month to less than $3,000 per month and was still improving. "One month we'd have a negative adjustment, the next a positive adjustment," William Chew, vice-president of finance said. At a time when the company was attempting to refine its cost system and implement standard costs under an activity-based cost system, the inventory problem was major. Chew commented, "Even our fork truck operators have gotten involved in helping solve the inventory adjustments problem."

To support the quality program and refine data for decision making, the company purchased a new computer system using Prism software on an IBM AS/400 mainframe. The conversion was implemented within one year. "We were able to do it because Paula released people from some of their regular jobs and put them on the project," Chew said. According to the consultants working with Bama, no company had ever been able to accomplish such a conversion in such a short period. The result was a system with world-class manufacturing software that supported an activity-based standard cost accounting system and electronic data interchange transactions.

DRUG POLICIES

Bama was a "drug-free" workplace; all applicants for employment were screened for drugs. According to company officials, approximately one in five applicants tested positive. In addition, all employees (including Paula) had been drug tested and random drug testing was administered within the company. The random sampling for drug tests was determined by a computer program. Urine samples were taken and tested in a lab. A positive result was grounds for immediate dismissal.

According to Marshall-Chapman, the company's drug policy was mainly aimed at reducing accidents. Since the program had been implemented, accidents had declined significantly. Any employee involved in accident at work was automatically drug tested.

BEBOPP

In 1990, Bama instituted the Bama Employees' Bonus on Profit Plan (BEBOPP) to provide bonus incentives to all employees in the company. The plan was based on an annual return on sales objective that was established by Marshall-Chapman. The goal was expressed as a percentage and for each 0.5 percent above the target, all employees shared in a bonus pool. The pool began at 2 percent of payroll and increased for each 0.5 percent above the target. For example, if Bama's return on sales topped the goal by 2 percent, the bonus pool would equal 3.5 percent of payroll. Even though the program was based on annual sales, quarterly payments were made to employees. All eligible employees received equal amounts from the pool.

CURRENT SITUATION

The company was attempting to decrease it reliance on McDonald's. The biscuit plant, which was also capable of producing cookies and other bread-type products, had underutilized capacity. The main plant also had open capacity where the prototype biscuit line was located and where another product was dropped. The new facility also had room for expansion.

Opportunities for new business were coming in faster than the company could deal with them. John Davsko, vice-president of operations, said, "We have people calling us all the time asking if we are interested in developing a product for them. Our reputation is bringing business. We had one potential customer referred to us by one of our suppliers."

However, there were problems with expansion. Management believed any expansion had to come mainly from new product development. Bama believed it could not seek additional customers for its fast-food pie product without putting its McDonald's account at risk. Likewise, it would be unwise to seek another customer for biscuits or bread sticks. According to Marshall-Chapman, about the only negative thing Paul Marshall had said regarding how Paula had handled the business since he left is, "He thinks we're expanding too fast, and he doesn't like us borrowing money."

RUBBERMAID CORP.

Bernard A. Deitzer, Alan G. Krigline, and Thomas C. Peterson
University of Akron

During 1990, we celebrated the 70th anniversary of the founding of the company. It has progressed through seven decades of successful growth from the results of innovation, diversification, the company's emphasis on quality, and the contributions of extremely dedicated associates. Those same strengths position Rubbermaid to continue its success into the 1990s.

Today, Rubbermaid is a growing and vital enterprise. We have modern manufacturing facilities, aggressive plans for the future, and, most importantly, experienced management with over 9,000 skilled and committed associates throughout the organization. We are confident that the company will continue to perform vigorously and effectively.

Stanley C. Gault

Rubbermaid, under Chairman and CEO Stanley Gault's leadership, enjoyed a banner year in 1990. The firm reported record net sales of $1.53 billion, a 6 percent increase over the $1.45 billion of 1989, and record earnings of $143.5 million, 15 percent above the $125.0 million earned in 1989. The fourth quarter of 1990 represented the 40th consecutive quarter in which both sales and earnings increased over those of the prior year's period. Since 1980, Rubbermaid's sales had quadrupled, and earnings had risen sixfold.

Consistent with its announced overall growth objectives, Rubbermaid acquired two companies in 1990. It also entered into a joint venture with a European housewares company to establish a base for marketing its rubber and plastic products in Europe when the European Community opened its markets in 1992.

COMPANY HISTORY

Rubbermaid's origins could be traced to events that transpired in the 1920s. In early May 1920, the Wooster Rubber Company began manufacturing its first product—the Sunshine brand of toy balloons. In the mid-1920s, Horatio B. Ebert and Errett M. Grable, executives of the Wear-Ever Division, Aluminum Company of America, purchased Wooster Rubber as a personal investment. They engaged Clyde C. Gault, Stanley Gault's father, who had been general manager of Wooster Rubber, to continue managing the business. By 1928, the company had prospered sufficiently to build a new factory and office building. However, the Great Depression caused sales to plummet.

Meanwhile, James R. Caldwell of New England, who had developed a rubber dustpan, was forced into selling it door to door since department store buyers turned it down, saying, "We have no calls for a $1 rubber dustpan. We can sell metal dustpans for 39 cents." Persistence paid, and eventually Caldwell, the door-to-door entrepreneur, persuaded department store buyers to carry rubber dustpans. He adopted the brand name Rubbermaid and developed three other rubber items—a drain board mat to protect countertops, a soap dish, and a sink stopper.

During this period, Ebert, while calling on New England department stores, saw and became interested in Caldwell's rubber housewares products. Subsequently, the two combined businesses, and in July 1934, the manufacture of rubber housewares products began at the Wooster Rubber Company.

During World War II, civilian use of rubber was frozen by the government. The company's consumer business became nonexistent. Survival came in the form of subcontracts to produce components for self-sealing fuel tanks for military aircraft, life jackets, and medical tourniquets. Following the war, the company resumed production and sale of rubber housewares products. Since coloring materials were not yet available, all products were produced in black. In 1950, the company established an operation in Canada and in 1955 issued its first public offering of stock, trading in the over-the-counter market.

The first plastic product, a dishpan, was introduced in 1956. In 1957, the firm officially changed its corporate name to Rubbermaid Incorporated to capitalize on an already widely accepted brand name. In 1958, a salesman was assigned to call on hotels and motels to sell doormats and bathtub mats. Thus was the beginning of today's successful institutional business, established as Rubbermaid Commercial Products Inc. in 1967.

When Caldwell retired as president in 1958, Donald E. Noble, who had joined Rubbermaid in 1941, was elected chief executive officer, serving first as president and later as chairman of the board. During Noble's 39 years of service, new businesses were entered, physical facilities were expanded, and an operation in West Germany was established. Rubbermaid's rite of passage from a small, rural Ohio company to a multinational firm with one of America's best-known brand names was under way.

THE BUSINESS

Rubbermaid in 1991 manufactured and marketed plastic and rubber products for both consumer and institutional markets worldwide. Its product line consisted of over 3,000 items including kitchenware, laundry and bath accessories, microwave ovenware, toys, and products for home horticulture, office, food-service, health-care, and industrial maintenance uses.

Rubbermaid operated one of the largest plastic and rubber houseware production facilities in the world: some 1.6 million square feet spread over a single floor. Half a million housewares products of all sizes, shapes, and colors were processed daily from plastic resin.

Corporate headquarters, as well as the housewares products and specialty products divisions, were located in Wooster, Ohio, (population about 21,000) some 50 miles from downtown Cleveland.

Redesigned versions of the early and ordinary dustpan along with drain board mats, sink mats, and soap dishes were among the most popular of the company's portfolio of rubber and plastic products. What set Rubbermaid products apart was the company's ability to transform ordinary, colorless kitchen utensils into appealing, colorful, upscale housewares. The Rubbermaid brand name was highly recognized by customers and was synonymous with quality household products. Stanley Gault had been regularly hailed by the media for his stunningly superior leadership, while Rubbermaid stood second only to Merck in *Fortune's* rankings of the most admired American corporations. Rubbermaid's growth and success was said to be the result of seven fundamental strengths (see Exhibit 1).

RUBBERMAID'S MANAGEMENT

Stanley Carleton Gault, 65, chairman of the board, chief executive officer, and director, joined Rubbermaid in 1980. He had just ended an illustrious 31-year career at General Electric, where he served as senior vice president and sector executive of the industrial products and components sector. He decided to leave GE when he realized he was being passed over in selecting GE's next CEO.

Walter W. Williams, 57, director, president, and chief operating officer, joined Rubbermaid in 1987. Like Gault, Williams left a 31-year career at General Electric where he was senior vice president of corporate marketing. Williams's strong marketing skills were considered by Gault to be critical to Rubbermaid's future success.

Wolfgang R. Schmitt, 47, executive vice president, began his Rubbermaid career in 1966 as a management trainee after graduating from Otterbein College in Westerville, Ohio. He had held numerous top marketing and management assignments.

Exhibit 2 lists the awards and honors given to Stanley Gault and to Rubbermaid during Gault's tenure as CEO.

GAULT'S INITIAL STRATEGY

When Stanley C. Gault became CEO of Rubbermaid in 1980, revenues were climbing steadily, and, while sales totaled $341 million, earnings had dipped to $21 million. In Gault's view, Rubbermaid was a slow-growth business with a growing overhead, a declining rate of productivity, and personnel that had grown comfortable and unaccustomed to change.[1] "Our product development lagged, our retail customers claimed we were arrogant, and our profit margins had fallen," summarized the new CEO.[2]

Gault immediately began to restructure the firm and its in-place management, stating, "You have to set the tone and pace, define objectives and strategies and demonstrate through personal example what you expect from others."[3] He reshuffled, hired, and fired. Ten percent of all salaried personnel were dismissed. Some two years later, only 2 of 172 Rubbermaid managers still held their original jobs.

While the housewares and commercial products divisions generated over 96 percent of total corporate income, the remaining units were "six weak soldiers." All operations were subsequently and rigorously evaluated to

---

[1]Kenneth Labich, "The Seven Keys to Business Leadership," *Fortune*, October 24, 1988, p. 60.
[2]Patricia Sellers, "Does the CEO Really Matter?" *Fortune*, April 22, 1991, p. 86.
[3]Labich, "The Seven Keys."

EXHIBIT 1   **Rubbermaid's Fundamental Strengths**

1. *A focused direction to maximize the value of Rubbermaid for its shareholders.* Each operating unit is well positioned in attractive markets, with quality products, a strong organization, and a well-defined mission for growth.

2. *The strength of its franchise with customers and consumers.* Its brand names are recognized and respected within each market segment it serves.

3. *A reputation for quality products.* All of its brand names connote quality and value within their respective markets.

4. *An emphasis on new products.* Its goal is to have 30% of sales each year come from products that were not in the line five years earlier.

5. *Marketing, sales, and manufacturing capabilities.* These organizations are among the strongest, best qualified in each of the industries it serves.

6. *Financial performance and strength.* Rubbermaid enjoys a strong finance position with very little debt. It has the capability to pursue its business objectives successfully.

7. *Human resources.* The company has capable and dedicated people throughout the organization who have demonstrated their ability to perform impressively and consistently.

Source: *Rubbermaid Corp. 1987 Annual Report.*

EXHIBIT 2   **Awards and Honors Given to Stanley Gault and Rubbermaid Since January 1980**   *(When Gault became Rubbermaid's CEO)*

1980	Elected to PPG Industries, Inc., Board of Directors.
1982	Honorary member, Beta Gamma Sigma, a national honorary society for business administrators, the University of Akron, Akron, Ohio.
1982	*Wall Street Transcript*, Best CEO/Gold Award Home Furnishings, Table and Ovenware.
1981–85	*Financial World* CEO of year awards. Certificate of Distinction, Bronze Award.
1983	The College of Wooster, Wooster, Ohio, Distinguished Alumni Award.
1983	Rubbermaid named to Fortune 500.
1984	*Sales and Marketing Management*, Special Citation.
1985–90	*Fortune Magazine*, Among the Top Ten of America's Most Admired Corporations (Rubbermaid is the smallest company ever to be listed; in 1987, 1988, and 1990 Rubbermaid's ranking was second.)
1985	Elected to board of directors of Avon Products, Inc., and International Paper Company.
1986	Rubbermaid named to Standard & Poor's 500.
1986–87	Chairman of the board for the National Association of Manufacturers.
1987	Member Advisory Committee on Trade, Policy, and Negotiations appointed by President Ronald Reagan.
1987	*Business Week*, Cited Rubbermaid as one of the Most Competitive Companies in America.
1987	American Manager of the Year Award, presented by the National Management Association and Sponsors of Management Week in America.
1988	Management Excellence Award presented by the Society for the Advancement of Management.
1988	*Wall Street Transcript*, Best CEO/Gold Award, Household Products Industry.
1988	Elected to the Timken Company Board of Directors.
1988	*Business Month*, Named Rubbermaid one of the Five Best Run Companies in America.
1987–present	Chairman of the Board of Trustees, The College of Wooster, Wooster, Ohio.
1989	Elected to Goodyear Tire and Rubber Company Board of Directors.
1990	Selected the Rubber Industry Executive of the Year by *Rubber and Plastic News*.
1990	Rubbermaid named among *Forbes Magazine*'s 25 "Most Profitable of the Giants."
1990	Named by President Bush to continue as a member of the Advisory Committee on Trade Policy and Negotiations.
1990	Inducted into the National Sales Hall of Fame and into the Entrepreneur's Hall of Fame.
1990	Elected to the New York Stock Exchange Board of Directors.
1991	Rubbermaid ranked 10th by *Fortune* among "The 10 Best Investments in the 1980s."

determine their strengths, weaknesses, and opportunities. Early on, Gault dramatically informed the organization he was aiming for a 15 percent average annual growth in sales, profits, and earnings per share, plus $1 billion in sales revenues by 1990.[4]

Gault's first strategic step in restructuring was to review Rubbermaid's eight lines of business and to cut out half of them. One casualty was its in-home party plan operation. Gault perceived that current demographics and the changing life-styles of working women allowed little time for after-hours houseware parties. Besides, Rubbermaid did not have a presence commensurate with its competitive arch rival, Tupperware.

In addition, Rubbermaid sold its domestic car mat and auto accessories business. Gault believed auto accessories were a commodity business with stiff price and volume elastic competition where automakers tended to pressure suppliers.[5]

RUBBERMAID'S ACQUISITION STRATEGY

Gault's relentless and unyielding commitment to controlled growth earmarked the firm's approach to expansion. Rubbermaid has consistently demonstrated an ability to expand its existing businesses. Both new product flow and new market entries have thrived via opportunistic and related acquisitions. Gault looked for small companies that fit, were No. 1 or 2 in their product category, and could benefit from Rubbermaid's manufacturing and marketing expertise. Exhibit 3 lists the company's acquisitions and joint ventures.

As Gault emphasized, "We are definitely receptive to good acquisition opportunities. We have made numerous acquisitions; they have all been top-notch companies. We want them to be companies that are well managed and where the management will want to stay and be part of the growing Rubbermaid family."[6]

RUBBERMAID'S GROWTH STRATEGIES

Gault strongly believed in developing strategies to control and direct new product activities to meet two types of ambitious growth objectives. The first was incremental growth, which concentrated on doing what Rubbermaid did best—only better. The second approach was leap growth, which involved a higher degree of risk since it created high visibility on the one hand yet high vulnerability on the other—the company won big or lost big. Within these two major classifications, there were eight strategic elements; four applied to incremental growth and four were leap approaches:[7]

---

[4]Ibid.

[5]James Braham, "The Billion Dollar Dustpan," *Industry Week*, August 1, 1988, p. 47.

[6]*Wall Street Transcript*, April 18, 1988, p. 89116.

[7]Adapted from remarks by Stanley C. Gault, chairman of the board and chief executive officer, Rubbermaid Incorporated, before the Conference Board of Canada's 15th Annual Marketing Conference, Hilton International, Toronto, Canada, March 29, 1990.

EXHIBIT 3   Rubbermaid's Acquisitions/Joint Ventures, 1981–1990

1981	Con-Tact Brand self-adhesive decorative coverings.
1984	The Little Tikes Company—leading quality manufacturer of preschool children's toys.
1985	Gott Corporation—high-quality consumer recreational products.
1986	SECO Industries—leading manufacturer of maintenance products.
1986	Micro Computer Accessories—accessories for the microcomputer market.
1987	Viking Brush Limited—household brushes.
1987	The Little Tikes Company (Ireland).
1987	MicroComputer Accessories Europe S.A.—computer related accessories.
1987	Reynolds, Inc.—Compression-molding facilities of Polymer Engineering.
1989	Rubbermaid Allibert—(joint venture) manufactures casual resin furniture for the North American market.
1990	Curver Rubbermaid Group, Breda, The Netherlands—(joint venture) manufactures plastics and rubber housewares and resin furniture.
1990	EWU AG, Switzerland—producer of floor care supplies and equipment.
1990	Eldon Industries—distributor of molded plastic office products and equipment.

Rubbermaid's Incremental Growth Strategies

- To increase the volume of Rubbermaid's existing products. The key to this growth area is in providing value to dealers, distributors, and consumers. The key to value is providing quality, low cost, and service.
- To upscale existing products to meet today's consumer and new designs preferences. Upscaling includes introducing new colors to existing lines.
- To extend existing lines to capitalize on product successes, increase retail shelf space, and boost sales volume.
- To expand Rubbermaid's international business as a significant growth opportunity during the 1990s.

Rubbermaid's Leap Growth Strategies

- To develop new products. Rubbermaid's goal is to have at least 30 percent of the annual sales coming from new products introduced during the past five years.
- To hone product lines and optimize the number of stock units retained to keep the lines manageable and provide proper customer service levels.
- To enter new markets. This is consistent with a corporate objective to enter a new market every 18 to 24 months.
- To engage in joint ventures or acquisitions to enter new markets by combining the capabilities of a strong outside partner with the many strengths of Rubbermaid.

Rubbermaid's Corporate Goals

Over the years, Rubbermaid had been widely recognized as an innovative company. The corporatewide drive for innovation mirrored Gault's efforts to implement corporate growth objectives and to expand the firm's markets. Rubbermaid's new products goal was to have 30 percent of sales each year come from products not in its product line five years earlier. Over 1,000 new products were introduced between 1985 and 1990. Rubbermaid also strived to be the lowest cost, highest quality producer in the household products industry. From 1981 through 1990, over $612 million was invested in facilities to increase productivity, develop new products, and achieve world-class manufacturing status. In 1989, Gault set a goal of achieving $2 billion in annual sales five years from 1987, the year in which Rubbermaid reached sales of $1 billion.

In 1991, Gault believed Rubbermaid could reach the $2 billion mark by the last quarter of 1992 simply by following its present course:

> We project our growth to come from a combination of areas. We'll see growth occur in the core product lines of Rubbermaid's domestic business; the effort under way to grow business internationally; from new product development in all our businesses; new product categories being added to existing businesses; and growth through a selective acquisition program.[8]

Rubbermaid's corporate mission was to offer exceptional value to its customers with high quality and cost-competitive products, excellent distribution, and a highly focused customer mentality. According to management, Rubbermaid's fundamental corporate strengths had served it effectively over the years with widely recognized and respected brand names, high-quality innovative products, strategic marketing direction, efficient and modern manufacturing facilities, an enviable financial performance record, dedicated associates, and a focused direction for growth and profitability.[9]

The company's objectives for the 1990s are shown in Exhibit 4. The company's key strategies are outlined in Exhibit 5.

Focus on Quality

Rubbermaid's hallmark was product quality. Senior executives stressed the importance of turning out top-quality products on a consistent basis and were willing to personally lead the company's drive to achieve product superiority. Stanley Gault did not hesitate to phone and placate disgruntled dealers. He functioned as Rubbermaid's top quality controller. Precise and methodical, Gault visited several stores a week to see how Rubbermaid products were displayed and to see that Rubbermaid's products on store shelves met his standard for quality and workmanship. If Gault spotted an ill-fitting lid or wrinkled label, he bought the offending goods and then later summoned his senior managers for a lecture. "He gets livid about defects," said Walter W. Williams, the chief operating officer.[10]

---

[8]*Rubbermaid Annual Report*, Rubbermaid Incorporated, Wooster, Ohio, 1986, pp. 4–6.
[9]*Wall Street Transcript*, March 23, 1987, p. 84964.
[10]Brian O'Reilly, "Leaders of the Most Admired Corporations," *Fortune*, January 29, 1990, p. 43.

EXHIBIT 4   **Rubbermaid's Objectives for the 1990s**

---

1. To increase sales, earnings, and earnings per share 15% per year, while achieving a 20% return on shareholders' equity.
2. To pay approximately 30% of current year's earnings as dividends to shareholders, while using the remainder to fund future growth opportunities.
3. Each year 30% of sales should come from new products introduced over the previous five years; an entirely new market should be entered every 12 to 18 months.
4. To offer the best value possible; to provide reasonably priced, high-quality products and exceptional service to customers.
5. To treat all constituents fairly and consider the interests of associates as individuals.
6. To be an environmentally responsible corporate citizen.

Source: *1990 Annual Report.*

EXHIBIT 5   **Rubbermaid's Strategies for the 1990s**

---

1. Continue a market-driven approach to product development and marketing. Listen to customers and consumers and effectively respond to the changes in needs, demographics, and life-styles. This outside-in strategy will help develop new markets and create unique, proprietary products and programs.
2. Continue to grow using both incremental and leap growth strategies. Incremental growth comes from continuous improvement in all aspects of the business such as line extensions, international expansion, and innovative marketing and sales programs. The leap approach involves new technologies, new market entries, acquisitions, and joint ventures.
3. Invest for future growth and keep facilities modern and efficient. It is the company's intention to continue to be the lowest cost, highest quality producer in its industry.
4. Build partnerships with customers, suppliers, associates, and communities to enhance the value of Rubbermaid for shareholders and other constituencies.
5. Increase the use of technology in manufacturing and communications, both internally and externally.
6. Pursue world-class status and compete on a global basis.

Source: *1990 Annual Report.*

When confronted by the claim that plastic was once synonymous with junk, Gault launched into an energetic speech on the mixture of polyethylene that Rubbermaid used and the intricacies of Rubbermaid's injection molding process. Gault, when comparing Rubbermaid's enormously popular garbage cans to flimsier competing versions, remarked, "On quality I'm a sonofabitch. No one surpasses our quality. We use more and better resin. We don't buy any scrap resin. And we use a thick gauge."[11] Sales of Rubbermaid's big garbage cans jumped 20 percent when Gault suggested to the design engineer that the cans be made in a specific shade of blue instead of chocolate brown.

---

[11]Ibid.

MANAGEMENT ENVIRONMENT

Stanley Gault's leadership philosophy reflected an ingrained belief that a leader has to be a living example, has to inspire the organization, and has to be part of the team while still being the manager. In Gault's view, leaders should be supportive and, when sensing the need for change, should genuinely communicate the need for it. Highly interactive and strong on interpersonal communications, Gault regularly toured Rubbermaid factories to talk one on one with managers and workers alike. Gault favored a lean and flat organization structure, believing, "Any incoming chief executive will need to be able to run a flatter organization. As companies continue to cut costs further, middle managers will be eliminated and the CEO will have more people reporting directly to him."[12]

Gault was regarded as a tireless, energetic leader who expected and rewarded hard work from his subordinates. He was an affable person, well liked by his staff despite the demands he placed on them. His personal schedule often included 12- to 14-hour workdays, six days a week. Gault was described by his associates as being a very involved manager who wanted to know everything that was going on in each of Rubbermaid's businesses.

Gault believed successful CEOs should set strategic direction, align employees behind that strategy so they would carry it out, and groom a successor. "I am very demanding and I know it. But I'm demanding of myself, first. I set high standards and I expect people to meet them. I want all the business we can get, provided we get it fairly. If people can't meet my standards after training and counseling, then a change has to be made. That's not saying they aren't good people but they are not cut out for the particular job."[13]

Rubbermaid sought out managers with a strong work ethic who were entrepreneurial, enthusiastic, competent, and ambitious. The company wanted its managers to be good team players as well as hard-working. Bonuses were based on both increase in profit and increase in the firm's shareholder value.

Hourly workers generally mirrored a belief that the Rubbermaid family comes first and that there is no other way. Regularly enjoying profit sharing since 1944, workers had offered over 12,000 cost-cutting suggestions in housewares alone. In 1987, the housewares and specialty products division saved $24.7 million from adopting worker suggestions.[14] Relations with the United Rubber Workers were good. In 1987's negotiations, a new contract froze wages for three years in return for the company's pledge to maintain existing jobs.[15] While doubling sales, Rubbermaid increased its work force by only 50 percent and had halved its number of sales representatives. It had held the line on prices; revenue and profit gains came mainly from increased volume and productivity improvement.[16]

---

[12]Jennifer Reese, "CEO's: More Churn at the Top," *Fortune*, March 11, 1991, p. 13.
[13]Braham, "The Billion Dollar Dustpan," p. 48.
[14]Ibid.
[15]Ibid.
[16]Ibid.

PRODUCT DEVELOPMENT AT RUBBERMAID

Rubbermaid practices the team approach to product development and product innovation. In 1987, Rubbermaid considered developing the so-called auto office, a portable plastic device that straps onto a car seat and holds files, pens, and other articles and provides a writing surface. A cross-functional team composed of, among others, engineers, designers, and marketers was assembled. They went out to do field research to determine what features customers desired. Rubbermaid brought the new product to the market in 1990; sales at last count were running 50 percent above projections.[17]

RUBBERMAID'S MARKETING STRATEGY

One of Gault's first moves on assuming leadership in 1980 was to revamp Rubbermaid's sales and marketing strategy. The key, according to Gault, was strict adherence to fundamentals. At the time, Rubbermaid's sales force traditionally sold every product category such as sinkware, household containers, and space organizers to all customers. Gault split the field sales function from marketing and put sales strategies in place to cover each market segment. As Gault explained it, "A distribution channel that would serve supermarkets and drugstores would not necessarily work for mass merchants or hardware stores or catalog showrooms." Marketing was organized around product categories and a product manager was put in charge of each category. Rubbermaid believed this allowed effective specialization and permitted a "more intense level of management involvement with customers."[18]

CUSTOMER RESEARCH

While the firm employed demographic and life-style analysis techniques to identify trends, the core of product development at Rubbermaid lay in the use of consumer research. Qualitative and quantitative methods were used to reveal shopper preferences. Rubbermaid never test marketed its products. Instead, it tested color preferences year-round through fact-finding consumer focus groups in five cities, and it regularly quizzed people in shopping malls. The company extensively used buyer panels, brand awareness studies, and diaries that consumers filled with notations about product use.[19]

Rubbermaid had some 150 competitors in home products alone, but no one rival competed with Rubbermaid across its entire product line. Rubbermaid was the only broadly recognized brand name. Since competing products often were not imprinted with the manufacturer's name, it was not unusual for Rubbermaid to receive complaints about some other manufacturer's product. Gault took advantage of this. "We're the only name they can think of, so they write *us* their complaint letters." It was Gault's practice to respond with a letter to the disgruntled writer, "Please make certain that every time you buy a plastic

---

[17]Brian Dunmaine, "Who Needs a Boss," *Fortune*, May 7, 1990, p. 53.
[18]Christy Marshall, "Rubbermaid, Yes, Plastic," *Business Month*, December 1988, p. 38.
[19]Alex Taylor III, "Why the Bounce at Rubbermaid?" *Fortune*, April 13, 1987, p. 78.

product you look for our name. If we make it, our name is on it. But because you did mean to buy ours and made a mistake and will not do so in the future, here, have one on us."[20]

RUBBERMAID'S PROMOTION STRATEGY

Rubbermaid supported its products with national television and radio commercials and magazine ads, along with allowances for promotion and co-op advertising. The company had boosted the number of outlets carrying Rubbermaid products from 60,000 in 1980 to over 100,000 in 1988. While Rubbermaid's prices tended to be higher than those of competitors, the company had a wider range of promotable products that commanded more shelf space. Rubbermaid's advertising and promotion budget for 1989 was about 3.6 percent of sales, or about $50 million.[21]

R&D AT RUBBERMAID

Rubbermaid was adept at searching out ways to grow. Designers continually tweaked mature products to provide incremental sales. Rubbermaid's recipe for R&D success was simple; according to Stanley Gault, "We absolutely watch the market and we work at it 24 hours a day."[22] Gault saw the key to effective R&D as being a student of demographics and current trends, forever listening to customers' stated and perceived needs.

Keeping a stream of new products and product improvements flowing took a deep commitment to research and development. Each of Rubbermaid's operating divisions had its own R&D team, and some divisions were expected to enter a new market segment every 18 to 24 months.[23] Rubbermaid had launched more than 250 new products in both 1989 and 1990, with a success rate of 90 percent. The company's goal of 30 percent of sales each year coming from products less than five years old had been consistently met and often exceeded.

Rubbermaid looked for fresh design ideas anywhere: from trying to apply the Ford Taurus-style soft look to garbage cans to successfully introducing stackable plastic chairs.[24] As Gault explained it, "We just keep bringing these new categories out while expanding categories we're already in, like bathware, sinkware, trash and refuse collection, and gadgets."[25]

Gault observed, "The primary reason for developing so many new products is to identify and develop entirely new categories that permit us to enter new areas and new sections within a retail store. New lines keep the products fresh, up to date, and highly salable."[26]

---

[20]Ibid.

[21]Ibid.

[22]Ibid.

[23]Marshall, "Rubbermaid, Yes, Plastic."

[24]"Masters of Innovation," *Business Week*, April 10, 1989, p. 10.

[25]Braham, "The Billion Dollar Dustpan," p. 46.

[26]Marshall, "Rubbermaid, Yes, Plastic," p. 38.

"I have this vision," he says, "that when you look down the aisle of a store, you see nothing except Rubbermaid products."[27]

Rubbermaid's R&D expenditures ran about 1 percent of sales, equal to about $16 million in 1990. R&D as a percentage of profits was about 7 percent.

CAPITAL INVESTMENTS

In 1990, the firm spent $104 million (6.8 percent of net sales) to update production processes and expand facilities. By upgrading plants, worker productivity had increased from 300 units per day in 1952 to 500 in 1980 and, under Gault, had risen beyond 900 units.[28] Between 1981 and 1991, Rubbermaid invested over $600 million to expand manufacturing and distribution facilities, modernize equipment, install process control systems and automatic packaging systems, purchase new tooling for new products, and increase capacity for existing products.

FINANCIAL PERFORMANCE

Stanley Gault personally made 20 to 25 formal presentations a year to financial analysts responsible for recommending Rubbermaid shares, all in the pursuit of satisfying the firm's overall financial objective of maximizing the shareholder's investment, an objective realized in the firm's 32.5 percent average annual return to investors between 1980 and 1990.[29]

Investment analysts see Rubbermaid as a big-capitalization company whose very bigness should inspire investor confidence. While rumored at times as a takeover target, Rubbermaid was considered a solid firm with little debt and recession-resistant "necessity products." Exhibit 6 presents an 11-year summary of Rubbermaid's financial performance.

Rubbermaid's daily stock price, posted prominently at corporate headquarters, had risen about 900 percent during Gault's tenure. According to company sources, had one invested $1,000 in Rubbermaid shares in 1980 and reinvested dividends, the investment would be worth over $25,000 as of April 1991.

RUBBERMAID'S ORGANIZATION STRUCTURE

Rubbermaid was organized into nine operating divisions, each with its own president who functioned as division CEO and general manager. In addition to the Housewares Product Division, the firm had a Specialty Products Division, the Little Tikes Company, Rubbermaid Commercial Products Inc., the Rubbermaid Office Products Group, Rubbermaid-Allibert, the International Division, Rubbermaid Canada, and Curver Rubbermaid Group. Each division operated independently of the others and pursued its own strategy, subject only to the need to conform to Rubbermaid's corporate objectives and corporate strategy.

---

[27]Sellers, "Does the CEO Really Matter?" p. 86.
[28]Taylor, "Why the Bounce at Rubbermaid?" p. 78.
[29]Braham, "The Billion Dollar Dustpan," p. 48.

EXHIBIT 6 Summary of Rubbermaid's Financial and Operating Performance, 1980–90
(Dollars in thousands except per share amounts)

	1990	1989	1988	1987	1986	1985	1984	1983	1982	1981	1980
Operating Results											
Net sales	$1,534,013	$1,452,365	$1,291,584	$1,096,055	$864,721	$747,858	$676,660	$555,789	$462,792	$434,021	$375,758
Cost of sales	1,014,526	967,563	886,850	727,927	554,421	488,169	458,803	366,425	306,190	289,748	261,448
Selling, general, administrative expenses	286,647	268,148	221,497	199,145	166,954	140,203	118,915	103,608	90,336	82,731	67,634
Other charges (credits), net	1,571	11,974	11,407	10,761	684	3,233	803	2,189	3,619	2,457	3,047
Earnings before income taxes	231,269	204,680	171,830	158,222	142,662	116,253	98,139	83,567	62,647	59,085	43,629
Income taxes	87,749	79,696	64,972	67,499	67,658	53,965	44,010	38,742	29,828	28,796	20,795
Net earnings	$ 143,520	$ 124,984	$ 106,858	$ 90,723	$ 75,004	$ 62,288	$ 54,129	$ 44,825	$ 32,819	$ 30,289	$ 22,834
Per Common Share	$ 1.80	$ 1.57	$ 1.34	$ 1.15	$ .95	$ .79	$ .69	$ .58	$ .44	$ .40	$ .30
Percentage of sales	9.4%	8.6%	8.3%	8.3%	8.7%	8.3%	8.0%	8.1%	7.1%	7.0%	6.1%
Financial Position											
Current assets	$ 602,697	$ 567,307	$ 452,639	$ 418,563	$332,655	$309,336	$270,989	$232,226	$169,879	$137,074	$111,055
Property, plant and equipment, net	405,520	379,107	347,677	310,017	248,224	210,929	171,836	138,078	138,003	138,858	142,917
Intangible and other assets, net	106,033	38,591	42,389	45,748	45,780	13,041	9,826	8,151	8,112	7,909	1,076
Total assets	$1,114,250	$ 985,005	$ 842,705	$ 774,328	$626,659	$533,306	$452,651	$378,455	$315,994	$283,841	$255,048
Current liabilities	$ 235,300	$ 215,121	$ 197,431	$ 209,771	$156,456	$133,116	$114,970	$ 87,061	$ 65,342	$ 65,821	$ 56,117
Deferred taxes, credits, and other liabilities	71,555	67,114	47,471	47,585	40,013	28,713	23,172	19,317	17,166	17,528	16,486
Long-term debt	39,191	50,294	39,023	40,042	35,668	34,071	27,559	28,589	29,873	24,400	25,266
Shareholders' equity	768,204	652,476	558,780	476,930	394,522	337,406	286,950	243,488	203,613	176,092	157,179
Total liabilities and shareholders' equity	$1,114,250	$ 985,005	$ 842,705	$ 774,328	$626,659	$533,306	$542,651	$378,455	$315,994	$283,841	$255,048
Long-term debt to total capitalization	5%	8%	7%	8%	9%	10%	9%	11%	13%	13%	15%
Working capital	$ 367,397	$ 352,186	$ 255,208	$ 208,792	$176,199	$176,220	$156,019	$145,165	$104,537	$ 71,253	$ 54,938
Current ratio	2.56	2.64	2.29	2.00	2.13	2.32	2.36	2.67	2.60	2.08	1.98
Other data											
Average common shares outstanding (000)	79,844	79,625	79,464	79,234	79,032	78,794	78,620	76,967	74,722	75,531	75,621
Return on average shareholders' equity	20.2%	20.6%	20.6%	20.8%	20.5%	20.0%	20.4%	20.1%	17.3%	18.2%	15.0%
Cash dividends paid	$ 42,621	$ 35,975	$ 29,520	$ 24,581	$ 19,771	$ 15,907	$ 13,224	$ 11,277	$ 9,995	$ 8,558	$ 7,408
Cash dividends paid per common share	$ .54	$ .46	$ .38	$ .32	$ .26	$ .225	$ .195	$ .175	$ .157	$ .135	$ .12
Shareholders' equity per common share	$ 9.60	$ 8.20	$ 7.04	$ 6.02	$ 5.00	$ 4.29	$ 3.66	$ 3.14	$ 2.76	$ 2.40	$ 2.10
NYSE stock price range, high-low	$ 45–31	$ 38–25	$ 27–21	$ 35–19	$ 29–17	$ 17–11	$ 11–8	$ 13–7	$ 8–4	$ 5–3	$ 4–3
Additions to property, plant and equipment	$ 103,720	$ 89,787	$ 87,333	$ 104,429	$ 71,587	$ 71,665	$ 55,615	$ 29,275	$ 21,433	$ 23,873	$ 37,370
Depreciation expense	$ 55,346	$ 57,341	$ 46,134	$ 44,155	$ 34,135	$ 31,607	$ 23,473	$ 20,054	$ 18,450	$ 17,280	$ 16,466
Number of shareholders at year end	13,305	11,225	10,482	10,104	8,379	6,332	5,722	5,168	4,775	4,305	4,711
Average number of associates	9,304	9,098	8,643	7,512	6,509	5,934	5,374	4,815	4,645	4,612	4,585

Source: Rubbermaid Inc. 1990 Annual Report.

Housewares Products Division

Formerly the Home Product Division, the Housewares Product Division was renamed to define more clearly its mission of serving the housewares industry. It manufactured and marketed sinkware, space organizers, household and refuse containers, food preparation utensils and gadgets, microwave cookware, food storage products, bathware, rubber gloves, casual dinnerware and drinkware, workshop organizers, Con-Tact brand decorative coverings, shelf liners, and vacuum cleaner bags.

Most recently, the division had entered the consumer recycling market with containers that made it easy to separate and collect recyclable materials in the home; the containers were manufactured using recycled post-consumer plastics such as milk and soft-drink containers.

Specialty Products Division

This division was responsible for aggressively manufacturing and marketing insulated products, home horticulture products, and outdoor casual resin furniture. The division's principal products were insulated chests, thermal jugs, water coolers, fuel containers, storage containers, Blue Ice refreezable ice substitute, planters, and bird feeders.

The Little Tikes Company

Many new products were introduced and added to this company's product lines in 1989, including three new categories—toy trucks, infant products, and a dollhouse line. The dollhouse category included Little Tikes Place and miniature accessories of such highly popular items as the Cozy Coupe, Party Kitchen, and Play Slide.

The infant product category consisted of 11 items, including a Stacking Clown, Baby Roller, Baby Mirror, and a variety of tub toys. The truck category featured Big Dump Truck and Big Loader.

The quality and integrity of Little Tikes products received favorable recognition as three products—Little Tikes Place, Little Tug, and Toddle Tots' child care center—were named first, second, and ninth among the top 10 nonvideo new toys for 1989 by the Consumer Affairs Committee of Americans for Democratic Action.

Rubbermaid's market share in preschool and infant toys and furnishings had gained steadily in the past three years:[30]

	1987	1990
Fisher Price	64%	44%
Rubbermaid (Little Tikes)	13%	22%
Hasbro (Playskool)	23%	22%
Mattel (Disney)	—	11%
Combined sales	$1.2 billion	$1.4 billion

---

[30] *Akron Beacon Journal*, March 15, 1989, p. 1.

Little Tikes enjoyed 40 percent annual growth and, since its founding in 1970, had doubled sales every three years to about $300 million, spending less than $2 million for advertising.

Little Tikes was expanding its capacity and had plants in California, Ohio, Missouri, Canada, and Ireland. Little Tikes, acquired in 1984 for $56 million in stock, in 1988 contributed more than $200 million of Rubbermaid's $1.2 billion in sales.

Rubbermaid Commercial Products

Rubbermaid Commercial Products was established in 1967 to design and manufacture lines of products for the commercial, industrial, and institutional markets. It sold a wide variety of products to the sanitary maintenance, food-service, industrial, and agricultural markets.

In June 1990, Rubbermaid acquired EWU AG, a Swiss-based manufacturer of mopping equipment and cleaning tools, to gain increased commercial distribution throughout Europe.

The municipal recycling market was viewed as having many growth opportunities for Commercial Products. The operation pioneered the use of recycled plastics in many of its containers and participated in national efforts to help raise awareness that containers manufactured with recycled materials were used widely in municipal curbside recycling programs.

Office Products Group

Located in Inglewood, California, this business was established in January 1991 to focus on the office products industry, which was growing faster than the gross national product.

The acquisition of Eldon Industries enhanced Rubbermaid's position in the office products market. Eldon was the leading manufacturer of office accessories and offered a wide range of products for the desk; Rubbermaid was the leader in chair mats, and MicroComputer Accessories had a strong market position in computer-related accessories for personal computer, word processor, and data terminal users. Other units in the of Office Products Group produced communication boards, building directories, signage, lecterns, wall cabinets, and tools for the assembly and repair of electronic circuits.

Rubbermaid-Allibert

During 1989, this operation was established as a joint venture with Allibert S.A. of Paris to manufacture and market resin casual furniture for the North American market. Rubbermaid had 50 percent ownership and management control of the venture. Allibert was a leading European manufacturer of casual furniture and had participated in international markets for years. It had extensive experience in materials technology, processing technologies, and furniture design.

Curver Rubbermaid

The Curver Rubbermaid Group became operational in January 1990 as a joint venture between Rubbermaid and the Dutch chemical conglomerate, DSM. The group manufactured and marketed plastic and rubber housewares and resin furniture for Europe, the Middle East, and North Africa. As its venture share, Rubbermaid contributed its European housewares manufacturing facilities and distribution centers in Germany, France, Austria, the Netherlands, and Switzerland. DSM contributed its Curver Housewares Group, which included its manufacturing and marketing subsidiaries scattered throughout Europe.

The integration of the two organizations, Rubbermaid and Curver, with their respective product lines, sales and marketing organizations, and manufacturing and distribution facilities, positioned Rubbermaid for a leadership role in the European Community of 1992 and the emerging eastern bloc markets.

Headquartered in Breda, the Netherlands, Curver Rubbermaid was expected to employ 1,700 people in Europe. Sales were expected to exceed $200 million in 1990 the first year of operation.

International Operations in 1990

Rubbermaid's international businesses achieved record sales and earnings growth in 1990, particularly in Europe, Latin America, Mexico, the Far East, and Canada. With the exception of the Far East, the management of Rubbermaid businesses around the world plus the coordination of sales and marketing in foreign markets were the responsibility of the respective U.S. operating companies.

To maximize return on existing investments, Rubbermaid emphasized exporting from its existing manufacturing facilities in the United States and Europe. Where market size and economies justified, local manufacturing facilities were established. Licensing agreements were employed in those markets where the costs of importing were prohibitive and where local company-owned manufacturing was economically justified.

MANAGEMENT IN THE COMING DECADE

On May 1, 1991, Stanley Carleton Gault retired from Rubbermaid as chairman of the board and chief executive officer. The board of directors selected Walter W. Williams, Rubbermaid's president and chief operating officer, as Gault's successor.

At the time he retired, Gault planned to maintain his association with Rubbermaid, stating, "I certainly won't be running the company anymore, but I'll be around to talk about it."[31] Gault was given a two-year consulting contract, an office at Rubbermaid headquarters, and membership on Rubbermaid's board of directors until he turned 70.[32] However, within a matter of months after his retirement at Rubbermaid, Goodyear's board of directors persuaded Gault to become chairman and CEO of Goodyear and lead Goodyear's effort to reclaim its long-held leadership status in the world tire industry.

---

[31] Alecia Swasy, *The Wall Street Journal*, April 2, 1990, p. 26.

[32] Yalinda Rhoden, "Sans Gault," *Akron Beacon Journal*, April 22, 1991, p. D2.

AMERICAN TEXTILE MACHINERY COMPANY*

Tracy Kramer, University of Alabama

In early 1992, Bill Owens, vice president of American Textile Machinery Company (ATM), was mulling over the issues confronting the Textile Services Division (TSD). Owens had recently replaced the previous vice president and was instructed to turn the division around—to take a faltering venture that began as an internal start-up five years ago and turn it into a money-making business.

Owens was finding this easier said than done. TSD represented a strategically important initiative; its task was to tap into an $80 billion dollar industry by providing installation, start-up, and repair service on all equipment manufactured by ATM and other textile machinery manufacturers. However, problems with overtime compensation, training, inventory control, and accounting procedures had plagued the division and hindered its success. Owens was uncertain of how best to overcome these and other problems and successfully implement the division's strategy.

TEXTILE SERVICES DIVISION—THE CONCEPT

The American Textile Machinery Company was a leading manufacturer of looms, frames, heddles, and large and small pieces of machinery that textile mills used to produce various materials ranging from cloth to plastic wrap. Some pieces were so large that certified personnel were required to correctly install them. ATM also produced hundreds of other textile machinery parts, components, and material consumed by the textile industry.

ATM was organized into five business units according to the different technologies used by each product. The Frames and Looms Division manufactured equipment primarily for the production of woven cloth using mechanical looms and heddles. The Water Technologies Division manufactured equipment that used water jets to propel fibers in the production of woven cloth. Knit Technologies equipment catered to the mills producing knitted fabrics, including polyester cloths. And the Plastics Division manufactured very large pieces of equipment that produced continuous rolls of plastic that varied in thickness from one inch to ultra-thin plastic wrap.

Before 1981, warranty service on ATM's more than 18,000 products was performed sporadically within the company. After-sale services were almost nonexistent. In general, products were serviced by the original manufacturing facility—each plant responsible for making the equipment would either dispatch plant personnel to where the equipment was installed, have the customer send the equipment to the plant for repair, or contract with someone locally to

---

make the repairs. Some plants had internal service because of the business requirements; others had dedicated service personnel to better serve their customers. Within ATM, service was very informal and decentralized. Service requests were routed to the various service technicians through the product field sales force that had offices in 190 locations throughout the United States.

In 1981, ATM began centralizing its service function. It formed the Field Service Organization, a group of about 20 technicians operating out of 11 plants. From 1981 through 1987, the service responsibilities of various plants were gradually assumed by the Field Service Organization, and by 1987 this group had grown to 30 technicians in 13 plants and seven field sales offices.

In 1987, ATM's CEO, James Williams, spearheaded an effort to establish centralized, corporatewide service with corporate commitment to aggressive growth plans. Williams believed service was an untapped potential for ATM. He had a vision of creating a service division within ATM that would generate a dependable revenue stream by capturing approximately 10 percent of an $800 million market for servicing the maintenance and repair needs of textiles customers. Williams wanted to generate $80 million in revenues within five years.

In early 1988, ATM formed the Textile Service Division (TSD) under the direction of Vice President Robert Patten. Williams was committed to the venture and provided significant financial support as well as positive internal and external communications. The mission statement developed for TSD was "We are committed to providing quality service products that consistently meet customer expectations, support our business sectors and contribute to the profitable growth of American Textile Machinery." TSD's financial goals were to break even within three years and to reach $80 million in revenues by 1992. The five-year sales forecast was as follows:

Year	Sales
1988	$ 4 million
1989	10 million
1990	25 million
1991	50 million
1992	80 million

The primary objective was to fully support ATM's 18,000 products and to offer installation and start-up service, testing/preventive maintenance services, upgrading and retrofitting capabilities, and time-based repair services.

The push for service was appropriate for several reasons. First, the type of equipment ATM manufactured often had a product life of 20 or more years. Most products had a life cycle that began with the sale of the product, which could be accompanied by installation and the initial start-up of the equipment; then periodic maintenance; repair of the equipment as needed; and finally, potential upgrading of the equipment before replacement was necessary. Without a service organization, American Textile was limited to new product sales, which meant revenues and customer contact only every 20 years or so, unless the field sales force actively maintained customer relations. However, James Williams envisioned ATM offering service to customers for each stage of the product life cycle—installation, start-up, maintenance, repair, and upgrading.

The potential revenues from a stream of services on the equipment far exceeded the onetime, lump-sum revenues from the product sale, and there was the added bonus of ongoing customer contact.

A second reason a service division was appropriate for American Textile was that the profit margins on service products were significantly greater than those on product sales. In 1988, TSD managers were striving to achieve gross profit margins of 35 percent and a 50 percent return on investment by 1992. Service calls also represented an opportunity to pull through additional product sales on jobs that required new parts and/or materials. Additionally, the company's competitors were using ATM's limited service capabilities as leverage against ATM to increase their sales.

GROWTH

The primary objective during 1988 was to develop an infrastructure to support the goals of the division. Robert Patten, vice president and general manager, hired Rick Harrison and John Thompson to assist with the development. Harrison was responsible for logistics, headquarters operations, and business development. Logistics concerned the practicalities of responding to a service call, including who to send and how to get both technicians and required parts to the job site. Headquarters facilities, a technical assistance center, and a service control center (SCC) were opened. At the SCC, a toll-free telephone number was established to provide a central communication point and phones were manned by service coordinators. An information system package, called SERVICEWATCH, was purchased to track all information pertaining to incoming calls, including billings and costs. The technical assistance center was established to provide technical support to the technicians; to act as a liaison among plant manufacturing, design engineering, and field service; and to assist end-users with minor problems that could be handled by phone.

Thompson was charged with field operations, with responsibilities for generating sales and recruiting, training, and managing service technicians. Beginning in 1988, technicians, called textile service representatives (TSRs), were dedicated to field locations and standards and procedures were developed. In February 1988, 37 TSRs were working out of 10 plants and 11 field locations, and the division planned an aggressive hiring campaign to increase the number of technicians. Thompson then hired five regional managers who had profit-and-loss responsibility for sales and service within a geographic area.

By early 1990, Patten had assembled a functioning senior management staff. In addition to Thompson and Harrison, members of the senior staff included Larry Strickland, controller; Art Brown, logistics; Greg Smith, human resources; and Gary Palmer, technical support. Thompson had five regional managers under his direct supervision and 113 TSRs and 21 sales representatives as indirect reports. Harrison had also added another level of management under his direct command, including a marketing manager, an SCC manager, and numerous indirect reports.

Growth at all costs was the overriding theme, starting in 1988 and continuing through 1990. By mid-1990, there were 120 TSRs, and the company had invested over $50 million to make the division a success. By January 1991, it had grown to 242 employees. The division had met its revenue and profit plans in 1988 and 1989, but by 1990 it began experiencing problems associated with its fast growth.

SALES

Pent-up demand for ATM to provide warranty and start-up service generated sufficient sales for TSD to meet its revenue goals in 1988 and most of 1989 without the use of a sales force (see Exhibit 1). A sales force was not created until mid-1989 when the account representative position was established. Account representatives were hired to solicit outside sales and to work with ATM's product field sales force.

John Thompson, manager for field operations, was responsible for overall sales and hired five regional managers to recruit sales personnel and coordinate their efforts, in addition to other field operations responsibilities including management of the TSRs. By January 1, 1991, TSD had 21 account representatives, but there were underlying problems in the sales organization. First, several of the regional managers did not have sales management experience. Furthermore, neither Thompson nor three of his five regional managers had experience in the textile equipment industry. These combined factors resulted in hiring unqualified or ineffective account representatives.

The second problem, possibly a result of the first, was that TSD did not attempt to capitalize on American Textile's greatest marketing strength—its field sales force and its distributor network. Over the years, ATM had cultivated relationships with distributors through which it sold the majority of its products. Additionally, ATM's field sales force was a large group of highly trained individuals, primarily engineers, that delivered excellent customer service, maintained customer and distributor relations, and contributed heavily to the company's quality reputation and success. However, rather than using the field sales force and pushing TSD's service products through established networks, TSD elected to have its own sales force. Rather than capitalizing on American Textile's distributor relations, TSD chose to market strictly to end-users, alienating distributors and locking out a large network of potential leads and sales.

MARKETING AND PLANNING

With the assistance of outside consultants, TSD managers developed a 1989 strategic plan. This plan involved the following:

- Concentrate service product development and marketing activities at those target markets with the best opportunities.
- Obtain business unit support in 1989.
- Use technology to enhance productivity and provide differentiation.
- Develop and market end-user service products

By mid-1990, TSD managers were finding this strategy difficult to implement because of its lack of specificity. For example, there was no indication of which markets represented the best opportunities; there was neither a plan nor

EXHIBIT 1	Financial Performance of ATM's Technical Services Division, 1988–91

(In millions of dollars)

	1988	**1989**	**1990**	**1991**
Revenue goals	$4.0	$10.0	$25.0	$50.0
Actual revenues	4.5	9.9	22.1	24.6
Cost of service	5.1	14.5	31.2	26.8
Gross profit	−0.6	−3.6	−9.1	−2.2
Net income	−1.9	−8.2	−14.0	−5.4

a liaison to build business unit support; and there was no indication of how and/or which technologies would enhance productivity or provide differentiation. During 1988 and 1989, marketing efforts primarily concentrated on marketing communications. Accomplishments during this period included putting stickers with TSD's toll-free number on each piece of equipment before it was shipped to inform customers of who to call for service. Marketing also instituted the issuance of warranty cards with new equipment to keep track of American Textile's warranty obligations. However, little, if any, market research had been accomplished before 1990. In March 1990, Rick Harrison hired Bradley Davis to head marketing activities.

According to Davis, who was promoted to national marketing manager in late 1990, there was "a lack of true sweating the details of business and marketing planning." Planning and marketing efforts were focused on achieving the "$80 million vision" and were very broad in scope. TSD managers had a good grasp of the big picture, but in general had not developed operations-level plans. It was not until the division's senior staff began to develop the 1991 business plan that the division addressed many of the fundamental strategic and marketing issues.

The original plan called for sales revenues of $50 million; however, the division had never questioned the source of these projected revenues. Davis, responsible for developing the overall plan, said,

> What we were trying to do was very complex, elaborate, and the systems and processes were not in place to support it. There were five to six different customer bases for the different product technologies that American Textile manufactured. There was no plan or idea of where revenues would come from until the 1991 business plan. Specific questions that remained unanswered were: Where were we going to get these sales? How much of each (service product) were we going to get from where? What markets were we going to compete in? What were our pricing levels going to be? What were going to be the channels to market?

TEXTILE SERVICE REPRESENTATIVES

A technical service representative was hired at a higher-than-marketplace guaranteed salary, provided corporate phone and American Express charge cards, issued a travel letter that would allow the TSR to write himself a reimbursement check for travel expenses up to $400 every two weeks, and given uniforms, tools, beepers, and an ATM/TSD van. He had the opportunity to earn overtime pay for hours worked outside of a normal 8 A.M. to 5 P.M., Monday through Friday workday, but was not required to be present at an ATM office if he was not on a job site. Subsequently, many TSRs worked out of their homes. TSRs could also participate in an incentive program that would award the TSR with a gift for providing leads that resulted in future sales.

Initially, the SCC would contact the TSR, inform him of a service customer, and leave the scheduling of the service visit to the TSR's discretion and convenience. By mid-1990, the number of TSRs employed far exceeded the number needed to service the calls received by the division, and TSD began to reduce the size of the service force from a peak of 120 technicians to 69 by the end of 1991. Even with the workforce reduction, the average utilization rate for the TSRs was only approximately 35 percent,[1] and the division was still paying significant amounts in overtime.

Thompson and his regional managers were confronted with many managerial and operational problems regarding the TSRs. The most distressing was the issue of overtime. TSD's human resources manager, Greg Smith, informed them that TSRs were classified as exempt employees, but the division's pay policies tended to categorize them and compensate them as nonexempt employees because they carried tools. Therefore, TSRs were eligible for overtime for any hours worked outside of the normal workweek—even if the hours worked during the normal workweek were less than 40. Smith pointed out the legal implications of the situation: TSD could not require its technicians to be available during the standard 40-hour workweek and also work nights and/or weekends as needed without additional pay. Furthermore, the job description for TSRs provided a guaranteed salary even if the TSR worked zero hours during the normal workweek.

TSRs also represented a training and skills challenge for management. American Textile manufactured over 18,000 products that were often customized at the time of purchase. As a result, the number of possible product permutations was practically infinite. TSD offered its technicians three weeks of training initially, as well as ongoing training sessions. However, it was virtually impossible for TSD's management to develop a skills data base that would track which products each TSR was qualified to start up, maintain, or repair. Due to possible customizing of the products, the individual TSRs might not learn if they were qualified to work on the equipment until they reached the job site. This represented a serious scheduling problem.

SYSTEMS AND CONTROLS

At TSD, the service delivery process began when a customer called the SCC. Service coordinators answered calls, obtained billing information, then relayed information on the customer's problem to the appropriate technician, and opened an account on the SERVICEWATCH information system. On receiving the call, the TSR contacted the customer, scheduled the visit, and made the service call. After completing the assignment, the TSR was required to close the

---

[1]Utilization is defined as the amount of straight-time billable work hours reported divided by the total number of available straight-time hours.

call by submitting to the SCC the number of hours to be billed to the customer, travel expenses, and the itemization of all material and/or parts, if any, used on the job. The accounting department would retrieve this information from the computer system and send invoices accordingly.

TSD's management found several glitches in this process, however. First, service coordinators did not always obtain the appropriate billing name and address, since the service contact and billing contact were not always the same. Additionally, TSRs often failed to report materials and/or parts used on the job. As a result, the division could not track its inventory shrinkage problems. Calls were not closed on a timely basis, which caused considerable problems when the accounting department attempted to issue invoices months after the service visit.

Because of misspecifications in billing contacts, accounts receivables were large. Larry Strickland took over as controller in early 1990 when receivables were hitting an all-time high of $7 million. The problem was compounded by a lack of established procedures for writing off uncollectible debts, so receivables continued to grow. Also contributing to this growth was a tendency to double or triple bill in attempts to collect. According to Strickland, "When I came on board TSD, there were no financial controls in place. Accounts receivable was growing by leaps and bounds because it was rerecorded as a collectible amount each time a payment notification was sent out. This also meant that the revenue figures were grossly overstated."

Purchasing and inventory control were presenting a managerial challenge for Art Brown. As logistics manager, Brown said, "Once a call comes in, my job is to insure that a qualified service technician arrives with the correct parts and materials needed to accurately and professionally perform the required service in an expedient manner." Brown's objective at TSD was to establish centralized purchasing for the division. However, this policy was not strictly enforced by field operations and, consequently, TSRs often purchased the parts and materials they needed directly from the plant, a distributor, or a local hardware store. Not only did this practice reduce TSD's buying power, but also the TSRs would submit expense statements for reimbursement that did not always report the cost as a billable expense to the customer. Therefore, costs and revenues were not always matched. Furthermore, if a TSR did not report the use of a part on a job, it remained on the records as still in inventory. Brown said, "Many TSRs had no concept of expense/revenue matching. If they needed a part that they didn't have and went next door to the local hardware store to get it—fine, do whatever it takes to do the job right. But they were very inconsistent in reporting the purchase as a billable expense. Sometimes, when I would ask a technician why he didn't report the expense when he closed the job, he would say he simply forgot or that it never occurred to him. It's funny though that they never forgot to request reimbursement."

CULTURE

Two cultures influenced TSD's success or failure—American Textile's corporate culture and the culture within TSD. The corporate culture, specifically the way ATM traditionally conducted business, was not conducive to a centralized service center. Typically, each business unit within the company was vertically integrated. It had its own manufacturing facilities, it own sales force, and its own service. TSD's 1988 business plan clarified the division's relationship with other business units: "In order to be successful and meet the plan, Textile Service needs the unqualified support of the business units and 'buy-in' of our charter in 1988. The current internal environment is one of reluctance to accept and support this change." By late 1991, the division still had not resolved relations with its internal customers. In an internal survey, business unit managers made the following statements regarding TSD: "Service costs too much; we can do it better/cheaper; response is slow; your personnel are not properly trained; you are aloof and get special treatment from corporate headquarters; you sit around and wait for the phone to ring; you steal our good people and our business."

The culture within TSD through the middle of 1990 was one of camaraderie, teamwork, and high employee morale. Employees believed the division was headed for great success and were proud to be a part of a winning team. The individuals hired were truly committed to customer service. James Williams's words of praise regarding TSD to other business units and in the annual report reinforced these sentiments. TSD also paid higher than market salaries across the board. But as the division grew, management's inept efforts to correct the emerging problems had devastating effects on morale.

TSD's policy had been to hire ahead of sales since the learning curve for TSRs was perceived to be very long. However, by late 1990, it became obvious that sales were not going to catch up with the structure in place in the near future. Strickland said, "As the business grew, rather than stretch the capabilities of existing personnel until new people could be hired and trained, TSD chose to hire ahead of demand. As a result, people were underutilized and the division was always larger—and more costly—than sales could sustain."

Not only was the division missing revenue targets, but also excessive costs were resulting in unplanned losses. By early 1991, it became apparent the division could not grow sales fast enough to cover costs and the division would have to downsize.

Employee layoffs and job eliminations occurred each quarter in 1991 (see Exhibit 2). Rick Harrison's position was eliminated, and his primary duties were absorbed by the marketing department. John Thompson and four of his five regional managers were laid off and the entire division was restructured. Ed Henderson, the surviving regional manager, was placed in charge of the TSRs and was asked to address the overtime and training issues. Bradley Davis was given responsibility for the account representatives and was asked to define the markets, set targets, and increase sales accordingly. Gary Palmer and most of his technical support staff of 18 were eliminated following charges that end-users were tying up the phone lines without resulting in revenues. In fact, the technical support group was accused of causing revenue losses—each time an end-user's needs were met by phone rather than requiring a service visit, a revenue opportunity was lost. Within the human resources department, the four-person training group was reduced to one.

Every department was scrutinized and cut to the bare minimum. Surviving employees feared their jobs were next. Morale hit an all-time low when the division discontinued the coffee and water service, considered perks by some and necessities by others. Employees and senior staff questioned Robert Pat-

EXHIBIT 2   **Employee Reductions in TSD in 1991**

	Jan. 1	Oct. 31	Dec. 31	Average
ESRs	113	72	72	93
Electrical support	11	10	10	11
Account reps	21	13	10	16
Other support	97	83	83	90
Total employees	242	178	175	210

ten's ability to spearhead a plan of action to turn the division around and return it to its previous stature. Brown said of Patten:

> Robert's management style was one of encouragement and delegation rather than direction and, in the right time and place, that's OK. But TSD's senior staff was looking to Robert for direction. Instead of setting a direction, he tended to agree with each executive, even if their recommendations were at odds. Consequently, very little got done due to lack of support. Robert was trying to practice the Japanese style of consensus building when what he probably should have been practicing was martial law.

In late 1991, Robert Patten was replaced by Bill Owens as vice president of TSD. Owens had previously been a sales vice president for American Textile's sales force and, therefore, was aware of the importance of capitalizing on ATM's strengths. After a period of observing and reviewing the situation, Owens was still undecided about the correct action for the division. Options ranged from dismantling the division to paring it back to only a few key services to generating renewed corporate senior management support. There was no question customers needed and wanted a single point of contact to receive warranty service on all ATM products. Furthermore, TSD's customers were extremely pleased with the service received. The issue was how could TSD continue to provide quality customer service while simultaneously achieving controlled growth and working within American Textile Machinery's corporate culture.

ELECTRIMEX*

Stephen Jenner, San Diego State University

Geraldo Ortiz, general manager of Electrimex, was frustrated and a little angry with his Mexican subordinates. The same pattern kept repeating itself: Geraldo would ask one of his managers to do something, they would agree, and when Geraldo checked on their progress, he found they had done nothing. They usually offered a good excuse, but it was often embarrassing to Geraldo when they mysteriously failed to perform and left him struggling to explain to his U.S. superiors at corporate headquarters why the plant was not progressing as fast as planned. Meanwhile, the pressure on Geraldo for better plant performance was increasing as Electrimex's parent company in the United States shifted new products to its Mexican plant, while at the same time pushing Geraldo and Electrimex to prepare for the comprehensive European quality management and quality systems guidelines known as ISO 9000. Company management assigned "monumental importance" to ISO 9000 as a means of getting a foothold in Central and South America.

ISO 9000

The International Organization for Standardization (ISO) was a worldwide federation of national standards bodies that drafted technical standards for the type of products made by Electrimex. International Standard 9000 had been prepared by a technical committee on quality assurance in 1987 and subsequently approved by a 75 percent majority of the members. ISO 9000 included requirements covering quality assurance, quality costs, marketing, design, procurement, production, product verification, control of measuring and test equipment, postproduction functions, quality documentation and records, personnel (including training, qualification, and motivation), product safety and liability, and the use of statistical methods. Unless the Electrimex plant could meet ISO 9000 standards, its products could not be sold in many of the countries being targeted as markets.

BACKGROUND OF COMPANY

Electrimex was one of three Mexican factories that operated as wholly owned subsidiaries of a U.S. manufacturer of household electrical products. The parent company had been in business for generations in the United States, but as competition from low-cost Asian sources intensified, high wages and labor costs at the company's unionized plants in the Northeast became a competitive

---

*The name of the real company that served as a basis for this case study is disguised, along with the names of the managers.

disadvantage. Wage and benefits, plus payroll taxes and workers compensation, were rising steadily and were not offset by increases in productivity or the depreciation of the U.S. dollar relative to the currencies of South Korea, Taiwan, Singapore, or Hong Kong. Meanwhile, entry-level wages in Mexico were between $1.20 and $1.65 per hour, and the Mexican peso was depreciating steadily against the U.S. dollar. The Mexican government's "maquiladora/in-bond program" allowed U.S.-based companies to open assembly plants in Mexico (usually just across the border) and ship in unassembled components free of duties, with the understanding that assembled finished products would be exported back to the United States. Often, the components were manufactured at plants close to the Mexican border to minimize shipping costs to the Mexican assembly plant. Usually the U.S. plant did high-skill, capital-intensive tasks, whereas the Mexican plant used low-cost labor to perform labor-intensive tasks. This type of production-sharing arrangement between U.S. plants and Mexican plants was also facilitated by U.S. government tariff policy, which required U.S. companies to pay import duties only on the value added abroad when the products returned.

In Electrimex's case, the labor cost savings associated with products assembled in Mexico were big enough to allow it to sell at a price low enough to supply major retailers such as Wal-Mart and Home Depot. The company claimed to have a product in virtually every American home in 1992.

Electrimex was established in Tijuana in January 1988 by Geraldo Ortiz, a U.S. national of Puerto Rican descent who was fluent in Spanish. Geraldo prepared a comprehensive plan to establish a plant in Tijuana, Baja California, which he implemented with great success, and Electrimex became the company's biggest plant worldwide. The family values of the parent corporation fit very well with Mexican culture. Even before the plant was established, Geraldo was clear about the importance of corporate culture:

> To develop a healthy company culture at the plant level, the individual must feel that he/she has and is getting respect, objectivity, and rewards for his/her contributions. We must undertake special care in Mexico not to develop a negative culture where favoritism, alienation and a "they and we" attitude prevails. We must foster the positive aspects of the Mexican idiosyncrasies, such as pride of workmanship, the hunger for recognition, the strong feelings for belonging and acceptance, strong family ties, and the desire to get ahead. Management must realize that it is not running a plant across a border, but is instead, a guest of a foreign country with a different culture and way of life, where difficult hardships tax the population. On the other hand, doing business in Mexico can be as easy or as difficult as one wants to make it. Progress, intelligently planned and managed, will add to the company culture positively since the Mexican national, with few exceptions, wants to learn and grow. The atmosphere we wish and should foster is one of problem solving, not blame placing, selling people on ideas, not ramming them down their throats, giving people the opportunity to learn from their mistakes, not threatening dismissal for failure.

DEVELOPING YOUNG MEXICAN MANAGERS

All of the managers and supervisors at the Electrimex plant in Tijuana seemed to have a clear understanding of the parent company's objectives and expectations for Electrimex, as well as great respect for the general manager. On a typical day, each of the eight top Electrimex managers received as many as 100 messages for the United States in English through the electronic mail computer system ("E-Mail"), as well as follow-up telephone calls. Many of the supervisors were unable to communicate in English and were spared this flood of communications; this created an additional burden for their managers, who had to translate. Also, these young and relatively inexperienced people lacked the maturity and discipline to work effectively on their own. Electrimex employees were very young, reflecting the youthful nature of Mexico's population (the average age of Mexicans was 15 years, and two thirds of the Mexican population was under the age of 25). The average age of Electrimex employees was 19, and most of the assembly line workers were teenage women.

Electrimex employee turnover was about 7 percent a month, while the average for other maquiladora plants in the area was 11 percent. Each employee turnover cost about $150, including indirect employees to recruit and interview new workers, compensation administration, the time required for inexperienced people to progress down the learning curve, and the supervisors' time to train the new workers. Given Electrimex's work force of 1,300, the 7 percent per month turnover rate cost about $13,650 per month. Proposals to overcome the turnover problem included better pay with more increases, better transportation service, child care, better facilities (work areas, bathrooms, cafeteria), and better supervisor relations. Some supervisors were responsible for 60 workers, but they had group leaders to help them manage each line of approximately 15 workers. One supervisor reported success in motivating workers with small gifts, such as pens and stamps. Another emphasized the need to "be nice," to laugh and be friendly and not strict all the time. There were cases of sexual harassment of young female workers by male supervisors, some of whom demanded sexual favors during off-duty hours.

Overall, many of the management problems at Electrimex seemed related to the plant's transition from an entrepreneurial, start-up organization in which Geraldo was the central management figure to a large plant run, by necessity, by a professional management team. Geraldo believed Electrimex should try to preserve the positive aspects of the entrepreneurial organization while seeking to achieve some of the positive characteristics of professional plant management. Exhibit 1 shows the current management organization chart at Electrimex. Exhibit 2 shows the pros and cons of the two management phases.

Young Mexican managers appreciated the confidence, respect, and trust of the general manager, but they were stressed and frustrated by their own lack of skills and understanding of other functions. In the future, it was expected that different department managers would need to work together in "tiger teams" or "task forces" to solve problems that crossed departmental boundaries. Geraldo Ortiz believed he had to accelerate the development of these young people as managers now to cope with the continuing growth and vertical integration of Electrimex.

Geraldo wanted Electrimex to be the first plant in the company and in Tijuana certified under ISO 9000, and he wanted to begin manufacturing components in the near future rather than importing them from the U.S. side of the border. However, he was well aware that the challenges he faced were daunting.

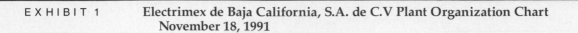

E X H I B I T 1   **Electrimex de Baja California, S.A. de C.V Plant Organization Chart**
                        November 18, 1991

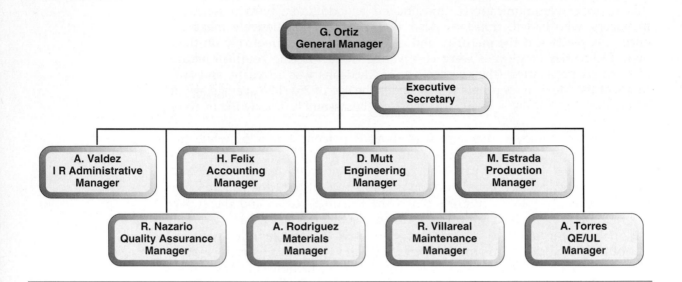

ELECTRIMEX OPERATING DEPARTMENTS

Production

According to Electrimex's production manager, Milton Estrada, the production department had three key problems: (1) inconsistent flow of the defect-free materials, (2) employee turnover (often the actual head count was even worse than the overall reported 7 percent average per month; for example at 7 A.M. Monday there were fewer workers than at any other time of the week), and (3) weak supervisory skills. According to Milton, the general manager was sometimes slow to respond or unable to react to requests for help in resolving these problems.

A key objective was to shift from batch to continuous-flow production, including assembly and packaging. For the products recently transferred for production at Electrimex, there was often a lack of good standards based on time- and-motion studies—many standards were estimated even though procedures called for new standards to be in place when transfers occurred. The assembly work was very repetitive and characterized by very short cycle times (5 to 25 seconds).

Milton was generally accepted as the most likely successor to the general manager and was seen by Geraldo as someone who needed to be developed by increasing his responsibilities relative to both the U.S. parent company and the other departments at Electrimex. Specifically, Geraldo believed that he and the corporate vice president responsible for Mexico should help Milton understand U.S. cost accounting and how Electrimex performance was measured and involve him in the planning process.

Geraldo could also see a need to encourage Milton to prepare and present more reports that integrated information now maintained in separate departments. The strongest interrelationships existed between production and qual-

EXHIBIT 2 **Pros and Cons of Electrimex's Transition from Entrepreneurial Management to Large-Plant Professional Management**

Start-up and Entrepreneurial Phase

Pros	Cons
• Entrepreneurial spirit	• Lack of professionalism ("rookie errors")
• Youth	• Fear of failure
• Enthusiasm	• High turnover of managers and supervisors
• Managers molded in the "Electrimex way"	• Lack of discipline
• Informality	• Need to remind managers of deadlines and commitments
• Strong technical skills	• Weak managerial skills
• Clear feedback from market	• Little time to correct problems
• High level of commitment	• Long hours and much stress
• Efficient in small groups	• Not suitable to larger factories
• Managers solve problems when told by general manager	• Lack of assertiveness, independence
	• Reactive "firefighting" and tendency to blame others versus proactive problem solving and "swimming upstream" to solve problems at source

Convergence to Professional Management Phase

Pros	Cons
• Greater stability	• More "red tape"
• Better documentation	• Limited horizons
• Division of labor	• Lack of understanding
• Lower costs due to scale	• Greater potential for errors
• Greater standardization	• Need discipline for quality
• More growth opportunities for people	• Need better selection, training and, reward systems
• Clearer objectives	• Lack of depth of "players"
• Greater emphasis on setting direction of units' day-to-day activities	• Greater distance from corporate goals
	• Greater risk of failure

ity engineering (these two managers were the informal leaders of the group of eight below the general manager) and to a lesser extent between production and quality assurance, maintenance, engineering, and materials. Geraldo considered the possibility that there needed to be more separate meetings of these managers and key supervisors, without the general manager and the other departments.

Geraldo tried to focus on providing clear standards and coaching individuals, especially Milton. According to Geraldo, Milton tended to be too loyal to his subordinates and often lacked the patience to see alternatives. Like many bright young people, Milton tended to expect others to grasp ideas quickly and implement policies with little more than a request from their boss.

Materials

The purchasing function was previously managed by the human resources manager and was now an additional burden for materials, which seemed to be struggling as a department. The materials manager, Alejandro Rodriguez, was responsible not only for purchasing, but also for making sure all materials arrived on time. Although he was always busy and typically spent two hours per day working directly with Geraldo, there continued to be failures due to problems with suppliers, U.S. and Mexican Customs, and transportation.

Trained as an engineer specializing in computer systems, Alejandro was frustrated by Electrimex's two computer systems, each with its problems. Now dependent on U.S. headquarters for computing software, he wanted to develop his own subsystem, complete with his own materials lists (with the correct part numbers and quantities). He also complained that frequent engineering changes often made materials obsolete. Electrimex E-Mail was very time consuming (he reviewed 100 documents per day).

The dependence on the U.S. parent corporation could make the materials department look worse; for example, the dumping of rework of bad products led to more scrap, which made Electrimex's performance look bad. Inconsistent performance of this vital function seemed to be causing a lot of problems at Electrimex. In addition to Alejandro's complaints about having too much on his plate and the criticisms of his subordinates, Geraldo noted that Alejandro was often unaware of his subordinates' activities. Alejandro often remarked about how much he would like more rest and vacation time.

Quality Engineering

Amilcar Torres managed the quality engineering department very informally. There was little documentation of engineering, testing, and pilot runs or of the history of equipment brought in from the United States. Due to a lack of planning, engineering projects were often rushed. There was no formal requisition process for equipment. Amilcar believed that because his subordinates lacked skills, he was unable to delegate. For example, Amilcar believed he was the only person in the plant who could translate U.S. training videos. Amilcar also spent a lot of time learning the technical details of the Electrimex computer network, and people always came to him for help.

In Geraldo's view, Amilcar was too dependent on his subordinates, so he needed to be coached frequently in this area. Geraldo thought there was also a need for better relations, linkages, and teamwork with other departments. Specifically, to maintain high quality, Geraldo believed there was a need to build relationships at the supervisory level between departments, such as materials and production. Amilcar was concerned about the overreliance on quality data provided by the production department.

Quality Assurance

To sell in Europe, Electrimex needed to achieve the ISO 9000 standards. There would be visits by inspection teams in the near future to evaluate the plant. The quality assurance manager, Raul Nazario, believed there was a critical need for training courses for supervisors in the area of statistical process control. Raul doubted that inspectors or workers were capable of understanding more than the detailed procedures of their own jobs since they lacked formal education. The department relied on on-the-job training and a library of English-language references on statistical process control.

At the present time, people from quality assurance sampled and tested throughout the plant and relied on the production department for some of the data on rejects. Meanwhile, pressure from the marketplace was growing; Electrimex needed to reduce customer complaints since only three mistakes were allowed by some key accounts. There had been major problems with different customer bar code systems causing confusion during the packaging process. Managers complained the workers were insensitive to the importance of these mistakes, and there was no direct consequence for individual errors. After taking many steps to ensure success and following the credo of positive enforcement, Electrimex became the plant with the least errors in the company.

Raul was a first-time manager with a background in industrial engineering, and Geraldo thought he needed both technical training and development as a manager. Raul described himself as "a volcano" with a quiet exterior but capable of an explosion.

Engineering

David Mutt, engineering manager, had just lost four of the eight engineers in his department. Like many young Mexicans, the engineers left to become entrepreneurs; one of them claimed he was making three times as much money selling clothing at the local swap meet. Since they had little work experience and the pay scale was low, these people believed they had nothing to lose. David was able to fill two of the positions by internal transfers from other departments, and he was looking for other candidates by networking with his friends at other maquiladoras and placing an advertisement in the local newspaper. However, he had just learned his packaging manager was pregnant and planning to leave the company.

David believed someone should be assigned primary responsibility for ISO 9000 certification. Given the complexity and high volume of production at Electrimex, the documentation required was overwhelming because every piece produced needed to be tested or inspected. Language differences further complicated the situation, since much of the existing documentation was in English. For example, the training course in methods time measurement, which was used to set production standards, had never been translated into Spanish. Meanwhile, there were plans to bring new products and new production lines to Electrimex, and a new computer-aided design and manufacturing system was to be brought on-line in two months.

Maintenance

The maintenance manager, Ramon Villareal, was strong technically, but he came up from a supervisor position and appeared to Geraldo to be struggling as a manager. His parents were tenant farmers in the interior of Mexico, and his intellectual development was remarkable considering his upbringing in rural poverty. However, Geraldo was concerned about a lack of delegation in this department, combined with a lack of clear orders. Ramon was prone to get angry at subordinates in front of their peers, which was very bad in the Mexican culture.

Geraldo wanted Ramon to pay more attention to the cause of machine failures so problems could be solved, instead of concentrating so heavily on a maintenance policy of "fix it quick." Preventive maintenance was rare, and there was little documentation of machine history. Many people in this department did not identify with Electrimex's objectives, especially at the lowest level. Maintenance department workers were more interested in the size of their paycheck than in improving maintenance practices, reducing machine downtime, or pride of workmanship. There had been a lot of resentment since Ramon cut overtime.

Accounting

This department and its manager, Humberto Felix, had the confidence of everyone and a reputation for making few errors. However, Humberto was somewhat inflexible, in Geraldo's opinion, and his department could have been more involved in supporting operational decision making by providing biweekly budgets for planning and control. There had never been an internal audit of production, inventory, or human resources. There was no common standard for payroll and other accounting systems throughout the organization in the United States and Mexico. In Tijuana, six people worked full time in the office to manually maintain records and process payroll.

No one at either Electrimex or the U.S. corporate office had any detailed knowledge of rapidly changing Mexican tax laws.

Industrial Relations/Administration

Anacleto Valdez was the manager in charge of industrial relations and administration. This department allocated most of its resources to the classic functions of a traditional personnel department: compensation administration, entry and exit of workers, and social activities for employees outside the workplace. There were classes in beauty, basketball, English, computers, and primary education, in addition to soldering and bobbin winding. Anacleto and his seven subordinates provided data for the accounting department on vacation time and other payroll inputs. They organized social events like the all-important Christmas party and published a monthly newsletter. Anacleto's second-in-command spent his time visiting different parts of the plant to gauge morale.

Electrimex was located near the outskirts of the rambling and rapidly growing city of Tijuana. To recruit new workers, technicians, and managers, the industrial relations department usually placed an advertisement in the local newspaper. Candidates responding to these ads were asked to complete application forms and sent home pending a decision by Electrimex to schedule an interview by someone from the industrial relations department and perhaps a manager or supervisor from the department where they would be working. New employee orientation consisted of reviewing booklets titled, "The Employee's Manual" and "The Internal Work Rules" of Electrimex.

RELATIONS WITH THE PARENT CORPORATION

In addition to the vertical reporting relationships through the general manager to the department managers in the United States, there were other "dotted line" reporting relationships. The Electrimex materials manager reported to a materials manager in the United States, and there were similar upward report-ing lines from the quality assurance manager, accounting manager, and the other department managers in Tijuana. They were often accountable to corpo-rate vice presidents of manufacturing or finance, as well.

The Mexican managers were concerned about and affected by the low morale up north as U.S. plants were downsized and production transferred to Electrimex. They often received incomplete training and instructions from their U.S. counterparts, yet were delegated little latitude to operate on their own—the common feeling among the Mexican managers was, "They don't think we have the capacity and they don't want to delegate." There were also instances of suspected sabotage by U.S. employees who resented the shift of production to Mexico.

The weekly meals the general manager had with small groups of production workers were usually eventful. Geraldo Ortiz enjoyed asking line workers for their concerns and suggestions and then dramatically calling his managers and office workers into the room and demanding they immediately resolve these issues.

Geraldo also enjoyed dining with his eight managers, and he convened a weekly general information meeting on Wednesday mornings. He used the weekly meeting to keep his managers informed of what was happening throughout the company and to coach his department managers, who generally seemed prepared for their individual reports. There was humor and consider-able explanation of U.S. parent company actions and vendor relationships. There seemed to be a clear understanding of Electrimex's objectives of rapid growth and vertical integration. However, the meeting was generally two hours long, and there was no shared written agenda, no visual aids, many inter-ruptions from outside, and much defensiveness. It was not clear that the accounting and industrial relations managers needed to attend, and many of the details discussed were irrelevant to more than one or two departments.

Facilities were cramped and split into two different buildings, and there were stored materials around production lines, a variety of different work-tables, not enough bathrooms, a cafeteria that was a constant source of com-plaints, and no child-care center. Management was convinced that day care for children was not a viable option. Parking was cramped, and much time was wasted looking for people to move cars blocking someone from leaving. How-ever, a new warehouse was in the final phase of construction.

GERALDO ORTIZ'S BUSINESS PHILOSOPHY

Geraldo Ortiz strongly believed "the ultimate management book" was a famous book of letters by an ancient Roman, Marcus Tullius Cicero, born January 3, 106 B.C. In *De Officiis*, Cicero instructed his son in the ways of the world as follows:

> Whatever is profitable must also be honest, and whatever is honest must also be profitable. The contrary opinion is the greatest source of all wickedness . . . .
> To separate profit from honesty is to pervert the first principle of nature.

Geraldo wanted a cohesive group of managers and supervisors who were (1) capable of accepting individual and collective responsibility for future planned expansions, (2) able to cope with internal stresses and to work out their daily problems in a "win-win" ambiance, (3) willing to assume a proactive attitude when faced with a dilemma, and (4) committed to meeting mutually agreed-on deadlines and schedules. He reflected on how hard this was going to be to achieve, given the turnover of managers and supervisors he had experienced during the first three years of operations. Could the lack of depth and experience in his management team be overcome with youth and enthusiasm? And what actions on his part were needed?

STRATEGY AND ETHICS MANAGEMENT

. . . .

RANDY HESS (A)*

Karen E. Moriarty, Stanford University
William C. Lazier, Stanford University
James C. Collins, Stanford University

In was January 1987. Randy Hess had joined 3R Corporation (3R) just four years ago at the age of 25. At the time, the prospect of joining the high-flying, young disk drive manufacturer had been tantalizing. Hess had been approached by a colleague at Storage Technology Corporation, where he had worked in the vendor quality assurance group. Through the colleague, he learned that 3R was searching for a division controller who would have responsibility for implementing a corporatewide business software system. Hess, who had a degree in finance and marketing from the University of Northern Colorado, was excited by the opportunity. 3R was extraordinarily well-positioned to capture the burgeoning growth in the microcomputer market. Hess jumped at the chance to be a part of the company's growing success.

By the time Hess joined 3R, the company had secured a major contract with IBM. As a direct result of the contract, the number of employees at 3R more than tripled from 344 to 1,457. The company was expanding its facilities in the United States and developing production facilities in Southeast Asia. In the aftermath of these dramatic events, 3R went public in November 1983. Hess, who had been given stock options on joining the company, congratulated himself on the timing and good fortune of his job decision.

3R CORPORATION: A BRIEF HISTORY

3R Corporation, a manufacturer of hard disk drives for the microcomputer market, was started by Terry Langston in his Lubbock, Texas, garage in 1979. With the tremendous proliferation of microcomputers in the business, education, and home-use markets, Langston recognized the growing need for hard disks as a primary storage medium. While there were other manufacturers in the market, Langston knew he could design a disk drive whose quality and reliability were superior to existing products. He also recognized the enormous potential demand that would soon be unleashed on the market; he believed this demand could not be satisfied by existing production. Langston's strategy was simple; he wanted to design and manufacture high-performance drives and then compete on the basis of performance features in selling to computer original equipment manufacturers (OEMs).

Langston started the company by developing a 10 megabyte (MB), 5$\frac{1}{4}$-inch drive. At the time, 10 MB was a huge amount of storage capacity for a personal computer (PC) disk drive. Sales were brisk as Langston's hunch about pent-up demand for disk drives proved to be correct. Sales to OEMs began to increase,

---

Income Statement and Balance Sheet Data for 3R Corporation, 1980–83   *(In thousands)*

	Fiscal Year Ended December 31,			
	1980[a]	**1981**	**1982**	**1983**
Income Statement				
Net sales	$ 0	$ 81	$ 5,043	$76,591
Cost of goods sold	0	383	5,757	62,571
Gross profit	$ 0	$ (302)	$ (714)	$14,020
Selling, general and administrative	10	255	1,738	5,191
Research and development	54	525	828	3,771
Total operating expenses	$ 64	$ 780	$ 2,566	$ 8,962
Income (loss) from operations	(64)	(1,082)	(3,280)	5,058
Interest income (expense)	0	42	33	(270)
Pretax income	(64)	(1,040)	(3,247)	4,788
Income taxes	0	0	0	1,971
Net income before extra. item	$(64)	$(1,040)	$(3,247)	$ 2,817
Extraordinary credit: tax loss carryforward	0	0	0	1,971
Net income	$(64)	$(1,040)	$(3,247)	$ 4,788

and in 1982, 3R increased facility space to 65,000 square feet. For the 1982 fiscal year, revenues were $5 million with net losses of $3.2 million.

In 1983, 3R's growth continued. By the time 3R won the IBM contract for the 10 MB drive, the company was riding high on the wave of success. To capitalize on its momentum and solidify its prospects for the future, 3R began development of a 20 MB product. Revenues for the year were $76.6 million and net income was $4.8 million (See Exhibit 1 for the historical financials.)

THE INDUSTRY

The Winchester or "hard" disk drive industry targeted at the microcomputer market was pioneered in the late 1970s by Alan Shugart, founder of Seagate Technology. A hard disk drive was essentially a box containing disks, or magnetic platters, onto which data could be written or read by movable heads. Hard disks offered a greater capacity, reliability and stability than did floppy disks. Shugart was among the first to recognize the significance of the new Winchester disks and to foresee the huge demand for the drives capable of operating the disks.

The industry's customers were organized in a hierarchical channel that operated much like a chronological pipeline (see Exhibit 2). At the beginning of the channel were the architects, the largest, most innovative, and powerful of the OEMs in the microcomputer industry. These included Apple Computer, IBM, and DEC. Architects wielded the most power over the disk drive manufacturers because they set de facto standards that signaled acceptance to the rest of the industry. They subjected new products to a rigorous qualification process during which a drive was repeatedly tested for its ability to meet performance, reliability, and length of life criteria. Often, qualification periods for

EXHIBIT 1   *(concluded)*

	1982	1983
Balance Sheet		
Assets		
Current assets		
Cash	$ 17	$ 967
Accounts receivable[b]	2,929	16,941
Inventories	3,181	29,133
Other current assets	60	137
Total current assets	6,187	47,178
Property and equipment, net	1,437	11,931
Other assets	8	10
Total assets	$7,632	$59,119
Liabilities and Owners' Equity		
Current liabilities		
Accounts payable	$3,573	$14,165
Notes payable	500	0
Accrued compensation	362	1,730
Other current liabilities	330	1,395
Total current liabilities	4,765	17,290
Convertible subordinated notes payable	1,800	0
Stockholders' equity		
Convertible Preferred, Series A[c]	108	0
Convertible Preferred, Series B[d]	977	0
Convertible Preferred, Series C[e]	4,299	0
Common stock	20	182
Paid-in capital	106	41,371
Notes receivable[f]	(92)	(161)
Retained earnings (deficit)	(4,351)	437
Total shareholders' equity	1,067	41,829
Total liabilities and owners' equity	$7,632	$59,119

[a] From inception on July 21, 1980.
[b] Net an allowance for doubtful accounts of $65 and $461, respectively.
[c] Each share of preferred converted into 1,800 shares of common at IPO.
[d] Each share of preferred converted into 300 shares of common at IPO.
[e] Each share of preferred converted into 109.09 shares of common at IPO.
[f] Owed to officers and secured by common stock.

new products could last as long as six months. Once a new product had been qualified by an architect OEM, however, acceptance by the rest of the market was virtually guaranteed. Additionally, because the qualification process was so lengthy, architects often became financial partners in the development of new products. The partnership helped defray the enormous research and development costs as well as ensure the manufacturer's commitment.

Next in the purchasing channel were the innovators, other OEM manufacturers that took existing computer products and modified or improved them. While not as critical to the acceptance of a new drive as the architects, innovators typically had extensive purchasing power. They also undertook rigorous qualification procedures of their own.

EXHIBIT 2   **Disk Drive Industry Customer Channel**

Architect OEMs	Both Architects and Innovators	Product/Systems Innovators	Innovators/ "Clone" Manufacturers	"Clone" Manufacturers	Aftermarket Suppliers
Apple	Apollo	AT&T	Altos	Convergent	Cal-Abco
Compaq	Hewlett Packard	ICL	AST	Data General	CBC
DEC	Novell	Multitech	Epson	ITT	Compuadd
IBM	Sun Microsystems	NCR	Everex	Kaypro	Microtech
	Tandem	Nixdorf	Mitsubishi	Leading Edge	Omicom
	3COM	Olivetti	Philips	PC Limited	Techdata
		Stellar	Prime	Televideo	Hamilton/Avnet
		Tandy	Siemens	TI	Arrow
		Tektronix	Wang	Unisys	Softsel
		Telex		Wyse	Microware
		Zenith		Xerox	Ingram Micro D

The last two segments of the sales channel were the "clone" manufacturers and the aftermarket suppliers. These customers were located at the back end of the channel and were less important to a product's success. Clone manufacturers typically copied the architecture and standards of the architects and innovators. They did little qualification of new products. The aftermarket consisted primarily of industrial distributors. They typically sold mature, end-of-life products in large volume.

To maintain a balance between new product introduction, with the associated R&D costs, and revenue generation, disk drive manufacturers tried to keep a percentage of sales flowing to all segments of the customer channel. However, to maintain a strong position in the industry, most manufacturers attempted to skew sales toward the architects, thus ensuring that new products remained in the pipeline to protect the long-term viability of the company.

THE ONSET OF A DOWNTURN

As 3R headed into the middle of 1984, the company began to experience problems. The market was becoming increasingly volatile as competition in the industry heated up. In the midst of this environment, the company was dealt a severe blow. Early in the third quarter, IBM, which had accounted for 61 percent of 3R's sales in 1983, cut its contract for the 10 MB drive. For 3R, the consequences were grave. Production that had reached 30,000 units per month at the end of 1983 fell below that amount for an entire *quarter* by the end of 1984. 3R no longer had any contracts of significance with industry architects.

Other problems began to appear. In mid-1983, 3R had introduced a new series of 10 MB half-height drives. Half-height drives contained a more compact arrangement of heads and platters than did the older drives, thus giving them significantly faster access times. At the same time, the company had also been pouring capital into the development of its first 10 MB 3½-inch product. This meant 3R was expending enormous financial resources on two concurrent 10 MB projects.

Unfortunately for 3R, the R&D efforts at the company were driven primarily by the engineers. As a result, the company was virtually blindsided by the introduction of a 20 MB half-height drive in mid-1984. Prices and unit sales of 10 MB drives deteriorated rapidly, as the market demand for the suddenly outdated technology plummeted. With only a 10 MB half-height product to offer its customers, 3R was soon facing a crisis.

The company began a frantic round of R&D activity in the search for new products and revenues. A 20 MB drive was rushed into production, but not before stiff competition had captured a significant part of the market. In addition, the engineers began working on the development of another series of drives. The new series would provide OEMs with an entire "family" of extraordinarily high-capacity drives. By creating more complex ways of combining disks and heads in a single box, the engineers had developed an 80 MB drive. Then 40 and 30 MB models evolved as "depopulated" versions (containing fewer platters) of the higher capacity model. The engineers and the R&D community hailed the development as the next major standard in the industry.

Technological excellence notwithstanding, 3R had one problem with the series: the marketing group could not find a customer for the product. None of the personal computer OEMs was at that time interested in an 80 MB drive. A glimmer of hope flickered when IBM expressed an interest in the 40 MB version. Even this hope died, however, when the drive, originally designed to hold 80 MB of capacity, failed to be cost competitive in a depopulated version. 3R lost the bid for the contract.

In addition to everything else, the company was facing continued price pressure. The second half of the 1984 was one of intense downward price pressure throughout the industry. Average unit prices declined 16 percent in 1984, down as much as 24 percent in the fourth quarter from the same period in 1983. 3R was also experiencing problems from a cost perspective. Extreme underutilization of the manufacturing capacity increased the cost of goods, while start-up costs for offshore production facilities in Singapore and Hong Kong also affected profitability. As a result, 3R lost $5.7 million for the 1984 fiscal year on revenues of $123.6 million.

Attempts to Get the Situation under Control

In an effort to stem the mounting losses, 3R rushed its remaining production offshore. By April 1985, 95 percent of 3R's production had been moved to its Far East operations. This resulted in the closing of some of the company's Lubbock facilities and reducing the number of employees to approximately 400. 3R was also forced to write off most of the 10 MB product it had continued to produce in 1984 despite the decline in demand.

In the middle of the turmoil, Terry Langston resigned in early 1985, recognizing he had reached the limits of both his ability and his interest in managing the company. He brought in Roger Glasser, another electrical engineer with management experience, to head the company. The downward slide continued, however, as 3R lost an additional $12.5 million in the first quarter of 1985.

3R's working capital situation rapidly approached a crisis point. The company was in violation of several covenants of its revolving bank line, precipitating extensive negotiations with the company's bank. George Pence, the CFO, knew the company was going broke at a rapid rate; in six months, it would be bankrupt. However, if the company could get a six-month financial bridge, Pence was convinced 3R could survive until the qualification process for several new products was completed. As the cash situation became critical, Pence initiated a three-month campaign to find a capital infusion for the company.

HARRISON & TAIN

By late April 1985, Pence was exhausted and frustrated by his unsuccessful search for capital. The major Wall Street investment banks had all refused to consider a new round of financing. Many of 3R's public shareholders had been hurt by the loss of the IBM contract; at the time, the company had been forced to halt trading as the stock price plummeted from $15 to $5 per share. As a result, Wall Street was certain investors would shy away from any subsequent offerings.

3R's luck changed, however, in the last week of April, when two offers appeared on Pence's desk. The first was a merger offer from Kodak, a major storage media manufacturer. Kodak had previously purchased Xidex, a floppy disk drive manufacturer, and was looking for a hard disk drive acquisition to complement its entry into the drive market. Unfortunately, Pence was certain 3R would be insolvent before the deal could be completed. Driven by the desperate cash situation, he was forced to accept the alternative offer, a $20 million convertible preferred stock private placement with Harrison & Tain. Harrison & Tain (H&T) was a well-known Los Angeles investment bank specializing in high technology. It also had a successful track record with troubled companies.

On May 3, 1985, less than one week after being approached by H&T, 3R signed a deal giving 133,331 shares of preferred stock at $145 per share to H&T. Each share was convertible into common stock at $1.45 per share. In conjunction with the offering, 3R also agreed to sell warrants, at $.01 per warrant, to purchase 1,455,972 shares of common stock at $1.60 per share to the new chairman of the board and CEO of 3R Corporation, Richard Whitney.

INITIAL REACTION TO THE NEW REGIME

Randy Hess was excited about the fresh talent and a new perspective for the company. As were many people at 3R, he had been increasingly disillusioned with the previous management's inability to run the company profitably. In addition, Hess believed the company had always been managed by engineers who were more interested in designing technically sophisticated products than in making what the customers wanted. In Hess's opinion:

> Whitney's operational people were like a breath of fresh air. They supported what all of us nontechnical people had been saying all along: if you can't pay for it and you can't sell it, don't build it.

The first wave of H&T managers arrived at 3R in late May 1985. The first order of business was a lengthy evaluative process involving numerous meetings with all levels of management. Throughout the process, the new management examined 3R's organization, products, and customers. It was a massive attempt

EXHIBIT 3   **The Organization and Disciplines of 3R Corporation**

Whitney's Method of Operation
1. **Identify** problems and opportunities.
2. **Prioritize** to see which ones to work on.
3. **Complete definition** of problems and/or opportunities.
4. **Plan** the solution or solutions.
5. **Organize** to implement solution.
6. **Start implementation** of solution.
7. **Measure** progress.
8. **Evaluate, redirect, discontinue,** etc.

Whitney's Method of Control
Charter
Help management at all levels run their business.

Operating Principles
1. Help management at all levels figure out the information they need to run their business.
2. Maintain an operations orientation when designing "systems" and solving problems.
3. Make sure the "systems" are keeping up with the changes in the business.
4. Make sure the interfaces between control and history are working.

Disciplines
1. Weekly business profit and loss statements.
2. Forecast and plan.

3. Five most important tasks.
4. Top 10 orders.
5. Reverse key account team (focuses on vendors, not customers).
6. Top 10 receivables.
7. Monthly headcount report.

Whitney's Method of Communication
Charter
Help management at all levels communicate and constantly work to ensure they are "the people's" communication tools.

Purpose
1. Provides better communication throughout the company.
2. Valuable tools to help run your business.
3. Measures your progress.

Disciplines
1. Weekly status reports
2. Quarterly dash meetings
3. "What I heard" memos
4. Monthly activity reports
5. Trip reports
6. Recruiting/priority list
7. Quarterly employee meetings

Excerpted from company memoranda.

to diagnose the company's problems and prevent it from careening headlong into bankruptcy.

Throughout June and July, initial steps were taken to implement controls on all aspects of the business. Efficiency and accountability were the new watchwords as employees were indoctrinated through a flood of materials into the new system (see Exhibit 3). The incoming management instituted a master scheduling process and required documentation such as purchase orders (POs) on all products scheduled for production. The marketing and customer service organizations were instructed to become more responsive to the customer service aspects of the business. Most importantly, however, there was no undue emphasis on immediate profitability. Rather, the new management focused on realistic projections that allowed for gradual, consistent improvement in 3R's financial position. As the company began moving forward, an air of excitement and renewal pervaded the company.

GETTING READY FOR THE DASH MEETING

As the early weeks of July flew by, the atmosphere at 3R began to change subtly to one of tension and anxiety. The source of this anxiety was the high-pressure preparation meetings that Whitney's managers held with all of the 3R management. The culmination of the early meetings was to be the first quarterly "dash" meeting in late July, which both Richard Whitney and Bill Harrison would attend. It would be Whitney's introduction to the employees and his first opportunity to review changes. According to Hess, even Whitney's "lieutenants" seemed nervous and "under the gun."

At the preliminary meetings in early July, each manager was told he was expected to present two sets of projections at the upcoming dash meeting: forecast and plan. Forecast was intended to be a feasible yet conservative target, while plan was a more optimistic set of projections. At these early meetings, managers were expected to present aggressive yet achievable projections. Though nervous about the process, Hess was comforted by the new strategic and operational discipline in the company. In addition, Hess knew that, although it would be a lot of work, the forecast and plan targets were definitely achievable.

Hess and his peers were much less comfortable, however, with the style and tactics Whitney was using to instill this new discipline. As the dash meeting grew closer, managers were being upbraided harshly in front of their peers if the quality or content of a meeting's presentation was judged deficient. Horror stories circulated about incensed H&T managers hurling presentation books that had been called "garbage" back in the face of the offending party. Hess related the story of one preliminary session, to which he was a witness, during which a manager was given the following "feedback" on his quarterly presentation: "If Whitney ever sees that namby-pamby MBA bullshit, your ass is going to be out on the street. Do you understand?"

Hess commented on the fundamental message he believed was being sent to the employees at 3R: "If you made forecast, you kept your job. If you made plan, you might make a little bonus money. If you didn't, you were out." Over time, the focus of the initial preparation became apparent. The financial projections were paramount. Explanations or rationalizations, it appeared, were superfluous.

THE JULY DASH MEETING

Ambiguity and anxiety about the process and the "sink or swim" mentality of the H&T management began to spread throughout 3R. On the one hand, most managers were relieved to have a renewed sense of focus instilled in the company. For many of 3R's employees, it was a matter of survival. Keeping their well-paying, stable jobs was foremost in everyone's minds. There was also the feeling, according to Hess, that "somehow, the 'old' situation just couldn't have gotten any worse." On the other hand, the pressure to perform was increasing noticeably. As the tension notched upward, internal struggles among the 3R managers began increasing. People began maneuvering for power and security in the new organization. Hess related the following story that occurred just before the July dash meeting:

> At this point, I was division controller for the $5\frac{1}{4}$-inch division. I was in Singapore at our facilities to install the financial accounting system that we had designed. I ran into some unexpected problems, but nothing major. I got a phone call one day out of nowhere from Ward Brently, the head of the division. "You're

fired, Hess," he said, with no explanation or elaboration. A couple of hours later, Brently called back. "I was just ****ing with your head, Hess. Just wanted you to know who was in control."

With tension at the breaking point in the midst of the maneuverings and power politics, the July dash meeting finally arrived. Whitney, Bill Harrison, and Gerald Gorman, the new president and chief operating officer, sat in front of the room at a long table. The rest of the company managers were also in the room, seated in a large, U-shaped audience in front of the table. In the center of the room was located the "hot" seat, where the individual currently presenting his plan sat. According to Hess, it was as if the new management was a tribunal sitting in judgment. And it soon became clear that the process was an inquisition.

One by one, the 3R managers were called to the center of the tension-filled room. Verbal tirades and humiliation were meted out to those who were judged to be lacking in preparation or the proper attitude. Individuals whose plans were inadequate or not aggressive enough were castigated bluntly in front of their peers. Word quickly circulated among the managers waiting outside the room as they prepared for their presentations. Whitney and the new managers only wanted to hear one thing; the new goal was abundantly clear. Whitney wanted short-term financial performance. The turnaround of the company, complete with highly visible improvements that could be easily demonstrated to the shareholders, was the immediate priority. There was no room for debate or argument, regardless of the rationale. As one engineer muttered on the way out of the meeting. "I understand now. It's form over substance."

Despite the inquisition-like atmosphere, Hess and many others thought two important directives had come out of the dash meeting. First, Whitney brought in several experienced marketing and operations managers to coordinate 3R's efforts and add manpower and organizational weight to these groups. Clearly, the new management believed a myopic emphasis on engineering and lack of attention to other areas had been responsible for many of 3R's previous problems. Indicative of the problem was the relative staffing of these departments: engineers outnumbered marketing and operations managers by the ratio of 10 to 1. The new management hoped to address this imbalance and give the company a stronger, more market-focused orientation.

Whitney and Gorman also decided to further divisionalize the company and split up all of the employees along product lines. The marketing, sales, and engineering groups, which had all previously been grouped by function, were assigned to the various product groups. The H&T rationale was a simple one: engineers and marketing people needed to be more in touch with the marketplace and thus the products. What better way to make people more responsive to market demands than to give them immediate responsibility for a product. To Whitney and the H&T managers, it was a clear-cut, well-proven strategy.

To Hess, the outcome of the charges was a bit more uncertain. With most of the "old" 3R people nervous and shaken up by the dash meeting process, people were eager to prove themselves and establish good reputations. However, Hess wondered about the ability of 3R's engineering-oriented culture to accept the new, more marketing-driven management team. In addition, he wasn't sure how the organization would react to the new divisionalization. Whether or not these new changes would be accepted and adopted effectively remained to be seen.

PROBLEMS FOLLOWING THE CHANGES

Hess's initial fears about the new changes at 3R proved to be well founded. The focus of the problem was the engineers. The engineers were the group hit hardest by both a loss of organizational power and the divisionalization. With the influx of new managers to augment the marketing and production functions, engineering's influence over the company's strategic course was greatly diminished. To make matters worse, the divisionalization had dispersed the engineers among different products and locations, a stark contrast to their previously elite environment. At the same time, money allocated for R&D expenditures was cut severely. For the first time, engineers found themselves competing against one another for dwindling resources. The combination of the changes had a dramatic effect on the engineers. They went from a creative and innovative community to a collection of fragmented, disenchanted groups.

As a result of engineering's new status, morale among the engineers plummeted. The new management did not understand the rarity of 3R's top engineers and their almost prima donna–like mentality. In at least one respect, the mishandling of the engineers would come back to haunt Whitney. One of the engineers, John Sire, went to Whitney to request more R&D money for a new project, a drive with "intelligent" interface that monitored and diagnosed its own problems. When Whitney refused and suggested Sire establish an independent start-up with Whitney as a major shareholder, the offended engineer resigned on the spot. John Sire left 3R and joined an effort to found Conners Peripherals, a company that would later become 3R's second largest competitor.

A TEXTBOOK TURNAROUND?

Despite the resistance among the engineers, Gorman and Whitney convinced most of them to remain with the company. They established a management by objectives (MBO) program and instituted large bonuses as an incentive to quell the dissent. Objections declined further as Whitney's connections with many of the industrial distributors in the aftermarket began generating new contracts for the company.

By the October 1985 dash meeting, 3R's prospects had brightened dramatically and both management and employees rebounded with new enthusiasm. This time, an air of excitement and cautious optimism pervaded the dash meeting. The company was once again gaining new customers and selling new products. Revenues for fiscal year 1985 were projected to be $114 million with net losses of $16.8 million. However, quarterly losses for 1985 had steadily decreased to the point where 3R actually expected to earn $2.5 million in net income on sales of $35.6 million in the fourth quarter. (See Exhibit 4 for 1984 and 1985 income statement and balance sheet.)

As the 1985 fiscal year ended, 3R reaped the results of H&T strategies undertaken earlier in the year. 3R maintained its emphasis on controls and discipline, cost-effective manufacturing processes, targeted marketing efforts and further divisionalization. Enhancements to older products extended their life and increased sales with relatively low R&D expenditures. In addition, the half-height 20MB drive, which was originally a stopgap product, had evolved into the major industry standard for its size and form factor. Whitney released a 10

EXHIBIT 4   Income Statement and Balance Sheet Data for 3R Corporation, 1984–85   (*In thousands*)

	Fiscal Year Ended December 31,	
	1984	1985
Income Statement		
Net sales	$123,606	$113,951
Cost of goods sold	110,577	111,445
Gross profit	$ 13,029	$ 2,506
Selling, general and administrative	9,798	12,217
Research and development	8,307	4,204
Total operating expenses	$ 18,105	$ 16,421
Income (loss) from operations	(5,076)	(13,915)
Other income	280	708
Interest income (expense)	(948)	(3,174)
Pretax income	(5,744)	(16,381)
Income taxes	0	392
Net income	$ (5,744)	$ (16,773)

Quarterly Information: 1985

Sales
First quarter	$ 23,868
Second quarter	25,961
Third quarter	28,520
Fourth quarter	35,602

Net income
First quarter	$(12,479)
Second quarter	(7,091)
Third quarter	329
Fourth quarter	2,468

percent profitability projection for the first quarter to industry analysts and the company seemed certain to achieve this target. 3R was beginning to look like a textbook turnaround in the Harrison & Tain portfolio.

THE PRESSURE TO PERFORM INCREASES

With the 10 percent profitability numbers already released to the financial community, managers were pushed very hard on their forecast and plan numbers at the January 1986 dash meeting. What the 3R managers found disconcerting and ominous, however, was that the push for sales was contrary to the reality they were encountering in the market. Once again, the drive market had begun to soften. Whitney, however, was not willing to accept a decline in 3R's sales. Ignoring the growing market weakness, Whitney was publicly committing the firm to aggressive financial projections by releasing them well in advance of the quarter's end.

EXHIBIT 4   *(concluded)*

	1984	1985
Balance Sheet		
Assets		
Current assets		
Cash	$ 1,025	$23,244
Accounts receivable*	19,290	16,041
Inventories	33,022	22,501
Other current assets	319	239
Total current assets	$53,656	$62,025
Property and equipment, net	20,942	19,588
Other assets	287	253
Total assets	$74,885	$81,866
Liabilities and Owners' Equity		
Current liabilities		
Accounts payable	$10,704	$12,228
Notes payable	875	1,742
Accrued compensation	2,418	1,746
Accrued warranty expense	508	2,083
Other current liabilities	1,667	3,274
Total current liabilities	$16,172	$21,073
Long-term debt	21,806	20,771
Stockholders' equity		
Convertible Preferred, Series E†	0	133
Common stock	187	193
Common stock warrants	0	15
Paid-in capital	42,394	62,021
Notes receivable‡	(367)	(260)
Retained earnings (deficit)	(5,307)	(22,080)
Total shareholders' equity	$36,907	$40,022
Total liabilities and owners' equity	$74,885	$81,866

*Net an allowance for doubtful accounts of $889 and $752, respectively.
†Each share converts into 100 shares of common at $1.45 per share.
‡Owed to officers and secured by common stock.

By the April dash meeting, Whitney began demanding even higher targets for the forecast and plan numbers to release to the analysts for the second quarter. In Hess's opinion, the new, more aggressive projections were now pushing the upper boundary of feasibility. Whereas people had previously been working harder and longer to achieve their targets, the new goals seemed unobtainable with *any* amount of effort.

Making sure the results were achieved, however, was a problem managers were stuck with. Implicit in the dash meeting atmosphere was the threat of what would happen if a manager couldn't make the new numbers. According to Hess:

> You weren't given the option to not make tight projections. Whitney's refrain would go something like this: "Boy, are you sure there's *nothing* that we can do to help you sell another 30,000 units? To help you be *successful*?" And you knew if you didn't, then somebody else would. So people would just go ahead and increase their numbers.

With overt pressure from the new management increasing almost daily, Hess began to perceive a precariousness in the general level of job security at 3R. Nonetheless, he was still confident in his own ability to succeed at his job. More importantly, however, Hess viewed the current status quo as necessary to the continued existence of the company. Once 3R had turned the financial corner, Hess was certain, the H&T management would ease their expectations and the company would gravitate toward stable, more realistic operating guidelines.

Instead, Whitney's management team became even more demanding. By the next dash meeting in early July 1986, the pressure on 3R's employees had increased tangibly. To deliver even greater financial progress to Whitney, top management began narrowing the previously existing gap between the forecast and the plan targets. In essence, the plan had *become* the forecast. This new reality left 3R's intimidated managers with no room for error.

Insecurity and stress among the employees skyrocketed. Hess and the other managers half-jokingly began to call their job security the "one-four body slam." As he explained the concept, Hess drew a square with four tiers or boxes, with each box designating relative power in the 3R organization. Hess and his colleagues were currently in the first box, with the highest salaries and influence in the company. But, as they had witnessed all too frequently, one misstep or failure to conform would get them "body slammed" down to the fourth level and sent to the organizational equivalent of Siberia.

As the work environment and internal morale deteriorated even further, Hess began noticing some unusual norms developing within the top management cabals of 3R. For example, management was exhibiting a somewhat cavalier attitude toward accounting. Accounting, according to Hess, was referred to disdainfully as the "history" department. Whitney and the new management considered it a relic of the past with very little relevance for current operations. On the other hand, the finance group, known as "control," was responsible for financial oversight of the company. As such, it was increasingly given broad discretionary power. If accounts didn't balance, for example, finance was soon telling the accountants to "find" the appropriate journal entry. As their power grew, the controllers were given carte blanche to make any "necessary" adjustments and to override the objections of the "bookkeepers."

With all of the uncertainty pervading most people's job security, Hess considered himself lucky to have a position in the finance group. Although he was disquieted by the ramifications of some of the accounting "adjustments," he pushed these feelings aside. For a change, it felt great to have the power to get things done and get the company on the right track. Hess was excited about his growing position of authority and influence in the company.

3R'S REACTION TO A WORSENING MARKET: THE MICRONET DEAL

Despite the efforts to drive the 3R managers to higher levels of performance, sales of many of 3R's established products, such as the half-height 20 MB drive, declined in the third quarter of 1986. Because of the slowdown, it was soon apparent to Hess and the rest of the 3R management that the company would not make the revenue plan. Unable to generate quick sales to the architect or innovator end of the distribution channel, the marketing people were pressured to dump product in the aftermarket and thereby make up the shortfall. With the recent dash meetings etched in everyone's mind, there was a frantic short-term focus on "making the books look good" for the investment community.

One distributor targeted in the new efforts was MicroNet Corporation (MicroNet). MicroNet already had a sufficient supply of 3R drives in stock given its anticipated level of sales. However, the CEO of the distributor was a very good friend of Richard Whitney. As in many previous instances, this connection came through for 3R. Over a round of golf with Whitney late in the third quarter, MicroNet's CEO agreed to place a relatively common order for $5 million of drives. What was unusual about the deal, though, was a clause in the contract that allowed MicroNet to return the drives to 3R if they could not be sold. In effect, the clause transformed the deal to a sale on a consignment basis only. This contingency notwithstanding, however, the sale was booked as revenue on the quarterly financial statements.

The fourth quarter of 1986 proved to be no better for 3R. Complicating matters was 3R's steadily worsening cash position. The general market conditions had softened even further, causing a backlog of inventory that had consumed cash at an alarming rate. Efforts to collect cash from customers, delinquent or not, were intensified toward the end of the quarter.

While working on these collections efforts, the finance department noticed MicroNet had still not paid its $5 million bill, now well past 90 days due. An unknowing finance manager sent a collection agent out to visit the distributor. To his surprise, the collection agent was shown the unusual clause in the purchase order.

The same collection agent was also sent out to visit the OEM customers in an attempt to collect early on certain accounts. What the agent found astonished him; not only was he unable to collect early on the accounts, but he also discovered some very unusual deals with the OEMs as well. For example, certain customers had contracts giving them as many as *60 days* until payment was due. After talking with the OEMs, the collection agent realized the special deals had been the salespeople's way of wringing otherwise impossible sales from the customers. The salespeople's goals were clear. Out of fear for their jobs, they were desperate to hit their revenue targets, and they were beginning to go to extraordinary lengths to do so.

Faced with the impossible task of collecting on these unusual deals, the collection agent returned to 3R empty-handed. Skeptical and unwilling to hear the collection agent's explanation, the CFO fired the agent. Angry at what he considered to be an unfair dismissal, the agent decided to exact his revenge and went to 3R's auditors with the story of the MicroNet deal.

In January 1987, the scheduled 1986 fiscal year audit arrived. Somewhat unusually, 3R's auditors immediately requested the MicroNet files. The auditors, a major firm, examined the transaction and revealed the consignment clause in the contract. Citing the open-ended nature of the sale, the auditors balked at treating the contract as a sale and, by extension, questioned their ability to issue a clean opinion on the financial statements as a whole.

Hess, who was aware of the circumstances surrounding the collection agent's dismissal, immediately suspected what had happened. By this time, he had been promoted to corporate controller and, as such, was charged with handling the situation. Hess was in a difficult position. Once again, Whitney had already released 3R's performance for the quarter publicly. Management made it clear it expected Randy Hess to produce nothing short of a clean opinion—and quickly.

Feeling the enormous pressure and vulnerability of his position, Hess pondered his alternatives. Obviously, he could go to Whitney and the CFO with the explanation of the MicroNet contract. It would be easy enough to reverse the sale to MicroNet and satisfy the auditors. On the other hand, Hess knew the $5 million in sales was essential to 3R's achievement of its financial projections, projections that Whitney had once again released as fact to the investment community.

Hess contemplated Whitney's probable reaction to the reversal of the Micro-Net contract. Rather than face Whitney's rage and potential exile from the corporate offices, Hess considered the possibility of quitting his job and leaving the company. In Hess's opinion, the tension and anxiety created by the new management's expectations had made the current work environment fairly unpleasant. He certainly would not mind leaving the strain of constantly living up to tougher performance standards. On the other hand, Hess knew he would be giving up a lot of the "perks" that came with being the corporate controller of a large company. Finding another job with a similarly high salary would be difficult, particularly in Lubbock. Besides, Hess really liked the power and influence he had in the 3R organization.

Perhaps, Hess thought, there was another alternative. He reasoned that, since the drive in question was a relatively new product and 3R needed to build up inventory to establish the product's viability, the FASB 48 revenue recognition rule might not directly apply. If he could persuade the auditors that the amounts inventoried would be reasonable and not indefinitely open-ended, Hess believed they might accept inventory as revenue under his interpretation of the surrounding circumstances. Hess thought he could make a convincing argument for the reasonableness for the $5 million deal given the expected run rate for the product. (See Exhibit 5 for FASB Statement 48.)

With this idea firmly in mind, Hess considered the possibility of visiting the auditors to try to convince them to accept his interpretation of the situation. 3R was a very significant account for the auditors' local office, and Hess was confident they would go to great lengths to retain 3R as a client. Furthermore, if the auditors agreed with his interpretation, he could feel comfortable that 3R was within the bounds of probity by FASB standards.

Whatever he decided, Hess knew he had to act immediately.

EXHIBIT 5   **Federal Accounting Standards Board Revenue Recognition Rule**

REVENUE RECOGNITION   **SECTION R75**

Sources: ARB 43, Chapter 1A; APB Opinion 10; FASB Statement 48

Summary

Profit ordinarily shall be recognized at the time a sale in the ordinary course of business is effected. Accordingly, revenues ordinarily shall be recognized at the time a transaction is completed, with appropriate provision for uncollectible accounts. The installment method of recognizing revenue is not acceptable unless collection of the sale price is not reasonably assured.

Revenue from sales transactions in which the buyer has a right to return the product shall be recognized at time of sale only if specified conditions are met. If those conditions are not met, revenue recognition is postponed; if they are met, sales revenue and cost of sales shall be reported in the income statement and shall be reduced to reflect estimated returns. Expected costs or losses relating to sales returns also shall be accrued.

Profit and Revenue Recognition

.101 Profit is realized when a sale in the ordinary course of business is effected, unless the circumstances are such that the collection of the sale price is not reasonably assured. [ARB43, ch1A, ¶1] [Accordingly,] revenues shall ordinarily be [recognized] at the time a transaction is completed, with appropriate provision for uncollectible accounts. [APB ¶12] An exception to the general [principle] may be made with respect to inventories in industries, such as [the] packing-house industry, in which, owing to the impossibility of determining costs, it is a trade custom to [account for] inventories at net selling prices, which may exceed cost. [ARB43, ch1A, ¶1]

.102 Unrealized profit shall not be credited to income of the enterprise either directly or indirectly, by charging against such unrealized profits amounts that ordinarily would be charged against income. [ARB43, ch1A, ¶1]

R75.103   *General Standards*

Installment Method of Accounting

.103 The installment method of recognizing revenue is not acceptable unless the circumstances[1] are such that the collection of the sale price is not reasonably assured. [APB10, ¶12]

Other Guidance on Revenue Recognition

.104 [Refer to Sections Co4, "Contractor Accounting: Construction-Type Contracts" and Co5, "Contractor Accounting: Government Contracts," for principles regarding accounting for profits on contracts. In addition, refer to Sections Fr3, "Franchising: Accounting by Franchisors," and L20, "Lending Activities," for accounting principles on recognition of franchisor and loan fee revenue.]

Revenue Recognition When Right of Return Exists

Applicability and Scope

.105 Paragraphs .107 through .109 specify criteria for recognizing revenue on a sale in which a product may be returned, whether as a matter of contract or as a matter of existing practice, either by the

---

[1]There are exceptional cases in which receivables are collectible over an extended period and, because of the terms of the transactions or other conditions, there is no reasonable basis for estimating the degree of collectibility. When those circumstances exist, and as long as they exist, either the installment method or the cost-recovery method of accounting may be used. (Under the cost-recovery method, equal amounts of revenue and expense are recognized as collections are made until all costs have been recovered, postponing any recognition of profit until that time.) [APB10, ¶12, fn8]

EXHIBIT 5   *(continued)*

ultimate customer or by a party who resells the product to others. The product may be returned for a refund of the purchase price, for a credit applied to amounts owed or to be owed for other purchases, or in exchange for other products. The purchase price or credit may include amounts related to incidental services, such as installation. [FAS48, ¶3]

.106 Paragraphs .107 through .109 do not apply to [the following]:

a. Accounting for revenue in service industries if part or all of the service revenue may be returned under cancellation privileges granted to the buyer

b. Transactions involving real estate or leases

c. Sales transactions in which a customer may return defective goods, such as under warranty provisions [FAS48, ¶4]

Criteria for Recognizing Revenue When Right of Return Exists

.107 If an enterprise sells its product but gives the buyer the right to return the product, revenue from the sales transaction shall be recognized at time of sale only if *all* of the following conditions are met:

Revenue Recognition   75.109

a. The seller's price to the buyer is substantially fixed or determinable at the date of sale.

b. The buyer has paid the seller, or the buyer is obligated to pay the seller and the obligation is not contingent on resale of the product.[2]

c. The buyer's obligation to the seller would not be changed in the event of theft or physical destruction or damage of the product.

d. The buyer acquiring the product for resale has economic substance apart from that provided by the seller.[3]

e. The seller does not have significant obligations for future performance to directly bring about resale of the product by the buyer.

f. The amount of future returns[4] can be reasonably estimated (refer to paragraph .109).[5]

Sales revenues and cost of sales that are not recognized at time of sale because the foregoing conditions are not met shall be recognized either when the return privilege has substantially expired or if those conditions subsequently are met, whichever occurs first. [FAS48, ¶6]

.108 If sales revenue is recognized because the conditions of paragraph .107 are met, any costs or losses that may be expected in connection with any returns shall be accrued in accordance with Section C59, "Contingencies." Sales revenue and cost of sales reported in the income statement shall be reduced to reflect estimated returns. [FAS48, ¶7]

.109 The ability to make a reasonable estimate of the amount of future returns depends on many factors and circumstances that will vary from one case to the next. However, the following factors may impair the ability to make a reasonable estimate:

---

[2]This condition is met if the buyer pays the seller at time of sale or if the buyer does not pay at time of sale but is obligated to pay at a specified date or dates. If, however, the buyer does not pay at time of sale and the buyer's obligation to pay is contractually or implicitly excused until the buyer resells the product, then the condition is not met. [FAS48, ¶22]

[3]This condition relates primarily to buyers that exist "on paper," that is, buyers that have little or no physical facilities or employees. It prevents enterprises from recognizing sales revenue on transactions with parties that the sellers have established primarily for the purpose of recognizing such sales revenue. [FAS48, ¶6, fn2]

[4]Exchanges by ultimate customers of one item for another of the same kind, quality, and price (for example, one color or size for another) are not considered returns for purposes of this section. [FAS48, ¶6, fn3]

[5][Because] detailed record keeping for returns for each product line might be costly in some cases, reasonable aggregations and approximations of product returns [are permitted]. [FAS48, ¶20]

EXHIBIT 5   *(concluded)*

R75.109   *General Standards*

a. The susceptibility of the product to significant external factors, such as technological obsolescence or changes in demand

b. Relatively long periods in which a particular product may be returned

c. Absence of historical experience with similar products, or inability to apply such experience because of changing circumstances, for example, changes in the selling enterprise's marketing policies or relationships with its customers

d. Absence of a large volume of relatively homogeneous transactions

The existence of one or more of the above factors, in light of the significance of other factors, may not be sufficient to prevent making a reasonable estimate; likewise, other factors may preclude a reasonable estimate. [FAS48, ¶8]

CITIZENS FOR CLEAN AIR (B)

William O. Boulton, Auburn University

The *Atlanta Constitution's* front page carried a picture of Union Camp's Savannah kraft mill on October 30, 1990. Under the caption "Pulp, paper and pollution," the description read, "Union Camp: The plant on the Savannah River is Georgia's largest polluter, last year dumping 13.2 million pounds of toxic chemicals into the air and water." John Northup, a Savannah doctor and major force behind the Citizens for Clean Air (CCA), an environmentalist group, elaborated on the nature of Union Camp's emissions:

> Union Camp is No. 8 in the nation in the emissions of toxic pollutants. *USA Today* on April 26, 1990, in an article entitled "Most Emissions in U.S.A. The 25 Plants That Emitted the Most Air Pollutants in 1988" showed the statistics. Union Camp was the eighth largest air polluting plant in America. *USA Today* got this report from the National Resources Defense Council. The companies are required by Congress to submit reports each year on toxic and potentially harmful emissions. These are what you would call toxic and potentially harmful emissions. Union Camp is the eighth largest emitter of such emissions in America.
>
> According to the data from the Environmental Protection Division of the state of Georgia, after they complete the rebuild, the largest nonelectric utility SO_2 emitter in the state of Georgia will be Union Camp of Savannah.

CCA was concerned with the Georgia Department of Natural Resources' adoption of the weakest dioxin standards for water emissions in the nation. However, CCA's primary concern was for clean air, and it wanted Union Camp to add a $27 million scrubber to its mill to reduce the level of toxic SO_2 emission into the air. With the company's refusal, CCA's aggressive attacks on Union Camp were getting increased media attention. According to CCA's public relations specialist, Linda Martin:

> Actually we laid off Union Camp for about two years. We kind of had them up against a wall in 1987, and a local ordinance was before the Chatham County Commission. Then Union Camp announced that there was going to be a $375 million improvement to the plant and that $40 million was strictly for environmental reasons. We felt we had achieved our objective and that there was no point in beating a dead horse. What they didn't tell us is that they were putting in new plants which fell under the federal government's new regulations, so they had to meet current regulations. But it's OK that they took credit for being good guys when essentially they had to do it.
>
> They said they were going to clean up the smell. What they did not tell us was that, when they burned TRS (total reduced sulfur) emission, they were also going to increase sulfur dioxide emissions. That moves us from a nuisance type emission to a class one type emission, one of only seven EPA-regulated toxic emissions. So we have essentially traded up in the seriousness of our emissions. Union Camp argues that the emissions are within federal guidelines.

CITIZENS FOR CLEAN AIR

The Citizens for Clean Air had been established in 1982 by a small group of Savannah professionals that were fed up with Union Camp's "bad breath"—the rotten egg odor coming from its kraft paper mill. They had attempted to influence federal, state, and local government to do something to help the community improve its air quality. In 1987, they had nearly gotten a local ordinance passed that would have set higher standards for Union Camp, but it had been dropped with the announcement of Union Camp's expansion plants. More recently, the group had shifted its concern to the problem of increased SO_2 emissions that had been approved for Union Camp's new plant.

Before returning to Savannah in 1986 with her son, Linda Martin had worked with AT&T in public relations. She now consulted with local business. She described CCA:

> We have a board of directors. We are a nonprofit organization. We are very careful to keep that data up to date, and we are very careful not to go outside the boundaries set up for nonprofit organizations. We cannot really get involved in political elections or nonelections. The Citizens can do whatever they want to do as individuals.
>
> There are 8 or 10 people who are on our board who meet on a regular basis. Now we have meetings where we call other members to come, and it is a good meeting when we have 20 people there. We are capable of getting out public rallies of 150 to 175 people, and we have done that before and will do it again. Our support is growing this year, but that is essentially the thumbnail sketch of the organization.
>
> Like the Sierra Club, there is a small cadre of people who do the work, other people who go out and spend money, others who are willing to attend meetings, and others who just have their name on the membership list. When I get disappointed that more people will not get involved, I remember what Sam Adler told me, and that was that the Russian revolution came about with about 10 people. There was a tremendous change in the government caused by a small amount of people. I know that is the way that change happens.
>
> We do have high levels of frustration. All of us get burned out except for John Northup. Essentially, he works every day. We all have different reasons. I have my six-year-old son and I have made a commitment to his future in coming back here, and I do not want to move again, and I do not want my son to have cancer. I do not want to question myself 20 or 30 years from now as to whether my decision was part of the problem. I think people's motivations are real important in understanding an organization like this, because you are giving some of your weekend time and your evening time and your lunch hours to the issue.

Ogden Doremus, an environmental lawyer of 45 years, talked about his motives:

> I am involved in every kind of environmental problem all over the state. It does not matter whether it is sanitary waste or landfills. I must get three or four calls a day trying to employ me in environmental litigation and I can only do so much. If someone is being fair and is doing their very best under the conditions, then I am interested in dealing with them.
>
> There is no justification for a corporation or individual to deliberately increase the health risk of people that live in the community. That is the basis of the whole movement here. This is not a bunch of wild-eyed people. Everyone that is involved in trying to clean up the air in Savannah is highly responsible

and highly successful in business. They are looking at it from a purely moral standpoint, not from a standpoint of dollars and cents. There has to be a point when dollars and cents are no longer relevant. That is why we are somewhat aggressive in dealing with Union Camp.

John Ross, a local businessman and member of the Citizens for Clean Air in Savannah, was involved in local organizations and was always available to help. He had been actively involved with the American Cancer Society at the local and state level. He commented on CCA's core:

> John Northup is well versed in everything. Linda Martin can write like crazy. Dr. Dickerson and some of the others are very intelligent. I will get out and do the work. Joe Anne and Shelly Dawn in Brunswick analyzed what was going on between locations and air flows in Chatham County. We know the problem; we have documented it. What do we do with it? Absolutely nothing. Where do we go with it? Nowhere, until the state wants to do source summations and not ambient measurements.

SAVANNAH CHAMBER OF COMMERCE

On the question of air quality in Chatham County, two of the most vocal groups making their opinions known were the Savannah Area Chamber of Commerce and Citizens for Clean Air. After the chamber issued a five-page statement on March 14, 1990, spelling out its views on air quality issues, the Citizens for Clean Air released a 13-page reply April 10. Both the chamber's and Citizens for Clean Air's responses were based on state and federal regulatory documents and interviews with officials in Jacksonville, Florida, which had an air quality ordinance. Citizens for Clean Air also cited *Savannah Morning News* and *Evening Press* articles as sources. The questions had been raised before the Chatham County Commission in recent months. The positions of the two groups are summarized below:

> **Q:** Has Georgia given Union Camp a permit to put 29 million pounds of sulfur dioxide into the air?
> **A Chamber:** Yes. But, when taken out of context, this number is misleading. The state Department of Natural Resources' permit allows Union Camp 11 million pounds for existing coal-burning furnace emissions and 18 million pounds of sulfur dioxide from the burning of total reduced sulfur (TRS) to eliminate odor. This sulfur dioxide should be compared with the 390 million pounds emitted into the air from all sources in the Savannah area, including natural sulfur emissions from salt marshes. When mixed with the 26,000 billion pounds of air above Chatham County, the air that each of us breathes is around 0.002 percent sulfur from all sources.
> **A CCA:** Yes, but we don't see anything misleading about this. The permit allows 29 million pounds of sulfur dioxide to be emitted, an increase of 161 percent. Sulfur dioxide is one of seven emissions classified as "health-related" by the federal Environmental Protection Agency (EPA). It is possible that Union Camp will not emit sulfur dioxide up to the allowable limit of the permit. However, the chamber did not state that this is the case.
> **Q:** Should the state require Union Camp to install a scrubber to remove sulfur dioxide?

A Chamber: The state and federal governments refuse to force businesses to use this particular type of technology because the governments do not believe they know as much about how a particular business can handle its emissions as the business does. Jacksonville, Florida, under its local air quality regulations, has not required the Jefferson-Smurfit Pulp and Paper Mill to install a scrubber in its overhauled plant because the plant has met emissions standards through other means. Technology can change from month to month. For example, Georgia Tech is working on an electro-chemical system that would remove sulfur dioxide at one fifth the cost of a scrubber. The scientist developing the system says the main advantage is that his method is self-contained.

A CCA: As citizens, we want the latest available technology to be used that will result in the lowest possible emissions. Scrubbers are the existing state-of-the-art technology for reducing sulfur dioxide emissions.

According to Georgia Tech's engineer who patented the electrochemical system, the system is a few years away. Research and development of any new technology frequently involves unexpected delays, and there are no guarantees that implementation and testing will be successful.

When we purchase new technology, we are aware that better, perhaps less costly, products will be available over time. However, we make the purchase of the latest available technology because we need the benefits of that technology now. Union Camp has estimated a scrubber will cost $27 million; this would be a 7 percent increase in Union Camp's $375 million modernization. For this marginal increase in Union Camp's costs, 95 percent of the sulfur dioxide emissions could be avoided. If Union Camp identifies more advanced technology that can be implemented now, without increasing other hazardous pollutants, we will support their efforts.

One of the greatest concerns for the Savannah Chamber was the economic well-being of the community. The Savannah Chamber, which promoted both tourism and industry, downplayed the negative aspects of the paper mill in support of the jobs and revenue it produced. The odor from the mill was often referred to as "the smell of money." However, according to John Ross, not everyone could smell the odor:

> We are led by a gentleman who is the mayor of Savannah who does a fine job in many areas, but he personally told me that he has never smelled any odor in our area. I said, "You are kidding me, you have never smelled Union Camp?" He said, "What about Union Camp. If there is an odor, I have never smelled it." I think he needs to retire, because we have some young Turks who can smell the odor. We also have individuals who do not want anything else coming into Chatham County that has odors.

Q: How is manufacturing important to the local economy?

A Chamber: There are 138 manufacturing firms in Chatham County employing 16,256 people at a payroll of $452 million per year. Manufacturing's total economic impact is 38,000 jobs with $909 million in income. Manufacturers annually purchase $434 million in goods and services, mostly from small businesses. They support government with $18.5 million in ad valorem taxes. They donate $1.6 million to the arts and human services. The tourist industry depends upon the 25,000 rooms booked in local hotels and motels. The port benefits from the 3.5 million tons of goods exported every year. Manufacturing provides 39 percent of the county's employment and almost 50 percent of local income.

A CCA: Stricter air quality standards would primarily affect the two manufacturing companies that account for 94 percent of Chatham County's industrial air pollution. Union Camp Corp. employs about 3,250 people, or about 3 percent of the 106,300 work force in the Savannah metropolitan area. The latest figures released by the Georgia Department of Natural Resources indicate that Union Camp is responsible for 88 percent of Chatham County's pollution emissions. Stone Container Corp. accounts for 6 percent of air pollution emissions in Chatham County.

A recent economic study of the Savannah metro area indicates manufacturing lags behind services, retail, and construction in new jobs. Manufacturing accounted for only 10 percent of new jobs generated from 1984 to 1989. We acknowledge the importance of manufacturing industries to our economy, but future economic growth depends on the ability to attract a diverse group of industries.

Q: Isn't tourism our No. 1 industry and the wave of the future?

A Chamber: Tourism is very important to the local economy, but its impact is much less than manufacturing. Tourist businesses employ 8,700 people with a direct payroll of $56 million. Although the number of tourism jobs is 53 percent of manufacturing jobs, the tourism payroll is only 12 percent of the manufacturing payroll because wages are much lower than those in industry. If we want Chatham County to rely on tourism as the basic way we earn a living in the future we will have to be content with low salaries. In terms of total direct and indirect payroll, tourism, at $112 million, is our fourth highest wage earner after manufacturing ($909 million), the port ($237 million), and the military ($170 million).

A CCA: The wave of the future apparently will continue on its present trajectory—manufacturing is becoming a smaller percentage of the total work force. If our community is to avoid stagnation in the coming decades, we must attract diverse industries, including service industries.

Service industries account for two thirds of the U.S. gross national product. Low-paying personal service jobs are far outnumbered by positions in information processing, financial services, communications, engineering, and medical technology. Some analysts predict that about 90 percent of the American work force will be in service jobs by the year 2000.

This does not mean we should not attract manufacturers. Our geographic location and deep-water port provide competitive advantages to companies distributing products to global markets. However, the manufacturing work force will shrink as fewer people are required to manufacture goods. Companies will continue introducing computer and robotics technologies in order to survive global competition. Union Camp is a good example of this competitive environment. In its last annual report, Union Camp indicated that 10+ percent of its work force in the kraft paper and board operation has been reduced within the last 10 years while productivity has increased. The Savannah plant is identified as one of the company's four mill locations for paper and paperboard production. So our community's work force already is experiencing the adjustments required for a company's survival in international markets.

Earlier in 1990, the Savannah Chamber, at the behest of paper mills, asked the state to soften discharge limits designed to protect the lower 27 miles of the Savannah River. Tough new standards were aimed mainly at four paper mills and one chemical company that discharge tons of organic wastes each year into the Savannah or its tributaries. Paper mill spokesmen argued that the new standards would have put them at an economic disadvantage with mills in other states.

POLLUTION CONCERNS

The forest products industry is one of Georgia's largest, most important, and most powerful industries, generating $10 billion worth of economic activity each year. Georgia tied Louisiana with the most kraft mills—those producing the rotten egg odor. An examination of state and federal records concerning the pulp and paper industry showed that of Georgia's 10 biggest air polluters, 7 were pulp and paper plants, and that 14 Georgia mills had discharged 35.3 million pounds of toxins into the air over the past year. Air discharges included 21.7 million pounds of methanol (damages the nervous system), 2.3 million pounds of chloroform (damages the nervous system), 560,000 pounds of toluene and chlorine dioxide (causes birth defects), and another 11.5 million pounds of other toxins that adversely affected reproduction, liver, and eyes or caused nausea or headaches.

Pulp and paper mills consumed 134 million gallons of groundwater daily, and the water withdrawals caused saltwater encroachment to threaten drinking water supplies in Savannah and Brunswick. The mills dumped 332,750 pounds of material toxic to aquatic life in the state's waterways. Four paper mills along the Savannah River dumped more wastewater into that river each day than Atlanta's 2 million people dumped into the Chattahoochee River. Federal EPA officials said oxygen levels in the lower Savannah River were so low that only the hardiest fish could survive.

John Ross described the results of a recent poll, called Vision 20–20:

> They asked the questions on a community poll that was televised. They set up 11 locations for people to call in to and to fill in blanks about concerns in our community. Clean air and the environment was No. 2 on their list of approximately 26 items. People were concerned primarily about education and clean air and the environment.

Q: Can we expect air quality to improve in the future?

A Chamber: Yes. Present TRS emissions are responsible for much of the industrial odor in our air. These emissions will be reduced by 84 percent by 1991. All air toxins will be reduced by 74 percent by the same time. To take Union Camp as an example, all chemical emissions will be reduced by 7,560 tons—from 9,488 to 1,928—a reduction of 80 percent. TRS will be reduced by 82 percent. Sulfur dioxide will increase by 36 percent as a result of the process used to decrease the TRS, but the net gain for clean air is 1,000 tons less of sulfur of all kinds per year. New federal standards in the Clean Air Act will require reduction of sulfur dioxide emissions in Chatham County primarily by tightening requirements on Savannah

Electric and Power Co., whose generators are the major sulfur dioxide source in Chatham County.

A CCA: Yes, no, and maybe. Odor should decrease, but at least one health-damaging emission will increase. The chamber states that sulfur dioxide emissions will increase by 36 percent. Information obtained from the U.S. Environmental Protection Agency indicates that emissions could increase by 161 percent according to Union Camp's permit. Even if we use the example provided by the chamber, we see that TRS, considered an odorous "nuisance" emission, should be reduced, but sulfur dioxide, classified by EPA as one of seven "health-related" emissions, will increase. This example illustrates the frustration encountered over the past 15 years of working toward cleaner air in Chatham County. In good faith, citizens accepted Union Camp's assurances that it would greatly reduce TRS. Now, with the state and federal governments' blessing, an even more health-damaging emission is going to be increased in Chatham County.

In terms of air toxic emissions, it is unclear whether Congress will require industry to use the best available technology to curb releases of 192 toxic chemicals including carcinogens. If this legislation does not pass, any clean air gains as a result of Union Camp's modernization could be wiped out by new or expanded industries in Chatham County.

Much of the debate in Congress has centered on a reduction in sulfur dioxide emissions from power plants. Power plants account for about 90 percent of sulfur dioxide emissions, excluding auto emissions. Lobbying continues, but if the legislation is passed, we may have some reduction in sulfur dioxide emissions at Savannah Electric's two plants in Port Wentworth and Effingham County.

INDUSTRY SUPPORT

In Savannah, the Union Camp paper mill had enjoyed tax breaks and other incentives since it was built in 1935. Savannah and Chatham County provided nearly $400,000 in incentives—as much as the city's total tax revenue for 1936—to encourage Union Camp's move to the area. Union Camp came in the middle of the Depression and, as far as Savannah was concerned, they saved it from bankruptcy.

In 1970, consumer advocate Ralph Nader sent a team of lawyers and students in law, medicine, and other fields to Georgia to review public records and interview officials and citizens to compare the concessions accorded local paper mills with other Savannah industries. The report titled, "The Water Lords," portrayed the industry as one whose pollution was "destroying the property and health of innocent neighbors" with little fear of retribution. Union Camp was singled out for special criticism for its "grim pursuit of profits" that had taken away the city's groundwater, polluted the river, and fouled the city's air. According to Nader's study, by 1970, Union Camp's local tax breaks were "shortchanging" Chatham County by $3 million to $4 million a year. At that time, Chatham's annual budget was $11 million. Today, "little has changed," said Ogden Doremus, a Metter, Georgia, lawyer who had advised the Nader group and was a member of the Citizens for Clean Air. Ogden Doremus expressed his opinion:

Without Union Camp, the port would have survived and the town would have been a lot better off. John Bouhan, the political boss here, represented Union Camp through his firm—a pretty powerful firm as far as Savannah went. He established a thing called the Savannah District Authority down on the river. It is an industrial zone in which the occupants pay taxes of only 5 mills, while the other people pay the rate of 45 mills. They changed the name of it to the Savannah Port Authority. In 1965, I was unable to get District Authority abolished. I got a bill through the legislature that abolished everybody that was on the District Authority, changed it from 10 to 20 men, and classified their function. It took them about two or three years to pack it.

They have their own fire department and police department, and they own everything. The education, police, fire, and all the services are given by the city while they pay low taxes in their little industrial zone. They did not even allow people to come in there to inspect their wells. They got a permit to drill a well, and we did not know if they were drilling a 4-inch well or a 40-inch well. All you knew was that the water level was dropping and the piezometric pressure was going to hell.

Linda Martin commented on CCA's growing attacks on Union Camp:

People are getting angry about the situation. They feel that Union Camp bought this town 50 years ago. The very boundaries of this town were rethought for the company. They bought it, they bought the air, they bought the water, they bought people, and who are we to now cause them problems. There is a lot of personal anger and resentment.

There are also water problems. I believe 40 million gallons of water a day are drawn from our fresh water aquifer by Union Camp. In the summer, when we need extra water for drinking, it comes out of the Savannah River, which has a known dioxin level from the pulp and paper industry and from the Savannah River Nuclear Plant, which is farther upstream.

The Savannah mill, which lost money in the early 1980s, launched a $375 million improvement project in 1988, but not before Union Camp hinted the company might close the plant and move its operations because of environmental opposition. The company was incensed by a 77-page citizens task force report in 1987 that accused state officials of delaying enforcement of emission controls at the plant. Union Camp's board of directors contended the grumbling was a sign that the community no longer wanted the plant. Local and state leaders, including Governor Joe Frank Harris and Georgia Trade Commissioner George Berry, quickly assured officials the plant was wanted, and local officials agreed to create a buffer area between company property and new development.

Q: Have other counties successfully regulated local air quality?
A Chamber: Jacksonville/Duval County is our nearest neighbor with local air quality regulations. It costs Jacksonville nearly $2.5 million per year to fund the section of its Bio-environmental Services Division that regulates local air quality. Of that budget, $500,000 is the cost of responding to citizen complaints. So $2 million and 40 city employees are devoted to monitoring, regulating, and enforcing air quality in Duval County. Jacksonville has not imposed standards stricter than federal and state requirements, but they are proud of their accomplishments in air quality. They have brought ambient air quality into compliance with federal standards in ozone and sulfur dioxide emissions. They do not regulate TRS emissions. They do not regulate TRS directly, but have imposed a nuisance ordinance to control industrial odors.

Like Chatham County, Duval County has two pulp paper mills. One, Seminole Kraft, has decided to shut down its power plant, chemical recovery, pulp mill and wood yard, drastically reducing its 500 jobs. The other mill, Jefferson-Smurfit, has rebuilt its plant, greatly reducing its TRS. Jefferson-Smurfit did not install a scrubber.

A CCA: More stringent regulations for sulfur dioxide provide good examples. The EPA ambient air standard for this emission is 0.14 parts per million as a 24-hour average. Jacksonville and Florida have set a more stringent standard of 0.10 parts per million. California has adopted a short-term standard for sulfur dioxide of 0.25 ppm for one hour.

The chamber's comments give the erroneous impression that Jacksonville/Duval County residents spend $2.5 million to regulate air quality. The Bio-environmental Services Division has many functions, and air quality is just one of them. Other responsibilities include water, water conservation, noise, nuisance abatement, hazardous materials, and mosquito control.

Florida counties choose if they want to perform EPA-mandated functions of monitoring, regulating, and enforcing air quality standards. Jacksonville/Duval has elected to perform these functions instead of Florida. Therefore, the county receives EPA monies to help fund its Bio-environmental Services Division.

The chamber creates the impression that 500 jobs are being endangered at Seminole Kraft because of Jacksonville's air quality standards. Seminole Kraft denies this claim. In March, a company representative said the company's work force reduction is the result of business decisions not related to air quality standards. Seminole Kraft is spending $130 million to install pollution control equipment, and parts of the plant are being shut down because recycled paper will be used to manufacture products. Jefferson-Smurfit also is modernizing its plant, installing pollution control equipment required by federal law.

Union Camp's name was well known in state circles. George Busby, the former governor, was on Union Camp's board of directors. State Senator Al Scott of Savannah was an employee—a production supervisor at the Union Camp mill. Ogden Doremus commented:

> If you dump your garbage in the cheapest possible way, which is straight up in the air, you obviously have to have the governor of Georgia in your hip pocket. Whenever we mentioned anything about Busby two weeks after he became a director of Union Camp, the people there acted morally outraged. Just for good measure, Governor Busby killed the participation of the state of Georgia in the Coastal Zone Management Act, so that we have no ability to require compliance in our coast zone with other federal laws. Obviously, the possible effects from the pollutants from Union Camp on the Coastal Zone were foremost in Mr. Busby's mind and Union Camp's mind while we were considering participating in the program.
>
> About the time that Busby was the governor, one of our organizations engaged in writing a monograph that is still available from the Georgia Conservancy. It is called Air Pollution in Savannah. We hired a young lady who is now an attorney to get affidavits from all the companies in Chatham County to find who is putting what into the air and all the statistical data, which is available in this monograph. Well, we found out that the big air polluter was Union Camp, which we knew, and that they were producing something like 50 percent of all

the toxic pollution, which we also knew. We anticipated, however, that the site implementation plan would start to correct this.

Q: Can Chatham County afford to follow Jacksonville down the path to a high technology and a service economy?
A Chamber: It is unrealistic to imagine that Chatham County can become a regional insurance and banking center on a par with Jacksonville, Atlanta, and Charlotte, North Carolina. High-technology businesses and service firms will not be attracted to Chatham County in large numbers until our work force is better educated and we have a university to support technology research. Other nonpolluting industries such as tourism and the arts are important to the Chatham County economy, but they cannot replace manufacturing in producing good jobs for the majority.
A CCA: We are already going down this path because this is the way the world economy is evolving. A recent economic study by the University of Georgia indicates the service industry in metro Savannah has been the primary source of new jobs over the past five years. Until our community leaders understand basic economic changes that are taking place, it seems we will have to follow cities like Jacksonville. Beginning in the early 1980s, Jacksonville decided to diversify its economy, and as a result it is creating jobs at a faster rate than Savannah (29 percent increase in jobs from 1980–88, versus a 19 percent increase in Savannah).

Educating the work force is recognized as a national problem. Savannah is not unique in its need to address this issue.

It is true that research universities attract high-tech industries. We are fortunate to have specialized research facilities in Georgia and the resources of institutions such as the University of Georgia and the Georgia Institute of Technology.

UNION CAMP, "BEING A GOOD NEIGHBOR"

Despite the fact that Union Camp reported dumping 13.2 million pounds of toxic chemicals into Savannah and Chatham County's air and water, company officials argued they have never violated environmental laws. They were operating within the guidelines established by state and federal laws. The company had spent $110 million since 1970 for environmental improvements. In addition, the plant's $375 million modernization program, beginning its operation in early 1991, would "bring the mill into full compliance with pending Georgia regulations governing pulp mill odor emissions." According to Gene Cartledge, chairman and chief executive officer of Union Camp: "These improvements will eliminate 95 percent of the emissions of the mill's sulfur odor and will ensure that the mill will be an economically viable contributor to the local economy well into the next century."

Union Camp's officials stated that $40 million of its latest $375 million improvement package was being spent for environmental protection. Union Camp spokesman Bill Binns said, "We are trying to be good neighbors, and have been good neighbors since 1935."

John Ross acknowledged Union Camp's community activities: "I have given 16 talks to civic organizations in the last year and a half. Union Camp employee Jerry Carter shows up for everything: openings of elementary schools, the

Rotary Club, the Kiwanis, homebuilders. No matter where I go, there he is. That has got to be expensive for them."

CONCERNED CITIZENS FOR CHATHAM INDUSTRY

The Savannah Chamber of Commerce was not the only group in support of Union Camp. A new organization, called Concerned Citizens for Chatham Industry, had been formed to also support Union Camp's position against the attacks of CCA. John Ross was surprised:

> It was founded on Monday morning and funded with some $12,000 to $18,000 by Friday afternoon in order to buy a full-page ad in the local newspaper. I can honestly tell you that I have never been able to collect money quite that fast in the form of donations from small businesses and in an economy such as ours. It was embarrassing to see a group spend $5,860 a day for a full-page ad saying, "The air is clean, there is no problem." Well, anytime you put 14,800 tons of undiluted toxins into the air, there is a problem.

CCA was also being attacked by the union for its attacks on Union Camp. Ross attempted to rationalize the strong union support

> I was quite shocked by the outcry from their union to our actions. Organized labor normally does not come out of the woodwork screaming. Finally I sat down with the union president in Chatham County and said, "Do you people feel very strongly about Union Camp? Do you believe they are good to you? Do you believe we are telling false stories? What is going on?" He said, "I don't believe a damn bit of it, but what I believe is page 37 of the union handbook," that says if Union Camp Corporation has to have a cutback in labor force which is caused by environmental impact and local ordinance, then they don't have to pay them. No wonder they were able to get the union so upset and so strong behind them. They have got them in a catch 22. But it is shocking that all the unions have the same clauses in their contracts.

ENVIRONMENTAL LEGISLATION

A decade ago, Georgia began responding to federal pressures to adopt the Clean Air Act regulations that would compel 11 paper mills to clean up noxious odors—the rotten egg smell that permeates cities along Georgia's coast. Ogden Doremus described his involvement:

> I was contacted in the 1970s, when the federal Clean Air Act was about to pass, by Richard Ayers, chairman of the Clean Air Coalition. He was with Natural Resources Defense Council (NRDC). Dick asked if I would make a comparison between the proposed federal act and the Georgia Clean Air Act. Union Camp and the other paper mills showed some interest, because at the time they were the big polluters; at least you could smell their pollution. Georgia's Clean Air Act turned out to be a "Dirty Air Act" in reality. It allowed any kind of pollution that you wanted.
>
> After comparing the acts, I went back to the NRDC and told Dick that the provisions of the federal Clean Air Act had to be put into Georgia's Clean Air Act. After some lobbying, we passed all the necessary provisions to conform the Georgia law to the federal law. All through that period, we were experiencing intense lobbying efforts in the Georgia General Assembly and in the governor's office against doing anything to improve the environment.

In 1980, the paper industry persuaded Georgia authorities to drop the enforcement timetable for new regulations that would force paper mills to control their odors. So after the state's Department of Natural Resources (DNR) adopted tough antipollution regulations, it reversed itself after industry representatives argued that the regulations threatened its economic and competitive well-being. Ogden Doremus was outraged:

> At the request of the pulp and paper industry, a meeting was held by Georgia's Department of Natural Resources in Savannah. So many people came that they had to take a wall out of the meeting room to accommodate them. The chief of DNR at the time, Bill Tanner, cut off the discussion and changed the agenda and said it would be discussed in Atlanta. People were livid. Leonard Ledbetter stood up and said because of federal law, there was no way the state of Georgia could do anything to control this pollution. We had the law in hand and knew this was a blatantly false statement coming from the state of Georgia. Nevertheless, they moved the meeting to Atlanta, withdrew the state implementation plan, and passed a ruling called the Ten State Trigger.
>
> The Ten State Trigger said Georgia would not do anything until 10 other states passed similar laws, otherwise Georgia would be noncompetitive in the pulp and paper industry. Of the 11 companies engaged in the production of pulp, only one was a Georgia company—the other 10 are run from out of state. Did they mean, "We will be noncompetitive unless you let us continue to pollute?" It is saying we must do something immoral in order to be competitive. At any rate, so went the state of Georgia.
>
> It took eight years before the Ten State Trigger was overturned, and we feel one of the things that overturned it was the Chatham County Air Quality Task Force. It was composed of individuals with no bias and no previous knowledge of this subject who said that the action of Union Camp was just immoral and ridiculous.

Q: How is air quality regulated now?

A Chamber: The federal EPA sets standards for allowable limits of various air emissions, including sulfur dioxide. The Environmental Protection Division (EPD) of the Georgia Department of Natural Resources regulates compliance in Georgia. Locally, the EPD maintains a full-time staff person in Chatham County. That person operates the local monitoring network of nine measuring sites and responds to citizens' air quality concerns. There are 99 facilities in Chatham County subject to air quality control rules. Unannounced air quality inspections of these facilities are made annually.

A CCA: It is misleading to state that the EPA sets limits for various air emissions, including sulfur dioxide. Ambient air standards set for sulfur dioxide allow 0.14 parts per million as a 24-hour average. What this averaging means is that much higher concentrations can occur, enough to impact health, without exceeding existing EPA ambient air standards.

There are no federal regulations for many of the chemicals defined as toxic by the EPA. However, the EPA must gather information about toxic chemicals being released into air, water, or land.

The U.S. Congress is debating revisions to the Clean Air Act. One proposal calls for industrial plants to use the best available technology to curb releases of 192 toxic chemicals, including carcinogens (cancer-causing agents). It is uncertain whether this proposal will become part of the Clean Air Act. If it is not passed, it may be decades before federal regulation is in place to assist in reducing toxic chemicals in Chatham County's air.

Q: Is the state doing a good job of protecting our air?

A Chamber: Under EPA air quality standards, Chatham County meets all air quality requirements. The compliance rates for the 27 major emissions sources in Chatham County are well below legal standards and below those of Atlanta and Jacksonville. Based on these findings, the state EPD is performing its duties of air protection in Chatham County as prescribed by law.

A CCA: Chatham County may be in compliance with federal regulations, but our standing as the most polluted county in the state and the 16th most polluted county in the country shows that our air is not being adequately protected. The county's total reduced sulfur (TRS) emissions is an example of how the state Department of Natural Resources chooses to protect the earnings of one industry instead of the interests of citizens.

Under provisions of the Georgia Clean Air Act of 1978, the department controls pollution which is injurious or unreasonably interferes with the enjoyment of life or use of property.

The Department of Natural Resources board adopted a regulation that required TRS controls by December 1984. After the Georgia Pulp and Paper Association requested a delay in the regulation's implementation, a 10-state triggering mechanism was adopted, allowing implementation to be delayed until the EPA adopted the plans of 10 states, or at least 25 percent of the kraft paper-producing mills in the nation.

In 1982, the EPA accepted Georgia's TRS plan except for the triggering mechanism. When the EPA approved the plans of seven states, environmental groups requested Georgia to implement its TRS regulations because the seven states exceeded 25 percent of the kraft mill industry. The Department of Natural Resources rejected those requests.

The state could have drastically reduced TRS emissions by December 1984. It chose not to do so. Now, TRS reductions are promised by 1991.

In 1988, the state ordered that TRS improvements under the Clean Air Act be enforced. It argued that it would no longer put the kraft mills in economic straits. The mills were ordered to reduce their odors by 80 to 90 percent by September 1992.

For Dr. John Northup, the longtime leader of CCA, the regulations were not strong enough:

> The government classifies TRS as only affecting your welfare. That is about as intelligent as saying, "If you are nauseated, vomiting, cannot eat breakfast, lunch or dinner, and are too weak to walk but you will recover, then you are not sick." That is the basis of their classification system.

For some asthma patients, odor control couldn't come soon enough: "When the wind blows from the direction of the Union Camp mill, the odor is terrible and the air is so heavy that I can hardly breathe," said Catherine Rotureau, 58, an asthma sufferer who lives in Thunderbolt, a few miles from the paper plant near Savannah. "I have to go in the house and cut on the air conditioner to get a breath of fresh air."

Regarding SO_2, Northup expressed his personal concerns:

> Some chemicals cause permanent and irreparable harm. Sulfur dioxide is one of them. When you take H_2S and incinerate it, it burns with oxygen and turns into SO_2, sulfur dioxide. Sulfur dioxide is what we are going to have more of after the

Union Camp modernization. Sulfur dioxide can turn into sulfurous and sulfuric acids when combined with a catalyst in the environment. These things can burn you. When your lungs are burned, the harm is permanent, like putting a flamethrower on my arm, and produces scars. If I move to the state of Washington, I take the scars with me and I do not recover, I don't get new skin back. The same thing is true with sulfur dioxide. When you get a lot of this stuff in you, the harm is permanent and irreparable.

CCA was arguing for even greater reduced SO_2 emissions from Union Camp's remodeled mill. Northup explained his position:

It is estimated 5 percent of the country may have asthma. Asthma is called a threshold disease. You get an inflammation in the airways and then you have asthma. Asthma can be a fatal disease, especially in children. You can produce an asthma attack 100 percent of the time with SO_2. If you get a little pollen plus a little dust plus a little bit humidity and then add a little bit of the SO_2 to it, bingo, you have an asthma attack. To treat asthma, you have to identify all of these risk factors. You put plastic sheets on the bed, get an air conditioner, you stay away from dust, try to block your antibodies with shots, and then you say, "Don't load up the atmosphere with all this crap." But industries are trying to figure out how much crap they can put in the atmosphere based on all these different kinds of studies, based on studies that so much SO_2 will not trigger an asthma attack all by itself. They are trying to decode how much sulfur dioxide we can load in the atmosphere before people suffer any permanent harm. There are studies where they have people in chambers and they are breathing sulfur dioxide and they are riding bicycles, and they are doing this and that. They are trying to measure how much of this stuff in the pure state you need to produce so much harm. That is what they are trying to do.

Q: Is sulfur dioxide dangerous to our health?

A Chamber: Yes, in high concentrations. There is no medical evidence that concentrations as low as those in Chatham County have any health effects. Sulfur dioxide in the air is measured in parts per million. The EPA has found annual, average sulfur dioxide concentrations of 0.04 ppm or more to be hazardous. The national standard is no more than 0.03 ppm. The average individual can smell sulfur dioxide at a concentration of 0.3 ppm (10 times higher than the national standard). Annual average sulfur dioxide concentrations in Chatham County, measured by EPD at the Farmers Market, are 0.00c (10 times less than the national standard).

A CCA: Industries' compliance with federal ambient air standards does not prevent much higher concentrations that impact citizens' health. Health hazards are masked by averaging sulfur dioxide levels across 24 hours.

A pulmonary research specialist testified recently before Congress that people with asthma and other lung diseases are most affected. Three to 5 percent of the American population suffers from asthma. Sulfur dioxide is a common pollutant, and even brief exposure can trigger attacks in asthmatics. National air quality standards for sulfur dioxide permit levels to greatly exceed those shown to cause attacks of bronchoconstriction in people with asthma.

Q: Does sulfur dioxide turn to sulfuric acid when mixed with water?

A Chamber: No. If it did, local industries could mix water with sulfur dioxide to make sulfuric acid to sell. There would be no need for a scrubber or other expensive chemical machinery. Sulfur dioxide must first be turned into sulfur trioxide before it will mix with water. When sulfuric acid is made in a lab or plant, this step requires the use of special catalysts.

A CCA: Yes. The process that results in the formation of acid rain generally begins with emissions into the atmosphere of sulfur dioxide and nitrogen oxide. These gasses, released by automobiles, certain industrial operations, and electric power plants that burn such fossil fuels as coal and oil, combine with water vapor in clouds to form sulfuric and nitric acids. The chamber may be referring to what happens in a laboratory. We are concerned about how sulfur dioxide reacts in our environment.

WHITE LUMBER COMPANY

Stewart C. Malone and Robert B. Brown, University of Virginia

What had started as a typically slow February day in the lumber business had turned into a moral dilemma. With 12 inches of snow covering the ground, construction (and lumber shipments) had ground to a halt and on the 26th of the month, the company was still $5,000 below break-even point. In the three years since he had been in the business, Bob Hopkins knew that a losing February was nothing unusual, but the country seemed to be headed for a recession, and as usual, housing starts were leading the way into the abyss.

Bob had gone to work for a commercial bank immediately after college, but he soon found the bureaucracy to be overwhelming and his career progress appeared to be written in stone. At the same time he was considering changing jobs, one of his customers, John White, offered him a job at White Lumber Company. The job was as a trader, a position that involved both buying and selling lumber. The compensation was incentive based, and there was no cap on how much a trader could earn. White Lumber, although small, was one of the bank's best accounts. John White was not only a director of the bank, but also one of the community's leading citizens.

It was a little after 8 A.M. when Bob had received a call from Stan Parrish, the lumber buyer at Quality Lumber. Quality was one of White Lumber's best retail dealer accounts, and Bob and Stan and established a good relationship.

"Bob, I need a price and availability on 600 pieces of 3 × 12 Douglas Fir-Rough-sawn-2 & Better grade—16 feet long," said Stan, after exchanging the usual pleasantries.

"No problem, Stan. We could have those ready for pickup tomorrow and the price would be $470 per thousand board feet."

"The price sounds good, Bob. I'll probably be getting back to you this afternoon with a firm order," Stan replied.

Bob poured a third cup of coffee and congratulated himself. Not bad, he thought, a two-truck order and a price that guaranteed full margin. It was only a half hour later that John, his partner, asked Bob if he had gotten any inquiries on a truck of 16-foot scaffold plank. As Bob said he hadn't, alarm bells began to go off in his brain. While Stan hadn't said anything about scaffold plank, the similarities between the inquiries seemed to be more than coincidence.

While almost all lumber undergoes some sort of grading, the grading rules on scaffold plank were unusually restrictive. Scaffold planks are the wooden planks suspended between metal supports, often many stories above the ground. When you see painters and window washers six stories in the air, they are generally standing on scaffold plank. The lumber had to be free of most of the natural defects found in ordinary construction lumber and had to have unusually high strength in flexing. Most people would not be able to tell certified scaffold plank from ordinary lumber, but it was covered by its own rules in the grading book, and if you were working 10 stories above the ground, you definitely wanted to have certified scaffold plank underneath you. White Lumber did not carry scaffold plank, but its rough 3 × 12s would certainly fool all but the expertly trained eye.

At lunch, Bob discussed his concerns about the inquiry with John.

"Look, Bob, I just don't see where we have a problem. Stan didn't specify scaffold plank, and you didn't quote him on scaffold plank," observed John. "We aren't even certain that the order is for the same material."

"I know all that, John," said Bob, "but we both know that four inquiries with the same tally is just too big a coincidence, and three of those inquiries were for Paragraph 171 scaffold plank. It seems reasonable to assume that Stan's quotation is for the same stuff."

"Well, it's obvious that our construction lumber is a good deal cheaper than the certified plank. If Stan is quoting based on our price for 2 & Better grade and the rest of his competition is quoting on scaffold plank, then he will certainly win the job," John said.

"Maybe I should call Stan back and get more information on the specifications on the job. It may turn out that this isn't a scaffold plank job, and all of these problems will just disappear."

The waitress slipped the check between the two lumbermen. "Well, that might not be such a great idea, hotshot. First, Stan may be a little ticked off if you were suggesting he might be doing something unethical. It could blow the relations between our companies. Second, suppose he does say that the material is going to be used for scaffolding. We would no longer be able to say we didn't know what it was going to be used for, and our best legal defense is out the window. I'd advise against calling him."

Bob thought about discussing the situation with John White, but White was out of town. Also, White prided himself on giving his traders a great deal of autonomy. Going to White too often for answers to questions was perceived as showing a lack of initiative and responsibility.

Against John's earlier warnings, Bob called Stan after lunch and discovered to his dismay that the material was going to be used as scaffold plank.

"Listen, Bob, I've been trying to sell this account for three months and this is the first inquiry that I've had a chance on. This is really important to me personally, and to my superior here at Quality. With this sale, we could land this account."

"But, Stan, we both know that our material doesn't meet the specs for scaffold plank."

"I know, I know," said Stan, "but I'm not selling it to the customer as scaffold plank. It's just regular construction lumber as far as we are both concerned. That's how I've sold it, and that's what will show on the invoices. We're completely protected. Now just between you and me, the foreman on the job kinda winked at me and told me it was going to be scaffolding, but they're interested in keeping their costs down too. Also, they need this lumber by Friday, and there just isn't any scaffold plank in the local market."

"It just doesn't seem right to me," replied Bob.

"Look, I don't particularly like it either. The actual specifications call for 2-inch thick material, but since it isn't actually scaffold plank, I'm going to order 3-inch planks. That is an extra inch of strength, and we both know that the load factors given in the engineering tables are too conservative to begin with. There's no chance that the material could fail in use. I happen to know that Haney Lumber is quoting a nonscaffold grade in a 2-inch material. If we don't grab this, someone else will and the material will be a lot worse than what we are going to supply."

When Bob continued to express hesitation, Stan said, "I won't hear about the status of the order until tomorrow, but we both know that your material will do this job OK—scaffold plank or not. The next year or two in this business are going to be lean for everyone, and our job—yours and mine—is putting lumber on job sites, not debating how many angels can dance on the head of a pin. Now if Quality can't count on you doing your job as a supplier, there are plenty of other wholesalers calling here very day who want our business. You better decide if you are going to be one of the survivors! I'll talk to you in the morning, Bob."

The next morning, Bob found a note at his desk telling him to see White ASAP. Bob entered White's oak-paneled office and described the conversation with Stan yesterday. White slid a company sales order across the desk, and Bob saw it was the order for the 3×12s to Quality Lumber. In the space for the salesman's name, Bob saw that White had filled in "Bob Hopkins." Struggling to control his anger, Bob said, "I don't want anything to do with this order. I thought White Lumber was an ethical company, and here we are doing the same thing that all the fly-by-nighters do."

John White looked at Bob and calmly puffed on his pipe. "The first thing you better do, Bob, is to calm down and put away your righteous superiority for a moment. You can't make or understand a good decision when you are lathered up as you are. You are beginning to sound like a religious nut. What makes you think that you have the monopoly on ethical behavior? You've been out of college for 4 or 5 years, while I've been making these decisions for 40 years. If you go into the industry or the community and compare your reputation with mine, you'll find out that you aren't even in the same league."

Bob knew White was right. He had, perhaps, overstated his case, and in doing so, sounded like a zealot. When he relaxed and felt as though he was once again capable of rational thought, he said, "We both know that this lumber is going to be used for a purpose for which it is probably not suitable. Granted, there is only a very small chance that it will fail, but I don't see how we can take that chance."

"Look, Bob, I've been in this business for a long time, and I've seen practices that would curl your hair. Undershipping (shipping 290 pieces when the order calls for 300), shipping material a grade below what was ordered, bribing building inspectors and receiving clerks, etc. We don't do those things at my company."

"Don't we have a responsibility to our customers, though?" asked Bob.

"Of course we do, Bob, but we aren't policemen either. Our job is to sell lumber that is up to specification. I can't and won't be responsible for how the lumber is used after it leaves our yard. Between the forest and the final user, lumber may pass through a dozen transactions before it reaches the ultimate user. If we were to assume responsibility for every one of those transactions, we would probably have time to sell about four boards a year. We have to assume, just like every other business, that our suppliers and customers are knowledgeable and will also act ethically—but whether they do or don't, it is not possible for us to be their keepers."

Bob interjected, "But we have reason to believe that this material will be used as scaffolding. I think we have an obligation to follow up on that information."

"Hold on, just a second, Bob. I told you once we are not the police. We don't even know who the final user is, so how are we going to follow up on this? If Stan is jerking us around, he certainly won't tell us. And even if we did know, what would we do? If we are going to do this consistently, that means we would have to ask every customer who the final end-user is. Most of our customers would interpret that as us trying to bypass them in the distribution channel. They won't tell us, and I can't blame them. If we carry your argument to its final conclusion, we'll have to start taking depositions on every invoice we sell.

"In the Quality Lumber instance, we are selling material to the customer as specified by the customer, Stan at Quality Lumber. The invoice will be marked, 'This material is not suitable for use as Scaffold Plank.' Although I'm not a lawyer, I believe that we have fulfilled our legal obligation. We have a signed purchase order and are supplying lumber that meets specifications. I know we have followed the practices that are customary in the industry. Finally, I believe that our material will be better than anything else that could conceivably go on the job. Right now, there is no 2-inch Dense 171 scaffold plank in this market, so it is not as though a better grade could be supplied in the time allotted. I would argue that we are ethically obligated to supply this lumber. If anyone is ethically at fault, it is probably the purchasing agent who specified a material that is not available."

When Bob still appeared to be unconvinced, John White asked him, "What about the other people here at the company? You're acting as though you are the only person who has a stake in this. It may be easy for you to turn this order down—you've got a college degree and a lot of career options. But I have to worry about all of the people at this company. Steve out there on the forklift never finished high school. He's worked here 30 years, and if he loses this job, he'll probably never find another one. Janet over in bookkeeping has a disabled husband. While I can't afford to pay her very much, our health insurance plan keeps their family together. With the bills her husband accumulates in a year, she could never get him on another group insurance plan if she lost this job."

"Bob, I'm not saying that we should do anything and then try to justify it, but business ethics in the real world is not the same thing you studied in the classroom. There it is easy to say, 'Oh, there is an ethical problem here. We better not do that.' In the classroom, you have nothing to lose by always taking the morally superior ground. Out here, companies close, people lose their jobs, lives can be destroyed. To always say 'No, we won't do that' is no better than having no ethics at all. Ethics involves making tough choices, weighing costs and benefits. There are no hard and fast answers in these cases. We just have to approach each situation individually."

As Bob left White's office, he was more confused than ever. When he first entered White's office, he had every intention of quitting in moral indignation, but White's arguments had made a lot of sense to him, and he both trusted and respected White. After all, John White had a great deal more experience than he did and was highly respected in both the community and the lumber industry. Yet, he was still uncomfortable with the decision. Was selling the lumber to Quality merely a necessary adjustment of his ivory tower ethics to the real world of business? Or was it the first fork in the road to a destination he didn't want to reach?

THE POSSUM CONNECTION, INC., AND ETHICAL EMPLOYMENT PRACTICES*

Margaret J. Naumes, University of New Hampshire

Drew Swensen, president of the Possum Connection, Inc., faced his two fellow officers. "In short, business has not been as good as we expected. The work is there, if we can just get the contracts. But as long as M 'n P, Ltd., continues to underbid us, we have a problem. They're not incorporated, so they don't worry about profits, only about paying themselves salaries. We also know that they're calling their workers 'subcontractors' so they don't have to pay benefits. That gives them a cost advantage—an illegal cost advantage! We could turn them in to the IRS. Should we do it or do you have a better option?"

BACKGROUND

The Possum Connection, Inc., was incorporated in March 1990 as a scenic construction company. Its board of directors was made up of its president, executive vice president, and vice president of finance. According to its mission statement: "The Possum Connection, Inc., designs and/or constructs sets and scenery for motion picture, television, commercial, and theme entertainment. It is striving to be the No. 1 company in the geographic areas it serves. To be No. 1, the Possum Connection, Inc., must supply the highest quality of work and services to its clients." Drew Swensen defined the key components as an equation:

$$\text{Quality} \times \text{Time} \times \text{Budget} = \text{Production value.}$$

He specified that quality meant the best possible value to the customers, which meant use of the highest quality of materials and personnel possible. It also required on time, or even before time, completion of projects.

An additional concern of the company's founders was for the quality of work life. In this area, the company's mission statement went on to say "The Possum Connection, Inc., should be a company that both management and employees want to work for. We intend to extend to all personnel a progressive program of benefits including health insurance, wage increases, and profit sharing. We feel that our employees are the key success factor to our growth."

The founders had considerable expertise in their fields. Drew Swensen, president, had an undergraduate degree in theater and an MBA. Since coming to Florida, he had served as a production assistant, construction coordinator for a feature-length film, crew chief, and lead carpenter for a scenic shop. Dan Hyde, executive vice president, had produced a number of commercials and served as location manager on two films, assistant director on two television

EXHIBIT 1   Sample Bid Estimate for Scenery Construction Jobs

Materials		Unit	Quantity Estimated	Unit Price Estimated	Total Estimated
Wood	1 × 6	foot	3,500	$ 0.50	$ 1,750.00
	1/8 bend birch	sheet	8	$ 20.00	$ 160.00
	3/4 B/C		65	$ 24.00	$ 1,560.00
	1/4 luan		110	$ 13.00	$ 1,430.00
	half round				$ 0.00
Plexi	1/4 × 3′ × 5′ milk		18	$ 4.00	$ 72.00
Hardware	hinges	each	30	$ 7.00	$ 210.00
	mounted hinges				$ 0.00
	mounted hinges				$ 0.00
	screws 3/4 × 10		200	$ 7.50	$ 1,500.00
	casters		48	$ 20.00	$ 960.00
	Home Depot stuff				$ 0.00
	hinges-double swing		6	$ 15.00	$ 90.00
	thomas stuff				$ 0.00
	thomas stuff again				$ 0.00
	bungy cord				$ 0.00
	springs		6	$ 9.00	$ 54.00
	bolts- 1/4 × 2″		200	$ 0.50	$ 100.00
	staples		1	$270.00	$ 270.00
	screws		10	$ 5.00	$ 50.00
	casters #2		96	$ 15.00	$ 1,440.00
	Scotty stuff				$ 0.00
Soft goods	velour	yard	6	$ 20.00	$ 120.00
Glue	yellow	gallon	2	$ 15.00	$ 30.00
	spray contact	can	12	$ 10.00	$ 120.00
Paint	primer	gallon	14	$ 35.00	$ 490.00
	base	gallon	12.5	$ 22.50	$ 281.25
	back	gallon	12.5	$ 15.00	$ 187.50
	glitter glaze				$ 0.00
	brushes	each	6	$ 8.00	$ 48.00
	rollers	each	11	$ 5.00	$ 55.00
	cellophane				$ 0.00
	white tape				$ 0.00
Steel sub contract					$ 0.00
Subtotal					$10,977.75

series and two films, and most recently production manager for two feature-length films. He had been a member of the Directors Guild of America since 1978. The vice president of finance, David S. "Sam" Francisco, had previously owned and operated two consulting companies specializing in product marketing and contracting. Additionally, he had extensive experience in data processing and accounting applications.

Initially, wood was the company's major raw material. "It is the medium with which we have the most expertise," according to Drew Swensen. Metal and sculpted foam products would be added as demand grew. These required larger capital investment, as well as extensive regulation by city, county, state, and federal bodies. The demand for these products was not very large and, in the officers' opinions, did not warrant emphasis for the first two years.

Contracts were based on a competitive bidding process. The price was arrived at individually for each job and included raw materials, labor, admin-

EXHIBIT 1   (*concluded*)

Labor		Hours Estimated	Cost Estimated	Total Estimated
Plate 30	construction	58	$15.00	$ 870.00
	supervisor	25	$22.50	$ 562.50
	prime	8	$15.00	$ 120.00
	base	8	$15.00	$ 120.00
	back	8	$15.00	$ 120.00
Plate 26	construction	63	$15.00	$ 945.00
	supervisor	35	$22.50	$ 787.50
	prime	4.5	$15.00	$ 67.50
	base	4.5	$15.00	$ 67.50
	back	5	$15.00	$ 75.00
	crafts	6	$15.00	$ 90.00
Plate 13	construction	24	$15.00	$ 360.00
	supervisor	20	$22.50	$ 450.00
	prime	6	$15.00	$ 90.00
	base	6	$15.00	$ 90.00
	back	6	$15.00	$ 90.00
Week ending 6-30-90				$ 0.00
Week ending 7-7-90				$ 0.00
Week ending 7-14-90				$ 0.00
Week ending 7-21-90				$ 0.00
		287	Subtotal	$4,905.00

Tools Needed for Job	Quantity Estimated	Cost Estimated	Total Estimated
Tools from F.E.M.S.			$0.00
Subtotal			$0.00

Equipment Rental	Days Estimated	Cost Estimated	Total Estimated
Truck	3	$125.00	$375.00
Subtotal			$375.00

Overhead		Hours Estimated	Cost Estimated	Total Estimated
Corp. Admin		310	$21.02	$ 6,516.20
Subtotal				$ 6,516.20
Grand subtotal				$22,773.95
Profit percentage	15.08%			$26,208.78

istrative overhead, and a profit percentage of all of the above. Examples of this process are shown in Exhibits 1 and 2. The Florida film industry, and therefore the scenic design and construction industry, was seasonal, with a one-month hiatus at Christmas and a summer vacation (when, as Swensen put it, "It's too damn hot to work"). The Possum Connection's work force fluctuated, depending on the number and size of projects in the shop. In May and June, the company had employed 25 people. In August, due to a lack of work, the payroll consisted of the three officers and the heads of technical operations and artistic operations.

EXHIBIT 2   **A Sample Proposal to Fabricate Submitted by the Possum Connection**

Client: Amusements, Inc.

Requestor: J.K. Thor

Project: Set for Amusement Park

The Possum Connection, Inc., is pleased to provide a quotation for the fabrication of the set for N.W. Amusement Park. This quotation, upon acceptance, will serve as a Contract of Services between the Possum Connection, Inc., and Amusements, Inc., for the services listed below.

Quotation

The total quotation is based upon a delivery to Amusements, Inc., of not later than 6:00 P.M., Thursday, 25 October, 1990. The breakdown for the bid is as follows:

Set for new attraction for N.W. Amusement Park	$ 9,813.83
Design/Painters Elevation	200.00
Total	$10,013.83

This quotation is based on 7 working days in our shop. If changes are made and/or a delay starting this project is encountered that the Possum Connection, Inc., is not liable for that affects the time needed to construct this project, quotation price will change if the delivery date remains the same. If the delivery date changes, then the price remains in effect.

Changes made to the specification listed at the time of the bid quotation cannot be guaranteed if they are made after 9:00 A.M. Friday, 7 September, 1990. The Possum Connection, Inc., cannot guarantee delivery as specified if changes in specifications are made after the date listed above, nor can delivery be guaranteed if payments are late in forthcoming.

SPECIFICATIONS OF QUOTATION

- Four (4) platforms will be constructed so as to be 6′ wide and 8′ deep from 2″ × 4″ stock with 5/8″ plywood lids.
- They will be covered with 1/4″ luan applied to simulate a hardwood floor.
- Each platform will have swivel, locking casters.
- The platforms will bolt together.
- Four (4) walls will be constructed from 1″ × 4″ #2 stock on edge covered with 1/4″ luan skin.

COMPETITION

The competition facing the Possum Connection, Inc., was separated into two groups that were not mutually exclusive: nationally recognized companies and central Florida production companies. In addition, the major studios operated their own in-house construction facilities.

Nationally recognized companies included: Adirondack Scenic from Glens Falls, New York, through its subsidiary, Adirondack Scenic South in Vero Beach; FM Productions from San Francisco; and Cinnibar from Los Angeles. All of these companies had national operations, but only Adirondack had been established in central Florida for some time. They all were full-spectrum scenic shops providing not only wooden scenery, but sculpted products and metal as well. FM Productions and Cinnibar were recent entrants, having opened shops in the second and third quarters of 1990, respectively. They also provided the full range of techniques and in addition offered construction of touring concert scenery.

All these companies had other profitable operations that could subsidize losses by their Florida operations. This financial base, combined with their

EXHIBIT 2   *(concluded)*

- One (1) window will be constructed in the wall that will have a 1/8″ acrylic windowpane.
- Total wall height from the floor will be 7′6″.
- Four (4) shelves will be constructed from 1″ × 6″ clear stock and have detailed brackets made from sculptured wood.
- Eight (8) jacks will be constructed for wall support.
- Chair rail and crown moulding are included in this quotation; baseboard moulding is not.
- A reliefed wainscot will be below the chair rail.
- All painting will be as drawn.
- Painters elevations are to be delivered to the Possum Connection, Inc., no later than 7 days from the acceptance of this bid. If they are not received, the design fee of $200.00 is immediately due.
- FLAME TREATMENT IS NOT INCLUDED IN THIS QUOTATION.
- Crating is not included.
- Shipping will be from the Possum Connection, Inc.'s, loading dock on 1 November, 1990.
- Shipping fees will be paid by the Client.
- A fee of $25.00 per week will be due for every week past 1 November, 1990, the set remains undelivered.

Payment Schedule

The amount due on acceptance of the bid will be $6,000.00
If the artwork is not supplied, then the amount of $200.00 is due seven (7) days from the acceptance of this bid. If artwork is supplied, this fee does not apply.
The remaining $3,813.83 will be due at the time of delivery.
All payments are due as specified. No materials will be ordered, nor will any delivery take place until the respective amounts above are paid.
The Possum Connection, Inc., shall not be held liable for any cost incurred and/or late delivery penalties, nor shall they be liable for any revenue lost because the above specified payments were not made at the times indicated.

Indemnification

Amusements, Inc., shall indemnify and hold harmless the Possum Connection, Inc., against any and all liability, loss, or damage the Possum Connection, Inc., may suffer as a result of claims, demands, costs, or judgments against it arising out of the construction, delivery, or use of the attraction set for N.W. Amusement Park.

national reputations and established clients, could pose a problem for the Possum Connection. "We can not bid competitively against them for large national contracts," stated Swensen. "We are not equipped to handle construction of projects costing in excess of $250,000. Instead, we feel we are in a position to subcontract scenic work from them, in our specialty—wood. In addition, their large physical plants create a large overhead that will prohibit them from bidding successfully on smaller contracts."

The second group of competitors included all other shops. This group ranged from Southern Scenic, a regional scenic and theatrical supply house, to local independent cabinetmakers who felt qualified to build scenery. This segment was characterized by the willingness to undercut price to get a project through the door. Because these were mostly "Mom and Pop" operations, undercutting could not continue for long.

Referring to the smaller local competitors, Swensen believed:

Our strength against this segment lies in two directions. First, we are film and television professionals. We speak the language of the business and have solid professional reputations. We know how to bid a project, similar to the national companies, and are not going to sacrifice quality. Quality is the unknown that the small operations are fighting to achieve. Because of our reputations, quality is not a limiting factor. If our price is slightly higher than theirs, we are more likely to be awarded a bid based on this.

The second factor is our limited financing. It will not allow us to undercut profitability for the sake of business. We are a lean operation. We cannot afford to cut profit to just above cost for any length of time. We feel that doing so not only is a bad business practice, since the market can get used to artificially lower prices, but also will hurt the quality of our product. If we are to provide the quality of product we want, we must use quality materials and labor, and these cost more. We could sacrifice on either or both, but we would ultimately hurt our solid reputation if we did.

It is our opinion these small operations will shake themselves out of the market because of either poor quality of product or lack of money to sustain operations. We have dedicated ourselves to putting together a management team of industry professionals who know how to run successful small businesses and who know the film and television industries. We feel this is another of our success factors.

Exhibits 3 and 4 show the Possum Connection's financial situation.

Both Walt Disney World and Universal Studios Florida had in-house construction facilities. In the past, these facilities had been responsible for all in-house designed projects. This was changing. At Disney, the marketing and promotion departments were no longer required to have their designs built by Disney's central shop; Disney's in-house facilities were frequently overloaded with work. Universal Studios was in the same position; it had a central shop, but only used it for maintenance on park facilities. The Universal shop was allowed to bid for projects that could be produced in its own soundstages, but this did not guarantee it would be awarded the contract.

In-house operations also typically had higher overhead. This is not to say the smaller independent operations did not take overhead into account, but the in-house shops had to cover not only their own costs, but also a share of general corporate overhead. On occasion, however, they would ignore overhead to submit the lowest possible bid.

INDUSTRY CHARACTERISTICS

Nationally, the scenic construction industry was characterized by unionization, independent contract labor, high material costs, and a mobile labor pool. Florida was a right-to-work state. Unions did not have the power to demand a closed-shop operation, as they did in either California or New York. As evidence that Florida had become a leading movie production site because of lower labor costs, unions in both California and New York had made major concessions to movie and film producers on wage and working condition issues. Unionization was notoriously heavy in scenic shops, however. Swensen thought the Possum Connection avoided having union representation in its shop by paying above-average wages and providing excellent working conditions: "We keep quality personnel in the area employed at a fair rate and are receiving quality products in return."

In part because of the higher cost of unionized labor, independent contract labor, rather than permanent employees, had become the industry norm.

EXHIBIT 3   **The Possum Connection's Profit (Loss) Statement, April–August**

	April	May	June	July	August	Year-to-Date
Income						
Sales	$ 8,041.32	$40,125.94	$61,136.97	$ 17,118.98	$ 0.00	$126,423.21
Rent from sublease	0.00	0.00	0.00	450.00	450.00	900.00
Total income	$ 8,041.32	$40,125.94	$61,136.97	$ 17,568.98	$ 450.00	$127,323.21
Operating expenses						
Project						
Wages	285.00	11,531.75	20,085.79	22,373.99	3,451.00	57,727.53
Materials	3,672.56	20,018.03	17,229.97	7,021.94	0.00	47,942.50
Rentals	103.29	1,965.20	1,095.82	468.96	169.60	3,802.87
SubContracts	0.00	650.00	4,005.21	0.00	0.00	4,655.21
Total projects	$ 4,060.85	$34,164.98	$42,416.79	$ 29,864.89	$ 3,620.60	$114,128.11
Shop						
Wages	0.00	0.00	206.00	485.50	0.00	692.50
Materials	1,352.89	212.25	35.00	0.00	0.00	1,600.14
Rentals	495.56	0.00	0.00	482.52	1,757.62	2,735.70
Misc.	170.97	327.16	1,769.38	453.57	134.68	2,855.76
Total shop	$ 2,019.42	$539.41	$ 2,010.38	$ 1,421.59	$ 1,892.30	$ 7,884.10
Rent	0.00	0.00	1,908.00	3,259.50	3,259.50	8,427.00
Utilities	0.00	156.94	257.47	349.65	505.75	1,269.81
Gross Profit	$ 1,961.05	$5,264.61	$14,544.33	$(17,327.65)	$ (8,828.15)	$ (4,385.81)
Administrative expenses						
Administrative salaries						
Corporation	2,100.00	4,770.00	4,537.50	4,663.50	6,709.50	22,780.50
Operations	1,000.00	(300.00)	(400.00)	(200.00)	0.00	100.00
Employee taxes	347.46	770.59	2,033.46	3,901.10	742.19	7,794.80
Office equipment leases	29.36	22.02	324.12	0.00	84.80	460.30
Dues & subscriptions	446.95	120.00	97.95	52.70	0.00	717.60
Office Supplies	614.88	336.17	338.73	251.64	0.00	1,541.42
Office expenses	121.97	519.97	585.81	395.72	141.17	1,764.64
Printing	716.48	93.33	182.32	0.00	0.00	992.13
Postage & freight	65.25	13.50	86.75	62.66	62.50	290.65
Telephone						
Office	0.00	451.92	483.85	734.47	349.77	2,020.01
Cellular	230.63	358.02	144.16	357.14	0.00	1,089.95
Legal & accounting	567.49	187.91	0.00	0.00	0.00	755.40
Licenses & fees	90.00	0.00	0.00	0.00	0.00	90.00
Insurance						
General	0.00	721.95	873.95	721.95	721.95	3,039.80
Medical	0.00	323.73	11.22	317.55	287.55	940.05
Advertisement	95.00	833.71	0.00	404.00	56.46	1,389.17
Travel & entertainment	1,132.52	351.74	217.41	571.51	59.46	2,332.64
Bank expenses	105.46	0.00	62.16	159.79	120.00	447.41
Misc. expenses	480.00	235.00	165.73	0.00	4.83	885.56
Marketing	0.00	366.19	350.81	421.70	468.52	1,607.22
Total administrative expenses	$ 8,143.45	$10,175.75	$10,095.93	$ 12,815.43	$ 9,808.70	$ 51,039.25
Net profit (loss)	$(6,182.40)	$(4,911.14)	$(4,448.40)	$(30,143.08)	$(18,636.85)	$(55,425.06)

This was still the case for location projects (those being produced outside the producers' home area). This practice had been severely curtailed, however, by changes in the Internal Revenue Service's tax codes. Classification of a worker as an independent contractor or as an employee depended on whether the company "has the right to control and direct the individual who performs

EXHIBIT 4   The Possum Connection's Balance Sheet as of August 31

Assets			
Cash			
General account	$ 6,674.46		
Interest account	506.82		
Petty cash	0.00	$7,181.28	
Accounts receivables	20.00	20.00	
Accrued insurance	980.00	980.00	
Furniture & fixtures			
Shop	480.00		
Office	2,950.27	3,430.27	
Leasehold improvement			
Labor	5,248.00		
Materials	5,154.19		
Subcontracts	4,950.65		
Equipment leases	1,219.96	16,572.80	
Deposits	5,920.00	5,920.00	
Total assets			$34,104.35
Liabilities and equity			
Accounts payable	0.00	0.00	
Accrued taxes			
Withholding taxes	702.00		
FICA	471.29	1,173.29	
Short-term notes payable			
Drew Swensen	252.58	252.58	
Long-term notes payable			
Investors	80,000.00		
Drew Swensen	9,568.73	89,568.73	
Total liabilities			90,994.70
Equity			
Retained earnings (loss)			(56,890.35)
Total liabilities and equity			$34,104.35

the services, not only as to the result to be accomplished by the work but also as to the details and means by which the result is accomplished."[1]

The guidelines for qualifying as independent contract labor had been stiffened in 1987. Two important questions, used to test whether someone qualifies, were: (1) Did the employer set the conditions of employment, in particular the starting, break, and quitting times and the precise nature of the task? (i.e., did the employer provide a supervisor) and (2) Did the employer provide the tools? A contractor had to be able to answer no to both questions. In addition, he or she had to have a federal tax ID number (not the same as a social security number), and pay his or her own income and employment (FICA) taxes.

Although use of independent contractors had been a recognized practice in the scenic construction industry, in 1989 the IRS began looking critically at the smaller firms in the industry. In general, contractor status was disallowed, unless the employer could prove justification. This typically meant the contrac-

---

[1]Reg. Sec. 31.3401(c)-(1)b.

tor had his or her own company that was hired by the employer and in turn employed the contractor and filed the necessary paperwork and taxes.

Using independent contract labor meant a shop did not have to pay hazard insurance, employer contributions to the state unemployment fund, or an employer portion of FICA. Employers, on the other hand, were required to cover all of these. Swensen estimated that this amounted to 21 percent of his payroll. Several shops in the Orlando area still continued to use independent contract labor, but they were being pressured by the government to change. This would push all the scenic shops onto a level playing field when it came to bidding labor on a job. The small scenic shops typically hired workers by the project, laying them off when the work was completed. Most of M 'n P, Ltd.'s work force was immediate family (the parents and three adult children). It collected the employee contributions to the benefit programs from the other workers it hired, but treated them as contractors for tax and bidding purposes.

The mobility of the work force was also changing. Florida technicians, in the past, had to travel to find work. With the increase in local production, experienced personnel were able to find adequate work in the state. Because of higher union labor costs in California and New York, productions were moving and the resident personnel were moving with them. Since Florida already had a qualified work force, these incoming technicians were having the same trouble finding work that Florida technicians had experienced in the past. The net effect was that Florida's qualified labor pool had grown, but at a greater rate than available jobs. This competition for jobs had kept labor rates down. As employers, the Possum Connection wanted the most qualified personnel at the lowest possible rates.

DECISION TIME

"OK," said Drew. "We estimate our costs as accurately as we can. We specify the quality of materials that we plan on using. If a customer feels that he can use something cheaper, we'll build it that way if we can. But even if we don't pay dividends, we still have our salaries to pay. And, more important, we have to pay wages and benefits for our crew. Like us, M 'n P, Ltd., just hires people when they need them, but they save on benefits by calling them independent contractors. But some of these guys have told us that M 'n P provides the tools, at least, and generally is supervising their work as well. With the money they save in benefits, they consistently underbid us. We don't have any firm contracts for September yet! We can't afford to stay in business if we don't get the contracts! So what do we do?"

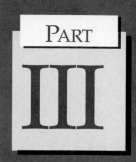
INSTRUCTIONS FOR USING THE STRAT-ANALYST™ SOFTWARE PACKAGE

Instructions for Using STRAT-ANALYST™

STRAT-ANALYST™ is user-friendly. Even if you are a novice on the personal computer, you can learn to use STRAT-ANALYST successfully in an hour or two. STRAT-ANALYST gives you the capability to *quickly* and *easily*:

1. Obtain calculations showing financial ratios, profit margins and rates of return, the percentage composition of income statements and balance sheets, annual compound growth rates, and Altman's bankruptcy index (a predictor of impending financial crisis).

2. Construct line graphs, bar graphs, pie charts, and scatter diagrams using any of the case data or calculations on file.

3. Make five-year financial projections of a company's performance.

4. Do "what-if" scenarios and compare the projected outcomes for one strategic option versus another.

5. Get report-ready printouts of all these calculations and graphs.

6. Go through an easy-to-use procedure for doing:

   - Industry and competitive situation analysis (as described in Chapter 3).
   - Company situation analysis (as described in Chapter 4).
   - Business portfolio analysis (as described in Chapter 8).

   Then get report-ready printouts of all your work.

7. Develop a set of action recommendations for:

   - Revising/improving a company's strategy and competitive position (a particularly useful option for Cases 1–20).
   - Improving strategy implementation and addressing internal problems/issues (a particularly useful option for Cases 1–6 and 26–37).

   Again, the software will generate report-ready printouts of your recommended action plan.

Complete step-by-step instructions for using all of these capabilities are provided on the STRAT-ANALYST screens as needed. You will find that the STRAT-ANALYST software package will give you a major assist in doing higher-caliber strategic analysis, and it will significantly cut the time it takes to do the number-crunching needed for first-rate preparation of a case assignment.

HARDWARE REQUIREMENTS

To successfully run STRAT-ANALYST, the computer setup you use must meet the following requirements:

- IBM or 100 percent IBM compatible.
- 640k of RAM with at least 550k of RAM available for program execution after DOS and any other memory-resident programming has been loaded. (The program will recognize expanded memory but not extended memory.)
- At least one normal or high-density removable disk drive ($3\frac{1}{2}$ or $5\frac{1}{4}$ inch).
- Printer access: IBM or Epson compatible dot-matrix printer, or HP LaserJet or compatible laser printer.
- DOS version 2.1 or later.

GETTING STARTED

Due to the variety of personal computer disk drive configurations that are available, we have provided separate start-up instructions for each of the three basic types of disk drive setups that will run STRAT-ANALYST.

Step 1: Determine which size and density disk you will be working from:

- High-density 3.5" dsk
- Low-density 3.5" disk
- Low-density 5.25" disk

Step 2: Determine which of the following modes of operation you will use to run the software:

- Run the program and access files from a hard disk
- Run the program from a hard disk but access files from floppy drive (Low-density 3.5" only)
- Run the program from a floppy disk but access files from a hard disk (5.25" only)
- Run from the floppy drive(s)

Step 3: Follow the appropriate directions in the Section number indicated in the table below

	Run the program and access files from a hard disk	Run the program from a hard disk but access files from floppy drive	Run the program from a floppy drive but access files from a hard disk	Run from the floppy drive(s) only
High-density 3.5" disk	Section 1	Not applicable	Not applicable	Section 2
Low-density 3.5" disk	Section 3	Section 4	Not applicable	Section 5
Low-density 5.25" disk	Section 6	Not applicable	Section 7	Section 8

NOTE: All of the following instructions that refer to a hard disk assume that the letter designation for the hard disk is C. If the letter designation of your hard disk is other than C, replace the letter C in the following directions with your letter designation.

All of the following instructions that refer to floppy disk drives assume that if you have only one floppy disk drive, its letter designation is A, and if you have two floppy disk drives, the primary drive is A and the secondary drive is B. If the letter designation(s) for your floppy drive(s) differ from these letter designations, replace the letters in the following directions with your letter designation(s).

SECTION 1: Installing from high-density 3.5" disk
       Running the program and accessing files from a hard disk

1. Start your computer with DOS. If you are not starting from the hard drive, at the DOS prompt type

```
C: <Enter>
```

2. Create a new directory on your hard drive called STRAT. To create a directory type

```
MD \STRAT <Enter>
```

3. Switch to the new directory you just created by typing

```
CD \STRAT <Enter>
```

4. Insert the STRAT-ANALYST disk into your A: drive
5. Type

```
COPY A:*.* <Enter>
```

6. After all files have been copied from the floppy disk you can begin using the program by typing

```
RUN SA <Enter>
```

SECTION 2: Installing from high-density 3.5" disk
       Running from high-density 3.5" disk

1. Start your computer with DOS. If you are not starting from the floppy drive, at the DOS prompt type

```
A: <Enter>
```

2. (If you started with the DOS disk in the A: drive remove it now.) Insert the STRAT-ANALYST disk in the A: drive and type

```
RUN SA <Enter>
```

SECTION 3: Installing from low-density 3.5" disks
       Running the program and accessing files from a hard disk

1. Start your computer with DOS. If you are not starting from the hard drive, at the DOS prompt type

```
C: <Enter>
```

2. Create a new directory on your hard drive called STRAT. To create a directory type

`MD \STRAT <Enter>`

3. Switch to the new directory you just created by typing

`CD \STRAT <Enter>`

4. Insert the STRAT-ANALYST **RUN DISK** into your A: drive
5. Type

`COPY A:*.* <Enter>`

6. After all files have been copied from the floppy disk remove the STRAT-ANALYST **RUN DISK** and insert the STRAT-ANALYST **CASE DISK** into your A: drive

7. Type

`COPY A:*.* <Enter>`

8. After all files have been copied from the floppy disk you can begin using the program by typing

`RUN SA <Enter>`

SECTION 4: Installing from low-density 3.5″ disks
Running the program from a hard disk and accessing files from a floppy drive

1. Start your computer with DOS. If you are not starting from the hard drive, at the DOS prompt type

`C: <Enter>`

2. Create a new directory on your hard drive called STRAT. To create a directory type

`MD \STRAT <Enter>`

3. Switch to the new directory you just created by typing

`CD \STRAT <Enter>`

4. Insert the STRAT-ANALYST **RUN DISK** into your A: drive
5. Type

`COPY A:*.* <Enter>`

(This copies all of the necessary run files into the STRAT directory on your hard drive.)

6. After all files have been copied from the floppy disk remove the STRAT-ANALYST **RUN DISK** and insert the STRAT-ANALYST **CASE DISK** into your A: drive

7. Type

`RUN A:SA <Enter>`

SECTION 5: Running the program and accessing files from 3.5" floppy drives
(requires two 3.5" floppy drives)

1. Start your computer with DOS.

2. (If you started with the DOS disk in the A: drive remove it now. If you started with DOS on your hard drive, after inserting the disks indicated, type

$$\text{A: }\texttt{<Enter>})$$

Insert the STRAT-ANALYST **RUN DISK** in the A: drive and the STRAT-ANALYST **CASE DISK** in the B: drive.

3. Type

$$\texttt{RUN B:SA <Enter>}$$

SECTION 6: Installing from 5.25" disks
Running the program and accessing files from a hard disk

1. Start your computer with DOS. If you are not starting from the hard drive, at the DOS prompt type

$$\texttt{C: <Enter>}$$

2. Insert the STRAT-ANALYST **DISK 4** in your A: drive

3. Type

$$\texttt{A: <Enter>}$$

4. Type

$$\texttt{INSTALL <Enter>}$$

5. Follow the instructions carefully as they appear on screen. You will need at least 1 megabyte of free storage space on your hard drive to install all of the files. During the installation process you will be prompted to insert other STRAT-ANALYST disks as they are required.

6. When the installation process is completed and you are returned to the DOS prompt, type

$$\texttt{RUN SA <Enter>}$$

SECTION 7: Installing from 5.25" disks
Running the program from a floppy disk and accessing files from a hard drive.

1. Start your computer with DOS. If you are not starting from the hard drive, at the DOS prompt type

$$\texttt{C: <Enter>}$$

2. Insert the STRAT-ANALYST **DISK 1** in your A: drive

3. Type

$$\texttt{A: <Enter>}$$

4. Type

$$\texttt{RUN SA <Enter>}$$

5. Follow the instructions carefully as they appear on screen. During the installation process you will be prompted to insert other STRAT-ANALYST disks as they are required.

SECTION 8: Running the program and accessing files from 5.25″ floppy drives (requires two 5.25″ floppy drives)

1. Start your computer with DOS.

2. (If you started with the DOS disk in the A: drive remove it now. If you started with DOS on your hard drive, after inserting the disks indicated, type

```
A: <Enter>)
```

Insert the STRAT-ANALYST **DISK 1** in the A: drive and the STRAT-ANALYST **DISK 2** in the B: drive.

3. Type

```
RUN B:SA <Enter>
```

The program will prompt you to insert STRAT-ANALYST **DISK 3** when it is needed.

STRAT-ANALYST MENUS

Moving from file to file from screen to screen is easy with STRAT-ANALYST menus. STRAT-ANALYST menus appear in two forms: (1) in a column on the screen or (2) in a line at the top of the screen. To make a menu selection from either of these types of menus, simply press the letter corresponding to your menu selection.

Some STRAT-ANALYST screens will have no menu. These screens will always present instructions as to how to proceed (the usual procedure is to press [Return]).

Unless otherwise indicated, the [Esc] key will send you to the first screen (usually the main menu) for the particular file you are in. Use the [Esc] key to "escape" from any screen you have accessed; it will return you to the Main Menu of the current file. [Esc] will NOT cause you to leave the STRAT-ANALYST file you are currently using.

When accessing files with the STRAT-ANALYST Main Menu, you will (if you have $5\frac{1}{4}$-inch disks) occasionally be prompted by STRAT-ANALYST to replace Disk 1 with Disk 2 or vice versa. This occurs when the computer needs to access a file stored on the other STRAT-ANALYST disk—i.e., the one NOT currently in the machine. When you encounter this screen, instructions for proceeding will appear.

> FIXED DISK USERS: If you have loaded all of the STRAT-ANALYST disks onto your hard disk and the program prompts you to exchange disks, simply press [Return] to continue the execution of your menu selection.

Important Notice. All other instructions you will need to use STRAT-ANALYST's capabilities successfully are self-contained on STRAT-ANALYST and will appear on the screen as needed.

MAKING A BACKUP COPY OF STRAT-ANALYST

It is always good practice to make backup copies of your working disks. In the event that your original STRAT-ANALYST disks are lost or damaged, your backup copies will serve as replacements. To make backup copies, simply use the normal procedure for whatever type of computer system you work with.

Needless to say, you should always observe safe disk-handling procedures.

INDEXES

Name Index

A

Aaker, David A., 124, 247
Abbott, Jon, 397
Abell, Derek F., 20, 199
Aburdne, Patricia, 801
Adams, Russell B., Jr., 526
Aiken, Miriam, 321
Allen, B., 649
Allen, George, 321, 334
Allen, Michael G., 200
Allio, Robert J., 200
Allison, Barbara J., 373, 415
Amara, Roy, 66
Anderson, M. J., Jr., 151, 152
Andrews, Kenneth R., 16, 17, 19, 45, 54, 55, 99
Angrist, S. W., 801
Ansoff, H. Igor, 189
Atchison, Michael D., 293
Augsburger, Robert R., 397
Austin, Nancy, 252, 256, 261, 267, 277

B

Bagamery, A., 444
Baldo, Anthony, 613
Bales, Carter E., 176
Bartlett, Christopher A., 230, 247
Baum, L., 526
Belford, Raymond E., 345, 821
Bennis, Warren, 269
Berg, Norman A., 164
Bettinger, Cass, 276
Bettis, Richard A., 214, 228, 247
Blackwell, Roger D., 45
Bleeke, Joel A., 159
Bolt, James F., 159
Bolwijn, Piet T., 189
Boulton, William O., 895
Bourgeois, L. J., 51

Bower, Joseph L., 276
Boyer, Mark A., 698
Braham, James, 843, 847, 849, 850
Bright, William M., 189
Brodwin, David R., 51
Brown, Lew G., 505
Brown, Robert B., 911
Buzzell, Robert D., 189

C

Caminiti, Susan, 526, 810
Cannon, J. Thomas, 220
Carlson, Ed, 267–68
Carroll, Glenn R., 47, 51, 159
Carroll, Lewis, 2
Carter, Richard L., 811
Chandler, Alfred D., 222, 247
Chapin, Kim, 337, 342
Christensen, H. Kurt, 99, 214
Christensen, Roland, 164
Cohen, Daniel, 691, 692
Cohen, William A., 124
Collins, James C., 877
Collins, John, 102
Cooper, Arnold C., 214
Corey, Raymond, 223, 225, 227
Cotter, Marion, 768
Coyne, Kevin P., 124
Cyert, R. M., 270

D

Daigle, Jules O., 766
Davies, Garret A., 214
Davis, Stanley M., 232
Deal, Terrence E., 254, 276
Deitzer, Bernard A., 839

Subject Index